THE **CMPTR** SOLU

Print
+
Online

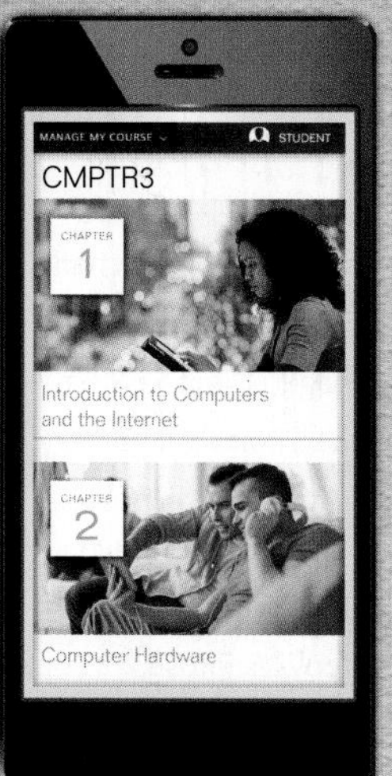

CMPTR³ delivers all the key terms and core concepts for the **Computer Applications and Concepts** course.

CMPTR Online provides the complete narrative from the printed text with additional interactive media and the unique functionality of **StudyBits**—all available on nearly any device!

What is a StudyBit™? Created through a deep investigation of students' challenges and workflows, the StudyBit™ functionality of **CMPTR Online** enables students of different generations and learning styles to study more effectively by allowing them to learn their way. Here's how they work:

Collect What's Important
Create StudyBits as you highlight text, images or take notes!

Rate and Organize StudyBits
Rate your understanding and use the color-coding to quickly organize your study time and personalize your flashcards and quizzes.

StudyBit™

Track/Monitor Progress
Use Concept Tracker to decide how you'll spend study time and study YOUR way!

Personalize Quizzes
Filter by your StudyBits to personalize quizzes or just take chapter quizzes off-the-shelf.

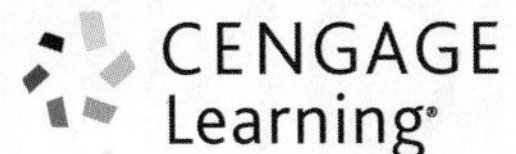

CMPTR³
Katherine T. Pinard
Robin M. Romer
Deborah Morley

Vice President, General Manager, 4LTR Press: Neil Marquardt

Product Director, 4LTR Press: Steven E. Joos

Content/Media Developer: Victoria Castrucci

Product Assistant: Lauren Dame

Marketing Manager: Jeffrey A. Tousignant

Marketing Coordinator: Cassie Cloutier

Content Project Manager: Darrell E. Frye

Manufacturing Planner: Ron Montgomery

Production Service: Prashant Kumar Das, MPS Limited

Sr. Art Director: Bethany Casey

Internal Designer: Tippy McIntosh

Cover Designer: Lisa Kuhn/Curio Press, LLC

Cover Image: © Shutterstock.com/VLADGRIN

Title Page Images: © Shutterstock.com/ VLADGRIN

Back Cover Images: Jetta Productions/Getty Images; JGI/Tom Grill/Blend/Corbis

Intellectual Property Analyst: Amber Hill

Intellectual Property Project Manager: Nick Barrows

Library of Congress Control Number: 2016933796

Student Edition with Online ISBN: 978-1-305-86287-6

Student Edition ISBN: 978-1-305-86286-9

Cengage Learning
20 Channel Center Street
Boston, MA 02210
USA

Printed in the United States of America
Print Number: 01 Print Year: 2016

PINARD / ROMER / MORLEY

CMPTR 3

BRIEF CONTENTS

© Shutterstock.com/VLADGRIN

BRIEF CONTENTS

CONTENTS

Part 1 CONCEPTS

© Jetta Productions/Getty Images

Part 2 NETWORKS and THE INTERNET

© John Fedele/AGE Fotostock

© Bloomberg/Getty Images

© Who is Danny/Shutterstock.com

Part 5
OFFICE 2016

© Andrey_Popov/Shutterstock.com

Part 6
WORD 2016

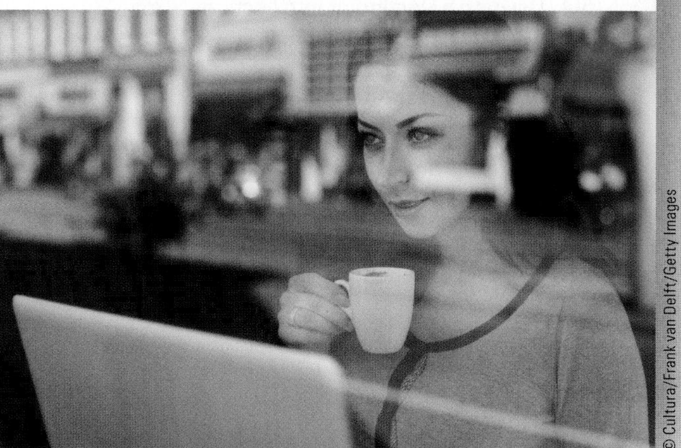

© Cultura/Frank van Delft/Getty Images

12 Enhancing a Document 346

Part 7 EXCEL 2016

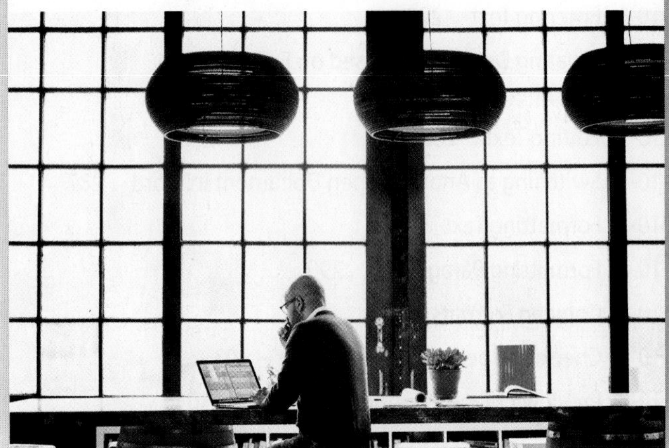
© Thomas Barwick/Getty Images

13 Creating a Workbook 382

14 Working with Formulas and Functions 412

15 Creating an Advanced Workbook 448

16 Inserting and Formatting Charts 472

Part 8 ACCESS 2016

© alphaspirit/Shutterstock.com

17 Creating a Database 506

18 Maintaining and Querying a Database 536

19 Creating Forms and Reports 566

Part 9 POWERPOINT 2016

© Hero Images/Getty Images

20 Creating a Presentation 590

Part 10 INTEGRATION

© nopporn/Shutterstock.com

CMPTR ONLINE

ACCESS TEXTBOOK CONTENT ONLINE—INCLUDING ON SMARTPHONES!

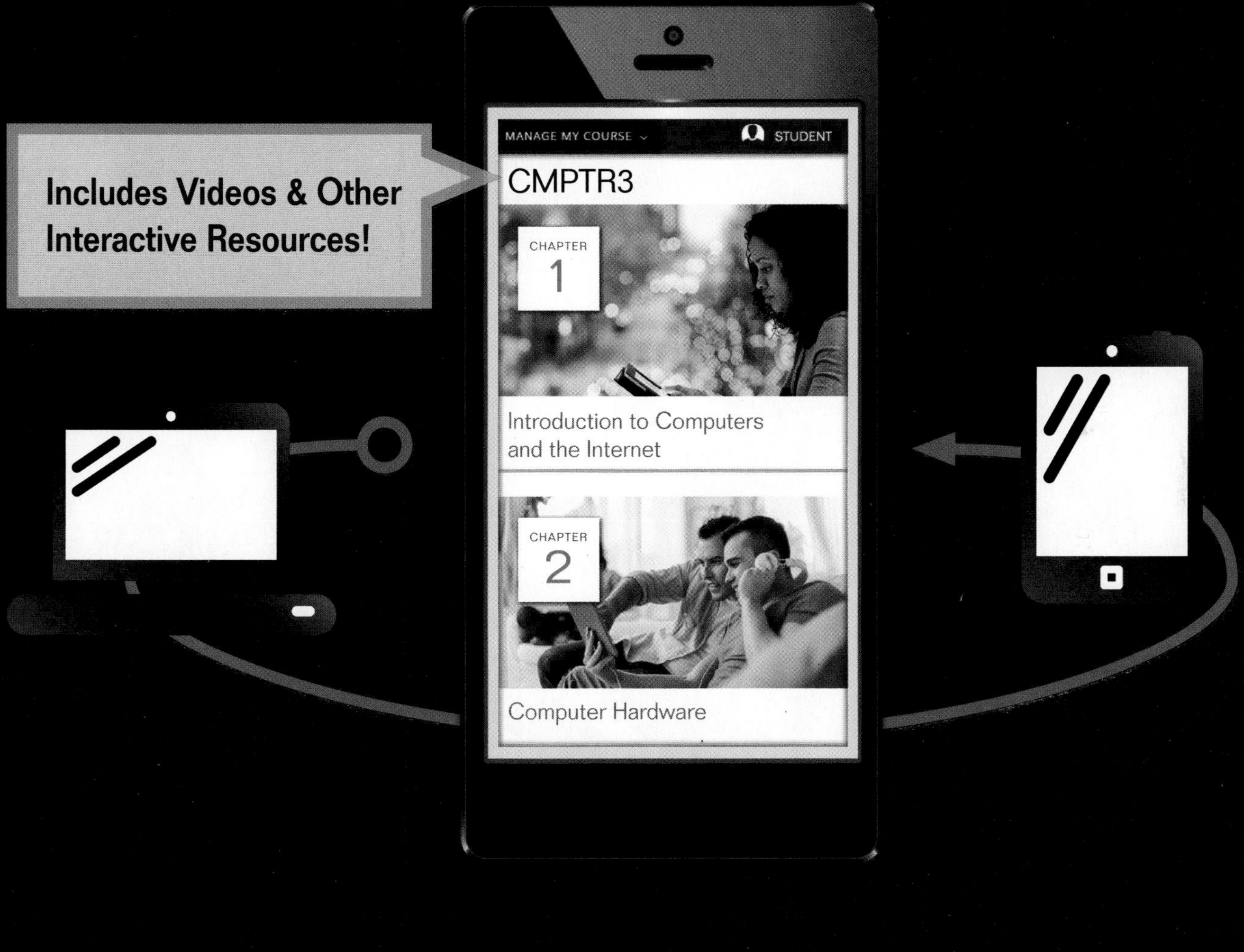

Includes Videos & Other Interactive Resources!

MANAGE MY COURSE

STUDENT

CMPTR3

CHAPTER 1

Introduction to Computers and the Internet

CHAPTER 2

Computer Hardware

Access CMPTR ONLINE at www.cengagebrain.com

Part 1
CONCEPTS

1 Introduction to Computers and the Internet

© Jetta Productions/Getty Images

LEARNING OBJECTIVES

After studying the material in this chapter, you will be able to:

1-1 Explain what computers do

1-2 Identify types of computers

1-3 Describe computer networks and the Internet

1-4 Understand how computers impact society

After finishing this chapter, go to **PAGE 26** for **STUDY TOOLS**.

1-1 WHAT IS A COMPUTER?

Computers and other forms of technology impact your daily life in many ways. You encounter computers in stores, restaurants, and other retail establishments. You probably use a computer or smartphone and the Internet regularly to obtain information, find entertainment, buy products and services, and communicate with others. Businesses also use computers extensively, such as to maintain employee and customer records, control robots and other machines in factories, and provide executives with the up-to-date information they need to make decisions. Finally, the government uses computers to support the nation's defense systems, for space exploration, and for law enforcement and military purposes. In short, computers and computing technology are used in an endless number of ways.

A **computer** is a programmable, electronic device that accepts data, performs operations on that data, presents the results, and stores the data or results as needed. Because a computer is programmable, it will do whatever the instructions (called **programs**) tell it to do. The programs used with a computer determine the tasks the computer is able to perform.

1-1a Primary Operations of a Computer

The four primary operations of a computer are referred to as input, processing, output, and storage. These operations can be defined as follows:

- **Input**—entering data into the computer
- **Processing**—performing operations on the data
- **Output**—presenting the results
- **Storage**—saving data, programs, or output for future use

The progression of input, processing, output, and storage is sometimes called the IPOS cycle or the information processing cycle.

For a computer that has been programmed to add two numbers, as shown in Exhibit 1-1, input occurs when data (in this example, the numbers 2 and 5) is entered into the computer, processing takes place when the computer program adds those two numbers, and output happens when the sum of 7 is displayed on the computer screen. The storage operation occurs any time the data, a change to a program, or the output is saved for future use.

Another example of a computer is a supermarket barcode reader. First, the grocery item being purchased is passed over the barcode reader—input. Next, the description and price of the item are looked up—processing. Then, the item description and price are displayed on the cash register and printed on the receipt—output. Finally, the inventory, ordering, and sales records are updated—storage.

Today's computers almost always also perform communications functions, such as sending or retrieving

EXHIBIT 1-1 IPOS CYCLE

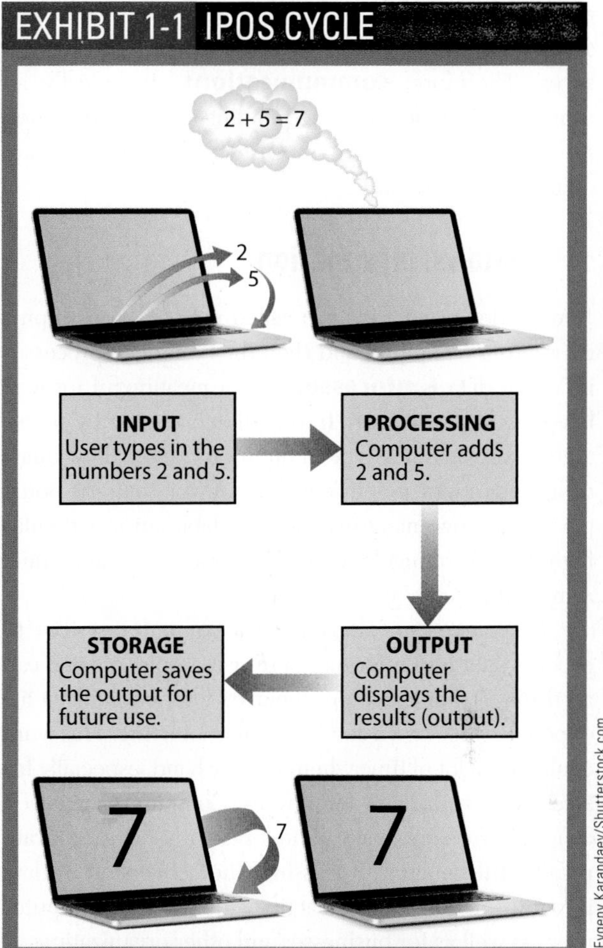

© Evgeny Karandaev/Shutterstock.com

computer A programmable, electronic device that accepts data input, performs processing operations on that data, and outputs and stores the results.

program Instructions used to tell the computer what to do to accomplish tasks; also called software.

input The process of entering data into a computer; can also refer to the data itself.

processing Performing operations on data that has been input into a computer, such as to convert that input to output.

output The process of presenting the results of processing; can also refer to the results themselves.

storage The operation of saving data, programs, or output for future use.

CONCEPTS

data via the Internet, accessing information located in a shared company database, or exchanging email messages. Therefore, **communications**—technically an input or output operation, depending on which direction the information is going—is considered the fifth primary computer operation.

1-1b Data vs. Information

Raw, unorganized facts are called **data**. A user inputs data into a computer, and then the computer processes it. When data is **processed** into a meaningful form, it becomes **information**. Information is frequently generated to answer some type of question, such as how many of a restaurant's employees work fewer than 20 hours per week, how many seats are available on a particular flight from Los Angeles to San Francisco, or what is Hank Aaron's lifetime home run total.

Of course, you don't need a computer system to process data into information. For example, anyone can go through time cards or employee files and make a list of people who work a certain number of hours. This work could take a lot of time when done by hand, especially for a company with many employees. Computers, however, can perform such tasks almost instantly, with accurate results. Information processing (the conversion of data into information) is a vital activity today for all computer users as well as for businesses and other organizations.

1-1c Hardware and Software

The physical parts of a computer (the parts you can touch) are called **hardware**. Hardware components can be internal (located inside the computer) or external (located outside the computer and connected to the computer via a wired or wireless connection). Exhibit 1-2 illustrates typical computer hardware.

The term **software** refers to the programs or instructions used to tell the computer hardware what to do. It runs the computer and allows people to use that computer to perform specific tasks, such as creating letters, preparing budgets, managing inventory and customer databases, playing games, watching videos, listening to music, scheduling appointments, editing digital photographs, designing homes, viewing Web pages, burning DVDs, and exchanging email. In Exhibit 1-2, the software being used allows you to look at information on the Internet.

FYI

DATA

Any fact or set of facts can become computer data, such as the words in a letter to a friend, the numbers in a monthly budget, the images in a photograph, the notes in a song, or the facts stored in an employee record.

© ymgerman/Shutterstock.com

1-1d Computer Users and Professionals

Computer users, often called **end users**, are the people who use computers to perform tasks or obtain information. This includes an accountant electronically preparing a client's taxes, an office worker using a word processing program to create a letter, a doctor updating a patient's electronic medical record, a parent emailing his or her child's teacher, a college student researching a topic online, a child playing a computer game, and a person shopping online.

Programmers, on the other hand, are computer professionals who write the programs that computers use. Other computer professionals include systems analysts, who design computer systems to be used within their companies; computer operations personnel, who are responsible for the day-to-day computer operations at a company, such as maintaining systems or troubleshooting user-related problems; and security specialists, who are responsible for securing the company computers and networks against hackers and other intruders.

communications The transmission of data from one device to another.

data Raw, unorganized facts.

process To perform useful operations, such as transforming data into information.

information Data that has been processed into a meaningful form.

hardware The physical parts of a computer.

software Programs or instructions used to tell the computer what to do.

end user A person who uses a computer to perform tasks or obtain information.

programmer A computer professional who writes the programs that computers use.

EXHIBIT 1-2 TYPICAL COMPUTER HARDWARE

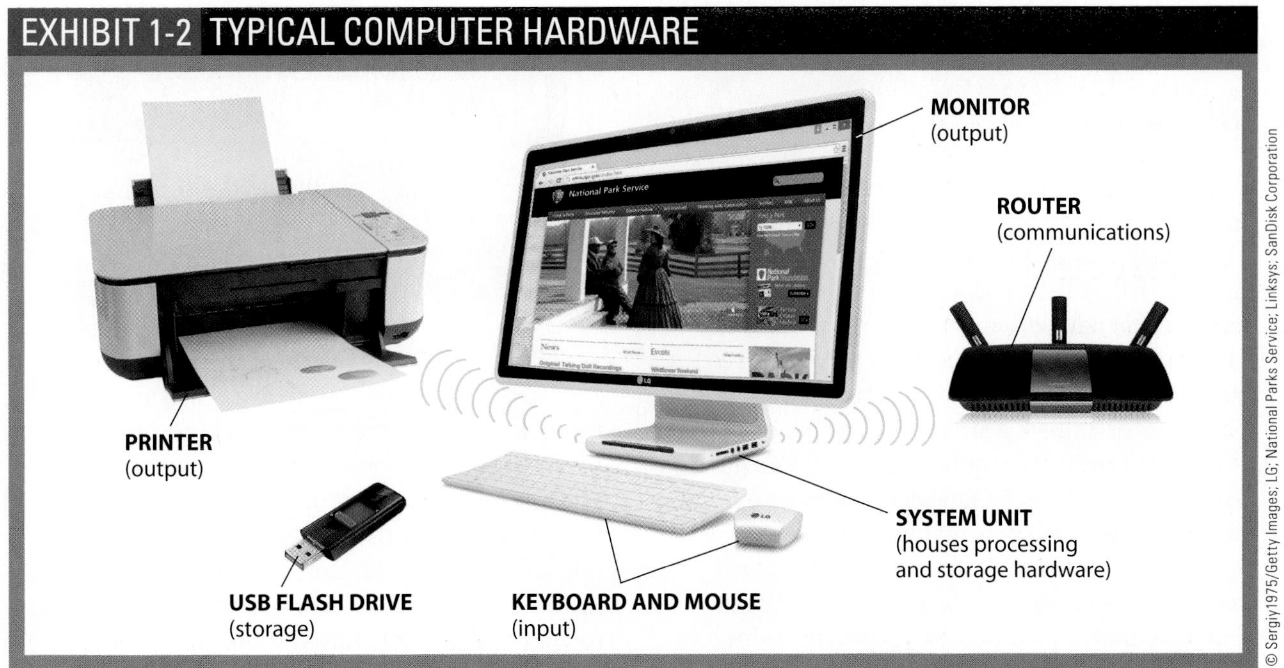

© Sergiy1975/Getty Images; LG; National Parks Service; Linksys; SanDisk Corporation

1-2 TYPES OF COMPUTERS

The types of computers available today vary from the tiny computers embedded in consumer products, to the pocket-sized mobile devices that do a limited number of computing tasks, to the powerful and versatile computers found in homes and businesses, to the superpowerful computers used for scientific research and to control critical government systems. Computers are generally classified by category, based on size, capability, and price.

1-2a Embedded Computers

An **embedded computer** is a tiny computer embedded into a product designed to perform specific tasks or functions for that product. For example, computers are often embedded into household appliances, such as dishwashers, microwaves, ovens, and coffee makers, as well as into other everyday objects, such as thermostats, treadmills, sewing machines, DVD players, and televisions, to help those appliances and objects perform their designated tasks. Cars also use many embedded computers to assist with diagnostics, to notify the user of important conditions (such as an underinflated tire or an oil filter that needs changing), to facilitate the car's navigational or entertainment systems, to help the driver perform tasks, and to control the use of the airbag and other safety devices, such as cameras that alert a driver that a vehicle is in his or her blind spot or that assist with parking. Self-driving cars (such as the one shown in Exhibit 1-3), which are currently being road tested, contain a large number of embedded computers and other technology to enable the car to safely operate without a driver. Because embedded computers are

EXHIBIT 1-3 GOOGLE'S SELF-DRIVING CAR

Source: Google Inc.

embedded computer A tiny computer embedded in a product and designed to perform specific tasks or functions for that product.

TRENDING...

TINY PCs

© cobalt88/Shutterstock.com; Roku, Inc.

Computers have shrunk again. Forget small notebooks, tablets, or even the small mini desktop computers available now. If you want portability, look no further than today's tiny PCs that are the size of a USB flash drive.

Tiny PCs typically connect to a TV via an HDMI port to turn that TV into a fully functional computer or at least a smart TV capable of delivering Internet content. Many tiny PCs have USB ports to connect a keyboard or mouse or to power the device if external power is required. Some include Bluetooth capabilities to more easily connect a keyboard or mouse. They may also have built-in storage and a microSD slot for transferring photos, videos, or other content to the device.

The capabilities of these devices vary from device to device. Some, such as Amazon Fire TV Stick and Roku Streaming Stick (shown in the accompanying illustration), are designed to transform a traditional TV into a smart TV capable of displaying Internet content, such as YouTube videos and Netflix movies, via apps installed on the device, as well as displaying photos and videos from a smartphone or tablet. Others, such as Google's Chromecast, are designed to stream videos, movies, and music, and other content from, and control the device via, a computer, smartphone, or tablet, though the latest version of Chromecast also includes support for Netflix, Hulu, Pandora, and other popular online media apps. The newest devices, such as Google Chromebit and Intel Compute Stick, go one step further and are fully functioning "computers-on-a-stick." After you plug one of these devices into the HDMI port on a TV and connect a USB or Bluetooth mouse and keyboard, you can use it as a traditional PC, accessing both Internet content and running software that you would typically run on a personal computer.

The flexibility of these tiny PCs and the apps they can run vary from device to device, based on the operating system and the amount of storage available. But for turning a TV at any location into your own personal computer, gaming device, or video player, tiny PCs are definitely the way to go.

designed for specific tasks and specific products, they cannot be used as general-purpose computers.

1-2b Mobile Devices

A **mobile device** is loosely defined as a small device, often pocket-sized, that has built-in computing or Internet capability. Mobile devices are commonly used to make voice and video calls, send text messages, view Web pages and documents, take digital photos, play games, download and play music, watch TV shows, and access calendars, social media, and other tools. Mobile devices today include **smartphones**, such as the one in Exhibit 1-4, and small tablet devices, such as iPads and Android tablets. Handheld gaming devices, such as the Nintendo 3DS, and portable digital media players, such as the iPod touch, that include Internet

EXHIBIT 1-4 SMARTPHONE

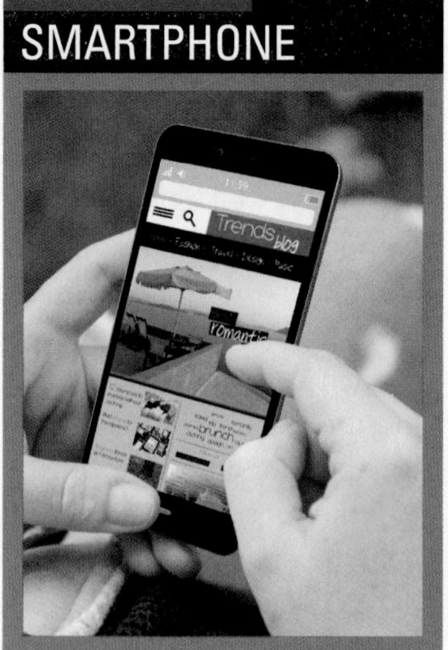

© Georgejmclittle/Shutterstock.com

mobile device A small device with built-in computing or Internet capability.

smartphone A mobile device based on a mobile phone that includes Internet capabilities and can run mobile apps.

capabilities can also be referred to as mobile devices; so can the Apple Watch and other smart watches and wearable devices. Mobile devices are powered by rechargeable batteries and typically include wireless connectivity to enable the device to connect to the Internet.

Mobile devices tend to have small screens and keyboards and so are more appropriate for individuals who want continual access to email and the ability to look up information online when needed, rather than individuals wanting general Web browsing or more extensive computing capabilities. This is beginning to change, however, as mobile devices continue to grow in capabilities, wireless communications continue to become faster, and as mobile input options, such as voice and touch input, continue to improve. For instance, many mobile devices can perform Internet searches and other tasks via voice commands, some can be used to pay for purchases while you are on the go, and many can view virtually any Web content as well as view and edit documents stored in a common format, such as Microsoft Office documents.

> Portable computers now outsell desktop computers in the United States.

1-2c Personal Computers (PCs)

A **personal computer (PC)** is a small computer designed to be used by one person at a time. Personal computers are widely used by individuals and businesses today.

Conventional personal computers that are designed to fit on or next to a desk, as shown in Exhibit 1-5, are often referred to as **desktop computers**. Desktop computers can be housed in different types of cases. A tower case is a system unit designed to sit vertically, typically on the floor. A desktop case is designed to be placed horizontally on a desk's surface and is often a mini desktop today, as in Exhibit 1-5, rather than a full-size desktop case. An all-in-one case, which was shown in Exhibit 1-2, incorporates the monitor and system unit into a single piece of hardware.

Desktop computers usually conform to one of two standards or platforms: PC-compatible or Mac. PC-compatible computers evolved from the original IBM PC—the first personal computer that was widely accepted for business use. They are made by companies such as Dell, Hewlett-Packard, Acer, Lenovo, and Gateway. These computers typically run the Microsoft Windows operating system, although some run an alternative operating system, such as Linux. Mac computers are made by Apple, run the OS X operating system, and typically use different software than PC-compatible computers. Mac computers are traditionally the computer of choice for artists, designers, and others who require advanced graphics capabilities.

Portable computers are small personal computers that are designed to be carried around easily. This portability makes them very flexible. For example, they enable individuals to use the same personal computer at home and at school, or the same work computer in the office, while on vacation, at off-site meetings, and at other locations. Portable computers are essential for many workers, such as salespeople who make presentations or take orders from clients off-site, agents who collect data at remote locations, and managers who need computing and communications resources as they travel. They are also typically the computer of choice for students and for individuals buying a new home computer. In fact, portable computers now outsell desktop computers in the United States.

EXHIBIT 1-5 DESKTOP COMPUTERS

PC-COMPATIBLE TOWER COMPUTER

MAC MINI DESKTOP COMPUTER

personal computer (PC)
A small computer designed to be used by one person at a time.

desktop computer
A personal computer designed to fit on or next to a desk.

portable computer
A small personal computer designed to be carried around easily.

TRENDING...

COMPUTERS THEN & NOW

The history of computers is often referred to in terms of generations, with each new generation characterized by a major technological development.

Precomputers and Early Computers (before approximately 1946)

Early computing devices include the abacus, the slide rule, the mechanical calculator, and Dr. Herman Hollerith's Punch Card Tabulating Machine and Sorter (shown here). This was the first electromechanical machine that could read punch cards. It was used to process the 1890 U.S. Census data. Hollerith's company eventually became International Business Machines (IBM).

Source: © IBM Corporate Archives

First-Generation Computers (approximately 1946–1957)

The first computers were enormous, often taking up entire rooms. First-generation computers could solve only one problem at a time because they needed to be physically rewired with cables to be reprogrammed. Paper punch cards and tape were used for input, and output was printed on paper. Completed in 1946, ENIAC (shown here) was the world's first large-scale, general-purpose computer. UNIVAC, released in 1951, was initially built for the U.S. Census Bureau and became the first computer to be mass produced for general commercial use.

Source: © U.S. Army

Second-Generation Computers (approximately 1958–1963)

The second generation of computers, such as the IBM 1401 mainframe (shown here), were smaller, less expensive, more powerful, and more reliable than first-generation computers. Programs and data were input on punch cards and magnetic tape, output was on punch cards and paper printouts, and magnetic tape was used for storage. Hard drives and programming languages, such as FORTRAN and COBOL, were developed during this generation.

Source: © IBM Corporate Archives

Third-Generation Computers (approximately 1964–1970)

Integrated circuits (ICs) marked the beginning of the third generation of computers, such as the IBM System/360 mainframe (shown here). Integrated circuits incorporate many transistors and electronic circuits on a single tiny silicon chip, making computers smaller and more reliable.

Source: © IBM Corporate Archives

Fourth-Generation Computers (approximately 1971–present)

The invention of the microprocessor in 1971 ushered in the fourth generation of computers. In essence, a microprocessor contains the core processing capabilities of an entire computer on one single chip. The original IBM PC (shown here) and Apple Macintosh computers, and most of today's traditional computers, fall into this category.

Source: IBM Corporate Archives

Fifth-Generation Computers (now and the future)

Fifth-generation computers are most commonly defined as those that are based on artificial intelligence, allowing them to think, reason, and learn, such as the IBM Watson supercomputer (shown here). Some aspects of fifth-generation computers—such as voice input, touch input, and speech recognition—are in use today. Future fifth-generation computers may be constructed in the form of optical computers that process data using light, tiny computers that utilize nanotechnology, or as computers built into desks, home appliances, and other everyday devices.

Source: © IBM Corporation

EXHIBIT 1-6 PORTABLE COMPUTERS

Source: © Courtesy of Dell Inc.; Lenovo

Portable computers (see Exhibit 1-6) are available in the following configurations:

- **Notebook computers (laptop computers)** are about the size of a paper notebook and open to reveal a screen on the top half of the computer and a keyboard on the bottom. They are comparable to desktop computers in features and capabilities.
- **Tablet computers** are about the size of a notebook computer and are designed to be used with a digital pen or touch input. Unlike notebooks, tablet computers don't have a physical keyboard but they can use an on-screen or attached keyboard as needed.
- **Hybrid notebook-tablet computers** (also called convertible tablets and 2-in-1 computers) can function as either a notebook or a tablet computer because they have a display screen that folds shut to resemble a tablet. Some are detachable—designed to separate the display part from the keyboard part when a tablet is needed.
- **Netbooks** are similar to notebook computers but are designed primarily for accessing Internet-based applications and resources.

Most personal computers today are sold as stand-alone, self-sufficient units that are equipped with all the hardware and software needed to operate independently. In other words, they can perform input, processing, output, and storage without being connected to a network, although they are often connected to the Internet or another network. In contrast, a device that must be connected to a network to function is referred to as a **dumb terminal**. Two types of personal computers that may be able to perform a limited amount of independent processing but are designed to be used with a network are thin clients and Internet appliances.

A **thin client** is designed to be used with a network, such as a company network, a school network, or the Internet. Instead of using local hard drives for storage, programs are accessed from and data is stored on a network server. Thin clients are often used in businesses, school computer labs, retail stores, and medical offices. Advantages of thin clients over desktop computers include lower initial cost, increased security because data is not stored locally, and easier maintenance because all software is located on a central server. Disadvantages include having limited or no local storage and not being able to function as a stand-alone computer when the network is not working.

Ordinary devices that can be used for accessing the Internet can be called **Internet appliances** (sometimes referred to as Internet-enabled devices or smart appliances). Some Internet appliances, such

notebook computer (laptop computer) A portable computer that opens to reveal a screen and keyboard and is comparable to a desktop computer in features and capabilities.

tablet computer A portable computer about the size of a notebook that is designed to be used with a digital pen or touch input.

hybrid notebook-tablet A portable computer designed to function as both a notebook and a tablet PC.

netbook A very small notebook computer that is designed to primarily access Internet applications and resources.

dumb terminal A computer that must be connected to a network to function.

thin client A device designed to access a network for processing and data storage instead of performing those tasks locally.

Internet appliance Ordinary devices that include Internet capabilities.

EXHIBIT 1-7 INTERNET APPLIANCES

Source: © LG; Netflix

as the smart refrigerator and smart TV shown in Exhibit 1-7, use apps to deliver news, sports scores, weather, music, and other Web-based information. Gaming consoles, such as the Nintendo Wii, the Xbox 360, and the Sony PlayStation 3, that can be used to view Internet content in addition to their gaming abilities can be classified as Internet appliances when they are used to access the Internet.

1-2d Servers

A **server** (sometimes called a minicomputer or midrange server) is a computer used to host programs and data for a network. Typically larger, more powerful, and more expensive than a desktop computer, a server is usually located in an out-of-the-way place and can serve many users at one time. Users connect to the server through a network, using a computer, thin client, or dumb terminal consisting of just a monitor and keyboard (see Exhibit 1-8). Servers are often used in small- to medium-sized businesses, such as medical or dental offices, as well as in schools, libraries, and other locations offering computer access. There are also special home servers designed for home use. Home servers are used to back up (make duplicate copies of) the content located on all the computers in a home and to host music, photos, movies, and other media to be shared via a home network. Some home servers also allow you to securely access your stored content remotely via the Internet—this is called creating a personal cloud.

One trend involving servers, as well as mainframe computers (discussed next), is **virtualization**—the creation of virtual (rather than actual) versions of a computing resource. Server virtualization uses separate server environments that are physically located on the same computer but function as separate servers and do not interact with each other. For instance, all applications for an organization can be installed in virtual environments on a single physical server instead of using a separate server for each application. This allows the organization to fulfill its computing needs with fewer servers, which results in lower costs for hardware and server management, as well as lower power and cooling costs. Desktop virtualization stores each user's desktop environment on a server and delivers it to each individual via any authorized device. This adds flexibility to where and how each worker performs daily tasks. Virtualization is also used in other computing areas, such as networking and storage.

server A computer used to host programs and data for a network.

virtualization The creation of virtual versions of a computing resource.

EXHIBIT 1-8 SERVER

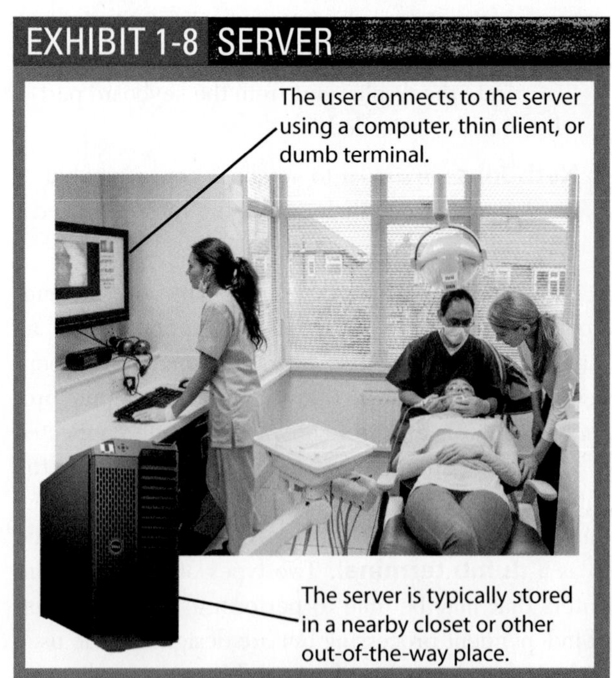

The user connects to the server using a computer, thin client, or dumb terminal.
The server is typically stored in a nearby closet or other out-of-the-way place.

© SolStock/Getty Images; Courtesy of Dell Inc.

1-2e Mainframe Computers

A **mainframe computer**, such as the one shown in Exhibit 1-9, is a powerful computer used in many large organizations that need to manage large amounts of centralized data. Larger, more expensive, and more powerful than ordinary servers, mainframes can serve thousands of users connected to the mainframe via personal computers, thin clients, or dumb terminals. Mainframe computers are typically located in climate-controlled data centers and are connected to the rest of the company computers via a computer network. During regular business hours, a mainframe runs the programs needed to meet the different needs of its wide variety of users. At night, it commonly performs large processing tasks, such as payroll and billing.

One recent focus for mainframes is ensuring that they can handle new and emerging needs, such as having the computational power to process data from smart meters and having the ability to run mobile and social networking applications. For example, the mainframe shown in Exhibit 1-9 is designed to process mobile data. It supports 8,000 virtual servers and can process 2.5 billion transactions per day.

EXHIBIT 1-9 MAINFRAME COMPUTER

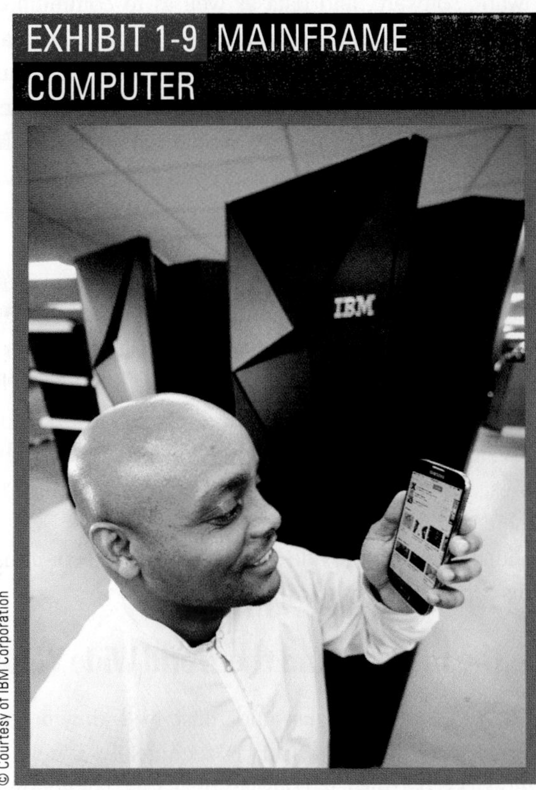

© Courtesy of IBM Corporation

1-2f Supercomputers

Some applications require extraordinary speed, accuracy, and processing capabilities—for example, sending astronauts into space, controlling missile guidance systems and satellites, forecasting the weather, exploring for oil, breaking codes, and designing and testing new products. **Supercomputers**—the most powerful and most expensive type of computer available—were developed to fill this need. Some relatively new supercomputing applications include hosting extremely complex Web sites, such as search sites and social networking sites, and three-dimensional applications, such as 3D medical imaging, 3D image projections, and 3D architectural modeling. Unlike mainframe computers, which typically run multiple applications simultaneously to serve a wide variety of users, supercomputers generally run one program at a time as fast as possible.

Conventional supercomputers can cost several million dollars each. They tend to be very large and have enormous processing power. For example, the Titan supercomputer, which is shown in Exhibit 1-10, occupies 4,352 square feet of floor space and contains more than 300,000 processors. Installed at the U.S. Department of

FYI

CLASSIFYING COMPUTERS
In practice, classifying a computer into one of the six categories described in this section is not always easy. For example, some personal computers are as powerful as servers, and some personal computers are as small as a mobile phone. And new devices, such as tablets, blur these categories. For example, small tablets running a mobile operating system are considered mobile devices, while more powerful tablets running a desktop operating system are considered personal computers. Nevertheless, these six categories are commonly used today to refer to groups of computers designed for similar purposes.

mainframe computer A powerful computer used in large organizations to manage large amounts of centralized data and run multiple programs simultaneously.

supercomputer The fastest, most expensive, and most powerful type of computer.

TRENDING...

GREEN BUSINESS PRACTICES

One issue facing businesses today is the high cost and environmental impact of the enormous amount of power that data centers consume. Many businesses are consolidating data centers and using virtualization to reduce power consumption and increase efficiency. Others, such as Google and Apple, use solar farms and other sources of renewable energy to power their campuses. Google, for example, has reduced its energy use by 50% through efficiency efforts. Google also produces or purchases enough renewable energy to supply 35% of its electricity needs, and funds projects to reduce carbon emission at sources outside Google in order to have a carbon footprint of zero since 2007.

© Vaclav Volrab Shutterstock.com

EXHIBIT 1-10 SUPERCOMPUTER

© DOE Photo/Alamy

Energy Oak Ridge National Laboratory, Titan is used for a variety of scientific research, including climate change and astrophysics. Its speed is expected to give researchers unparalleled accuracy in their simulations and facilitate faster research breakthroughs. With a peak speed of 27,000 trillion calculations per second, Titan is one of the fastest computers in the world.

computer network Computers and other devices that are connected to share hardware, software, and data.

Internet The largest and most well-known computer network, linking billions of computers all over the world.

Internet service provider (ISP) A business or other organization that provides Internet access to others, usually for a fee.

1-3 COMPUTER NETWORKS AND THE INTERNET

A **computer network** is a collection of computers and other devices that are connected to enable users to share hardware, software, and data as well as to communicate electronically. Computer networks exist in many sizes and types. For instance, home networks are commonly used to allow home computers to share a single printer and Internet connection as well as to exchange files. Small office networks enable workers to access company records stored on a network server, communicate with other employees, share a high-speed printer, and access the Internet, as shown in Exhibit 1-11. School networks allow students and teachers to access the Internet and school resources, and large corporate networks often connect all of the offices or retail stores in the corporation, creating a network that spans several cities or states. Public wireless networks, such as those available at some coffeehouses, restaurants, public libraries, and parks, provide Internet access to individuals via their portable computers and mobile devices. Mobile telephone networks provide Internet access and communications capabilities to smartphone users.

1-3a The Internet and the World Wide Web

The **Internet**, the largest and most well-known computer network in the world, is technically a network of networks because it consists of a vast collection of networks that can access each other. Individual users connect to the Internet by connecting their computers or mobile devices to servers belonging to an **Internet service provider (ISP)**—a company that

EXHIBIT 1-11 EXAMPLE OF A COMPUTER NETWORK

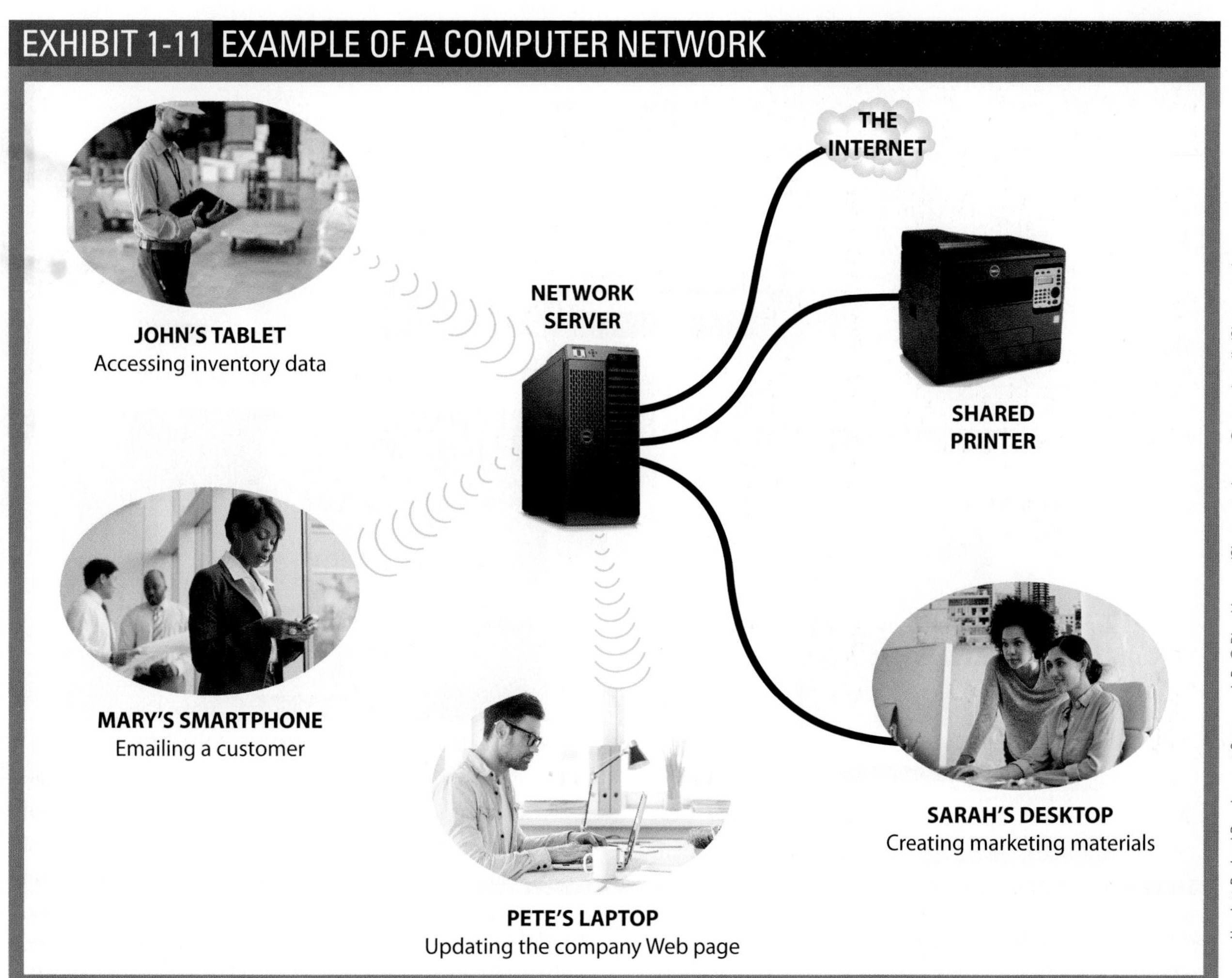

Source: Hewlett-Packard Development Company, L.P.; © Blend Images/Shutterstock.com; © g-stockstudio/Shutterstock.com; © Peopleimages/Getty Images; Courtesy of Dell Inc.

provides Internet access. ISPs—which include conventional and mobile telephone companies like AT&T, Verizon, and Sprint; cable providers like Comcast and Time Warner; and stand-alone ISPs like NetZero and EarthLink—function as onramps to the Internet, providing Internet access to their subscribers. ISP servers are continually connected to a larger network, called a regional network, which, in turn, is connected to one of the major high-speed networks within a country, called a backbone network. Backbone networks within a country are connected to each other and to backbone networks in other countries, forming the Internet.

While the term *Internet* refers to the physical structure of that network, the **World Wide Web** (often just called the **Web**) refers to one resource—an enormous collection of documents called **Web pages**—available through the Internet. Web pages typically contain **hyperlinks**—text or images that are linked to Web pages or other Web resources that you can click to access those pages or resources. A group of Web pages belonging to one individual or company is called a **Web site**. Web pages are stored on computers called **Web servers** that are continually connected to the Internet; they can be accessed at any time by anyone with a computer or other Web-enabled device and an Internet connection. A wide variety of information is available via Web pages, such as company and product information, government forms and publications, maps, school assignments and resources, news, weather, sports results, airline schedules, and much, much more. You can also

World Wide Web (Web) The collection of Web pages available through the Internet.

Web page A document, typically containing hyperlinks, located on a Web server.

hyperlink Text or an image linked to a Web page or other Web resource.

Web site A collection of related Web pages.

Web server A computer continually connected to the Internet that stores Web pages accessible through the Internet.

EXHIBIT 1-12 EXAMPLES OF COMMON WEB ACTIVITIES

use Web pages to shop and perform other types of online financial transactions; access social media like Facebook and Twitter; and listen to music, play games, watch television shows, and perform other entertainment-oriented activities (see Exhibit 1-12). Web pages are viewed using a **Web browser**, such as Edge, Internet Explorer (IE), Chrome, Safari, Opera, or Firefox.

1-3b Accessing a Network or the Internet

To access a network, you need to use a network adapter, typically built into your computer or other device being used, to connect your device to that network. With many networks you need to supply a username and a password to connect to the network. After you are connected to the network, you can access network resources, including the network's Internet connection. If you are connecting to the Internet without going through a computer network, your computer needs to use a modem to connect to the communications media, such as a telephone line, a cable connection, or a wireless signal, used by your ISP to deliver Internet content.

To request a Web page or other resource located on the Internet, its **Internet address**—a unique numeric or text-based address—is used. The most common types of Internet addresses are IP addresses and domain names (to identify computers), URLs (to identify Web pages), and email addresses (to identify people).

IP addresses and their corresponding **domain names** are used to identify computers available through the Internet. IP (short for Internet Protocol) addresses are numeric, such as 134.170.185.46, and are commonly used by computers to refer to other computers. A computer that hosts information available through the Internet, such as a Web server hosting Web pages, usually has a unique text-based domain

Web browser A program used to view Web pages.

Internet address A unique address that identifies a computer, person, or Web page on the Internet, such as an IP address, a domain name, a URL, or an email address.

IP address A numeric Internet address that uniquely identifies a computer on the Internet.

domain name A text-based Internet address that uniquely identifies a computer on the Internet.

Uniform Resource Locator (URL) An Internet address that uniquely identifies a Web page.

name, such as microsoft.com, that corresponds to that computer's IP address to make it easier for people to request Web pages located on that computer.

IP addresses and domain names are unique so no two computers on the Internet use the exact same IP address or domain name. To ensure this, specific IP addresses are allocated to each network, such as a company network or an ISP, to be used with the computers on that network. There is a worldwide registration system for domain name registration. When a domain name is registered, the IP address of the computer that will be hosting the Web site associated with that domain name is also registered. The Web site can be accessed using either its domain name or the corresponding IP address. When a Web site is requested by its domain name, the corresponding IP address is looked up using one of the Internet's domain name system (DNS) servers, and then the appropriate Web page is displayed.

Although most IP addresses (called IPv4) have four parts separated by periods, the newer IPv6 addresses have eight parts separated by colons. The transition from IPv4 to IPv6 is necessary because of the vast number of devices now connecting to the Internet.

Domain names typically reflect the name of the individual or organization associated with that Web site. The different parts of a domain name are separated by a period. The far right part of the domain name (which begins with the rightmost period) is called the top-level domain (TLD) and traditionally identifies the type of organization or its location, such as .com for businesses, .edu for educational institutions, .jp for Web sites located in Japan, or .fr for Web sites located in France. The part of the domain name that precedes the TLD is called the second-level domain name and typically reflects the name of a company or an organization, a product, or an individual. Only the legitimate holder of a trademarked name, such as Microsoft, can use that trademarked name as a domain name, such as microsoft.com. There were seven original TLDs used in the United States; additional TLDs and numerous two-letter country code TLDs have since been created and more are in the works. See Exhibit 1-13 for some examples.

Similar to the way an IP address or domain name uniquely identifies a computer on the Internet, a **Uniform Resource Locator (URL)** uniquely identifies a Web page by specifying the protocol—or standard—being used to display the Web page, the Web server hosting the Web page, the name of any folders on the Web server in which the Web page file is stored, and, finally, the Web page's file name, if needed.

EXHIBIT 1-13 SAMPLE TOP-LEVEL DOMAINS (TLDs)

Original TLDs	Intended use
.com	Commercial businesses
.edu	Educational institutions
.gov	Government organizations
.int	International treaty organizations
.mil	Military organizations
.net	Network providers and ISPs
.org	Noncommercial organizations
Newer TLDs	**Intended use**
.biz	Entrepreneurs and growing businesses
.fr	French businesses
.info	Information sites
.mobi	Sites optimized for mobile devices
.name	Individuals (personal branding)
.nyc	New York City businesses
.us	United States businesses

FYI

IPv6

IPv4 was never designed to be used with the vast number of devices that access the Internet today. Because the maximum number of IPv4 unique addresses—2^{32} or 4.3 billion—are expected to run out soon, a newer version of IP—IPv6—was developed. IPv6 allows for 2^{128} unique addresses—enough to provide a unique address to each and every device connected to the Internet now and in the foreseeable future. Although IPv4 and IPv6 will coexist for several years until IPv6 eventually replaces IPv4, the U.S. government has mandated that all federal agencies purchase only IPv6-compatible new hardware and software. Experts suggest that businesses determine what hardware and software changes will be needed to switch to IPv6 so that they are prepared.

EXHIBIT 1-14 URL FOR A WEB PAGE

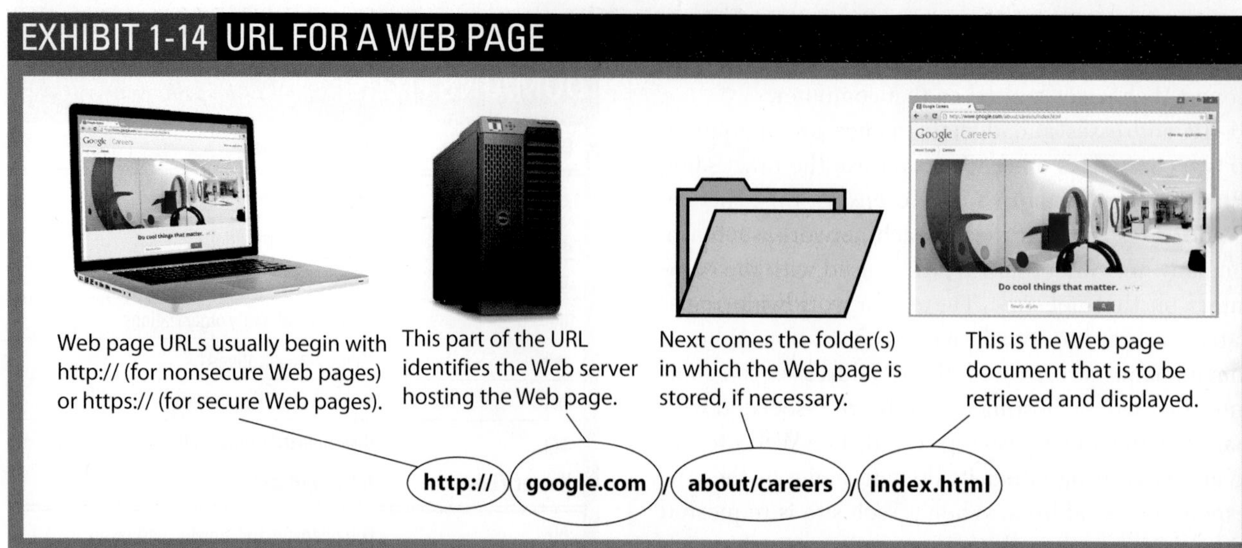
Web page URLs usually begin with http:// (for nonsecure Web pages) or https:// (for secure Web pages).
This part of the URL identifies the Web server hosting the Web page.
Next comes the folder(s) in which the Web page is stored, if necessary.
This is the Web page document that is to be retrieved and displayed.
http://
google.com
/
about/careers
/
index.html
Do cool things that matter.

The most common Web page protocols are Hypertext Transfer Protocol (http://) for regular Web pages or Hypertext Transfer Protocol Secure (https://) for secure Web pages that can be used to safely transmit sensitive information, such as credit card numbers. File Transfer Protocol (ftp://) is sometimes used to upload and download files. The file extension used in the Web page file name, such as .html or .htm for standard Web pages, indicates the type of Web page that will be displayed. For example, looking at the URL for the Web page shown in Exhibit 1-14 from right to left, you can see that the Web page called *index.html* is stored in a folder called *careers* inside another folder called *about* on the Web server associated with the *google.com* domain, and is a regular (nonsecure) Web page because the standard *http://* protocol is being used.

1-3c Using Email

An **email** message is a message sent between individuals over a network—usually the Internet. Email is one of the most widely used Internet applications—Americans alone send billions of email messages daily—and email sent via a mobile device is growing at an astounding rate. You can send an email message from any Internet-enabled device, such as a desktop computer, portable computer, or smartphone, to anyone who has an Internet email address.

To contact someone using the Internet, you most often use his or her **email address**. An email address consists of a **username** (a unique identifying name), followed by the @ symbol, followed by the domain name for the computer that will be handling that person's email

FYI

PRONOUNCING INTERNET ADDRESSES

Because Internet addresses are frequently given verbally, it is important to know how to pronounce them. Keep in mind the following tips when you say an Internet address:

- If a portion of the address forms a recognizable word or name, it is spoken; otherwise, it is spelled out.
- The @ sign is pronounced *at*.
- The period (.) is pronounced *dot*.
- The forward slash (/) is pronounced *slash*.

Type of address	Sample address	Pronunciation
Domain name	berkeley.edu	berkeley dot e d u
URL	irs.gov/freefile	irs dot gov slash free file
Email address	president@whitehouse.gov	president at white house dot gov

email Messages sent from one user to another over the Internet or other network.

email address An Internet address consisting of a username and domain name that uniquely identifies a person on the Internet.

username A name that uniquely identifies a user on a specific computer network.

EXHIBIT 1-15 GOOGLE WEB PAGE OPEN IN THE CHROME WEB BROWSER

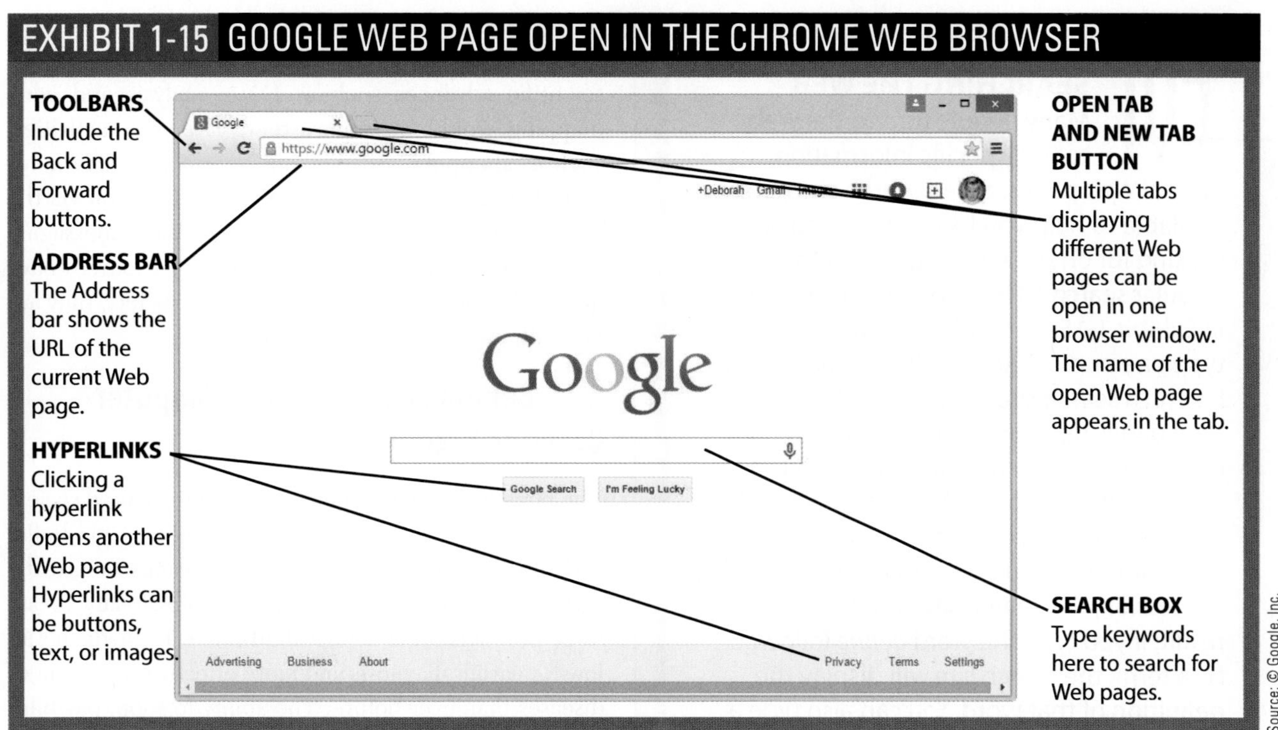
TOOLBARS
Include the Back and Forward buttons.
ADDRESS BAR
The Address bar shows the URL of the current Web page.
HYPERLINKS
Clicking a hyperlink opens another Web page. Hyperlinks can be buttons, text, or images.
OPEN TAB AND NEW TAB BUTTON
Multiple tabs displaying different Web pages can be open in one browser window. The name of the open Web page appears in the tab.
SEARCH BOX
Type keywords here to search for Web pages.
Google
https://www.google.com
+Deborah
Gmail
Google Search
I'm Feeling Lucky
Advertising
Business
About
Privacy
Terms
Settings

Source: © Google, Inc.

(called a mail server). For example, jsmith@cengage.com is the email address assigned to John Smith, a hypothetical employee at Cengage Learning, the publisher of this textbook.

1-3d Surfing the Web

Once you have an Internet connection, you are ready to begin **surfing the Web**—that is, using a Web browser to view Web pages. The first page that your Web browser displays when it is opened is your browser's starting page, or home page. From your browser's home page, you can move to other Web pages.

To navigate to a new Web page for which you know the URL, type that URL in the browser's Address bar, as shown in Exhibit 1-15, and then press the Enter key.

CAUTION CAUTION CAUTION
https://

SAFE SURFING
If you provide sensitive information, such as your Social Security number or credit card information, on a Web page, make sure that it is a secure Web page.

© seanbear/Shutterstock.com

After that page is displayed, you can use the hyperlinks on that page to display other Web pages or access other resources, such as to play a video or download a software program.

Most browsers include tabbed browsing so you can open multiple Web pages at the same time and the ability to type search terms into the Address bar. In addition, all Web browsers have a feature (usually called Favorites or Bookmarks that is accessed via a Favorites or Bookmarks menu, button, or bar) that you can use to save Web page URLs. Once a Web page is saved as a favorite or a bookmark, you can redisplay that page without typing its URL—you simply select its link from the Favorites or Bookmarks list. Web browsers also maintain a History list, which is a record of all Web pages visited during the period of time specified in the browser settings. You can revisit a Web page located on the History list by displaying the History list and selecting that page. If you use a browser in conjunction with an online account, such as Google, your bookmarks and history can be synced to your mobile device. If there is email associated with your account, such as Gmail for Google users, your contacts and email can be synced as well.

surf the Web To use a Web browser to view Web pages.

FYI SEARCHING THE WEB

Many people turn to the Web to find specific information. Special Web pages, called search sites, are available to help you locate what you are looking for on the Internet. One of the most popular search sites—Google—is shown in Exhibit 1-15. To conduct a search, you type one or more keywords into the search box on a search site, and a list of links to Web pages matching your search criteria is displayed. With some search sites, you can also use the search box to access a variety of tools, such as a calculator and dictionary. For example, if you type a mathematical expression, the search site will display the result; if you type the word *define* followed by a term, the search site will display the definition of that word. You can also type a tracking number to track a package or type a flight number to see the current status of that flight.

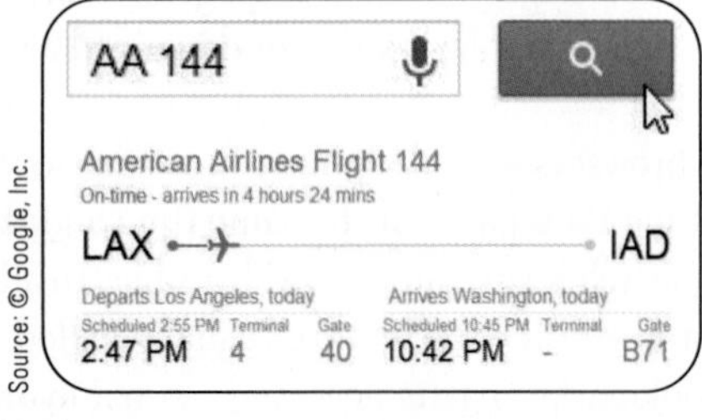

Source: © Google, Inc.

1-4 COMPUTERS AND SOCIETY

The vast improvements in technology over the past decade have had a distinct impact on daily life. Computers have become indispensable tools at home, at work, and while on the go. Related technological advancements have changed the way everyday items—cars, microwaves, coffee pots, toys, exercise bikes, telephones, televisions, and more—look and function. As computers and everyday devices become smarter, they work faster, better, and more reliably than ever before as well as take on additional capabilities. Computerization and technological advances have also changed society as a whole. Without computers, banks would be overwhelmed by the job of tracking all the transactions they process, moon exploration and the International Space Station would still belong to science fiction, and scientific advances such as DNA analysis and gene mapping would be nonexistent. Everyday activities, such as shopping and banking, are increasingly automated, and fast and easy access to information via the Internet and communication via email and messaging is expected. While the Internet and its resources have quickly become an integral part of our society, they are not without risks.

1-4a Benefits and Risks of a Computer-Oriented Society

The benefits of having such a computer-oriented society are numerous. The capability to virtually design, build, and test new buildings, cars, and airplanes before the actual construction begins helps professionals create safer products. Technological advances in medicine allow for earlier diagnosis and more effective treatment of diseases than ever before. The ability to shop, pay bills, research products, participate in online classes, and look up vast amounts of information 24 hours a day, 7 days a week, 365 days a year via the Internet is a huge convenience. In addition, a computer-oriented society generates new opportunities. For example, technologies, such as speech recognition software and Braille input and output devices, enable physically or visually challenged individuals to perform necessary job tasks and to communicate with others more easily.

Technology has also made a huge number of tasks in our lives go much faster. Instead of experiencing a long delay for a credit check, an applicant can get approved for a purchase, loan, or credit card almost immediately. Documents and photographs can be emailed in moments, instead of taking at least a day to be mailed physically. Viewers can watch favorite TV shows online and access up-to-the-minute news at their convenience. And we can download information, programs, music, files, movies, and more on demand when we want or need them, instead of having to order them and then wait for delivery or go to a physical store to purchase the items.

Although there are a great number of benefits from having a computer-oriented society, there are risks as well. A variety of problems have emerged from our extensive computer use, ranging from stress and health concerns, to the proliferation of unsolicited emails and harmful programs that can be installed on our computers without our knowledge, to security and privacy issues, to legal and ethical dilemmas. Many security and privacy concerns stem from the fact that so much personal

TRENDING...

ETHICAL USE OF DIGITAL MUSIC AND MOVIES

As digital music and movies have become widely available over the Internet, legal and ethical issues about their use have emerged. For example, is it legal and ethical to copy digital movies or music to other devices or share them with others? Similar to their offline counterparts, online digital content is protected by copyright law, and sharing or downloading unauthorized music or movies is both illegal and unethical. However, some use is generally viewed as fair use, such as transferring a legally obtained music file to more than one device as long as it is for personal, noncommercial use and does not violate a user agreement. And many purchased movie discs support digital copies—the purchaser either uploads the movie to a specified online service to stream to their personal devices as needed or copies the movie to a single personal device. Also, many online services, such as Netflix shown in the accompanying illustration, can be used to easily and legally download or stream movies, TV shows, and other digital content to your devices as needed.

Source: © Netflix

A tool that can be used to control how a digital work can be used is **digital rights management (DRM) software**. For instance, DRM software can control if a work may be copied, viewed, or printed. DRM controls are also used to make a movie or ebook rental unviewable after the rental period expires.

business takes place online—or at least the personal data ends up as data in a computer database somewhere—and the potential for misuse of this data is enormous.

CAUTION CAUTION CAUTION

PROTECT YOUR COMPUTER

To help protect your computer, never open an email attachment from someone you do not know or that has an executable file extension (the last three letters in the file name preceded by a period), such as .exe, .com, or .vbs, without first checking with the sender if you aren't sure the attachment is legitimate. You should never click a link in an email message. You should also be careful about what files you download from the Internet. In addition, it is crucial to install security software on your computer and to set up the program to monitor your computer on a continual basis and detect or block any harmful programs.

Another concern is the repercussions of collecting such vast amounts of information electronically. Some people worry about creating a "Big Brother" situation, in which the government or another organization is watching everything that we do. And some Internet behavior, such as downloading music or movies from an unauthorized source, can get you arrested or fired.

Some people view the potential risk to personal privacy as one of the most important societal issues. As more and more data about our everyday activities is collected and stored on computers accessible via the Internet, our privacy is at risk because the potential for privacy violations increases. Today, data is collected about practically anything we buy online or offline, although offline purchases may not be associated with our identity unless we use a credit card or a membership or loyalty card. The issue is not that data is collected—with virtually all organizations using computers for recordkeeping, that is unavoidable—but how the collected data is used and how secure it is. Other issues related to computer use include the ethical use of intellectual property, health implications, and the impact of technology on the environment. These topics are discussed next.

digital rights management (DRM) software
Software used to control how a digital work can be used.

1-4b Understanding Intellectual Property Rights

All computer users should be aware of **intellectual property rights**, which are the legal rights to which the creators of intellectual property—original creative works—are entitled. Examples of intellectual property include music and movies; paintings, computer graphics, and other works of art; poetry, books, and other types of written works; symbols, names, and designs used in conjunction with a business; architectural drawings; and inventions. The three main types of intellectual property rights are copyrights, trademarks, and patents.

A **copyright** is a form of protection available to the creator of an original artistic, musical, or literary work, such as a book, movie, software program, song, or painting. It gives the copyright holder the exclusive right to publish, reproduce, distribute, perform, or display the work. Immediately after creating a work in some type of material form, the creator automatically owns the copyright of that work. Copyrights apply to both published and unpublished works and remain in effect until 70 years after the creator's death. Copyrights for works registered by an organization or as anonymous works last 95 years from the date of publication or 120 years from the date of creation, whichever is shorter. Although works created in the United States after March 1, 1989, are not required to display a copyright notice to retain their copyright protection, displaying a copyright statement on a published work, such as the ones shown in Exhibit 1-16, reminds others that the work is protected by copyright law and that any use must comply with copyright law.

Anyone wishing to use copyrighted materials must first obtain permission from the copyright holder and pay any required fee. One exception is the legal concept of **fair use**, which permits limited duplication and use of a portion of copyrighted material for specific purposes, such as criticism, commentary, news reporting, teaching, and research. For example, a teacher may legally read a copyrighted poem for discussion in a poetry class, and a news crew may videotape a small portion of a song at a concert to include in a news report of that concert.

EXHIBIT 1-16 COPYRIGHT STATEMENTS

© 2015, 2013 Cengage Learning
ALL RIGHTS RESERVED. No part of this work covered by the copyright herein may be reproduced, transmitted, stored, or used in any form or by any means graphic, electronic, or mechanical, including but not limited to photocopying, recording, scanning, digitizing, taping, Web distribution, information networks, or information storage and retrieval systems, except as permitted under Section 107 or 108 of the 1976 United States Copyright Act, without the prior written permission of the publisher.

BOOK COPYRIGHT NOTICES

©2015 San Diego Zoo Global

WEB SITE COPYRIGHT NOTICES

Source: © Cengage Learning; San Diego Zoo Global

A **trademark** is a word, phrase, symbol, or design (or a combination of words, phrases, symbols, or designs) that identifies one product or service. A trademark used to identify a service is also called a service mark. Trademarks that are claimed but not registered with the U.S. Patent and Trademark Office (USPTO) can use the mark™; nonregistered service marks can use the symbol℠. The symbol ® is reserved for registered trademarks. Trademarked words and phrases—such as iPhone ®, Chicken McNuggets ®, Google Earth™, and FedEx 1Day℠—are widely used today. Trademarked logos are also common.

i'm lovin' it
ebay
skype
SONIC America's Drive-In.

Source: © McDonald's Corporation; imageBROKER/Alamy; Microsoft; SONIC

A **patent** protects inventions by granting exclusive rights of an invention to its inventor for a period of 20 years. Patents typically protect a unique product, but they can also protect a process or procedure.

1-4c Computer and Business Ethics

The term **ethics** refers to standards of moral conduct. For example, telling the truth is a matter of ethics. An unethical act is not always illegal, but an illegal act is

intellectual property rights The legal rights to which creators of original creative works are entitled.

copyright The legal right to sell, publish, or distribute an original artistic or literary work; it is held by the creator of a work as soon as it exists in physical form.

fair use The legal concept that permits limited duplication and use of a portion of copyrighted material for specific allowable purposes.

trademark A word, phrase, symbol, or design that identifies a good or service.

patent A form of protection for an invention.

ethics Overall standards of moral conduct.

usually viewed as unethical by most people. For example, purposely lying to a friend is unethical but usually not illegal, whereas perjuring oneself in a courtroom as a witness is both illegal and unethical.

Ethical beliefs can vary widely from one individual to another. Ethical beliefs can also vary based on religion, country, race, or culture. In addition, different ethical standards can apply to different areas of one's life. **Computer ethics** are ethics related to an individual's computer use. Computer ethics are significant because the proliferation of computers and mobile devices in the home and workplace provides many opportunities for unethical acts. The Internet also makes it easy to distribute harmful content to others as well as to distribute copies of software, movies, music, and other digital content in an illegal and unethical manner.

Whether at home, at work, or at school, ethical issues crop up every day. For example, you may need to decide whether to accept a relative's offer of a free copy of a downloaded song or movie, whether to have a friend help you take an online exam, whether to upload a photo of your friend to Facebook without asking permission, or whether to post a rumor on a campus gossip site.

Employees may need to decide whether to print their birthday party invitations on the office color printer, whether to correct their boss for giving them credit for another employee's idea, or whether to sneak a look at information that they can access but have no legitimate reason to view. IT employees, in particular, often face this latter ethical dilemma because they typically have both access and the technical ability to retrieve a wide variety of personal and professional information about other employees, such as their salary information, Web surfing history, and email.

Businesses also deal with a variety of ethical issues in the course of normal business activities—from determining how many computers a particular software program should be installed on; to identifying how customer and employee information should be obtained, used, and shared; to deciding business practices. **Business ethics** are the standards of conduct that guide a business's policies, decisions, and actions.

Both businesses and individuals should be very careful when copying, sharing, or otherwise using copyrighted material to ensure that the material is used in both a legal and an ethical manner. Students, researchers, authors, and other writers need to be especially careful when using literary material as a resource for papers, articles, books, and so forth, to ensure that the material is used appropriately and is properly credited to the original author. To present someone else's work as your own is **plagiarism**, which is a violation of copyright law and an unethical act. It can also get you fired, as some reporters have found out after faking quotes or plagiarizing content from other newspapers. Examples of acts that would normally be considered plagiarism or not considered plagiarism are shown in Exhibit 1-17.

With the widespread availability of online articles and fee-based online term paper services, some students might be tempted to create their papers by copying and pasting

EXHIBIT 1-17 EXAMPLES OF WHAT IS AND WHAT IS NOT PLAGIARISM

Plagiarism	Not plagiarism
A student including a few sentences or a few paragraphs written by another author in his essay without crediting the original author.	A student including a few sentences or a few paragraphs written by another author in his essay, either indenting the quotation or placing it inside quotation marks, and crediting the original author with a citation in the text or with a footnote or endnote.
A newspaper reporter changing a few words in a sentence or paragraph written by another author and including the revised text in an article without crediting the original author.	A newspaper reporter paraphrasing a few sentences or paragraphs written by another author without changing the meaning of the text, including the revised text in an article, and crediting the original author with a proper citiation.
A student copying and pasting information from various online documents to create her research paper without crediting the original authors.	A student copying and pasting information from various online documents and using those quotes in her research paper either indented or enclosed in quotation marks with the proper citations for each author.
A teacher sharing a poem with a class, leading the class to believe the poem was his original work.	A teacher sharing a poem with a class, clearly identifying the poet.

computer ethics Standards of moral conduct as they relate to computer use.

business ethics Standards of moral conduct that guide a business's policies, decisions, and actions.

plagiarism Presenting someone else's work as your own.

excerpts of online content into their documents to pass off as their original work. But these students should realize that this is plagiarism, and instructors can usually tell when a paper is created in this manner. There are also online resources that instructors can use to test the originality of student papers. Most colleges and universities have strict consequences for plagiarism, such as automatically failing the assignment or course or being expelled from the institution. As Internet-based plagiarism continues to expand to younger and younger students, many middle schools and high schools are developing strict plagiarism policies as well.

1-4d Computers and Health

Despite their many benefits, computers can pose a threat to a user's physical and mental well-being. Common physical conditions caused by computer use include eyestrain, blurred vision, fatigue, headaches, backaches, and wrist and finger pain. Some conditions are classified as **repetitive stress injuries (RSIs)**, in which hand, wrist, shoulder, or neck pain is caused by performing the same physical movements over and over again. For instance, extensive keyboard and mouse use has been associated with RSIs, although RSIs can be caused by non-computer-related activities as well. One RSI related to the repetitive movements made when using a keyboard is **carpal tunnel syndrome (CTS)**—a painful and crippling condition affecting the hands and wrists. CTS occurs when the nerve in the carpal tunnel located on the underside of the wrist is compressed. An RSI associated with typing on the tiny keyboards commonly found on smartphones and other mobile devices is **De Quervain's tendonitis**—a painful condition affecting the tendons on the thumb side of the wrists. Computer vision syndrome (CVS) is a collection of eye and vision problems, including eyestrain or eye fatigue, dry eyes, burning eyes, light sensitivity, and blurred vision. Extensive computer use can also lead to headaches and pain in the shoulders, neck, arms, or back.

Some recent physical health concerns center on the heat from devices commonly held in the hands or lap. For instance, studies have indicated that the temperature on the underside of a notebook computer can exceed 139° Fahrenheit and an iPad can reach 116° Fahrenheit. Laptop desks or notebook cooling stands can help protect your lap when it must be used as your work surface. Noise-induced hearing loss from extensive use of earbud headsets connected to mobile devices is another growing concern. One of the newest dangers is using a mobile device to text or talk while driving. One possible solution is using a service or app to disable the driver's phone while the car is in motion (see Exhibit 1-18).

EXHIBIT 1-18 A SAFE DRIVING APP

Source: © CellControl™

Emotional health is another concern. While many individuals view the ability to always be available as a benefit, it can be a source of stress to employees who feel they are always "on the job." In addition, computer use can lead to **Internet addiction**—the problem of overusing, or being unable to stop using, the Internet. Teenagers, in particular, tend to take their devices to bed with them, raising concerns about addiction, sleep deprivation, and the associated consequences.

repetitive stress injury (RSI) A type of injury, such as carpal tunnel syndrome, that is caused by performing the same physical movements over and over again.

carpal tunnel syndrome (CTS) A painful and crippling condition affecting the hands and wrists that can be caused by computer use.

De Quervain's tendonitis A painful condition affecting the tendons on the thumb side of the wrist that can be caused by mobile device keyboard use.

Internet addiction The problem of overusing, or being unable to stop using, the Internet.

ergonomics The science of fitting a work environment to the people who work there.

TRENDING...

ERGONOMICS & WORKSPACE DESIGN

Ergonomics is the science of fitting a work environment to the people who work there. With respect to computer use, it involves designing a safe and effective workspace, which includes properly adjusting furniture and hardware and using ergonomic hardware when needed. A proper work environment (see the illustration)—used in conjunction with good user habits and procedures—can prevent many physical problems caused by computer use. Proper placement and adjustment of furniture is a good place to start when evaluating a workspace.

The desk should be placed where the sun and other sources of light cannot shine directly onto the screen or into the user's eyes. The monitor should be placed directly in front of the user about an arm's length away, and the top of the screen should be no more than 3 inches above the user's eyes once the user's chair is adjusted. The desk chair should be adjusted so that the keyboard is at, or slightly below, the height at which the user's forearms are horizontal to the floor (special ergonomic chairs are also available). A footrest should be used, if needed, to keep the user's feet flat on the floor. The monitor settings should be adjusted to make the screen brightness match the brightness of the room and to have a high amount of contrast; the screen should also be periodically wiped clean of dust. An emerging ergonomic trend is sit/stand desks that allow the user to work while sitting or standing.

Portable computer users should work at a desk, use a separate keyboard and mouse, and either connect their computer to a secondary monitor or use a notebook stand to elevate the display screen of a notebook computer to the proper height. Docking stations can also be used to easily connect and disconnect peripheral devices, such as a keyboard and monitor. The devices remain connected to the docking station and are available to the user whenever the computer is connected to the docking station.

In addition to workspace devices, a variety of ergonomic hardware can be used to help users avoid or alleviate physical problems associated with computer use. These include:

- Ergonomic keyboards designed to lessen the strain on the hands and wrist.
- Trackballs or ergonomic mice that can be more comfortable to use than a conventional mouse.
- Document holders that allow the user to see both the document and the monitor.
- Tablet arms that connect to a desk or monitor to hold a tablet device at the proper height for comfortable viewing.
- Keyboard drawers that lower the keyboard and enable the user to keep his or her forearms parallel to the floor.
- Computer gloves that are designed to prevent and relieve RSIs by supporting the wrist and thumb while allowing the full use of hands.

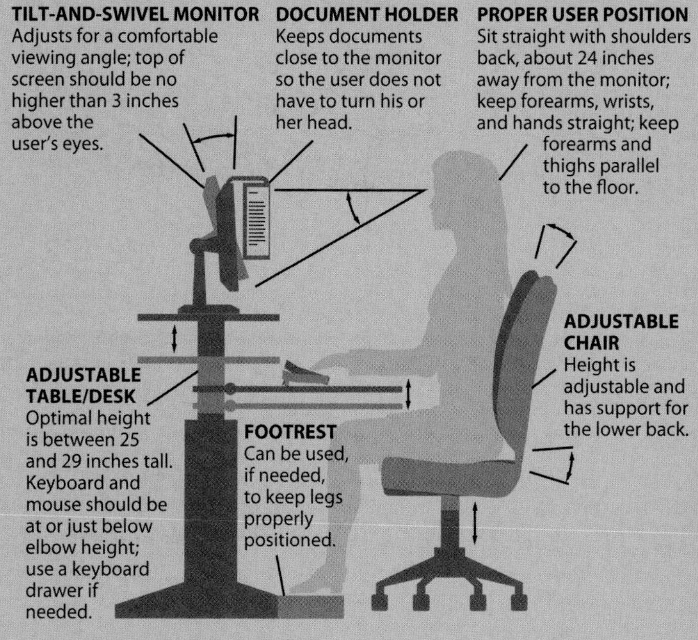

TILT-AND-SWIVEL MONITOR
Adjusts for a comfortable viewing angle; top of screen should be no higher than 3 inches above the user's eyes.
DOCUMENT HOLDER
Keeps documents close to the monitor so the user does not have to turn his or her head.
PROPER USER POSITION
Sit straight with shoulders back, about 24 inches away from the monitor; keep forearms, wrists, and hands straight; keep forearms and thighs parallel to the floor.
ADJUSTABLE CHAIR
Height is adjustable and has support for the lower back.
ADJUSTABLE TABLE/DESK
Optimal height is between 25 and 29 inches tall. Keyboard and mouse should be at or just below elbow height; use a keyboard drawer if needed.
FOOTREST
Can be used, if needed, to keep legs properly positioned.

In addition, computer users should take frequent breaks from typing, alternate computer work with other work, use good posture, stretch from time to time, and periodically refocus their eyes on a distant object for a minute or so. Mobile device users should also limit the duration of use of the device, reduce keystrokes by using text shortcuts and voice input, avoid looking down at the device excessively, and switch hands periodically.

1-4e Environmental Concerns

The increasing use of computers in our society has created a variety of environmental concerns. The term **green computing** refers to the use of computers in an environmentally friendly manner. Minimizing the use of natural resources, such as energy and paper, is one aspect of green computing. In 1992, the U.S. Environmental Protection Agency (EPA) introduced ENERGY STAR as a voluntary labeling program designed to identify and promote energy-efficient products in an effort to reduce greenhouse gas emissions. An ENERGY STAR-qualified computer will use between 30% and 75% less energy, depending on how it is used. Today, the ENERGY STAR label appears on computers, office equipment, residential heating and cooling equipment, major appliances, lighting, home electronics, and more. **Eco-labels**—environmental performance certifications—are used in other countries as well.

Source: © U.S. Environmental Protection Agency, ENERGY STAR program; European Commission

The high cost of electricity has made power consumption and heat generation by computers key concerns for businesses and individuals. Although computers have become more energy efficient, they can still draw quite a bit of power when they are not being used. For example, servers use 60% of their maximum power while idle. In addition, computers, home electronics, and home appliances often draw power even when they are turned off. Consolidating servers can help businesses reduce energy cost; turning off devices and unplugging mobile device chargers when they are not being used can help individuals save power.

In addition to more energy-efficient hardware, alternate power sources are being developed for greener computing. For instance, solar power is a growing alternative for powering electronic devices, including computers and mobile devices. With solar power, solar panels convert sunlight into electricity, which is then stored in an external battery or directly in the battery of a connected device. Solar charging capabilities are being built into a variety of mobile accessories, such as computer and tablet cases and backpacks (see Exhibit 1-19).

EXHIBIT 1-19 SOLAR POWER BACKPACK

Source: Voltaic Systems, Inc.

Another environmental concern is the amount of trash—and sometimes toxic trash—generated by computer use. One concern is paper waste. Despite the increase in the use of electronic communications and digital media, it now appears that the so-called paperless office that many visionaries predicted would arrive is largely a myth. Instead, research indicates that global paper use is still increasing, and at least 40% of all wood harvested in the world today ends up as paper. North Americans alone consume more than 500 pounds of paper per person per year. In addition to paper-based waste, computing refuse **(e-waste)** includes electronic trash such as used toner cartridges, obsolete or broken hardware, and discarded CDs, DVDs, and other storage media.

Compounding the problem of the amount of e-waste generated is that computers, mobile phones, and related hardware contain a variety of toxic and hazardous materials. For instance, a desktop computer may contain up to 700 different chemical elements and compounds, many of which (such as arsenic, lead, mercury, and cadmium) are hazardous and expensive to dispose of properly.

A global concern regarding e-waste is where it all eventually ends up. Much of it ends up in municipal

green computing The use of computers in an environmentally friendly manner.

eco-label An environmental performance certification, usually issued by a government agency, that identifies a device as meeting minimal environmental performance specifications.

e-waste Electronic trash, such as discarded computer components.

TRENDING...

PORTABLE POWER

Tired of your smartphone, laptop, or fitness band running out of power at inopportune times? Portable power devices are now available to let you bring additional power with you. The amount of power supplied by these devices varies depending on the device being used, from a single phone charge or one-quarter of a tablet charge, as in the device shown in the accompanying illustration, to six phone charges or more. Nearly all portable power devices charge via a USB power source, such as with a wall plug or a laptop, and some also include a solar panel.

Source: © PNY

landfills that are not designed for toxic waste. Even worse, the majority of all computer equipment sent to recyclers in developed countries (at least 80%, according to most estimates) ends up being exported to developing countries, such as China, India, and Nigeria, with more lax environmental standards, legislation, or enforcement than in the United States. Much of the e-waste exported to these countries is simply dumped into fields or processed with primitive and dangerous technologies that release toxins into the air and water. Unaware of the potential danger of these components, rural villagers are often employed to try to repair equipment or to reclaim metals or plastic (see Exhibit 1-20). Hardware that cannot be repaired or reclaimed is often burned or treated with acid baths to try to recover precious metals, but such processes release very dangerous pollutants.

Recycling computer equipment is difficult because of toxic materials and poor product design; however, proper recycling is essential to avoid pollution and health hazards. Some recycling centers will accept computer equipment, but many charge a fee for this service. Many computer manufacturers have voluntary take-back programs that will accept obsolete or broken computer equipment from consumers at a minimal cost. Expired toner cartridges and ink cartridges can sometimes be returned to the manufacturer or exchanged when ordering new cartridges; the cartridges are then refilled and resold. Cartridges that cannot be refilled can be sent to a recycling facility. In addition to helping to reduce e-waste in landfills, using refilled or recycled printer cartridges saves the consumer money because they are less expensive than new cartridges. Other computer components—such as CDs, DVDs, USB flash drives, and hard drives—can also be recycled through some organizations, such as GreenDisk, that reuse salvageable items and recycle the rest.

EXHIBIT 1-20 E-WASTE

© Courtesy Basel Action Network

In lieu of recycling, older equipment that is still functioning can be used for alternate purposes, such as for a child's computer, a personal Web server, or a DVR. Or it can be donated to schools and nonprofit groups. Some organizations accept and repair donated equipment and then distribute it to disadvantaged groups or other individuals in need of the hardware. However, be sure to completely remove any data stored on computer equipment before you dispose of, recycle, or donate it so that someone else cannot recover your information from that device.

STUDY TOOLS 1

READY TO STUDY? IN THE BOOK, YOU CAN:

- ☐ Rip out the Chapter Review Card, which includes key chapter concepts and important key terms.

ONLINE AT WWW.CENGAGEBRAIN.COM, YOU CAN:

- ☐ Review key concepts from the chapter in a short video.
- ☐ Explore computer networks with the interactive infographic.
- ☐ Practice what you've learned with more Practice It and On Your Own exercises.
- ☐ Prepare for tests with quizzes.
- ☐ Review the key terms with flashcards.

QUIZ YOURSELF

1. Define the term *computer*.
2. What are the four primary operations of a computer?
3. What is the difference between data and information?
4. Is a Web browser hardware and software? Explain why.
5. What does a programmer do?
6. What is a smart TV?
7. What is a smartphone?
8. Is a notebook computer a personal computer? Explain why or why not.
9. What is the difference between a mainframe computer and a supercomputer?
10. List three things a home network might be used for.
11. What is the largest and most well-known computer network in the world?
12. Explain the difference between the Internet and the World Wide Web.
13. List the most common types of Internet addresses, and explain what they identify.
14. In the email address jsmith@cengage.com, what is jsmith and what is cengage.com?
15. What types of works do copyrights protect?
16. Are unethical acts always illegal? Explain why or why not.
17. Why are repetitive stress injuries associated with computer use?
18. List three examples of e-waste related to computer usage.

PRACTICE IT

Practice It 1-1

A computer along with the Internet and World Wide Web are handy tools that you can use to research topics covered in this book, complete projects, and perform the online activities available at the book's Web site that are designed to enhance your learning and understanding of the content. Use an Internet-enabled computer to access CMPTR³ Online located at www.cengagebrain.com.

1. What types of information and activities are available on CMPTR³ Online?
2. Click the Chapter 1 image tile to access the tiles for the Chapter 1 Highlight boxes. View at least two of these Highlight boxes to explore more about this chapter. After viewing the content, click the link in the Highlight box to enter the eBook and explore other activities and videos within the narrative.
3. Evaluate the usefulness of the available resources in enhancing your learning experience.
4. Evaluate your overall experience using CMPTR³ Online.
5. Prepare a one-page summary of your experience and that answers these questions, and then submit it to your instructor.

Practice It 1-2

A great deal of obsolete computing equipment eventually ends up in a landfill, even though there may be alternative actions that could be taken instead.

1. Research what options are available to discard the following:
   a. a 5-year-old computer that is no longer functioning
   b. an older smart phone that still works but doesn't have as many features as today's smartphones
   c. a used-up toner cartridge for a laser printer
2. By making phone calls or researching online, determine if there are any schools and charitable organizations that would accept any of these items.
3. By making phone calls or researching online, research one computer manufacturer and one recycling company to see if they would accept the items. If so, what would the procedure and cost be?
4. By making phone calls or researching online, research one ink supply company or one office supply store to see if they accept used toner cartridges for credit toward new ones.
5. Prepare a one-page summary that answers these questions and then submit it to your instructor.

ON YOUR OWN

Portable power devices are handy when your smartphone's battery is running low and you are not near an electrical outlet.

1. Research portable power devices to determine the types of products available and what purposes they are designed for. Select one type that appeals to you to research more thoroughly.
2. Find three possible products for the type of portable power device you are researching. Either online or in person, determine the main features of each product, what devices each product is compatible with, how much power they provide, how they connect to devices, retail price, and other specifications.
3. Summarize your findings into a table to compare the main features of each product and the differences between them. Select the product you like the best and locate two places where you could purchase that device. Include the total cost (product plus tax and shipping, if applicable) and a statement explaining whether or not you would recommend buying this product in your summary and then submit it to your instructor.

Part 1
CONCEPTS

2 | Computer Hardware

© JGI/Tom Grill/Blend/Corbis

LEARNING OBJECTIVES

After studying the material in this chapter, you will be able to…

- 2-1 Understand how data is represented to a computer
- 2-2 Identify the hardware located inside the system unit
- 2-3 Explain how the CPU works
- 2-4 Describe different types of storage systems
- 2-5 Identify and describe common input devices
- 2-6 Identify and describe common output devices

After finishing this chapter, go to **PAGE 69** for **STUDY TOOLS**.

2-1 DIGITAL DATA REPRESENTATION

Virtually all computers today are digital computers which can understand only two states, represented by the digits 0 and 1 and usually thought of as off and on. Consequently, all data processed by a computer must be in **binary** form, which can only use two states, such as 0 and 1. Consequently, when you enter data into a computer, the computer translates the natural-language symbols you input into binary 0s and 1s, processes that data, and then translates and outputs the results in a form that you can understand. The 0s and 1s used to represent data can be represented in a variety of ways, such as with an open or closed circuit, the absence or presence of electronic current, two different types of magnetic alignment on a storage medium, and so on, as shown in Exhibit 2-1.

EXHIBIT 2-1 EXAMPLES OF WAYS OF REPRESENTING 0 AND 1

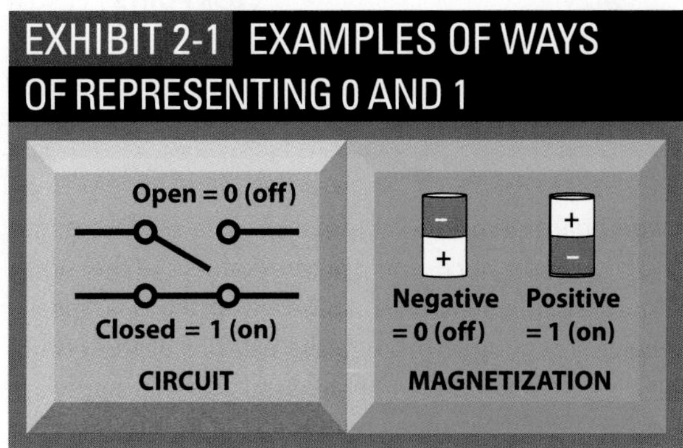

Regardless of their physical representations, these 0s and 1s are commonly referred to as bits, a computing term derived from the phrase *binary digits*. A **bit** is the smallest unit of data that a computer can recognize. The input you enter via a keyboard, the software program you use to play your music collection, the term paper stored on your USB flash drive, and the digital photos located on your smartphone are all just groups of bits. A bit by itself typically represents only a fraction of a piece of data. Eight bits grouped together are collectively referred to as a **byte**. A named collection of bytes that represent something, such as a written document, a computer program, a digital photo, or a song, and is stored on a computer or other piece of hardware is called a **file**. Because the number of bytes in a file can be in the thousands or millions of bytes, prefixes are commonly used with the term *byte* to represent larger amounts of data.

FYI A BIT ABOUT BYTES

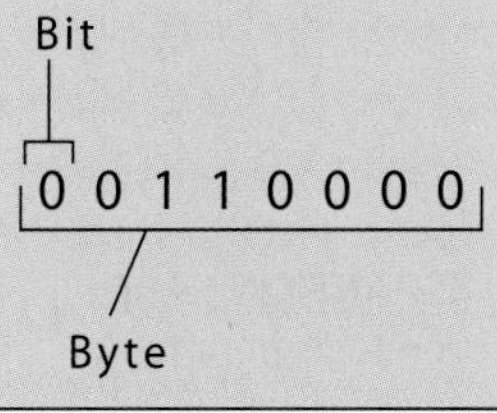

- 1 kilobyte (KB) is about 1,000 bytes.
- 1 megabyte (MB) is about 1 million bytes.
- 1 gigabyte (GB) is about 1 billion bytes.
- 1 terabyte (TB) is about 1 trillion bytes.
- 1 petabyte (PB) is about 1,000 terabytes.
- 1 exabyte (EB) is about 1,000 petabytes.
- 1 zettabyte (ZB) is about 1,000 exabytes.
- 1 yottabyte (YB) is about 1,000 zettabytes.

2-2 INSIDE THE SYSTEM UNIT

There is a variety of hardware used with a computer. Some hardware is external. Other hardware is located inside the **system unit**—the main case of a computer or mobile device. The system unit houses the processing hardware for that device, as well as a few other components, such as storage devices, the power supply, and cooling fans. The system unit for a desktop computer is typically a rectangular box, as in Exhibit 2-2. System units for portable computers and mobile devices are smaller and combined with the device's display screen. Their components, which are similar to a desktop computer, are just smaller.

binary Having only two states, such as representing data with only 0s and 1s.

bit The smallest unit of data that a computer can recognize.

byte Eight bits grouped together.

file A named collection of bytes that is stored on computer hardware.

system unit The main case of a computer or mobile device.

EXHIBIT 2-2 INSIDE A DESKTOP SYSTEM UNIT

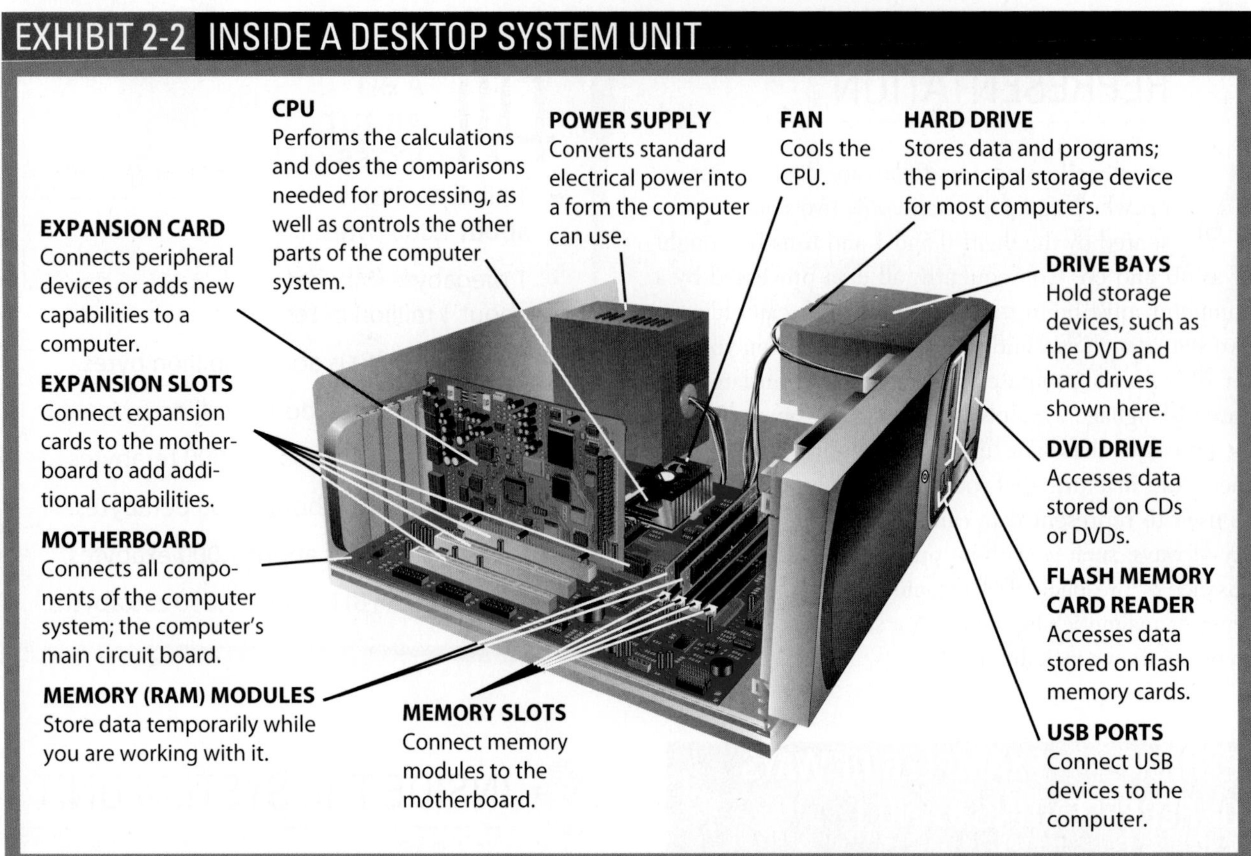
CPU
Performs the calculations and does the comparisons needed for processing, as well as controls the other parts of the computer system.
POWER SUPPLY
Converts standard electrical power into a form the computer can use.
FAN
Cools the CPU.
HARD DRIVE
Stores data and programs; the principal storage device for most computers.
EXPANSION CARD
Connects peripheral devices or adds new capabilities to a computer.
EXPANSION SLOTS
Connect expansion cards to the motherboard to add additional capabilities.
MOTHERBOARD
Connects all components of the computer system; the computer's main circuit board.
MEMORY (RAM) MODULES
Store data temporarily while you are working with it.
MEMORY SLOTS
Connect memory modules to the motherboard.
DRIVE BAYS
Hold storage devices, such as the DVD and hard drives shown here.
DVD DRIVE
Accesses data stored on CDs or DVDs.
FLASH MEMORY CARD READER
Accesses data stored on flash memory cards.
USB PORTS
Connect USB devices to the computer.

2-2a The Motherboard

A **circuit board** is a thin board containing computer chips and other electronic components. **Computer chips** (also called **integrated circuits**) are very small pieces of silicon or other semiconducting material that contain interconnected components that enable electrical current to perform particular functions. The main circuit board inside the system unit is called the **motherboard**.

All devices used with a computer need to be connected via a wired or wireless connection to the motherboard. Typically, external devices such as monitors, keyboards, mice, and printers connect to the motherboard by plugging into a port. A **port** is a special connector accessible through the exterior of the system unit case that is used to connect an external hardware device. The port is either built into the motherboard or created with an expansion card inserted into an expansion slot on the motherboard. Wireless external devices either use a transceiver that plugs into a port on the computer to transmit data between the wireless device and the motherboard, or they use wireless networking technology, such as Bluetooth or Wi-Fi, that is integrated into the system unit.

circuit board A thin board containing computer chips and other electronic components.

computer chip (integrated circuit) A very small piece of silicon or other semiconducting material that contains interconnected electronic components.

motherboard The main circuit board inside the system unit.

port A connector on the exterior of the system unit case that is used to connect an external hardware device.

processor A computer chip that performs processing functions.

2-2b The Power Supply

The power supply inside a computer delivers electricity to the computer via a power cord. Portable computers and mobile devices contain rechargeable battery packs that can be charged via a power outlet; some devices can be charged via a computer as well.

2-2c The CPU

Computers and mobile devices today contain one or more **processors** to perform processing functions. The

TRENDING...

WIRELESS POWER

After many years of development, wireless charging is here. With wireless charging, you simply place your device on a charging surface to have it automatically start charging. Mobile devices are beginning to be shipped with built-in wireless charging capabilities, and several new CPUs support wireless power to enable portable computers using those CPUs to be charged wirelessly. Stand-alone wireless chargers are available, and wireless charging capability is being built into locations where people normally place their devices during the day, such as in cars, on IKEA furniture, and on customer tables at McDonald's and Starbucks, as shown in the accompanying illustration. In the future, wireless charging could even be built into the walls of buildings to automatically power all the devices located inside them.

Source: © Powermat Technologies Ltd.

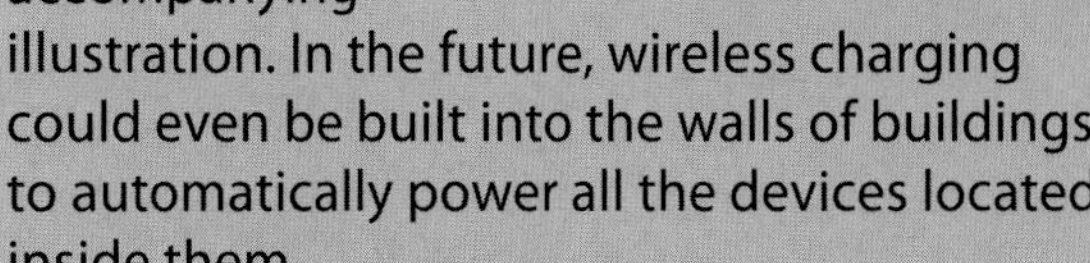

One limitation at the moment is the existence of two wireless charging standards, PMA and WPC Qi, though it is expected that one standard will eventually prevail. While the two standards are incompatible, some products, such as Samsung phones, support both standards so consumers can use wireless chargers based on either technology.

main processor is the **central processing unit (CPU)**, which performs most of the processing and controls the computer's operations. CPUs are usually designed for a specific type of computer, such as for desktop computers, servers, portable computers, or mobile devices. Most desktop computers and servers today use Intel or Advanced Micro Devices (AMD) CPUs. Portable computers and mobile devices often use an Intel or AMD mobile CPU or a mobile CPU manufactured by another company, such as ARM. Two common CPUs are shown in Exhibit 2-3.

EXHIBIT 2-3 CPUs

Source: © Intel Corporation; © ARM

Most CPUs today are **multi-core CPUs**, which are CPUs that contain the processing components or cores of multiple independent processors in a single CPU. For example, dual-core CPUs contain two cores and quad-core CPUs contain four cores. Multi-core CPUs allow computers to work on more than one task simultaneously, such as burning a DVD while surfing the Web, as well as to work faster within a single application. Multi-core CPUs also increase the performance of mobile devices while at the same time delivering better battery life.

One measurement of the processing speed of a CPU is **clock speed**, which measures the number of instructions that can be processed per second. Clock speed is typically rated in megahertz (MHz) or gigahertz (GHz). A CPU with a higher clock speed can process more instructions per second than the same CPU with a lower clock speed. CPUs for the earliest personal computers ran at less than 5 MHz; the fastest CPUs today have a clock speed of more than 5 GHz.

Although clock speed is important to computer performance, factors such as the number of cores, the amount of memory, the speed of external storage devices, and the bus width and bus speed greatly affect the overall processing speed of the computer. As a result, computers are beginning to be classified less by clock speed and more by the computer's overall processing speed or performance.

central processing unit (CPU) The main processor for a computer.

multi-core CPU A CPU that contains the processing components or cores of more than one processor in a single CPU.

clock speed A measurement of the number of instructions that a CPU can process per second.

FYI **GPUs** Computers and mobile devices usually contain two processors: a CPU and a GPU. GPU stands for graphics processing unit and is the chip that takes care of the processing needed to display images and video on the screen. While GPUs can be located on the motherboard or on a video card, a growing trend is to integrate both the CPU and GPU into the CPU package. For instance, the Intel Core i7, Intel Core M, Qualcomm Snapdragon, and AMD FX processors all have integrated GPUs. (AMD calls its integrated processors APUs, or accelerated processing units.)

Source: © NVIDIA

A computer **word** is the amount of data (typically measured in bits or bytes) that a CPU can manipulate at one time. In the past, CPUs used 32-bit words (referred to as 32-bit processors). Today, most CPUs are 64-bit processors, which means that they can simultaneously process 64 bits, or eight bytes, at one time. Usually, a larger word size allows for faster processing, provided the software being used is written to take advantage of 64-bit processing.

Cache memory is a special group of very fast memory circuitry, usually built into the CPU, that is used to speed up processing. It does this by storing the data and instructions that may be needed next by the CPU in a location from which it can be retrieved quickly. Typically, more cache memory results in faster processing. Most multi-core CPUs today have some cache memory dedicated to each core. They may also have a larger shared cache memory that can be accessed by any core as needed.

word The amount of data (typically measured in bits or bytes) that a CPU can manipulate at one time.

cache memory A group of very fast memory circuitry usually built into the CPU and used to speed up processing.

memory Locations, typically inside the system unit, that the computer uses for temporary storage.

RAM (random access memory) Memory used to store data and instructions that the computer is using.

2-2d Memory

In a computer, **memory** refers to locations, usually inside the system unit, that the computer uses to store data on a temporary basis. Most often, the term *memory* refers to **RAM (random access memory)**, which is used to store the essential parts of the operating system while the computer is running as well as the programs and data that the computer is currently using. RAM is volatile, so its content is erased when the computer is shut off. Data in RAM is also deleted when it is no longer needed, such as when the program using that data is closed.

Like the CPU, RAM consists of electronic circuits etched onto chips. Mobile devices usually have embedded memory chips. The memory chips for personal computers and servers are arranged onto circuit boards called memory modules, which, in turn, are plugged into the motherboard (see Exhibit 2-4). Most personal computers sold today have slots for two to four memory modules, and at least one slot is filled. For example, the motherboard shown in Exhibit 2-2 has two memory modules installed and room to add two more

EXHIBIT 2-4 INSERTING RAM MEMORY MODULES

DESKTOP RAM

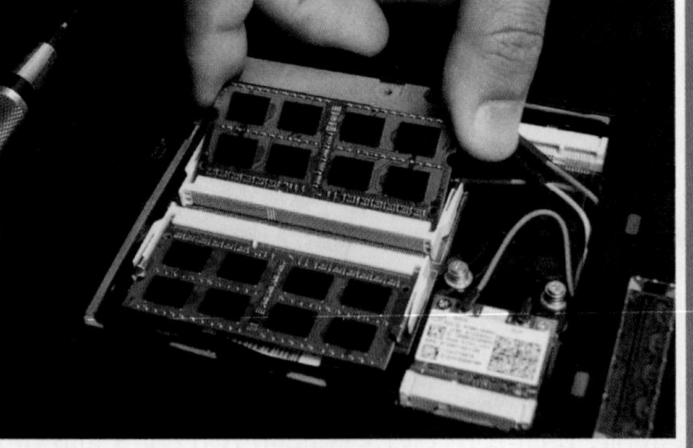

NOTEBOOK RAM

Source: © Kingston Technology Corporation

modules. If you want to add more RAM to a computer and no empty slots are available, you must replace at least one of the existing memory modules with a higher capacity module.

RAM capacity is measured in bytes. The amount of RAM that can be installed in a computer system depends on the CPU in that computer and the operating system being used. For instance, while computers with older 32-bit CPUs can use up to only 4 GB of RAM, computers with 64-bit CPUs and a 64-bit operating system can use significantly more RAM. In addition, different versions of a 64-bit operating system might support different amounts of RAM. Consequently, when adding RAM to a computer, it is important to determine whether the computer can support it. Having more RAM allows more applications to run at one time and the computer to respond more quickly when a user switches from task to task. Most computers sold today for personal use have between 4 and 16 GB of RAM. Smartphones and other mobile devices typically have between 1 and 4 GB of RAM, which usually cannot be replaced or expanded.

When adding new memory to a computer, it is also important to select the proper type and speed of RAM. Most personal computers today use SDRAM (synchronous dynamic RAM). SDRAM is available in several DDR (double-data rate) versions; the versions most commonly used today are DDR3 and the even faster DDR4. Each type of SDRAM is typically available in a variety of speeds (measured in MHz). For optimal performance, you should use the type and speed of RAM that your computer was designed to use.

To further improve memory performance, memory typically uses a dual-channel memory architecture, which has two paths that go to and from memory, so it can transfer twice as much data at one time as single-channel memory architecture of the same speed. Tri-channel (three paths) and quad-channel (four paths) memory architecture are also used for higher performance. Multichannel RAM is usually installed in matched sets, such as two 4 GB dual-channel memory modules instead of a single 8 GB dual-channel memory module.

To help users find the RAM that will work best with their computer, most memory manufacturer Web sites include a search feature that shows the available options for a particular device. Some sites also include a memory scanner feature that scans your computer to give you a custom recommendation.

A **register** is high-speed memory built into the CPU that temporarily stores data during processing. Registers are used by the CPU to store data and intermediary results temporarily during processing. Registers are the fastest type of memory used by the CPU. Generally, more registers and larger registers result in increased CPU performance. Most CPUs contain multiple registers that are used for specific purposes, such as to store data and intermediary calculations during processing.

ROM (read-only memory) consists of nonvolatile chips that permanently store data or programs.

FYI

MEMORY ADDRESSES

Regardless of the type of RAM used, the CPU must be able to find data and programs located in memory when they are needed. To accomplish this, each location in memory has an address. Each address typically holds only one byte. When the computer has finished using a program or set of data, it frees up that memory space to hold other programs and data. As a result, the content of each memory location constantly changes. This process can be roughly compared with the handling of the mailboxes in your local post office: the number on each P.O. box (memory location) remains the same, but the mail (data) stored inside changes as patrons remove their mail and as new mail arrives.

Each location in memory has a unique address, just like mailboxes at the post office.

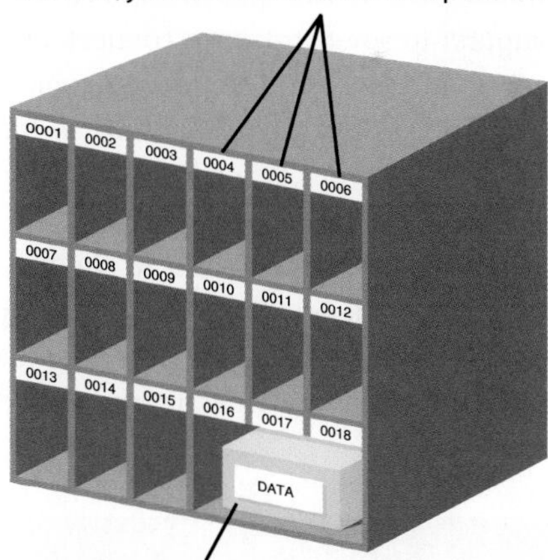

Programs and blocks of data are almost always too big to fit in a single address. A directory keeps track of the first address used to store each program and data block, as well as the number of addresses each block spans.

register High-speed memory built into a CPU.

ROM (read-only memory) Nonvolatile chips on the motherboard that permanently store data or programs.

Like RAM, these chips are attached to the motherboard inside the system unit, and the data or programs are retrieved by the computer when they are needed. An important difference, however, is that you can neither write over the data or programs in ROM chips (which is the reason ROM chips are called read-only) nor erase their content when you shut off the computer's power. Traditionally, ROM was used to store permanent instructions used by a computer (referred to as firmware).

Flash memory consists of nonvolatile memory chips that the user or computer can use for storage. Flash memory chips have begun to replace ROM for storing system information, such as a computer's **BIOS**, or **basic input/output system**—the sequence of instructions the computer follows as it is starting up. By storing this information in flash memory instead of ROM, it can be updated as needed.

Flash memory chips are also built into many types of devices, such as smartphones and tablets, as well as built into storage media and devices, such as flash memory cards and USB flash drives.

2-2e Expansion Slots and Expansion Cards

Expansion slots are locations on the motherboard into which expansion cards can be inserted to connect those cards to the motherboard. **Expansion cards** (also called **interface cards**) are circuit boards that are used to give computers additional capabilities, such as to connect the computer to a network or to connect a monitor to the computer. Most desktop computers come with a few empty expansion slots so new expansion cards can be added as needed. Each type of expansion slot is designed for a specific type of expansion card.

It is much less common for a user to add an expansion card to a notebook or other portable computers because most necessary capabilities are integrated directly into the motherboard or CPU or are added during manufacturing using a smaller interface card designed for smaller devices (see Exhibit 2-5). If you need to add new functionality to a portable computer or mobile device that has a USB port, you can plug an adapter into that port.

EXHIBIT 2-5 EXPANSION CARDS AND ADAPTERS

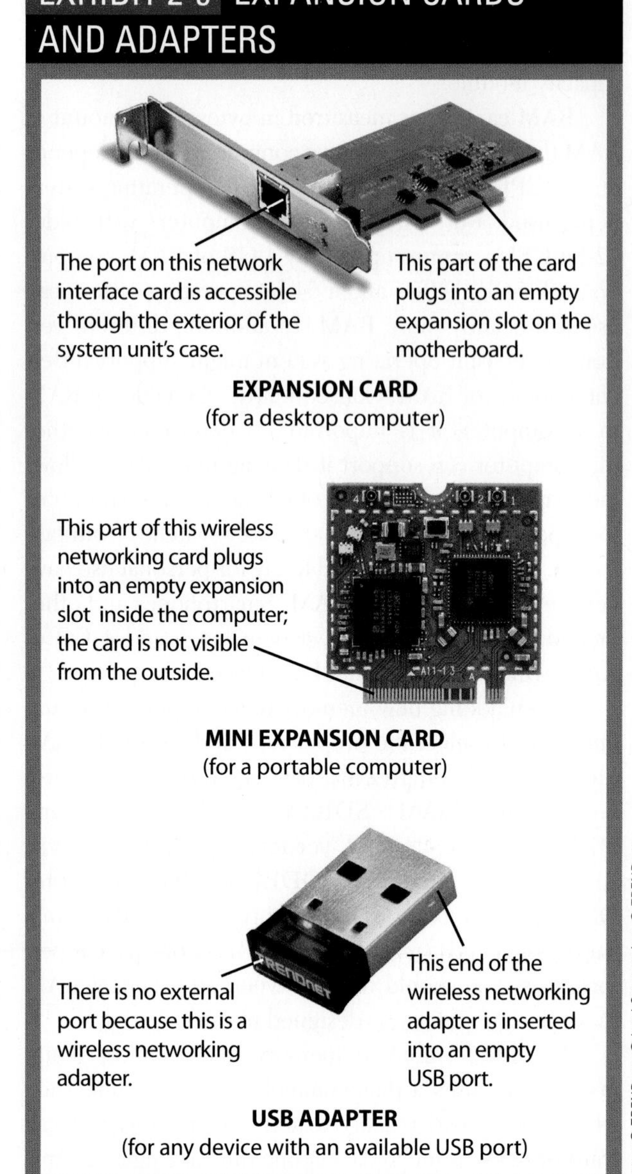
The port on this network interface card is accessible through the exterior of the system unit's case.
This part of the card plugs into an empty expansion slot on the motherboard.
EXPANSION CARD
(for a desktop computer)
This part of this wireless networking card plugs into an empty expansion slot inside the computer; the card is not visible from the outside.
MINI EXPANSION CARD
(for a portable computer)
There is no external port because this is a wireless networking adapter.
This end of the wireless networking adapter is inserted into an empty USB port.
USB ADAPTER
(for any device with an available USB port)

Source: © TRENDnet; © Intel Corporation; © TRENDnet

2-2f Buses

A **bus** is an electronic path over which data can travel. Buses are located within the CPU to move data between CPU components. A variety of buses are also etched onto the motherboard to tie the CPU to memory and to peripheral devices.

You can picture a bus as a highway with several lanes; each wire in the bus acts as a separate lane, transmitting

flash memory Nonvolatile memory chips that can be used for storage by a computer or a user.

BIOS (basic input/output system) The sequence of instructions the computer follows as it is starting up.

expansion slot A location on the motherboard into which an expansion card is inserted to connect it to the motherboard.

expansion card (interface card) A circuit board used to give computers additional capabilities.

bus An electronic path over which data travels.

EXHIBIT 2-6 BUS WIDTH

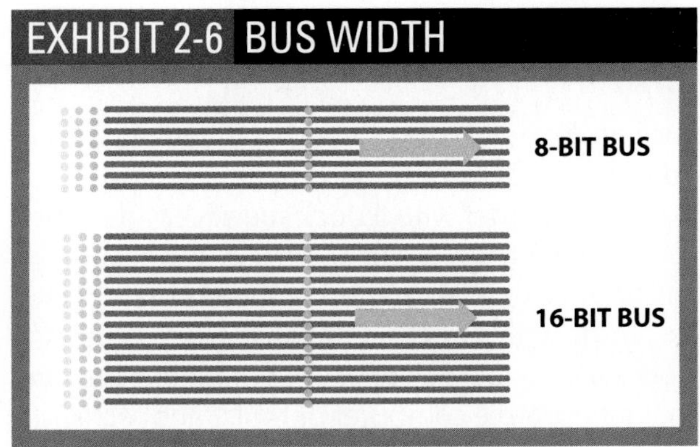
8-BIT BUS
16-BIT BUS

one bit at a time. The number of bits being transmitted at one time depends on the bus width, which is the number of wires in the bus over which data can travel (see Exhibit 2-6). The bus width and bus speed together determine the bus's **bandwidth**, which is the amount of data that can be transferred via the bus in a given time period. The amount of data actually transferred under real-life conditions is called **throughput**.

The buses that connect peripheral (typically input and output) devices to the motherboard are often called **expansion buses**. Expansion buses connect directly to ports on the system unit case or to expansion slots on the motherboard. Some of the most common expansion buses and expansion slots for a desktop computer are illustrated in Exhibit 2-7. As shown in this exhibit, the memory bus connects the CPU directly to RAM. The frontside bus connects the CPU to the chipset that connects the various buses together and connects the CPU to the rest of the bus architecture. The PCIe buses connect expansion slots to the chipset.

One of the more versatile bus architectures is the **Universal Serial Bus (USB)**. The USB standard allows 127 different devices to connect to a computer via a single USB port on the computer's system unit. The original USB standards, called USB 1.0 and 2.0, are relatively slow. They transfer data at 12 megabits per second (Mbps) and 480 Mbps, respectively. (Megabits means millions of bits.) The newest USB standards, called SuperSpeed USB 3.0 and 3.1, are much faster. They transfer data at 5 gigabits per second (Gbps) and 10 Gbps, respectively. (Gigabits means billions of bits.) USB 3 also supports faster and more powerful charging so it can be used to charge larger devices, such as laptops and monitors, in addition to smartphones and other mobile devices. The convenience and universal support of USB have made it the most widely used wired standard for connecting peripheral devices, such as keyboards, mice,

EXHIBIT 2-7 BUSES AND EXPANSION SLOTS

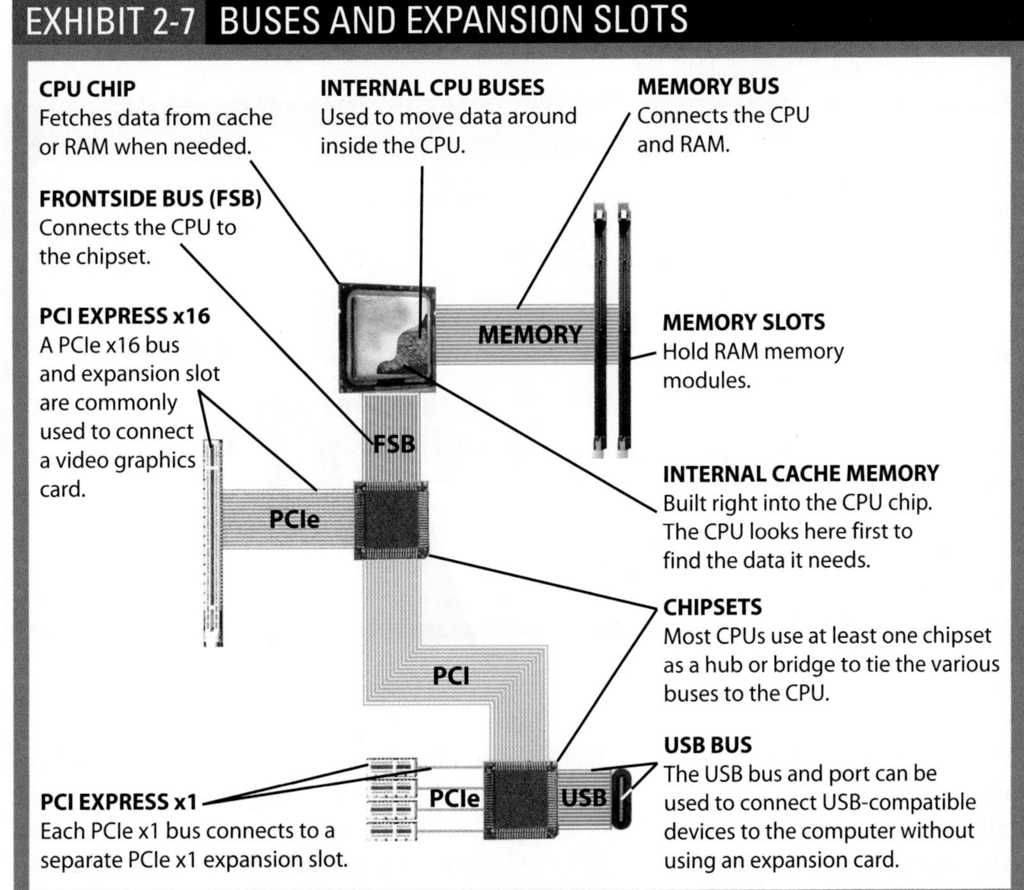
CPU CHIP
Fetches data from cache or RAM when needed.
INTERNAL CPU BUSES
Used to move data around inside the CPU.
MEMORY BUS
Connects the CPU and RAM.
FRONTSIDE BUS (FSB)
Connects the CPU to the chipset.
PCI EXPRESS x16
A PCIe x16 bus and expansion slot are commonly used to connect a video graphics card.
MEMORY
MEMORY SLOTS
Hold RAM memory modules.
FSB
PCIe
INTERNAL CACHE MEMORY
Built right into the CPU chip. The CPU looks here first to find the data it needs.
CHIPSETS
Most CPUs use at least one chipset as a hub or bridge to tie the various buses to the CPU.
PCI
USB BUS
The USB bus and port can be used to connect USB-compatible devices to the computer without using an expansion card.
PCI EXPRESS x1
Each PCIe x1 bus connects to a separate PCIe x1 expansion slot.
PCIe
USB

bandwidth The amount of data that can be transferred, such as via a bus, in a given time period.

throughput The amount of data that is transferred under real-life conditions.

expansion bus A bus on the motherboard used to connect peripheral devices.

Universal Serial Bus (USB) A versatile bus architecture widely used for connecting peripheral devices.

TRENDING...

TABLET DOCKS

Docking stations make it easier to connect portable computers and mobile devices to hardware, such as a second monitor or a wired printer, that stays at the home or office. Docking stations are widely used with notebook computers and are now available for tablets as well. Tablet docks give tablet users the flexibility and mobility of using a stand-alone tablet when needed as well as the productivity of a desktop setup. After connecting a tablet to a tablet dock, users have access to any hardware built into or connected to the dock, such as a keyboard and mouse for easier data entry, a monitor for easier viewing, and an external hard drive for additional storage. Some tablet docks include a second battery to extend the battery life of the device; others incorporate battery-charging capabilities into the dock so that the tablet can be recharged while it is docked. Some tablets, such as the detachable hybrid notebook-tablet computer shown in the accompanying illustration, are sold together with a dock specifically designed for that tablet. Other tablet docks are available as add-ons for iPads and other tablets that do not come with a dock. In the near future, wireless docks will connect all of your peripheral hardware to your portable computer or tablet and recharge that device by just being in communication range of the dock.

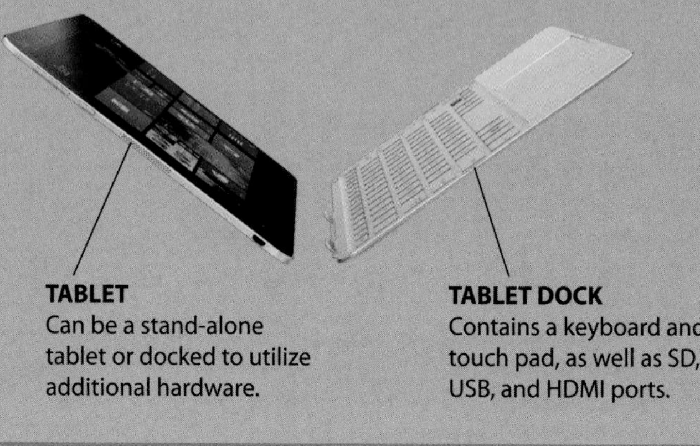

TABLET
Can be a stand-alone tablet or docked to utilize additional hardware.

TABLET DOCK
Contains a keyboard and touch pad, as well as SD, USB, and HDMI ports.

Source: © ASUSTeK Computer Inc.

printers, and storage devices. In fact, some portable computers now come with only USB ports for connecting devices to the computer as well as to power the computer. To help you identify USB 3 ports, they are colored blue.

2-2g Ports and Connectors

As already mentioned, ports are the connectors located on the exterior of a system unit that are used to connect external hardware devices. Each port is attached to the appropriate bus on the motherboard so that when a device is plugged into a port, the device can communicate with the CPU and other computer components. Typical ports for a desktop or notebook computer are shown in Exhibit 2-8.

EXHIBIT 2-8 TYPICAL PORTS

USB ports
Flash memory card slot
Audio port
Network port
USB ports
HDMI port
DisplayPort port

Source: © Hewlett-Packard Development Company, L.P.

Smartphones and other mobile devices have a more limited amount of expandability. However, these devices typically have a USB port and an audio port. They may also have an HDMI port and a flash memory card slot. Apple mobile devices usually have a proprietary Lightning port that is used to both power the device and connect it to other devices. Some of the most common connectors are shown in Exhibit 2-9. Instead of these full-sized connectors, mobile devices often use smaller versions, such as micro USB and micro HDMI.

TRENDING...

USB-C

The USB cables used with traditional USB ports are USB-A (the end that goes into the computer) and USB-B (the end that goes into the device being connected to the computer). The newest type of USB port and cable is **USB-C**. USB-C has many advantages over traditional USB and is expected to eventually replace it. One advantage is its flexibility—both ends of a USB-C cable are the same so it doesn't matter which end goes into which device, and the ends have no up or down orientation so you don't have to flip the connector in order to have it line up properly. Another advantage is speed and power. Because many USB-C ports support the USB 3.1 standard, they are very fast and can be used to charge portable computers.

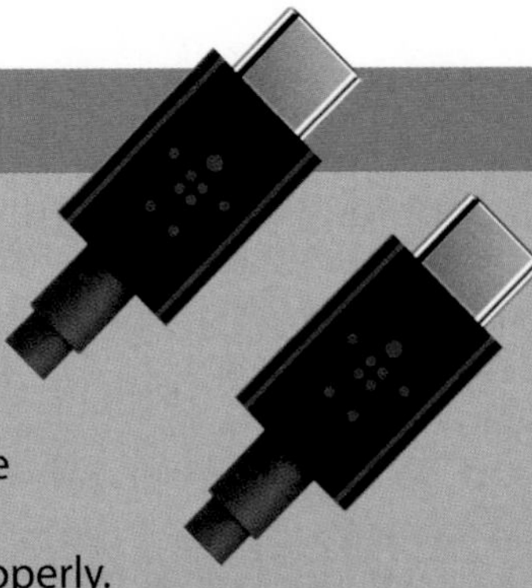

Source: © Belkin International, Inc.

EXHIBIT 2-9 TYPICAL CONNECTORS

USB-C

USB-A

Monitor (HDMI)

Network (RJ-45)

Audio (3.5 mm)

Source: © Belkin International, Inc.

2-3 HOW THE CPU WORKS

A CPU consists of a variety of circuitry and components packaged together. The key element of the CPU is the **transistor**—a device made of semiconductor material that controls the flow of electrons inside a chip. CPUs contain hundreds of millions of transistors.

2-3a Typical CPU Components

To begin to understand how a CPU works, you need to know how the CPU is organized and what components it includes. A simplified example of the principal components that might be included in a single core of a typical CPU is shown in Exhibit 2-10. Additional components are also typically located inside the CPU, but not within each core. For instance, there are buses to connect the CPU cores to each other, buses to connect each core to the CPU's memory controller (which controls the communication between the CPU cores and RAM), and buses to connect each core to any cache memory that is shared between the cores. If the CPU contains a graphics processing unit (GPU), as many do today, it would be located inside the CPU package as well.

The **arithmetic/logic unit (ALU)** is the section of a CPU core that performs arithmetic (addition, subtraction, multiplication, and division) involving integers and logical operations (such as comparing two pieces of data to see if they are equal or determining if a specific condition is true or false). Arithmetic requiring decimals is usually performed by the **floating point unit (FPU)**. Arithmetic operations are performed when mathematical calculations are requested by the user as well as when

USB-C The newest, and most versatile, type of USB connector.

transistor A device made of semiconductor material that controls the flow of electrons inside a chip.

arithmetic/logic unit (ALU) The part of a CPU core that performs integer arithmetic and logical operations.

floating point unit (FPU) The part of a CPU core that performs decimal arithmetic.

EXHIBIT 2-10 CPU COMPONENTS

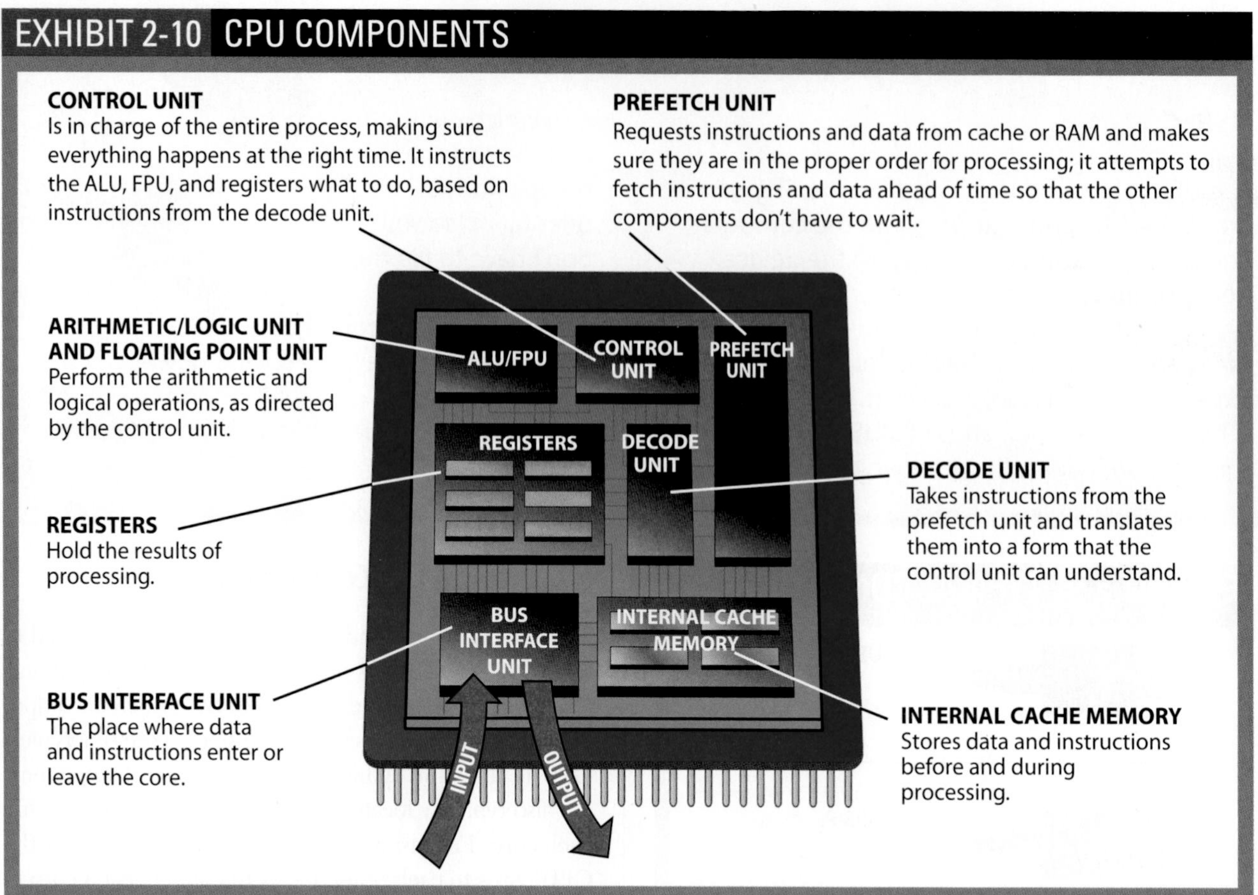
CONTROL UNIT
Is in charge of the entire process, making sure everything happens at the right time. It instructs the ALU, FPU, and registers what to do, based on instructions from the decode unit.
PREFETCH UNIT
Requests instructions and data from cache or RAM and makes sure they are in the proper order for processing; it attempts to fetch instructions and data ahead of time so that the other components don't have to wait.
ARITHMETIC/LOGIC UNIT AND FLOATING POINT UNIT
Perform the arithmetic and logical operations, as directed by the control unit.
ALU/FPU
CONTROL UNIT
PREFETCH UNIT
REGISTERS
DECODE UNIT
DECODE UNIT
Takes instructions from the prefetch unit and translates them into a form that the control unit can understand.
REGISTERS
Hold the results of processing.
BUS INTERFACE UNIT
INTERNAL CACHE MEMORY
BUS INTERFACE UNIT
The place where data and instructions enter or leave the core.
INPUT
OUTPUT
INTERNAL CACHE MEMORY
Stores data and instructions before and during processing.

many other common computing tasks are performed. For example, editing a digital photograph in an image editing program, running the spell checker in a word processing program, and burning a music CD are all performed by the ALU, with help from the FPU when needed, using only arithmetic and logical operations. Most CPUs today have multiple ALUs and FPUs that work together to perform the necessary operations.

The **control unit** coordinates and controls the operations and activities taking place within a CPU core, such as retrieving data and instructions and passing them on to the ALU or FPU for execution. In other words, it directs the flow of electronic traffic within the core, much like a traffic cop controls the flow of vehicles on a roadway. Essentially, the control unit tells the ALU and FPU what to do and makes sure that everything happens at the right time in order for the appropriate processing to take place.

The **prefetch unit** orders data and instructions from cache or RAM based on the current task. The prefetch unit tries to predict what data and instructions will be needed and retrieves them ahead of time to help avoid delays in processing.

The **decode unit** takes the instructions fetched by the prefetch unit and translates them into a form that can be understood by the control unit, ALU, and FPU. The decoded instructions go to the control unit for processing.

The **bus interface unit** allows the core to communicate with other CPU components, such as the memory controller and other cores. As previously mentioned, registers and cache memory are two types of memory used by the CPU.

2-3b The System Clock and the Machine Cycle

To synchronize all of a computer's operations, a **system clock**—a small quartz crystal located on the

control unit The part of a CPU core that coordinates its operations.

prefetch unit The part of a CPU core that attempts to retrieve data and instructions before they are needed for processing to avoid delays.

decode unit The part of a CPU core that translates instructions into a form that can be processed by the ALU and FPU.

bus interface unit The part of a CPU core that allows the core to communicate with other CPU components.

system clock The timing mechanism within a computer that synchronizes the computer's operations.

FYI COOLING COMPONENTS

One by-product of packing an increasing amount of technology into a smaller system unit is heat, an ongoing problem for CPU and computer manufacturers. Because heat can damage components and because cooler chips run faster, system units traditionally included fans and heat sinks (small components made of aluminum that help to dissipate heat) to cool the CPU and the system unit. As devices continue to shrink in size, however, finding room for cooling components is an issue. For example, the newest and thinnest notebook computers, such as the Macbook shown in the accompanying illustration, as well as smartphones and other mobile devices, don't include a fan. Instead, these devices use mobile CPUs, such as the Intel Core M, that run cooler than desktop CPUs. In addition, many of these devices use thermal transfer materials, such as sheets of metal or graphite, inside the case to spread out the heat generated by chips. In the future, new cooler materials, such as graphene, that generate less heat than silicon may be used for CPUs and other computer components.

Source: Apple, Inc.

motherboard—is used. The system clock sends out a signal on a regular basis to all other computer components, similar to a musician's metronome or a person's heartbeat. Each signal is referred to as a cycle. The number of cycles per second is measured in hertz (Hz). One megahertz (MHz) is equal to one million ticks of the system clock. Many personal computers have system clocks that run at 200 MHz, and all devices (such as CPUs) that are synchronized with the system clock run at either the system clock speed or at a multiple of or a fraction of the system clock speed. When you issue an instruction to a computer, such as by typing a command or clicking something with the mouse, it is converted into a set of small basic instructions that the CPU is able to execute. During each clock tick, the CPU executes one or more of these basic instructions.

Whenever the CPU processes a single basic instruction, it is referred to as a **machine cycle**. Each machine cycle consists of four general operations, as shown in Exhibit 2-11.

EXHIBIT 2-11 MACHINE CYCLE

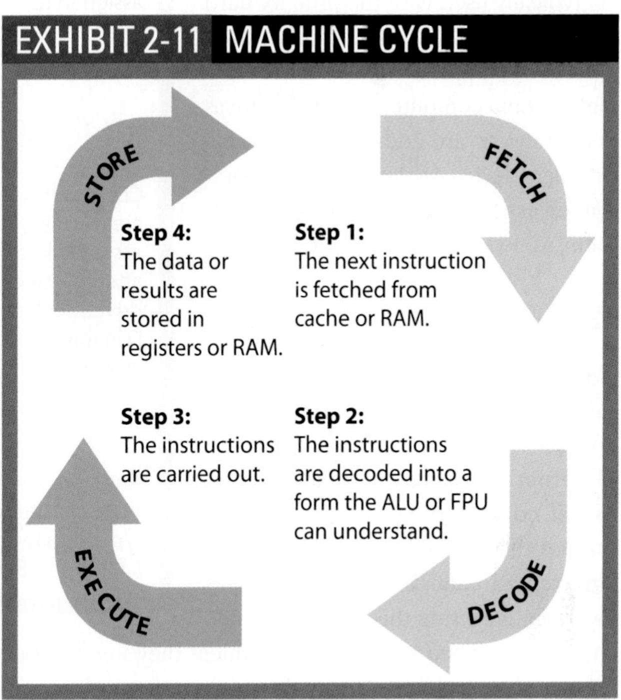

FETCH
Step 1:
The next instruction is fetched from cache or RAM.
DECODE
Step 2:
The instructions are decoded into a form the ALU or FPU can understand.
EXECUTE
Step 3:
The instructions are carried out.
STORE
Step 4:
The data or results are stored in registers or RAM.

2-4 STORAGE SYSTEMS

When you first create a document on a computer, both the program you are using to create the document and the document itself are temporarily stored in RAM. But when the program is closed, both are erased from RAM. Consequently, anything that needs to be preserved for future use must be stored on a more permanent medium.

Storage systems make it possible to save programs, data, and processing results for later use. They provide nonvolatile storage, so that when the power is shut off, the data stored on the storage medium remains intact. All storage systems involve two physical parts: a **storage medium**, which is the hardware where data is actually stored, and its corresponding **storage device**, which is the hardware into which the storage medium is inserted to be read from or written to.

machine cycle The series of steps performed by a computer when the CPU processes a single basic instruction.

storage medium The hardware where data is actually stored.

storage device The hardware used to read from or write to a storage medium.

Letters or names are assigned to each storage device so that the user can identify a device (see Exhibit 2-12). Some drive letters, such as the letter C typically used with the primary hard drive, are usually consistent from computer to computer. The rest of the drive letters on a computer might change as new devices are added. When a new storage device is detected, the computer assigns and reassigns drive letters, as needed.

EXHIBIT 2-12 STORAGE DEVICE IDENTIFIERS

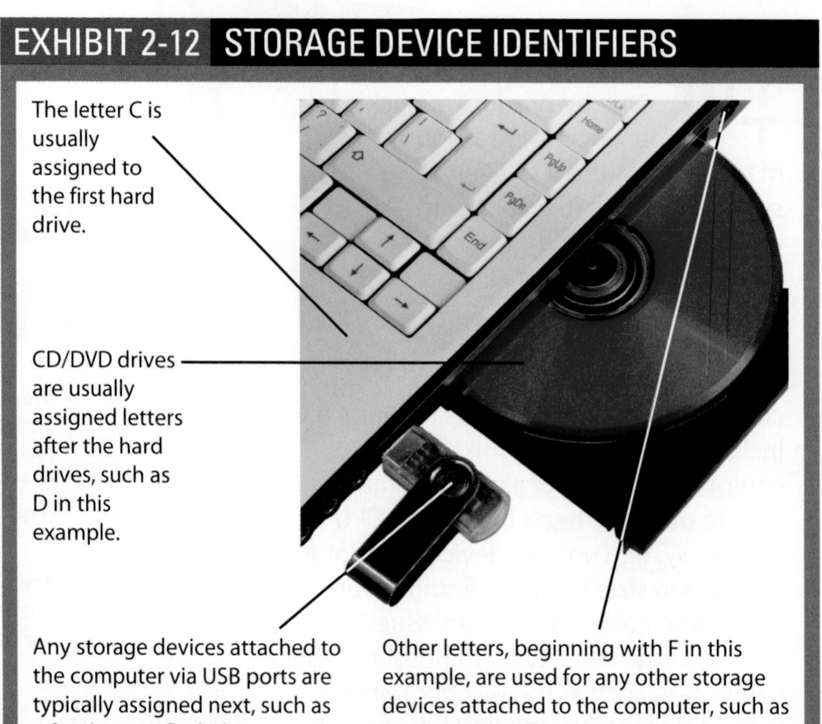

The letter C is usually assigned to the first hard drive.
CD/DVD drives are usually assigned letters after the hard drives, such as D in this example.
Any storage devices attached to the computer via USB ports are typically assigned next, such as E for this USB flash drive.
Other letters, beginning with F in this example, are used for any other storage devices attached to the computer, such as via this built-in flash memory card reader.

2-4a Hard Drives

With the exception of computers designed to use only network storage devices, such as thin clients and some Internet appliances, virtually all personal computers come with a **hard drive** that is used to store most programs and data. Internal hard drives are located inside the system unit and are not designed to be removed unless they need to be repaired or replaced. External hard drives typically connect to a computer via a USB port or a wireless connection and are frequently used for additional storage (such as for digital photos, videos, and other large multimedia files), to move files between computers, and for backup purposes.

Many hard drives are magnetic. **Magnetic hard drives** contain one or more metal hard disks that are coated with a magnetizable substance. These hard disks are permanently sealed inside the hard drive case, along with the read/write heads used to store (write) and retrieve (read) data and an access mechanism used to move the read/write heads in and out over the surface of the hard disks (see Exhibit 2-13). One hard drive usually contains a stack of two or more hard disks. If so, there is a read/write head for each hard disk surface (top and bottom), as illustrated in Exhibit 2-14, and these heads move in and out over the disk surfaces simultaneously.

EXHIBIT 2-13 HOW DATA IS STORED ON MAGNETIC DISKS

Disk surface

The read/write head inscribes data by aligning each of the magnetic particles in one of two ways.

Particles aligned one way represent 0s; the other way represent 1s.

A magnetic hard drive's read/write heads never touch the surface of the hard disks at any time, even during reading and writing. If the read/write heads do touch the surface—for example, if a desktop computer is bumped while the hard drive is spinning or if a foreign object gets onto the surface of a hard disk—a head crash occurs, which can permanently damage the hard drive. Because the read/write heads are located extremely close to the surface of the hard disks, the presence of any

hard drive Hardware used to store most programs and data on a computer.

magnetic hard drive A hard drive consisting of metal magnetic disks permanently sealed, along with an access mechanism and read/write heads, inside its drive.

EXHIBIT 2-14 MAGNETIC HARD DRIVES

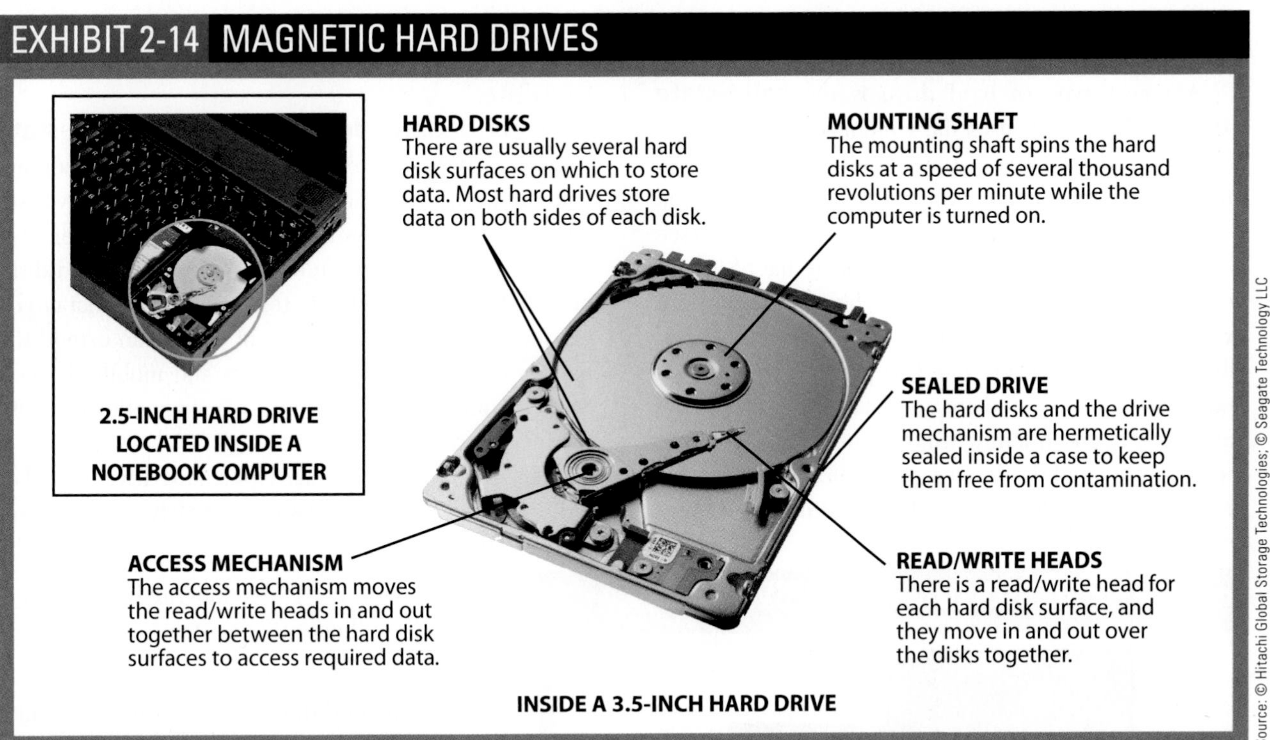

HARD DISKS
There are usually several hard disk surfaces on which to store data. Most hard drives store data on both sides of each disk.
MOUNTING SHAFT
The mounting shaft spins the hard disks at a speed of several thousand revolutions per minute while the computer is turned on.
2.5-INCH HARD DRIVE LOCATED INSIDE A NOTEBOOK COMPUTER
SEALED DRIVE
The hard disks and the drive mechanism are hermetically sealed inside a case to keep them free from contamination.
ACCESS MECHANISM
The access mechanism moves the read/write heads in and out together between the hard disk surfaces to access required data.
READ/WRITE HEADS
There is a read/write head for each hard disk surface, and they move in and out over the disks together.
INSIDE A 3.5-INCH HARD DRIVE

Source: © Hitachi Global Storage Technologies; © Seagate Technology LLC

foreign object on the surface of a hard disk is like placing a huge boulder on a road and then trying to drive over it with your car.

The surface of a hard disk is organized into **tracks** (concentric rings) and pie-shaped groups of **sectors** (pieces of a track), as shown in Exhibit 2-15. On most computer systems, the smallest amount of space on a hard disk that can be used to store a file is a **cluster**—one or more adjacent sectors. Because of this, everything stored on a hard disk always takes up at least one cluster. In addition to tracks, sectors, and clusters, hard disks are also organized into cylinders (refer again to Exhibit 2-15). A **cylinder** is

EXHIBIT 2-15 ORGANIZATION OF A MAGNETIC HARD DISK

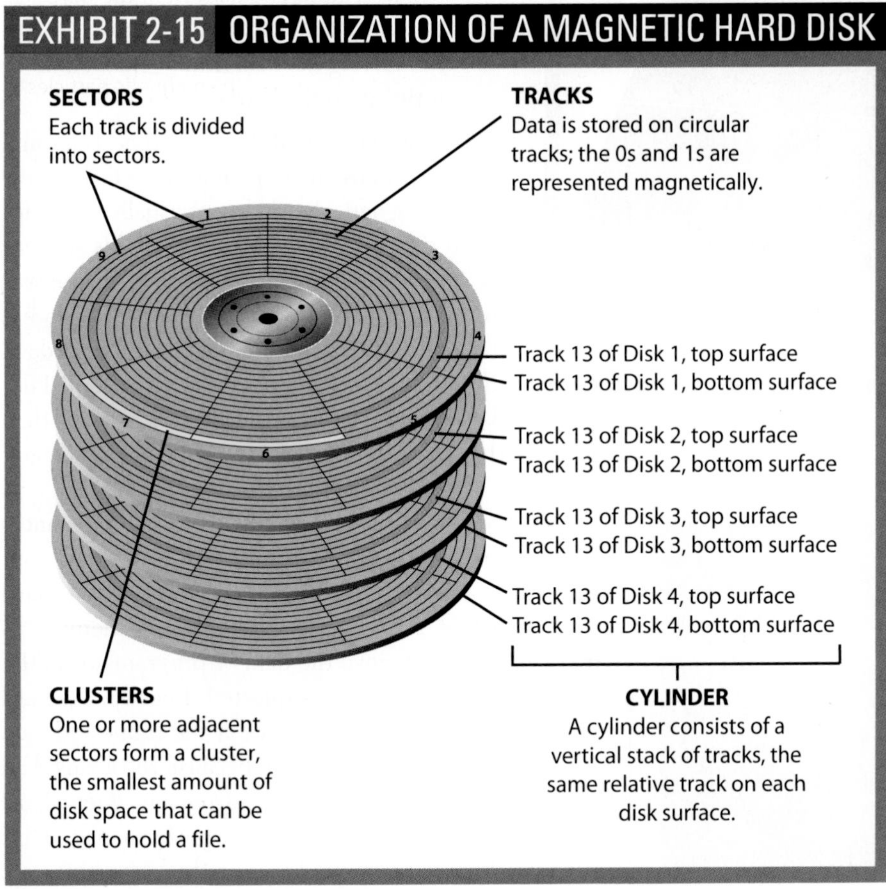

track A concentric ring on the surface of a hard disk where data is recorded.

sector A piece of a hard disk track.

cluster One or more adjacent sectors on a hard disk.

cylinder The collection of one specific track located on each hard disk surface.

the collection of one specific track located on each hard disk surface.

A newer type of hard drive is the **solid-state drive (SSD)**, which uses flash memory chips instead of magnetic hard disks. Consequently, SSDs have no moving parts and data is stored as electrical charges on the flash memory media located within the SSDs (see Exhibit 2-16). These characteristics mean that SSDs are not subject to mechanical failures like magnetic hard drives and are, therefore, more resistant to shock and vibration. They also consume less power, generate less heat, make no noise, and are much faster than magnetic hard drives. Consequently, SSDs are becoming the norm for netbooks, mobile devices, and other very portable devices as well as for devices designed for rugged use. They are also being used with notebooks and other portable computers instead of, or in addition to, a magnetic hard drive.

Hybrid hard drives (also called **solid-state hybrid drives** or **SSHDs**) contain both flash memory chips and a magnetic hard drive. The flash memory (usually up to 8 GB) allows the hard drive to be faster. It is also used to reduce the number of times the hard disks need to be read as well as to temporarily store data to be written to the hard disks, both of which can extend the battery life of portable computers and mobile devices. SSHDs combine the lower price of a magnetic drive with the increased performance of an SSD.

The total time that it takes for a hard drive to read or write data is called the **disk access time** and requires the following:

1. **Seek time**—The read/write heads move to the cylinder that contains (or will contain) the desired data.
2. **Rotational delay**—The hard disks rotate into the proper position so that the read/write heads are located over the part of the cylinder to be used.
3. **Data movement time**—The data moves, such as reading the data from the hard disk and transferring it to memory, or transferring the data from memory and storing it on the hard disk.

A typical magnetic disk access time is around 8 milliseconds (ms). To minimize disk access time, magnetic hard drives usually store related data on the same cylinder. This strategy reduces seek time and, therefore, improves the overall access time. Because SSDs do not have to move any parts to store or retrieve data, they do not require seek time or rotational delay, and their access time is much faster than magnetic hard drives—essentially instantaneous at about 0.1 ms.

To speed up magnetic hard drive performance, disk caching is often used. A **disk cache** stores copies of data or programs that are located on the hard drive and that might be needed soon in memory to avoid having to retrieve the data or programs from the hard drive when they are requested. Because the hard disks do not have to be accessed if the requested data is located in the disk cache, and because retrieving data from memory is much faster than from a magnetic hard disk, disk caching can speed up performance. Disk caching also saves wear and tear on the hard drive and,

EXHIBIT 2-16 SOLID-STATE DRIVE (SSD)

Transcend
Data is stored in flash memory chips located inside the drive; unlike magnetic drives, there are no moving parts.

Source: © Transcend Information USA

solid-state drive (SSD) A hard drive that uses flash memory chips instead of magnetic hard disks.

hybrid hard drive (solid-state hybrid drive or **SSHD)** A hard drive that uses a combination of flash memory chips and magnetic hard disks.

disk access time The total time that it takes for a hard drive to read or write data.

disk cache Memory used in conjunction with a magnetic hard drive to improve system performance.

EXHIBIT 2-17 EXTERNAL HARD DRIVES

FULL-SIZED EXTERNAL HARD DRIVE
This drive is about the size of a 5 by 7-inch picture frame, but thicker, and holds 6 TB.

PORTABLE HARD DRIVE
This drive is about the size of a 3 by 5-inch index card, but thicker, and holds 2 TB.

WIRELESS HARD DRIVE
This drive connects via Wi-Fi and holds 500 GB.

Source: © Western Digital Technologies, Inc.; © Seagate Technology LLC

in portable computers, can extend battery life. Memory used for disk caching typically consists of memory chips located on a circuit board inside the hard drive case. Hybrid hard drives use the flash memory inside the drive as a disk cache.

Hard drives can be internal or external. Internal hard drives are permanently located inside a computer's system unit and are not removed unless a problem occurs with them. External hard drives are located outside of the system unit and are connected when they are needed. A variety of external hard drives are available, as shown in Exhibit 2-17. External hard drives are commonly used for transporting a large amount of data from one computer to another, for backup purposes, and for additional storage. They usually connect via a USB or wireless connection. Wireless drives are becoming more common because they can be accessed by multiple devices at one time as well as extend the storage capabilities of a tablet or smartphone.

For security purposes, both internal and external hard drives often have built-in encryption that automatically encrypts (essentially scrambles) the data stored on the hard drive and limits access to the hard drive to only authorized users (see Exhibit 2-18).

EXHIBIT 2-18 ENCRYPTED HARD DRIVE

Source: © Apricorn

CAUTION CAUTION CAUTION CAUTION

BACK UP DATA

Because you never know when a head crash or other hard drive failure will occur—there may be no warning whatsoever—be sure to back up the data on your hard drive on a regular, frequent basis. Backing up data—that is, creating a second copy of important files on another storage medium, such as an external hard drive, a USB flash drive, or an online storage site—is critical not only for businesses but also for individuals. If a hard drive containing critical data that was not backed up becomes damaged, a data recovery firm might be able to retrieve the data, but it is expensive and inconvenient.

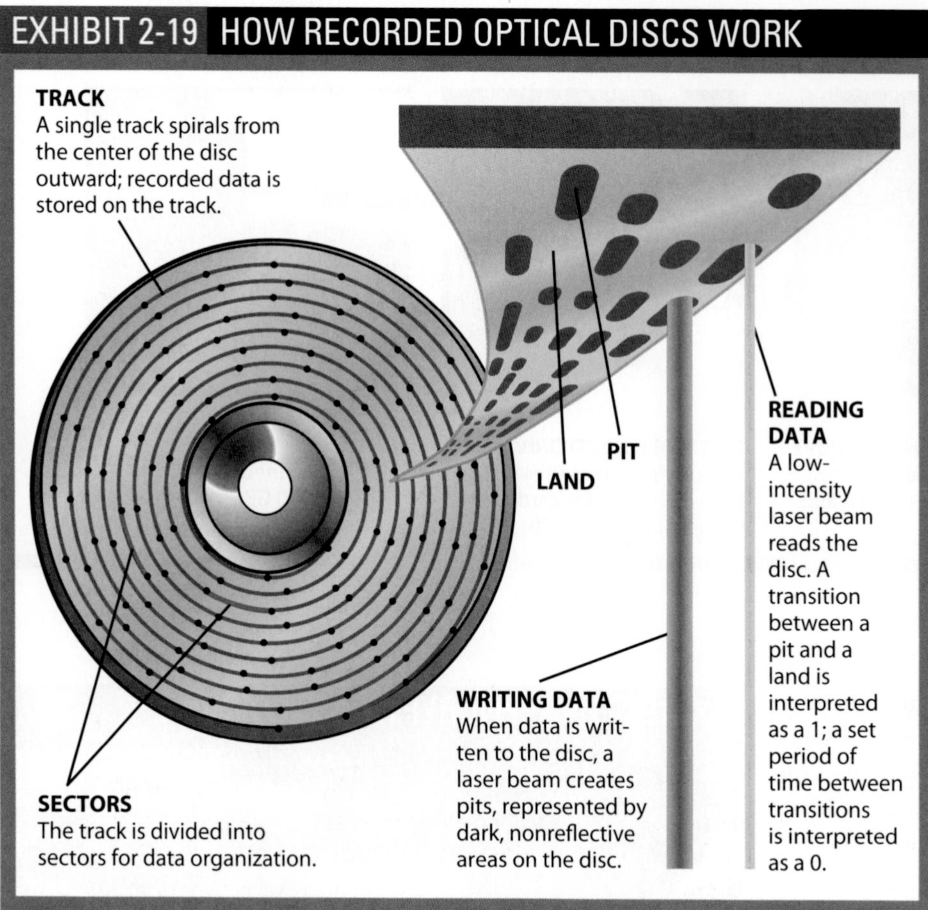

TRACK
A single track spirals from the center of the disc outward; recorded data is stored on the track.
PIT
LAND
READING DATA
A low-intensity laser beam reads the disc. A transition between a pit and a land is interpreted as a 1; a set period of time between transitions is interpreted as a 0.
WRITING DATA
When data is written to the disc, a laser beam creates pits, represented by dark, nonreflective areas on the disc.
SECTORS
The track is divided into sectors for data organization.

EXHIBIT 2-19 HOW RECORDED OPTICAL DISCS WORK

2-4b Optical Discs

Optical discs are thin circular plastic discs that are topped with layers of other materials and coatings used to store data and protect the disc. Data on optical discs is stored and read optically using laser beams. Data can be stored on one or both sides of an optical disc, depending on the disc design, and some types of discs use multiple recording layers on each side of the disc to increase capacity. An optical disc contains a single spiral track (instead of multiple tracks like magnetic disks), and the track is divided into sectors to keep data organized. As shown in Exhibit 2-19, this track (sometimes referred to as a *groove* to avoid confusion with the term *tracks* that refers to songs on an audio CD) begins at the center of the disc and spirals out to the edge of the disc. Optical discs include CDs, DVDs, and high-capacity Blu-ray Discs (BD), and discs can be read-only, recordable (can be written to once), or rewritable (can be written to, erased, and rewritten as needed). Optical discs are the current standard for packaged software. They are also commonly used for backup purposes and for storing and/or transporting music, photo, video, and other large files.

Standard-sized optical discs are 120 mm (approximately 4.7 inches) in diameter. There are also smaller mini discs (see Exhibit 2-20) that are 80 mm (approximately 3 inches) in diameter.

EXHIBIT 2-20 OPTICAL DISCS

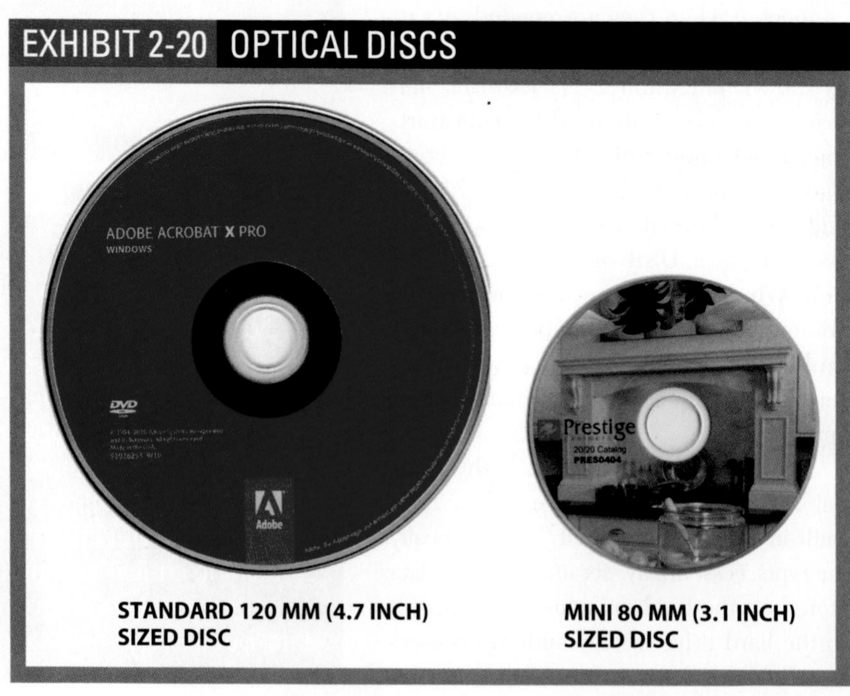

STANDARD 120 MM (4.7 INCH) SIZED DISC

MINI 80 MM (3.1 INCH) SIZED DISC

Source: © Adobe

optical disc A circular plastic disc used to store data and that is read from and written to using a laser beam.

The capacity of an optical disc varies with the type of disc being used and how many layers of data are stored on each side of the disc. For example, standard-sized CDs hold 700 MB, standard-sized, single-layer DVD discs hold 4.7 GB, and standard-sized, dual-layer DVD discs hold 8.5 GB. Standard-sized BD discs hold 25 GB on single-layer discs, 50 GB on dual-layer discs, or 100 GB on triple-layer BDXL discs.

Discs can be double sided, which doubles the capacity, but the disc must be turned over to access the second side. Double-sided discs are most often used with movies and other prerecorded content, such as to store a widescreen version of a movie on one side of a DVD disc and a standard version on the other side. Optical discs can also use the + or – standard.

Optical discs are more durable than magnetic media and do not degrade with use, as some magnetic media does. However, the discs should be handled carefully and stored in their cases when not in use to protect the recorded surfaces of the discs from scratches, fingerprints, and other marks that can interfere with the usability of the discs.

To use an optical disc, it is inserted into an appropriate **optical drive**, such as a CD, DVD, or BD drive. Most optical drives today support multiple types of optical discs—some support all possible types. Optical drives are almost always backward-compatible, meaning they can be used with lower (older) types of discs but not higher (newer) ones. So, while a DVD drive would likely support all types of CDs and DVDs, it cannot be used with BDs; but most BD drives today support all types of CDs, DVDs, and BDs. To use an optical disc with a computer that doesn't include an optical drive, external drives that connect via a USB port are available (see Exhibit 2-21).

The process of recording data onto a recordable or rewritable optical disc is called burning. To burn an optical disc, the optical drive being used must support burning and the type of disc being used. In addition, CD-burning or DVD-burning software is required. Many burning programs are available commercially, and recent versions of operating systems (including Windows and OS X) include burning capabilities.

EXHIBIT 2-21 EXTERNAL OPTICAL DRIVE

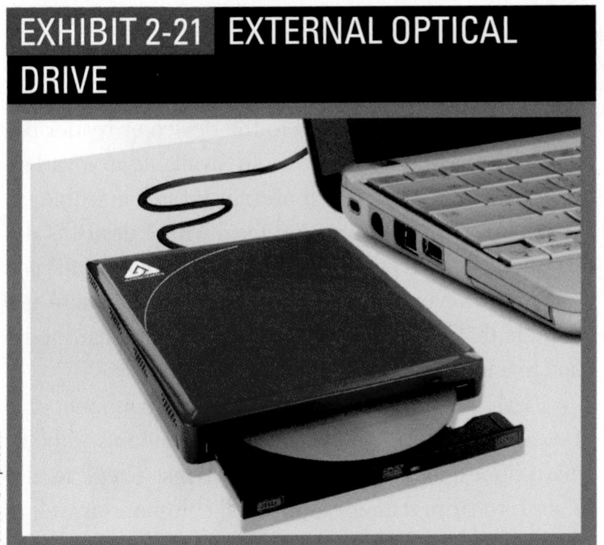

Source: © Apricorn

FYI

ULTRA HD (4K)

© Nerthuz/Shutterstock.com

Ultra HD (Ultra High Definition or 4K) is the next big step in high-definition (HD) TVs and digital content. It has four times the resolution of ordinary HD and is changing how HD content is delivered to the consumer.

Currently, many movies, TV shows, and sporting events are filmed and delivered in HD. While much of this content will be filmed in 4K in the near future, today's hardware and streaming services are not designed to support 4K content because it requires four times as much data as regular HD video. Cable and satellite providers already compress content to enable it to be delivered more efficiently, and some online streaming services, such as Netflix, allow subscribers to reduce the quality of the content they stream in order to speed up delivery and save Internet bandwidth. In addition, many Internet connections are not fast enough to support the large amounts of data required for 4K quality. So, for the time being, expect full-quality 4K content to be delivered via high-capacity (100 GB) Ultra HD (4K) Blu-ray Discs.

Data is written to an optical disc in one of two ways. With read-only optical discs like movie, music, and software CDs and DVDs, the surface of the disc is molded or stamped appropriately to represent the data. To accomplish this, tiny depressions (when viewed from the top side of the disc) or bumps (when viewed from the bottom) are created on the disc's surface. These bumps are called pits; the areas on the disc that are not changed

optical drive A storage device designed to read optical discs.

are called lands. With recordable or rewritable optical discs that can be written to using an optical drive such as a DVD drive, the reflectivity of the disc is changed using a laser to represent the data stored there—dark, nonreflective areas are pits; reflective areas are lands, as was illustrated in Exhibit 2-19. In either case, the disc is read with a laser and the computer interprets the reflection of the laser off the disc surface as 1s and 0s.

Most recordable optical discs have a recording layer containing organic light-sensitive dye embedded between the disc's plastic and reflective layers. One exception to this is the BD-R, which has a recording layer consisting of inorganic material. When data is written to a recordable disc, the recording laser inside the recordable optical drive burns the dye (for CDs and DVDs) or melts and combines the inorganic material (for BD-Rs), creating nonreflective areas that function as pits. In either case, the marks are permanent, so data on the disc cannot be erased or rewritten.

To write to, erase, or overwrite rewritable optical discs, phase change technology is used. With this technology, the rewritable CD or DVD is coated with layers of a special metal alloy compound that can have two different appearances after it has been heated and then cooled, depending on the heating and cooling process used. With one process, the material crystallizes and that area of the disc is reflective. With another process, the area cools to a nonreflective state. Before any data is written to a rewritable optical disc, the disc is completely reflective. To write data to the disc, the recording laser heats the metal alloy in the appropriate locations on the spiral track and then uses the appropriate cooling process to create either the nonreflective areas (pits) or the reflective areas (lands). To erase the disc, the appropriate heating and cooling process is used to change the areas to be erased back to their original reflective state.

2-4c Flash Memory Storage Systems

As discussed previously, flash memory is a chip-based storage medium that represents data using electrical charges. It is used in a variety of storage systems, such as the SSDs and hybrid hard drives already discussed and the additional storage systems discussed next.

Because flash memory media are physically very small, they are increasingly being embedded directly into a variety of consumer products—such as smartphones, tablets, smart watches, and even sunglasses—to provide built-in data storage. **Embedded flash memory** refers to flash memory chips embedded into products. Embedded flash memory is usually the primary storage for mobile devices, such as tablet and smartphones. Although embedded flash memory can take the form of small SSDs or memory cards, it is increasingly being implemented with small stand-alone chips, such as the one shown in Exhibit 2-22.

EXHIBIT 2-22 EMBEDDED FLASH MEMORY

TABLET
Contains 64 GB of embedded flash memory.

EMBEDDED FLASH MEMORY

Source: © Samsung Electronics Co., Ltd; © SanDisk Corporation

One of the most common types of flash memory media is the **flash memory card**—a small, rectangular card containing one or more flash memory chips, a controller chip, other electrical components, and metal contacts to connect the card to the device or reader being used. Flash memory cards are available in a variety of formats and sizes, which are not interchangeable, so the type of flash memory card used with a device is determined by the type of flash media card that device can accept. However, as shown in Exhibit 2-23, there are adapters that can be used to enable a smaller card to be used in a larger slot of the same type.

Flash memory cards are the most common type of external storage media for digital cameras, tablets, smartphones, and other portable devices. They can also be used to store data for a personal computer as well as to transfer data from a portable device to a computer.

embedded flash memory Flash memory chips embedded into products.

flash memory card A small, rectangular storage medium containing flash memory chips.

EXHIBIT 2-23 FLASH MEMORY CARDS, READERS, AND ADAPTERS

Source: © Micron Consumer Products Group, Inc.; © SanDisk Corporation

Consequently, most personal computers and many mobile devices have a built-in flash memory card reader capable of reading flash memory cards; an external flash memory card reader (such as the ones shown in Exhibit 2-23) that connects via a USB port can be used when the destination device doesn't have a built-in reader. Flash memory cards are available in capacities up to 512 GB.

USB flash drives (sometimes called just USB drives or flash drives) consist of flash memory media integrated into a self-contained unit that connects to a computer or other device via a USB port and is powered by that port. As shown in Exhibit 2-24, USB flash drives are available in a variety of formats to be appropriate for a wide variety of applications and are designed to be very small and very portable. USB flash drives are available in custom shapes for novelty or promotional purposes as well as in low-profile

EXHIBIT 2-24 USB FLASH DRIVES

Source: © Kingston Technology Corporation; © CustomUSB.com

USB flash drive A small storage device that contains flash memory media and plugs into a USB port.

TRENDING...

CLOUD COMPUTING

In general, **cloud computing** refers to accessing data, applications, and other resources stored on computers available via the Internet—in a "cloud" of computers—rather than on users' computers. With cloud computing, you can access Web-based software and apps, store and retrieve data via a cloud storage provider, and print documents to a cloud printer located anywhere in the world. While most individuals use cloud computing to some extent, users of Chromebooks (such as the one in the accompanying photo) are full-time cloud users. Chromebooks are designed to be used with online Google Apps, such as Google Docs, Gmail, and Google Play Music, and all documents, mail, photos, music, and more are stored in the cloud.

Source: © Intel Corporation

The biggest advantage of cloud computing is the ability to access data with any device, from anywhere the user has an Internet connection. In addition, because data is stored online instead of on the device being used, the data is safe if the device is lost, stolen, or damaged. Disadvantages of cloud computing include no or reduced functionality without an Internet connection and the potentially high expense related to data transfer for companies and individuals using high-bandwidth applications. Like any other data, data stored in the cloud should be backed up on a regular basis.

designs that can remain in a computer at all times. Micro USB flash drives are also available for use with smartphones and other mobile devices that have a micro USB port.

To read from or write to a USB flash drive, you just plug it into a USB port. If the USB flash drive is being used with a computer, it is assigned a drive letter by the computer, just like any other type of attached drive, and files can be read from or written to the USB flash drive until it is unplugged from the USB port. The capacity of most USB flash drives today ranges from 8 GB to 1 TB.

2-4d Network and Cloud Storage Systems

Network storage refers to using a storage device that is accessed through a local network. Using a network storage device works in much the same way as using local storage (the storage devices and media that are directly attached to the user's computer). To read data from or write data to a network storage device (such as a hard drive being accessed via a network), the user just selects it and then performs the necessary tasks in the usual fashion. Network storage is common in businesses. It is also used by individuals with home networks for backup purposes or to share files with other devices in the home.

Because of the vast amount of data shared and made available over networks, network storage has become increasingly important. There are two common types of network storage. **Network attached storage (NAS)** consists of high-performance storage systems that are connected individually to a network to provide storage for the computers connected to that network. They can be large storage systems designed for a large business, or smaller NAS devices designed for a home or a small business. A growing trend, in fact, is home NAS devices designed to store multimedia data to be distributed over a home entertainment network. A **storage area network (SAN)** also provides storage for a network, but it consists of a separate network of hard drives or other storage devices, which is connected to the main network.

The primary difference between an NAS and an SAN is how the storage devices interface with the network—that is, whether the storage devices act as individual network nodes, just like computers, printers, and other devices on the network (NAS), or whether they are located in a completely separate network of storage devices that is accessible via the main network (SAN).

cloud computing To use Internet-based computing resources, such as data, software, and storage.

network storage The use of a storage device that is accessed through a local network.

network attached storage (NAS) A high-performance storage system connected individually to a network to provide storage for computers on that network.

storage area network (SAN) A network of hard drives or other storage devices that provide storage for another network.

SANs can be more appropriate when a larger amount of network storage is needed; however, in terms of functionality, the distinction between NAS and SANs is blurring because they both provide storage services to the network. Typically, both NAS and SAN systems are scalable, which means that new devices can be added as more storage is needed and devices can be added or removed without disrupting the network.

Remote storage services accessed via the Internet are often referred to as **cloud storage** or **online storage**. Cloud storage can be provided either as a stand-alone service or as part of a cloud computing service. For instance, most online applications, such as Google Docs, the Flickr photo-sharing service, and social networking sites like Facebook, provide online storage for these services. There are also sites whose primary objective is to allow users to store documents online, such as Dropbox, iCloud, Google Drive, and Microsoft OneDrive. Cloud storage sites allow users to share files with others. For security purposes, cloud storage sites are usually password protected and you can specify the individuals who are allowed to view shared files.

EXHIBIT 2-25 SMART CARD USES

LOGGING ONTO A COMPUTER

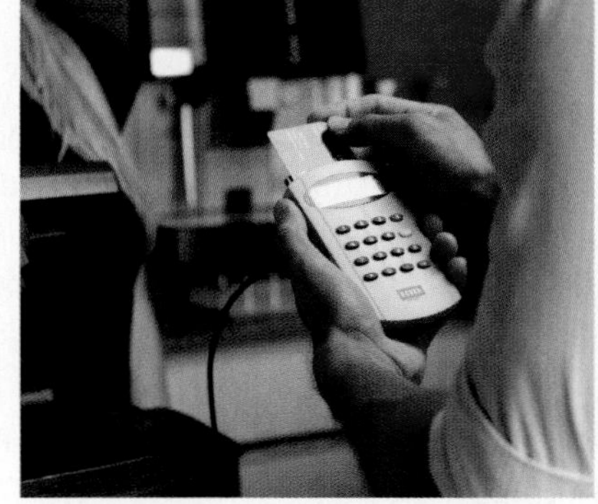

MAKING A STORE PURCHASE

ACCESSING A SECURE FACILITY

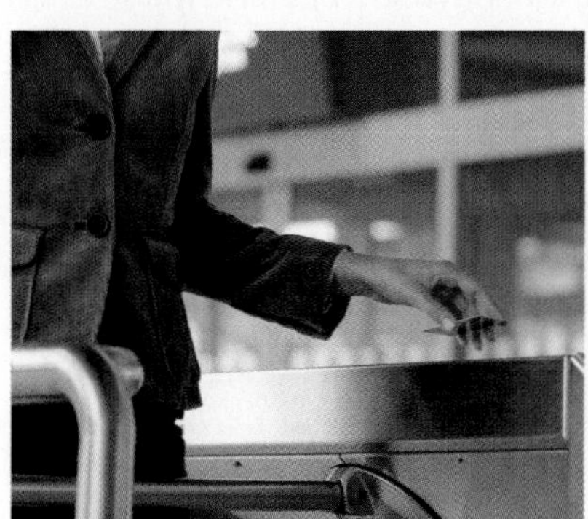

USING TRANSIT TICKETS

Source: © HID Global Corporation

2-4e Smart Cards

A **smart card** is a credit card–sized piece of plastic that has built-in computer circuitry and components—typically a processor, memory, and storage. Smart cards store a relatively small amount of data (typically 64 KB or less), most commonly personal identification data or funds. Smart cards are frequently used for national and student ID cards, credit and debit cards, transit fare cards, and access cards for facilities or computers.

To use a smart card, it must either be inserted into a smart card reader (if it is the type of card that requires contact) or placed close to a smart card reader (if it is a contactless card) built into or attached to a computer, door lock, ATM machine, vending machine, or other device (see Exhibit 2-25). Once a smart card has been verified by the card reader, the transaction—such as making a purchase or unlocking a door—can be completed. For an even higher level of security, some smart cards store biometric data in the card and use that data to ensure the authenticity of the card's user before authorizing the smart card transaction.

2-4f Storage Systems for Large Computer Systems

Businesses and other organizations have tremendous storage needs that are growing exponentially. In fact, the amount of digital data produced is expected to double every two years through 2020, according to one estimate. In addition to regular business data storage (such

cloud storage (online storage) The use of remote storage device that are accessed via the Internet.

smart card A storage medium consisting of a credit card–sized piece of plastic with built-in computer circuitry and components.

TRENDING...

MOBILE DIGITAL WALLETS

Digital wallets like Apple Pay and Google Wallet store payment information to help individuals pay for purchases more conveniently. Mobile digital wallets are stored on smartphones, smart watches, and other mobile devices. Some mobile digital wallet transactions use **Near Field Communications (NFC)** technology, a wireless technology used to facilitate communication between devices. If an NFC-enabled smartphone is used, payments can be made by simply touching the payment terminal with the phone (for security purposes, your can often choose to require a fingerprint swipe or PIN code in order to authorize the purchase). Mobile digital wallets can also be used when shopping online with a mobile device. Because many smartphones in use today are not yet NFC-enabled, other technology needs to be used in conjunction with some digital wallets. For example, several banks, including Bank of America, are testing contactless microSD cards that, when inserted into a smartphone, enable that phone to make payments via a Visa payWave payment terminal. In addition, online payment mobile apps like PayPal can often be used for mobile purchases.

Pay
Your wallet.
Without the
wallet.

© Bloomua/Shutterstock.com

as employee files, customer and order data, business documents, and Web site content), new regulations are continually increasing the types of and amounts of data that many businesses need to archive. These documents must be stored in a manner in which they can be readily retrieved as needed.

With large computer systems, instead of finding a single hard drive installed within the system unit, you will likely find a large storage system (sometimes called a storage server)—a separate piece of hardware containing multiple high-speed hard drives—connected to the computer system or network. While some NAS devices today are classified as storage servers, large storage systems typically contain drawers of hard drives for a significantly larger total capacity. For instance, the storage system shown in Exhibit 2-26 can include up to 240 hard drives for a total capacity of 432 TB.

In addition to being used as stand-alone storage for large computer systems, large storage systems may also be used in NAS, SAN, and RAID systems. **RAID (redundant array of independent disks)** is a method of storing data on two or more hard drives that work together. Although RAID can be used to increase performance, it is most often used to

EXHIBIT 2-26 LARGE STORAGE SYSTEMS

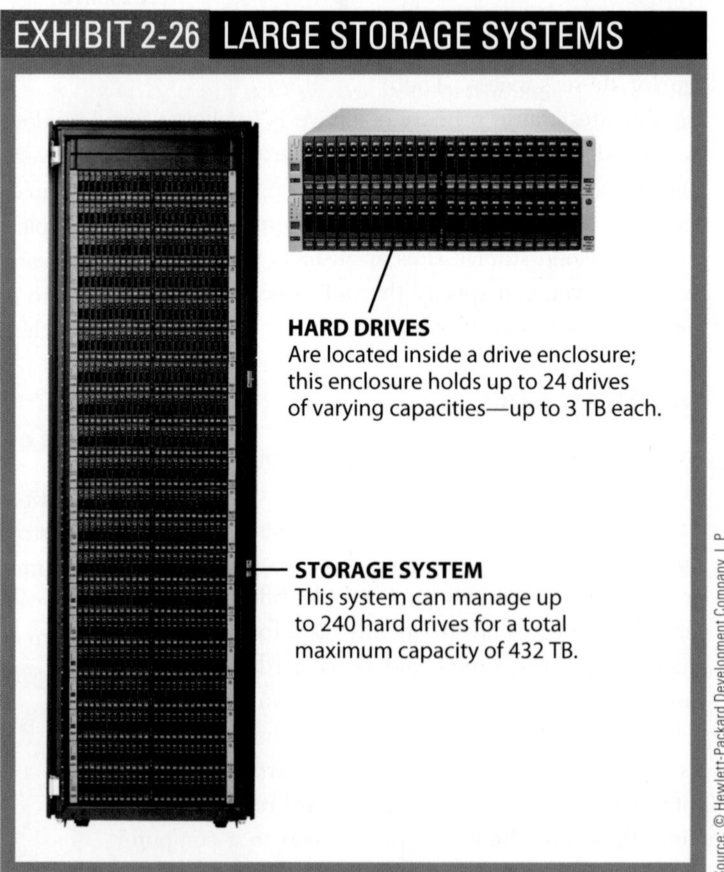

HARD DRIVES
Are located inside a drive enclosure; this enclosure holds up to 24 drives of varying capacities—up to 3 TB each.
STORAGE SYSTEM
This system can manage up to 240 hard drives for a total maximum capacity of 432 TB.

Source: © Hewlett-Packard Development Company, L.P.

Near Field Communications (NFC) A wireless technology used to facilitate communications between devices.

RAID (redundant array of independent disks) A storage method that uses several hard drives working together.

FYI

WHICH TYPE OF STORAGE DO YOU NEED?

With so many storage alternatives available, it can be overwhelming to decide which devices and media are most appropriate to use with your personal devices. In general, most computer users need a hard drive for storing programs and data; some type of recordable or rewritable optical drive for installing programs, backing up files, and sharing files with others; and a flash memory card reader for transferring photos, music, and other content between portable devices and the computer. If you are using flash memory cards with your devices, you will want to select and use the flash memory media that are compatible with those devices as well as any necessary adapters for your computer. In addition, you will need at least one convenient free USB port to use to connect external hard drives, USB flash drives, keyboards, mice, printers, and other USB-based storage hardware as well as USB devices that contain storage media, such as digital cameras and smartphones. Fewer storage options are available for mobile devices, so evaluate the available options when selecting a mobile device to ensure that it can perform the functions you need, such as the ability to back up data and contacts in the cloud or on a medium you can access with another device, the ability to transfer photos and other data to a computer or printer, and the ability to connect to any desired storage devices or other hardware.

protect critical data on a large storage system. Because RAID usually involves recording redundant (duplicate) copies of stored data, the copies can be used, when necessary, to reconstruct lost data. This helps to increase the fault tolerance—the ability to recover from an unexpected hardware or software failure, such as a system crash—of a storage system.

Most large storage systems are based on hard disks, although magnetic tape storage systems are also possible. **Magnetic tape** consists of plastic tape coated with a magnetizable substance that represents the bits and bytes of digital data, similar to magnetic hard disks. Although magnetic tape is no longer used for everyday storage applications, it is still used today for business data archiving and backup. One advantage of magnetic tape is its low cost per terabyte.

2-5 INPUT DEVICES

An **input device** is any hardware that is used to enter data into the computer. The most common input devices used with computers and mobile devices are keyboards, pointing devices (such as a mouse), touch input, and voice input. There are also input devices designed for capturing and reading data in electronic form, and for inputting audio data. In addition, **assistive hardware** is specifically designed for users with physical disabilities to make it easier for those individuals to use a computer. For example, Braille keyboards contain Braille overlays for use by visually impaired individuals, and one-handed keyboards and eye-tracking systems benefit individuals with limited dexterity.

2-5a Keyboards

Most computers are designed to be used with a **keyboard**—a device containing keys used to enter characters on the screen. Keyboards can be built into a device, attached using a wired cable, or connected via a wireless connection. Most keyboards contain standard alphanumeric keys to input text and numbers along with a variety of special keys for specific purposes. However, the order and layout of the keys on a mobile device is often different from the order and layout on a conventional keyboard. Keyboards used with desktop and notebook computers are similar, but notebook keyboards may contain fewer keys. Tablets, smartphones, and other mobile devices often have just an on-screen keyboard (see Exhibit 2-27). However, external keyboards, either built into a carrying case or stand-alone, as in Exhibit 2-27, can be used with many mobile devices.

magnetic tape Storage media consisting of plastic tape coated with a magnetizable substance.

input device Any hardware that is used to enter data into the computer.

assistive hardware Hardware designed for use by individuals with physical disabilities.

keyboard An input device containing keys used to enter characters on the screen.

EXHIBIT 2-27 KEYBOARDS

ON-SCREEN KEYBOARD
This keyboard is using the Swype app in which the user continuously drags through the letters in a word for faster input.

UNIVERSAL KEYBOARD
Can be used with computers, tablets, and smartphones. This keyboard can connect wirelessly to three devices at once and the user can switch between them.

Source: © Nuance Communications, Inc; © Logitech

FYI WEARABLE INPUT

Wearable devices, such as smart watches, present an input challenge because of their small size. Typically, these devices use a combination of touch screen buttons, physical buttons, and voice input. Some devices also include a modified on-screen keyboard. For example, the smart watch shown here has a tiny one-row keyboard at the bottom of the watch that is used in conjunction with software that tries to understand and predict what the user is typing. In addition, it can zoom in on the part of the keyboard you are touching to allow you to touch a larger key for your final selection if needed.

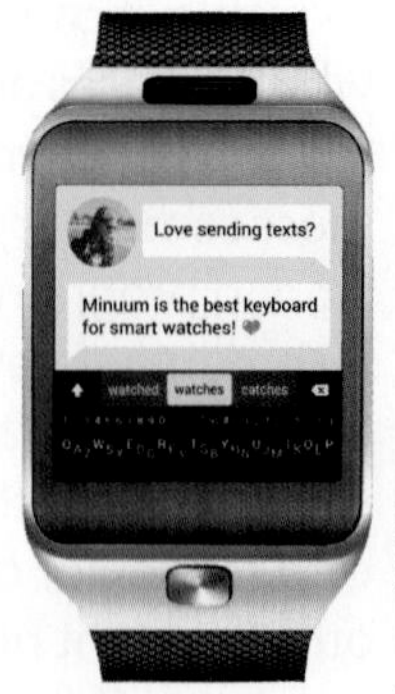

Source: © Whirlscape

2-5b Pointing Devices

In addition to a keyboard, most computers are used in conjunction with some type of pointing device. **Pointing devices** are used to select and manipulate objects, to input certain types of data, such as handwritten data, and to issue commands to the computer. The **mouse** is a common pointing device for desktop and notebook computers. It typically rests on the desk or other flat surface close to the computer, and the user slides it across the surface in the appropriate direction to point to and select objects on the screen. As it moves, the on-screen mouse pointer—usually an arrow—moves accordingly. Once the mouse pointer is pointing to the desired object on the screen, the user clicks the buttons on the mouse to perform actions on that object (such as to open a hyperlink, to select text, or to resize an image). In addition to the traditional type of mouse, there are mice that include a touch surface on top of the mouse in order to support finger swipes and other movements for convenient navigation. Exhibit 2-28 shows both a

pointing device An input device used to move the on-screen pointer to enable the user to select and manipulate objects.

mouse A common pointing device that the user slides along a flat surface to move the on-screen pointer and manipulate objects.

EXHIBIT 2-28 MICE

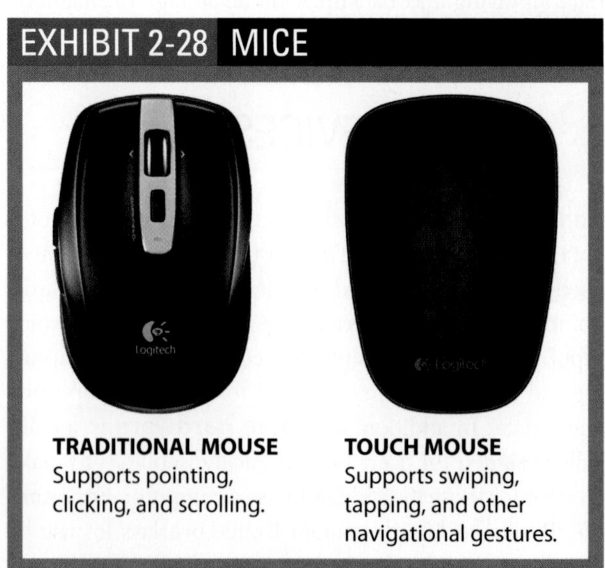

TRADITIONAL MOUSE
Supports pointing, clicking, and scrolling.

TOUCH MOUSE
Supports swiping, tapping, and other navigational gestures.

Source: © Logitech

traditional and a touch mouse. Similar to keyboards, mice typically connect via a USB port or via a wireless connection.

Many computers and mobile devices can accept pen input, which is input by writing, drawing, or tapping on the screen with a penlike device called a **stylus**. Sometimes, the stylus (also just called a pen) is simply a plastic device with no additional functionality. Other times, it is a pressure-sensitive device that transmits the pressure applied by the user to the device that the stylus is being used with to allow more precise input. These more sophisticated styluses also are typically powered by the device with which they are being used; have a smooth, rounded tip so they do not scratch the screen; and contain buttons or switches to perform actions such as erasing content or right-clicking. Although the capabilities depend on the type of device and software being used, pen input can be used with a variety of computers and mobile devices (see one example in Exhibit 2-29). In addition to being used as pointing devices, pens can also be used to input handwritten text and sketches.

EXHIBIT 2-30 GAMING DEVICES

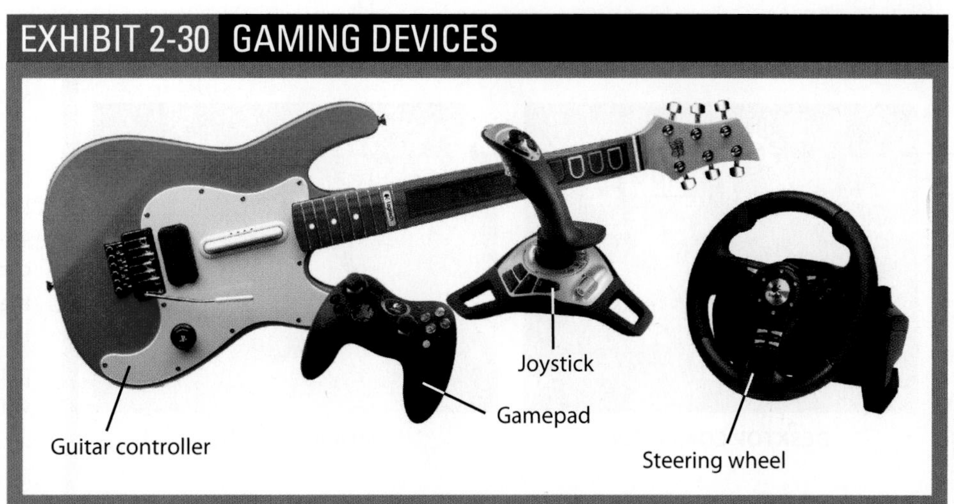

Source: © Logitech

EXHIBIT 2-29 PEN-BASED DEVICE

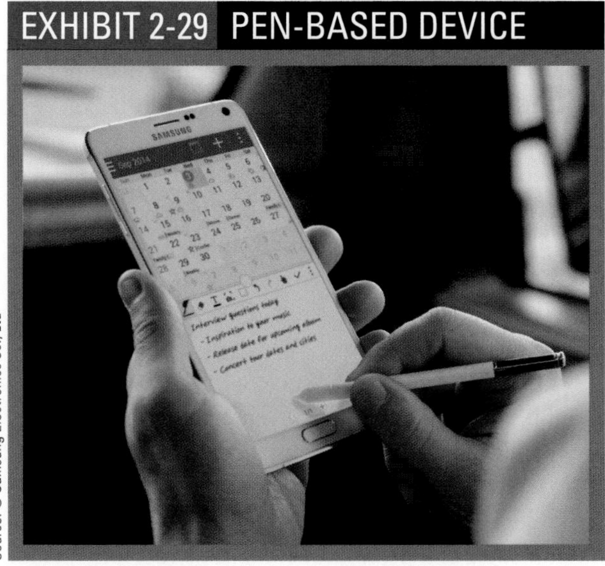

Source: © Samsung Electronics Co., Ltd

A variety of gaming devices today, such as the joystick, gamepad, and steering wheels shown in Exhibit 2-30, can be used as controllers to supply input to a computer. Other input devices are intended to be used with gaming devices, such as Wii, Xbox, and PlayStation gaming consoles. These devices include guitars, drums, and other musical instruments; dance pads and balance boards, and other motion-sensitive controllers; and proprietary controllers such as the Wii Remote, Xbox Kinect, and PlayStation Move.

2-5c Touch Devices

Touch screens are display screens that can be touched to select commands or otherwise provide input to the computer associated with the touch screen. Touch screens are common on personal computers as well as on smartphones and other mobile devices (see Exhibit 2-31) to provide easy input.

Many touch screens are multi-touch, which means they can recognize input from more than one finger at a time, such as using two fingers to enlarge or rotate an image on the screen. Similar multi-touch products are used for large wall displays, such as for use in museums, government command centers, and newsrooms. One new trend in touch screens is the table PC, which allows multi-touch input from multiple users so they can play games together, work together on a project, or otherwise interact. Table PCs can be either built into a table or designed to be used on a table, such as the 27-inch table PC shown in Exhibit 2-31.

Touch screens are also used in consumer kiosks, restaurant order systems, and other point-of-sale (POS)

stylus A penlike pointing device used to write electronically on the screen.

touch screen A display device that can be touched to select commands or otherwise provide input to the computer.

EXHIBIT 2-31 TOUCH DEVICES

DESKTOP COMPUTER

MOBILE DEVICE

TABLE PC

TOUCH PADS

Source: © Courtesy of Dell Inc.; © Amazon.com, Inc.; © Lenovo; © byggarn.se/Shutterstock.com; © Logitech

systems. They are also useful for on-the-job applications (such as factory work) where it might be impractical to use a keyboard or mouse. A growing trend is to use touch screens that provide tactile feedback—a slight movement or other physical sensation in response to the users' touch so they know their input has been received by the computer. Although touch screens make many devices more convenient for most people to use, these devices and their applications are not accessible to blind individuals, users with limited mobility, and other individuals with a disability.

A **touch pad** is a touch-sensitive pointing device. A touch pad is used with a fingertip or thumb to move the on-screen pointer; tapping the touch pad or one of its associated buttons performs clicks and other mouse actions. Touch pads are the most common pointing device for notebook and netbook computers. Because touch is so integrated into the newest operating systems, there are stand-alone touch pads available that can be used with computers that don't have a touch screen. Touch pads are also built into some keyboards.

touch pad A touch-sensitive pointing device used with a fingertip or thumb to control the on-screen pointer or manipulate objects.

scanner An input device that captures an image of an object and then transfers that data to a computer.

flatbed scanner A scanner that scans flat objects one page at a time.

portable scanner A scanner that captures text and other data while on the go.

2-5d Scanners, Readers, and Digital Cameras

A variety of input devices are designed to capture data in digital form so a computer can manipulate it. Some devices convert data that already exists in physical form to digital form; others capture data initially in digital form. Recording or capturing data initially in digital form helps reduce data input errors and saves time. A **scanner**, more officially called an optical scanner, captures an image of an object—usually a flat object, such as a printed document or photograph—in digital form and then transfers that data to a computer. Typically, the entire document is input as a single graphical image that can be resized, inserted into other documents, posted on a Web page, emailed to someone, printed, or otherwise treated like any other graphical image. The text in the scanned image, however, cannot be edited unless optical character recognition (OCR) software is used in conjunction with the scanner to input the scanned text as individual text characters.

Flatbed scanners, such as the one shown in Exhibit 2-32, scan flat objects one page at a time. They are the most common type of scanner. **Portable scanners** capture text and other data while on the go. Some portable scanners can capture images of an entire document, such as a printed document or receipt; smaller portable scanners capture text one line at a time. Some multimedia, medical, and business applications require the use of a three-dimensional (3D) scanner, which scans an item or person in 3D. In addition, scanning hardware is being incorporated into a growing number

TRENDING...

MODULAR PHONES

Source: © Google ATAP

Want to easily replace your cracked smartphone screen or add a new feature? You may soon be in luck if modular phones become a reality. Currently in the development and testing stages, modular phones (such as Google's Project Ara prototype shown here) allow individuals to create custom phones with the functions, modules, and appearance they wish. Modules can be safely inserted and removed from the phone's basic endoskeleton, even while the device is powered on. In addition to enabling individuals to build the phone they want, modular phones give the user flexibility to add new modules whenever they are needed for only as long as they are needed. Modular phones also reduce electronic waste by enabling individuals to upgrade just the modules they need or replace only the module that is broken instead of discarding an old phone for an entirely new one.

EXHIBIT 2-32 FLATBED SCANNER

© BlueSkyImage/Shutterstock.com

EXHIBIT 2-33 COMMON TYPES OF BARCODES

Source: © Motorola Solutions

of products. For example, ATMs have a built-in scanner to scan the images of checks as they are deposited.

A variety of readers are available to read the different types of codes and marks used to represent data on products, advertising material, packages, and other items. A **barcode** is an optical code that represents data with bars of varying widths or heights (see Exhibit 2-33). Two of the most familiar barcodes are UPC (Universal Product Code), the type of barcode found on packaged goods in supermarkets and other retail stores, and ISBN (International Standard Book Number), the barcode used with printed books. Businesses and organizations can also create and use custom barcodes to fulfill their unique needs. For instance, shipping organizations such as FedEx and UPS use custom barcodes to mark and track packages, retailers such as Target and Walmart use custom barcodes added to customer receipts to facilitate returns, hospitals use custom barcodes to match patients with their charts and medicines, libraries use custom barcodes for checking out and checking in books, and law enforcement agencies use custom barcodes to mark evidence.

Another type of barcode is the QR (Quick Response) code that represents data with a matrix of small squares. Most QR codes are designed to be used by consumers with smartphones. For instance, capturing the image of a printed QR barcode (such as the one shown in Exhibit 2-34) with a smartphone's camera could enable

barcode An optical code that represents data as a set of bars.

EXHIBIT 2-34 BARCODE READERS

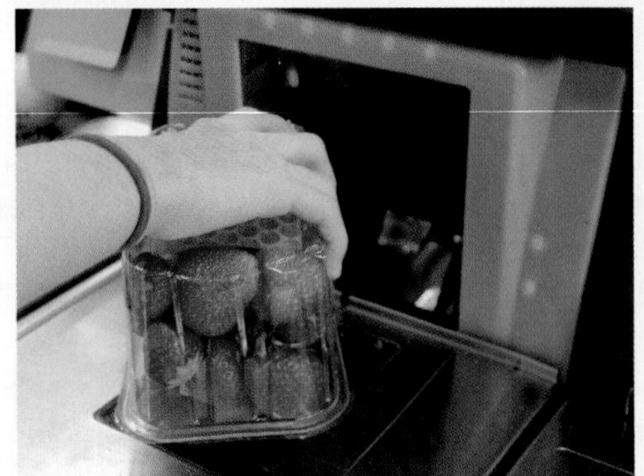

FIXED BARCODE READER
Used most often in retail point-of-sale applications.

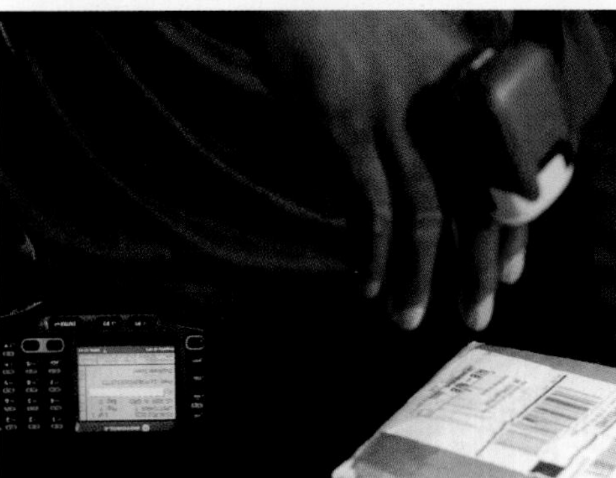

PORTABLE BARCODE READER
Used when portability is needed.

INTEGRATED BARCODE READER
Used most often for consumer applications.

the consumer's smartphone to load a Web page, display a video clip, like a Facebook page, or download a coupon or ticket. QR codes can also be used to transfer contact information to a phone or add an event to an online calendar.

Barcodes are read with **barcode readers** (see Exhibit 2-34). Barcode readers use either light reflected from the barcode or imaging technology to interpret the bars contained in the barcode as the numbers or letters they represent. Then, data associated with that barcode—typically identifying data, such as to uniquely identify a product, shipped package, or other item—can be retrieved. Fixed barcode readers are frequently used in point-of-sale (POS) systems (refer again to Exhibit 2-34). Portable barcode readers are also available for people who need to scan barcodes while on the go, such as while walking through a warehouse, retail store, hospital, or other facility. In addition, most smartphones and tablets today have barcode-reading capabilities.

Radio frequency identification (RFID) is a technology that can store, read, and transmit data located in RFID tags. **RFID tags** traditionally contain tiny chips and radio antennas, as shown in Exhibit 2-35, although newer chipless RFID tags are in development. RFID tags can be attached to objects, such as products, price tags, shipping labels, ID cards, assets (such as livestock, vehicles, computers, and other expensive items), and identification bracelets. Some of the initial RFID applications were tracking inventory, shipping containers, and livestock. RFID is also used for tracking patients at hospitals, speeding up border crossing identification, and for more efficient ticketing applications, such as ski lift tickets (see Exhibit 2-36).

The data in RFID tags is read by **RFID readers**, which are available in a number of different sizes and formats. Whenever an RFID-tagged item is within range of an RFID reader (from one inch to up to 300 feet or

EXHIBIT 2-35 RFID TAG

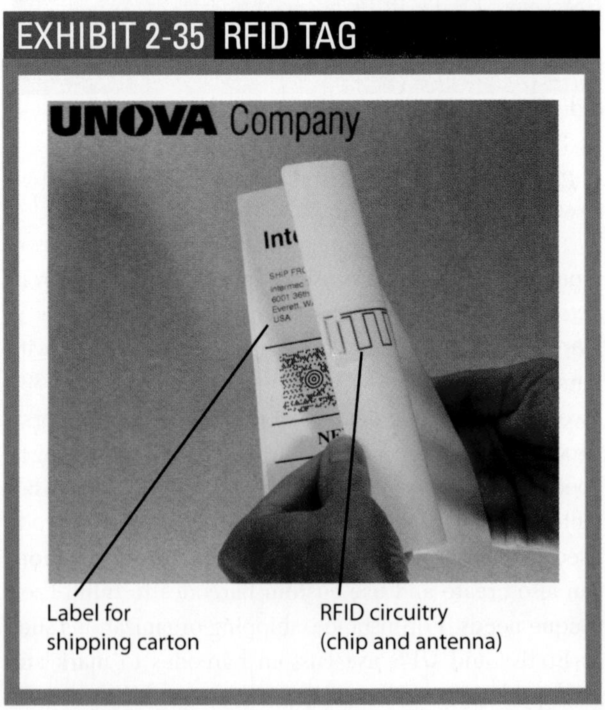

EXHIBIT 2-36 RFID APPLICATIONS

INVENTORY TRACKING
This portal RFID reader reads RFID tags attached to the shipping container or to items inside the container as it passes through the portal.

TICKETING APPLICATION
This stationary RFID reader is used to automatically open ski lift entry gates for valid lift ticket holders at a ski resort in Utah.

Source: © Honeywell International Inc.; © teamaxess.com

more, depending on the type of tag and the radio frequency being used), the tag's built-in antenna allows the information located within the RFID tag to be sent to the reader. Unlike barcodes, RFID readers can read the data stored in multiple RFID tags at the same time and can scan the tags through cardboard and other materials. Each RFID tag has a unique identifying number, and the data can be updated if needed. One disadvantage of RFID tags is cost, though the chipless, printable RFID tags in development are expected to eventually drop the cost to less than a tenth of a cent.

There are some privacy and security issues related to RFID. For example, there is concern that unauthorized individuals might be able to read the data contained in an RFID tag attached to clothing or a passport, or they might be able to make fraudulent charges via someone else's smartphone. Precautions against fraudulent use of RFID payment systems include using high-frequency tags that need to be within a few inches of the reader and requiring a PIN code, a signature, or another type of authorization when an RFID payment system is used. For example, when iPhone 6 users make a payment with Apple Pay, they can authorize it via a fingerprint swipe. To prevent RFID-enabled documents, such as credit cards, drivers licenses, and passports, from being read, shielded wallets are available.

Optical mark readers (OMRs) input data from optical mark forms to score or tally exams, questionnaires, ballots, and so forth. Typically, people use a pencil to fill in small circles or other shapes on the form to indicate their selections, and then the form is inserted into an optical mark reader, such as the one shown in Exhibit 2-37, to be scored or tallied. The results can be input into a computer system if the optical mark reader is connected to a computer.

Optical character recognition (OCR) refers to the ability of a computer to recognize text characters printed on a document. The characters are read by a compatible scanning device, such as a scanner, barcode reader, or dedicated OCR reader, and then OCR software is used to identify each character and convert it to editable text. While OCR systems can recognize many different types of printed characters, optical characters—which are characters specifically designed to be identifiable by humans as well as by an OCR device—are often used in documents intended to be processed by an OCR system. For example, optical characters are

barcode reader An input device that reads barcodes.

radio frequency identification (RFID) A technology used to store, read, and transmit data located in RFID tags.

RFID tag A tag that can be attached to an object so it can be identified using RFID technology.

RFID reader An input device that reads RFID tags.

optical mark reader (OMR) An input device that reads data from optical mark forms.

optical character recognition (OCR) The ability of a computer to recognize scanned characters as text.

widely used in processing turnaround documents, such as the monthly bills for credit card and utility companies (see Exhibit 2-38). These documents contain optical characters in certain places on the bill to aid processing when consumers send it back with payment—or "turn it around."

Magnetic ink character recognition (MICR) is a technology used primarily by the banking industry to facilitate check processing. MICR characters, such as those located on the bottom of a check that represent the bank routing number, check number, and account number, are inscribed on checks with magnetic ink when the checks are first printed. These characters can be read, and new characters, such as to reflect the check's amount, can be added by an MICR reader (also called a check scanner) when needed. High-volume MICR readers are used by banks to process checks deposited at the bank. Smaller units can be used by many businesses to deposit paper checks remotely, although small businesses may prefer remote deposits via a smartphone app and camera instead. MICR readers are also incorporated in most ATMs, such as the one in Exhibit 2-39, to enable the MICR information located on checks inserted into the ATM to be read at the time of the deposit.

Biometrics is the science of identifying individuals based on measurable biological characteristics. **Biometric readers** are used to read biometric data about a person so that the individual's identity can be verified based on a particular unique physiological characteristic, such as a fingerprint or a face, or personal trait, such as a voice or a signature. Biometric readers can

EXHIBIT 2-37 OPTICAL MARK READER

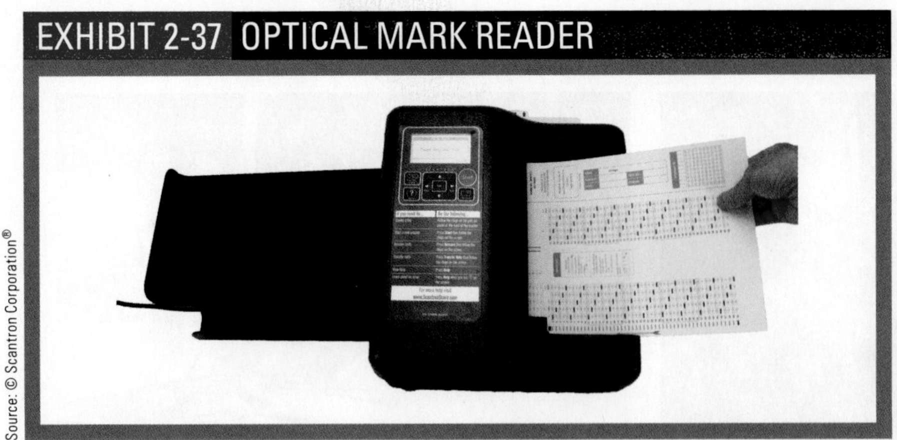

Source: © Scantron Corporation®

EXHIBIT 2-38 OPTICAL CHARACTERS

PLEASE RETURN THIS PORTION WITH PAYMENT

MAKE CHECKS PAYABLE TO NV ENERGY

NVEnergy

ACCOUNT NUMBER:
3000111111311111139

BALANCE FORWARD	.00
CURRENT CHARGES	135.86
TOTAL AMOUNT DUE	**$135.86**
Current Charges due by Apr 5, 2017	

Service Address: 123 MAPLE ST.
LAS VEGAS NV 89135

Please enter amount paid below
$

9965.3.86.18458 1 AV 0.324 oz 0.733

JOHN SMITH
123 MAPLE ST.
LAS VEGAS NV 89135

89520-3086

3000111111311111139 0000013586 0000013586 0 000

OPTICAL CHARACTERS
These OCR characters indicate the customer account number and amount due and can be read by both computers and humans.

Source: © NV Energy

EXHIBIT 2-39 MICR READER INCORPORATED INTO AN ATM

Source: © NCR Corporation

biometric reader An input device that reads biometric data, such as an individual's fingerprint or voice.

TRENDING...

BIOMETRIC SMARTPHONE KEYS

Think a password or even a pattern to unlock your smartphone takes too long? Well, you're in luck—a number of new biometric keys that can be used to unlock your smartphone are available. For newer iPhones, Touch ID can be used to unlock the phone simply by placing a finger on the Home button. Android users can enable Face Unlock to have their smartphones unlock by simply looking at the screen. For security purposes, users can choose to include a liveness check, which requires an eye blink before unlocking the phone. For an even more secure option, iris recognition unlocking systems are becoming available. All of these biometric key systems require an initial enrollment where your fingerprint, face image, or iris characteristics are recorded. For back up, you can often set up a password or pattern that can be used if the smartphone doesn't recognize you.

be stand-alone or built into a computer or mobile device, such as the Apple iPhone shown in Exhibit 2-40. They can also be built into another piece of hardware, such as a keyboard, an external hard drive, or a USB flash drive. Biometric readers can be used to allow only authorized users access to a computer or facility or to the data stored on a storage device as well as to authorize electronic payments, log on to secure Web sites, or punch into and out of work.

EXHIBIT 2-40 BIOMETRIC READER

Digital cameras (see Exhibit 2-41) record images on a digital storage medium, such as a flash memory card, an embedded flash memory, or a built-in hard drive. Digital cameras can take still photos or moving video images, or both. In addition to stand-alone digital cameras, digital cameras are integrated into many portable computers and mobile devices. The images taken with a digital camera can be sent to others or posted on social media; they can also be transferred to a computer for editing, printing, or inclusion in a document as needed.

EXHIBIT 2-41 DIGITAL CAMERA

2-5e Audio Input

Audio input is the process of entering audio data into the computer. The most common types of audio input are voice and music. Voice input—inputting spoken words and converting them to digital form—is typically performed via a microphone, which is often

digital camera An input device that records images on a digital storage medium.

EXHIBIT 2-42 SPEECH RECOGNITION SYSTEM

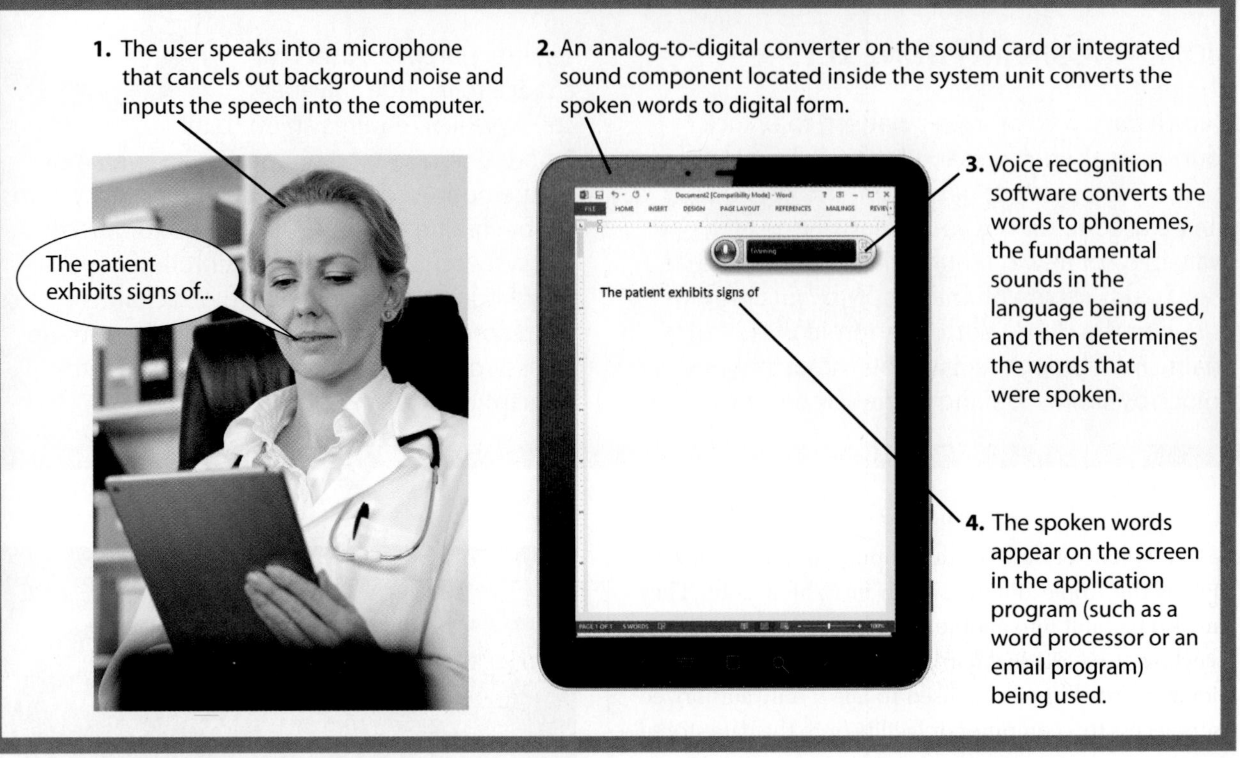

1. The user speaks into a microphone that cancels out background noise and inputs the speech into the computer.
2. An analog-to-digital converter on the sound card or integrated sound component located inside the system unit converts the spoken words to digital form.
The patient exhibits signs of...
The patient exhibits signs of
3. Voice recognition software converts the words to phonemes, the fundamental sounds in the language being used, and then determines the words that were spoken.
4. The spoken words appear on the screen in the application program (such as a word processor or an email program) being used.

© Sebastian Gauert/Shutterstock.com; © OmniArt/Shutterstock.com

built into the computer or mobile device being used. Voice input can be used in conjunction with sound recorder software to store the voice in an audio file, such as to create a podcast or perform legal or medical dictation (see Exhibit 2-42). It can also be used to provide spoken instructions to a computer or mobile device. **Speech recognition systems** enable the device being used to recognize voice input as spoken words. It requires appropriate software in addition to a microphone. To enable hands-free operation, speech recognition capabilities are commonly built into cars for hands-free control of navigation systems and sound systems as well as to allow hands-free mobile phone calls to take place via the car's voice interface. Specialty speech recognition systems are frequently used to control machines, robots, and other electronic equipment, such as by surgeons during surgical procedures. They can also be used by individuals who cannot use a keyboard to input data and control the computer.

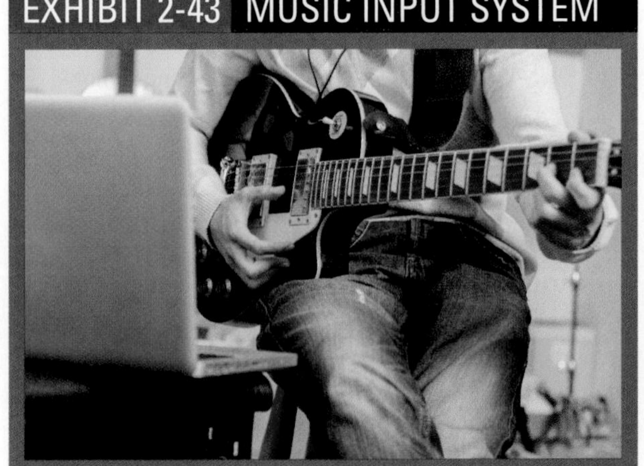

speech recognition system An input system that enables a computer to recognize voice input.

Music input systems are used to input music into a computer, such as to create an original music composition or arrangement or to create a custom music CD. Existing music can be input into a computer via a music CD or a Web download. For original compositions, microphones, keyboard controllers, and guitar controllers can be used to input the music into the computer (see Exhibit 2-43). Once music is input into a computer, it can be saved, modified, played, inserted into other programs, or burned to a CD or DVD.

EXHIBIT 2-43 MUSIC INPUT SYSTEM

© Gines Romero/Shutterstock.com

EXHIBIT 2-44 USES FOR DISPLAY DEVICES

PORTABLE COMPUTER

SMART WATCH

DIGITAL VIDEO CAMERA

E-READER

SMARTPHONE

DIGITAL SIGNAGE SYSTEM

Source: © Apple, Inc.; © Samsung Electronics Co., Ltd; © Sony Electronics; © Barnesandnoble.com llc; © HTC; © Clear Channel Spectacolor

2-6 OUTPUT DEVICES

An **output device** accepts processed data from the computer and presents the results to the user, most of the time on the computer screen, on paper, or through a speaker. In addition to conventional output devices, there are assistive output devices, such as screen readers, for visually impaired users that read all text information display on a screen aloud; Braille displays that convert screen input into Braille; and Braille printers that emboss output in Braille format on paper instead of, or in addition to, conventional ink output.

2-6a Display Devices

A **display device**—the most common form of output device—presents output visually on some type of screen. The display device for a desktop computer is more formally called a **monitor**. The display device for a notebook computer, tablet, smartphone, or other device for which the screen is built into the device is typically called a **display screen**. In addition to being used with computers and mobile devices, display screens are also built into handheld gaming devices, home entertainment devices, automobiles, and kitchen appliances. They are also an important component in digital photo frames, e-readers, digital cameras, wearable devices, and other consumer products as well as in digital signage systems used outdoors and in retail establishments (see Exhibit 2-44).

The **CRT monitor** used to be the norm for desktop computers. CRT monitors use the same cathode-ray tube

output device A device that accepts processed data from the computer and presents the results to the user.

display device An output device that presents visual output on a screen.

monitor A display device for a desktop computer.

display screen A display device built into a notebook computer, smartphone, or other device.

CRT monitor A display device that uses cathode-ray tube technology.

technology used in conventional televisions in which an electron gun sealed inside a large glass tube projects an electron beam at a screen coated with red, green, and blue phosphor dots; the beam lights up the appropriate colors in each **pixel** (the smallest colorable areas on a display device—essentially tiny dots on a display screen) to display the image. As a result, CRTs are large, bulky, and heavy.

Most computers (as well as most television sets, mobile phones, and other consumer devices containing a display screen) use the thinner and lighter **flat panel displays**. Flat panel displays form images by manipulating electronically charged chemicals or gases sandwiched between thin panes of glass or other transparent material. Flat panel displays take up less desk space, which makes it possible to use multiple monitors working together to increase the amount of data the user can view at one time (see Exhibit 2-45), increasing productivity. Flat panel displays also consume less power than CRTs and most use digital signals to display images (instead of the analog signals used with CRT monitors), which allows for sharper images. To use multiple monitors, you must have the necessary hardware to support them, such as a monitor port on a notebook computer or an appropriate video adapter, as discussed shortly. One disadvantage to a flat panel display is that the images sometimes cannot be seen clearly when viewed from a wide angle. To correct this, some newer monitors today are curved.

EXHIBIT 2-45 FLAT PANEL DISPLAYS

One of the most common flat panel technologies is **LCD (liquid crystal display)**, which uses charged liquid crystals located between two sheets of clear material (usually glass or plastic) to light up the appropriate pixels to form the image on the screen. Several layers of liquid crystals are used, and, in their normal state, the liquid crystals are aligned so that light passes through the display. When an electrical charge is applied to the liquid crystals (via an electrode grid layer contained within the LCD panel), the liquid crystals change their orientation, or "twist," so that light cannot pass through the display, and the liquid crystals at the charged intersections of the electrode grid appear dark. Color LCD displays use a color filter that consists of a pattern of red, green, and blue subpixels for each pixel. The voltage used controls the orientation (twisting) of the liquid crystals and the amount of light that gets through, affecting the color and shade of that pixel—the three different colors blend to make the pixel the appropriate color.

LCD displays can be viewed only with reflective light, unless light is built into the display. Consequently, LCD panels used with computer monitors typically include a light inside the panel, usually at the rear of the display—a technique referred to as backlighting.

LED (light-emitting diode) displays are another common type of flat panel display. LED displays consist of LCD displays that are backlit with LEDs, which are the same type of lights that are commonly used with consumer products, such as alarm clocks and Christmas lights. **OLED (organic light-emitting diode) displays** are even newer and use layers of organic material that emit a visible light when electric current is applied. Because they emit a visible light, OLED displays do not use backlighting. This characteristic makes OLEDs more energy efficient than LCDs and lengthens the battery life of portable devices using OLED displays. Other advantages of OLEDs are that they are thinner than LCDs, they have a wider viewing angle than LCDs so displayed content is visible from virtually all directions, and their images are brighter and sharper than LCDs. OLED displays are incorporated into many consumer devices, including digital cameras, smartphones (see Exhibit 2-46), and television.

Plasma displays use a layered technology like LCDs and OLEDs and look similar to LCD displays,

pixel The smallest colorable area in an electronic image.

flat panel display A slim display device that that uses electronically charged chemicals or gases to display images.

LCD (liquid crystal display) A type of flat panel display that uses charged liquid crystals to display images.

LED (light-emitting diode) display An LCD that is backlit with LEDs.

(OLED) organic light-emitting diode display A type of flat panel display that uses layers of organic material to display brighter and sharper images.

plasma display A type of flat panel display that uses a layer of gas between two plates of glass to display images.

EXHIBIT 2-46 HOW OLED DISPLAYS WORK

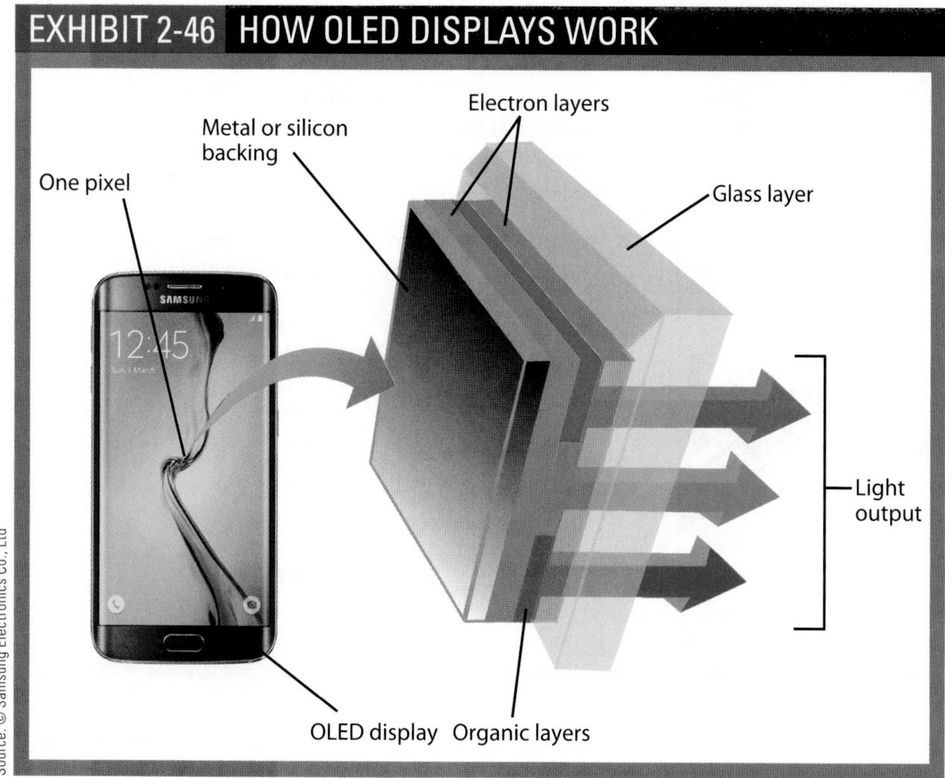

but they use a layer of gas between two plates of glass instead of a layer of liquid crystals or organic material. A phosphor-coated screen (with red, green, and blue phosphors for each pixel) is used, and an electrode grid layer and electronic charges are used to make the gas atoms light up the appropriate phosphors to create the image on the screen. Although plasma technology has traditionally been used with the very large displays used by businesses and many large screen televisions, it is being replaced by LEDs.

Regardless of the technology being used, display devices form images by lighting up the proper configurations of pixels in order to display a particular image. Display devices can be monochromatic displays, in which each pixel can only be one of two colors, such as black or white, or color displays, in which each pixel can display a combination of three colors—red, green, and blue—in order to display a large range of colors.

The number of pixels used on a display screen determines the screen resolution, which affects the amount of information that can be displayed on the screen at one time. When a higher resolution is selected, such as 1,920 pixels horizontally by 1,080 pixels vertically for a standard computer monitor (written as 1,920 × 1,080), more information can fit on the screen, but everything will be displayed smaller than with a lower resolution, such as 1,024 × 768. The screen resolution on many computers can be changed by users to match their preferences and the software being used.

Display device size is measured diagonally from corner to corner. Most desktop computer monitors today are between 19 inches and 30 inches (though larger screens—up to 80 inches and more—are becoming increasingly common); notebook displays are usually between 10 inches and 17 inches; and tablet displays are typically between 7 inches and 11 inches. To better view DVDs and other multimedia content, many monitors are widescreen, which conforms to the 16:9 aspect ratio of widescreen televisions, instead of the conventional 4:3 aspect ratio.

The video graphics card installed inside a computer or the integrated graphics component built directly into the motherboard of the CPU of a computer houses the graphics processing unit (GPU)—the chip devoted to rendering images on a display device. The video graphics card or the integrated graphics component determines the graphics capabilities of the computer, including the screen resolutions available, the number of bits used to store color information about each pixel (called the bit depth), the total number of colors that can be used to display images, the number of monitors that can be connected to the computer via that video card or component, and the types of connectors that can be used to connect a monitor to the computer. Video cards typically contain a fan and other cooling components to cool the card. Many video cards also contain memory chips (typically called video RAM or VRAM) to support graphics display. If a video graphics card does not contain memory chips, that device will use a portion of the computer's regular RAM as video RAM instead. Most video graphics cards today contain between 512 MB and 12 GB of video RAM. A typical video graphics card is shown in Exhibit 2-47.

The three most common types of interfaces used to connect a monitor to a computer are VGA (Video Graphics Array), DVI (Digital Visual Interface), and HDMI (High-Definition Multimedia Interface), all shown in Exhibit 2-47. VGA is an older connection

EXHIBIT 2-47 VIDEO GRAPHICS CARD

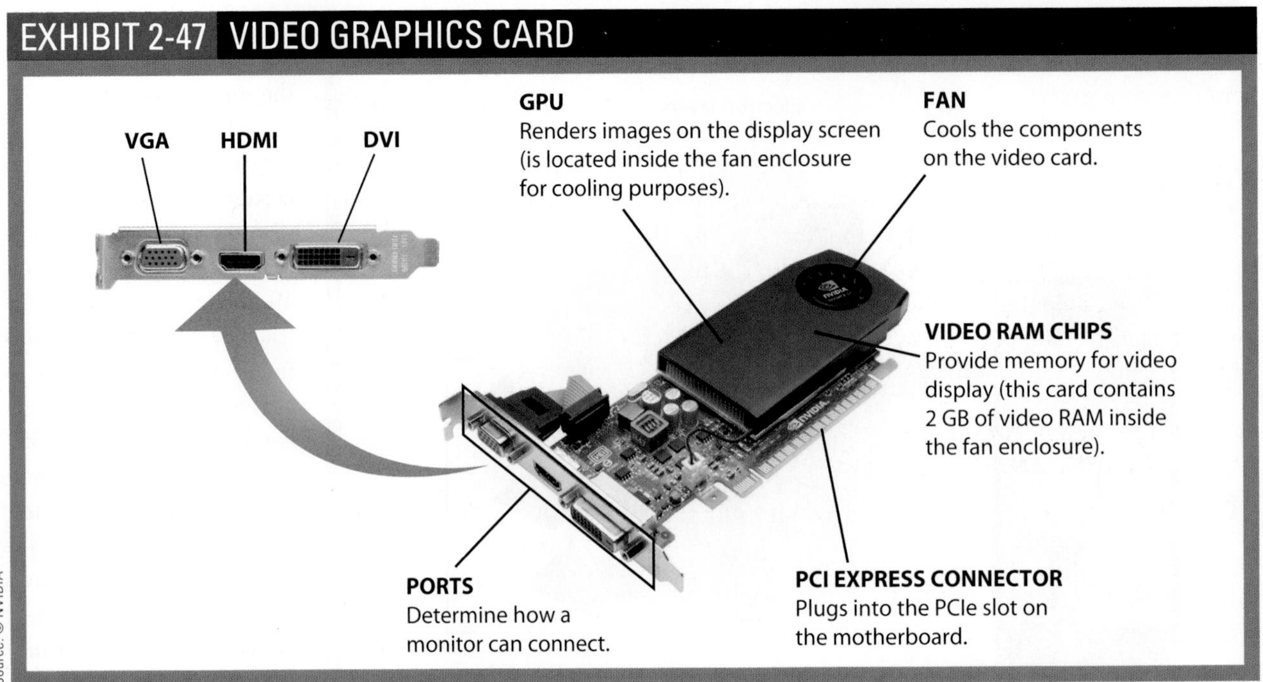
VGA
HDMI
DVI
GPU
Renders images on the display screen (is located inside the fan enclosure for cooling purposes).
FAN
Cools the components on the video card.
VIDEO RAM CHIPS
Provide memory for video display (this card contains 2 GB of video RAM inside the fan enclosure).
PORTS
Determine how a monitor can connect.
PCI EXPRESS CONNECTOR
Plugs into the PCIe slot on the motherboard.

Source: © NVIDIA

traditionally used with CRT monitors and many flat panel monitors to transfer analog images to the monitor. DVI uses a more rectangular connector and it is used with flat panel displays to allow the monitor to receive clearer, more reliable digital signals than is possible with a VGA interface. HDMI uses a smaller connector and can transfer audio signals as well as video signals to high-definition displays. A newer option is the USB monitor, which connects via a USB port.

A video card or integrated video component in a desktop computer has at least one port exposed through the system unit case to connect a monitor. Notebook

TRENDING...

WEARABLE HOLOGRAPHIC DISPLAYS

Recent improvements in flat panel display technology and graphics processing have led to the development of wearable display devices that project images in front of the user. Typically, the images are overlaid on top of what the user is seeing in real time, which is referred to as augmented reality. Smart glasses are one type of wearable display. They usually look like a pair of eyeglasses with a built-in display and connect to a smartphone to display content from that device. Some smart glasses, such as Google Glass, can also display content via a built-in Web browser. Other wearable displays are larger headset-based displays. For example, Microsoft HoloLens (shown in the accompanying photo) is essentially a Windows computer built into a headset. The headset can project 3D images throughout an entire room. It can even project images via video chat to another individual who can then draw on top of the images that the HoloLens wearer also sees in real time. While still in the development stages, HoloLens has great potential for training and customer support as well as for entertainment and productivity.

Source: © Microsoft Corporation

computers and other computers with a built-in display often contain a monitor port to connect a second monitor to the computer.

Traditionally, computer monitors are physically connected to the system unit via a cable. However, an increasing number of display devices, including digital photo frames, e-readers, computer monitors, and television sets, are designed to be wireless. Wireless displays connect to a computer or other device, such as to a smartphone (see Exhibit 2-48), using a wireless networking connection.

EXHIBIT 2-48 WIRELESS DISPLAY

Source: © HTC

2-6b Data and Multimedia Projectors

A **data projector** is used to display output from a computer onto a wall or projection screen. Projectors that are designed primarily to display movies and other multimedia are sometimes called multimedia projectors. Data projectors are often found in classrooms, conference rooms, and similar locations and can be portable units, freestanding larger units, or units that are permanently mounted onto the ceiling. Larger data projectors usually connect via cable to a computer. Wireless projectors connect via a wireless connection and are often used to more easily project content located on a company network, the Internet, a smartphone, or a tablet.

For projecting content to a small audience while on the go, small pico projectors are available. These pocket-sized projectors typically connect to a smartphone, a portable computer, or other device to project an image from the device onto a wall or other flat surface from up to 12 feet away. Pico projectors typically create a display up to about 10 feet wide in order to easily share information stored on the device without everyone having to crowd around a tiny screen. Projection capabilities are also beginning to be integrated directly into smartphones.

Another type of data projector is designed to project actual 3D projections or holograms. For instance, holograms of individuals and objects can be projected onto a stage for a presentation. Hologram display devices can be used in retail stores, exhibitions, and other locations to showcase products or other items in 3D.

2-6c Printers

Instead of the temporary, ever-changing output that a monitor produces, **printers** produce output on paper. Most desktop computers are connected to a printer. Portable computers and some mobile devices can use printers as well.

Printers produce images through either impact or nonimpact technologies. Impact printers, like old ribbon typewriters, have a print mechanism that actually strikes the paper to transfer ink to the paper. For example, a dot-matrix printer such as the one shown in Exhibit 2-49 uses a print head consisting of pins that strike an inked ribbon to transfer the ink to the paper—the appropriate pins are extended (and, consequently, strike the ribbon) as the print head moves across the paper to form the appropriate words or images. Impact printers are used primarily for producing multipart forms, such as invoices, packing slips, and credit card receipts.

EXHIBIT 2-49 DOT-MATRIX PRINTER

Source: © InfoPrint Solutions Company

data projector A display device that projects computer output onto a wall or projection screen.

printer An output device that produces a permanent copy of output on paper.

Most printers today are nonimpact printers, meaning they form images without the print mechanism actually touching the paper. Nonimpact printers usually produce higher-quality images and are much quieter than impact printers. The two most common types of printers—laser printers and ink-jet printers—are both nonimpact printers. Both impact and nonimpact printers form images with dots, in a manner similar to the way monitors display images with pixels. (Laser printers use flecks of powdered ink called toner powder and ink-jet printers use dots of liquid ink.) Because of this, printers are very versatile and can print text in virtually any size as well as print photos and other graphical images. Print quality is measured in dots per inch (dpi). The higher the dpi, the more dots are used and the better the quality of the output. In addition to paper, both impact and nonimpact printers can print on transparencies, envelopes, mailing labels, and more. Both color and black-and-white printers are available.

Print speed is traditionally measured in pages per minute (ppm). How long it takes a document to print depends on the actual printer being used, the selected print resolution, the amount of memory inside the printer, and the content being printed. For instance, pages containing photographs or other images usually take longer to print than pages containing only text, and full-color pages take longer to print than black-and-white pages. Because of this, the ISO standard of images per minute (IPM) was developed as a more uniform measurement of print speed to allow consumers to more easily compare printers from different manufacturers.

Most printers connect to a single computer via a USB connection or to a home or an office network via a networking cable or a wireless connection. Networked printers can be accessed by any computer or device on the same network. They can also be accessed via the Internet using an appropriate app, an assigned e-mail address for that printer, or a cloud printing service such as Google Cloud Print. For instance, if your printer has Internet access, you can print content from your smartphone or tablet to your home or office printer (see Exhibit 2-50) via the Internet from any location.

Laser printers form images with toner powder and are the standard for business documents. Laser printers come in a variety of sizes from home laser printers to enterprise laser printers, such as the one shown in Exhibit 2-51. They are also available as both color and black-and-white printers. To print a document, a laser printer uses a laser beam to charge the appropriate locations on a drum to form the page's image, and then toner powder is released from a toner cartridge and sticks to the drum. The toner is transferred to a piece of paper when the paper is rolled over the drum, and a heating unit fuses the toner powder to the paper to permanently form the image. Laser printers print an entire page at a time and so are typically faster than ink-jet printers.

Ink-jet printers form images by spraying tiny drops of liquid ink from one or more ink cartridges onto

laser printer A printer that forms images with toner powder (essentially ink powder).

ink-jet printer A printer that forms images by spraying tiny drops of liquid ink from one or more ink cartridges onto paper.

EXHIBIT 2-50 CLOUD PRINTING

Source: © Epson America

EXHIBIT 2-51 ENTERPRISE LASER PRINTER

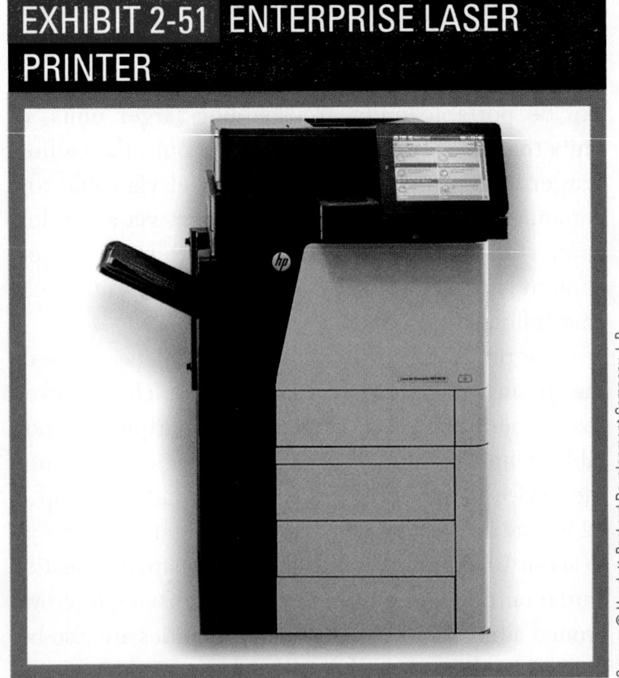

Source: © Hewlett-Packard Development Company, L.P.

EXHIBIT 2-52 HOW INK-JET PRINTERS WORK

Each ink cartridge is made up of multiple tiny ink-filled firing chambers; to print images, the appropriate color ink is ejected through the appropriate firing chamber.

INK-JET PRINTER

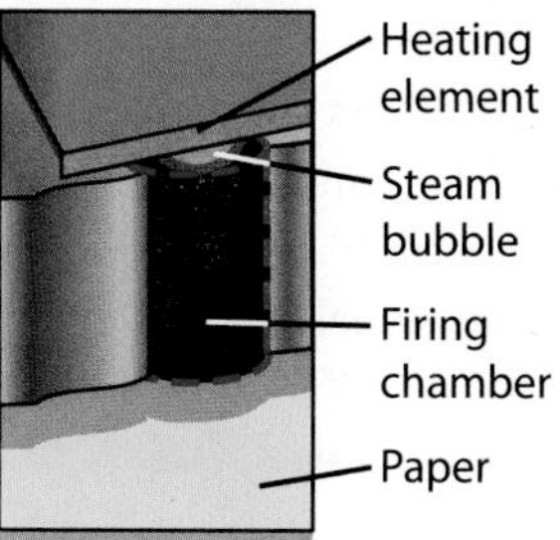

1. A heating element makes the ink boil, which causes a steam bubble to form.

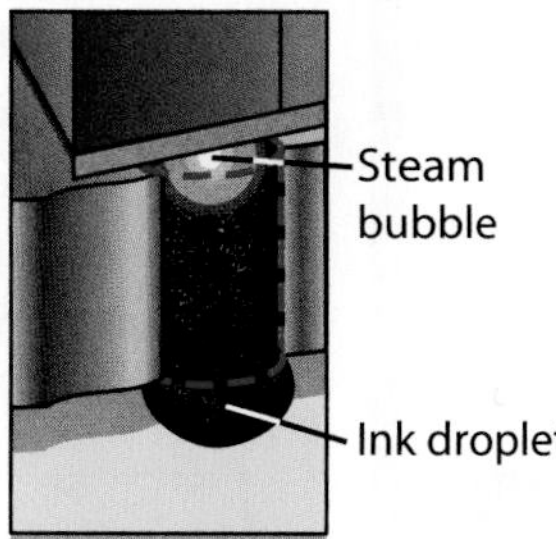

2. As the steam bubble expands, it pushes ink through the firing chamber.

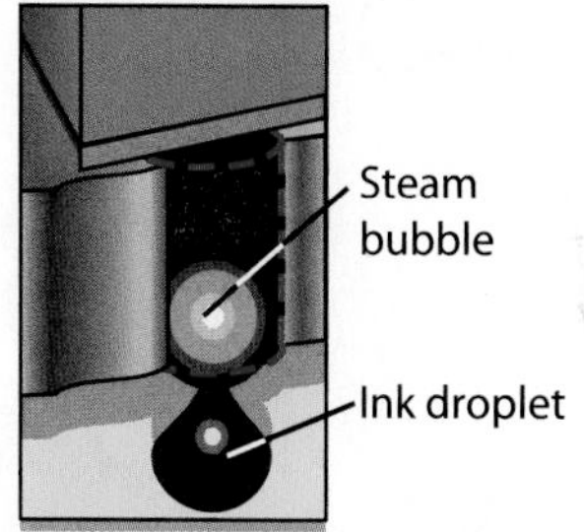

3. The ink droplet is ejected onto the paper and the steam bubble collapses, pulling more ink into the firing chamber.

the page, one line at a time, as illustrated in Exhibit 2-52. Some printers print with one single-sized ink droplet; others print using different-sized ink droplets and using multiple nozzles or varying electrical charges for more precise printing. The printhead for an ink-jet printer typically travels back and forth across the page, which is one reason why ink-jet printers are slower than laser printers. However, some ink-jet printers use a printhead that is the full width of the paper, which allows the printhead to remain stationary while the paper feeds past it, significantly increasing the speed.

Because ink-jet printers are relatively inexpensive, have good-quality output, and can print in color, ink-jet printers are often the printer of choice for home use. With the use of special photo paper, ink-jet printers can also print photograph-quality digital photos. Starting at less than $50 for a simple home printer, ink-jet printers are affordable, although the cost of the replaceable ink cartridges can add up, especially if you do a lot of color printing.

Barcode printers enable businesses and other organizations to print custom barcodes on price tags, shipping labels, and other documents for identification or pricing purposes. Most barcode printers can print labels in a variety of barcode standards; some can also encode RFID tags embedded in labels.

Portable printers are small, lightweight printers that can be used on the go, usually with a notebook computer or a mobile device, and they connect via either a wired or wireless connection. Portable printers that can print on letter-sized (8½ by 11-inch) paper are used by businesspeople while traveling. Portable receipt, label, and barcode printers are used in some service

barcode printer A printer used to print barcodes.

portable printer A small, lightweight printer that can be used on the go, such as with a notebook computer or a mobile device.

professions. Printers can also be integrated into other devices, such as smartphone cases and digital cameras. Some portable printers don't use conventional ink-jet or laser technology. For instance, some portable printers use a technology developed by ZINK (for "zero ink") Imaging. ZINK printers (see Exhibit 2-53) use no ink; instead, they use special paper that is coated with color dye crystals. Before printing, the embedded dye crystals are clear, so ZINK Paper looks like regular white photo paper. The ZINK printer uses heat to activate and colorize these dye crystals when a photo is printed, creating a full-color image.

EXHIBIT 2-53 ZINK PORTABLE PRINTER

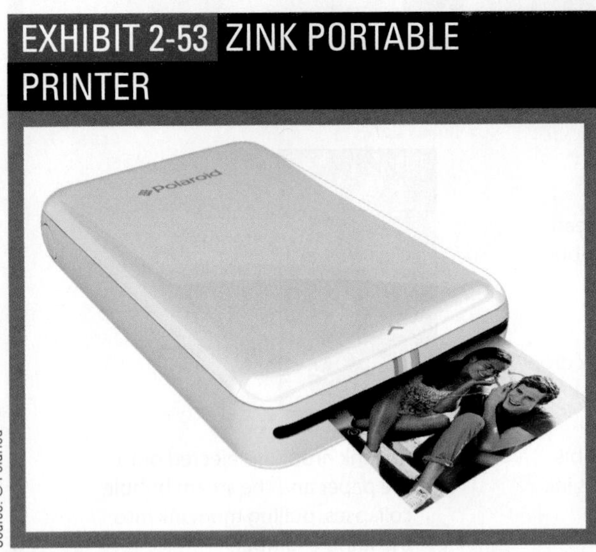

Source: © Polaroid

To print charts, drawings, maps, blueprints, posters, signs, advertising banners, and other large documents in one piece, a larger printer is needed. Most large-format printers (sometimes called plotters) are wide-format ink-jet printers, which are designed to print documents from around 24 inches to 60 inches in width. Although typically used to print on paper, some wide-format ink-jet printers can print directly on fabric and other types of materials.

3D printers produce three-dimensional (3D) objects. They can create a wide variety of objects, such as a 3D model of a new building, a prototype of a new product, custom medical and dental implants, and edible products printed from sugar or chocolate. They can also print objects containing moving parts (such as joints or gears as shown in Exhibit 2-54), so 3D printers are very versatile. Instead of printing on paper, 3D printers form

EXHIBIT 2-54 3D PRINTER

Source: © 3D Systems, Inc.

output in layers using materials such as plastic, metal, ceramic, or glass during a series of passes to build a 3D version of the desired output. Some printers can produce multicolor output; others print in only one color and need to be painted by hand, if color output is desired. 3D printers are available in a variety of sizes, from personal printers to professional printers.

FYI

MULTIFUNCTION DEVICES

Some printers today offer more than just printing capabilities. These units—referred to as **multifunction devices (MFDs)**, or all-in-ones—typically copy, scan, fax, and print documents. MFDs can be based on ink-jet printer or laser printer technology, and they are available as both color and black-and-white devices. Although multi-function devices have traditionally been desktop units used in small offices and home offices, it is common today for enterprise printers (such as the one shown here) to be multifunction devices.

Source: © Epson America, Inc.

3D printer A printer that produces three-dimensional (3D) output.

multifunction device (MFD) An output device that can copy, scan, fax, and print documents.

The ability of 3D printers to print customized objects on demand is a big advantage. For example, NASA has installed a 3D printer at the International Space Station and is testing its ability to print tools and other objects that astronauts may need on demand. In the future, it is possible that 3D printers will be used by consumers on a regular basis to print everyday items on demand. One issue with the increased availability of 3D printers is the risk of them being used to print dangerous or illegal items, such as working plastic guns. In fact, the first 3D-printed gun firing standard bullets was demonstrated in 2013 and more than 100,000 copies of the open-source blueprint were downloaded before the file was taken offline per a U.S. State Department request.

2-6d Audio Output

Audio output includes voice, music, and other audible sounds. Computer speakers, the most common type of audio output device, are either connected to or built into a computer and provide audio output for computer games, music, video clips and TV shows, Web conferencing, and other applications.

While desktop computers often use external speakers connected to the system unit, portable computers and mobile devices typically have speakers integrated into the device. These devices can also be connected to a home or car stereo system, portable speakers, or a consumer device such as a treadmill that contains a compatible dock and integrated speakers in order to play music stored on the device. Typically, mobile devices are connected to a speaker system via the device's headphone jack, dock connection, USB port, or wireless connection. For example, the portable wireless speaker shown in Exhibit 2-55 can play music from a smartphone whenever that phone is within range.

EXHIBIT 2-55 PORTABLE WIRELESS SPEAKER

Source: © Mova Systems SAS

Headphones can be used instead of speakers when you do not want the audio output to disturb others (such as in a school computer lab or public library). Headsets are headphones with a built-in microphone and are often used when dictating to a computer and when making telephone calls or participating in Web conferences using a computer; wireless headsets are commonly used in conjunction with mobile phones. Even smaller than headphones are the earphones and earbuds often used to listen to music via a mobile device.

STUDY TOOLS 2

READY TO STUDY? IN THE BOOK, YOU CAN:

- ☐ Rip out the Chapter Review Card, which includes key chapter concepts and important key terms.

ONLINE AT WWW.CENGAGEBRAIN.COM, YOU CAN:

- ☐ Review key concepts from the chapter in a short video.
- ☐ Explore computer hardware with the interactive infographic.
- ☐ Practice what you've learned with more Practice It and On Your Own exercises.
- ☐ Prepare for tests with quizzes.
- ☐ Review the key terms with flashcards.

QUIZ YOURSELF

1. In what form does data need to be in to be understood by a computer?
2. What is a bit?
3. What is a byte?
4. What is the main circuit board inside the system unit?
5. What is the main processing device for a computer?
6. What is a multi-core CPU?
7. Explain the purpose of RAM.
8. What does a blue USB port mean?
9. What does the ALU do?
10. Describe the difference between a storage medium and a storage device.
11. Describe the advantages of using an SSD instead of a hard drive.
12. What types of storage media does a hybrid hard drive contain?
13. What is the most common type of external storage media for smartphones and other mobile devices?
14. What is the biggest advantage of cloud computing?
15. What is the most common pointing device?
16. What device is typically used to read a QR barcode?
17. Which screen is more energy efficient, an LCD or an OLED screen? Explain why.
18. Are laser and ink-jet printers impact or nonimpact printers?

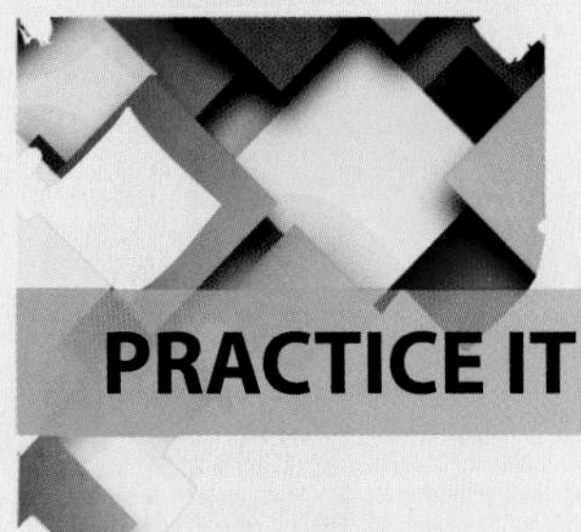

PRACTICE IT

Practice It 2-1

Adding additional RAM to a computer is one of the most common computer upgrades. Before purchasing additional memory, however, it is important to make sure that the memory about to be purchased is compatible with the computer.

1. Select a computer (your own computer, a school computer, or a computer at a local store), and then determine the manufacturer and model number, the CPU, the operating system, the current amount of memory, the total number of memory slots, and the number of available memory slots. (You can look at the computer, research online, or ask an appropriate individual, such as a lab aide in a school computer lab or a salesperson at a local store.)
2. Use the information you learned and a memory supplier's Web site to determine the appropriate type of memory needed for your selected computer. If you are using your own computer, you may wish to use the scanning tool available on some sites to analyze your computer and present you with upgrade options.
3. What choices do you have in terms of capacity and configuration?
4. Can you add just one memory module, or do you have to add memory in pairs?
5. Can you keep the old memory modules, or do they have to be removed?
6. Prepare a one-page summary of your findings and recommendations and submit it to your instructor.

Practice It 2-2

There are a variety of keyboard options for PCs and smartphones today. These options include built-in physical keyboards, on-screen keyboards, and external keyboards.

1. Locate one PC and one smartphone to investigate. Determine the types of keyboards integrated into your two selected devices. Do they have a physical keyboard or an on-screen keyboard, or both?
2. For your selected devices, evaluate the usefulness and ease of use of each keyboard options. Are there any that you would prefer to use on a regular basis?
3. Research additional keyboard options that could be used with your selected devices. For each option, determine the type of keyboard, how it connects to the device, the cost, and what advantages or additional features it provides over the built-in keyboard options.
4. Prepare a one-page summary of your findings and opinions, including whether or not you would recommend any of the keyboard options, and submit it to your instructor.

ON YOUR OWN

On Your Own 2-1

Wireless charging is an emerging option for recharging smartphones and other devices. Wireless charging capabilities are integrated into some devices; if not, it can sometimes be added.

1. Select a type of device, such as a smartphone or tablet, and research the wireless power options. Locate at least one device that has built-in wireless charging capabilities.
2. How does the wireless power feature work? Where can the device be recharged? How long does it take to charge the device?
3. Next, locate at least one add-on product, if it exists, that could be used to add wireless charging capabilities to your chosen type of device. How does it work? How long does it take to charge the device? How much does it cost?
4. Prepare a one-page summary of your findings, as well as your opinion regarding the usefulness of these products, and submit it to your instructor.

Part 1
CONCEPTS

3 | Computer Software

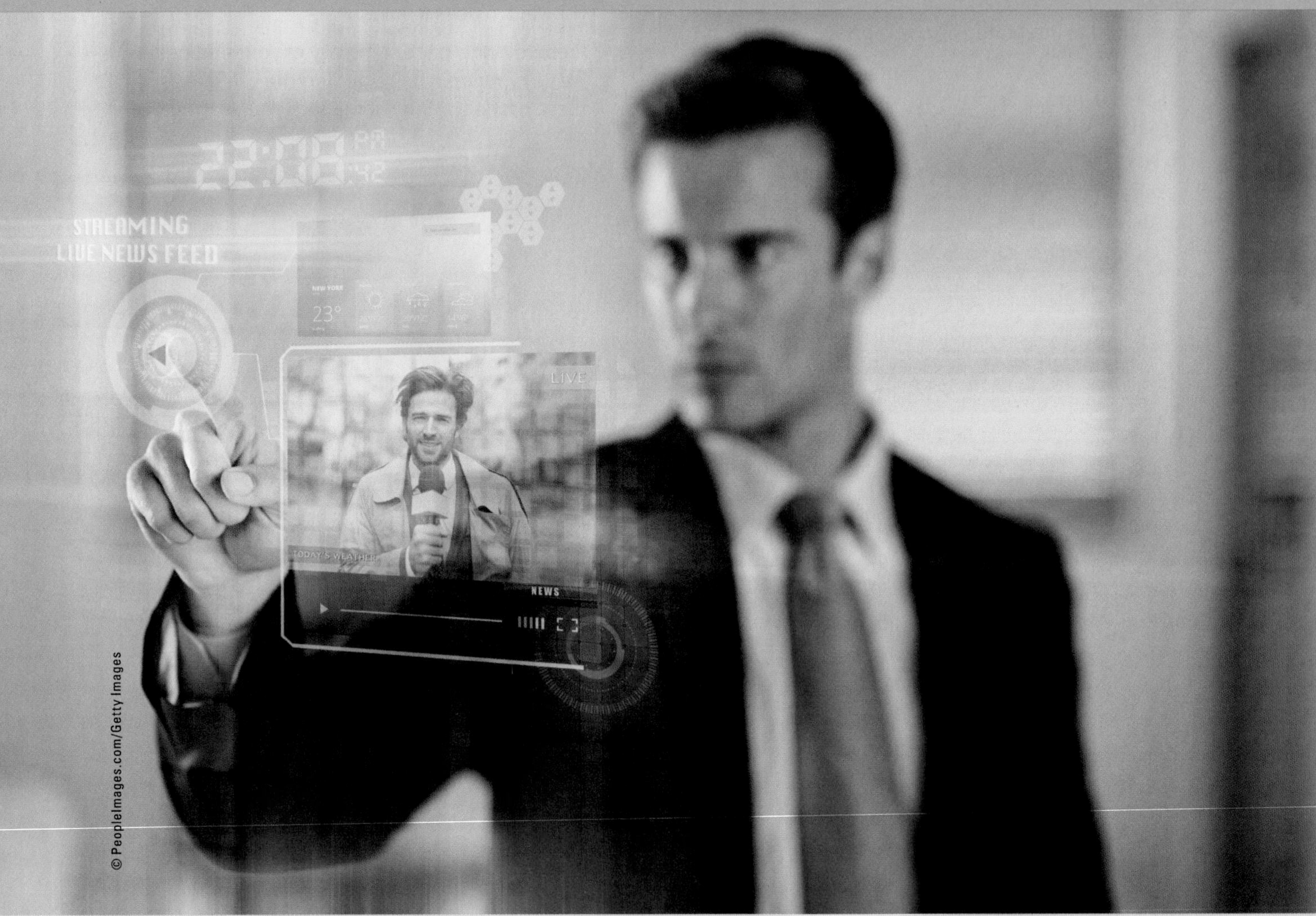

LEARNING OBJECTIVES

After studying the material in this chapter, you will be able to…

- 3-1 Explain system software and operating systems
- 3-2 Identify operating systems used with personal computers, mobile devices, and servers
- 3-3 Identify types of utility programs and explain their purpose
- 3-4 Describe common characteristics of application software
- 3-5 Describe application software used for business
- 3-6 Identify types of software used for working with multimedia
- 3-7 Describe other types of application software

After finishing this chapter, go to **PAGE 98** for **STUDY TOOLS**.

3-1 INTRODUCTION TO SYSTEM SOFTWARE AND OPERATING SYSTEMS

All computers require software to operate and perform basic tasks. **System software** is the software that controls a computer and allows you to use it. Systems software consists of the operating system and utility programs. These programs enable the computer to boot, to launch application programs, and to facilitate important jobs, such as transferring files from one storage medium to another, configuring the computer to work with the hardware connected to it, connecting the computer to a network, and protecting the computer from unauthorized use. All computers require software to operate and perform basic tasks.

A computer's **operating system** is a collection of programs that manages and coordinates the activities taking place within the computer; it is the most critical piece of software installed on the computer. The operating system is loaded into memory during the **boot process**, which gets a computer ready to be used and occurs when you power up a computer. After the boot process, the operating system provides access to application software and ensures that all actions requested by a user are valid and processed in an orderly fashion. For example, when you issue the command for your computer to store a document on your hard drive, the operating system must perform the following steps:

1. Make sure that the specified hard drive exists.
2. Verify that there is adequate space on the hard drive to store the document, and then store the document in that location.
3. Update the hard drive's directory with the file name and disk location for that file so that the document can be retrieved when needed.

In addition to managing all of the resources associated with your computer, the operating system also facilitates connections to the Internet and other networks.

3-1a Functions of the Operating System

In general, the operating system serves as an intermediary between the user and the computer, as well as between application programs and the computer's hardware, as shown in Exhibit 3-1. Without an operating system, no other program can run, and the computer cannot function. Many tasks performed by the operating system, however, go unnoticed by the user because the operating system works in the background much of the time.

As Exhibit 3-1 illustrates, one principal role of every operating system is to translate user instructions into a form the computer can understand. It also translates any feedback from hardware—such as a signal that the printer has run out of paper or that a new hardware

EXHIBIT 3-1 INTERMEDIARY ROLE OF THE OPERATING SYSTEM

1. **USER** The user instructs the operating system to start an application program.
2. **OPERATING SYSTEM** The operating system starts the requested program.
3. **USER** The user instructs the application program to open a document and then print it.
4. **APPLICATION PROGRAM** The application program hands the document over to the operating system for printing.
5. **OPERATING SYSTEM** The operating system sends the document to the printer.
6. **PRINTER** The printer prints the document.

system software Programs, such as the operating system and utility programs, that control a computer and its devices and enable it to run application software.

operating system A collection of programs that manages and coordinates the activities taking place within the computer.

boot process The actions taken, including loading the operating system, when a computer is powered up.

device has been connected to the computer—into a form that the user can understand. The means by which an operating system or any other program interacts with the user is called the **user interface**.

During the boot process, the essential portion, or core, of the operating system (called the **kernel**) is loaded into memory. The kernel remains in memory while the computer is on so that it is always available, and other parts of the operating system are retrieved from the hard drive and loaded into memory when needed. Before the boot process ends, the operating system determines the hardware devices that are connected to the computer and whether they are configured properly, and reads an opening batch of instructions. These start-up instructions are tasks the operating system carries out each time the computer boots, such as launching a security program to run continually in the background to detect possible threats.

Typically, many programs are running in the background at any one time, even before the user launches any application software. On Windows computers, the Task Manager (shown in Exhibit 3-2) lists all running programs and how much memory they are using. The programs listed on the Startup tab are launched automatically by the operating system when the computer boots. In Windows, users can also see some of the programs that are running in the background by looking at the icons in the notification area of the taskbar.

The operating system also configures all devices connected to a computer. Small programs called **device drivers** (or simply **drivers**) are used to communicate with peripheral devices, such as monitors, printers, portable storage devices, and keyboards. Most operating systems include the drivers needed for the most common peripheral devices. In addition, drivers often come on a CD packaged with the peripheral device, or they can be downloaded from the manufacturer's Web site. Most operating systems look for and recognize new devices each time the computer boots; USB devices are recognized as soon as they are connected to the computer. When a new device is found, the operating system tries to install the appropriate driver to get the new hardware ready to use. For instance, Exhibit 3-3 shows the message displayed when a new USB device is connected to a Windows computer.

EXHIBIT 3-2 WINDOWS TASK MANAGER

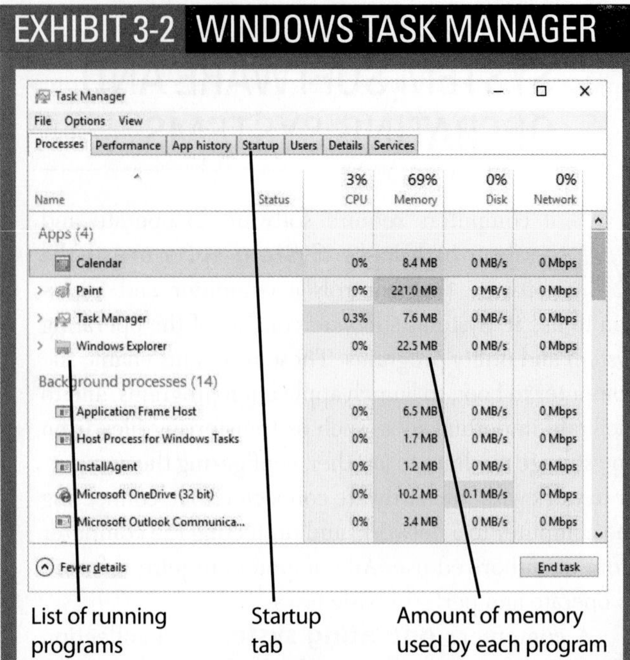

As you work on a computer, the operating system continuously manages the computer's resources and makes them available to devices and programs when needed. If a problem occurs—such as if a program stops functioning or too many programs are open for the amount of memory installed—the operating system notifies you and tries to correct the problem, often by closing the offending program. If the problem cannot be corrected by the operating system, you typically need to reboot the computer.

Other important tasks the operating system performs are file management, which involves keeping track of the files stored on a computer so that they can be retrieved when needed, and security, which protects the

EXHIBIT 3-3 FINDING NEW HARDWARE

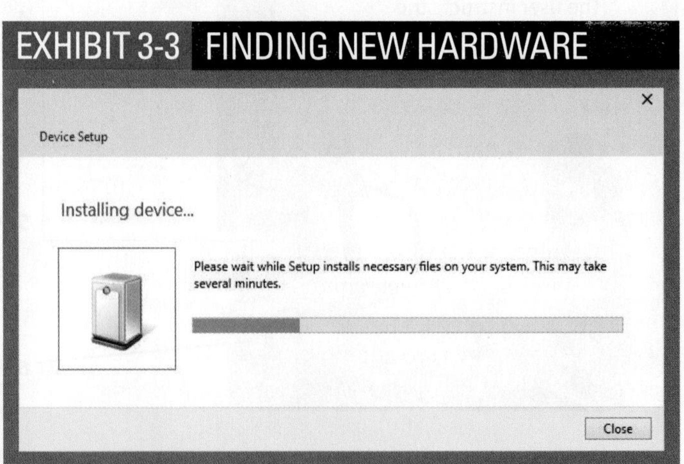

user interface The means by which an operating system or other program interacts with the user.

kernel The essential portion, or core, of the operating system.

device driver (driver) A small program used to communicate with a peripheral device, such as a monitor, printer, portable storage device, or keyboard.

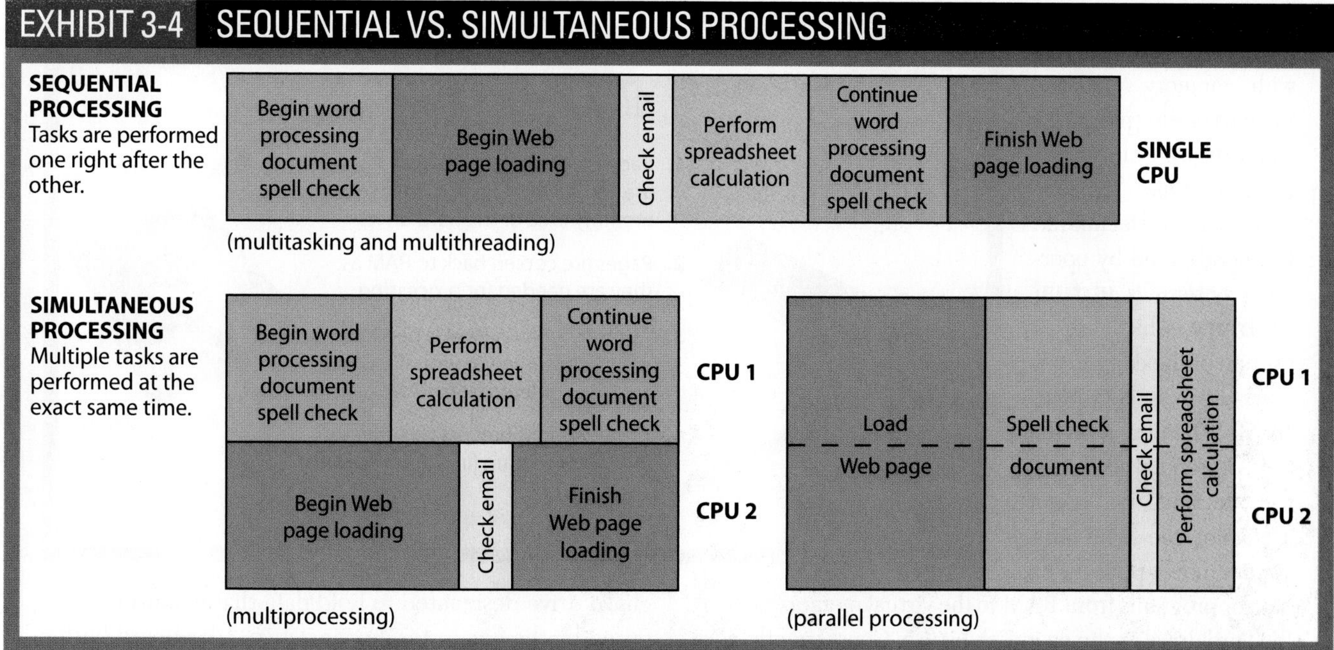

computer against outside threats and limits access to only authorized users.

3-1b Processing Techniques for Increased Efficiency

Operating systems often utilize various processing techniques to operate more efficiently and increase the amount of processing the computer can perform in any given time period. One way computers operate more efficiently is to multitask. **Multitasking** refers to the ability of an operating system to have more than one program (also called a task) open at one time. For example, multitasking allows you to edit a spreadsheet file in one window while loading a Web page in another window, or to retrieve new email messages in one window while a word processing document is open in another window.

A **thread** is a sequence of instructions within a program that is independent of other threads. For example, spell checking, printing, and opening documents might be threads in a word processing program. Operating systems that support multithreading can rotate between multiple threads so that processing is completed faster and more efficiently, even though only one thread is executed by a single core at one time.

If a computer has two or more CPUs (or multiple cores in a single CPU), techniques that perform operations simultaneously are possible. **Multiprocessing** and **parallel processing** are both techniques that use multiple processors or cores that work together to perform tasks more efficiently. With multiprocessing, each CPU or core typically works on a different job. With parallel processing, the CPUs or cores usually work together to complete one job more quickly. In either case, tasks are performed simultaneously (at exactly the same time). In contrast, with multitasking and multithreading, a single CPU or core processes tasks sequentially (by rotating through tasks). Exhibit 3-4 illustrates the difference between simultaneous and sequential processing, using tasks typical of a desktop computer.

Multiprocessing is supported by most operating systems and is used with personal computers that have multi-core CPUs as well as with servers and mainframe computers that have multi-core CPUs and/or multiple CPUs. Parallel processing is used most often with supercomputers.

Because many programs are memory-intensive, good memory management, which involves optimizing the use of main memory (RAM), can also help speed up processing. The operating system allocates RAM to programs as needed and then reclaims that memory when the program is closed. Because each additional running program or

multitasking The ability of an operating system to have more than one program open at one time.

thread A sequence of instructions within a program that is independent of other threads.

multiprocessing A processing technique in which multiple processors or multiple processing cores in a single computer each work on a different job.

parallel processing A processing technique in which multiple processors or multiple processing cores in a single computer work together to complete one job more quickly.

open window consumes memory, users can help with memory management by closing programs when they are no longer needed. One memory management technique frequently used by operating systems is **virtual memory**, which uses a portion of the computer's hard drive as additional RAM. When the amount of RAM required exceeds the amount of RAM available, the operating system moves portions of data or programs from RAM to the virtual memory area of the hard drive, as shown in Exhibit 3-5. Consequently, as a program is executed, some of the program may be stored in RAM and some in virtual memory. Virtual memory allows you to use more memory than is physically available on your computer, but using virtual memory is slower than using just RAM.

EXHIBIT 3-5 HOW VIRTUAL MEMORY WORKS

1. Pages of programs or data are copied from RAM to the virtual memory area of the hard drive.
2. Pages are copied back to RAM as they are needed for processing.
3. As more room in RAM is needed, pages are copied to virtual memory and then deleted from RAM.
4. The swapping process continues until the program finishes executing.

Source: © Kingston Technology Corporation; © Seagate Technology LLC

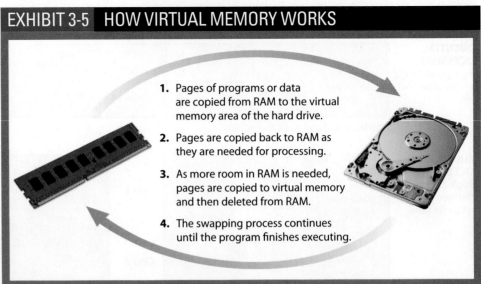

Some input and output devices are exceedingly slow compared to CPUs. If the CPU had to wait for these slower devices to finish their work, the computer system would experience a horrendous bottleneck. To avoid this problem, most operating systems use buffering and spooling. A **buffer** is an area in RAM or on the hard drive designated to hold data that is waiting to be used by the computer. For instance, a keyboard buffer stores characters as they are entered via the keyboard, and a print buffer stores documents that are waiting to be printed. The process of placing items in a buffer so they can be retrieved by the appropriate device when needed is called **buffering** or **spooling**. One common use of buffering and spooling is print spooling. Print spooling allows multiple documents to be sent to the printer at one time and to print, one after the other, in the background while the computer and user are performing other tasks. The documents waiting to be printed are in a print queue, which designates the order in which the documents will be printed. It is also common for computers to use buffers to assist in redisplaying images on the screen and to temporarily store data that is in the process of being burned onto a CD or DVD or being streamed from the Internet.

virtual memory A memory management technique that uses a portion of the computer's hard drive as additional RAM.

buffer An area in RAM or on the hard drive designated to hold data that is waiting to be used by the computer.

buffering (spooling) The process of placing items in a buffer so they can be retrieved by the appropriate device when needed.

graphical user interface (GUI) A graphics-based interface that allows a user to communicate instructions to the computer by clicking icons or other objects.

command line interface A text-based user interface that requires the user to communicate instructions to the computer by typing commands.

personal operating system (desktop operating system) An operating system designed to be installed on a single computer.

server operating system (network operating system) An operating system designed to be installed on a network server.

3-1c Differences Among Operating Systems

Different types of operating systems are available to meet different needs. Some of the major distinctions among operating systems include the type of user interface utilized and the category of device with which the operating system will be used.

Most operating systems today use a **graphical user interface (GUI)** in which users click icons, buttons, menu items, and other graphical objects to issue instructions to the computer. The older DOS operating system and some versions of other operating systems use a **command line interface**, which requires users to type commands to issue instructions to the computer. See Exhibit 3-6 for an example of the Windows 10 GUI, as well as a command line interface.

EXHIBIT 3-6 GRAPHICAL USER INTERFACE VS. COMMAND LINE INTERFACE

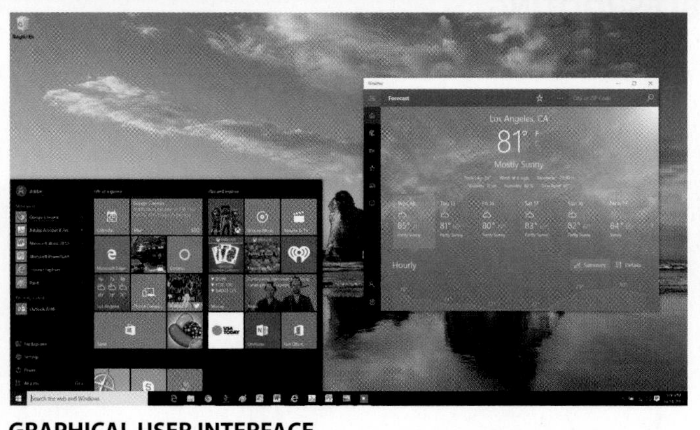

GRAPHICAL USER INTERFACE
Objects such as tiles, icons, buttons, and menus are selected with the mouse, pen, or finger to issue commands to the computer.

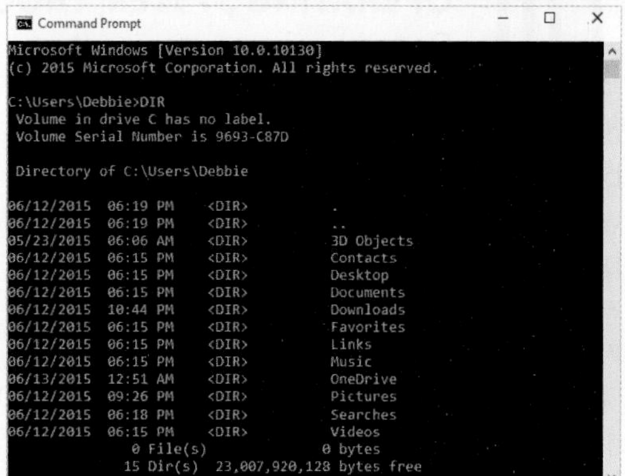
Command Prompt
Microsoft Windows [Version 10.0.10130]
(c) 2015 Microsoft Corporation. All rights reserved.
C:\Users\Debbie>DIR
Volume in drive C has no label.
Volume Serial Number is 9693-C87D
Directory of C:\Users\Debbie
06/12/2015 06:19 PM <DIR> .
06/12/2015 06:19 PM <DIR> ..
05/23/2015 06:06 AM <DIR> 3D Objects
06/12/2015 06:15 PM <DIR> Contacts
06/12/2015 06:15 PM <DIR> Desktop
06/12/2015 06:15 PM <DIR> Documents
06/12/2015 10:44 PM <DIR> Downloads
06/12/2015 06:15 PM <DIR> Favorites
06/12/2015 06:15 PM <DIR> Links
06/12/2015 06:15 PM <DIR> Music
06/13/2015 12:51 AM <DIR> OneDrive
06/12/2015 09:26 PM <DIR> Pictures
06/12/2015 06:18 PM <DIR> Searches
06/12/2015 06:15 PM <DIR> Videos
0 File(s) 0 bytes
15 Dir(s) 23,007,920,128 bytes free

COMMAND LINE INTERFACE
Commands are entered using the keyboard.

Operating systems used with personal computers are typically referred to as **personal operating systems** (also called **desktop operating systems**), and they are designed to be installed on a single computer. In contrast, **server operating systems** (also called **network operating systems**) are designed to be installed on a network server to grant multiple users access to a network and its resources. Each computer on a network has its own personal operating system installed (just as with a stand-alone computer), and that operating system controls the activity on that computer, while the server operating system controls access to network resources. Computers on a network may also need special client software to access the network and issue requests to the server. An overview of how a typical personal operating system and a server operating system interact on a business computer network is illustrated in Exhibit 3-7.

EXHIBIT 3-7 HOW OPERATING SYSTEMS ARE USED IN A NETWORK ENVIRONMENT

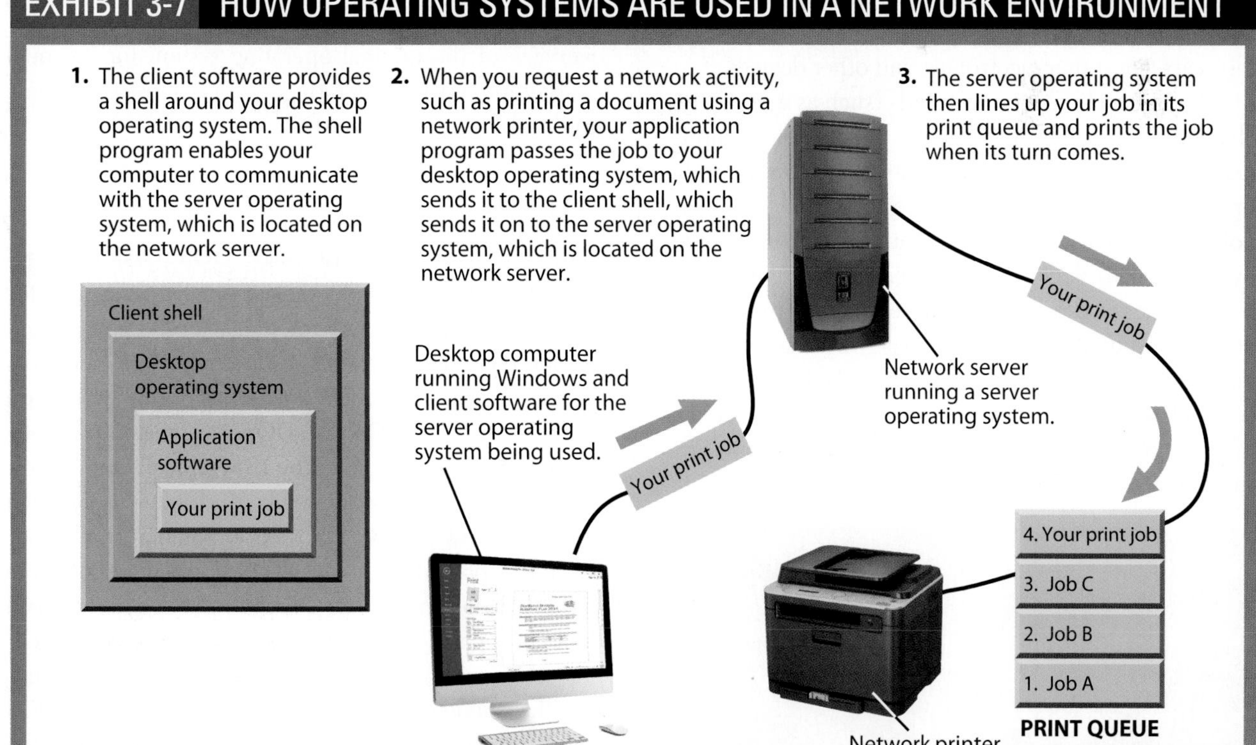
1. The client software provides a shell around your desktop operating system. The shell program enables your computer to communicate with the server operating system, which is located on the network server.
2. When you request a network activity, such as printing a document using a network printer, your application program passes the job to your desktop operating system, which sends it to the client shell, which sends it on to the server operating system, which is located on the network server.
3. The server operating system then lines up your job in its print queue and prints the job when its turn comes.
Client shell
Desktop operating system
Application software
Your print job
Desktop computer running Windows and client software for the server operating system being used.
Your print job
Network server running a server operating system.
Your print job
4. Your print job
3. Job C
2. Job B
1. Job A
PRINT QUEUE
Network printer

© prism68/Shutterstock.com; © Igor Klimov/Shutterstock.com; © kavione/Shutterstock.com

FYI OPERATING SYSTEM TROUBLESHOOTING

Once your computer is set up with your regular peripheral devices and the necessary drivers have been installed properly, they usually work fine. If a device driver file is deleted, becomes corrupted, or has a conflict with another piece of software, then the device will no longer work. A hardware problem can also be caused by a faulty setting, such as a disabled network adapter. Usually, the operating system detects problems like this during the boot process and then notifies you and tries to reinstall the driver automatically. Many operating systems, such as Windows, have troubleshooters that can be launched to help determine what the trouble is and correct it (see the accompanying illustration). To keep your system up to date, many operating systems have an option to check for operating system updates automatically—including updated driver files—on a regular basis. Enabling these automatic updates is a good idea to keep your system running smoothly and protected from new threats, such as computer viruses.

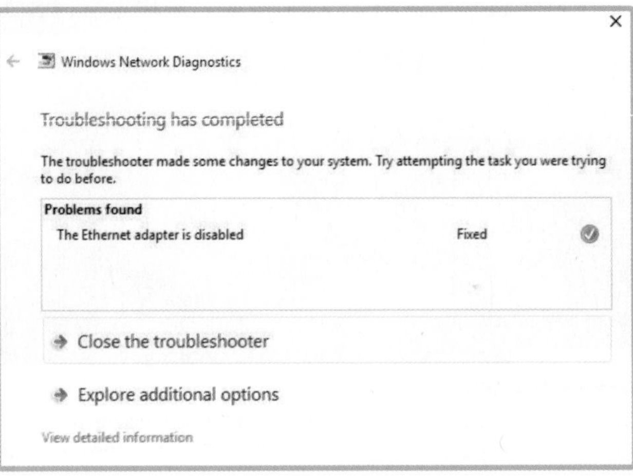

In addition to personal operating systems and server operating systems, there are **mobile operating systems** that are designed to be used with smartphones and other mobile devices, and **embedded operating systems** that are built into consumer kiosks, cash registers, cars, consumer electronics, and other devices.

As new technologies or trends (such as a new CPU characteristic or the development of wearable computers, for example) emerge, operating systems must be updated to support them. On the other hand, as technologies become obsolete, operating system manufacturers need to decide when to end support for those technologies. Likewise, hardware manufacturers also need to respond to new technologies introduced by operating systems. For instance, because the latest versions of Windows and OS X support multi-touch input, a flurry of new devices with touch screens and that support gesture input have been introduced.

mobile operating system An operating system designed to be used with mobile phones and other mobile devices.

embedded operating system An operating system that is built into devices such as cars and consumer electronics.

DOS (Disk Operating System) The dominant operating system for personal computers during the 1980s and early 1990s.

3-2 OPERATING SYSTEMS

A variety of operating systems are available for personal computers, network servers, and mobile devices. An overview of the original operating system for personal computers and the operating systems most commonly used today is provided next.

3-2a DOS

During the 1980s and early 1990s, **DOS (Disk Operating System)** was the dominant operating system for personal computers. DOS traditionally used a command line interface, although later versions of DOS supported a menu-driven interface. The two primary forms of DOS are PC-DOS and MS-DOS. PC-DOS was created originally for IBM PCs (and is owned by IBM); MS-DOS was created for use with IBM-compatible PCs. Both versions were originally developed by Microsoft Corporation, but neither version is updated any longer. DOS is considered obsolete because it does not utilize a graphical user interface and does not support modern processors and processing techniques. However, some computers, such as computers running the Windows operating system, can still execute DOS commands and users can issue these commands using the Command Prompt window, as shown in Exhibit 3-8.

EXHIBIT 3-8 DOS COMMANDS ISSUED VIA THE WINDOWS COMMAND PROMPT

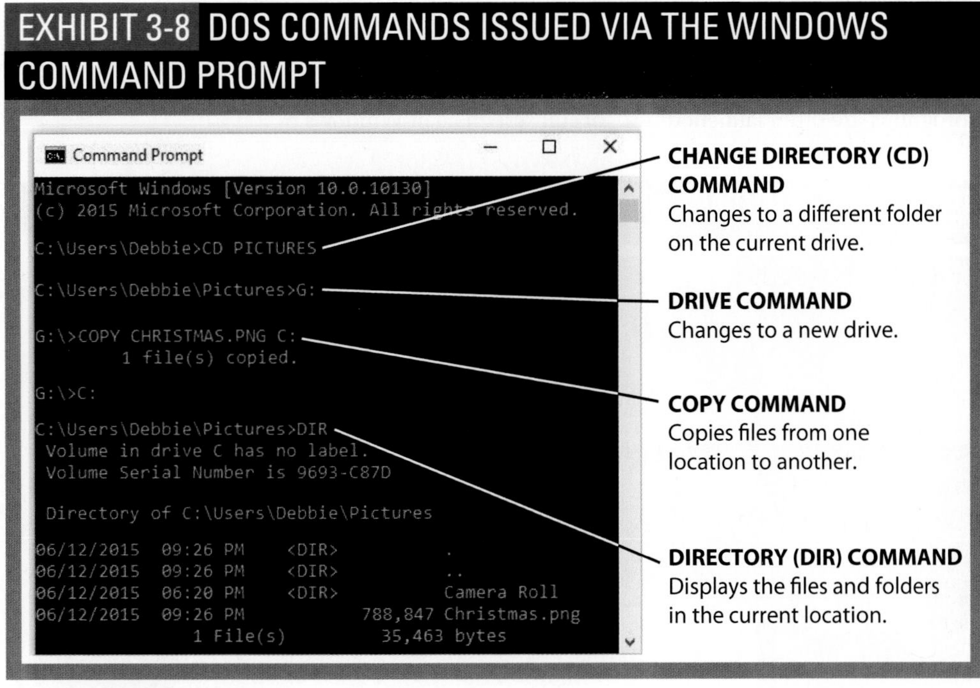

3-2b Windows

Windows has been the predominant operating system for personal computers for many years, and holds about 90% of the market. Microsoft created the original version of Windows—Windows 1.0—in 1985 in an effort to meet the needs of users frustrated by having to learn and use DOS commands. Windows 1.0 through Windows 3.x (where *x* stands for the version number of the software, such as Windows 3.0, 3.1, or 3.11) were not, however, full-fledged operating systems. Instead, they were operating environments for the DOS operating system—that is, they were graphical shells that operated around the DOS operating system—which were designed to make DOS easier to use.

In 1994, Microsoft announced that all versions of Windows after 3.11 would be full-fledged operating systems instead of just operating environments. The next three versions of Windows designed for personal computers were Windows 95, Windows 98, and Windows Me (Millennium Edition). Windows NT (New Technology) was the first 32-bit version of Windows designed for high-end workstations and servers. It was built from the ground up using a different kernel than the other versions of Windows and was eventually replaced by Windows 2000. Windows XP replaced both Windows 2000 (for business use) and Windows Me (for home use). Throughout this progression of Windows releases, support for new hardware (such as DVD drives and USB devices), networking and the Internet, multimedia applications, and voice and pen input were included. Support for all of these early versions of Windows has been discontinued.

Windows Vista replaced Windows XP. One of the most obvious changes in Windows Vista was the Aero interface, a visual graphical user interface that uses transparent windows and dynamic elements. Windows Vista also introduced the Sidebar feature, which contains gadgets—small applications that are used to perform a variety of tasks, such as displaying weather information, a calendar, and news headlines. Other features new to Vista included the Windows Media Center and Windows Speech Recognition. Support for Windows Vista is scheduled to end in 2017.

Windows 7 was released next. It requires less memory and processing power than previous versions of Windows, and it is designed to start up and respond faster than Vista so it can run well on netbooks and tablets. Windows 7 also added jump lists that show your most recent documents, live thumbnails of open programs that can be displayed by pointing to the taskbar buttons, and virtual folders called Libraries that display together in one location the content the user specifies, regardless of where those files are physically located on the hard drive.

The next version of Windows is Windows 8, which was released in 2012. According to Microsoft, it is a "reimaging of Windows, from the chip to the interface." Windows 8 is designed to be used with a wide range of devices, from smartphones to full-size desktop systems, as well as with or without a keyboard or mouse because it supports touch input. Windows 8 introduced Charm shortcuts for common tasks, as well as the Start screen—a tile-based alternative to the traditional Windows Start menu. Tiles on the Start screen represent conventional programs, apps downloaded from the new Windows

Windows The predominant operating system for personal computers.

Store, Web sites, and more. Tiles are selected with the mouse or finger to launch the corresponding content. Some tiles are live tiles that show up-to-date information and notifications. Although programs are often launched via the Start screen, users can work with the more traditional Windows desktop if they prefer.

In addition to desktop versions of Windows 8 and earlier designed for personal computers, there are versions of Windows designed for other devices. For example, Windows Server is the server version of Windows, Windows Phone is designed for smartphones, and Windows Embedded is designed for consumer and industrial devices.

The latest version of Windows is **Windows 10**. The most significant change is that Windows 10 is a universal operating system that will run on any device, from smartphones to tablets to personal computers to servers. Consequently, Windows 10 replaces all previous versions of Windows. The look and features of Windows 10 are consistent regardless of the device being used, although the experience is automatically adjusted to be optimized for each device and screen size. In addition, apps developed for Windows 10 can run on any device that has Windows 10 installed.

Windows 10 looks similar to Windows 8. However, some features have been adjusted to make them work better with both touch devices and conventional computers. For example, the Start menu has returned and is combined with the live tiles of the Windows 8 Start screen, as shown in Exhibit 3-9. In addition, apps downloaded from the Windows Store run in a window instead of full screen as in Windows 8.

EXHIBIT 3-9 WINDOWS 10

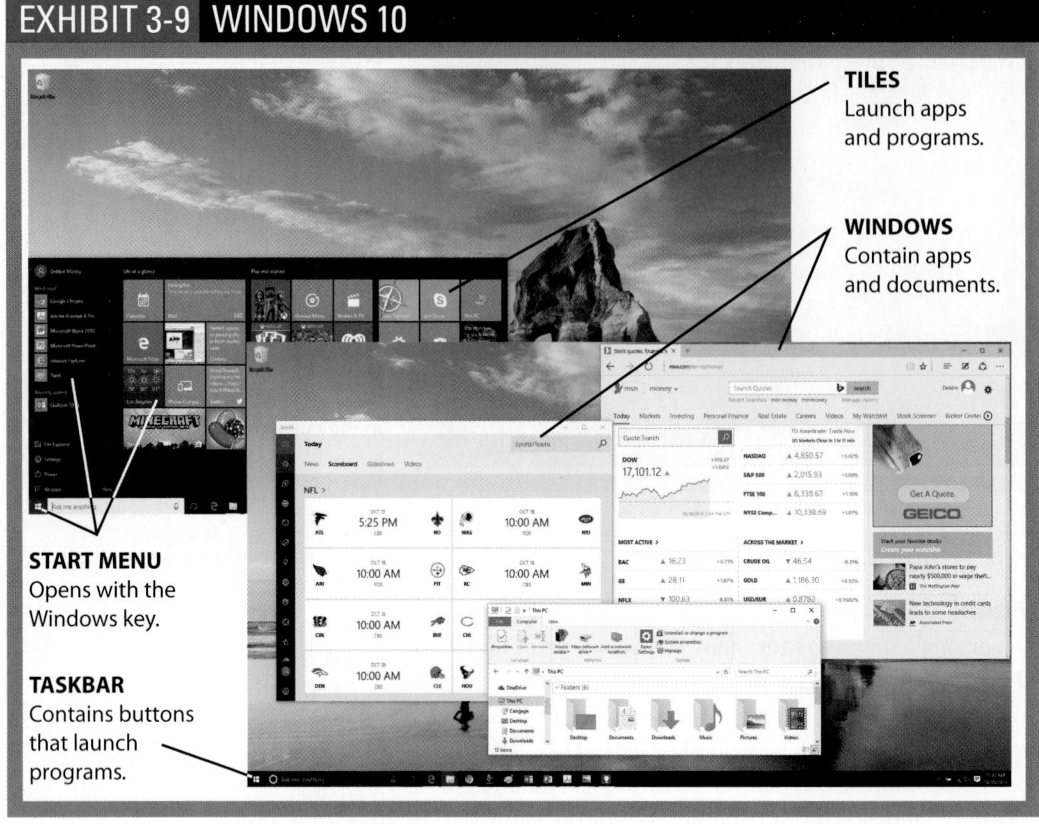
TILES
Launch apps and programs.
WINDOWS
Contain apps and documents.
START MENU
Opens with the Windows key.
TASKBAR
Contains buttons that launch programs.

One new feature of Windows 10 is Task View, which enables each user to create personalized desktops. Each desktop includes the programs the user specifies, such as programs used for work in one desktop and programs for gaming and other personal activities in another desktop, and the user can switch between them as needed. Windows 10 includes a new Web browser called Edge which replaces Internet Explorer. Edge includes Cortana, a virtual assistant, that can offer additional information as you browse the Web.

Windows 10 is being offered as a free upgrade for one year for all Windows 7 and 8 users. Consequently, it is expected that individuals and businesses will transition to Windows 10 much faster than they have upgraded to a new version of Windows in the past.

3-2c OS X

OS X (formerly called Mac OS X) is the proprietary operating system for Mac computers made by Apple. It is based on the UNIX operating system and set the original

Windows 10 The latest version of Windows; it runs on devices from smartphones to servers.

OS X The operating system used on Apple computers.

standard for graphical user interfaces. Many of today's operating systems follow the trend that this operating system started and, in fact, have GUIs that highly resemble it.

The most recent versions of OS X are OS X El Capitan and OS X Yosemite (shown in Exhibit 3-10). They include the Safari Web browser and a Dock from which you can launch programs. New features include a cleaner look and a new Notification Center that displays your calendar and widgets to provide you updated information. In addition, you can now place iPhone calls or send and receive texts via your Mac. You can also switch from one device to another and continue your work seamlessly, as long as the two devices are within range, and you can sync all your Apple devices via iCloud. **OS X Server** is the server version of OS X.

EXHIBIT 3-10 OS X YOSEMITE

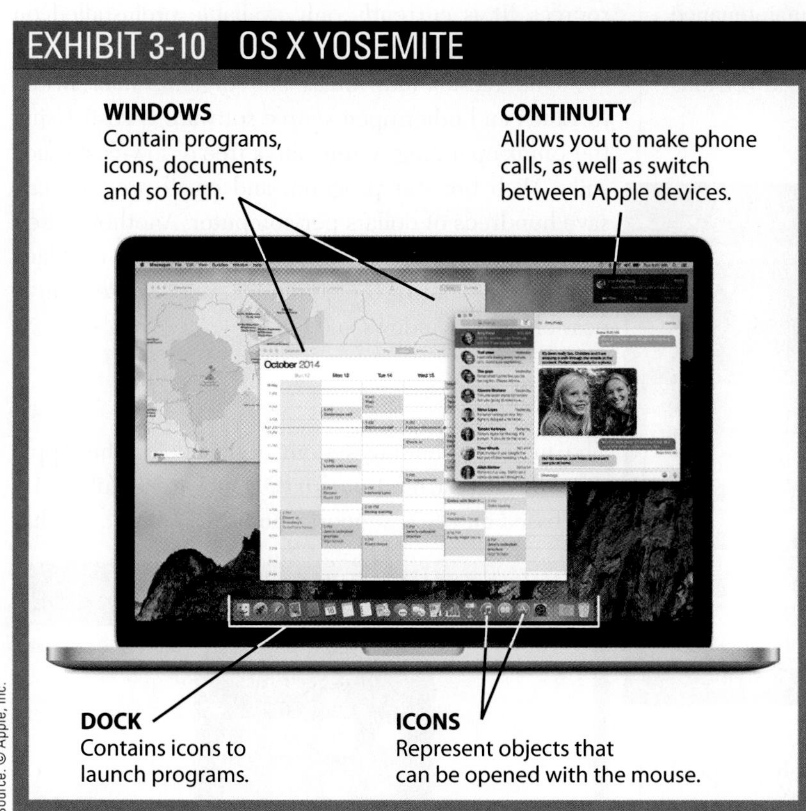
WINDOWS
Contain programs, icons, documents, and so forth.
CONTINUITY
Allows you to make phone calls, as well as switch between Apple devices.
October 2014
DOCK
Contains icons to launch programs.
ICONS
Represent objects that can be opened with the mouse.

Source: © Apple, Inc.

3-2d UNIX

UNIX was developed in the late 1960s at AT&T Bell Laboratories as an operating system for midrange servers. Computer systems ranging from personal computers to mainframes can run UNIX, and it can support a variety of devices from different manufacturers. This flexibility gives UNIX an advantage over competing operating systems in some situations. However, UNIX is more expensive, requires a higher level of technical knowledge, and tends to be harder to install, maintain, and upgrade than most other commonly used operating systems.

Many versions of UNIX are available, as are many operating systems based on UNIX. These operating systems—such as OS X—are sometimes referred to as UNIX flavors. In fact, the term *UNIX,* which initially referred to the original UNIX operating system, has evolved to refer to a group of similar operating systems based on UNIX. Many UNIX flavors are incompatible, which creates some problems when a program written for one UNIX computer system is moved to another computer system running a different flavor of UNIX. To avoid this incompatibility problem, the Open Group consortium has overseen the development of the Single UNIX Specification—a standardized programming environment for UNIX applications—and certifies UNIX systems if they conform to the Single UNIX Specification.

3-2e Linux

Linux (pronounced with a short *i* sound) is an operating system developed by Linus Torvalds in 1991 when he was a student at the University of Helsinki in Finland. Though Linux resembles UNIX, Linux was developed independently from it. Linux was released to the public as **open source software**, which is a program whose source code is available to the public and may be modified to improve it or customize it. Over the years, the number of Linux users has grown, and volunteer programmers from all over the world have collaborated to improve it, sharing their modified code with others over the Internet. Although Linux originally used a command line interface, most recent versions of Linux programs use a graphical user interface and operate similarly to other desktop operating

OS X Server The server version of OS X.

UNIX An operating system developed in the late 1960s for servers and mainframes; many variations of this operating system are in use today.

Linux An open source operating system that is available without charge over the Internet.

open source software A program whose source code is available to the public.

TRENDING...

Firefox OS, shown in the accompanying illustration, is a relatively new Linux-based operating system developed by Mozilla, the developers of the Firefox Web browser. Firefox OS includes a customizable Home screen consisting of panels that can include Web content, as well as feeds such as Instagram. It has a number of built-in apps, such as the Firefox Web browser, Calendar, E-Mail, and Messages, with additional apps available via the Firefox Marketplace. In addition to being used with smartphones, Firefox OS is used with some tablets and smart TVs.

Source: © Mozilla

systems, such as Windows and OS X. For instance, the version of Linux shown in Exhibit 3-11 has icons, menus, windows, and an app dock. Linux is widely available as a free download via the Internet. Companies are also permitted to customize Linux and sell it as a retail product. Commercial Linux distributions come with maintenance and support materials (something that many of the free versions do not offer), making the commercial versions more attractive for corporate users.

EXHIBIT 3-11 LINUX

Source: © Canonical Ltd.

Over the years, Linux has become a widely accepted operating system with strong support from mainstream companies such as IBM, HP, Dell, and NVIDIA. Versions of Linux are available for a wide variety of computers, from personal computers to servers to mobile devices. For example, Android, an operating system widely used with smartphones, is based on Linux. So is Chrome OS, the first cloud operating system designed for devices that will be used primarily online. Chrome OS is essentially the Chrome Web browser redesigned to run a computer in addition to accessing Web resources. It is currently only available preinstalled on Chromebook devices.

One reason individuals and organizations switch to Linux and other open source software is cost. Using the Linux operating system and a free or low-cost office suite, Web browser program, and email program can save hundreds of dollars per computer. Another reason is that Linux allows users to customize the user interface and directly control the computer much more than is possible with Windows and OS X.

3-2f iOS

The mobile operating system designed for the Apple iPhone, iPad, and iPod touch is **iOS**, shown in Exhibit 3-12. It is based on OS X, supports multi-touch input, and has

EXHIBIT 3-12 iOS

Source: © Apple, Inc.

Firefox OS A Linux-based operating system developed by Mozilla and designed for mobile devices.

iOS The operating system designed for Apple smartphones and mobile devices.

TRENDING...

APPLE WATCH

Smart watches and other wearables are one of the hottest trends today. One example is the Apple Watch shown in the accompanying photo. While it does contain a computer on a chip and has some built-in features, including Maps, the Passbook digital wallet, a heart rate sensor, and Activity and Workout apps, Apple Watch is designed to work in conjunction with your iPhone for much of its functionality. For example, you can answer phone calls via your Watch and then instantly transfer them to your iPhone for longer conversations. You can also get real-time notifications for incoming email or messages, as well as reminders of upcoming calendar items.

Source: © Apple, Inc.

For input, Apple Watch uses a unique Digital Crown button as a pointing device to zoom and scroll; pressing the button returns to the Home screen. From the Home screen, you can launch apps and select options via touch and a light touch on the screen issues different commands than a deep press. Apple Watch also supports voice input. For output, Apple Watch has the display screen on the face of the watch, the ability to tap you on your wrist to indicate an alert or notification, and audio output.

a variety of built-in apps and features; the current version is iOS 9. The most recent versions of iOS include Touch ID and Apple Pay for secure purchases, Facetime for video calls, and iCloud for online storage. They also include a Find My iPhone app to help users locate, lock, or remotely wipe a lost or stolen iPhone, as well as support for the Apple Watch.

3-2g Android

Android (shown in Exhibit 3-13) is a Linux-based operating system developed by the Open Handset Alliance, a group that includes Google and more than 30 technology and mobile companies. Android is essentially tied with iOS as the most widely used mobile operating system in the United States. It was built from the ground up with current mobile device capabilities in mind, which enables developers to create mobile applications that take full advantage of all the features a mobile device has to offer. It is an open platform, so anyone can download and use Android, although hardware manufacturers must adhere to certain specifications to be called "Android compatible."

EXHIBIT 3-13 ANDROID

© Zeynep Demir/Shutterstock.com

The current version of Android is Android 6.0, also known as Marshmallow. Similar to previous versions of Android, Android Marshmallow supports multi-touch input and has a variety of built-in apps with more than one million additional apps available via the Google Play store. It also includes the Android Device Manager to help users locate, lock, or remotely wipe a lost or stolen Android phone, as well as support for unlocking the phone via a PIN, password, pattern, or face recognition. One feature new to Marshmallow is the ability to access Google Now from any screen (called Google on Tap). In addition to being used with Android smartphones, Android is the operating system used with Android tablets, Android Wear smart watches, and some smart TVs.

Android A Linux-based operating system developed by the Open Handset Alliance and designed for mobile devices.

3-2h Operating Systems for Larger Computers

Larger computers—such as high-end servers, mainframes, and supercomputers—sometimes use operating systems designed solely for that type of system. For instance, IBM's z/OS is designed for IBM mainframes. In addition, many servers and mainframes today run conventional operating systems, such as Windows, UNIX, and Linux. Linux in particular is increasingly being used with both mainframes and supercomputers. Larger computers may also use a customized operating system based on a conventional operating system. For instance, many IBM mainframes and Cray supercomputers use versions of UNIX developed specifically for those computers.

3-3 UTILITY PROGRAMS

A **utility program** is a software program that performs a specific task, usually related to managing or maintaining the computer system. For example, there are utility programs designed to find files, diagnose and repair system problems, clean up a hard drive, back up files, and detect and correct security risks. Some utility programs are built into operating systems. There are also stand-alone utility programs available as alternatives to the operating system's utility programs or to provide additional features.

3-3a File Management Programs

File management programs allow you to perform file management tasks including looking at the files that are stored on a storage medium and copying, moving, deleting, and renaming folders and files. The file management program incorporated into the latest versions of Windows is File Explorer. Most file management programs can also be used to search for stored files that meet specified criteria, such as having certain characters in the file name or being modified since a particular date.

3-3b Diagnostic and Disk Management Programs

Diagnostic programs evaluate your computer and make recommendations for fixing any errors that are discovered. **Disk management programs** diagnose and repair problems related to your hard drive. Diagnostic and disk management utilities built into the Windows operating system can check your hard drive for errors and optimize your hard drive (see Exhibit 3-14). Optimization (also called disk defragmentation) is the process of rearranging data on a hard drive so it works more efficiently. System cleaners are another type of disk management utility. These programs delete temporary files, delete browsing history,

EXHIBIT 3-14 WINDOWS DISK TOOL

utility program A type of software that performs a specific task, usually related to managing or maintaining a computer system.

file management program A utility program that enables the user to perform file management tasks, such as copying and deleting files.

diagnostic program A utility program that evaluates your system and make recommendations for fixing any errors that are discovered.

disk management program A utility program that diagnoses and repairs problems related to your hard drive.

and remove other clutter taking up hard drive space. Many can also safely uninstall programs you no longer need to free up disk space.

3-3c Backup and Recovery Programs

A **backup program** makes a duplicate copy of files. Backing up files is critical so you don't lose important files to due to a hardware failure, a major disaster, or a user error. Performing a backup can consist of backing up an entire computer so it can be restored at a later date, backing up all data files, or backing up only certain selected files.

Recovery programs can be used to undo recent system changes without deleting your data files, or to roll back your system to the settings it used on a previous date. This is a useful tool if a change to your computer causes it to not function properly.

3-3d Security Programs

Security software protects your computer from threats such as programs that attempt to harm a computer and Web sites that try to trick users into supplying personal information that can be used for criminal acts. Many operating systems contain security programs that monitor your device and either remove or block suspicious activities. Stand-alone programs, such as the one shown in Exhibit 3-15, are available as well.

EXHIBIT 3-15 SECURITY SCAN

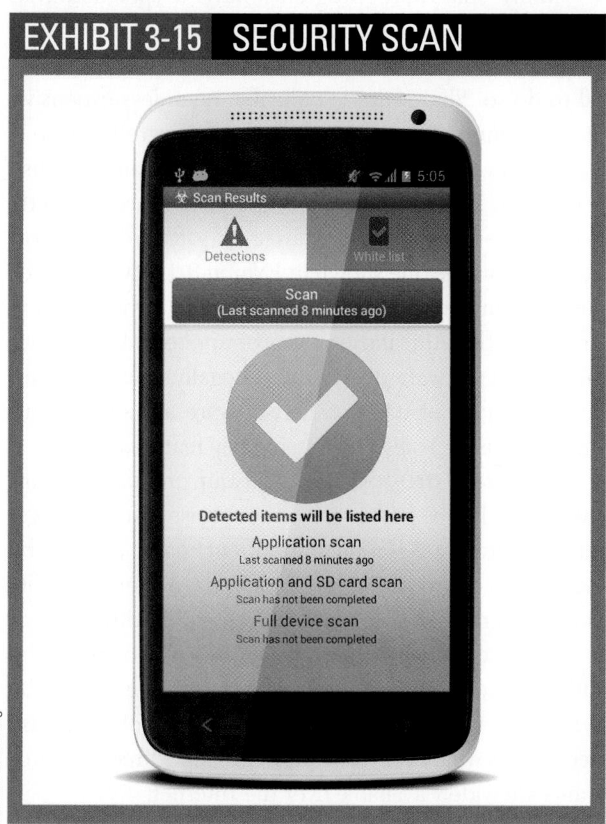

Source: © Bulldog

3-4 INTRODUCTION TO APPLICATION SOFTWARE

Application software (apps) includes all the programs that allow you to perform specific tasks or applications on a computer. Individuals and businesses use software to write letters, keep track of finances, participate in videoconferences, watch videos, make business presentations, process orders, access Web-based resources, and many other tasks.

3-4a Software Ownership Rights

The ownership rights of a software program specify the allowable use of that program, including whether or not the program can be sold, shared with others, or otherwise distributed. When a software program is purchased, the buyer is not actually buying the software. Instead, the buyer is acquiring a **software license** that permits him or her to use the software. This license specifies the conditions under which a buyer can use the software, such as the number of computers on which it may be installed.

The four basic types of software are commercial software, shareware, freeware, and public domain software, which are described in Exhibit 3-16. Each type of software has different ownership rights. In addition, any software can also be open source software. An open source program can be copyrighted, but individuals and businesses are allowed to modify the program and redistribute it—the only restrictions are that changes must be shared with the open source community and the original copyright notice must remain intact.

Commercial software includes any software program that is developed and sold for a profit. When you buy a commercial software program (such as Microsoft Office, TurboTax, or GarageBand), it typically comes with a single-user license, which means you cannot legally make copies of the installation program to give to your friends and you cannot legally install the software on their computers using

backup program A utility program that makes a duplicate copy of files in case the original files are destroyed.

security software Software, typically a suite of programs, used to protect a computer against a variety of threats.

application software (apps) The programs that allow you to perform specific tasks on a computer.

software license An agreement that specifies the conditions under which a program can be used.

commercial software A software program that is developed and sold for a profit.

EXHIBIT 3-16 SOFTWARE OWNERSHIP RIGHTS

Category	Description	Examples
Commercial software	A software program that is developed and sold for a profit.	Microsoft Office (office suite) Norton AntiVirus (antivirus program) Adobe Photoshop CC (image editing program) Minecraft - Pocket Edition (game)
Shareware	A software program that is distributed on the honor system; typically available free of charge but may require a small registration fee.	WinZip (file compression program) Video Edit Magic (video editing program) Image Shrinker (image optimizer) Deluxe Ski Jump 3 (game)
Freeware	A software program that is given away by the author for others to use free of charge.	Chrome (Web browser) LibreOffice (office suite) QuickTime Player (media player) Evernote Basic (note taking/archiving software)
Public domain software	A software program that is not copyrighted.	Lynx (text-based Web browser) Quake 3 (game)

your copy of the installation program. You cannot even install the software on a second computer that you own, unless allowed by the license. For example, some software licenses state that the program can be installed on one desktop computer and one portable computer belonging to the same individual. Schools or businesses that need to install software on a large number of computers or need to have the software available to multiple users over a network can usually obtain a site license or network license for the number of users needed.

In addition to their full versions, some commercial software is available in a demo or trial version. Typically, these versions can be used free of charge and distributed to others, but often they are missing key features, such as the ability to save or print a document, or they will not run after the trial period expires. Because these programs are not designed as replacements for the fee-based version, it is ethical to use them only to determine whether you want to buy the full program. If the decision is made against purchasing the product, you should uninstall the demo or trial version from your computer.

Recent trends in computing—such as multiprocessing, virtualization, mobile computing, and cloud computing—are leading to new software licensing issues for commercial software companies. For example, software companies must decide whether the number of installations allowed by the license is counted by the number of computers on which the software is installed, by the total number of CPU cores used by those computers, or by the number of individuals using installed or virtual copies of the software at any given time. Software vendors are expected to continue to develop and implement new licensing models to address these and other trends in the future.

Shareware programs are software programs that are distributed on the honor system. Most shareware programs are available to try free of charge but typically require a small fee if you choose to use the program regularly. By paying the requested registration fee, you can use the program for as long as you want to use it and may be entitled to product support, updates, and other benefits. You can legally and ethically copy shareware programs to pass along to friends and colleagues for evaluation purposes, but those individuals are expected to pay the shareware fee if they decide to keep the product.

Many shareware programs have a specified trial period, such as one month. Although it is not illegal to use shareware past the specified trial period, it is unethical to do so. Shareware is typically much less expensive than commercial versions of similar software because it is often developed by a single programmer and because it uses the shareware marketing system to sell directly to consumers (usually via a variety of software download sites, such as the one shown in Exhibit 3-17) with little or no packaging or advertising expenses. Shareware authors stress that the ethical use of shareware helps to cultivate this type of software distribution. Legally, shareware and demo versions of commercial software are similar, but shareware is typically not missing key features.

Freeware programs are software programs that are given away by the author for others to use free of charge. Although freeware is available without charge and can be shared with others, the author retains the ownership rights to the program, so you cannot do anything with it—such as sell it or modify it—that is not expressly allowed by the author. Freeware programs are frequently developed by individuals. Commercial software companies often release freeware as well. Like shareware programs, freeware programs are widely available over the Internet.

shareware program Software that is distributed on the honor system; consumers should either pay for it or uninstall it after the trial period.

freeware program Software that may be used free of charge.

EXHIBIT 3-17 SOFTWARE DOWNLOAD SITE

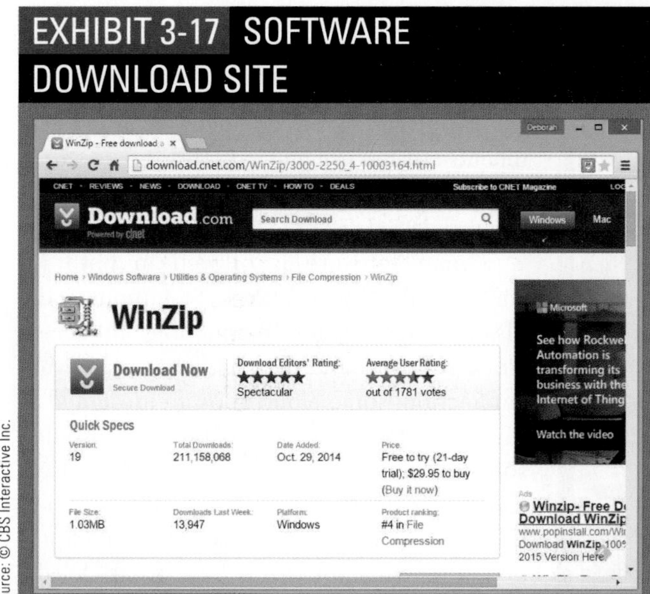

Source: © CBS Interactive Inc.

Public domain software is not copyrighted; instead, the ownership rights to the program have been donated to the public domain. Consequently, it is free and can be used, copied, modified, and distributed to others without restrictions.

3-4b Desktop vs. Mobile Software

Notebook computers and other portable computers typically run the same application software as desktop computers. However, smartphones and other mobile devices usually require mobile software, also called mobile apps. Mobile apps are software programs designed for a specific type of mobile device and operating system, such as an iPhone or an Android tablet.

In addition to having a more compact, efficient appearance, many mobile apps include features for easier data input, such as an on-screen keyboard, a phrase list, voice input capabilities, or handwriting recognition capabilities. Some mobile apps are designed to be compatible with popular desktop software, such as Microsoft Office, to facilitate sharing documents between the two platforms. See Exhibit 3-18 for some examples of mobile apps. The number of mobile applications is growing all the time, and many are available free of charge.

3-4c Installed vs. Cloud Software

Software also differs in how it is accessed by the end user. It can be installed on and run from the end user's computer (or installed on and run from a network server in a network setting), or it can be cloud software that is accessed by the end user over the Internet.

Installed software must be installed on the device being used before it is run. Desktop software can be purchased in physical form (such as on a CD or DVD) or downloaded from the Internet (see Exhibit 3-19). Mobile software is almost always downloaded from an app store. In either case, the program is installed using its installation program, which typically runs automatically when the software CD or DVD is inserted into the drive or when the downloaded program is opened. After the software is installed, it is ready to use. Whether installed software requires a fee depends on whether the program is a commercial, demo/trial, shareware, freeware, or public domain program.

Instead of being available in an installed format, some software is run directly from the Internet as **cloud software**, also referred to as Web-based software and

EXHIBIT 3-18 MOBILE APPS

Source: © Pandora; © Duck Duck Moose, Inc.; © Facebook; © Instagram; © DataViz Inc.

public domain software A software program that is not copyrighted.

installed software A software program that must be installed on a computer before it is run.

cloud software Software that is delivered on demand via the Web.

EXHIBIT 3-19 INSTALLED SOFTWARE IS OFTEN DOWNLOADED

Source: © Norton by Symantec; © Google Inc.

Software as a Service (SaaS) (see Exhibit 3-20). Cloud software is delivered on demand via the Web to wherever the user is at the moment, provided he or she has an Internet connection (and has paid to use the software if a payment is required). The use of cloud software is growing rapidly. Typically, documents created using cloud software are stored online so that they are accessible via any Internet-enabled device.

Some software is offered in both installed and cloud versions. To eliminate the disadvantage of not being able to access cloud software and data without an Internet connection, some cloud apps are designed to function, at least in part, offline like installed software. For example, Google Docs users can access the Google Docs applications and their documents locally on their computers, when needed. Edits are stored locally on the computer when a user is offline and, when the user reconnects to the Internet, the changes are synchronized with the documents stored on the Google Docs servers.

EXHIBIT 3-20 CLOUD SOFTWARE

WEB DATABASE APPLICATION
This application allows you to retrieve property information, such as home values and homes for sale.

Google Docs

Office Online

CLOUD PRODUCTIVITY APPLICATIONS
These programs allow you to create documents online.

BUSINESS SAAS APPLICATION
This program allows you to share documents and collaborate on projects online.

Source: © Google Inc.; © Zillow; © Soonr

TRENDING...

DRONES

Source: © Airwave

A drone is an unmanned aircraft. Drones usually look like small airplanes or multirotor helicopters (for example, a drone with four rotors is called a quadcopter). Most drones are remote controlled. Drones used for aerial filming are equipped with cameras and transmit video to the operator's base station. For example, they can capture video footage for feature films and real estate marketing, as well as enable farmers and ranchers to remotely check the conditions of crops, irrigation, cattle, and other resources. Drones can also be programmed to fly predetermined paths via an onboard computer and GPS in order to create 3D maps, perform surveillance for firefighters, or assist with search and rescue operations, as shown in the accompanying illustration.

The use of drones for both personal and business use is skyrocketing. In response, many countries, including the United States, are developing regulations for use of unmanned aircraft. While flying a drone for personal use in the United States currently doesn't require a license, operators must register their drones with the government, as well as follow safety rules including flying no higher than 400 feet and always being in sight of the drone. In addition, there are regulations regarding how close drones can get to airports, sporting arenas, and other no-fly zones. Use of drones is expected to keep growing as the potential uses for these aircraft are discovered. In fact, Amazon is currently testing a drone-based Amazon Prime Air delivery system. In the United States, the FAA is charged with regulating drone use and is drafting new policies to address both current and future use of drones.

3-5 APPLICATION SOFTWARE FOR BUSINESS

Related software programs (such as a group of graphics programs, utility programs, or office-related software) are sometimes sold bundled together as a **software suite**. The primary advantages of using a software suite include a common interface among programs in the suite and a total cost that is often lower than buying the programs individually. Businesses and individuals often use office suites, sometimes called productivity software suites, to produce written documents. Office suites are used to create, modify, save, and print documents, as well as share them via the Web. Typically, office suites contain the following programs, and many also contain additional productivity tools—such as a calendar, an email or a messaging program, or collaboration tools:

- **Word processing software**—allows users to create and edit complex text-based documents that can also include images and other content.
- **Spreadsheet software**—provides users with a convenient means of

Office

LibreOffice

Apache OpenOffice™

Source: © Microsoft Corporation; © The Document Foundation; © The Apache Software Foundation

software suite A collection of related software programs bundled together and sold as a single software package.

word processing software The type of software used to create, edit, save, and print written documents.

spreadsheet software The type of software used to create spreadsheets.

creating documents containing complex mathematical calculations.

- **Database software**—allows users to store and organize vast amounts of data and retrieve specific information when needed.
- **Presentation graphics software**—allows users to create visual presentations to convey information more easily to others.

One of the most widely used office software suites is Microsoft Office. Similar suites are available from Corel (WordPerfect Office) and Apple (iWork). Free alternative installed office suites are LibreOffice and Apache OpenOffice; a free cloud office suite is Google Docs. Many office suites are available in a variety of versions, such as a home or student version that contains fewer programs than a professional version. Not all software suites are available for all operating systems. For example, Microsoft Office is available for both Windows and OS X computers; iWork is available only for OS X computers; and both LibreOffice and Apache OpenOffice are available for Windows, Linux, and OS X computers.

3-5a Word Processing Concepts

Virtually all formal writing today is performed using a word processing program, such as the one shown in Exhibit 3-21. Word processing refers to using a computer

EXHIBIT 3-21 WORD PROCESSING SOFTWARE

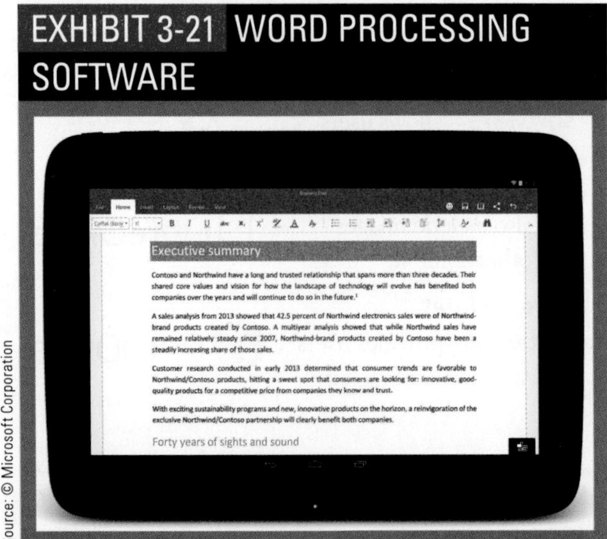

Source: © Microsoft Corporation

database software The type of software used to create and manipulate an electronic database.

presentation graphics software The type of software used to create presentation graphics, such as electronic slide shows.

and word processing software to create, edit, save, and print written documents, such as letters, contracts, newsletters, invoices, and reports. In addition to text, many documents created with word processing software also include photos, drawn objects, clip art images, hyperlinks, video clips, and tables. Like any document created with software instead of paper and pencil, word processing documents can be retrieved, modified, and printed as many times as needed. Some of the most frequently used word processing programs are Microsoft Word, Corel WordPerfect, Google Docs, and Apple Pages.

Word processing programs typically include collaboration, security, and rights-management tools (tools used to protect original content from misuse by others). They also often support speech and pen input. In addition, they frequently include Web-related features such as the ability to send a document as an email message via the word processing program, the inclusion of hyperlinks in documents, and the ability to create or modify Web pages or blogs.

3-5b Spreadsheet Concepts

Another widely used application program is spreadsheet software, which is the type of application software used to create computerized spreadsheets. A spreadsheet is a group of values and other data organized into rows and columns. Most spreadsheets include formulas that are used to compute calculations based on data entered into the spreadsheet. The results of all formulas are updated automatically whenever any changes are made to the data. Consequently, no manual computations are required, which increases accuracy. In addition, the automatic recalculation of formulas allows individuals to modify spreadsheet data as often as necessary either to create new spreadsheets or to experiment with various possible scenarios (called what-if analysis) to help make business decisions. Some of the most widely used spreadsheet programs today are Microsoft Excel, Corel Quattro Pro, Google Sheets, and Apple Numbers.

Spreadsheet software typically includes a variety of data analysis tools, as well as the ability to generate charts. In addition, most have built-in Web capabilities, such as the option to save the current spreadsheet as a Web page and to include hyperlinks in a spreadsheet.

3-5c Database Concepts

People often need to retrieve specific data rapidly while on the job. For example, a customer service representative may need to locate a customer's order status quickly while the customer is on the telephone. A database is a collection of related data that is stored on a computer and organized in a way that enables information to be retrieved as needed. Database software is the type of program used to create, maintain, and organize data in a database as well as to retrieve information from it. The most commonly used database management systems include Microsoft Access, Corel Paradox, Oracle Database, and IBM DB2.

Databases are often used on the Web. For instance, many Web sites use one or more databases to keep track of inventory; to allow searching for people, documents, or other information; and to place real-time orders. In fact, any time you type keywords in a search box on a search site or hunt for a product on a retail store's Web site using its search feature, you are using a Web database.

EXHIBIT 3-22 EXAMPLES OF PRESENTATION GRAPHICS

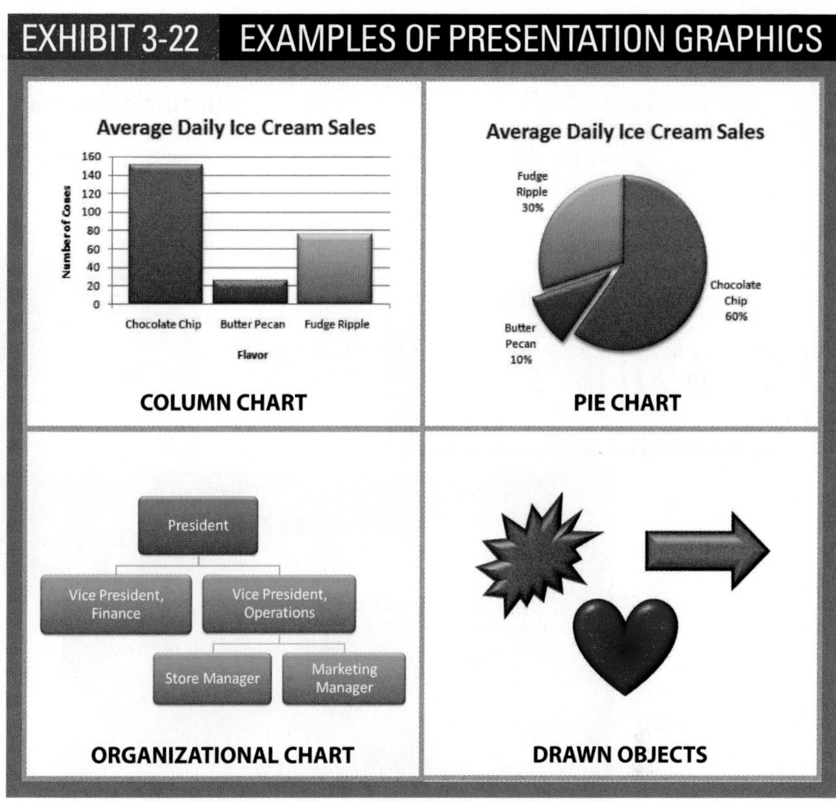

3-5d Presentation Graphics Concepts

If you try to explain to others what you look like, it may take several minutes. Show them a color photograph, on the other hand, and you can convey the same information within seconds. The saying "a picture is worth a thousand words" is the cornerstone of presentation graphics. A presentation graphic (see Exhibit 3-22) is an image designed to visually enhance a presentation, such as an electronic slide show or a printed report, to convey information more easily to people. A variety of software, including spreadsheet programs, image editing programs, and presentation graphics software, can be used to create presentation graphics. Presentation graphics often take the form of electronic slides containing images, text, video, and more that are displayed one after the other in an electronic slide show. Electronic slide shows are created with presentation graphics software and can be run on individual computers or presented to a large group using a data projector; for instance, they are frequently used for business and educational presentations. Some of the most common presentation graphics programs are Microsoft PowerPoint, Corel Presentations, Google Slides, and Apple Keynote.

Presentation graphics programs can also be used to generate Web pages or Web page content, and slides can include hyperlinks.

3-6 APPLICATION SOFTWARE FOR WORKING WITH MULTIMEDIA

Graphics are digital representations of images. Examples of graphics include digital photos, clip art, scanned drawings, and original images created using a software program. **Multimedia** technically refers to any application that contains more than one type of media but usually means audio and video content. A variety of software programs are designed to help individuals create or modify graphics, edit digital audio or video files,

graphic A digital representation of a graphical image, such as a digital photo, clip art, a scanned drawing, or an original image created using a software program.

multimedia Any application that contains more than one type of media; often used to refer to audio and video content.

EXHIBIT 3-23 GRAPHICS SOFTWARE

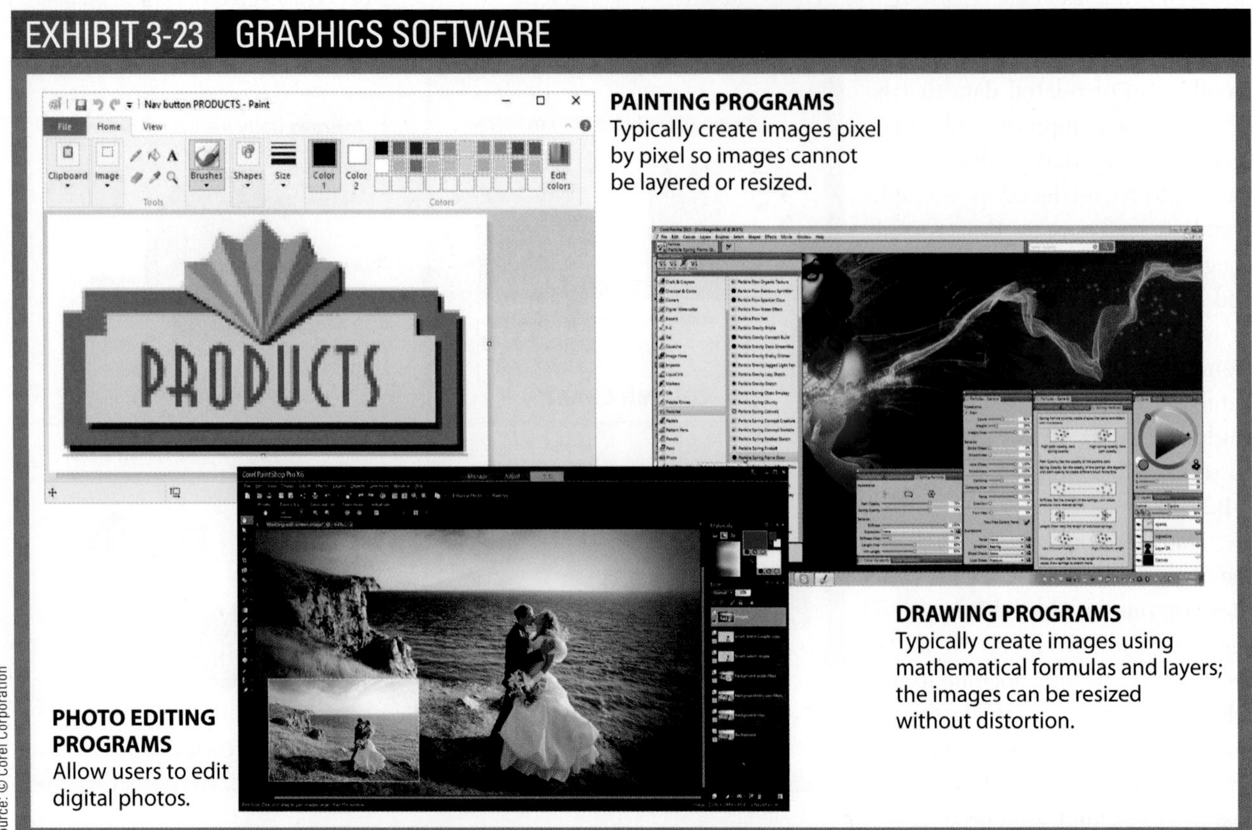

Nav button PRODUCTS - Paint
PRODUCTS
PAINTING PROGRAMS
Typically create images pixel by pixel so images cannot be layered or resized.
DRAWING PROGRAMS
Typically create images using mathematical formulas and layers; the images can be resized without distortion.
PHOTO EDITING PROGRAMS
Allow users to edit digital photos.

Source: © Corel Corporation

play media files, burn CDs and DVDs, and so forth, as discussed next. Some programs focus on just one task; others are designed to perform multiple tasks, such as to import and edit images, audio, and video, and then create a finished DVD.

3-6a Graphics Software

Graphics software—also called digital imaging software—is used to create or modify images. Graphics software programs are commonly distinguished by whether they are primarily oriented toward painting, drawing, or image editing, although these are general categories, not strict classifications, and some programs fit into more than one category. See Exhibit 3-23 for some examples of graphics software.

graphics software A program used to create or modify images; also called digital imaging software.

bitmap image A graphic created by coloring the individual pixels in an image.

vector graphic A graphic that uses mathematical formulas to represent image content instead of pixels.

Painting programs traditionally create **bitmap images**, which are created by coloring the individual pixels in an image. One of the most common painting programs is Microsoft Paint. Painting programs are often used to create and modify simple images, but, unless the painting program supports layers and other tools discussed shortly, use for these programs is relatively limited. This is because when something is drawn or placed on top of a bitmap image, the pixels in the image are recolored to reflect the new content, and whatever was beneath the new content is lost. In addition, bitmapped images cannot be enlarged and still maintain their quality because the pixels in the images just get larger, which makes the edges of the images look jagged. Painting tools are also increasingly included in other types of software, such as in office suites and drawing programs.

Drawing programs (also referred to as illustration programs) typically create **vector graphics**, which use mathematical formulas to represent image content instead of pixels. Unlike bitmap images, vector images can be resized and otherwise manipulated without loss of quality. Objects in drawing programs can also typically be layered so, if you place one object on top of another, you can later separate the two images if desired. Drawing programs are often used by individuals and small business owners to create original art, logos, business cards, and more. They are also used by professionals to create corporate images, Web site graphics, and so forth. Popular drawing programs include Adobe Illustrator CC, Corel Painter, and CorelDRAW.

Image editing or photo editing programs are drawing or painting programs that are specifically designed for touching up or modifying images, such as original digital images and digital photos. Some widely used consumer image editing and photo editing programs are Adobe Photoshop Elements, Apple Photos, Corel Paint Shop Photo Pro, and the free Picasa program. For professional image editing, the full Adobe Photoshop CC program is the leading program.

3-6b Audio Capture and Editing Software

For creating and editing audio files, audio capture and audio editing software is used. To capture sound from a microphone, sound recorder software is used; to capture sound from a CD, ripping software is used. In either case, after the audio is captured, it can then be modified as needed with audio editing software. For instance, background noise or pauses can be removed, portions of the selection can be edited out, multiple segments can be spliced together, and special effects such as fade-ins and fade-outs can be applied. Also available are specialized audio capture and editing programs designed for specific applications, such as creating podcasts or musical compositions. Professional audio capture and editing software (such as Sony Creative Software Sound Forge Pro and Adobe Audition CC) is used to create professional audio for end products, Web pages, presentations, and so forth. Common consumer audio capture and editing programs include Windows Sound Recorder, Apple GarageBand, and the free Audacity program. The WavePad Free Audio Editor mobile app is shown in Exhibit 3-24.

3-6c Video Editing and DVD Authoring Software

Digital video can be taken using many computers and virtually all smartphones today. If video is taken with a stand-alone video camera, it can be imported by connecting the camera to a computer or by inserting the storage media containing the video (such as a DVD) into a computer. Video editing tasks, such as deleting or rearranging scenes, adding voice-overs, and adding other special effects, can then be performed, as shown in Exhibit 3-25. Some

EXHIBIT 3-24 AUDIO EDITING SOFTWARE

Source: © NCH Software

EXHIBIT 3-25 VIDEO EDITING SOFTWARE

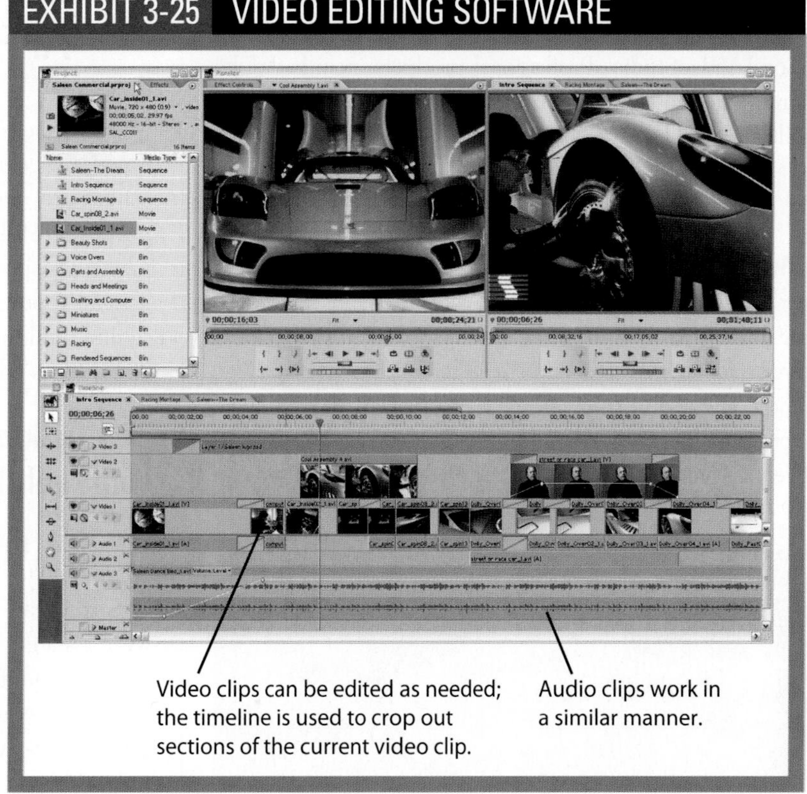

Video clips can be edited as needed; the timeline is used to crop out sections of the current video clip.
Audio clips work in a similar manner.

Source: © Adobe Systems Incorporated

EXHIBIT 3-26 TYPICAL MEDIA PLAYER PROGRAM

Current library content is listed here.
Additional music and videos can be purchased via the iTunes Store.

Source: © Apple, Inc.

video editing software today can edit HD and 4K video, as well as standard definition video.

DVD authoring refers to organizing content to be transferred to DVD, such as importing video clips and then creating the desired menu structure for the DVD to control the playback of those videos. DVD burning refers to recording data (such as a collection of songs or a finished video) on a recordable or rewritable DVD. DVD authoring and burning capabilities can be included in video editing software; there are also stand-alone DVD authoring programs and DVD burning capabilities are often preinstalled on computers containing a recordable or rewritable optical drive. Some file management programs include CD and DVD burning capabilities as well. Consumer video editing software includes Adobe Premiere Elements, Roxio Creator, Apple iMovie, Windows Movie Maker, and Corel VideoStudio. Professional products include Adobe Premiere Pro CC, Roxio Creator Pro, Corel VideoStudio Ultimate, and Sony Creative Software Vegas Pro.

3-6d Media Players

Media players are programs designed to play audio and video files, such as music CDs, downloaded music, or video or music streamed from the Internet. Many media players are available for free, such as RealPlayer, VLC Media Player, and iTunes (see Exhibit 3-26). Media players typically allow you to include both music you have purchased on CD, as well as music you have purchased and downloaded via an associated music store, in your library. They also often allow you to arrange your stored music and videos into playlists and then transfer them to a CD or mobile phone.

media player A program designed to play audio and video files.

desktop publishing The use of a personal computer to combine and manipulate text and images to create attractive documents that look as if they were created by a professional printer.

OTHER TYPES OF APPLICATION SOFTWARE

Many other types of application software are available. Some are geared for business or personal productivity; others are designed for entertainment or educational purposes. Still others are intended to help users with a particular specialized application, such as preparing financial reports, issuing prescriptions electronically, designing buildings, controlling machinery, or monitoring your fitness goals.

3-7a Desktop, Personal, and Web Publishing Software

Desktop publishing refers to using a personal computer to combine and manipulate text and images to create attractive documents that look as if they were created by a professional printer. Although many desktop publishing effects can be produced using a word processing program, users who frequently create publication-style documents usually find a desktop publishing program more efficient. Some popular

EXHIBIT 3-27 WEB SITE BUILDER

Source: © Webs

desktop publishing programs are Adobe InDesign, Microsoft Publisher, and Serif PagePlus. Personal publishing refers to creating desktop publishing-type documents—such as greeting cards, invitations, flyers, and certificates—for personal use. Specialized personal publishing programs are available for particular purposes, such as to create scrapbook pages, cross-stitch patterns, and CD and DVD labels.

Web publishing software (also called **Web site builders** when referring to a cloud service) is used to create complete Web sites. Most of these programs automatically generate Web pages as the user specifies what content each Web page should contain and what it should look like. They also typically allow users to choose a theme for the Web site to ensure it has a consistent appearance from page to page. After a site is created, most programs have the option of publishing it directly to a Web server. Web publishing programs include Adobe DreamWeaver CC, Adobe Contribute, and cloud software such as Webs, shown in Exhibit 3-27.

3-7b Educational, Entertainment, and Reference Software

A wide variety of educational and entertainment application programs are available. **Educational software** is designed to teach one or more skills, such as reading, math, spelling, a foreign language, or world geography, or to help prepare for standardized tests. **Entertainment software** includes games, simulations, and other programs that provide amusement. A hybrid of these two categories is called edutainment—educational software that also entertains. **Reference software** includes encyclopedias, dictionaries, atlases, mapping/travel programs, cookbook programs, nutrition or fitness programs, and other software designed to provide valuable information. Although still available as stand-alone programs, reference information today is often cloud software or obtained via reference Web sites.

Web publishing software (Web site builder) A program designed to create Web pages and entire Web sites.

educational software A program designed to teach one or more skills.

entertainment software A program that provides amusement, such as a game or simulation.

reference software A program designed to provide information, such as an encyclopedia, a dictionary, or an atlas.

3-7c Note Taking Software and Web Notebooks

Note taking software is used by both students and businesspeople to take notes during class lectures, meetings, and similar settings. It is used most often with tablet computers and other devices designed to accept pen input. Typically, note taking software, such as Microsoft OneNote or Circus Ponies NoteBook, supports both typed and handwritten input; handwritten input can usually be saved in its handwritten form as an image or converted to typed text. The NoteBook program, shown in Exhibit 3-28, also includes a voice recorder so you can record a lecture or meeting—tapping the speaker icon next to a note replays the voice recorded at the time that particular note was taken. Note taking software typically contains features designed specifically to make note taking—and, particularly, retrieving information from the notes—easier. Like a paper notebook, you can usually create tabbed sections (such as one tab per course); files, notes, Web links, and any other data are then stored under the appropriate tabs. In addition, search tools that allow you to find the information you need quickly and easily are usually included. Online versions of these programs, such as Zoho Notebook and Evernote, are sometimes referred to as **Web notebooks** and are designed to help organize your online research. Web notebooks can include text, images, Web links, search results, and other Web page resources, as well as other content you might want to save, such as notes, documents, and scanned images.

EXHIBIT 3-28 NOTE TAKING SOFTWARE

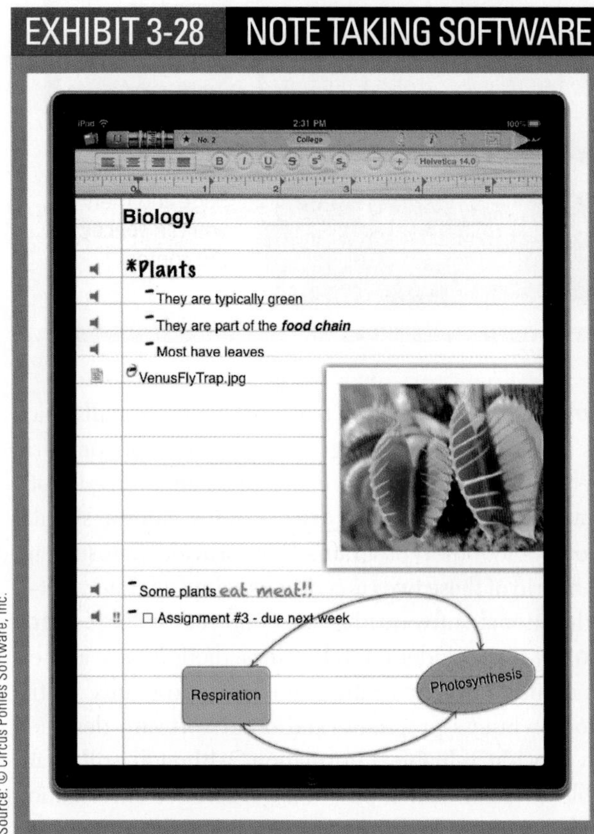

Source: © Circus Ponies Software, Inc.

3-7d CAD and Other Types of Design Software

Computer-aided design (CAD) software enables users to design objects on the computer. For example, engineers or architects can create designs of buildings or other objects and modify the designs as often as needed. Increasingly, CAD programs are including capabilities to analyze designs in terms of how well they meet a number of design criteria, such as testing how a building design will hold up during an earthquake or how a car will perform under certain conditions. Besides playing an important role in the design of finished products, CAD is also useful in fields such as art, advertising, architecture, and movie production. In addition to the powerful CAD programs used in business, design programs are available for home and small business use, such as for designing new homes and for making remodeling plans, interior designs, and landscape designs.

3-7e Accounting and Personal Finance Software

Accounting software is used to automate common accounting activities, such as creating payroll documents and checks, preparing financial statements, tracking business expenses, and managing customer accounts and invoices (see Exhibit 3-29). **Personal finance software** is commonly used at home by individuals to write checks and balance checking accounts,

note taking software A program used by both students and businesspeople to take notes during class lectures, meetings, and similar settings.

Web notebook An online version of a note taking program.

computer-aided design (CAD) software A program that enables users to design objects on the computer.

accounting software A program that is used to automate common accounting activities.

personal finance software Accounting software that is commonly used at home by individuals.

EXHIBIT 3-29 ACCOUNTING SOFTWARE

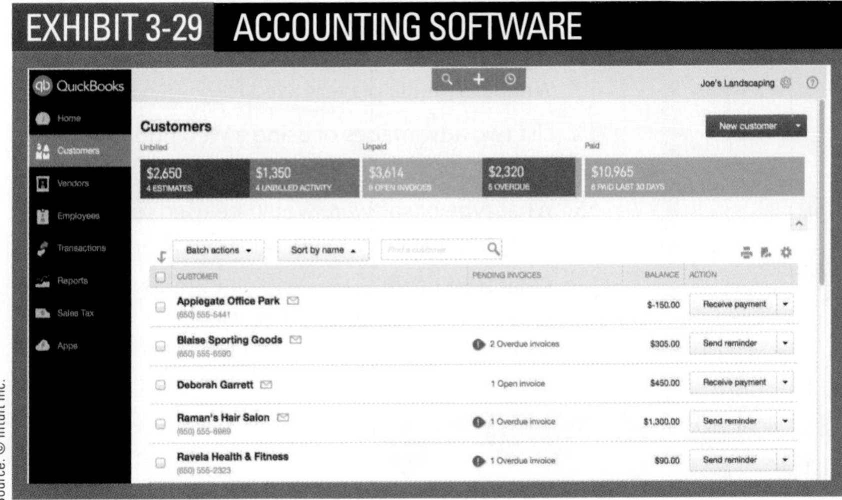

Source: © Intuit Inc.

track personal expenses, manage stock portfolios, and prepare income taxes. Increasingly, personal finance activities are becoming Web-based, such as the online banking and online portfolio management services available through many banks and brokerage firms.

3-7f Project Management, Collaboration, and Remote Access Software

Project management software is used to plan, schedule, track, and analyze the tasks involved in a project, such as the construction of a building or a large advertising campaign for a client. Project management capabilities are often included in **collaboration software**—software that enables a group of individuals to work together on a project—and are increasingly available as cloud software programs.

Remote access software enables individuals to access content on another computer they are authorized to access, via the Internet. Some programs allow you to control the remote computer directly; others allow you to access your media files (such as recorded TV shows or music) from any Web-enabled device while you are away from home. For instance, the Slingbox product gives you access to and control over your cable box and DVR via the Internet, and TeamViewer software (shown in Exhibit 3-30) allows you to access a computer (such as a home or an office PC) from any Web-enabled device while you are away from home provided you have the remote access software running on your PC. Other remote access software automatically backs up all data files on your main computer to a secure Web server so they can be accessed from any Web-enabled device (such as a portable computer or mobile device) as well as shared with others for collaboration purposes. Technical support is also sometimes offered via remote access feature—once you grant permission, the technician can access your computer remotely to resolve your problem.

EXHIBIT 3-30 REMOTE ACCESS SOFTWARE

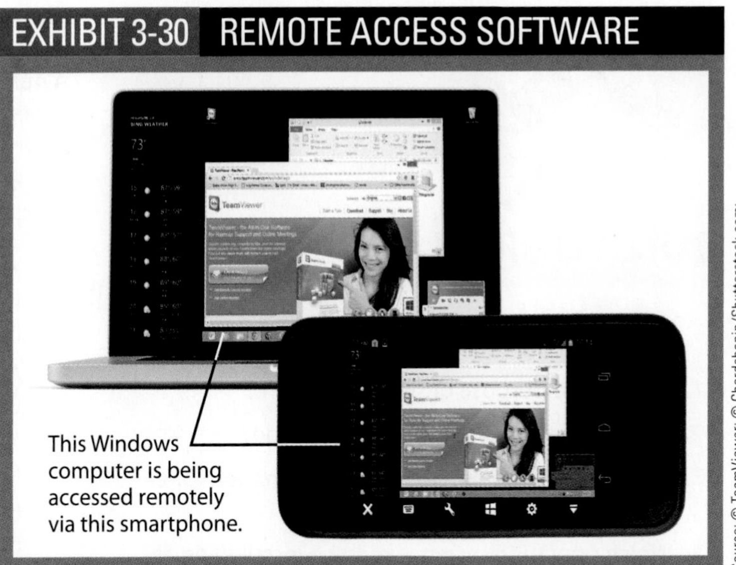

This Windows computer is being accessed remotely via this smartphone.

Source: © TeamViewer; © Chardchanin/Shutterstock.com; © Bombaert Patrick/Shutterstock.com

project management software A program used to plan, schedule, track, and analyze the tasks involved in a project.

collaboration software A program that enables a group of individuals to work together on a project.

remote access software A program that enables individuals to access content on another computer they are authorized to access, via the Internet.

STUDY TOOLS 3

READY TO STUDY? IN THE BOOK, YOU CAN:

- ☐ Rip out the Chapter Review Card, which includes key chapter concepts and important key terms.

ONLINE AT WWW.CENGAGEBRAIN.COM, YOU CAN:

- ☐ Review key concepts from the chapter in a short video.
- ☐ Explore the role of the operating system with the Interactive Infographic.
- ☐ Practice what you've learned with more Practice It and On Your Own exercises.
- ☐ Prepare for tests with quizzes.
- ☐ Review the key terms with flashcards.

QUIZ YOURSELF

1. What is the purpose of system software?
2. What does multitasking allow you to do?
3. What type of user interface do most modern operating systems use?
4. Which operating system would be installed on an iPhone?
5. What type of utility program is designed to make duplicate copies of files?
6. What is application software?
7. Explain the function of a software license.
8. Are shareware and freeware software the same? Explain.
9. What is the difference between installed and cloud software?
10. List the four types of programs that office suites typically contain.
11. Which Microsoft Office program is most appropriate for creating a memo?
12. What type of software programs are painting and drawing programs?
13. What are media players used for?
14. List two advantages of using a Web publishing program or Web site builder to create a Web site.
15. What type of software would be used to create a design of a new building or product?
16. What type of software enables a group of people to work together on a project?

PRACTICE IT

Practice It 3-1

A number of new operating systems have been developed in the past few years, such as Windows 10, Android, Firefox OS, and Google Chrome OS.

1. Select one new or emerging operating system and research it.
2. What is the purpose and targeted market for this operating system? What devices can it be installed on?
3. Are there other operating systems that could be used instead of your selected operating system? If so, what advantages does your selected operating system have over its competitors?
4. If the operating system was developed to fulfill a new need, are there other operating systems that are being adapted or being developed as a result?
5. Do you think your selected operating system will succeed? Why or why not?
6. Prepare a one-page summary that answers these questions and submit it to your instructor.

Practice It 3-2

Many online tours and tutorials are available for application programs. Some are available through the software company's Web site; others are located on third-party Web sites.

1. Select one common software program, such as Word, Excel, PowerPoint, Chrome, Google Docs, or Paint. Locate a free online tour or tutorial for the

program you selected, and then work your way through one tour or tutorial.

2. What features of the application program do you think are most interesting?
3. How helpful is the tour or tutorial? Is the tour or tutorial easy to use and understand?
4. Did you encounter any errors or other problems as you worked through the tour or tutorial?
5. Are there multiple versions for varying levels of difficulty? If so, how did you choose which version to review?
6. Would you recommend this tour or tutorial to others? Why or why not?
7. Prepare a one-page summary that answers these questions and submit it to your instructor.

ON YOUR OWN

On Your Own 3-1

Wearables, such as smart watches like the Apple Watch and fitness bands like Fitbit, are a hot trend. Some of these devices are designed to be used with smartphones, though they may also have stand-alone features.

1. Select smart watches, fitness bands, or another type of wearable device. Research three available products including the functions and features they offer, their prices, and the devices with which they are compatible.
2. If you were to buy this type of device, determine your budget as well as the functions and features that are most important to you. Separate the functions and features into mandatory versus desired specifications.
3. Evaluate the products you researched, weighing their price, functions, and features with your budget and specifications.
4. Prepare a one-page summary that includes the features, functions, and price of each product you researched, as well as the main differences between the products and their cost. Include a statement regarding which of these products you would choose and submit the summary to your instructor.

Part 2 NETWORKS and THE INTERNET

4 | Computer Networks

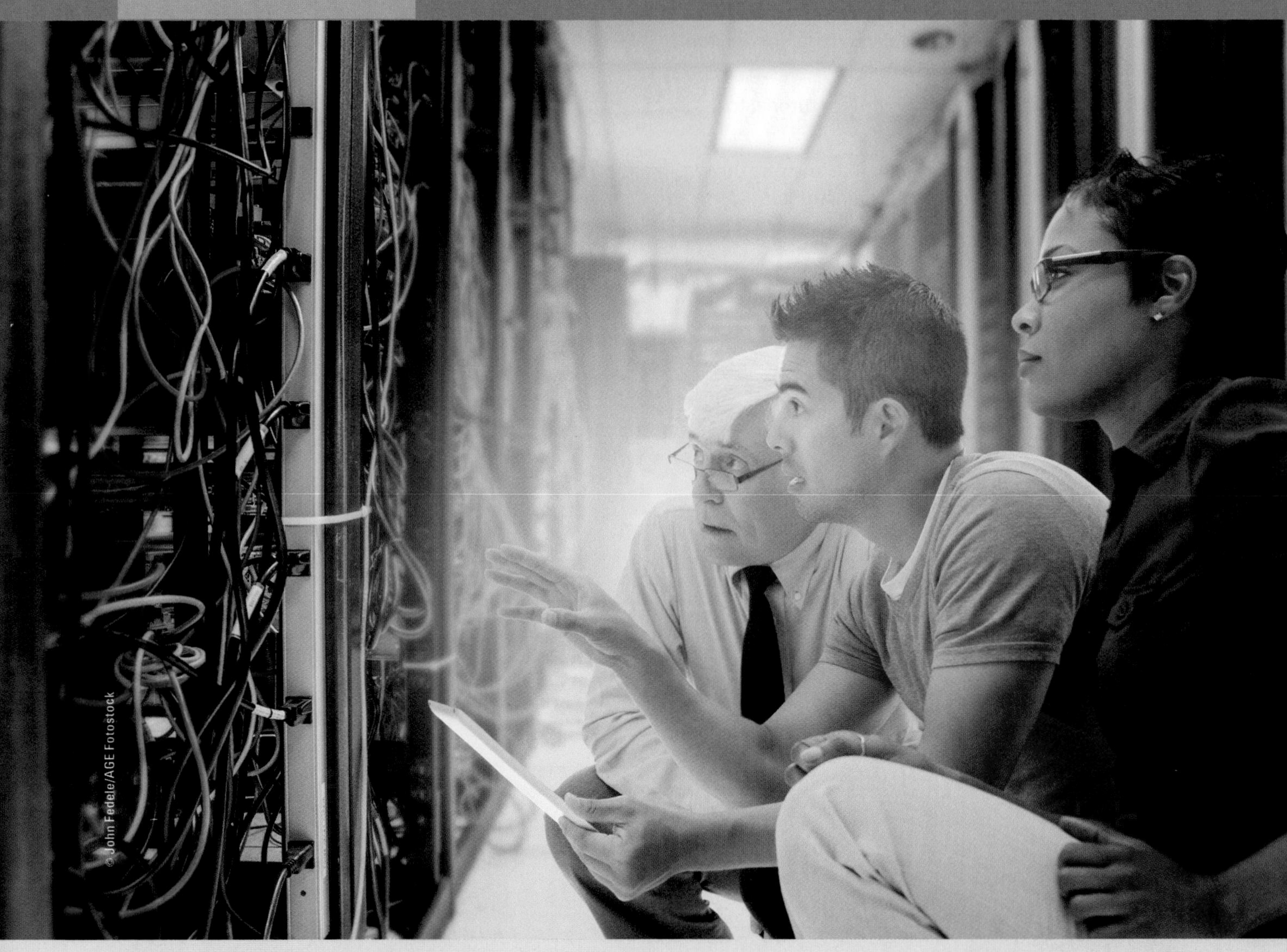

LEARNING OBJECTIVES

After studying the material in this chapter, you will be able to:

4-1 Explain what networks are and some common networking applications

4-2 Identify network characteristics

4-3 Understand how data is transmitted over a network

4-4 Describe common types of networking media

4-5 Identify communications protocols and networking standards

4-6 Describe networking hardware

After finishing this chapter, go to **PAGE 126** for **STUDY TOOLS**.

4-1 WHAT IS A NETWORK?

From telephone calls to home and business networks to Web surfing and online shopping, networking and the Internet are deeply embedded in our society. Because of this, it is important to be familiar with basic networking concepts and terminology as well as with the variety of activities that take place today via networks.

A **computer network** is a collection of computers and other hardware devices that are connected so users can share hardware, software, and data as well as communicate with each other electronically. Today, computer networks are converging with telephone networks and other communications networks with both data and voice being sent over these networks. Computer networks range from small private networks to the Internet and are widely used by businesses and individuals.

4-1a Business Use of Computer Networks

In most businesses, computer networks are essential. They enable employees to share expensive hardware, access the Internet, and communicate with each other, business partners, and customers. They facilitate the exchange and collaboration of documents, and they are often a key component of the ordering, inventory, and fulfillment systems used to process customer orders. In addition, there are specialty networking applications used for business purposes. For example, **videoconferencing** is the use of networking technology to conduct real-time, face-to-face meetings between individuals physically located in different places. It often takes place via personal computers or mobile devices. It can also take place via videoconferencing robots or telepresence videoconferencing rooms where individuals appear life-sized, as shown in Exhibit 4-1.

The availability of videoconferencing, email, and other communication technology has made **telecommuting** a viable option for many individuals. With telecommuting, individuals work from their homes or another remote location and communicate with their places of business and with clients via networking technologies. A networking application used in the medical field is **telemedicine**, which is the use of networking technology to provide medical information and services. At its simplest level, it includes Web sites that patients can access to contact their physicians, make appointments, view lab results, and more. However, more complex telemedicine systems are also used to provide care to individuals who may not otherwise have access to that care, such as to enable an individual living in a remote area to consult with a specialist.

4-1b Personal Use of Computer Networks

In homes, computer networks enable individuals to share resources, access the Internet, and communicate with others. In addition, they allow people to create a multimedia network to share digital photos, downloaded movies, and music among the networked devices in a home. On the go, networks enable individuals to work from remote locations, locate information whenever and wherever it is needed, and stay in touch with others.

4-1c Other Types of Networks

Some of the first communications networks were those used for television and radio broadcasting and to deliver telephone service. Many of these networks are still in use today. For example, the conventional telephone network is used to provide telephone service to landline phones as well as for some types of Internet connections. **Mobile phones** use a wireless telephone network for

EXHIBIT 4-1 TELEPRESENCE VIDEOCONFERENCING

Source: © Cisco

computer network Computers and other devices that are connected to share hardware, software, and data.

videoconference A real-time, face-to-face meeting between individuals physically located in different places conducted through the use of networking technology.

telecommute The act of working from a remote location by using computers and networking technology.

telemedicine The use of networking technology to provide medical information and services.

mobile phone A phone, such as a cellular or satellite phone, that uses a wireless network.

communications instead of the regular telephone network. The most common type of mobile phone is the **cellular (cell) phone**, which communicates via a cellular network. Increasingly, cell phones today are **dual-mode phones**, which are phones that allow users to make telephone calls using more than one communications network, such as via both a cellular and a Wi-Fi network. A less common type of mobile phone is the **satellite phone**, shown in Exhibit 4-2, which communicates via satellite technology. Although more expensive than cellular service, satellite phone coverage is much broader, often on a country-by-country basis, and some satellite phone services cover the entire earth. Consequently, satellite phones are most often used by individuals traveling in remote areas where continuous cellular service might not be available. Another communications network is the **global positioning system (GPS)**, which consists of GPS satellites that are used in conjunction with GPS receivers to determine the receiver's exact geographic location.

EXHIBIT 4-2 SATELLITE PHONE

cellular (cell) phone A type of mobile phone that communicates via cellular networks.

dual-mode phone A mobile phone that can be used with more than one communications network, such as with both a cellular and a Wi-Fi network.

satellite phone A type of mobile phone that communicates via satellite networks.

global positioning system (GPS) A system that uses satellites and a receiver to determine the exact geographic location of the receiver.

wired network A network in which computers and other devices are connected to the network via physical cables.

wireless network A network in which computers and other devices are connected to the network without physical cables.

hotspot A location that provides wireless Internet access.

4-2 NETWORK CHARACTERISTICS

Networks can be identified by a variety of characteristics, including whether they are designed for wired or wireless access, their topology, their architecture, and their size or coverage area.

4-2a Wired vs. Wireless Networks

Networks can be designed for access via wired and/or wireless connections. With a **wired network** connection, the computers and other devices on the network are physically connected via cabling to the network. With a **wireless network** connection, wireless (usually radio) signals are used to send data through the air between devices instead of using physical cables. Wired networks include conventional telephone networks, cable TV networks, and the wired networks commonly found in schools, businesses, and government facilities. Wireless networks include conventional television and radio networks, cellular telephone networks, satellite TV networks, and the wireless networks commonly found in homes, schools, and businesses. Wireless networks are also found in many public locations, such as coffeehouses, businesses, airports, hotels, and libraries, to provide Internet access to users while they are on the go via public wireless **hotspots**.

Many networks are accessible via both wired and wireless connections. For instance, a business may have a wired main company network to which the computers in employee offices are always connected as well as a wireless network for visitors and employees to use while inside the office building. A home network may have a wired connection between the devices needed to connect the home to the Internet, plus wireless access for the devices in the home that will access the home network wirelessly.

Wired networks tend to be faster and more secure than wireless networks. Wireless networks, however, allow easy connections in locations where physical wiring is impractical or inconvenient as well as provide much more freedom about where you can use your computer. With wireless networking, for example, you can surf the Web on your notebook or tablet from anywhere in your house or backyard, access the Internet with your portable computer or smartphone while on the go, and create a home network without having to run wires among the rooms in your house.

4-2b **Network Topologies**

The physical topology of a computer network indicates how the devices in the network are arranged. The three most common physical topologies are star, bus, and mesh, as shown in Exhibit 4-3.

EXHIBIT 4-3 COMMON NETWORK TOPOLOGIES

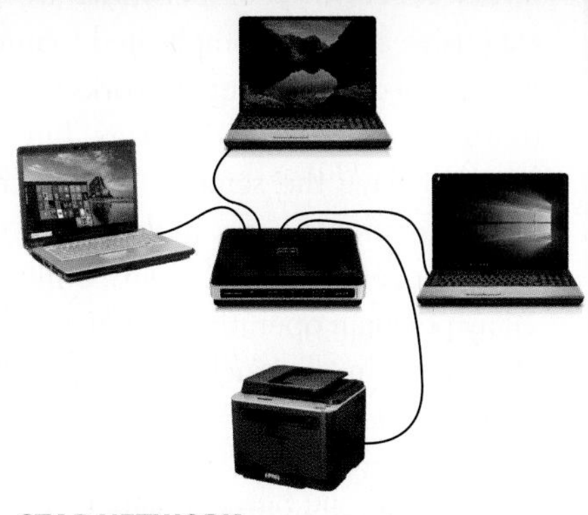

STAR NETWORK
Uses a central device to connect each device directly to the network.

BUS NETWORK
Uses a central cable to connect each device in a linear fashion.

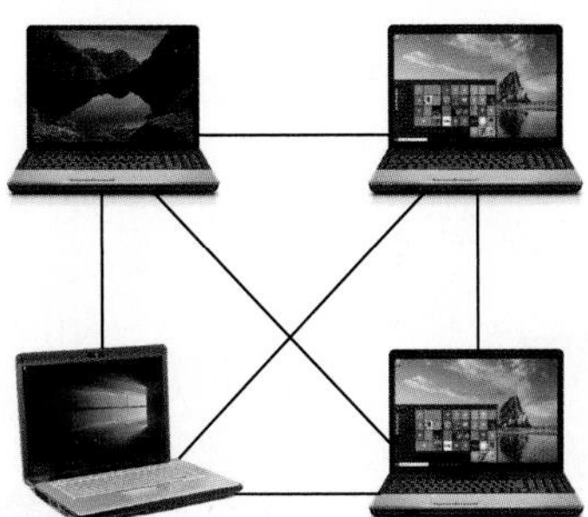

MESH NETWORK
Each computer or device is connected to multiple (sometimes all of the other) devices on the network.

- **Star network**—A network that uses a central device through which all data is sent. If the central device fails, the network cannot function.
- **Bus network**—A network that uses a central cable to which all network devices connect. All data is transmitted down the bus line from one device to another so, if the bus line fails, the network cannot function.
- **Mesh network**—A network that uses a number of different connections between network devices so that data can take any of several possible paths from source to destination. Consequently, if one device on a mesh network fails, the network can still function, assuming an alternate path is available. Mesh networks are used most often with wireless networks.

Many networks, however, do not conform to a standard topology. Some networks combine topologies and connect multiple smaller networks, in effect turning several smaller networks into one larger one. For example, two star networks may be joined together using a bus line.

4-2c **Network Architectures**

Networks also vary by their **network architecture**; that is, the way they are designed to communicate. The two most common network architectures are client-server and peer-to-peer.

Client-server networks include both **clients**, which are computers and other devices on the network that request and use network resources, and **servers**, which are computers that are dedicated to processing client requests. Network servers are typically powerful

star network A network that uses a central device connected directly to several other devices.

bus network A network that uses a central cable to which all network devices connect.

mesh network A network that uses multiple connections among network devices so that data can take any of several paths.

network architecture The way a network is designed to communicate.

client-server network A network that includes both client devices and the servers that process client requests.

client In a client-server network, a computer or other device that requests and uses network resources.

server In a client-server network, a computer that is dedicated to processing client requests.

computers with lots of memory and a very large hard drive. They provide access to software, files, and other resources that are being shared via the network. Servers typically perform a variety of tasks. For example, a single server can act as a network server to manage network traffic, a file server to manage shared files, a print server to handle printing-related activities, and/or a mail server or Web server to manage email and Web page requests, respectively. Only one server appears in the network illustrated in Exhibit 4-4, and it is capable of performing all server tasks for that network. When a client retrieves files from a server, it is called **downloading**; transferring data from a client to a server is called **uploading**.

With a **peer-to-peer (P2P) network**, a central server is not used. As shown in Exhibit 4-5, all the computers on the network work at the same functional level, and users have direct access to the computers and other devices attached to the network. For instance, users can access files stored on a peer computer's hard drive and print using a peer computer's printer, provided those devices have been designated as shared devices. Peer-to-peer networks are less expensive and less complicated to implement than client-server networks because there are no dedicated servers, but they may not have the same performance as client-server networks under heavy use. Peer-to-peer capabilities are built into many personal operating systems and are often used in conjunction with small office or home networks.

Another type of peer-to-peer networking—sometimes called Internet peer-to-peer (Internet P2P) computing—is performed via the Internet. Instead of placing content on a Web server for others to view via the Internet, content is exchanged over the Internet directly between individual users via a peer-to-peer network. For instance, one user can copy a file from another user's hard drive to his or her own computer via the Internet. Internet P2P networking is commonly used for exchanging music and video files with

EXHIBIT 4-4 CLIENT-SERVER NETWORK

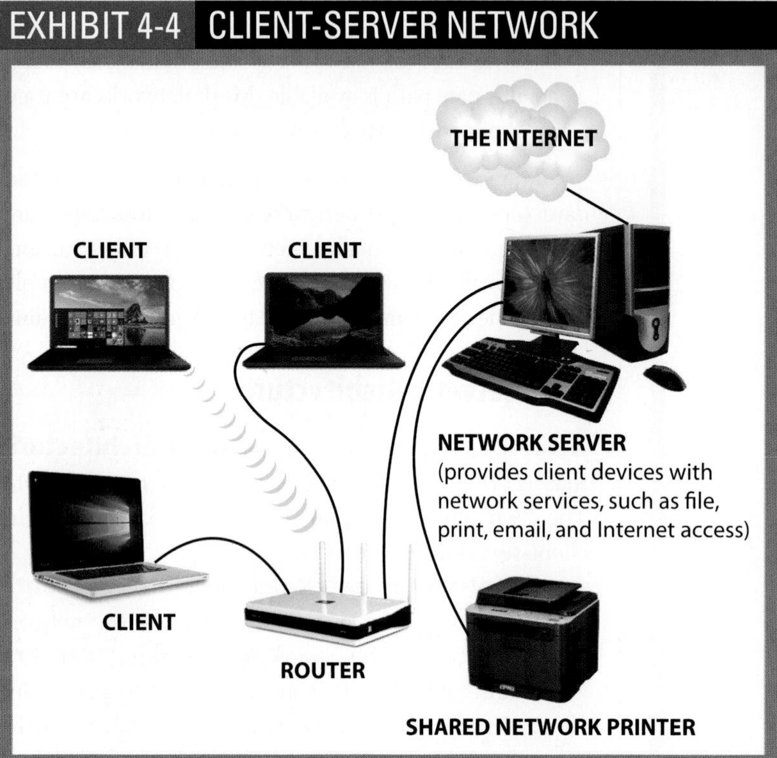

EXHIBIT 4-5 PEER-TO-PEER NETWORK

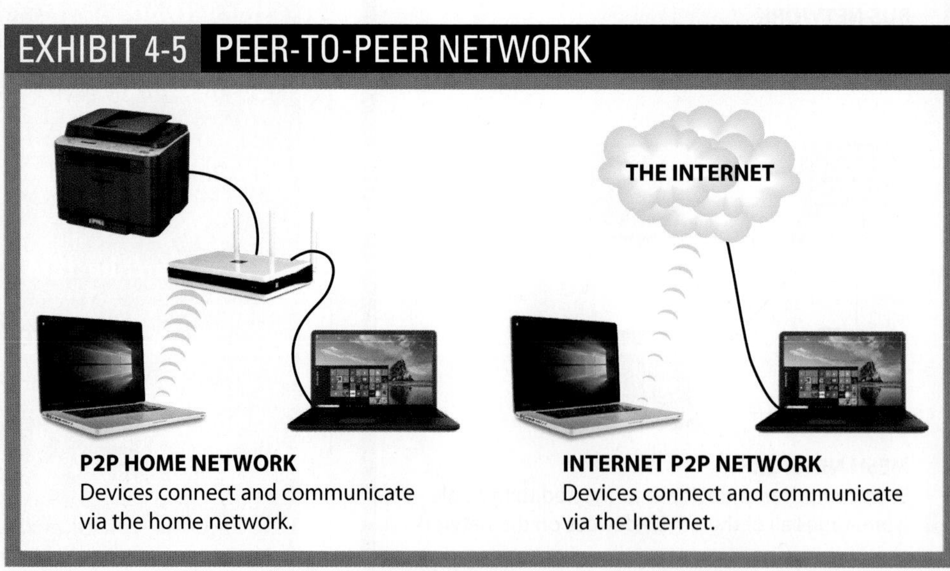

download To retrieve files from a server.

upload To transfer files to a server.

peer-to-peer (P2P) network A network configured to allow files and folders stored on the networked computers to be shared directly with other computers on that network.

others over the Internet—an illegal act if the content is copyright-protected and the exchange is unauthorized, although legal Internet P2P networks exist.

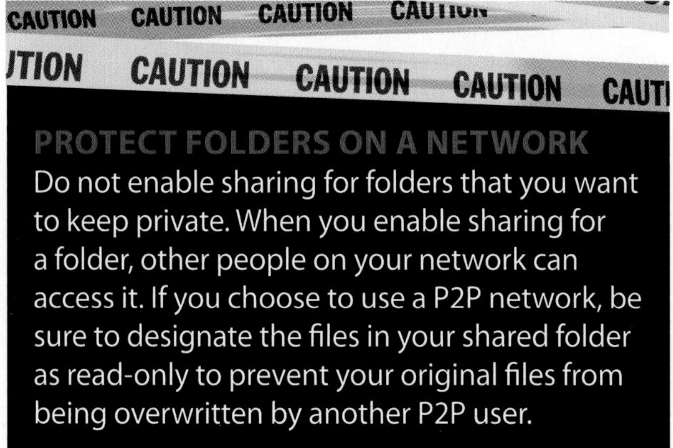

PROTECT FOLDERS ON A NETWORK

Do not enable sharing for folders that you want to keep private. When you enable sharing for a folder, other people on your network can access it. If you choose to use a P2P network, be sure to designate the files in your shared folder as read-only to prevent your original files from being overwritten by another P2P user.

4-2d Network Size and Coverage Area

Networks are also classified by their size and their coverage area. This classification impacts the types of users the network is designed to service. The most common categories of networks are discussed next; these networks can use both wired and wireless connections.

A **personal area network (PAN)** is a small network of personal devices for one individual (such as a portable computer, smartphone, headset, tablet, smart watch, and printer) that is designed to enable those devices to communicate and share data. PANs are typically wireless and set up to work together automatically as soon as the devices get within a certain physical distance of each other. For instance, a PAN can be used to synchronize a mobile device automatically with a personal computer whenever the devices are in range of each other or to connect a smartphone and other devices to a smart watch or fitness band (see Exhibit 4-6).

A **local area network (LAN)** is a network that covers a relatively small geographical area, such as a home, an office building, or a school. LANs allow users on the network to exchange files and email, share printers and other hardware, and access the Internet. The client-server network shown in Exhibit 4-4 is an example of a LAN.

A **metropolitan area network (MAN)** is a network designed to service a metropolitan area, typically a city or county. Most MANs are owned and operated by a city or by a network provider in order to provide individuals in that location access to the MAN. Some wireless MANs are created by cities or large organizations (such as Google in downtown Mountain View, California) to provide free or low-cost Internet access to area residents. In addition, some Internet service providers have free wireless MANs or hotspots in select metropolitan areas for their subscribers to use when they are on the go.

A **wide area network (WAN)** is a network that covers a large geographical area. Typically, a WAN consists of two or more LANs that are connected together using communications technology. The Internet, by this definition, is the world's largest WAN. WANs may be publicly accessible, like the Internet, or they may be privately owned and operated. For instance, a company may have a private WAN to transfer data from one location to another, such as from each retail store to the corporate headquarters. Large WANs, like the Internet, typically use a mesh topology.

An **intranet** is a private network, such as a company LAN, that is designed to be used by an organization's employees and is set up like the Internet with data posted on Web pages that are accessed with a Web

EXHIBIT 4-6 FITNESS PAN

Source: © Microsoft Corporation

personal area network (PAN) A network that connects an individual's personal devices when they are located close together.

local area network (LAN) A network that connects devices located in a small geographical area.

metropolitan area network (MAN) A network designed to service a metropolitan area.

wide area network (WAN) A network that connects devices located in a large geographical area.

intranet A private network that is set up similarly to the Internet and is accessed via a Web browser.

TRENDING...

SMART HOMES AND APPLIANCES

Increasingly, appliances today are becoming **smart appliances**; that is, traditional appliances, such as refrigerators, ovens, and coffee makers, with some type of built-in computing or communications technology that allows them to be controlled remotely by the user or to display information on demand. A **smart home** contains smart appliances and other features that automate household tasks. For instance, tasks such as watering the lawn, turning the air conditioning on or off, making coffee, and monitoring the security of the home and grounds are controlled by a main computer in the home or by the homeowner remotely via a smartphone or other computing device.

There are both stand-alone smart appliances (like smart refrigerators and smart TVs) and smart home automation systems (such as the one in the accompanying illustration) that give the homeowner control of a large number of devices via a single interface.

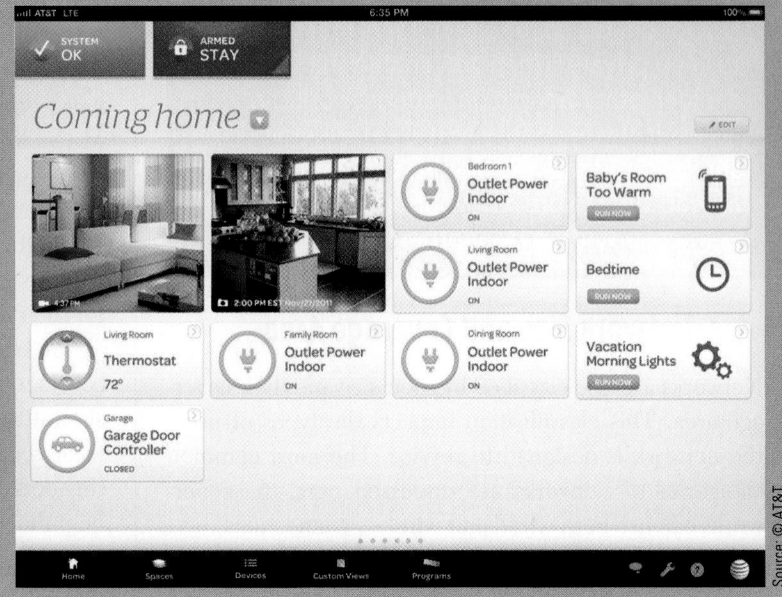

Source: © AT&T

browser. Consequently, little or no employee training is required to use an intranet, and intranet content can be accessed using a variety of devices. Intranets are used for many purposes including coordinating internal email and communications, making company publications available to employees, facilitating collaborative computing, and providing access to shared calendars and schedules.

A company network that is accessible to authorized outsiders is called an **extranet**. Extranets are usually accessed via the Internet, and they can be used to provide customers and business partners with access to the data they need. Access to intranets and extranets is typically restricted to employees and other authorized users, similar to other company networks.

A **virtual private network (VPN)** is a private, secure path across a public network (usually the Internet) that is set up to allow authorized users private, secure access to a network. VPNs allow an organization to provide secure, remote access to the company network without the cost of physically extending the private network. For instance, a VPN can allow a traveling employee, a business partner, or an employee located at a satellite office or public wireless hotspot to connect securely to the company network via the Internet. A process called tunneling is typically used to carry the data over the Internet; special encryption technology is used to protect the data so it cannot be understood if it is intercepted during transit. Personal VPNs, such as the one shown in Exhibit 4-7, can be used by individuals to provide a secure path to a public hotspot. Without a VPN, passwords, credit card numbers, and other sensitive data sent to the hotspot could be intercepted. VPNs can be used to protect any device that connects to a hotspot via Wi-Fi, including notebook computers, tablets, and smartphones.

smart appliance A traditional appliance with built-in computing or communications functions.

smart home A home that uses smart appliances and/or other smart features to automate household tasks.

extranet An intranet that is at least partially accessible to authorized outsiders.

virtual private network (VPN) A private, secure path over the Internet used for accessing a private network.

EXHIBIT 4-7 VPN FOR A LAPTOP COMPUTER

Source: AnchorFree, Inc.

4-3 DATA TRANSMISSION

Data transmitted over a network has specific characteristics, and it can travel over a network in various ways. The most common data transmission characteristics are discussed next.

4-3a Bandwidth

Bandwidth is the amount of data that can be transferred in a given time period, such as via a bus or over a certain type of networking medium. Just as a wide fire hose allows more water to pass through it per unit of time than a narrow garden hose allows, a networking medium with a high bandwidth allows more data to pass through it per unit of time than one with a low bandwidth. Text data requires the least amount of bandwidth; video data requires the most. Bandwidth is usually measured in the number of bps (bits per second), Kbps (thousands of bits per second), Mbps (millions of bits per second), or Gbps (billions of bits per second). The amount of data that is actually transferred under real-life conditions is called **throughput**.

4-3b Analog vs. Digital Signals

Data can be represented as either analog or digital signals. Voice and music data in its natural form, for instance, is analog. Data stored on a computer is digital. Most networking media send data using **digital signals**, in which data is represented by only two discrete states: 0s and 1s. **Analog signals**, such as those used by the conventional telephone system, represent data with continuous waves. The data to be transmitted over a networking medium must match the type of signal—analog or digital—that the medium supports. If it doesn't, then the data must be converted before it is transmitted. For instance, analog data that is to be sent using digital signals, such as analog music broadcast by a digital radio station, must first be converted into digital form. Likewise, digital data to be sent using analog signals, such as computer data sent over a conventional analog telephone network, must first be converted into analog form. The conversion of data between analog and digital form is performed by networking hardware.

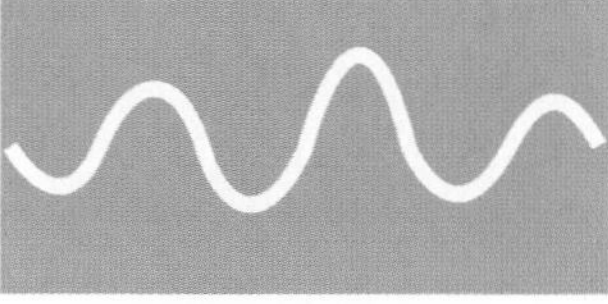

ANALOG SIGNALS

DIGITAL SIGNALS

4-3c Transmission Type and Timing

Networking media can also use either serial transmission or parallel transmission. With **serial transmission**, data is sent one bit at a time, one after the other along a single path. When **parallel transmission** is used, a group of bits is sent at the same time and each bit takes a separate path, as shown in Exhibit 4-8. Although parallel transmission is frequently used within computer components, such as buses, and is used for some wireless networking applications, networking media typically use serial transmission.

bandwidth The amount of data that can be can be transferred, such as via a bus or over a networking medium, in a given time period.

throughput The amount of data that is transferred under real-life conditions.

digital signal A type of signal where the data is represented by 0s and 1s.

analog signal A type of signal where the data is represented by continuous waves.

serial transmission A type of data transmission in which the bits in a byte travel down the same path one after the other.

parallel transmission A type of data transmission in which a group of bits is transmitted at one time and each bit takes a separate path.

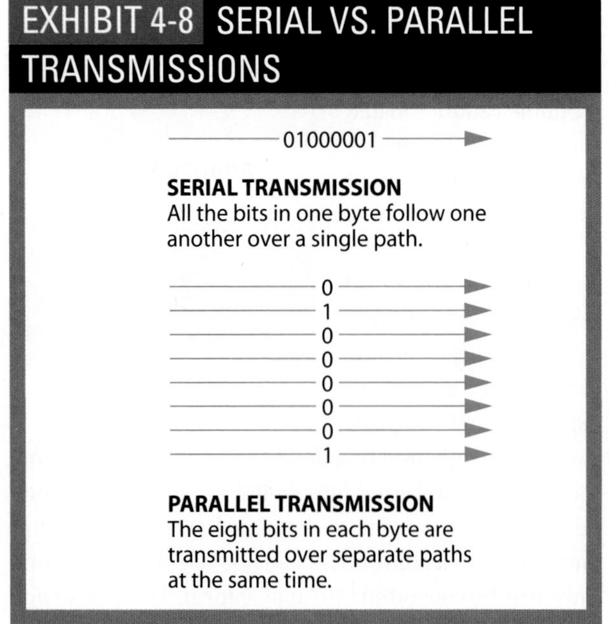

EXHIBIT 4-8 SERIAL VS. PARALLEL TRANSMISSIONS
01000001
SERIAL TRANSMISSION
All the bits in one byte follow one another over a single path.
0
1
0
0
0
0
0
1
PARALLEL TRANSMISSION
The eight bits in each byte are transmitted over separate paths at the same time.

When data is sent using serial transmission, one of the following three techniques is usually used to organize and time the bits being transferred so the data can be reconstructed after it is received.

- **Synchronous transmission**—Data is organized into groups or blocks of data, which are transferred at regular, specified intervals. Because the transmissions are synchronized, both devices know when data can be sent and when it should arrive. Most data transmissions within a computer and over a network are synchronous transmissions.
- **Asynchronous transmission**—Data is sent when it is ready to be sent, without being synchronized. To identify the bits that belong in each byte, a start bit and stop bit are used at the beginning and end of the byte, respectively. This overhead makes asynchronous transmission less efficient than synchronous transmission, and so it is not as widely used as synchronous transmission.
- **Isochronous transmission**—Data is sent when it is ready but all data must be delivered at the time it is needed. For example, when transmitting a video file, the audio data must be received at the proper time in order for it to be played with its corresponding video data. To accomplish this with isochronous transmission, the sending and receiving devices first communicate to determine the bandwidth and other factors needed for the transmission, and then the necessary bandwidth is reserved just for that transmission.

Although all three of these techniques send data one bit at a time, they vary with respect to how the bits are organized for transfer, as shown in Exhibit 4-9.

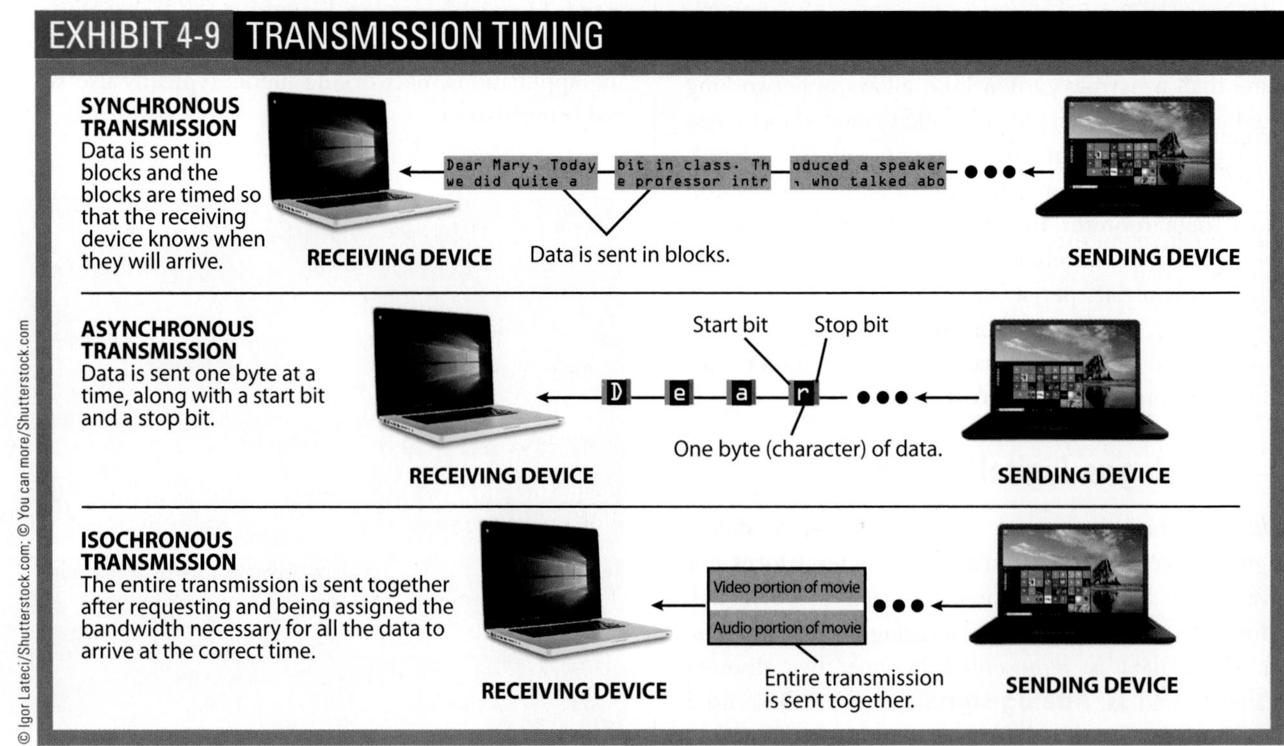

Data is sent in blocks and the blocks are timed so that the receiving device knows when they will arrive.
Dear Mary, Today we did quite a
bit in class. The professor intr
oduced a speaker, who talked abo

One byte (character) of data.

The entire transmission is sent together after requesting and being assigned the bandwidth necessary for all the data to arrive at the correct time.
Video portion of movie
Audio portion of movie

Another distinction between the different types of transmissions is the direction in which transmitted data can move.

- **Simplex transmission**—Data travels in a single direction only (like a doorbell). Simplex transmission is relatively uncommon in data transmissions because most devices that are mainly one-directional, such as a printer, can still transmit error messages and other data back to the computer.

EXHIBIT 4-10 CIRCUIT-SWITCHED, PACKET-SWITCHED, AND BROADCAST NETWORKS

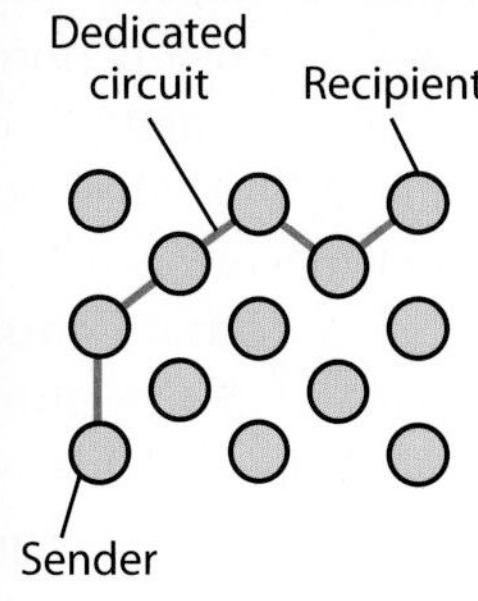

CIRCUIT-SWITCHED NETWORK
Data uses a dedicated path from the sender to the recipient.

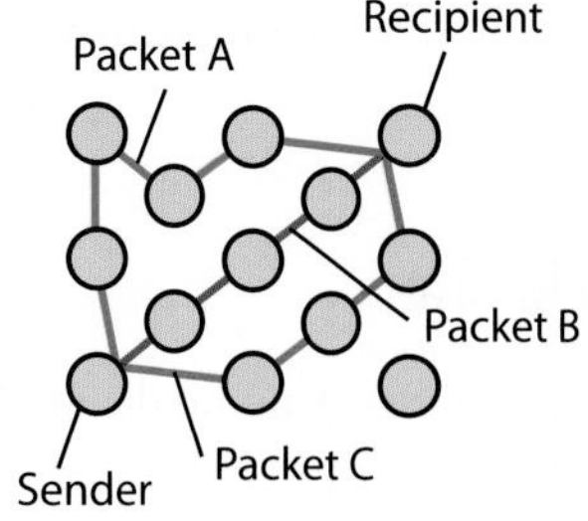

PACKET-SWITCHED NETWORK
Data is sent as individual packets, which are assembled at the recipient's destination.

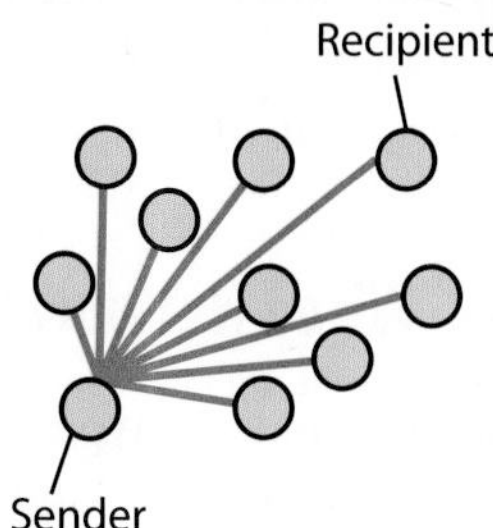

BROADCAST NETWORK
Data is broadcast to all nodes within range; the designated recipient retrieves the data.

- **Half-duplex transmission**—Data can travel in either direction, but only in one direction at a time (like a walkie-talkie where only one person can talk at a time). Some network transmissions are half-duplex.
- **Full-duplex transmission**—Data can move in both directions at the same time (like a telephone). Many network and most Internet connections are full-duplex; sometimes two connections between the sending device and receiving device are needed to support full-duplex transmissions.

4-3d Delivery Method

When data needs to travel across a large network, one of the three methods shown in Exhibit 4-10 is typically used. With **circuit switching**, a dedicated path over a network is established between the sender and receiver, and all data follows that path from the sender to the receiver. Once the connection is established, the physical path or circuit is dedicated to that connection and cannot be used by any other device until the transmission is finished. The most common example of a circuit-switched network is a conventional telephone system.

The delivery method used for data sent over the Internet is packet switching. With **packet switching**, messages are separated into small units called packets. Packets contain information about the sender and the receiver, the actual data being sent, and information about how to reassemble the packets to reconstruct the original message. Packets travel along the network separately, based on their final destination, network traffic, and other network conditions. When the packets reach their destination, they are reassembled in the proper order. Another alternative is **broadcasting**, in which data is sent out, typically in packets, to all nodes on a network and is retrieved only by the intended recipient. Broadcasting is used primarily with LANs.

synchronous transmission A type of serial data transmission in which data is organized into groups or blocks that are transferred at regular, specified intervals.

asynchronous transmission A type of serial data transmission in which data is sent when it is ready to be sent without being synchronized.

isochronous transmission A type of serial data transmission in which data must be delivered at the time it is needed.

simplex transmission A type of data transmission in which data travels in a single direction only.

half-duplex transmission A type of data transmission in which data can travel in either direction but only in one direction at a time.

full-duplex transmission A type of data transmission in which data can move in both directions at the same time.

circuit switching A method of transmitting data in which messages travel along a dedicated network path.

packet switching A method of transmitting data in which messages are separated into packets that travel along the network separately and then are reassembled in the proper order at the destination.

broadcasting A method of transmitting data in which data is sent out to all nodes on a network and is retrieved only by the intended recipient.

NETWORKING MEDIA

To connect the devices in a network, either wired media (physical cables) or wireless media (typically radio signals) can be used. The most common wired and wireless networking media are discussed next.

4-4a Wired Networking Media

The most common types of wired networking media are twisted-pair, coaxial, and fiber-optic cable, which are shown in Exhibit 4-11.

A **twisted-pair cable** is made up of pairs of thin strands of insulated wire twisted together. Twisted-pair is the least expensive type of networking cable and has been in use the longest. In fact, it is the same type of cabling used inside most homes for telephone communications. Twisted-pair cabling can be used with both analog and digital data transmission and is commonly used for LANs. Twisted-pair cable is rated by category, which indicates the type of data, speed, distance, and other factors that the cable supports. Category 3 (Cat 3) twisted-pair cabling is regular telephone cable; higher speed and quality cabling—such as Category 5 (Cat 5), Category 6 (Cat 6), and Category 7 (Cat 7)—is frequently used for home or business networks. The pairs of wires in twisted-pair cabling are twisted together to reduce interference and improve performance. To further improve performance, twisted-pair cabling can be shielded with a metal lining. Twisted-pair cables used for networks have different connectors than those used for telephones.

A **coaxial cable** (also known as a **coax cable**) consists of a relatively thick center wire surrounded by insulation and then covered with a shield of braided wire to block electromagnetic signals from entering the cable. Coaxial cable was originally developed to carry a large number of high-speed video transmissions at one time, such as to deliver cable TV service. It is commonly used today in computer networks, for short-run telephone transmissions outside of the home, and for cable television delivery. Although more expensive than twisted-pair cabling, it is much less susceptible to interference and can carry more data more quickly. Although not used extensively for networking home computers at the moment, that may change with the relatively new option of networking via the existing coax in a home. Coax is also used with home multimedia networks.

EXHIBIT 4-11 WIRED NETWORK TRANSMISSION MEDIA

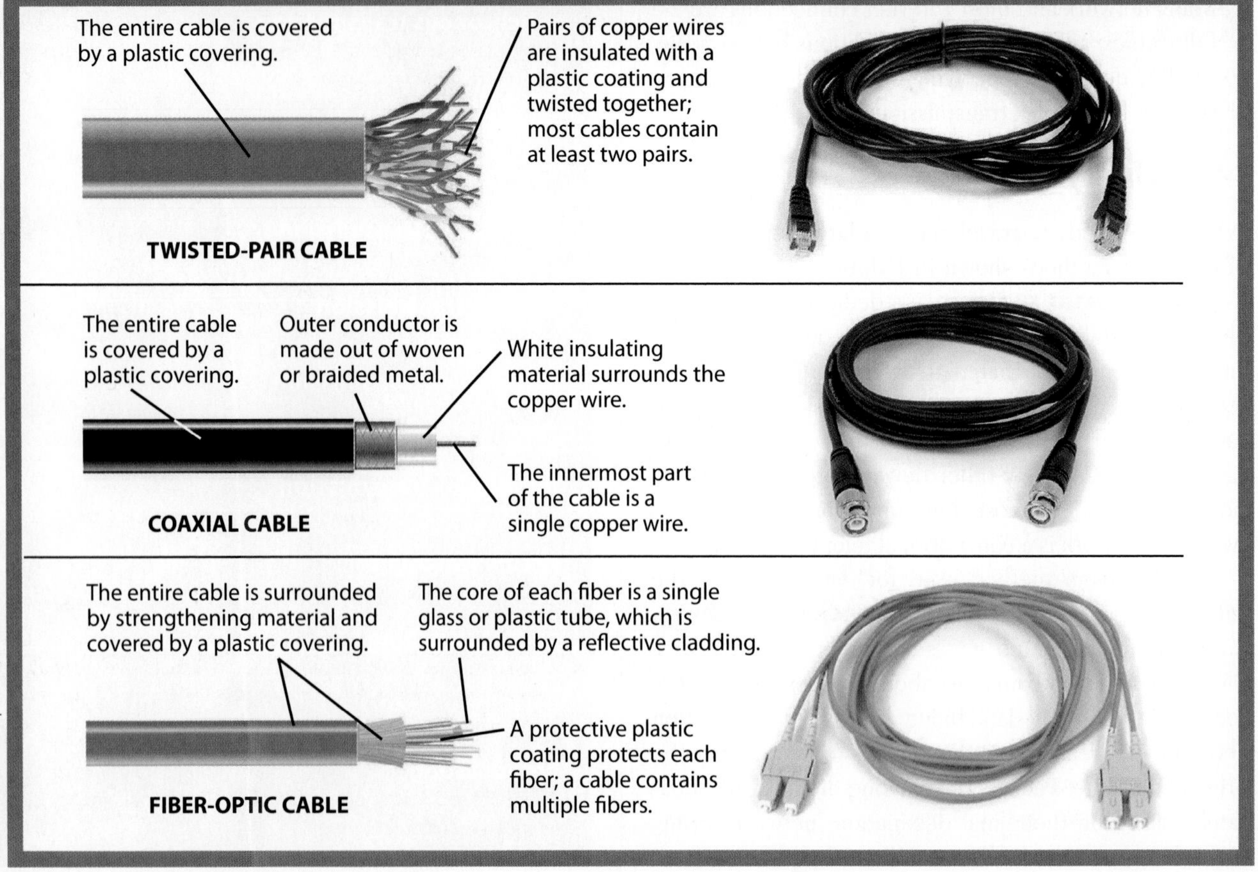

The entire cable is covered by a plastic covering.

Pairs of copper wires are insulated with a plastic coating and twisted together; most cables contain at least two pairs.

TWISTED-PAIR CABLE

The entire cable is covered by a plastic covering.

Outer conductor is made out of woven or braided metal.

White insulating material surrounds the copper wire.

The innermost part of the cable is a single copper wire.

COAXIAL CABLE

The entire cable is surrounded by strengthening material and covered by a plastic covering.

The core of each fiber is a single glass or plastic tube, which is surrounded by a reflective cladding.

A protective plastic coating protects each fiber; a cable contains multiple fibers.

FIBER-OPTIC CABLE

Source: © Black Box Corporation; Belkin International, Inc.

Fiber-optic cable is the newest and fastest of these three types of wired transmission media. It contains multiple—sometimes several hundred—clear glass or plastic fiber strands, each about the thickness of a human hair. Fiber-optic cable transfers data represented by light pulses at speeds of billions of bits per second. Each strand has the capacity to carry data for several television stations or thousands of voice conversations. However, each strand can send data in only one direction, so two strands are needed for full-duplex data transmissions. There are different connectors that can be used with fiber-optic cable—one example is shown in Exhibit 4-11.

Wireless networks usually use radio signals to send data through the airwaves.

Fiber-optic cable is commonly used for the high-speed backbone lines of a network, such as to connect networks housed in separate buildings or for the Internet infrastructure. It is also used for telephone backbone lines and, increasingly, is being installed by telephone companies all the way to the home or business to provide super-fast connections directly to the end user. The biggest advantage of fiber-optic cabling is speed; the main disadvantage of fiber-optic cabling is the initial expense of both the cable and the installation.

4-4b Wireless Networking Media

Wireless networks usually use radio signals to send data through the airwaves. All wireless applications in the United States—such as wireless networks, mobile phones, radio and TV broadcasts, sonar and radar applications, and GPS systems—use specific frequencies as assigned by the Federal Communications Commission (FCC). Frequencies are measured in hertz (Hz). The frequencies that make up the electromagnetic spectrum—the range of common electromagnetic radiation—are shown in Exhibit 4-12. Different parts of the spectrum have different properties including the distance a signal can travel, the amount of data a signal can transmit in a given period of time, and the types of objects a signal can pass through. These properties make certain frequencies more appropriate for certain applications. Each type of communication is assigned specific frequencies within which to operate. As illustrated in Exhibit 4-12, most wireless networking applications use frequencies located in the radio frequency (RF) band at the low end of the electromagnetic spectrum. This range—up to 300 GHz—is sometimes referred to as the wireless spectrum.

The frequencies assigned to an application, such as FM radio or cell phone service, typically consist of a range of frequencies to be used as needed for that

EXHIBIT 4-12 THE ELECTROMAGNETIC SPECTRUM

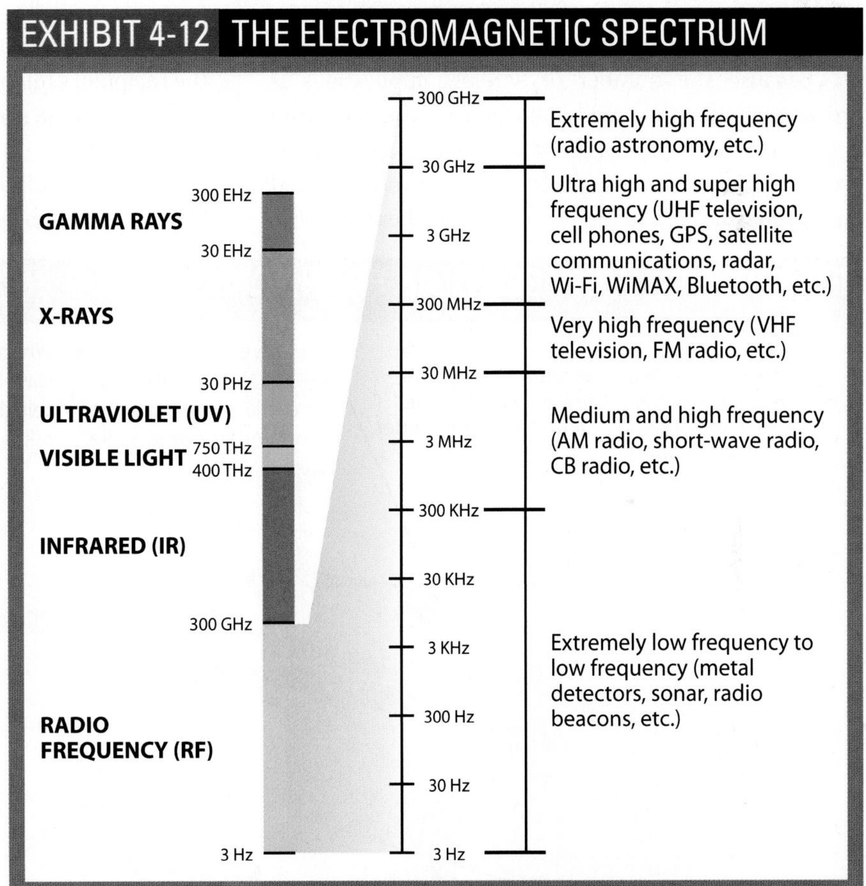

twisted-pair cable A networking cable consisting of insulated wire strands twisted in sets of two and bound into a cable.

coaxial (coax) cable A networking cable consisting of a center wire inside a grounded, cylindrical shield, capable of sending data at high speeds.

fiber-optic cable A networking cable that contains hundreds of thin, transparent fibers over which lasers transmit data as light.

application. For instance, FM radio stations broadcast on frequencies from 88 MHz to 108 MHz, and each radio station in a particular geographic area is assigned its own frequency. Most radio frequencies in the United States are licensed by the FCC and can be used only for that specific application by the licensed individuals in their specified geographic areas. However, frequencies within an unlicensed part of the spectrum can be used by any product or individual. For example, cordless landline phones typically use the 900 MHz frequency and wireless networking often uses frequencies in the 2.4 GHz and 5 GHz bands. A frequency range can be further broken down into multiple channels, each of which can be used simultaneously by different users. There are also ways to combine multiple signals to send them over a transmission medium at one time to allow more users than would otherwise be possible.

Because the number of wireless applications is growing all the time and the parts of the spectrum appropriate for today's wireless networking applications are limited, the wireless spectrum is relatively crowded and frequencies are in high demand. One benefit of the switch from analog to digital television broadcasts that occurred in 2009 is that it freed up some of the VHF and UHF frequencies for other applications. As a new part of the wireless spectrum becomes available, it is either assigned a function by the FCC or auctioned off (typically to wireless providers).

Cellular radio transmissions are radio signals sent to and from cell phones. They are sent and received via cellular (cell) towers—tall metal poles with antennas on top. Cellular service areas are divided into overlapping honeycomb-shaped zones called cells; each cell contains one cell tower. When a cell phone user begins to make a call, it is picked up by the cell tower located in the cell in which the cell phone is located and that belongs to the user's wireless provider. That cell tower then forwards the call to the wireless provider's Mobile Telephone Switching Office (MTSO), which routes the call to the recipient's telephone via his or her mobile or conventional telephone service provider, depending on the type of phone being used by the recipient. A simplified example of how cell phones work is shown in Exhibit 4-13. When a cell phone user moves out of the current cell into

EXHIBIT 4-13 HOW CELLULAR PHONE CALLS WORK

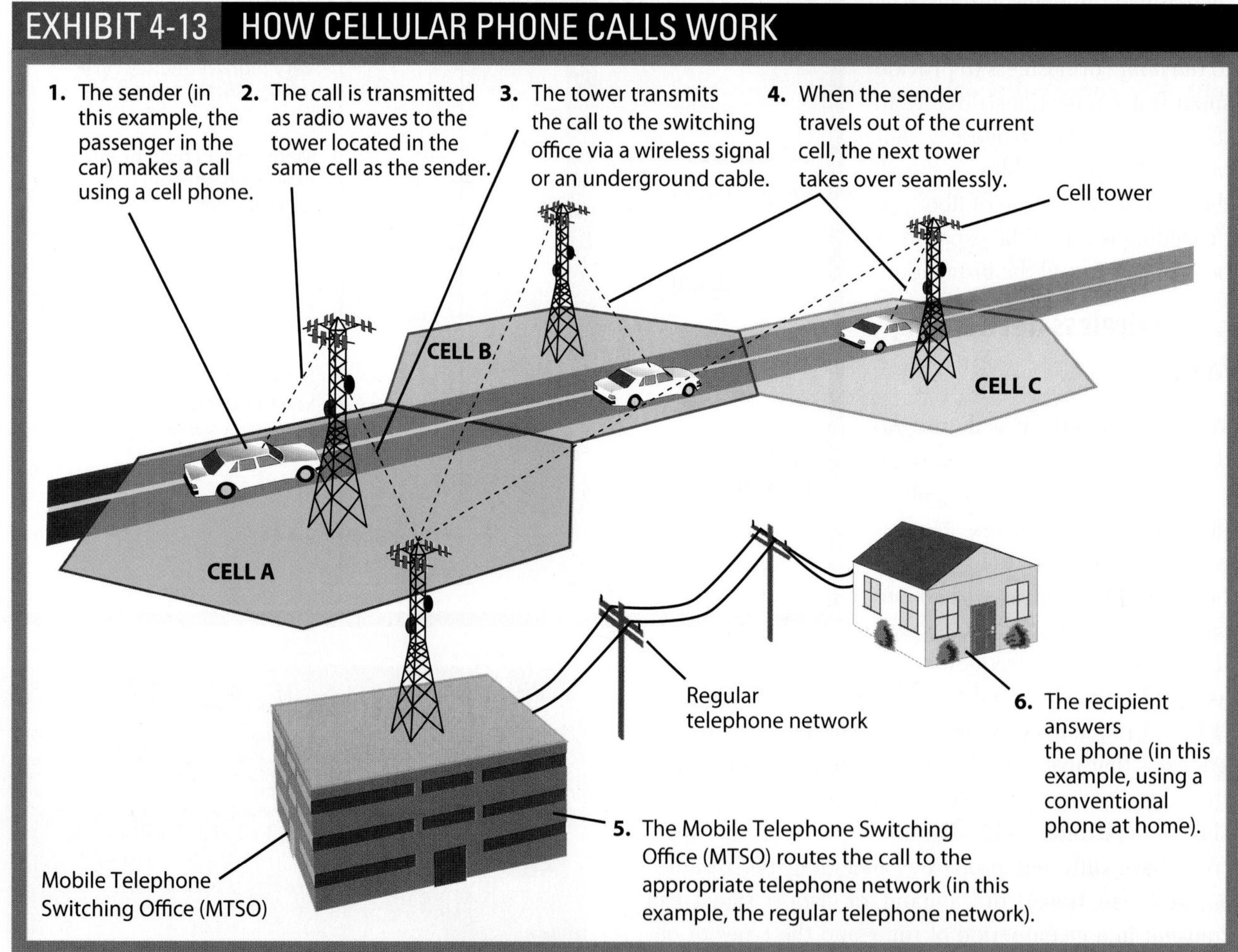
1. The sender (in this example, the passenger in the car) makes a call using a cell phone.
2. The call is transmitted as radio waves to the tower located in the same cell as the sender.
3. The tower transmits the call to the switching office via a wireless signal or an underground cable.
4. When the sender travels out of the current cell, the next tower takes over seamlessly.
Cell tower
CELL A
CELL B
CELL C
Regular telephone network
6. The recipient answers the phone (in this example, using a conventional phone at home).
5. The Mobile Telephone Switching Office (MTSO) routes the call to the appropriate telephone network (in this example, the regular telephone network).
Mobile Telephone Switching Office (MTSO)

a new cell, the call is passed automatically to the appropriate cell tower in the cell that the user is entering. The transmission of data, such as email and Web page requests, sent via cell phones works in a similar manner. The speed of cellular radio transmissions depends on the type of cellular standard being used.

Microwaves are high-frequency radio signals that can send large quantities of data at high speeds over long distances. Microwave signals can be sent or received using microwave stations or communications satellites, but they must travel in a straight line from one station or satellite to another without encountering any obstacles because microwave signals are line of sight. **Microwave stations** are Earth-based stations that can transmit microwave signals directly to each other over distances of up to about 30 miles. To avoid buildings, mountains, and the curvature of the earth obstructing the signal, microwave stations are usually placed on tall buildings, towers, and mountaintops. Microwave stations typically contain both a dish-shaped microwave antenna and a transceiver. When one station receives a transmission from another, it amplifies it and passes it on to the next station. Microwave stations can exchange data transmissions with communications satellites as well as with other microwave stations. Microwave stations designed specifically to communicate with satellites, such as for satellite TV and Internet services, are referred to as satellite dishes.

Communications satellites are space-based devices launched into orbit around the earth to receive and transmit microwave signals to and from Earth (see the satellite Internet example in Exhibit 4-14). Communications satellites were originally used to facilitate microwave transmission when microwave stations were not economically viable, such as over large, sparsely populated areas, or were physically impractical, such as over large bodies of water. They were used primarily by the military and communications companies, such as for remote television news broadcasts. Today, communications satellites are used to send and receive transmissions to and from a variety of other devices, such as personal satellite dishes used for satellite television and Internet service, GPS receivers, satellite radio receivers, and satellite phones. They are also used for Earth observation (EO) applications, including weather observation, mapping, and government surveillance.

Traditional communications satellites maintain a geosynchronous orbit 22,300 miles above the earth. Because these satellites are so far above the surface of the earth, there is a slight delay while the signals travel from Earth, to the satellite, and back to Earth again. This delay—less than one half-second—is not normally noticed by most users, such as individuals who receive Internet or TV service via satellite. However, it makes

EXHIBIT 4-14 HOW SATELLITE INTERNET WORKS

1. Data, such as a Web page request, is sent from the individual's computer to the satellite dish via a satellite modem.

2. The request is sent up to a satellite from the individual's satellite dish.

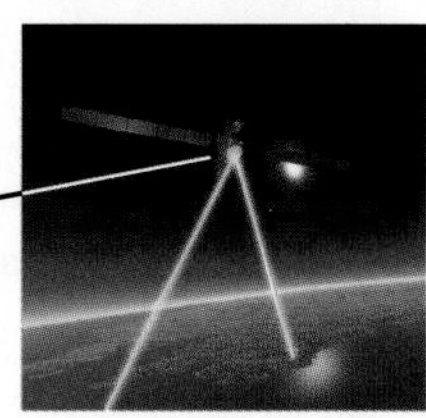

3. An orbiting satellite receives the request and beams it down to the satellite dish at the ISP's operations center.

4. The ISP's operations center receives the request (via its satellite dish) and transfers it to the Internet.

THE INTERNET

5. The request travels over the Internet as usual. The requested information takes a reverse route back to the individual.

cellular radio transmission Broadcast radio signals sent to and from cell phones via cell towers.

microwaves High-frequency radio signals that can send large quantities of data at high speeds over long distances.

microwave station An Earth-based device that sends and receives microwave signals.

communications satellite A device that orbits the earth and relays communications signals over long distances.

geosynchronous satellite transmissions less practical for voice, gaming, and other real-time communications. Because of this delay factor, low Earth orbit (LEO) satellite systems were developed for use with satellite telephone systems. LEO satellites typically are located anywhere from 100 to 1,000 miles above the earth and, consequently, provide faster transmission than traditional satellites. Medium Earth orbit (MEO) systems typically use satellites located about 1,000 to 12,000 miles above the earth and are used most often for GPS.

One type of wireless networking that does not use signals in the RF band of the electromagnetic spectrum is **infrared (IR) transmission**, which sends data as infrared light rays over relatively short distances. Like an infrared television remote control, infrared technology requires line-of-sight transmission. Because of this limitation, many formerly infrared devices, such as wireless mice and keyboards, now use RF radio signals instead. Infrared transmissions are still used with some remote controls. They are also sometimes used to beam data between mobile devices as well as between game consoles, handheld gaming devices, and other home entertainment devices.

FYI RADIO SIGNALS Radio signals can be short range (such as when used to connect a wireless keyboard or mouse to a computer), medium range (such as when used to connect a computer to a wireless LAN or public hotspot), or long range (such as when used to provide Internet access to a large geographic area or to broadcast a TV show).

iconmonstr/Shutterstock

infrared (IR) transmission A wireless networking medium that sends data as infrared light rays.

communications protocol A set of rules that determine how devices on a network communicate.

TCP/IP A networking protocol that uses packet switching to facilitate the transmission of messages; the protocol used with the Internet.

4-5 COMMUNICATIONS PROTOCOLS AND NETWORKING STANDARDS

A protocol is a set of rules to be followed in a specific situation. In networking, for instance, **communications protocols** determine how devices on a network communicate. The term *standard* refers to a set of criteria or requirements that has been approved by a recognized standards organization, such as the American National Standards Institute (ANSI), which helps to develop standards used in business and industry, or the Institute of Electrical and Electronics Engineers (IEEE), which develops networking standards, or is accepted as a de facto standard by the industry. Standards help manufacturers ensure that their hardware and software products work with other computing products.

Networking standards typically address both how the devices in a network physically connect, such as the types of cabling that can be used, and how the devices communicate, such as the communications protocols that can be used.

4-5a TCP/IP and Other Communications Protocols

The most widely used communications protocol today is TCP/IP. **TCP/IP** is used for transferring data over the Internet and actually consists of two protocols: Transmission Control Protocol (TCP), which is responsible for the delivery of data, and Internet Protocol (IP), which provides addresses and routing information. TCP/IP uses packet switching to transmit data; when the packets reach their destination, they are reassembled in the proper order (see Exhibit 4-15). Support for TCP/IP is built into operating systems, and IP addresses are commonly used to identify the various devices on computer networks.

The first widely used version of IP—Internet Protocol Version 4 (IPv4)—was standardized in the early 1980s. IPv4 uses 32-bit addresses, which allows for 2^{32} (or 4.3 billion) unique addresses. The newer IPv6 standard uses 128-bit addresses, which allows for 2^{128} possible unique addresses. It provides enough unique addresses so that all devices in a home or business can be accessible on the Internet directly by their own IP address, rather than by the address of the router to which they are connected as in IPv4. Consequently, the use of IPv6 addressing will make home automation

EXHIBIT 4-15 HOW TCP/IP WORKS

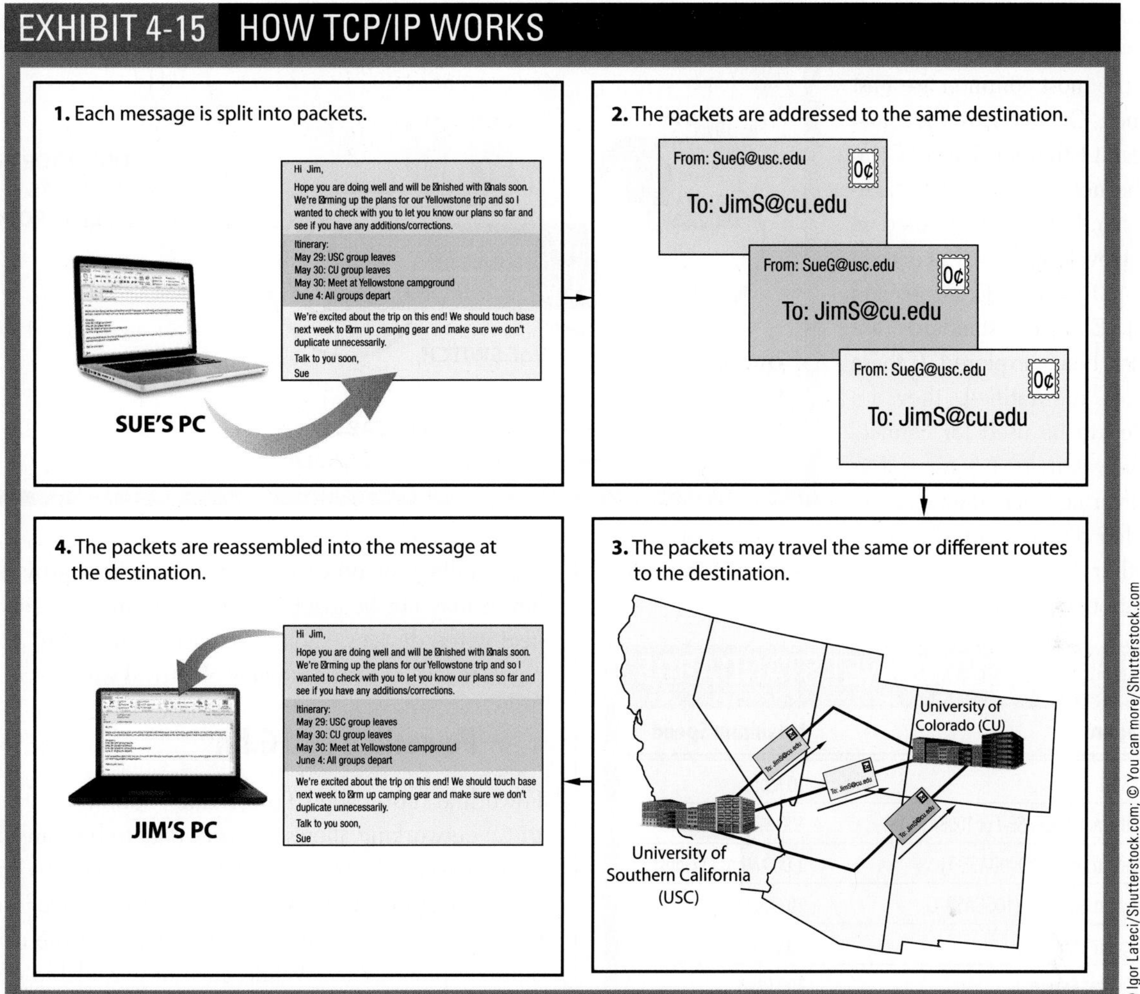
1. Each message is split into packets.
SUE'S PC
2. The packets are addressed to the same destination.
From: SueG@usc.edu
To: JimS@cu.edu
0¢
3. The packets may travel the same or different routes to the destination.
University of Colorado (CU)
University of Southern California (USC)
4. The packets are reassembled into the message at the destination.
JIM'S PC

and other applications involving smart devices easier to implement. It is expected that IPv4 and IPv6 will coexist for several years and businesses in the United States will switch over to IPv6 first. However, in some countries, such as China, where IPv4 addresses are scarce, end users are expected to switch over to IPv6 faster.

While TCP/IP is used to connect to and communicate with the Internet, other protocols are used for specific Internet applications. Some examples are:

- **HTTP (Hypertext Transfer Protocol)**—used to display Web pages
- **HTTPS (Secure Hypertext Transfer Protocol)**—used to display secure Web pages
- **FTP (File Transfer Protocol)**—used to transfer files over the Internet
- **SFTP (Secure File Transfer Protocol)**—used to transfer files over the Internet using a secure connection
- **SMTP (Simple Mail Transfer Protocol)**—used to send email
- **POP3 (Post Office Protocol)**—used to retrieve email

4-5b Ethernet (802.3)

Ethernet (802.3) is the most widely used standard for wired networks. It is typically used with LANs that have a star topology, though it can also be used with WANs and MANs. It can be used in conjunction with twisted-pair, coaxial, or fiber-optic cabling.

Ethernet has continued to evolve since it was invented in the mid-1970s. About every three years, the new approved amendments are incorporated into the existing IEEE 802.3 Ethernet standard to keep it up to

Ethernet (802.3) The most widely used standard for wired networks.

date. Exhibit 4-16 summarizes the various Ethernet standards. Of these, the most common are Fast Ethernet, Gigabit Ethernet, and 10 Gigabit Ethernet. The 40 Gigabit Ethernet and 100 Gigabit Ethernet standards were ratified in 2010. Development of the even faster 400 Gigabit Ethernet and Terabit Ethernet standards are currently being explored. If these standards are ratified, they are expected to be used for connections between servers as well as for delivering video, digital X-rays and other digital medical images, and other high-speed, bandwidth-intensive networking applications.

EXHIBIT 4-17 POWER OVER ETHERNET (PoE)

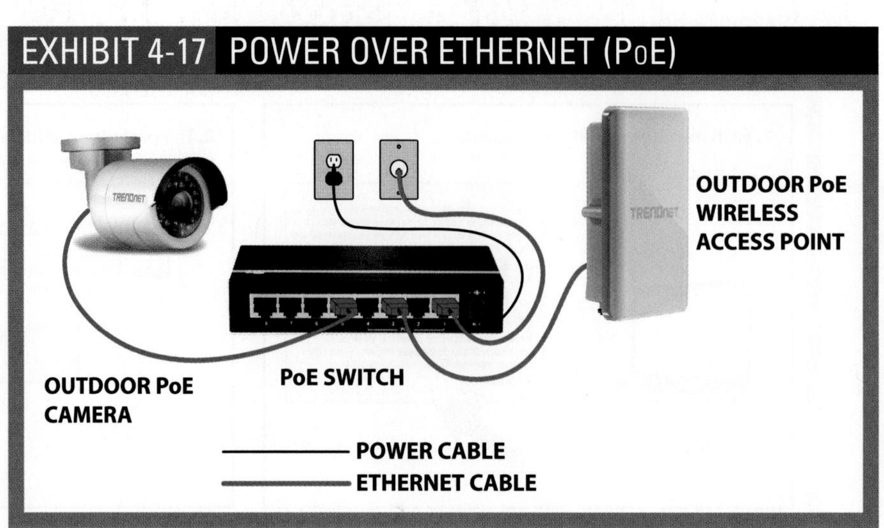

Source: © TRENDnet

EXHIBIT 4-16 ETHERNET STANDARDS

Standard	Maximum Speed
10BASE-T	10 Mbps
Fast Ethernet (100BASE-T or 100BASE-TX)	100 Mbps
Gigabit Ethernet (1000BASE-T)	1,000 Mbps (1 Gbps)
10 Gigabit Ethernet (10GBASE-T)	10 Gbps
40 Gigabit Ethernet	40 Gbps
100 Gigabit Ethernet	100 Gbps
400 Gigabit Ethernet*	400 Gbps
Terabit Ethernet*	1,000 Gbps (1 Tbps)
* Under consideration for development	

Devices connected to an Ethernet network need to have an Ethernet port either built in or added using an expansion card. Ethernet networks can contain devices using multiple Ethernet speeds, but the slower devices will operate only at their respective speeds.

A relatively new Ethernet development is Power over Ethernet (PoE), which allows electrical power to be sent along with data over the cables in an Ethernet network. Consequently, PoE devices are not plugged into an electrical outlet (see Exhibit 4-17), as long as they are connected to an Ethernet port that supports PoE. If the device is connected to a non-PoE port, a PoE injector is used to send power to the device over an Ethernet cable.

PoE is most often used in business networks with remote devices, such as outdoor networking hardware or security cameras that are often not located near a power outlet. It can also be used to place networked devices near ceilings or other locations where a nearby power outlet may not be available as well as in homes to connect wired devices (such as security cameras) to a home network without running new electrical wiring.

4-5c Powerline and G.hn

Powerline (also called Power Line Communications or PLC) networking allows network data to be transmitted over existing electrical wiring. One example is broadband over powerline (BPL), which can deliver broadband Internet to homes and businesses via the existing outdoor power lines. While currently available only in very limited areas in the United States through power companies, BPL has potential for delivering broadband Internet access to remote locations, although momentum for BPL appears to be slowing. One Powerline alternative to the Ethernet standard for wired home networks is the HomePlug Powerline standard, which allows computers to be networked over existing power lines within a home using conventional electrical outlets. HomePlug Powerline networks are quick and easy to set up (see Exhibit 4-18). They are also fast (up to 1 Gbps for the newest HomePlug AV2 standard). In addition to networking computers, HomePlug AV2 can be used to network home entertainment devices and it is fast enough to support streaming HD video. HomePlug is also used to extend Wi-Fi networks to locations (such as basements) that are otherwise hard to reach.

The G.hn standard was developed as a unified worldwide standard for creating home networks over any existing home wiring, including phone lines, power lines, and coaxial cable. While it will coexist with the HomePlug standard for the near future, G.hn supporters view it as the future standard for wired home networking. G.hn products are just starting to become available.

EXHIBIT 4-18 HOMEPLUG POWERLINE NETWORK

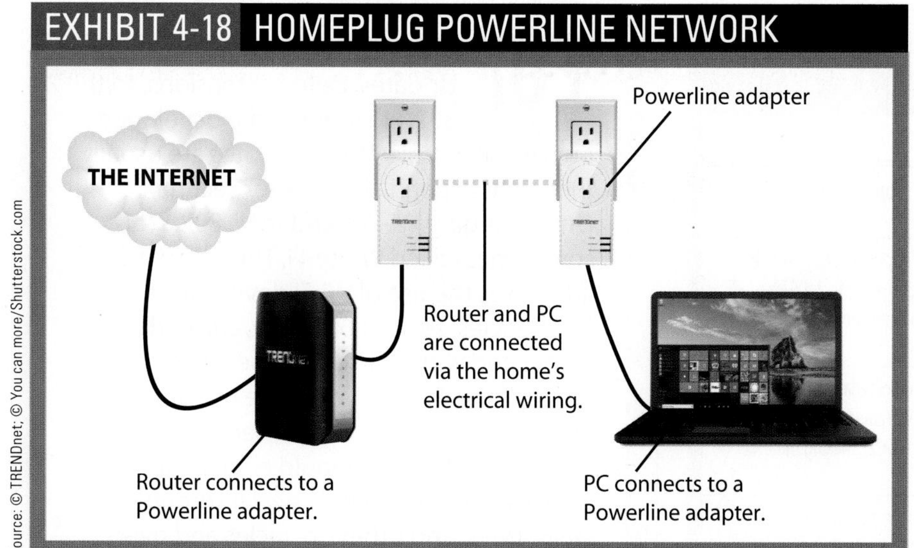

A summary of Wi-Fi standards is shown in Exhibit 4-20. Of these, the most widely used are 802.11n and 802.11ac.

Beginning with the 802.11n standard, MIMO (multiple in, multiple out) antennas are used to transfer multiple streams of data at one time. As a result of this and other improvements, 802.11n allows for data transmissions typically about five times as fast as 802.11g and about twice the range. The newer 802.11ac standard supports speeds up to about 1.3 Gbps—about three times faster than 802.11n—to better support high-speed file transfers and HD video streaming.

Typically, products using the various types of Wi-Fi can be used on the same network as long as they operate on the same frequencies. Wi-Fi products are backward compatible (so 802.11ac devices can be used on

4-5d Wi-Fi (802.11)

One of the most common networking standards used with wireless LANs is **Wi-Fi (802.11)**, which is a family of wireless networking standards that use the IEEE 802.11 standard. Wi-Fi is the current standard for wireless networks in the home or office as well as for public Wi-Fi hotspots. Wi-Fi hardware is built into virtually all portable computers and most mobile devices today. Wi-Fi capabilities are also becoming increasingly integrated into everyday products, such as printers, external hard drives, home appliances, gaming consoles, and Blu-ray Disc players, to allow those devices to wirelessly network with other devices or to access the Internet. For example, the coffee maker shown in Exhibit 4-19 is wirelessly controlled, via Wi-Fi, by a smartphone.

The speed of a Wi-Fi network and the area it can cover depend on a variety of factors, including the Wi-Fi standard and hardware being used, the number of solid objects—such as walls, trees, or buildings—between the access point and the computer or other device being used, and the amount of interference from cordless phones, baby monitors, microwave ovens, and other devices that also operate on the same radio frequencies as some Wi-Fi devices. In general, Wi-Fi is designed for medium-range data transfers—typically between 100 and 300 feet indoors and 300 to 900 feet outdoors. Usually both speed and distance degrade with interference. The distance of a Wi-Fi network can be extended using additional antennas and other hardware designed for that purpose.

EXHIBIT 4-19 WI-FI COFFEE MAKER

Wi-Fi (802.11) A widely used networking standard for medium-range wireless networks.

EXHIBIT 4-20 COMMON WI-FI STANDARDS

Wi-Fi Standard	Description
802.11b	An early Wi-Fi standard; supports data transfer rates of 11 Mbps.
802.11g	An older Wi-Fi standard; supports data transfer rates of 54 Mbps and uses the same 2.4 GHz frequency as 802.11b, so their products are compatible.
802.11a	An older Wi-Fi standard; supports data transfer rates of 54 Mbps, but uses a different radio frequency (5 GHz) than 802.11g/b (2.4 GHz), making the standards incompatible.
802.11n	A current Wi-Fi standard; supports speeds up to about 450 Mbps and has twice the range of 802.11g. It can use either the 2.4 GHz or 5 GHz frequency.
802.11ac	The newest Wi-Fi standard; supports speed up to about three times faster than 802.11n and uses the 5 GHz frequency (most 802.11ac routers are dual band to also support 2.4 GHz devices for backward compatibility).
802.11ax*	A proposed Wi-Fi standard; expected to support speed of more than 2 Gbps.

* Expected by 2018

an 802.11n network, for example, but they will work at 802.11n speeds). To ensure that hardware from various vendors will work together, consumers can look for products that are certified by the Wi-Fi Alliance.

Wi-Fi is very widely used, but it does have some limitations—particularly its relatively limited range. For instance, a person using a Wi-Fi hotspot inside a coffeehouse will lose that Internet connection when he or she moves out of range of that network and will need to locate another hotspot at his or her next location. In addition, many businesses may be physically too large for a Wi-Fi network to span the entire organization. Although hardware can be used to extend a Wi-Fi network, larger wireless networks may use WiMAX or a cellular standard instead. There are also short-range Wi-Fi standards under development, as discussed later in this chapter.

Source: © Wi-Fi Alliance.

WiMAX (802.16) A wireless networking standard that is faster and has a greater range than Wi-Fi.

FYI

WHITE-FI (802.11AF)

Updates, called extensions, to the 802.11 standard are developed on a regular basis. These updates are usually to increase speed, distance, or security. One emerging Wi-Fi standard is 802.11af, sometimes called White-Fi. This standard addresses the use of Wi-Fi devices in lower frequencies, such as 600 MHz, currently associated with unused TV spectrum or white space. If the FCC approves the use of some of this frequency for unlicensed devices, the lower frequency would enable 802.11af devices to communicate better through walls, trees, and other obstacles and over longer distances.

4-5e WiMAX (802.16)

WiMAX (802.16) is a series of standards designed for longer range wireless networking connections, typically MANs. Similar to Wi-Fi, fixed WiMAX (also known as 802.16a) is designed to provide Internet access to fixed locations, sometimes called hotzones. However, at a typical radius of two to six miles, WiMAX hotzones are significantly larger than Wi-Fi hotspots. With fixed WiMAX, it is feasible to provide coverage to an entire city or other geographical area by using multiple WiMAX towers and overlapping hotzones, similar to the way cell phone cells overlap to provide continuous cell phone service. In the United States, WiMAX is most often used in rural areas.

Mobile WiMAX (802.16e) is the mobile version of the WiMAX wireless networking standard. It is designed to deliver broadband wireless networking to mobile users via a smartphone, portable computer, or other WiMAX-enabled device. While still in existence, many mobile WiMAX services (such as from the leading supporter, Sprint) are moving to cellular standards (such as LTE) instead.

4-5f Cellular Standards

Cellular standards have evolved over the years to better fulfill the demand for mobile Internet, mobile multimedia delivery, and other relatively recent mobile trends. The original first-generation phones were analog and designed for voice only. Second-generation (2G) cell phones are digital, support both data and voice, and are faster. Common 2G wireless standards included GSM (Global System for Mobile communications) and CDMA (Code Division Multiple Access).

The current standards for cellular networks today in the United States and many other countries are 3G (third generation) and 4G (fourth generation). 3G and 4G networks use packet switching (like TCP/IP) instead of circuit switching (like conventional telephones and earlier mobile phones). Many mobile devices today can switch between 3G and 4G, such as to use a 3G network in a location where a 4G network is not within range or to use 3G if 4G usage exceeds the individual's 4G limit. Internet access via a 3G or 4G network is often referred to as mobile broadband because 3G and 4G speeds are equivalent to the speeds many home broadband Internet users experience. 4G capabilities are integrated into some portable computers, tablets, and other devices to enable users to connect to the Internet via their wireless provider when needed (see Exhibit 4-21). Devices without built-in 4G can connect to a cellular network via a mobile hotspot.

Cellular standards for 3G networks depend on the type of cellular network being used. For instance, GSM mobile networks, such as AT&T Wireless and T-Mobile, typically use the HSDPA (High Speed Downlink Packet Access)/UMTS (Universal Mobile Telecommunications System) 3G standards; CDMA networks, such as Verizon Wireless and Cricket Wireless, typically use the EV-DO (Evolution Data Optimized) 3G standard instead.

EXHIBIT 4-21 CONNECTING A NOTEBOOK TO A 4G NETWORK

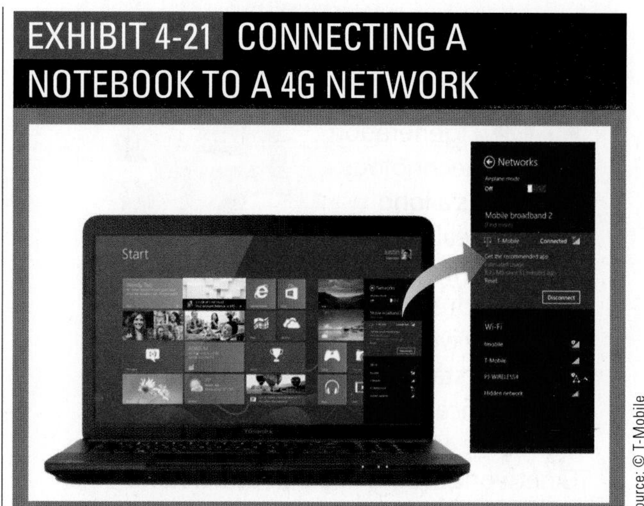

Source: © T-Mobile

The primary standard for 4G networks today is Long Term Evolution (LTE), although mobile WiMAX has been used by some companies. Currently, the LTE-Advanced standard is the fastest cellular standard, though new standards are always in the works. For example, the next 4G development is expected to be LTE-Unlicensed (LTE-U), also referred to as Licensed-Assisted Access (LAA), which uses both the regular licensed cellular frequencies and part of the 5 GHz band of unlicensed spectrum in order to enable wireless providers to offer better coverage and faster speeds.

TRENDING...

MOBILE DATA CAPS

Mobile data use has increased tremendously recently due to individuals streaming TV and videos from the Internet, participating in video phone calls, and otherwise performing high-bandwidth activities using their smartphones and tablets. In response, many wireless providers have implemented data caps. With a data cap, customers have a download limit for data (such as 3 GB per month) and either temporarily lose high-speed Internet access (such as being slowed down from 4G to 3G speeds) or are charged an additional fee if they exceed that limit.

To avoid going over your data cap, use Wi-Fi instead of your cellular service whenever possible. You can also monitor your data usage to make sure you stay under your data cap. In addition, third-party apps can help you manage your data usage. For example, Onavo Extend (shown in the accompanying illustration) compresses your incoming data by up to 500 percent so you can do up to five times more with your data plan without going over.

Source: © Onavo

FYI **5G** The next generation of cellular technology, called 5G, is a long way from reality, but companies in the wireless industry are already working to define what it will be. The 5G standard is expected to be both significantly faster and smarter than the current 4G standard. For example, 5G networks may be able to understand situations and respond accordingly, such as providing a connection with a faster response time to a smart car while providing a slower, less responsive connection to a smart thermostat. In addition, 5G is expected to open up new possibilities, such as road sensors communicating with smart cars to adjust car speed in response to upcoming road or traffic conditions. It is expected that 5G will operate on higher frequencies than 4G, so new infrastructure will be required because higher frequency signals do not travel as far as lower frequency signals. The speed of 5G connections may reach 10 Gbps—fast enough to download an HD movie in mere seconds. And companies are getting close already. For example, Nokia Networks has demonstrated speeds of up to 10 Gbps in 5G tests, while Samsung recently achieved 7.5 Gbps.

© kurtcan/Shutterstock

4-5g Bluetooth and Other Short-Range Wireless Standards

Several wireless networking standards are in existence or being developed that are designed for short-range wireless networking connections. Most of these are used to facilitate PANs or very small, special-purpose home networks, such as connecting home entertainment devices or appliances within a home.

Bluetooth A networking standard for very short-range wireless connections.

Bluetooth is a wireless standard that was originally designed for very short-range connections (about 33 feet or less). Bluetooth is designed to replace cables between devices, such as to connect a wireless keyboard or mouse to a desktop computer, as shown in Exhibit 4-22, or to connect a mobile phone to a wireless headset. Bluetooth devices automatically recognize and network with each other when they get within transmission range. Bluetooth signals can transmit through clothing and other nonmetallic objects, so a mobile phone or other device in a pocket or briefcase can connect with Bluetooth hardware, such as a headset, without having to be removed from the pocket or briefcase. The newest Bluetooth specification is Bluetooth 4.0, also called Bluetooth Smart.

EXHIBIT 4-22 BLUETOOTH PICONET

The desktop computer, keyboard, and mouse form a piconet.

© lightwavemedia/Shutterstock

One of the key enhancements of Bluetooth 4.0 is energy efficiency, which enables small devices to run for years on a single button-sized battery. Consequently, Bluetooth is increasingly being used with consumer devices, such as to connect a smartphone to a portable speaker or smart watch, or to connect a pedometer, heart rate monitor, and other health and fitness devices together. For example, the smart tennis racket shown in Exhibit 4-23 includes Bluetooth capabilities to transfer data about swing speed, ball speed, and more to a connected device via the app also shown in Exhibit 4-23.

Bluetooth works using radio signals in the frequency band of 2.4 GHz, the same as some Wi-Fi devices, and supports transfers up to 246 Mbps. Bluetooth 4.0 devices can also use their low-energy

EXHIBIT 4-23 BLUETOOTH TENNIS RACKET

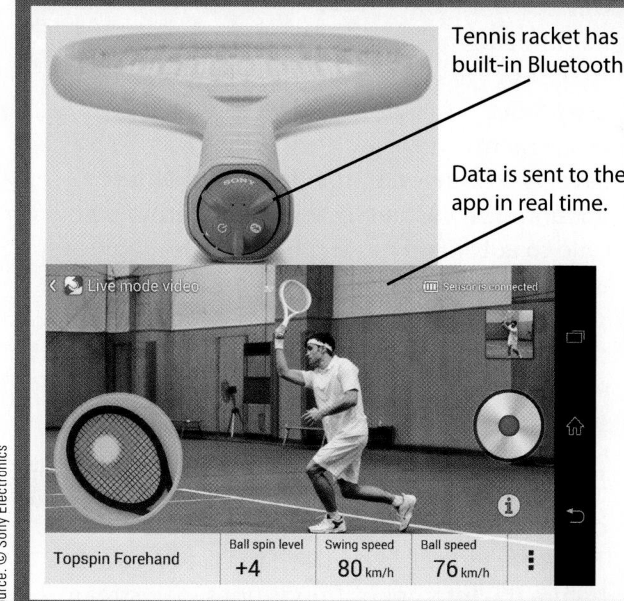

Source: © Sony Electronics

EXHIBIT 4-24 WI-FI DIRECT HOTSPOT

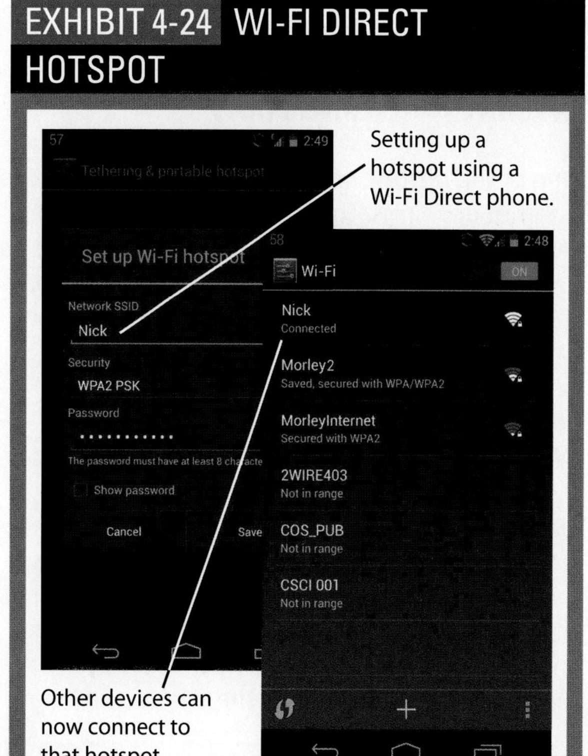

© Nick Morley

capabilities to wirelessly connect to other devices while being powered (potentially for years) by a single battery. When two Bluetooth-enabled devices come within range of each other, their software identifies each other using their unique identification numbers and establishes a link. Because there may be many Bluetooth devices within range, up to 10 individual Bluetooth networks (called **piconets**) can be in place within the same physical area at one time. Each piconet can connect up to eight devices, for a maximum of 80 devices within any 10-meter radius. To facilitate this, Bluetooth divides its allocated radio spectrum into multiple channels of 1 MHz each. Each Bluetooth device can use the entire range of frequencies, jumping randomly (in unison with the other devices in that piconet) on a regular basis to minimize interference between piconets, as well as from other devices, such as garage door openers, Wi-Fi networks, and some cordless phones and baby monitors, that use the same frequencies.

Other standards that are designed to connect nearby peripheral devices but that transfer data more quickly are Wi-Fi Direct, Wi-Gig, and Wireless HD. Wi-Fi Direct enables Wi-Fi devices, such as computers, smartphones, printers, and gaming devices, to connect directly to each other using Wi-Fi signals at speeds of up to 250 Mbps without needing a router or an access point. A compatible app is required for many tasks, but a Wi-Fi Direct device can often create a Wi-Fi hotspot for other Wi-Fi devices by using the phone's Wi-Fi settings, as shown in Exhibit 4-24. The Wi-Gig (802.11ad) and Wireless HD (WiHD) standards are most often used to wirelessly connect computers and home entertainment devices together, such as to stream video from a computer or Blu-ray player to an HDTV. Both Wi-Gig and WiHD operate in the 60 GHz frequency band, which allows for faster speeds (up to about 7 Gbps and 28 Gbps, respectively) within a single room.

For inexpensive and simple short-range networking, such as those that include sensors that monitor temperature and other factors, smart appliances, and other smart devices, usually low-power, low-bandwidth, short-range wireless networking standards are used. In addition to Bluetooth Smart, networking options include ZigBee and Z-Wave. ZigBee (802.15) is intended for applications that require low data transfer rates and several years of battery life. For instance, ZigBee can be used for home and commercial automation systems to connect a wide variety of devices (such as appliances and lighting, heating, cooling, water, filtration, and security systems) and allows for their control from

piconet A network of Bluetooth devices.

TRENDING...

INTERNET OF THINGS (IoT)

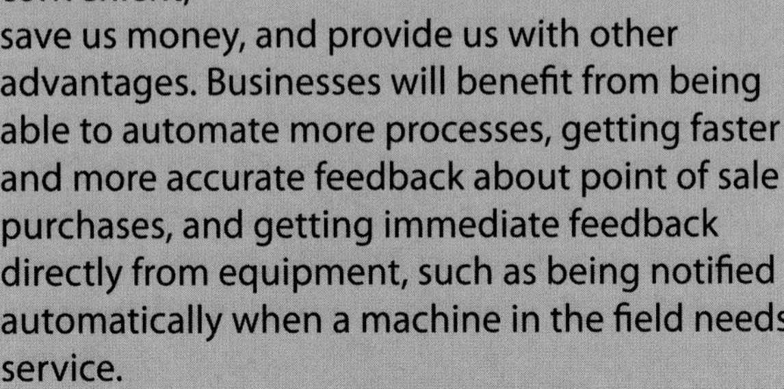
© aslysun/Shutterstock

One of the hottest networking topics today is the Internet of Things. The **Internet of Things (IoT)** refers to a world where everyday physical objects are connected to, and uniquely identifiable on, the Internet so they can communicate with each other. Because the Internet of Things involves primarily machines talking directly to one another, it is also called Machine-to-Machine (M2M) networking. Devices included in the Internet of Things can range from sensors in your shoes, to home automation systems, to smart farm equipment, to smart freeways, cars, and traffic lights. While still in the early stages, some aspects of the Internet of Things, such as smart homes and fitness PANs, exist today. As the Internet of Things matures, the connected smart devices will continue to make our lives more convenient, save us money, and provide us with other advantages. Businesses will benefit from being able to automate more processes, getting faster and more accurate feedback about point of sale purchases, and getting immediate feedback directly from equipment, such as being notified automatically when a machine in the field needs service.

One concern about the Internet of Things is how best to protect the security and privacy of individuals from hackers and data leaks. That concern will likely need to be addressed before the Internet of Things goes mainstream.

anywhere in the world. ZigBee is also used in industrial plant manufacturing, personal home healthcare, device tracking, telecommunications, and wireless sensor networks. ZigBee is designed to accommodate more than 65,000 devices on a single network and supports speeds up to 250 Kbps. ZigBee networks have a range of 10 to 50 meters (about 33 to 164 feet).

Z-Wave is designed primarily for home automation. Devices with built-in Z-Wave capabilities or an attached Z-Wave module can communicate with each other and be controlled via home control modules as well as remotely via a computer or smartphone. There can be up to 232 devices on a single Z-Wave network, and each device has its own unique code. Devices can control each other, such as having your garage door opener programmed to turn on your house lights when you arrive home, and sequences of actions can be programmed to be performed with a single button, such as turning off the house lights, activating the security system, locking the doors, and programming the coffee maker for breakfast when a single button designated for bedtime is pressed. Z-Wave signals have a range of about 90 feet indoors.

For a summary of wireless networking standards, see Exhibit 4-25.

Internet of Things (IoT) The network of everyday physical objects that can communicate with each other via the Internet.

network adapter A device used to connect a computer to a network.

network interface card (NIC) A network adapter in the form of an expansion card.

modem A device that is used to connect a computer to a network over telephone lines.

FYI

LOW POWER WI-FI (802.11AH)

Low Power Wi-Fi (802.11ah) is a Wi-Fi standard under development that is designed to network sensors and other devices in home automation networks. It operates in the 900 MHz band and is expected to have speeds of around 150 Kbps. Whether it will replace other standards with similar purposes (such as ZigBee) remains to be seen.

EXHIBIT 4-25 EXAMPLES OF WIRELESS NETWORKING STANDARDS

Category	Application	Wireless Standard	Approximate Range
Short range	To connect peripheral devices to a computer or mobile device or to connect devices together.	Bluetooth WiGig	33 feet
	To connect and transfer multimedia content between home consumer electronic devices (computers, TVs, DVD players, printers, etc.).	WiGig WirelessHD (WiHD)	33 feet
	To connect a variety of home, personal, and automation devices.	ZigBee Z-Wave Low Power Wi-Fi (802.11ah)	33–164 feet
Medium range	To connect computers and other devices to a local area network.	Wi-Fi (802.11)	100–300 feet indoors; 300–900 feet outdoors
	To connect computers and other devices directly together.	Wi-Fi Direct	600 feet
Long range	To provide Internet access to a large geographic area for fixed and/or mobile users.	WiMAX Mobile WiMAX	6 miles non-line of sight; 30 miles line of sight
	To connect mobile phones and other devices to a cellular network for telephone and Internet service.	Cellular standards (3G/4G)	10 miles

4-6 NETWORKING HARDWARE

Various types of hardware are necessary to create a computer network, to connect multiple networks together, or to connect a computer or network to the Internet. The following sections discuss the most common types of networking hardware used in home and small office networks.

4-6a Network Adapters and Modems

A **network adapter**, also called a **network interface card (NIC)** when it is in the form of an expansion card, is used to connect a computer to a network (such as a home or business network). A **modem** (derived from the terms *modulate* and *demodulate*) is used to connect a computer to a network over telephone lines. Technically, to be called a modem, a device must convert digital signals, such as those used by a computer, to modulated analog signals, such as those used by conventional telephone lines, and vice versa. However, in everyday use, the term *modem* is also used to refer to any device that connects a computer to a broadband Internet connection, such as a cable modem used for cable Internet service. In addition, the term *modem* is often used interchangeably with the term *network adapter* when describing devices used to obtain Internet access via certain networks, such as cellular networks.

Most computers and mobile devices come with a network adapter or a modem, or both, built into the device, typically as a network interface card, as a chip included on the motherboard, or as circuitry built directly into the CPU. The type of network adapter and modem needed depends on the type of network and Internet access being used. When a new type of networking connectivity is needed, an external adapter or modem can be obtained. The network adapter or modem needs to be for the appropriate type of network as well as support the type of networking media, such as twisted-pair cabling, coaxial cabling, or wireless signal, being used. Some examples of network adapters and modems are shown in Exhibit 4-26.

If your Internet connection slows down or stops working altogether, try power cycling your modem and router. Unplug the modem and router for 30 seconds, then plug in the modem and wait 30 seconds, then plug in the router.

4-6b Switches, Routers, and Other Hardware for Connecting Devices and Networks

A variety of networking hardware is used to connect the devices on a network as well as to connect multiple networks together. For instance, as mentioned earlier in this

EXHIBIT 4-26 NETWORK ADAPTERS AND MODEMS

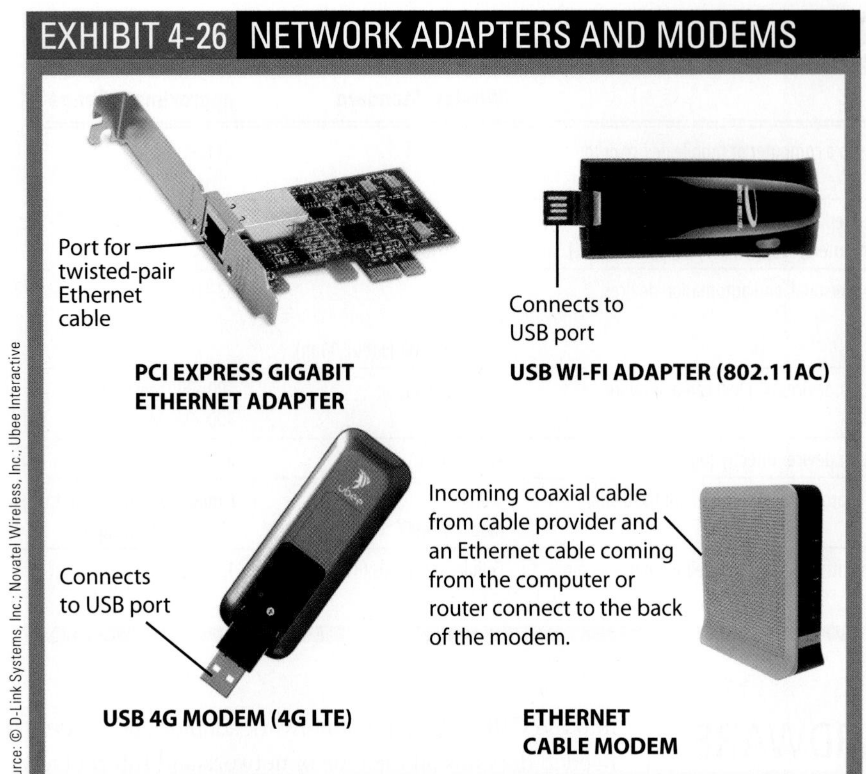
Port for twisted-pair Ethernet cable
Connects to USB port
PCI EXPRESS GIGABIT ETHERNET ADAPTER
USB WI-FI ADAPTER (802.11AC)
Incoming coaxial cable from cable provider and an Ethernet cable coming from the computer or router connect to the back of the modem.
Connects to USB port
USB 4G MODEM (4G LTE)
ETHERNET CABLE MODEM

Source: © D-Link Systems, Inc.; Novatel Wireless, Inc.; Ubee Interactive

chapter, networks using the star topology need a central device to connect all of the devices on the network. In a wired network, this device was originally a hub. A hub transmits all data received to all network devices connected to the hub, regardless of which device the data is being sent to, so the bandwidth of the network is shared and the network is not extremely efficient. Today, the central device in a wired network is usually a switch. A **switch** contains ports to which the devices on the network connect (typically via networking cables) and facilitates communications between the devices, similar to a hub. But, unlike a hub, a switch identifies which device connected to the switch is the one the data is intended for and sends the data only to that device, rather than sending data out to all connected devices. Consequently, switches are more efficient than hubs.

To connect multiple networks (such as two LANs, two WANs, or a LAN and the Internet), a **router** is used. Routers pass data on to the intended recipient only and can plan a path through the network to ensure that the data reaches its destination in the most efficient manner possible. They are also used to route traffic over the Internet.

A **wireless access point** is a device on a wireless network used to grant network access to wireless devices. In home and small business networks, typically the capabilities of a switch, router, and wireless access point are integrated into a single device. For example, a **wireless router** is a router with a built-in wireless access point and, often, a switch. If so, it can be used to connect both wireless (via Wi-Fi) and wired (via Ethernet cables) devices to a network as well as connect that network to an Internet connection. The wireless router shown in Exhibit 4-27 supports three different wireless connections (two 802.11ac streams and one 802.11n stream) at one time, has four Gigabit Ethernet ports, and can connect shared USB devices as well as a broadband modem. Some broadband modems today include wireless router capabilities, which you can use to create a wireless network and obtain Internet access

switch A device that connects multiple devices on a wired network and forwards data only to the intended recipient.

router A device that connects multiple networks together and passes data to the intended recipient using the most efficient route.

wireless access point A device on a wireless network that connects wireless devices to that network and to the Internet.

wireless router A router with a built-in wireless access point.

EXHIBIT 4-27 WIRELESS ROUTER

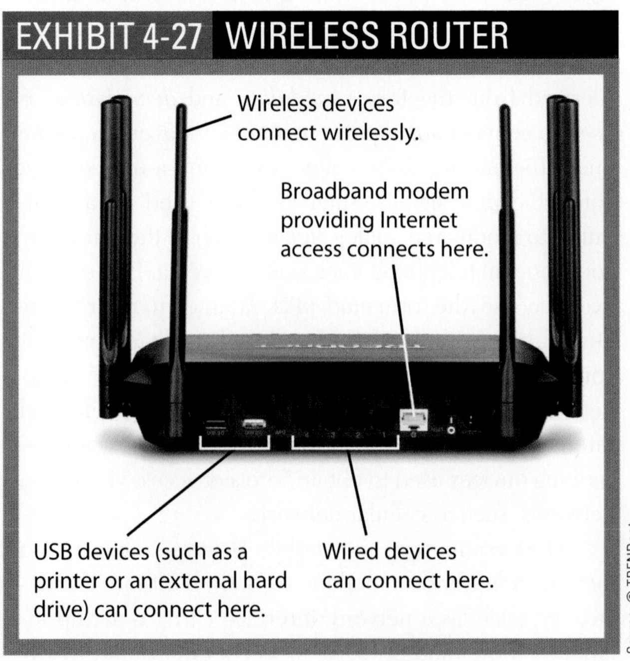
Wireless devices connect wirelessly.
Broadband modem providing Internet access connects here.
USB devices (such as a printer or an external hard drive) can connect here.
Wired devices can connect here.

Source: © TRENDnet

EXHIBIT 4-28 NETWORKING HARDWARE

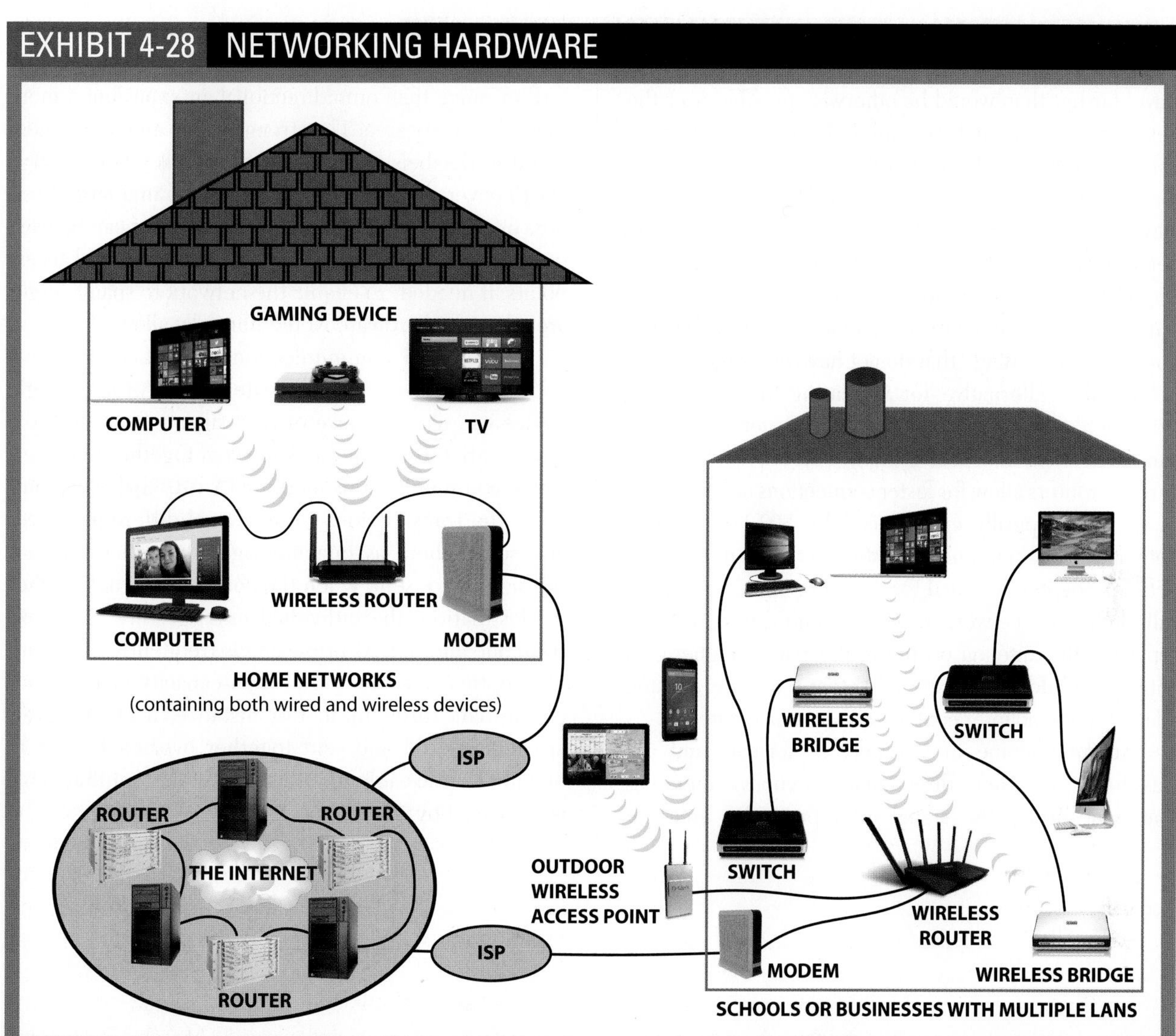

Source: © ASUSTeK Computer Inc.; © Denys Prykhodov/Shutterstock.com; Roku, Inc.; Courtesy of Dell Inc.; TRENDnet; Ubee Interactive; DCB; © Sergey Furtaev/Shutterstock.com; DCB; Samsung Electronics Co., Ltd.; Sony Electronics; © Julia Ivantsova/Shutterstock.com; Apple, Inc.

using a single piece of hardware. To connect just two LANs together, a **bridge** can be used. The most common use for a bridge in a home network is to wirelessly connect a wired device (such as a home audio/video system, DVR, or gaming console) to a home network via a wireless connection.

There are also routers and other devices used to connect multiple devices to a cellular network. For instance, mobile broadband routers are used to share a mobile wireless Internet connection with multiple devices (such as a smartphone, personal computer, and tablet)—essentially creating a Wi-Fi hotspot that connects to your 3G or 4G Internet connection.

Exhibit 4-28 provides an example of how the devices discussed in this section might be used in a network.

4-6c Other Networking Hardware

Additional networking hardware is often needed to extend the range of a network and to share networking media.

FYI

FIRMWARE

The firmware—embedded instructions—for a router impact its performance and capabilities. Firmware updates are often performed automatically. If not, you can usually download the most recent firmware file from the manufacturer's Web site and install it manually using a computer connected to the device via a wired, not wireless, connection.

bridge A device used to connect two LANs.

Repeaters are devices that amplify signals along a network. They are necessary whenever signals have to travel farther than would be otherwise possible over the networking medium being used. Repeaters are available for both wired and wireless networks; repeaters for a wireless network are often called range extenders. **Range extenders** usually connect wirelessly to the network and repeat the wireless signal to extend coverage of that network outside or to an additional floor of a building, or to eliminate dead spots—areas within the normal network range that do not have coverage.

Another alternative for increasing the range of a Wi-Fi network is using a higher-gain (stronger) **antenna**. The MIMO antennas used by many 802.11n and 802.11ac wireless routers allow for faster connections and a greater range than typically experienced by 802.11g wireless networks, but sometimes this still isn't enough. Using a network adapter designed for the router being used typically helps the network range to some extent; so does replacing the antenna on the router with a higher-gain antenna or adding an external antenna to a networking adapter, if the adapter contains an antenna connector.

Antennas come in a variety of formats and are classified as either directional antennas (antennas that concentrate the signal in a particular area) or omnidirectional antennas (antennas that are equally effective in all directions). Directional antennas have a farther range than omnidirectional antennas but a more limited delivery area. The strength of an antenna is measured in decibels (dB). For applications where a large Wi-Fi coverage area is needed (such as in a large business or a hotel), high-gain outdoor antennas can be used (in conjunction with outdoor range extenders and access points, if needed) to enable the network to span a larger area than the hardware would normally allow.

High-speed communications lines are expensive and almost always have far greater capacity than a single device can use. Because of this, signals from multiple devices are often combined and sent together to share a single communications medium. A **multiplexer** combines the transmissions from several different devices and sends them as one message. Regardless of how the signals are sent, when the combined signal reaches its destination, the individual messages are separated from one another. Multiplexing is frequently used with fiber-optic cables and other high-capacity media to increase data throughput. For instance, if eight signals are multiplexed and sent together over each fiber in one fiber-optic cable, then the throughput of that cable is increased by a factor of eight.

STUDY TOOLS 4

READY TO STUDY? IN THE BOOK, YOU CAN:

- ☐ Rip out the Chapter Review Card, which includes key terms and key chapter concepts.

ONLINE AT WWW.CENGAGEBRAIN.COM, YOU CAN:

- ☐ Review key concepts from the chapter in a short video.
- ☐ Explore networking hardware with the interactive infographic.
- ☐ Practice what you've learned with more Practice It and On Your Own exercises.
- ☐ Prepare for tests with quizzes.
- ☐ Review the key terms with flashcards.

repeater A device on a network that amplifies signals for that network.

range extender A repeater for a wireless network.

antenna A device used for receiving or sending radio signals and often used to increase the range of a network.

multiplexer A device that combines the transmissions from several different devices and sends them as one message.

QUIZ YOURSELF

1. Describe what a computer network is and what it is used for.
2. Describe telecommuting.
3. What are the three most common network topologies?
4. What is the difference between a client-server network and a peer-to-peer network?
5. What is a small network designed to connect the personal devices for an individual called?
6. What is the world's largest WAN?
7. What is a virtual private network (VPN), and when is it used?
8. Describe the difference between digital and analog signals, and identify which is most often used with computers.
9. What are the three most common types of cables used to create wired networks?
10. What is TCP/IP?
11. What is the most widely used standard for wired networks?
12. What is Wi-Fi used for?
13. What type of network is the 4G standard designed for?
14. Is Bluetooth a short-range or long-range networking standard? Explain.
15. What is the purpose of a wireless router?
16. What is the purpose of a bridge?
17. What is a repeater?
18. What is the purpose of an antenna?

PRACTICE IT

Practice It 4-1

Home networks—particularly wireless home networks—are becoming very common. Suppose that you have a notebook computer and a tablet, and you want to network the two devices wirelessly. You also want to use a printer with both devices.

1. Determine the hardware you will need to wirelessly network the two computers and the printer.
2. Create a labeled sketch of the network.
3. Create a list of the hardware you need to acquire.
4. Research the approximate cost of the hardware to determine the overall cost of creating the wireless network (excluding the cost of the computers and the printer). Record the model numbers of the hardware items and the sources where you found the prices.
5. Prepare a one-page summary of your findings that includes your sketch and submit it to your instructor.

Practice It 4-2

New Wi-Fi standards are being developed all the time to increase speed or add other improvements. The current standard is 802.11ac, which is replacing 802.11n.

1. Research the 802.11ac and 802.11n standards and determine their primary differences.
2. What benefits does 802.11ac provide over 802.11n? Is hardware currently available for both standards? Are devices for these standards compatible with one another?
3. If you were buying a new computer or networking device today, which standard would you choose? Explain your answer.
4. Prepare a one-page summary that answers these questions and submit it to your instructor.

ON YOUR OWN

On Your Own 4-1

Internet peer-to-peer (P2P) networking involves sharing files and other resources directly with other computers via the Internet. While some content is legally exchanged via an Internet P2P network, some content (such as movies and music) is exchanged illegally.

1. Should Internet P2P networks be regulated to ensure that they are used only for legal activities? Why or why not?

2. If a P2P network set up for legitimate use is used for illegal purposes, should the organization or person who set up the P2P network be responsible? Explain your answer.
3. Use the Web to research more about a P2P service, such as BitTorrent. Are there legitimate reasons for using your selected P2P network? If so, what are they?
4. To share files with others, would you rather use a P2P service or an online file sharing service such as Dropbox? Explain. Why or why not?
5. Prepare a one-page summary that answers these questions, and submit it to your instructor.

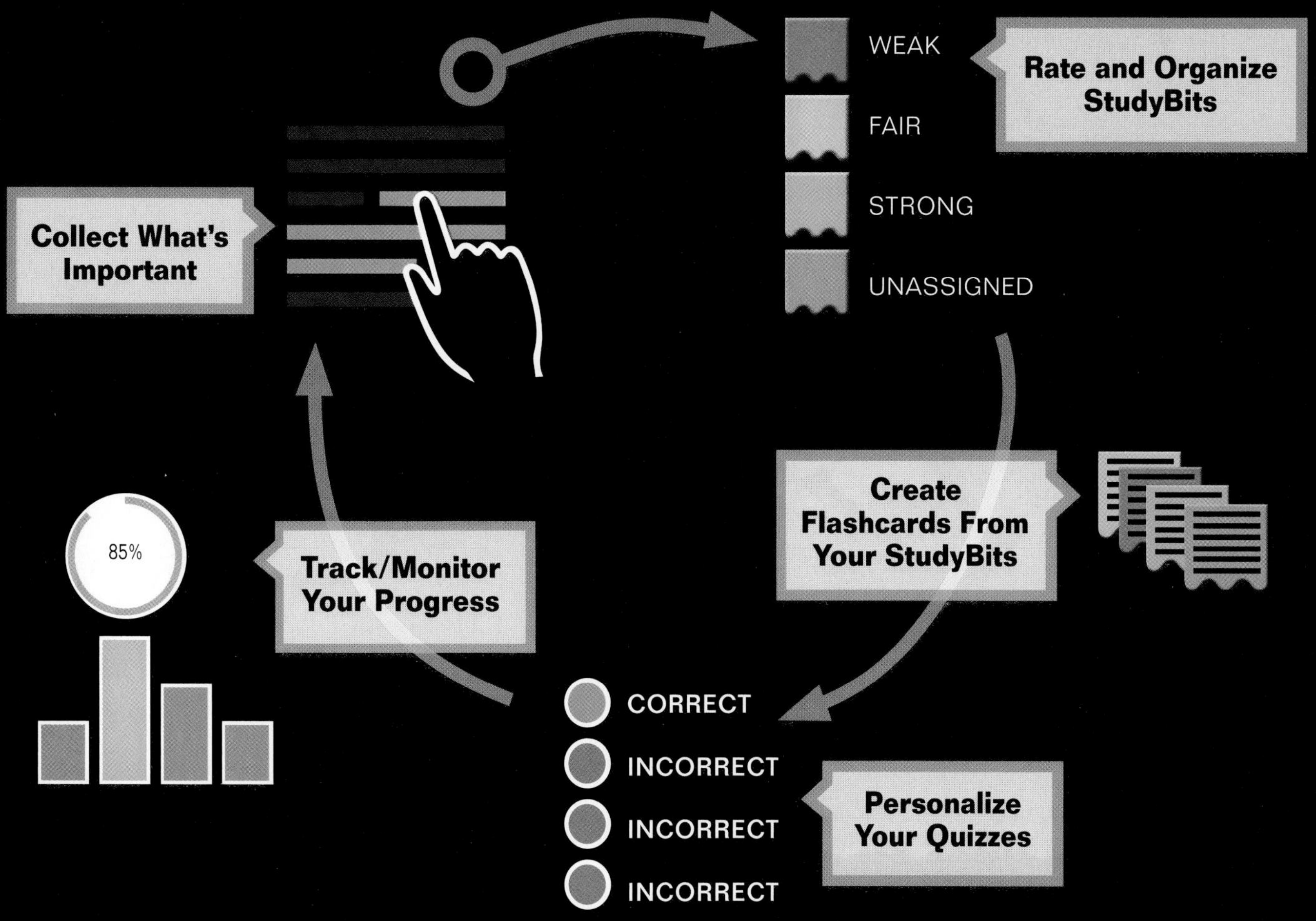

Part 2
NETWORKS
and
THE
INTERNET

5 | The Internet and Email

LEARNING OBJECTIVES

After studying the material in this chapter, you will be able to:

- 5-1 Understand how the Internet evolved
- 5-2 Set up your computer to use the Internet
- 5-3 Understand how to search the Internet for information
- 5-4 Understand email and other types of messaging
- 5-5 Describe common Internet activities

After finishing this chapter, go to **PAGE 149** for **STUDY TOOLS**.

5-1 EVOLUTION OF THE INTERNET

The **Internet** is a worldwide collection of separate, but interconnected, networks accessed by billions of people using a variety of devices to obtain information, disseminate information, access entertainment, or communicate with others. As it has evolved over the past two decades or so, it has redefined how people think about computers, communications, and the availability of news and information.

5-1a From ARPANET to Internet2

The roots of the Internet began with an experimental project called **ARPANET** created in 1969 by the U.S. Department of Defense Advanced Research Projects Agency (ARPA). Initially, ARPANET connected four supercomputers (a sketch of ARPANET drawn in 1969 is shown in Exhibit 5-1).

EXHIBIT 5-1 HAND-DRAWN SKETCH OF ARPANET FROM 1969

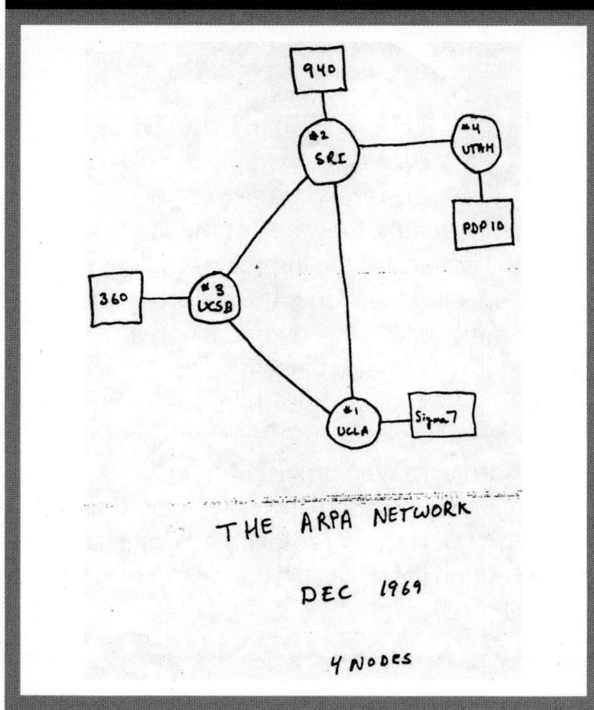

© Courtesy DARPA

One objective of the ARPANET project was to create a computer network that would allow researchers located in different places to communicate with each other. Another objective was to build a computer network capable of sending or receiving data over a variety of paths to ensure that network communications could continue even if part of the network was destroyed, such as in a nuclear attack or by a natural disaster.

As ARPANET grew during the next decade, networks at hundreds of colleges and universities were connected to it. These networks consisted of a mixture of different computers so, over the years, protocols were developed for tying this mix of computers and networks together, for transferring data over the network, and for ensuring that data was transferred intact. In 1972, electronic mail (email) was introduced and immediately became the largest network application for more than a decade. Additional networks were created and connected to ARPANET, and this internet—or network of networks—eventually evolved into the present-day Internet.

The Internet infrastructure is used for a variety of purposes, such as researching topics of interest; exchanging email and other messages; participating in videoconferences and making telephone calls; downloading software, music, and movies; purchasing goods and services; watching TV shows and videos; accessing computers remotely; and sharing files with others. Most of these activities are available through the primary Internet resource—the World Wide Web.

5-1b The World Wide Web

In its early years, the Internet was used primarily by the government, scientists, and educational institutions. Despite its popularity in academia and with government researchers, the Internet went virtually unnoticed by the public and the business community for over two decades because (1) it required a computer and (2) it was hard to use (see the left image in Exhibit 5-2). As always, however, computer and networking technology improved, and new applications quickly followed. Then, in 1989, a researcher named Tim Berners-Lee proposed the idea of the **World Wide Web (Web)**. He envisioned the Web as a way to organize information in the form of pages linked together through selectable text or images (today's hyperlinks) on the screen. Although the introduction of Web pages did not replace all other Internet resources,

Internet The largest and most well-known computer network, linking billions of computers all over the world.

ARPANET The predecessor to the Internet; named after the Advanced Research Projects Agency (ARPA), which sponsored its development.

World Wide Web (Web) The collection of Web pages available through the Internet.

EXHIBIT 5-2 THE INTERNET: THEN AND NOW

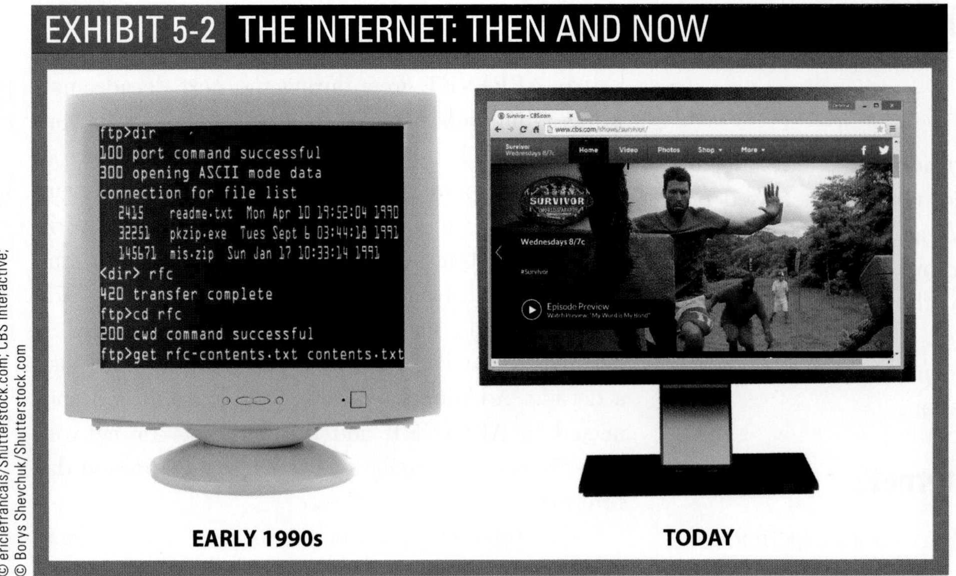

such as email and collections of downloadable files, it became a popular way for researchers to provide written information to others.

In 1993, a group of professors and students at the University of Illinois National Center for Supercomputing Applications (NCSA) released the Mosaic Web browser. Soon after, use of the Web began to increase dramatically because Mosaic's graphical user interface (GUI) and its ability to display images on Web pages made using the Web both easier and more fun than in the past. Today's Web pages are a true multimedia, interactive experience (see the *Survivor* Web site shown in Exhibit 5-2). They can contain text, graphics, animation, sound, video, and three-dimensional virtual reality objects.

A growing number of today's Web-based applications and services are referred to as Web 2.0 applications. Although there is no precise definition, Web 2.0 generally refers to applications and services that use the Web as a platform to deliver rich applications that enable people to collaborate, socialize, and share information online. Some Web 2.0 applications include cloud computing, social media, podcasts, blogs, and wikis.

The Web is only part of the Internet, but it is by far the most widely used part. Today, most companies regard their use of the Internet and their Web presence as indispensable competitive business tools, and many individuals view the Internet—and especially the Web—as a vital research, communications, and entertainment medium.

5-1c Internet2

Internet2 is a consortium of researchers, educators, and technology leaders from industry, government, and the international community who are dedicated to the development of revolutionary Internet technologies. Internet2 uses high-performance networks linking over 500 member institutions to deploy and test new network applications and technologies. Designed as a research and development tool to help create technologies that ensure the Internet can handle tomorrow's applications, Internet2 is working to deploy advanced applications and technologies that might not be possible otherwise with today's Internet. Much of Internet2 research is focused on speed. In fact, the Internet2 backbone network was recently upgraded to support 8.8 Tbps. This network is the first national network to use 100 Gigabit Ethernet over its entire footprint; it will be used to support high bandwidth applications, such as telemedicine and distance learning, to schools, libraries, hospitals, and other organizations.

> **FYI** **THE INTERNET VS. THE WEB**
> Even though many people use the terms *Internet* and *Web* interchangeably, they are not the same thing. Technically, the Internet is the physical network, and the Web is the collection of Web pages accessible over that network. A majority of Internet activities today take place via Web pages, but there are Internet resources other than the Web that are not accessed via a Web browser. For instance, files can be uploaded and downloaded using an FTP (File Transfer Protocol) program, and conventional email can be accessed using an email program.

5-1d The Internet Community Today

The Internet community today consists of individuals, businesses, and a variety of organizations located throughout the world. Virtually anyone with a computer or other Internet-enabled device can be part of the Internet, either as a user or as a supplier of information or services. Most members of the Internet community fall into one or more of the following groups:

- **Users**—people who use the Internet to retrieve content or perform online activities, such as to look up a telephone number, read the day's news headlines or top stories, browse through an online catalog, make an online purchase, download a music file, watch an online video, make a phone call, or send an email message.
- **Internet service providers (ISPs)**—businesses or other organizations, including telephone, cable, and satellite companies (see Exhibit 5-3), that provide Internet access to others, typically for a fee. Regardless of their delivery method and geographical coverage, ISPs are the onramp to the Internet, providing their subscribers with access to the Web, email, and other Internet resources.

EXHIBIT 5-3 EXAMPLES OF ISPs

Source: © AT&T; © Verizon Communications; © Comcast; © T-Mobile USA, Inc.; © EarthLink, Inc.; © ViaSat, Inc.

- **Internet content providers**—the suppliers of the information that is available through the Internet. Internet content providers can be commercial businesses, nonprofit organizations, educational institutions, individuals, and more. For example, a musician posting his music video on YouTube, a photographer posting her best photos on her Web site, and a TV network supplying the latest episodes of a TV show to Hulu are all Internet content providers. While a great deal of Internet content is free (and typically supported by ads), a growing amount is fee based.
- **Application service providers (ASPs)**—the companies that manage and distribute Web-based software services to customers over the Internet. Instead of providing access to the Internet like ISPs do, ASPs provide access to software applications via the Internet. Common ASP applications for businesses include office suites, collaboration and communications software, accounting programs, and e-commerce software.
- **Infrastructure companies**—the enterprises that own or operate the paths or "roadways" along which Internet data travels, such as the Internet backbone and the communications networks connected to it. Examples of infrastructure companies include conventional and wireless telephone providers, cable companies, and satellite Internet providers.
- **Hardware and software companies**—the organizations that make and distribute the products used with the Internet and Internet activities. For example, companies that create or sell the software used in conjunction with the Internet, such as Web browsers, email programs, e-commerce and multimedia software, and Web development tools, fall into this category. So, too, do the companies that make the hardware, such as network adapters, modems, cables, routers, servers, computers, and smartphones, that is used with the Internet.
- **Governments**—the ruling bodies of countries can pass laws that impact both the information available via the Web and the access their citizens have to the Internet. For example, in France, it is illegal to sell items or post online content related to racist groups or activities. In China, tight controls are imposed on what information is published on Web servers located in China as well as on the information available to its citizens. And in the United States, anything illegal offline is illegal online.
- **Key Internet organizations**—other organizations that are responsible for many aspects of the Internet. For example, the Internet Society provides leadership in addressing issues that may impact the future of the Internet. It also oversees the groups responsible for Internet infrastructure standards,

Internet service provider (ISP) A business or other organization that provides Internet access to others, usually for a fee.

Internet content provider A person or an organization that provides Internet content.

application service provider (ASP) A company that manages and distributes software-based services over the Internet.

FYI WHO'S IN CHARGE?

One remarkable characteristic of both the Internet and Web is that they are not owned by any person or business, and no single person, business, or organization is in charge. Each network connected to the Internet is privately owned and managed individually by that network's administrator; the primary infrastructure that makes up the Internet backbone is typically owned by communications companies, such as telephone and cable companies. The closest the Internet comes to having a governing body are the organizations that are involved with issues such as establishing the protocols used on the Internet, making recommendations for changes, and encouraging cooperation between and coordinating communications among the networks connected to the Internet. Governments in each country have the power to regulate the content and use of the Internet within their borders, as allowed by their laws. However, legislators often face serious obstacles getting legislation passed into law—let alone getting it enforced. Making governmental control even harder is the "bombproof" design of the Internet itself. If a government tries to block access to or from a specific country or Web site, for example, users can use a third party, such as an individual located in another country or a different Web site, to circumvent the block.

© Oleksiy Mark/Shutterstock.com

such as determining the protocols that can be used and how Internet addresses are constructed, as well as facilitating and coordinating Internet-related initiatives around the world. ICANN (Internet Corporation for Assigned Names and Numbers) coordinates activities related to the Internet's naming system, such as IP address allocation and domain name management. The World Wide Web Consortium (W3C) is an international community of over 450 organizations dedicated to developing new protocols and specifications to be used with the Web and to ensure its interoperability. In addition, many colleges and universities support Internet research and manage blocks of the Internet's resources.

5-2 CONNECTING TO THE INTERNET

Getting connected to the Internet typically involves three decisions—determining the type of device you will use to access the Internet, deciding which type of connection you want, and selecting the Internet service provider to use. Once you have made these determinations, you can set up your Internet access and your devices.

5-2a Selecting the Type of Device

You can access the Internet using a variety of devices. The type of device you use depends on a combination of factors, such as the devices available to you, whether you need access just at home or while on the go, and what types of Internet content you want to access. Some possible devices are shown in Exhibit 5-4.

One advantage of using personal computers for Internet access is that they have relatively large screens for viewing Internet content and keyboards for easier data entry. They can also be used to view or otherwise access virtually any Web page content, such as graphics, animation, music files, games, and videos. In addition, they typically have a large hard drive and are connected to a printer so Web pages, email messages, and downloaded files can be saved or printed easily.

Smartphones and other mobile devices are also frequently used to view Web page content, exchange email and other messages, and download music and other online content. Although smartphones are convenient to use on the go, they have a relatively small display screen; tablets typically have a larger screen size for easier viewing. Some mobile devices include a built-in or sliding keyboard for easier data entry; others utilize pen, voice, or touch input instead.

Another option is using a gaming console or handheld gaming device to access Web content. Many gaming devices have Web browsers that can be used to

EXHIBIT 5-4 DEVICES USED TO ACCESS THE INTERNET

PERSONAL COMPUTER

SMARTPHONE

SMART TV

TRENDING...

NET NEUTRALITY

Net neutrality is the basic concept that all content on the Internet is equal; that is, all packets traveling over the Internet are delivered on a first-come, first-served basis regardless of where they originated. The Internet has operated under this assumption since it began, enabling small start-up companies to compete with major Internet players. Controversy about net neutrality started when multimedia became more widely available online and ISPs began to carry content that directly competed with their own products, such as a cable ISP delivering Netflix to its customers or a telephone ISP delivering video calling services to its customers. Consequently, for the past several years, some major ISPs, such as Verizon, have been challenging net neutrality regulations. Some ISPs have attempted to block or slow the speed of data coming from competitors to its customers. For example, cable giant Comcast once blocked the use of P2P sites like BitTorrent that are used to download movies and music. In addition, some content providers want the option of buying the right to have their content delivered faster than smaller competitors.

The issue of net neutrality came to the forefront in 2014 when Verizon challenged the FCC's regulations barring broadband providers from slowing or blocking selected Web traffic. After the U.S. Court of Appeals ruled that the FCC did not have the appropriate authority to enact such restrictions, the FCC, in 2015, reclassified broadband ISPs as common carriers, which means they are treated essentially as public utilities. The FCC also defined "Open Internet," which prohibits broadband providers from blocking access to legal Internet content, slowing down any legal Internet content, or favoring some Internet traffic over others in exchange for money or other considerations. In response, a number of ISPs are challenging the FCCs decision in court. Consequently, while the FCC's decision appears to be a victory for net neutrality, the issue may still be debated for quite some time.

access general Web content in addition to online gaming resources. Smart TVs can also be used to display Web content. The type of Web content available depends on the smart TV being used and the installed apps.

net neutrality The basic concept that all content on the Internet is equal.

5-2b Choosing a Type of Internet Connection

To access the Internet, you need to connect a computer or other device to it. Typically, this occurs by connecting the device you are using to a computer or network, usually belonging to your ISP, school, or employer, that is continually connected to the Internet. Most types of Internet connections today are broadband, or high-speed, connections. Broadband is defined by the FCC as 25 Mbps or faster, although many Internet connections considered broadband today are slower than 25 Mbps. As applications requiring high-speed connections continue to grow in popularity, access to broadband Internet speeds are needed to take full advantage of these applications (see Exhibit 5-5). Most connections today are also direct connections (which are always connected to the Internet). With a direct connection, you access the Internet simply by opening a Web browser, such as Chrome or Edge, using your chosen device. Direct Internet connections are commonly used in homes and businesses and are often connected to a LAN to share the Internet connection with multiple devices within the home or business. In contrast, dial-up connections are typically used with only one computer and are not connected to the Internet until the user directs his or her computer to dial up and connect to the Internet. The most common types of Internet connections for personal use are summarized in Exhibit 5-6 and are described next.

Conventional dial-up Internet access works over standard telephone lines. It uses a conventional dial-up modem connected to a standard telephone jack with regular twisted-pair telephone cabling. Conventional dial-up Internet service is most often used with the home desktop computers of users who do not need, or do not want to pay for, faster broadband Internet service. Advantages include inexpensive hardware, ease of setup and use, widespread availability (including remote areas), and increased security

EXHIBIT 5-5 LENGTH OF TIME TO DOWNLOAD A 2.7 GB (ABOUT 2-HOUR HD) MOVIE

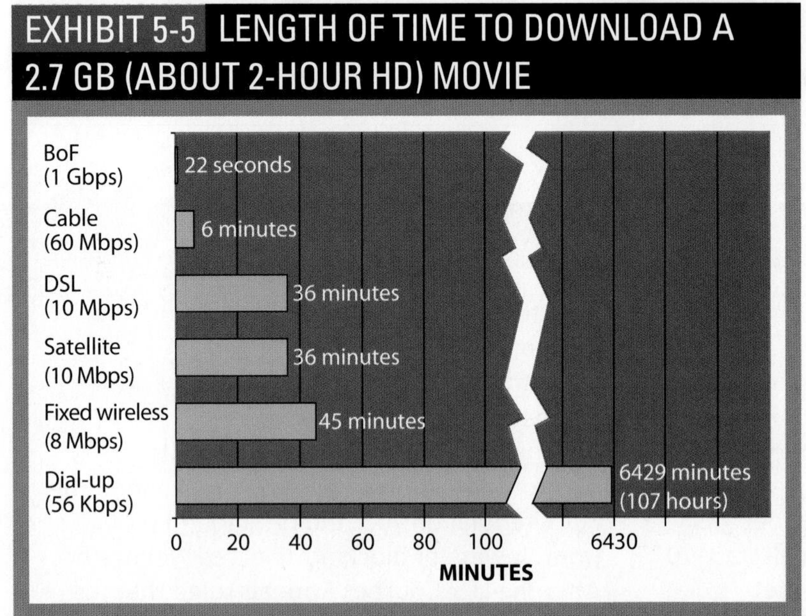

EXHIBIT 5-6 TYPICAL HOME INTERNET CONNECTION OPTIONS

Type of Internet Connection	Availability	Approximate Maximum Speed*	Approximate Monthly Price
Conventional dial-up	Anywhere there is telephone service	56 Kbps	Free–$30
Cable	Virtually anywhere cable TV service is available	6–200 Mbps	$30–110
DSL	Within three miles of a switching station that supports DSL	3–15 Mbps	$30–40
Satellite	Anywhere there is a clear view of the southern sky and where a satellite dish can be mounted and receive a signal	5–15 Mbps	$40–80
Fixed wireless	Selected areas where service is available	2–12 Mbps	$60–250
Broadband over fiber (BoF)	Anywhere fiber has been installed to the building	5 Mbps–1 Gbps	$30–70
Mobile wireless (4G)	Virtually anywhere cellular phone service	3–100 Mbps	Varies greatly depending on data plan

* Download speed; most connections have slower upload speeds.

(because the computer is not continually connected to the Internet). The primary disadvantage is a much slower connection speed than other types of connections—a maximum of 56 Kbps.

Cable Internet access uses a direct connection and is one of the most widely used types of home broadband connections. Cable Internet is very fast, typically around 25 Mbps, and is available wherever cable TV access is offered as long as the local cable provider supports Internet access. Consequently, cable Internet is not widely available in rural areas. Cable Internet service requires a cable modem.

DSL (Digital Subscriber Line) Internet access is a direct connection that transmits via standard telephone lines, but it does not tie up your telephone line. DSL requires a DSL modem and is available only to users who are relatively close (within three miles) to a telephone switching station and who have telephone lines capable of handling DSL. DSL speeds are slower than cable speeds, and the speed of the connection degrades as the distance between the modem and the switching station gets closer and closer to the three-mile limit. Consequently, DSL is usually available only in urban areas. Download speeds can be up to about 25 Mbps, but are more typically around 10 Mbps.

Satellite Internet access also uses a direct connection and has speeds similar to DSL access, but it is more expensive than both DSL and cable and almost always has a data cap. However, it is often the only broadband option for rural areas. In addition to a satellite modem, it requires a transceiver satellite dish mounted outside the home or building to receive and transmit data to and from the satellites being used. Installation requires an unobstructed view of the southern sky to have a clear line of sight between the transceiver and appropriate satellite. Performance might degrade or stop altogether during very heavy rain or snowstorms.

Fixed wireless Internet access uses a direct connection and is similar to satellite Internet in that it uses wireless signals, but it uses radio transmission towers—either stand-alone towers like the one shown in Exhibit 5-7 or transmitters placed on existing cell towers—instead of satellites. Fixed wireless Internet access requires a modem and, sometimes, an outside-mounted transceiver. Fixed wireless companies typically use Wi-Fi or WiMAX technology to broadcast the wireless signals to customers. Speeds are typically between 2 and 10 Mbps, though the speed depends somewhat on the distance between the tower and the customer, the type and number of obstacles in the path, and the type and speed of the connection between the wireless transmitter and the Internet.

In areas where fiber-optic cabling runs all the way to the building, a relatively new type of very fast direct Internet connection is available to homes and businesses. This type of Internet connection is generically called **broadband over fiber (BoF)** or **fiber-to-the-premises (FTTP)**, with other names being used by

EXHIBIT 5-7 WIMAX TOWER AT THE PEAK OF WHISTLER MOUNTAIN IN BRITISH COLUMBIA

Source: © Tranzeo Wireless USA

conventional dial-up Internet access Dial-up Internet access via standard telephone lines.

cable Internet access Fast, direct Internet access via cable TV lines.

DSL (Digital Subscriber Line) Internet access Fast, direct Internet access via standard telephone lines.

satellite Internet access Fast, direct Internet access via the airwaves and a satellite dish.

fixed wireless Internet access Fast, direct Internet access available in some areas via the airwaves.

broadband over fiber (BoF) or **fiber-to-the-premises (FTTP)** Very fast, direct Internet access via fiber-optic networks.

TRENDING...

AUGMENTED REALITY

While virtual reality (VR) immerses you in a virtual world and blocks out the real world, **augmented reality (AR)** overlays computer-generated images on top of real-time, real life images. Some of the earliest AR applications were industrial, such as displaying wiring diagrams on top of the actual wiring of an airplane via a technician's headset. Today, augmented reality is being used with mobile devices like smartphones, Google Glass, and Microsoft HoloLens. To accomplish this, content is displayed over the images seen through the smartphone's camera or the lenses of the glasses or headset. Some content is based on the user's location, such as overlaying information about the location the user is currently viewing. Other content is based on the physical objects being viewed, such as overlaying a movie trailer or a 3D image over a magazine ad or book page being viewed.

Some examples of location-based AR apps designed for consumers include overlaying home listing information, such as pricing and photos, when a phone is pointed at a neighborhood; displaying information, such as real-time game stats and player information, when a phone is pointed at a sporting event; displaying information about an exhibit at a museum, when a phone is pointed at that exhibit; and displaying activity opportunities, such as restaurant, movie, museum, or shopping information, when a phone is pointed at a business district (see the accompanying illustration).

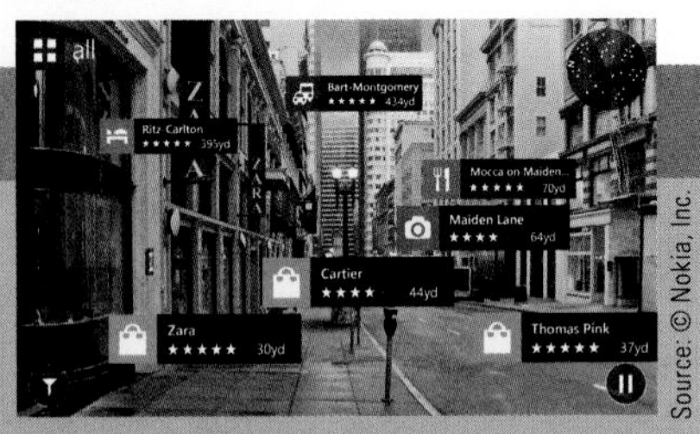

Source: © Nokia, Inc.

Other AR apps are being developed to allow businesses to display information or promotional offers when an individual points his or her phone in the vicinity of the business. For example, a hotel could display room photos and pricing, a restaurant could display dining room photos and menus, and a retail store could display merchandise photos and specials. Another emerging consumer application is AR car navigation systems. Already in the testing stages, these systems work with voice commands and overlay a virtual route on the car windshield over the actual road in the driver's line of vision—no glasses, headphones, or smartphone required.

individual providers, such as Verizon Fios and Google Fiber. These fiber-optic networks are often used to deliver telephone and TV service in addition to Internet service. Where available, BoF is very fast—up to 1 Gbps. BoF requires a special networking terminal installed at the building to convert the optical signals into electrical signals that can be sent to a computer or over a LAN.

Mobile wireless Internet access is the type of direct connection most commonly used with smartphones and tablets to keep them connected to the Internet via a mobile phone (typically cell) network, even as they are carried from place to place. Some mobile wireless services can be used with portable computers as well. The speed depends on the cellular standard and specific network being used, but 4G networks are often between 3 and 15 Mbps, with speeds up to 100 Mbps available in some areas. Costs for mobile wireless Internet access vary widely. Many plans available today from wireless providers offer unlimited voice and text but have a data cap and so charge by the amount of data used or are included in the plan. A growing trend is prepaid mobile Internet, in which you purchase service month to month (and can buy additional data as needed), instead of committing to a lengthy contract.

A **Wi-Fi hotspot** is a location with a direct Internet connection and a wireless access point that allows users to connect wirelessly (via Wi-Fi) to the hotspot to use its Internet connection (see Exhibit 5-8). Public Wi-Fi hotspots are widely available today, including at many coffeehouses and restaurants; at hotels, airports, and other locations frequented by business travelers; and in or near public areas such as libraries, subway stations, and parks. Some public Wi-Fi hotspots are free; others charge per hour, per day, or

augmented reality A technology that overlays computer-generated images on top of real-time, real life images.

mobile wireless Internet access Internet access via a mobile phone network.

Wi-Fi hotspot A location that provides wireless Internet access to the public.

on a subscription basis. College campuses also typically have Wi-Fi hotspots to provide Internet access to students. Businesses and other organizations may have Wi-Fi hotspots for use by employees in their offices as well as by employees and guests in conference rooms, waiting rooms, lunchrooms, and other onsite locations.

EXHIBIT 5-8 WI-FI HOTSPOTS

COFFEEHOUSES AND OTHER PUBLIC LOCATIONS
Often fee-based, though some are available for free.

HOTELS AND CONFERENCE CENTERS
Often free for guests.

HOSPITALS, BUSINESSES, AND OTHER ORGANIZATIONS
Usually designed for employees but are sometimes also available free to visitors.

COLLEGE CAMPUSES
Usually designed for students and faculty; sometimes used directly in class, as shown here.

5-2c Selecting an ISP

The type of device you will use (such as a personal computer or smartphone), the type of Internet connection and service you want (such as cable Internet or mobile wireless), and your geographical location (such as metropolitan or rural) determine your ISP options. The pricing and services available often vary within a single ISP as well as from one ISP to the next. The questions listed in Exhibit 5-9 can help you narrow

EXHIBIT 5-9 QUESTIONS TO ASK BEFORE CHOOSING AN ISP

Area	Questions to Ask
Services	Is the service compatible with my selected device? Is there a monthly data cap? If so, do I have a choice of tiers? How many email addresses can I have? What is the size limit on incoming and outgoing email messages and attachments? Do I have a choice between conventional and Web-based email? Are there any special member features or benefits? Does the service include Web site hosting, Wi-Fi hotspots, or other benefits?
Speed	How fast are the maximum and usual downstream (ISP to my device) speeds? How fast are the maximum and usual upstream (my device to ISP) speeds? How much does the service slow down under adverse conditions, such as high traffic or poor weather?
Support	Is telephone-based technical support available? Is Web-based technical support (such as via email) available? Is there ever a charge for technical support?
Cost	What is the monthly cost for the service? Is it lower if I prepay a few months in advance? Are different tiers available? Is there a setup fee? If so, can it be waived with a 6-month or 12-month agreement? What is the cost of any additional hardware needed, such as modem? Are there any other services (telephone service or TV, for instance) available from this provider that can be combined with Internet access for a lower total cost?

your ISP choices and determine the questions you want answered before you decide on an ISP and a service package. A growing trend is for ISPs to offer a number of tiers, or different combinations of speeds and/or data caps for different prices, so users requiring faster service or more data can get it but at a higher price.

5-2d Setting Up Your Internet Connection and Devices

The specific steps for setting up your Internet connection depend on the type of device, the type of connection, and the ISP you have chosen to use. Some types of Internet connections, such as satellite and broadband over fiber, require professional installation. With other types, you can install the necessary hardware—typically a modem that connects to your computer or wireless router via an Ethernet cable—yourself. You may be asked to select a username and a password at some point during the setup process to either log on to the Internet connection or log on to a Web site to access your billing information, usage data, and so forth. During the process of setting up your Internet connection, you may wish to connect your broadband modem to a wireless router or Wi-Fi connection if the modem does not contain a built-in switch or wireless router in order to share the Internet connection with those devices via Wi-Fi. If you are only setting up a smartphone or other mobile device to a mobile wireless Internet connection, you typically only need to power up the activated device, download any necessary apps, and sign into an email account if desired in order to be set up.

SEARCHING THE INTERNET

Most people use the Internet to find specific information. For instance, you might want to find the lowest price for the latest *Star Trek* Blu-ray movie, flights available from Los Angeles to New York on a particular day, a recipe for clam chowder, the weather forecast for the upcoming weekend, a video of the previous presidential inaugural address, or a map of hiking trails in the Grand Tetons. The Internet provides access to a vast array of interesting and useful information, but that information is worthless if you cannot find it when you need it. Consequently, one of the most important skills an Internet user can acquire today is how to successfully search for and locate information on the Internet.

search site A Web site designed to help users search for Web pages that match specified keywords.

search engine A software program used by a search site to retrieve matching Web pages from a search database.

keyword A word typed in a search box on a search site or other Web page to locate information related to that keyword.

hit A link displayed in a search site's results, that matches the supplied search criteria.

search phrase A search using multiple keywords.

5-3a Using Search Sites

Search sites are Web sites designed specifically to help users find information on the Web. Some popular search sites are Google and Bing. Most search sites use a **search engine**—a software program—in conjunction with a huge database of information about Web pages to help visitors find Web pages that contain the information they are seeking.

Search site databases are updated on a regular basis; for example, Google estimates that its entire index is updated about once per month. Typically, this occurs using small, automated programs (often called spiders or web crawlers) that use the hyperlinks located on Web pages to crawl (jump continually) from page to page. At each Web page, the spider program records important data about the page into the search site's database, such as the page's URL, its title, the words that appear frequently on the page, and the keywords and descriptive information added to the page's code by the Web page author at the time the page was created. In addition to spiders, search site databases also obtain information from Web page authors who submit Web page URLs and keywords associated with their Web sites to the search site.

To conduct a search, type an appropriate **keyword**—a word describing what you are looking for—into a search box on a search site. Many Web browsers allow you to type keywords directly in the Address bar of your browser and then perform the search using whichever search site is specified as your browser's default search site. The site's search engine then uses those keywords to return a list of links to Web pages (called **hits**) that match your search criteria (see Exhibit 5-10). Search sites differ in determining how close a match must be between the specified search criteria and a Web page before a link to that page is displayed, so the number of hits returned typically varies from one search site to another.

Often, a search returns millions of hits. To narrow the search, you can use multiple keywords, called a **search phrase**. For example, the keyword *cooking* might return links to recipe sites, sites with definitions of cooking, links to books about cooking, and so on. To

EXHIBIT 5-10 USING A SEARCH SITE

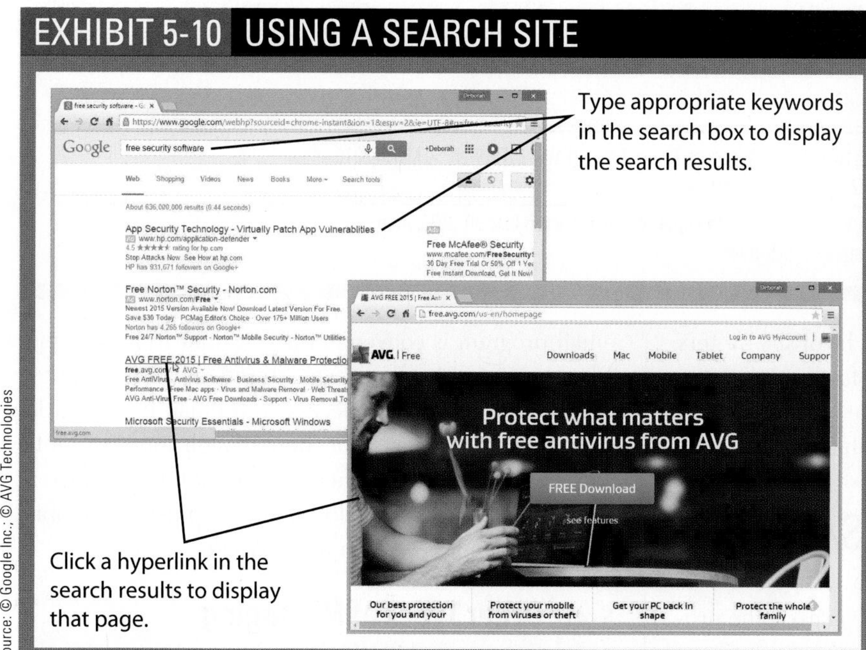
Type appropriate keywords in the search box to display the search results.
Click a hyperlink in the search results to display that page.
Protect what matters with free antivirus from AVG
FREE Download

Source: © Google Inc.; © AVG Technologies

restrict the list of results to only Web sites that contain recipes for appetizers made with shrimp, you can use the search phrase *shrimp appetizer recipes*. In addition, many search sites have other tools to help you narrow down the number of hits returned. For example, you can often use quotation marks around a search phrase to indicate that you want to only search for those keywords in the order you typed them. Some search sites allow you to restrict your search to specific top-level domains or even to specific Web sites. For example, if you type *tax tips site:.gov* as your search phrase, the results will include only government Web pages related to tax tips. If you type *tax tips site:irs.gov*, the results will only include IRS Web pages related to tax tips. You can look up the search tips for your favorite search site or look for an Advanced Search option at that site to find out what search options are possible.

5-3b Citing Internet Resources

According to the online version of the Merriam-Webster Dictionary, the term *plagiarize* means "to steal and pass off the ideas or words of another as one's own" or to "use another's production without crediting the source." To avoid plagiarizing Web page content, you need to credit Web page sources—as well as any other Internet resources—when you use them in papers, on Web pages, or in other documents.

The guidelines for citing Web page content are similar to those for written sources. In general, the author, date of publication, and article or Web page title are listed along with a "Retrieved" or "Accessed" statement listing the date the article was retrieved from the Internet and the URL of the Web page used to retrieve the article (while including the URL isn't always required, it is acceptable to include it). If in doubt when preparing a research paper, check with your instructor as to the style

FYI

EVALUATING SEARCH RESULTS

When you are presented with a list of hits, you need to determine if those Web sites are likely to contain information that is relevant and that can be trusted. To help evaluate the usefulness of a site or Web page, you can:

- Review the page title and description to make sure it's appropriate before loading the page.
- Look at the URL to see if it's from an appropriate source.
- Evaluate both the author and the source to determine if the information is reliable and unbiased.
- Check for a date to see how current the information is—many online articles are years old.
- Verify the information with a second source, if possible, if the information is important or you will be quoting it in a document.
- If the hits don't contain the information you need, try another search site or an advanced search using a search phrase or search operator.

EXHIBIT 5-11 CITING ONLINE ARTICLES

Style Format	Citation Example
MLA	Kedmey, Dan. "Why Thieves Love the Apple Watch." *Time*. Time, 14 May 2015. Web. 30 March 2016. <http://time.com/3858762/apple-watch-theft/>.
APA	Kedmey, D. (2015, May 14). Why Thieves Love the Apple Watch. Retrieved June 30, 2015, from http://time.com/3858762/apple-watch-theft/

format, such as APA, MLA, or Chicago, he or she prefers you to follow and refer to that guide for direction. An example of how to cite an online article using the MLA and APA style formats is shown in Exhibit 5-11.

5-4 EMAIL AND MESSAGING

Email (more formally called electronic mail) is the process of exchanging electronic messages (emails) over a network, typically the Internet. Other types of electronic messages include instant messages (IM), social messages, and text messages.

5-4a How Email Works

Email messages can be sent from any Internet-enabled device, such as a personal computer or smartphone, to anyone who has an email address. As illustrated in Exhibit 5-12, when you send an email message, it travels from your device, through a network (such as a LAN or the Internet) to your designated mail server, and then through the Internet to the mail server being used by the recipient. When the recipient's device retrieves new email, the email message is displayed on the device he or she is using. In addition to text, email messages can include attached files, such as documents, photos, and videos.

Email can be sent and received via an installed email program, such as OS X Mail or via a Web mail service or app, such as Gmail. Using an installed email program is convenient if you want to have copies of sent and received messages stored on your computer. Web mail allows you to access your email from any device with an Internet connection, though you may not be able to see your email when you are offline. Email sent via a smartphone is typically counted against your mobile data usage, unless you are using Wi-Fi.

5-4b Other Types of Messaging

Instant messaging (IM), also commonly referred to as **chat**, allows you to exchange real-time messages with others. Instant messages can be sent via computers and smartphones using installed messaging programs or apps such as Hangouts, Kik, and What's App. Messaging capabilities are also connected with some social networks, such as Facebook's Messenger app that enables you to chat directly with your Facebook

EXHIBIT 5-12 HOW EMAIL WORKS

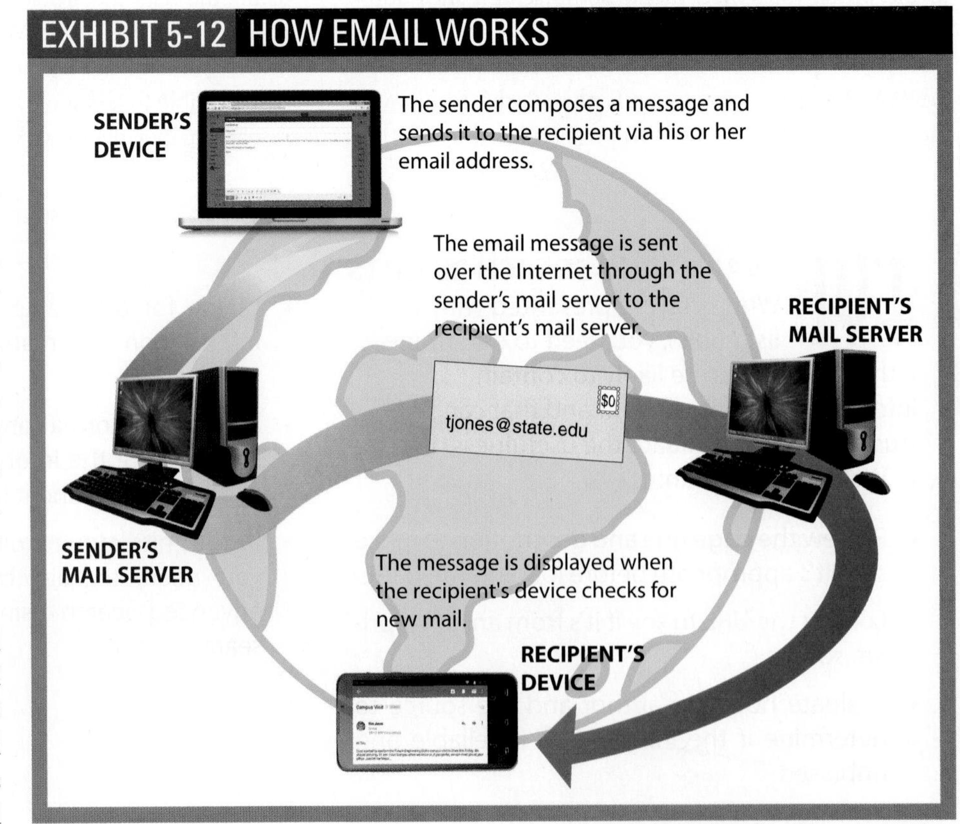
SENDER'S DEVICE
The sender composes a message and sends it to the recipient via his or her email address.
The email message is sent over the Internet through the sender's mail server to the recipient's mail server.
RECIPIENT'S MAIL SERVER
$0
tjones@state.edu
SENDER'S MAIL SERVER
The message is displayed when the recipient's device checks for new mail.
RECIPIENT'S DEVICE

TRENDING...

SMART POSTING

Once you send an email or text message or post something online, you lose control of it. Consequently, it is wise to think twice before you send a message or post something to social media. For example, a private message that you send to someone can be forwarded to others without your knowledge and can be archived on a mail server indefinitely. In addition, social media posts are frequently reviewed by employers and colleges. For example, the majority of employees include a social media review when evaluating job candidates and some monitor the activities of current employees. It is not uncommon for individuals to lose out on job offers because their social media presence is viewed as undesirable by a company, and employees have even been fired based on their social media activity. Colleges are increasingly monitoring social media to find inappropriate behavior by current students and hold them accountable for that behavior as well as to research college applicants. Consequently, it is a good idea to be smart about what you post online and not post anything that might be potentially embarrassing if viewed by an employer, a business associate, or a future partner. Finally, you should not post any content while you are angry or upset—wait until you cool off first.

© Oleksiy Mark/Shutterstock.com

friends. Some messaging apps support group messaging (see Exhibit 5-13) as well as voice and video calls. There are also social messaging apps and Web sites that enable you to send a message, photo, or video to a large number of individuals at one time. For example, SnapChat lets you post self-destructing photos that can be viewed only for a very short time (up to 10 seconds or 24 hours, depending on how you post them), and Twitter lets you post updates called tweets of up to 140 characters that anyone can view. Chat capabilities are also integrated into Web pages, such as to enable customers to ask questions of a customer service representative.

EXHIBIT 5-13 GROUP MESSAGING

Source: © WhatsApp Inc.

Source: © Kik Interactive Inc.; © Facebook; © SnapChat

Text messaging is a form of messaging used to send messages from one mobile phone to another. It is also called Short Message Service (SMS) when the message contains only text or Multimedia Message Service

email The process of sending electronic messages over the Internet or other network.

instant messaging (IM) or **chat** A way of exchanging real-time typed messages with other individuals.

text messaging A way of exchanging real-time typed messages with other individuals via a cellular network and cell phones.

(MMS) when the message includes a photo, an audio, or a video. In either case, the messages are sent to the recipient via his or her mobile phone number and are delivered to the recipient's mobile phone immediately. While some smartphones can text over Wi-Fi, most texts are sent via a cellular network and so text or data charges may apply.

FYI **UNIQUE EMAIL ADDRESSES** To ensure a unique email address for everyone in the world, usernames must be unique within each domain name. So, even though there could be a *jsmith* at Cengage Learning using the email address *jsmith@cengage.com* and a *jsmith* at Stanford University using the email address *jsmith@stanford.edu*, the two email addresses are unique. It is up to each organization with a registered domain name to ensure that one—and only one—exact same username is assigned to its domain.

© Anita Ponne/Shutterstock.com

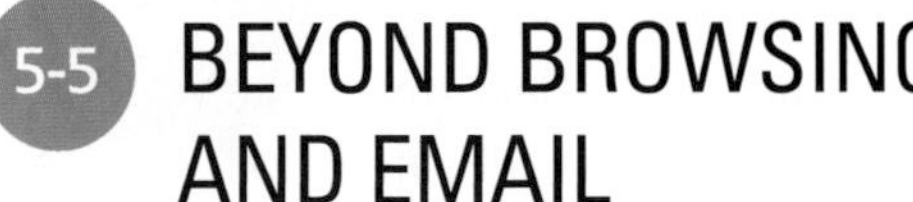

5-5 BEYOND BROWSING AND EMAIL

In addition to basic browsing and email and other types of messaging, many other activities can take place via the Internet. Some of the most common of these Web-based activities are discussed next.

5-5a Other Types of Online Communication

A **blog**—also called a Web log—is a Web page that contains short, frequently updated entries in chronological order, typically as a means of expression or communication (see the food blog shown in Exhibit 5-14). In essence, a blog is an online personal journal accessible to the public that is usually created and updated by one individual. Blogs are written by a wide variety of individuals—including ordinary people as well as celebrities, writers, students, and experts on particular subjects—and can be used to post personal commentary, research updates, comments on current events, political opinions, celebrity gossip, travel diaries, television show recaps, and more.

EXHIBIT 5-14 AN EXAMPLE OF A BLOG

Source: © Amy Sherman

Blogs are most often created via blogging sites such as Blogger and WordPress.com. Blogs are also frequently published on school, business, and personal Web sites. Blogs tend to be updated frequently, and entries can be posted via computers, email, and smartphones. Blogs often contain text, photos, and video clips.

With their growing use and audiences, bloggers are beginning to have increasing influence on businesses, politicians, and individuals. An ethical issue surrounding blogging relates to bloggers who are paid to blog about certain products. Although some Web sites that match bloggers with advertisers require that the blogger reveal that he or she receives payment for "sponsored" posts, some believe that commercializing blogging will corrupt the blogosphere. Others, however, view it as a natural evolution of word-of-mouth advertising.

Another form of online writing similar to a blog is a wiki. However, where blogs are typically edited by an individual, a **wiki** is collaborative and intended to be modified by multiple individuals. For example, Wikipedia is an online encyclopedia that is updated by contributors from all over the world. To protect the content of a wiki

blog A Web page that contains short, frequently updated entries in chronological order, typically by just one individual.

wiki A collaborative Web page that is edited and republished by a variety of individuals.

from sabotage, the entire wiki or editing privileges for a wiki can be password protected.

For asking questions of, making comments to, or initiating discussions on specific subjects with a large group of individuals, **forums** (also called discussion groups and message boards) can be used. When a participant posts a message on a forum Web page, the message is displayed for anyone accessing the forum to read and respond to. Messages are usually organized by topics called threads; participants can post new messages in response to an existing message and stay within that thread, or they can start a new thread. Forum participants do not have to be online at the same time so participants can post and respond to messages at their convenience.

In addition to written online communication, there are some types of online communications that utilize audio or video. For example, a **podcast** is a recorded audio or video file that can be downloaded via the Internet. The term *podcast* is derived from the iPod (the first widely used device for playing digital audio files), although you can also listen to podcasts today using a computer or mobile phone.

Podcasting (creating a podcast) enables individuals to create self-published, inexpensive Internet broadcasts in order to share their knowledge, express their opinions, or present their original poems, songs, or short stories. Podcasts are also created and distributed by businesses. For instance, some commercial radio stations make portions of their broadcasts available via podcasts, and a growing number of news sites and corporate sites have regular podcasts available. Podcasts are also used for educational purposes. Podcasts are typically uploaded to the Web on a regular basis.

Internet telephony is the original industry term for the process of placing telephone calls over the Internet. Today, placing telephone calls over the Internet is called **Voice over Internet Protocol (VoIP)** and it can take many forms. At its simplest level, VoIP calls can take place from one device to another, such as by starting a voice conversation using a messaging program such as Skype or a smartphone app like Hangouts Dialer or FaceTime.

More permanent VoIP setups—sometimes referred to as digital voice or broadband phone—are designed to replace conventional landline phones in homes and businesses. VoIP is offered through some ISPs; it is also offered through dedicated VoIP providers, such as Vonage. Permanent VoIP setups require a broadband Internet connection and a VoIP phone adapter, which goes between a conventional phone and a broadband router, as shown in Exhibit 5-15. Once your phone calls are routed through your phone adapter and router to the Internet, they travel to the recipient's phone, which can be another VoIP phone, a mobile phone, or a landline phone. VoIP phone adapters are typically designed for a specific VoIP provider. With these more permanent VoIP setups, most users switching from landline phone service can keep their existing telephone number.

EXHIBIT 5-15 HOW VoIP WORKS

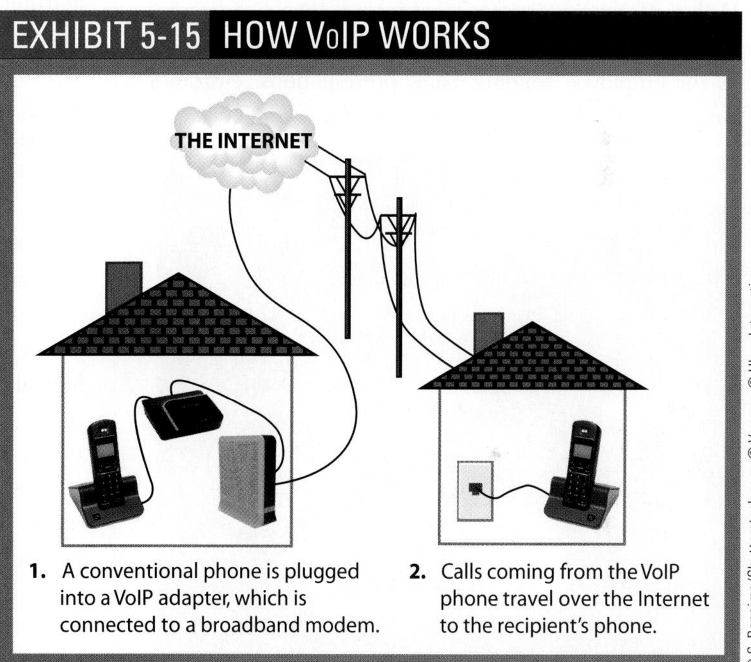

THE INTERNET
1. A conventional phone is plugged into a VoIP adapter, which is connected to a broadband modem.
2. Calls coming from the VoIP phone travel over the Internet to the recipient's phone.

© S. Bonaime/Shutterstock.com; © Vonage; © Ubee Interactive

The biggest advantage of VoIP is cost savings, such as unlimited local and long-distance calls for as little as $25 per month, or basic cable and VoIP services bundled together for about $50 per month. One of the biggest disadvantages of VoIP is that it does not function during a power outage or if your Internet connection goes down, though some VoIP services are able to forward calls to a landline or mobile phone during outages.

forum A Web page where individuals can post messages on specific subjects to initiate a discussion with a large group of individuals.

podcast A recorded audio or video file that can be played or downloaded via the Web.

Voice over Internet Protocol (VoIP) The process of placing telephone calls via the Internet.

Web conferences typically include both audio and video, take place via a personal computer or mobile device, and are used by businesses and individuals. A basic Web conference, such as a video call between individuals, can be performed via any online communications program or app that supports video phone calls. While some of these programs support multiple participants (see Exhibit 5-16), business Web conferences that require multiple participants or other communications tools, such as a shared whiteboard or the ability for attendees to share the content of their computer screens, may need to use a Web conferencing service, such as WebEx, or a premium service from Skype or another messaging service instead. Business Web conferencing is often used for meetings between individuals located in different geographical locations as well as for employee training, sales presentations, customer support, and other business applications.

EXHIBIT 5-16 WEB CONFERENCING

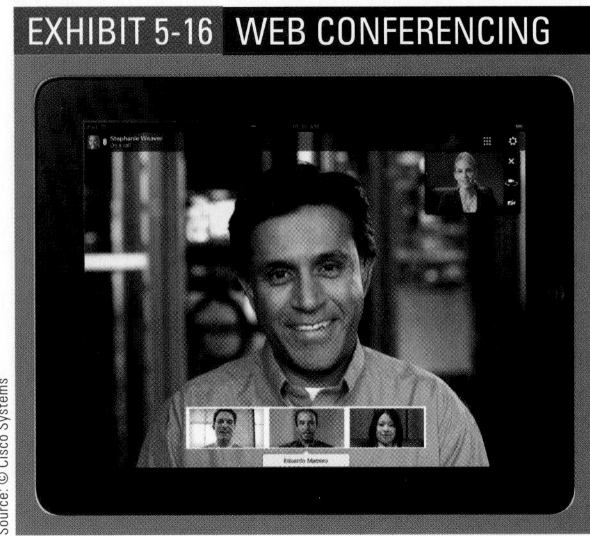

Source: © Cisco Systems

Webinars (Web seminars) are similar to Web conferences but typically have a designated presenter and an audience. Although interaction with the audience is usually included, a Webinar is typically more one-way communication than a Web conference.

Web conference A face-to-face meeting that takes place via the Web.

Webinar A seminar presented via the Web.

Web-based training (WBT) Instruction delivered on an individual basis via the Web.

distance learning An online learning environment in which the student is physically located away from the instructor and other students.

social networking site A site that enables individuals to connect and interact with other individuals.

5-5b Online Education

Online education is a rapidly growing Internet activity. For example, **Web-based training (WBT)** refers to any instruction delivered via the Web. It is commonly used for employee training as well as for delivering instruction in an educational setting. **Distance learning** occurs whenever students take classes from a location that is different from the one where the delivery of instruction takes place. Distance learning typically includes Web-based training and is available through many high schools, colleges, and universities as well as organizations that provide professional certifications. Distance learning can be used to learn just one task or new skill or it can be used to complete a college course or an entire degree program. Online education can also include using online syllabi and assignments, forums for class discussions, and learning management systems (such as Blackboard) to deliver course content, manage assignments and grades, and more.

One advantage of Web-based training and distance learning is that each user can learn at his or her own pace. Another advantage is that content can be updated as needed. One disadvantage is the possibility of technological problems. Because students need a working computer and Internet connection to access the material, they cannot participate if their computer, their Internet connection, or the Web server hosting the material goes down. Some educators have concerns about the lack of face-to-face contact with Web-based training and distance learning. They also have concerns related to security, such as the difficulty in ensuring that the appropriate student is completing assignments or taking exams. To try to prevent cheating, some distance learning programs require students to go physically to a testing center to take a test or to find an acceptable test proctor, such as an educator at a nearby school or a commanding officer for military personnel. Other options are using smart cards, fingerprint scans, and other means to authenticate students taking an online exam from a remote location.

5-5c Social Media

A **social networking site** can be loosely defined as any site that enables individuals to connect and interact with other individuals, such as by following each other's activities and posting messages. Some examples are Facebook and Google+, which allow users to post information about themselves for others to read; Meetup, which connects people in specific geographic areas with common hobbies and interests; and LinkedIn, which is used for business networking. The collection of social networking sites and other online platforms used to transmit or share information with a broad audience is referred to as **social media**. In addition to social networks, social media includes media sharing sites like YouTube and Flickr, microblogging sites like Twitter, and social curation sites like Digg, Reddit, and Pinterest that allow individuals to share Web content with others. Social media activities can be performed via personal computers, though the use of mobile social networking—social networks accessed with a smartphone or other mobile device—is more common today, making social networking a real-time, on-the-go activity. Some reasons for this include that most individuals carry a smartphone with them all the time, many individuals like to communicate with others via the Web while they are on the go, and smartphones enable location applications to be integrated into the social media experience.

Social networking sites are used most often to communicate with existing friends. Facebook, for instance, allows you to post photos, videos, music, status updates, and other content. You can also chat with Facebook friends who are currently online and comment on the posts shown on your friends' Facebook pages. For privacy purposes, you can limit access to your Facebook page to the individuals you identify, such as just to your Facebook friends.

In addition to being used for personal activities, social media is also viewed as a business marketing tool. For instance, Facebook and YouTube are often used by businesses, political candidates, emerging musicians, and other professionals or professional organizations to increase their online presence (see Exhibit 5-17). There are also social networking sites designed for children and families, such as to exchange messages, view online task lists, and access a shared family calendar.

Social media is also increasingly being integrated with other online activities. For example, you can exchange messages or have video calls with your friends from within Google+ or Facebook; you can share YouTube videos via an e-mail message, a video call, or one of your social networking pages from a YouTube video page; and you can view your friends' Facebook updates in Skype. In addition, many Web sites include buttons to allow visitors to easily access the business's Facebook page or log in to the site using the visitor's social media logon credentials.

5-5d Online Entertainment

There are an ever-growing number of ways to use the Web for entertainment purposes, such as listening to music, watching TV and videos, and playing online games. Music can be listened to or downloaded via a computer or mobile device. Downloaded music can be played directly from that device. However, online music is often accessed via streaming online music, such as via Pandora or iHeartRadio (see Exhibit 5-18).

EXHIBIT 5-17 FACEBOOK

Source: © Throw the Fight www.facebook.com/throwthefight, www.throwthefight.com

EXHIBIT 5-18 ONLINE ENTERTAINMENT

© Roman Samokhin/Shutterstock.com; © iHeartMedia, Inc.; © Barnesandnoble.com llc

social media The collection of social networking sites and other online platforms used to transmit or share information with a broad audience.

Watching TV shows, videos, and movies online is another very popular type of online entertainment. Online videos are widely available. For example, YouTube alone streams one billion video views per day. A wide variety of TV shows and movies are also available online. Some, such as news broadcasts and sporting events, can be watched live, but most are streamed on demand at the user's convenience. For example, you can watch episodes of your favorite network shows via Web sites for ABC, CBS, FOX, and other TV networks; you can also watch TV shows and movies via third-party streaming services such as Amazon Instant Video, Netflix, and Hulu Plus (shown in Exhibit 5-18). These services may include some free content; other content is typically available via a monthly subscription or a fee for each TV episode or movie watched. A new trend is the development of TV shows that are only available online, such as *Alpha House* on Amazon and *Arrested Development* and *House of Cards* on Netflix.

Online gaming is another common online entertainment activity. Many Web sites—especially children's Web sites—include games for visitors to play. There are also sites whose sole purpose is hosting games that can be played online. Some of the games are designed to be played alone or with just one other person. Others, called online multiplayer games, are designed to be played online against many other online gamers. Online multiplayer games, such as Doom, EverQuest, and Final Fantasy, are especially popular in countries such as South Korea that have readily available high-speed Internet connections and high levels of Internet use in general. Internet-enabled gaming consoles, such as recent versions of the PlayStation, Xbox, and Wii consoles, can also be used for multiplayer online gaming. For individuals who find reading relaxing, there is also a huge amount of online books and magazines that can be downloaded and read via a personal computer, tablet, or mobile device.

5-5e E-Commerce

Online shopping and online investing are examples of **e-commerce**—performing financial transactions online. It is very common today to order products, buy and sell stock, pay bills, and manage financial accounts online. However, because online fraud, credit card fraud, and identity theft (a situation in which someone gains enough personal information to pose as another person) are continuing to grow rapidly, it is important to be cautious when participating in online financial activities. To protect yourself, use a credit card or online payment service such as PayPal whenever possible when purchasing goods or services online so that any fraudulent activities can be disputed. Also, be sure to enter your payment information only on a secure Web page (look for a URL that begins with *https* instead of *http*) and don't perform any financial transactions via a public Wi-Fi hotspot unless you are using a VPN. Online financial accounts should also be protected with strong user passwords that are changed frequently.

e-commerce The act of performing financial transactions online.

Online shopping is commonly used to purchase both physical products—such as clothing, shoes, and furniture—as well as downloadable products—such as software, movies, and e-books—via Web pages like the L.L.Bean Web page shown in Exhibit 5-19.

EXHIBIT 5-19 AN ONLINE SHOPPING SITE

Source: © L.L.Bean® is a registered trademark of L.L.Bean Inc.

Online auctions are the most common ways to purchase items online from other individuals. Sellers list items for sale on an auction site, such as eBay, and sometimes pay a small listing fee as well as a commission to the auction site when the item is sold. Individuals can visit the auction site and enter bids on auction items until the end of the auction. Another common way to purchase items from other individuals is via online classified ads, such as those posted on the popular Craigslist site.

Many banks today offer online banking as a free service to their customers to enable customers to check balances on all their accounts, view cashed checks and other transactions, deposit checks remotely, pay bills electronically, and perform other activities related to their bank accounts. Online banking is continually growing and can be performed via a computer or smartphone. Online banking is typically performed via the bank's Web site or mobile app, though some activities at some banks can be carried out via text message.

Buying and selling stocks, bonds, mutual funds, and other types of securities is referred to as online investing and is another common e-commerce application. Although stock quotes are available on many search and news sites, trading stocks and other securities requires an online broker. Common online investing services include the ability to order sales and purchases; access performance histories, corporate news, and other useful investment information; and set up an online portfolio that displays the status of the stocks you specify.

5-5f **Product, Corporate, Government, and Other Information**

The Web is a very useful tool for locating product and corporate information. Manufacturer and retailer Web sites often include product specifications, instruction manuals, and other information that is useful to consumers before or after they purchase a product. Numerous consumer review sites, such as Epinions.com, are also available to help purchasers evaluate their options before buying a product online or in a physical store. For investors and consumers, a variety of corporate information is available online, from both company Web sites and sites, such as hoovers.com, that offer free or fee-based corporate information.

Government information is also widely available on the Internet. Most state and federal agencies have Web sites to provide information to citizens, such as government publications and forms. You can also perform a variety of tasks, such as downloading tax forms and filing your tax returns online. In addition, many cities, counties, and states allow you to register to vote, view property tax information, or renew your driver's license or car registration online (see Exhibit 5-20).

Other information available online includes online newspapers and news sites that provide access to up-to-the minute news, and reference sites that provide access to maps, dictionaries, and other reference resources.

EXHIBIT 5-20 A GOVERNMENT SITE

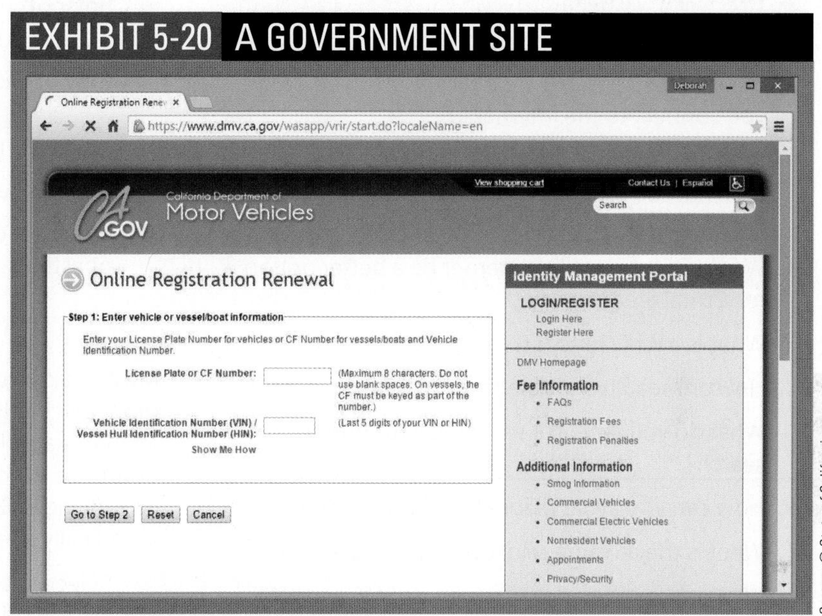

Source: © State of California

STUDY TOOLS 5

READY TO STUDY? IN THE BOOK, YOU CAN:

- ☐ Rip out the Chapter Review Card, which includes key terms and key chapter concepts.

ONLINE AT WWW.CENGAGEBRAIN.COM, YOU CAN:

- ☐ Review key concepts from the chapter in a short video.
- ☐ Explore how email works with the interactive infographic.
- ☐ Practice what you've learned with more Practice It and On Your Own exercises.
- ☐ Prepare for tests with quizzes.
- ☐ Review the key terms with flashcards.

QUIZ YOURSELF

1. What is ARPANET?
2. What is an Internet service provider?
3. What three decisions are typically involved before you connect to the Internet?
4. Are all Internet connections direct Internet connections? If not, list one type of Internet connection that is not a direct connection.
5. Would DSL or satellite Internet be a better option for a rural area? Explain.
6. What is a Wi-Fi hotspot?
7. How are search site databases typically updated?
8. What do you type in a search box to conduct a search?
9. How can you avoid plagiarizing Web content?
10. What is the advantage of using Web-based email?
11. What is the difference between an SMS and MMS text message?
12. What is the difference between a blog and a wiki?
13. What is a podcast?
14. List the biggest advantage and the biggest disadvantage of VoIP.
15. What is a Webinar?
16. What type of Web site is Facebook?
17. Does all online music need to be downloaded to your device in order to be listened to? Explain.
18. What is e-commerce?

PRACTICE IT

Practice It 5-1

An increasing number of public locations offer Wi-Fi hotspots for public use. You can often find them in public libraries, coffee shops, bookstores, and some restaurants.

1. Find one location in your local area that offers public Wi-Fi access, and then either visit the location or research it online to find out how the hotspot works.
2. Is there a fee to use the hotspot?
3. If not, do you have to make a purchase to use the hotspot?
4. If so, how much does it cost, how long can you use the hotspot for that fee, and how is payment made?
5. Do you need to be assigned a username or key (such as a WPA or WPA2 key) before you can use the service?
6. Prepare a one-page summary that answers these questions and submit it to your instructor.

Practice It 5-2

Most search sites include advanced features to help you more efficiently find the information you are searching for. For example, some allow special operators or symbols to be used with a search phrase, and some include an Advanced Search form you can complete to more specifically state what you are searching for.

1. Select one search site, such as Google or Bing, and research the advanced search options available on that site.
2. Does the site support special characters or search operators? If so, what are they and how do they work?
3. Does the site offer an Advanced Search page? If so, what options are available? For instance, can you search for specific types of files or recently updated Web pages?
4. Try out the advanced search options available on your site. Do you find them useful? Why or why not?
5. Prepare a one-page summary that answers these questions and submit it to your instructor.

ON YOUR OWN

On Your Own 5-1

Social networks (such as Facebook and Google+) are very popular with individuals. However, some individuals are moving from casual social networking use to compulsive or addictive behavior.

1. Investigate either Facebook addiction or Internet addiction.
2. What is it? How common is it?
3. What are some of the warning signs?
4. Is there an actual medical disorder associated with it? If so, what is it and how is it treated?
5. Find one example in a news or journal article of a person who was "addicted" to using a social networking site or other online activity. Why was that person's behavior considered addictive? Was that person able to modify his or her behavior?
6. Have you ever been concerned about becoming addicted to any Internet activities? Why or why not?
7. Prepare a one-page summary that answers these questions and submit it to your instructor.

Part 2
NETWORKS and THE INTERNET

6 | Security and Privacy

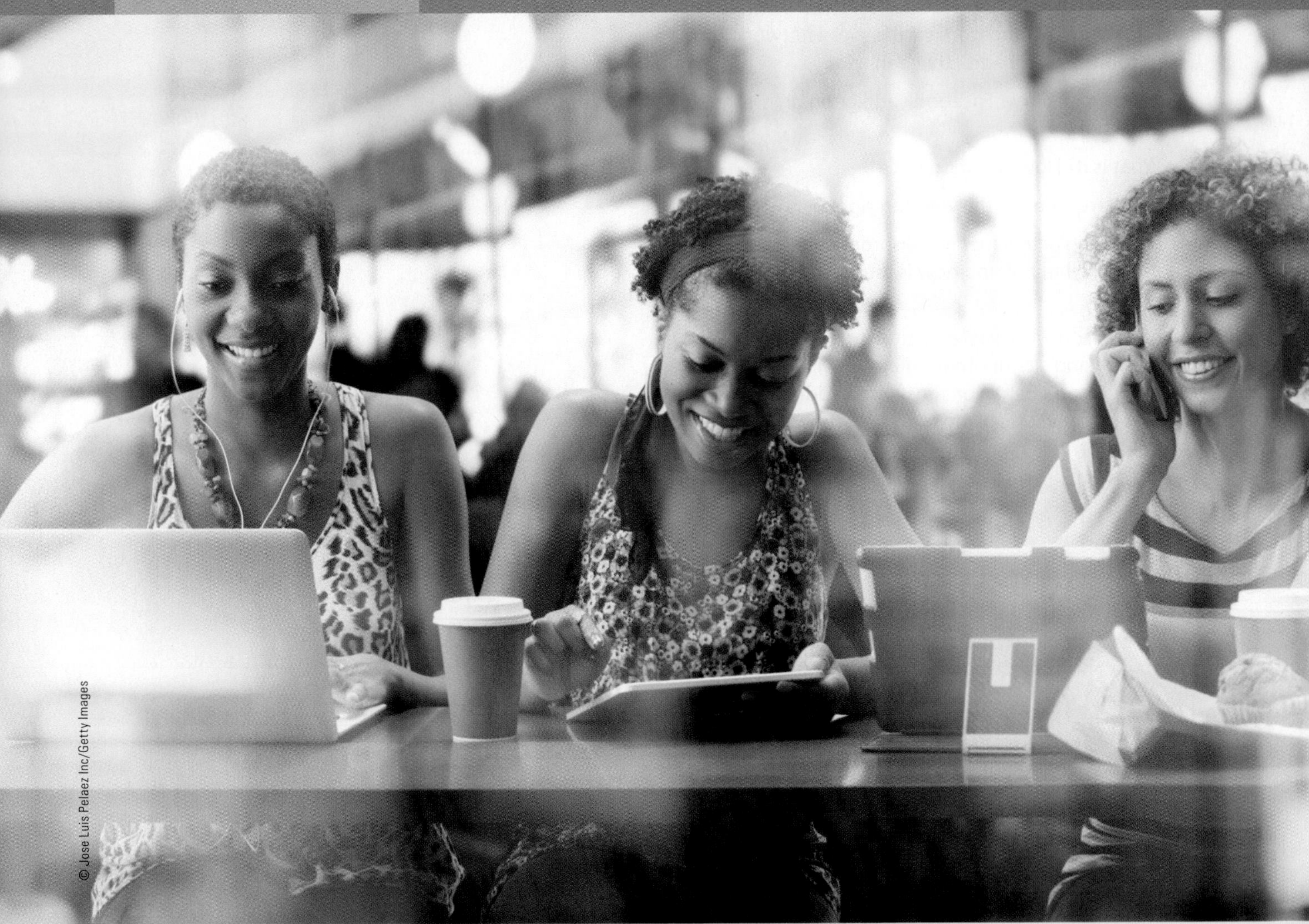

LEARNING OBJECTIVES

After studying the material in this chapter, you will be able to:

6-1 Explain the importance of network and Internet security

6-2 Define unauthorized access and use and list some precautions

6-3 Define computer sabotage and list some precautions

6-4 Describe online theft, online fraud, and other dot cons and list some precautions

6-5 Describe cyberstalking and other personal safety concerns and list some precautions

6-6 List some personal computer security risks and identify some precautions

6-7 Identify privacy concerns and list some precautions

6-8 Discuss current security and privacy legislation

After finishing this chapter, go to **PAGE 183** for **STUDY TOOLS**.

6-1 UNDERSTANDING SECURITY CONCERNS

Computers, networks, and the Internet help many workers be more efficient and effective as well as add convenience and enjoyment to our personal lives. However, they also open up new possibilities for problems, such as hardware or data loss due to a system malfunction, hardware theft, or a security breach. Security concerns related to computers, networks, and the Internet range from someone stealing your computer or mobile device, to a malicious program making your computer function abnormally, to a hacker using your personal information to make fraudulent purchases, to someone harassing you online.

Many of these security concerns can be categorized as computer crimes. **Computer crime**—sometimes referred to as **cybercrime**—includes any illegal act involving a computer. Cybercrime is frequently committed using the Internet or another computer network and many include theft of financial assets or information, manipulating data, and acts of sabotage. It is a multibillion-dollar business that is often conducted by seasoned criminals. According to the FBI, organized crime organizations in many countries are increasingly turning to computer crime to target millions of potential victims.

With some security concerns, such as when a program changes your browser's home page, the consequence may be just an annoyance. In other cases, such as when someone steals your laptop containing all your passwords and other sensitive data or steals your identity and purchases items using your name and credit card number, the consequences are much more serious. In addition, with the growing use of wireless networks, social media, cloud computing, mobile computing, and individuals accessing company networks remotely, paired with an increasing number of security and privacy regulations that businesses need to comply with, computer, network, and Internet security has never been more important or more challenging. All computer users should be aware of the security concerns surrounding computer, network, and Internet use, and they should take appropriate precautions.

6-2 UNAUTHORIZED ACCESS AND UNAUTHORIZED USE

Unauthorized access occurs whenever an individual gains access to a computer, network, file, or other computing resource without permission. **Unauthorized use** is using a computing resource for unauthorized activities, even if the user is authorized to access that resource. For instance, students may be authorized to access the Internet via a campus computer lab, but some use, such as viewing pornography, would likely be deemed off-limits and, consequently, unauthorized use. For employees, checking personal email or visiting personal Facebook pages using work devices might be classified as unauthorized use.

Unauthorized access and many types of unauthorized use are criminal offenses in the United States and many other countries. Whether a specific act constitutes unauthorized use or is illegal depends on the circumstances as well as the specific company or institution involved. To explain acceptable computer use to their employees, students, or other users, many organizations and educational institutions publish guidelines for behavior, often called **codes of conduct**.

6-2a Hacking

Hacking refers to the act of breaking into a computer or network. It can be performed in person if the hacker has physical access to the computer or network being hacked, but it is more often performed via the Internet or another network. Hacking in the United States and many other countries is a crime.

Typically, the motivation for hacking is to steal data, sabotage a computer system, or perform some other type of illegal act. In particular, the theft of consumer data, such as credit card numbers, has increased dramatically over the past several years. A growing trend is to hack into

computer crime (cybercrime) Any illegal act involving a computer.

unauthorized access Access gained to a computer, network, file, or other computing resource without permission.

unauthorized use Use of a computing resource for unauthorized activities.

code of conduct Guidelines for behavior for students, employees, or other users that explain acceptable computer use.

hacking The act of breaking into a computing resource.

TRENDING...

SECURING A WIRELESS HOME ROUTER

Securing a home wireless network prevents unauthorized individuals from using it. Security settings are specified in the router's configuration screen, such as the one shown here. To open this screen, type the IP address assigned to your router (such as 192.168.0.1—check your router's documentation for its default IP address and username) in your browser's Address bar. Use the default password to log on the first time, and then change the password using the configuration screen to prevent unauthorized individuals from changing your router settings. To secure the router, first enter the network name (called the SSID) that you want associated with the router. Then, select the appropriate security mode, such as WPA or WPA2, and type a secure passphrase to be used to access the network. For additional security you can disable SSID broadcast to hide your router name from view or use MAC address filtering to specify the only devices (via their MAC addresses) that are allowed to access the network.

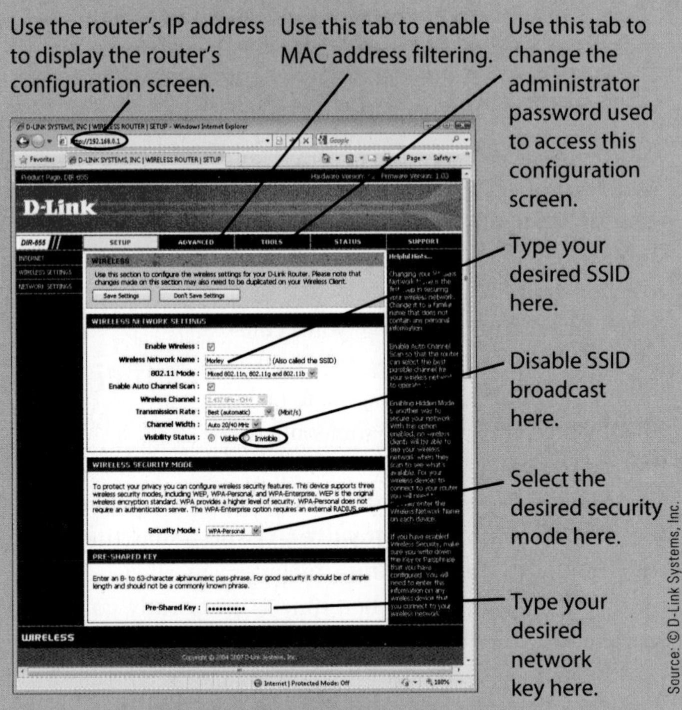

Use the router's IP address to display the router's configuration screen.
Use this tab to enable MAC address filtering.
Use this tab to change the administrator password used to access this configuration screen.
Type your desired SSID here.
Disable SSID broadcast here.
Select the desired security mode here.
Type your desired network key here.
D-Link

Source: © D-Link Systems, Inc.

a computer and use it in an illegal or unethical act, such as taking over an individual's computer, spying via a Web cam, generating spam, or hosting pornographic Web sites.

In addition to being a threat to individuals and businesses, hacking is also considered a serious threat to national security in the United States. The increased number of systems that are controlled by computers and are connected to the Internet, along with the continually improving abilities of hackers, has led to an increased risk of **cyberterrorism**—where terrorists launch attacks via the Internet. Current concerns include attacks by individual terrorists, as well as by other countries, against the computers controlling vital systems, such as those controlling the nation's power grids, banks, and water filtration facilities, as well as computers related to national defense, the airlines, and the stock market.

cyberterrorism An attack launched by terrorists via the Internet.

war driving Driving around an area with a Wi-Fi-enabled computer or mobile device to find a Wi-Fi network to access and use without authorization.

Wi-Fi piggybacking Accessing an unsecured Wi-Fi network without authorization.

Hackers often gain access via a wireless network. This is because wireless networks are widely used and they are easier to hack into than wired networks. In fact, it is possible to gain access to a wireless network just by being within range of a wireless access point, unless the access point is sufficiently protected. Although security features are built into wireless routers and other networking hardware, they are typically not enabled by default. As a result, many wireless networks belonging to businesses and individuals are left unsecured.

6-2b War Driving and Wi-Fi Piggybacking

Unauthorized use of a Wi-Fi network is called war driving or Wi-Fi piggybacking, depending on the location of the hacker at the time. **War driving** involves driving in a car with a portable device looking for unsecured Wi-Fi networks to connect to. **Wi-Fi piggybacking** is accessing someone else's unsecured Wi-Fi network from the hacker's current location without authorization. Both war driving and Wi-Fi piggybacking are ethically—if not legally—questionable acts. They can also lead to illegal behavior, such as individuals deciding to use credit card numbers or other data they run across for fraudulent purposes.

6-2c Interception of Communications

Instead of hacking into a computer or network, some criminals gain unauthorized access to data, files, messages, and other content as it is being sent over the Internet. For instance, unencrypted messages, files, logon information, and more sent over an unsecured wireless network can be captured and read by anyone within range using software designed for that purpose. In particular, proprietary corporate information and sensitive personal information is at risk if it is sent unsecured over the Internet or over a wireless home or corporate network. In addition, data on mobile devices with Bluetooth capabilities enabled can be accessed by other Bluetooth devices that are within range and any sensitive data stored on a smartphone can be accessed by a hacker if the phone is connected to an unsecured Wi-Fi network. With an increasing number of smartphone owners storing sensitive data (such as passwords for online banking and social media accounts and credit card numbers) on their devices, the risk of that data being intercepted is increasing.

Another way criminals can intercept credit and debit card information is during the card verification process; that is, intercepting the data from a card in real time as a purchase is being authorized. Often this occurs via packetsniffing software installed by hackers at payment terminals, such as restaurant cash registers or gas station credit/debit card readers. The software gathers credit card data during transactions and then sends it to the hacker.

6-2d Protecting Against Unauthorized Access and Unauthorized Use

The first step in protecting against unauthorized access and unauthorized use of a computer system is to ensure that only authorized individuals can access an organization's facilities and computer networks. In addition, organizations must ensure that authorized individuals can access only the resources that they are supposed to access. Access control systems are used for these purposes. They can be identification systems, which verify that the person trying to access the facility or system is listed as an authorized user, or authentication systems, which determine whether or not the person attempting access is actually who he or she claims to be. Specific types of access control systems include the following:

- **Possessed knowledge access system**—requires the person requesting access to provide information that only the authorized user is supposed to know, such as a username and its corresponding **password**, which is a secret combination of characters.
- **Possessed object access system**—requires the person requesting access to present an appropriate physical object, such as a smart card or a smartphone containing an appropriate micro SD card or NFC capability—see Exhibit 6-1).
- **Biometric access system**—requires the person requesting access to provide a particular unique biological characteristic (such as a fingerprint, a hand, or his or her voice or face, as shown in Exhibit 6-1) for identification.

EXHIBIT 6-1 ACCESS CONTROL SYSTEMS

USING A POSSESSED OBJECT

USING A BIOMETRIC CHARACTERISTIC

Source: HID Global Corporation; © Roman Samokhin/Shutterstock.com; Sensible Vision, Inc.

Another way to control access to a computer or network is to use a **firewall**, which is a security system that essentially creates a barrier between a computer or a network and the Internet. Firewalls are typically two-way, so they check all incoming and outgoing traffic and only allow authorized traffic through. Personal firewalls are software programs designed to protect home computers from hackers attempting to access those computers through their Internet connections. Personal firewalls can be stand-alone programs, such as the free Comodo Firewall program shown in Exhibit 6-2. They are also built into many operating systems, such as the Windows Firewall program. Many routers, modems, and other pieces of networking hardware also include built-in firewall capabilities to help secure the networks these devices are used with. Firewalls designed to protect business networks may be software-based, hardware-based, or a combination of the two. They can be used to prevent network access by hackers and other outsiders as well as to control employee Internet access.

password A secret combination of characters used to gain access to a computer, network, Web site, or other resource.

firewall A collection of hardware and/or software that protects a computer or computer network from unauthorized access.

EXHIBIT 6-2 PERSONAL FIREWALL

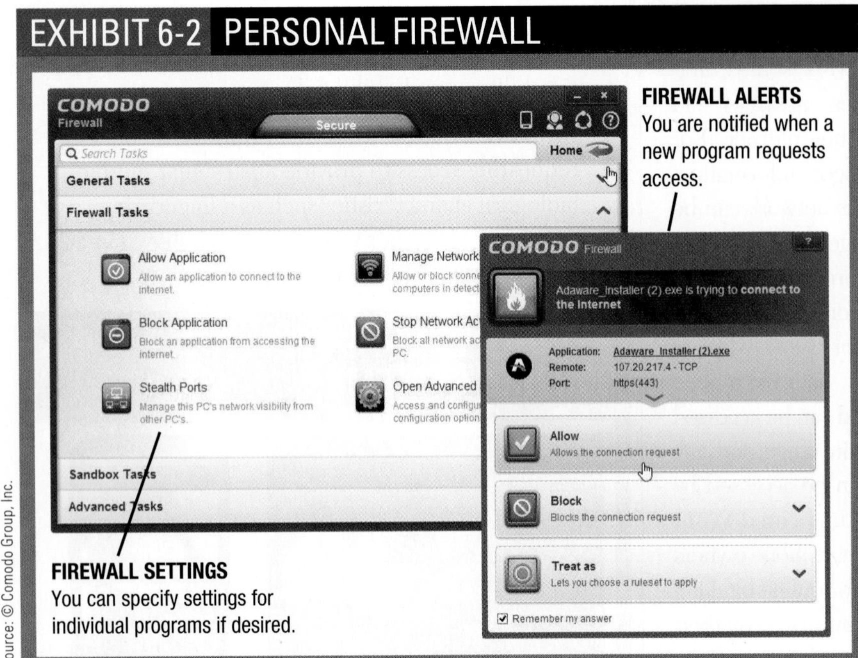

Source: © Comodo Group, Inc.

Firewalls work by closing down all external communications to unauthorized computers and programs. Business firewalls are set up by the network administrator and so those settings cannot be changed by end users. Individuals can change the settings for their personal firewall. For example, a user can choose to be notified when an application program on the computer is trying to access the Internet, to specify the programs that are allowed to access the Internet, or to block all incoming connections temporarily.

To protect data from being viewed by unauthorized individuals, you can use **encryption**, which is a way of temporarily converting data into a form that is unreadable until it is decrypted. Secure Wi-Fi networks and VPNs use encryption to secure data transferred over those networks. Encryption is also used with secure Web pages and can be used to secure files.

The most common security protocol used with secure Web pages is Transport Layer Protocol (TLP), though this protocol is still commonly referred to by the name of its predecessors Secure Sockets Layer (SSL) and Extended Validation Secure Sockets Layer (EV SSL). The URL for Web pages using TPL/SSL begins with *https:* instead of *http:*. Sensitive data, such as credit card numbers and Web site passwords, should be entered only on secure Web pages so that it is protected as it travels over the Internet.

Some Internet services, such as Skype calls and Hushmail email, are automatically encrypted. Encryption can also be added manually to a file or an email message before it is sent over the Internet to ensure that the content is unreadable if the file or message is

TRENDING...

TWO-FACTOR AUTHENTICATION

Two-factor authentication is the use of two different access control methods to authenticate a user. It usually combines some type of possessed knowledge (something you know) along with either a possessed object (something you have) or a biometric feature (something you are). Two-factor authentication adds an additional level of security because hackers are much less likely to be able to gain access to two different required factors.

One type of two-factor authentication uses a conventional username and password combination in conjunction with a one-time password (OTP) that is generated and sent to your smartphone when you are ready to log on to an account. In order to finish logging on to the account, you must enter the OTP sent to your smartphone (see the Facebook example in the accompanying illustration). Two-factor authentication systems are common in many countries, and their use is growing in the United States.

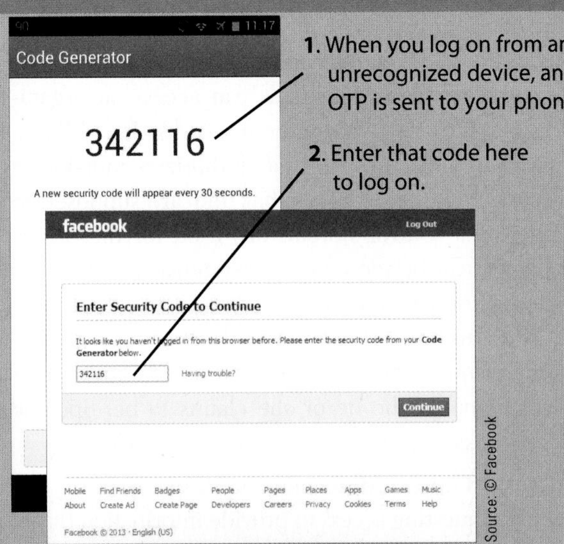

Source: © Facebook

EXHIBIT 6-3 HOW PUBLIC KEY ENCRYPTION WORKS

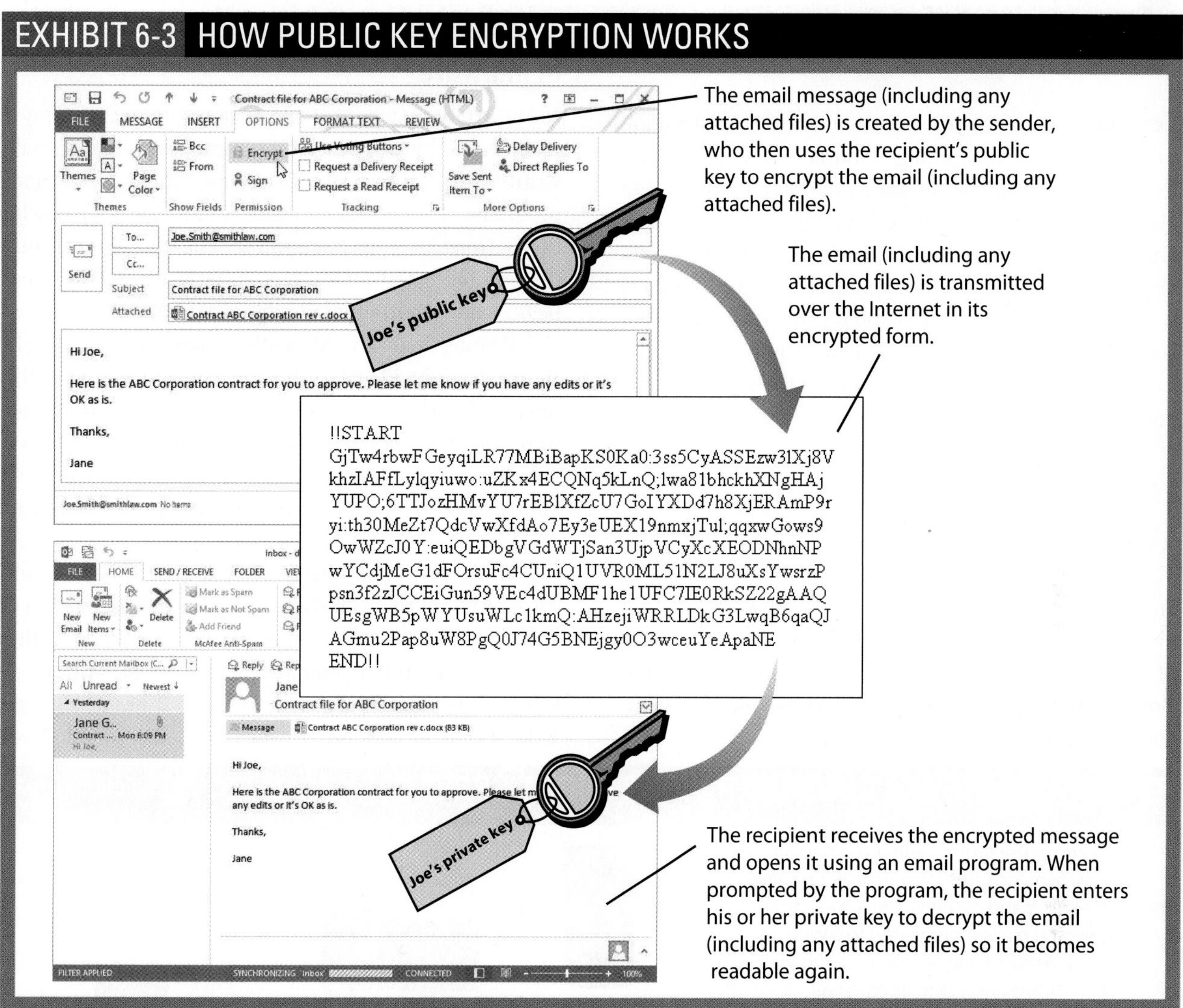

intercepted during transit. In addition to securing files during transit, encryption can be used to protect the files stored on a hard drive or other storage medium so they will be unreadable if opened by an unauthorized person. Increasingly, computers and storage devices, particularly those used with portable computers, are self-encrypting, which means they encrypt all data automatically and invisibly to the user.

The email message (including any attached files) is created by the sender, who then uses the recipient's public key to encrypt the email (including any attached files).
Joe's public key
The email (including any attached files) is transmitted over the Internet in its encrypted form.
!!START
END!!
Joe's private key
The recipient receives the encrypted message and opens it using an email program. When prompted by the program, the recipient enters his or her private key to decrypt the email (including any attached files) so it becomes readable again.

The two most common types of encryption are private key encryption and public key encryption. **Private key encryption** uses a single, secret private key, which is essentially a password, to both encrypt and decrypt a file or message. Private key encryption can be used to send files securely to others, but the recipient must know the private key. Private key encryption is most often used to encrypt files on a computer or storage medium.

Public key encryption uses two encryption keys to encrypt and decrypt documents. Specifically, public key encryption uses a private key and a public key that are related mathematically to each other and have been assigned to a particular individual. An individual's public key is not secret and is available for anyone to use, but the corresponding private key is secret and is used only by the individual to whom it was assigned. The recipient's public key is used to encrypt a file or email message; the recipient's private key is used to decrypt the encrypted contents (see Exhibit 6-3 for an example of sending an encrypted email).

two-factor authentication Using two different methods to authenticate a user.

encryption A method of scrambling content to make it unreadable if an unauthorized user intercepts it.

private key encryption A type of encryption that uses a single key to encrypt and decrypt a file or message.

public key encryption A type of encryption that uses a key pair to encrypt and decrypt a file or message.

6-3 COMPUTER SABOTAGE

Computer sabotage—acts of malicious destruction to a computer or computing resource—is another common type of computer crime. Computer sabotage can take several forms, including launching a harmful program, altering the content of a Web site, or changing data or programs located on a computer. Computer sabotage is illegal in the United States and is estimated to cost billions of dollars per year, primarily for labor costs related to correcting the problems caused by the sabotage, lost productivity, and lost sales.

6-3a Botnets

A computer that is controlled by a hacker or other computer criminal is referred to as a **bot**; a group of bots that are controlled by one individual and can work together in a coordinated fashion is called a **botnet**. Millions of U.S. computers are unknowingly part of a botnet. Botnets are frequently set up to perform computer sabotage as well as to steal personal data.

6-3b Computer Viruses and Other Types of Malware

Malware is a generic term that refers to any type of malicious software. Malware programs are intentionally written to perform destructive acts, such as damaging programs, deleting files, erasing a hard drive, or slowing the performance of a computer. This damage can take place immediately after a computer is infected, or it can begin when a particular condition is met.

Writing malware or posting malware code on the Internet is not illegal, although it is considered highly unethical and irresponsible behavior. Distributing malware, on the other hand, is illegal. Malware can infect any device, including personal computers, smartphones, tablets, and printers, that contain computing hardware and software.

One type of malware is a **computer virus**—a software program that is installed without the permission or knowledge of the computer user, that is designed to alter the way a computer operates, and that can replicate itself to infect any new media to which it has access (see Exhibit 6-4). Computer viruses are often embedded into

EXHIBIT 6-4 HOW A COMPUTER VIRUS MIGHT SPREAD

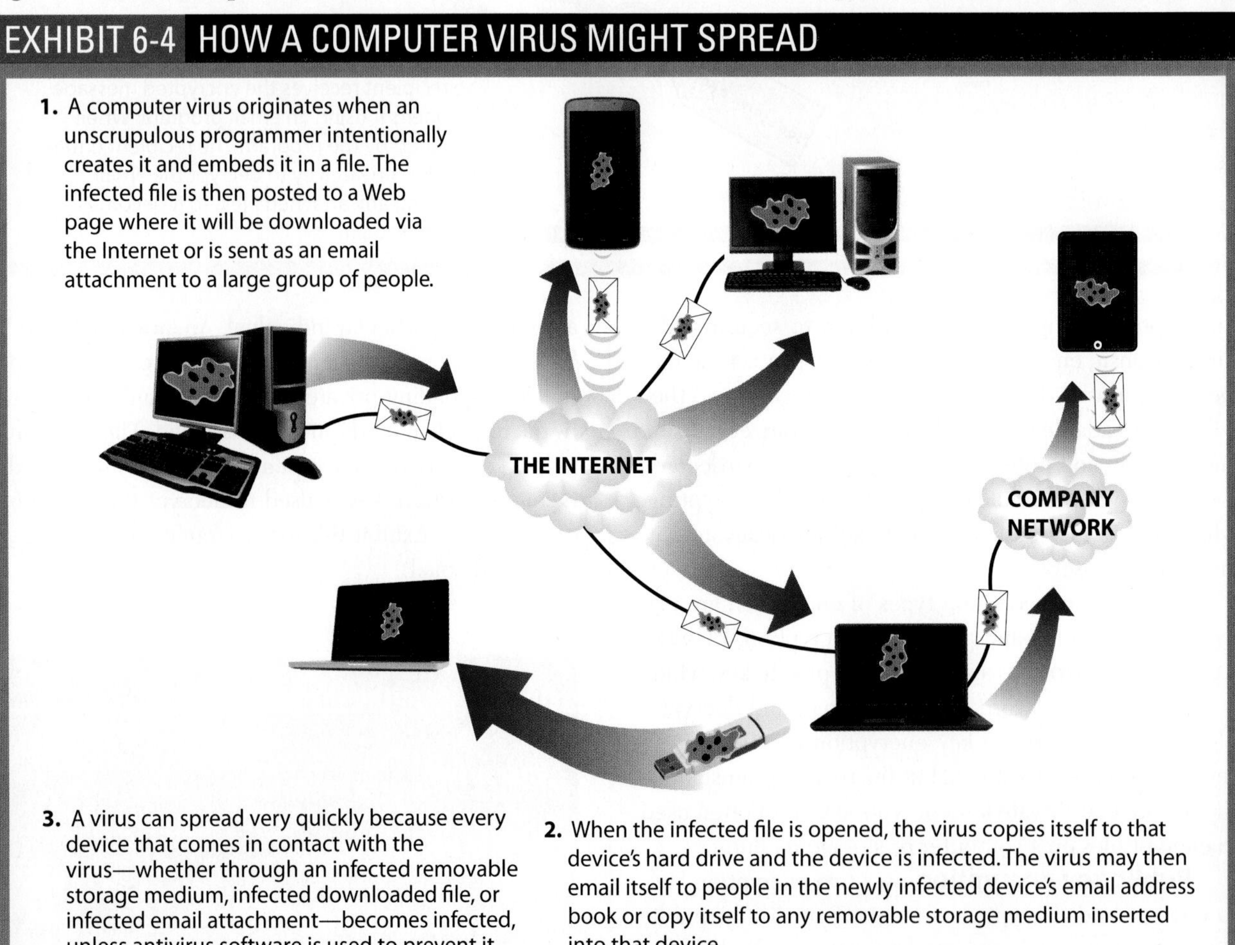
1. A computer virus originates when an unscrupulous programmer intentionally creates it and embeds it in a file. The infected file is then posted to a Web page where it will be downloaded via the Internet or is sent as an email attachment to a large group of people.
THE INTERNET
COMPANY NETWORK
2. When the infected file is opened, the virus copies itself to that device's hard drive and the device is infected. The virus may then email itself to people in the newly infected device's email address book or copy itself to any removable storage medium inserted into that device.
3. A virus can spread very quickly because every device that comes in contact with the virus—whether through an infected removable storage medium, infected downloaded file, or infected email attachment—becomes infected, unless antivirus software is used to prevent it.

program or data files, such as games, videos, and music files downloaded from Web pages or shared via a P2P service. They are spread when an infected file is downloaded, transferred to a new device via an infected removable storage medium, or emailed to another device. Viruses can also be installed when a recipient clicks a link in an instant message or an email or loads a Web page that contains a malicious advertisement that installs malware. Once a copy of the infected file reaches a new device, the virus embeds itself into program, data, or system files on the new device and remains there, affecting that device according to its programmed instructions, until it is discovered and removed.

Another common form of malware is a **computer worm**, which is a malicious program that is designed to cause damage by creating copies of its code and sending those copies to other devices via a network. Often, a worm is sent to other devices as an email attachment. Usually, after the infected email attachment is opened by an individual, the worm inflicts its damage and then automatically sends copies of itself to other devices via the Internet or a private network, using addresses in the email address book located on the newly infected device.

Typically, worms do not require any user action to infect the user's device. Instead, a worm scans the Internet looking for computers and other devices that are vulnerable to that particular worm and sends a copy of itself to those devices to infect them. Other worms just require the user to view an infected email message or insert an infected removable storage medium into the device to infect that device. Still other worms are specifically written to take advantage of newly discovered security holes in operating systems and email programs.

A **Trojan horse** is a type of malware that masquerades as something else—usually an application program. When the seemingly legitimate program is downloaded or installed, the Trojan horse infects the device. Many recent Trojan horses masquerade as normal, ongoing activities, such as the Windows Update service or a warning from a security program, to try to trick unsuspecting users into downloading another malware program or buying a useless program. For instance, after a rogue antimalware app like the one shown in Exhibit 6-5 is installed, the malware takes over the device, displaying bogus warning messages or scan results indicating that the device is infected with malware and prompting the user to buy a fake protection program to get rid of the "malware." These rogue programs also often interfere with normal activities, such as blocking access to Web sites and changing the computer settings, and they can be difficult to remove.

EXHIBIT 6-5 ROGUE ANTIMALWARE APP

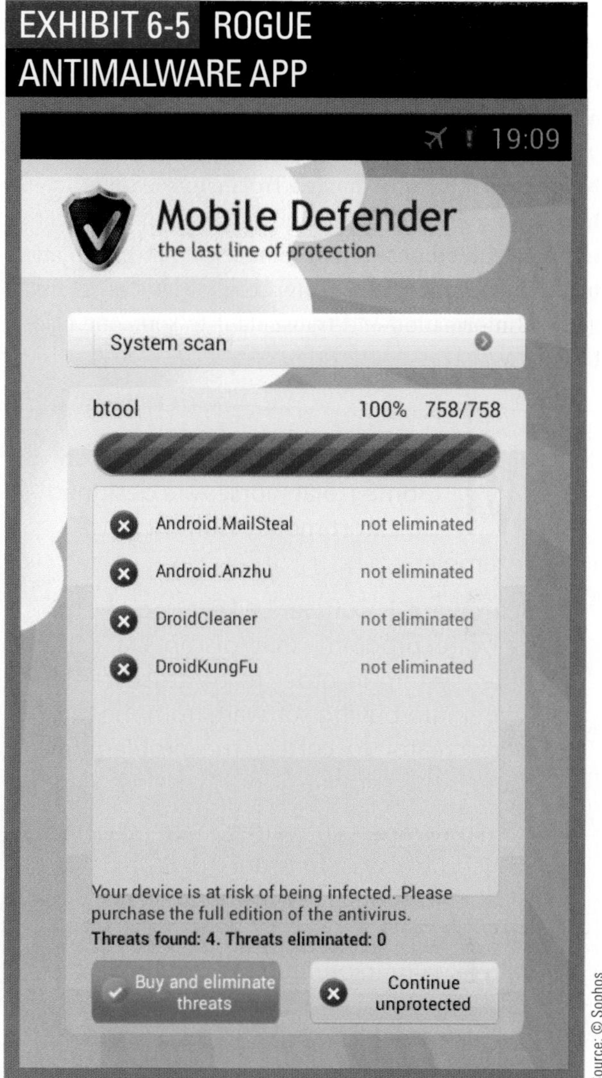

Source: © Sophos

computer sabotage An act of malicious destruction to a computer or computing resource.

bot A computer that is controlled by a hacker or other computer criminal.

botnet A group of bots that are controlled by one individual.

malware Any type of malicious software.

computer virus A software program installed without the user's knowledge that is designed to alter the way a computer operates or to cause harm to the computer system.

computer worm A malicious program designed to spread rapidly to a large number of computers by sending copies of itself to other computers.

Trojan horse A malicious program that masquerades as something else.

Unlike viruses and worms, Trojan horses cannot replicate themselves. Trojan horses are usually spread by being downloaded from the Internet, though they may also be sent as an email attachment, either from the Trojan horse author or from individuals who forward it, not realizing that the program is a Trojan horse. Some Trojan horses are designed to find private information located on infected computers and then send that information to the malware creator. Software like this that secretly gathers information and transmits it to someone else is called **spyware**.

FYI

TYPES OF TROJAN HORSES

Some Trojan horses are designed to extort money from victims. For example:

- **Scareware** is software, like a rogue anti-malware program, that disrupts a computer system in order to try to scare the owner into buying software from the malware creator to correct the problem, although this software is often useless.
- **Ransomware** is software that freezes up a device, displays a message that the device has been used for illegal activity, and demands that the user pay a fine to the malware creator in order to unlock the device.

6-3c Denial of Service (DoS) Attacks

A **denial of service (DoS)** attack is an act of sabotage that attempts to flood a network server or Web server with so many requests for action that the server shuts down or simply can no longer handle requests. If enough useless traffic is generated, the server has no resources left to deal with legitimate requests, as illustrated in Exhibit 6-6.

DoS attacks today are often directed toward popular or controversial sites and typically are carried out via multiple computers. This is known as a **distributed denial of service (DDoS) attack**. DDoS attacks are often performed by botnets created by hackers; the computers in the botnet participate in the attacks without the owners' knowledge.

6-3d Data, Program, or Web Site Alteration

Another type of computer sabotage occurs when a hacker breaches a computer system to delete or alter the data and programs located there. For example, a student might try to hack into a school database to change his or her grade, or a hacker might change a program located on a company server to steal money or information.

Data on Web sites can also be altered by hackers. For instance, social media accounts are being increasingly targeted by hackers. It is also becoming more common for hackers to compromise legitimate Web sites and then use those sites to perform malware attacks. For example, a hacker can alter a Web site to display an official-looking message that informs the user that a particular software program must be downloaded to use the site, or a hacker might post a rogue ad on a legitimate site that redirects the user to a malware site instead of the site for the product featured in the ad. According to a report by security company Websense, more than half of the Web sites classified as malicious are actually legitimate Web sites that have been compromised.

6-3e Protecting Against Computer Sabotage

One of the most important protections against computer sabotage is using up-to-date **security software**. Security software typically includes a variety of security features, such as a firewall; protection against viruses, spyware, and bots; and protection against some types of online fraud. One of the most important components of security software is **antivirus software**, which protects against computer viruses and other types of malware. Like most security software components, antivirus software runs continuously to monitor the computer or other device being used, including monitoring incoming messages, Web page content, and downloaded files to prevent malicious software from executing. Many antivirus programs also automatically scan devices when they are connected to a USB port. Another component of security software is antispyware software, which is used to find and remove spyware.

spyware A program designed to find private information on a computer and then send that information to the creator of the malware program.

denial of service (DoS) attack An act of sabotage that attempts to flood a network server or a Web server with so much activity that it is unable to function.

distributed denial of service (DDoS) attack A DoS attack carried out by multiple computers.

security software Software, typically a suite of programs, used to protect a device against a variety of threats.

antivirus software Software used to detect and eliminate computer viruses and other types of malware.

EXHIBIT 6-6 HOW A DoS ATTACK MIGHT WORK

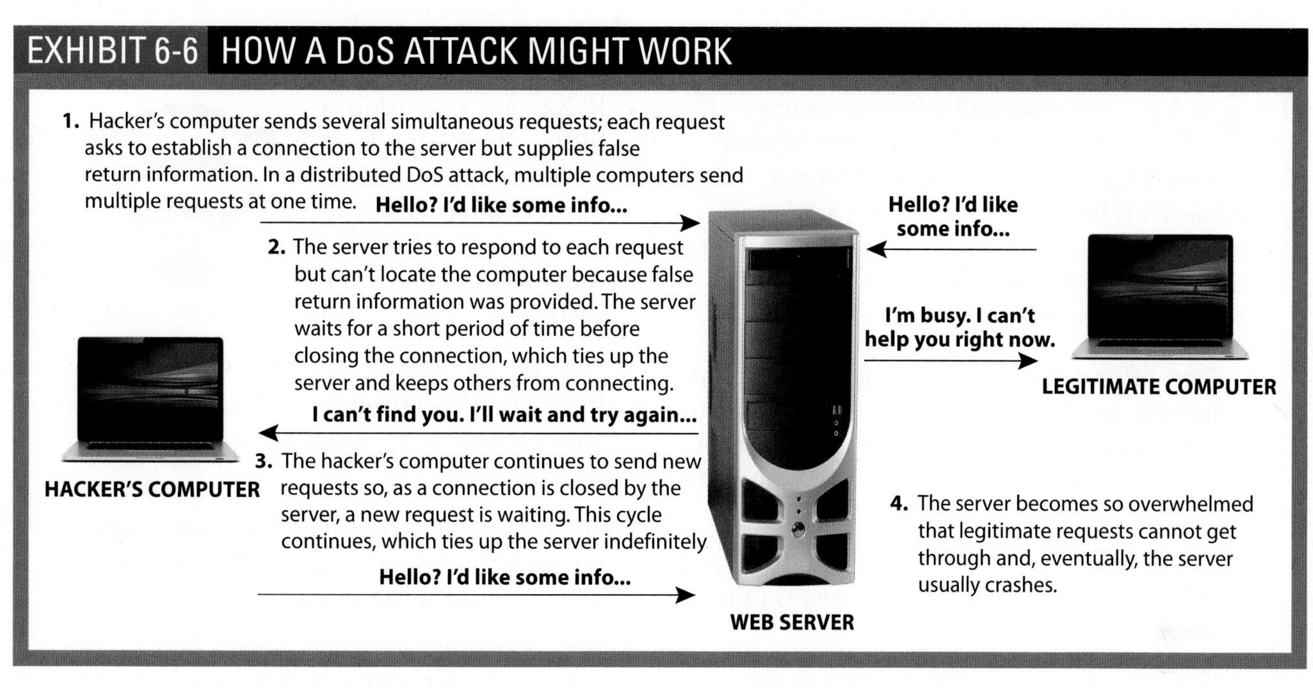

1. Hacker's computer sends several simultaneous requests; each request asks to establish a connection to the server but supplies false return information. In a distributed DoS attack, multiple computers send multiple requests at one time.
Hello? I'd like some info...
2. The server tries to respond to each request but can't locate the computer because false return information was provided. The server waits for a short period of time before closing the connection, which ties up the server and keeps others from connecting.
I can't find you. I'll wait and try again...
3. The hacker's computer continues to send new requests so, as a connection is closed by the server, a new request is waiting. This cycle continues, which ties up the server indefinitely
Hello? I'd like some info...
HACKER'S COMPUTER
WEB SERVER
Hello? I'd like some info...
I'm busy. I can't help you right now.
LEGITIMATE COMPUTER
4. The server becomes so overwhelmed that legitimate requests cannot get through and, eventually, the server usually crashes.

© Digital Genetics/Shutterstock.com; © karam Miri/Shutterstock.com

Security software helps prevent malware from being installed on your devices because it deletes or quarantines any suspicious content as it arrives. Regular full-system scans can detect and remove any threats that find their way onto your computer. Refer to Exhibit 6-7 for some examples of security software. Because new threats are introduced all the time, it is essential for all devices to have security software installed as well as to make sure that the software is updated regularly. In addition, only download apps from trusted sources, such as Google Play, Apple iTunes, and Windows Store, because many third-party app stores host malicious apps.

EXHIBIT 6-7 SECURITY SOFTWARE

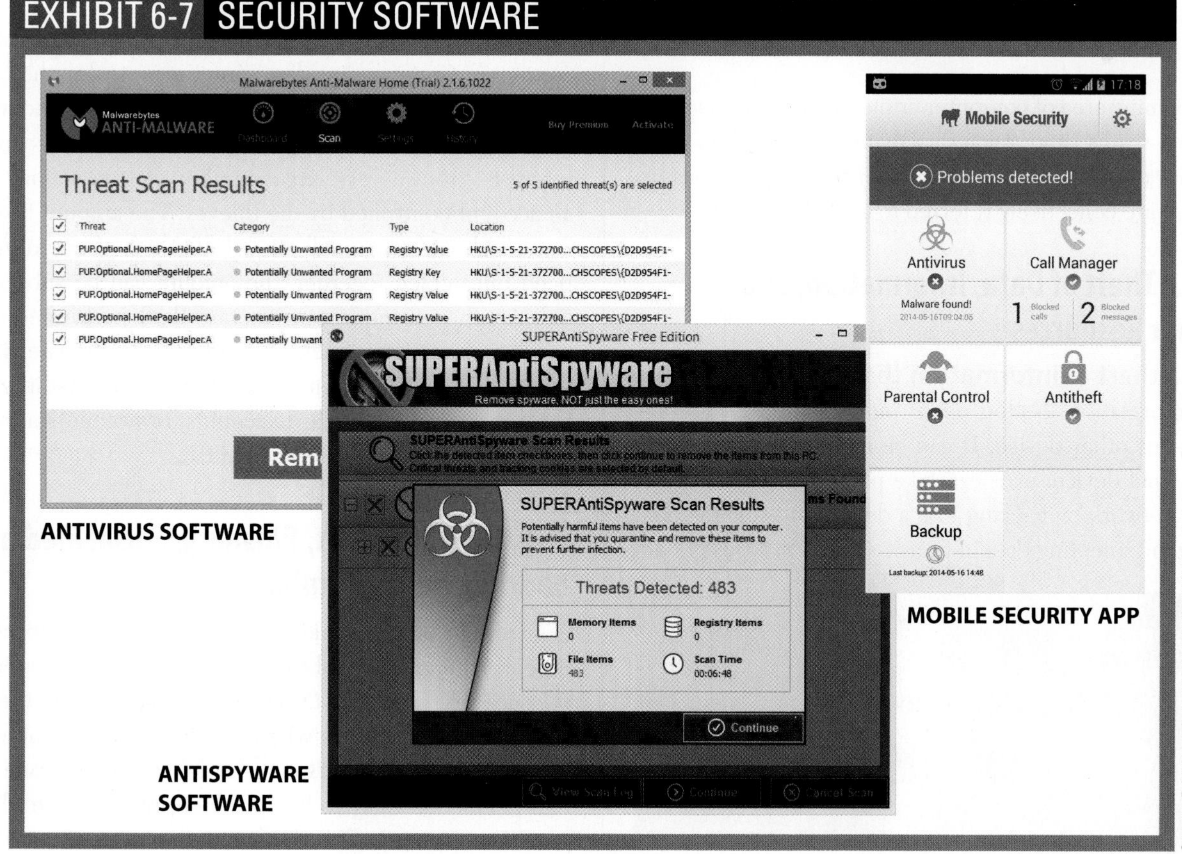

Source: © MalwareBytes; Bullguard; SUPERAntispyware

PUBLIC HOTSPOT PRECAUTIONS

Using firewall software, secure Web pages, VPNs, and encryption is a good start for protecting yourself at a public Wi-Fi hotspot. The following additional precautions can help you to avoid data on your computer or data sent over the Internet from being compromised:

- Turn off automatic connections, and pay attention to the list of available hotspots to make sure you connect to a legitimate access point, not one masquerading as a legitimate hotspot.
- Enter passwords, credit card numbers, and other data only on secure Web pages using a VPN.
- If you are not using a VPN, encrypt all sensitive files before transferring or emailing them.
- If you are not using a VPN, don't perform online shopping, banking, or other sensitive transactions that require you to log on to a Web site.

© Gazlast/Shutterstock.com

- Turn off file sharing so others cannot access the files on your device.
- Turn off Bluetooth and Wi-Fi when you are not using them.
- Disable ad hoc capabilities to prevent another device from connecting to your device directly without using an access point.
- Use antivirus software, and make sure your operating system and browser are up to date.

6-4 ONLINE THEFT, ONLINE FRAUD, AND OTHER DOT CONS

A booming area of computer crime involves online theft, fraud, scams, and related activities designed to steal money or other resources from individuals or businesses. These are collectively referred to as **dot cons**.

6-4a Theft of Data, Information, and Other Resources

Data theft or **information theft** is the theft of data or information located on or being sent from a computer or other device. It can be committed by stealing an actual device, or it can take place over the Internet or a network by hacking into a device and stealing data or by intercepting data in transit. Common types of data and information stolen via the Internet or another network include customer data (such as Web site passwords or credit card information) and proprietary corporate information.

dot con A fraud or scam carried out through the Internet.

data theft (information theft) The theft of data or information located on or being sent from a computer.

identity theft Using someone else's identity to purchase goods or services or otherwise illegally masquerade as that individual.

Money is another resource that can be stolen via a computer. Company insiders sometimes steal money by altering company programs to transfer small amounts of money—for example, a few cents of bank account interest—from a very large number of transactions to an account controlled by the thieves. The amount taken from each victim is small enough that it is often not noticed but, added together, the amount can be substantial. Another example of monetary theft performed via computers involves hackers electronically transferring money illegally from online bank accounts, traditional bank accounts, credit card accounts, or accounts at online payment services such as PayPal.

6-4b Identity Theft, Phishing, Social Media Hacking, and Pharming

A growing dot con trend is obtaining enough information about an individual to perform fraudulent financial transactions. Often, this is carried out via identity theft. **Identity theft** occurs when someone obtains enough information about a person to be able to masquerade as that person—usually to buy products or services in that person's name, as illustrated in Exhibit 6-8. Typically,

EXHIBIT 6-8 HOW IDENTITY THEFT WORKS

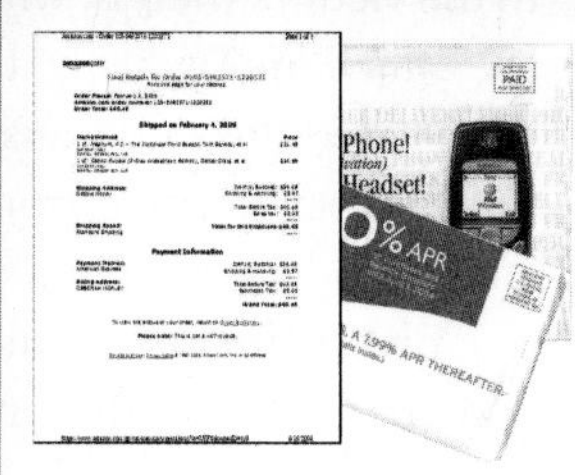

1. The thief obtains information about an individual from discarded mail, employee records, credit card transactions, Web server files, or some other method.

2. The thief makes purchases, opens new credit card accounts, and more in the victim's name. Often, the thief changes the address on the account to delay discovery.

3. The victim usually finds out by being denied credit or by being contacted about overdue bills generated by the thief. Clearing one's name after identity theft is time consuming and can be very difficult and frustrating for the victim.

identity theft begins when a thief obtains a person's name, address, and Social Security number, often from a discarded or stolen document, such as a preapproved credit card application that was sent in the mail; from information obtained via the Internet, such as a résumé posted online; from information located on a device, such as a stolen computer or hacked server; or from information sent from a device via a computer virus or spyware program installed on that device. The thief may then order a copy of the individual's birth certificate, obtain a "replacement" driver's license, make purchases and charge them to the victim, or open credit or bank accounts in the victim's name. Assuming that the thief requests a change of address for new accounts after they are opened, it may take some time—often until a company or collections agency contacts the victim about overdue bills—for the victim to become aware that his or her identity has been stolen. Although identity theft often takes place via a computer, information used in identity theft can also be gathered from trash dumpsters, mailboxes, and other offline locations.

Other techniques commonly used for identity theft are skimming and social engineering. Skimmers steal credit card or debit card numbers by attaching an illegal device to a credit card reader or an ATM that reads and stores the card numbers. They sometimes also position a hidden camera to capture ATM PINs. Social engineering involves pretending—typically via phone or email—to be a bank officer, a potential employer, an IT employee, or other trusted individual to get the potential victim to supply personal information.

Phishing (pronounced "fishing") is the use of an email message that appears to come from a legitimate organization, such as PayPal or a bank, but is actually sent from a phisher to trick the recipient into revealing sensitive personal information, such as Web site logon information or credit card numbers. Once obtained, this information is used in identity theft and other fraudulent activities. A phishing email often looks legitimate and contains links that appear to go to the Web site of the legitimate business. However, these links go to the phisher's Web site, which is set up to look like the legitimate site. Phishing emails are typically sent to a wide group of individuals and usually include an urgent message stating that the individual's credit card or account information needs to be updated and instructing the individual to click the link provided in the email to keep the account active, as shown in Exhibit 6-9. If the victim clicks the link and supplies the requested information via the phisher's bogus site, the criminal gains access to all information provided by the victim. Phishing attempts can also occur via instant messages, text messages, fake messages sent via eBay or Facebook, tweets, pop-up security alert windows, and even links in YouTube videos. Phishers also frequently use spyware; clicking the link in the phishing email installs the spyware on the victim's computer where it remains, transmitting sensitive data to the phisher, until it is detected and removed.

phishing The use of electronic communications (typically email messages) to gain credit card numbers and other personal data to be used for fraudulent purposes.

EXHIBIT 6-9 PHISHING EMAIL

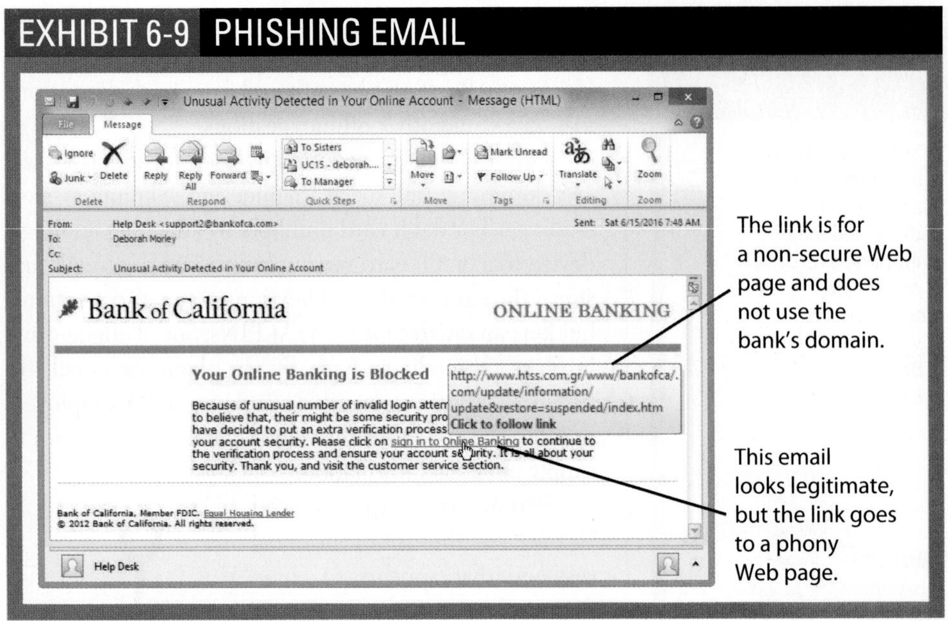

Spear phishing occurs when phishing emails are targeted to a specific individual and appear to come from an organization or person that the targeted individual has an association with. These emails often include personalized information, such as the potential victim's name, employer, and other information frequently found on social media and other public resources to make them seem more legitimate. Spear phishers target employees of selected organizations by posing as someone within the company, such as a human resources or technical support employee. These spear phishing emails often request confidential information or direct the employee to click a link to validate an account. The goal of corporate spear phishing attacks is usually to steal intellectual property, such as software source code, design documents, or schematics.

A more recent trend is **social media hacking**, in which a hacker obtains access to a victim's social media account in order to post comments or send messages as that individual. The messages typically contain phishing links and are sent to the victim's friends, who are much more likely to click the links because they appear to come from a friend.

Pharming is a scam that redirects traffic intended for a commonly used Web site to a bogus Web site set up by the pharmer in an effort to obtain users' personal information. Sometimes pharming takes place using malicious code sent to a computer or other device via an email message. More often, however, it takes place through changes made to a DNS server—a computer that translates URLs into the appropriate IP addresses needed to display Web pages. Pharming most often takes place via a company's DNS server, which routes Web page requests corresponding to company URLs. The pharmer changes the IP addresses used in conjunction with a particular company's URL (called DNS poisoning) so any Web page requests made to the legitimate company URL are routed via the company's poisoned DNS server to a phony Web page located on the pharmer's Web server. So, even though a user types the proper URL to display the legitimate company Web page in his or her browser, the bogus page is displayed instead. Because these bogus sites are set up to look like the legitimate sites, the user typically does not notice any difference, and passwords or any information sent via that site are captured by the pharmer.

6-4c Online Auction Fraud and Other Internet Scams

Online auction fraud occurs when an online auction buyer pays for merchandise that is never delivered or that is delivered but is not as represented. It can also occur when an online buyer receives the proper items but falsely claims that they never arrived. Other scams that can occur via Web sites or unsolicited emails include loan scams, work-at-home cons, pyramid schemes, bogus credit card offers and prize promotions, and fraudulent business opportunities. These offers try to sell potential victims nonexistent services or worthless information, or they try to convince potential victims

spear phishing A personalized phishing scheme targeted at an individual.

social media hacking The act of accessing someone else's social media account to make changes to the content or to perform an activity as that individual, often for phishing purposes.

pharming The use of redirection and a bogus Web site to obtain personal information to use in fraudulent activities.

online auction fraud When an item purchased through an online auction is never delivered or delivered but not as represented by the seller.

TRENDING...

DIGITAL IDs

The purpose of a **digital ID** (also called a **digital certificate**) is to authenticate the identity of an individual or organization. Digital certificates are granted by certificate authorities and contain the name of the person, organization, or Web site being certified along with a certificate serial number, an expiration date, and a public/private key pair. The digital certificate is used with secure Web pages to guarantee that the Web pages are secure and actually belong to the stated organization (see the accompanying illustration), in order to protect against phishing and other online scams that use phony sites set up to look like legitimate sites.

The keys included in a digital certificate can be used to digitally sign an email message or other document to authenticate that document. The sender's private key is used to sign the document, and that key, along with the contents of the document, generates a unique **digital signature**. When a digitally signed document is received, the recipient's device uses the sender's public key to verify the digital signature. Because the digital signature will be deemed invalid if the content of the document is changed, digital signatures guarantee that the document was sent by a specific individual and that it was not altered after it was signed.

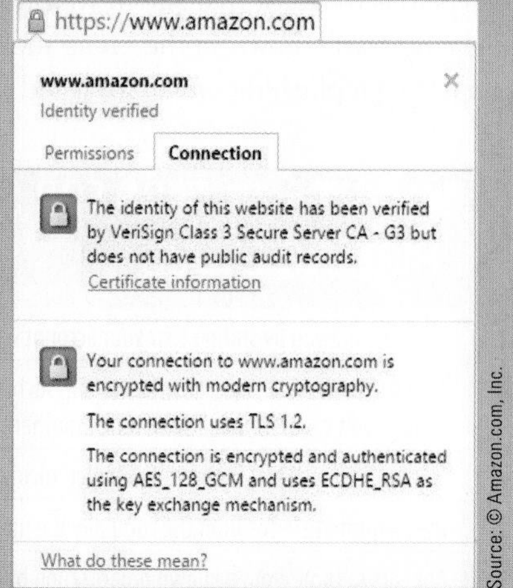

Source: © Amazon.com, Inc.

to voluntarily supply their credit card details and other personal information.

One ongoing Internet scam is the Nigerian letter fraud scheme. This scheme involves an email message that appears to come from the Nigerian government and that promises the potential victim a share of a substantial amount of money in exchange for the use of the victim's bank account. Supposedly the victim's bank account information is needed to facilitate a wire transfer, but the victim's account is emptied instead, or up-front cash is needed to pay for nonexistent fees, which the con artist keeps while giving nothing in return. Other scams include con artists who solicit charitable donations after disasters and other tragic events but who keep the donations instead, or who post fake job listings to elicit personal information from job seekers.

6-4d Protecting Against Identity Theft and Online Threats

The best protection against many dot cons is protecting your identity—that is, protecting any identifying information about you that could be used in fraudulent activities.

To protect yourself against information theft and identity theft, send sensitive information via secure Web servers only and don't disclose personal information—especially a Social Security number or your mother's maiden name—unless it is absolutely necessary and you know how the information will be used and that it will not be shared with others. Never give out sensitive personal information to anyone who requests it over the phone or by email; businesses that legitimately need personal information will not request it via phone or email. Be sure to also shred preapproved credit card offers and other sensitive documents before disposing of them, and keep a close eye on your credit card bills and credit history in order to catch any fraudulent charges or new accounts as soon as possible. In addition, you should use security software and keep it up to date to guard against malware that can send information from your device or about your activities to a criminal.

digital ID (digital certificate) Electronic data used to verify the identity of a person or an organization; includes a key pair that can be used for encryption and digital signatures.

digital signature A unique digital code that can be attached to a file or an email message to verify the identity of the sender and guarantee that the file or message has not been changed since it was signed.

To avoid phishing schemes, never click a link in an email message to go to a secure Web site; instead, always type the URL for that site in your browser (not necessarily the URL shown in the email message). Some tips for spotting a phishing email are listed in Exhibit 6-10.

EXHIBIT 6-10 TIPS FOR SPOTTING A PHISHING EMAIL

Tries to scare you by stating that your account will be closed or that you are a victim of fraud.
Asks you to provide personal information, such as your bank account number, an account password, credit card number, PIN number, mother's maiden name, or Social Security number.
Contains a bogus link (point to the hyperlink in the message to view the URL for that link).
Uses legitimate logos from the company the phisher is posing as.
Appears to come from a known organization but one you do not have an association with.
Contains spelling or grammatical errors (see the following example). THIS IS TO OFFICIALY INFORM YOU THAT WE HAVE OPEN YOUR PAYMENT FILE WHICH WORTH ABOUT EIGHT HUNDERED THOUSAND DOLLARS (US$800.000.00).WE ALSO FOUND OUT THAT YOU HAVE NOT RECEIVED ANY PAYMENT.

You can also use the antiphishing tools built into some browsers and security programs to help identify possible phishing Web sites (see the warning message in Exhibit 6-11). Some secure Web sites display an image or word preselected by the user and stored on the bank's server to prove to the user that the site being viewed is the legitimate, not a phishing, site. In addition, many secure Web sites require the user to correctly supply answers to the authentication questions that were asked when the account was set up if the system does not recognize the user's device.

EXHIBIT 6-11 POSSIBLE PHISHING WARNING

Warning: Dangerous Site

Whoa!

Are you sure you want to go there?

http://go.spktrk.com/aff_r?offer_id=1160&aff_i... may be risky to visit.

Why were you redirected to this page?

When we visited this site, we found it exhibited one or more risky behaviors.

« Back Visit anyway

Source: © McAfee, Inc.

The best protection against many dot cons is common sense. Be extremely cautious of any unsolicited email messages you receive. Realize that if an offer sounds too good to be true, it probably is. Before bidding on an auction item, check out the feedback rating of the seller to see comments written by other auction sellers and buyers as well as the seller's return policy. Always pay for auctions and other online purchases using a credit card or an online payment service such as PayPal that accepts credit card payments so you can dispute the transaction through your credit card company, if needed. To protect buyers of expensive items, PayPal also temporarily holds payments to ensure that the merchandise is as specified before the payment is released to the seller.

It is important to act quickly if you think you have been a victim of any type of fraud or con. For instance, you should work with your local law enforcement agency, credit card companies, and the three major consumer credit bureaus—TransUnion, Equifax, and Experian—to close any accessed or fraudulent accounts, place fraud alerts on your credit report, and take other actions to prevent additional fraudulent activity while the fraud is being investigated.

Source: © TransUnion LLC; Equifax Inc.; Experian Information Solutions, Inc.

6-5 CYBERSTALKING AND OTHER PERSONAL SAFETY CONCERNS

Cybercrime, in addition to being expensive and inconvenient, can also be physically dangerous. Although most of us may not ordinarily view using the Internet as a potentially dangerous activity, cases of physical harm due to Internet activity do happen. For example, children and teenagers have become the victims of pedophiles who arranged face-to-face meetings by using information gathered via email, online games, social media, or other online sources. In addition, many children and teens are threatened by classmates via email, posts on social media sites, or text messages. Adults may fall victim to unscrupulous or dangerous individuals who misrepresent themselves online, and the availability of personal information online has made it more difficult for individuals to hide from people who may want to do them harm, such as abused women trying to hide from their abusive husbands.

TRENDING...

PASSWORD STRATEGIES

To protect against some types of online theft and fraud, it is critical to use strong passwords that are easy to remember without writing them down. Some strategies include the following:

Use strong passwords. Passwords should be at least eight characters; use a combination of upper- and lowercase letters, numbers, and symbols; are not words found in a dictionary; and do not include words that others might know, such as your kids' or pets' names, your address, or your birthday.

I'm A Current Online Customer
Email Address janedoe@example.com
Password: •••••••••
(Password is case sensitive.)
log in

Create a strong passphrase. A passphrase is a statement that you can remember and use corresponding letters and symbols, such as the first letter of each word, for your password. For instance, the passphrase "My son John is five years older than my daughter Abby" could be used to remember the corresponding strong password "Msji5yotMd@".

Use unique passwords. Ideally, each password you use will be unique for that site. As a minimum, be sure that passwords for high-security sites, such as online banking, are different from passwords for your lower-security sites, such as social media accounts. If you use the same password for all accounts and a hacker determines it, he or she can use it for any of your accounts. To create a strong unique password for each site, you can develop a strong basic password or passphrase and then add site-specific information for each site, such as the first two letters of the site followed by a number that is significant to you, such as Msji5yotMd@Am17 for Amazon.

Protect your passwords. Do not keep a written copy of the password in your desk or taped to your monitor. If you need to keep a record of your passwords, create a password-protected file on your computer or use a password manager program.

Change your passwords frequently. It is a good idea to change your passwords every three to six months.

6-5a Cyberbullying and Cyberstalking

Two of the most common ways individuals are harassed online are cyberbullying and cyberstalking. Bullying others via the Internet, such as through email, text messaging, a social networking site, or other online communications method, is referred to as **cyberbullying**. Cyberbullying can take place openly, but often it occurs anonymously, such as a bully sending messages via a hacked social media or email account, or a bully hacking a victim's social media account and changing the content. Unfortunately, cyberbullying is common and is especially prevalent among teens—about one-quarter of all U.S. teenagers have been cyberbullied, according to recent estimates. And some of the victims have committed suicide because of it. Consequently, many states and schools have implemented antibullying policies and campaigns. Some states have also introduced new laws or amended existing harassment laws to address cyberbullying.

Source: © National Crime Prevention Council

Repeated threats or other malicious behavior that pose a credible threat of harm carried out online is referred to as **cyberstalking**. Cyberstalkers sometimes find their victims online—for instance, someone who posts a comment that the cyberstalker does not like on a social media site, or bloggers who are harassed and threatened because of their blogging activities.

cyberbullying The use of online communications to bully another person.

cyberstalking Repeated threats or harassing behavior between adults carried out via email or another Internet communications method.

Other times the attack is more personal, such as employers who are stalked online by former employees who were fired and celebrities who are stalked online by fans. Cyberstalking typically begins with online harassment, such as sending harassing or threatening email messages to the victim, posing as the victim to sign the victim up for pornographic or otherwise offensive email newsletters, publicizing the victim's home address and telephone number, or hacking into the victim's social media pages to alter the content. Cyberstalking can also lead to offline stalking and possibly physical harm to, and sometimes the death of, the victim.

Although there are as yet no specific federal laws against cyberstalking, all states have made it illegal, and some federal laws do apply if the online actions include computer fraud or another type of computer crime, suggest a threat of personal injury, or involve sending obscene email messages.

6-5b Online Pornography

A variety of controversial and potentially objectionable material is available on the Internet. Although there have been attempts to ban this type of material from the Internet, they have not been successful due to free speech and constitutional challenges. Like its printed counterpart, however, online pornography involving minors is illegal. Because of the strong link that experts believe exists between child pornography and child molestation, many experts are very concerned about the amount of child pornography that can be found and distributed via the Internet. They also believe that the Internet makes it easier for sexual predators to act out, such as by striking up "friendships" with children online and convincing these children to meet them in real life.

6-5c Protecting Personal Safety

The increasing amount of attention paid to cyberbullying and cyberstalking is leading to more efforts to improve safeguards. For instance, social networking sites have privacy features that can be used to protect the private information of their members. In addition, numerous states in the United States have implemented cyberbullying and cyberstalking laws. Although no surefire way exists to completely protect against cyberbullying, cyberstalking, and other online dangers, some common-sense precautions can reduce the chance of a serious personal safety problem occurring due to online activities. The following can help you protect yourself against cyberstalking and other types of online harassment:

- Be discreet online and use gender-neutral, nonprovocative identifying names, such as *jsmith*, instead of *janesmith* or *iamcute*.
- Be careful about the types of photos you post of yourself online or email to others, and do not reveal personal information, such as your real name, address, or telephone number, to people you meet online.
- Do not respond to any insults or other harassing comments you receive online.
- Consider requesting that your personal information be removed from online directories, especially those associated with your email address or other online identifiers.
- If you are a parent, protect your children by monitoring their computer and smartphone activities as well as making sure that they know what activities are off-limits and that they cannot reveal personal information online without your permission.

6-6 PERSONAL COMPUTER SECURITY

Some computer security issues are not related to networks and the Internet. These include having your computer stolen, losing a document because the storage medium it was stored on becomes unreadable, or losing your mobile phone containing your entire contact list and calendar.

6-6a Hardware Loss and Damage

Hardware loss can occur when a personal computer, USB flash drive, mobile device, or other piece of hardware is stolen or is lost by the owner. Hardware loss, as well as other security issues, can also result from hardware damage—both intentional and accidental—and system failure.

One of the most obvious types of hardware loss is hardware theft, which occurs when hardware is stolen from an individual or from a business, school, or other organization. Although security experts stress that the vast majority of hardware is stolen to obtain the value of the hardware itself, corporate executives and government employees may be targeted by thieves for the information contained on their devices. Even if the data on a device is not the primary reason for a theft, any unencrypted sensitive data stored on the stolen device is at risk of being exposed or used for fraudulent purposes.

Hardware loss also occurs when luggage or a package containing hardware is lost by an airline or shipping

TRENDING...

DISASTER RECOVERY PLANS

To supplement backup procedures, businesses and other organizations should have a **disaster recovery plan** (also called a **business continuity plan**)—a plan that spells out what the organization will do to prepare for and recover from a disruptive event, such as a fire, natural disaster, terrorist attack, or computer failure. Disaster recovery plans should include information about who will be in charge immediately after the disaster has occurred, what alternate facilities and equipment can be used, where backup media is located, the priority of getting each operation back online, disaster insurance coverage information, emergency communications methods, and so forth.

Traditionally, alternate locations equipped with the computers, cabling, desks, and other equipment necessary to keep a business's operations going were used when resuming business operations immediately after a disaster was critical. Today, it is more common to have alternative sites that can be used following a disaster but that require the business to provide the needed equipment. In either case, cloud data recovery services can be used to replicate operations at a lower cost and the site and resources to be used should be included in the disaster recovery plan. Businesses that host their email onsite should also consider making arrangements with an emergency mail system provider to act as a temporary mail server if the company mail server is not functioning. Copies of the disaster recovery plan should be located off-site.

© Sashkin/Shutterstock.com

company, or when an individual misplaces or otherwise loses a piece of hardware. In addition to the inconvenience and expense of having to replace lost hardware, individuals risk identity theft if the lost hardware contains any sensitive data. Businesses hosting sensitive data that is breached have to deal with the numerous issues and potential consequences of that loss, such as notifying customers that their personal information was exposed, responding to potential lawsuits, and trying to repair damage to the company's reputation.

Computer hardware can also be damaged by power fluctuations, heat, dust, static electricity, water, and abuse. For instance, fans clogged by dust can cause a computer to overheat; dropping a device will often break it; and spilling a drink on a keyboard or leaving a smartphone in the pocket of your jeans while they go through the wash will likely damage or ruin it.

6-6b System Failure and Other Disasters

Although many of us may prefer not to think about it, **system failure**—the complete malfunction of a computer system—and other types of computer-related disasters do happen. From accidentally deleting a file to having your computer just stop working, computer problems can be a huge inconvenience as well as cost a great deal of time and money. System failure can occur because of a hardware problem, software problem, or computer sabotage. It can also occur because of a natural disaster or terrorist attack.

6-6c Protecting Against Hardware Loss, Hardware Damage, and System Failure

Locked doors and other access control methods can be simple deterrents to hardware theft. To secure computers and other hardware to a table or other object that is difficult to move, you can use cable locks, such as the one shown in Exhibit 6-12. As an additional precaution

EXHIBIT 6-12 CABLE LOCK

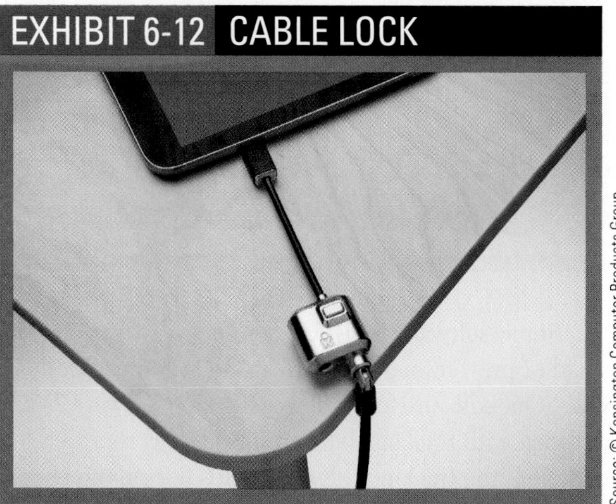

Source: © Kensington Computer Products Group

disaster recovery plan (business continuity plan) A written plan that describes the steps a company will take following the occurrence of a disaster.

system failure The complete malfunction of a computer system.

with portable computers, you can use laptop alarm software that emits a very loud alarm noise if the computer is unplugged, if USB devices are removed, or if the computer is shut down without the owner's permission. For smartphones, proximity key fob devices that are paired with your smartphone and sound an alarm if the distance between your keys and phone exceeds a preset distance can be used to help you keep your phone with you when you are in a public location.

To protect the data on a device from being readable if the device is stolen, encryption can be used. **Full disk encryption (FDE)** provides an easy way to protect data because it automatically encrypts everything stored on a drive, so users do not have to remember to encrypt sensitive documents. A hard drive that uses FDE, often referred to as a **self-encrypting hard drive**, cannot be accessed without providing the appropriate username and password, biometric characteristic, or other authentication control.

Encryption can also be used to protect the data stored on removable storage media; a strong password, a biometric feature, or a PIN (such as is used with the device shown in Exhibit 6-13) is used to provide access to the data on the drive. Many businesses today are requiring that all portable computers, portable storage devices, tablets, and smartphones issued to employees be encrypted in order to protect against a data breach.

EXHIBIT 6-13 ENCRYPTED USB FLASH DRIVE

Source: © Apricorn

Some software tools are designed for recovery, instead of prevention; that is, to locate stolen or lost hardware. One software tool is device tracking software. When a device with tracking software installed is reported lost or stolen, the tracking software sends information about the location of the device, typically determined by GPS or the nearest Wi-Fi network, to the tracking software company on a regular basis so that the information can be provided to law enforcement agencies to help them recover the device. Some tracking software can even take video or photos with the device's camera of the person using the stolen device to help identify and prosecute the thief.

To protect itself, most tracking software can also survive operating system reinstallations and hard drive reformats. Some can also display a message on the screen when the device is reported lost or stolen, such as a plea to return the device for a reward or a simple statement of "THIS DEVICE IS STOLEN" on the desktop or lock screen to call attention to the fact that the device is stolen. Another common option is the ability to remotely lock the device and display a message that the device is locked and will not function without the appropriate password (see Exhibit 6-14).

EXHIBIT 6-14 A REMOTE LOCK MESSAGE

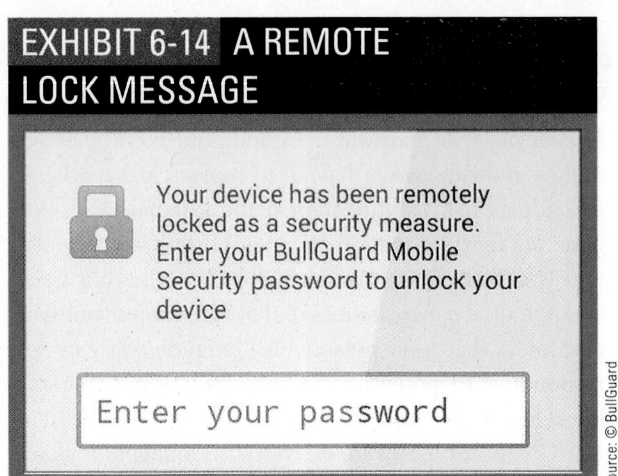

Your device has been remotely locked as a security measure. Enter your BullGuard Mobile Security password to unlock your device
Enter your password

Source: © BullGuard

Keep in mind the following precautions when using portable computers, smartphones, and other devices while on the go:

- Install and use encryption, antivirus, antispyware, and firewall software.
- Secure computers with boot passwords; set your smartphone to autolock the screen after a short period of time, and require a passcode to unlock it.
- Use only secure Wi-Fi connections, and disable Wi-Fi and Bluetooth when they are not needed.
- Do not store usernames or passwords attached to a computer or inside its case.
- Use a plain case to make a portable computer less conspicuous.

full disk encryption (FDE) A technology that encrypts everything stored on a storage medium without any user interaction.

self-encrypting hard drive A hard drive that uses full disk encryption (FDE).

- Keep an eye on your devices at all times, especially when traveling.
- Use a cable lock to secure devices to a desk or other object whenever you must leave them unattended.
- Regularly back up your data.
- Install tracking software to remotely locate and wipe your device if it is lost or stolen.

Proper care of hardware can help prevent serious damage to devices. An obvious precaution is to not harm your hardware physically, such as by dropping a device. To help protect a portable device against minor abuse, use a protective case, such as the one shown in Exhibit 6-15. These cases are typically padded or made from protective material; they also often have a thin, protective layer over the device's display to protect against scratches.

EXHIBIT 6-15 PROTECTIVE SMARTPHONE CASE

Source: © Griffin Technology

If you need more protection than a case can provide, **ruggedized devices**, such as the ones in Exhibit 6-16, that are designed to withstand much more physical abuse than conventional devices can be used. Ruggedized devices range from semirugged, such as devices that can withstand being submerged in water, to ultrarugged, such as devices that can withstand drops over concrete or extreme temperature variations. Ultrarugged devices are used most often by individuals who work outside of an office, such as field workers, construction workers, outdoor technicians, military personnel, police officers, and firefighters.

EXHIBIT 6-16 RUGGEDIZED DEVICES

SEMIRUGGED (WATERPROOF) SMARTPHONE

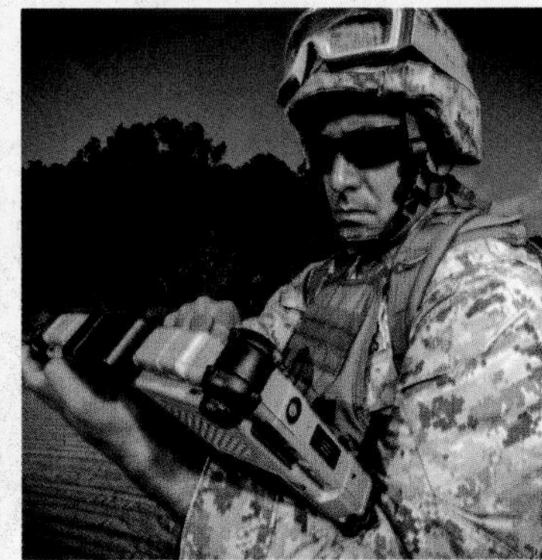

RUGGED TABLET

Source: © Sony Electronics; Xplore Technologies Corp.

To protect hardware from damage due to power fluctuations, use a **surge suppressor** with a computer whenever it is plugged into a power outlet. The surge suppressor prevents electrical power spikes from harming your system. For the best protection, surge suppressors should be used with all of the powered components that have a wired connection to the computer. Small surge suppressors designed for use on the go are also available, as are more powerful surge suppressors designed for business and industrial use.

Users who want their desktop computers to remain powered up when the electricity goes off should use an **uninterruptible power supply (UPS)**, which contains a built-in battery. The length of time that a UPS

ruggedized device A device that is designed to withstand much more physical abuse than a conventional device.

surge suppressor A device that protects a computer system from damage due to electrical fluctuations.

uninterruptible power supply (UPS) A device containing a built-in battery that provides continuous power to a computer and other connected components when the electricity goes out.

TRENDING...

KILL SWITCHES

Due to the rising number of violent thefts of smartphones in major U.S. cities, **kill switches**—software that enables owners to render stolen devices inoperable—have been getting increased attention. In fact, Michigan and California recently passed laws requiring all smartphones sold in those states to include a kill switch.

Some features of kill switches are included in many device tracking apps. For example, the Android Device Manager shown in the accompanying illustration displays the current location of a selected device after a user logs on to his or her account. It also has the ability to ring the device, lock the device and display a message on the lock screen, or erase the device. Some stand-alone kill switches go one step further and actually destroy the device. For example, some encrypted hard drives automatically delete the encryption key, which leaves the device inaccessible, after a specific number of unsuccessful password entry attempts.

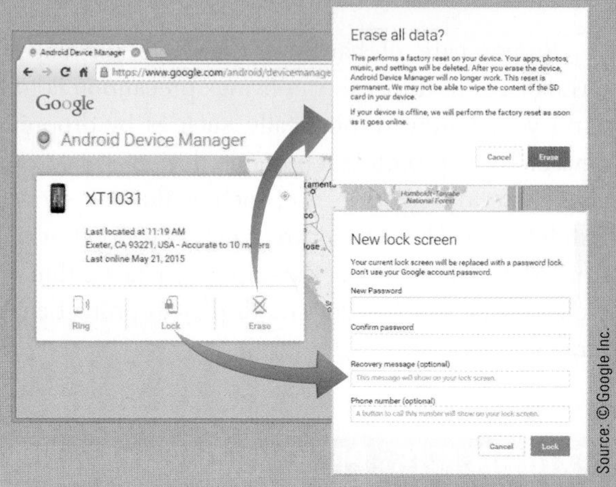

Source: © Google Inc.

can power a system depends on the type and number of devices connected to the UPS, the power capacity of the UPS device, and the age of the battery. Most UPS devices also protect against power fluctuations. UPSs designed for use by individuals typically provide power for a few minutes to keep the system powered up during short power blips as well as to allow the user to save open documents and shut down the computer properly in case the electricity remains off. Industrial-level UPSs typically run for a significantly longer time (up to a few hours). For extended power outages, generators are needed.

Dust, heat, static electricity, and moisture can also be dangerous to hardware, so do not place your devices in direct sunlight or in a dusty area. You can periodically use a small, handheld vacuum made for electrical equipment to remove the dust from the keyboard and from inside the system unit of a computer, but be very careful when vacuuming inside the system unit. Also, be sure that the system unit has plenty of ventilation, especially around the fan vents and avoid placing a portable computer on a soft surface, such as a couch or blanket, to help prevent overheating. Unless your computer is ruggedized, do not get it wet or otherwise expose it to adverse conditions.

6-7 UNDERSTANDING PRIVACY CONCERNS

Privacy is usually defined as the state of being concealed or free from unauthorized intrusion. The term **information privacy** refers to the rights of individuals and companies to control how information about them is collected and used. Computers, with their ability to store, duplicate, and manipulate large quantities of data, combined with the fact that databases containing our personal information can be accessed and shared via the Internet, present challenges for protecting personal privacy.

Many people are concerned about the privacy of their Web site activities and email messages. Recently,

kill switch A software program or app that enables a device owner to disable that device remotely.

privacy The state of being concealed or free from unauthorized intrusion.

information privacy The rights of individuals and companies to control how information about them is collected and used.

an unprecedented number of high-profile data breaches have occurred—some via hacking and other network intrusions; others due to lost or stolen hardware, or carelessness with papers or storage media containing Social Security numbers or other sensitive data. Every data breach is a risk to information privacy. Consequently, protecting the data stored in databases is an important concern for everyone. Additional privacy concerns are spam and other marketing activities, electronic surveillance, and electronic monitoring.

> Every data breach is a risk to information privacy.

FYI

BIG DATA

The vast collection of data gathered by many organizations today is collectively referred to as big data. It usually exists in a variety of formats and arrives often—frequently in real time. Big data collected today by businesses and the government includes transaction data, viewed Web pages and browsing habits, data from sensors and smart devices, social media activity, purchasing habits, phone call and email records, and more. The use of big data is expected to increase as the use of smartphones and other smart devices continues to grow. As it does, new techniques to process—and safeguard the privacy of—this vast amount of data will need to be developed.

© Novelo/Shutterstock.com

CAUTION CAUTION CAUTION CAUTION

BE CAREFUL WITH LOCATION SERVICES

Be selective when deciding which smartphone apps you allow to use location services. While popular with many individuals for checking in and other activities, there is concern about location information being used inappropriately (such as by stalkers and home burglars) as well as if and for how long location data is stored.

6-7a Databases, Electronic Profiling, Spam, and Other Marketing Activities

Information about individuals can be located in many different databases. For example, educational institutions have databases containing student information, organizations use databases to hold employee information, and most physicians and health insurance providers maintain databases containing individuals' medical information. If these databases are adequately protected from hackers and other unauthorized individuals, and if the data is not transported on a portable computer or other device that may be vulnerable to loss or theft, then these databases do not pose a significant privacy concern to consumers because the information can rarely be shared without the individuals' permission. However, the data stored in these types of databases is not always sufficiently protected and has been breached quite often in the past. Consequently, these databases, along with marketing databases and government databases that are typically associated with a higher risk of personal privacy violations, are of growing concern to privacy advocates.

Marketing databases contain marketing and demographic data about people, such as where they live and what products they buy. This information is used for marketing purposes, including sending advertisements that fit each individual's interests via regular mail or email or trying to sign up people over the phone for some type of service. Almost any time you provide information about yourself online or offline—when you subscribe to a magazine, fill out a product registration card, or buy something using a credit card—there is a good chance that the information will find its way into a marketing database.

Marketing databases are also used in conjunction with Web activities, such as social media activities and Web searches. For instance, the data stored on Facebook, Google+, and other social networking sites can be gathered and used for advertising purposes by marketing companies, and the activities of users of personalized search services (where users log in to use the service) can be tracked and that data can be used for marketing purposes. And companies with services that collect a wide variety of data, such as Google with its Chrome, Gmail, Calendar, Hangouts, Checkout, and Google+ services, worry some privacy advocates.

marketing database A collection of data about people that is stored in a large database and used for marketing purposes.

Information about individuals is also available in **government databases**. Some information, such as Social Security earnings and income tax returns, is confidential and can legally be seen only by authorized individuals. Other information, such as birth records, marriage certificates, and divorce information, as well as property purchases, assessments, liens, and tax values, is available to the public, including to the marketing companies that specialize in creating marketing databases.

EXHIBIT 6-17 SEARCHABLE DATABASES AVAILABLE VIA THE INTERNET

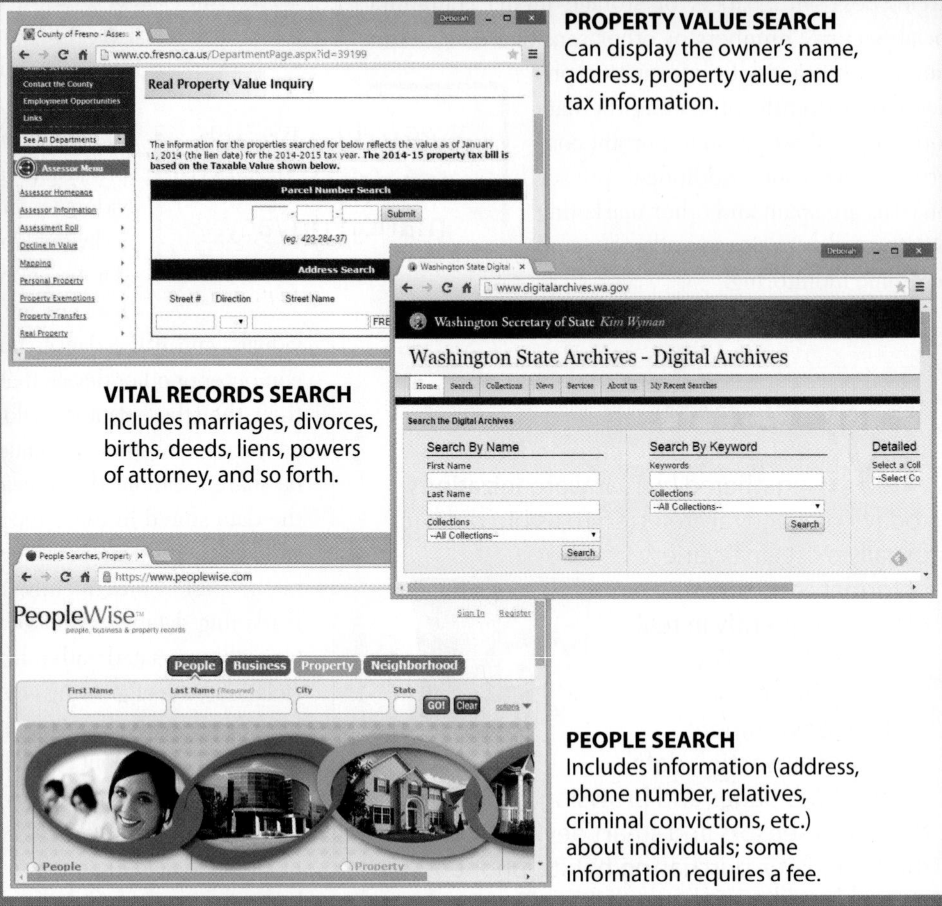

Source: © County of Fresno; Washington State Archives; LexisNexis Risk Solutions

In the past, the data about any one individual was stored in a variety of separate locations, such as at different government agencies, individual retail stores, and the person's bank and credit card companies. Because it would be extremely time consuming to locate all the information about one person from all these different places, there was a fairly high level of information privacy. Today, however, most of an individual's data is stored on computers that can communicate with each other, and some database search services are available online for free or for a fee (see some examples in Exhibit 6-17). Although this ability to search online databases can be an advantage—such as checking the background of a potential employee—it does raise privacy concerns. In response to the increased occurrence of identity theft, some local governments have removed birth and death information from their available online database records.

Collecting in-depth information about an individual is known as **electronic profiling**. Electronic profiles are generally designed to provide specific information and can include an individual's name, current and previous addresses, telephone number, marital status, number and age of children, spending habits, and product preferences. The information retrieved from electronic profiles is then sold to companies upon request to be used for marketing purposes, as illustrated in Exhibit 6-18. For example, one company might request a list of all individuals in a particular state whose street addresses are considered to be in an affluent area and who buy baby products. Another company might request a list of all SUV owners in a particular city who have not purchased a car in five years.

Most businesses and Web sites that collect personal information have a **privacy policy** that discloses how

government database A collection of data about people that is collected and maintained by the government.

electronic profiling Using electronic means to collect a variety of in-depth information about an individual, such as name, address, income, and buying habits.

privacy policy A policy, commonly posted on a company's Web site, that explains how personal information provided to that company will be used.

EXHIBIT 6-18 HOW ELECTRONIC PROFILING MIGHT WORK

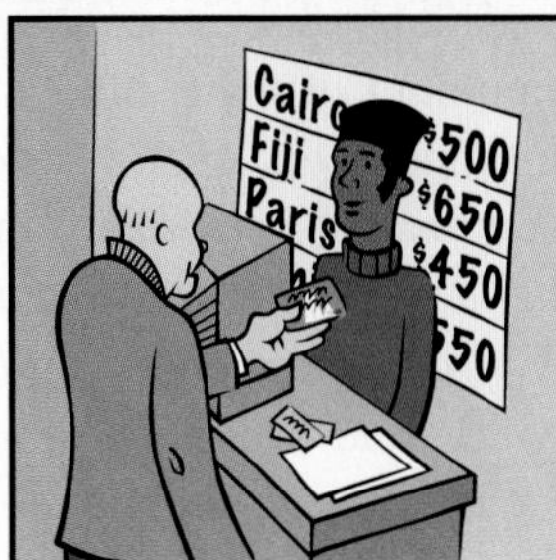

When you make an electronic transaction, information about who you are and what you buy is recorded, usually in a database.

Databases containing the identities of people and what they buy are sold to marketing companies.

The marketing companies add the new data to their marketing databases; they can then reorganize the data in ways that might be valuable to other companies.

The marketing companies create lists of individuals matching the specific needs of companies; the companies buy the lists for their own marketing purposes.

the personal information you provide will be used (see the Facebook privacy policy in Exhibit 6-19). As long as their actions do not violate their privacy policy, it is legal for businesses to sell the personal data that they collect. However, privacy policies are sometimes difficult to decipher, and most people do not take the time to read them before using a site. In addition, many businesses periodically change their privacy policies without warning, requiring consumers to reread privacy policies frequently or risk their personal information being used in a manner that they did not agree to when the information was initially provided.

EXHIBIT 6-19 WEB SITE PRIVACY POLICY

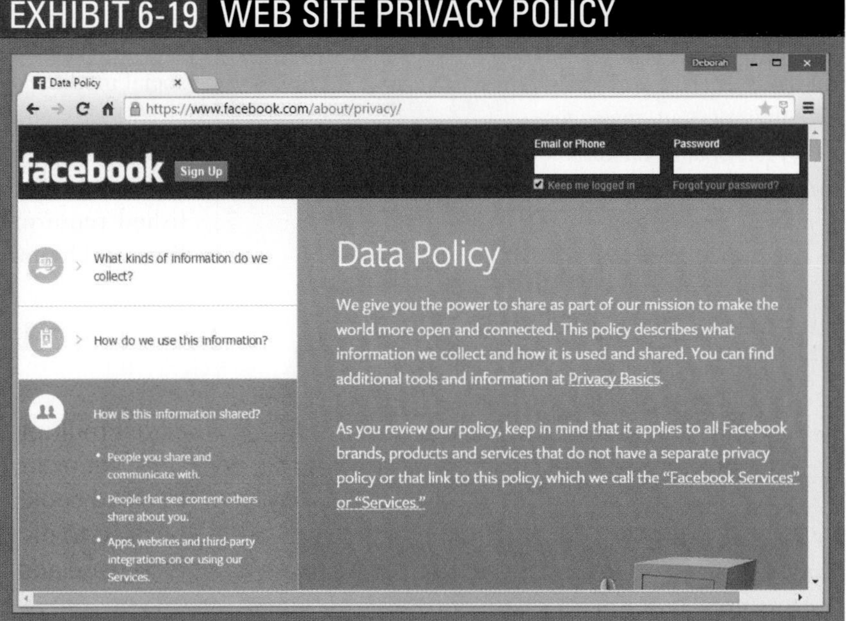

Source: © Facebook

Spam refers to unsolicited email sent to a large group of individuals at one time. The electronic equivalent of junk mail (see Exhibit 6-20), spam is most often used to sell products or services to individuals and can be sent via email, text, instant, or social media messages. Spam is also used in phishing schemes and other dot cons and is sent frequently via botnets. A great deal of spam involves health-related products, counterfeit products, pornography, and fraudulent business opportunities and stock deals. Spam can also be generated by individuals forwarding email messages they receive to everyone in their address books. In addition to spam, most individuals receive marketing emails either from companies they directly provided with their email addresses or from other companies that acquired their email addresses from a third party, such as from a partner site or via a purchased mailing list. While these latter types of marketing email messages do not technically fit the definition of spam because they were permission-based, many individuals consider them to be spam.

While email spam is decreasing as a result of better spam filters and other protections that are discussed shortly, it is still a problem. In fact, Kaspersky Labs

spam Unsolicited, bulk email sent over the Internet.

EXHIBIT 6-20 EXAMPLES OF SPAM

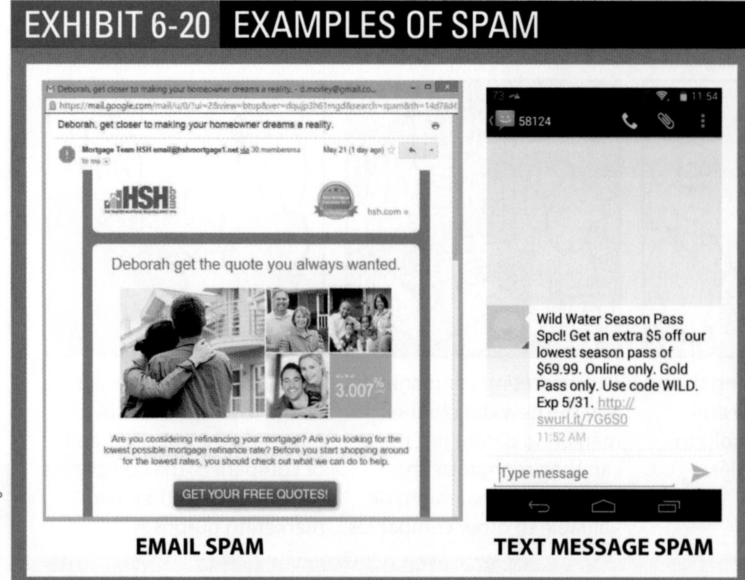

EMAIL SPAM **TEXT MESSAGE SPAM**

Source: © Google Inc.

recently estimated that about 66% of all email messages are spam. At best, spam is an annoyance to recipients and can slow a mail server's delivery of important messages. At worst, spam can disable a mail network completely, or it can cause recipients to miss or lose important email messages because those messages were caught in a spam filter or were accidentally deleted by the recipient while he or she was deleting a large number of spam email messages. Most Internet users spend several minutes each day dealing with spam, making spam expensive for businesses in terms of lost productivity, consumption of communications bandwidth, and drain of technical support. Spam sent to a smartphone, either via text message or email, is also expensive for end users who have a limited data or text message allowance.

© gfdunt/Shutterstock.com

One of the most common ways of getting on a spam mailing list is by having your email address entered into a marketing database, which can happen when you sign up for a free online service or use your email address to register a product or make an online purchase. Spammers also use software to gather email addresses from Web pages, forum posts, and social media.

Most spam is legal, but there are requirements that must be adhered to in order for it to be legal. For instance, the CAN-SPAM Act of 2003 established requirements, such as using truthful subject lines and honoring remove requests, for commercial

FYI COOKIES

Many Web pages today use cookies—small text files that are stored on your hard drive by a Web server—to identify return visitors and their preferences. Cookies can be session based (that only last until your browser is closed) or persistent (that are stored on your hard drive). About half of persistent cookies are first-party cookies that belong to the Web site you are visiting and are only read by that site. These cookies can provide some benefits to consumers, such as saving a shopping cart or remembering personalized settings. Third-party cookies (cookies placed on your hard drive by a company other than the one associated with the Web page that you are viewing—typically a Web advertising company) are typically viewed as a higher privacy risk. Many of these are tracking cookies, which can track your activities across multiple Web sites. For example, tracking cookies can be used to display Web page ads based on your browsing activities, and Facebook receives information each time you visit a Web page with a Like button on it if you have a Facebook cookie on your hard drive.

© Dani Vincek/Shutterstock.com

To notify you about cookie use, many sites display a notification on your first visit so you can choose not to use the site if you object to the usage. To control overall cookie use, you can use your browser's privacy settings to delete all cookies stored on your hard drive as well as to block third-party cookies. In addition, security software typically scans for tracking cookies and will quarantine those cookie files at your request.

TRENDING...

WEARABLES AND PRIVACY

Source: © Kapture

The demand for wearables is huge and growing every day but, similar to when mobile phones with cameras first became available, there are privacy concerns. One privacy concern is the ability of some wearable devices to discreetly gather data about individuals. For example, people wearing Google Glass can take photos or record video of others, and people with audio recording devices like Kapture (shown in the accompanying illustration) can record the conversations of others. Because the recording capabilities of these wearable devices can be activated much less conspicuously than a smartphone, data can often be recorded about an individual without his or her knowledge.

Another privacy concern is what is being done with the vast amount of data our wearables gather about us. While many devices have privacy settings that can control how data is shared, they often enable sharing by default. Consequently, data about our health, location, and activities could inadvertently be shared with others, opening up the risk of stalking, burglary, extortion, or employment or health insurance ramifications.

The ethical and legal use of wearables will likely be debated for some time. In the meantime, the legal system must apply current laws to wearables and other new technology as it is introduced and businesses may determine policies that are appropriate for that business. For example, similar to smartphones being banned from some locker rooms and other sensitive public locations for privacy reasons, some restaurants and bars have banned Google Glass on the basis that it may make some customers uncomfortable.

emailers as well as specified penalties for companies and individuals that break the law. To comply with truth-in-advertising laws, an unsubscribe email address included in an unsolicited email must be a working address. However, because spam from less-legitimate sources may include an unsubscribe link only to verify that your email address is genuine—a very valuable piece of information—some privacy experts recommend never trying to unsubscribe from spam.

6-7b Electronic Surveillance and Monitoring

Electronic tools can be used in many ways to watch individuals, listen in on their conversations, or monitor their activities. Some of these tools, such as devices used by individuals to eavesdrop on wireless telephone conversations, are not legal for individuals to use. Other products and technologies, such as GPS devices that are built into some cars so they can be located if stolen or monitoring ankle bracelets used for offenders sentenced to house arrest, are used solely for law enforcement purposes. Other electronic tools can be used legally by individuals, by businesses in conjunction with employee monitoring, and by law enforcement agencies.

Computer-monitoring software records keystrokes, logs the programs or Web sites accessed, or otherwise monitors someone's computer activity. Some can also block specific Web sites as well as notify a designated party if the individual using the computer being monitored uses specified keywords or visits a Web site deemed inappropriate. Computer-monitoring programs are typically marketed toward parents, spouses, law enforcement agencies, or employers. Although it is legal to use this type of software on your own computer or on the computers of your employees, installing it on other computers without the owners' knowledge to monitor their computer activity is usually illegal.

Video surveillance is the use of closed-circuit security cameras to monitor activities taking place at

computer-monitoring software Software that can be used to record an individual's computer usage, such as recording the actual keystrokes used or creating a summary of Web sites and programs accessed.

video surveillance The use of video cameras to monitor activities of individuals, typically for work-related or crime-prevention purposes.

facilities for security purposes. It is routinely used for security purposes at retail stores, banks, office buildings, and other privately owned facilities that are open to the public. It is also used for law enforcement purposes in public locations such as streets, parks, airports, sporting arenas, and subway systems.

© Leonard Zhukovsky/Shutterstock.com

Public video surveillance systems are often used in conjunction with face recognition technology to try to identify known terrorists and other criminals, to identify criminals when their crimes are caught on tape, and to prevent crimes from occurring. Some public video surveillance systems are also beginning to be used in conjunction with software to try to identify suspicious behavior, such as a person leaving a bag unattended in a public location, and alert authorities to these possible threats before any damage occurs. Many privacy advocates object to the use of video surveillance and face recognition technology in public locations; their concerns are primarily based on how the video captured by these systems will be used. However, law enforcement agencies view this technology as just one more tool to be used to protect the public, similar to scanning luggage at the airport.

Employee monitoring is the act of recording or observing the actions of employees while on the job. Common employee-monitoring activities include screening telephone calls, reviewing email, and tracking computer and Internet usage. The primary reason employers monitor Internet usage is for legal liability, but monitoring employee productivity is another motivating factor. Although many employees feel that being watched at work is an invasion of their personal privacy, it is legal and very common in many countries, including the United States.

Presence technology is the ability of one computing device, such as a computer or smartphone, to identify another device on the same network, such as the Internet, and determine its status. It can be used to tell when someone is using his or her computer or smartphone as well as the individual's availability for communications, such as whether the individual is able and willing to take a voice or video call. Presence capabilities are integrated into many messaging programs; for example, they let you see when your Facebook friends are online. Presence capabilities are also used in some business communications programs.

employee monitoring Observing or reviewing employees' actions while they are on the job.

presence technology Technology that enables one computing device to locate and identify the current status of another device via the Internet or other network.

wipe To permanently destroy the data on a device so it cannot be recovered.

6-7c Protecting Personal Privacy

Any business that stores personal information about employees, customers, or other individuals must take adequate security measures to protect the privacy of that information. Secure servers and encryption can protect the data stored on a server; firewalls and access control systems can protect against unauthorized access. To prevent personal information from being sent intentionally or inadvertently in an email message, organizations can use email encryption systems that automatically encrypt or block email messages containing certain keywords.

Both individuals and businesses need to protect the information located on paper documents and hardware that are to be disposed of. Papers, CDs, DVDs, and other media containing sensitive data should be shredded. Because data deleted from a hard drive remains on the drive and can be recovered using special software, the hard drives of devices to be disposed of should be **wiped**—overwritten several times using disk-wiping or disk-erasing software so that the data on it cannot be recovered—before they are sold or recycled. Unlike the data on a drive that has merely been erased or even reformatted, data on a properly wiped drive is very difficult or impossible to recover.

Wiping is typically viewed as an acceptable precaution for deleting sensitive data such as Web site passwords and tax returns from hard drives and other storage media. However, before disposing of storage media containing sensitive data, businesses should consider physically destroying the media, such as by shredding or melting the hardware. To help with this process, a data destruction service is often used. Once a hard drive has been shredded (see Exhibit 6-21), it is virtually impossible for any data to be recovered from the pieces.

There are a number of precautions that can be taken to protect the privacy of personal information. For example, protecting your email address is one of the best ways to avoid spam. One way to accomplish this is to use one private email address for family, friends, colleagues, and other trusted sources. For online shopping, signing up for free offers, forums, product registration, and other

EXHIBIT 6-21 SHREDDED HARD DRIVE

Source: © Data Killers

activities that typically lead to junk email, use a disposable or **throw-away email address** (a second address obtained from your ISP or a free email address from a service such as Outlook.com or Gmail that you can check as needed). Another advantage of using a throw-away email address for only noncritical applications is that you can quit using it and obtain a new one if spam begins to get overwhelming or too annoying.

In addition to protecting your email address, protecting your personal data is a critical step toward safeguarding your privacy. Consequently, it makes sense to be cautious about revealing private information to anyone. You can use the following tips to help limit the exposure of your personal data.

- Read a Web site's privacy policy, if one exists, before providing any personal information. If the Web site reserves the right to share your information unless you specifically notify them otherwise, it is best to assume that any information you provide will eventually be shared with others.
- Avoid putting too many personal details on your Web site or on social media. Although complete anonymity would defeat the purpose of using social media, it is a good idea to be careful about what content you post and who can view it. Review the privacy settings of each site you use and make adjustments as needed. If you want to post photos or other personal documents on a Web site for friends and family members to see, use a photo-sharing site, such as Flickr or Snapfish, that allows you to restrict access to your photos. Avoid using location-based services that share your location information with strangers.
- When you sign up for free trials or other services that may result in spam, use a throw-away email address.
- Consider using privacy software, such as Privacy Guardian, to hide your personal information as you browse the Web so it is not revealed and your activities cannot be tracked by marketers. Also check the privacy settings of the cloud services that you use to see what control you have over what personal data is collected and shared.
- Supply only the required information when completing an online form. Just because a Web site or registration form asks for personal information, that does not mean you have to give it.
- If you are using a public computer, remove any personal information and settings stored on the computer during your session. You can use browser options to delete this data manually from the computer before you leave. An easier option is using the private browsing mode offered by some browsers (see Exhibit 6-22) that allows you to browse the Web without leaving any history on the computer you are using. In either case, be sure to log out of any Web sites you were using before leaving the computer.

EXHIBIT 6-22 PRIVATE BROWSING

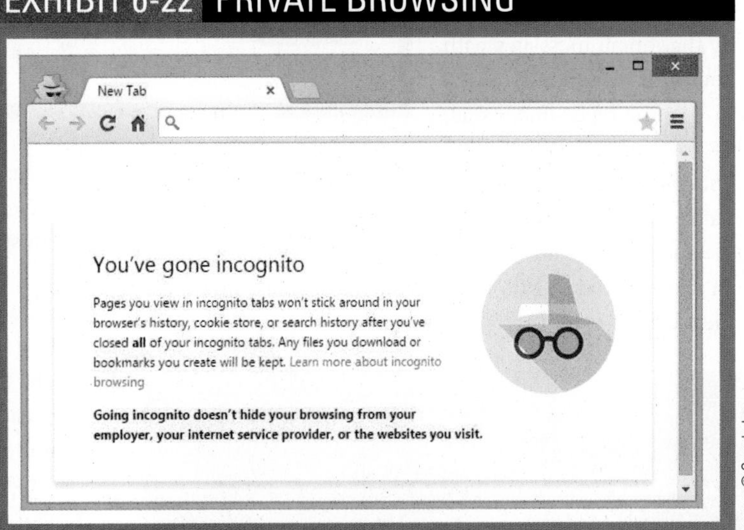

Source: © Google Inc.

throw-away email address An email address used only for nonessential purposes and activities that may result in spam; the address can be disposed of and replaced if spam becomes a problem.

To avoid seeing and having to deal with the spam that arrives in your Inbox, various tools can be used. For example, some ISPs automatically block all email messages originating from known or suspected spammers, as well as block messages containing possible viruses, so those email messages never reach individuals' mailboxes. Other ISPs flag suspicious email messages as possible spam or malicious emails, based on their content or subject lines, to warn individuals. To deal with spam that does make it to your device, you can use an **email filter**—a tool for automatically sorting incoming email messages. Email filters used to capture spam are called **spam filters**. Many email programs and services have built-in spam filters that identify possible spam and either flag it or move it to a Spam folder.

Custom email filters are used to route messages automatically to particular folders based on stated criteria. For example, you can specify that email messages with keywords frequently used in spam subject lines, such as *free*, *porn*, *opportunity*, *last chance*, *weight*, and *pharmacy*, be routed into a folder named Possible Spam, and you can specify that all email messages from your boss's email address be routed into an Urgent folder. Filtering can help you find important messages in your Inbox by preventing it from becoming cluttered with spam. However, be sure to check your Spam folder periodically to locate any email messages mistakenly filed there—especially before you permanently delete those messages. Creating a new email filter in Gmail is shown in Exhibit 6-23.

EXHIBIT 6-23 CREATING A FILTER IN GMAIL

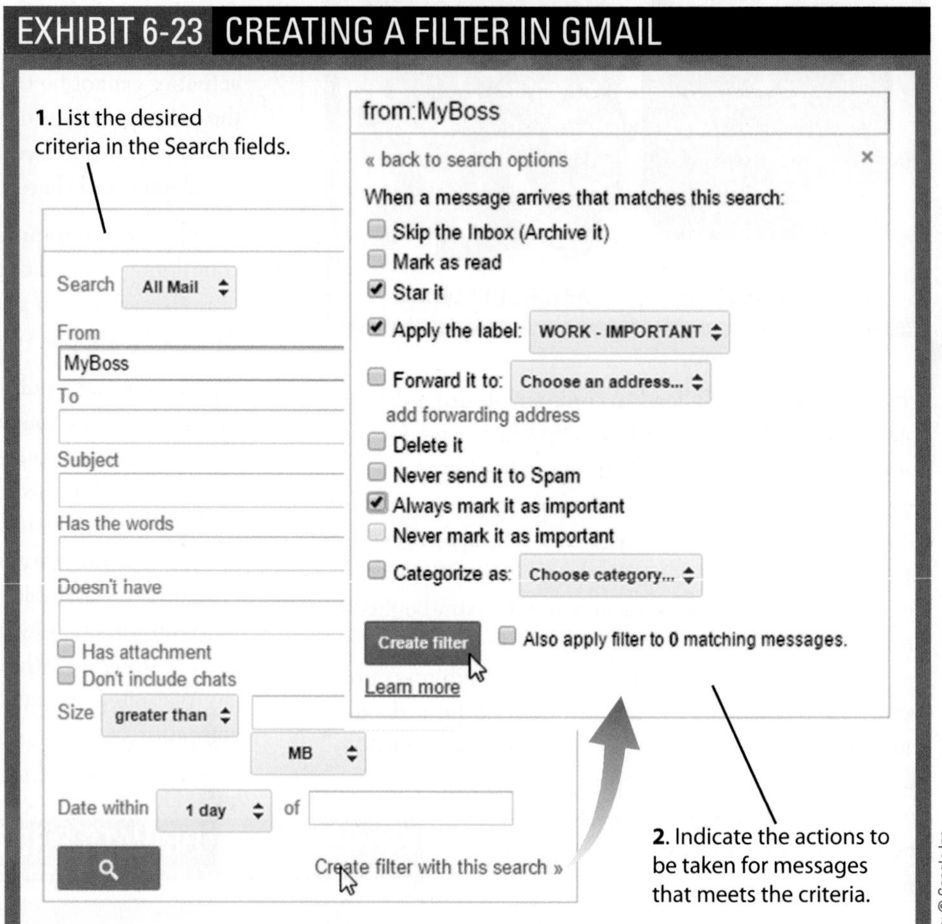

Source: © Google Inc.

Another way to reduce the amount of spam you receive is to opt out. **Opting out** refers to following a predesignated procedure to remove yourself from marketing lists or otherwise preventing your personal information from being obtained by or shared with others. By opting out, you instruct companies you do business with not to share your personal information with third parties. You can also opt out of being contacted by direct and online marketing companies.

Opting-out procedures are somewhat confusing and time consuming, and they do not always work well. Consequently, some privacy groups are pushing to change to an **opt-in** process, in which individuals would need to opt in—request participation in—to a particular marketing activity before companies can collect or share any personal data. This is already the case in the European Union. In fact, Walmart recently changed its privacy

email filter A tool that automatically sorts incoming email messages based on specific criteria.

spam filter An email filter used to redirect possible spam into a special folder.

opt out To request that you be removed from marketing activities or that your information not be shared with other companies.

opt in To request that you be included in marketing activities or that your information be shared with other companies.

policy to share information with third parties only if customers opt in. However, the general practice in the U.S. business community is to use your information as allowed for by each privacy policy unless you specifically opt out.

There are few options for protecting yourself against computer monitoring by your employer or the government or against video surveillance systems. However, businesses should take the necessary security measures to ensure that employee activities are not being monitored by a hacker or other unauthorized individual. People should also secure their home computers to protect against computer-monitoring software that may be inadvertently installed via a game or other downloaded file.

Strong security measures can help to protect against unauthorized access by hackers.

Businesses and organizations are responsible for keeping private information about their employees, the company, and their customers safe. Strong security measures can help to protect against unauthorized access by hackers. Businesses and organizations should take precautions against both intentional and accidental breaches of privacy by employees. In general, businesses must maintain a safe and productive workplace environment and protect the privacy of their customers and employees, while at the same time ensure that the company is not vulnerable to lawsuits.

Employees are responsible for reading a company's employee policy that specifies what personal activities are allowed during company time or on company equipment, as well as what activities, such as Web surfing, email, telephone calls, and file downloads, may be monitored when initially hired. They should review it periodically to ensure that they understand the policy and do not violate any company rules while working for that organization. Because employers can legally monitor at-work activities, it is wise—from a privacy standpoint—to avoid personal activities at work.

6-8 SECURITY AND PRIVACY LEGISLATION

The high level of concern regarding computer security, Internet security, and personal privacy has led state and federal legislators to pass a variety of laws since the 1970s. Internet privacy is viewed as one of the top policy issues facing Congress today, and numerous bills have been proposed in the last several years regarding spam, telemarketing, spyware, online profiling, and other important privacy issues. However, despite a renewed interest in privacy legislation, due to the recent leak of NSA surveillance operations, Congress has had difficulty passing new legislation. One reason is jurisdictional issues because many computer crimes affect businesses and individuals in geographic areas other than the one in which the computer criminal is located, and hackers can make it appear that activity is coming from a different location than it really is. Another reason is that the speed at which technology changes makes it difficult for the legal system to keep up. In addition, privacy is difficult to define, and there is a struggle to balance protection with freedom of speech and other civil liberties.

Another issue is weighing the need to implement legislation versus the use of voluntary methods to protect computer security and personal privacy. For instance, the *Child Online Protection Act (COPA)* has been controversial since it was passed in 1998, and, in fact, it has never been implemented. This legislation prohibited making pornography or any other content deemed harmful to minors available to minors via the Internet. This law was blocked by the U.S. Supreme Court several times, based on the likelihood that it violates the First Amendment and that less restrictive alternatives such as Internet filtering can be used instead to prevent the access of inappropriate materials by minors. A list of selected federal laws related to computer and Internet security and privacy is shown in Exhibit 6-24.

FYI

CHIEF PRIVACY OFFICER Ensuring that the private data stored by a business is adequately protected is increasingly the responsibility of a chief privacy officer (CPO)—a rapidly growing position in business. CPOs are responsible for ensuring that privacy laws are complied with, identifying the data in a company that needs to be protected, developing policies to protect that data, and responding to any incidents that occur. CPOs must also deal with the changing definition of what information is regarded as personal and, therefore, needs to be safeguarded.

EXHIBIT 6-24 EXAMPLES OF FEDERAL COMPUTER AND INTERNET SECURITY AND PRIVACY LEGISLATION

Date	Law and Description
2009	**American Recovery and Reinvestment Act** Requires HIPAA covered entities to notify patients when protected health information has been compromised.
2006	**U.S. SAFE WEB Act of 2006** Grants additional authority to the FTC to help protect consumers from spam, spyware, and Internet fraud and deception.
2005	**Real ID Act** Establishes national standards for state-issued driver's licenses and identification cards.
2004	**Identity Theft Penalty Enhancement Act** Adds extra years to prison sentences for criminals who use identity theft (including the use of stolen credit card numbers) to commit other crimes, including credit card fraud and terrorism.
2003	**Do Not Call Implementation Act** Amends the Telephone Consumer Protection Act to implement the National Do Not Call Registry.
2003	**CAN-SPAM Act** Implements regulations for unsolicited email messages.
2003	**Fair and Accurate Credit Transactions Act (FACTA)** Requires, among other things, that the three nationwide consumer reporting agencies (Equifax, Experian, and TransUnion) provide to consumers, upon request, a free copy of their credit report once every 12 months.
2003	**PROTECT Act** Includes provisions to prohibit virtual child pornography.
2003	**Health Insurance Portability and Accountability Act (HIPAA)** Includes a Security Rule that sets minimum security standards to protect health information stored electronically.
2002	**Homeland Security Act** Includes provisions to combat cyberterrorism, including protecting ISPs against lawsuits from customers for revealing private information to law enforcement agencies.
2002	**Sarbanes-Oxley Act** Requires archiving a variety of electronic records and protecting the integrity of corporate financial data.
2001	**USA PATRIOT Act** Grants federal authorities expanded surveillance and intelligence-gathering powers, such as broadening the ability of federal agents to obtain the real identity of Internet users, intercept email and other types of Internet communications, follow online activity of suspects, expand their wiretapping authority, and more.
2000	**Children's Internet Protection Act (CIPA)** Requires schools and libraries that receive discounts through the E-rate program to enact Internet safety policies, including filtering for obscene content.
1999	**Financial Modernization (Gramm-Leach-Bliley) Act** Extends the ability of banks, securities firms, and insurance companies to share consumers' non-public personal information, but requires them to notify consumers and give them the opportunity to opt out before disclosing any information.
1998	**Child Online Protection Act (COPA)** Prohibits online pornography and other content deemed harmful to minors; has been blocked by the Supreme Court.
1998	**Children's Online Privacy Protection Act (COPPA)** Regulates how Web sites can collect information from minors and communicate with them.
1998	**Telephone Anti-Spamming Amendments Act** Applies restrictions to unsolicited, bulk commercial email.
1998	**Identity Theft and Assumption Deterrence Act of 1998** Makes it a federal crime to knowingly use someone else's means of identification to commit any unlawful activity.
1997	**No Electronic Theft (NET) Act** Expands computer piracy laws to include distribution of copyrighted materials over the Internet.
1996	**National Information Infrastructure Protection Act** Amends the Computer Fraud and Abuse Act of 1984 to cover information theft crossing state lines and network trespassing.
1984	**Computer Fraud and Abuse Act of 1984** Makes it a crime to break into computers owned by the federal government. This act is regularly amended.

STUDY TOOLS 6

READY TO STUDY? IN THE BOOK, YOU CAN:

- ☐ Rip out the Chapter Review Card, which includes key terms and key chapter concepts.

ONLINE AT WWW.CENGAGEBRAIN.COM, YOU CAN:

- ☐ Review key concepts from the chapter in a short video.
- ☐ Explore how computer viruses spread with the interactive infographic.
- ☐ Practice what you've learned with more Practice It and On Your Own exercises.
- ☐ Prepare for tests with quizzes.
- ☐ Review the key terms with flashcards.

QUIZ YOURSELF

1. What is the difference between unauthorized access and unauthorized use?
2. What is the typical motivation for hacking?
3. What is war driving?
4. What type of access system uses a physical characteristic, such as a fingerprint?
5. What is the purpose of a firewall?
6. When would you encrypt a file?
7. What is malware?
8. What is a Trojan horse?
9. What does phishing attempt to do?
10. What is the best way to avoid phishing schemes?
11. What are the two most common ways individuals are harrassed online?
12. What is a full-disk encryption?
13. When would a ruggedized device be used?
14. What does information privacy refer to?
15. What is electronic profiling?
16. What does computer-monitoring software do?
17. Why would you use a throw-away email address?
18. What is the difference between opting out and opting in?

PRACTICE IT

Practice It 6-1

New computer viruses and other types of malware are released all the time. In addition to malware targeted toward computers, there is also mobile malware targeted to smartphones, tablets, and other Internet-enabled devices. Many security companies, such as Symantec and McAfee, list the most recent security threats on their Web sites.

1. Visit the Web site of a security company, and then identify a current virus or worm.
2. When was that virus or worm introduced? What does it do? How is it spread? To what types of devices is it targeted?
3. How many devices have been affected so far?
4. Is there an estimated cost associated with that virus or worm?
5. Is that virus or worm still in existence?
6. Have security programs been updated to locate and remove this malware? If not, is there a procedure for removing this virus or worm from an infected device?
7. Prepare a one-page summary of your findings and submit it to your instructor.

Practice It 6-2

Some people view using live surveillance cameras as a valid crime-prevention tool; other people think it is an invasion of privacy.

1. Is it ethical for businesses to use video cameras to record customers' activities? If so, for what purposes?
2. Does a government have the responsibility to use every means possible to protect the country and its inhabitants, or do people have the right not to be watched in public? Explain.

3. One objection stated about these systems is, "It is not the same as a cop on the corner. This is a cop on every corner." What if it were a live police officer at each public video camera location instead of a camera? Would that be more acceptable from a privacy standpoint? Why or why not?
4. If people do not plan to commit criminal acts in public, should they be concerned that law enforcement personnel may see them? Why or why not?
5. Do you think the risk of being recorded deters some illegal or unethical acts? Why or why not?
6. Prepare a one-page summary that answers these questions and submit it to your instructor.

ON YOUR OWN

On Your Own 6-1

Phishing and spear phishing attacks are still common and put individuals at risk. One of the newest twists is the use of social media. After a phisher hacks into a person's social media account, he or she posts comments or sends messages containing phishing links in hopes that the person's friends will click one of the links.

1. Find one example of a recent phishing, spear phishing, or social media hacking scheme. Was the attack targeted to a specific individual or a large number of people? Explain.
2. How many people fell victim to the scheme? What were the ramifications for the victims? Did they lose money? Explain.
3. Has the phisher been identified? If so, was he or she apprehended? If so, was the individual charged with a crime or prosecuted? Why or why not?
4. What precautions could the victims in this case taken to protect themselves or not fall victim to the scheme?
5. If the attack had been targeted to you, do you think you would have fallen for it? Why or why not? If so, are there any precautions you will now take to protect yourself in the future?
6. Prepare a one-page summary that answers these questions and submit it to your instructor.

CAPSTONE

COMPUTER CONCEPTS

Technology is changing our world at an explosive pace. Older technology becomes obsolete very quickly, and new technology is being introduced all the time. Think about some of the technological advances you have seen in the last several months, as well as technologies that have recently become obsolete.

1. Discuss the impact of the speed of new technological developments and the regular introduction of new technology. Be sure to consider the personal, business, societal, economic, global, and environmental impacts of new technology.
2. Select two recent examples of new technology. What benefit does the new technology provide? Be sure to consider the impact of that technology on individuals, businesses, local communities, the country, and the world.
3. Are there any risks related to these new technologies? If so, who is affected by these risks? Can these risks be minimized? If so, how? If not, why not?
4. In general, do the benefits of new technology outweigh the risks? Who should have the ultimate decision about whether the benefits of a new product outweigh the risks—Consumers? Government? Businesses? Explain your answer.
5. Are there ever ethical concerns related to the introduction of new technology? If so, list an example and explain the concerns surrounding that technology or product. If not, list an example of a new technology and explain why there are no ethical issues surrounding that technology or product.
6. Prepare a two- or three-page summary that answers these questions and submit it to your instructor.

Part 3
WINDOWS 10

7 | Exploring Windows 10 and Managing Files

© Bloomberg/Getty Images

LEARNING OBJECTIVES After studying the material in this chapter, you will be able to:

7-1 Use the Windows 10 desktop

7-2 Work with windows on the desktop

7-3 Work with the Windows file system

7-4 Work with files

7-5 Delete files and work with the Recycle Bin

7-6 Close apps and windows

7-7 Get help in Windows

7-8 Shut down Windows

After finishing this chapter, go to **PAGE 215** for **STUDY TOOLS**.

7-1 USING THE WINDOWS 10 DESKTOP

Many personal computers use the Microsoft **Windows 10** operating system—Windows 10 for short. Windows is the name of the operating system; 10 indicates the version. Windows 10 manages and coordinates activities on your computer and helps your computer perform essential tasks. As the operating system, Windows 10 is the starting point of everything you do on your computer.

7-1a Starting Windows 10

To start Windows 10, you simply turn your computer on. After completing the boot process, you need to sign in to your Windows 10 account. Once you do that, the desktop appears, as shown in Exhibit 7-1. The **desktop** is the work area for using apps and where you manage files and folders.

FYI USING A MICROSOFT ACCOUNT

A **Microsoft account** is a free account that associates an email address and password with Microsoft cloud services, such as Outlook.com for email, OneDrive for file storage, and Xbox Live for games. If you sign into Windows 10 with an email address and password, you are using a Microsoft account. If you sign in to Windows 10 with a user name that is not an email address and you do not have a password, you are not using a Microsoft account as your Windows 10 account. If you are not signed in to Windows 10 with a Microsoft account, you can sign in to your Microsoft account to use apps that require it, such as Mail (an app used to send and receive email messages) and Messaging (an app used to send and receive instant messages). You can also sign in to your Microsoft account to access and share files and other data stored on OneDrive. For example, you can store photos in a folder on your OneDrive, and you can use the Photos app to display those photos on your PC.

Begin Activity

Start Windows 10.

1. Turn on your computer. After a moment, Windows 10 starts. You will see either the lock screen or the Sign in screen. The lock screen displays a picture along with the current date and time. The Sign in screen lists all of the user names for accounts added to this PC.
2. If the lock screen appears, click anywhere on the screen or press any key to display the Sign in screen.
3. If your user name does not appear in the center of the Sign in screen, click your user name. If you do not have a password associated with your account, the Sign in button appears. If you have a password associated with your account, the Password box appears.
4. If you do not have a password, click **Sign in**. If you have a password, type the password associated with your user account in the Password box, and then press the **Enter key**. The desktop appears. Refer again to Exhibit 7-1.

End Activity

FYI MAKING WINDOWS 10 ACCESSIBLE

You can make Windows 10 more accessible to someone with physical limitations. Click the Start button ⊞ in the lower-left corner of the screen, and then click Settings. In the Settings window, click Ease of Access. In the EASE OF ACCESS window, you can turn on the Narrator (the screen reader), increase the size of items on the screen, change the colors to high contrast colors, display closed captions in apps, show the on-screen keyboard, adjust what happens when keys are pressed, change how the pointer looks, add keyboard control for the pointer, set the items to flash when a sound is played, and more.

Windows 10 The latest version of windows.

desktop The work area for using apps designed to run in Windows and for managing files and folders.

Microsoft account A free account that associates an email address and password with Microsoft cloud services.

EXHIBIT 7-1 WINDOWS 10 DESKTOP

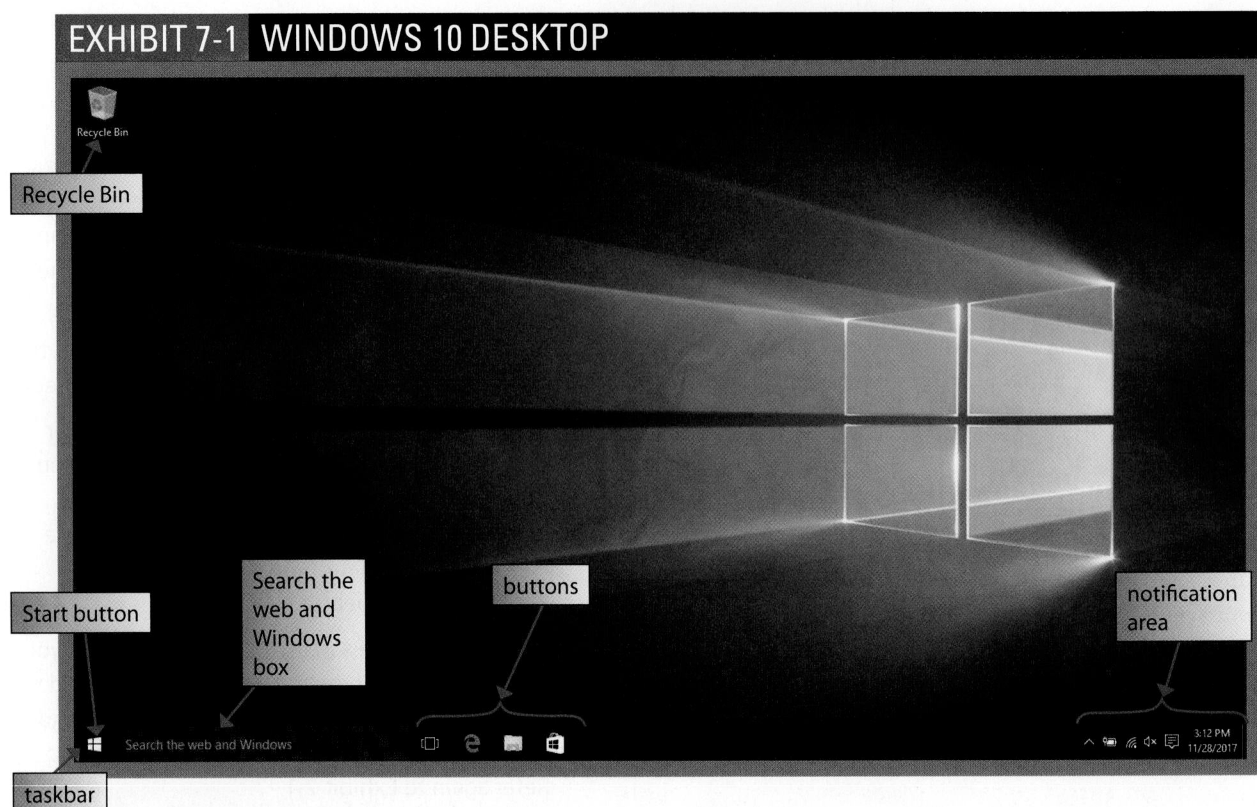

7-1b Exploring the Desktop

The desktop is the whole workspace on the screen. It includes the following features (refer to Exhibit 7-1):

- **Taskbar**—the horizontal bar containing buttons that provide quick access to common tools, running apps, and buttons to start some apps.
- **Button**—an object that you click to execute a command or perform a task.
- **Start button**—a button you use to start apps, access files, adjust settings on your computer, and other tasks.
- **Search the web and Windows box** or **Ask me anything box**—a box on the taskbar that you type text in or use to interact verbally with Windows using Cortana to search for anything stored on your computer, including apps, files such as documents, pictures, music, and videos, and settings, as well as search the Web for pages related to your search text.
- **Notification area**—the area on the right end of the taskbar containing icons that provide information about the computer and some of the apps that are running, as well as display the current date and time.
- **Recycle Bin**—a folder that stores items deleted from the hard drive until you remove them permanently.

To interact with the desktop, you use the keyboard and the pointing device. The most common pointing device is the mouse, so this book uses that term. If you are using a different pointing device, such as a trackball, or if you are using a touch pad or touch screen and your finger is the pointing device, substitute your device whenever you see the term *mouse*.

taskbar The horizontal bar containing buttons that provide quick access to common tools, running apps, and buttons to start some apps.

button An object that you click to execute a command or perform a task.

Start button A button you use to start apps, access files, adjust settings on your computer, and other tasks.

Search the web and Windows box/Ask me anything box A box on the taskbar that you type text in to search for anything stored on your computer, as well as search the Web for pages related to your search text.

notification area The part of the taskbar that displays icons that provide information about the computer and apps that are running, as well as display the current date and time.

Recycle Bin A folder that stores items deleted from the hard drive until you remove them permanently.

The **pointer** is a small object, such as an arrow, that moves on the screen when you move your mouse. The pointer is usually shaped like an arrow, although it changes shape depending on the pointer's location on the screen and the tasks you are performing. When you drag the mouse on a surface (or roll the trackball or slide your finger on a touch pad), the pointer on the screen moves in the corresponding direction. If you are using a touch screen, no pointer appears on the screen; you simply touch the part of the screen you want to interact with.

You use the mouse to perform specific actions:

- **Point**—to position the pointer directly on top of an item.
- **Click**—to press the left mouse button and immediately release it. (On a touch pad or touch screen, tap the screen with your finger.)
- **Right-click**—to click the right mouse button and immediately release it. (On a touch screen, press and hold your finger in a spot on the screen.)
- **Double-click**—to click the left mouse button twice in quick succession. (On a touch pad or touch screen, double-tap the screen with your finger.)
- **Drag**—to position the pointer on top of an item, and then press and hold the left mouse button while moving the pointer. (On a touch screen, swipe your finger over the item or items you want to drag to select them, and then press and hold your finger over the selected item or items and slide your finger on the screen.)

When you want more information about an item on the desktop, you can use the mouse to point to that item to make a **ScreenTip** appear, which identifies the name or purpose of the item. (ScreenTips do not appear on a touch screen.) In Exhibit 7-2, the ScreenTip for the date on the taskbar is displayed.

FYI USING CORTANA

Cortana is a feature of Windows 10 that allows you to search for apps and start them, search the Web for pages containing information about specific topics, and run certain apps, such as maintaining a list of items or appointments to remind you of using Cortana's Notebook. When you use Cortana, the history of the things you ask it to do is collected both on your computer and on a Microsoft server. This means the more you use it, the more Cortana will "get to know you" and be able to produce more relevant results.

To use Cortana, you need to set it up. After you set it up, you can type questions or commands using the keyboard, or if your computer has a microphone (most laptops have a built-in microphone) you can ask questions or issue commands verbally. When you first start to use Windows 10, dialog boxes appear asking you if you want to set up Cortana. If you did not set it up at that point, click in the Search the web and Windows box, click the circle above the Start button, and then follow the instructions that appear. After you set up Cortana, the Search the web and Windows box changes to the Ask me box. To use Cortana verbally, you click the microphone icon in the Ask me box, or you can say, "Hey, Cortana," if you have set it up to respond to that verbal command.

EXHIBIT 7-2 SCREENTIP DISPLAYED ON DESKTOP

pointer A small object, such as an arrow, that moves on the screen when you move your mouse.

point To position the pointer directly on top of an item.

click To press the left mouse button and immediately release it.

Cortana A Windows 10 feature that allows you to interact with Windows verbally.

right-click To click the right mouse button and immediately release it.

double-click To click the left mouse button twice in quick succession.

drag To position the pointer on top of an item, and then press and hold the left mouse button while moving the pointer.

ScreenTip A box that appears when you point to an item and that displays information about the item, such as its name or purpose.

FYI PERSONALIZING THE DESKTOP

The default desktop you see after you first install Windows 10 is a dark blue background with a picture of light streaming through four squares that represent a window, as shown in Exhibit 7-1. You can easily change the appearance of the desktop. To do this, right-click a blank area of the desktop to open the desktop shortcut menu, and then click Personalize to open the PERSONALIZATION screen in the Settings window. Here, you can change the background, the highlight colors (for example, the colors of the title bars in windows), what is displayed on the lock screen, how the Start menu looks, and the Windows theme used. A **Windows theme** is a set of desktop backgrounds, colors, sounds, and screen savers.

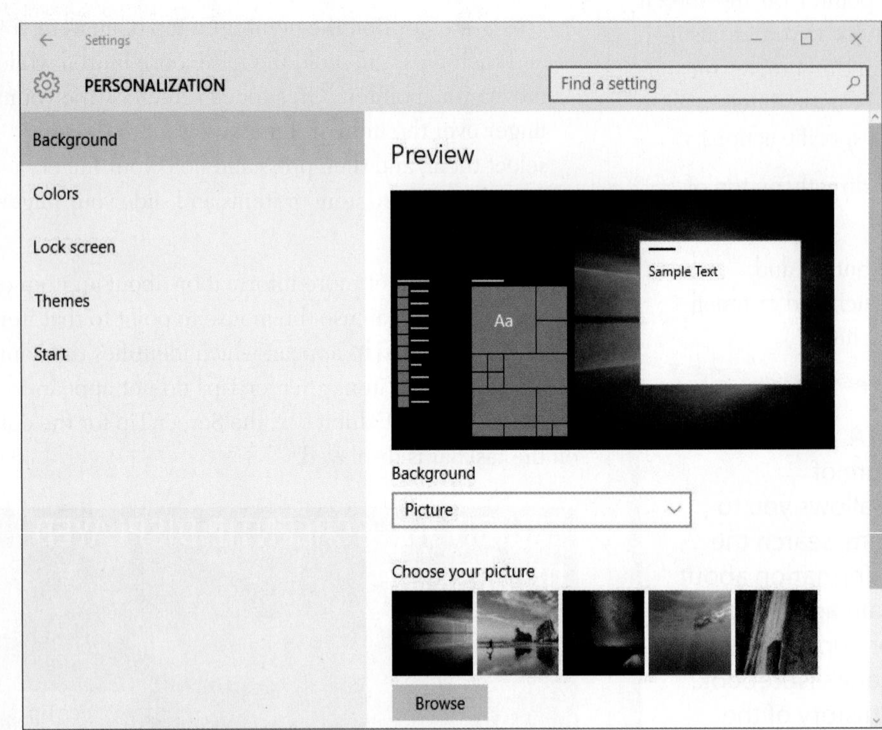

When you want to work with an item on the desktop, you need to select that item by clicking it. Clicking sends a signal to the computer that you want to perform an action on the object you clicked. When you right-click an item, the object is selected and a shortcut menu opens. A **menu** is a group or list of commands that you click to complete tasks. A **shortcut menu** lists actions you can take with the item you right-clicked. You can right-click practically anything on the desktop, including a blank area of the desktop, to view commands associated with that item. Shortcut menus provide the commands you need where you need them. Exhibit 7-3 shows the shortcut menu for the Recycle Bin.

EXHIBIT 7-3 RECYCLE BIN SHORTCUT MENU

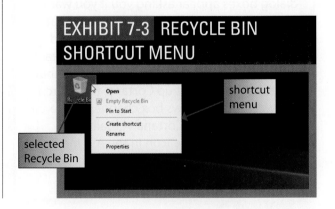

Open
Empty Recycle Bin
Pin to Start
Create shortcut
Rename
Properties

shortcut menu

selected Recycle Bin

menu A group or list of commands that you click to complete tasks.

shortcut menu A menu that lists actions you can take with the item you right-clicked.

Windows theme A set of desktop backgrounds, colors, sounds, and screen savers.

Begin Activity

Explore the desktop.

1 On the taskbar, in the notification area, point to the **date and time**. Its ScreenTip appears showing the long version of the current date. Refer again to Exhibit 7-2.

2 On your desktop, point to the **Recycle Bin icon**. A light shaded box appears around it.

3 Point to the **desktop**. The box disappears from around the Recycle Bin.

4 Click the **Recycle Bin**, and then point to the **desktop**. The Recycle Bin is selected as indicated by the shaded box around it.

5 Right-click the **Recycle Bin**. The Recycle Bin shortcut menu opens. Refer again to Exhibit 7-3. The commands on this menu are actions you can take with the Recycle Bin.

6 Click a **blank area of the desktop**. The shortcut menu closes without you selecting a command.

7 Right-click a **blank area of the desktop**. The desktop shortcut menu opens. The commands differ from the commands that you saw on the Recycle Bin shortcut menu.

8 Press the **Esc key**. The shortcut menu closes without selecting a command.

End Activity

7-1c Starting Apps

An **app** is a program designed to run on the desktop in a window. A **window** is a rectangular work area on the desktop that contains an app, text, files, or other data and tools for performing tasks.

To start an app, you use the Start menu or the Search the web and Windows box on the taskbar. You open the Start menu by clicking the Start button or pressing the Windows key on the keyboard. Pressing the Windows key is an example of using a **keyboard shortcut**, which means you press one or more keys on the keyboard to perform an action.

The Start menu is organized into two panes, as shown in Exhibit 7-4. A **pane** is a separate area of a menu or window. Each pane lists items you can point to or click.

EXHIBIT 7-4 START MENU

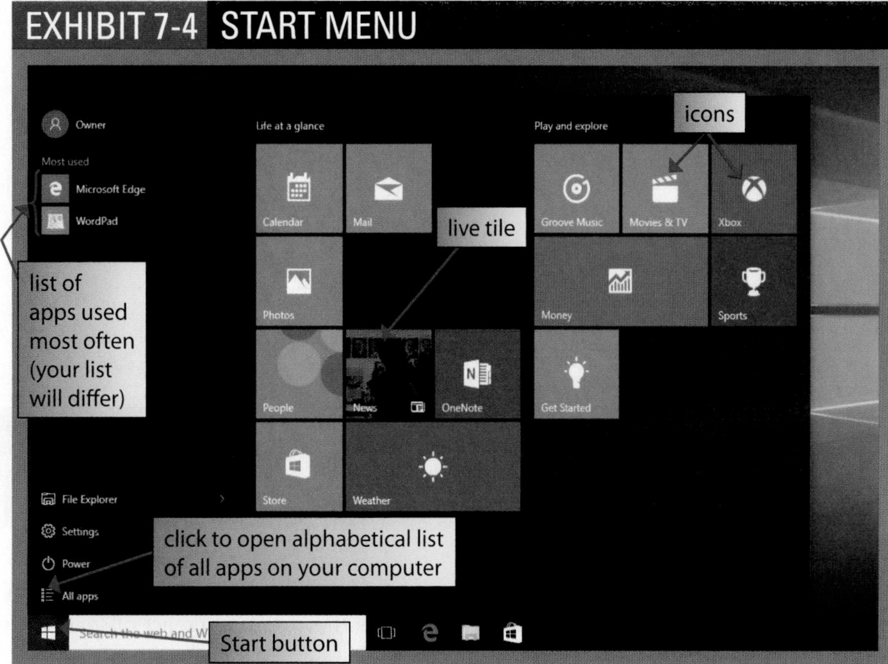

The left pane of the Start menu contains links to the apps you use most often, commands for opening specific windows on your computer, a command for turning off your computer, and a command to list all the apps on your computer. The right pane of the Start menu includes multicolored rectangles called **tiles**, which represent apps or other resources, such as Web pages. Some tiles display only an **icon**, a small picture that represents a resource available on your computer, such as an

app A program designed to run on the desktop in a window.

window A rectangular work area on the desktop that contains an app, text, files, or other data and tools for performing tasks.

keyboard shortcut A key or combination of keys that when pressed performs a command.

pane A separate area of a menu or window.

tile A rectangle on the Windows 10 Start screen that represents an app or another resource.

icon A small picture that represents a resource on your computer.

EXHIBIT 7-5 PAINT AND CALCULATOR APP WINDOWS OPEN ON THE DESKTOP

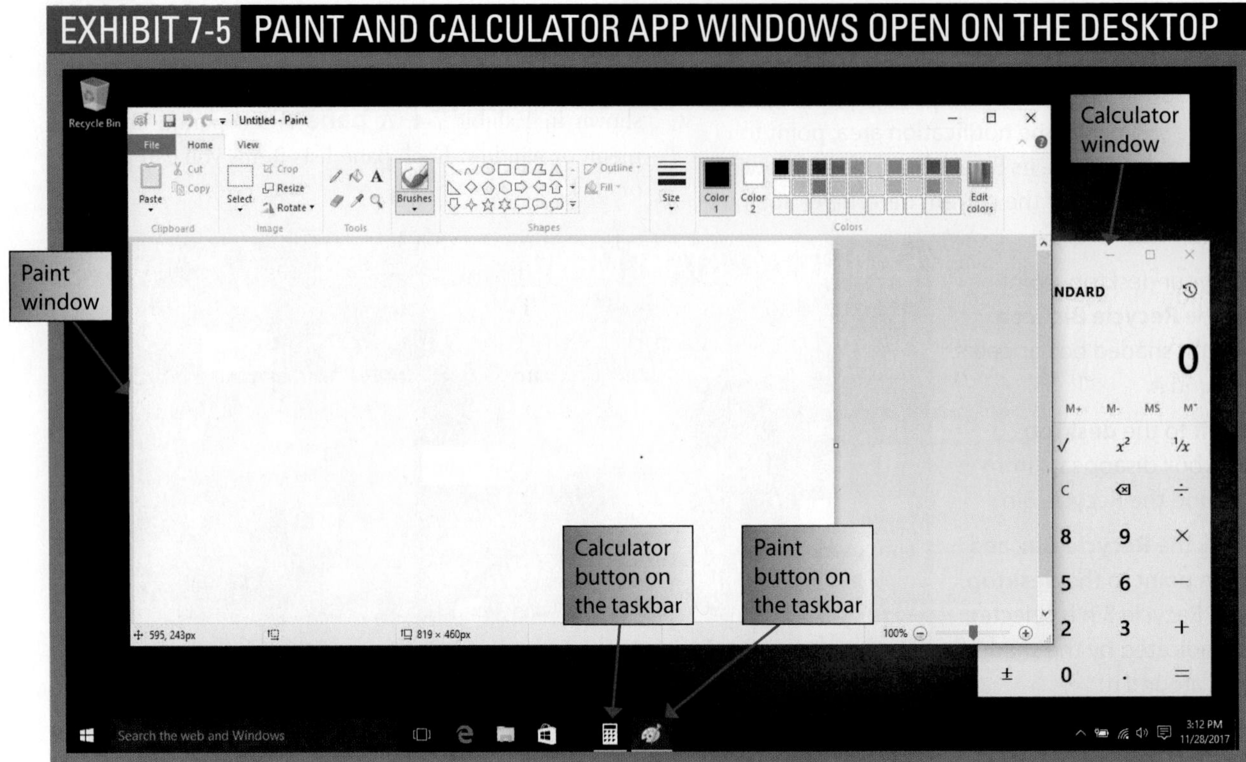

application or a file. Other tiles display pictures that preview the contents of the tile. For example, the Weather tile might display current weather conditions in cities around the world. A tile that displays content that is updated on a regular basis is called a **live tile**.

To start an app, you click a link in the left pane or a tile in the right pane on the Start menu. If you don't see the app you want to start, you can click All apps on the start menu to display a list of many of the apps installed on your computer. You can also click in the Search the web and Windows box and type the app name to display it in a list above the box.

When you click a link or tile on the Start menu or in the list of search results after typing in the Search the web or Windows box, the corresponding app starts and opens in a window on the desktop. Exhibit 7-5 shows the Paint and Calculator windows open on the desktop.

FYI

CUSTOMIZING THE START MENU AND THE TASKBAR

You can add tiles to the Start menu for any app, folder, or file on your computer. This is called **pinning**, which means the app name or tile is permanently displayed, as if it were pinned in place. Removing a tile from the Start menu is called **unpinning**. To pin an app as a tile on the Start menu, right-click the app in the All apps list, and then on the shortcut menu, click Pin to Start. To unpin a tile, right-click the tile, and then click Unpin from Start on the shortcut menu. To pin an app as a button on the taskbar, right-click it in the All apps list or right-click the tile, point to More, and then click Pin to taskbar.

You can also rearrange and group tiles on the Start menu. For example, you might want to keep folders in one group, entertainment apps such as Music and Games in another group, and apps for keeping in touch with people, such as Mail, Messaging, and People, in a different group. To create or rename a group, click the space or current group name between rows of tiles. In the box that appears, type the group name you want, and then press Enter. To rearrange tiles, drag a tile to another location on the Start menu. If you need more room for tiles, you can drag the top or right edge of the Start menu to resize it.

live tile A tile that displays content that is regularly updated.

pin To permanently display an item.

unpin To remove a pinned item so that it is no longer displayed.

Begin Activity

Start apps.

1 On the taskbar, click the **Start button** ⊞. The Start menu opens. Refer again to Exhibit 7-4.

2 Click **All apps**. An alphabetized list of apps installed on your computer appears.

TIP: Click a letter in the All apps list to display the complete alphabet, and then click the letter you want to scroll to.

3 In the All apps list, click **Calculator**. The Calculator app starts and opens in a window. A button corresponding to the app appears on the taskbar.

4 On the keyboard, press the **Windows key**. The Start menu opens.

5 Type **Paint**. Paint is an app that you use to draw, color, and edit pictures. The text you type appears in the Search the web and Windows box, and a search results pane appears in place of most of the Start menu with Paint at the top of the list.

6 In the search results, click **Paint Desktop app**. The Paint app window opens on the desktop. The text *Untitled – Paint* appears at the top of the open window. A button corresponding to the Paint window appears on the taskbar. Refer again to Exhibit 7-5.

PROBLEM?
If the app windows are in a different position on your screen, or if the Paint window covers the Calculator window, don't worry about this.

End Activity

FYI **DESKTOP APPS AND TRUSTED WINDOWS STORE APPS**

Some apps are categorized as desktop apps and some are categorized as trusted Windows Store apps. Either type of app runs on computers that run Windows 10, so you don't need to worry about the difference between them if you are using a computer running Windows 10. Trusted Windows Store apps also run on mobile devices such as smartphones and tablets.

7-2 WORKING WITH WINDOWS ON THE DESKTOP

When you work on the desktop, you interact with windows. There are three types of windows: app windows, File Explorer windows, and dialog boxes. **App windows** display commands for working with the app and its workspace. You opened two app windows when you started Paint and Calculator. You use **File Explorer windows** to navigate, view, and work with the contents and resources on your computer. **Dialog boxes** are a special kind of window in which you enter or choose settings for how you want to perform a task. When a File Explorer or app window is open, a corresponding button appears on the taskbar. If more than one window is open in an app or if more than one File Explorer window is open, the windows are grouped together in one button representing the app or File Explorer on the taskbar.

All windows have a **title bar** at the top of the window that displays the name of the window. They also have a Close button ☒ at the right end of the title bar that you can click to close the window. App windows and File Explorer windows also have **sizing buttons**, located to the left of the Close button on the title bar, to enlarge or shrink a window. Most app and File Explorer windows have a **status bar** at the bottom of the window that displays information or messages about the task you are performing or the selected item. See Exhibit 7-6.

app window A window that opens when an app starts and displays commands for working with the app and the app's workspace.

File Explorer window A window you use to navigate, view, and work with the contents and resources on your computer.

dialog box A window that opens when you need to enter or choose settings for how you want to perform a task.

title bar A banner at the top of a window that displays the window title and contains the Close button and sizing buttons.

sizing buttons The buttons used to enlarge or shrink a window.

status bar A banner at the bottom of a window that displays information or messages about the task you are performing or the selected item.

EXHIBIT 7-6 COMMON WINDOW ELEMENTS

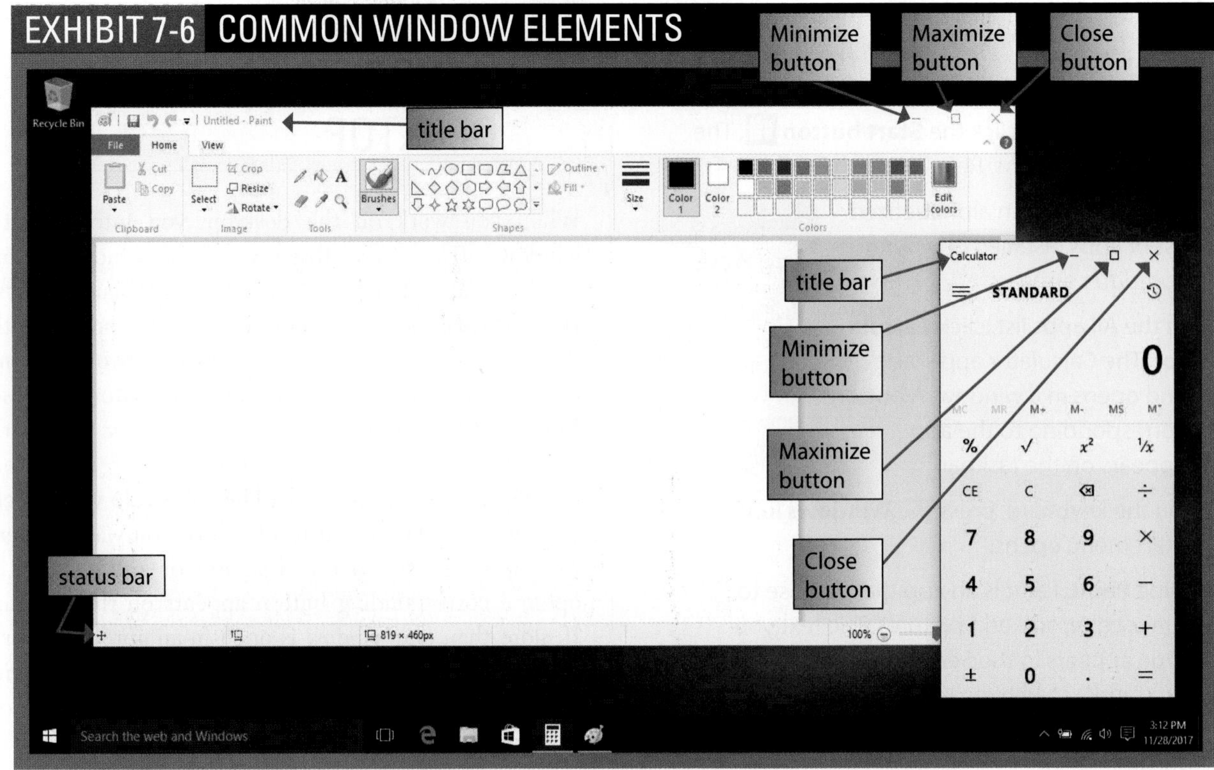

7-2a Switching Between Open Windows

When more than one window is open on the desktop, only one can be the **active window**, the window to which the next keystroke or command is applied. If two or more windows overlap, the active window appears in front of the other windows. The button for the active window is highlighted on the taskbar.

To make a window active, you can click in it or you can click its button on the taskbar. If more than one window is open in an app or if more than one File Explorer window is open, when you click the corresponding button on the taskbar, **thumbnails** (miniature images) for each window appear above the button, and you click the thumbnail of the window you want to switch to. Exhibit 7-7 shows the one open window in the running Paint app displayed as a thumbnail above the button on the taskbar.

Another way to switch between open windows is to use **Task View**, which displays all of the open windows on the desktop. See Exhibit 7-8. You can click a window in Task View to make it the active window.

active window The window to which the next keystroke or command is applied.

thumbnail A miniature image.

Task View A display of all of the open windows on the desktop.

Begin Activity

Switch between open windows.

1. On the taskbar, point to the **Calculator button** . A thumbnail of the Calculator window appears above the taskbar. Refer to Exhibit 7-7.
2. Move the **pointer** on top of the Calculator window thumbnail. A Close button appears on the thumbnail, and only the Calculator window appears on the desktop.
3. On the taskbar, click the **Calculator button** . The Calculator window is the active window.
4. On the taskbar, click the **Task View button** . All of the open windows appear on the desktop at a reduced size. Refer again to Exhibit 7-8.
5. Click the **Paint window**. The Paint window becomes the active window and returns to the size it was previously.

TIP: You can also press and hold the Alt key, and then press and release the Tab key to display all open windows as thumbnails; press the Tab key to cycle through the thumbnails.

End Activity

EXHIBIT 7-7 THUMBNAIL OF AN OPEN WINDOW DISPLAYED ABOVE THE TASKBAR

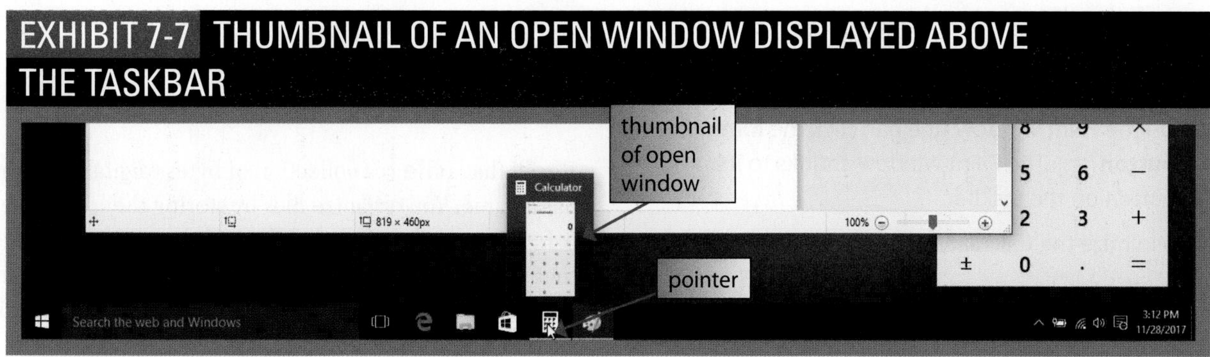

EXHIBIT 7-8 TASK VIEW SHOWING OPEN WINDOWS

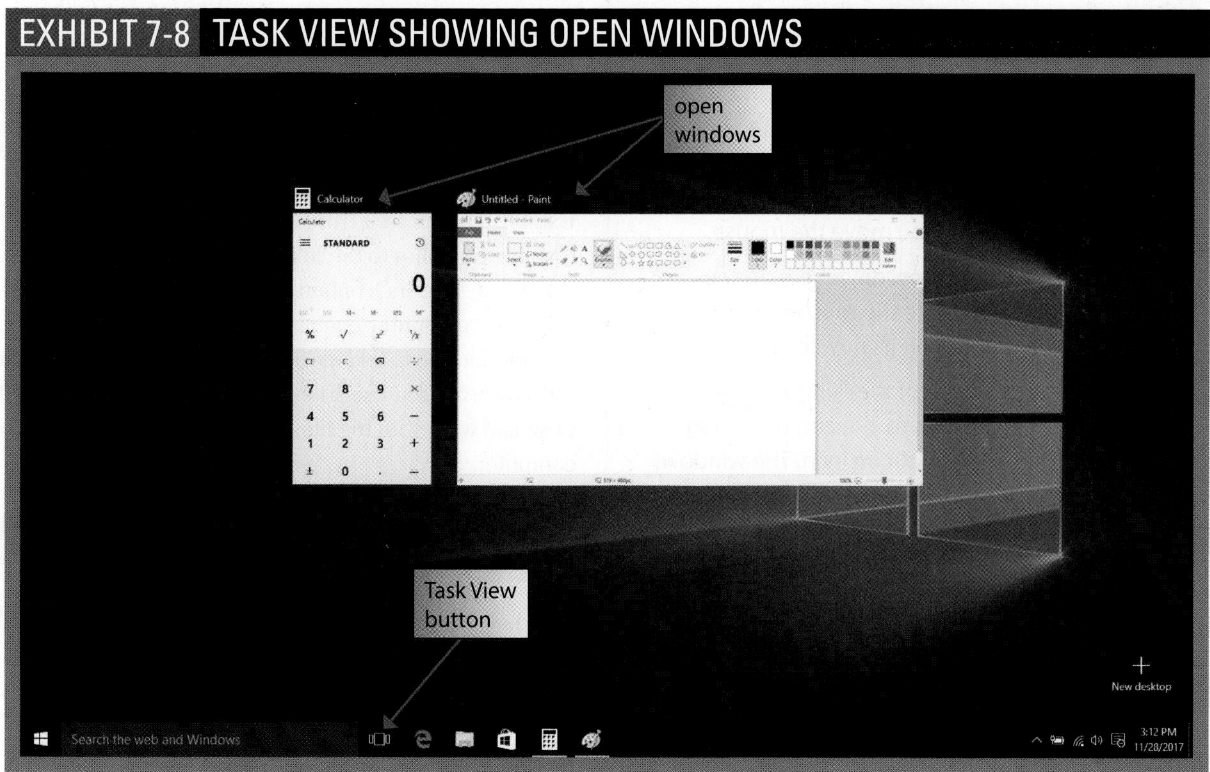

7-2b Resizing and Moving Windows

You can change the size and position of the active window. The sizing buttons appear on the right end of the title bar. The first button is the Minimize button [—], which shrinks a window to its button on the taskbar. A minimized window is still open. You can redisplay a minimized window by clicking the window's button on the taskbar or by pointing to the button on the taskbar and then clicking the thumbnail that appears.

The next sizing button changes depending on the state of the window. If the window is not as large as it can be on the screen, the button is the Maximize button [□]. When you click the Maximize button, the window resizes to fill the screen. When the window is maximized, the button is the Restore Down button [🗗]. Clicking the Restore Down button returns the window to the size it was before you maximized it.

You can also resize a window manually, if it is not maximized. When you point to a window border, the pointer changes to a two-headed arrow. Using the two-headed arrow pointer, you drag the window border until the window is the size you want. To move a window to a new position on the screen, you drag the window by its title bar. You cannot reposition a maximized window.

Begin Activity

Resize and move windows.

1 On the Paint window title bar, click the **Minimize button** [—]. The Paint window shrinks to its button on the taskbar.

2 Minimize the Calculator window.

3 On the taskbar, click the **Paint button**. The Paint window reappears on the desktop.

4 On the Paint window title bar, click the **Maximize button** [□]. The Paint window expands to fill the screen.

5 On the Paint window title bar, click the **Restore Down button**. The Paint window returns to its previous size.

6 Point to the **Paint window title bar** (the pointer should still be), press and hold down the **left mouse button**, and then drag in one direction. The window moves as you move the mouse.

7 Position the **Paint window** anywhere on the desktop, and then release the **mouse button**. The Paint window stays in its new location.

8 Point to the **left border** of the Paint window so that the pointer changes to ⇔, and then drag the border to the left about an inch. The window widens by the amount you dragged.

9 Drag the **left border** of the Paint window to the right about an inch to return the window to its previous size.

10 Drag the **Paint window** by its title bar to reposition it in its original location.

11 Minimize the Paint window.

End Activity

file A named collection of bytes stored on a drive.

folder A container that helps to organize files on a computer.

file system The hierarchy of how files and folders are organized.

root directory The top of the file system where folders and files that Windows needs when you turn on the computer are stored.

subfolder A folder contained within another folder.

7-3 WORKING WITH THE WINDOWS FILE SYSTEM

Recall that a **file** is a collection of bytes (digital data) that has a name. You organize files by storing them in folders. A **folder** is a container for files, similar to a paper folder that is used to organize files in a file cabinet. Files and folders are stored on disks, including removable media, such as USB drives and hard disks.

Windows stores thousands of files in many folders on the hard disk of your computer. The folders and files on your drives are organized in a hierarchy, or **file system**. At the top of the hierarchy, Windows stores folders and files that it needs when you turn on the computer. This location is called the **root directory** and is usually drive C (the hard disk). The term *root* refers to a popular metaphor for visualizing a file system—an upside-down tree, which reflects the file hierarchy that Windows uses. In Exhibit 7-9, the tree trunk corresponds to the root directory, the branches to the folders, and the leaves to the files.

Some folders contain other folders. An effectively organized computer contains a few folders in the root directory, and those folders contain other folders, also called **subfolders**. You use File Explorer windows to navigate, view, and work with the files, folders, and resources on your computer.

EXHIBIT 7-9 WINDOWS FILE HIERARCHY

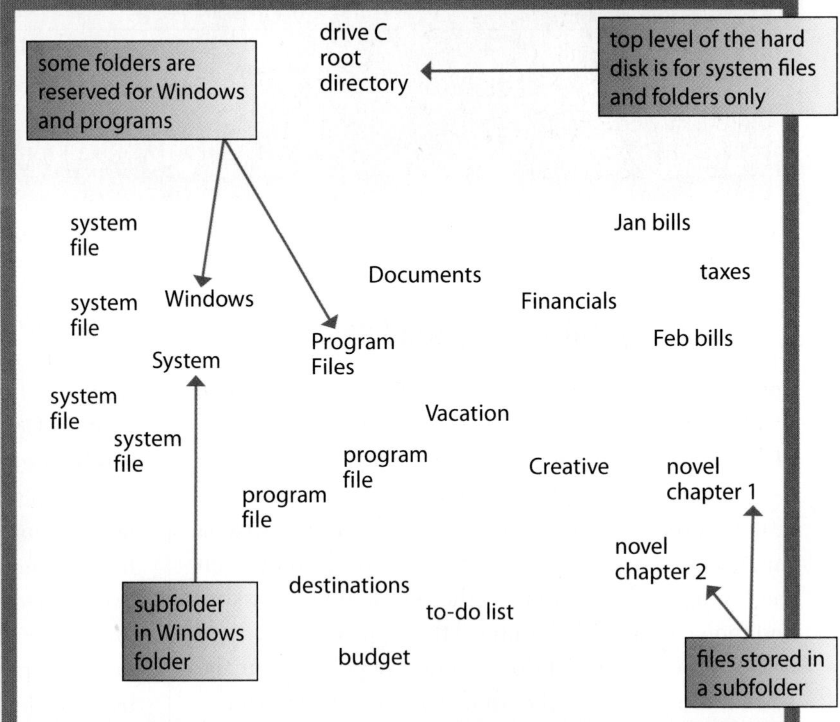

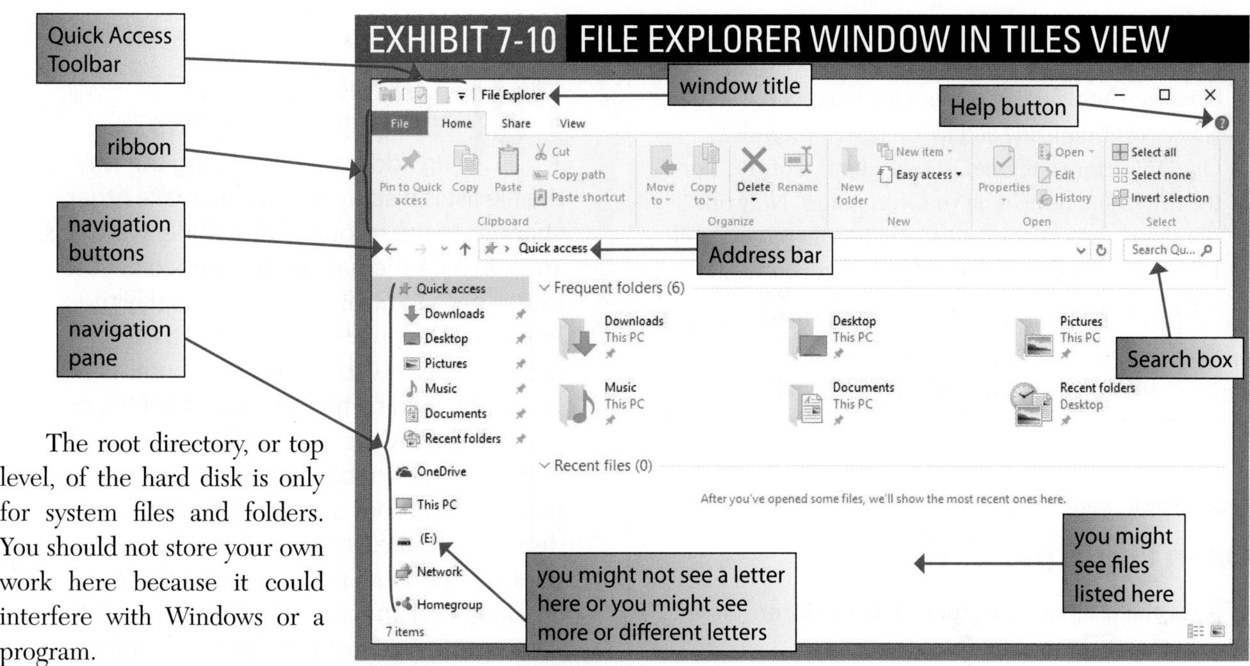

The root directory, or top level, of the hard disk is only for system files and folders. You should not store your own work here because it could interfere with Windows or a program.

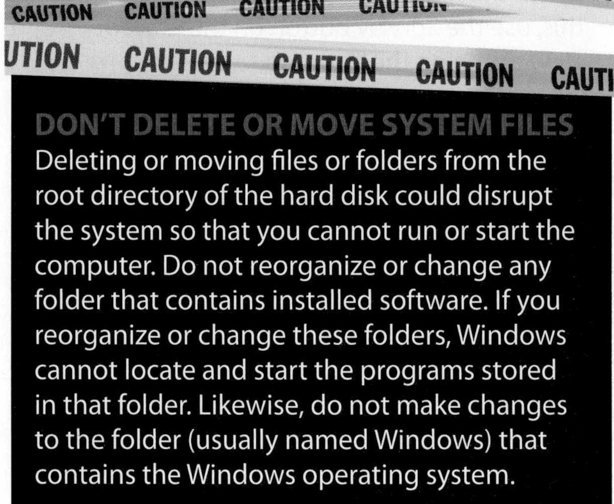

DON'T DELETE OR MOVE SYSTEM FILES
Deleting or moving files or folders from the root directory of the hard disk could disrupt the system so that you cannot run or start the computer. Do not reorganize or change any folder that contains installed software. If you reorganize or change these folders, Windows cannot locate and start the programs stored in that folder. Likewise, do not make changes to the folder (usually named Windows) that contains the Windows operating system.

7-3a Opening a File Explorer Window

When you open a Files Explorer window, you are looking at the contents of the computer, a drive, or a folder. In addition to the title bar, sizing buttons, and status bar, File Explorer windows contain the following elements, which are called out in Exhibit 7-10:

- **Quick Access Toolbar**—contains buttons for frequently used commands.
- **Ribbon**—contains commands for working with the contents of the window organized into tabs of related activities or tasks. Each tab is organized into groups of related commands. As you open different folders and navigate with File Explorer, new tabs appear at the top of the window to the right of the existing tabs. This type of tab is called a contextual tab, and it contains options related to your current task. For example, the Picture Tools Manage tab appears when you navigate to the Pictures library and contains options for working with pictures.
- **Help button**—opens a Web page in your browser listing search results in the Bing search engine for the search phrase "get help with file explorer in windows 10."
- **Navigation buttons**—returns the display to a previously viewed window.
- **Address bar**—lists the location of the currently displayed folder.
- **Search box**—locates an item in the current location that matches the key words you typed in it.

Quick Access Toolbar An area at the left side of the title bar that contains buttons for frequently used commands.

ribbon An area at the top of File Explorer and some application windows that contains commands for working with the contents of the window.

Address bar A bar in a File Explorer window that lists the location of the currently displayed folder.

Search box A box near the top of a File Explorer window that you can use to search for items containing key words.

- **Navigation pane**—contains icons and links to locations on your computer and your network organized into five categories: Quick access (for folders you access frequently and files accessed recently), OneDrive (for your OneDrive location), This PC (for the drives and devices on your computer), Network (for network locations your computer can access), and Homegroup (for your shared home network, if any).

When you open a new File Explorer window, it opens with Quick access selected in the navigation pane and with the 10 most frequently accessed folders and the 20 most recently accessed files listed in the window.

Begin Activity

Open File Explorer windows.

1. On the taskbar, point to the **File Explorer button** to see its ScreenTip.
2. Click the **File Explorer button**. A File Explorer window opens with Quick access selected in the navigation pane. Refer again to Exhibit 7-10.
3. On the taskbar, right-click the **File Explorer button**. A shortcut menu opens.
4. Click **File Explorer**. A second File Explorer window opens with Quick access selected in the navigation pane.

End Activity

TIP: You can also click the File tab on the ribbon, and then click Open new window.

7-3b Changing the View of File Explorer Windows

The File Explorer window provides a variety of ways to view the contents of a folder—Extra large icons, Large icons, Medium icons, Small icons, List, Details, Tiles, and Content. Exhibit 7-10 in the previous section shows a folder in Tiles view, and Exhibit 7-11 shows a folder in Details view.

navigation pane An area on the left side of File Explorer windows that contains icons and links to locations on your computer and your network.

FYI

CUSTOMIZING FILE EXPLORER WINDOWS

In addition to changing the way the file list is displayed, you can make other changes to the layout of your folder windows. You can hide the navigation pane to devote more space to file lists. You can display the Preview pane on the right side of a File Explorer window to display the contents of a picture file and some other types of files, or you can display the Details pane on the right to display information about a selected file, such as the author and file type. (You cannot display both the Details and the Preview panes at the same time.) To make these changes, click the appropriate buttons in the Panes group on the View tab on the ribbon. In some views, you can change the order in which the files and folders are listed. To do this, use the Sort by button on the Current view group on the View tab.

EXHIBIT 7-11 FILE EXPLORER FOLDER IN DETAILS VIEW

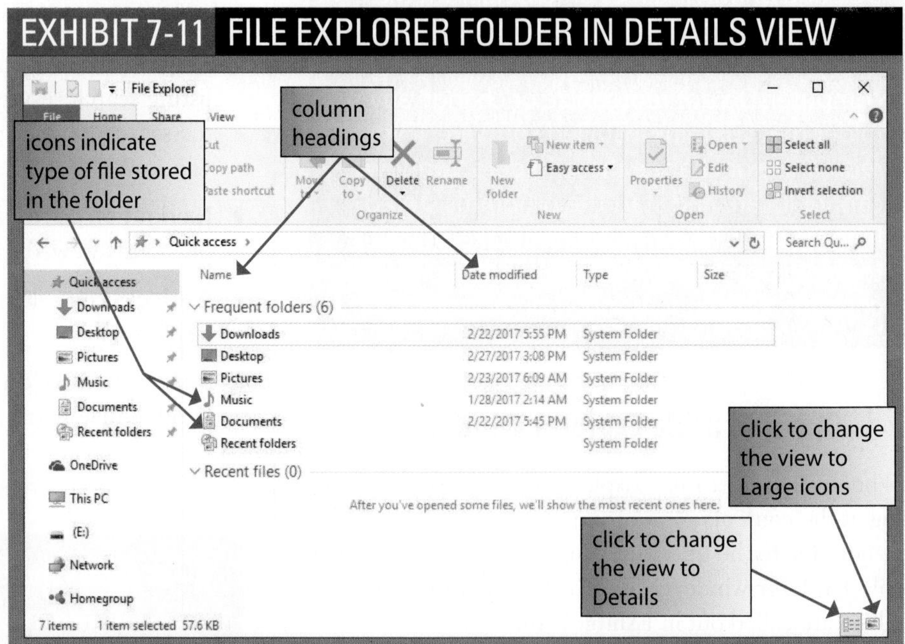

Exhibit 7-12 shows a File Explorer window with the View tab on the ribbon selected. To change the view, click one of the buttons in the status bar of the window, right-click a blank area of the window and then point to View, or use the View tab on the ribbon in the window.

EXHIBIT 7-12 FILE EXPLORER WINDOW WITH THE VIEW TAB SELECTED

Begin Activity

Change the view in aFile Explorer window.

1 In the active File Explorer window, click the **View tab** on the ribbon. The commands on the View tab appear. Refer again to Exhibit 7-12.

2 In the Layout group on the View tab, click the **List button.** The folders in the File Explorer window are displayed as a list. If files are listed in the File Explorer window on your screen, the files are also displayed as a list next to the folders.

3 On the status bar, click the **Large icons button** [icon]. The folder now shows the contents of the window as large icons.

4 On the status bar, click the **Details button** [icon]. The file list is displayed in Details view. Refer again to Exhibit 7-11.

End Activity

7-3c Developing an Organizational Strategy

Having well-organized files and folders makes it easier and faster to find the files you want. To develop a strategy for organizing your folders and files, first, determine which files seem to belong together. Then, develop an appropriate file structure. Exhibit 7-13 shows how you could organize your files on a hard disk if you were taking distance-learning classes. To duplicate this organization, you would open the main folder for your documents, create four folders—one each for the Accounting, Computer Concepts, Management Skills, and Business Writing courses—and then store the writing assignments you complete in the Business Writing folder.

FYI DETERMINING WHERE TO STORE FILES

When you create and save files on your computer's hard disk, you should store them in subfolders. The top level of the hard disk is off-limits for your files because they could interfere with system files. If you are working on your own computer, store your files within the Documents folder, which is where many programs save files by default. When you use a computer that has access to a network, you might be assigned a folder to you for storing your work. In either case, if you simply store all your files in one folder, you will soon have trouble finding the files you want. Instead, you should create subfolders within a main folder to separate files in a way that makes sense for you. Even if you store most of your files on removable media, such as USB drives, you should organize those files into folders and subfolders.

Spectral-Design/Shutterstock.com

EXHIBIT 7-13 FOLDERS AND FILES ORGANIZED ON A HARD DISK

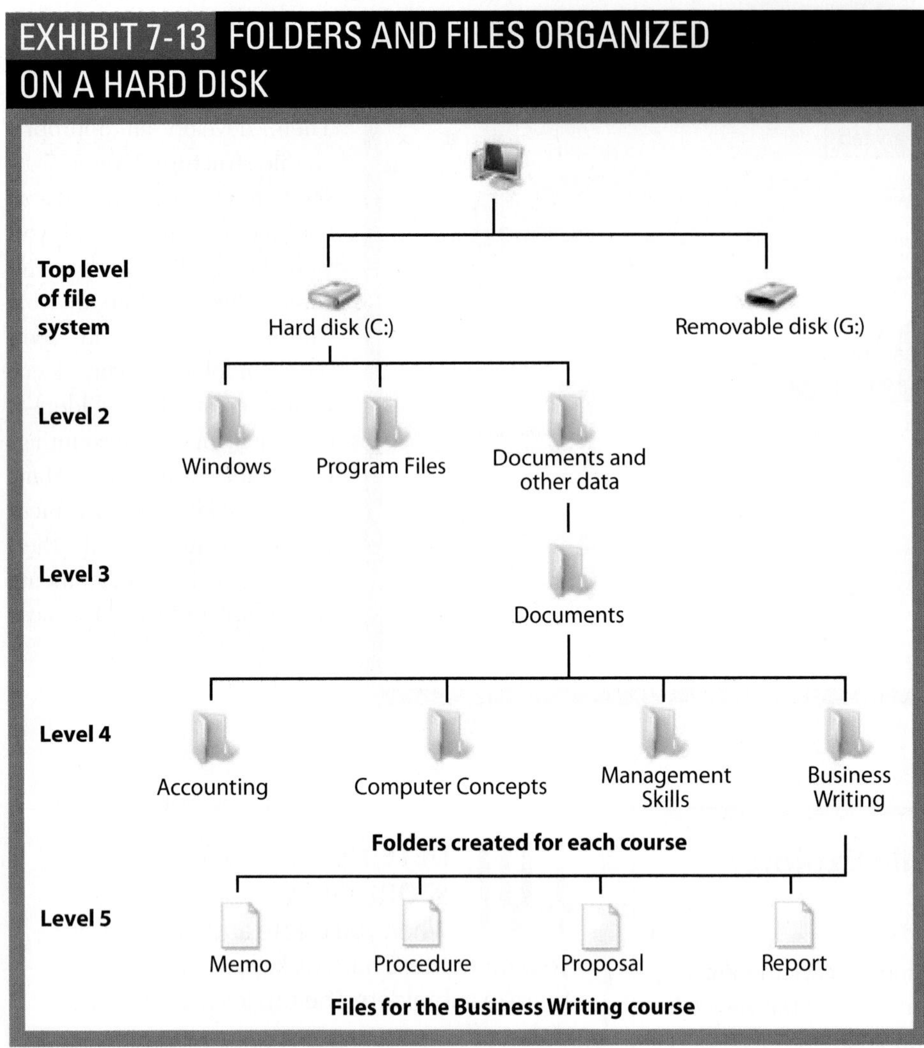

If you store your files on removable media, such as a USB drive, you can use a simpler organization because you do not have to account for system files. In general, the larger the medium, the more levels of folders you should use because large media can store more files and, therefore, need better organization. For example, if you are organizing files on a USB drive, you could create folders in the top level of the USB drive for each general category of documents you store—one each for Courses, Creative, Financials, and Vacation. The Courses folder could then include one folder for each course, and each of those folders could contain the appropriate files.

navigate To move from one location to another on your computer.

path The notation that indicates a file's location on a computer.

7-3d Navigating to Folders

You explore, or navigate, your computer to work with its contents and resources. In this context, **navigate** means to move from one location to another on your computer, such as from one window or folder to another. To successfully navigate your computer, you need to understand a bit about how your computer is organized.

The contents of the Quick access folder, the folder that is selected when you first open a File Explorer window, changes as you use your computer. The Quick access folder lists up to the 10 most frequently used folders and up to the 20 most recently accessed files. If you click This PC in the navigation pane, you see the drives on your computer, network locations, and the six folders in the This PC folder: Desktop, Documents, Downloads, Music, Pictures, and Videos.

You can display the storage devices on your computer by displaying the This PC folder. See Exhibit 7-14. Recall that a computer distinguishes one disk drive from another by assigning each a drive letter, and the first hard drive in a computer is usually drive C. If you add additional hard drives, they are usually designated D, E, and so on. If you have a DVD drive or a USB flash drive plugged into a USB port, it usually has the next letter in the alphabetic sequence. For example, your USB drive might be drive E, as in Exhibit 7-14, or drive G. If you can access hard drives on other computers in a network, those drives sometimes (although not always) have letters associated with them as well.

To navigate to the files you want, it helps to know the file path. The **path** shows the location of a file on a computer and leads you through the file and folder organization to the file. For example, a file named Letterhead is stored in the Chapter subfolder of the Chapter 7 folder

EXHIBIT 7-14 RELATIONSHIP BETWEEN YOUR COMPUTER AND THE THIS PC WINDOW

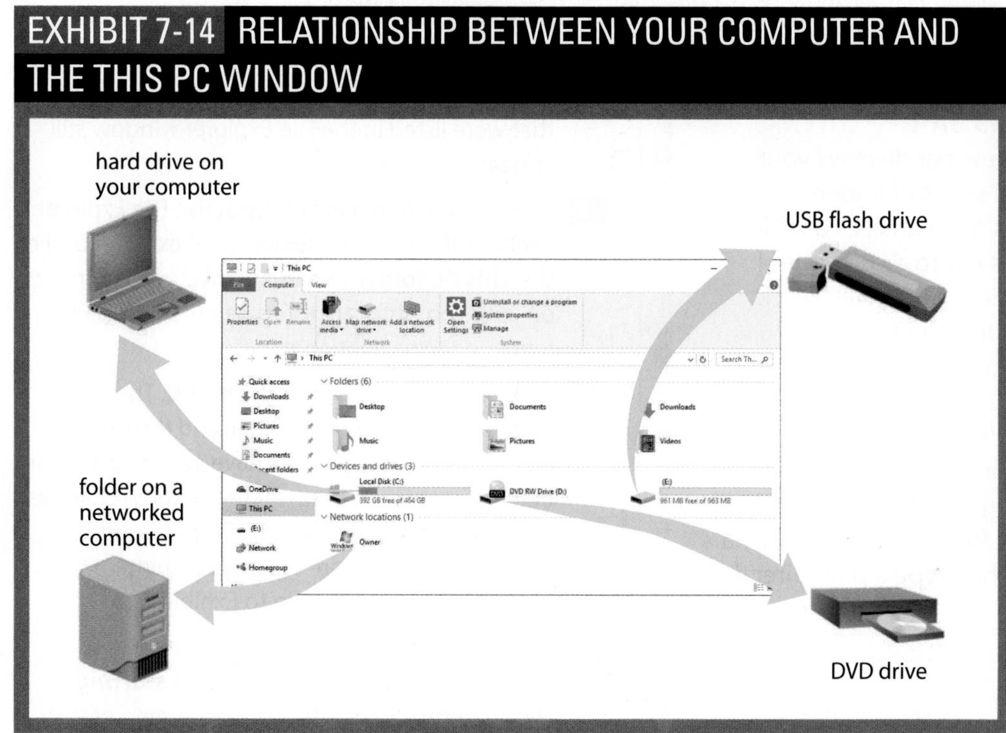

the contents of that folder or drive, or you can click a folder or drive in the navigation pane to navigate directly to that folder or drive and display its contents in the window. When you move the pointer into the navigation pane or when a folder is selected in the navigation pane, arrows appear next to some of the names, as shown in Exhibit 7-15. Right-pointing arrows [>]—called expand arrows—indicate that the location contains other folders that are not currently displayed in the navigation pane. Downward-pointing arrows [v]—collapse arrows—indicate the folder is expanded, and its subfolders are listed below the folder name. Exhibit 7-15 shows This PC selected and expanded in the navigation pane.

included with your data files. If you are working on a USB drive, the path to this file might be:

G:\Chapter 7\Chapter\Letterhead.docx

This path has four parts, and each part is separated by a backslash (\ ):

- **G:**—the drive name
- **Chapter 7**—a top-level folder on drive G
- **Chapter**—a subfolder in the Chapter 7 folder
- **Letterhead.docx**—the name of the file

To find the file G:\Chapter 7\Chapter\Letterhead.docx, you must navigate to drive G, open the Chapter 7 folder, and then open the Chapter folder to find the Letterhead file.

You can use any File Explorer window to navigate to the data files you need for the rest of these chapters. You can double-click a folder or drive in the window to display

EXHIBIT 7-15 COLLAPSED AND EXPANDED FOLDERS IN THE NAVIGATION PANE

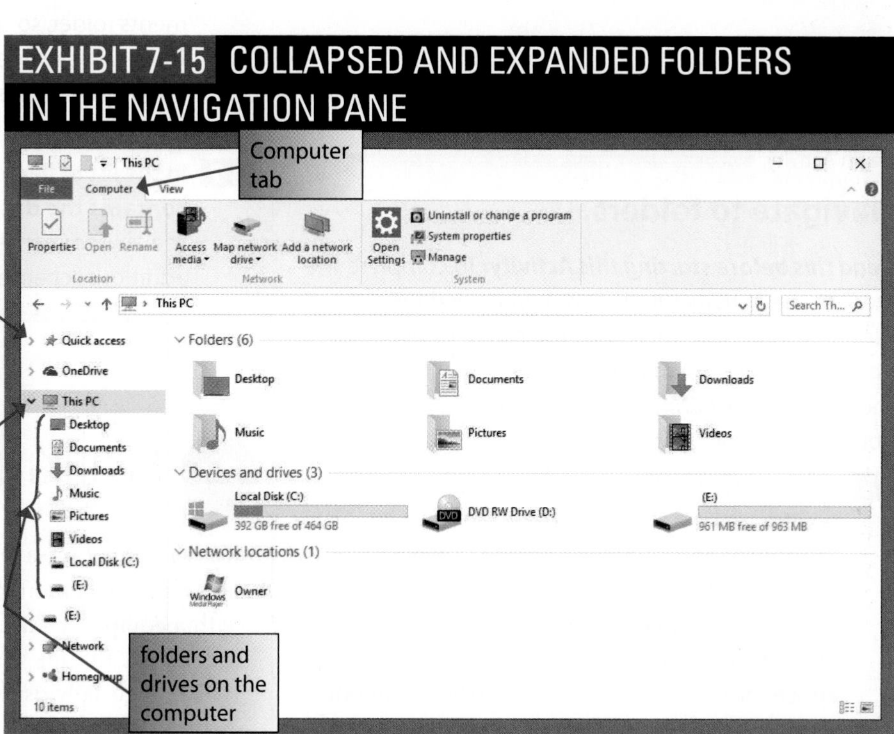

FYI

NAVIGATING WITH THE ADDRESS BAR

The Address bar displays your current location as a series of folders separated by arrows. You can click a folder name in the Address bar to display the contents of that folder. You can also click an arrow to open a drop-down list with the names of each folder in that location. To display the contents of one of those folders, click the folder name in the list. You can also click the icon at the left end of the Address bar to change the hierarchy in the Address bar so each folder is separated by a backslash. You can then type a path directly in the Address bar.

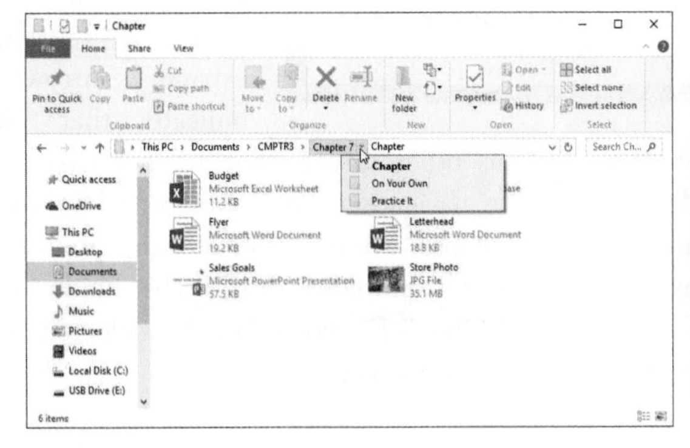

Begin Activity

Navigate to folders.

Read this before starting this Activity: To complete the steps in the Activities in this book, you need the data files that come with this book. You can get them from your instructor, who may include them in the Assignment Calendar of CMPTR Online or provide them to you another way.

1 In the active File Explorer window, move the pointer to the **navigation pane**. Collapse arrows [v] appear next to drives and folders whose contents is displayed in the pane, and OneDrive, This PC, Network, and Homegroup, and next to any other drives on your computer. Expand arrows [>] appear next to drives and folders whose contents is not listed in the pane.

2 Next to Quick access, click the **collapse arrow** [v] if it appears. The Quick access list collapses in the navigation pane, but the folders and any files that were listed in the File Explorer window still appear.

3 In the navigation pane of the active File Explorer window, if the This PC folder is not expanded, click the **This PC folder expand arrow** [>]. The drives on your computer are listed below the This PC folder in the navigation pane.

4 In the navigation pane, click **This PC**. The six folders in the This PC folder, and the drives and network locations you have access to appear in the window. The name of the window changes to This PC and the Home and Share tabs that were on the ribbon are replaced with the Computer tab. Refer again to Exhibit 7-15.

5 Make sure you know where your data files are stored. See the ***Read this before starting this Activity*** paragraph at the beginning of this Activity.

6 In the This PC window, double-click the **drive or folder containing your data files**, if necessary. For example, if your data files are on a USB drive, double-click the drive letter corresponding to your removable drive, such as E, F, or G. If your data files are on a network drive, double-click the drive under **Network locations**. If your data files are on your hard drive, they are probably in the Documents folder, so double-click the **Documents folder**. The window now shows the list of folders on the drive you selected or the list of folders and files stored in the Documents folder.

7 In the list of folders, double-click the **folder that contains the data files**, if necessary. You should see an item named Chapter 7. (You might see additional chapter folders as well.)

End Activity

7-4 WORKING WITH FILES

Knowing how to save, locate, and organize computer files makes you more productive when you are working with a computer. After you create a file, you can open it and edit the file's contents, print the file, and save it again—usually using the same program you used to create it.

7-4a Extracting Compressed Data Files

If you transfer files from one location to another, such as from your hard disk to a removable disk or vice versa, or from one computer to another via email, you can store the files in a compressed (zipped) folder. A **compressed (zipped) folder** stores files in a compact format. In File Explorer windows, Windows displays a zipper on the folder icon of compressed folders.

To work with a file in a compressed folder, you need to **extract** it, which means that you create an uncompressed copy of the file in a folder you specify. To do this, you right-click the compressed folder, and then click Extract All on the shortcut menu, or you select the compressed folder, click the Compressed Folder Tools Extract tab on the ribbon, and then click the Extract all button to open the Extract Compressed (Zipped) Folders dialog box. See Exhibit 7-16. The path to the folder in which the compressed folder is stored and a suggested folder name for the new uncompressed folder appears in the box. You can keep this path and suggested name or change it.

EXHIBIT 7-16 EXTRACT COMPRESSED (ZIPPED) FOLDERS DIALOG BOX

Extract Compressed (Zipped) Folders

Select a Destination and Extract Files

Files will be extracted to this folder:

C:\Users\Owner\Documents\CMPTR3\Chapter 7 | Browse...

Show extracted files when complete

Extract | Cancel

file path

keep selected to display File Explorer window containing the extracted files when the extraction process is complete

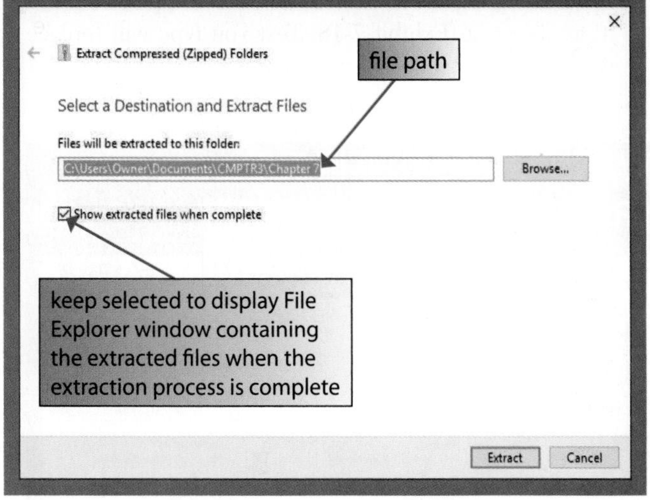

Begin Activity

Extract compressed files.

1. Right-click the **Chapter 7 compressed folder**. On the shortcut menu, click **Extract All**. The Extract Compressed (Zipped) Folders dialog box opens. The path to the folder the compressed folder is in and a suggested folder name of Chapter 7 is selected in the box in the middle of the dialog box. Refer again to Exhibit 7-16.
2. If you do not need to change the location of the data files, skip to Step 3. If you need to change the location of the data files, click **Browse** to open the Select a destination dialog box, navigate to the folder in which you want to store the Chapter 7 folder, and then click **Select Folder** to close the Select a destination dialog box. The Extract Compressed (Zipped) Folders dialog box is the active window again.
3. Click **Extract**. A dialog box showing the progress of the extraction appears, and then the Chapter 7 File Explorer window opens listing the Chapter, On Your Own, and Practice It folders that are contained in the Chapter 7 folder.
4. If necessary, extract the files from the compressed folders containing the data files for Chapters 8 through Chapter 22.

PROBLEM? If you need to create a new folder inside the currently selected folder, in the Select a destination box, click the **New folder button** in the bar below the Address bar, and then type the name of the new folder to replace the highlighted text *New folder*.

TIP: You can also select the compressed folder, click the Compressed Folder Tools Extract tab on the ribbon, and then click the Extract all button.

End Activity

7-4b Creating a Folder or Subfolder

After you devise a plan for storing your files, you are ready to get organized by creating folders and subfolders that will hold your files and then moving the files into the appropriate folders. When you create a folder, you give it a name, preferably one that describes its contents. A folder name can have up to 255 characters but cannot include the / \ : * ? " < > or | characters. Exhibit 7-17 shows the files in the Chapter 7\Chapter folder. All of these files

compressed (zipped) folder A folder that stores files in a compact format.

extract To create an uncompressed copy of a compressed file.

EXHIBIT 7-17 FILES IN THE CHAPTER 7\CHAPTER FOLDER IN TILES VIEW

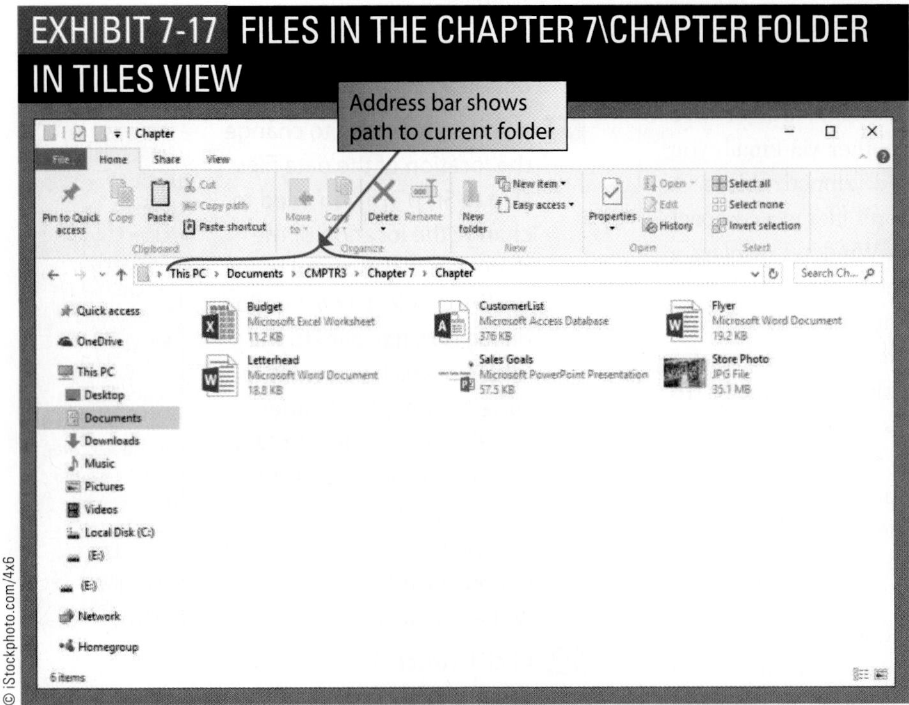

for marketing—and then move the files into the appropriate folders:

- **Images folder**—Store Photo
- **Finances folder**—Budget and Sales Goals
- **Marketing folder**—Customer List, Flyer, and Letterhead

When you are working on your own computer, you usually create folders within the Documents folder, which is in the This PC folder, and other standard folders, such as Music and Pictures. If you are saving your files on a USB drive, you can create folders on it.

are related to a business named Cathy's Candy Shoppe. The files in this folder are described here:

- **Budget**—an Excel file that lists projected expenses for the store.
- **CustomerList**—an Access file listing customer names and addresses.
- **Flyer**—a Word file that contains a flyer to announce the grand opening of the store.
- **Letterhead**—a Word file containing (as the name implies) letterhead for the store.
- **Sales Goals**—a PowerPoint file that contains the beginnings of a presentation to describe the business's sales goals for the next year.
- **Store Photo**—a graphic file that contains a photo of a female clerk in a candy store.

One way to organize these files is to create the following three folders—one for images, one for the finances, and one

To create a new folder, you can click the New folder button on the Quick Access Toolbar in the File Explorer window, or click the New folder button in the New group on the Home tab on the ribbon. When the new folder is created, the temporary folder name *New folder* is highlighted (selected), and a box appears around it, as shown in Exhibit 7-18. Text you type will replace the temporary name.

EXHIBIT 7-18 NEW FOLDER CREATED IN THE CHAPTER\CHAPTER 7 FOLDER

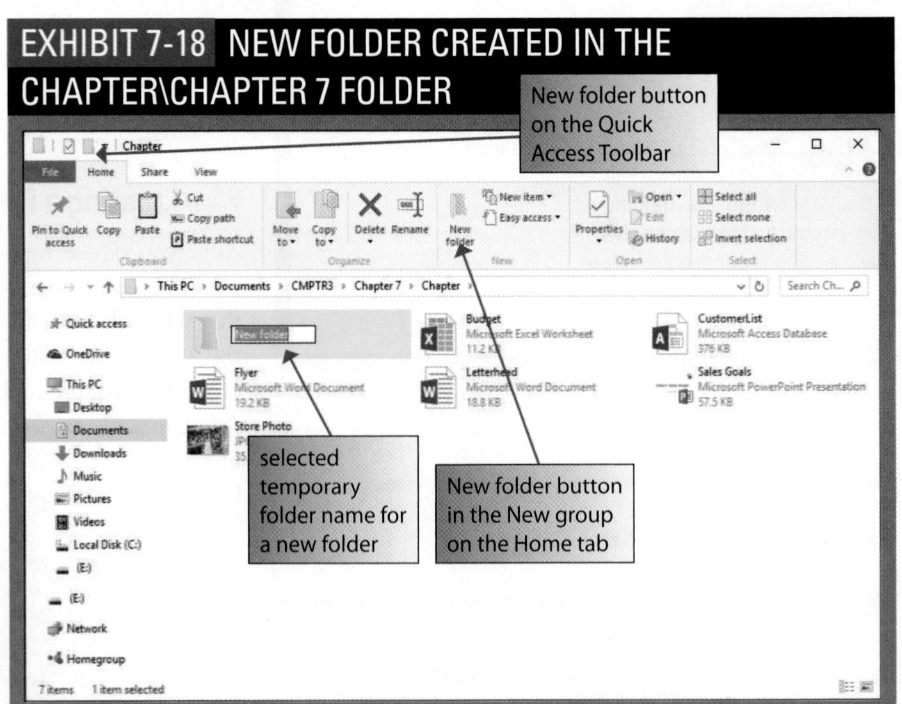

FYI **GUIDELINES FOR FOLDERS** As you organize your files by creating folders, keep in mind the following guidelines to ensure that you and others who might later work with your files can quickly and easily find the files needed:

- **Keep folder names short and familiar.** Long names can be cut off in a folder window, so use names that are short but meaningful, such as project names or categories.
- **Develop standards for naming folders.** Use a consistent naming scheme that is logical to you and others. For example, you could use a project name as the name of the main folder and include step numbers in each subfolder name, such as 01Plan, 02Approvals, 03Prelim, and so on.
- **Create subfolders to organize files.** If a folder contains so many files that you must scroll the folder window to see them all, consider organizing those files into subfolders.

Begin Activity

Create folders.

1 Navigate to the **Chapter 7\Chapter folder window** using the techniques you learned earlier. This folder is included with your data files.

2 If the Chapter 7\Chapter folder window is not in Tiles view, click the **View tab** on the ribbon. In the Layout group, click the **scroll up or down arrow** if needed, and then click the **Tiles button**.

3 On the Quick Access Toolbar, click the **New folder button**. A folder icon with the selected temporary folder name *New folder* appears in the window. Refer again to Exhibit 7-18.

4 Type **Images** and then press the **Enter key**. *Images* replaces the temporary folder name, and the new Images folder is selected in the window.

5 On the ribbon, click the **Home tab**. In the New group, click the **New folder button**. Another new folder is created.

6 Type **Finances** to replace the temporary folder name, and then press the **Enter key**. The new folder is renamed.

7 Create a new folder named **Marketing**. The Chapter 7\Chapter folder now contains three subfolders.

End Activity

7-4c Moving or Copying Files and Folders

If you want to place a file into a folder from another location, you can move the file or copy it. Moving a file removes it from its current location and places it in a new location you specify. Copying also places the file in a new location but does not remove it from its current location. You can move and copy folders in the same way that you move and copy files. When you do, you move or copy all the files contained in the folder.

The easiest way to move files or folders is to drag them from one location to another. When you drag a file or folder from one location to another on the same drive, the file or folder is moved from its original location to the new location. Exhibit 7-19 shows the Budget

EXHIBIT 7-19 FILE BEING MOVED BETWEEN FOLDERS ON THE SAME DRIVE

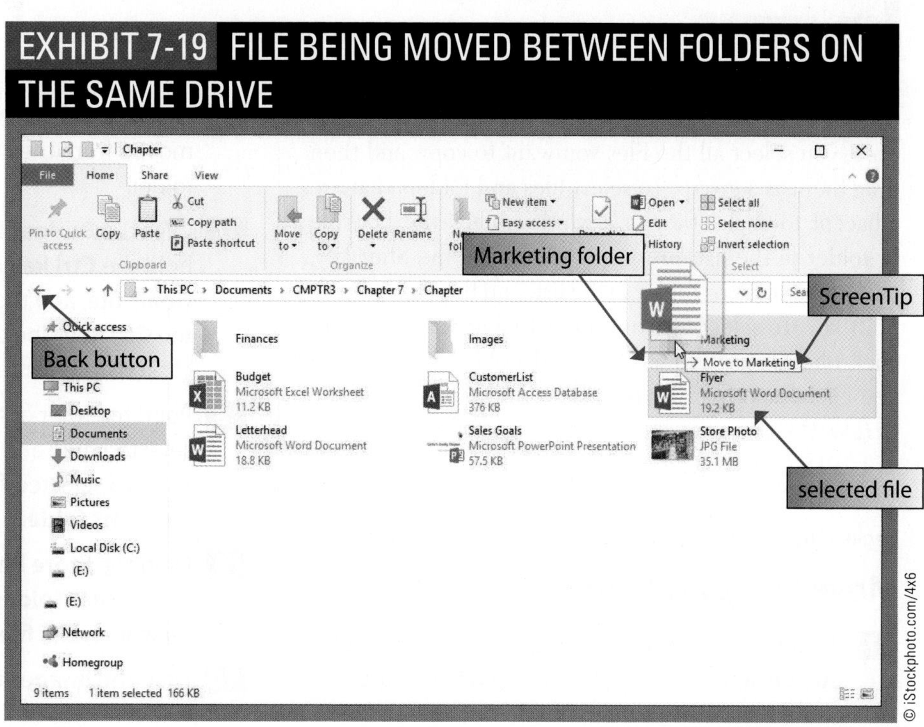

© iStockphoto.com/4x6

file being moved from the Chapter 7\Chapter folder to the Chapter 7\Chapter\Finances folder. When you drag a file or folder from one drive to another drive, the file or folder is copied instead of moved.

You can override the default behavior by dragging a file using the right mouse button (also referred to as right-dragging). When you drag a file or folder using the right mouse button, a shortcut menu appears as shown in Exhibit 7-20, and you can choose the Move here or the Copy here command, depending on what you want to do.

EXHIBIT 7-20 SHORTCUT MENU AFTER RIGHT-DRAGGING A FILE BETWEEN FOLDERS

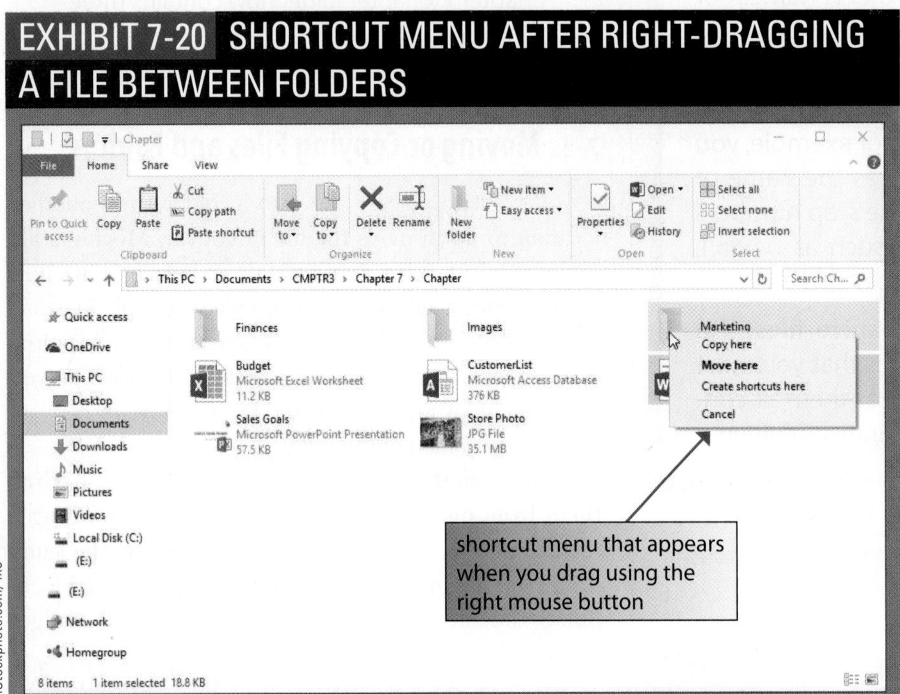

© iStockphoto.com/4x6

To move or copy more than one file at the same time, you select all the files you want to copy, and then drag them as a group. To select files and folders that are adjacent to each other in a window, click the first file or folder in the list, press and hold down the Shift key, click the last file or folder in the list, and then release the Shift key. To select files or folders that are not adjacent, click one file or folder, press and hold down the Ctrl key, click the other files or folders, and then release the Ctrl key.

Begin Activity

Move files or folders.

1 Point to the **Flyer file**, press and hold the **mouse button**, and then drag the selected file on top of the **Marketing folder**, but do not release the mouse button. The ScreenTip identifies the action as moving the file to the Marketing folder. Refer again to Exhibit 7-19.

2 Release the **mouse button**. A dialog box might briefly appear showing the progress as the file is moved. When the move is complete, the dialog box closes and the Flyer file no longer appears in the window because you moved it to the Marketing folder.

3 Double-click the **Marketing folder**. The window changes to display the contents of the Marketing folder, which now contains the Flyer file.

4 To the left of the Address bar, click the **Back button** [←]. The contents of the Chapter folder appear in the window.

5 Right-click the **Letterhead file**, but do not release the mouse button. Drag the **Letterhead file** to the **Marketing folder**, and then release the **mouse button.** A shortcut menu opens. Refer again to Exhibit 7-20.

6 On the shortcut menu, click **Move here.** The file is moved from the current folder to the Marketing folder.

7 Click the **Budget file**, press and hold the **Ctrl key** click the **Sales Goals file**, and then release the **Ctrl key**. The two files you clicked are selected.

8 Point to either of the two selected files, and then drag the two selected files into the **Finances folder**.

9 Drag the **Store Photo file** into the **Images folder**. Drag the **CustomerList file** into the **Marketing folder**.

10 Drag the **Images folder** into the **Marketing folder**.

TIP: You can press and hold the Shift key, click the first file in the list, click the last file in the list, and then release the Shift key to select the files you clicked as well as all of the files between them.

11 In the navigation pane, expand the drive or folder containing your data files, expand subfolders until you have expanded the **Chapter 7\Chapter folder**, and then expand the **Marketing folder**. The Images folder is listed below the Marketing folder in the navigation pane.

End Activity

If you want to copy a file or folder from one location to another on the same drive, you can right-click and drag and then click Copy here, or you can press and hold the Ctrl key while you drag. The ScreenTip that appears indicates that you are copying the item. See Exhibit 7-21.

EXHIBIT 7-21 SCREENTIP WHEN PRESSING THE CTRL KEY WHILE DRAGGING A FILE

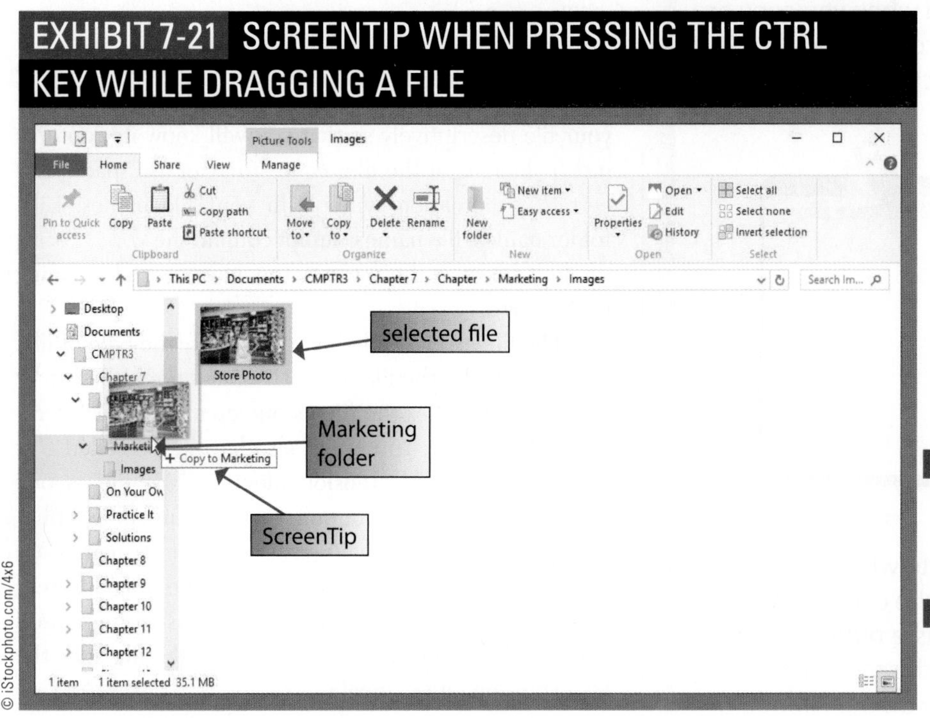

© iStockphoto.com/4x6

Begin Activity

Copy files or folders.

1 In the navigation pane, click the **Images folder**. The file in the Images folder appear in the folder window.

2 Press and hold the **Ctrl key**, and then drag the **Store Photo file** to the **Marketing folder** in the navigation pane, but do not release the Ctrl key. The ScreenTip indicates that the file will be copied to the Marketing folder. Refer again to Exhibit 7-21.

3 Release the **mouse button**, and then release the **Ctrl key**. The file is copied to the Marketing folder. Notice that the Store Photo file still appears in the Images folder.

4 In the navigation pane, click the **Marketing folder**. The Store Photo file is listed in the folder window along with the Images folder and the other three files in the Marketing folder.

5 In the Address bar, after Chapter, click the **right-pointing arrow** to display the list of folders in the Chapter folder, and then click **Finances.** The contents of the Finances folder appear in the folder window.

6 Right-click the **Sales Goals file**, and then drag it to the **Marketing folder** in the navigation pane. When you release the mouse button, the same shortcut menu you saw when you were moving files appears.

PROBLEM?
Even though you intend to copy the file, the ScreenTip *Move to Marketing* appears. You can still choose the Copy here command on the shortcut menu when it appears.

7 On the shortcut menu, click **Copy here**. The file is copied to the Marketing folder.

8 To the left of the Address bar, click the **Back button**. The contents of the previously viewed folder, the Marketing folder, appear in the window, including the Sales Goals file.

9 Press and hold the **Ctrl key**. In the navigation pane, drag the **Images folder** on top of the **Chapter folder**. Release the **mouse button**, and then release the **Ctrl key**. The Images folder is copied to the Chapter folder and appears after the Finances folder in the folders list.

10 In the navigation pane, click the **Images folder** in the Chapter folder (not the original Images folder in the Marketing folder). The file in the original Images folder appears in the File Explorer window because the file was copied along with the folder.

End Activity

FYI MOVING AND COPYING USING THE RIBBON AND THE CLIPBOARD

To move or copy files and folders, you can also use the Cut, Copy, and Paste commands in the Clipboard group on the Home tab on the ribbon, or the Move to and Copy to commands in the Organize group on the Home tab. When you use the Cut, Copy, and Paste commands in the Clipboard group, you use the **Clipboard**, a temporary storage area in Windows on which files, folders, text, or other objects are stored when you copy or move them. To use these commands, click a file or folder to select it, click the Home tab, and then click the Cut command to remove the item from its current location and place it on the Clipboard, or click the Copy command to place a copy of the file or folder on the Clipboard. To paste the contents of the Clipboard, display the contents of the folder to which you want to place the item or the copy of the item, and then click the Paste button. If you cut or copy another item, the second item replaces the item currently on the Clipboard. Using the Move to or Copy to buttons is an alternative to dragging the items from one folder to another and nothing is placed on the Clipboard.

TRINACRIA PHOTO/Shutterstock.com

Clipboard A temporary storage area in Windows on which objects are stored when you copy or move them.

file name Information about a file, including its title and file extension.

file extension Three or four characters that follow the dot in a file name and that identify the file type.

7-4d Naming and Renaming Files and Folders

As you work with files, pay attention to **file names**—they provide information about the file, including its contents and purpose. A file name such as *Car Sales.docx* has three parts:

- **Title**—text that you provide when you create a file that describes the content of the file and its purpose
- **Dot**—the period (.) that separates the main part of the file name from the file extension
- **File extension**—three or four characters that follow the dot in the file name and that identify the file type

The main part of a file name can have up to 255 characters, which gives you plenty of space to name your file descriptively so that you will know its contents just by looking at the file name. You can use spaces and certain punctuation symbols in your file names. Like folder names, file names cannot contain the \ / ? : * " < > | symbols because these characters have special meaning in Windows.

The file extension helps you identify the type of file. For example, in the file name *Car Sales.docx*, the extension *docx* identifies the file as one created using Microsoft Office Word. You might also have a file called *Car Sales.jpg*—the *jpg* extension identifies the file as one created in a graphics program, such as Paint, or as a photograph. Though the main parts of these file names are identical, their extensions distinguish them as different files. You do not need to add extensions to file names because the program you use to create the file adds the file extension automatically.

Although Windows keeps track of extensions, not all computers are set to display them. The screenshots in this book do not show file extensions. You can, however, identify the file type of a file in a file list in a File Explorer window by changing the view to Tiles, Details, or Content.

If you need to rename a file, right-click it in the File Explorer window, and then click Rename on the shortcut menu. You can also select a file, click the Home tab on the ribbon, and then click the Rename button in the Organize group. Taking either of these actions selects the file name. Type the new name to replace the selected text. You do not need to type the file extension.

As you have already seen, folder names are also important. You might find that you need to rename an existing folder. You can do this using the same methods you use to rename files.

FYI **GUIDELINES FOR NAMING FILES AND FOLDERS**

Be sure to give your files and folders meaningful names that help you remember their purpose and contents. You can easily rename a file or folder by using the Rename command on the file's shortcut menu. The following are a few suggestions for naming your files:

- **Use common names.** Avoid cryptic names that might make sense now but could cause confusion later, such as nonstandard abbreviations or imprecise names like Stuff2013.
- **Find a balance between too short and too long.** Use names that are long enough to be meaningful but short enough to read easily on the screen.
- **Don't change the file extension.** When renaming a file, don't change the file extension. If you do, Windows might not be able to find a program that can open the file.

Begin Activity

Rename files or folders.

1. Display the contents of the **Marketing folder** in the window.
2. Right-click the **Flyer file**. On the shortcut menu, click **Rename**. The shortcut menu closes, and the file name is highlighted in the same manner as it was when you created a new folder.
3. Type **Grand Opening Flyer** and then press the **Enter key**. The file name changes to the name you typed.

TIP: You can also select a file or folder, click the Home tab on the ribbon, and then in the Organize group, click the Rename button.

PROBLEM?
If your computer is set to display file extensions, only the file name is selected. The .docx file extension is not selected. If a dialog box opens asking if you are sure you want to change the file extension, click **No**, and then repeat Steps 2 and 3.

4. Click the **Letterhead file**, pause for a moment, and then click the **Letterhead file name**. The file name becomes highlighted.
5. Click immediately before the **L** in the file name, type **Store**, press the **Spacebar**, and then press the **Enter key**. The file is renamed to Store Letterhead.
6. On the Marketing folder title bar, click the **Minimize button** [–]. The Marketing folder window minimizes to the File Explorer button on the taskbar.
7. Minimize the other open File Explorer window.

End Activity

7-4e Working with Compressed Folders

You compress a folder so that the files it contains use less space on the disk. For example, a folder named Photos might contain 8.6 MB of files. But if you compress that folder, those same files will require only 6.5 MB of disk space. In this case, the compressed files use about 25 percent less disk space than the uncompressed files. You can also transfer the smaller compressed files more quickly.

To create a compressed folder, select all the files and folders you want to compress, click the Share tab on the ribbon, and then in the Send group, click the Zip button. The new, compressed folder appears in the same folder as the files and folders you compressed with a temporary folder name selected so that you can type a new name if you want. See Exhibit 7-22. You can also right-click one of the selected files or folders, point to Send to on the shortcut menu, and then click Compressed (zipped) folder. You can also right-click a single folder and use the same command to compress all the files stored in that folder. Finally, you can add additional files or folders to the compressed folder by dragging the files or folders to the compressed folder. Note that when you compress folders, the original folders are not removed.

You can open a file from a compressed folder, although you cannot modify the compressed file. You can also move and copy files and folders in a compressed folder. To rename or edit a compressed file or folder, you must extract it first.

If a different compression program, such as WinZip or WinRAR, has been installed on your computer, the Send to Compressed (zipped) folder command might not appear on the shortcut menu. Instead, it might be replaced by the name of your compression program. In this case, refer to your compression program's Help information for instructions on working with compressed files.

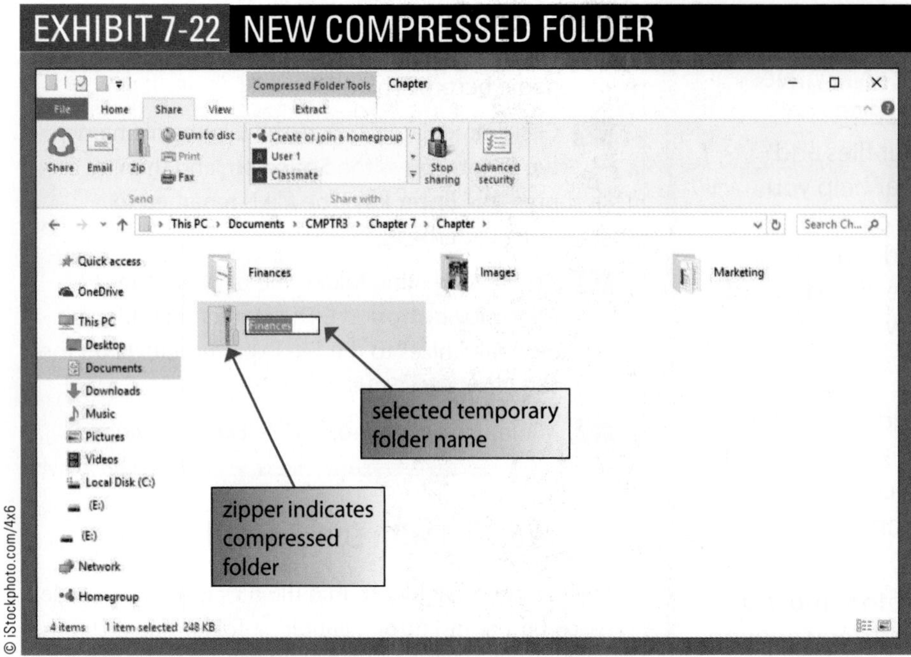

EXHIBIT 7-22 NEW COMPRESSED FOLDER

© iStockphoto.com/4x6

As you have already seen, you can easily extract all the files from a compressed folder either by using the Extract All command on the shortcut menu or by clicking the Extract all button on the Compressed Folder Tools Extract tab on the ribbon. To extract one file from a compressed folder, open the compressed folder, click the file you want to extract, and then in the Extract To group on the Compressed Folder Tools Extract tab on the ribbon, click the button corresponding to the folder you want to put the extracted file into. If you do not see the folder you want, click the Desktop button, and the file will be extracted to the Desktop. Then you can open a File Explorer window and drag the extracted file into the correct folder or you can drag the compressed file from the compressed folder window into the window for the folder to which you want to extract the file. When you extract a file from a compressed folder, the compressed file remains in the compressed folder.

Begin Activity

Work with compressed folders.

1. On the taskbar, point to the **File Explorer button** . Thumbnails of the open File Explorer windows appear.
2. Click the **Marketing thumbnail**. The Marketing File Explorer window appears on the desktop.
3. In the Address bar, click **Chapter**, and then in the Chapter folder window, select the **Finances folder** and the **Marketing folder**.
4. Click the **Share tab** on the ribbon. In the Send group, click the **Zip button**. A dialog box might open showing you the progress of the compression. After a few moments, the dialog box closes and a new compressed folder with a zipper icon appears in the window with its temporary folder name selected. The temporary folder name is the same as the first folder you clicked when you selected the folders, so it will be Finances if you selected that folder first, and Marketing if you selected that folder first. The Finances and Marketing folders remain in the file list.
5. Type **My Compressed Folders** and then press the **Enter key** to rename the compressed folder.
6. Double-click the **My Compressed Folders folder**. The Finances and Marketing folders are listed in the window.
7. Double-click the **Finances folder**, and then click the **Sales Goals file** to select it.
8. Click the **Compressed Folder Tools Extract tab** on the ribbon, if necessary. The Extract To group includes buttons for the folders in the This PC folder, and folders you recently opened.
9. Scroll the list of buttons in the Extract To group if necessary, and then click the **Desktop button**. The selected Sales Goals file is extracted to the desktop. The compressed Sales Goals file is still in the My Compressed Folders folder.
10. If you can't see the extracted Sales Goals file on the desktop, drag the **Finances window** by its title bar until you can see the Sales Goals file on the desktop.

TIP: You can also display the My Compressed Folders folder and the Chapter folder windows side by side, and then drag the Sales Goals file from the Compressed Folders File Explorer window to the Chapter File Explorer window.

End Activity

FYI **BACKING UP YOUR DATA**
You should back up your data regularly so that you can restore the files if something happens to your computer. Performing a backup can include backing up an entire computer (so it can be restored at a later date, if needed), backing up all data files (so they can be restored if the computer is lost or damaged), or backing up only selected files (so you have a clean copy of each selected file if the original is lost or destroyed). Depending on their size, backup data files can be placed on an external hard drive, a USB flash drive, or virtually any other storage medium. To protect against fires and other natural disasters, you should store backup media in a physical location other than where your computer is located or inside a fire-resistant safe. You can perform backups by manually copying files that change, but backup utility programs make the backup process easier. For convenience, many backup programs can be scheduled to back up specified files, folders, or drives on a regular basis (such as every night or once a week). You can also back up to the cloud using an online backup service, such as Carbonite or Mozy. These services back up your files automatically to a secure Web server on a regular basis provided you have a broadband Internet connection.

7-5 DELETING FILES AND WORKING WITH THE RECYCLE BIN

When you delete a file from a hard drive, it is not removed from your computer. Instead, it is moved to the Recycle Bin. The Recycle Bin is located on the desktop.

7-5a Deleting Files and Folders

You should periodically delete unneeded files and folders so that your folders and drives do not get cluttered. When you delete a file or folder from the hard drive, the file or folder and all of its contents are moved to the Recycle Bin. When you delete a file or folder from removable media, such as a USB drive, or from a network drive, it is not moved to the Recycle Bin; instead, it is permanently deleted and cannot be recovered.

Begin Activity

Delete files or folders.

1. Drag the **Sales Goals file** on the desktop on top of the Recycle Bin so that the ScreenTip Move to Recycle Bin appears, and then release the **mouse button**. If your data files are stored on the hard drive, the file is moved to the Recycle Bin. If your data files are stored on removable media or a network drive, the Delete File dialog box opens asking if you are sure you want to permanently delete the file.

PROBLEM?
If you cannot see the Recycle Bin, drag the File Explorer window covering it to a new location by its title bar.

2. If the Delete File dialog box is open, click **Yes**. The dialog box closes, and the file is deleted.
3. In the navigation pane, click the **Finances folder**. In the Finances File Explorer window, right-click the **Sales Goals file**. On the shortcut menu, click **Delete**. The Delete File dialog box opens. If your data files are stored on the hard drive, the dialog box asks if you're sure you want to move the file to the Recycle Bin. If your data files are stored on re-movable media or a network drive, the dialog box asks if you want to permanently delete the file.
4. In the Delete File dialog box, click **Yes**. The file is either moved to the Recycle Bin or permanently deleted.
5. Minimize the Finances File Explorer window.

End Activity

7-5b Working with the Recycle Bin

You can double-click the Recycle Bin to open the Recycle Bin window and see the files that are ready to be permanently deleted. See Exhibit 7-23.

If you want to keep a file that is in the Recycle Bin instead of permanently deleting it, you can return the file to its previous location. To do this, right-click a file in the Recycle Bin window and then click Restore on the shortcut menu, or click the Recycle Bin Tools Manage tab on the Ribbon, and then click the Restore the selected items button.

EXHIBIT 7-23 RECYCLE BIN AND RECYCLE BIN WINDOW

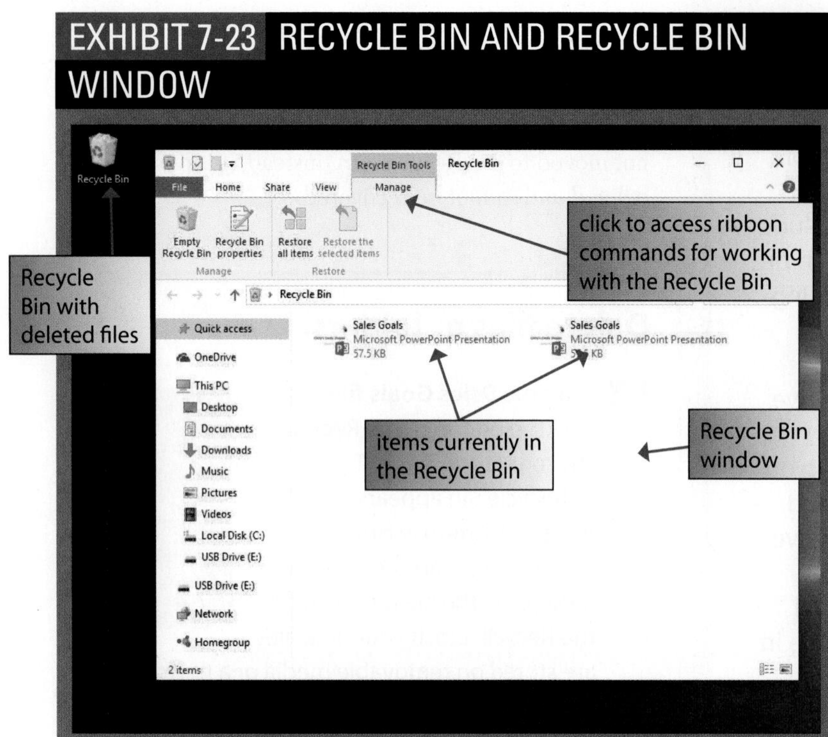

When you no longer need the files stored in the Recycle Bin, you can permanently delete them. To do this, right-click the Recycle Bin and then click Empty Recycle Bin on the shortcut menu, or click the Empty Recycle Bin button on the Recycle Bin Tools Manage tab on the ribbon. Keep in mind that you cannot retrieve files that have been emptied from the Recycle Bin.

Make it a practice to regularly empty the Recycle Bin. Storing files in the Recycle Bin can slow down your computer's start-up time. The unneeded files also take up space on your computer. Files you want to keep should be stored in other folders, not in the Recycle Bin. Remember, permanently deleted files cannot be retrieved from the Recycle Bin.

Begin Activity

Work with the Recycle Bin.

1. Right-click the **Recycle Bin**. The Recycle Bin shortcut menu opens. If no files are currently in the Recycle Bin, the Empty Recycle Bin command will be gray, which means it is unavailable.
2. Press the **Esc key** to close the shortcut menu.
3. Double-click the **Recycle Bin**. The Recycle Bin window opens. Any files or folders currently in the Recycle Bin are listed in this window. Refer again to Exhibit 7-23.
4. If the Recycle Bin contains files, click the **Recycle Bin Tools Manage tab** on the ribbon, and then click the **Empty Recycle Bin button**. A dialog box opens asking if you are sure you want to permanently delete the items.

TIP: To retrieve a file or folder from the Recycle Bin, in the Recycle Bin window, click the item you want to retrieve, click the Recycle Bin Tools Manage tab on the ribbon, and then click Restore the selected items button.

5. Click **Yes**. The dialog box closes, and the files in the Recycle Bin are permanently deleted. They also disappear from the file list in the Recycle Bin window.

End Activity

7-6 CLOSING APPS AND WINDOWS

You should close an application when you are finished using it. Each application uses computer resources, such as memory, so Windows works more efficiently when only the applications you need are open. You should also close File Explorer windows that you are not using to keep your desktop uncluttered. You click the Close button at the right end of the title bar to close windows. If the window is a program window, clicking the Close button can also stop the program from running. (This is called *exiting* or *closing* the program.) You can also right-click a window's taskbar button, and then click Close window on the shortcut menu or point to a taskbar button, point to the thumbnail, and then click the Close button that appears.

Begin Activity

Close apps and windows.

1. On the taskbar, click the **Paint button**. The Paint window is restored to its original size and becomes the active window.

2 On the Paint window title bar, click the **Close button** ☒. The Paint window and application close, and its button no longer appears on the taskbar.

PROBLEM? If a dialog box opens asking if you want to save changes to Untitled, click **Don't Save.**

3 On the taskbar, right-click the **Calculator button**. The shortcut menu for the Calculator taskbar button opens.

4 Click **Close window** on the shortcut menu. The Calculator window closes, and its button no longer appears on the taskbar.

TIP: To close windows from Task View, point to the window you want to close, and then click the Close button that appears.

5 On the taskbar, point to the **File Explorer button**.

6 Point to the **Finances thumbnail**, and then click the **Close button** ☒ that appears in the upper-right corner of the thumbnail.

7 Right-click the **File Explorer button**, and then on the shortcut menu, click **Close all windows.** The rest of the open File Explorer windows (including the Recycle Bin window) close.

End Activity

7-7 GETTING HELP IN WINDOWS

As you work, you might need more information about Windows or one of its apps. You can click the Help button at the right end of File Explorer windows to start your browser and display search results for the search phrase "get help with file explorer in windows 10" in the Bing search engine. You can also type terms in the Search the web and Windows box or the Ask me anything box on the taskbar to search for anything stored on your computer or for information about the terms your typed on Web pages. If you type help in the Search the web and Windows box, Get Started, a Windows app appears in the list of results. You can click this to open a window displaying a list of videos you can watch about using Windows 10.

In addition, there is a Contact Support app installed with Windows 10. When you start this app, the Contact support window opens, as shown in Exhibit 7-24.

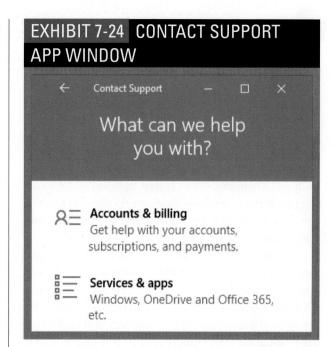

To obtain assistance with Windows, click Services & apps, and then click Windows. Then you can click Setting up, Technical support, or Protecting my PC, as shown to display a window listing support options, as shown in Exhibit 7-25. To continue with support, click one of the support links, and then follow the instructions on the screen.

EXHIBIT 7-24 CONTACT SUPPORT APP WINDOW

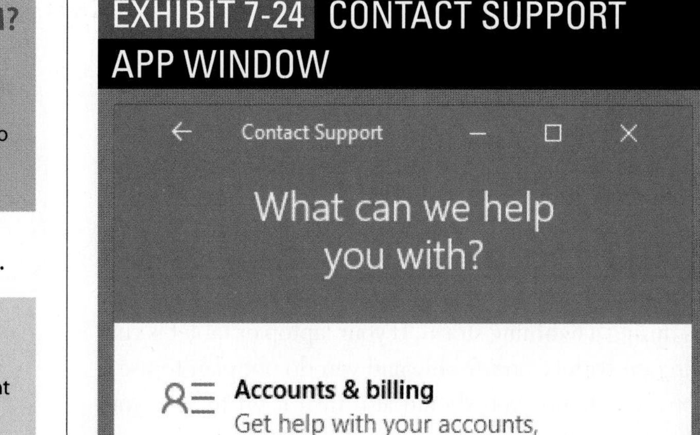

EXHIBIT 7-25 WAYS YOU CAN ASK FOR HELP IN THE CONTACT SUPPORT APP

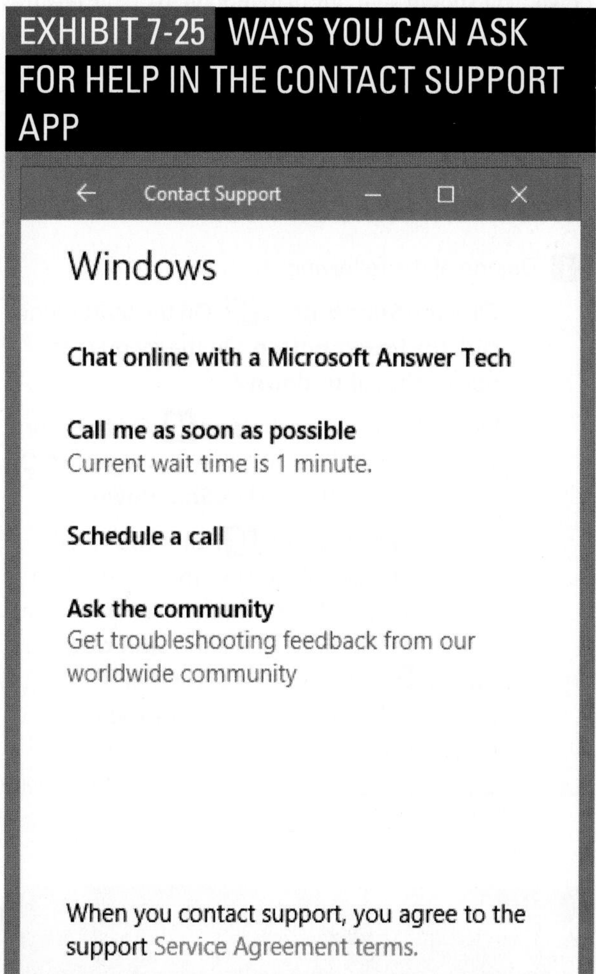

7-8 SHUTTING DOWN WINDOWS

If your computer is plugged in to a power outlet and you do not plan to use the computer for more than a day, turning it off saves wear and tear on your electronic components and conserves energy. You should also turn off the computer when it is susceptible to electrical damage, such as during a lightning storm. If your laptop or tablet is running on battery power only and you do not plan to use it for a few hours, you should also turn it off to save your battery charge.

You should always shut down Windows before you turn off your computer. **Shutting down** closes all open apps, including Windows itself, and then completely turns off your computer. Shutting down your computer saves energy, preserves your data and settings, and makes sure your computer starts quickly the next time you use it. Shutting down does not automatically save your work, so be sure to save your files before clicking the Shut down button. If you are share a computer, before shutting down, you should sign out of Windows 10. This ensures that no one else who uses that computer has access to your files.

Begin Activity

Shut down Windows 10.

1 Do one of the following:

- Click the **Start button** ⊞. On the Start menu, click the **Power button**. On the menu that opens, click **Shut down**.
- Right-click the **Start button** ⊞. On the shortcut menu, point to **Shut down or sign out**. On the menu that opens, click **Shut down**.
- Click the **Start button** ⊞, Click your user name at the top of the Start menu, and then click **Sign out**. Click the **lock screen** to display the list of user names, click the **Shut down button** ⏻ in the lower-right corner, and then click **Shut down** on the menu that opens.

End Activity

shut down To close all running apps and Windows before completely turning off power to the computer.

FYI SIGN OUT, SLEEP, OR SHUT DOWN

When you are finished working on the computer, you need to decide whether to log off the computer, put the computer to sleep, or shut down. If you are using a computer that belongs to someone else, follow that person's policy. Otherwise, the best approach depends on who uses the computer and how long it will be idle. Consider the following as you make your decision:

- **Sign out**—closes all programs and signs you out of Windows 10 but leaves the computer turned on. If another person might use the computer shortly, log off Windows to protect your data and prepare the computer for someone else to use.
- **Sleep**—saves your work and then turns down the power to your monitor and computer. A light on the outside of the computer case blinks or turns yellow to indicate that the computer is sleeping. Because your work is saved, you do not need to close your programs or files before putting your computer to sleep. By default, Windows 10 is set to sleep after 15 to 30 minutes of idle time, depending on whether you are using a mobile or desktop computer. If you will be away from the computer for more than 15 minutes but less than a day, you can generally let the computer go to sleep on its own. To wake a desktop computer, you press any key or move the mouse. To wake a laptop computer, you might need to press the hardware power button on your computer case instead. After you wake a computer, the screen looks exactly as it did when you turned off your computer.
- **Shut down**—turns off the computer. If your computer is plugged in to a power outlet and you do not plan to use the computer for more than a day, shutting down saves wear and tear on your electronic components and conserves energy. You should also turn off the computer when it is susceptible to electrical damage, such as during a lightning storm, and when you need to install new hardware or disconnect the computer from a power source. If your mobile computer is running on battery power only and you do not plan to use it for a few hours, you should also shut it down to save your battery charge.

STUDY TOOLS 7

READY TO STUDY? IN THE BOOK, YOU CAN:

- ☐ Rip out the Chapter Review Card, which includes key terms and key chapter concepts.

ONLINE AT WWW.CENGAGEBRAIN.COM, YOU CAN:

- ☐ Review key concepts from the chapter in a short video.
- ☐ Explore Windows 10 with the interactive infographic.
- ☐ Practice what you've learned with more Practice It and On Your Own exercises.
- ☐ Prepare for tests with quizzes.
- ☐ Review the key terms with flashcards.

QUIZ YOURSELF

1. How do you start an app?
2. How do you manually resize a window?
3. How do you switch between open windows?
4. What is the left pane in a File Explorer window called?
5. How do you change the view in a File Explorer window?
6. What is the root directory?
7. What is a path?
8. When you use the left mouse button to drag a file or folder from one location to another on a drive, what happens? What happens when you drag a file or folder from one drive to another drive?
9. Describe two ways to copy a file or folder from one location to another on the same drive using the mouse.
10. How many characters can a file name have?
11. How can you identify a compressed folder?
12. Is a file deleted from a compressed folder when you extract it?
13. How do you permanently delete files in the Recycle Bin from a drive?
14. How do you close a window?
15. What does shutting down Windows do?

PRACTICE IT

Practice It 7-1

1. Start Windows 10, and sign in, if necessary.
2. Start the Photos app and the Maps app.
3. Open the File Explorer window.
4. Start the WordPad app.

5. Minimize the WordPad window.
6. Change the view of the File Explorer window to Extra large icons.
7. Display the data files located in the Chapter 7\Practice It folder in a new folder window, and then display the files as Large icons.
8. In the Chapter 7\Practice It folder window, create three folders: **Marketing, Sales Department,** and **Sales Meeting**.
9. Move the Brochure Photo1 and Brochure Photo2 files from the Chapter 7\Practice It folder into the Marketing folder.
10. Move the Agenda, Sales Meeting Evaluation Form, and 2016 Sales files from the Chapter 7\Practice It folder into the Sales Meeting folder.
11. Move the Bonus Plan file from the Chapter 7\Practice It folder into the Sales Department folder.
12. Move the Sales Meeting folder from the Chapter 7\Practice It folder into the Sales Department folder.
13. Copy the Bonus Plan file located in the Sales Department folder into the Sales Meeting folder, and then copy the 2016 Sales file located in the Sales Meeting folder into the Sales Department folder.
14. Rename the Sales Meeting folder as **Annual Sales Meeting**.
15. In the Sales Department folder, create a compressed (zipped) folder named **Annual Sales Meeting Zipped** that contains the Annual Sales Meeting folder, and then move the zipped folder into the Chapter 7\Practice It folder.
16. Extract the contents of the Annual Sales Meeting Zipped folder to a new folder named **Annual Sales Meeting Extracted** in the Chapter 7\Practice It folder.
17. Delete the 2016 Sales file from the Annual Sales Meeting folder located in the Sales Department folder.
18. Open the Recycle Bin window.
19. Empty the Recycle Bin, if necessary, and then close the Recycle Bin window.
20. Close all open windows and all running apps.
21. Sign out if needed, and then shut down Windows 10.

Practice It 7-2

1. Start Windows 10, and sign in, if necessary.
2. Start the News app, and then start the Notepad app.
3. Open a File Explorer window, and then open the This PC window. Identify the names of the drives on the computer.
4. In the navigation pane, expand the This PC folder, and then expand the hard disk, such as Local Disk (C:) or OS (C:). Expand the Users folder, and then expand the Public folder.
5. Open a second File Explorer window, and display the contents of the Chapter 7\Practice It folder.
6. Change the view of the Practice It window to Details view.
7. Create a copy of the One-Day Sale Flyer file located in the Chapter 7\Practice It folder in the same folder. (*Hint*: Use the right mouse button to drag the file to a blank area of the File Explorer window.) Rename the One-Day Sale Flyer - Copy file as **Flyer for Ad**.
8. Create three copies of the First Quarter Sales file located in the Chapter 7\Practice It folder to the same folder. Rename the copies as **Second Quarter Sales, Third Quarter Sales,** and **Fourth Quarter Sales**.
9. Create two folders in the Chapter 7\Practice It folder: **Sales** and **Advertising**.
10. Move the One-Day Sale Flyer and Flyer for Ad files into the Advertising folder, and then move the Advertising folder and the four Quarter Sales files into the Sales folder.
11. Compress the four Quarter Sales files in the Sales folder to a folder named **Quarter Sales Compressed** in the Sales folder.
12. Extract only the First Quarter Sales file from the Quarter Sales Compressed folder to a folder named **Quarter Sales Extracted** folder located in the Chapter 7\Practice It folder.
13. Delete the One-Day Sale Flyer file from the Sales\Advertising folder.
14. Rename the Advertising folder as **Advertising Info**.
15. Locate the Get Started app and open it. Review the information available in this app.
16. Close all open windows and all running apps.
17. Sign out if needed, and then shut down Windows 10.

ON YOUR OWN

On Your Own 7-1

1. Start the Windows Media Player app, which is an app that plays digital media.
2. Start the Sticky Notes app.
3. Use ScreenTips to identify the two buttons on the note created on the desktop when you started the app in Step 3.
4. Close the Sticky Notes window.
5. Open a File Explorer window. Experiment with using the Search box and answer the following questions:

   a. Where is the Search box located?

   b. What is the name of the contextual tab that appears on the ribbon when you start searching?

   c. Do you need to type the entire file name to find a specific file?

   d. How do you clear your search history?
6. Display the contents of the Chapter 7\Chapter folder, and then display the full path in the Address bar. (*Hint*: Click the icon in the Address bar.) What is the full path?
7. Try to compress the Chapter 7\On Your Own folder. Describe what happens.
8. Close all open windows and running apps.
9. Sign out if needed, and then shut down Windows 10.

Part 4
BROWSER and EMAIL

8 | Using Edge, Mail, and People

LEARNING OBJECTIVES After studying the material in this chapter, you will be able to:

8-1 Browse the Web with Edge

8-2 Save links to Web pages

8-3 Create Web notes

8-4 Print Web pages and Web notes

8-5 Delete items from the Hub and unpin Web pages from the Start menu

8-6 Exit Edge

8-7 Use the Mail app

8-8 Add information to the People app

After finishing this chapter, go to **PAGE 245** for **STUDY TOOLS**.

8-1 BROWSING THE WEB WITH EDGE

You use a Web browser to view and interact with Web pages. In other words, a Web browser lets you access, retrieve, and display Web pages from a computer that is connected to the Internet. **Microsoft Edge** (or simply **Edge**) is the default web browser in Windows 10. Edge provides all of the tools you need to communicate, access, and share information on the web.

8-1a Starting Edge and Navigating to Web Pages

To start Edge, you click the Microsoft Edge button on the taskbar. After it starts, Edge appears in an application window and displays the **start page**, similar to Exhibit 8-1.

The start page in Edge contains the Search or enter web address box. To display a specific Web page when the Edge start page is open, you type its Web address in the Search or enter web address box. (Recall from Chapter 1 that the address of a Web page is its URL.)

The main page of a Web site is called the **home page**. The home page appears when you type the domain name and top-level domain of a Web site, such as *nasa.gov*. You don't need to type *www* when you type a Web address because Edge recognizes the entry as a Web address. As you type, the names or Web addresses of other Web pages that start with the same characters and suggested keywords to search for other Web pages appear. See Exhibit 8-2. To display the Web page whose Web address you typed, you press the Enter key or click the Go button if it appears to load the Web page in the browser window. When a Web page **loads**, it is copied from the Web server to your computer. The Edge browser window changes and the Web address for

CAUTION CAUTION CAUTION CAUTION

THE DYNAMIC WEB

Because the Web is a dynamic medium, the Web pages shown in the exhibits will most likely differ from the Web pages that you see on your screen. You should still be able to identify the elements called out in the exhibits.

FYI

CHANGING YOUR START PAGE

You can change the start page in Edge. Near the top-right corner of the Edge application window, click the More button, and then click the Settings at the bottom of the menu to open the SETTINGS pane. The Open with list contains four options for setting the start page. If you want to specify a particular Web page, click the A specific page or pages option button, click the box that appears, and then click Custom in the list. Next to the current start page that appears below Custom, click the Delete button. In the Enter a web address box, type the address of the Web page you want to use as your start page, and then click the Add button. Click a blank area of the window to close the SETTINGS pane. The next time you start Edge, the Web page you specified will appear as the start page.

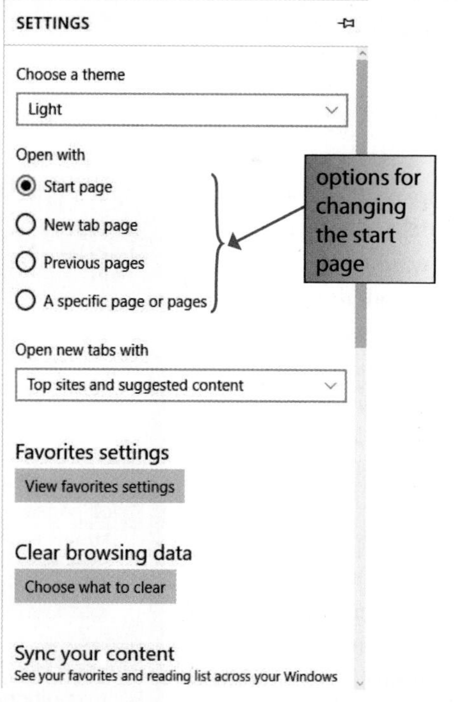

Microsoft Edge (Edge) The default Web browser in Windows 10.

start page The page that appears when Edge starts.

home page The main page of a Web site.

load To copy a Web page from a server to a computer.

BROWSER AND EMAIL

EXHIBIT 8-1 EDGE START PAGE

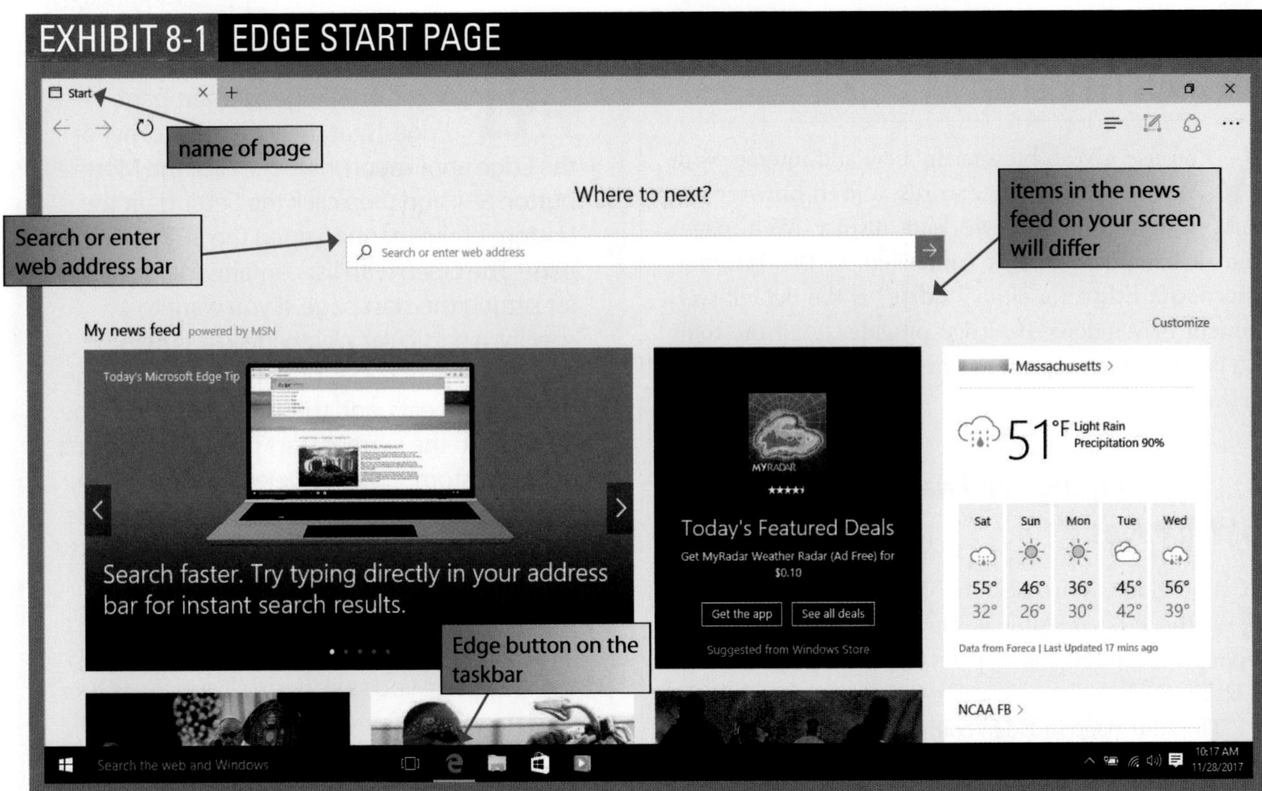

the displayed page appears in the **Address bar** at the top of the window.

Web addresses are generally not case-sensitive, although some longer Web addresses use a mix of uppercase and lowercase letters to distinguish the different words in the address. However, some operating systems used by Web servers do distinguish between uppercase and lowercase letters. So, if you are entering a Web address that includes mixed cases, it is safer to enter the address exactly as it was provided.

Address bar The bar at the top of the Edge window that contains the Web address of the displayed Web page.

EXHIBIT 8-2 START PAGE AFTER TYPING A WEB PAGE ADDRESS

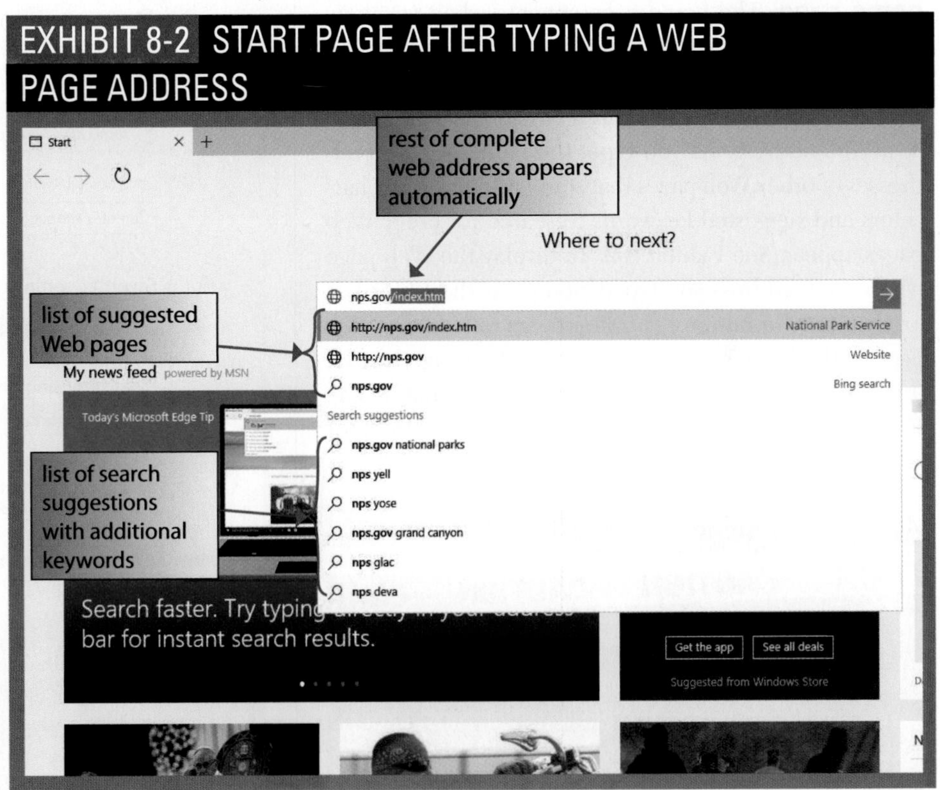

EXHIBIT 8-3 HOME PAGE ON THE NATIONAL PARK SERVICE WEB SITE

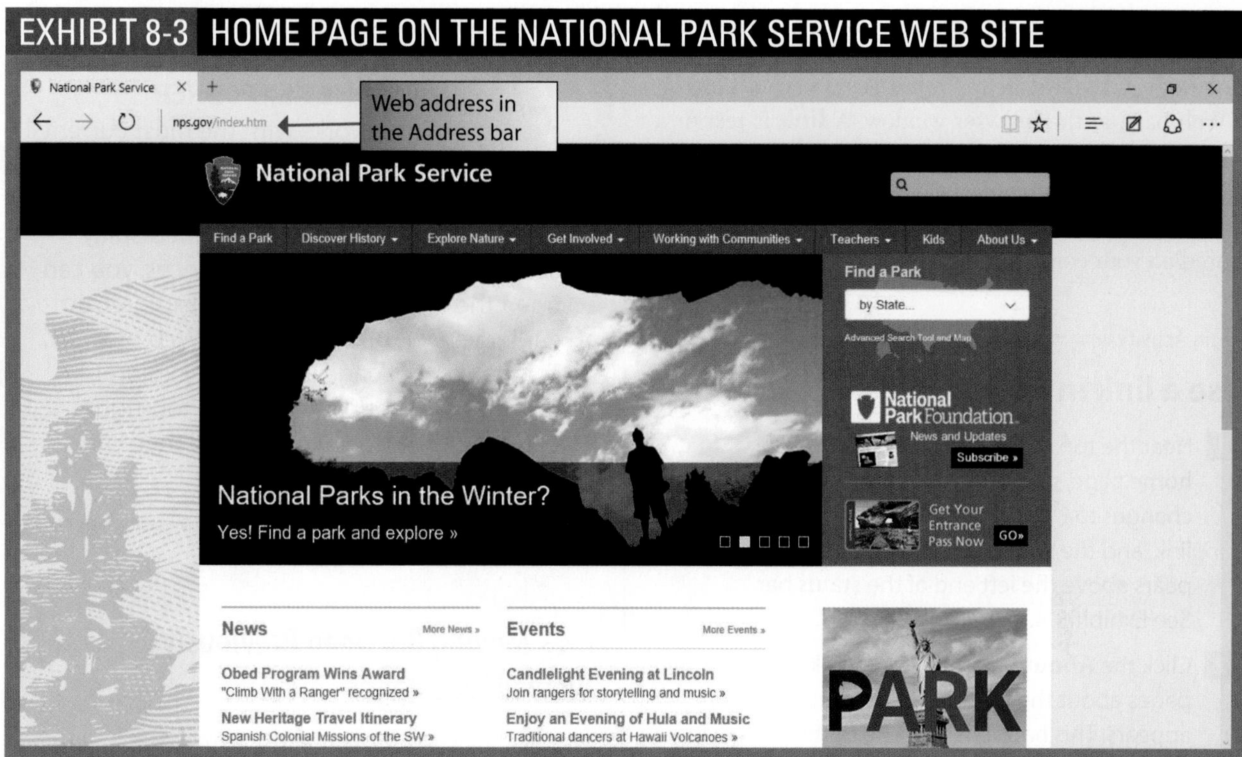

Begin Activity

Start Edge and go to a Web page.

1 On the Windows taskbar, click the **Microsoft Edge button** . The Edge Web browser starts and the start page appears.

2 If the browser window does not fill the screen, click the **Maximize button** in the top-right corner of the title bar. The insertion point is in the Search or web address box. Refer again to Exhibit 8-1.

> **PROBLEM?**
> If your screen does not look similar to Exhibit 8-1, the start page for Edge on your computer was changed. Continue with Step 3.
> If your screen contains the message *Welcome to Microsoft Edge* and contains links to import your favorites, meet Cortana, and write on the Web, you can click each of these links. When you are finished, at the top-left of the window, next to Get Started, click the **Close tab button** . You can import favorites or bookmarks from another browser at any time by clicking the **More button** , clicking **Settings**, clicking **View favorites settings**, and then clicking **Import**.

3 Click in the **Search or enter web address box**, and then type **nps.gov**. This is the Web address for the home page for the U.S. National Park Service Web site. As you type, a list of Web sites that contain the same characters you are typing appears. If you see the Web address you are typing, you can click it to display that Web page instead of finishing typing the address. After you type *gov*, */index.htm* appears after *nps.gov*. This is the full Web address of the National Park Service Web site home page. Refer again to Exhibit 8-2.

> **PROBLEM?**
> If your start page does not include the Search or enter web address box, click in the bar at the top of the window that displays the Web address of the page shown to select the whole address, type **nps.gov**, and then continue with Step 4.

4 Press the **Enter key**. Edge displays the page, in this case, the home page for the National Park Service Web site, and the Web page address appears in the Address bar at the top of the window. Your screen will look similar to Exhibit 8-3.

> **PROBLEM?**
> If a box appears on top of the Web page asking you to sign up to receive news or to take a survey, click the **Close button** (an X) in the top-right corner of the box.

End Activity

8-1b Using Links in Edge

Another way to navigate to Web pages is to click links on a Web page in the browser window. A **link** is text or a graphic formatted so that when you click it, another Web page loads in the browser window, you jump to another location on the same Web page, or you open a document stored on your computer or on a Web server.

Begin Activity

Use a link in Edge.

1. Near the top of the National Park Service home page, point to **About Us**. The pointer changes to 👆 to indicate that this text is a link, and the Web address of the linked page appears above the left end of the status bar. See Exhibit 8-4.
2. Click the **About Us link**. A list of links to Web pages about the National Park Service appears. This happens because of the underlying design of this Web page; this does not always happen.
3. Click the **Overview link**. The About Us page loads, and the Web address in the Address bar changes to the address for that page.

End Activity

FYI

OPENING WEB PAGES IN INTERNET EXPLORER

Edge works with the most current versions of Web pages. Web pages that were created using earlier accepted standards for creating Web pages might not display correctly in Edge. In those instances, you can open the Web page in Internet Explorer, an earlier version of the Microsoft Web browser. To open a Web page in Internet Explorer, click the More button ··· in the top-right corner of the Edge window, and then click Open with Internet Explorer.

8-1c Moving Between Previously Viewed Web Pages

You can move back and forth between the different Web pages you have recently viewed. The Back button and the Forward button are at the top of the window to the left of the Address bar. Clicking the Back button redisplays the previous Web page you viewed. You can continue backward through the viewed pages until you reach the first page that opened when you started Edge.

EXHIBIT 8-4 POINTING TO A LINK ON A WEB PAGE IN THE EDGE APP

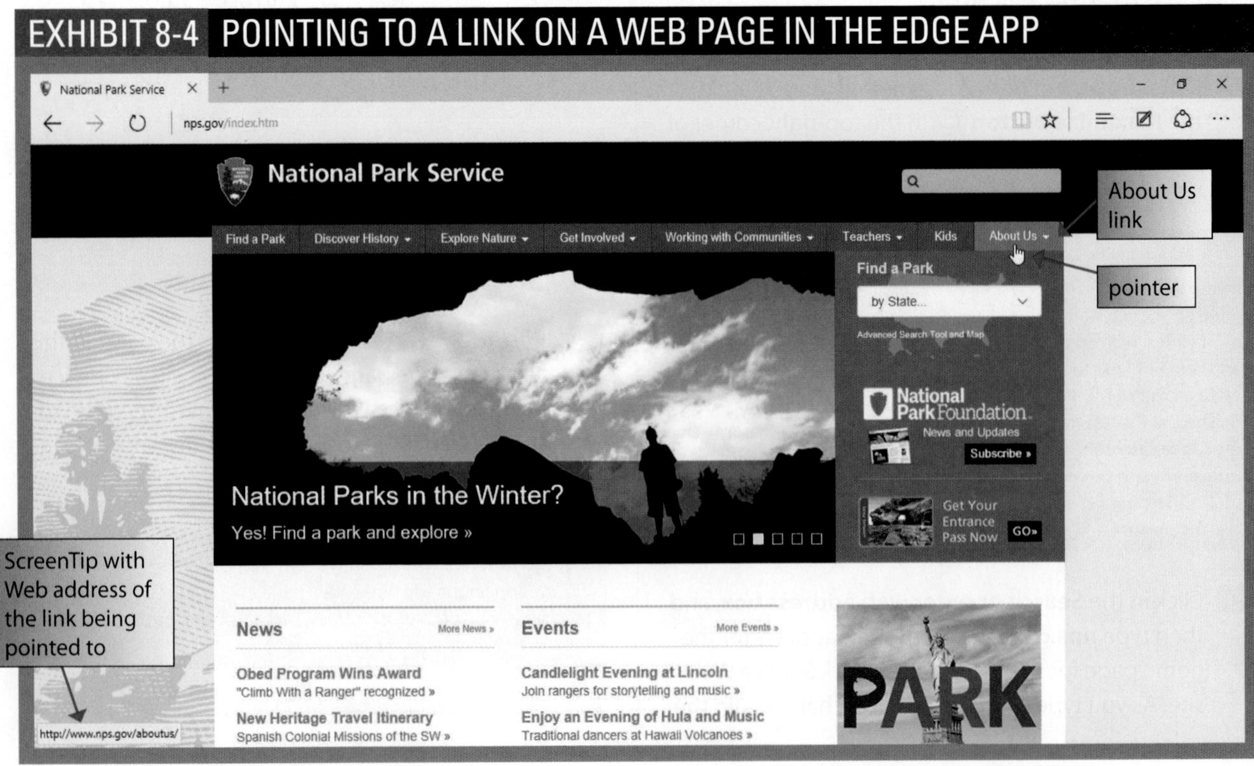

Once you navigate back a page, the Forward button becomes available so you can return to the more recent pages you viewed. See Exhibit 8-5.

EXHIBIT 8-5 BACK BUTTON AND FORWARD BUTTON

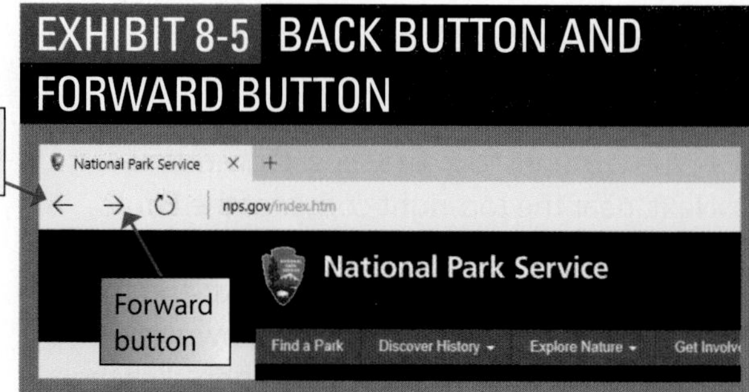

If the Back or Forward button on the navigation bar is dimmed, it means that there is no recently viewed Web page. The Back and Forward buttons and arrows track only your current browser session.

Begin Activity

Go to previously viewed Web pages.

1. To the left of the Address bar, click the **Back button** ←. The previously viewed Web page—the National Park Service Web site home page—appears on the screen. Now the Forward button is available. Refer again to Exhibit 8-5.
2. To the left of the Address bar, click the **Forward button** →. The About Us page loads again. The Forward button is again unavailable (dimmed) because you have not viewed any more pages after the current page.

End Activity

8-1d Accessing a Search Site from the Address Bar

Finding information on the Internet is made easier with search engines, which are available through search sites. **Search sites** are Web sites designed specifically to help you find information on the Web. Some popular search sites are Bing and Google. Most search sites use a **search engine**—a software program that uses a huge database of information about Web pages to help users find Web pages that contain the information they are seeking.

You can use the Address bar to conduct a search using the default search site for Edge. Unless it has been changed, the default search engine for Edge is Bing. To conduct a search, type appropriate **keywords**—one or more words describing what you are looking for—in the Address bar or the Search or enter web address bar. (Multiple keywords are sometimes called a **search phrase**.) As you type the keywords, a list of suggested search phrases appears. You can continue typing, and then press the Enter key, or you can click one of the suggested search phrases to open the default search site displaying the **search results**—a list of links to Web pages that contain the keywords. The results are arranged in descending order by relevancy—the pages that seem more related to your search term appear at the top of the list. Each result includes a link you can click to display that Web page and a few lines from the Web page that describe the result. Usually, the text of the link is blue and underlined, and the keywords are bold in the both the links and the descriptions. Exhibit 8-6 shows search results for the keywords *green living* in the Bing search site.

Begin Activity

Search the Internet using the default search engine.

1. Click in the **Address bar**. The entire Web address appears and is selected.
2. Type **green living**. The text you type replaces the selected Web address and a list appears below the Address bar displaying Search suggestions.
3. Press the **Enter key**. A list of Web pages that contain the keywords *green living* appears in your default search engine. Refer again to Exhibit 8-6 (keep in mind that your results will not match those shown in Exhibit 8-6 exactly). In most search engines, links to additional pages of results appear at the bottom of the page.

TIP: If the keywords you want to use appear in the Search suggestions list below the Address bar, you can click that entry to select it and run the search.

link Text or a graphic formatted to load a Web page, jump to another location on the same Web page, or open a document when it is clicked.

search site A Web site designed to help users search for Web pages that contain keywords.

search engine A software program used by a search site to retrieve Web pages containing the keywords from a search database.

keyword A word typed in a search box on a search site or other Web page to locate information related to that keyword.

search phrase Multiple keywords.

search results A list of links to Web pages that contain the keywords entered in a search engine.

EXHIBIT 8-6 SEARCH RESULTS FOR THE KEYWORDS *GREEN LIVING* IN THE BING SEARCH SITE

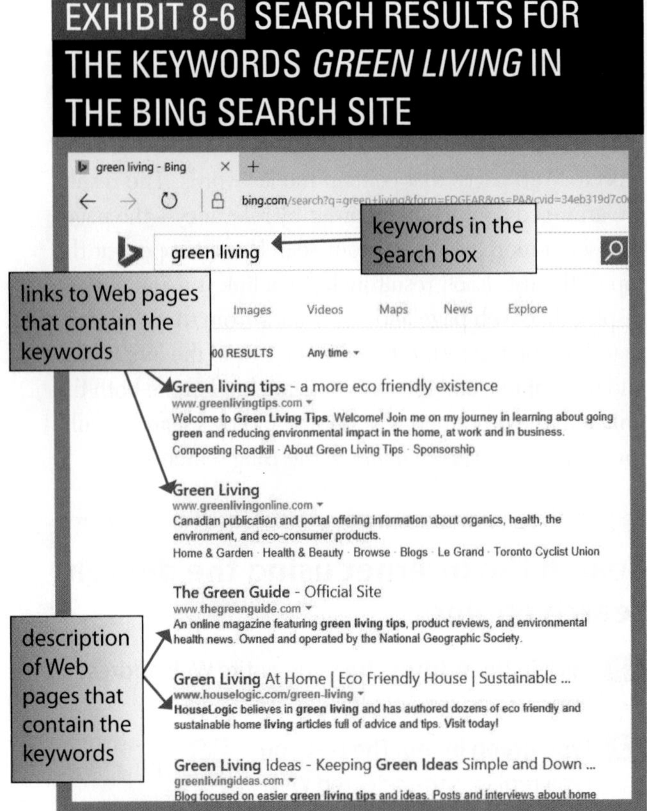

4. At the right edge of the screen, use the **vertical scroll bar** to scroll down the page to examine the first page of search results.
5. Scroll back up to the top of the page, and then click in the **Search box** at the top of the page after the keyword *living*.
6. Press the **Spacebar**, type **on a budget** and then press the **Enter key**. The list of results narrows to include only Web sites that contain all of the keywords *green living on a budget*.
7. Scroll down the list on the first page of results, and click a link that interests you. The Web page you clicked loads, replacing the list of results.
8. Click the **Back button** to return to the list of search results. The link you clicked is now a different color from the other links to indicate that you visited that Web page.
9. Click the **Back button** twice to return to the About Us page on the National Park Service Web site.

End Activity

tab An object that displays a Web page within Edge.

FYI CHANGING THE DEFAULT SEARCH ENGINE

You can choose the search engine you want to use to search from the Search of enter web address bar or the Address bar. First, display the search site you want to use in the current tab in the browser window. Next, near the top-right corner of the Edge window, click the More button ···, and then click Settings at the bottom of the menu to open the SETTINGS pane. Scroll down to the Advanced settings section, and then click the View advanced settings button. Scroll down to the Privacy and services section. Below the Search in the address bar with label, click the Change button to display the Change search engine pane. Below the Choose one label, click the search site you want to use, and then click the Set as default button. Click in a blank area of the current Web page to close the SETTINGS pane.

8-1e Using Tabs

Web pages are displayed on **tabs** in Edge. You can open multiple tabs to display different Web pages at the same time. Each tab remembers the Web pages that you have viewed on that tab, so that the Back and Forward buttons move you between only those Web pages you viewed on that tab.

When you start Edge, the start page appears in a tab in the application window. To open a second tab, you click the New tab button to the right of the current tabs. The new tab that opens is the same as the start page, except it lists frequently or recently visited Web pages above the news feed, which you can click to display that Web page in the new tab. See Exhibit 8-7.

If you want to open a linked Web page in a new tab, you can right-click the link on a Web page, and then click Open link in new tab on the shortcut menu.

Exhibit 8-8 shows three tabs open in the browser window. When multiple tabs are open, the tab on top containing the Web page you can see is the current tab. To switch to another tab, you click it. You can close tabs by clicking the Close button on the right end of the tab. If you are trying to close a tab other than the current tab, point to that tab to make its Close button visible.

EXHIBIT 8-7 NEW TAB IN EDGE

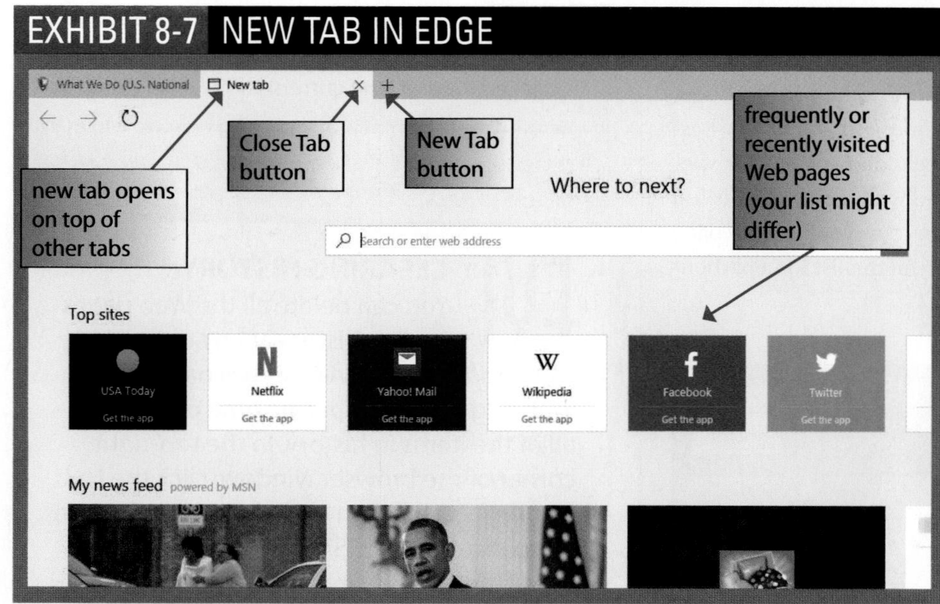

3 In the Search or enter web address box, type **usa.gov** and then press the **Enter key**. The home page for the USA.gov Web site appears in the new tab.

4 Scroll down to the bottom of the page.

5 Right-click the **About Us link**. On the shortcut menu, click **Open in new tab**. A new tab opens to the right of the USA.gov home page tab.

EXHIBIT 8-8 THREE TABS OPEN IN EDGE

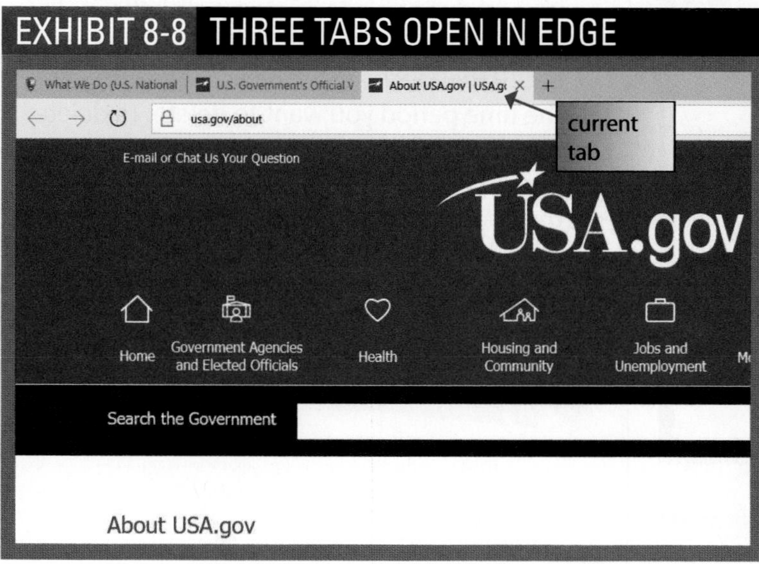

TIP: You can also press and hold the Ctrl key while you click a link to open the linked page in a new tab.

6 Click the **About USA.gov | USA.gov tab**. The About USA.gov page becomes the current tab in the window. Refer again to Exhibit 8-8.

7 On the About USA.gov | USA.gov tab, click the **Close tab button** [X]. The tab closes, and the USA.gov home page is the current tab.

8 Right-click the **U.S. Government's Offic tab**. On the shortcut menu, click **Close other tabs**. The National Park Service tab closes, and the USA.gov tab becomes the current tab.

End Activity

Begin Activity

Use tabs.

1 To the right of the National Park Service tab, point to the **New tab button** [+]. The ScreenTip that appears identifies the button name.

2 Click the **New tab button** [+]. A new tab appears with the insertion point blinking in the Search or enter web address box. Refer again to Exhibit 8-7.

TIP: To change new tab settings, click the More button [...], click Settings, click the Open new tabs with box, click the option you want, and then click a blank area of the current web page to close the SETTINGS pane.

8-1f Using the History List

History tracks the Web pages you visit over multiple browsing sessions. You can display the complete history by opening a pane called the Hub, and then clicking

history A list that tracks the Web pages you visit over multiple browsing sessions.

the History button [History icon]. See Exhibit 8-9. In the Hub, the HISTORY pane lists the web addresses for the Web sites and Web pages that you have visited using Edge. The entries are grouped into time and date lists (Last hour, Today, Yesterday, Last week, and sometimes specific days). Each list contains the web pages you visited in chronological order. To return to a specific Web page listed in the history, click its entry in the list for a particular day or time.

EXHIBIT 8-9 HISTORY LIST IN THE HUB

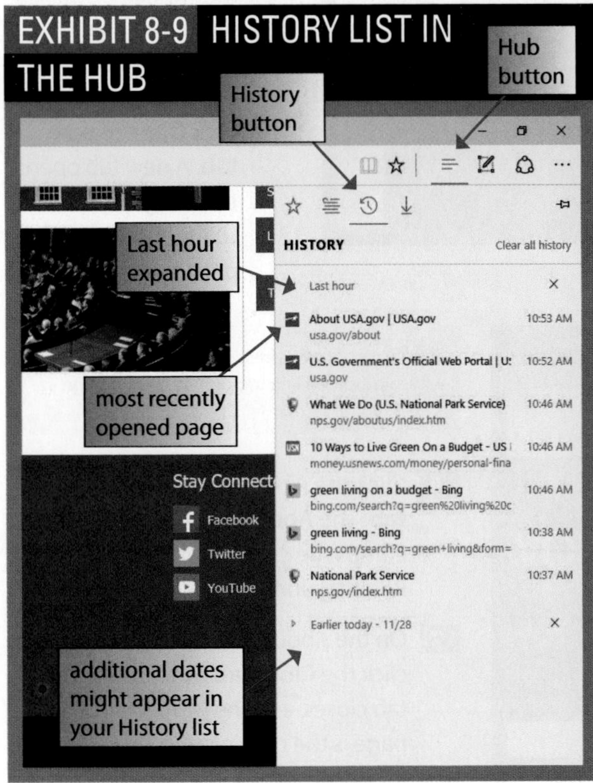

Begin Activity

Return to a page in the history.

1 At the right end of the Address bar, click the **Hub button** [Hub icon]. The Hub opens on the right side of the screen displaying the HISTORY pane. At the top of the pane, the History button [History icon] is blue to indicate that it is selected.

> **PROBLEM?**
> If the HISTORY pane is not displayed, click the **History button** [History icon] at the top of the pane.

2 If the Expand button [Expand icon] appears next to Last hour, click **Last hour** to expand that group. A list of the Web sites you viewed in the past 60 minutes appears in chronological order with the most recently visited listed first. Refer again to Exhibit 8-9.

3 In the HISTORY pane, click the **What We Do (U.S. National Park Service) link**. The Web page you clicked loads in the current tab.

End Activity

> **FYI**
> **CLEARING HISTORY**
> You can delete all the Web pages in your history at any time. You can remove an individual Web page, all the Web pages from a specific time period, or all of the items in history. In the top-right corner of the browser window, click the Hub button [Hub icon], and then click the History button [History icon] to display the HISTORY pane. To clear a specific Web page from the history, point to it, and then click the Delete button [X] to the right of its entry. To clear all the Web pages viewed during a specific time, click the Delete button [X] to the right of the time or date label, such as Last hour or Yesterday, for the time period you want to delete. To delete the history of any visits to a specific Web site, right-click any Web page in the history list on that Web site, and then click Delete all visits to <*Web site name*> on the shortcut menu. To clear all of the Web pages in the history, click the Clear all history link near the top-right corner of the HISTORY pane.

8-2 SAVING LINKS TO WEB PAGES

To make it easier to display the Web pages you view the most frequently, you can pin Web pages to the Start menu. You can also save Web pages as links in the Favorites and Reading lists.

8-2a Pinning Web Pages to the Start Menu

If you visit a Web page frequently, you can pin it to the Start menu for easy access. When you pin a Web page to the Start menu, it appears as a tile on the right side of the menu. You can then open the Web page directly from the Start menu without first starting Edge.

To pin a Web page to the Start menu, first display that Web page in Edge. Next, click the More button [...] to open the menu of actions you can perform in Edge. See Exhibit 8-10. On the menu, click Pin this page to Start. A tile for that Web page appears as a tile at the bottom of the right pane of the Start menu.

EXHIBIT 8-10 MORE MENU

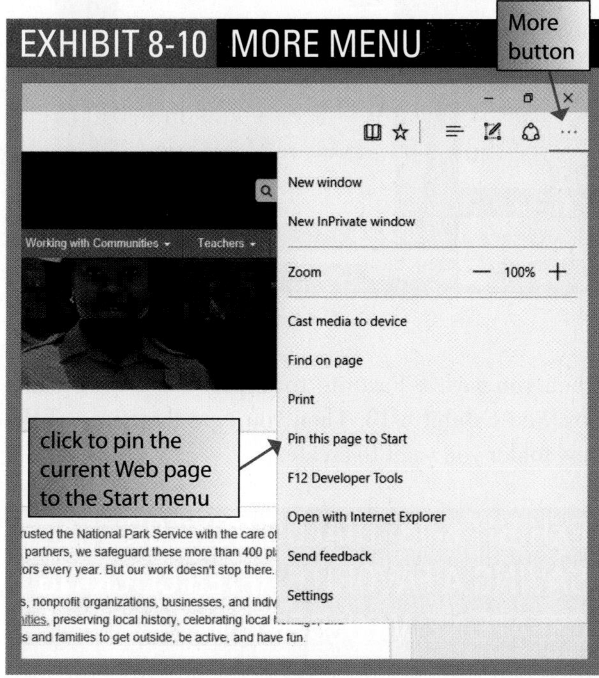

Exhibit 8-11 shows a Web page pinned to the Start menu. When you click the tile for the pinned page, the Web page opens in a new tab.

EXHIBIT 8-11 WEB PAGE PINNED TO THE START MENU

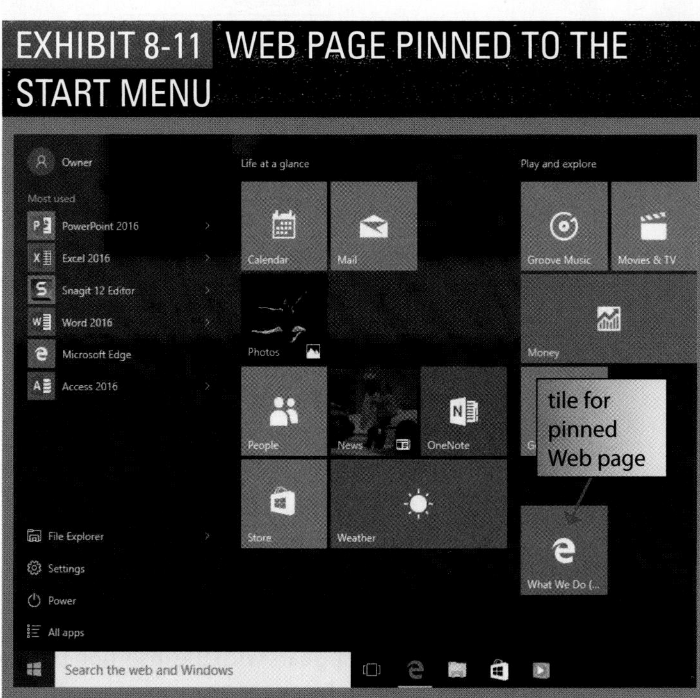

Begin Activity

Pin a Web page to the Start menu.

1. Make sure the **What We Do (U.S. Natio tab** is the active tab.
2. To the right of the Address bar, click the **More button** [...]. A menu of actions that you can perform in Edge opens. Refer again to Exhibit 8-10.
3. On the menu, click the **Pin this page to Start**. A dialog box opens asking if you want to pin this tile to Start.
4. Click **Yes**. The dialog box closes and the tile for the Web page is added to the Start menu.
5. Click the **Back button** [←]. The USA.gov home page appears.
6. Click the **Start button** [⊞], and then scroll the right pane down until you see the tile for the pinned site. Refer again to Exhibit 8-11.
7. Click the **What We Do tile**. The What We Do page on the National Park Service Web site opens in a new tab.

End Activity

8-2b Saving Web Pages as Favorites

Similar to pinning a Web page to the Start menu, you can save a Web page as a favorite. A **favorite** is a link to a Web page saved in the Favorites list.

To add a Web page as a favorite, click the Add to favorites or reading list button [☆] in the top-right corner of the Edge window, and then click the Favorites button at the top of the dialog box that opens. See Exhibit 8-12. You can keep the suggested name or change it to something shorter and more understandable to you. The Save in box displays the name of the folder in which the favorite will be stored. Favorites is the default folder, and this means that the favorite will be stored in the main Favorites list. You can also add favorites to the Favorites bar, which you can display below the Address bar, or you can create or select a different folder. After you select the folder you want to save the favorite in, click the Add button.

favorite A link to a Web page saved in the Favorites list.

EXHIBIT 8-12 DIALOG BOX FOR SAVING A FAVORITE

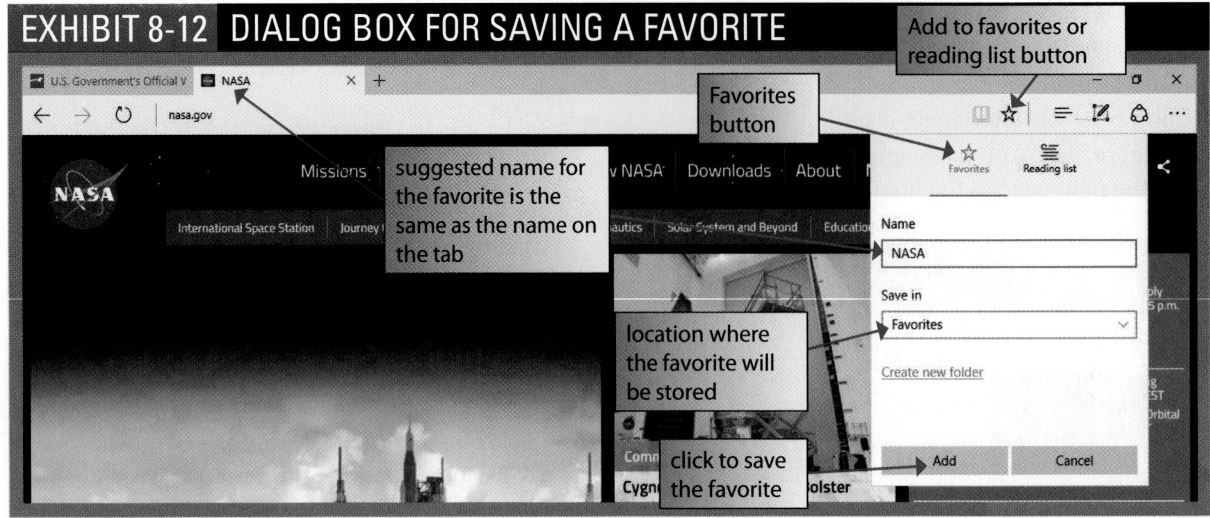

Begin Activity

Add a Web page as a favorite in the Favorites folder.

1. Click in the **Address bar**, type **nasa.gov** and then press the **Enter key**. The NASA home page opens in the current tab.
2. To the right of the Address bar, click the **Add to favorites or reading list button** ☆. A dialog box opens.
3. If it is not already blue to indicate that it is selected, click the **Favorites button** at the top of the dialog box. The text in the Name box is the name of the currently displayed Web page, as it appears on the page tab at the top of the screen, and Favorites appears in the Save in box. Refer again to Exhibit 8-12.

> **TIP:** To see the full name of the Web page, point to the tab to display a ScreenTip.

4. Click in the **Name box** after *NASA*, press the **Spacebar**, and then type **home page**.
5. In the dialog box, click **Add**. The dialog box closes, and the home page of the NASA Web site is saved as a favorite in the main Favorites folder with the name you typed. The Add to favorites or reading list button changes to ★ to indicate that this page was saved as a favorite.

End Activity

To help you organize your favorites, you can create folders within the Favorites folder. To do this, you click the Create new folder link in the dialog box that opens when you save a Favorite to display the Folder name box. See Exhibit 8-13. Then you type the name of the new folder you want to create.

EXHIBIT 8-13 DIALOG BOX FOR SAVING A FAVORITE AFTER CLICKING CREATE NEW FOLDER LINK

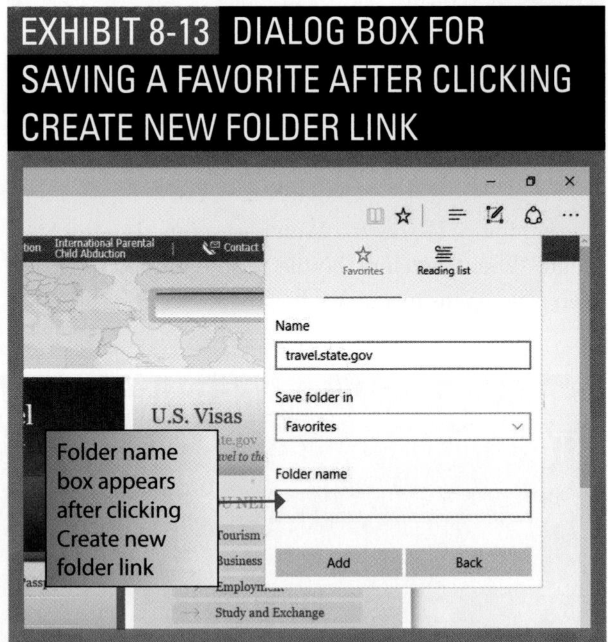

Begin Activity

Add a Web page as a favorite in a new folder.

1. Click in the **Address bar**, type **travel.state.gov**, and then press the **Enter key**.
2. Click the **Add to favorites or reading list** button ☆, and then click the **Create new folder** link. The Folder name box appears with the insertion point in it. Refer again to Exhibit 8-13.

3 Type **Travel Sites** in the Folder name box, and then click **Add**. The dialog box closes and the Add to favorites or reading list button changes to ★ to indicate that the page was added as a favorite.

End Activity

Finally, you can save a favorite to the Favorites bar. The Favorites bar is a good place to save favorites you want to access frequently.

You can change the Favorites settings so that the Favorites bar appears below the Address bar at the top of the Edge window. You do this by clicking the More button ··· and then clicking Settings to open the SETTINGS pane. See Exhibit 8-14.

EXHIBIT 8-14 SETTINGS PANE

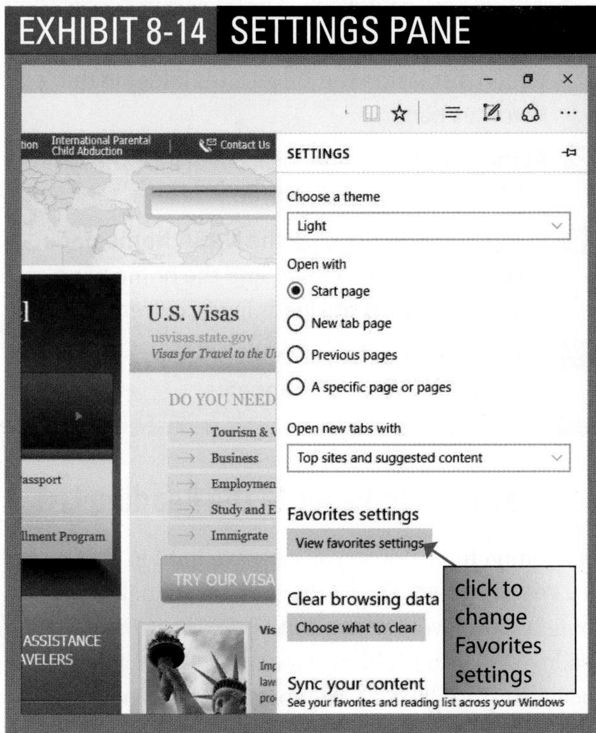

In the SETTINGS pane, click the View favorites settings button to change the pane to the Favorites settings pane. Then you click the Show the favorites bar switch to change it to On and display the Favorites bar. See Exhibit 8-15.

Begin Activity

Add a favorite to the Favorites bar.

1 To the right of the Address bar, click the **More** button ···, and then click **Settings**. The SETTINGS pane opens. Refer again to Exhibit 8-14.

2 Below Favorites settings, click the **View favorites settings button**. The pane changes to the Favorites settings pane. Near the top of the pane, the Show the favorites bar switch is set to Off.

TIP: If you want to import favorites from another browser, click Import in the Favorites settings pane.

3 Click the **Show the favorites bar switch** to change it to On. The Favorites bar appears below the Address bar in the Edge window. Refer again to Exhibit 8-15.

4 Click a **blank area of the Web page** to close the SETTINGS pane, click in the **Address bar**, type **usa.gov**, and then press the **Enter key**.

5 Click the **Add to favorites or reading list** button ☆, and then type **USA.gov** to replace the selected text in the Name box in the Favorites dialog box.

6 Click the **Save in box**. A menu opens listing three folders: Favorites with Favorites Bar and Travel Sites folder indented below it.

7 Click **Favorites Bar**, and then click **Add**. The dialog box closes and the current page is added to the Favorites bar. Compare your screen to Exhibit 8-16.

End Activity

EXHIBIT 8-15 FAVORITES BAR DISPLAYED IN EDGE WINDOW

EXHIBIT 8-16 USA.GOV FAVORITE IN FAVORITES BAR

After you have added a Web page as a favorite, it is available on the Favorites list. See Exhibit 8-17. When you click its link in the Favorites list, that page will load in the current tab.

EXHIBIT 8-17 LIST OF FAVORITES IN FAVORITES PANE

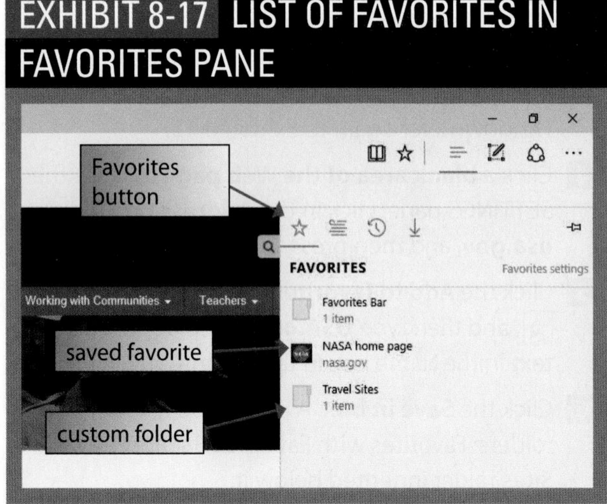

Begin Activity

Go to a favorite.

1 Click the **Back button** [←] three times to return to the About Us page on the National Park Service Web site.

2 To the right of the Address bar, click the **Hub button** [≡]. The Hub opens on the right side of the screen displaying the HISTORY pane.

3 In the HISTORY pane, click the **Favorites button** [☆]. In the FAVORITES pane, the NASA home page favorite and the Travel Sites folder you created are listed below the Favorites Bar folder. Refer again to Exhibit 8-17.

4 Click the **Travel Sites folder**. The pane changes to list the contents of the Travel Sites folder.

5 In the FAVORITES pane, click the **travel.state.gov favorite**. The pane closes and the Travel.State.Gov Web page appears in the current tab.

> **TIP:** You can click the Pin this pane button [⊣¤] in the top-right corner of the Hub so that the Hub pane remains open until you click the Close this pane button [X].

6 At the right end of the Address bar, click the **Hub button** [≡]. The Hub opens on the right side of the screen displaying the Travel Sites folder in the Favorites pane.

7 At the top of the pane, click **Favorites**. The main FAVORITES folder is displayed.

8 In the Favorites list, click the **NASA home page favorite**. The pane closes, and the home page of the NASA Web site loads in the current tab.

9 On the Favorites bar, click the **USA.gov favorite**. The USA.gov Web page appears.

End Activity

8-2c Saving Web Pages to the Reading List

In addition to favorites, you can save links to Web pages in a **reading list**. The reading list is essentially the same thing as the favorites list, but you cannot organize the reading list using folders. Generally, the reading list is meant to store links to Web pages you intend to return to shortly, rather than permanently saved links for Web pages that you intend to visit many times in the future.

To add a Web page to your reading list, click the Add to favorites or reading list button [☆] to the right of the Address bar. Click the reading list button in the dialog box that opens. You can keep the suggested name or replace that with one you choose. See Exhibit 8-18. When you click the Add button, the current Web page is saved to your reading list as a static Web page.

Begin Activity

Add a Web page to the reading list.

1 On the USA.gov home page, click the **Travel and Immigration button**, and then click the **Recreation and Travel within the U.S. link**.

reading list A collection of links to Web pages.

EXHIBIT 8-18 DIALOG BOX FOR SAVING A WEB PAGE TO THE READING LIST

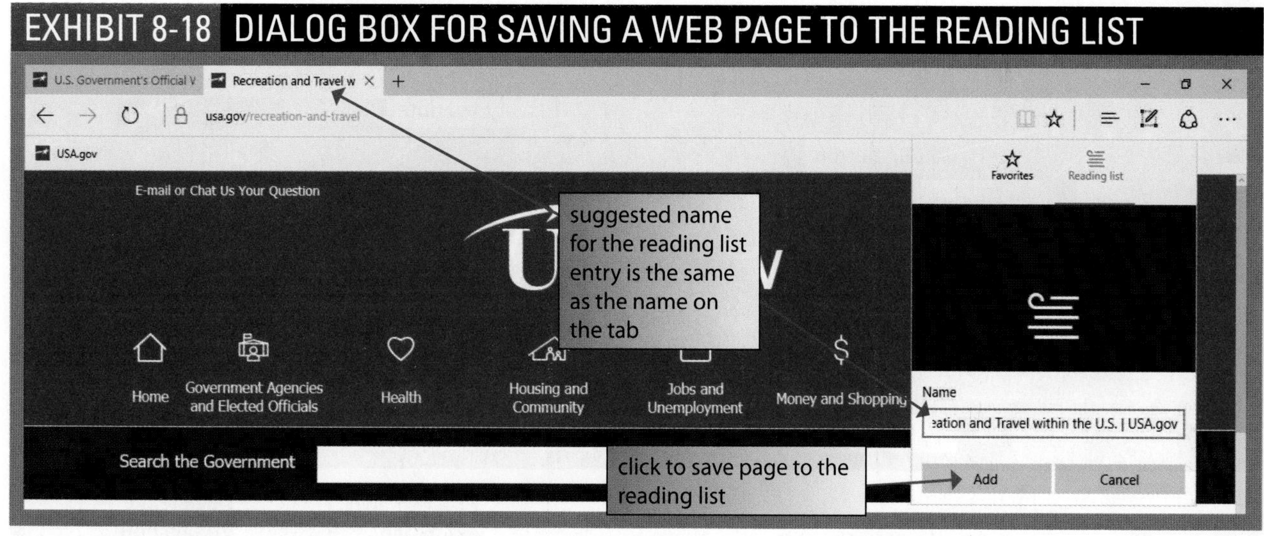

2 Click the **Add to favorites or reading list button** ☆ to the right of the Address bar. The dialog box opens with the Favorites button selected at the top of the dialog box.

3 Click the **Reading list button**. The reading list button is blue to indicate that it is selected, and the name of the Web page appears in the Name box in the dialog box. Refer again to Exhibit 8-18.

4 In the dialog box, click **Add**. The link to the current Web page is saved in your reading list using the suggested name.

End Activity

You can return to a reading list entry at any time. Just open the reading list in the Hub to see all of your reading list entries. See Exhibit 8-19. Then, you can click an entry in the list to open the Web page in the current tab.

EXHIBIT 8-19 READING LIST IN READING LIST PANE

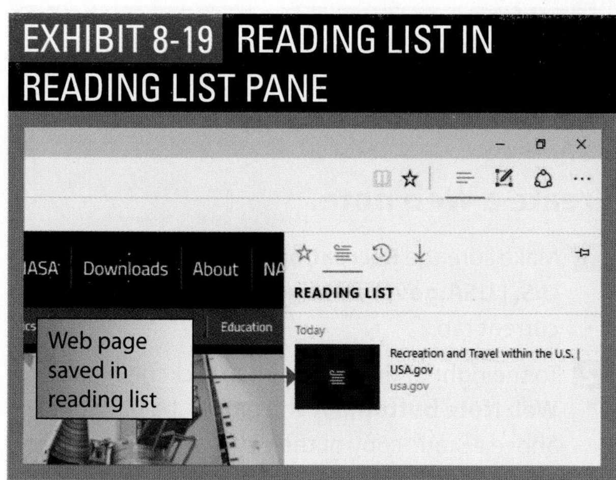

Begin Activity

View a reading list entry.

1 Click the **Back button** ← three times to return to the NASA home page.

2 Click the **Hub button** , and then click the **Reading list button**. The link to the Web page you just saved appears at the top of your reading list. Refer again to Exhibit 8-19.

3 Click the **Recreation and Travel within the U.S. | USA.gov link** at the top of the reading list. The page is displayed again in the browser window.

End Activity

8-3 CREATING WEB NOTES

Web pages are regularly and continually updated and changed. However, at times you may want to look at the Web page as it was when you first viewed it. You may also want to write notes on that page. Rather than using the resources to print a Web page, you can create a **Web note**, which saves, a static version of the Web page in a file with notes and highlights you added to particular sections, phrases, or images. You can even clip a section of the Web page to save. See Exhibit 8-20.

Web note A Web page that you save as an image with drawn or typed notes and highlights.

EXHIBIT 8-20 WEB PAGE DISPLAYED AS A WEB NOTE

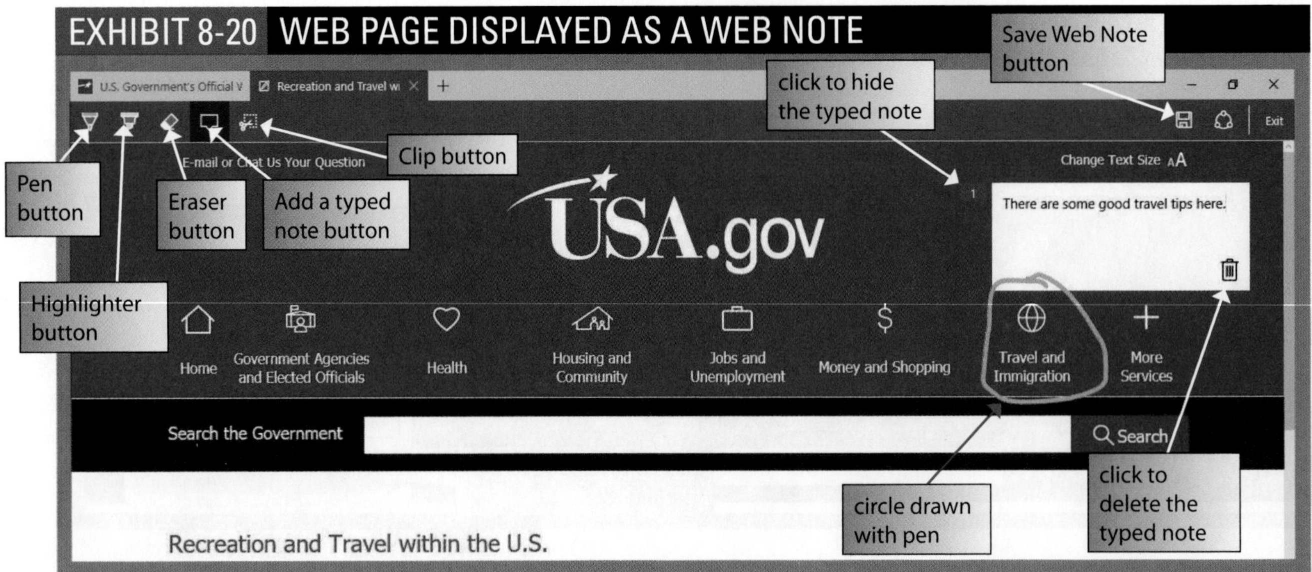

You can save the Web note to OneNote, as a favorite, or to your reading list. You do this from the dialog box that opens when you click the Save Web Note button on the toolbar. See Exhibit 8-21.

> **FYI**
>
> **SHARING A WEB PAGE AS A WEB NOTE**
>
> You can share a link to a Web page, a Web note, or a screenshot of a Web page with other people or apps. The Share pane lists all of the ways you can share the current Web page. To open the Share pane, click the Share button to the right of the Address bar. If a Web page is displayed, you will share a link to the Web page; if a Web note is displayed, you will share the Web note as an image. In either case, you can click the Web page or Web note name at the top of the Share pane, and then click Screenshot to take a picture of the currently displayed Web page or Web note to share. Decide which of the listed methods you want to use to share the item. For example, you can share the item via the Mail or Messaging app, or you can save it to a OneNote notebook.

EXHIBIT 8-21 DIALOG BOX FOR SAVING A WEB NOTE TO THE READING LIST

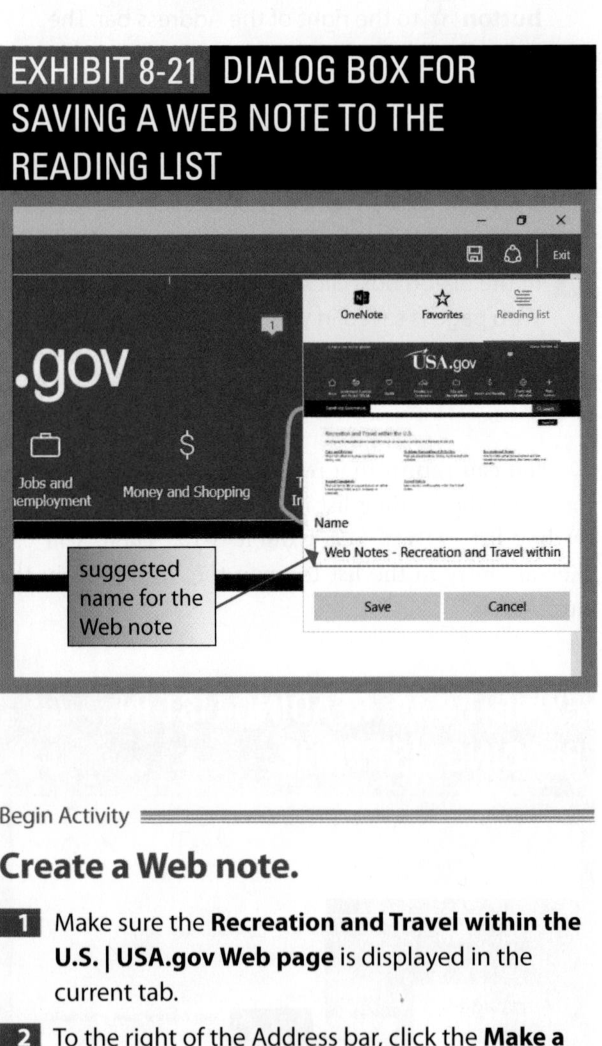

Begin Activity

Create a Web note.

1. Make sure the **Recreation and Travel within the U.S. | USA.gov Web page** is displayed in the current tab.
2. To the right of the Address bar, click the **Make a Web Note button**. The purple bar appears above a static copy of the page with buttons for

adding and erasing notes and highlights, clipping a section of the page, and saving or sharing the Web Note page. The Pen button is selected.

3 On the purple bar, click the **Pen button**, and then click the **orange square**.

> **TIP:** To remove pen or highlighter marks from the Web page, click the Eraser button, and then click or drag the pointer over the drawn mark to remove it.

4 Point to the area next to the Travel and Immigration button, press and hold the **mouse button**, drag the **pointer** to draw an orange circle around the button, and then release the **mouse button**. An orange circle is drawn around the Travel and Immigration button.

5 On the purple bar, click the **Add a typed note button**, and then click above the circled Travel and Immigration button. A white box appears with the insertion point in it and to the left of the white box.

> **TIP:** You can use the Clip button to save only part of the Web page in the Web note.

6 Type **There are some good travel tips here.** as the note. Refer again to Exhibit 8-20.

7 Next to the typed note, click the **Collapse typed note 1 button**. The typed note closes.

8 On the purple bar, click the **Save Web Note button** to open a dialog box so you can choose where to save and what to name the Web note.

9 Click the **Reading list button** at the top of the dialog box. Refer back to Exhibit 8-21.

10 Click the **Save button**. The Web notes Web page is saved to the reading list with the suggested name.

11 On the purple bar, click the **Exit button**. The Web note closes.

End Activity

You access Web notes you saved as favorites or added to your reading list from the Hub just like any other favorite or reading list entry. From the Hub, you can open the Web note. The open Web note includes options to hide the notes you added and to go to the original page. See Exhibit 8-22.

Begin Activity

Open a Web note.

1 In the top-right corner of the browser window, click the **Hub button**. The READING LIST Pane opens and Web Notes — Recreation and Travel within the U.S. | USA.gov is the first entry in the reading list.

2 Click the **Web Notes — Recreation and Travel within the U.S. | USA.gov**. The Web note with your notes and highlights opens in the current tab. The purple bar above the Web page contains the Hide notes button and a link that you can click to display the actual Web page from which the Web note was created. Refer again to Exhibit 8-22.

EXHIBIT 8-22 WEB NOTE OPENED IN EDGE WINDOW

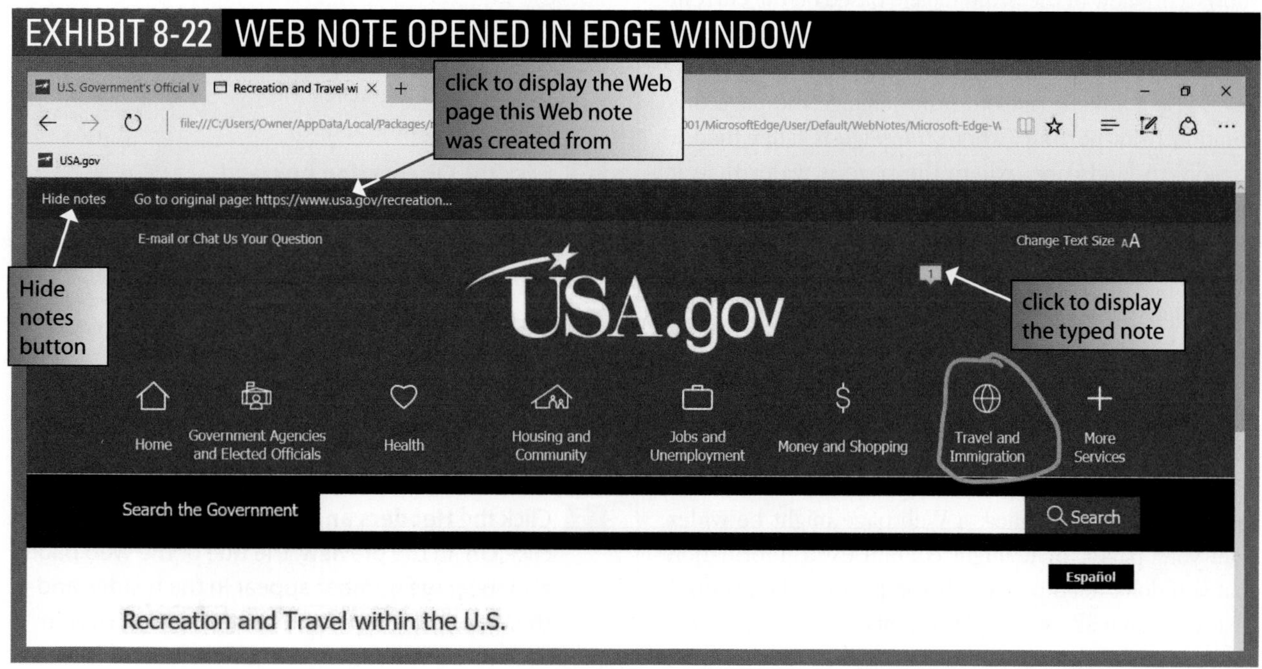

3 Click the **Expand typed note 1 button** on the Web Note page. The white box containing the typed note appears.

4 On the purple bar at the top of the Web page, click the **Hide notes button**. The typed note and the orange circle disappear, and the Hide notes button changes to the Show notes button.

5 On the purple bar, click the **Go to original page: link**. The Web note closes and the Recreation and Travel Web Page on USA.gov reappears.

End Activity

8-4 PRINTING WEB PAGES AND WEB NOTES

You might need to print a Web page occasionally. For example, you might want to print the receipt for an item you purchased on a shopping Web site or you might want to print copies of Web pages that you have used when researching a topic to document the information. Many Web pages provide a link to a separate printer-friendly version of the page. This version prints only essential information in an appropriate format.

When you are ready to preview and print a Web page, you open the Print dialog box. The Print dialog box shows a preview of the printed page based on the current print settings. You can change any of these settings. For example, you might select a different printer or print to PDF, select which pages to print, change the page orientation from portrait (where the page is taller than it is wide) to landscape (where the page is wider than it is tall), change the scale to force the content to fit on a specific number of pages, adjust the margins, display or hide the text that prints at the top and bottom of the page (called headers and footers), and change the paper size. Exhibit 8-23 shows the Print dialog box for the Microsoft Print to PDF printer.

It is a good idea to examine the preview of a Web page that appears in the Print dialog box before you print it because Web pages are not always designed with printing in mind. For instance, a Web page might be wider than your paper, or it might contain extra information that you don't need printed. If you preview the printout first, you can make some adjustments when you preview the page.

EXHIBIT 8-23 PRINT DIALOG BOX IN EDGE

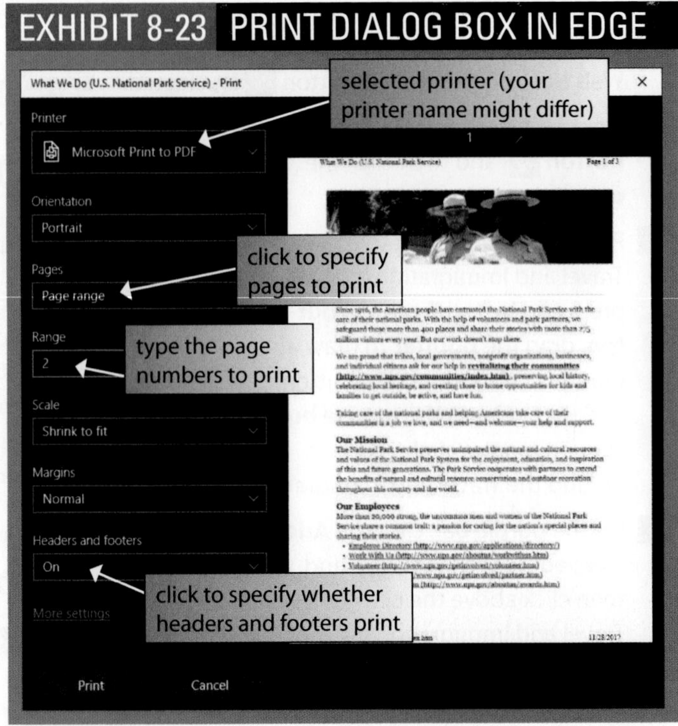

Begin Activity

Preview and print a Web page.

1 On the taskbar, click the **Start button**, and then click the **What We Do tile**. The page opens in a new tab.

2 To the right of the Address bar, click the **More button** ···, and then click **Print** on the menu. The Print dialog box opens.

3 If necessary, click the **Printer button**, and then click the printer you want to use.

4 Click the **Orientation box**, and then click **Landscape**. The orientation of the page in the preview changes to landscape.

5 Click the **Pages button**, and then click **Page Range**. The Range box appears below the Pages box.

6 Click in the **Range box**, and then type **2**. Now only the second page will print.

7 Click the **Headers and footers button**, and then click **On**. In the preview, the title of the Web page and the page number appear in the header, and the Web address and the current date appear in the footer. Refer again to Exhibit 8-23.

TIP: To print only the main contents of a Web page, click the Reading view button to the right of the Address bar before you open the Print dialog box.

8 If you are instructed to print, click the **Print button**; the dialog box closes, and page 2 of the What We Do (U.S. National Park Service) Web page prints. If you are instructed not to print, click the **Cancel button** to close the Print dialog box.

End Activity

8-5 CLEANING UP THE HUB AND UNPINNING WEB PAGES

When you no longer need Web pages and Web notes you saved as favorites or added to your reading list, you can delete them from the Hub. This keeps the entries current and streamlined. You can also clear your history so that Edge no longer remembers Web pages that you have viewed.

Begin Activity

Delete items from the Hub.

1 In the top-right corner of the browser window, click the **Hub button** . The Hub pane opens.

2 At the top of the pane, click the **Favorites button** .

3 Right-click the **NASA favorite**. On the shortcut menu, click **Delete**. The favorite is deleted.

4 Right-click the **Travel Sites** folder, and then on the shortcut menu, click **Delete**. The Travel Sites folder and the favorite it contains is deleted from the FAVORITES pane.

TIP: You can also display the favorite Web page, click the Add to favorites or reading list button, and then click Delete in the dialog box.

5 At the top of the pane, click the **Reading list button** . The Web note and the Web page you added earlier appear at the top of your reading list.

6 Right-click **Web Notes — Recreation and Travel within the U.S. | USA.gov**. On the shortcut menu, click **Delete**. The Web note is deleted from your reading list.

7 Right-click **Recreation and Travel within the U.S. | USA.gov**. On the shortcut menu, click **Delete**. The Web page is deleted from your reading list.

8 At the top of the pane, click the **History button** to display your history.

9 At the top of the HISTORY pane, click the **Clear all history link**. The pane changes to the Clear browsing data pane.

10 In the Clear browsing data pane, click **check boxes** as needed so that the **Browsing history check box** is checked and none of the other check boxes are selected.

11 At the bottom of the pane, click **Clear**. When the history is completely clear, the message "All clear!" appears briefly near the top of the pane.

12 Press the **Esc key** to close the pane.

13 In the Favorites bar, right-click the **USA.gov favorite**, and then click **Delete**. The favorite is removed from the Favorites bar.

14 Click the **More button** , click **Settings**, click **View favorite settings**, and then click the **Show the favorites bar switch.** The switch changes to Off and the Favorites bar disappears.

15 Press the **Esc key** to close the pane.

End Activity

You can unpin any site that you no longer need from the Start screen. You unpin the page directly from the Start menu. On the shortcut menu, click Unpin this program from taskbar. Even though the command uses the word "program," it is referring to only the button for the pinned page that you right-clicked.

Begin Activity

Unpin a Web page from the Start menu.

1 Click the **Start button** , and then right-click the **What We Do (U.S. National Park Service) tile.** A shortcut menu opens with options to unpin the page from Start, resize the tile, or turn off the live tile.

2 On the shortcut menu, click **Unpin from Start.** The What We Do tile is removed from the Start menu.

3 Click the **Start button** to close the Start menu.

End Activity

8-6 EXITING EDGE

You can close Edge when you are finished using it. If you have only one tab open, you exit the Edge the same way you do any other program, using the Close button on the title bar. However, if more than one tab is open, a dialog box opens, asking if you want to close all the tabs or only the current tab. See Exhibit 8-24. If you click Close all, the Edge application closes.

EXHIBIT 8-24 DIALOG BOX ASKING IF YOU WANT TO CLOSE ALL TABS

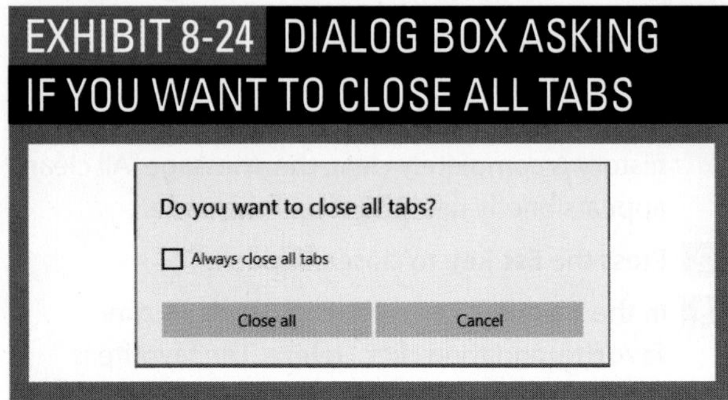

Begin Activity

Exit Edge.

1. In the top-right corner of the title bar, click the **Close button**. A dialog box opens, asking whether you want to close all tabs. Refer again to Exhibit 8-24.
2. Click **Close all** to close any open tabs and exit Edge.

End Activity

8-7 USING THE MAIL APP

Email allows you to communicate with other users on a network such as the Internet. If you are like most computer users, you exchange many email messages every day with friends, family, colleagues, and other contacts. You probably also receive newsletters, coupons, offers, and other types of messages from companies and organizations. You can also attach files, such as word processing documents, graphics, or spreadsheets, to an email message.

Windows 10 includes **Mail**, an app you use to send, receive, and manage email. Using Mail, you can send email to and receive email from anyone in the world who has an email address, regardless of the operating system or type of computer the person is using. Although this section provides steps for using the Mail app, these concepts and activities apply to any email application, including Microsoft Outlook, which comes with Microsoft Office.

Mail A Windows 10 app used to send, receive, and manage email.

8-7a Starting Mail

To use Mail (or any other email program), you need an Internet connection and an email address. Having an email address means you have an email account, which is space on an email server reserved for your messages. You set up an account with an email service provider, which can be an ISP, an employer or school, or a Web service such as Outlook.com, Hotmail, or Gmail.

The first time you start Mail, it looks for the email associated with your Microsoft account. After you have added one or more accounts, the Mail window opens. The elements on the Mail window are labeled in Exhibit 8-25.

Begin Activity

Start Mail.

1. On the taskbar, click the **Start button**, and then in the right pane, click the **Mail tile.** If this is the first time you have started Mail, the Welcome screen opens. If the main Mail window opens, you already have an associated account; skip the rest of this Activity and go to the section 8-7b, "Creating and Sending Email Using Mail."
2. Click the **Get started button**. After a moment, the Accounts window opens. It includes the email for the Microsoft account that you used to sign into Windows 10.

PROBLEM?
If you are not signed into Windows with a Microsoft account or if you do not have a Microsoft account, click **Add account.** If your Microsoft account is listed, click it. If it is not listed or if you do not have one, click **Outlook.com.** On the next screen, type your Microsoft account user name and password if you have a Microsoft account, or if you do not have a Microsoft account, click the **Create one! link**, follow the instructions to create a Microsoft account. When the Accounts window appears, continue with Step 4.

3. Click the **Ready to go button.** The Mail window opens, the app connects to your account and displays any messages received in that account. The next time you start Mail, it will open directly to this window.
4. If the Mail window does not fill your screen, click the **Maximize button** on the title bar. Refer again to Exhibit 8-25.

End Activity

EXHIBIT 8-25 MAIL WINDOW

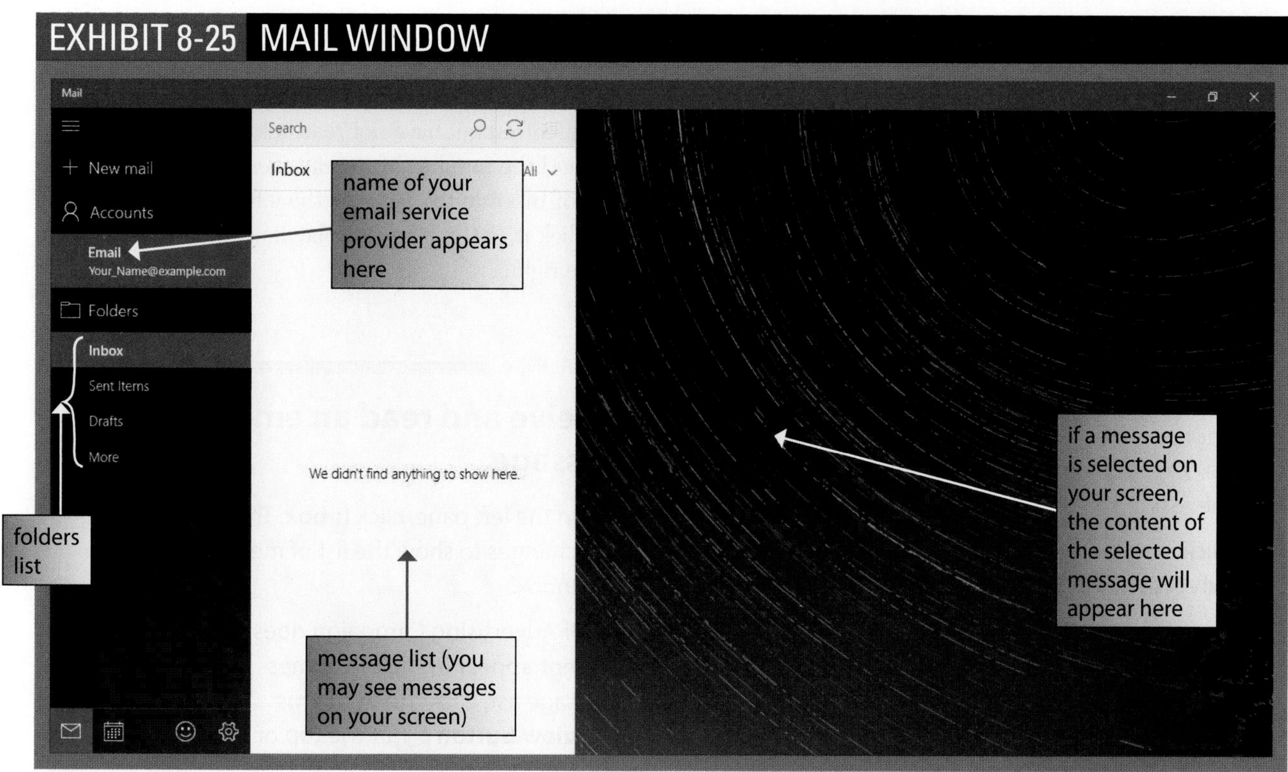

8-7b Creating and Sending Email Using Mail

EXHIBIT 8-26 NEW MAIL MESSAGE

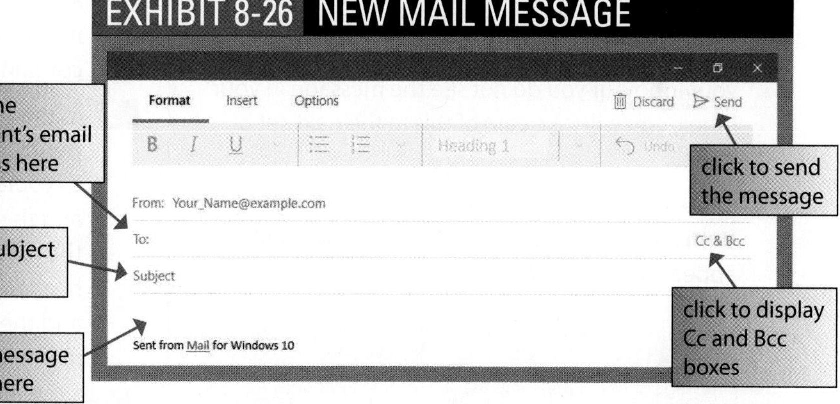

An email message contains lines for Date, From, To, and Subject, followed by the body of the message. The Date line shows the date on which you send the message (as set in your computer's clock) and is not visible in the pane in which you create your email message. The From line lists the name or email address associated with that email account. You complete the other lines. The To line lists the email addresses of one or more recipients. You can click the Cc & Bcc link to add lines to list the email addresses of anyone who will receive a courtesy copy or blind courtesy copy of the message. Bcc recipients are not visible to each other or to the To and Cc recipients. The Subject line provides a quick overview of the message topic, similar to a headline. The main part of the email is the message body. See Exhibit 8-26.

When you click the Send button, Mail moves the message from your computer to your email server, which routes it to the recipient. It also keeps a copy

> **FYI**
>
> **CORRECTING SPELLING**
> Mail includes a built-in spelling dictionary. As you type the text of a message, Mail corrects any words it flags as misspelled according to its dictionary. If a word is not in the Mail spelling dictionary, a red wavy line appears under it. You can right-click the word to display a shortcut menu of suggested spellings, as well as options to add the word to the dictionary or ignore it.

of the message in the Sent Items folder, which you can open to see all the messages you have sent or replied to.

Begin Activity

Create and send an email message.

1 In the top-left corner of the screen, click the **New mail button**. A new, blank message appears in the right pane. Refer again to Exhibit 8-26.

2 Click in the **To box**, and then type your email address. As you type, if your email appears in a list below the To box, you can click it instead of typing the rest of the address.

3 Click in the **Subject box**, and then type **Advertising Campaign**.

4 Press the **Tab key** to move the insertion point into the message area.

5 Type **Let's meet soon to discuss the new advertising campaign.** as the message, press the **Enter key** twice, and then type your name.

6 In the top-right corner of the screen, click the **Send button**. The message screen closes, and the main Mail screen appears again. The message is immediately sent to your email server, and then, because you addressed it to yourself, it arrives in your Inbox. (If you do not see the message in your Inbox, you will take care of this in the next set of steps.)

7 In the left pane, in the Folders list, click **Sent Items**. The list of messages that you have sent appears in the right pane.

PROBLEM?
If the message does not appear in the Sent Items folder, click **More** in the Folders list, click **Outbox** in the All folders list, and then click the **Sync this view button** at the top of the pane to send the message.

End Activity

8-7c Receiving and Reading Email Using Mail

Mail transfers, or downloads, messages addressed to you from your email server to your Inbox whenever you start the program and periodically after that. You can also check for received email by clicking the Sync this view button at the top of the message list. When the Inbox folder is selected in the left pane, messages downloaded to your Inbox appear in a list in the message list in the center pane on the screen. The subject of messages you have received but have not read yet appears in blue, bold text, and the number of unread messages appears to the right of Inbox in the pane on the left. To read a message, you click it in the list to display its contents in the pane on the right.

Begin Activity

Receive and read an email message.

1 In the left pane, click **Inbox**. The message list changes to show the list of messages in your Inbox.

2 If Advertising Campaign does not appear in the Inbox message list, click the **Sync this view button** at the top of the pane to send the message at the top of the Inbox pane. Mail downloads your email messages from the email server, and the message appears in the message list. Your Inbox might contain additional email messages.

PROBLEM?
If the message still doesn't appear in your Inbox, wait a few minutes, and then click the **Sync this view button** again.

3 In the message list, click the **Advertising Campaign message**. Because you sent this message to yourself, the message is part of a conversation, and the Advertising message expands to show the messages in the conversation. The message header of the message you received is highlighted and the content of the selected message appears in the right pane.

End Activity

8-7d Replying to and Forwarding Email Messages

Some of the email you receive will ask you to provide information, answer questions, or confirm decisions. Instead of creating a new email message, you can reply directly to a message that you received.

As part of the reply, Mail fills in the To and Subject boxes and includes the text of the original message. If the original message was sent to more than one person, the Reply command creates a response to only the original sender; the Reply all command creates a response to the original sender as well as all of the other recipients.

With both the reply to and forward features, you can add a new message above the original message. Exhibit 8-27 shows a message being replied to.

EXHIBIT 8-27 REPLYING TO A MESSAGE

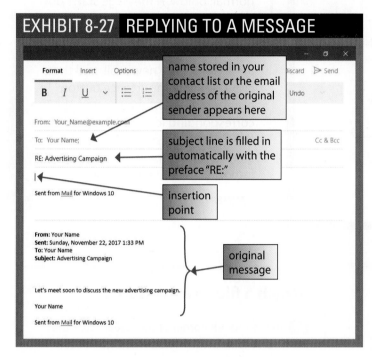

When you reply to or forward an email, you should place your response at the top of the message above any text from the original message so that the recipients can find it easily. If you respond to questions or insert comments in the original message, you should use a contrasting text color to clearly identify your additions and mention that you have done this in your response at the top of the message.

The running list of an original email and its replies is called a **conversation**. In the message list, emails are grouped by conversation—that is, replies to an email are listed below the original message.

Begin Activity

Reply to an email message.

1. Make sure the message you received is selected in the message list. The Reply, Reply all, and Forward buttons appear at the top of the right pane.
2. At the top of the right pane, click the **Reply button**. In the message list, a new message in the conversation appears with *[Draft]* in red. In the right pane, a new message is created and the reply message header and body appear above the original message. Your name or email address appears in the To box because you sent the original message. The letters *RE:* are inserted before the original Advertising Campaign subject to indicate a reply. The insertion point is in the message body above the original message. Refer again to Exhibit 8-27.
3. Type **Are you available to meet on Tuesday?** to add a reply.
4. In the top-right corner of the right pane, click the **Send button**. The message is sent. In the message list, a left-pointing arrow appears above the time in the original message, indicating that you replied to this message.

End Activity

You can also forward a message to someone who wasn't included on the original message. The Forward feature creates a copy of the original message subject and body, but leaves the To, Cc, and Bcc boxes blank. You can enter the recipient or recipients who will receive a copy of the message. Exhibit 8-28 shows a message being forwarded.

FYI

REPLY ALL AND FORWARD CAREFULLY

Use the Reply feature if only some of the original message recipients need to read your response. This ensures that you do not clutter others' Inboxes unnecessarily, and more important, that you don't inadvertently send a reply meant for one person to many people. Use the Reply All feature only if everyone who received the original email needs to remain in the "conversation." When you forward a message, be aware that the original message header may contain private email addresses that you may want to delete before sending. Finally, remember that email is not private. Anyone you send a message to can forward it to others, including people you don't know, without your knowledge or permission.

conversation In Mail, an original email and its replies.

EXHIBIT 8-28 FORWARDING A MESSAGE

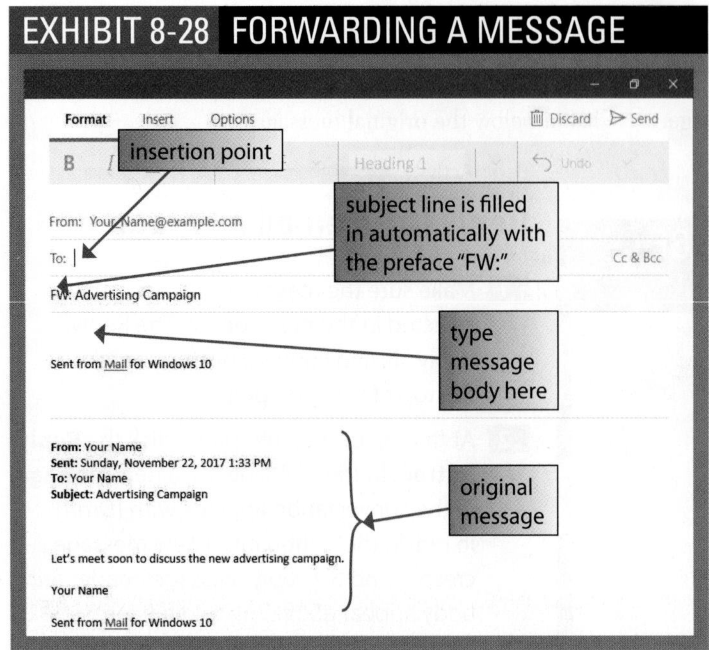

FYI CHANGING THE MESSAGE IMPORTANCE

The priority conveys the message's importance—high, normal, or low. A message starts out as normal unless you change it to high or low importance. To change the importance level, click Options at the top of the new mail, and then click the High Importance button or the Low Importance button. The corresponding icon appears above the time the message was received alerting the recipient about the importance of that message.

Begin Activity

Forward a message.

1 In the message list, make sure the original message that you received is selected.

2 At the top of the right pane, click the **Forward button**. *FW:* is inserted before the subject to indicate this is a forwarded message. As with a reply, the original message appears in the bottom portion of the message body. The insertion point appears in the To box, which is empty. Refer again to Exhibit 8-28.

3 In the **To box**, type your email address.

4 In the message area, click above the copied original message, and then type **Please join us for the discussion.** as the message.

5 Click the **Send button**. The message is sent.

End Activity

8-7e Working with Attachments

An **attachment** is a file that you send with an email message. The file content does not appear within the message body, and the recipients can save the file to their computer and then open, edit, and print it just as they can with a file they created.

attachment A file that is sent with an email message.

Begin Activity

Attach a file to a message.

1 In the top-left corner of the screen, click the **New mail button**. A new message screen opens.

2 In the To box, type your email address, press the **Tab key** twice, and then type **First Quarter Sales** as the subject.

3 Press the **Tab key** to move the insertion point to the message area.

4 Type **Hello,** as the greeting, press the **Enter key** twice, type **The attached workbook contains our first quarter sales. Let me know if you have any questions.** as the message, press the **Enter key** twice, and then type your name.

5 At the top of the right pane, click **Insert**, and then click the **Attach button**. The Open dialog box appears.

6 Navigate to the **Chapter 8\Chapter folder** included with the data files. The data files in the Chapter folder appear in the Open dialog box.

7 Click the data file **Quarterly Sales** to select the file.

PROBLEM? If you do not have the data files, you can get them from your instructor who may include them in the Assignment Calendar on CMPTR Online or provide them to you another way.

8 At the bottom of the dialog box, click **Open**. The dialog box closes, and the Quarterly Sales file is listed as an attachment below the subject and above the message. The file name and size of the attachment appear next to its file icon. See Exhibit 8-29.

9 Send the message. The message is sent, along with the attached file.

End Activity

EXHIBIT 8-29 MESSAGE CREATED WITH AN ATTACHMENT

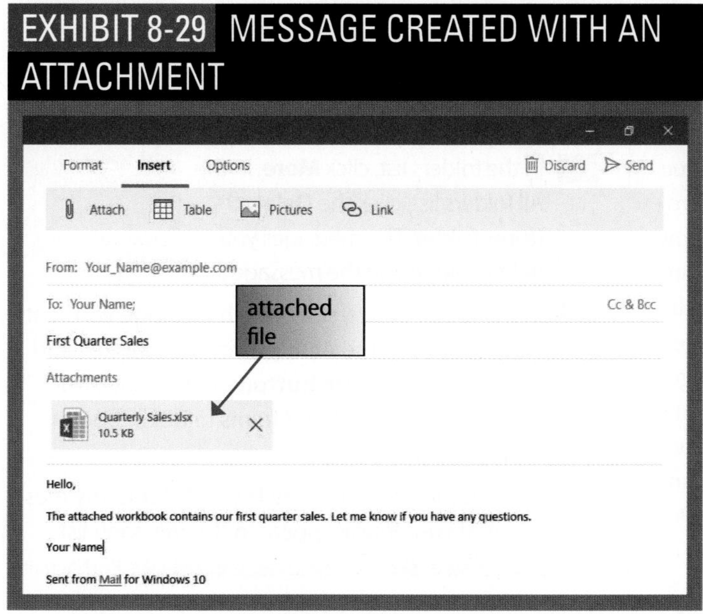

When you receive a message that contains an attachment, a paperclip appears in the message list above the time that the message was received to indicate that the message includes an attachment. When the message is selected in the list and displayed in the right pane, the file name of the attachment appears below the subject line. Exhibit 8-30 shows a message with an attachment selected in the Inbox.

You can choose to open or save the attachment. To open the attachment, the program used to create the attachment must be installed on your computer. If the program is not installed, sometimes you can use a text editor, such as WordPad or Notepad, to open the attached file.

If you open an attachment that causes a Microsoft Office program, such as Word, Excel, or PowerPoint, to open, the attachment is displayed in Protected View. In Protected View, you can read but not edit or save the file. This helps protect your computer from viruses that may be embedded in the attached file.

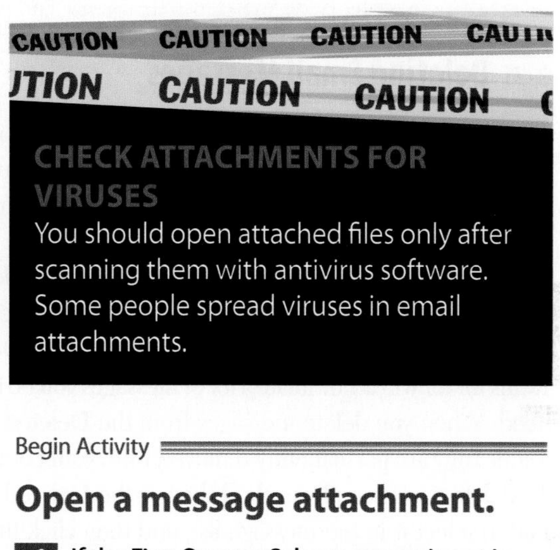

CHECK ATTACHMENTS FOR VIRUSES

You should open attached files only after scanning them with antivirus software. Some people spread viruses in email attachments.

Begin Activity

Open a message attachment.

1 If the First Quarter Sales message is not in your Inbox, click the **Sync this view button** at the top of the message list. The First Quarter Sales message appears in the message list with a paperclip above the time.

2 In the message list, click the **First Quarter Sales message**. The conversation expands, the message you received is selected, the content of the message appears in the right pane, and the attached file is listed below the subject. Refer again to Exhibit 8-30.

EXHIBIT 8-30 RECEIVED MESSAGE WITH AN ATTACHMENT

3 In the message, click the **Quarterly Sales.xlsx attachment**. Microsoft Excel starts, and the attached file opens in Protected View.

TIP: If you want to save the attachment, right-click the attachment, and then click Save on the shortcut menu.

4 In the top-right corner of the Excel window title bar, click the **Close button**. The Excel application window closes, and the Mail app reappears.

End Activity

8-7f Deleting Email Messages

After you read and respond to your messages, you can delete any messages that you no longer need. When you delete a message from the Inbox, it is not permanently removed from the Inbox; it is moved to the Deleted Items folder. Messages remain in the Deleted Items folder until you delete that folder's contents. You should delete the contents of this folder periodically; otherwise the Deleted Items folder will accumulate a lot of messages you no longer need. When you delete messages from the Deleted Items folder, they are permanently removed from your computer. To delete a message from the Inbox or the Deleted Items folder, select it in the message list, and then click the Delete button that appears at the top of the right pane or in the message header. If you want to delete all of the messages sent and received about a particular subject, click the Delete button in the message header for the latest message in the message list to delete the entire chain of messages.

Begin Activity

Delete email messages.

1 In the message list, click the original **Advertising Campaign** message to select it.

2 At the top of the right pane, click the **Delete button**. The selected message is moved to the Deleted Items folder.

3 In the message list, click the **FW: Advertising Campaign conversation header** to select the entire chain of messages.

4 Point to the **selected conversation header**, and then in the message header, click the **Delete button**. All of the messages in the conversation are moved to the Deleted Items folder.

People A Windows 10 app used to store information about the people and businesses with whom you communicate.

contact Each person or organization with whom you communicate and about whom you store information.

5 In the message list, delete the **First Quarter Sales conversation.**

6 In the folders list, click the **Sent Items folder**. The messages you sent appear in the message list. The First Quarter Sales message is selected because it is at the top of the list as the most recent message sent.

7 For each message you sent in the Activities in this chapter, select that message and then click the **Delete button**. The selected messages are moved to the Deleted Items folder.

TIP: You can also right-click a message header, click Move on the shortcut menu, and then click the folder you want to move the selected messages into.

8 In the folders list, click **More**. In the All folders list, click the **Deleted Items folder**. The messages you deleted appear in the message list.

9 In the message list, select each message you sent and received in the Activities in this chapter, and then click the **Delete button**. The selected messages in the Deleted Items folder are permanently deleted.

10 In the folders list, click the **Inbox folder**. Any messages in your Inbox appear in the message list.

End Activity

8-7g Closing Mail

You close Mail the same way you close any other app. You can click the Close button in the top-right corner of the title bar. You can also right-click the app's icon in the taskbar, and then click Close window on the shortcut menu.

Begin Activity

Close Mail.

1 Click the **Close button** in the top-right corner of the title bar. The Mail app closes.

End Activity

8-8 ADDING INFORMATION TO THE PEOPLE APP

The **People** app is a communication tool in Windows 10 that you use to store information about the people and businesses with whom you communicate. Each person or organization is called a **contact**. Exhibit 8-31 shows the People app.

EXHIBIT 8-31 PEOPLE APP

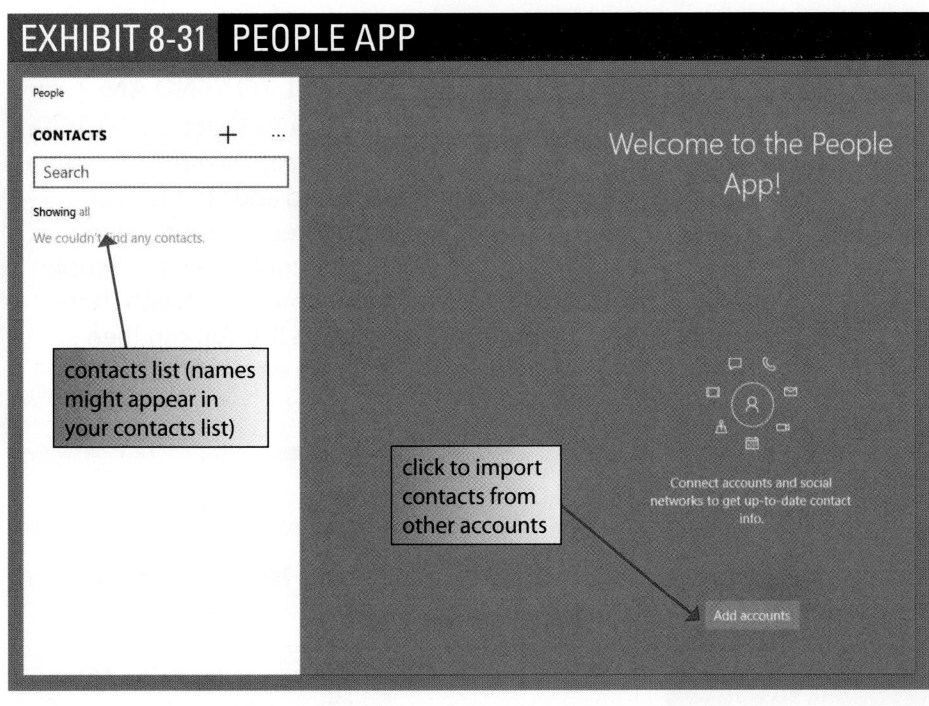

Begin Activity

Start the People app.

1. On the taskbar, click the **Start button** ⊞, and then on the Start menu, click **All apps**.
2. Scroll down the **All apps pane** to the P section, and then click **People**. The People app opens, listing any contacts added to the app in the pane on the left. Refer again to Exhibit 8-31. If this is the first time you are starting People, the main screen lists contact sources, including Facebook, Twitter, Exchange, Outlook, and LinkedIn.

End Activity

You store information about each contact, including a name, nickname, company, email addresses, phone and fax numbers, and postal addresses, as well as other information, such as job title, significant other, Web site, and notes. The collected information about a contact is sometimes called a **profile**. You can create a new contact and then enter as much information as you want about that contact on the New contact screen, as shown in Exhibit 8-32.

Begin Activity

Add a contact to the People app.

1. In the left pane, click the **New contact button** ⊞. The New contact window in which you can enter basic contact information appears. Refer again to Exhibit 8-32.
2. Click in the **Name box**, and then type **Fabia Afnan**.
3. Click in the **Mobile phone box**, and then type **978-555-2399**.
4. Click in the **Personal email label** to open a shortcut menu with other email labels, and then click **Work**.

TIP: To add information for a contact, click the labels with the plus sign next to them.

5. In the Work email box, type **fabia_afnan@ example.com**. This sets Fabia's work email address as the default email address.

EXHIBIT 8-32 NEW CONTACT SCREEN

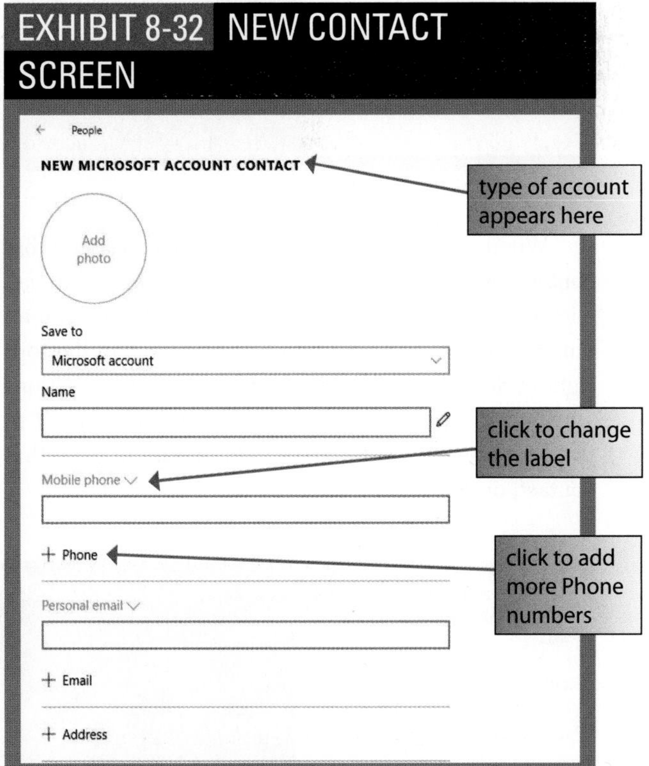

profile The collected information about a contact.

6 In the top-right corner of the window, click the **Save button** . The New contact screen closes, and the Fabia Afnan contact appears in the Contacts list in the left pane and her information appears in the right pane. See Exhibit 8-33.

End Activity

EXHIBIT 8-33 INFORMATION FOR A SELECTED CONTACT

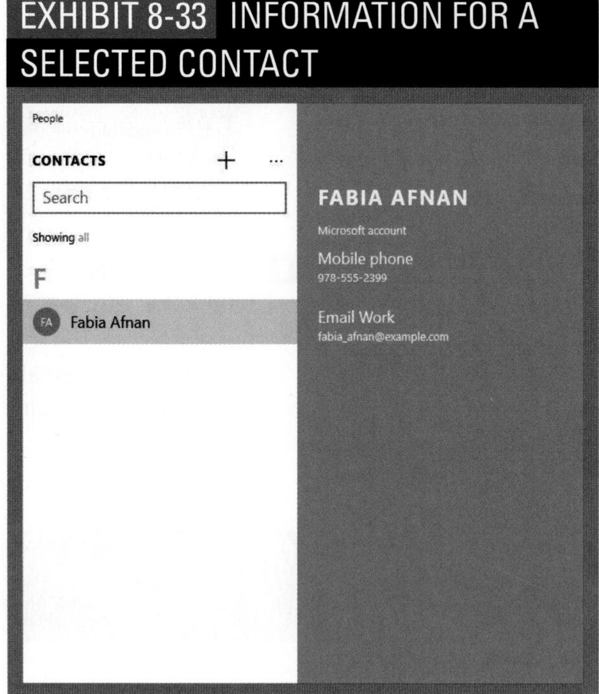

When you select a name in the Contact list and that contact's information appears in the right pane, you can click the contact's email address to send that person an email message. You can also use the buttons in the top-right corner of the right pane to take additional actions with the contact. For instance, you can pin a contact to the Start menu, edit the contact's information, share that contact, or delete the contact. See Exhibit 8-34.

FYI

USING MAIL TO SEND AN EMAIL TO A PEOPLE CONTACT

When you create an email message in the Mail app and start to type the name or email address of a contact in the To, Cc, or Bcc lines, contacts in the People app whose names or emails start with those same letters appear in a list. You can then click the contact whose email address you want to insert in the box.

Begin Activity

Display the actions for a contact and delete a contact.

1 In the Contacts list, make sure the **Fabia Afnan contact** is selected. The profile for the selected contact appears. Buttons corresponding to the actions you can take with the contact appear in the top-right corner of the window. You can delete contacts if you no longer need them.

2 In the top-right corner of the window, click the **See more button** . A menu opens with two additional actions you can take with the contact. Refer again to Exhibit 8-34.

3 On the menu, click **Delete**. The Delete contact? dialog box appears, asking if you want to delete this contact from the People and Mail apps.

4 In the dialog box, click **Delete**. The Fabia Afnan contact is deleted, and the main screen for the People app reappears.

5 Click the **Close button** to exit the People app.

End Activity

EXHIBIT 8-34 ACTIONS YOU CAN TAKE WITH A SELECTED CONTACT

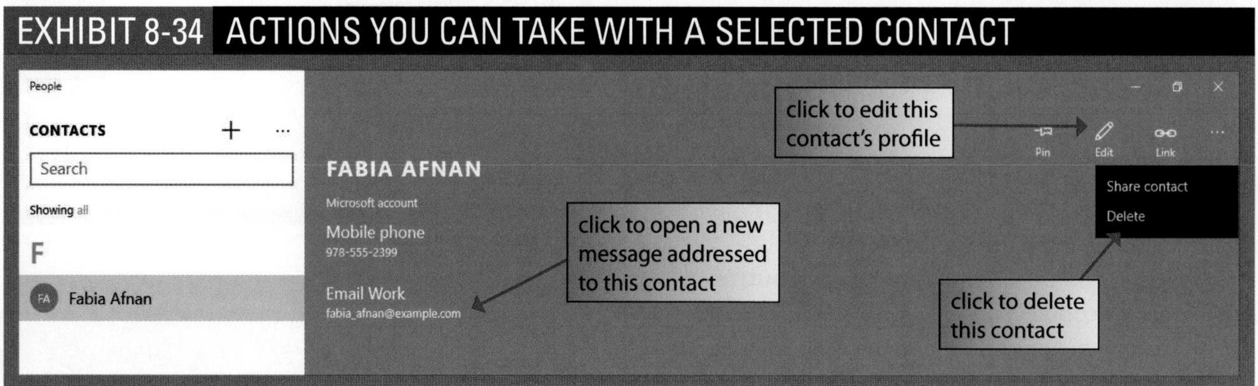

STUDY TOOLS 8

READY TO STUDY? IN THE BOOK, YOU CAN:

- ☐ Rip out the Chapter Review Card, which includes key terms and key chapter concepts

ONLINE AT WWW.CENGAGEBRAIN.COM, YOU CAN:

- ☐ Review key concepts from the chapter in a short video.
- ☐ Explore working in Edge with the interactive infographic.
- ☐ Practice what you've learned with more Practice It and On Your Own Exercises.
- ☐ Prepare for tests with quizzes.
- ☐ Review the key terms with flashcards.

QUIZ YOURSELF

1. What is the start page?
2. What is a home page on a Web site?
3. How do you conduct a search using the default search engine in Edge?
4. What is a tab?
5. What is the history in Edge?
6. Why would you pin a Web page to the Start menu?
7. What is a favorite?
8. What is a reading list?
9. What is a Web note?
10. Why is it a good idea to preview a Web page before you print it?
11. What is the difference between replying to an email message and forwarding it?
12. What is an attachment?
13. What happens when you delete an email message?
14. Which app do you use to store information about the people and businesses with whom you communicate?

PRACTICE IT

Practice It 8-1

1. Start Edge. Maximize the window if it does not already fill the screen.
2. Type **computerhistory.org** in the Search or enter web address bar, and then press the Enter key to go to the home page of the Computer History Museum Web site.
3. Click the Exhibits link, and then click the Internet History 1962 to 1992 link. Examine this Web page.
4. Use the Back button as many times as needed to return to the home page on the Computer History Museum Web site.
5. Open a new tab, and then go to **archive.org**, the home page of the Internet Archive Web site.
6. Pin the home page of the Internet Archive site to the Start screen.
7. Open any link on the current Web page in a new tab.
8. Open a new tab as the fourth tab, and then conduct a search using **computer history** as the search phrase. In the list of results, click the link

to the History of Computers page on the Web site computersciencelab.com.

9. Save the History of Computers page as a favorite in the Favorites folder named **History of Computers**.
10. Close all the tabs except the home page on the Computer History Museum Web site.
11. Use the Internet Archive tile on the Start menu to open that page in new tab.
12. Save the home page of the Internet Archive Web site in a new folder in the Favorites list named **Archive**.
13. Create a Web note based on the home page of the Internet Archive Web site. Add **Very interesting Web site!** as a typed note next to the title *Wayback Machine* at the top of the page, and then collapse the typed note. Circle the title Wayback Machine using the red pen. Save the Web note as a favorite named **Internet Archive Web note**. Exit the Web note.
14. Open a new tab, and then use the History of Computers favorite to open that page in the new tab.
15. Open a new tab, and then use the History list to open the Internet History 1962 to 1992 page on the Computer History Museum Web site in the new tab.
16. Save the Internet History 1962 to 1992 Web page as an entry on the reading list.
17. Display the Internet History 1962 to 1992 Web page in the Print Preview window, switch the orientation to portrait, if necessary, and then display headers and footers. If instructed, print page 1.
18. Unpin the home page of the Internet Archive site from the Start screen.
19. Delete the Internet History 1962 to 1992 Web page entry from the reading list.
20. Delete the History of Computers and the Internet Archive Web note favorites, and then delete the Archive folder from the Favorites list.
21. Delete all the entries in the History list that were added as a result of completing the steps in this Practice It. Close Edge.
22. Start the Mail app, and then create a new email message. Address it to yourself.
23. Type **Computer History Web Sites** as the subject.
24. Type the following as the message body:

    Hi,

    You can use the Computer History Museum Web site to learn about the history of computers.

    Your Name
25. Send the email, and then download messages from your server to your Inbox, if necessary.
26. Reply to the Computer History Web Sites message, typing the following as the message:

    Thank you! I will look into this.
27. Forward the RE: Computer History Web Sites message to yourself. Type the following as the message:

    The Internet Archive Web site stores historical, digital collections.
28. Reply to the FW: Computer History Web Sites message. Attach the data file **Computer History Sites** located in the Chapter 8/Practice It folder included with this book. Type the following as the message body:

    Please review the attached list.
29. When the message with the attachment arrives in your Inbox, open the attachment in Microsoft Word. Exit Word after reading the document.
30. Move the four messages you sent and received from your Inbox to the Deleted Items folder. Delete the four messages from the Deleted Items folder. Close the Mail app.
31. Start the People app. Add the following person as a new contact:

First name:	**Meg**
Last name:	**Chopra**
Work email:	**meg_chopra@example.com**
Mobile phone:	**501-555-3209**
32. Delete the contact Meg Chopra. Close the People app.

Practice It 8-2

1. Start Edge, and then go to **zagat.com**. If the Web address in the Address bar doesn't change to include a large city near your location at the end of the address, click the city name below the Zagat name at the top of the page, and then click the city closest to your location.
2. In the large Search box in the center of the home page, type **restaurants,** and then press the Enter key to display a list of reviewed restaurants in your city.
3. Click one of the links to read a review of that restaurant.
4. Open a new tab, and then go to **citysearch.com** in the new tab. If the site doesn't automatically display the Citysearch page for a large city near you, click in the right Search box on the Citysearch page, start typing type your city and state, and then click the appropriate link when it appears.
5. Display the Restaurants category in the current tab, and then click links to find reviews of the same restaurant you read about on Zagat. (*Hint*: If you cannot find the same restaurant by clicking links, at the top of the

Citysearch page, click in the left Search box, type the restaurant name, and then click the Search button.)

6. Pin the pages with reviews on each site to the Start menu or add them as favorites.
7. Print one review of the restaurant you chose, changing the orientation if needed.
8. Start the People app. Add a friend, classmate, or your instructor as a contact.
9. Start the Mail app. Create a new email message addressed to the person you added as a contact. Type your email address in the Cc box. (*Hint*: Click the Cc & Bcc link to the right of the To box in the new message.)
10. Type **Restaurant Suggestion** as the subject. Type the following as the message body, replacing the italicized text with the name of the restaurant about which you read reviews and with your name:

    Hi,

    I read a review of *restaurant*, and I think we should meet there for lunch next week.

    Your Name
11. If a friend or classmate sent you the message, reply to it; otherwise, reply to the copy that you sent to yourself. Type **See the attached list of Web sites that contain reviews of restaurants.** as the message body, and then attach the data file **Restaurant Review Sites** located in the Chapter 8/Practice It folder included with this book.
12. Unpin the Web pages from the Start menu or delete the entries you added to the favorites list, delete your browsing history, and then exit Edge.
13. Delete the messages you sent and received, and then exit Mail.
14. Delete the contact you added to the People app, and then exit People.

ON YOUR OWN

On Your Own 8-1

1. Start Edge, and then search for information on Internet hoaxes.
2. Display a result in the current tab, examine the site, and then return to the list of results. Display three more sites in the same manner, returning to the list of results after examining each site.
3. Use the History list to display the home pages of two of the sites you examined in separate tabs. Add these pages as favorites in the Favorites folder.
4. Close all but one tab, and then search for sites that contain information about Internet scams. Display three results from the results list in new tabs. (Do not display the pages of any Web sites you already visited.) Add these three Web pages as entries in the reading list.
5. Open the Hub, and then display the FAVORITES pane. Move the two Web sites about Internet hoaxes into a new folder named **Internet Hoax Info**. (*Hint*: Right-click a blank area of the FAVORITES pane to create the folder, and then drag the favorites into it.)
6. Display one of the Web pages about Internet scams that you saved as an entry in your reading list, and then change it to a Web note.
7. Use the Highlighter to highlight any sentence on the Web note.
8. Share the Web note using the Mail app. (*Hint*: Use the Share Web Note button at the right end of the purple bar.)
9. Address the message to your instructor, and add your email address to the Cc box. (*Hint*: Click the Cc & Bcc link to the right of the To box in the new message.)
10. Type **Helpful Site** as the subject, and then type the following as the message body, replacing the italicized text with the name of the Web site with information about Internet hoaxes that you liked the best:

    Hi,

    The Web site *Scam Site* contains useful information about avoiding Internet scams.

    Your Name
11. Send the email message.
12. When the message arrives in your Inbox, save the attachment (the Web note) to the location where you saving your files.
13. Delete the messages you sent and received, and then exit Mail.
14. In the Edge application, close all but one tab, and then go to the site that you identified as containing useful information about Internet hoaxes.
15. Display the Web page in Print Preview, and then examine the page in landscape orientation.
16. Display the header and footer, and then print the page if instructed.
17. Delete the favorites folder that you created, and then delete the entries in the reading list.
18. Delete your browsing history from this exercise.
19. Exit Edge.

Part 5
OFFICE 2016

9 | Introducing Microsoft Office 2016

LEARNING OBJECTIVES After studying the material in this chapter, you will be able to:

9-1 Explore common elements of Office application windows

9-2 Use the ribbon

9-3 Select text and use the Mini toolbar

9-4 Undo and redo

9-5 Zoom and scroll

9-6 Work with Office files

9-7 Use the Clipboard

9-8 Get Help

9-9 Close Office applications

After finishing this chapter, go to **PAGE 272** for **STUDY TOOLS**.

EXPLORING COMMON ELEMENTS OF OFFICE APPLICATION WINDOWS

Microsoft Office 2016, or **Office**, is a collection of Microsoft applications, including Word, Excel, Access, and PowerPoint. Word is used to enter, edit, and format text. Excel is used to enter, calculate, analyze, and present charts of numerical data. Access enables you to enter, maintain, and retrieve related information (or data) in a format known as a database. PowerPoint is used to create a collection of slides that can contain text, charts, pictures, sound, movies, multimedia, and so on. These four Office applications are designed to work together and have common features that work similarly in all of them.

Each Office application creates different types of files. The files you create in Word are called **documents**, although many people use the term *document* to refer to any file created on a computer. The files you create in Excel are called **workbooks** (commonly referred to as *spreadsheets*). Access files are **databases**, and PowerPoint files are **presentations**.

Although the file types are different, the Office applications have many common elements and features. To learn about some of the features the applications share, you will start a few Office applications and examine the application windows.

You start Office applications the same way you start any Windows 10 application. You can click in the Search the web and Windows box on the taskbar or click the Start button and then type the first few letters of the application name. When the application name appears in the list of search results, you can click it to start that application. You can also click the Start button, click All apps, locate the application you want to start in the alphabetical list, and then click it to start that application. After an application starts on the desktop, and its application button appears on the taskbar.

When Word, Excel, Access, and PowerPoint start, the Recent screen in Backstage view appears. **Backstage view** contains commands that allow you to manage application files and options. The only actions available on the Recent screen are to open an existing application file or create a new file. Exhibit 9-1 shows the Recent screen in Backstage view of Word. After you create or open a file, the document, workbook, database, or presentation appears in the application window, ready for you to work.

FYI **OFFICE 365 VS. OFFICE 2016 ONE-TIME PURCHASE** You can purchase Microsoft Office as a one-time purchase or as a monthly or annual subscription. When you purchase it as a one-time purchase, the software that you install on your computer is not updated when new features become available. When you purchase a subscription, you subscribe to the Office 365 service and the software installed on your computer is updated when new features become available. (If you are a college student, you might be able to get a free subscription to Office 365 through your school. Check with your school's IT department.)

Begin Activity

Start Office applications and examine the application windows.

1. On the taskbar, click the **Start button**, and then type **Word**. The text you typed appears in the Search the web and Windows box on the taskbar, and a list of search results appears.
2. In the list of search results, click **Word 2016 Desktop app**. Word starts, and the Recent screen in Backstage view appears. Refer again to Exhibit 9-1. Also, note that a Word button appears on the taskbar.

Microsoft Office 2016 (Office) A collection of Microsoft applications.

document A Word file.

workbook An Excel file.

database An Access file.

presentation A PowerPoint file.

Backstage view The screen that contains commands to manage application files and options.

OFFICE 2016

EXHIBIT 9-1 RECENT SCREEN IN BACKSTAGE VIEW IN WORD

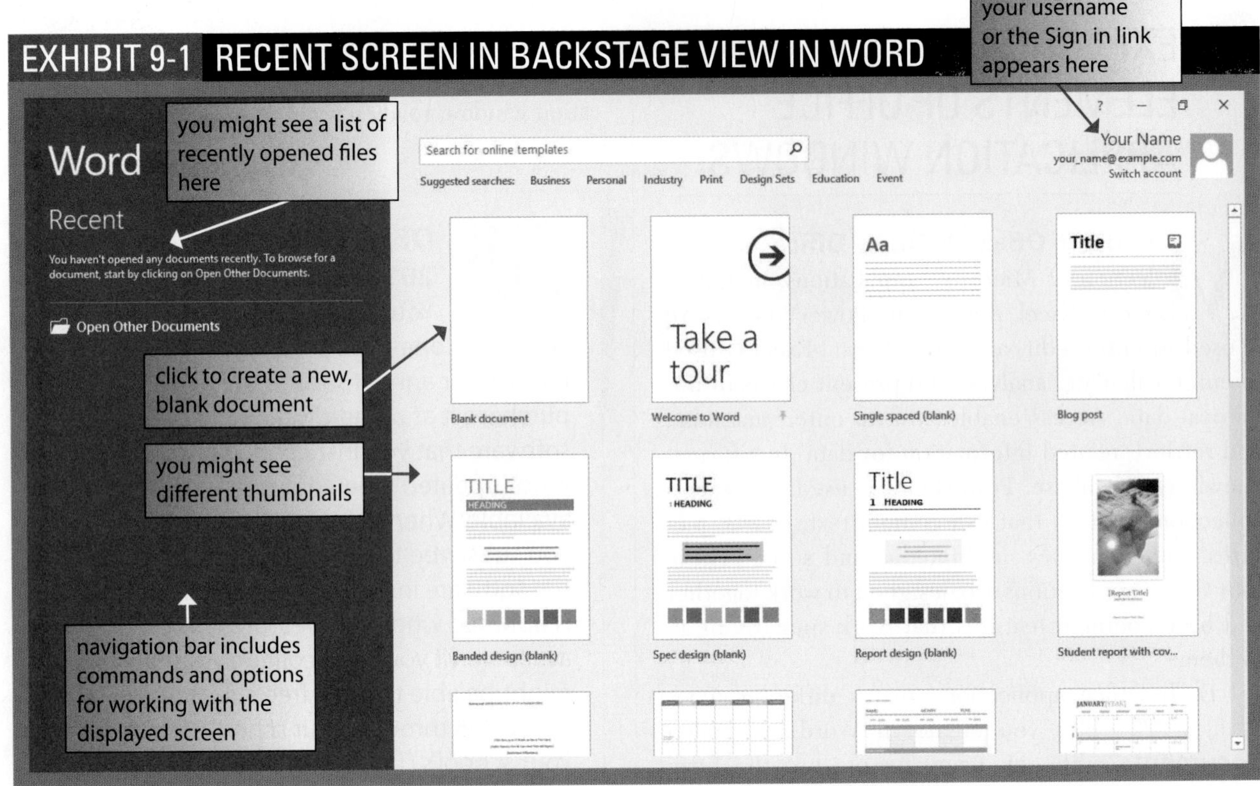

3 If the application window doesn't fill your screen as shown in Exhibit 9-1, click the **Maximize button** ☐ on the title bar.

4 Click the **Blank document tile**. Backstage view closes, and a new, blank document opens. See Exhibit 9-2. The elements labeled in Exhibit 9-2 are found in all of the Office applications.

PROBLEM? If the ribbon is not fully displayed, as shown in Exhibits 9-2 and 9-3, refer to the FYI box titled "Showing and Hiding the Ribbon".

5 On the taskbar, click the **Start button** ⊞.

6 On the Start menu, click **All apps**. An alphabetical list of the apps installed on your computer appears.

TIP: If the app you want to start is listed at the top of the Start menu or as a tile on the right side of the Start menu, you can click it to start the app.

7 Point to the **list of apps** so that the scroll bar appears, scroll down the list to the letter *E*, and then click **Excel 2016.** Excel starts on the desktop with the Recent screen displayed, and an Excel button appears on the taskbar.

8 Click the **Blank workbook tile.** Backstage view closes, and a new, blank workbook opens. See Exhibit 9-3.

9 Start **PowerPoint 2016**, and then on the Recent screen, click the **Blank Presentation tile.** Backstage view closes, and a new, blank presentation opens. The PowerPoint window contains the same elements labeled in the Word and Excel windows shown in Exhibits 9-2 and 9-3.

TIP: The Recent screen in Access is similar to the Recent screens in the other applications. To start creating a new, blank database, you click the Blank desktop database tile.

10 On the taskbar, click the **Excel button**. The Excel window is the active window and appears on top of the other windows.

End Activity

As you can see in Exhibits 9-2 and 9-3, many of the elements in the Word and Excel windows are the same. Exhibit 9-4 lists elements common to all of the Office applications. Because these elements are the same in each application, after you have learned one application, it is easy to learn the others.

EXHIBIT 9-2 WORD WINDOW WITH A NEW, BLANK DOCUMENT

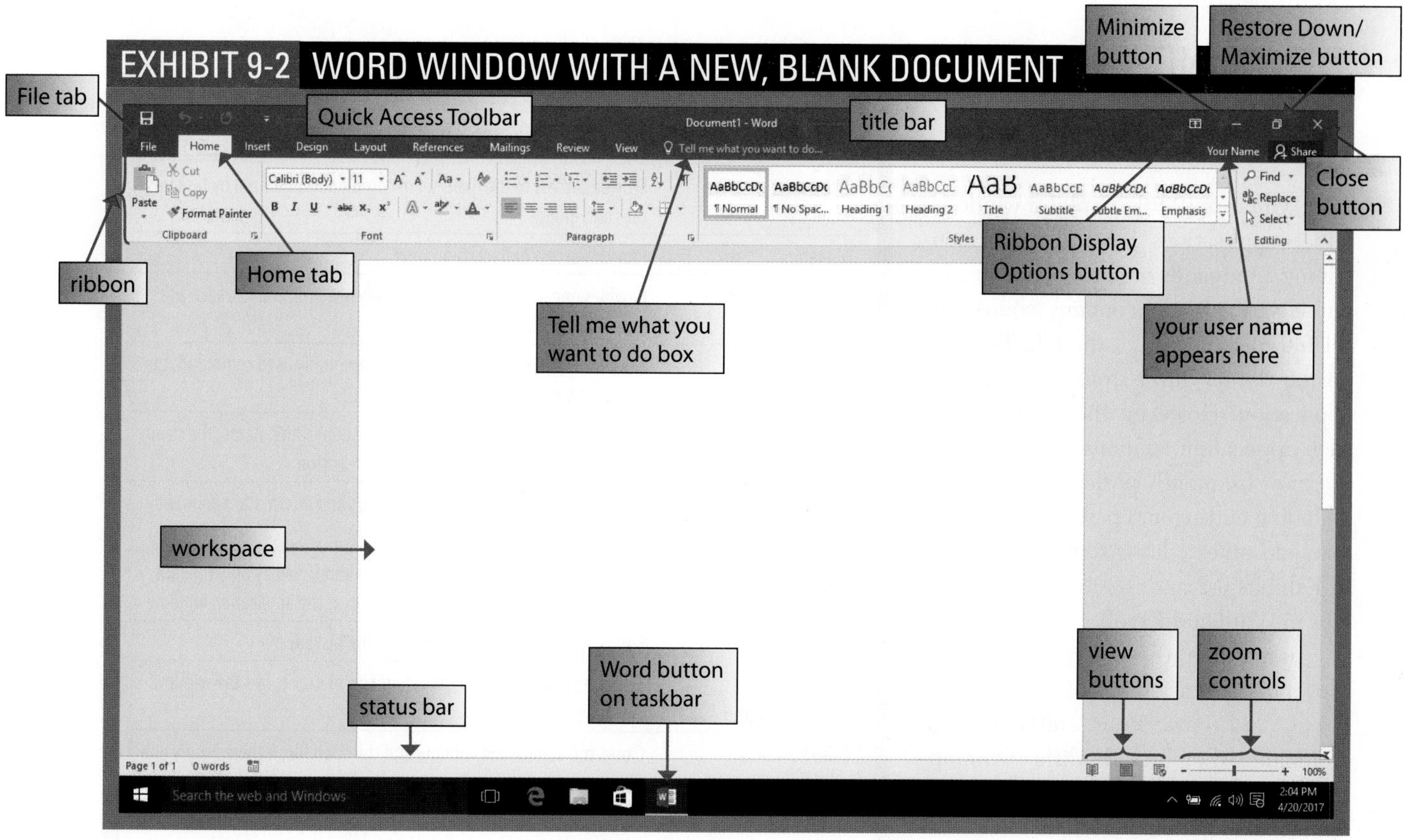

EXHIBIT 9-3 EXCEL WINDOW WITH A NEW, BLANK WORKBOOK

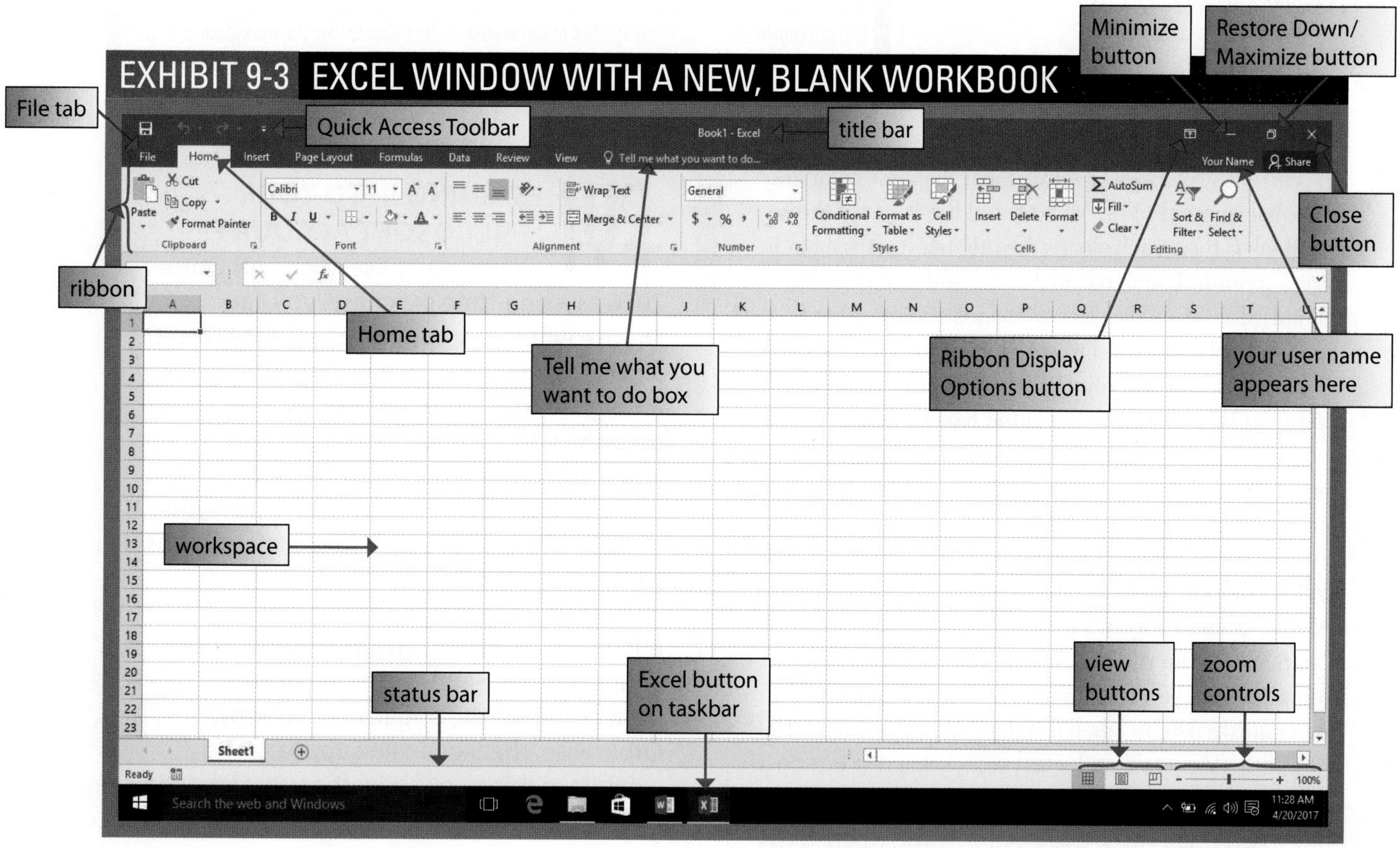

9-2 USING THE RIBBON

Like Windows 10 File Explorer windows, Office applications have a ribbon containing commands organized into groups on tabs. Each tab contains commands related to the name of the tab. The tabs on the ribbon differ from application to application. However, the Home tab in each application contains commands for the most frequently performed activities, including cutting and pasting, formatting text, and other editing tools. Refer again to Exhibits 9-2 and 9-3 to see the Home tabs in Word and Excel.

In addition, the Insert, Review, and View tabs appear on the ribbon in Word, Excel, and PowerPoint, although the commands they include differ from application to application. Other tabs are application specific, such as the Formulas tab in Excel, the Database Tools tab in Access, and the Slide Show tab in PowerPoint.

EXHIBIT 9-4 COMMON OFFICE ELEMENTS

Element	Description
Ribbon	Provides access to the main set of commands organized by task into tabs and groups
File tab	Provides access to Backstage view
Quick Access Toolbar	Provides one-click access to commonly used commands, such as Save, Undo, and Redo
Home tab	Contains buttons to access the most commonly used commands in each application
Title bar	Contains the name of the open file, the application name, the sizing buttons, the Help button, and the Close button
Tell me what you want to do box	Type key words to search for commands and information about how to use specific commands
Ribbon Display Options button	Provides options to display the entire ribbon, display only the tabs, or hide the ribbon until you click the top of the application window
Minimize button	Shrinks the window to its button on the taskbar
Restore Down/ Maximize button	Restores the window to its previous size or maximizes the window to fill the screen
Close button	Closes the application window and the open file; if there is only one file open in the application, also exits the program
Status bar	Provides information about the application, open file, or current task as well as the view buttons and zoom controls
Workspace	Displays the file you are working on (Word document, Excel workbook, Access database, or PowerPoint slide)
Zoom controls	Magnifies or shrinks the content displayed in the workspace

9-2a Switching Tabs and Displaying Contextual Tabs

The currently selected, or active, tab is the same color gray as the background of the ribbon, and the name of the selected tab is the same color as the title bar (that is, blue in Word, green in Excel, red in Access, and orange in PowerPoint). To see and access commands on tabs other than the Home tab, you need to select another tab to make it active. To select a tab, you click the tab name. Exhibit 9-5 shows the Insert tab selected in the Excel window.

Like the ribbon in File Explorer windows, the ribbon in Office applications contains contextual tabs. Remember that contextual tabs contain commands related to your current task or object. An **object** is anything that can be manipulated as a whole, such as a table, a picture, a shape, a chart, or an equation. Contextual tabs usually appear to the right of the standard ribbon tabs. For example, when you click in a table in a Word document, two contextual tabs labeled Table Tools appear to the right of the View tab, and when you click a text box on a

object Anything in a file that can be manipulated as a whole.

FYI

SIGNING IN TO YOUR MICROSOFT ACCOUNT

If you purchase Microsoft Office 2016 as a one-time purchase, you can choose whether to sign in to your Microsoft account while you use the software. (If you are signed into Windows 10 with a Microsoft account, you are automatically signed in when you open an Office application.) If you buy a subscription through Office 365, you must be signed in to your Microsoft account to use the software.

When you are signed in to your Microsoft account in an Office application, your user name appears in the upper-right corner of the application window. Otherwise, the Sign in link appears. The exhibits in this book show the user signed in to a Microsoft account.

EXHIBIT 9-5 INSERT TAB ON THE RIBBON IN EXCEL

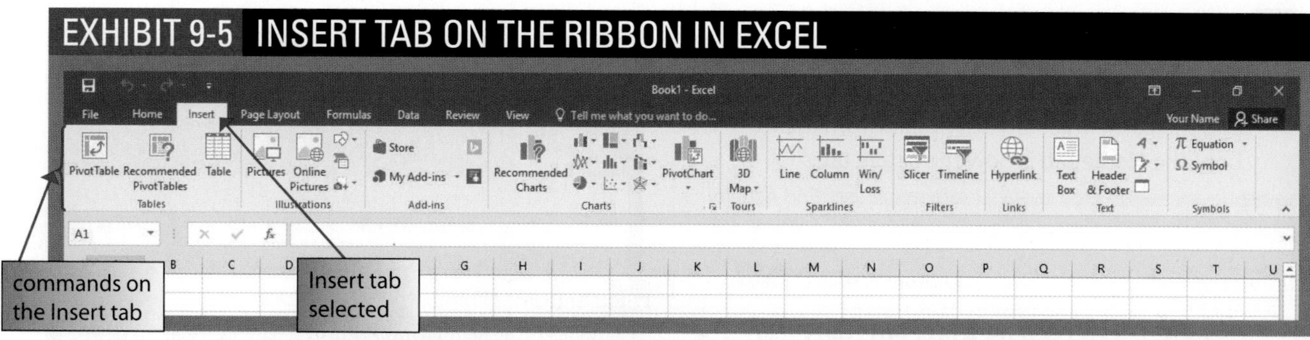

EXHIBIT 9-6 CONTEXTUAL DRAWING TOOLS FORMAT TAB IN POWERPOINT

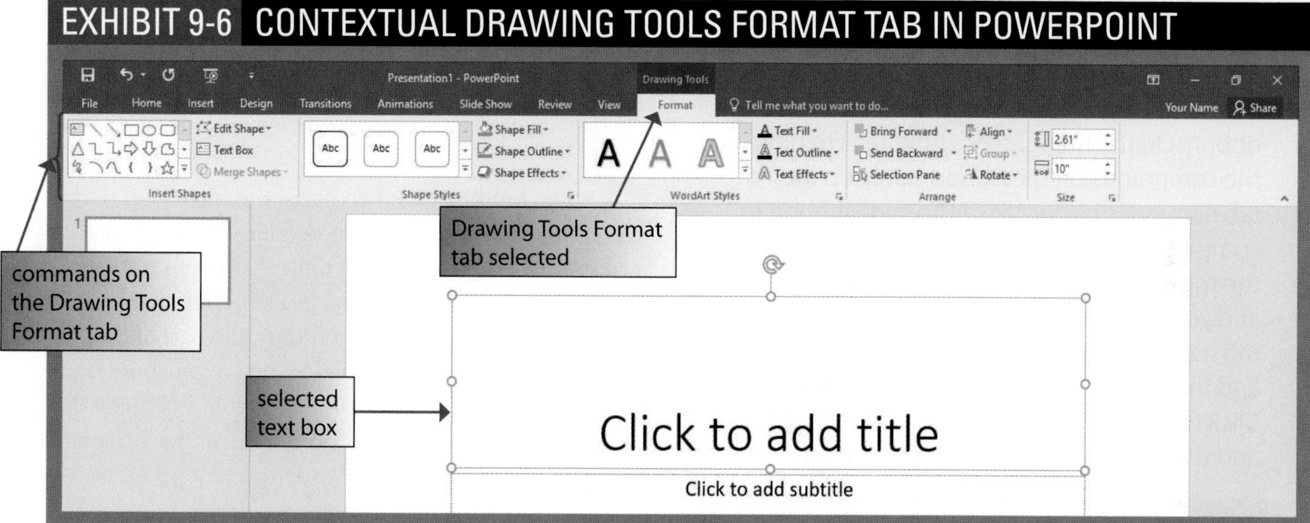

PowerPoint slide, the Drawing Tools Format tab appears (see Exhibit 9-6). **Text boxes** are object that contain text. Contextual tabs disappear when you click elsewhere on the screen, deselecting the object.

Begin Activity

Switch tabs, and display and close a contextual tab.

1. On the ribbon in the Excel window, click the **Insert tab**. The color of the Insert tab changes to gray, the color of the label *Insert* on the tab changes to green to indicate that it is selected, and the commands on the Insert tab appear.
2. On the ribbon, click the **Formulas tab**. The color of the Formulas tab changes to gray, the label *Formulas* on the tab changes to green, and the commands on the Formulas tab appear. The Formulas tab appears only on the Excel ribbon.
3. On the taskbar, click the **PowerPoint button** . PowerPoint is now the active application.
4. On the ribbon, click the **Insert tab**. The color of the Insert tab changes to gray, the label *Insert* on the tab changes to orange, and the commands on the Insert tab appear. The commands on the Insert tab on the PowerPoint ribbon are similar to, but not exactly the same as, the commands on the Insert tab on the Excel ribbon.
5. On the ribbon, click the **Slide Show tab**. The Slide Show tab is unique to PowerPoint.
6. In the center of the window, position the **pointer** directly on top of the dotted line around *Click to add title* so that the pointer changes to ✥.
7. With the pointer as ✥, click the **dotted line**. A solid line appears in place of the dotted line because the text box object is now selected, and the Drawing Tools Format tab appears on the ribbon.
8. Click the **Drawing Tools Format tab** to make it the active tab on the ribbon. Refer again to Exhibit 9-6.

TIP: Sometimes when you select an object, a contextual tab becomes the active tab on the ribbon automatically.

text box An object that contains text.

9 In the middle of the PowerPoint window, click anywhere in the white space outside of the selected text box object. The object is no longer selected, and the contextual tab disappears from the ribbon. The Home tab is now the active tab.

End Activity

> **FYI**
> **SHOWING AND HIDING THE RIBBON**
> If the ribbon is visible and you want to hide it, click the Ribbon Display Options button at the right end of the ribbon. On the menu, click Show Tabs to hide the commands on the ribbon but keep the tab names visible, or click Auto-hide Ribbon to completely hide the ribbon until you point to the top of the window. If the ribbon is hidden and you want to make it visible again, click a tab name or point to the top of the window and then click the colored bar that appears. Click the Ribbon Display Options button, and then click Show Tabs and Commands.

EXHIBIT 9-7 BOLD BUTTON TOGGLED ON IN WORD

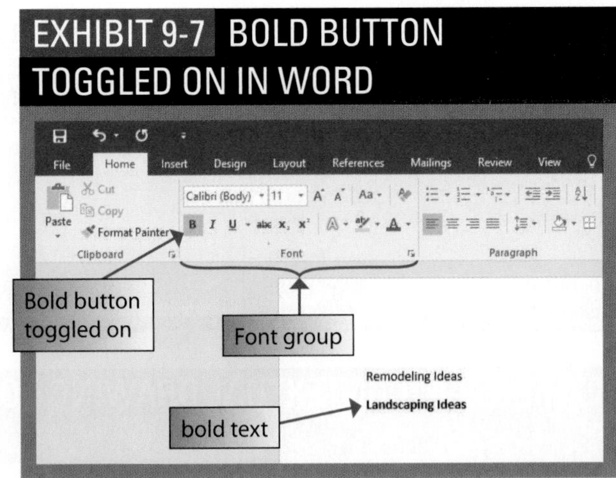

Some buttons have two parts: the top or left part of the button that executes the default command, and an arrow on the bottom or the right that opens a menu of all the commands or options available for that button. When you point to two-part buttons, the part of the button you are pointing to is shaded, and a gray border appears around the other part of the button. In Exhibit 9-8, the pointer is on the Bullets button in the Paragraph group on the Home tab in Word.

9-2b Using Buttons

As with the ribbon in File Explorer windows, the group names appear at the bottom of the ribbon below the buttons. For the most part, when you click a button in a group on a ribbon tab, something happens in the file. For example, the Clipboard group on the Home tab in Word, Excel, Access, and PowerPoint includes the Cut, Copy, and Format Painter buttons, which you can click to cut or copy text or objects, or copy formatting.

Some buttons on the ribbon are **toggle buttons**: one click turns the feature on and the next click turns the feature off. While the feature is on, the button remains shaded or highlighted to indicate that it is selected. For example, when you click the Bold button **B** in the Font group on the Word Home tab to select it, the currently selected text is formatted as bold and the Bold button changes to **B**, as shown in Exhibit 9-7. Clicking the Bold button again removes the bold formatting.

toggle button A button that you click once to turn a feature on and click again to turn it off.

EXHIBIT 9-8 A TWO-PART BUTTON

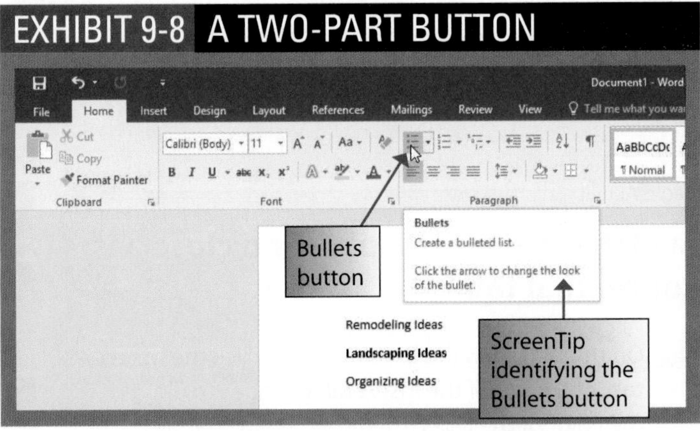

To use the default command for a two-part button, you click the top or left part of the button—the part of the button with the icon on it. To use a command other than the default, you click the arrow part of the button, and then click one of the commands or options that appear. Exhibit 9-9 shows the options available when you click the arrow part of the Bullets button in the Paragraph group on the Home tab in Word.

Note that some buttons have an arrow on them, but they are not two-part buttons, such as the Line and Paragraph Spacing button in the Paragraph group

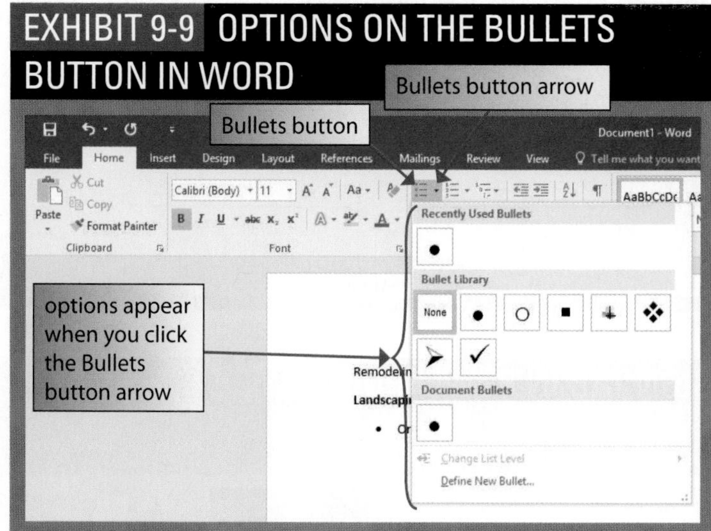

on the Home tab in Word. When you point to this type of button, the entire button is shaded, and clicking any part of this type of button always opens a list of commands or options.

Begin Activity

Use buttons on the ribbon.

Read this before starting this Activity: In this book, when you need to click the icon part of a two-part button (the top or the left part of the button), the step will instruct you to simply *click the button*. When you need to click the arrow part of a two-part button (below or to the right of the button), the step will instruct you to *click the button arrow*.

1 Make **Word** the active application.

2 Type **Remodeling Ideas** and then press the **Enter key**. The text appears in the first line of the document, and the insertion point moves to the second line.

> **PROBLEM?**
> If you make a typing error, press the **Backspace key** to delete the incorrect letters and then retype the text.

3 On the Home tab, in the Font group, point to the **Bold button** B. The button changes to B and its ScreenTip appears.

4 Click the **Bold button** B. The button stays shaded to indicate that it is selected.

5 Type **Landscaping Ideas**. The text you typed is in bold. Refer again to Exhibit 9-7.

6 Click the **Bold button** B. The button toggles off and changes to B.

7 Press the **Enter key**, and then type **Organizing Ideas**. The text in the third line is not bold because you toggled the command off before you started typing.

8 On the Home tab, in the Paragraph group, point to the **Bullets button**, but do not click. The part of the button with the icon is shaded, and a border surrounds the arrow, indicating that this is a two-part button. Refer again to Exhibit 9-8.

> **PROBLEM?**
> If the arrow part of the Bullets button is shaded, you are pointing to the arrow part of the button. Move the pointer so it is pointing to the left part of the Bullets button.

9 Click the **Bullets button** (the icon part of the Bullets button). A bullet is added in front of the third line of text and the line is indented.

10 Click in the second line of text, and then click the **Bullets button arrow** (the arrow part of the Bullets button). A list of types of bullets appears. Refer again to Exhibit 9-9.

11 In the list, click the **check mark bullet style** ✓. A check mark bullet is added in front of the second line of text, and the line is indented.

12 On the Home tab, in the Paragraph group, point to the **Line and Paragraph Spacing button**. Although this button has an arrow next to its icon, the arrow part of the button is shaded along with the icon part of the button and there is no line separating the icon from the arrow, so it is not a two-part button.

13 Click the **Line and Paragraph Spacing button**. A list of options opens.

14 On the list, click **3.0**. The spacing after the second line of text—the line that the insertion point is currently in—changes to three lines.

End Activity

9-2c Using Galleries and Live Preview

A **menu** is a list of commands that appears when you click a button. A **gallery** is a grid that shows visual

menu A list of commands that appears when you click a button.

gallery A menu or grid that shows visual representations of the options available for a button.

EXHIBIT 9-10 GALLERY ON THE HOME TAB IN WORD

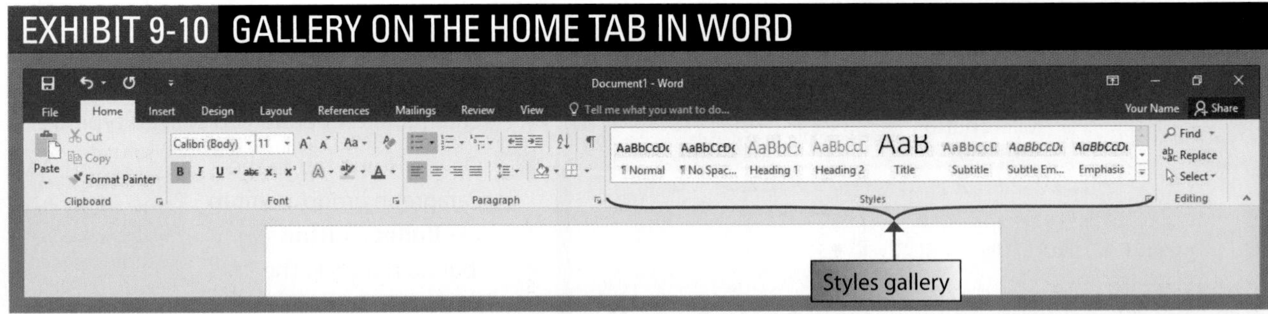

EXHIBIT 9-11 GALLERIES ON THE DESIGN TAB IN POWERPOINT

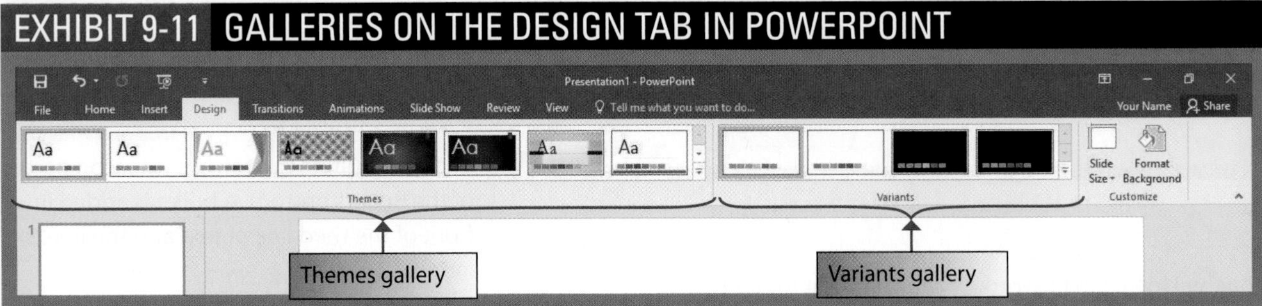

representations of the options available. When you clicked the Bullets button arrow in the previous Activity, the Bullets gallery and menu appeared (refer again to Exhibit 9-9). The gallery shows the bullet styles you can select. The menu at the bottom contains additional commands for working with bullets.

Galleries can appear when you click a button, such as the gallery on the Bullets button, or they are displayed in a group on the ribbon. An example of a gallery displayed in a group on the ribbon is the gallery in the Styles group on the Home tab in Word (shown in Exhibit 9-10) and the galleries in the Themes and Variants groups on the Design tab in PowerPoint (shown in Exhibit 9-11). These types of galleries usually have scroll arrows on the right to allow you to shift up or down a row, and a More button below the scroll arrows that you can click to expand the gallery to see all the options it contains.

In many galleries and on some menus, when you point to an option, **Live Preview** shows the results that would occur in your file if you clicked that option. To continue the bullets example, when you point to a bullet style in the Bullets gallery, a bullet in the style you are pointing to appears before the paragraph in which the insertion point is located. By moving the pointer from option to option, you can quickly see the text formatted with different bullet styles, making it easier to select the style you want.

Live Preview A feature that shows the results that would occur if you clicked the option to which you are pointing in a gallery.

Begin Activity

Use galleries and Live Preview.

1. In the Word window, double-click **Landscaping**. The entire word is highlighted with gray to indicate that it is selected.
2. On the Home tab, in the Font group, click the **Font Size button arrow**. A menu of font sizes (text sizes) opens.
3. In the menu, point to **26**. Live Preview shows the selected text formatted in the larger size. See Exhibit 9-12.

EXHIBIT 9-12 LIVE PREVIEW OF A NEW FONT SIZE IN WORD

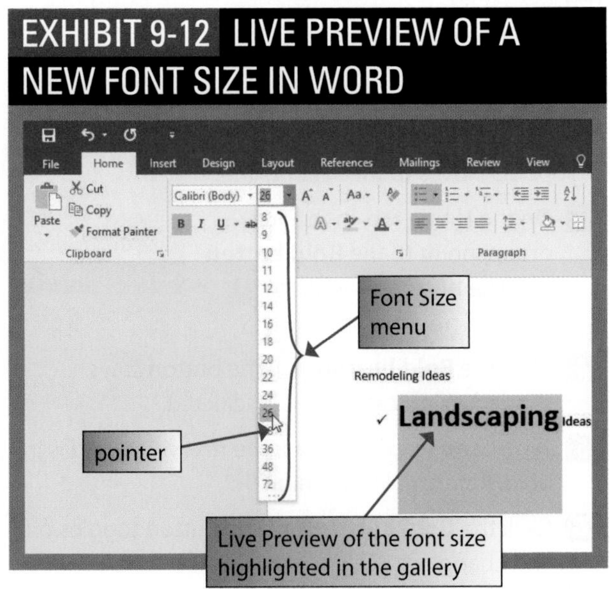

FYI

HOW BUTTONS, GROUPS, AND GALLERIES APPEAR ON THE RIBBON

The buttons and groups on the ribbon change based on your monitor size, your screen resolution, and the size of the application window. With smaller monitors, lower screen resolutions, and resized application windows, buttons can appear as icons without labels and some groups are condensed into a button that you click to display the commands in the group. The instructions and figures in this book were created using a screen resolution of 1366 × 768 and, unless otherwise specified, the maximized application windows. If you are using a different screen resolution or window size, the buttons on the ribbon might show more or fewer button names, and some groups might be wider or narrower than described in the steps. Some groups might even be reduced to a button; for example, at the lower resolution of 1024 × 768, the Pages group, the Links group, and the Symbols group on the Insert tab are each collapsed into a single button. If you cannot find a button referenced in the steps, you might need to click the group button first; for example, if the instruction in a step is, "In the Pages group, click the Page Break button," you would need to click the Pages button, and then click the Page Break button. Also be aware that button icons are shown in this book only when the button name is not visible at the resolution of 1366 × 768. For example, the buttons in the Text group on the Insert tab all show the name of the button on the ribbon when displayed at 1366 × 768, so the icons are not pictured in the steps in this book. However, most of the buttons in the Text group on the Insert tab do not show the name of the button when displayed at 1024 × 768. If you cannot find a button in a group on a tab, use the ScreenTips to find the correct button. Using different resolutions also affects the instructions for galleries. At lower resolutions, fewer choices are displayed in a gallery on the ribbon, and at higher resolutions, more choices are displayed. This means that if you are working with a lower resolution and the step instruction says to click a style or button in a gallery on the ribbon and you don't see it, you will need to click the More button first. Likewise, if you are working with a higher resolution, you might not need to click the More button to access the specific style or button in the step; however, you can still follow the step instruction as written.

Ribbon at 1024 × 768

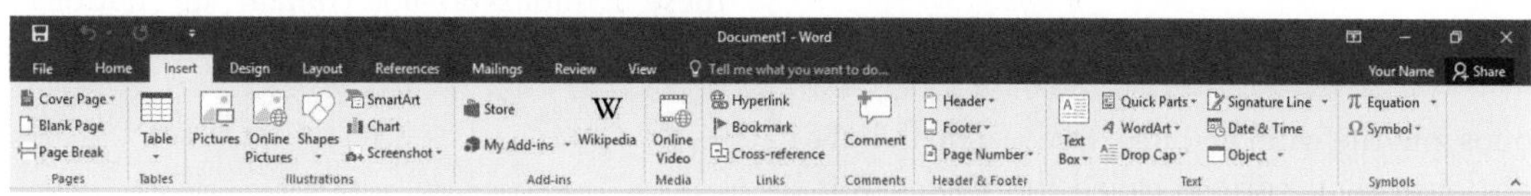

Ribbon at 1366 × 768 (resolution used in this book)

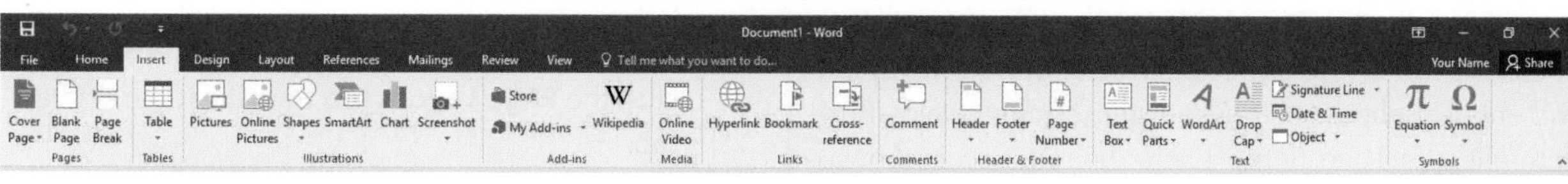

Ribbon at 1600 × 900

4. Click a **blank area** of the document to close the gallery without selecting anything.
5. Make **Excel** the active application.
6. Type **Budget** and then press the **Enter key**. The text you typed appears in the first box in column A and the second box in column A has a green border.
7. Click the box containing the word you just typed. The box containing *Budget* now has the green border.
8. On the ribbon, click the **Home tab** to make it the active tab. In the Font group, click the **Font button arrow** [Calibri] to display the Font gallery.
9. Point to several of the fonts (the design of text) to preview the effect on the text you just typed.
10. In the gallery, click **Algerian**. The gallery closes, and the text you typed is formatted with the Algerian font.
11. Make **Word** the active application. On the Home tab, in the Styles group, click the **down scroll arrow** to the right of the Styles gallery. The gallery scrolls down one row.
12. In the Styles group, click the **More button**. The Styles gallery opens so that you can see all of the options in the gallery.
13. Press the **Esc key**. The gallery closes without making a selection.

End Activity

EXHIBIT 9-13 PAGE TAB IN THE PAGE SETUP DIALOG BOX IN EXCEL

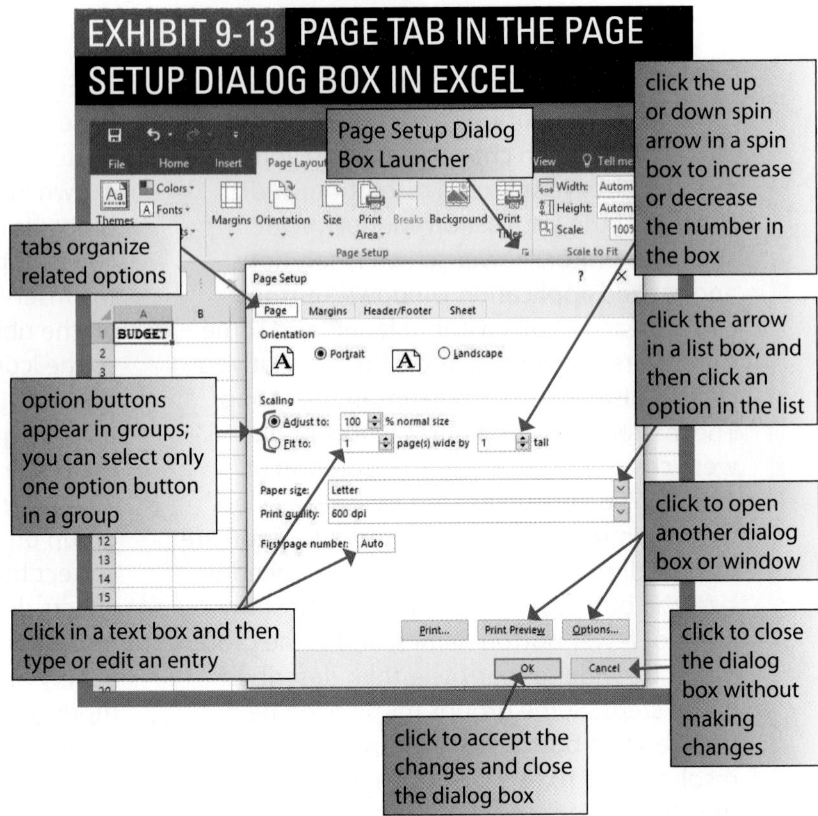

Page Setup Dialog Box Launcher
click the up or down spin arrow in a spin box to increase or decrease the number in the box
tabs organize related options
click the arrow in a list box, and then click an option in the list
option buttons appear in groups; you can select only one option button in a group
click to open another dialog box or window
click in a text box and then type or edit an entry
click to close the dialog box without making changes
click to accept the changes and close the dialog box

9-2d Using Commands in Dialog Boxes

Some groups on the ribbon tabs have a small button in their lower-right corners called the Dialog Box Launcher. Most of the time, when you click a Dialog Box Launcher, a dialog box related to that group of buttons opens. Recall that a dialog box is a window that opens on top of the application window and in which you enter or choose settings for performing a task. For example, the Page Setup dialog box in Excel, shown in Exhibit 9-13, contains options to change how the printed document looks. Some dialog boxes open as a result of you clicking a command on a menu or a button on the ribbon.

Most dialog boxes organize related information into tabs with related options and settings are organized into sections or groups, just as they are on the ribbon. Exhibit 9-13 shows the Page tab selected in the Excel Page Setup dialog box, and Exhibit 9-14 shows the Sheet tab in the same dialog box. You select settings in a dialog box using buttons similar to the buttons on the ribbon, command buttons, option buttons, check boxes, text and spin boxes, lists, and sliders to specify how you want to perform a task. These controls are all labeled in Exhibits 9-13 and 9-14. (Note that the tabs shown in these Exhibits do not contain any buttons similar to those on the ribbon or sliders.)

Begin Activity

Use commands in a dialog box.

1. Make **Excel** the active application. On the ribbon, click the **Page Layout tab** to make it the active tab.
2. In the Page Setup group, click the **Dialog Box Launcher**. The Page Setup dialog box opens with the Page tab as the active tab in the dialog box. Refer again to Exhibit 9-13.

EXHIBIT 9-14 SHEET TAB IN THE PAGE SETUP DIALOG BOX IN EXCEL

check boxes appear in groups; you can select more than one check box in a group

a check indicates that the check box is selected

3 In the Orientation section, click the **Landscape option button**. The black dot moves from the Portrait option button to the Landscape option button, indicating that the Landscape option is now selected. Landscape means that when you print, the page will be wider than it is long.

4 Click the **Paper size arrow**. A list of paper sizes opens. The size that appeared in the box before you clicked the arrow (Letter 8.5×11in.) is selected. A scroll bar appears on the right side of the list because you need to scroll to see the additional choices in the list.

5 Drag the **scroll box** to the bottom of the scroll bar to see some of the additional choices, and then click a **blank area** of the dialog box to close the list without selecting anything.

6 Click the **Sheet tab** to make it the active tab in the dialog box.

7 In the Print section of the dialog box, click the **Black and white check box**. A check mark appears in the check box, indicating that it is selected.

8 Click the **Draft quality check box**. A check mark appears in this check box as well.

9 Click the **Margins tab** to make it the active tab in the dialog box.

10 Click the **Top up arrow** three times. The value in the Top box changes from .75 to 1.5.

11 In the Bottom box, click after the 5. The insertion point appears in the Bottom box after the 5.

12 Press the **Backspace key** four times, and then type **2**. The value in the Bottom box is now 2.

13 Click **Cancel**. The dialog box closes without changing the page setup in the workbook.

End Activity

FYI USING KEY TIPS

You can use keyboard shortcuts to perform commands instead of clicking buttons on the ribbon. To access the options on the ribbon using the keyboard, press the Alt key. A label, called a Key Tip, appears with a single letter over each tab on the ribbon and with a number over each button on the Quick Access Toolbar. To select a tab or a button, press the key identified by the Key Tip. After you select a tab, new Key Tips appear over each button on that tab. Press the appropriate key or keys to select a button.

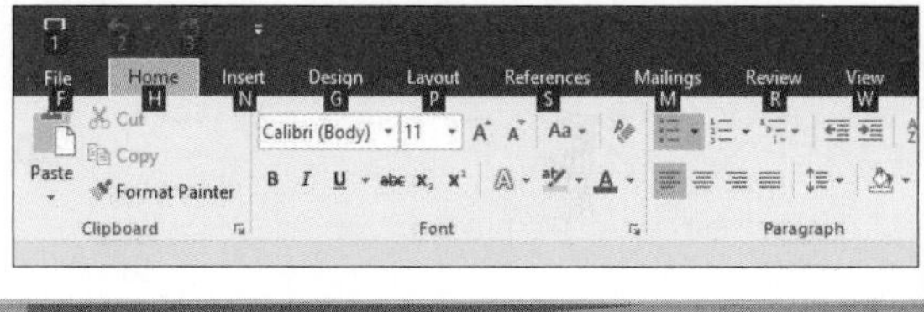

9-2e Open and Close Panes

Sometimes when you click a Dialog Box Launcher or a button, a pane appears to the right or left of the workspace instead of a dialog box. For example, clicking the Thesaurus button in the Proofing group on the Review tabs in Word, Excel, and PowerPoint opens the Thesaurus pane to the right of the window. Exhibit 9-15 shows the Thesaurus pane in Excel listing synonyms for the word *Budget*. Likewise, when a shape or a text box is selected, clicking the Dialog Box Launcher in the Shape Styles group on the Drawing Tools Format tab opens the Format Shape pane. The Format Shape pane in PowerPoint is shown in Exhibit 9-16. Like dialog boxes, you open some task panes by clicking a command on a menu or a button on the ribbon.

As in a dialog box, the commands and options available in a pane vary depending on the purpose of the pane. Some panes, like the Format Shape pane shown in Exhibit 9-16, contain labels and buttons that are similar

EXHIBIT 9-15 THESAURUS PANE IN EXCEL SHOWING SYNONYMS FOR *BUDGET*

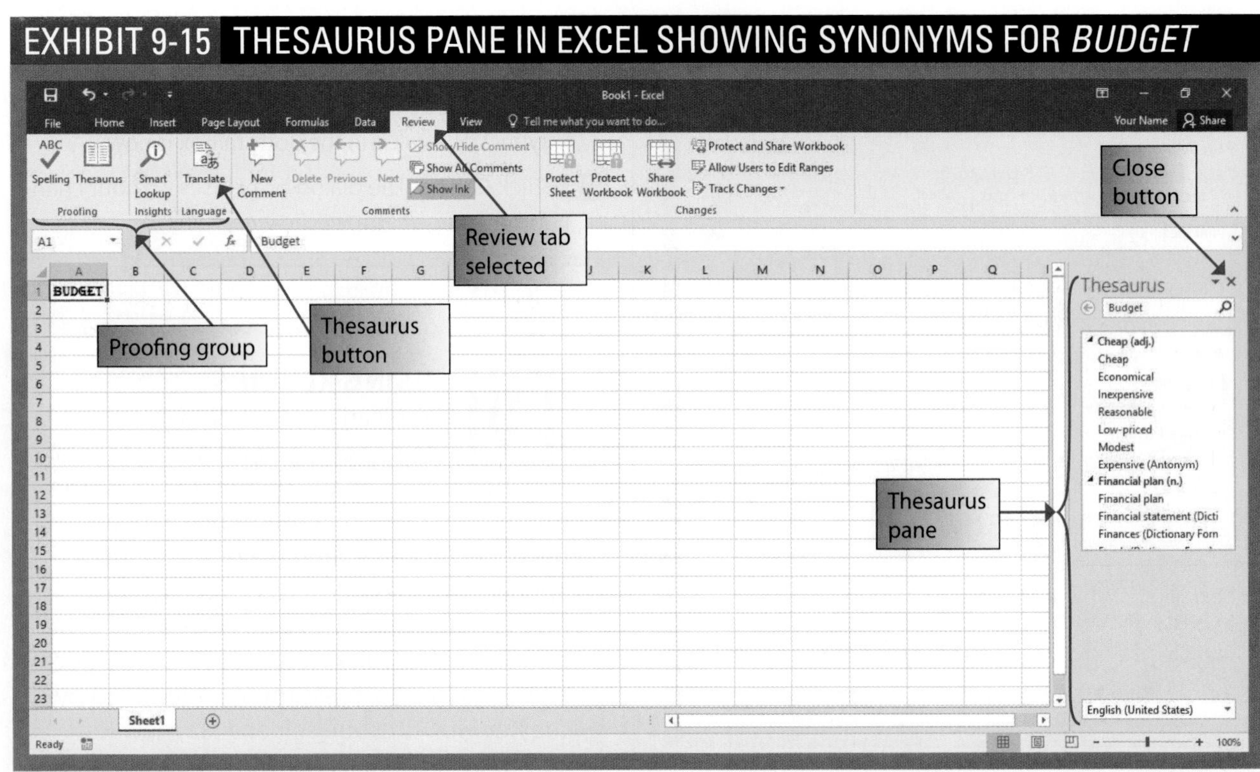

EXHIBIT 9-16 FORMAT SHAPE PANE IN POWERPOINT

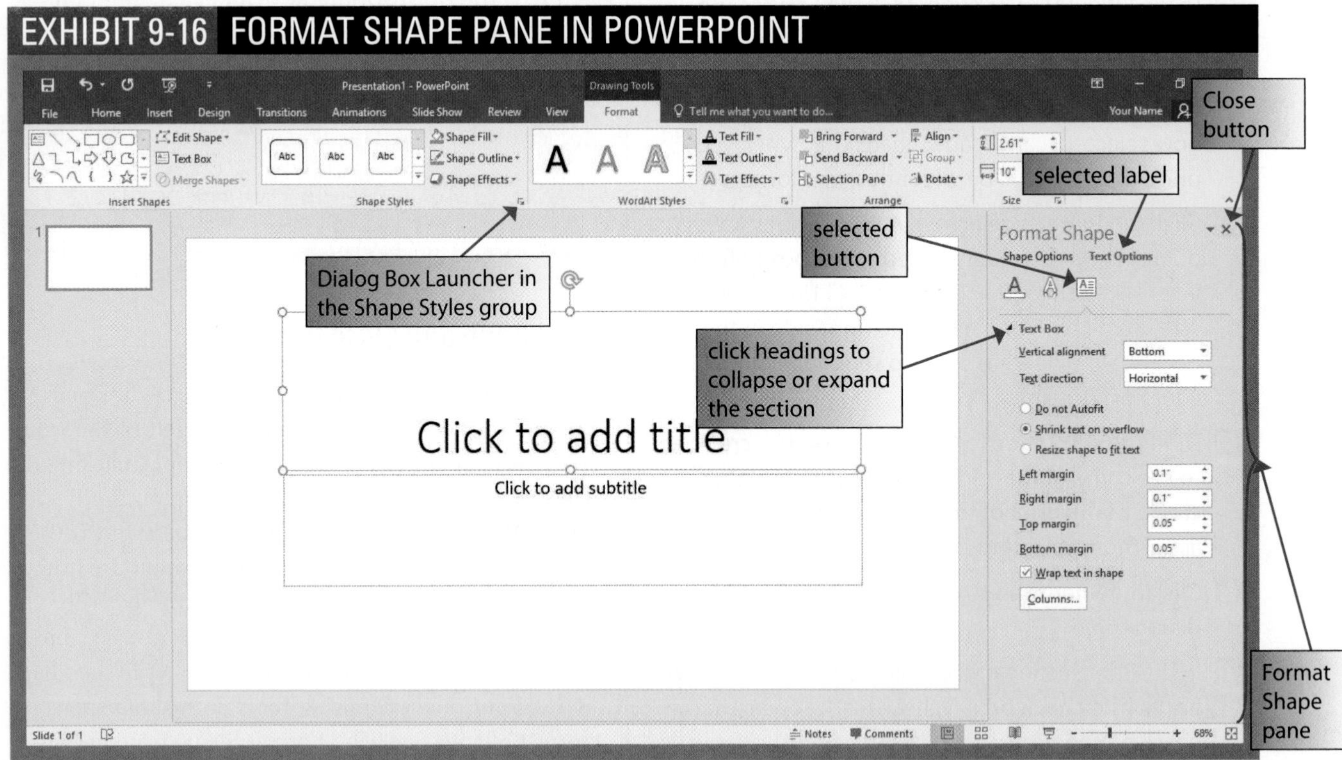

to tabs in a dialog box. Click each label to display a different, related set of buttons, and click each button to display a different set of commands or options. You can then click the commands with expand arrows (▷) next to them to display the options or commands related to that command. In the Format Shape pane in Exhibit 9-16, the Text Options label is selected, and the Textbox button (▤) is selected on the Text Options tab. The Text Box commands are expanded. Panes can contain all the types of commands available in dialog boxes.

When you are finished working in a pane, you can click its Close button ✕ in the top-right corner to close it.

Begin Activity

Open and close a pane.

1 On the Excel ribbon, click the **Review tab**. If a green outline does not surround the box containing the word *Budget* that you typed earlier, click **Budget**.

2 In the Proofing group, click the **Thesaurus button**. The Thesaurus pane opens to the right of the workspace. Refer again to Exhibit 9-15. Because the box with the word *Budget* is selected, this task pane contains synonyms for *Budget*.

3 In the Thesaurus pane, in the upper-right corner, click the **Close button** ☒. The Thesaurus pane closes.

4 Make **PowerPoint** the active application. Position the **pointer** directly on top of the dotted line around *Click to add title* so that the pointer changes to ✥, and then click the **dotted line**. A solid line appears in place of the dotted line indicating that the text box object is now selected.

5 On the ribbon, click the **Drawing Tools Format tab**. In the Shape Styles group, point to the **Dialog Box Launcher** ⧉. The ScreenTip identifies this Dialog Box Launcher as Format Shape.

6 Click the **Format Shape Dialog Box Launcher** ⧉. The Format Shape pane opens on the right side of the window. The Shape Options label at the top of the pane is orange, indicating it is selected.

7 In the pane, click the **Text Options label**. The buttons below the labels change.

8 In the pane, click the **Textbox button** ▤. The commands in the task pane change to include commands for modifying the selected text box.

9 If the Text Box list is not expanded, click the **expand arrow** ▷ next to Text Box. Refer again to Exhibit 9-16.

10 In the pane, click the **Vertical alignment arrow**, and then on the menu, click **Middle**. The text in the selected text box is centered.

11 In the pane, click the **Resize shape to fit text option button**. The selected text box is resized smaller to just fit the height of the text.

12 In the Format Shape pane title bar, click the **Close button** ☒. The Format Shape pane closes.

End Activity

9-2f Exploring Backstage View

The first tab on the ribbon, in both Office applications and in Windows 10 File Explorer windows, is the File tab. Instead of displaying a different set of commands on the ribbon, clicking the File tab opens Backstage view. Remember that when you start an Office application, Backstage view offers only the Recent screen. After you open a file, you can access all of the commands available in Backstage view. The left pane in Backstage view is the **navigation bar** and it contains commands you click to display different screens or perform an action. Exhibit 9-17 shows the Info screen in Backstage view in PowerPoint.

EXHIBIT 9-17 BACKSTAGE VIEW IN POWERPOINT WITH THE INFO SCREEN DISPLAYED

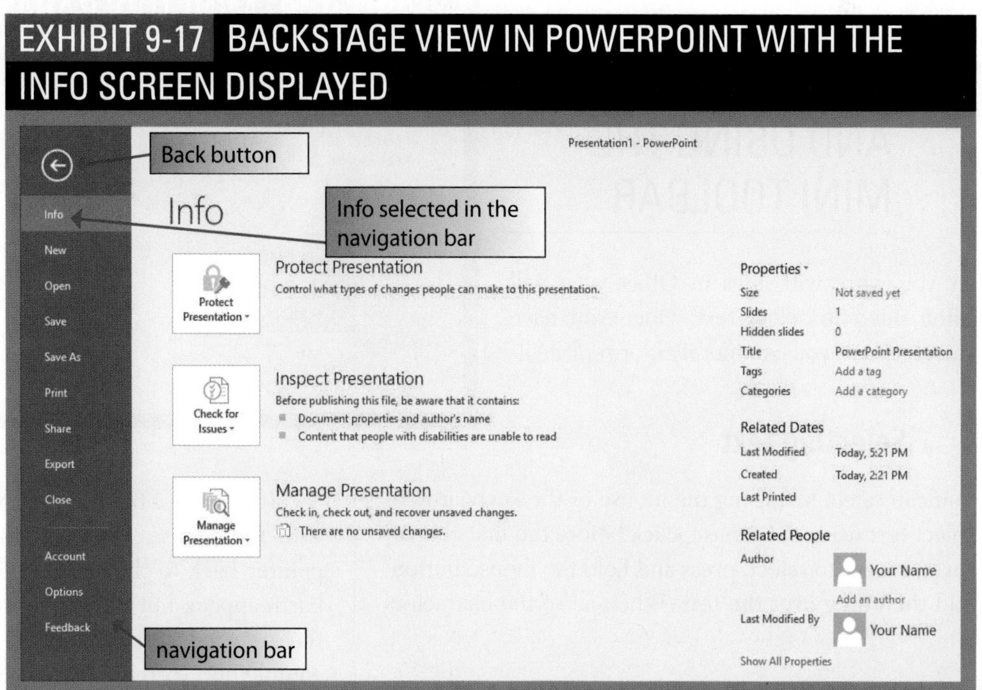

navigation bar The left pane in Backstage view.

Backstage view hides the window containing the open file, including the ribbon. If you need to leave Backstage view and display the commands on a different tab on the ribbon, you click the Back button at the top of the navigation bar.

Begin Activity

Explore Backstage view.

1 On the PowerPoint ribbon, click the **File tab**. Backstage view in PowerPoint appears, replacing the blank presentation in the workspace. The Info screen, which contains information about the current file is displayed. Refer again to Exhibit 9-17.

2 In the navigation bar, click the **Back button**. Backstage view closes, and the PowerPoint window and ribbon are visible again.

3 Make **Word** the active application, and then click the **File tab**. Backstage view in Word appears with the Info screen displayed.

4 In the navigation bar, click the **Back button**. Backstage view closes, and the Word window and ribbon are visible again.

End Activity

9-3 SELECTING TEXT AND USING THE MINI TOOLBAR

As you work with files in Office, you will often need to select text. Once you have selected text, you can modify it or replace it.

9-3a Selecting Text

You can select text using the mouse or the keyboard. To select text using the mouse, click before the first character you want to select, press and hold the mouse button, and then drag over the text. When all of the characters that you want to select are highlighted, release the mouse button. To select text using the keyboard, position the insertion point before the first character you want to select (you can click or use the arrow keys on the keyboard), press and hold the Shift key, and then press the arrow key pointing in the direction in which you want to select text. To combine using the mouse and the keyboard to select text. Click before the first character you want to select, press and hold the Shift key, and then click after the last character you want to select.

In addition, you can select nonadjacent text. To do this, use any method to select the first block of text, press and hold the Ctrl key, and then use the mouse and drag to select as many other blocks of text as you want.

9-3b Using the Mini Toolbar

The **Mini toolbar** contains buttons for the most commonly used formatting commands, such as font, font size, styles, color, alignment, and indents. Exhibit 9-18 shows the Mini toolbar in Word. The exact buttons on the Mini toolbar differ in each application, and all of the commands on the Mini toolbar appear somewhere on the ribbon in that application. The Mini toolbar appears whenever you select text with the mouse or right-click in Word, Excel, or PowerPoint.

EXHIBIT 9-18 MINI TOOLBAR IN WORD

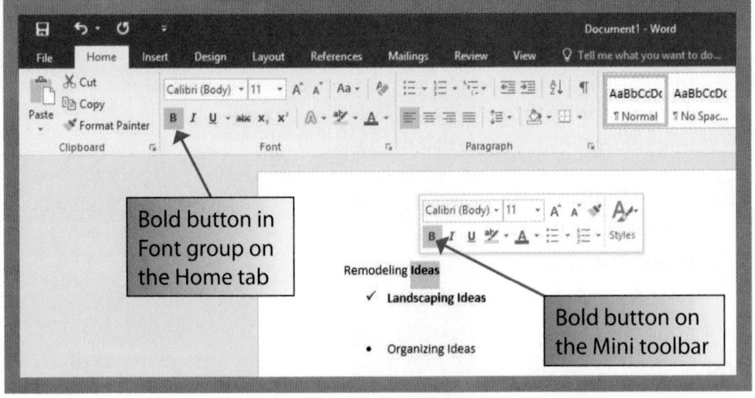

Bold button in Font group on the Home tab

Bold button on the Mini toolbar

If you move the pointer away from text you selected with the mouse, the Mini toolbar fades. Moving the pointer back to the selected text makes the Mini toolbar reappear, but moving the mouse farther away from the selected text makes the Mini toolbar disappear completely. To redisplay it, you need to right-click the selected text or deselect and then reselect the text.

Note: The Activity steps in this book instruct you to use the ribbon. You can click the correct button on the Mini toolbar if you prefer.

Mini toolbar A toolbar with buttons for commonly used formatting commands that appears next to the pointer when you select text with the mouse or you right-click.

Begin Activity

Select text and use the Mini toolbar.

1 In the Word window, position the **pointer** (which looks like I) before the word *Ideas*. Press and hold the **mouse button**, drag the pointer across **Ideas**, and then release the **mouse button**. The word is shaded with gray to indicate that it is selected, and the Mini toolbar appears above selected text.

2 On the Mini toolbar, click the **Bold button** B. The Bold button on the Mini toolbar and the Bold button in the Font group on the Home tab are shaded, and the selected text is formatted with bold. Refer again to Exhibit 9-18.

> **PROBLEM?**
> If the Mini toolbar disappears, you moved the pointer away from the selected text. Move the pointer back to the selected text or repeat Step 1.

3 Click a **blank area** of the document to deselect the text.

End Activity

9-4 UNDOING AND REDOING

If you make a mistake or change your mind about an action as you are working, you can reverse the action by clicking the Undo button on the Quick Access Toolbar or by pressing the Ctrl+Z keys. You can continue to click the Undo button or press the Ctrl+Z keys to undo more actions, or you can click the Undo button arrow and then select as many actions in the list that appears as you want. Exhibit 9-19 shows the Undo button menu in Word with a list of actions on it. You can also Redo an action that you undid by clicking the Redo button on the Quick Access Toolbar or by pressing the Ctrl+Y keys.

EXHIBIT 9-19 UNDO BUTTON MENU IN WORD

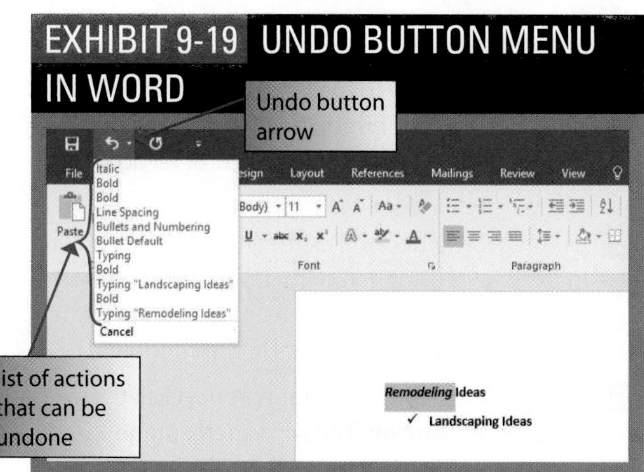

Begin Activity

Undo and redo actions.

1 In the Word window, in the first line of text, double-click **Remodeling** to select it.

2 On the Home tab on the ribbon, in the Font group, click the **Bold button** B, and then click the **Italic button** I.

3 On the Quick Access Toolbar, point to the **Undo button**. The ScreenTip identifies the action that will be undone if you click the button, in this case, *Undo Italic*.

4 Click the **Undo button arrow**. A list of actions that can be undone appears. Refer again to Exhibit 9-19. The list of actions on your screen might differ.

5 On the menu, click **Italic**. The italic formatting is removed from the word *Remodeling*.

6 Click the **Undo button**. The bold formatting is removed from the word *Remodeling*.

7 On the Quick Access Toolbar, click the **Redo button**. The bold action you just undid is redone, and the word *Remodeling* is bold again.

8 Click a **blank area** of the document to deselect the text.

End Activity

> **FYI**
> **REDO/REPEAT BUTTON**
> When no actions can be redone, the Redo button on the Quick Access Toolbar changes to the Repeat button. When the Repeat button appears, you can click it to repeat the most recent action. For instance, if you apply bold formatting to one word, you can select another word and then click the Repeat button to apply bold formatting to the second word.

9-5 ZOOMING AND SCROLLING

You can zoom and scroll in the Office applications. To change the zoom level, you can drag the Zoom slider button on the Zoom slider at the right end of the status

EXHIBIT 9-20 VIEW TAB AND THE ZOOM PERCENTAGE SET TO 10% IN WORD

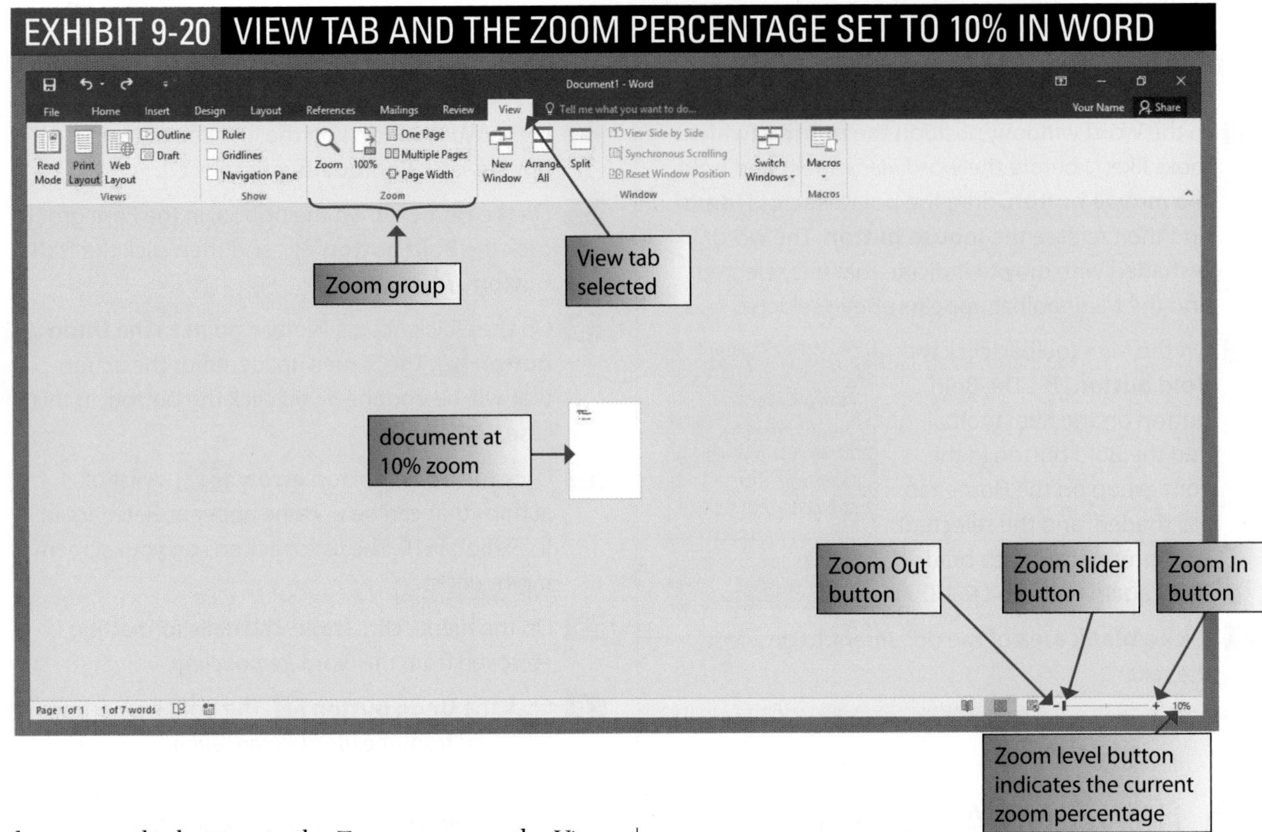

bar or use the buttons in the Zoom group on the View tab on the ribbon. The buttons in the Zoom group on the View tab in each application differ somewhat. Exhibit 9-20 shows the Word window with the View tab selected and a document zoomed to 10%. Exhibit 9-21 shows the Excel window with the View tab selected and the Zoom dialog box open.

EXHIBIT 9-21 VIEW TAB AND THE ZOOM DIALOG BOX IN EXCEL

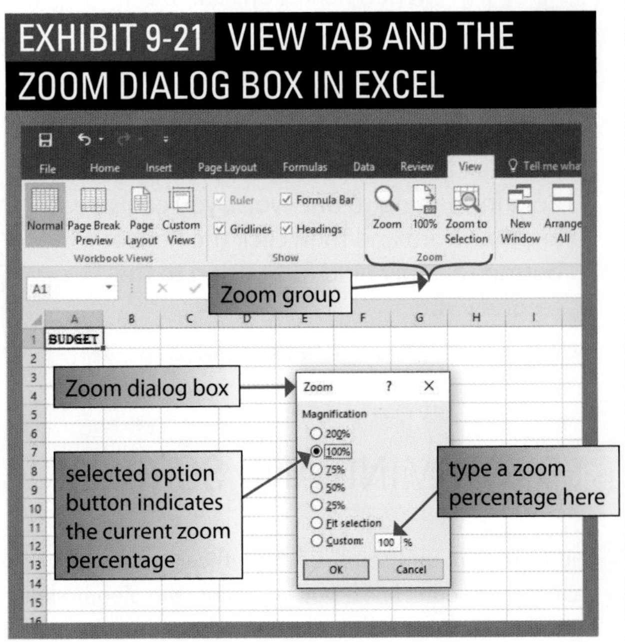

9-5a Zooming

Zooming resizes the content in the workspace. You can zoom in to get a closer look at the content of an open document, workbook, or presentation, or of a database report. Likewise, you can zoom out to see more of the content at a smaller size. The Word and Excel figures in this book show the workspace zoomed in to enhance readability.

Begin Activity

Zoom an application window.

1. On the Word status bar, drag the **Zoom slider button** all the way to the left. The percentage on the Zoom level button is 10%, and the document is reduced to its smallest size. Refer again to Exhibit 9-20.
2. On the Word ribbon, click the **View tab**, as shown in Exhibit 9-20. In the Zoom group, click the **One Page button**. The zoom percentage changes so that the entire page appears in the window.
3. On the View tab, in the Zoom group, click the **Page Width button**. The zoom percentage changes so that the page width fills the window.

4 On the status bar, click the **Zoom out button** [−] as many times as needed so that the Zoom level button to the right of the Zoom slider is 100%.

5 Make **Excel** the active application.

6 On the ribbon, click the **View tab**. In the Zoom group, click the **Zoom button**. The Zoom dialog box opens. Refer again to Exhibit 9-21.

7 Click in the **Custom box** after *100*, press the **Backspace key** three times to delete the text in the box, and then type **60**. The Custom option button becomes selected instead of the 100% option button.

8 Click **OK**. The dialog box closes, and the zoom percentage in the Excel window changes to 60%.

9 On the View tab, in the Zoom group, click the **100% button**. The zoom percentage in the Excel window changes to 100%.

End Activity

9-5b Scrolling

To change which area of the workspace is visible in the application window, you can use the scroll bars. To scroll in a window, you can click the scroll arrows at either end of the scroll bar to scroll one line at a time; you can drag the scroll box the length of the scroll bar to scroll a longer distance; or you can click above or below the scroll box to jump a screen at a time.

Scroll bars appear in Office application windows when the workspace is taller or wider than the window. Depending on the application and zoom level, you might see a vertical scroll bar, a horizontal scroll bar, or both. Exhibit 9-22 shows the scroll bars in the Excel window.

Begin Activity

Scroll in an application window.

1 In the Excel window, on the horizontal scroll bar, click the **right scroll arrow** [▸] twice. The worksheet shifts two columns to the right. The first two columns (columns A and B, labeled by letters at the top of the columns) shift out of view and two additional columns shift into view on the right side of the window.

2 On the horizontal scroll bar, drag the **scroll box** all the way to the left. The worksheet shifts left to display columns A and B again.

3 On the vertical scroll bar, click the **down scroll arrow** [▾] three times. The first three rows (rows 1, 2, and 3, labeled by numbers to the left of the rows) scroll up out of view, and three new rows appear at the bottom of the window.

EXHIBIT 9-22 SCROLL BARS IN EXCEL

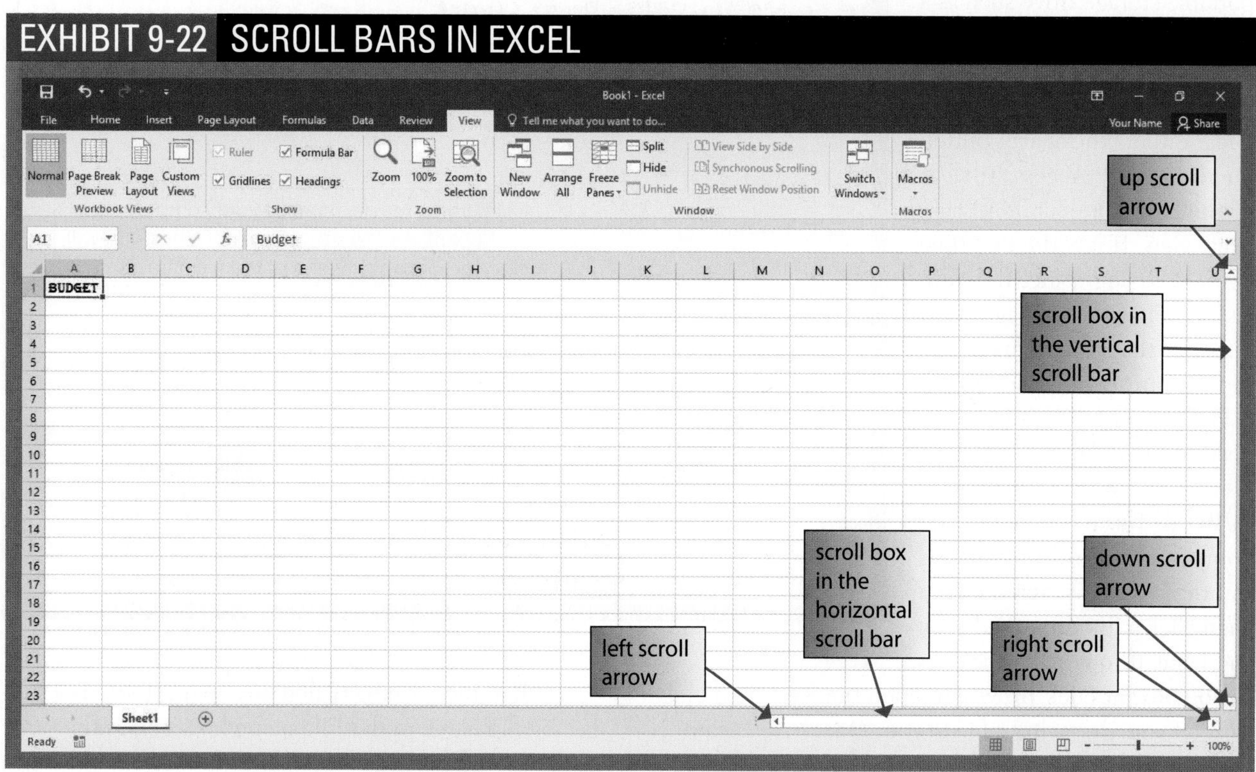

4 On the vertical scroll bar, drag the **scroll box** up to the top of the scroll bar. Rows 1, 2, and 3 scroll back into view.

End Activity

EXHIBIT 9-23 SAVE AS SCREEN IN BACKSTAGE VIEW IN WORD

9-6 WORKING WITH OFFICE FILES

The most common tasks you perform in any Office application are to create, open, save, and close files. All of these tasks can be done from Backstage view, and the processes for these tasks are basically the same in all Office applications.

9-6a Saving a File for the First Time

As you create and modify an Office file, your work is stored only in the computer's temporary memory. If you were to close the application without saving, turn off your computer, or experience a power failure, your work would be lost. You can save files to the hard drive located inside your computer, an external hard drive, a network storage drive, a portable storage drive such as a USB flash drive, or a folder on a Web site.

To save a file, you can click either the Save button on the Quick Access Toolbar or the Save command in Backstage view. If it is the first time you are saving a file, the Save As screen in Backstage view opens so that you can name the file you are saving and specify a location in which to save it. Exhibit 9-23 shows the Save As screen in Backstage view in Word. To save a file on your computer, you select This PC on the Save As screen, and then click a folder in the list on the right to open the Save As dialog box, or click Browse to open the Save As dialog box. (If you are saving a file to your OneDrive account, refer to the Office Online section titled "Saving a File to OneDrive" at the end of this chapter.) Exhibit 9-24 shows the Save As dialog box in Word. The Save As dialog box looks similar to a File Explorer folder window, and you navigate through it in the same manner so you can choose a location in which to store your file.

EXHIBIT 9-24 SAVE AS DIALOG BOX IN WORD

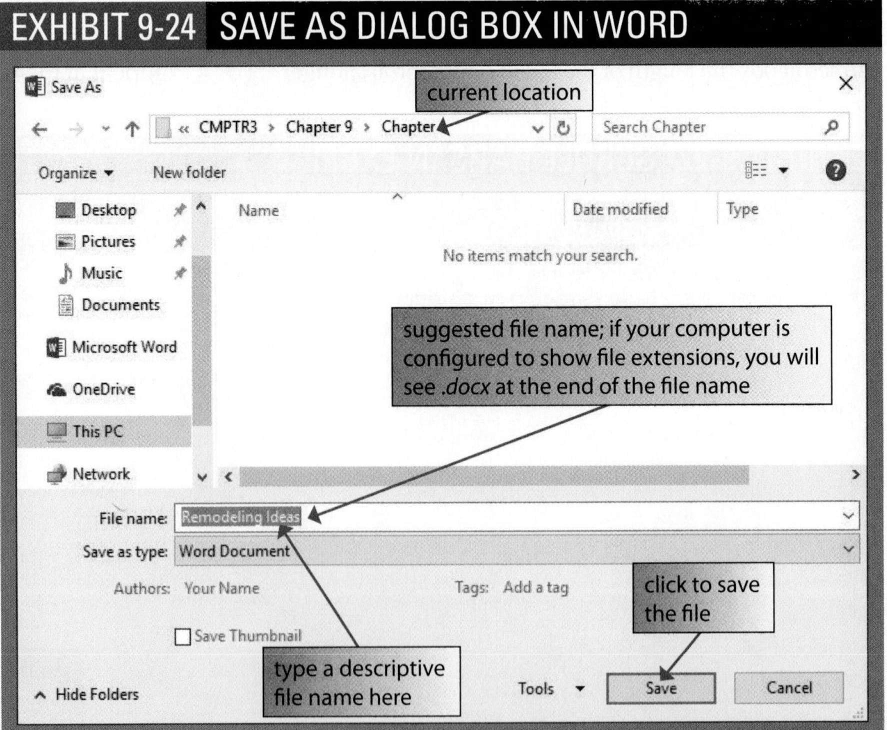

When the Save As dialog box opens, there is a suggested file name in the File name box. This is the same as the first few words in the file. The first time you save a file, you need to name it. Remember that file names include a title you specify and a file extension assigned by Office to indicate the file type and that file names can include uppercase and lowercase letters, numbers, hyphens, and spaces in any combination, but not the special characters ? " / \ < > * |. The file extensions for Office 2016 files are *.docx* for Word, *.xlsx* for Excel, *.accdb* for Access, and *.pptx* for PowerPoint. File names can include a maximum of 255 characters (including the file extension).

After you save a file, the file name appears in the title bar of the application window. Exhibit 9-25 shows a file name in the Word window title bar. If your computer is configured to show file extensions, you will see the file extension after the file name in the title bar. This book does not show file extensions.

EXHIBIT 9-25 FILE NAME IN THE WORD WINDOW TITLE BAR

file name in the title bar

if your computer is configured to show file extensions, you will see *.docx* at the end of the file name

Begin Activity

Save a file for the first time.

1 Make **Word** the active application.

2 On the Quick Access Toolbar, click the **Save button**. Backstage view opens displaying the Save As screen. Refer again to Exhibit 9-23.

TIP: You can click a folder in the list on the right to open the Save As dialog box to that location.

3 If necessary, click **This PC**. The list of of folders changes to a list of recently used folders on your computer.

4 Click **Browse**. The Save As dialog box opens. Refer again to Exhibit 9-24. The text in the File name box is the suggested file name.

PROBLEM? If you plan to save your files to your OneDrive account, see the Office Online section titled "Saving a File to OneDrive" at the end of this chapter.

5 Use the techniques you learned in Chapter 7 to navigate to the drive and folder where you plan to store the files you create as you work through the Activities in this book.

6 Click in the **File name box**. The suggested file name is selected.

7 Type **Bulleted List Example** in the File name box.

8 Click **Save**. The Save As dialog box and Backstage view close, and the file name you entered for the file appears in the Word window title bar. Refer again to Exhibit 9-25.

End Activity

9-6b Saving a File after Making Changes

The saved file includes everything in the document at the time you last saved it. If you make changes to the file, you need to save the file again. Until you do, any new edits or additions you make to the document exist only in the computer's memory and are not saved in the file. To save the file again, you click the Save button or use the Save command in Backstage view. Because you already named the document and selected a storage location, the Save As dialog box does not open.

To save a copy of the file with a different file name so that the original version remains unchanged, or to save the file to a different location, you click the File tab on the ribbon, and then in the navigation bar, click the Save As command to open the Save As dialog box again. When you save the file with a new name or to a new location, the original version of the file remains unchanged and in its original location. Be sure to save frequently as you work so that the file reflects the latest content in case the application or your computer shuts down unexpectedly.

Begin Activity

Modify a file and save your changes.

1 In the Word window, in the third line of the document, click immediately after *Ideas*. The insertion point blinks at the location where you clicked.

2 Press the **Backspace key** five times to delete *Ideas*, and then type **Suggestions**.

3 On the Quick Access Toolbar, click the **Save button** . The changes you made to the document are saved in the file stored on the drive.

TIP: You can also press the Ctrl+S keys to save the file.

End Activity

9-6c Closing a File

Although you can keep multiple files open at one time, you should close any file you are no longer working on to conserve system resources and prevent changes to the file. You can close a file by clicking the Close command in Backstage view or by clicking the Close button in the upper-right corner of the title bar. Note, however, that if the file is the only file open in that application, clicking the Close button also exits the application.

If you try to close a file that you have modified but haven't saved, a dialog box, similar to the one shown in Exhibit 9-26, opens, asking whether you want to save your changes. If the file has been saved at least once, clicking Save in this dialog box saves the changes to the file, closes the file, and then exits the application. If the file is not named, clicking Save opens the Save As dialog box so that you can name the file, choose a save location, and save it. The application would then close after you click Save in the Save As dialog box. If you don't want to save the file, you click Don't Save.

EXHIBIT 9-26 DIALOG BOX ASKING WHETHER TO SAVE CHANGES

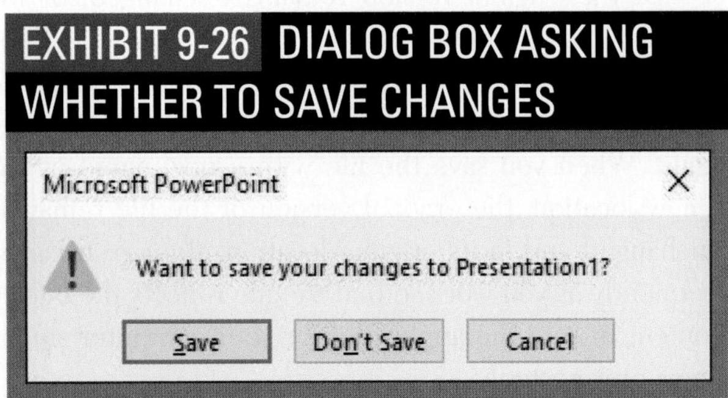

Begin Activity

Close a file.

1 On the Word ribbon, click the **File tab**. Backstage view opens.

2 In the navigation bar, click **Close**. Backstage view closes and the document closes, but the Word window stays open.

3 Make **PowerPoint** the active application.

4 In the title bar, click the **Close button** . A dialog box opens, asking if you want to save changes to the file. Refer again to Exhibit 9-26.

5 Click **Don't Save**. The file closes without saving, and the application exits. Word is the active application again.

End Activity

9-6d Opening a File

When you want to view or edit a previously created file, you must first open it. Opening a file transfers a copy of the file from the storage location to the computer's memory and displays it on your screen.

To open a file, display Backstage view, click Open in the navigation bar to display the Open screen, and then click the Browse button to open the Open dialog box. The Open dialog box is very similar to the Save As dialog box.

Begin Activity

Open a file.

1 On the Word ribbon, click the **File tab** to open Backstage view. Because no files are open, the Open screen appears. Recent is selected, and a list of recently opened documents appears on the right. If the document you want to open is in this list, you can click it to open it. Even though the Bulleted List Example file appears in this list, do not click it so that you can see the Open dialog box.

2 Click **Browse**. The Open dialog box opens. Navigate to the drive and folder in which you saved the file Bulleted List Example.

3 In the list of files, click **Bulleted List Example**, and then click **Open**. The file opens in the Word window.

End Activity

FYI **PROTECTED VIEW**

Any file you open that was downloaded from the Internet, accessed from a shared network, or received as an email attachment might open in Protected View. In **Protected View**, you can see the file contents, but you cannot edit, save, or print until you enable editing. To do so, click the Enable Editing button on the Protected View bar. If the Protected View bar is red and the Enable Editing button does not appear on the bar, that means a bigger potential security problem was detected, and something in the file might harm your computer.

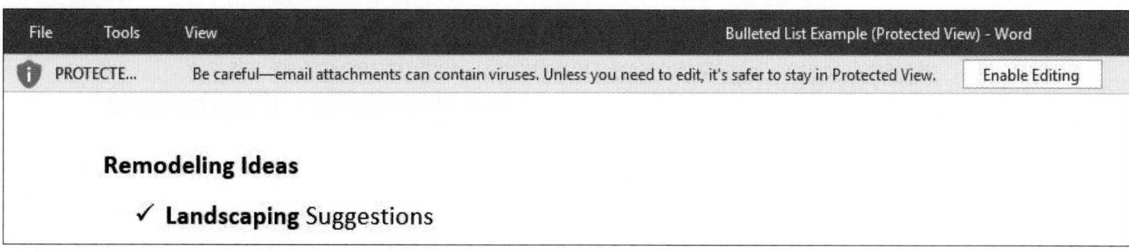

9-7 USING THE CLIPBOARD

The **Clipboard** is a temporary storage area in Windows on which text or other objects are stored when you copy or cut them. To **copy** text or an object, you select it, and then use the Copy command to duplicate it on the Clipboard so that you can paste it somewhere else. If you want to move text from one location and paste it somewhere else, you first need to **cut** it—that is, remove it from the original location and place it on the Clipboard using the Cut command. Once something is on the Clipboard, you can then **paste** it—that is, insert a copy of the text or object on the Clipboard somewhere in the current document or in another document.

9-7a Using the System Clipboard

The system Clipboard is a feature of Windows and is available to all Windows 10 apps and applications. Only one item can be on the system Clipboard at a time. The text or object on the Clipboard stays on the Clipboard until you cut or copy something else or until you shut down your computer. So if you cut text in a Word document and then switch to a File Explorer window and cut a file, the cut file replaces the Word text on the system Clipboard.

In all of the Office applications, you can click the Cut button in the Clipboard group on the Home tab to cut selected text or objects and place them on the system Clipboard, click the Copy button in the same group to copy selected text or objects and place them on the system Clipboard, and click the Paste button to paste the text or objects on the system Clipboard. (Note that the Paste button is a two-part button.) When you press the Delete or Backspace key, the deleted text or object is not placed on the Clipboard.

Begin Activity

Cut, copy, and paste with the system Clipboard.

1. In the third line of text in the Word window, double-click **Suggestions** to select it.
2. On the Home tab, in the Clipboard group, click the **Copy button**. The selected text remains in the document and is placed on the Clipboard.
3. In the second line of text, click before the word *Ideas*. The text will be pasted at the insertion point.
4. On the Home tab, in the Clipboard group, click the **Paste button**. The copied text, *Suggestions*, appears between *Landscaping* and *Ideas*. Another button appears below the pasted text; ignore this for now.

Protected View A view of a file in an Office application in which you can see the file contents, but you cannot edit, save, or print them until you enable editing.

Clipboard A temporary storage area in Windows on which text or other objects are stored when you copy or cut them.

copy To duplicate selected text or an object and place it on the Clipboard.

cut To remove selected text or an object from the original location and place it on the Clipboard.

paste To insert a copy of the text or object on the Clipboard in a file.

5 In the second line of text, double-click **Ideas**.

6 In the Clipboard group, click the **Cut button**. The selected text is removed from the document and replaces the previously copied item on the Clipboard.

7 Make **Excel** the active application, and then click the box to the right of the box containing *Budget*.

8 On the ribbon, click the **Home tab**. In the Clipboard group, click the **Paste button**. The text you cut, *Ideas*, appears in the current box.

End Activity

9-7b Using the Office Clipboard

The Office Clipboard is a special Clipboard available only to Office applications. Unlike the system Clipboard, which can contain only the most recently cut or copied item, the Office Clipboard can hold up to 24 items cut or copied from Office applications. You can then paste these items as needed in any order into any Office document. The last item cut or copied is the first item listed in the Clipboard pane. Exhibit 9-27 shows the Clipboard pane open in Word. It contains cut or copied items from Word and Excel files.

EXHIBIT 9-27 CLIPBOARD PANE IN WORD

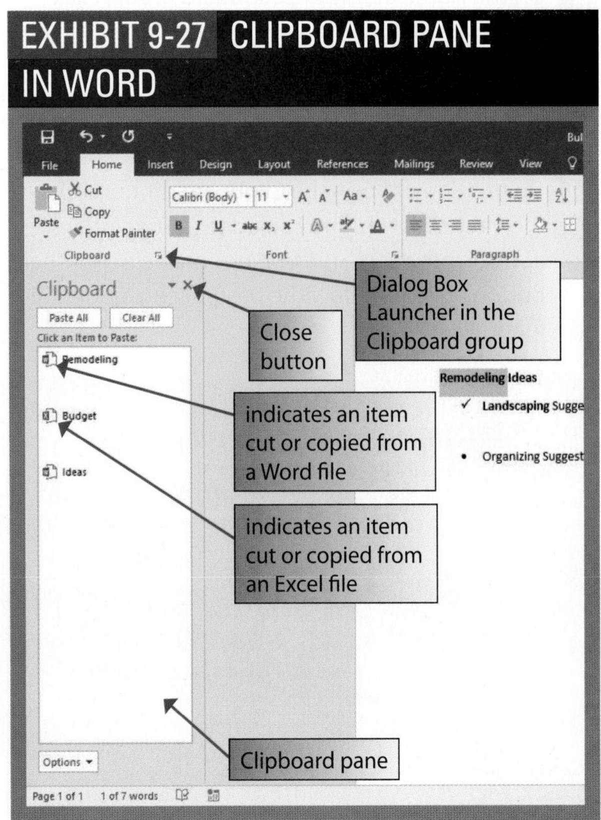

To use the Office Clipboard, you need to activate it by opening the Clipboard pane in an Office application. If you do not open the Clipboard pane, the Office Clipboard is not available, and the system Clipboard is used when you cut or copy items. (When the Clipboard task pane is open, the system Clipboard continues to store the latest cut or copied item.) If the Office Clipboard is open in one application, it is available to all of the Office applications.

Begin Activity

Use the Office Clipboard.

1 On the Home tab of the Excel ribbon, in the Clipboard group, point to the **Dialog Box Launcher**. The ScreenTip identifies this Dialog Box Launcher as Clipboard.

2 Click the **Clipboard Dialog Box Launcher**. The Clipboard pane opens on the left side of the window and shows items on the Office Clipboard. As you can see, the Office Clipboard already contains the last item you placed on the system Clipboard—the text *Ideas* that you cut from the Word document.

3 Click the box that contains the word *Budget*.

4 On the Home tab, in the Clipboard group, click the **Copy button**. The text *Budget* appears at the top of the Clipboard pane.

5 Make **Word** the active application.

6 In the first line of text, double-click **Remodeling** to select it.

7 On the Home tab, in the Clipboard group, click the **Copy button**.

8 On the Home tab, in the Clipboard group, click the **Clipboard Dialog Box Launcher**. The Clipboard pane opens with the text you just copied listed at the top of the task pane. Refer again to Exhibit 9-27.

9 In the third line of text in the document, click after *Suggestions*, and then press the **Enter key** twice.

10 In the Clipboard pane, click **Budget**. The text you copied from the Excel document appears in the Word document.

11 In the Clipboard pane title bar, click the **Close button**.

12 On the Quick Access Toolbar, click the **Save button**.

TIP: To delete an item from the Office Clipboard, point to the item, click the arrow that appears, and then click Delete.

End Activity

FYI
KEYBOARD SHORTCUTS FOR CUT, COPY, AND PASTE
When you cut, copy, and paste frequently, the keyboard shortcuts for the Cut, Copy, and Paste commands can save you time. To cut selected text or objects, press the Ctrl+X keys. To copy the selected text or objects, press the Ctrl+C keys. To paste the contents of the Clipboard, press the Ctrl+V keys.
Ctrl
X
V
C
© deepspacedave/Shutterstock.com; © pryzmat/Shutterstock.com

9-8 GETTING HELP

If you don't know how to perform a task or if you want more information about a feature, you can use the Tell me what you want to do box. First, click the Tell me what you want to do box on the ribbon in any of the Office applications, and then type key words to describe the topic you want help with. When you do this, a menu opens listing commands available in the application related to the key words you typed, as shown in Exhibit 9-28. If you want to use one of those commands, you can click it to execute it. If you want more information about the topic, click Get Help on "*key words*" to open the Word 2016 Help window. See Exhibit 9-29. To access all of the Help topics, your computer must be connected to the Internet.

EXHIBIT 9-29 WORD HELP WINDOW

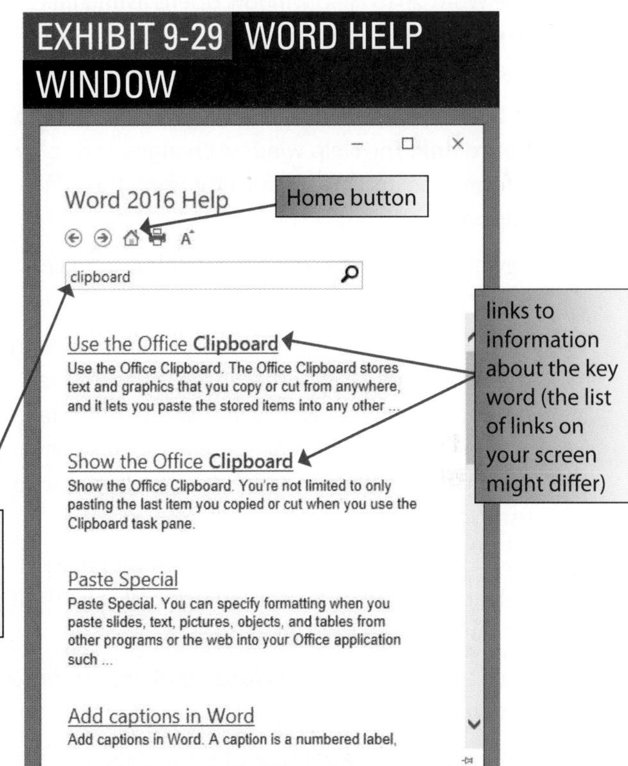

Begin Activity

Use Help.

1 In the Word window, on the ribbon, click the **Tell me what you want to do box.** The text *Tell me what you want to do* disappears and several topics appear below the box.

2 Type **clipboard.** The menu below the box changes to list commands on the ribbon associated with the word *clipboard*. Refer again to Exhibit 9-28.

3 On the menu, click **Clipboard.** The Clipboard pane opens.

EXHIBIT 9-28 WORD WINDOW WITH KEY WORD IN TELL ME WHAT YOU WANT TO DO BOX

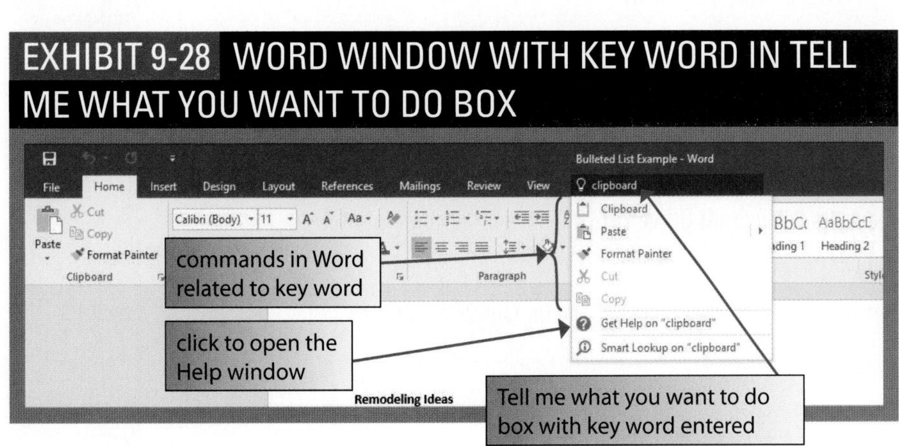

4 Close the **Clipboard pane**, click the **Tell me what you want to do box**, and then type **clipboard** again.

5 On the menu, click **Get Help on "clipboard"**. The Word 2016 Help window opens listing links to information about using the Clipboard. Refer again to Exhibit 9-29.

6 In the Help window, click the **Use the Office Clipboard link**. The Help window changes to display information and instructions for using the Office Clipboard.

7 Review the information in the window, scrolling down as needed.

8 When you are finished reading the information in the Help window, click the **Home button** at the top of the Word Help window. The Help start screen (or the Help Home screen) appears containing a list of links to topics that explain how to use Word features.

9 Click the **Get started link**. A list of topics related to learning how to get started using Word 2016 is displayed in the Help window.

10 Click the **What's new in Word 2016 link**, and then read the information in the Help window.

11 On the Word Help window title bar, click the **Close button** . The Word Help window closes.

End Activity

9-9 EXITING OFFICE APPLICATIONS

When you finish working with an application, you should exit it. You exit an application by closing the application window the same way you close any window on the desktop—by clicking its Close button on the title bar. As you saw when you closed the PowerPoint window, when only one file, or no file, is open, clicking the Close button closes the file and exits the application. If more than one file is open in an application, you will need to click the Close button in each file's window to exit the application.

Begin Activity

Exit Office applications.

1 On the Word window title bar, click the **Close button** . The file closes, and the application exits. The Excel window is the active window on the desktop.

2 Close the Clipboard pane.

3 On the Excel window title bar, click the **Close button** . Because you have not saved this file, a dialog box opens asking whether you want to save the changes you made to the workbook.

4 Click **Don't Save**. The file closes without being saved, and the Excel application exits.

End Activity

STUDY TOOLS 9

READY TO STUDY? IN THE BOOK, YOU CAN:

- ☐ Rip out the Chapter Review Card, which includes key terms and key chapter concepts.

ONLINE AT WWW.CENGAGEBRAIN.COM, YOU CAN:

- ☐ Review key concepts from the chapter in a short video.
- ☐ Explore common elements in Microsoft Office 2016 application windows with the interactive infographic.
- ☐ Practice what you've learned with more Practice It and On Your Own exercises.
- ☐ Prepare for tests with quizzes.
- ☐ Review the key terms with flashcards.

QUIZ YOURSELF

1. What is Backstage view?
2. How is the ribbon organized?
3. What is an object?
4. What is a text box?
5. What is a toggle button?
6. What is Live Preview?
7. What is a dialog box?
8. What is a task pane?
9. When does the Mini toolbar appear?
10. How do you undo your most recent action?
11. Why do you need to save files that you create in Office applications?
12. How do you close a file without exiting the application?
13. Describe the difference between the system Clipboard and the Office Clipboard.
14. What happens when you click the Tell me what you want to do box and then type key words?
15. How do you exit an Office application?

PRACTICE IT

Practice It 9-1

1. Start Word, start Excel, and then start PowerPoint, opening a new, blank file in each application.
2. Make Excel the active application, and then make the Data tab the active tab.
3. Make PowerPoint the active application, and then click directly on the border of the box around *Click to add subtitle*. Make the Drawing Tools Format tab the active tab on the ribbon. Make the Drawing Tools Format tab disappear from the ribbon.
4. In the PowerPoint window, click in the box labeled *Click to add title*, and then type your first and last name.
5. Select your first name, and then on the Home tab, in the Font group, click the Bold button.
6. On the Home tab, in the Font group, use the ScreenTips to identify the Font Color button, and then click the Font Color button arrow to open the Font Color gallery.
7. Use Live Preview to preview several colors, and then change the color of the selected text to Green (under Standard Colors).
8. In the Font group, click the Font Dialog Box Launcher to open the Font dialog box with the Font tab selected. Click the Font style arrow, and then click Bold Italic. Click after 60 in the Size box, press the Backspace key twice to delete the value, and then type **40**. In the Effects section, select the All Caps check box. Click OK.
9. Select your whole name, and then copy it to the Clipboard.
10. Make Word the active application. Paste your name from the Clipboard. (Note that your name will be pasted as all black text, smaller than in the PowerPoint window, and your first name will not be in all capital letters.)
11. Press the Enter key, type your street address, press the Enter key, and then type your city, state, and ZIP code. Use the mouse to select your name, and then use the Underline button on the Mini toolbar to underline the line of text containing your name. Use the Strikethrough button in the Font group on the Home tab to draw a line through your name.
12. Undo the actions to strikethrough your name, and make it underlined. Redo the underline action.
13. Scroll down to the bottom of the page in the Word window.
14. Save the Word file to the drive and folder where you are storing your files using the file name **My Info**.
15. Close the My Info file without exiting Word, and then re-open the **My Info** file.
16. Open the Clipboard pane. (Your name, which you copied from the PowerPoint file, is on the Office Clipboard.) Select the lines in the document containing your street and city, state, and ZIP code, and then copy those lines to the Clipboard.
17. Make Excel the active application, and then open the Clipboard pane in Excel. Paste your name that you copied from the PowerPoint file. (Note that

your name will look like it did in the PowerPoint file.) Press the Down Arrow key, and then paste the address information you copied from the Word document. Close the Clipboard pane.

18. Use the Zoom slider in Excel to zoom to 150%. Make the View tab the active tab, and then in the Zoom group, click the 100% button.
19. Save the Excel file as **Excel Contact Info** in the location where you are saving your files.
20. Make PowerPoint the active application. Save the PowerPoint file to the location where you are storing your files using the file name **My Name**.
21. Use the Tell me what you want to do box to search for commands and topics that contain the word **themes**. Open the PowerPoint 2016 Help window and read the Help topic "Add color and design to my slides with themes." Close the Help window.
22. Exit PowerPoint, saving changes if asked. Close the Clipboard pane in the Word window, and then exit Word, saving changes if prompted. Exit Excel.

Practice It 9-2

1. Start Excel. Open the data file named **Budget** located in the Chapter 9\Practice It folder. (You should have data files if you completed the steps in Chapter 7. If you do not have data files, you can get them from your instructor who may include them in the Assignment Calendar of CMPTR Online or provide them to you another way.)
2. Use a button in the Font group on the Home tab to make the text in the top box bold.
3. Use a button in the Font group on the Home tab to add a fill color of Gray 50% – Accent 3 to the top box.
4. Click in the first white box (to the right of "2"), type your name, and then press the Enter key. Save the changed file as **Budget Revised** to the drive and folder where you are storing your files.
5. In the chart, click a blank area to the right of the bars to select the chart, and then copy it to the Clipboard.
6. Start Word. Open the data file named **Stockholder** located in the Chapter 9\Practice It folder.
7. Replace the name *Mark Sullivan* in the signature with your name, and then save the file as **Stockholder Letter** to the drive and folder where you are storing your files.
8. Scroll down so you can see the large space between the body of the letter and the signature block, and then click in the middle of this space.
9. Paste the chart you copied. (Note that it will be pasted with orange and blue bars.)
10. Click the chart to select it. Make the Chart Tools Design tab the active tab. In the Chart Styles group, click the More button to display all of the chart styles, point to several styles to see the Live Preview, and then click Style 8.
11. Make the Layout tab the active tab. In the Page Setup group, click the Margins button, and then click Wide to change the margins.
12. In the Page Setup group, click the Dialog Box Launcher to open the Page Setup dialog box. Make the Layout tab the active tab, and then use the Vertical alignment box in the Page section to change the vertical alignment to centered.
13. Close the Stockholder Letter file without closing Word, saving changes when asked.
14. Exit both open applications.

ON YOUR OWN

On Your Own 9-1

1. Open the PowerPoint data file named **Music** located in the Chapter 9\On Your Own folder. (You should have data files if you completed the steps in Chapter 7. If you do not have data files, you can get them from your instructor who may include them in the Assignment Calendar of CMPTR Online or provide them to you another way.)
2. Click after "Categories" in the title, type --, and then type your name. Save the file as **Music Data** to the drive and folder where you are storing your files.
3. Click anywhere on the bulleted list, and then click directly on top of the dotted-line border.
4. Use the Font button in the Font group on the Home tab to change the font to Bodoni MT Black.
5. Use the Text Shadow button in the Font group on the Home tab to add a shadow effect to the text.
6. Copy the selected box.
7. Open a new Word document, and then paste the text box you copied into the document.
8. Use the Bullets gallery to change the bullet symbols to squares.

9. Click after the word Rock, press the Enter key, and then type your name. Remove the bullet symbol from the line containing your name.
10. Use the appropriate button on the Design tab to change the page color to Orange, Accent 2, Lighter 80%. (Note that the page color formatting only appears when you are looking at the document on a computer. It will not appear if you print the document.)
11. Save the file as **Music List** to the drive and folder where you are storing your files.
12. Exit Word and PowerPoint.

CAPSTONE

WINDOWS 10 AND OFFICE 2016: ORGANIZE YOUR FILES

1. Develop an organization strategy for storing the files you create and work with. Consider various folder and subfolder structures, and evaluate which one best fits your needs. Plan your approach for naming the files and folders so that you can easily remember their purposes.
2. Use Word to record your plan for organizing the files on your computer.
   a. List the types of files stored on your computer.
   b. Determine where to store the files: on your hard drive or on removable media.
   c. Sketch the folders and subfolders you will use to manage your files. If you choose a hard drive as your storage medium, plan to store your work files and folders in a subfolder of the Documents folder.
   d. Save the file with an appropriate file name, and then close it.
3. Implement your organization strategy:
   a. Create or rename the main and subfolders you want to use for your files.
   b. Move and copy files to the appropriate folders; rename and delete files as necessary.
4. Create a backup copy of your work files by creating a compressed file of the folders and files, and then copying the compressed file to a removable medium, such as a USB flash drive.
5. Open Edge, and then search for information about backing up your files to the cloud using an online backup service such as Carbonite or Mozy. Decide which service you might use.
6. In the Word document you created, add a description of the service you would choose and explain why.

Office Online

SAVING A FILE TO ONEDRIVE

OneDrive is online storage provided by Microsoft. All you need to access your workspace on OneDrive is a Microsoft account. To obtain a Microsoft account, go to **account.live.com**, click the Sign up now link (or something similar), and fill in the requested information. You can also click the Sign in link in the upper-right corner of any Office application or open the Save As screen in Backstage view, click OneDrive, and then click the Sign up button. When you sign up, you can use an existing email address or you can sign up for a new Outlook.com or Hotmail.com email address.

When you are working in Word, Excel, and PowerPoint and you are signed into your Microsoft account, the OneDrive command on the Save As screen in Backstage view includes the email address associated with your Microsoft account below it. Click OneDrive, and then click Browse to open the Save As dialog box with the current location as your OneDrive. Exhibit 1 shows the Save As dialog box open on the Save As screen in Backstage view in Word. (Note that you cannot save to OneDrive from Backstage view in Access.) You can also access your OneDrive by clicking OneDrive in the navigation bar in a File Explorer window or by opening a browser window, going to **www.onedrive.com**, and signing in to your Microsoft account from that Web page. On your OneDrive page, you can click the Upload button at the top to choose a file to upload from your computer.

EXHIBIT 1 SAVE AS DIALOG BOX OPEN ON THE SAVE AS SCREEN IN BACKSTAGE VIEW IN WORD

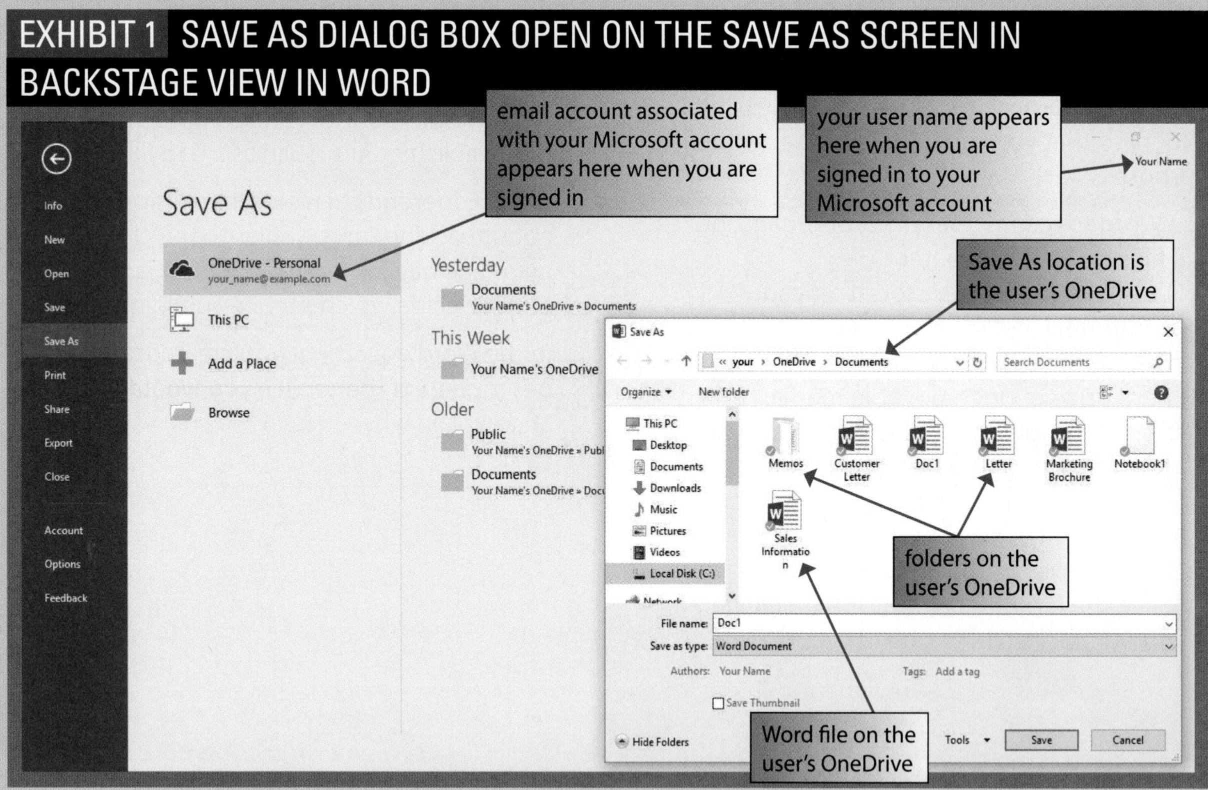

Important Note: OneDrive and Office Online are dynamic Web pages and might change over time, including the way they are organized and how actions are performed. The information provided here was accurate at the time this book was published.

Each of the tiles in your OneDrive window represents a file or folder. See Exhibit 2. You can choose to share access to the files and folders on your OneDrive. If you do, the people with whom you share the folder can access, view, and download the files stored in those folders. To share a file or folder, point to it to display a round check box in the upper-right corner, and then click the round check box to insert a check mark, indicating that the file or folder is selected. If you are sharing a folder, you can also click the folder tile to open the folder, and then on the blue bar at the top, click the Share button. A dialog box opens in which you enter the email addresses of the people with whom you want to share the file or folder. See Exhibit 3. After you click Share in the dialog box, a message containing a link to the file or folder is sent to the people whose email addresses you entered.

EXHIBIT 2 FOLDERS AND FILES ON A USER'S ONEDRIVE IN A BROWSER WINDOW

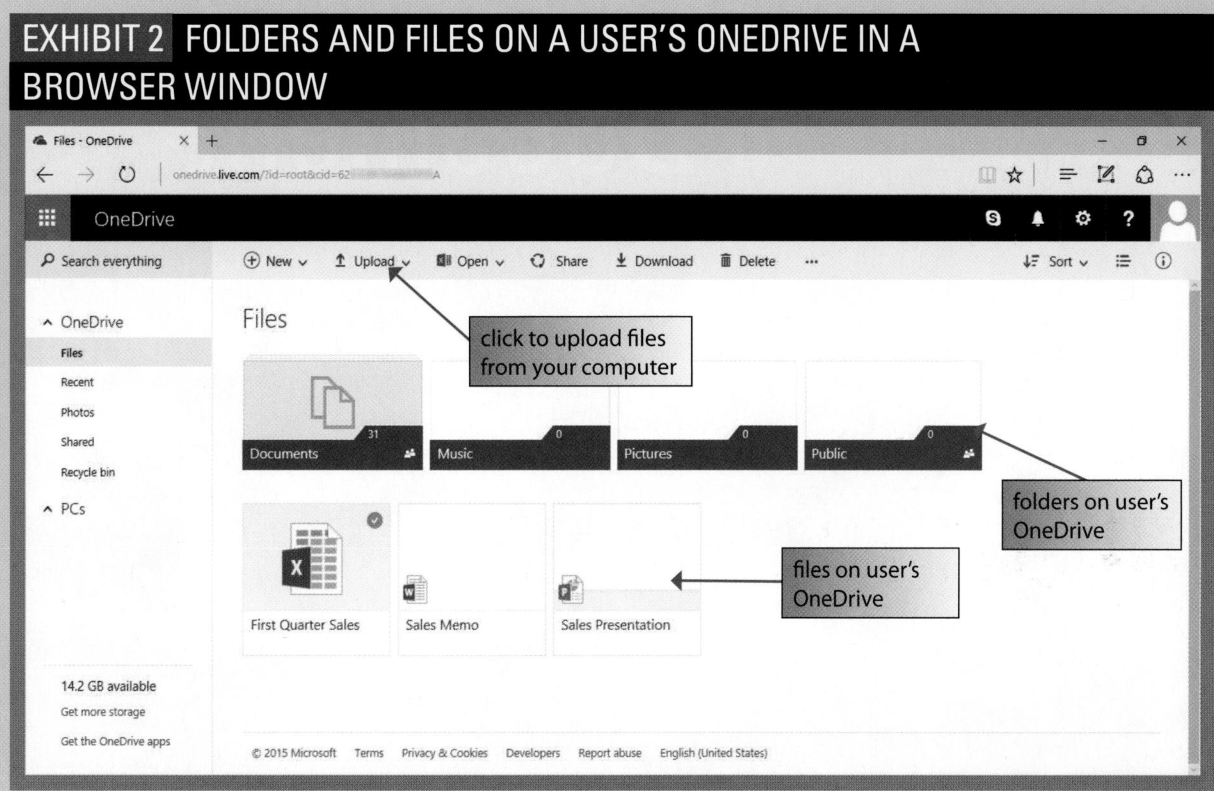

The people you send the link to do not need to be signed in to their Microsoft accounts to access your OneDrive folder, although you can force them to by clicking the Recipients can edit link in the Share dialog box, clicking the Recipients don't need a Microsoft account box, and then clicking Recipients need to sign in with a Microsoft account.

EXHIBIT 3 SHARING A FILE OR FOLDER ON A ONEDRIVE

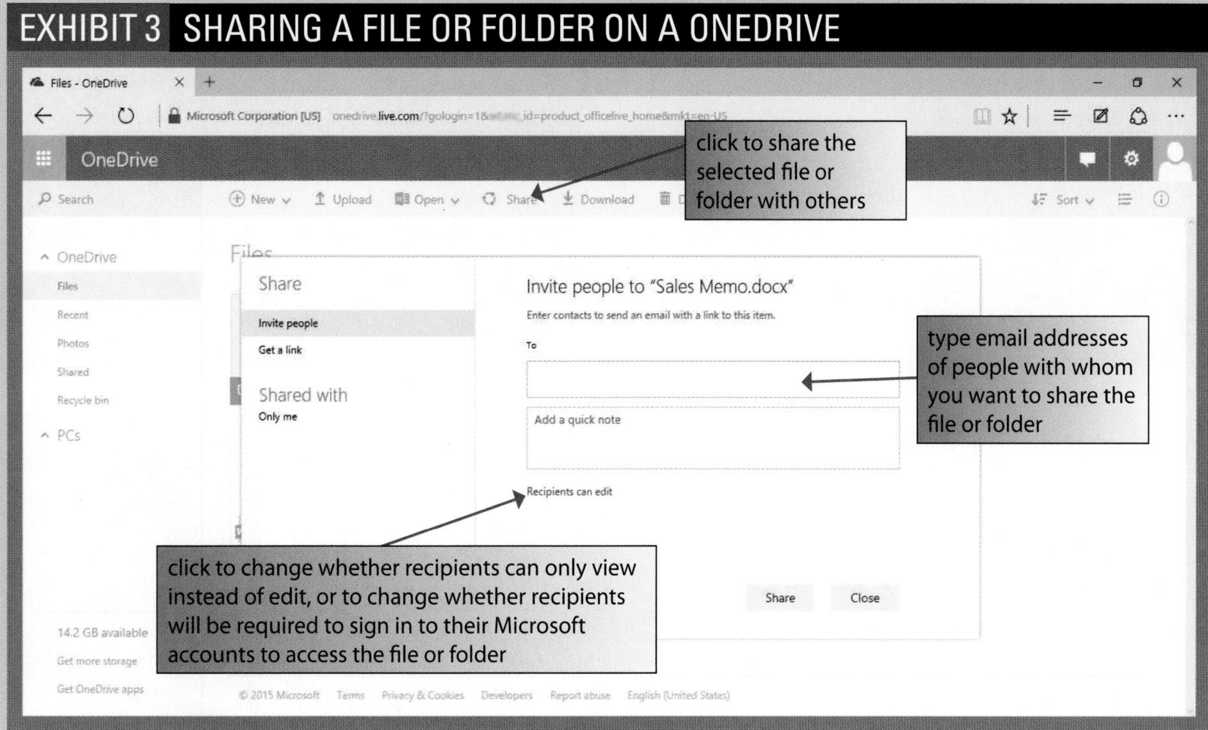

Part 6
WORD 2016

10 | Creating a Document

© Cultura/Frank van Delft/Getty Images

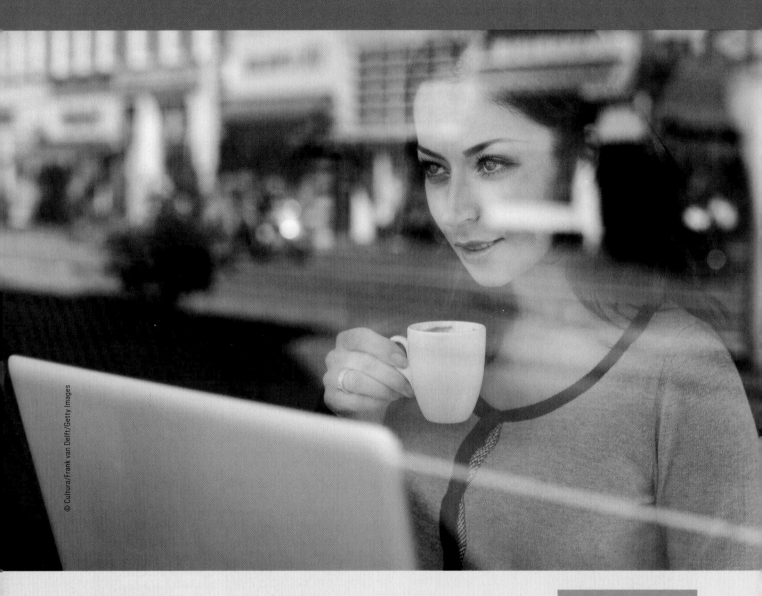

LEARNING OBJECTIVES After studying the material in this chapter, you will be able to:

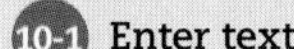
10-1 Enter text

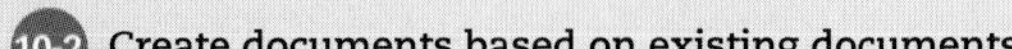
10-2 Create documents based on existing documents

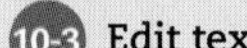
10-3 Edit text

10-4 Switch to another open document in Word

10-5 Format text

10-6 Format paragraphs

10-7 Copy formats

10-8 Check spelling and grammar

10-9 Preview and print documents

After finishing this chapter, go to **PAGE 306** for **STUDY TOOLS**.

10-1 ENTERING TEXT

Microsoft Word 2016 (or simply **Word**) is a word processing program used to enter, edit, and change the appearance of text. Using Word, you can create all types of documents and make them attractive and easy to read.

When you work in Word, you can customize the workspace to suit your work style. One thing you can do is show or hide nonprinting characters in your documents. **Nonprinting characters** are characters that do not print and that control the way the document looks. For example, the ¶ character marks the end of a paragraph, and the • character marks the space between words. It is helpful to display nonprinting characters so you can see whether you have typed an extra space, ended a paragraph, and so on.

The first time you start Word, nonprinting characters are not displayed. To show them, you click the Show/Hide ¶ button in the Paragraph group on the Home tab. If you exit Word and nonprinting characters are displayed, they will appear again the next time you start Word. To hide nonprinting characters, click the Show/Hide ¶ button to toggle it off.

Another helpful tool in Word is the ruler. To display a horizontal ruler along the top of the workspace and a vertical ruler along the left side of the workspace, select the Ruler check box in the Show group on the View tab.

Figures of documents in the Word window in this book show the document window maximized, rulers visible, the zoom level set to 120% (unless specified otherwise), and with nonprinting characters displayed, as shown in Exhibit 10-1.

Begin Activity

Start Word and set up the document window.

1. Start **Word**. Word starts, and the Recent screen appears in Backstage view.
2. Click the **Blank document tile**. A new blank document appears in the Word window.
3. If the Word program window is not maximized, click the **Maximize button** ☐.
4. If the rulers are not displayed along the top and left sides of the window, click the **View tab** on the ribbon. In the Show group, click the **Ruler check box** to select it.

TIP: To create a new blank document when Word is running, click the File tab, click New in the navigation bar, and then click Blank document in the right pane.

5. On the status bar, use the **Zoom slider** and the **Zoom in** + and **Zoom out** – buttons to change the zoom percentage to **120%**.
6. On the ribbon, click the **Home tab**, if necessary. In the Paragraph group, click the **Show/Hide ¶ button** ¶ if it is not already selected. (When it is selected, it is shaded (¶). Compare your screen to Exhibit 10-1.

End Activity

Now you need to save the document with a name. You will be creating a letter.

Begin Activity

Save a document for the first time.

1. On the Quick Access Toolbar, click the **Save button** 💾. Because this is the first time this document is being saved, the Save As screen opens in Backstage view.
2. Click **Browse**. The Save As dialog box opens with the temporary file name selected in the File name box.
3. Type **Letter** to replace the temporary file name in the File name box.
4. Navigate to the drive and folder where you are saving the files you create as you complete the steps in this book.
5. Click **Save**. The dialog box closes, and the file name *Letter* appears in the title bar of the Word window.

End Activity

10-1a Entering Text and Correcting Errors as You Type

To enter text in a Word document, simply start typing. The characters you type appear at the insertion point. As you type, the text wraps to new lines as needed to accommodate the text. If you make errors as you type, you can press the Backspace key, which deletes the characters and spaces to the left of the insertion point one at a time. You can also press the Delete key, which deletes characters to the right of the insertion point one at a time.

Microsoft Word 2016 (Word) Application software used to create and format documents.

nonprinting character A character that does not print and that controls the format of a document.

EXHIBIT 10-1 WORD WINDOW WITH RULERS AND NONPRINTING CHARACTERS DISPLAYED AT 120% ZOOM

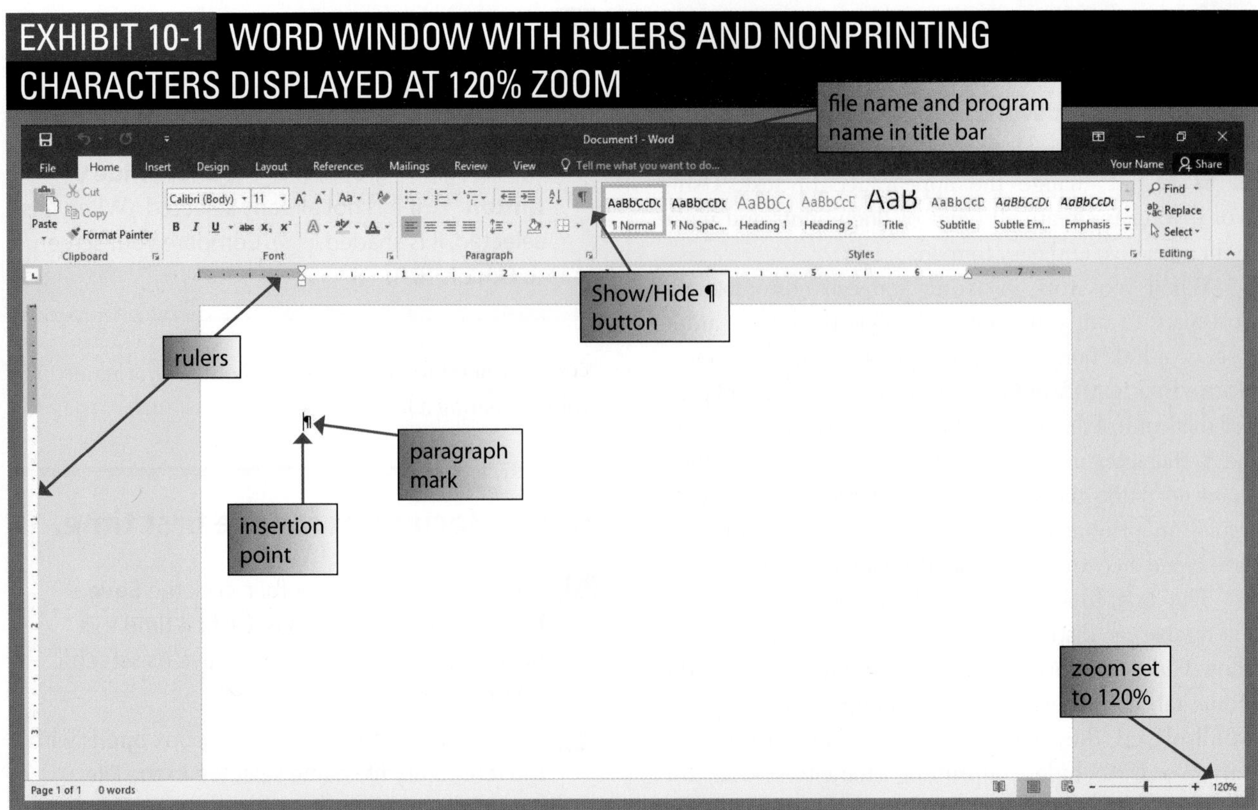

When you press the Enter key, a new paragraph is created. In Word, a "paragraph" can be several lines, one line, a single word, or blank (or empty). For example, the main heading for this section, "10-1 Entering Text," would be a paragraph in a Word document.

SAVE YOUR FILES

Remember to click the **Save button** on the Quick Access Toolbar to save changes to your files as you complete the steps in this book. Also, be sure to save frequently as you go.

Begin Activity

Enter text and correct errors as you type.

1 Move the **pointer** into the workspace. The pointer changes to I. Depending on exactly where the pointer is positioned in the workspace, you might see several horizontal lines next to it.

2 Type **21490 North Parker Ave.** (including the period). The text you typed appears on the screen, and the paragraph mark moves to the right as you type.

3 Press the **Backspace** key four times. The four characters to the left of the insertion point, *Ave.*, are deleted.

4 Type **St.** (including the period).

5 Press the **Left Arrow key** six times. The insertion point moves six characters to the left and is positioned between the *k* and the *e* in *Parker*.

6 Press the **Delete key** twice. The two characters to the right of the insertion point are deleted, and the street address is now *21490 North Park St.*

7 Click after **St.** The insertion point appears at the end of the line.

8 Press the **Enter key**. The insertion point moves to a new line, creating a new paragraph.

9 Type **Chicago, IL 60601** and then press the **Enter key**. A third paragraph is created.

End Activity

AutoComplete A feature that automatically inserts dates and other regularly used items.

10-1b Inserting a Date with AutoComplete

When you insert dates, you can take advantage of **AutoComplete**, a feature that automatically inserts

FYI MOVING THE INSERTION POINT

The insertion point indicates where text will be inserted in the document. You can click anywhere in a document to place the insertion point at the location where you clicked. You can also use the keyboard to move the insertion point in the document, which may be faster when your hands are already on the keyboard. Pressing the arrow keys moves the insertion point one character in the direction of the arrow key you pressed. If you combine other keys with the arrow keys, you can move the insertion point quickly to different locations. The table below summarizes the most common keystrokes for moving the insertion point in a document.

To move insertion point	Press
Left or right one character at a time	Left Arrow key or Right Arrow key
Up or down one line at a time	Up Arrow key or Down Arrow key
Left or right one word at a time	Ctrl+Left Arrow keys or Ctrl+Right Arrow keys
Up or down one paragraph at a time	Ctrl+Up Arrow keys or Ctrl+Down Arrow keys
To the beginning or to the end of the current line	Home key or End key
To the beginning or to the end of the document	Ctrl+Home keys or Ctrl+End keys
To the previous screen or to the next screen	Page Up key or Page Down key
To the top or to the bottom of the document window	Alt+Ctrl+Page Up keys or Alt+Ctrl+Page Down keys

dates and other regularly used items. To insert the date with AutoComplete, type the first four characters of any month whose name contains more than five letters. A ScreenTip appears, telling you that you can press the Enter key to insert the month name into the document. See Exhibit 10-2. If you want to type something other than the month name suggested in the ScreenTip, or if you don't want to use the AutoComplete feature, simply continue typing and the ScreenTip will disappear. If you type the current month, another ScreenTip appears after you press the Spacebar, instructing you to press the Enter key to insert the current date in the form MMMM dd, yyyy (for example, October 12, 2017). You can press Enter to accept the AutoComplete entry, or you can type any text you want to override the AutoComplete suggestion.

Begin Activity

Insert the date with AutoComplete.

1 Type **Octo** (the first four letters of October). A ScreenTip appears above the letters suggesting *October* as the complete word. Refer to Exhibit 10-2.

EXHIBIT 10-2 AUTOCOMPLETE SUGGESTION FOR A MONTH NAME

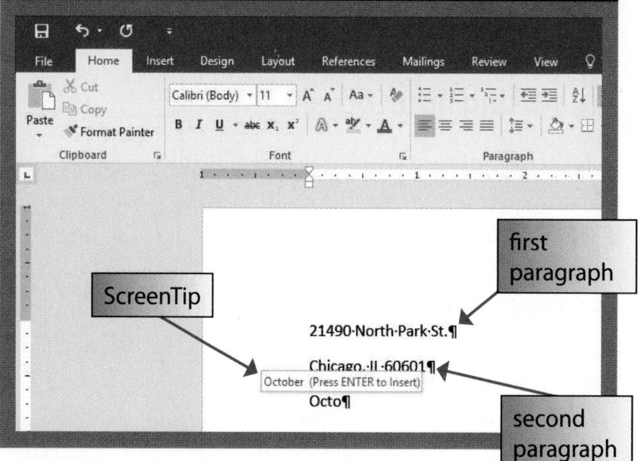

2 Press the **Enter key**. The rest of the word *October* is inserted in the document.

3 Press the **Spacebar**. If the current month is October, another ScreenTip appears displaying the current date.

4 Type **12, 2017**.

End Activity

FYI **INSERTING THE CURRENT DATE**

You can quickly insert the current date into a document in a variety of formats. Position the insertion point in the location where you want to insert the current date. Click the Insert tab. In the Text group, click the Date & Time button to open the Date and Time dialog box. Click one of the date formats in the Available formats box. If you want the current date to appear every time you open the document, select the Update automatically check box. If you want the date to remain unchanged, deselect the Update automatically check box. Click OK. The current date is inserted in the format you specified.

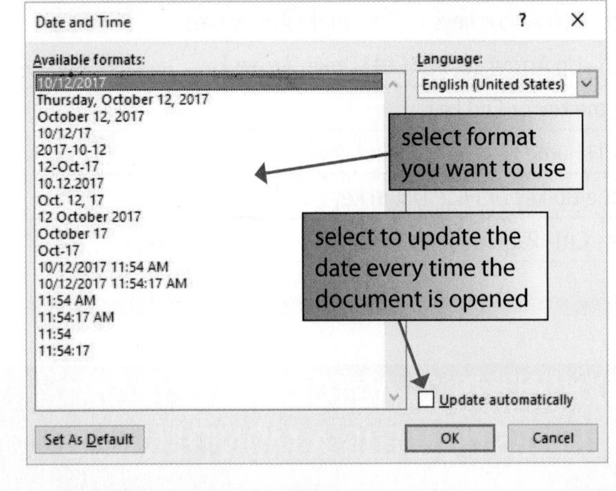

10-1c Using AutoCorrect

The **AutoCorrect** feature automatically corrects certain misspelled words and typing errors. For example, if you type *teh* instead of *the*, as soon as you press the Spacebar or the Enter key, AutoCorrect changes it to *the*. AutoCorrect also fixes capitalization errors, including changing the first character in the first word of a sentence to an uppercase letter.

The AutoCorrect feature also automatically converts some standard characters into symbols as you type. For example, AutoCorrect changes (c) to the standard copyright symbol © as soon as you type the closing parenthesis. Exhibit 10-3 lists some of the other character combinations that AutoCorrect converts to symbols.

AutoCorrect A feature that automatically corrects certain misspelled words and typing errors and changes some characters into symbols.

EXHIBIT 10-3 COMMON SYMBOLS INSERTED WITH AUTOCORRECT

To insert	Type	AutoCorrect converts to
em dash	word--word	word—word
smiley	:) or :-)	☺
copyright symbol	(c)	©
trademark symbol	(tm)	™
registered trademark symbol	(r)	®
ordinal numbers	1st, 2nd, 3rd, etc.	1st, 2nd, 3rd, etc.
fractions	1/2, 1/4	½, ¼
arrows	--> or <--	→ or ←

Begin Activity

Use AutoCorrect.

1. With the insertion point positioned after 2017, press the **Enter key** twice, and then type **DEar**. Make sure you type this word with the two uppercase letters as shown here.
2. Press the **Spacebar**. The incorrect capitalization is automatically corrected.
3. Type **Ms. Gutierrez:** and then press the **Enter key**.
4. Type **from** and then press the **Spacebar**. The capitalization of the first word in the sentence is corrected.
5. Type **the information on your Web site, i** and then press the **Spacebar**. The capitalization of the word *I* is corrected. In the next step, watch as AutoCorrect corrects the misspelled word *you* when you press the Spacebar.
6. Type **understand that yuo** and then press the **Spacebar**. The misspelled word automatically corrects to *you*.
7. Type **are looking for a Marketing Assistant. I gained experience working at Zisk Media Corporation** (do not type a period).
8. Type **(r)**. As soon as you type the closing parenthesis, the characters *(r)* change to the registered trademark symbol ®, and the symbol is changed to a superscript.
9. Type **.** (a period) to complete the sentence. Compare your screen to Exhibit 10-4.

End Activity

EXHIBIT 10-4 AUTOCORRECTED TEXT IN DOCUMENT

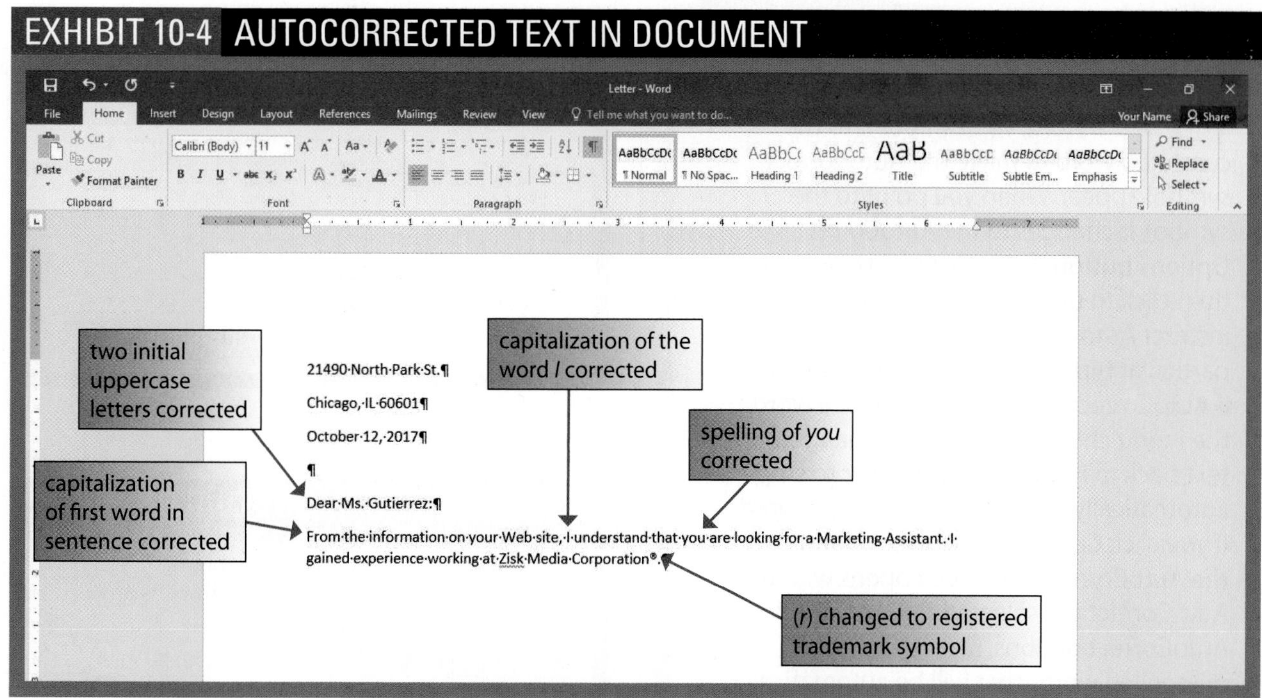

AutoCorrect also formats Web site addresses that start with *http* and *www* and email addresses as hyperlinks, or links. To indicate that the text is a link, the text is changed to a color and is underlined. When text is formatted as a link, you can click it to open your browser and go to that Web page or open a new email message addressed to the email address you clicked. You rarely want to retain link formatting in printed documents. To remove the link formatting, you right-click the link to display a shortcut menu that includes commands for working with the link. See Exhibit 10-5. Click Remove Hyperlink on the shortcut menu to remove the link formatting.

EXHIBIT 10-5 REMOVING LINK FORMATTING

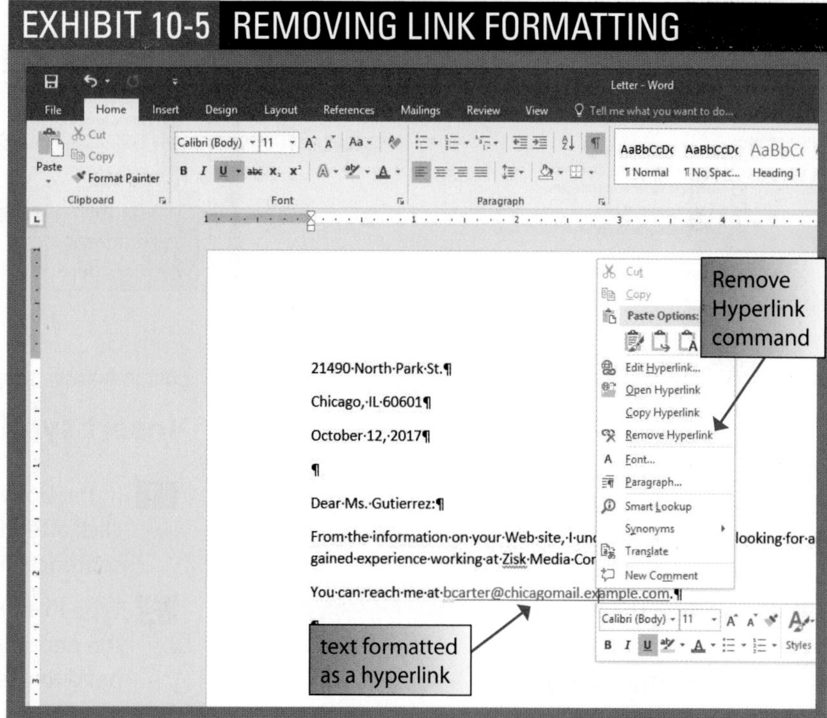

Begin Activity

Format text as a link and remove the link.

1 Press the **Enter key**, type **You can reach me at bcarter@chicagomail.example.com.** and then press the **Enter key**. AutoCorrect changes the email address you typed to blue and underlined and changes it to a hyperlink.

2 Right-click the **hyperlink**. Refer to Exhibit 10-5.

3 On the shortcut menu, click **Remove Hyperlink**. The text is changed to ordinary black text and is no longer a hyperlink.

End Activity

FYI **CUSTOMIZING AUTOCORRECT** When AutoCorrect changes a word, you can point to the corrected word to make the AutoCorrect symbol appear. When you point to the symbol, it changes to the AutoCorrect Options button, which you can then click to undo the AutoCorrection or instruct AutoCorrect to stop making that particular type of correction. For example, if AutoCorrect fixed the spelling of a word, the menu choices would be to change the text back to its original spelling or to stop automatically correcting that specific word. If you click Control AutoCorrect Options, the AutoCorrect dialog box opens with the AutoCorrect tab selected. You can deselect AutoCorrect options, review the list of misspelled words that will be automatically corrected, or add words that you frequently misspell to the list.

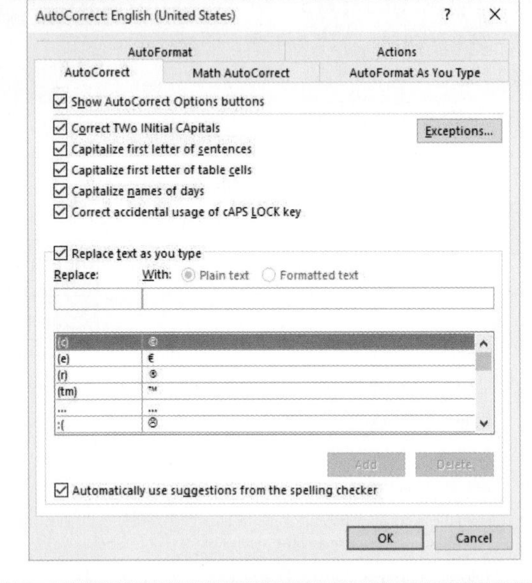

10-1d Inserting Symbols

Sometimes you need to insert a character or symbol that is not automatically entered with AutoCorrect. To do this, click the Symbol button in the Symbols group on the Insert tab to display the Symbol gallery, as shown in Exhibit 10-6. If the symbol you want to use appears in the Symbol gallery, simply click it to insert it. If the symbol doesn't appear there, click More Symbols to open the Symbol dialog box, shown in Exhibit 10-7, and then choose the symbol you want in there.

EXHIBIT 10-6 SYMBOL GALLERY

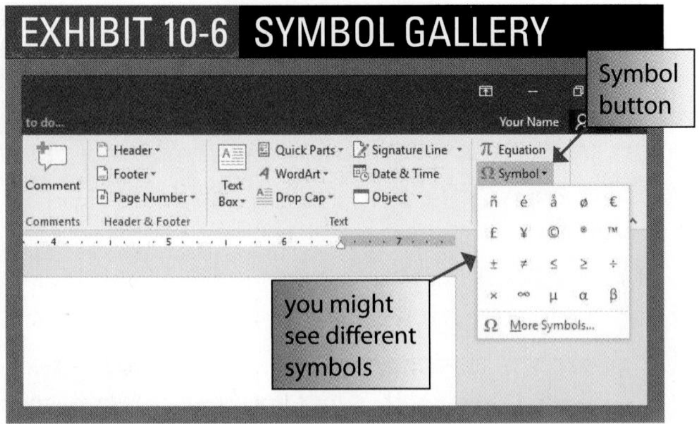

EXHIBIT 10-7 SYMBOL DIALOG BOX

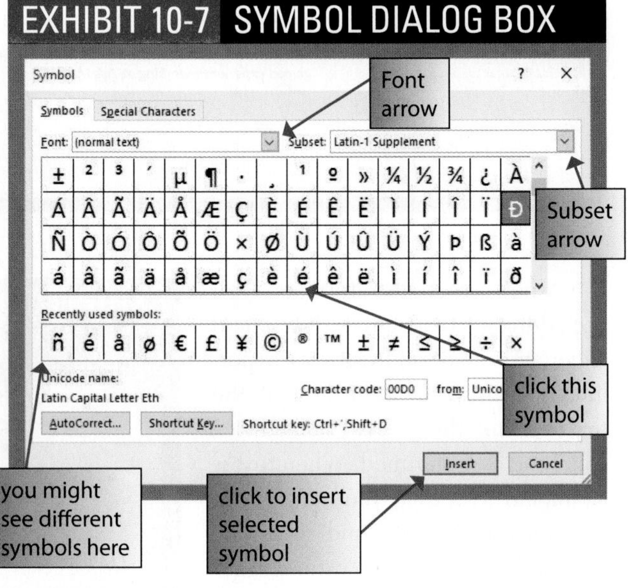

Begin Activity

Insert symbols.

1. In the body of the letter, in the first paragraph, click after the period at the end of the second sentence (after ®), and then press the **Spacebar**.
2. Type **I've enclosed a copy of my r**. (Do not type the period.) To finish typing the word *résumé*, you need to use the Symbol dialog box.
3. On the ribbon, click the **Insert tab**. In the Symbols group, click the **Symbol button**. The Symbol gallery opens. Refer back to Exhibit 10-6.
4. Below the gallery, click **More Symbols**. The Symbol dialog box opens. Refer back to Exhibit 10-7. First you'll examine the types of symbols you can insert.
5. Scroll through the list of symbols to see the types of symbols you can insert.

6 Click the **Font arrow**, scroll to the bottom of the list, and then click **Wingdings**. The symbols change to display the symbols in the Wingdings font.

7 Click the **Special Characters tab**. A list of special characters appears, including the paragraph symbol. Now you'll insert the correct character.

8 Click the **Symbols tab**, click the **Font arrow**, scroll to the top of the Font list, and then click **(normal text)**.

9 Click the **Subset arrow**, scroll up, and then click **Latin-1 Supplement**. The list scrolls to display the first row in the Latin-1 Supplement subset.

10 Click the **down scroll arrow** three times to scroll the list three rows. Lowercase characters appear in the bottom row. Refer back to Exhibit 10-7.

11 In the last row of symbols, click the **é character**, and then click **Insert**. The symbol is inserted in the document.

PROBLEM? If the é symbol does not appear, your dialog box might have been resized. Use Exhibit 10-7 as a guide to help you locate the symbol.

12 In the dialog box, click **Close**.

13 Type **sum**.

14 On the Insert tab, in the Symbols group, click the **Symbol button**. The é symbol appears as the first symbol in the gallery now.

15 In the gallery, click the **é symbol**. The gallery closes, and the symbol is inserted in the document.

16 Type a **period**. The last sentence in the first paragraph is now *I've enclosed a copy of my résumé*.

17 Click the blank paragraph at the end of the document, type your name, and then save the document.

18 Click the **File tab**, and then click **Close** in the navigation bar to close the document. Word is still open.

End Activity

10-2 CREATING DOCUMENTS BASED ON EXISTING DOCUMENTS

When you create a new document, you can start with a new blank document as you did when you started typing the letter, or you can start with an existing document. For example, if you saved and closed a document, you can re-open that document and continue working on it. If you simply open a document, make changes, and then save the document, the original document is modified. If you want the original document to remain unchanged, you can create a copy of the original document. One way to do this is to open the original document, and then use the Save As command to save it with a new name.

Begin Activity

Open documents and save copies with new names.

1 Click the **File tab**. The Open screen in Backstage view appears.

TIP: To use a document in the Recent Documents list on the Open screen, click it to open it, or right-click it, and then click Open a copy on the shortcut menu.

2 Click **Browse** to display the Open dialog box.

3 Navigate to the **Chapter 10\Chapter folder** included with the data files. (If you do not have the data files, you can get them from your instructor who may include them in the Assignment Calendar on CMPTR Online or provide them to you another way.)

4 Click **Resume**, and then click **Open**. The Resume document opens in the Word window.

5 Click the **File tab**, and then click **Save As** in the navigation pane. The Save As screen appears in Backstage view.

6 Click **Browse** to open the Save As dialog box. The current folder is Chapter 10\Chapter, and the file name Resume is selected in the File name box.

7 Type **Resume Final** in the File name box.

8 If necessary, navigate to the drive and folder where you are saving the files you create as you work through these steps.

9 Click **Save**. The dialog box closes, and a copy of the Resume document is saved with the name Resume Final.

10 Open the document **Letter2** located in the **Chapter 10\Chapter folder** included with the data files.

TIP: Remember to save periodically as you work through the steps in this chapter.

11 Save Letter2 as **Cover Letter** in the drive and folder where you are saving the files you create as you work through these steps.

End Activity

10-3 EDITING TEXT

One of the fundamental features of a word processor is the ability to easily edit text without retyping an entire document. When you edit a document, you can type additional text in the document, delete existing text from the document, replace text already in the document, and copy or move text within the document.

10-3a Replacing Selected Text

To replace existing text, you select the text you no longer want and then start typing. The text you type replaces the selected text, no matter how much text is selected. There is no need to press the Delete key to remove the selected text first.

Begin Activity

Replace selected text.

1 In the Cover Letter document, in the body of the letter, in the first sentence in the first paragraph, click before the word *From*, but do not release the mouse button.

2 Drag across the text **From the information on your Web site, I understand** and then release the **mouse button**. The text you dragged across is selected.

3 Type **L**. The selected text is replaced with the character you typed.

4 Type **arry Cohen told me**. The first sentence now reads *Larry Cohen told me that you are looking for an assistant.*

End Activity

drag and drop A technique for moving or copying selected text or objects to a new location.

10-3b Using Drag and Drop

You learned how to use the Cut, Copy, and Paste commands in Chapter 9. Another technique for moving and copying text is drag and drop. **Drag and drop** means to select text and then drag the selected text to a new location. As you drag, a vertical line follows the pointer, indicating where the selected text will be placed when you release the mouse button. See Exhibit 10-8. Unlike the Cut or Copy commands, when you use drag and drop, the text you drag is not placed on the Clipboard. If you want to paste the text you dragged to another location, you need to drag it again or use the Cut or Copy command.

EXHIBIT 10-8 TEXT BEING MOVED USING DRAG AND DROP

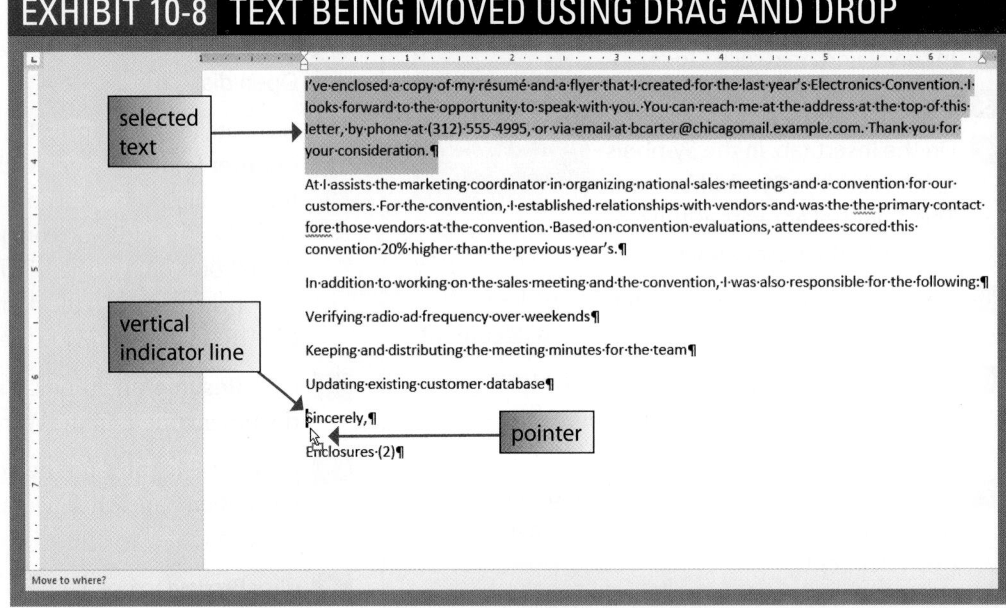

Begin Activity

Use drag and drop to move text.

1 Scroll the document until you can see both the second paragraph in the body of the letter and the closing *Sincerely* at the end of the letter.

2 In the body of the letter, move the **pointer** to the left of the first line of the second paragraph so that the pointer changes to .

3 Press and hold the **mouse button**. The first line in the second paragraph is selected.

4 Still pressing the mouse button, drag down until all four lines in the second paragraph are selected, and then release the **mouse button**.

5 Point to the **selected text** so that the pointer changes to .

6 Press and hold the **mouse button**, and then move the pointer slightly in any direction (but do not release the mouse button). The pointer changes to and a dotted vertical line appears within the selected text.

7 Drag down to the closing until the vertical line is positioned before the word *Sincerely*. Refer back to Exhibit 10-8. This shows that the selected text will be positioned before the word *Sincerely*.

8 Release the **mouse button**. The selected paragraph is now the last paragraph in the body of the letter.

9 In the body of the letter, in the third sentence in the first paragraph, select **Zisk Media Corporation**.

10 Point to the **selected text**, press and hold the **Ctrl key**, press and hold the **mouse button**, and then move the pointer slightly. The pointer changes to to indicate that the text you are dragging is being copied instead of moved.

11 Drag the **selected text** down to the beginning of the second paragraph in the body of the letter until the vertical indicator line appears between the words *At* and *I*. Release the **mouse button**, and then release the **Ctrl key**. The text you copied, *Zisk Media Corporation*, appears after the word *At*.

> **PROBLEM?**
> If the selected text moves instead of copies, you released the Ctrl key before the mouse button. Undo your last action, then repeat Steps 10 and 11.

12 In the second paragraph, click to the right of *Corporation*, and then type **,** (a comma). The beginning of the second paragraph is now *At Zisk Media Corporation, I assists*.

End Activity

10-4 SWITCHING TO ANOTHER OPEN DOCUMENT IN WORD

When more than one document is open in a program window, there are several ways you can switch to the other open document. One way to switch to another open file in a program is to point to the program button on the taskbar to display thumbnails of the open files in that program, and then click the thumbnail. In Word, Excel, and PowerPoint, you can also use the Switch Windows button on the View tab. See Exhibit 10-9.

EXHIBIT 10-9 SWITCH WINDOWS BUTTON MENU

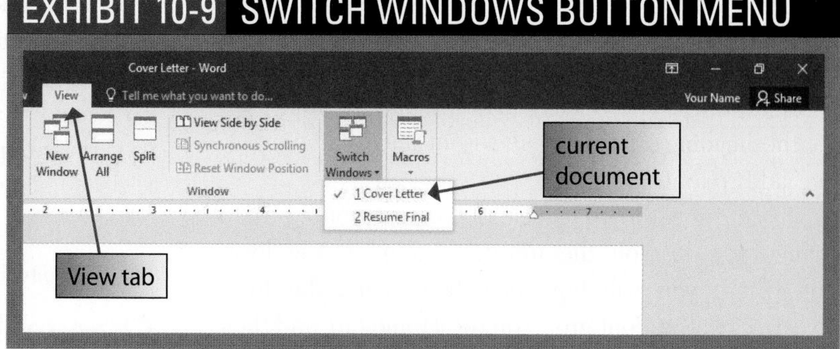

Begin Activity

Switch to another open Word document.

1 On the ribbon, click the **View tab**. In the Window group, click the **Switch Windows button**. The two open documents are listed on the menu that appears. There is a check mark next to Cover Letter because that is the current document. Refer back to Exhibit 10-9.

2 Click **Resume Final**. The menu closes, and the Resume Final document is now the active document.

End Activity

10-5 FORMATTING TEXT

Once you have entered the text of a document, you can change how it looks—that is, you can **format** the document. The purpose of formatting is to make the document attractive, emphasize certain points in the document, and make the organization and flow of the document clear to readers. You can format the document by changing the style of the text, adding color to text or as shading behind text, adding borders, and adding and removing space between lines and paragraphs.

format To change the appearance of a file's content.

To format text, you can either select text that is already entered and then change the format, or you can change the format and then type, and all the text from that point on will retain the new formatting.

10-5a Changing the Font and Font Size

An easy way to change the look of a document is to change the font. A **font** is the design of a set of characters. For example, the font used for the text you are reading right now is New Caledonia font, and the font used for the heading "Changing the Font and Font Size" is Myriad Pro font.

To change the font, select the text you want to change (or position the insertion point at the location where you will type new text), click the Font box arrow in the Font group on the Home tab, and then select a font. See Exhibit 10-10. The first font listed is the font Word suggests using for headings in the document. The second font listed is the font used for ordinary text in a document, or body text. The list of All Fonts is a complete alphabetical list of all available fonts. Each font name in the list is shown in the font that it names. For example, Arial appears in the Arial font, and Times New Roman appears in the Times New Roman font.

Fonts are measured in **points**, which are units of measurement. One point equals 1/72 of an inch. Text in a book is typically printed in 10- or 12-point type. The font size of this text is 10 points, and the font size of the "Changing the Font and Font Size" heading is 15 points. To change the font size, click the Font Size box arrow in the Font group on the Home tab, and then select a size, or click in the Font Size box and type the size you want to use.

EXHIBIT 10-10 FONT MENU

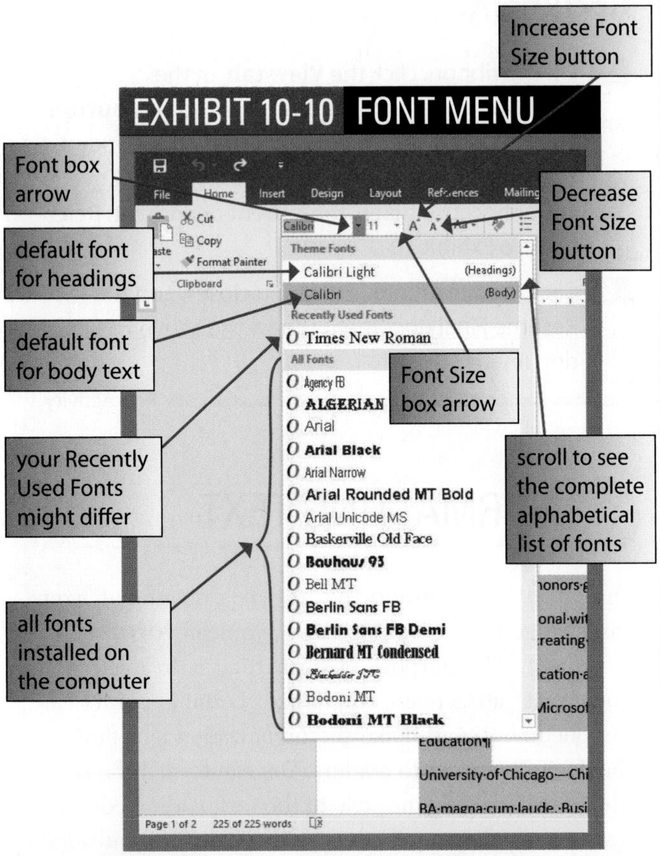

Increase Font Size button
Font box arrow
default font for headings
default font for body text
your Recently Used Fonts might differ
all fonts installed on the computer
Decrease Font Size button
Font Size box arrow
scroll to see the complete alphabetical list of fonts

font The design of a set of characters.

point The unit of measurement used for type; equal to 1/72 of an inch.

Begin Activity

Change the font and font size.

1. In the Resume Final document, press the **Ctrl+A keys**. All the text in the document is selected.
2. On the Home tab, in the Font group, click the **Font box arrow** [Calibri (Body)]. A list of available fonts appears. Refer back to Exhibit 10-10. Calibri (Body) is shaded, indicating that this font is currently applied to the selected text.
3. Scroll down the list, and then click **Century Gothic**. The Font gallery closes, and the selected text is formatted in Century Gothic.
4. Click the **Font box arrow**, and then click **Calibri (Body)**. The selected text is changed back to the Calibri font.
5. With all the text in the document still selected, on the Home tab, in the Font group, look at the Font Size box [11] to see that the font size of the selected text is 11 points.
6. On the Home tab, in the Font group, click the **Decrease Font Size button**. The font size of the selected text changes from 11 points to 10 points.
7. Click a blank area of the document to deselect the text.
8. In the fourth paragraph, double-click **Qualifications** to select it. Press and hold the **Ctrl key**, drag across **Education** in the ninth paragraph near the bottom of the window, and then release the **Ctrl key**. *Qualifications* and *Education* are selected.
9. In the Font group, click the **Increase Font Size button** twice. The point size of the selected text increases from 10 points to 12 points.
10. At the top of the document, select **Brian T. Carter**.

11 On the Home tab, in the Font group, click the **Font Size box arrow** [10 ▾], and then click **20**. The size of the selected text changes to 20 points.

End Activity

TIP: You can also click the number in the Font Size box, type a point size, and then press the Enter key.

10-5b Changing Font Styles

To make text stand out, you can change the style of a font, such as by applying bold and italics. To change the style, use the formatting commands in the Font group on the Home tab. Exhibit 10-11 shows text formatted with bold and italics.

Begin Activity

Change the font style.

1 With *Brian T. Carter* still selected, press and hold the **Ctrl key**, use the mouse to select **Qualifications** and **Education**, and then release the **Ctrl key**. The three nonsequential paragraphs are selected.

2 On the Home tab, in the Font group, click the **Bold button** [B]. The button toggles on and changes to [B], and the selected text is formatted in bold.

3 Scroll down so that you can see the first two paragraphs under Education. In the second line below that heading, select **magna cum laude**.

4 In the Font group, click the **Italic button** [*I*]. The button toggles on, and the selected text is italicized.

5 Scroll down a few more lines, and then select the line that starts with **Internship Zisk Media Corporation**. Format this line so it is **bold**. Refer back to Exhibit 10-11.

End Activity

10-5c Changing Text Color

Another way to emphasize text is to use color. Judicious use of color makes headings or other important text stand out. To apply color to text, click the Font Color button arrow in the Font group on the Home tab to open the document's color palette. See Exhibit 10-12. The color palette contains a top row of colors labeled Theme Colors. The next five rows under the theme colors are lighter and darker variations of the theme colors. The specific theme colors available might change from one document to another. The row of colors under the Standard Colors label does not change from one document to the next—this row of colors is always available.

EXHIBIT 10-11 NONADJACENT TEXT FORMATTED AS BOLD

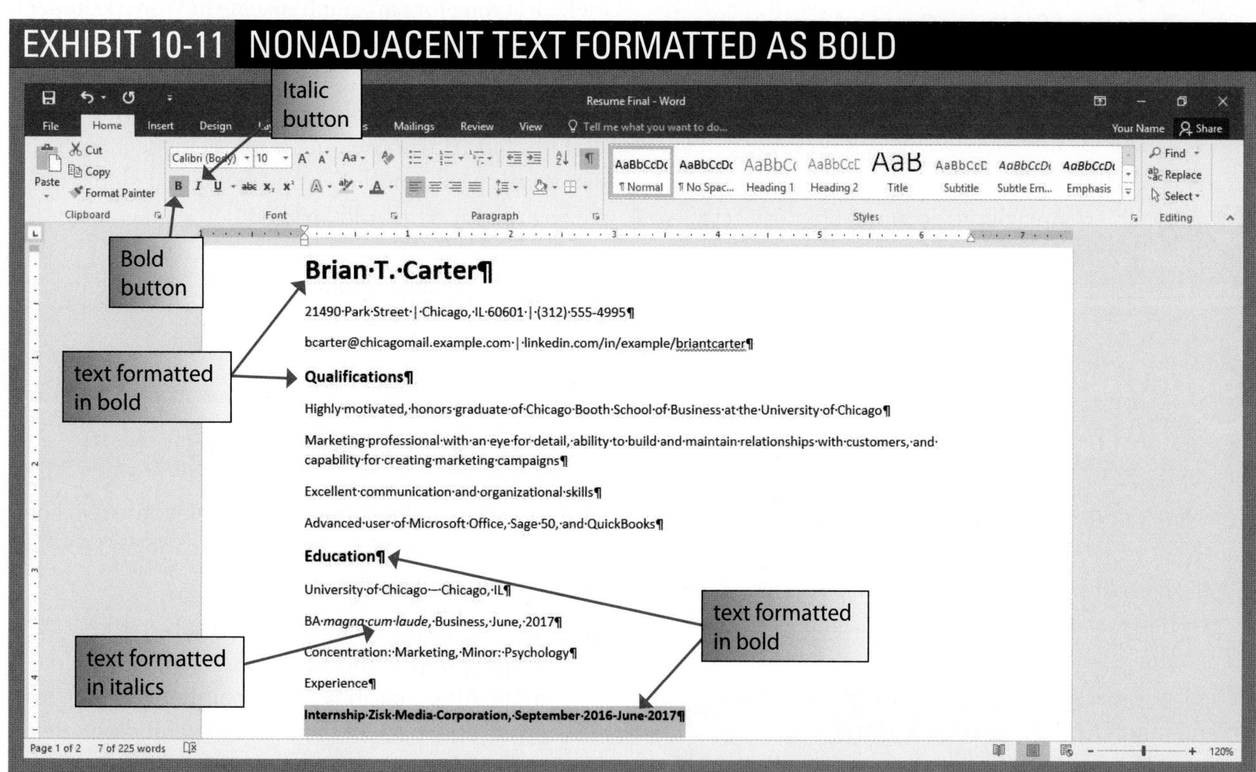

EXHIBIT 10-12 COLOR PALETTE IN THE FONT COLOR BUTTON GALLERY

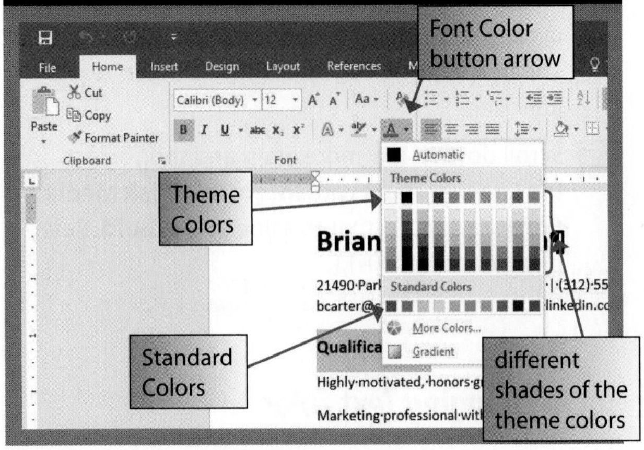

Begin Activity

Change the color of text.

1. Select the **Qualifications** and the **Education headings**.
2. On the Home tab, in the Font group, click the **Font Color button arrow** [A]. The color palette appears. Refer back to Exhibit 10-12.
3. In the Theme Colors section, in the first row, point to the **orange color**. The ScreenTip that appears identifies this as Orange, Accent 2.
4. In the Theme Colors section, in the first row, click the **Gray-50%, Accent 3 color**, using the ScreenTip to identify the color name. The selected headings are now gray.
5. Click a blank area of the document to deselect the headings. Compare your screen to Exhibit 10-13.

TIP: To restore selected text to the default font, size, and color, click the Clear All Formatting button in the Font group on the Home tab.

End Activity

10-6 FORMATTING PARAGRAPHS

In addition to formatting text, you can also apply formatting to entire paragraphs. For example, you can change the amount of space before or after a paragraph or between the lines within a paragraph, change the alignment of a paragraph from left-aligned to centered, or indent a paragraph.

paragraph spacing The space above and below a paragraph.

EXHIBIT 10-13 HEADINGS FORMATTED WITH A COLOR

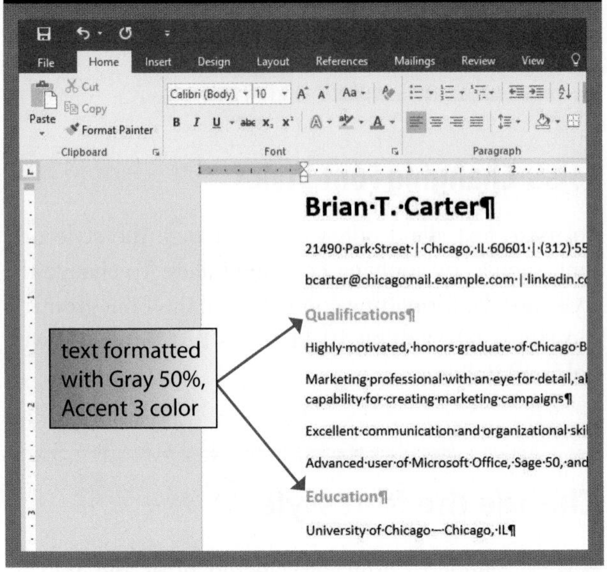

10-6a Adjusting Paragraph Spacing

Paragraph spacing refers to the space that appears between paragraphs. Remember, in Word, any text that ends with ¶ (a paragraph mark symbol) is a paragraph. So, a paragraph can be a group of words that is many lines long, a single word, or even a blank line, in which case the only character on the line is the paragraph mark symbol. Paragraph spacing is measured in points. The default setting for paragraph spacing in Word documents is 0 points before each paragraph and 8 points after each paragraph.

To adjust paragraph spacing in Word, you use the Before and After boxes in the Spacing section in the Paragraph group on the Layout tab. See Exhibit 10-14. You can also use the Add Space Before Paragraph or Remove Space After Paragraph commands on the Line and Paragraph Spacing button menu in the Paragraph group on the Home tab. See Exhibit 10-15.

Begin Activity

Adjust paragraph spacing.

1. Under the Education heading, select the two lines that start with **University of Chicago** and **BA *magna cum laude***.
2. On the ribbon, click the **Layout tab.** In the Paragraph group, in the Spacing section, 8 pt appears in the After box, indicating that there is 8 points of space after each of the selected paragraphs. Refer to Exhibit 10-14.

EXHIBIT 10-14 PARAGRAPH SPACING SETTINGS

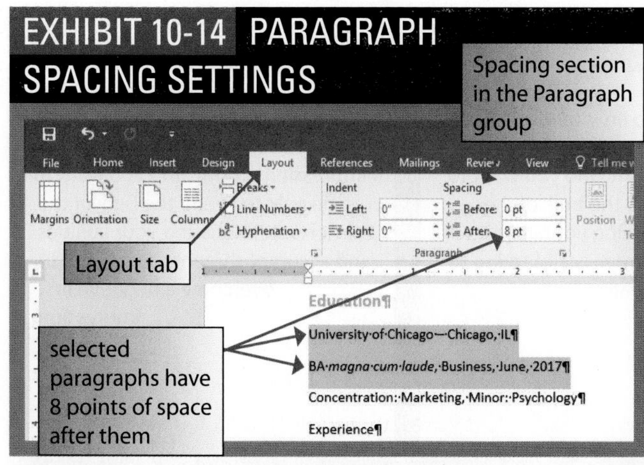

EXHIBIT 10-15 LINE AND PARAGRAPH SPACING BUTTON MENU

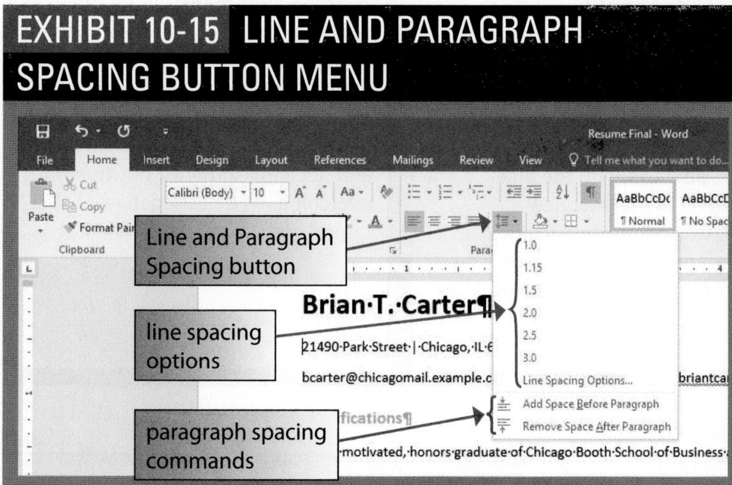

3 In the Paragraph group, in the Spacing section, click the **After box down arrow** twice. The value in the After box changes to 0 pt, and the extra space is removed after the selected paragraphs.

4 Select the **Qualifications** and the **Education headings**.

5 On the Layout tab, in the Paragraph group, in the Spacing section, click the **Before box up arrow** twice. The space above the selected paragraph increases to 12 points.

6 Click anywhere in the **second line** (the line containing Brian's address).

7 On the ribbon, click the **Home tab**. In the Paragraph group, click the **Line and Paragraph Spacing button** . A menu of line spacing options appears, with two paragraph spacing commands at the bottom. Refer back to Exhibit 10-15.

> **TIP:** You can press the Shift+Enter keys to move the insertion point to a new line without starting a new paragraph, which creates new lines without the paragraph spacing.

8 At the bottom of the menu, click **Remove Space After Paragraph.** The menu closes, and the 8 points of space are removed after the selected paragraph.

9 Switch to the **Cover Letter document.**

10 Select the first three lines in the inside address (from **Maria Gutierrez** through **19 Canal St.**).

11 On the **Home tab,** in the Paragraph group, click the **Line and Spacing Paragraph button** , and then click **Remove Space After Paragraph.**

12 Click anywhere in the first paragraph (the first line in the return address), and then remove the space after it.

End Activity

10-6b Adjusting Line Spacing

Line spacing is the amount of space that appears between lines of text within a paragraph. Word offers a number of preset line spacing options. Paragraphs formatted with the 1.0 setting are called **single spaced**. Single spacing allows the least amount of space between lines—essentially no extra space. Paragraphs formatted with the 2.0 setting are called **double spaced** and have a blank line of space between each line of text in the paragraph. The default line spacing setting is 1.08, which allows a little more space between lines than 1.0 spacing. The 1.08 line spacing setting makes it easier to read text on a computer screen.

Begin Activity

Adjust line spacing.

1 On the Home tab on the ribbon, in the Editing group, click the **Select button**, and then click **Select All.** All the text in the document is selected.

line spacing The amount of space between lines of text within a paragraph.

single spaced Line spacing that has no extra space between lines of text in a paragraph.

double spaced Line spacing that has a blank line between each line of text in a paragraph.

2 On the Home tab, in the Paragraph group, click the **Line and Paragraph Spacing button**. Refer back to Exhibit 10-15. None of the line spacing commands have a check mark next to them. This is because the default line spacing setting for the selected text is 1.08, and this option does not appear on the menu.

TIP: To see the exact spacing, click Line Spacing Options on the Line and Paragraph Spacing button menu to open the Indents and Spacing tab in the Paragraph dialog box.

3 On the menu, click **1.0**. The spacing between lines in each paragraph is changed to single spacing.

End Activity

10-6c Aligning Paragraphs

Normal paragraphs are **left-aligned**—they are flush with the left margin and **ragged**, or uneven, along the right margin. **Right-aligned** paragraphs are aligned along the right margin and ragged along the left margin. Paragraphs that are **centered** are positioned midway between the left and right margins and ragged along both margins. **Justified** paragraphs are flush with both the left and right margins. Text in newspaper columns is often justified. See Exhibit 10-16.

The Paragraph group on the Home tab includes a button for each of the four types of alignment described in Exhibit 10-16. To align a single paragraph, click anywhere in that paragraph, and then click the appropriate alignment button. To align multiple paragraphs, select the paragraphs, and then click an alignment button.

EXHIBIT 10-16 PARAGRAPH ALIGNMENTS

left alignment
When you go to an interview, don't forget about your appearance. First impressions count, and you want to be able to spend the bulk of the interview discussing your abilities and accomplishments, not trying to overcome a negative first impression.

right alignment
When you go to an interview, don't forget about your appearance. First impressions count, and you want to be able to spend the bulk of the interview discussing your abilities and accomplishments, not trying to overcome a negative first impression.

center alignment
When you go to an interview, don't forget about your appearance. First impressions count, and you want to be able to spend the bulk of the interview discussing your abilities and accomplishments, not trying to overcome a negative first impression.

justified alignment
When you go to an interview, don't forget about your appearance. First impressions count, and you want to be able to spend the bulk of the interview discussing your abilities and accomplishments, not trying to overcome a negative first impression.

left-align To align paragraph text along the left margin with ragged edges along the right margin.

ragged Uneven, such as text with an uneven appearance along a margin.

right-align To align paragraph text along the right margin with ragged edges along the left margin.

center To position paragraph text evenly between the left and right margins with ragged edges along both margins.

justify To align paragraph text along both the left and right margins.

Begin Activity

Change the alignment of paragraphs.

1 Switch to the **Resume Final document**.

2 At the top of the document, select the first three lines of text (Brian's name and contact information).

3 On the ribbon, on the Home tab, locate the Align Left button in the Paragraph group. It is shaded to indicate that it is selected.

4 On the Home tab, in the Paragraph group, click the **Center button**. The selected paragraphs are centered horizontally on the page.

5 Select the **Qualifications** and the **Education headings**.

6 In the Paragraph group, click the **Align Right button**. The Align Right button toggles on, and the selected paragraphs are right-aligned. Compare your screen to Exhibit 10-17.

7 In the Paragraph group, click the **Align Left button**. The selected headings are left-aligned again.

End Activity

EXHIBIT 10-17 PARAGRAPHS WITH DIFFERENT ALIGNMENTS

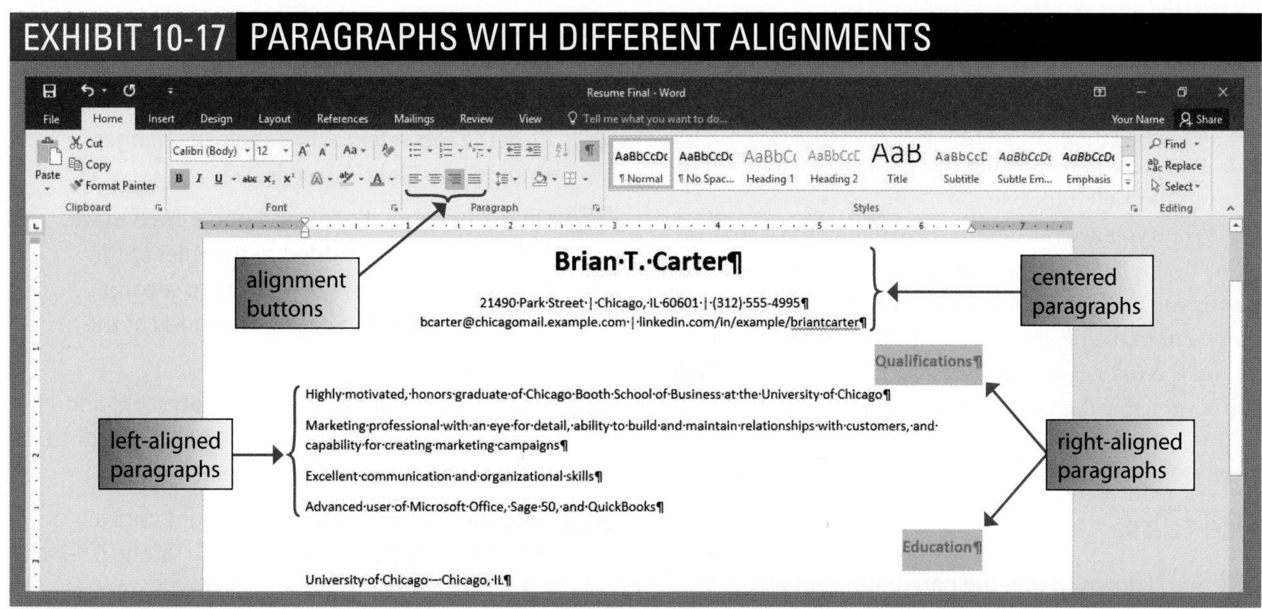

EXHIBIT 10-18 TAB STOP ALIGNMENT STYLES

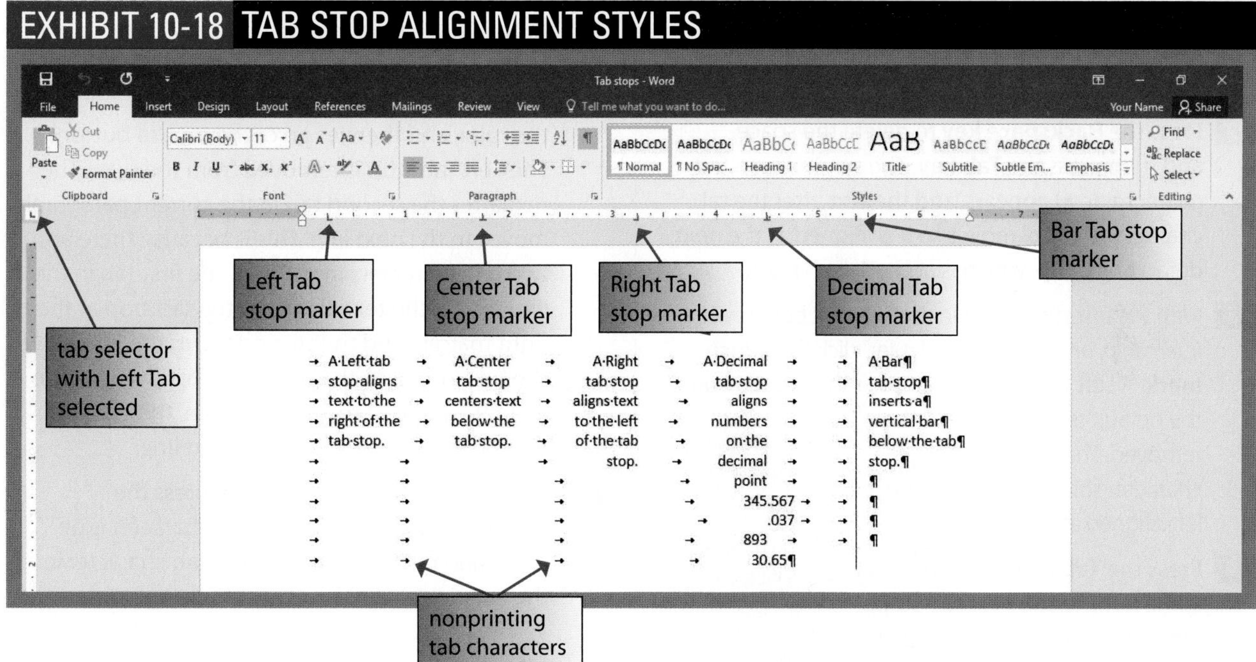

10-6d Using Tabs

A **tab stop** is a location on the horizontal ruler where the insertion point moves when you press the Tab key. Tab stops are useful for aligning small amounts of data in columns and for positioning some of the text on a line so it is centered or right-aligned while leaving the beginning of the line left-aligned. If the Show/Hide ¶ button ¶ is selected, you can see the nonprinting tab character (→) that is inserted when you press the Tab key. A tab is just like any other character you type; you can delete it by pressing the Backspace key or the Delete key.

The default tab stops appear every one-half inch on the horizontal ruler. You can override the default tab stops by setting custom tab stops. The four types of tab stops are Left, Center, Right, and Decimal. (The default tab stops are all Left Tab stops.) Exhibit 10-18 shows the different tab stop styles in a document. Exhibit 10-18 also includes the Bar Tab stop. This is not actually a tab stop—it simply inserts a vertical line (bar) in the document at the location of the stop placed on the ruler.

To set a tab stop, first select a tab stop style using the tab selector, located to the left of the horizontal ruler, and then click on the horizontal ruler where you want to

tab stop A location on the horizontal ruler where the insertion point moves when you press the Tab key.

insert the tab stop. The default tab stop style is the Left Tab. When you click the tab selector, you cycle through the four types of tab stops, and then through two markers that can be used to set indents. To return to the Left Tab style, continue clicking the tab selector until it returns to the Left Tab style.

When you insert a tab stop (except the Bar Tab stop), all of the default tab stops to its left are removed. This means you press the Tab key only once to move the insertion point to the newly created tab stop, no matter where it is on the ruler. The Left Tab style is selected by default and is probably the tab style you will use most often.

Begin Activity

Use tabs.

1 Scroll down so that the paragraph containing *Experience* is at the top of the document window. In the line beginning with *Internship* (below the Experience paragraph), click immediately before the word *Zisk*.

2 Press the **Backspace key** to delete the space, and then press the **Tab key**. The symbol for a tab character (→) appears, and the text after the tab character symbol moves so it is aligned at the next default tab stop, which is at the 1-inch mark.

3 With the insertion point in the line that begins with *Internship*, on the horizontal ruler, click the **2-inch mark**. A Left Tab stop is inserted at that location and the default tab stops to its left are removed. The text after the tab character shifts to the right and is left-aligned at the 2-inch mark.

4 Press the **Tab key** again. The text shifts right to the next tab stop, which is the default tab stop at 2.5 inches.

TIP: One way to align columns of text is to separate the text in each row with tabs, and then add the appropriate tab stops.

5 To the left of the horizontal ruler, click the **tab selector** [L]. It changes to show the Center Tab style [⊥].

6 Click the **tab selector** [⊥] again. It changes to show the Right Tab style [┘].

7 On the horizontal ruler, click the **6-inch mark**. A Right Tab stop is added to the ruler at the 6-inch mark, and the text after the second tab symbol shifts so it is right-aligned at the 6-inch mark.

8 On the ruler, point to the **Right Tab stop**, and then press and hold the **mouse button**. A dotted vertical line appears. See Exhibit 10-19.

9 Drag the **Right Tab stop** to the right until it is on top of the small triangle marker △ at the 6.5-inch mark on the ruler, and then release the mouse button. The Right Tab stop is repositioned.

10 At the 2-inch mark on the horizontal ruler, point to the **Left Tab stop**, press and hold the **mouse button**, drag down so the pointer is no longer on the ruler, and then let go of the mouse button. The Left Tab stop is removed from the ruler. The text after the second tab in the current paragraph moves to the next line. This is because there are two tab characters in the line. The first tab in the line moves the text after it to the tab stop at the right margin, and the second tab in the line moves the text after it to the next tab stop. Because the first tab stop is at the right margin, the text after that tab stop is moved to the next line.

11 Click to the left of *Zisk*, and then press the **Backspace key**. The second tab character is deleted, and the text after the only tab character in the line right-aligns properly at the Right Tab stop you inserted.

End Activity

EXHIBIT 10-19 TEXT RIGHT-ALIGNED AT NEW RIGHT TAB STOP

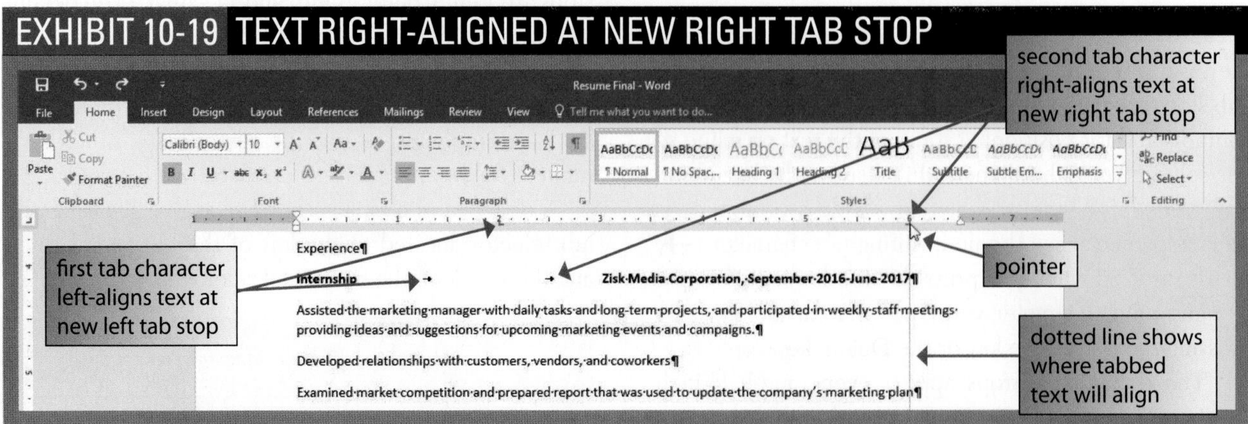
second tab character right-aligns text at new right tab stop
Resume Final - Word
first tab character left-aligns text at new left tab stop
Experience¶
Internship
Zisk·Media·Corporation,·September·2016-June·2017¶
pointer
Assisted·the·marketing·manager·with·daily·tasks·and·long-term·projects,·and·participated·in·weekly·staff·meetings·providing·ideas·and·suggestions·for·upcoming·marketing·events·and·campaigns.¶
Developed·relationships·with·customers,·vendors,·and·coworkers¶
Examined·market·competition·and·prepared·report·that·was·used·to·update·the·company's·marketing·plan¶
dotted line shows where tabbed text will align

FYI TABS DIALOG BOX

The Tabs dialog box lets you add a leader line and set tabs at precise positions. A **leader line** is a line or row of dots or dashes that appears in the space between tabbed text. To open the Tabs dialog box, double-click a tab stop on the ruler. To create a tab stop at a precise position, click in the Tab stop position box, and then type the location on the ruler where you want to insert the tab—for example, 4.15. To change the alignment, click an option button in the Alignment section. To set a leader line, click an option button in the Leader section. To change a tab stop, select it in the list, and then modify it as needed. Make sure you click Set to set the tab stop or the changes; clicking OK only closes the dialog box.

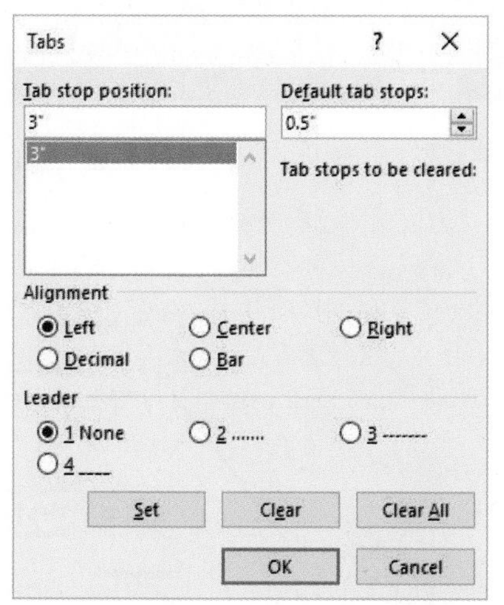

10-6e Creating a Bulleted List

A **bulleted list** is a group of related paragraphs with a symbol, such as a dot, dash, or other character, that appears to the left of each paragraph. When you create a bulleted list, the bullet symbol is placed at the beginning of the paragraph and a tab character is inserted between the bullet symbol and the text in the paragraph. You can click the Bullets button to create a bulleted list using the default or last-used bullet symbol, or you can click the Bullets button arrow to select a different symbol from the gallery. See Exhibit 10-20.

EXHIBIT 10-20 BULLETS GALLERY

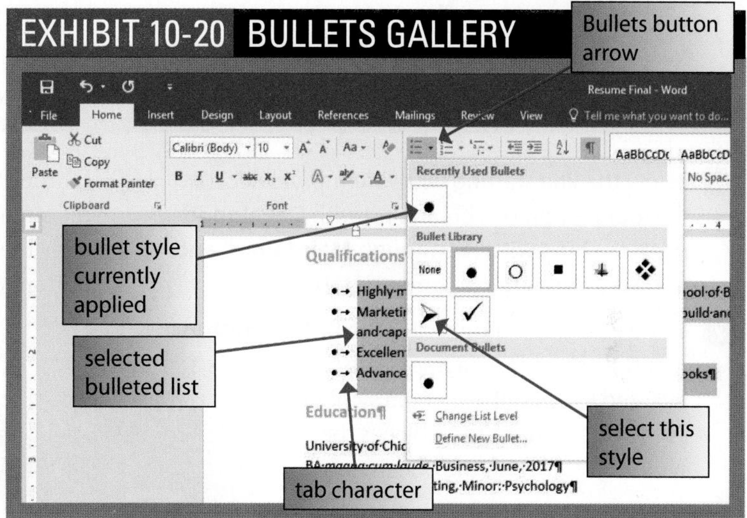

Begin Activity

Create bulleted lists.

1. Scroll up so that the Qualifications heading is at the top of the window. Below the Qualifications heading, select the next four paragraphs beginning with **Highly motivated . . .** through **Advanced user . . .**.
2. On the Home tab, in the Paragraph group, click the **Bullets button**. The Bullets button is selected, black circles appear as bullets before each selected paragraph, and the bulleted list is indented.
3. In the Paragraph group, click the **Bullets button arrow**. A gallery of bullet styles opens. Refer back to Exhibit 10-20.
4. In the Bullet Library section of the gallery, point to the bullet styles to see a Live Preview of the bullet styles in the document.
5. In the Bullet Library section, click **first shape in the second row** (refer to Exhibit 10-20). The round bullets are replaced with the bullet symbol you selected.

TIP: To find additional bullet symbols, click the Bullets button arrow, click Define New Bullet to open the Define New Bullet dialog box, and then click Symbol or Picture.

leader line A line that appears between two elements, such as between tabbed text.

bulleted list A group of related paragraphs with a symbol to the left of each paragraph.

EXHIBIT 10-21 RÉSUMÉ AFTER FORMATTING TEXT AS BULLETED LISTS

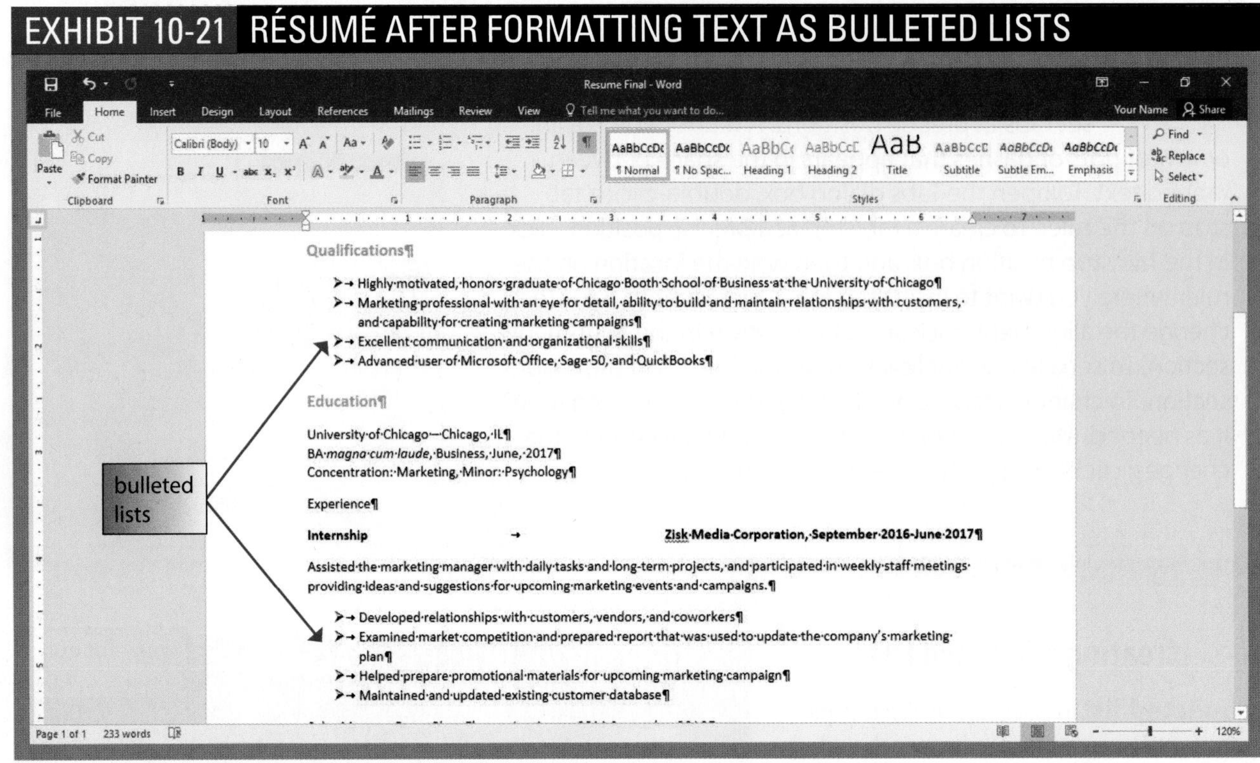

Resume Final - Word
bulleted lists
Qualifications¶
Highly·motivated,·honors·graduate·of·Chicago·Booth·School·of·Business·at·the·University·of·Chicago¶
Marketing·professional·with·an·eye·for·detail,·ability·to·build·and·maintain·relationships·with·customers,·and·capability·for·creating·marketing·campaigns¶
Excellent·communication·and·organizational·skills¶
Advanced·user·of·Microsoft·Office,·Sage·50,·and·QuickBooks¶
Education¶
University·of·Chicago—Chicago,·IL¶
BA·magna·cum·laude,·Business,·June,·2017¶
Concentration:·Marketing,·Minor:·Psychology¶
Experience¶
Internship
Zisk·Media·Corporation,·September·2016-June·2017¶
Assisted·the·marketing·manager·with·daily·tasks·and·long-term·projects,·and·participated·in·weekly·staff·meetings·providing·ideas·and·suggestions·for·upcoming·marketing·events·and·campaigns.¶
Developed·relationships·with·customers,·vendors,·and·coworkers¶
Examined·market·competition·and·prepared·report·that·was·used·to·update·the·company's·marketing·plan¶
Helped·prepare·promotional·materials·for·upcoming·marketing·campaign¶
Maintained·and·updated·existing·customer·database¶
Page 1 of 1 233 words

6 Below the line starting with *Internship*, select the four paragraphs beginning with **Developed relationships with . . .** through **Maintained and updated existing customer database**.

7 In the Paragraph group, click the **Bullets button** . The selected paragraphs are formatted as a bulleted list with the triangle symbol as the bullet character, which is the last symbol you used in the document.

8 Click anywhere in the document to deselect the text, and then scroll so that the Qualifications heading is at the top of the window. Compare your screen to Exhibit 10-21.

End Activity

10-6f Creating a Numbered List

For a group of related paragraphs that have a particular order (such as steps in a procedure), you can use numbers instead of bullets to create a **numbered list.** If you insert a new paragraph, delete a paragraph, or reorder the paragraphs in a numbered list, Word adjusts the numbers to make sure they remain consecutive. As with the Bullets button, you can click the Numbering button to apply the default or last-used number style, or you can click the Numbering button arrow to open a gallery of number styles, as shown in Exhibit 10-22.

numbered list A group of related paragraphs that have a particular order with sequential numbers to the left of each paragraph.

EXHIBIT 10-22 NUMBERING GALLERY

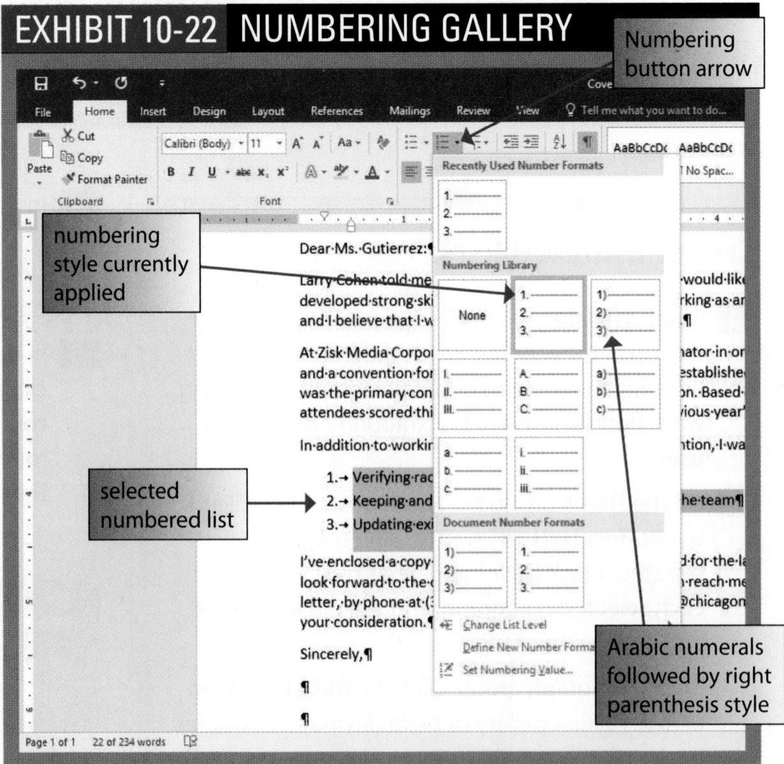

FYI CREATING BULLETED OR NUMBERED LISTS AS YOU TYPE

To create a bulleted list as you type, click the Bullets button in the Paragraph group on the Home tab, type the first item in the list, and then press the Enter key. The next paragraph is formatted with the bullet symbol and the Tab character.

To create a numbered list as you type, click the Numbering button in the Paragraph group on the Home tab, and then start typing. You can use the AutoCorrect feature to create a numbered list. To do this, type the number 1 followed by a period, and then press the Tab key. AutoCorrect formats the paragraph as the first item in a numbered list, and the Numbering button in the Paragraph group on the Home tab is selected. After you type the first item and then press the Enter key, the number 2 automatically appears in the next paragraph, and the insertion point appears after a Tab character, ready for you to type the second item.

To end both a bulleted and numbered list as you type, press the Enter key twice after you type the last item in the list. This creates a new blank paragraph at the left margin without a bullet or number.

Begin Activity

Create a numbered list.

1. Switch to the **Cover Letter document**.
2. In the body of the letter, below the third paragraph, select the three paragraphs starting with **Verifying radio ad frequency . . .** through **Updating existing customer database**.
3. On the Home tab, in the Paragraph group, click the **Numbering button** . The selected paragraphs are changed to a numbered list.
4. On the Home tab, in the Paragraph group, click the **Numbering button arrow** . A gallery of numbering formats appears. Refer to Exhibit 10-22.
5. In the gallery, click the numbering style that shows **Arabic numerals followed by a right parenthesis**. The gallery closes, and the style of numbers in the selected paragraphs is changed.
6. In the Paragraph group, click the **Bullets button** . The selected text is changed to a bulleted list with default bullet symbols.

End Activity

10-6g Indenting a Paragraph

Word offers a number of options for indenting a paragraph. You can shift the left edge of an entire paragraph to the right. This is called increasing the left indent. You can also shift the right edge of an entire paragraph to the left. This is called increasing the right indent. You can also create specialized indents. A **first-line indent** shifts the first line of a paragraph from the left margin, and a **hanging indent** shifts all the lines of a paragraph from the left margin except the first line.

To create indents, drag the indent markers on the ruler. The marker on the left end of the ruler contains three parts: the First Line Indent marker , the Hanging Indent marker , and the Left Indent marker . When the three parts are aligned, the marker looks like . The Right Indent marker is the only marker on the right end of the ruler. ScreenTips appear as you point to each marker so that you can drag the correct marker.

To quickly indent an entire paragraph one-half inch, you can also use the Increase Indent button in the Paragraph group on the Home tab. (Note that if you use the Increase Indent button to indent a bulleted list, it will indent the list one-quarter inch at a time.) To move an indented paragraph back to the left one-half inch, click the Decrease Indent button .

Begin Activity

Change paragraph indents.

1. Switch to the **Resume Final document**. Below the *Internship* line, click anywhere in the paragraph that begins with **Assisted the marketing manager**.
2. On the horizontal ruler, point to the **Left Indent marker** , which is the rectangle at the bottom

first-line indent A paragraph in which the first line is indented from the left margin.

hanging indent A paragraph in which all the lines are indented from the left margin except the first line.

of the marker at the left margin on the horizontal ruler. Use the ScreenTip to make sure you are pointing to the correct section of the marker.

3 While still pointing to the **Left Indent marker**, press and hold the **mouse button**. A dotted vertical line appears over the document.

4 Drag the **Left Indent marker** right to the **0.5-inch mark** on the horizontal ruler.

5 Let go of the **mouse button**. All three sections of the marker move when you drag the Left Indent marker. The entire paragraph containing the insertion point indents from the left one-half inch.

6 Below the *Sales Manager* line (which is the first line below the bulleted list under *Internship*), select the paragraph that begins **Managed staff of five cashiers**.

7 On the Home tab, in the Paragraph group, click the **Increase Indent button**. The selected paragraph is indented one-half inch.

8 Under the *Internship* line, select the four items in the bulleted list. On the ruler, notice that the First Line Indent marker is at the 0.25-inch mark and the Hanging Indent marker is at the 0.5-inch mark. Paragraphs in bulleted lists are formatted with a hanging indent. The first line of each of the selected paragraphs is indented one-quarter inch, and for the item that is longer than one line, the second line is indented one-half inch.

9 In the Paragraph group, click the **Increase Indent button**. Because the selected paragraphs are a bulleted list, they are indented one-quarter inch from their original position instead of one-half inch. Now the bullet symbols are aligned with the indented paragraph above the list. Compare your screen to Exhibit 10-23.

10 Scroll down and indent the line that begins *Staffed sales register* one-half inch from the left margin.

End Activity

TIP: You can also click in the paragraph you want to indent or select multiple paragraphs, click the Dialog Box Launcher in the Paragraph group, and then adjust the settings in the Indentation section.

EXHIBIT 10-23 PARAGRAPHS INDENTED

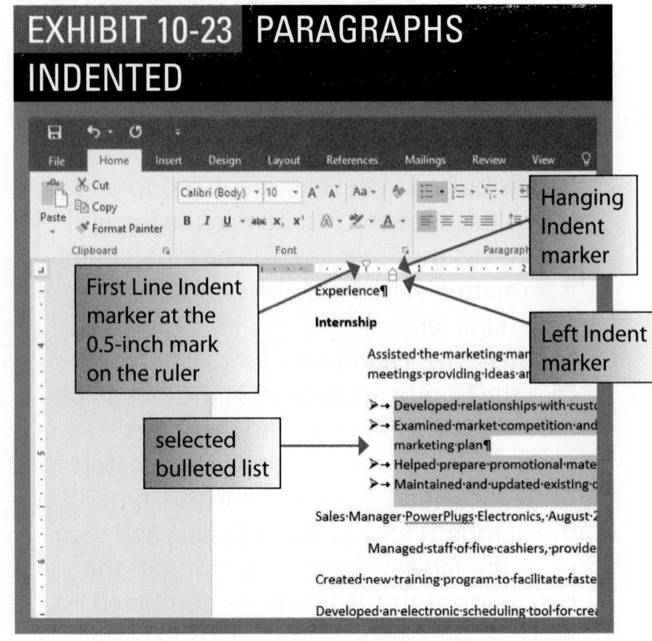

10-6h Adding a Paragraph Border

You can add borders around paragraphs, or you can add only part of a border—for example, a bottom border that appears below the last line of text in a paragraph. You can select different colors and line weights for the border as well, making the border more or less prominent, as needed. To add a border, you click the Borders button arrow to open a menu of border options, as shown in Exhibit 10-24. If you click one of the options in the menu, you add a border using the default style, color, and width, which is a solid ½-point black line. Or you

EXHIBIT 10-24 BORDERS BUTTON MENU

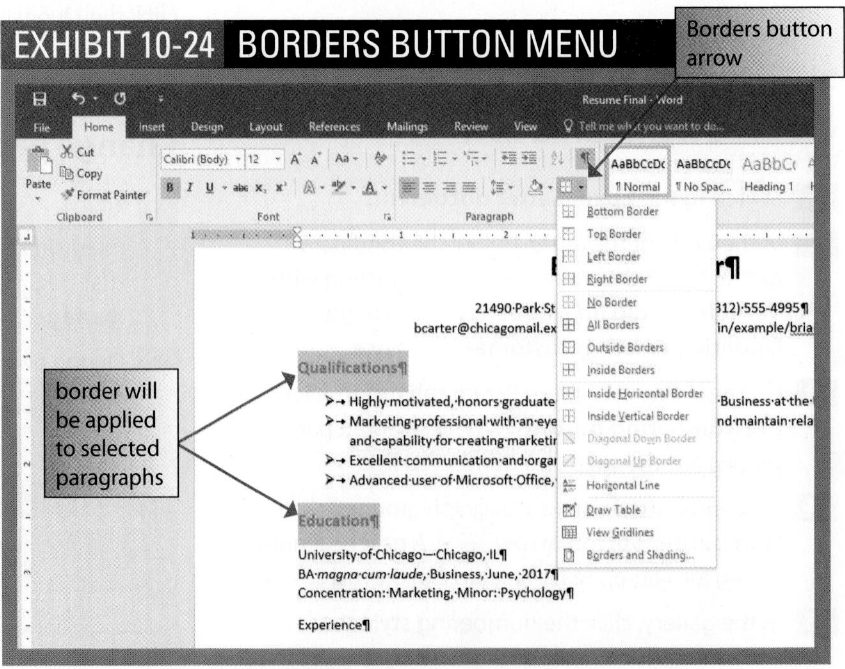

can open the Borders and Shading dialog box and use the commands on the Borders tab as shown in Exhibit 10-25 to create a custom border. Note that you must click the Custom button in the Setting list to apply a custom border; otherwise, the border will be applied to all four sides of the selected text or paragraph.

EXHIBIT 10-25 BORDERS TAB IN THE BORDERS AND SHADING DIALOG BOX

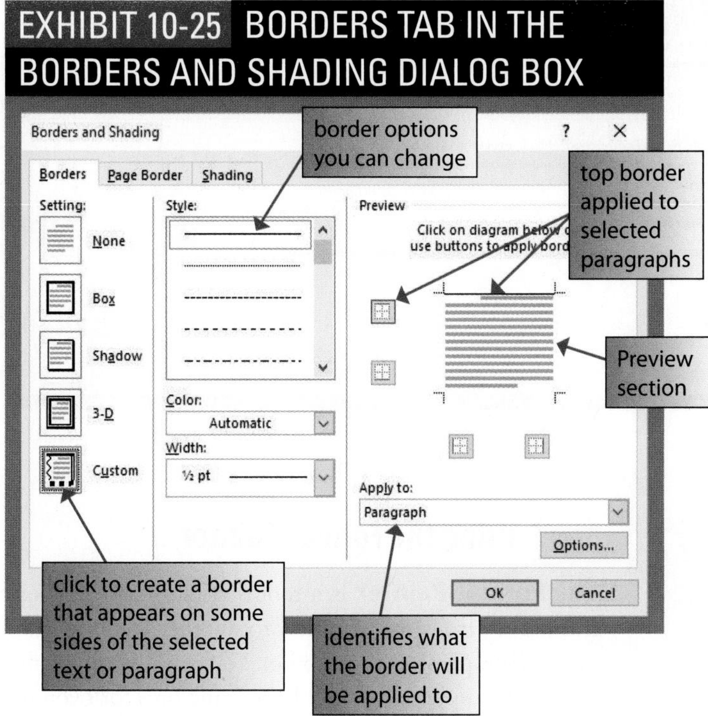

Begin Activity

Add a paragraph border.

1. Scroll so you can see the top of the page.
2. Select the **Qualifications** and **Education paragraphs**, including the **paragraph marks**.
3. On the Home tab, in the Paragraph group, click the **Borders button arrow**. A menu of border options opens. Refer back to Exhibit 10-24.
4. On the Borders menu, click **Top Border**. The menu closes, and a solid line, one-half point wide, black border appears above the selected paragraph. The Borders button now shows the Top Border option.

> **PROBLEM?** If a box appears around either heading, you did not select the paragraph mark before applying the border. Undo the action, and then repeat Steps 2 through 4.

5. In the Paragraph group, click the **Border button arrow**, and then click **Borders and Shading**. The Borders and Shading dialog box opens with the Borders tab selected. Refer back to Exhibit 10-25. Custom is selected in the Setting list because the border is not applied to all four sides of the paragraph. The Preview section shows the current settings.
6. In the Style list, click the **down scroll arrow** six times, and then click the line style that shows a **thick line with thin lines above and below it**.
7. Click the **Color arrow**. The same color palette you used when you changed the font color appears.
8. In the color palette, under Theme Colors, click the **Gray-50%, Accent 3, Darker 25% color**. The selected line style in the Style box and the sample in the Width box change to the gray color.
9. Click the **Width arrow**, and then click **1 ½ pt**. Do not close the dialog box yet; you still need to apply the selected border style.
10. In the Preview section, click the **top of the paragraph**. The solid black border is replaced with the triple-line gray border. Below the Preview section, the Apply to box contains Paragraph, indicating that the border will be applied to the entire paragraph, not just selected text.

> **PROBLEM?** If you click the wrong side in the Preview section, click the border you applied to remove it.

11. Click **OK**. The dialog box closes, and the borders above the Qualifications and Education headings change to the 1 ½-point, dark gray border you selected.

End Activity

10-6i Adding Paragraph Shading

You can add shading as background color to paragraphs. You can use shading in conjunction with a border for a more defined effect.

Begin Activity

Add shading to a paragraph.

1. At the top of the document, select **Brian T. Carter** and the **paragraph mark** at the end of the line.
2. On the Home tab, in the Paragraph group, click the **Shading button arrow**. The color palette appears.

EXHIBIT 10-26 SHADING APPLIED TO A PARAGRAPH

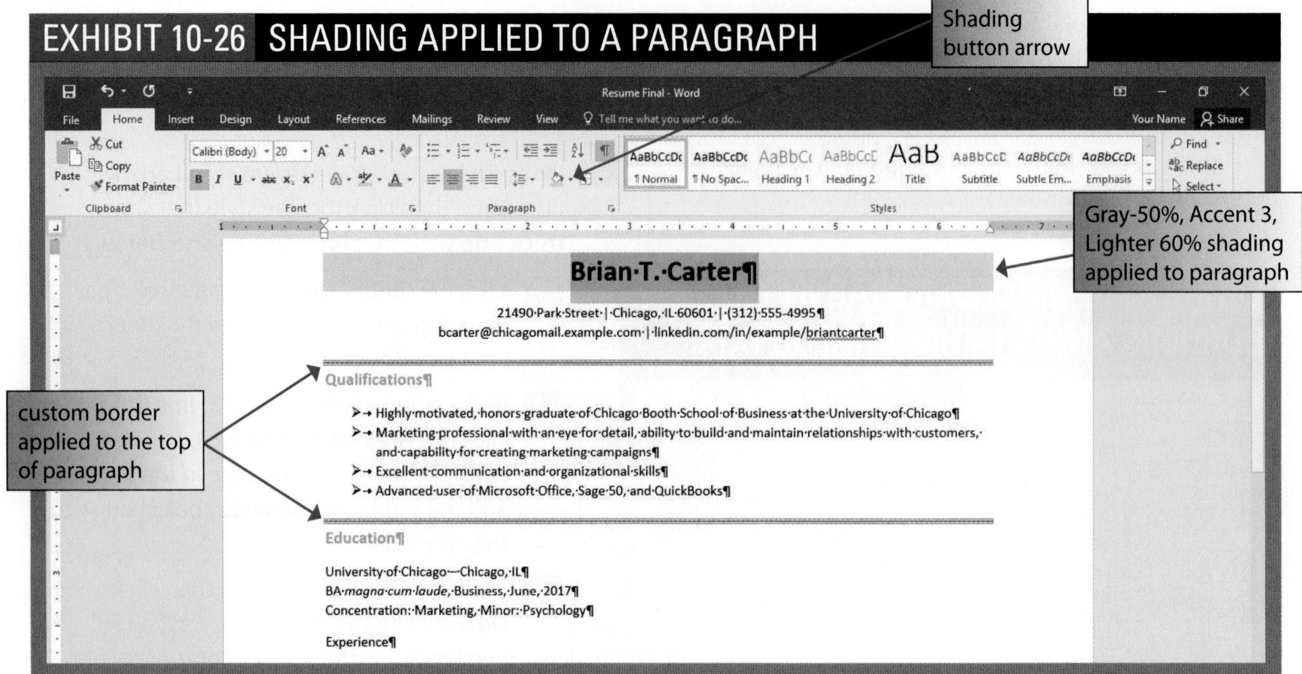

3 In the second row of variants under the Theme Colors, click the **Gray-50%, Accent 3, Lighter 60% color**. The color palette closes, and light gray shading is applied across the width of the page to the paragraph containing Brian's name. Compare your screen to Exhibit 10-26.

PROBLEM? If the shading was applied only behind Brian's name, you did not select the paragraph mark. Undo the action, and then repeat Steps 1 through 3.

End Activity

10-7 COPYING FORMATS

If you are working with a document that contains a lot of formatting, it can be easier to copy the formatting rather than trying to re-create it on a different block of text. Likewise, if you are pasting text that is formatted differently from the text in the location where you are pasting it, you can control whether the formatting is pasted.

Format Painter A tool that is used to copy formatting from one location to another, such as from one block of text to another.

10-7a Using the Format Painter

The **Format Painter** is a tool that allows you to copy formatting from one location to another, such as from one paragraph of text to another. You can use the Format Painter to apply the copied formatting once or over and over again until you toggle it off.

Begin Activity

Use the Format Painter.

1 Select the **Qualifications paragraph**, including the **paragraph mark**.

2 On the Home tab, in the Clipboard group, click the **Format Painter button**, and then move the pointer on top of text in the document (but do not click). The Format Painter button toggles on, and the pointer changes to [pointer icon].

3 Below the Education heading and above the *Internship* line, position the pointer to the left of the paragraph containing **Experience** so that it changes to [pointer icon], and then click. The font and paragraph formatting applied to the *Qualifications* paragraph is copied to the *Experience* paragraph, the Format Painter button toggles off, and the pointer returns to its usual shape. The paragraph formatting is copied because you selected the paragraph mark before using the Format Painter.

4. Copy the formatting applied to the **Experience paragraph** to the **Activities paragraph**, which is three lines from the end of the document.
5. Scroll up, and then under the Experience heading, select the paragraph beginning with **Internship**, including the **paragraph mark**. In the Clipboard group, double-click the **Format Painter button**.
6. Below the bulleted list, drag all the way across the line beginning with **Sales Manager**. The formatting from the *Internship* line is copied to this line. Notice on the ruler that the custom Right Tab stop you set was copied as well. Because you double-clicked the Format Painter button, the button is still selected, and the pointer is still .
7. Two lines above the *Activities* heading, drag all the way across the line beginning with **Sales Clerk**. The formatting copied from the *Internship* line is applied to the *Sales Clerk* line.
8. In the Clipboard group, click the **Format Painter button**. The Format Painter button is no longer selected, and the pointer returns to its usual shape. Now you need to add tab characters between the job titles and the companies in the two lines you just applied the copied format to.
9. In the lines beginning with *Sales Manager* and *Sales Clerk*, delete the space before *Power-Plugs*, and insert a tab character in its place.
10. Use the **Format Painter** to copy the formatting of the bulleted list under *Internship* to the three paragraphs under *Sales Manager*, beginning with **Created new training program . . .** through **Awarded Employee of the Month . . . .** The paragraph formatting, including the bullet characters and the indent level, is copied to the three paragraphs you selected, and the Format Painter is no longer selected.
11. Use the **Format Painter** to copy the formatting of the bulleted list under *Qualifications* near the beginning of the document to the two paragraphs below the *Activities* paragraph at the end of the document. Compare your document to the one shown in Exhibit 10-27.

TIP: To see the entire document at once, click the One Page button in the Zoom group on the View tab.

End Activity

EXHIBIT 10-27 COMPLETED RÉSUMÉ

Brian T. Carter

21490 Park Street | Chicago, IL 60601 | (312) 555-4995
bcarter@chicagomail.example.com | linkedin.com/in/example/briantcarter

Qualifications

- Highly motivated, honors graduate of Chicago Booth School of Business at the University of Chicago
- Marketing professional with an eye for detail, ability to build and maintain relationships with customers, and capability for creating marketing campaigns
- Excellent communication and organizational skills
- Advanced user of Microsoft Office, Sage 50, and QuickBooks

Education

University of Chicago – Chicago, IL
BA *magna cum laude*, Business, June, 2017
Concentration: Marketing, Minor: Psychology

Experience

Internship **Zisk Media Corporation, September 2016-June 2017**

Assisted the marketing manager with daily tasks and long-term projects, and participated in weekly staff meetings providing ideas and suggestions for upcoming marketing events and campaigns.

- Developed relationships with customers, vendors, and coworkers
- Examined market competition and prepared report that was used to update the company's marketing plan
- Helped prepare promotional materials for upcoming marketing campaign
- Maintained and updated existing customer database

Sales Manager **PowerPlugs Electronics, August 2014-September 2016**

Managed staff of five cashiers, provided training, resolved conflicts, and scheduled shifts.

- Created new training program to facilitate faster start up
- Developed an electronic scheduling tool for creating weekly employee work hours
- Awarded Employee of the Month eight times

Sales Clerk **PowerPlugs Electronics, August 2012-August 2014**

Staffed sales register during peak store hours.

Activities

- American Marketing Association, collegiate member
- Chicago Crew Team, four years

10-7b Using Paste Options

When you paste text or objects in Office programs, you can click the Paste button arrow instead of the Paste button in the Clipboard group on the Home tab to display a menu of options for pasting the contents of the Clipboard. The buttons on the menu change depending on what you are pasting. The buttons that you will use most often are Keep Source Formatting and Keep Text Only. The Keep Source Formatting button pastes the contents of the Clipboard in the new location but retains the formatting that the copied or cut item had in its original location. The Keep Text Only button pastes the contents of the Clipboard using the formatting of the surrounding text in the new location. Another button that commonly appears is the Merge Formatting button, which combines the formatting from the original location with the formatting of the new location. When other buttons are available, they will have similar descriptive names that appear in a ScreenTip when you point to them.

You can point to each button on the Paste button menu to see a Live Preview of the formatted Clipboard item in the document. See Exhibit 10-28. If you click the Paste button, the contents of the Clipboard is pasted with the default option, which is the first button on the menu. When you paste anything, a Paste Options button (Ctrl) appears below and to the right of the pasted item. You can click the Paste Options button to display the same menu of buttons that appears on the Paste button menu, and you can click these to change how the pasted item is formatted.

Begin Activity

Use paste options.

1. At the top of the document, select **Brian T. Carter** and the **paragraph mark** at the end of the line.
2. On the Home tab, in the Clipboard group, click the **Copy button**.
3. Switch to the **Cover Letter document**. At the bottom of the letter, click after the comma after the word *Sincerely*, and then press the **Enter key** three times.
4. On the Home tab, in the Clipboard group, click the **Paste button arrow**. The menu of paste options appears.
5. On the menu, point to the **Keep Source Formatting button**. Brian's name appears in the document with the same formatting it had in the résumé. Refer to Exhibit 10-28.
6. Point to the **Merge Formatting button**. Live Preview changes the pasted text so it merges the formatting used in the résumé with that of the letter; that is, it changes the text to 11-point Calibri and removes the gray shading but retains the bold formatting.
7. On the Paste Options menu, click the **Keep Text Only button**. The menu closes, and the text is pasted as plain, unformatted text. The Paste Options button (Ctrl) appears below the lower-right corner of the pasted text.

End Activity

EXHIBIT 10-28 PASTED TEXT WITH SOURCE FORMATTING

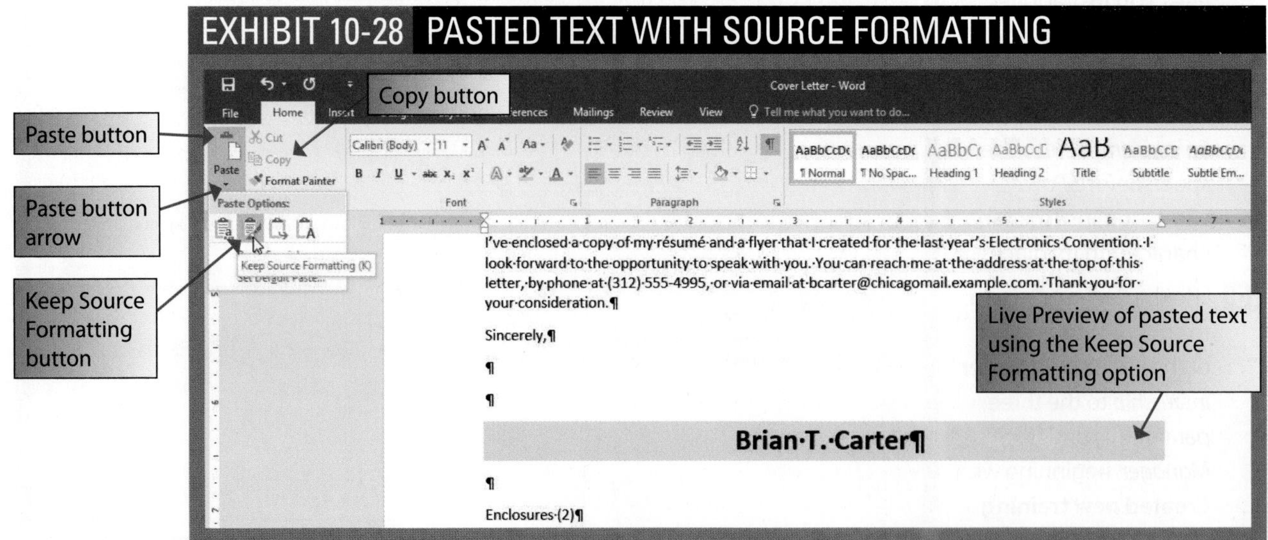

10-8 CHECKING SPELLING AND GRAMMAR

Before you print or send a document, you should always perform a final check of the spelling using the Spelling and Grammar Checker. This is commonly called using the spell checker or **spell checking.** The spell checker continually checks your document against the Office built-in dictionary. If it finds a word that doesn't match the correct spelling in the Office dictionary and was not fixed by AutoCorrect, or if a word, such as a last name, is not in the dictionary, a red, wavy line appears beneath it. A red, wavy underline also appears if the same word appears twice in a row. The context in which words are used can also be checked, so words that are spelled correctly but might be used incorrectly are underlined with a blue, wavy line. For example, if you type *their* when you mean *there*, the word would be flagged. Of course, a computer program won't be completely accurate in determining the correct context, so Word doesn't catch every instance of this type of error. Finally, Word also checks the grammar in a document and flags potential grammatical errors with a blue, wavy underline.

Sometimes grammatical errors are not flagged no matter what is selected in the Grammar Settings dialog box. To ensure an error-free document, you should always read your documents carefully even after using the spelling and grammar tools because nothing beats a human proofread.

There are three ways to correct misspelled words. You can correct words individually by right-clicking flagged words and then using options on the shortcut menu that opens. You can check the entire document by opening the Spelling task pane. Or, you can simply delete the misspelled word and retype it.

10-8a Checking Flagged Words Individually

You can right-click a word flagged with a colored, wavy underline to open a shortcut menu containing suggestions for alternate spellings or a correction for a grammatical error. The shortcut menu also includes commands for ignoring the misspelled word or grammatical error. See Exhibit 10-29.

EXHIBIT 10-29 SHORTCUT MENU FOR A MISSPELLED WORD

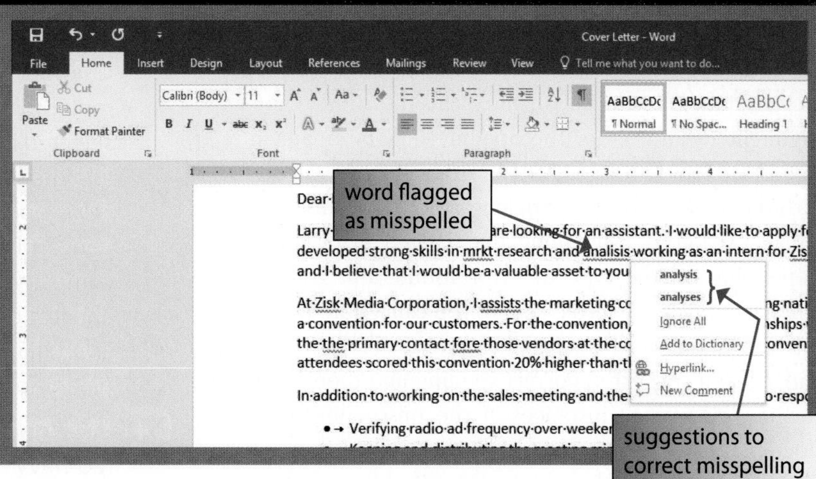

Begin Activity

Check flagged words individually.

1 In the body of the letter, in the first paragraph, in the last sentence, right-click the flagged spelling error **analisis**. A shortcut menu opens. Refer back to Exhibit 10-29.

2 On the shortcut menu, click **analysis**. The spelling of the word is corrected, and the red, wavy underline is removed.

3 In the second paragraph, in the first sentence, right-click the flagged grammar error **assists.** Only one word appears at the top of the shortcut menu as a suggested replacement, *assist*, and this is incorrect.

PROBLEM?
If the word *assists* doesn't have a blue, wavy underline, click the word *assists* to make the underline appear, and then do Step 3. If it still doesn't have a blue, wavy underline, click File, click Options, click Proofing in the navigation bar, click Settings next to Writing Style: Grammar in the "When correcting spelling and grammar in Word" section, select all of the check boxes in the Grammar Settings dialog box, and then click OK in both dialog boxes.

4 Click a blank area of the window to close the shortcut menu without selecting anything.

5 Click after the word *assists*, press the **Backspace key**, and then type **ed**. The word is changed to *assisted*, and the blue, wavy underline is removed.

End Activity

spell check To check a file for spelling and grammatical errors using the Spelling and Grammar Checker.

10-8b Checking the Spelling and Grammar in the Entire Document

To spell-check the entire document, click the Spelling & Grammar button in the Proofing group on the Review tab. The first error after the insertion point is highlighted, and either the Spelling or Grammar pane opens, depending on what type of error is highlighted. Exhibit 10-30 shows the Spelling pane for a misspelled word. Options for handling the flagged error change depending on the type of error found. For example, when a duplicated word is found, you can ignore it or delete it; when a word is flagged as a misspelled word, you can select a suggested correct spelling and then change it once, change all instances of the misspelling in the document, ignore this instance or ignore all instances, or add the flagged word to the built-in dictionary or to the AutoCorrect list.

Begin Activity

Check the spelling and grammar in the entire document.

1. Press the **Ctrl+Home keys**. The insertion point moves to the beginning of the document.
2. On the ribbon, click the **Review tab**. In the Proofing group, click the **Spelling & Grammar button**. The first flagged word in the document, *mrkt*, is highlighted. The Spelling pane opens with a list of suggested correct spellings. The correct spelling—*market*—is selected in the list. Refer to Exhibit 10-30.
3. In the Spelling pane, click **Change**. The highlighted word is replaced with the word that was selected in the Spelling pane, and the next flagged word—*Zisk*—appears in the Spelling pane. This is the name of a company, so it is not misspelled and it should not be changed. The company name is also flagged at the beginning of the second paragraph in the body of the document.

TIP: You can also click [icon] on the status bar to open the Spelling task pane. If the button is [icon], there are no flagged errors.

4. Click **Ignore All**. The word is not changed, and the red wavy underline under both instances of Zisk in the document is removed. In the document, the next flagged word is selected. In this case, the word *the* appears twice in a row. No suggested alternate spellings appear in the Spelling pane because the only choice here is to delete the repeated word or leave it as is.
5. In the Spelling pane, click **Delete**. The repeated word is deleted, and the next flagged word, *fore*, is highlighted. This is a misused word, so the Spelling pane changes to the Grammar pane. The list of synonyms at the bottom includes synonyms for both the misused word and for the selected correction.

EXHIBIT 10-30 SPELLING PANE SHOWING A MISSPELLED WORD

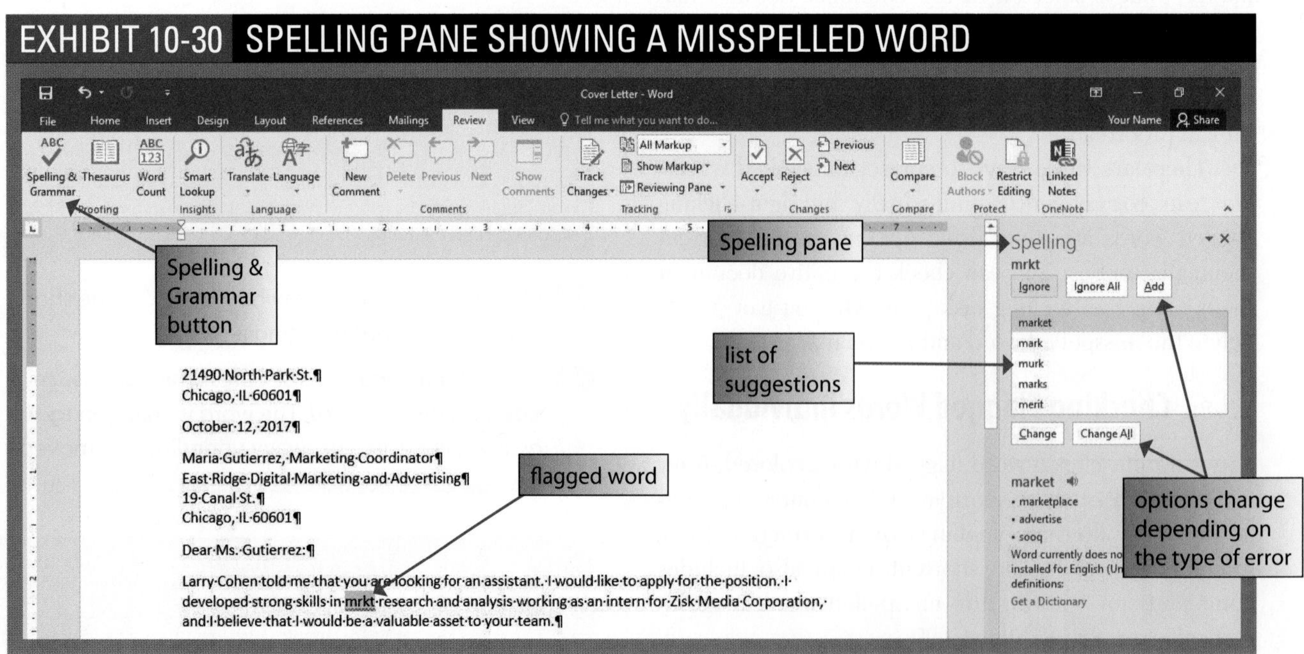

6 Click **Change**. The word is corrected in the document. This is the last flagged word in the document, so the Grammar pane closes, and dialog box opens telling you that the spelling and grammar check is complete.

7 In the dialog box, click **OK**. The dialog box closes.

PROBLEM? If another word is flagged as misspelled, select the correct spelling in the Suggestions list, and then click **Change**.

End Activity

10-9 PREVIEWING AND PRINTING DOCUMENTS

To be sure the document is ready to print, and to avoid wasting paper and time, you should first review it on the Print screen in Backstage view to make sure it will appear as you want when printed. See Exhibit 10-31.

The Print screen contains options for printing the document and a preview displaying a full-page version of the document in the right pane. However, you cannot edit the document from the Print screen; it simply provides a way to look at the document page by page before printing. The Print settings in the left pane allow you to control a variety of print options. For example, you can change the number of copies or which pages to print. If your document has more than one page, you can scroll from page to page by clicking the Next Page ▶ and Previous Page ◀ buttons at the bottom of the preview or dragging the scroll bar to the right of the preview.

Begin Activity

Preview the document.

1 Proof the Cover Letter document one last time, and correct any remaining errors.

2 In the inside address, replace *Maria Gutierrez* with your name.

3 Save the Cover Letter document.

4 On the ribbon, click the **File tab** to open Backstage view. In the navigation bar, click **Print**. The Print screen appears.

5 Review your document, and make sure its overall layout matches the document in Exhibit 10-31. If you notice a problem with paragraph breaks or spacing, click the **Back button** at the top of the navigation pane, edit the document, and then repeat Step 4.

6 Make sure your printer is turned on and contains paper.

7 In the left pane of the Print screen, click **Print**. Backstage view closes, and the letter prints.

PROBLEM? If the document doesn't appear to fill the preview pane, at the bottom-right corner of the window, click the **Zoom to Page button**.

EXHIBIT 10-31 PRINT SCREEN IN BACKSTAGE VIEW

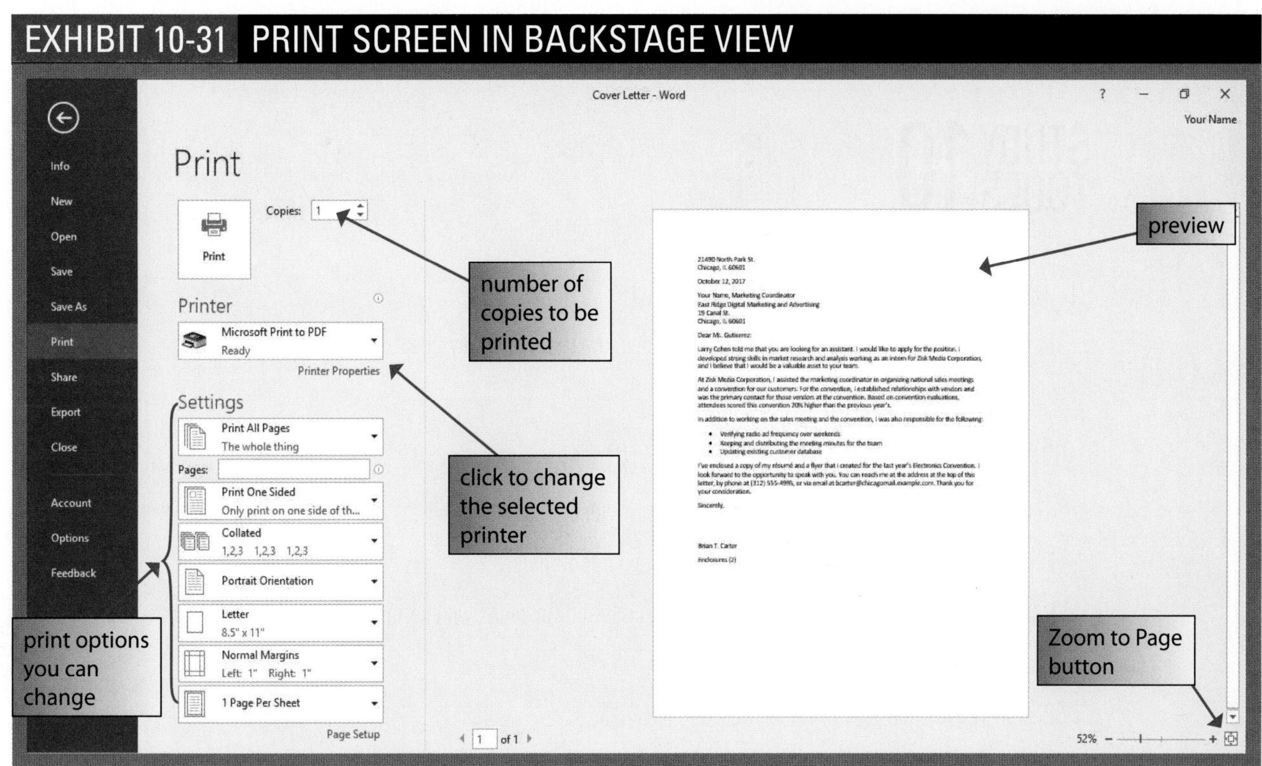

8 On the ribbon, click the **File tab**. In the navigation bar, click **Close**. The Cover Letter document closes, and the Resume Final document is the current document.

9 Proof the Resume Final document one last time, and correct any remaining errors.

10 Replace Brian's name at the top of the document with your name, and then save the document.

11 View the Resume Final document on the Print screen in Backstage view.

TIP: If a document almost fits on one page, click the 1 Page Per Sheet button near the bottom of the Print screen in Backstage view, point to Scale to Paper Size, scroll down the submenu, and then click Letter 8.5×11in.

12 Print the document, and then close it.

End Activity

FYI

CREATING AN ENVELOPE

Most printers are capable of printing envelopes. To create an envelope, you need to create a document with the address and return address sized and positioned correctly. To do this, click the Envelopes button in the Create group on the Mailings tab to open the Envelopes and Labels dialog box with the Envelopes tab selected. Type the recipient's name and address in the Delivery address box, type your return address in the Return address box, load an envelope in the printer, and then print it. If you click Add to Document instead of Print, the envelope will be added as a new page to the current document. Alternatively, if a letter is open in the document window, select the inside address, and then open the Envelopes and Labels dialog box to have the recipient's name and address pasted in the Delivery address box.

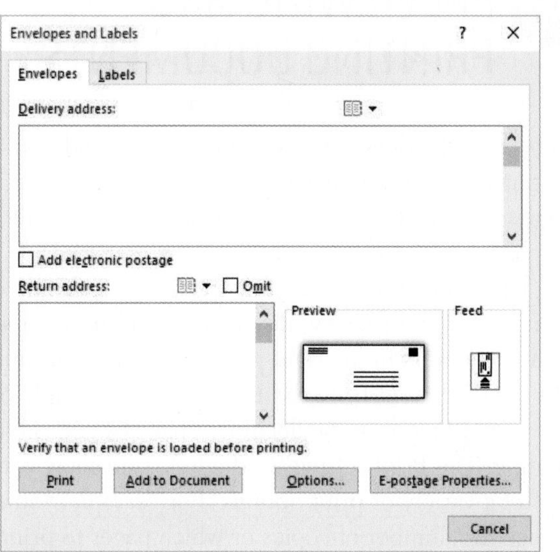

STUDY TOOLS 10

READY TO STUDY? IN THE BOOK, YOU CAN:

- ☐ Rip out the Chapter Review Card, which includes key terms and key chapter concepts.

ONLINE AT WWW.CENGAGEBRAIN.COM, YOU CAN:

- ☐ Review key concepts from the chapter in a short video.
- ☐ Explore creating a document with the interactive infographic.
- ☐ Practice what you've learned with more Practice It and On Your Own exercises.
- ☐ Prepare for tests with quizzes.
- ☐ Review the key terms with flashcards.

QUIZ YOURSELF

1. What are nonprinting characters, and how do you display them?
2. How do you insert symbols that are not included in the AutoCorrect list?
3. When you use drag and drop to move text, can you next use the Paste command to paste that text somewhere else? Why or why not?
4. What is a font?
5. According to the chapter, what is a point?
6. What is the default paragraph spacing in a Word document? What is the default line spacing?
7. What is justified text?
8. Where are the default tab stops? What happens to them when you insert a new tab stop?
9. When you create a bulleted or a numbered list, what character is inserted after the bullet symbol or the number, and what type of indent is applied to the paragraph?
10. Describe two ways to indent a paragraph one-half inch from the left margin.
11. What do the buttons on the Paste Options menu do?
12. What tool do you use to copy the format of a block of text to another block of text?
13. What happens when you type text in the Search Document box in the Navigation Pane?
14. How are possible spelling errors, contextual spelling errors, and grammatical errors flagged in a document?
15. What does the Print screen in Backstage view show?

PRACTICE IT

Practice It 10-1

1. Start Word and open a new, blank document. Display the rulers, show nonprinting characters, and then save the blank document as **Complaint Draft**.
2. Type the date **February 18, 2017** using AutoComplete for *February*.
3. Press the Enter key, and then type the following inside address, using the default paragraph spacing and allowing AutoCorrect to change *Cafe* to *Café*:

   Todd Huang, Manager

   Plaza Café

   21 Main St.

   Atlanta, GA 30032

   Dear Mr. Huang:

   I am writing to express my disappointment at the service my colleagues and I received during our celebration of the launch of our new product EasyGo.
4. After *EasyGo* and before the period, type **(tm)** allowing AutoCorrect to change it to ™.
5. Position the insertion point after the period, and then press the Spacebar. Type **You can reach me at** and then type your email address followed by a period. Press the Enter key, and then type your name.
6. Remove the hyperlink formatting from your email address.
7. Remove the spacing after the first three paragraphs in the inside address.
8. Save and close the document.
9. Open the data file **Menu** located in the Chapter 10\Practice It folder. Use the Save As command to save the file as **Cafe Menu**. Open the file **Complaint** located in the Chapter 10\Practice It folder. Save this file as **Complaint Letter**.
10. Switch to the Cafe Menu document. In the third line, delete the *e* from *Fixe* and use the Symbol button to insert **é** so the word is *Fixé*.
11. Select all the text in the document, change the font to Bradley Hand ITC, and change the font size to 14 points. Change the font size of the text in the second paragraph to 12 points, and then change the font size of the text in the third paragraph to 20 points.
12. In the first line, make *Plaza Café* bold, increase the font size to 36 points, and change the font color to Olive Green, Accent 3, Darker 50%.
13. Center-align the first two paragraphs.
14. In the third paragraph, add a Right Tab stop at the 6-inch mark on the ruler, and then drag it to the 6.5-inch mark. Insert a tab character after *Prix Fixé Meal*, and then type **$38**.
15. Increase the spacing before and after the third paragraph to 24 points.

16. Select all the text and the paragraph mark in the lines starting with *Appetizer*, *Entrée*, and *Dessert*. Format the lines as bold, and then format them as a numbered list using Arabic numerals followed by a period. Decrease the indent so they are aligned at the left margin. (*Hint*: You will need to drag the Left Indent marker on the ruler.)
17. Format the three paragraphs under *Appetizer*, the four paragraphs under *Entrée*, and the first three paragraphs under *Dessert* as bulleted lists using the right-pointing arrowhead in the Bullet Library.
18. Add a custom border to the top and bottom of the paragraph containing *Prix Fixé Meal*. Use the style that appears at the bottom of the Style list after scrolling the Style list on the Borders tab in the Borders and Shading dialog box down one row (a line composed of a dash followed by two dots); the Olive Green, Accent 3, Darker 50% color; and a width of 1½ points. (*Hint*: Make sure you click the Custom button in the Setting list in the dialog box.)
19. Add Olive Green, Accent 3, Lighter 60% shading to the first paragraph.
20. Copy the formatting of the first paragraph to the last paragraph containing text (*Make your reservation today!*). Change the spacing before the last paragraph containing text to 48 points and after this paragraph to 30 points.
21. Copy the first paragraph to the Clipboard. Switch to the Complaint Letter document. Paste the copied text in the empty paragraph in the second line in the inside address as text only.
22. Select all the text in the document, and then change the line spacing to single spacing.
23. At the end of the letter, replace *Your Name* in the closing with your name.
24. In the body of the letter, move the second paragraph (which begins with *As the person*) after the third paragraph so it becomes the third paragraph. Then copy *Plaza Café* from the second sentence in the first paragraph to the end of the last sentence in the first paragraph after *expect from* and before the period.
25. In the first paragraph, correct the spelling of the misspelled word *colleagues*. Then check the rest of the document, and make any corrections needed. If a word is flagged but spelled correctly, ignore it.
26. Save the Complaint Letter document, examine it in the preview pane on the Print tab in Backstage view, and then print it. Close the Complaint Letter document.
27. In the Cafe Menu document, add your name in the last, blank paragraph at the end of the document. Save the document.
28. Examine the Cafe Menu document in the preview pane on the Print tab in Backstage view, and then print it. Close the Cafe Menu document.

Practice It 10-2

1. Open a new blank document, and then save the document as **Thank You Letter**.
2. Change the font to Century, change the font size to 12 points, and change the line spacing to single spaced.
3. Type the following as the return address:

   Columbus Community Center

   114 27th St.

   Columbus, OH 43002
4. Press the Enter key, and then add **October 21, 2017** as the date.
5. Press the Enter key, and then type the following as the inside address:

   Kevin Moore

   Career Counseling

   12 Grove St.

   Columbus, OH 43002
6. Press the Enter key, type the salutation **Dear Mr. Moore:** and then press the Enter key.
7. Type the following paragraph: **Thank you for agreeing to give a presentation describing job search strategies. We are hoping that you can address the following questions as part of your presentation:**
8. Press the Enter key, and then type the following questions as separate paragraphs:

   What is the best way to find job listings?

   How do I learn how to network?

   How do I prepare for an interview?

   Do I need to dress in a business suit?
9. Insert a new paragraph after the last question, and then type **Thank you again for your time.** Press the Enter key, and then type the complimentary closing **Sincerely,** (including the comma).
10. Press the Enter key three times, and then type your name.
11. Format the four questions as a numbered list, and then increase the indent so that the numbers are aligned at the 1-inch mark.
12. Format the four questions as bold.

13. Remove the extra space after the first two lines in the return address and after the first three lines in the inside address.
14. Increase the space before the first line in the letter (the first line in the return address) to 42 points.
15. Change the alignment of the return address, the date, and the closing ("Sincerely," the two blank paragraphs following "Sincerely," and your name) to right-aligned.
16. Check the spelling and grammar in the document, and correct any errors.
17. Save the document, preview and print it, and then close it.

ON YOUR OWN

On Your Own 10-1

1. Create a new document based on the Modern Fax Cover template—the version that does not include the eFax app. (*Hint*: You must be connected to the Internet to use templates. In the Search box on the New screen, type **modern fax**, and then click the Search button to filter the templates to show fax templates.) This template contains placeholders that you click once to select and replace with text.
2. Save the document as **Price Quote**.
3. Select all the text in the document, and then change the font size of all the text to 12 points. Select *Fax* in the first line, and then change the font size of the selected text to 48 points.
4. Next to *To:*, click [Name] to select the placeholder. Type your instructor's name.
5. Next to *From:*, if the name is not your name, select the name, delete it, and then type your name.
6. Next to *Pages:*, replace the placeholder with **2**.
7. Next to *Subject:*, type **Remodeling project quote**.
8. Next to *Date:*, click the placeholder, click the arrow that appears, and then click Today below the calendar.
9. Next to *Cc:*, select the placeholder, and then delete it. Then delete Cc:. (There will be a blank line between the *Subject* and the *Date* lines.)
10. Select all four phone number labels and placeholder text, and then press the Delete key to delete that text.
11. In the last line, click the "[Start text here]" placeholder, and then type the following. In the paragraphs containing prices, press the Tab key instead of the Spacebar before the price.

    Per your request, here is my quote for completing your remodeling project:

    5 Windows $1,625.79

    Skylight $451.99

    Labor $1,100.00

    Total $3,177.78

    Please let me know if you have any questions.
12. Change the font color of *Fax* in the first line to Gray-25%, Accent 2. (Note that this document uses a different color palette than the other documents you have created.)
13. Format the dollar amounts at the bottom of the page in bold.
14. Indent all the text under *Comments* one inch from the left margin, and then indent the same text one inch from the right margin.
15. Add shading using the Gray-25%, Accent 2, Lighter 80% color behind all the text below *Comments*.
16. Indent the four paragraphs containing prices another half-inch. Notice that the shading is no longer a rectangle behind all the text.
17. Decrease the indent of the four paragraphs containing prices one-half inch so it again matches the indent of the first and last paragraphs below *Comments*.
18. In the four paragraphs containing the prices, set a Left Tab stop at the 1.75-inch mark on the ruler, and set a Decimal Tab stop at the 3.5-inch mark on the ruler. Insert a tab before the first character in each of the four lines containing prices.
19. Save the document, examine it in the preview pane on the Print tab in Backstage view, print it, and then close the document.

Part 6
WORD 2016

11 | Formatting a Long Document

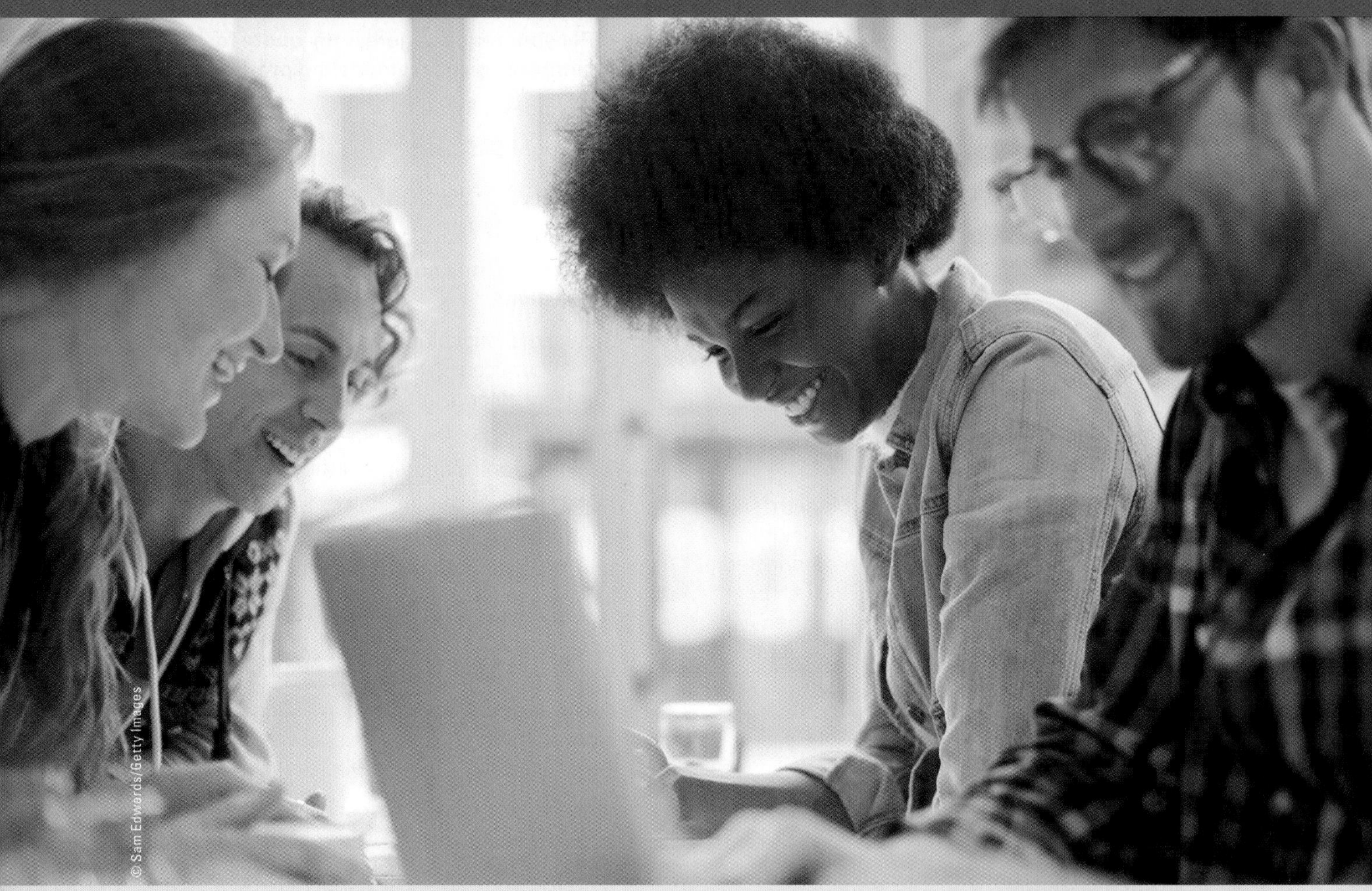

LEARNING OBJECTIVES After studying the material in this chapter, you will be able to:

- 11-1 Find and replace text
- 11-2 Work with styles
- 11-3 Work with themes
- 11-4 Scroll through a long document
- 11-5 Work with the document outline
- 11-6 Change the margins
- 11-7 Insert a manual page break
- 11-8 Add page numbers, headers, and footers
- 11-9 Create citations and a list of works cited
- 11-10 Create footnotes and endnotes

After finishing this chapter, go to **PAGE 342** for **STUDY TOOLS**.

11-1 FINDING AND REPLACING TEXT

Although a shorter document is useful for providing a summary or snapshot view, longer documents are a fact of life in the business world, the government arena, academia, and personal life. Long documents are created for developing business plans, proposing new ideas or products, evaluating current strategies, and explaining new products or approaches. In academia, long documents are commonly used when applying for grants, documenting research, submitting journal articles, and even writing books.

When working with a longer document, you can spend a lot of time reading through the text to locate a particular word or phrase. The Find command provides a faster way to locate a word or phrase. The Find and Replace dialog box makes it simple to replace a word or phrase throughout a document.

11-1a Finding Text

To find specific text in a document, you can use the Results tab in the Navigation pane, which you open by clicking the Find button in the Editing group on the Home tab. In the Search document box, you type the text for which you are searching. As you type, Word highlights every instance of the search text in the document and displays the corresponding text snippets in the Navigation pane. See Exhibit 11-1. You can click a snippet to go immediately to its location in the document.

Begin Activity

Find text.

1 Open the data file **Biking** located in the Chapter 11\Chapter folder. Save the document as **Biking Proposal**. Change the zoom percentage to **120%**, if necessary.

2 On the Home tab, in the Editing group, click the **Find button**. The Navigation pane opens on the left side of the document window with the Results tab selected. The empty, white box at the top of the Navigation pane is the Search document box.

3 At the top of the Navigation pane, click in the **Search document box**, and then type **r**. Every letter *r* in the document is highlighted with yellow.

PROBLEM?
If the Search document box contains text, delete it and then do Step 3.

4 Continue typing **oute** to complete the word *route*. As you continue typing, the highlighting is removed from words that do not match the search text. The six instances of the word *route* are highlighted in the document. Refer to Exhibit 11-1.

EXHIBIT 11-1 RESULTS TAB IN THE NAVIGATION PANE WITH SEARCH RESULTS FOR *ROUTE*

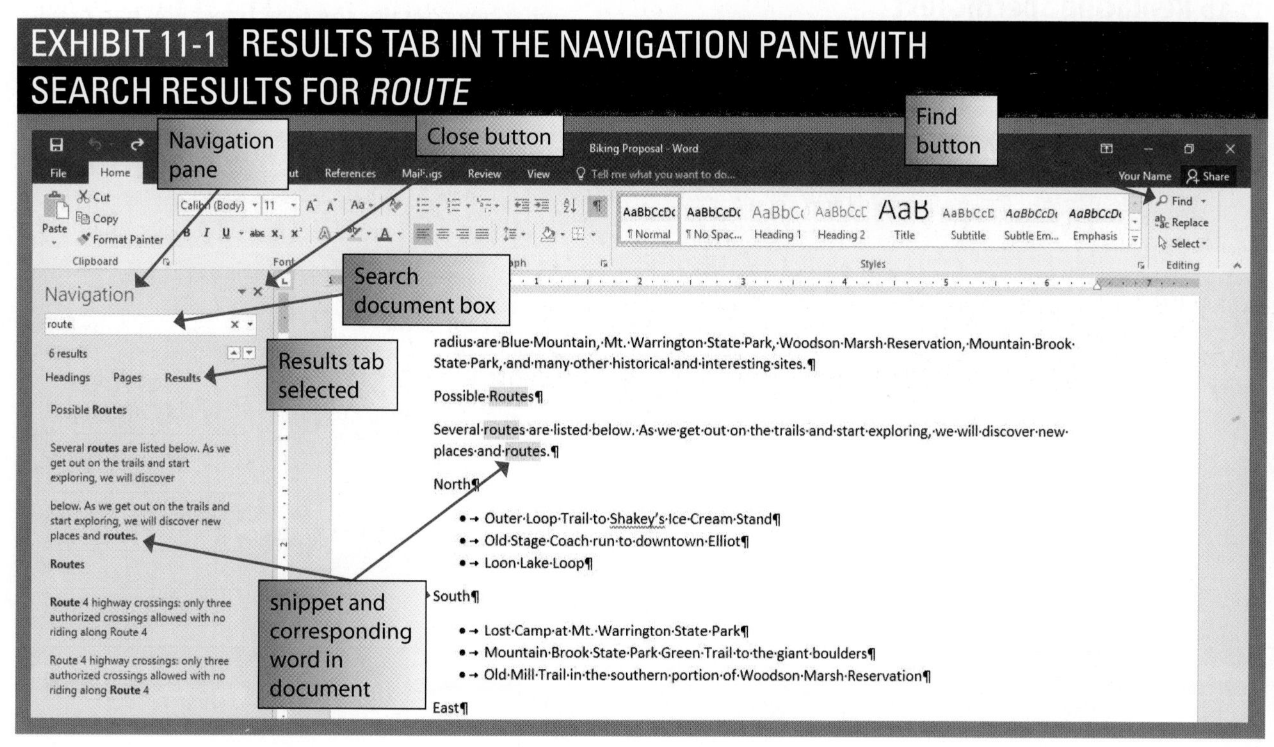

5. In the Navigation pane, click the **first snippet.** In the document, the first instance of the word *route* is highlighted with gray shading on top of the yellow highlight. Note that the word containing *route* is *Routes* (with an *s*), but only *Route* is selected. Also note that *Route*, with an uppercase *R*, is highlighted as a found word, even though you typed the word with all lowercase letters.
6. Click in the document window, select the first instance of *route*, and then type **Course**. (If you selected the entire word including the *s*, add an **s** to *Course* so that the final word is *Courses*.) The text you type replaces the selected text, and the snippets in the Navigation pane and the highlighting in the document disappear.
7. In the Navigation pane, click the **Next Search Result button** ▾. The search is performed again, and the remaining instances of *route* are highlighted in the document and listed as snippets in the Navigation pane. In the document, the next instance of *route* is selected.
8. In the Navigation pane title bar, click the **Close button** ✕. The Navigation pane closes.
9. Save the document.

> **TIP:** Remember to save frequently as you work through the chapter. A good practice is to save after every Activity.

End Activity

11-1b Replacing Specific Text

You can replace specific text using the Replace tab in the Find and Replace dialog box. To open the Replace tab in the Find and Replace dialog box, click the Replace button in the Editing group on the Home tab. On the Replace tab, you type the text you want to locate in the Find what box and the text you want to substitute in the Replace with box. Click Find Next to locate the next instance of the text in the Find what box. Click Replace to replace just that instance, or click Replace All to replace all instances of the text. See Exhibit 11-2.

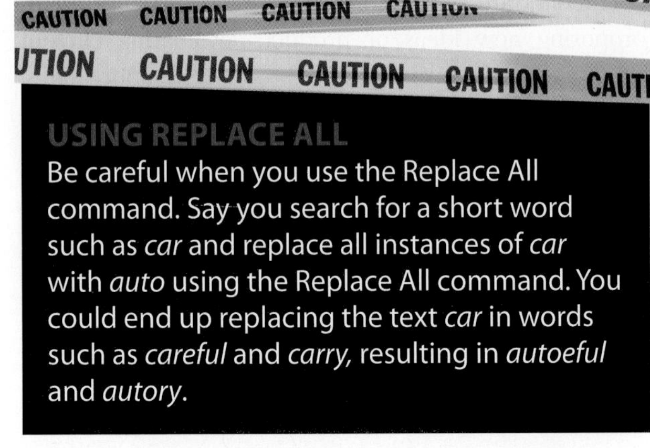

USING REPLACE ALL

Be careful when you use the Replace All command. Say you search for a short word such as *car* and replace all instances of *car* with *auto* using the Replace All command. You could end up replacing the text *car* in words such as *careful* and *carry*, resulting in *autoeful* and *autory*.

Begin Activity

Replace specific text.

1. Press the **Ctrl+Home keys**. The insertion point moves to the beginning of the document.
2. On the Home tab, in the Editing group, click the **Replace button**. The Find and Replace dialog box opens, with the Replace tab selected. The Find what box contains the search text you had previously typed in the Search document box in the Navigation pane—*route*.

EXHIBIT 11-2 REPLACE TAB IN THE FIND AND REPLACE DIALOG BOX

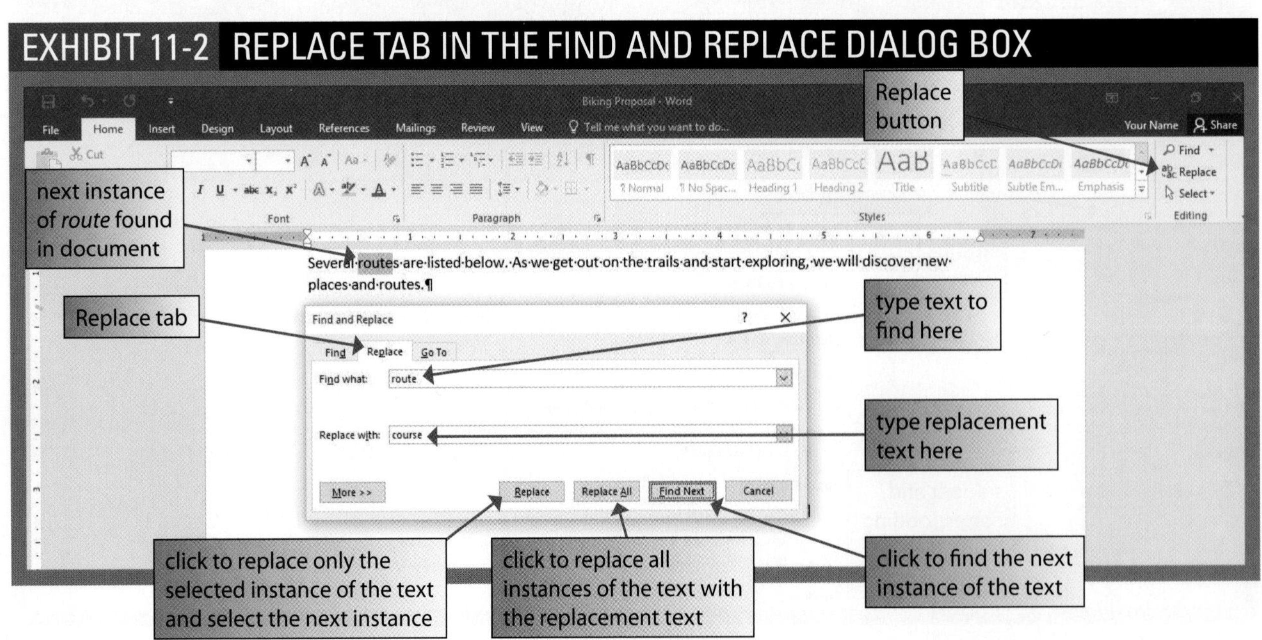

3 Click in the **Replace with box**, and then type **course**.

4 Click **Find Next.** The dialog box stays open, and the next instance of *route* is highlighted in the document. Refer back to Exhibit 11-2.

PROBLEM? If the dialog box displays more options than shown in Exhibit 11-2, click Less in the dialog box to collapse it.

5 In the dialog box, click **Replace**. The selected text in the document changes to *course*, and the next instance of the text *course* is selected.

6 In the dialog box, click **Replace**. The selected text is changed to *course*, and the next instance of *route* is selected. This time, the selected text has an uppercase *R*.

7 In the dialog box, click **Replace**. The selected text is changed to *Course* with an uppercase first letter because the found text had an uppercase first letter. The next instance of *route* is selected in the bulleted item that starts with *Route 4 highway crossings*. In this case, the selected text should not be replaced because it is part of the name of a road, not a synonym for *course*.

8 In the dialog box, click **Find Next**. The selected text is left unchanged and the next instance of *route* is selected. Again, the selected text should not be replaced.

9 In the dialog box, click **Find Next**. The selected text is left unchanged and a dialog box opens telling you that Word has finished searching the document.

10 Click **OK**. The dialog box closes, and the document scrolls back to the beginning. The Find and Replace dialog box is still open.

11 Click **Close**. The Find and Replace dialog box closes.

End Activity

11-2 WORKING WITH STYLES

A **style** is a named set of formatting instructions, or definitions. All text has a style applied to it. Unless you change to a different style, text is formatted with the Normal style, which, as you have seen, is text formatted as 11-point Calibri in a left-aligned paragraph with line spacing set to 1.08 and 8 points of space after the paragraph.

The Normal style is part of the Normal template. A **template** is a file that contains a set of styles that can be used to format documents based on that template. The **Normal template** is the template on which all new, blank Word documents are based. The Normal template does not contain any placeholder text or graphics, but it does include the Normal style and other built-in styles.

Using styles saves time and makes the elements in a document consistent. For example, if you want all the headings in a document to be bold, dark red, 14-point Cambria and centered, you could create a style named Heading that includes all of those formatting instructions and apply it to every heading in

FYI

NARROWING A SEARCH

You can customize a search to narrow the results. First, open the Find Options dialog box, and then select the ways you want to narrow the search. For example, you can select the Find whole words only check box to search for complete words, or you can select the Match case check box to find text with the same case (upper or lower) as the search text. To open the dialog box, you can click the Search for more things arrow to the right of the Search document box in the Navigation Pane, and then click Options. These same options are also available in the Find and Replace dialog box when you click the More button to display the Search Options section.

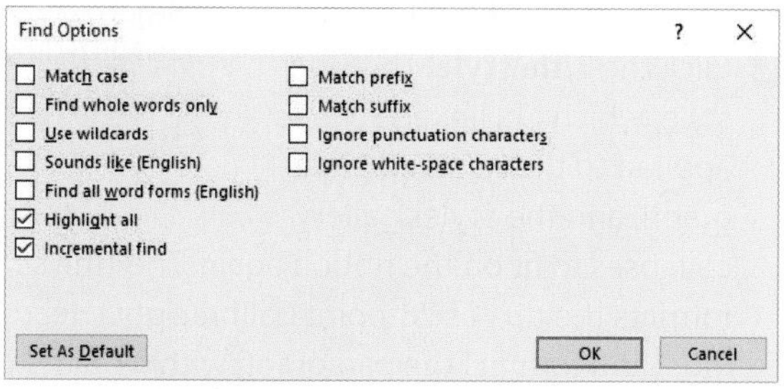

Find Options ? X

- [ ] Match case
- [ ] Find whole words only
- [ ] Use wildcards
- [ ] Sounds like (English)
- [ ] Find all word forms (English)
- [x] Highlight all
- [x] Incremental find
- [ ] Match prefix
- [ ] Match suffix
- [ ] Ignore punctuation characters
- [ ] Ignore white-space characters

Set As Default | OK | Cancel

style A named set of formatting instructions.

template A file that contains a set of styles that can be used to format documents based on that template.

Normal template The template on which all Word documents are based.

the document. If you later decide the headings should be 16-point Arial on a shaded blue background, you simply change the style definition, which updates all text that has the Heading style applied to the new style definition. When you change the text or paragraph formatting of a single instance, such as by applying bold or changing the alignment, you are applying direct formatting. **Direct formatting** overrides the style currently applied, but it does not change the style definition.

There are five types of styles. A **paragraph style** formats an entire paragraph and can include formatting instructions for both paragraphs and text. The Heading style described in the previous paragraph would be a paragraph style. Another commonly used style type is the character style. **Character style** definitions include only text-formatting instructions. A third style type, the **linked style**, behaves as a paragraph or a character style depending on what is selected when you apply the style. If you select only a character or a few words, the style is applied as a character style, and any paragraph formatting included in the style definition is ignored. If you apply a linked style to a paragraph, it is treated as a paragraph style—in other words, it applies both paragraph and text formatting. The other two style types are table and list styles, which are used to format, as the names indicate, tables and lists. Usually, you don't need to worry about identifying the type of a style. Just be sure to correctly select the text to which you want to apply the style.

Style definitions include more than formatting instructions and the style type. They also specify which style the style is based on—often the Normal style. Paragraph and linked style definitions also specify which style will be applied to the next paragraph created when you press the Enter key. For paragraphs formatted with the Normal style, the next paragraph created is also formatted with the Normal style. For some styles, such as a style that is intended to format headings, the style for the next paragraph is usually the Normal style or another style created for body text. That makes sense, because you typically want to format only a single paragraph with a heading style.

direct formatting Formatting that overrides the style currently applied.

paragraph style A style type that includes instructions for formatting text and paragraphs.

character style A style type that includes instructions for formatting only text.

linked style A style type that acts as a paragraph style if applied to a paragraph and as a character style if applied to text.

11-2a Applying a Style from the Styles Gallery

Word comes with many built-in styles. Each built-in style has a name that reflects its suggested use. For example, the Title style is intended for formatting the title at the beginning of a document, and the various Heading styles are intended to format different levels of headings.

The most commonly used styles are listed in the Styles gallery in the Styles group on the Home tab. In the Styles gallery, a paragraph symbol (¶) appears next to the names of the styles that are paragraph styles. Styles without the paragraph symbol next to their names are either character or linked styles.

To apply a style from the Styles gallery, select the text or paragraph to which you want to apply the style, and then click the style in the Styles gallery. When you apply a style, that style is selected in the Styles gallery. In Exhibit 11-3, the Normal style in the Styles gallery has a border, indicating that it is selected; that is, it is the style applied to the currently selected text.

When you create a new document, only two built-in heading styles, Heading 1 and Heading 2, appear in the Styles gallery. If you apply the Heading 2 style to text, the Heading 3 style is added to the Styles gallery. As you apply each more subordinate heading style, the next level of heading style is added to the gallery.

Begin Activity

Apply styles from the Styles gallery.

1. Select the first paragraph in the document (the title line). On the Home tab, in the Styles group, the Normal style—the default style—is selected.
2. On the Home tab, in the Styles group, click the **More button** . The Styles gallery opens. Refer back to Exhibit 11-3.
3. Point to several of the styles in the gallery to see the Live Preview of those styles applied to the selected paragraph.
4. Click the **Title style**. The Title style, which is a linked style, is applied to the selected paragraph, and the Styles gallery collapses to fit on the ribbon again. The Title style formats the text as 28-point Calibri Light (Headings) and formats the paragraph with 0 points of space before and after and single-spaced line spacing.

TIP: To apply a style that does not appear in the Styles gallery, open the Styles pane by clicking the Dialog Box Launcher in the Styles group, and then click the style in the list.

EXHIBIT 11-3 STYLES IN THE STYLES GALLERY

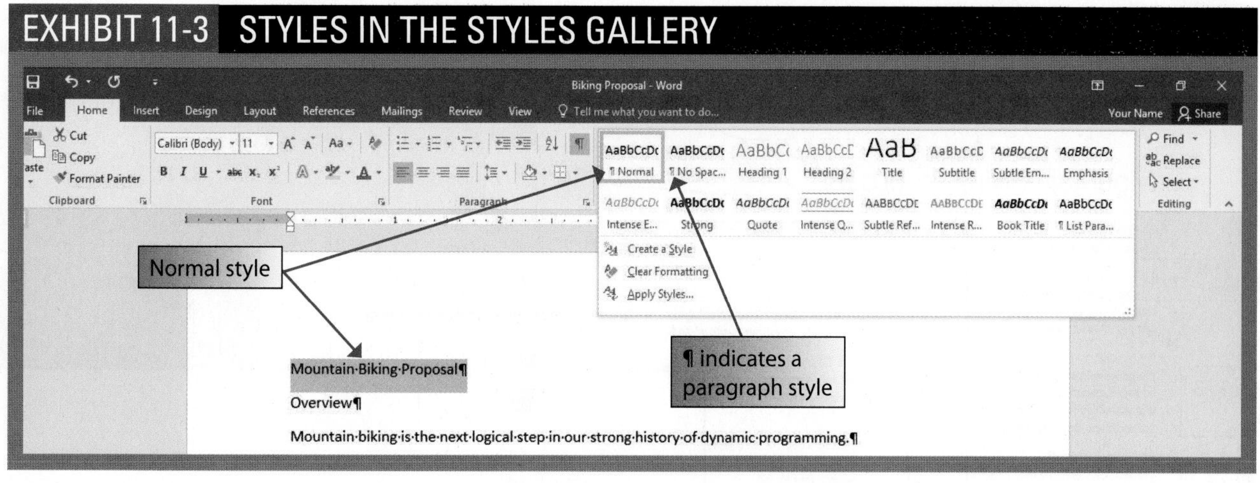

5 Select the **Overview paragraph** (the second paragraph in the document).

6 In the Styles group, click the **Heading 1 style**. The Heading 1 style formats the selected paragraph as 16-point Calibri Light (Headings), changes the color of the text to Blue, Accent 1, Darker 25%, removes the space after the paragraph, and changes the space before the paragraph to 12 points.

7 Select the **Finances paragraph** (the fifth paragraph). In the Styles group, only two Heading styles—Heading 1 and Heading 2—are listed in the gallery.

8 In the Styles gallery, click the **Heading 2 style**. The selected text is formatted with the Heading 2 style, which is similar to the Heading 1 style, but the size of the text is 13 points and the space before the paragraph is only 2 points. Because you applied the Heading 2 style, the Heading 3 style is now listed in the gallery.

9 Scroll down in the document and apply Heading styles to the following paragraphs:

Minimum Funding	**Heading 3**
Moderate Funding	**Heading 3**
Description	**Heading 1**
Area for Setting Up Trails	**Heading 2**
Possible Courses	**Heading 2**
North	**Heading 3**
South	**Heading 3**
East	**Heading 3**
West	**Heading 3**
Outstanding Questions	**Heading 2**
Potential Issues	**Heading 1**
Conclusion	**Heading 1**

10 At the beginning of the document, select all of the text in the first paragraph in the Overview section (starts with **Mountain biking is the...**).

11 In the Styles gallery, click the **More button**, and then click the **Emphasis style**. The selected text is formatted with the Emphasis style, a character style that applies italic formatting to text. Exhibit 11-4 shows the three pages of the document with the title and heading styles applied.

End Activity

FYI HEADING STYLES

The highest level heading style, Heading 1, is for major headings and applies the most noticeable formatting, with a larger font than the other heading styles. (In heading styles, the highest level has the lowest number.) The Heading 2 style is for headings subordinate to the highest level headings; it applies slightly less prominent formatting than the Heading 1 style. When you apply a heading style, the font labeled (Headings) in the Font list is applied to the text.

Heading 1

Heading 2

Heading 3

EXHIBIT 11-4 STYLES APPLIED TO THE TITLE AND HEADINGS

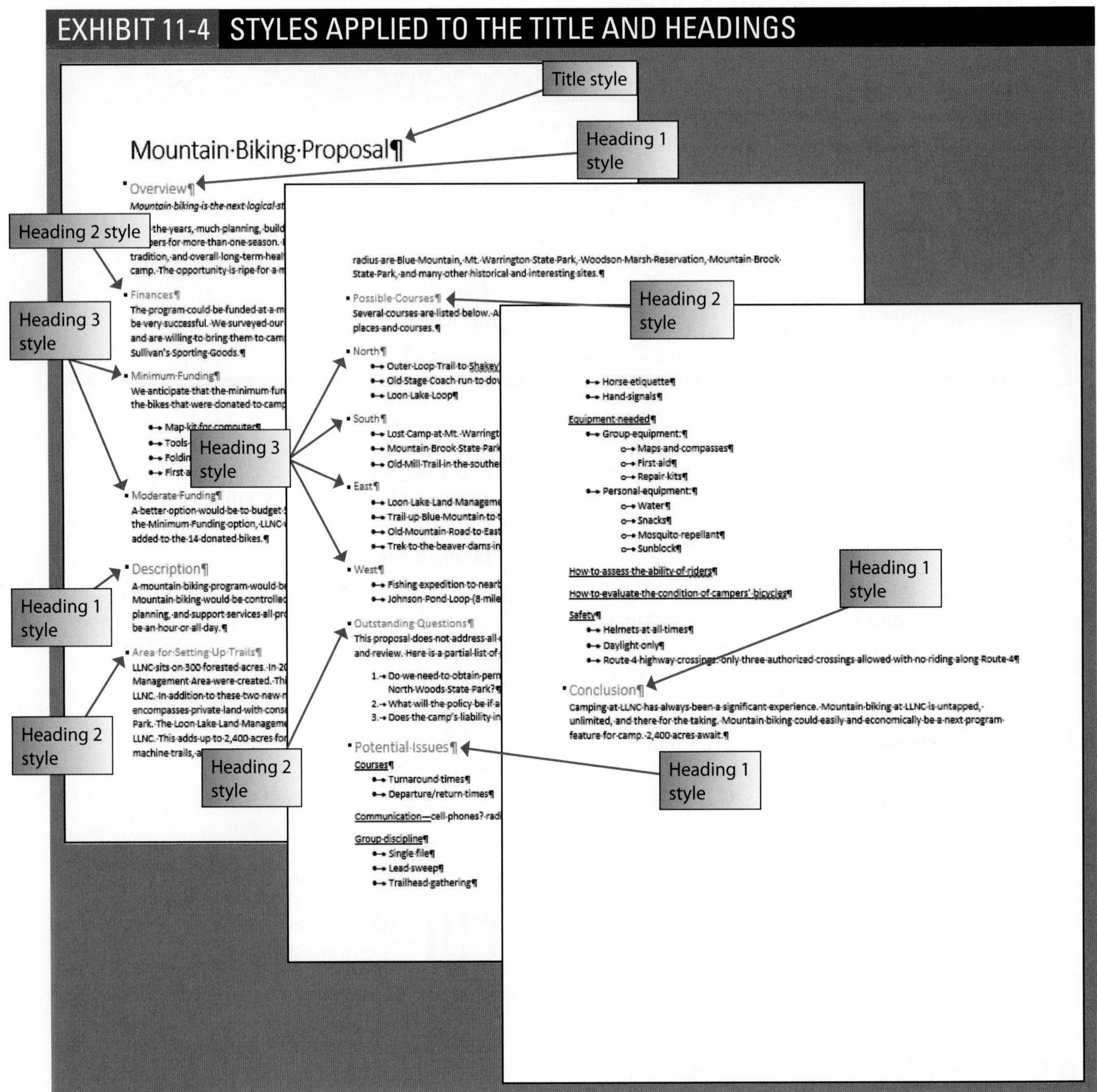

11-2b Changing the Style Set

A **style set** is a coordinated group of style definitions. The style set used in new documents is the default style set. If you change the style set, the style definitions are changed. You can change the style set before or after you apply styles. Exhibit 11-5 shows the Live Preview of the Basic (Stylish) style set applied to the Biking Proposal document.

When you change the style set, the parts of the style definitions that are changed are the size of the text, the font style—that is, whether text is bold, italic, and so on—the spacing before and after paragraphs, the alignment of paragraphs, and whether paragraphs have borders. The fonts and set of colors used to format text does not change when you change the style set.

style set A coordinated group of style definitions.

Begin Activity

Change the style set.

1. On the ribbon, click the **Design tab**. In the Document Formatting group, point to the **first style set** in the gallery. This is always the current style set.

EXHIBIT 11-5 LIVE PREVIEW OF BASIC (STYLISH) STYLE SET

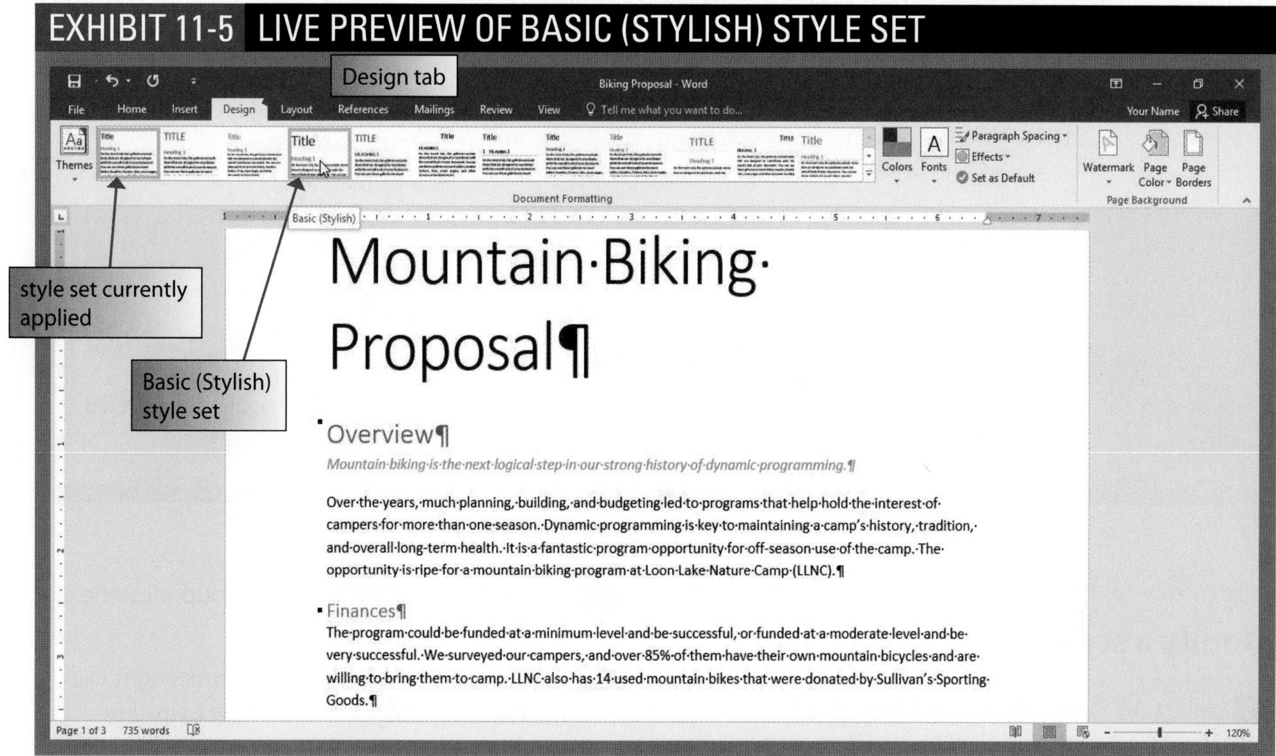

2 Point to the **fourth style set** in the gallery. Its ScreenTip identifies it as the Basic (Stylish) style set. The Live Preview shows the changes to the titles and headings. For example, the Heading 1 style is still formatted with the Calibri Light (Headings) font, but the font size in the Basic (Stylish) style set is 20 points instead of 16 points in the default style set, and the font color is green instead of blue. Refer to Exhibit 11-5.

TIP: To switch back to the default style set, on the Design tab, in the Document Formatting group, click the More button, and then click Reset to the Default Style Set.

3 In the gallery, click the **Basic (Stylish) style set.** The Basic (Stylish) style set is applied to the document.

End Activity

11-2c Modifying a Style in the Styles Gallery

If you want to change some parts of the definition of a style, you can modify it. To modify a style, first apply the style to text or a paragraph, and then apply direct formatting. Next, right-click the style in the Styles gallery, and then on the shortcut menu, click Update *Style Name* to Match Selection (where *Style Name* is the actual name of the style). Exhibit 11-6 shows the shortcut menu for the Heading 2 style.

Modifications you make to styles are saved only within the document. Also, if you change the style set after you modify the definition of a built-in style, the changes are not retained and the style definition from the new style set is applied.

FYI

SAVING A STYLE TO THE TEMPLATE

Changes to a style definition and new styles that you create are saved only with the current document. To make the modified style available to all documents based on the current template (even if it is the Normal template), right-click the style name, and then click Modify on the shortcut menu to open the Modify Style dialog box. At the bottom of the dialog box, click the New documents based on this template option button, and then click OK.

EXHIBIT 11-6 SHORTCUT MENU FOR THE HEADING 1 STYLE

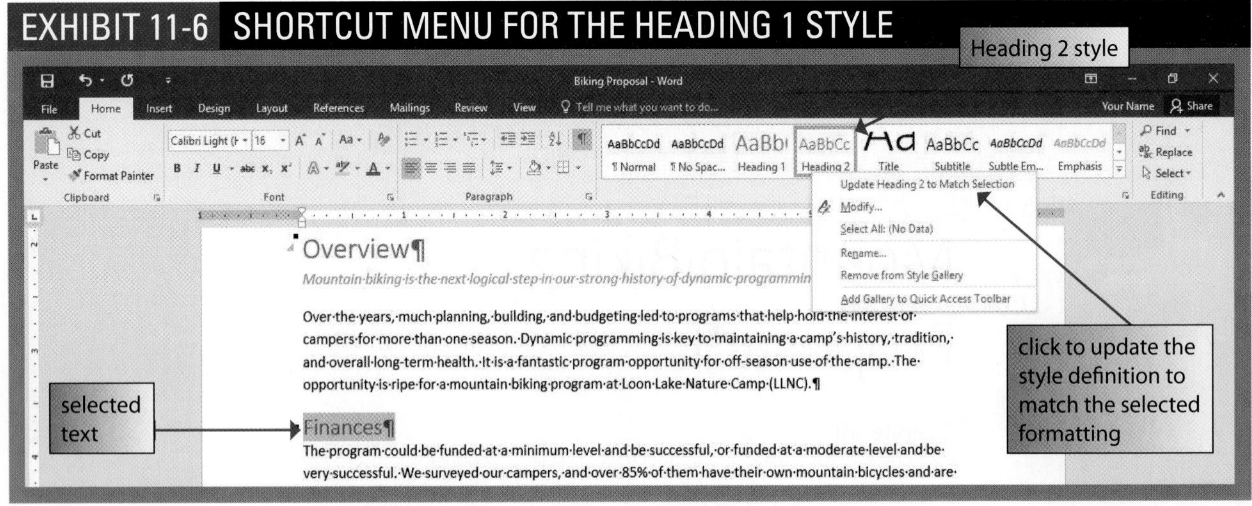

Begin Activity

Modify a style in the Styles gallery.

1. Select the **Finances heading paragraph**. The Heading 2 style is applied to the Finances heading.
2. Increase the font size of the selected text to **16 points**.
3. On the Home tab, in the Styles gallery, right-click the selected **Heading 2 style**. A shortcut menu opens. Refer to Exhibit 11-6.
4. On the shortcut menu, click **Update Heading 2 to Match Selection**. The style is redefined to match the formatting change you made to the Finances heading, and all the headings with the Heading 2 style applied now match this modified style.
5. Scroll down to the top of page 2, and then click in the **Area for Setting Up Trails heading paragraph**. This paragraph has the Heading 2 style applied to it. The change you made to the style—changing the font size to 16 points—was made to this heading as well.
6. Scroll back up to page 1 so that you can see both the Minimum Funding and Moderate Funding heading paragraphs, and then select the **Minimum Funding heading paragraph**. This paragraph has the Heading 3 style applied to it.
7. On the Home tab, in the Font group, click the **Underline button** U.
8. On the Home tab, in the Styles group, right-click the **Heading 3 style**, and then click **Update Heading 3 to Match Selection**. The style definition is modified, and all the text formatted with the Heading 3 style changes to reflect the new style definition. You can see the change to the Moderate Funding heading.

End Activity

TIP: To modify a style that does not appear in the Styles gallery, open the Styles pane by clicking the Dialog Box Launcher in the Styles group, point to the style you want to modify, click the arrow that appears, and then click Update *Style Name* to Match Selection.

11-2d Creating a New Style

You might need to create a new style for a document. The easiest way to create a new style is to format text in the way that you want, and then create the style based on the formatted text. To do this, select the formatted text, click the More button in the Styles group, and then click Create a Style to open the Create New Style from Formatting dialog box, which is shown in Exhibit 11-7. You can name and save the style from this dialog box.

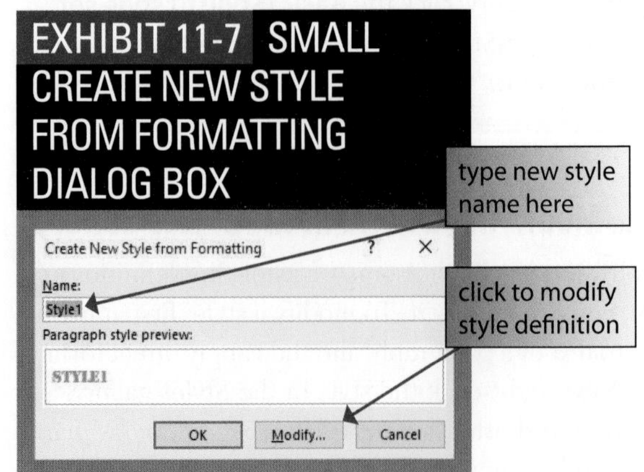
EXHIBIT 11-7 SMALL CREATE NEW STYLE FROM FORMATTING DIALOG BOX

New styles are created as linked styles. If you want to change the style to another type of style, in the Create New Style from Formatting dialog box, click Modify to open a larger version of the Create New Style from Formatting dialog box, which is shown in Exhibit 11-8. Click the Style type arrow, and then select the style type from the list.

If you create a new style and then change the style set, the new style will not be redefined. However, the style you created will no longer appear in the Styles gallery. The new style you created will still be available in the list of styles available to the document; it just no longer appears in the Styles gallery. To see the complete list of styles available for a document, you click the Dialog Box Launcher in the Styles group on the Home tab to open the Styles pane. In the Styles pane, you can click the custom style, and then click Add to Styles Gallery to add it to the Styles gallery in the new Quick Style set.

EXHIBIT 11-8 LARGE CREATE NEW STYLE FROM FORMATTING DIALOG BOX

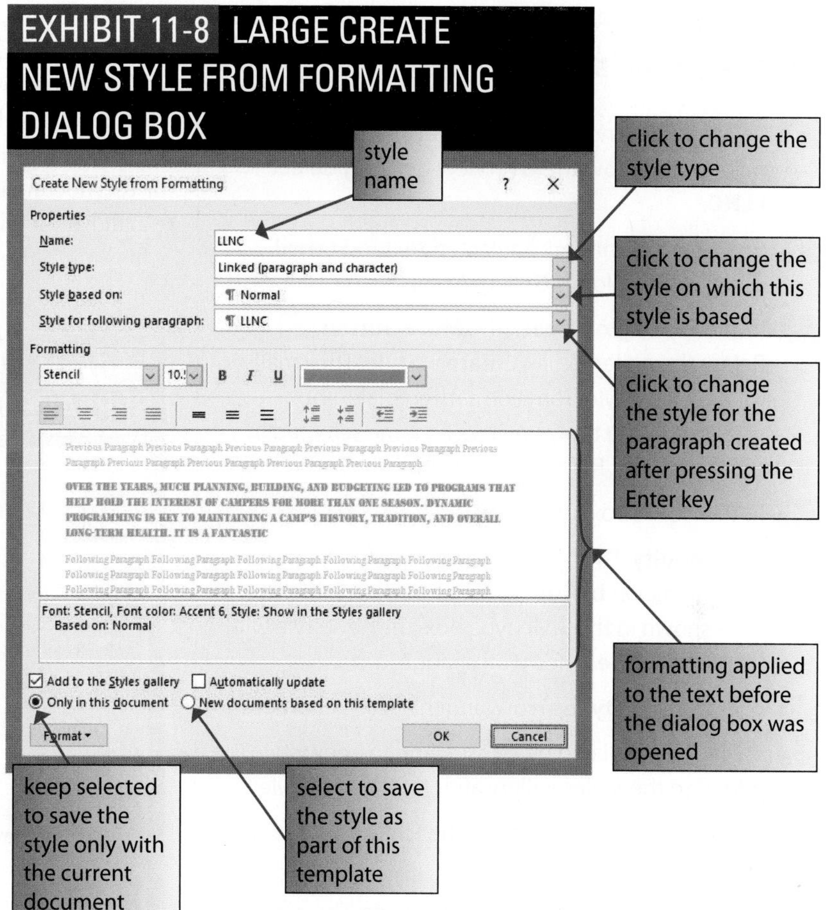

FYI MODIFYING THE STYLE BASED ON AND STYLE FOR FOLLOWING PARAGRAPH SETTINGS

Part of a style definition is the style on which the style is based. When you create a new style based on the formatting of selected text, the new style retains a connection to the original style. If you modify the original style, these changes will also be applied to the new style. For example, suppose you need to create a new style that will be used exclusively for formatting the heading Budget in all reports. You could start by selecting text formatted with the Heading 1 style, change the font color of the selected text to purple, and then save the formatting of the selected text as a new style named Budget. If you then modify the Heading 1 style—perhaps by adding italics—the text in the document that is formatted with the Budget style will also have italics, because it is based on the Heading 1 style. This connection between a new style and the style on which it is based enforces a consistent look among styles, helping to create a document with a coherent design. If, on the other hand, you don't want the new style to change when the style it is based on changes, open the larger Create from New Style Formatting dialog box, click the Style based on arrow, and then click Normal or (no style).

When you create a new paragraph or linked style, the style for the next paragraph created when you press the Enter key is that new style. To change this, open the larger version of the Create New Style from Formatting dialog box, as described above, click the Style for following paragraph arrow, and then select the style you want.

Begin Activity

Create a new style.

1. At the beginning of the document, in the second paragraph below the Overview heading, select **LLNC**.
2. Change the font of the selected text to **Stencil**. Change the color to **Green, Accent 6**.
3. In the Styles group, click the **More button** . Below the gallery, click **Create a Style**. The small Create New Style from Formatting dialog box opens with the temporary style name selected in the Name box. Refer back to Exhibit 11-7.
4. In the Name box, type **LLNC**.
5. Click **Modify**. The larger Create New Style from Formatting dialog box opens. Refer back to Exhibit 11-8. As shown in the Style type box, the new style will be a linked style unless you change it.
6. Click the **Style type arrow**, and then click **Character**.
7. Click **OK**. The dialog box closes, and the new style is added to the Styles gallery after the Normal style.
8. In the first paragraph below the Finances heading, select **LLNC**.
9. In the Styles group, click the **LLNC style**. The new style is applied to the selected text. See Exhibit 11-9.

End Activity

You could apply the new LLNC style to each instance of LLNC in the document, one at a time. A faster way to do this is to use the Replace tab in the Find and Replace dialog box. This is the same dialog box you used when you replaced instances of the text *route* with *course* in the document. To replace formatting, click More to expand the dialog box, and then specify the formatting you want to use. See Exhibit 11-10.

EXHIBIT 11-10 EXPANDED FIND AND REPLACE DIALOG BOX

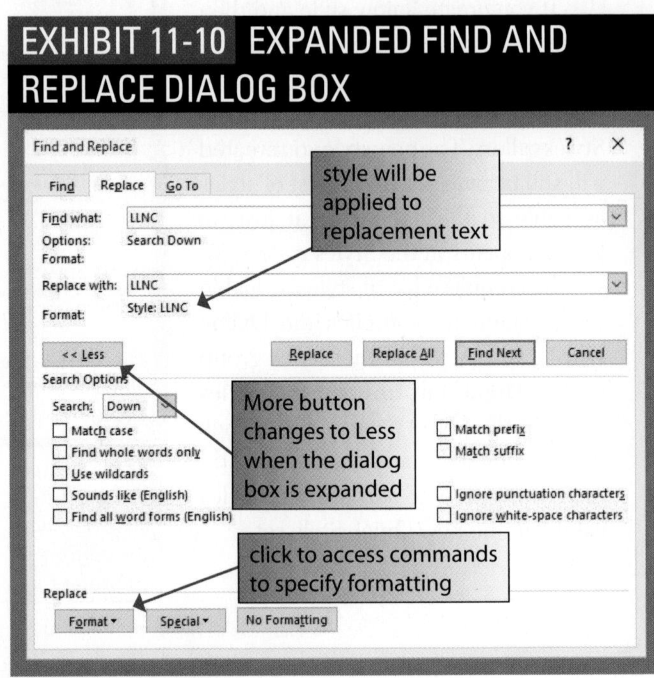

EXHIBIT 11-9 CUSTOM STYLE APPLIED TO TEXT

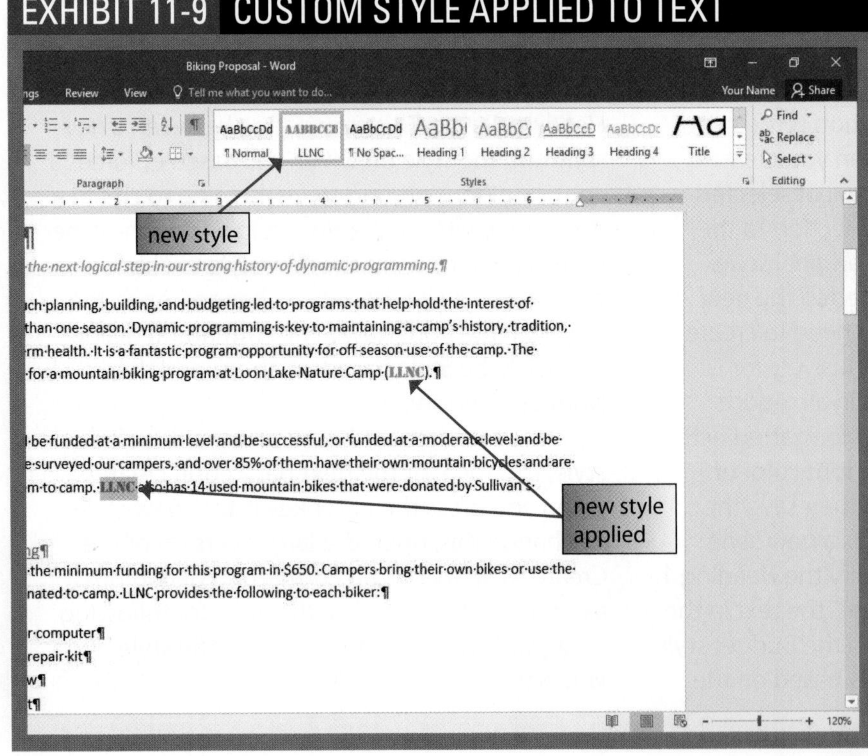

Begin Activity

Replace formatting.

1. On the Home tab, in the Editing group, click the **Replace button**. The Find and Replace dialog box opens. Because *LLNC* was selected before you opened the dialog box, *LLNC* appears in the Find what box.
2. Click in the **Replace with box**, delete **course** if necessary, and then type **LLNC**.
3. At the bottom of the dialog box, click **More**. The dialog box expands to show additional options, and the More button you just clicked changes to Less.

4 With the insertion point in the Replace with box, click **Format** at the bottom of the dialog box. On the menu, click **Style**. The Replace Style dialog box opens.

5 In the list, select **LLNC**, and then click **OK**. The Replace Style dialog box closes, and *Style: LLNC* appears under the Replace with box. Refer back to Exhibit 11-10.

6 Click **Replace All**. A dialog box opens telling you that 8 replacements were made and asking if you want to continue searching from the beginning.

7 In the dialog box, click **Yes**. Another dialog box opens telling you that 10 replacements were made.

8 Click **OK** in the dialog box that tells you that 10 replacements were made. All instances of *LLNC* formatted with the Normal style are replaced with *LLNC* formatted with the LLNC style.

9 In the Find and Replace dialog box, click **Close**.

End Activity

11-3 WORKING WITH THEMES

You can alter the look of the document by changing the document's theme. A **theme** is a coordinated set of colors, fonts, and effects. Created by professional designers, themes ensure that a document has a polished, coherent look. Several themes are included in Office, and many more are available in the templates stored on Office.com. The default theme for new documents is the Office theme.

Every theme assigns one font to headings and one to body text. These two theme fonts are always listed at the top of the Fonts menu with the labels *(Headings)* and *(Body)*. You have already seen this when you opened the Fonts menu to apply a different font to text and when you examined the fonts applied to documents. Some themes use one font for headings and another for body text; other themes use the same font for both elements. In the Office theme, the heading font is Calibri Light, and the body font is Calibri. If you change the theme, the theme fonts in the Font list change to match the fonts for the new theme.

This is the Office theme's heading font, Calibri Light.

This is the Office theme's body font, Calibri.

This is the Integral theme's heading font, Tw Cen MT Condensed.

This is the Integral theme's body font, Tw Cen MT.

When you type text in a new document, the text is formatted with the body text font. If you change the theme, text formatted with the theme fonts changes to the new theme's fonts. Text formatted with a non-theme font will not change.

Each theme also has a color palette. You saw the colors associated with the Office theme when you changed the color of text and the color of paragraph borders and shading. The Theme Colors are the coordinated colors of the current theme. This set of colors changes from theme to theme. Exhibit 11-11 shows the color palettes for the Office, Facet, and Integral themes. If you change the theme, text or objects formatted with a theme color will change based on the new theme's color palette. Text or objects formatted with one of the Standard Colors, or another color you select after clicking More Colors, will not change.

The Theme Colors are coordinated to look good together, so if you are going to use multiple colors in a document (perhaps for paragraph shading and font color), it's a good idea to stick with the Theme Colors.

EXHIBIT 11-11 THEME COLOR PALETTES

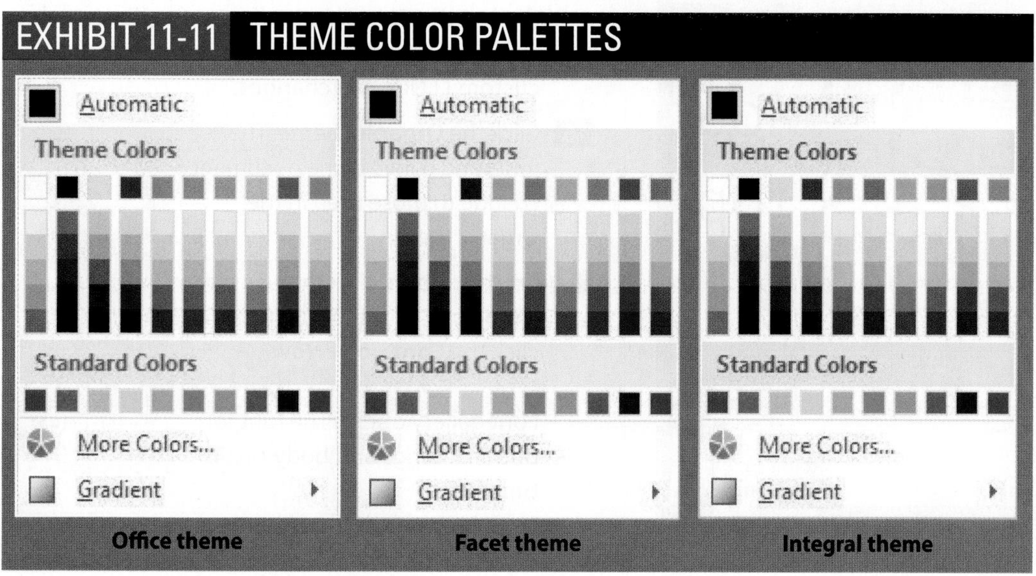

theme A coordinated set of colors, fonts, and effects.

FYI **CUSTOMIZING THE NORMAL TEMPLATE** The combination of themes and style sets provides an almost dizzying number of choices. You can select a theme; change the theme fonts, colors, or effects; change the style set; change the paragraph and line spacing; and redefine or create new styles to create a document quickly formatted with a distinctive look. If you come up with a combination you want to save and use when you create new documents—in other words, if you want to save changes to the Normal template—click the Set as Default button in the Document Formatting group on the Design tab.

11-3a Changing the Theme

You change the theme using the Themes gallery, which you open by clicking the Themes button in the Themes group on the Design tab. See Exhibit 11-12. Select the theme you want in the gallery. The new theme is applied to the entire document, and the colors and fonts change to match the colors and fonts of the new theme.

EXHIBIT 11-12 THEMES GALLERY

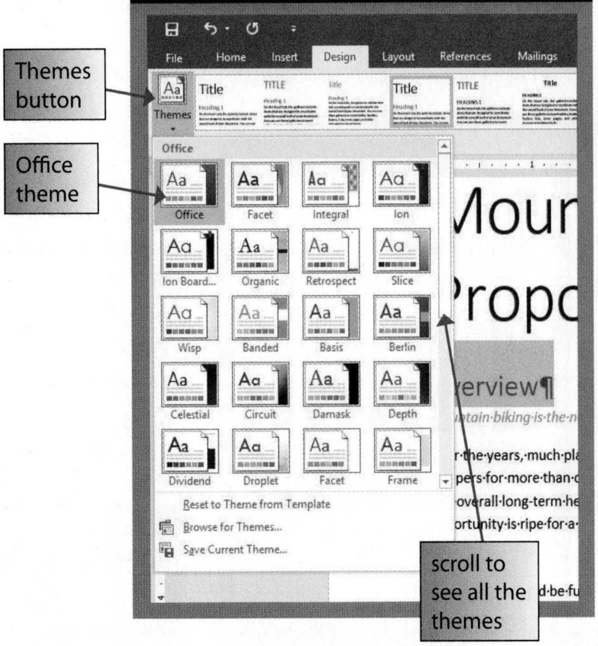

Begin Activity

Change the document's theme.

1 At the beginning of the document, select the **Overview heading**. This paragraph is formatted with the Heading 1 style.

2 On the Home tab, in the Font group, click the **Font Color button arrow**. The color selected is in the last column, second to last row in the theme colors. This is the Accent 6 color, Darker 25% shade. In the Office theme (the current theme), this is a shade of green. In a different theme, the Heading 1 font color will be in the same position, but might be a different color. In a different style set, the Heading 1 font color might be in a different position in the color palette.

3 Press the **Esc key** to close the palette. On the ribbon, click the **Design tab**. In the Document Formatting group, point to the **Themes button**. The ScreenTip indicates that Office is the current theme.

4 Click the **Themes button**. The Themes gallery opens. The Office theme is shaded to indicate that it is the current theme. Refer back to Exhibit 11-12.

5 In the gallery, point to several themes, and then point to the **Facet theme** to see a Live Preview in the document. The fonts in the document change, and the color of the text formatted with the built-in Title, Headings, and Emphasis styles, and the color of the text formatted with the custom LLNC style changes.

6 Click the **Organic theme**. The fonts and colors in the document change to those used in the Organic theme.

7 On the ribbon, click the **Home tab**. In the Font group, click the **Font box arrow** Garamond (Headings). The Font gallery opens. The font for both headings and body text is Garamond.

8 Press the **Esc key** to close the Font list.

TIP: To create a style that uses a theme font that doesn't change if the theme is changed, use the font in the alphabetical list rather than the theme fonts at the top of the Fonts list.

9 Select the **Overview heading**, if necessary. In the Font group, click the **Font Color button arrow** [A]. The color palette opens. The Theme Colors in the palette are the Organic theme colors. The selected color for the Overview heading is still in the last column, second to last row of the theme colors, and it is still the Accent 6, Darker 25% color, but in the Organic theme, this color is a shade of gold.

10 Press the **Esc key** to close the color palette, and then scroll through the document. The changes you made to the Heading 2 and Heading 3 style definition are retained. Text formatted with the LLNC style is now gold because you used a theme color in the style definition.

11 In the last line under the Overview heading, select **LLNC**. In the Font group, click the **Font Color button arrow** [A]. The selected color is in the same position in the palette as the theme color you selected when you created the style; but now it is a shade of gold, not green. (The font is unchanged because you did not select a theme font when you created the style.)

12 At the bottom of the color palette, click **More Colors**. The Colors dialog box opens with the Custom tab selected.

13 Click the **Standard tab**, and then click the same **dark green color** that is selected in Exhibit 11-13.

EXHIBIT 11-13 STANDARD TAB IN THE COLORS DIALOG BOX

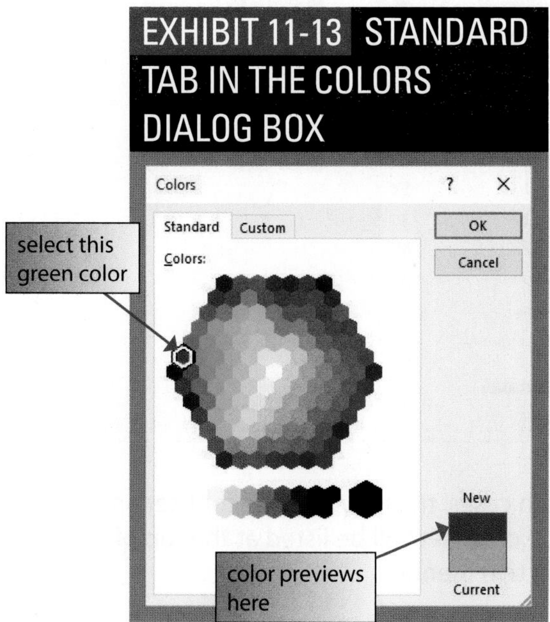

14 Click **OK**. The selected text is reformatted with the dark green color.

15 In the Styles group, right-click the **LLNC style**, and then click **Update LLNC to Match Selection**. The style definition is updated. All the text with that style applied changes color to match the new definition.

16 In the Font group, click the **Font Color button arrow** [A]. The custom color you selected appears in a new Recent Colors row below the Standard Colors row. Because this color is not a theme color, text formatted with this color will not change if the theme is changed.

17 Press the **Esc key** to close the color palette.

End Activity

11-3b Modifying a Theme

Once you have chosen a theme, you can change any of the elements that make up the theme, including the color palette, the theme fonts, the style of the effects, and the default paragraph spacing. To change the theme fonts, you select from font sets on the Fonts button menu in the Document Formatting group on the Design tab. See Exhibit 11-14. To change the theme colors, select from the palettes in the Document Formatting group. See Exhibit 11-15.

EXHIBIT 11-14 FONTS BUTTON MENU

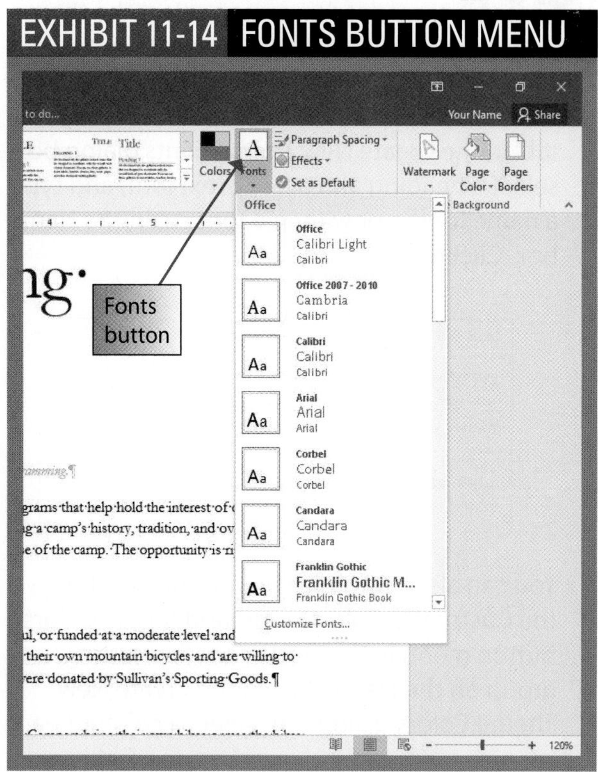

EXHIBIT 11-15 COLORS BUTTON MENU

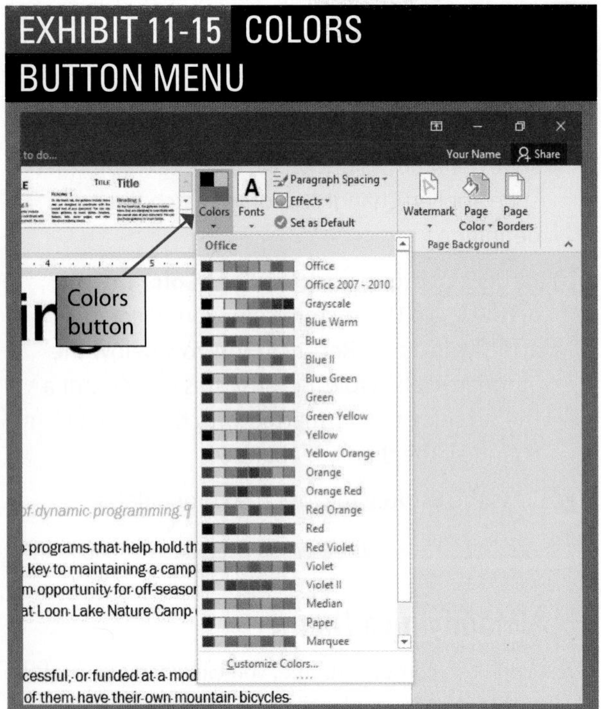

Begin Activity

Modify the theme fonts and colors.

1 On the ribbon, click the **Design tab**. In the Document Formatting group, click the **Fonts button**. The Fonts menu opens, listing sets of coordinated fonts for headings and body text. Refer back to Exhibit 11-14.

2 Point to several of the font sets to see the Live Preview.

3 Click the **Franklin Gothic font set**. Those fonts (Franklin Gothic Medium for the headings and Franklin Gothic Book for the body text) are applied to the document. The font of the text with the LLNC style applied did not change because it was not formatted with a theme font.

4 In the Document Formatting group, click the **Colors button**. Refer back to Exhibit 11-15. The palettes in the list are provided in addition to the

FYI

CREATING NEW THEME FONTS AND COLORS

If none of the theme font sets suits your needs, you can select the theme fonts you want. Click the Customize Fonts command on the Fonts button menu in the Document Formatting group on the Design tab. In the Create New Theme Fonts dialog box, select a heading and a body text font, and type a name for the new theme font set in the Name box. Click Save.

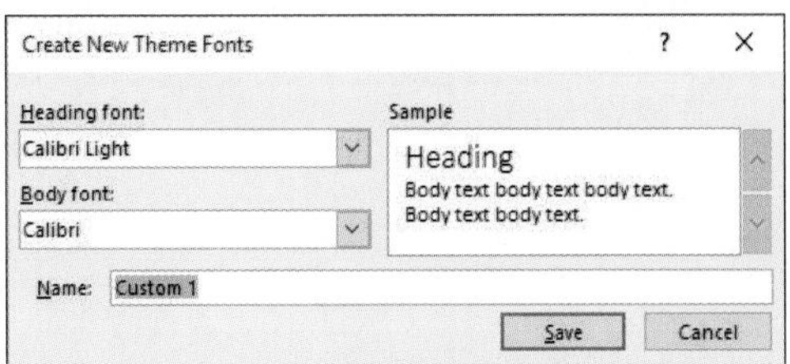

You can also customize theme colors. Click the Customize Colors command on the Colors button menu in the Document Formatting group on the Design tab. In the Create New Theme Colors dialog box, select a color for each theme element listed, and then type a name for the new color set in the Name box. Click Save.

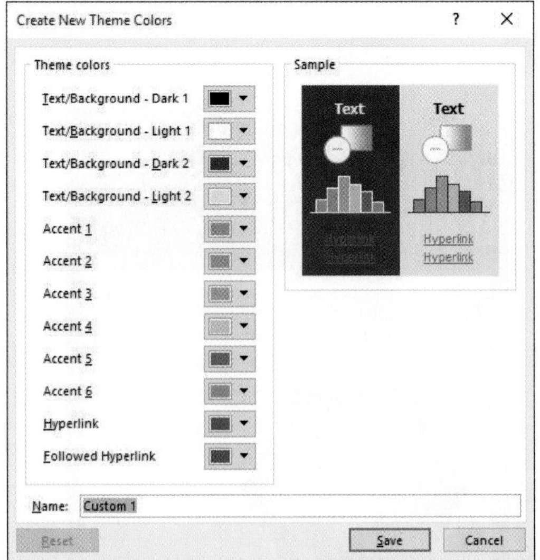

In both cases, the new, custom font set and theme color set will be listed at the top of their respective menus.

palettes used by the themes. The only theme palette that appears in this gallery is the Office theme color palette. (To use the color palettes of any of the other themes, you need to apply that theme.)

5 Point to several of the palettes to see the Live Preview.

6 Click the **Yellow color palette**. The elements in the document formatted with theme colors change to the corresponding theme colors of the Yellow color palette.

End Activity

SCROLLING THROUGH A LONG DOCUMENT

One way to move among the pages in a multiple-page document is to drag the scroll box in the vertical scroll bar. As you drag, a ScreenTip appears, identifying the current page number. If paragraphs are formatted with the built-in heading styles, the first heading on the page also appears in the ScreenTip. (Pressing the Page Up and Page Down keys scrolls the document one screen at a time unless the document is displayed at One Page zoom.)

Another way to move to another page in the document is to use the Pages tab in the Navigation pane. To open the Navigation pane, you can click the page count indicator button at the left end of the status bar; you can select the Navigation pane check box in the Show group on the View tab; or you can click the Find button in the Editing group on the Home tab. After you open the Navigation pane, you need to click the Pages tab to see thumbnails of the pages in the document in a scrollable list. See Exhibit 11-16. You click a thumbnail to instantly move to that page in the document.

Begin Activity

View different pages in a multiple-page document.

1 In the vertical scroll bar, point to the **scroll box**, and then press and hold the mouse button. A ScreenTip appears identifying the page as page 1. The first heading on the page, *Overview*, also appears in the ScreenTip.

EXHIBIT 11-16 PAGES TAB IN THE NAVIGATION PANE

Pages tab selected

selected thumbnail

page count indicator button

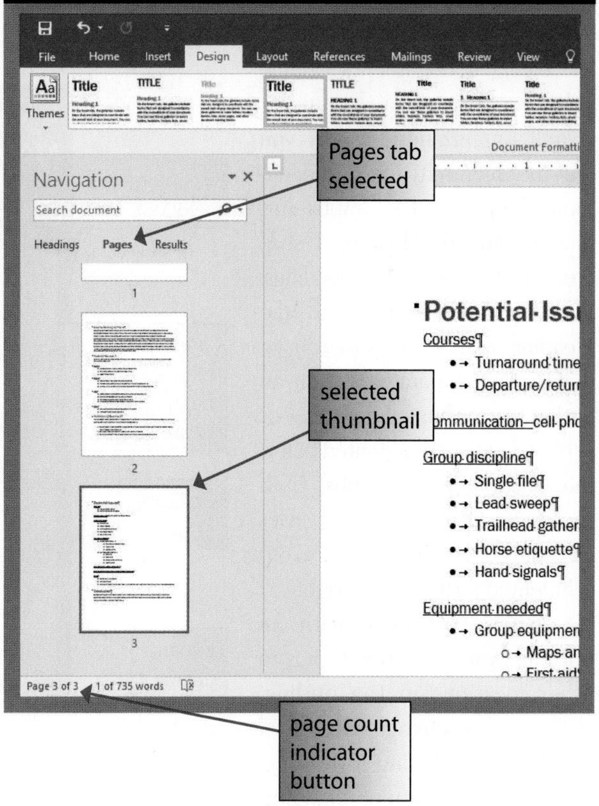

2 Drag the **scroll box** slowly down the vertical scroll bar until the ScreenTip identifies the current page as page 3, and then release the mouse button. Page 3 appears in the document window, and the page number indicator on the status bar identifies the page as Page 3 of 3.

3 On the status bar, click the **page count indicator** Page 3 of 3. The Navigation pane opens with the Pages tab selected. Thumbnails of the pages in the document appear in the Navigation pane. The blue border around the page 3 thumbnail indicates it is the current page. Refer back to Exhibit 11-16.

4 Point to the Navigation pane. A vertical scroll bar appears.

5 In the Navigation pane, scroll to the top of the list, and then click the **page 1 thumbnail**. The document scrolls to page 1.

6 At the top of the Navigation pane, click the **Close button** ✕. The Navigation pane closes.

End Activity

11-5 WORKING WITH THE DOCUMENT OUTLINE

Reviewing a document's outline helps you manage a document's overall organization. It lets you see the hierarchy of the document headings. Paragraphs formatted with the Heading 1 style are the highest level headings. Paragraphs formatted with the Heading 2 style are subordinate to Heading 1 paragraphs. In an outline, subordinate headings—or subheadings—are indented below the Heading 1 paragraphs. Each successive level of heading styles (Heading 3, Heading 4, and so on) is indented farther to the right.

When you work with an outline, you can move topics to other locations in the outline, or you can change the level of headings. Moving a heading to a higher level in the outline—for example, changing a Heading 2 paragraph into a Heading 1 paragraph—is called **promoting** the heading. Moving an item to a lower level in the outline is called **demoting** the heading. If you used the built-in heading styles to format the headings in your document, when you promote or demote a heading, the next higher or lower level of heading style is automatically applied.

There are two ways to work with a document outline: in the Navigation pane and in Outline view.

11-5a Using the Navigation Pane

To work with a document outline, you use the Headings tab in the Navigation pane. When you click a heading in the Navigation pane, the document scrolls to display that heading at the top of the document window. You can also promote and demote headings in the Navigation pane. When you change the level of a heading, subheadings are promoted or demoted one level as well. Headings with subheadings have either a Collapse arrow ◢ or an Expand arrow ▷ next to them in the Navigation pane. You can also drag a heading up or down in the Navigation pane to position it in a new location in the outline. When you do this, any subheadings and body text under the heading move to the new location with the heading you drag. See Exhibit 11-17.

EXHIBIT 11-17 HEADINGS TAB IN THE NAVIGATION PANE WHILE MOVING A HEADING

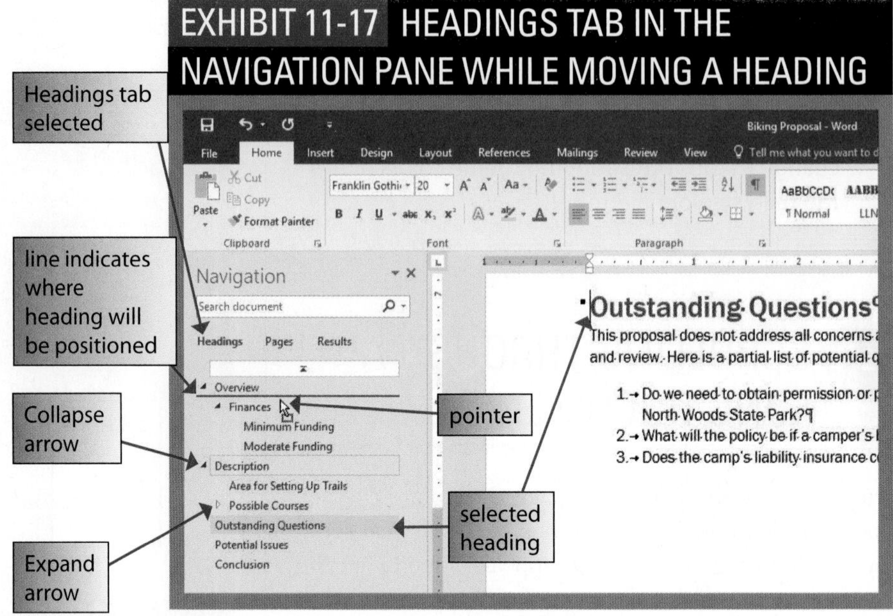

promote To move an item to a higher level in an outline.

demote To move an item to a lower level in an outline.

Begin Activity

Change the outline in the Navigation pane.

1. On the ribbon, click the **View tab**. In the Show group, click the **Navigation Pane check box**. The Navigation pane opens.
2. At the top of the Navigation pane, click the **Headings tab**. The document headings are displayed in the Navigation pane.
3. In the Navigation pane, click the **Possible Courses heading**. The document scrolls to display that heading at the top of the document window with the insertion point at the beginning of the heading.
4. In the Navigation pane, next to the Possible Courses heading, click the **Collapse arrow** ◢. The headings formatted as Heading 3 headings under the Possible Courses heading are hidden, and the arrow next to the Possible Courses heading changes to an Expand arrow ▷.
5. In the Navigation pane, click the **Outstanding Questions heading**.
6. On the ribbon, click the **Home tab**. In the Styles group, the Heading 2 style is selected.

7 In the Navigation pane, right-click the **Outstanding Questions heading**. On the shortcut menu, click **Promote**. The heading moves to the left in the Navigation pane so it aligns below the other headings formatted with the Heading 1 style. In the Styles group on the Home tab, the style applied to this heading is now Heading 1.

8 In the Navigation pane, point to the **Description heading**. A box appears around the heading.

9 Press and hold the mouse button, and drag the **Description heading** up, but do not release the mouse button. As you drag the heading, the pointer changes to , which is the same pointer you saw when you used the drag-and-drop technique, and a horizontal line appears indicating the position of the heading when you release the mouse button. Refer back to Exhibit 11-17.

10 When the horizontal line is positioned above *Finances* and below *Overview*, as shown in Exhibit 11-17, release the mouse button. The Description heading and all the subheadings below it are moved to the new position in the document.

11 In the Navigation pane, click the **Close button** to close it.

End Activity

11-5b Using Outline View

Outline view displays the various heading levels in a document as an outline in the document window instead of in a pane. If you create an outline in Outline view, the built-in heading styles are applied automatically. Working with the outline in Outline view is similar to viewing the structure of a document in the Navigation pane. However, in Outline view, you can see the body text below the headings if you want.

In Outline view, outline symbols appear to the left of each paragraph. See Exhibit 11-18. The plus sign symbol appears next to headings that have subheadings or body text below the heading. The minus sign symbol appears next to headings that do not have any subordinate text. A small gray circle next to a paragraph indicates the text is body text and not a heading. A horizontal line below a heading indicates that there is body text below that heading.

EXHIBIT 11-18 OUTLINE VIEW WITH THREE LEVELS OF HEADINGS DISPLAYED

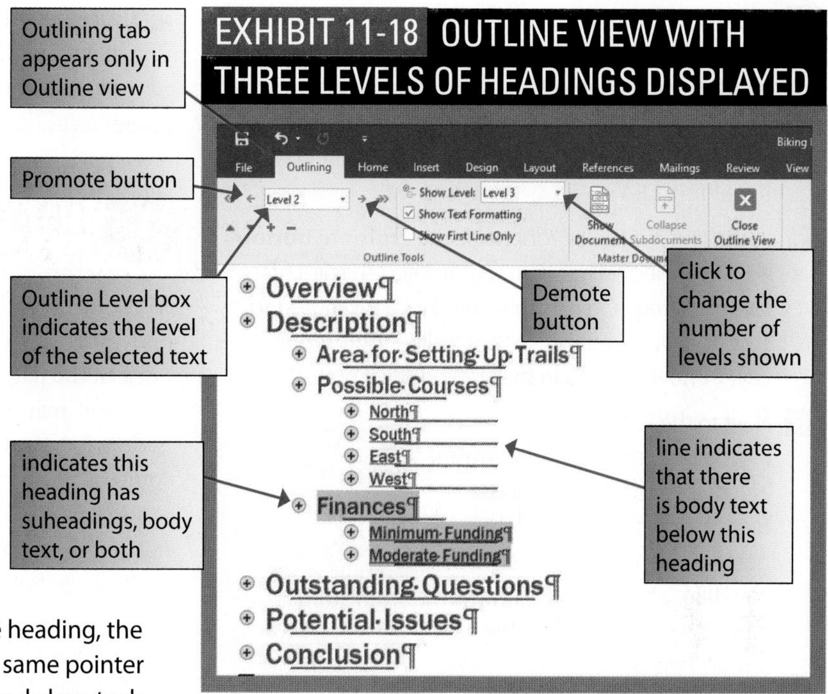

When you click the outline symbol next to a heading, you select the heading and all of its subordinate text, or a section. To move a section after you select it, you can drag it or click the Move Up or Move Down button in the Outline Tools group on the Outlining tab, which is visible only in Outline view. You can also use buttons on the Outlining tab to promote or demote headings or to demote text from a heading to body text.

Begin Activity

Change the outline in Outline view.

1 On the ribbon, click the **View tab**. In the Views group, click the **Outline button**. The document switches to Outline view, and a new tab, Outlining, appears on the ribbon and is the active tab.

2 If necessary, change the zoom level to **120%** to match the figures in this section.

3 On the Outlining tab, in the Outline Tools group, click the **Show Level box arrow**, and then click **Level 3**. Scroll to the top of the window. Now only text formatted with the Heading 1, Heading 2, and Heading 3 styles appears.

TIP: If the formatting makes the headings difficult to read in Outline view, click the Show Text Formatting check box in the Outline Tools group on the Outlining tab to deselect it and show all the text as black.

4 Next to the Finances heading, click the **plus sign symbol** ⊕. The Finances heading and its subheadings are selected. In the Outline Tools group, Level 2 appears in the Outline Level box. This is the level of the selected Funding heading. Refer back to Exhibit 11-18.

5 In the Outline Tools group, click the **Promote button** ←. The selected heading is promoted so it is a first-level heading, and its subheadings are promoted to second-level headings. In the Outline Tools group, Level 1 now appears in the Outline Level box.

6 Next to the Potential Issues heading, point to the **plus sign symbol** ⊕, press and hold the **mouse button,** and then drag up, but do not release the mouse button. As you drag, a horizontal line appears, indicating the position of the heading, and the pointer changes to ⇕.

TIP: You can also click the Move Up button ▲ and the Move Down button ▼ in the Outline Tools group to move paragraphs in an outline.

7 When the horizontal line is above the Outstanding Questions heading, release the **mouse button.** The Potential Issues heading and its subheads move to just above the Outstanding Questions heading. Compare your screen to Exhibit 11-19.

EXHIBIT 11-19 FINAL OUTLINE OF BIKING PROPOSAL DOCUMENT

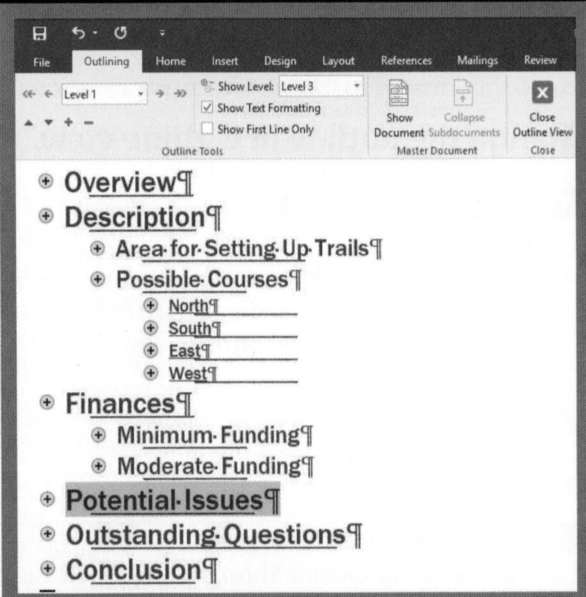

margin The blank area above or below text, or to the left or right of text between the text and the edge of the page.

8 On the Outlining tab, in the Close group, click the **Close Outline View button** to close Outline view.

End Activity

11-6 CHANGING THE MARGINS

Margins are the blank areas at the top, bottom, left, and right sides of the page between the text and the edge of the page. The default settings for documents are one-inch margins on all sides. See Exhibit 11-20. This is fine for most documents. But sometimes you might want to change the margins. For example, you might want to provide additional space to allow readers to take notes. To change the margins, click the Margins button in the Page Setup group on the Layout tab to display the menu, as shown in Exhibit 11-21. You can choose from the predefined margins on the menu, or you can click the Custom Margins command to open the Margins tab in the Page Setup dialog box to select your own settings. See Exhibit 11-22. After you create custom margin settings, the most recent set appears as an option at the top of the menu.

FYI

WORKING WITH CUSTOM MARGINS

If you need to use a specific custom margin for all your documents, on the Margins tab of the Page Setup dialog box, click the Set As Default button. Keep in mind that most printers cannot print to the edge of the page. If you create custom margins that are too narrow for your printer, a dialog box opens warning you of this and advising you to change the margin settings.

Begin Activity

Change the page margins.

1 Press the **Ctrl+Home keys** to move the insertion point to the beginning of the document.

2 On the ribbon, click the **View tab**. In the Zoom group, click the **One Page button**. The current page of the document, page 1, appears completely in the Word window, and you can easily see the margins. Refer to Exhibit 11-20.

EXHIBIT 11-20 ONE-INCH MARGINS IN DOCUMENT

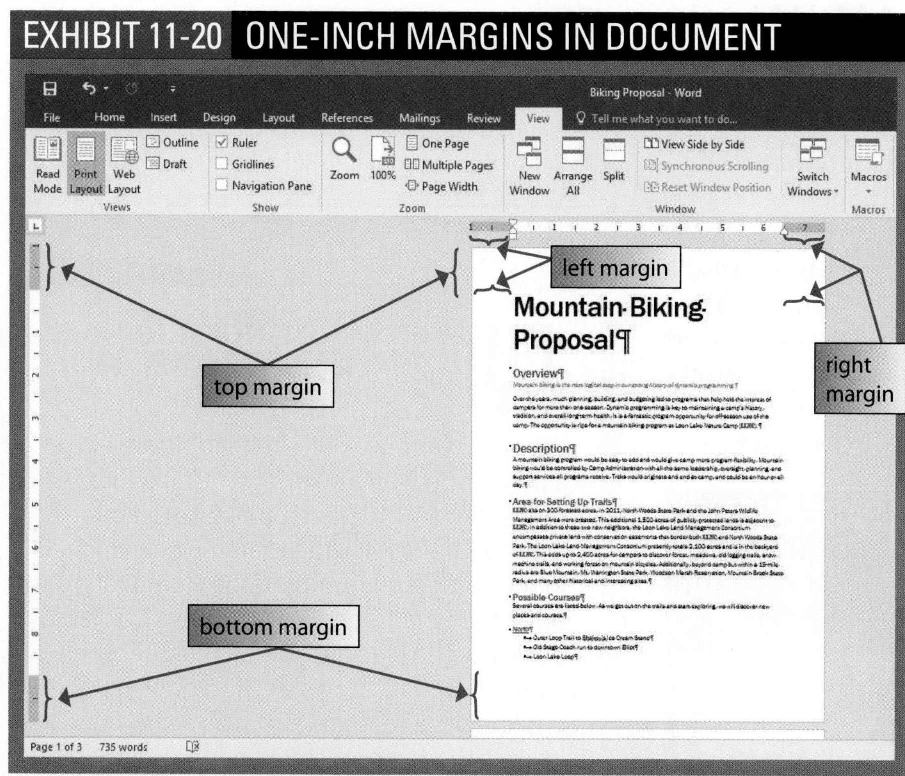

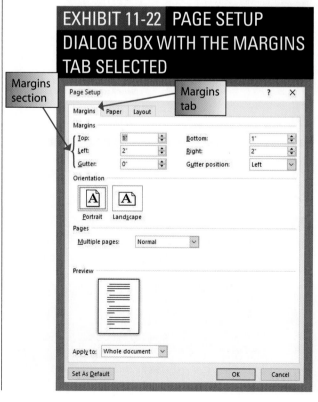

5 In the Page Setup group, click the **Margins button**. At the bottom of the menu, click **Custom Margins.** The Page Setup dialog box opens with the Margins tab selected. Refer to Exhibit 11-22. The current margin settings are displayed in the boxes in the Margins section at the top of the Margins tab. The value in the Top box is selected.

6 Press the **Tab key** twice to select the value in the **Left box**, and then type **1.5**.

7 In the Right box, click the **down arrow** five times to change the value to 1.5".

EXHIBIT 11-21 MARGINS MENU

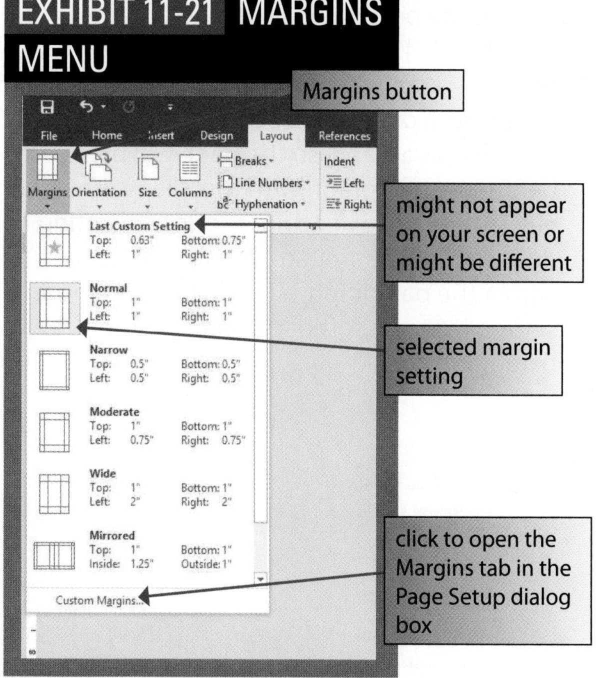

might not appear on your screen or might be different

3 On the ribbon, click the **Layout tab**. In the Page Setup group, click the **Margins button**. The Margins menu opens. Refer to Exhibit 11-21.

4 Click **Wide**. The menu closes, and the margins in the document are changed to the Wide setting, which keeps the one-inch margin at the top and bottom but changes both the left and right margins to two inches.

8 Click **OK**. The margins are changed to the custom settings.

9 Change the zoom level back to **120%**.

End Activity

EXHIBIT 11-22 PAGE SETUP DIALOG BOX WITH THE MARGINS TAB SELECTED

Margins section

Margins tab

11-7 INSERTING A MANUAL PAGE BREAK

As you add text to a document, **automatic page breaks** (sometimes called **soft page breaks**) are inserted. You can create a new page manually by inserting a **manual page break** (sometimes called a **hard page break**). To insert a manual page break, use the Page Break button in the Pages group on the Insert tab. When nonprinting characters are displayed, manual page breaks appear as a dotted line with the words *Page Break* in the center of the line. See Exhibit 11-23.

EXHIBIT 11-23 MANUAL PAGE BREAK IN DOCUMENT

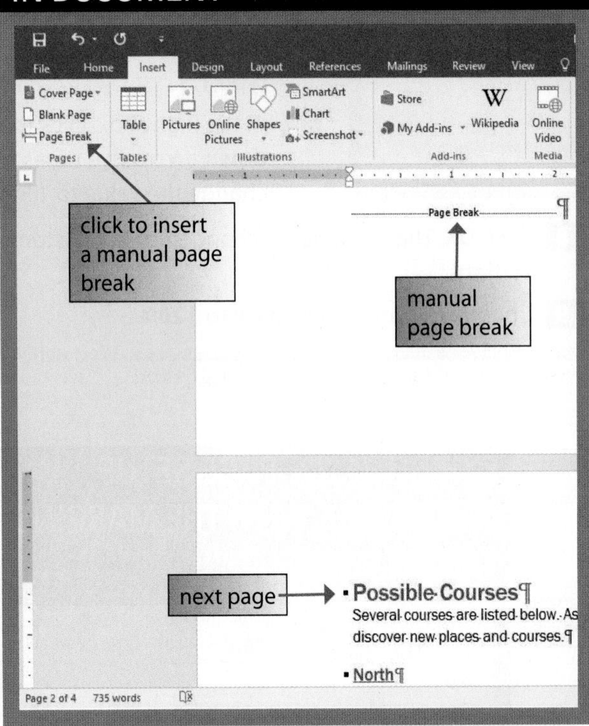

Begin Activity

To insert a manual page break.

1 Scroll so that you can see the bottom of page 1 and the top of page 2, and then click before the Possible Courses heading at the bottom of page 1.

2 On the ribbon, click the **Insert tab**. In the Pages group, click the **Page Break button**. A manual page break is inserted before the insertion point, and the Possible Courses heading moves to the top of the next page. Refer back to Exhibit 11-23.

End Activity

automatic page break (soft page break) A page break that is created when content fills a page and a new page is created automatically.

manual page break (hard page break) A page break that you insert to force content after the break to appear on a new page.

FYI CONTROLLING PAGE BREAKS WITH PARAGRAPH SETTINGS

When you apply a built-in heading style to a paragraph, you also apply settings that prevent awkward page breaks. To examine these settings, click the Dialog Box Launcher in the Paragraph group on the Home tab to open the Paragraph dialog box. In the dialog box, click the Line and Page Breaks tab. The Widow/Orphan control setting prevents the last line of a paragraph from appearing by itself at the top of the next page, and the first line of a paragraph from appearing by itself at the bottom of a page before the page break. The Keep with next setting prevents a paragraph from appearing at the bottom of a page by connecting it to the next paragraph, so the page will break before the paragraph with the Keep with next setting. The Keep lines together setting doesn't allow a soft page break to appear within the paragraph. The Page break before setting inserts a soft page break before the paragraph.

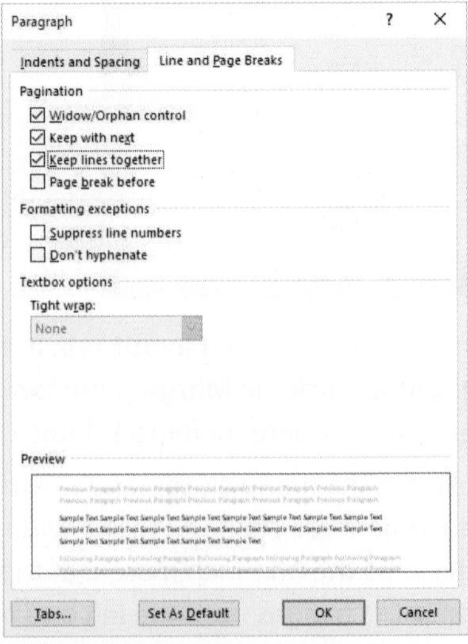

11-8 ADDING PAGE NUMBERS, HEADERS, AND FOOTERS

To add page numbers in a document, you use a page number field. A **field** is a placeholder for variable information that includes an instruction to insert the specific information. A page number field inserts the correct page number on each page. Usually, page numbers appear in the top or bottom margin. You can also insert page numbers in the side margins; although for business or academic documents, it's customary to place them at the top or bottom of a document.

When you insert a page number field, the document switches to Header and Footer view. A **header** is text that appears at the top of every page in a document; a **footer** is text that appears at the bottom of every page. In this book, the chapter number and title appear in the right page footer. In Header and Footer view, the body of the document is dimmed, indicating that it cannot be edited, and you can type only in the header or footer area.

11-8a Inserting Page Numbers

To add page numbers to a document, click the Page Number button in the Header & Footer group on the Insert tab. On the menu that opens, point to the position on the page where you want to insert the page number to open a menu of page number styles. See Exhibit 11-24.

You can choose to insert the page number in the header or footer area, in the left or right margin, or at the current position of the insertion point.

> **FYI**
> **FORMAT PAGE NUMBERS**
> To change the numbering style for a page number or to specify a number to use as the first page number, click the Page Number button in the Header & Footer group on the Header & Footer Tools Design tab, and then click Format Page Numbers.

Begin Activity

Add page numbers.

1. If necessary, click anywhere on page 2 to position the insertion point.
2. On the ribbon, click the **Insert tab**, if necessary. In the Header & Footer group, click the **Page Number button** to open the Page Number menu.
3. Point to **Bottom of Page**. A gallery of page number styles opens. Refer to Exhibit 11-24.

EXHIBIT 11-24 GALLERY OF PAGE NUMBER STYLES

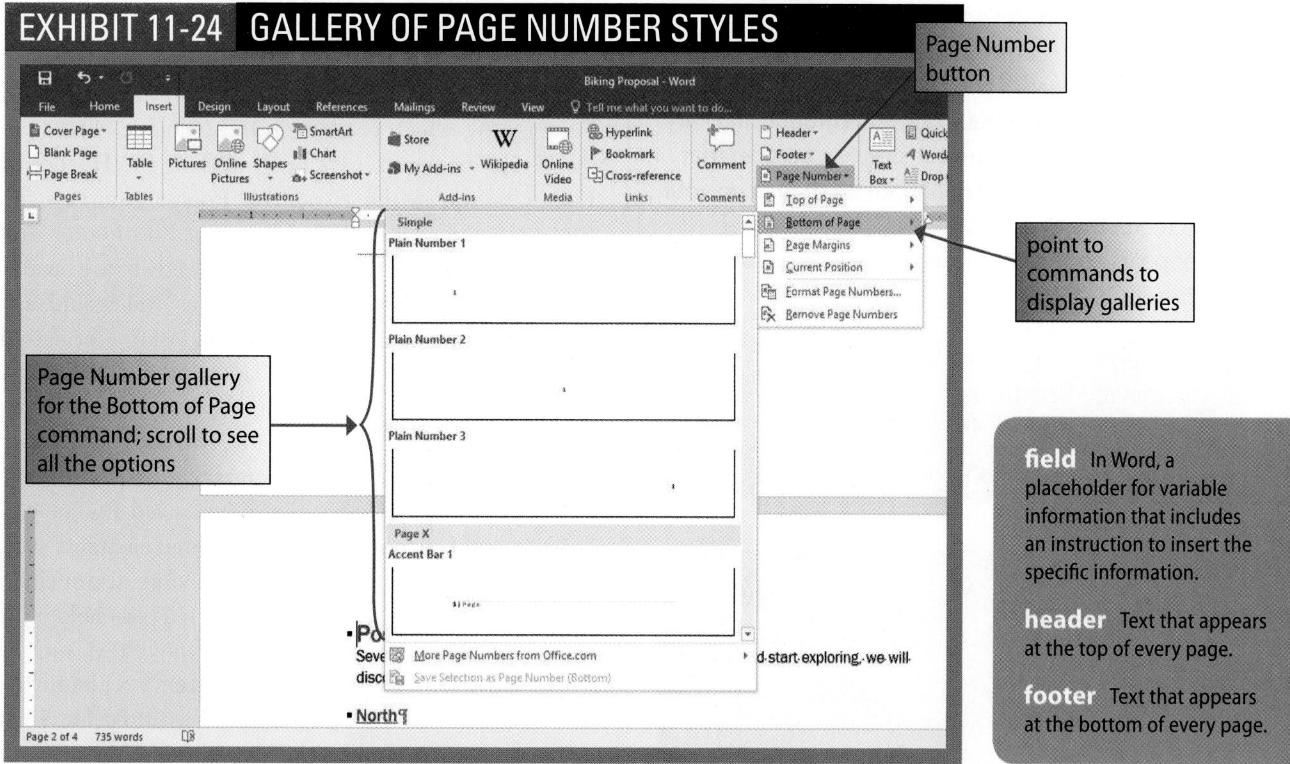

field In Word, a placeholder for variable information that includes an instruction to insert the specific information.

header Text that appears at the top of every page.

footer Text that appears at the bottom of every page.

EXHIBIT 11-25 PAGE NUMBER INSERTED IN FOOTER

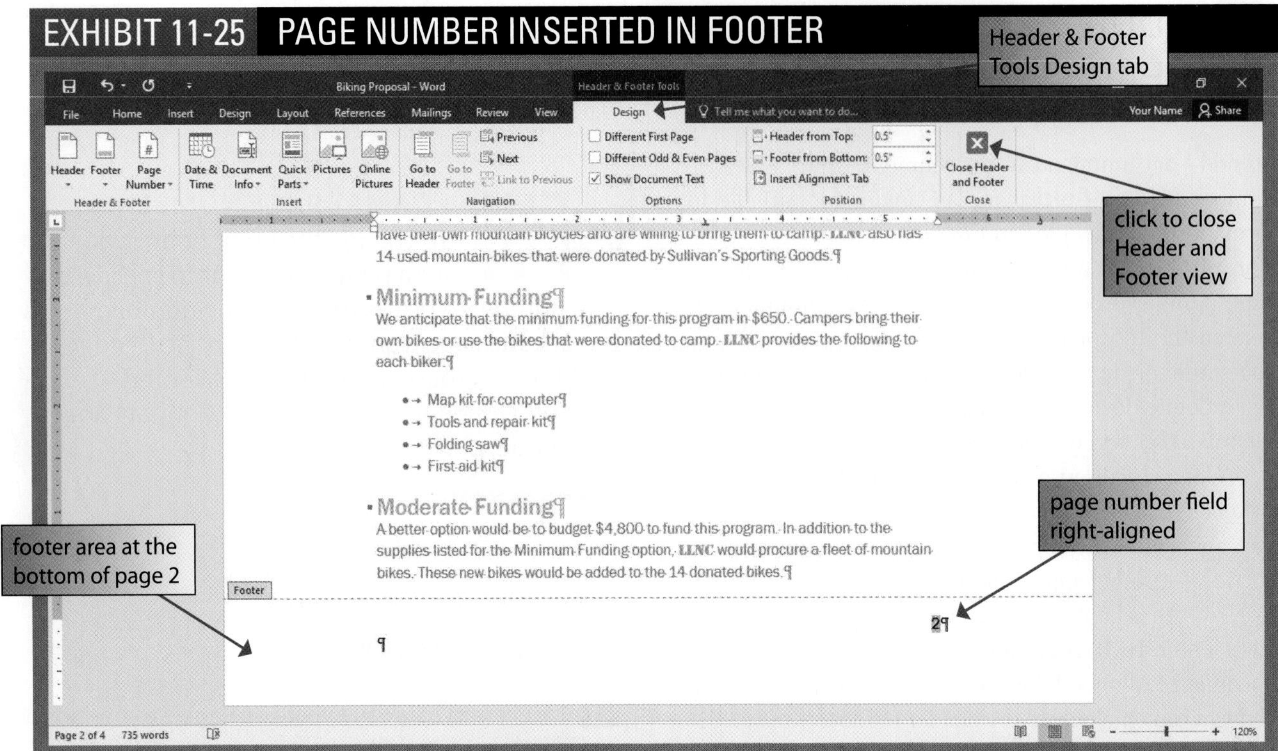

4 Scroll down and examine the styles of page number that you can insert.

5 Scroll back to the top of the list, and then click the **Plain Number 3 style**. The document switches to Header and Footer view, and the page number for the current page (page 2) appears right-aligned in the footer area. The page number has a gray background, indicating that it is a field and not simply a number that you typed. (The field might not be shaded on your screen.) The Header & Footer Tools Design tab appears on the ribbon and is the active tab. See Exhibit 11-25.

TIP: To remove page numbers, click the Remove Page Numbers command on the Page Number button menu.

PROBLEM?
If you see {PAGE * MERGEFORMAT} instead of a page number, click the **FILE tab**, click **Options**, click **Advanced**, scroll down to the "Show document content" section. Click the **Show field codes instead of their values check box** to deselect it. Click **OK**.

content control A special field either used as a placeholder for text you insert or designed to contain a specific type of text.

property Identifying information about a file that is saved with the file.

6 On the Header & Footer Tools Design tab, in the Close group, click the **Close Header and Footer button**. Header and Footer view closes, and the Header & Footer Tools Design tab no longer appears on the ribbon.

End Activity

11-8b Adding a Header and Footer

You can insert a simple header or footer in Header and Footer view, which you switch to by double-clicking in the header or footer area, or by clicking the Header or Footer button in the Header & Footer group on the Insert tab and clicking Edit Header or Edit Footer. You then type the header or footer text directly in the header or footer area, formatting the text as you would any other text in a document. You can also insert a formatted header or footer by using the Header and Footer buttons in the Header & Footer group on the Insert tab or on the Header & Footer Tools Design tab, and then click a style in the gallery of headers and footers that opens.

Many of the styles in the Header and Footer galleries include page numbers and graphic elements such as horizontal lines or shaded boxes. Some also include content controls. A **content control** is a placeholder for text you insert; it can store a specific type of text, such as a date or a document property. A **property** is identifying information about a file that is saved with the file, such as the author's name and the date the file was created.

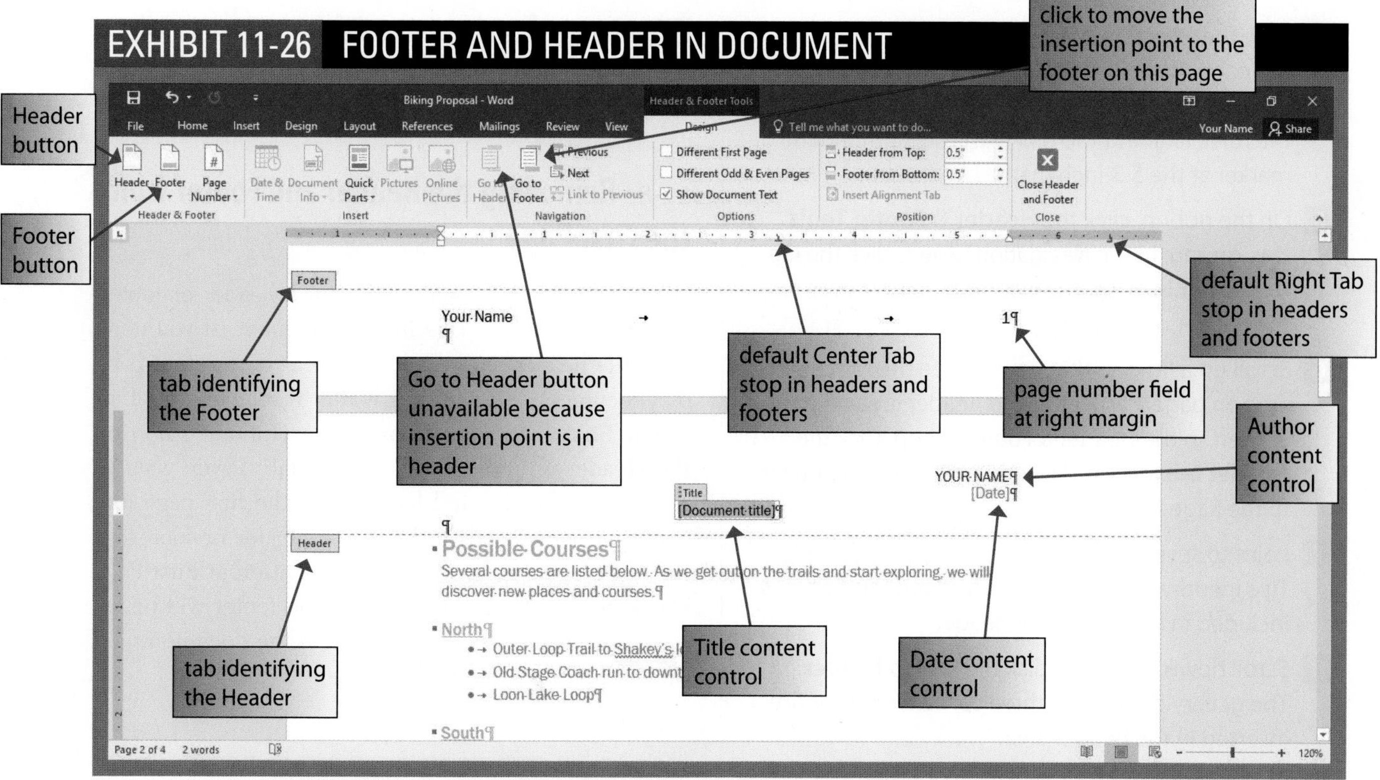

Information entered in a content control associated with a property will appear in any other content control that is associated with that property. For example, if you enter the company name in a Company content control in the header, and the Company content control also appears in the footer, the company name that you typed in the header will appear automatically in the footer. Some content controls are associated with properties that appear automatically in the content control. For example, the registered user's name is saved as the document author property every time you create a document, so that name will appear in a content control that displays the author name.

Most of the content controls that appear in headers and footers are text placeholders. You click the text placeholder once to make it active, and then type the text to replace the placeholder. Date content controls are formatted so that you can click an arrow to display a calendar and then select a date from the calendar. You can delete a content control that you don't want to use.

When a content control is active, its title tab appears. The **title tab** usually contains a label identifying the content control.

Headers and footers have a Center Tab stop at the 3.25-inch mark and a Right Tab stop at the 6.5-inch mark. These tab stops center and right-align text based on the Normal margins. If you change the margin settings, consider changing the tab settings to better align the header or footer text. If the Right Tab stop is outside of the right margin, the second tab stop is at the right margin instead of at 6.5-inch mark.

When a header or footer area is active, the Header & Footer Tools Design tab is available on the ribbon, and tabs identifying the header and footer areas appear in the left margin. Exhibit 11-26 shows a header with content controls and a footer with a page number.

Begin Activity

Add a header and a footer.

1 On page 2, double-click in the **footer area.** The document switches to Header and Footer view, and the Header & Footer Tools Design tab appears on the ribbon and is the active tab. The insertion point is positioned before the page number field in the footer area, ready for you to begin typing.

2 Type your name.

3 On the ribbon, click the **Home tab.** In the Paragraph group, click the **Align Left button**. The text in the footer is now left-aligned.

title tab A tab on a content control that indicates the control is selected and usually contains the name of the content control.

4 With the insertion point between your name and the page number field, press the **Tab key** twice. The page number moves to the 5.5-inch mark on the ruler, aligning the text with the Right Indent marker at the 5.5-inch mark.

5 On the ribbon, click the **Header & Footer Tools Design tab**. In the Navigation group, click the **Go to Header button**. The insertion point moves to the header on page 2.

6 Scroll up a little so that you can see the footer area on page 1 as well as the header area on page 2. Then, in the Header & Footer group, click the **Header button**. The Header gallery opens, similar to the Page Number gallery.

7 Point to several of the header styles. The ScreenTips identify the header style and describe what is included in that particular header.

8 Scroll down, and then click the **Whisp header**. The gallery closes, and three content controls are inserted in the header area.

9 Click the **Document title content control**. The entire content control becomes selected and the title tab—in this case, with the label *Title*—appears. Refer back to Exhibit 11-26.

10 Type **Mountain Biking Proposal**. The placeholder text is replaced by the text you typed. (The text in the Whisp heading is formatted to appear as all uppercase letters, even if you type lowercase letters.)

11 Click the **Date content control**. The entire content control is selected, and the title tab with the label *Date* appears. An arrow appears on the right side of the control.

> **TIP:** You can click the arrows to the right and left of the month name to scroll to other months.

12 Click the **arrow**. At the bottom of the calendar that appears, click **Today**. The calendar closes, and today's date replaces the placeholder text in the Date content control.

13 Click the **control above the Date control**. The Title tab appears with the label *Author*. The contents of the control will be your Windows 10 user name.

14 Click the **Author title tab**. The entire control is selected.

15 Press the **Delete key** to delete the Author content control, and then press the **Delete key** again to delete the empty paragraph.

16 Double-click in the document area. Header and Footer view closes.

End Activity

11-8c Removing the Header and Footer from the First Page

When you insert a page number or a header or footer, it appears on every page in the document. If you don't want the header and footer to appear on the first page of a document, you can specify this by selecting the Different First Page check box in the Options group on the Header & Footer Tools Design tab. If you want to remove the header and footer from the first page, the insertion point needs to be in the header or footer on the first page when you deselect the Different First Page check box; otherwise, the header and footer will be removed from the rest of the pages in the document and they will reamain on the first page.

Begin Activity

Remove the header and footer from the first page.

1 Change the view to **One Page view**, scroll so that you can see all of page 1, and then click anywhere on page 1.

2 On the ribbon, click the **Insert tab**. In the Header & Footer group, click the **Header button**. At the bottom of the menu, click **Edit Header**. The view changes to Header & Footer view with the Header & Footer Tools Design tab selected, and the insertion point is blinking in the selected Date content control in the header on page 1. This is the same thing that would have happened if you had double-clicked in the Header area of page 1.

3 On the Header & Footer Tools Design tab, in the Options group, click the **Different First Page check box**. The content of the header and footer, including the page number, disappears from page 1 because the insertion point was on the first page. The tabs labeling the header and footer area on page 1 change to First Page Header and First Page Footer.

4 Scroll down to page 2, and confirm that the header and footer still appear on that page.

5 On the Header & Footer Tools Design tab, in the Close group, click the **Close Header and Footer button**, and then change the zoom back to **120%**.

End Activity

FYI

PREFORMATTED COVER PAGES

A document's cover page typically includes the title and the name of the author. Some people also include a summary of the report on the cover page; this is commonly referred to as an abstract. In addition, you might include the date, the name and possibly the logo of your company or organization, and a subtitle. A cover page should not include the document header or footer. You can create your own cover page, or you can use one of the preformatted cover pages included with Word. To use a preformatted cover page, click the Cover Page button in the Pages group on the Insert tab, and then click a cover page in the gallery. The cover page includes content controls in which you can enter the document title and author, the date, and so on.

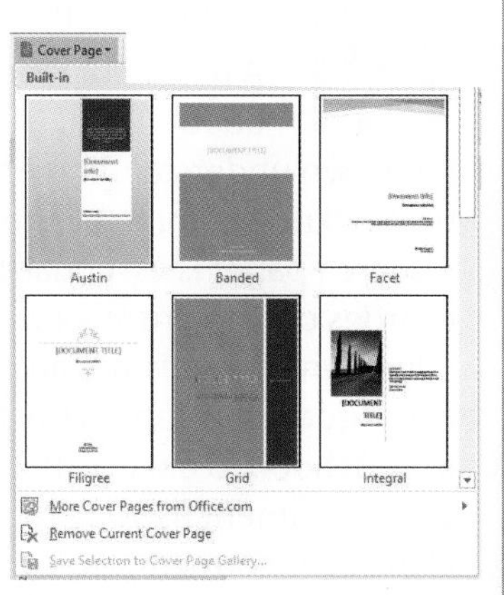

11-9 CREATING CITATIONS AND A LIST OF WORKS CITED

When you write a research paper, you should always cite your sources. A **source** is anything you use to research your topic, including books, magazines, Web sites, and movies. Every time you quote or refer to a source within the research paper itself, you need to include a **citation**, a formal reference to the work of others, usually as a parenthetical reference to the author and page number of a source. A citation should include enough information to identify the quote or referenced material so that the reader can easily locate the source in the accompanying works cited list.

Every source you cite needs to be included in a **list of works cited**, sometimes called **references** or a **bibliography**. In common usage, the list of works cited, references, and the bibliography are the same thing: a list of the sources cited in a document. Sometimes, the list of works cited and the bibliography are different, where the list of works cited is a list only of the works cited in the document, and the bibliography is a complete list of all the sources consulted when researching a topic, even sources that are not cited in the document. Sometimes, this complete list of sources is called a *complete bibliography* or a *complete list of works cited*, and the shorter list of works actually cited is called a *works consulted list* or a *selected bibliography*.

11-9a Selecting a Citation Style

The exact form for citations and the list of works cited varies, depending on the style guide you are using and the type of material you are referencing. People in different fields use different style guides, with each style guide designed to suit the needs of a specific discipline. For example, journalists commonly use the Associated Press (AP) style, which focuses on the concise writing style common in magazines and newspapers. Researchers in the social and behavioral sciences use the American Psychological Association (APA) style, which is designed to help readers scan an article quickly for key points and emphasizes the date of publication in citations. Other scientific and technical fields have their own specialized style guides. In the humanities, the Modern Language Association (MLA) style is widely used. Refer to the style guide you are using to see exactly what information you need to include in citations and the list of works cited, as well as how to format this information. Note that some style guides require both a list of works cited and a complete bibliography.

In Word documents, you can specify the style you want to use from a list of 12 styles. Then, when you insert citations and create the list of works cited, they are formatted appropriately for the selected style. You can change the style you select at any time, and if any citations already exist, or if the list of works cited is already created, they are reformatted using the new style.

Begin Activity

Select a citation style.

1. On the ribbon, click the **References tab.**
2. In the Citations & Bibliography group, click the **Style box arrow**, and then click **MLA Seventh Edition** in the list of styles.

End Activity

source Anything you use to research your topic.

citation A formal reference to the work of others.

list of works cited, **references**, or **bibliography** A list of sources cited in a document or consulted while researching a topic.

FYI

ACKNOWLEDGING YOUR SOURCES

A research paper is a way to explore the available information about a subject and then present this information, along with your own understanding of the subject, in an organized and interesting way. Acknowledging all the sources of the information presented in your research paper is essential. If you don't do this, you might be subject to charges of plagiarism, or trying to pass off someone else's thoughts as your own. Plagiarism is an extremely serious accusation and has academic consequences ranging from failing an assignment to being expelled from school. To ensure that you cite all your sources, create citations in your document as you type it. It is very easy to forget to go back and cite all sources correctly after you have finished typing a paper. Forgetting to cite a source could lead to accusations of plagiarism and all of the consequences that entails.

Source: © silver-john/Shutterstock.com

11-9b Creating a New Source and Inserting a Citation

To create a new source and insert a citation to it, click the Insert Citation button in the Citations & Bibliography group on the References tab, and then click Add New Source to open the Create Source dialog box. See Exhibit 11-27. In the dialog box, you choose the type of source—book, Web site, sound recording, and so on—and the dialog box changes to contain the appropriate boxes for gathering the information about the source type you selected according to the style guide you selected prior to opening this dialog box. When you close the dialog box, the citation will be inserted in the style you chose inside a Citation content control. For example, if you chose the MLA style, the author's last name will be inserted between parentheses. In Exhibit 11-27, Book is selected in the Type of Source box, and the boxes shown in the dialog box collect the information needed to document the source when the source is a book and the style is MLA.

EXHIBIT 11-27 CREATE SOURCE DIALOG BOX

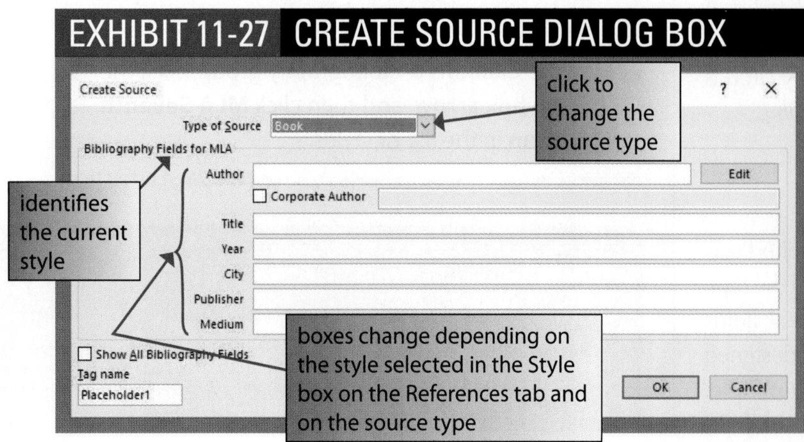

Begin Activity

Create a new source, and insert a citation.

1. On page 1, below the Area for Setting Up Trails heading, place the insertion point immediately before the period at the end of the fourth sentence (after *North Woods State Park*).
2. On the References tab, in the Citations & Bibliography group, click the **Insert Citation button**, and then click **Add New Source**. The Create Source dialog box opens. Refer back to Exhibit 11-27.
3. Click the **Type of Source arrow**, scroll down one line, if necessary, and then click **Web site**. The boxes in the dialog box change to collect the information needed when the source is a Web site and the style is MLA.

TIP: Web sites don't always provide all the information used to create a citation; include as much information as you can.

4. Click in the **Author box**, and then type **Alan Wilson**.
5. Click in the **Name of Web Page box**, and then type **Protected Land in the Loon Lake Area**.
6. Click in the **Year box**, and then type **2013**.
7. Click in the **Year Accessed box**, and then type **2017**. Click in the **Month Accessed box**, and then type **May**. Click in the **Day Accessed box**, and then type **5**.

8 Click in the **Medium box**, and then type **Web**.

9 Click **OK**. The dialog box closes, and the citation *(Wilson)* is inserted at the insertion point.

10 Click anywhere on the **(Wilson) citation**. The Citation content control is now visible.

11 Locate the Finances heading on page 2. In the first paragraph under the Finances heading, position the insertion point at the end of the second sentence before the period (after *bring them to camp*).

12 On the References tab, in the Citations & Bibliography group, click the **Insert Citation button**. The source you just added is listed on the Insert Citation menu.

13 Click **Add New Source**.

14 Click the **Type of Source arrow**, and then click **Report**. The boxes in the dialog box change to collect the information needed when the source is a report using MLA style.

15 Below the Author box, click the **Corporate Author check box** to select it. Click in the empty box to the right of the Corporate Author label, and then type **Loon Lake Nature Camp Program Committee**.

16 Add the following information:

Title:	**2016 Report on Survey Results**
Year:	**2016**
City:	**Elliot**
Medium:	**Print**

17 Click **OK**. The dialog box closes, and the citation is inserted.

End Activity

11-9c Inserting a Citation to an Existing Source

If you need to insert a citation to a source you have already added to your source list, you simply select the source from the Insert Citation menu. Exhibit 11-28 shows two sources listed on the menu.

Begin Activity

Insert a citation to an existing source.

1 On page 2, below the Possible Courses heading, place the insertion point immediately before the period after the first sentence in the paragraph (after the word *below*).

EXHIBIT 11-28 INSERT CITATION MENU WITH SOURCES

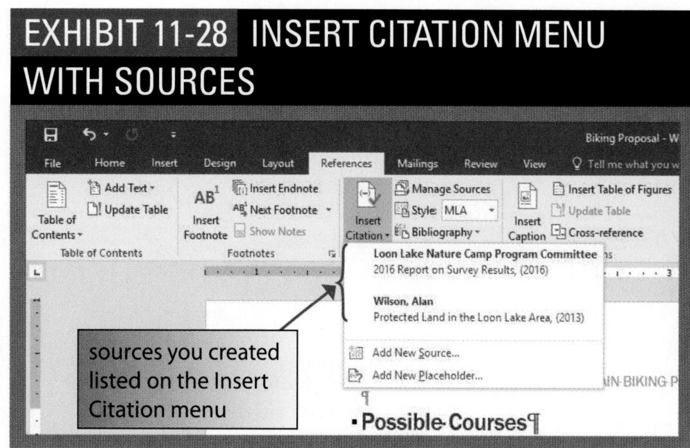

2 On the References tab, in the Citations & Bibliography group, click the **Insert Citation button**. The two sources you added are listed at the top of the menu. Refer back to Exhibit 11-28.

3 Click **Loon Lake Nature Camp Program Committee**. The citation is inserted at the insertion point.

End Activity

11-9d Using the Source Manager

The Current List is the list of sources associated with the current document. The Master List is available for use with any document created using the same user account on that computer. Both the Master List and the Current List are accessible via the Source Manager dialog box, which you open by clicking the Manage Sources button in the Citations & Bibliography group on the References tab. See Exhibit 11-29. You can use the Source Manager dialog box to copy sources from one list to the other, delete and edit existing sources, or create new sources without adding a citation in the document. Sources in the Current List that have a check mark next to them are cited in the document; those without a check mark are not cited.

Begin Activity

Use the Source Manager dialog box.

1 On the References tab, in the Citations & Bibliography group, click the **Manage Sources button**. The Source Manager dialog box opens with the Master List of sources on the left and the Current List on the right.

2 Click **New**. The Create Source dialog box opens.

3 Click the **Type of Source arrow**, and then click **Book**.

EXHIBIT 11-29 SOURCE MANAGER DIALOG BOX

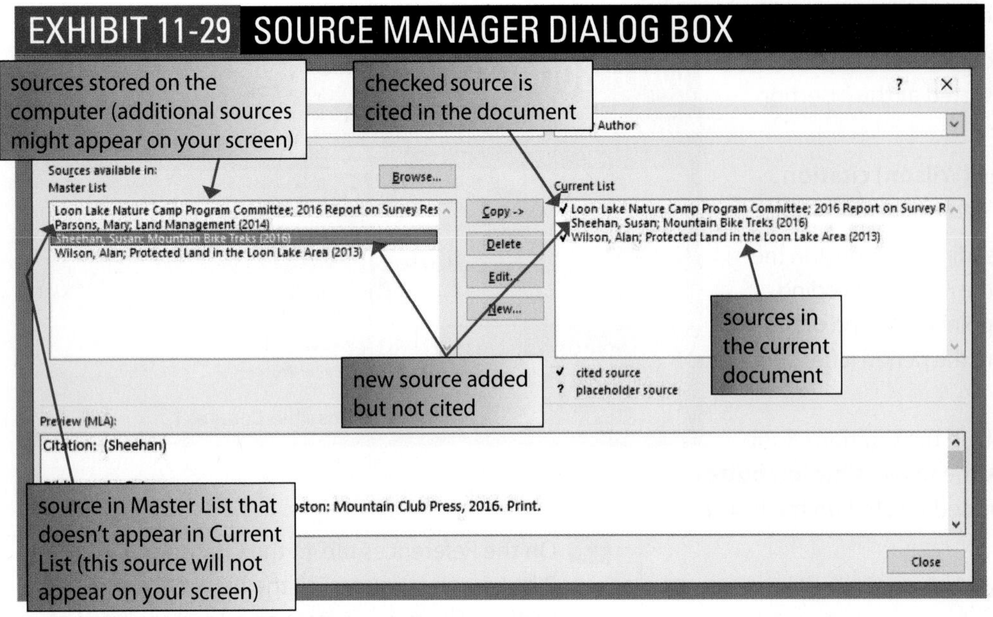

4 Add the following information:

Author:	**Susan Sheehan**
Title:	**Mountain Bike Treks**
Year:	**2016**
City:	**Boston**
Publisher:	**Mountain Club Press**
Medium:	**Print**

5 Click **OK**. The Create Source dialog box closes, and the book you added appears in both the Master List and the Current List. In the Current List, there is no check mark next to it, indicating that the book is not cited in the document. Refer back to Exhibit 11-29.

6 Click **Close**. The Source Manager dialog box closes.

End Activity

11-9e Editing Citations

If you need to add additional information to the citation, such as a page number, click the citation to display the Citation content control, click the Citation Options arrow that appears, and then click Edit Citation to open the Edit Citation dialog box. Exhibit 11-30 shows a selected citation content control and the Edit Citation dialog box. If your style guide allows it, you can also use the Edit Citation dialog box to remove, or suppress, the author's name, the year, and the title from the citation by selecting the appropriate check boxes in the Edit Citation dialog box, so that only the page number appears in the citation. Note that with the MLA style selected, if you suppress the author, Word will replace the suppressed author name with the title of the source.

Begin Activity

Edit citations to include the page number.

1 Below the Possible Courses heading on page 2, click the **Loon Lake Nature Camp Program Committee citation**. The content control containing the citation appears.

2 Click the **Citation Options arrow** ▾, and then click **Edit Citation**. The Edit Citation dialog box opens with the insertion point in the Pages box. Refer to Exhibit 11-30.

TIP: To delete a citation, click the citation to display the content control, click the title tab (the tab with the three dots) on the left side of the content control, and then press the Delete key.

EXHIBIT 11-30 EDITING A CITATION

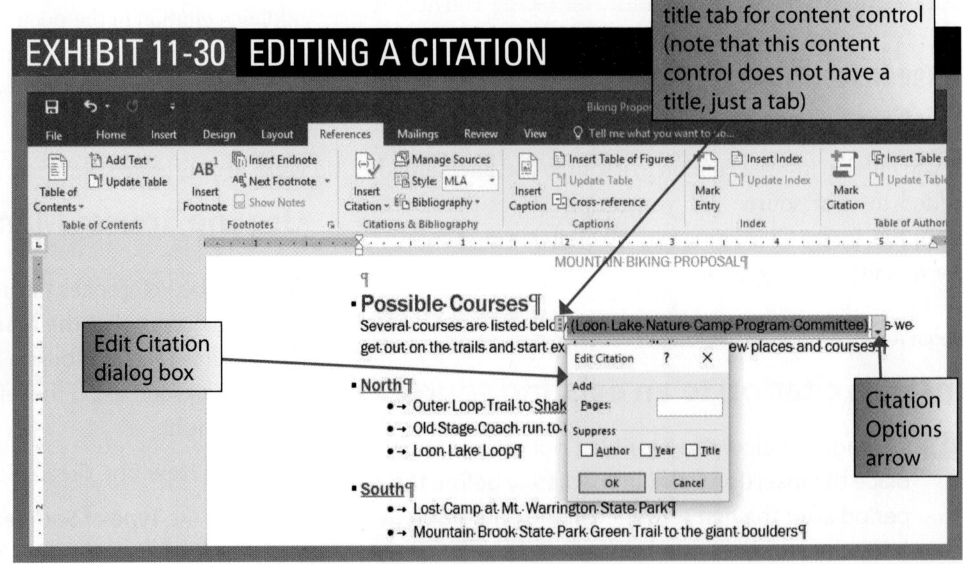

3 Type **7**, and then click **OK**. The dialog box closes, and the citation changes to include the referenced page number from the report.

4 On page 2, in the paragraph below the Finances heading in page 2, modify the Loon Lake Nature Camp Program Committee citation to include the page reference **12**.

5 On page 1, in the paragraph below the Area for Setting Up Trails heading, edit the Wilson citation to include the page number **56**.

End Activity

11-9f Generating a List of Works Cited

To create a list of works cited for a document, click the Bibliography button in the Citations & Bibliography group on the References tab, and then click one of the options in the list. See Exhibit 11-31. This creates a field that lists all the works in the Current List in the Source Manager dialog box. If you select the Works Cited, References, or Bibliography style in the gallery, the appropriate title is inserted along with the field inside a content control. If you select Insert Bibliography at the bottom, the list of sources in the Current List in the Source Manger is inserted as a field without a content control and title.

The format of the entries in the list of works cited matches the style selected in the Style box in the Citations & Bibliography group on the References tab. Because the list is a field, you can update the list later to reflect changes to the source list.

Begin Activity

Generate the bibliography.

1 Press the **Ctrl+End keys**. The insertion point moves to the end of the document.

2 Insert a **manual page break**. A new page 5 is created.

3 On the References tab, in the Citations & Bibliography group, click the **Bibliography button**. The Bibliography menu opens. Refer to Exhibit 11-31.

4 Click **Works Cited**. The list of works cited is inserted below the Works Cited heading in the style selected in the Style box in the Citations & Bibliography group on the References tab—in this case, in the MLA style. The text is formatted in the body font, and the Works Cited heading is formatted with the Heading 1 style. Compare your screen to Exhibit 11-32.

TIP: If there are no sources in the Current List in the Source Manager when you try to create a list of works cited, a message is inserted telling you that there are no sources in the current document.

End Activity

EXHIBIT 11-31 BIBLIOGRAPHY BUTTON MENU

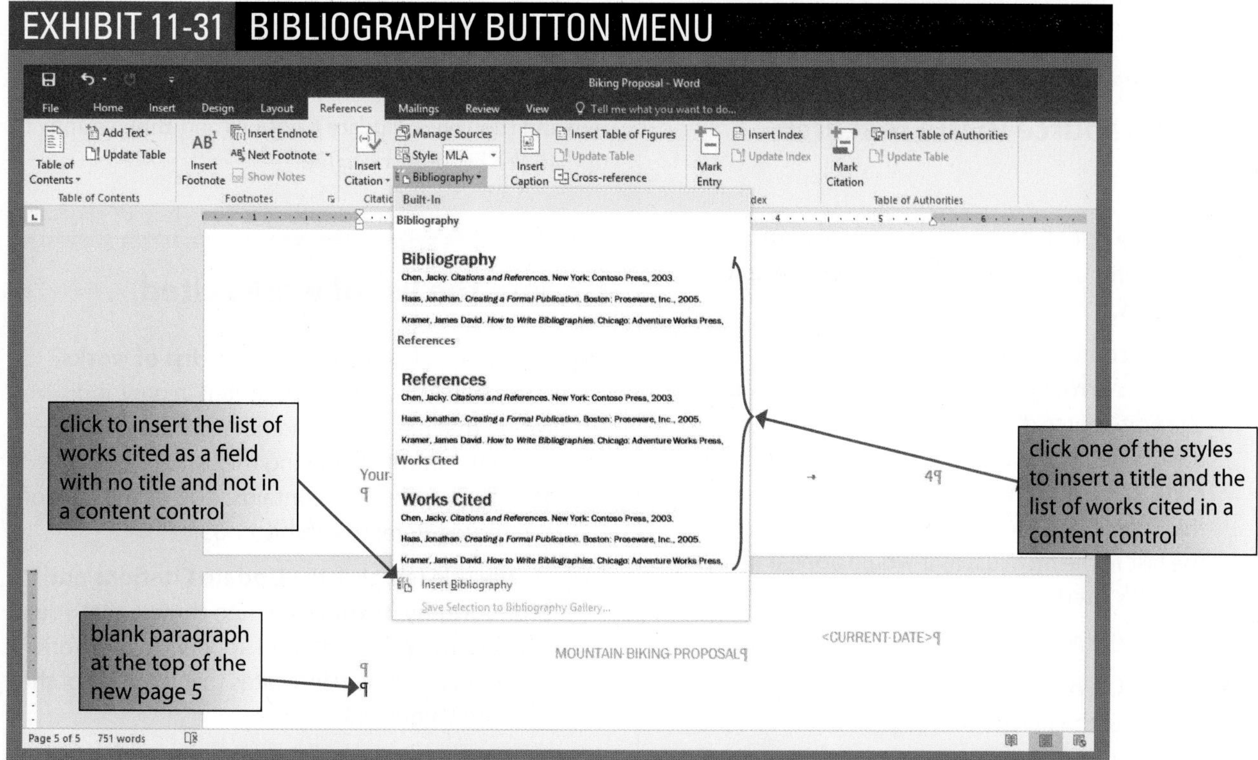

EXHIBIT 11-32 WORKS CITED LIST

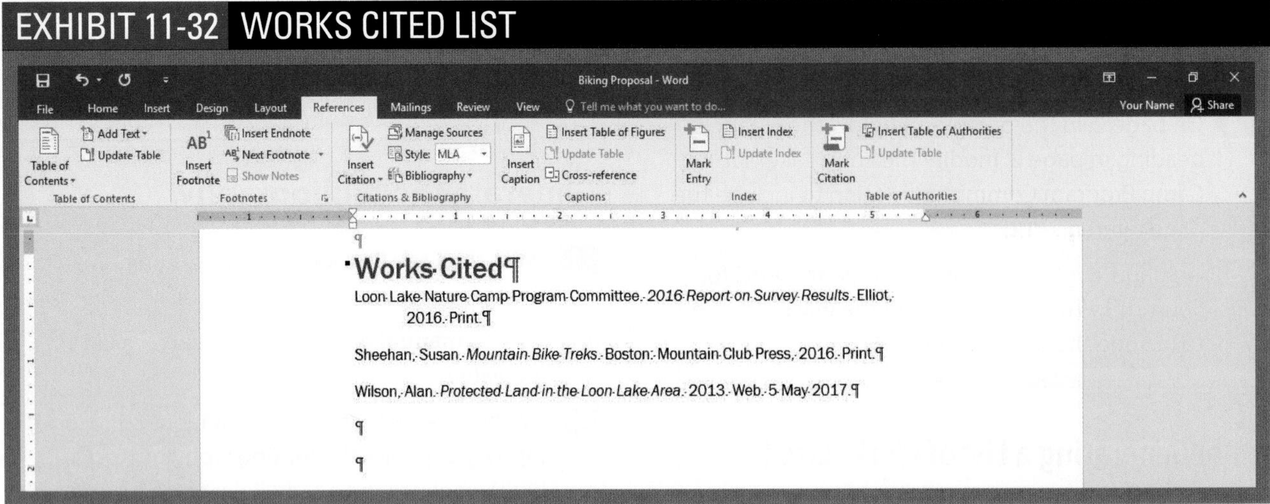

11-9g **Modifying a Source**

To modify information about a source, you need to open the Edit Source dialog box for that source. To do this, click a citation to that source in the document to display the content control, click the Citation Options arrow on the content control, and then click Edit Source; or in the Source Manager dialog box, select the source in either the Master List or the Current List, and then click Edit. After you are finished editing the source, if the source is listed in both the Master List and the Current List, a dialog box opens prompting you to update both lists. In almost all cases, you should click Yes to ensure that the source information is correct in all places it is stored on your computer.

Begin Activity

To edit a source in the research paper.

1 On page 1, in the paragraph below the Area for Setting Up Trails heading, click the **Wilson citation**.

2 On the content control, click the **Citation Options arrow** , and then click **Edit Source**. The Edit Source dialog box opens. It is identical to the Create Source dialog box, but, obviously, contains all the information you already entered for this source. The name in the Author box displays the last name first, just as it would appear in a list of works cited.

3 Click in the **Month box**, and then type **August**.

4 Click **OK**. A dialog box opens asking if you want to update the master source list and the current document.

5 Click **Yes**. The dialog box closes, and the source is modified, although the citation remains unchanged.

End Activity

11-9h **Updating the List of Works Cited**

Because the list of works cited is a field, you can update the bibliography to reflect new or edited sources. If you created the list of works cited using the Insert Bibliography command, to update the field, you need to right-click it, and then on the shortcut menu, click Update Field. If you used one of the styles in the gallery and the list of works cited is in a content control, click the list to display the content control (see Exhibit 11-33), and then on the title tab, click the Update Citations and Bibliography button. You can also click the Citation Options arrow on a citation and then click Update Citations and Bibliography to update the list of works cited.

Begin Activity

Update the list of works cited.

1 On page 5, click anywhere in the **list of works cited**. The list itself is highlighted in gray, indicating that it is a field and not regular text. The content control containing the list is also visible. The Wilson reference contains 2013 as the date of the source. Refer to Exhibit 11-33.

2 On the title tab, click the **Update Citations and Bibliography button**. The date change that you made to the Wilson citation appears in the Works Cited list, and it now indicates that the date of the source is August 2013.

End Activity

EXHIBIT 11-33 WORKS CITED DISPLAYED IN A CONTENT CONTROL

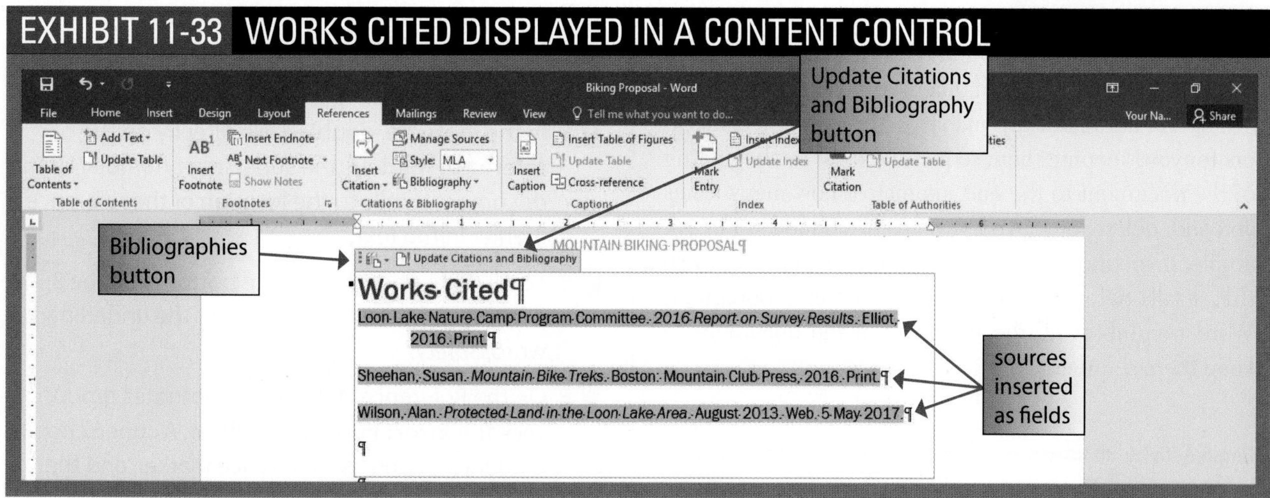

FYI CONVERTING A LIST OF WORKS CITED AND CITATIONS TO STATIC TEXT

You should always double-check the format of the citations and the list of works cited to make sure that they are formatted correctly in the style prescribed by the style guide you are using. For example, papers in the MLA style should not have colored headings. Style guides are updated from time to time, or your company or instructor might require you to use a modified style. If you need to adjust the style of the list of works cited, you can select the text and paragraphs as usual and add formatting, but if you then update the list, the formatting will revert to the selected citation style. When you are sure that you are finished updating the list of works cited, click the list to display the content control, click the Bibliographies button in the content control title tab, and then click Convert bibliography to static text to convert the list from a field that can be updated automatically to static text—that is, text that cannot be updated automatically. Then you can modify the format of the list as desired. For example, you can change the format of titles from underlined to italics or modify the indent.

You can also convert citations to static text. To do this, click the citation to display the content control and the Citation Options arrow, click the Citation Options arrow, and then click Convert citation to static text.

11-10 CREATING FOOTNOTES AND ENDNOTES

A **footnote** is an explanatory comment or reference that appears at the bottom of a page. When you create a footnote, Word inserts a small, superscript number called a **reference marker** in the text and in the bottom margin of the page and positions the insertion point next to it so you can type the text of the footnote. See Exhibit 11-34. **Endnotes** are similar, except that the

EXHIBIT 11-34 INSERTION POINT IN A NEW FOOTNOTE

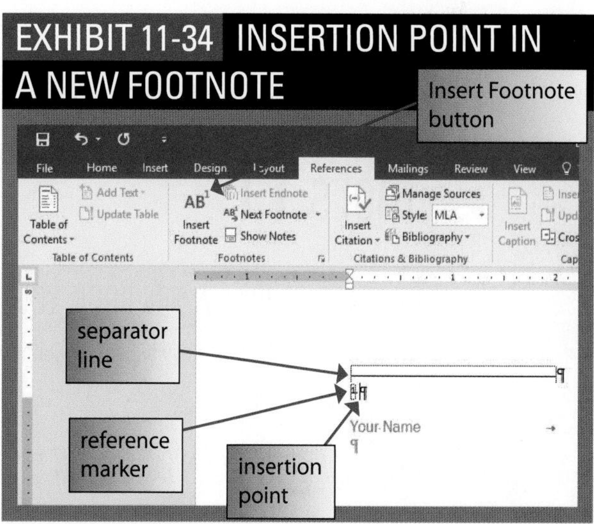

footnote An explanatory comment or reference that appears at the bottom of a page.

reference marker A small, superscript number to the right of text that corresponds to the footnote or endnote.

endnote An explanatory comment or reference that appears at the end of a section or at the end of a document.

text of an endnote appears at the end of a section or at the end of the document, and the reference marker is a lowercase Roman numeral unless you change it.

Word automatically manages the reference markers for you, keeping them sequential from the beginning of the document to the end, no matter how many times you add, delete, or move footnotes or endnotes. For example, if you move a paragraph containing footnote 4 so that it falls before the paragraph containing footnote 1, Word renumbers all the footnotes in the document to keep them sequential.

Begin Activity

Add a footnote.

1 On page 4, position the insertion point after the question mark after question number 3.

2 On the References tab, in the Footnotes group, click the **Insert Footnote button**. A superscript 1 is inserted as a reference marker at the insertion point, and the same reference marker—the superscript number 1—appears just above the bottom margin below a separator line. The insertion point is next to the number at the bottom of the page ready for you to type the text of the footnote. Refer back to Exhibit 11-34.

3 Type **If we need to increase our liability insurance, it will affect the budget.** (including the period).

4 In the footnote, double-click directly on the **reference marker** (the superscript number 1). The document scrolls to the location of the reference marker in the text.

5 Scroll up to page 3. Near the bottom of page 3, position the insertion point after the underlined word, *Safety*.

6 On the References tab, in the Footnotes group, click the **Insert Footnote button**. A superscript 1 is again inserted as a reference marker, and the insertion point moves to the new footnote.

7 Type **Each participant must sign a contract agreeing to these terms.** (including the period).

8 On the References tab, in the Footnotes group, click the **Next Footnote button**. The document scrolls, and the footnote you typed previously on page 4 appears. This footnote has been renumbered to 2 because it appears in the document after the footnote you added on page 3.

9 Save the document, and then close it.

End Activity

STUDY TOOLS 11

READY TO STUDY? IN THE BOOK, YOU CAN:

- ☐ Rip out the Chapter Review Card, which includes key terms and key chapter concepts.

ONLINE AT WWW.CENGAGEBRAIN.COM, YOU CAN:

- ☐ Review key concepts from the chapter in a short video.
- ☐ Explore formatting a long document in Word with the interactive infographic.
- ☐ Practice what you've learned with more Practice It and On Your Own exercises.
- ☐ Prepare for tests with quizzes
- ☐ Review the key terms with flashcards.

QUIZ YOURSELF

1. What happens when you use the Replace All command?
2. What style is applied to text if you do nothing to change it?
3. What is the template on which all Word documents are based?
4. How is a linked style different from a paragraph or character style?
5. How do you apply a style from the Styles gallery to text already in a document?
6. What is a theme?
7. What happens when you apply a different style set to a document?
8. What happens when you promote a paragraph in an outline?
9. How do you move a heading up or down in a document in both the Navigation pane and in Outline view?
10. What is the default setting for margins in a new document?
11. Explain the difference between an automatic and a manual page break.
12. What do you actually insert when you use the Page Number command to insert page numbers in a document?
13. Define *header* and *footer*.
14. What is a content control?
15. What is a source?
16. Why do you need to cite your sources?
17. What is included in the list of works cited when you use the Bibliography command to create the list?
18. What is the difference between a footnote and an endnote?

PRACTICE IT

Practice It 11-1

1. Open the data file **Report** located in the Chapter 11\Practice It folder. Save the document as **Annual Report**.
2. Replace all instances of the word *endowment* with **asset**.
3. Find the three instances of the phrase *Asset Fund*. Replace those instances of *Asset* with **Endowment**.
4. Apply the Title style to the first paragraph.
5. Apply the Heading 1 style to the following paragraphs: Overview, Community Collaboration, Professional Advisors Group, and Investment Committee.
6. Apply the Heading 2 style to the following paragraphs: Fiscal Year Outcome and Community Impact.
7. Apply the Heading 3 style to the following paragraphs: Community Endowment Fund, Books for All, and Young Adult Outreach.
8. Change the style set to Lines (Stylish).
9. At the beginning of the document, select the Overview heading paragraph, change its font size to 22 points, and change its color to Green, Accent 6. Then update the definition of the Heading 1 style to match the formatting of the Overview paragraph.
10. At the beginning of the document, select the first paragraph under the Overview heading, change the line spacing to single-spacing, and change the space after the paragraph to 12 points. Then create a new paragraph style based on this paragraph named **Body**, and apply this new style to all the body text in the document.
11. Change the theme to the Damask theme.
12. Change the theme colors to the Marquee color palette, and then change the theme fonts to the Calibri-Cambria font set.
13. In the Navigation pane, promote the Fiscal Year Outcome heading to a Level 1 heading, and then

move the Fiscal Year Outcome heading down so it follows the Investment Committee heading (above the Community Impact heading).

14. In Outline view, promote the Community Impact heading and its subheadings one level so that the Community Impact heading is a Level 1 heading. Then move the Community Impact heading and its subheadings up to precede the Professional Advisors Group heading.
15. Change the left and right margins to 1.5 inches.
16. At the end of the document, create a manual page break to create a new, blank page 4.
17. Use the Plain Number 2 page number style to insert a page number in the center of the footer area.
18. Insert the Filigree header from the Header gallery. In the Title content control, type **Annual Report**. In the other content control—the Author content control—type your name, replacing the user name that's there, if necessary.
19. Don't show the headers and footers on page 1.
20. Change the style for citations and the list of works cited to the APA style.
21. On page 1, in the first paragraph below the Overview heading, delete the highlighted text *[citation]*, and then insert the following citation:

Type of Source:	**Book**
Author:	**Robert L. Simmons**
Title:	**Community Foundation: A History**
Year:	**2012**
City:	**Boston**
Publisher:	**Anson Press**

22. On page 2, in the first paragraph below the Community Endowment Fund heading, replace the highlighted text *[citation]* with a citation to *Community Foundation: A History* by Robert L. Simmons.
23. On page 2, in the first paragraph below the Books for All heading, replace the highlighted text *[citation]* with the following citation:

Type of Source:	**Web site**
Name of Web Page:	**Books for All**
Name of Web Site:	**Reading Initiative**
Year:	**2017**
Month:	**June**
Day:	**4**

URL: **http://www.readinginit.example.org/outreach/booksforall.html**

24. Add the page reference **45** to the Simmons citation on page 2, and then add the page reference **15** to the Simmons citation on page 1.
25. On page 4, generate a list of works cited using the built-in Bibliography style.
26. Create the following source without inserting a citation to it:

Type of Source:	**Book**
Author:	**Sam Blackwater**
Title:	**Community-Based Aid**
Year:	**2012**
City:	**New York**
Publisher:	**Messier Publishing**

27. Update the bibliography to include the new source.
28. On page 2, after the last sentence in the first paragraph below the Community Endowment Fund heading, insert the following footnote: **The complete list of donors is on file.** (including the period). Then, on page 1, below the Overview heading, after the last sentence in the first paragraph, insert the following footnote: **The Profit and Loss statement is available on our Web site.** (including the period).
29. Save and close the document.

Practice It 11-2

1. Open the data file **Functions** located in the Chapter 11\Practice It folder. Save the document as **Hotel Functions**.
2. Replace all five instances of the word *galas* with the word **parties**.
3. Apply the Title style to the first paragraph, reduce the font size of the text in this paragraph to 24 points, and then update the Title style definition to match this change.
4. Apply the Heading 1 style to the following paragraphs: Social Events and Business Functions, Recommended Vendors, Getting Started, Select the Food, Additional Options, Choose an Event Space, and Hotel Accommodations.
5. Adjust the outline as follows:
   Social Events and Business Functions
   Getting Started
      Choose an Event Space
      Select the Food
      Additional Options
   Hotel Accommodations
   Recommended Vendors
6. Change the theme to Slice, and then change the theme color palette to Violet II.

7. At the beginning of the document, change the size of the text in the first paragraph below the Social Events and Business Functions heading to 12 points, change the line spacing to 1.15, and then create a new linked style named **Regular Text**. Apply this style to all of the body text in the document, but do *not* apply it to the three bulleted lists.
8. Change the size of the text in a paragraph formatted with the Heading 1 style to 20 points, and then update the Heading 1 style definition to match this formatting. Change the size of the text in a paragraph formatted with the Heading 2 style to 16 points, and then update the Heading 2 style to match this formatting.
9. Change the top margin to two inches and the bottom margin to 1.5 inches.
10. Insert a manual page break before the Choose an Event Space heading on page 1.
11. Insert the Sideline footer.
12. Add the Blank header, and then replace the placeholder text with your name.
13. On page 3, after the Additional Options heading, insert the following footnote: **Contact John Henderson at the main office for pricing information.**
14. Save and close the document.

ON YOUR OWN

On Your Own 11-1

1. Open the data file **Photography** located in the Chapter 11\On Your Own folder. Save the document as **Photography Flyer**.
2. Change the style set to Centered.
3. Apply the Heading 1 style to the first paragraph (*What We Do*). Use the Font dialog box to change the format of this text to Small caps. (*Hint*: On the Home tab, in the Font group, click the Dialog Box Launcher.) Change the space before the paragraph to 24 points. Update the Heading 1 style to match this formatting.
4. Apply the redefined Heading 1 style to the following paragraphs: Services, Ordering, Who We Are, Kid Perfect Picture Tips, and What Others Say About Us.
5. Apply the Heading 2 style to the following paragraphs: Show Your Support at Home, Hair, Clothing, Hats, Attitude, and Eyeglasses.
6. Move the section titled Who We Are so it is the first section in the document.
7. Use the Cover Page button in the Pages group on the Insert tab to insert the Austin cover page. On the cover page, in the Title content control, type **Kid Perfect Photography for Schools**. In the Author content control, replace the content with your name, if necessary. Delete the Subtitle content control, and then delete the Abstract content control above the title.
8. Using the APA style, add the following sources without inserting a citation. (*Hint*: Select the Show All Bibliography Fields check box in the Create Source dialog box.)

Type of Source:	**Article in a Periodical**
Author:	**Jeremy Walsh**
Title:	**Tips for Perfect Portraits**
Periodical Title:	**Photography Today**
Year:	**2016**
Month:	**September**
Pages:	**35–42**
Volume:	**21**
Issue:	**2**

9. Insert a footnote to the right of the Kid Perfect Picture Tips heading. Add a citation to the Jeremy Walsh article in the footnote.
10. Insert a manual page break before the What Others Say About Us heading on page 4.
11. Insert the Grid footer. Insert the Blank header, and then replace the placeholder with your name. Do not show the header and footer on the title page.
12. Replace all instances of **picture** with **photo**, but do not replace instances of *Picture*. (*Hint*: Expand the Find and Replace dialog box by clicking More in the dialog box.)
13. Save and close the document.

Part 6
WORD 2016

12 | Enhancing a Document

© Westend61/Getty Images

LEARNING OBJECTIVES After studying the material in this chapter, you will be able to:

- 12-1 Organize information in tables
- 12-2 Change the page orientation
- 12-3 Divide a document into sections
- 12-4 Insert and modify graphics
- 12-5 Wrap text around graphics
- 12-6 Move graphics
- 12-7 Add text effects and WordArt text boxes
- 12-8 Work with columns
- 12-9 Work with building blocks

After finishing this chapter, go to **PAGE 375** for **STUDY TOOLS**.

12-1 ORGANIZING INFORMATION IN TABLES

Word documents can contain much more than text. Elements such as tables, illustrations, graphical headlines, and formatted headings can be used to enhance documents. Some documents are formatted in multiple columns. Other documents have decorative borders around the entire page. Word provides many tools for creating these types of elements and more.

A **table**, a grid of horizontal rows and vertical columns, is a useful way to present information that is organized into categories. For example, you can use a table to organize contact information for a list of clients. For each client, you could include the following information: first name, last name, street address, city, state, and ZIP code.

Tables are organized into columns and rows. The box at the intersection of a column and a row is a **cell**. The row at the top of the table, called the **header row**, typically contains the labels for the columns so you know what type of data appears in each column.

12-1a Creating a Table

When you create a table in Word, you specify how many rows and columns to include in the table. You do this with the Table button in the Tables group on the Insert tab. When you click the Table button, you can drag across the grid that appears to select the number of columns and rows to include in the table, as shown in Exhibit 12-1. You can also click the Insert Table command to open the Insert Table dialog box in which you can specify the number of columns and rows.

Begin Activity

Create a table.

1. Open the data file **Table** located in the Chapter 12\Chapter folder. Save the document as **Class Table**.
2. If necessary, change the zoom to **120%** and display the **nonprinting characters** and the **rulers**.
3. In the body of the letter, position the insertion point in the **second paragraph** (the blank paragraph).
4. On the ribbon, click the **Insert tab**. In the Tables group, click the **Table button**. A table grid opens, with a menu at the bottom.
5. Point to the **grid** to highlight two columns and five rows. (The outline of a cell turns orange when it is highlighted.) As you move the pointer across the grid, the size of the table (columns by rows) appears above the grid. A Live Preview of the table structure appears in the document. Refer to Exhibit 12-1.
6. When **2×5 Table** appears at the top of the grid, click the **grid**. An empty table with two columns and five rows is inserted in the document, and the insertion point is in the upper-left cell. The two columns are the same widths. Because nonprinting characters are displayed, each cell contains an end-of-cell mark, and each row contains an end-of-row mark. The Table Tools Design and Layout contextual tabs appear on the ribbon. See Exhibit 12-2.

End Activity

EXHIBIT 12-1 TABLE SELECTED ON THE TABLE BUTTON MENU GRID

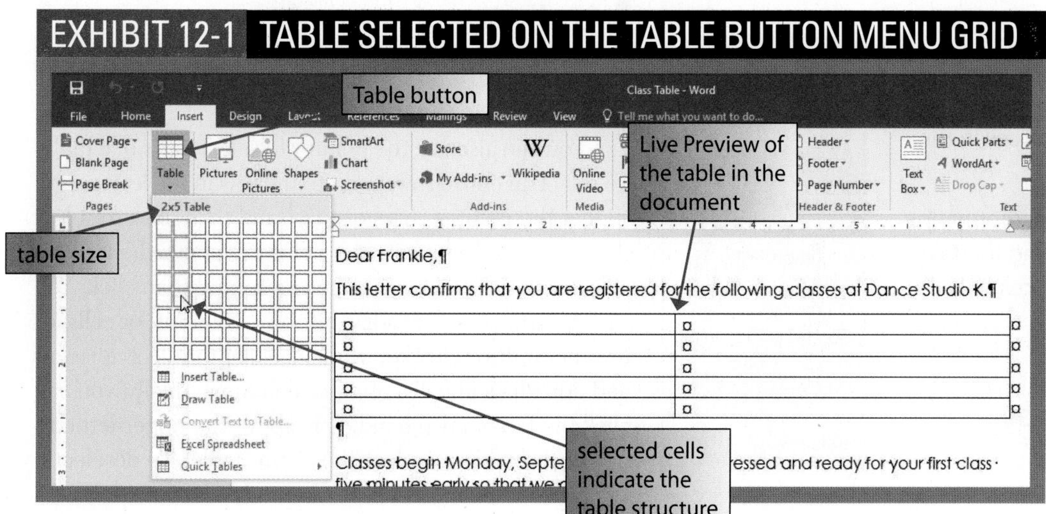

table A grid of horizontal rows and vertical columns.

cell The intersection of a column and a row.

header row The top row in a table that contains the labels for the columns.

WORD 2016

EXHIBIT 12-2 BLANK TABLE WITH TWO COLUMNS AND FIVE ROWS

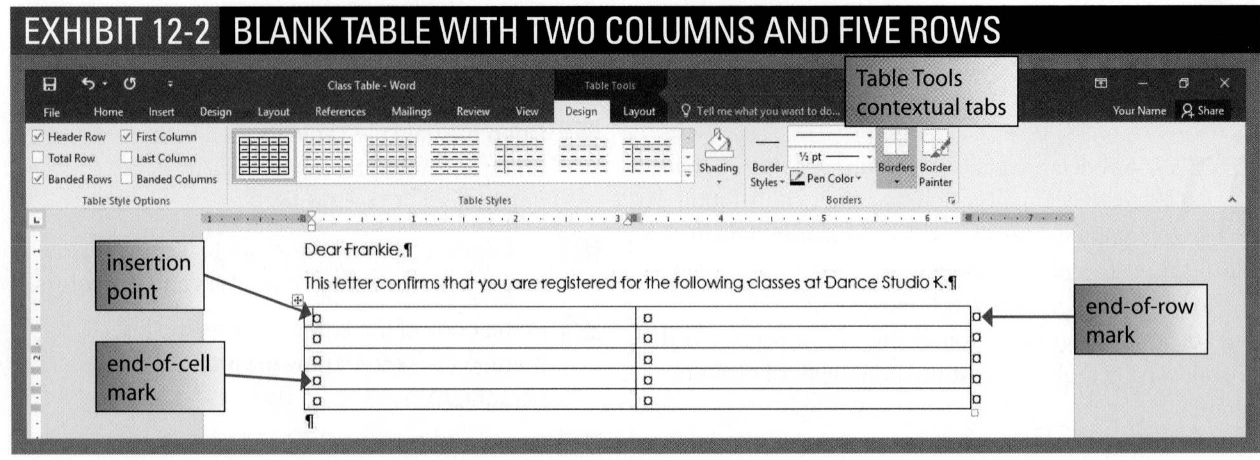

12-1b Entering Data in a Table

To enter data in a table, simply move the insertion point to a cell and type. You can move the insertion point to a cell by clicking in that cell. You can also use the keyboard to move the insertion point between cells. To move to the next cell to the right, press the Tab key. To move to the next cell to the left, press the Shift+Tab keys. You can also press the arrow keys to move between cells. If the data takes up more than one line in the cell, Word automatically wraps the text to the next line and increases the height of that cell as well as all of the cells in that row.

Begin Activity

Enter data into a table.

1. With the insertion point in the upper-left cell in the table, type **Class**. As you type, the end-of-cell mark moves to the right to accommodate the text.
2. Press the **Tab key** to move the insertion point to the next cell to the right.
3. Type **Time** and then press the **Tab key**. Because the insertion point was in the last column, it moves to the first cell in the next row.
4. Type the following information in the table, pressing the **Tab key** to move from cell to cell:

Ballet	**5-6**
Jazz	**6-7**
Modern	**6-7:30**
Tap	**6–8**

PROBLEM? If a new row is added to your table, you pressed the Tab key when the insertion point was in the last cell in the table. On the Quick Access Toolbar, click the **Undo button** to remove the extra row.

End Activity

12-1c Selecting Parts of a Table

As you work with tables, you need to be able to select their parts. You can select a cell, a row or column, multiple rows or columns, or the entire table. To select parts of a table from the ribbon, position the insertion point in a cell, click the Select button in the Table group on the Table Tools Layout tab, and then click the appropriate command—Select Cell, Select Column, Select Row, or Select Table. See Exhibit 12-3.

EXHIBIT 12-3 SELECT BUTTON AND TABLE MOVE HANDLE

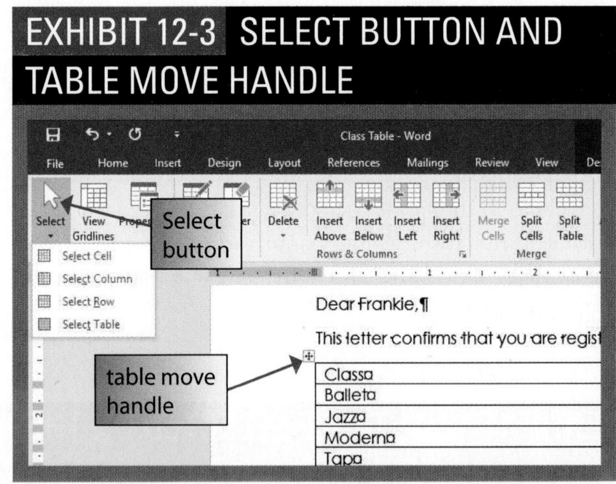

You can also use the pointer to select parts of a table. To select an entire row, point to the row in the left margin so that the pointer changes to ⇗, and then click to select that row; to select a column, point just above the top of a column so the pointer changes to ⬇, and then click. You can also drag to select adjacent rows, columns, or cells, or use the Shift or Ctrl key while clicking to select adjacent and nonadjacent cells, rows, or columns. Finally, you can click the table move handle ✥ above the upper-left corner of the table to select the entire table. To deselect a cell or table, click anywhere else in the document.

Begin Activity

Select parts of a table.

1 Move the pointer to the **left of the top row** in the table so it changes to ↗, and then click. The top row is selected.

2 Point to the **top of the first column** so that the pointer changes to ⬇, and then click. The first column is selected. The table move handle ⊞ appears above the upper-left corner of the table.

3 Point to the **table move handle** ⊞ so that the pointer changes to ✥, and then click the **table move handle** ⊞. The entire table is selected.

4 Click **any cell** in the table to deselect the table and place the insertion point in that cell.

End Activity

PROBLEM? If you have a hard time making the pointer change to ⬇, point above the table, and then slowly move the pointer down on top of the column.

TIP: Press the Shift key as you select more rows or columns to select adjacent rows or columns; use the Ctrl key to select nonadjacent rows or columns.

12-1d Inserting a Row or Column

You can modify the structure of a table by adding or removing rows and columns. To insert a row or column, move the pointer to the left of a row divider or above a column divider to display an Insert control. Exhibit 12-4 shows an Insert control for a column. Click the Insert control ⊕ to insert a row above or a column to the left of the control. You can also use the Insert Above, Insert Below, Insert Left, or Insert Right buttons in the Rows & Columns group on the Table Tools Layout tab.

FYI

CREATING A QUICK TABLE

A **Quick Table** is a table template that contains sample text and formatting. To insert a Quick Table, point to the Quick Tables command on the Table button menu, and then scroll through the gallery of Quick Tables that appears. You can insert a calendar, a simple list, tables with subheads, and other types of formatted tables. You can then replace the text in the Quick Table with your own text.

ITEM	NEEDED
Books	1
Magazines	3
Notebooks	1
Paper pads	1
Pens	3
Pencils	2
Highlighter	2 colors
Scissors	1 pair

Begin Activity

Insert rows and columns in a table.

1 Point above the column border between the Class and Time columns. The Insert control ⊕ appears. Refer back to Exhibit 12-4.

2 Click the **Insert control** ⊕. A new column is inserted to the left of the Insert control—between the Class and Time columns. The overall width of the table did not change. The original two columns decreased in width, making all three columns the same width.

3 In the new column, click in the **top cell**, and then type **Day**.

EXHIBIT 12-4 COMMANDS TO INSERT ROWS AND COLUMNS

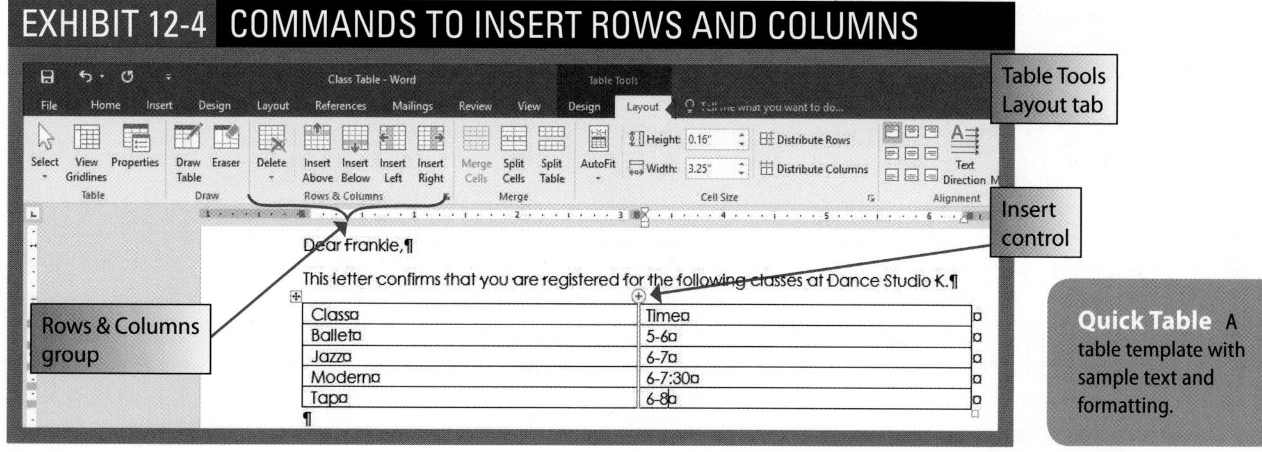

Quick Table A table template with sample text and formatting.

4 Press the **Down Arrow key**. The insertion point moves down one row.

5 Type the following information in the new column, pressing the **Down Arrow key** to move from cell to cell:

Monday
Monday
Thursday
Wednesday

6 Make sure the insertion point is in the **second cell in the last row**.

7 Click the **Table Tools Layout tab** if necessary. In the Rows & Columns group, click the **Insert Above button.** A new row is inserted above the row containing the insertion point.

TIP: To create a new bottom row in a table, place the insertion point in the rightmost cell in the bottom row, and then press the Tab key.

8 Click in the **first cell in the new row**, type **Contemporary**, press the **Tab key**, type **Thursday**, press the **Tab key**, and then type **7:30–8:30**.

9 With the insertion point in the **last column**, in the Rows & Columns group, click the **Insert Right button**. A new column is inserted to the right of the Time column, and all of the columns are resized.

10 In the new column, click in the **top cell**, and then type **Price**. Compare your screen to Exhibit 12-5.

End Activity

12-1e Deleting a Row, Column, or Table

To delete the structure of a row, column, or the entire table—including its contents—you click in the row or column you want to delete—or anywhere in the table if you want to delete the whole table—and then click the Delete button in the Rows & Columns group on the Table Tools Layout tab. This opens the menu of commands shown in Exhibit 12-6. To delete multiple rows or columns, start by selecting all the rows or columns you want to delete.

EXHIBIT 12-6 DELETE BUTTON MENU

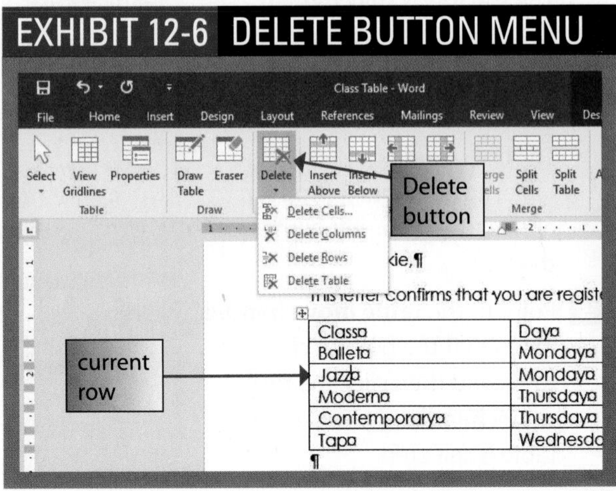

Begin Activity

Delete a row and a column in a table.

1 Position the insertion point anywhere in the **Jazz row** in the table.

2 On the Table Tools Layout tab, in the Rows & Columns group, click the **Delete button**. The Delete menu opens, displaying options for deleting cells, columns, rows, or the entire table. Refer back to Exhibit 12-6.

TIP: To delete the contents of a cell, row, column, or table, select the parts of the table containing the contents you want to delete, and then press the Delete key.

EXHIBIT 12-5 TABLE WITH NEW COLUMNS AND NEW ROW

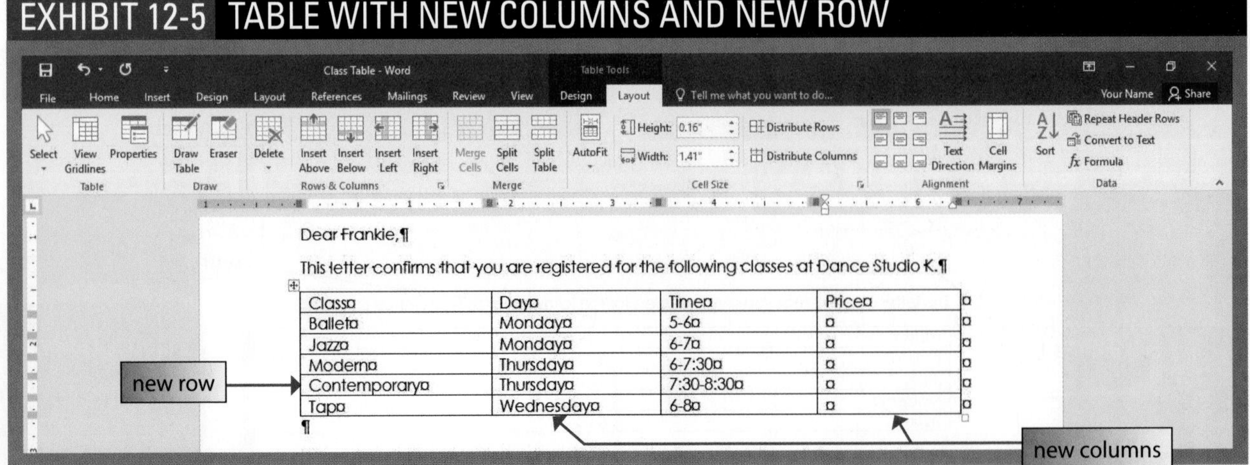

3 Click **Delete Rows.** The Jazz row is deleted.

4 Position the insertion point anywhere in the **Price column.**

5 In the Rows & Columns group, click the **Delete button**, and then click **Delete Columns.** The Price column is deleted. The width of the three remaining columns does not change and the table no longer fills the width of the page.

End Activity

12-1f Changing Table Column Widths

Columns that are too narrow or too wide for the material they contain can make a table hard to read. When the insertion point is positioned in a table, Move Table Column markers appear on the horizontal ruler above each column border to indicate the column widths. See Exhibit 12-7. You can make column widths adjust automatically to accommodate the widest entry in the column. To adjust the width of all the columns at once to match their widest entries, click the AutoFit button in the Cell Size group on the Table Tools Layout tab, and then click AutoFit Contents. To adjust the width of a single column to fit its widest entry, double-click its right column border. To change a column's width to a specific width, drag the column's right border to a new position, as shown in Exhibit 12-7, or type a measurement in the Width box in the Cell Size group on the Table Tools Layout tab.

EXHIBIT 12-7 IDENTIFYING AND CHANGING COLUMN WIDTHS IN TABLES

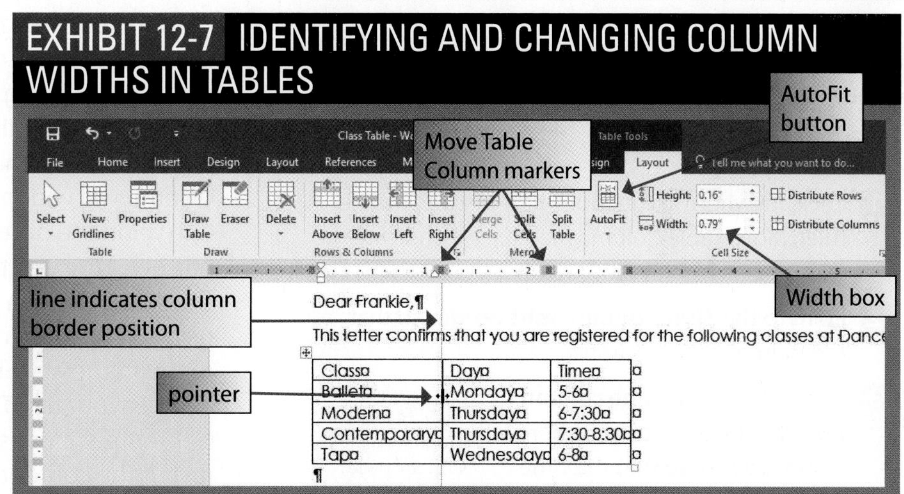

FYI SORTING ROWS IN A TABLE

You can sort a table based on the contents of one of the columns in alphabetical, numerical, or chronological order. For example, you could sort the table you just created based on the contents of the Class column. When you sort, you can choose to sort either in ascending (alphabetical or lowest to highest) or descending (reverse alphabetical or highest to lowest) order. You can also sort a table based on more than one column. For example, if a table included a list of items purchased at several stores, you could sort the table first on the store names, and then on the item names so that the list would be alphabetized by store name and then by item name within each store. To sort a table, select the table, and then click the Sort button in the Data group on the Table Tools Layout tab to open the Sort dialog box (shown here).

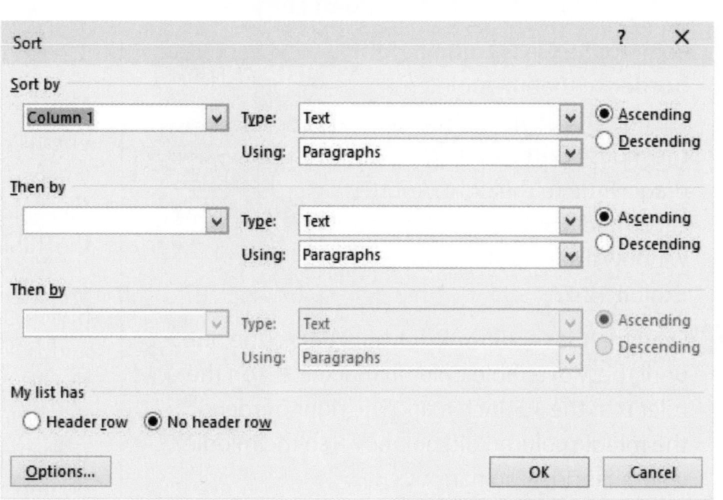

CAUTION CAUTION CAUTION CAUTION

CAUTION CAUTION CAUTION CAUTION CAUTION

DON'T SELECT TEXT BEFORE RESIZING COLUMNS

When you adjust the width of a table column, make sure that none of the text or cells in the table is selected. If a cell is selected when you change the column width, only the width of the selected cell will be changed.

Begin Activity

Change the width of columns in a table.

1 Click anywhere in the **table**, if necessary. On the ruler, Move Table Column markers ▦ indicate the width of each column.

2 Point to the **Time column right border** so that the pointer changes to ⇹.

3 Double-click the **Time column right border**. The column border moves left so that the Time column is just wide enough to accommodate the widest entry in the column.

TIP: To make the entire table span the page width, click the AutoFit button in the Cell Size group on the Table Tools Layout tab, and then click AutoFit Window.

4 On the Table Tools Layout tab, in the Cell Size group, click the **AutoFit button**. A menu opens.

5 On the menu, click **AutoFit Contents**. All the columns in the table adjust so that each is just wide enough to accommodate its widest entry.

6 Point to the **Class column right border** so that the pointer changes to ⇹, press and hold the mouse button, and then drag a little to the right. A vertical dotted line the length of the window appears. Refer back to Exhibit 12-7.

TIP: To change the height of a row, point to the bottom row border and drag the border up or down.

7 Drag the **Class column right border** to the right until the Move Table Column marker ▦ on the ruler is at the 1.5-inch mark. The right border of the middle column did not move, so the middle column is now too narrow.

8 Drag the **Time column right border** to the right until the Move Table Column marker on the ruler is at the 3.75-inch mark on the ruler.

9 Drag the **Day right column border** to the right to the 2.75-inch mark on the ruler.

End Activity

FYI

USING AUTOFIT IN TABLES

The default setting for tables in Word is for the table width to be the same width as the page, for text to wrap within cells, and for the columns to automatically resize as you enter text. This means that if you enter text in a cell with a natural breaking point, such as between words, the text will wrap within the cell. But if there is no natural breaking point, the column will widen to accommodate the long entry and the other columns will become narrower to keep the total width of the table the same. You can control this behavior using the commands on the AutoFit button menu in the Cell Size group on the Table Tools Layout tab. The first command, AutoFit Contents, changes the column widths to just fit the contents of each cell, including shrinking the width of empty columns. The second command, AutoFit Window, returns the table to the default behavior. The third command, Fixed Column Width, causes the column widths to stay the same no matter how wide an entry is.

12-1g Formatting Tables with Table Styles

You have already used styles to format text and paragraphs. Word also includes a variety of built-in styles that you can use to add borders, shading, and color to tables. You select a table style from the Table Styles gallery on the Table Tools Design tab. See Exhibit 12-8.

As shown in Exhibit 12-8, the first row in the Table Styles gallery contains styles in the Plain Tables section, and below that is the Grid Tables section. If you scroll the list of styles, you see the List Tables section. Styles in the Grid Tables section include visible vertical borders between the columns; styles in the List Tables section do not.

When you apply a style to a table, you can select or deselect the check boxes in the Table Style Options group on the Table Tools Design tab to format

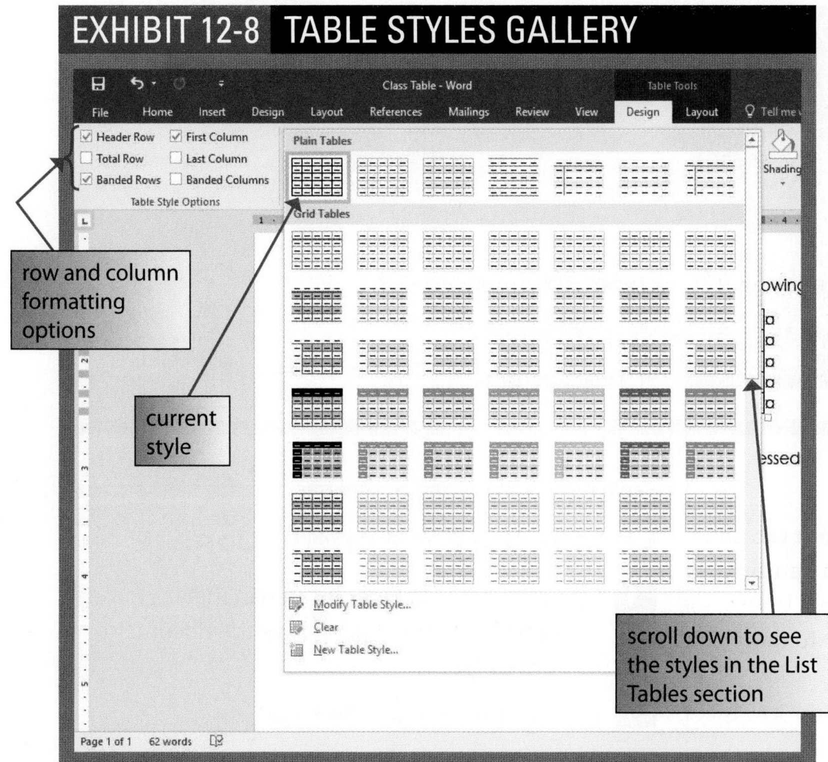

EXHIBIT 12-8 TABLE STYLES GALLERY

Begin Activity

Apply a table style.

1 On the ribbon, click the **Table Tools Design tab**. In the Table Styles group, click the **More button** . The Table Styles gallery opens. Refer back to Exhibit 12-8. The first style in the Plain Tables section is selected.

2 Scroll down to display the styles in the List Tables section. Click the **List Table 1 Light style** (use the ScreenTips to locate this style). The Table Styles gallery closes, and the table is formatted with the style you selected.

3 On the Table Tools Design tab, in the Table Style Options group, click the **First Column check box** to deselect it. The bold formatting is removed from the first column in the table.

End Activity

additional rows and columns with the table style. For example, you can specify that the first and last rows—the header and total rows—and the first and last columns be formatted differently from the rest of the rows and columns in the table. Some styles format the rows in alternating colors, called **banded rows**, while others format the columns in alternating colors, called **banded columns**.

FYI FINE-TUNING TABLE STYLES

After you apply a table style to a table, you might like the look of the table but find that it no longer effectively conveys the information or is not quite as easy to read. To solve this problem, you can, of course, apply a different style to the table. You can also customize the table formatting by using the Shading and Borders buttons on the Table Tools Design tab. Remember that built-in styles and shading and border colors that you choose from the Theme Colors in the color palette will change if you change the theme.

12-1h Aligning Tables and Text in Tables

You can change the alignment of the entire table on the page, and you can change the alignment of text in cells. To change the alignment of the table on the page, align it the same way you align a paragraph by using the paragraph alignment buttons in the Paragraph group on the Home tab. To change the alignment of text in cells, use the alignment buttons in the Alignment group on the Table Tools Layout tab.

Begin Activity

Align a table and the text in a table.

1 Click the **table move handle** to select the entire table.

2 On the ribbon, click the **Home tab**. In the Paragraph group, click the **Center button** . The table is centered horizontally on the page.

TIP: You can also click the Select button in the Table group on the Table Tools Layout tab, and then click Select Table.

banded rows/banded columns Formatting that displays alternate rows or columns in a table with different fill colors.

EXHIBIT 12-9 FINAL FORMATTED TABLE

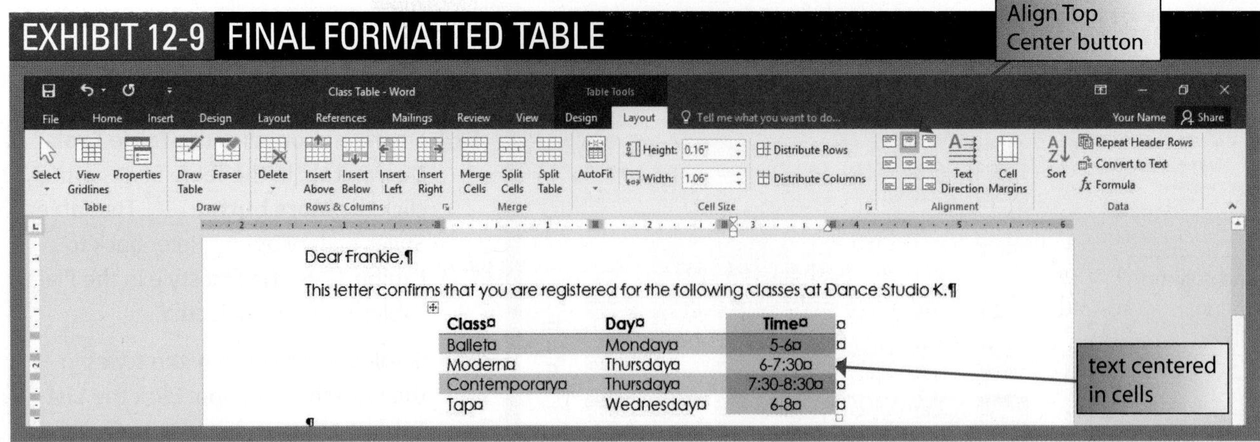

Class	Day	Time
Ballet	Monday	5-6
Modern	Thursday	6-7:30
Contemporary	Thursday	7:30-8:30
Tap	Wednesday	6-8

3 Select the **Time column.**

4 On the ribbon, click the **Table Tools Layout tab**. In the Alignment group, click the **Align Top Center button** . All the text in the Time column is centered in the cells. Compare your table to the one shown in Exhibit 12-9.

End Activity

12-2 CHANGING THE PAGE ORIENTATION

You can set the **orientation**—the way a page is turned—for the pages in a document. A page set to **portrait orientation** is taller than it is wide. This orientation, most commonly used for letters, reports, and other formal documents, is the usual orientation for most Word documents. **Landscape orientation** is a page that is wider than it is tall. You can easily change the orientation of a document using the Orientation button in the Page Setup group on the Layout tab.

orientation The way a page is turned.

portrait orientation A page that is taller than it is wide.

landscape orientation A page that is wider than it is tall.

section A part of a document that can have its own page-level formatting and properties.

section break A formatting mark in a document that indicates the start of a new section.

Begin Activity

Change the page orientation.

1 Open the data file **Flyer** located in the Chapter 12\Chapter folder. Save the document as **Dance Flyer**.

2 Change the zoom to **One Page**.

3 On the ribbon, click the **Layout tab**. In the Page Setup group, click the **Orientation button**. The Orientation menu opens with Portrait selected.

4 On the menu, click **Landscape**. The document changes to landscape orientation, with the page wider than it is tall. Compare your screen to Exhibit 12-10.

End Activity

EXHIBIT 12-10 DOCUMENT IN LANDSCAPE ORIENTATION

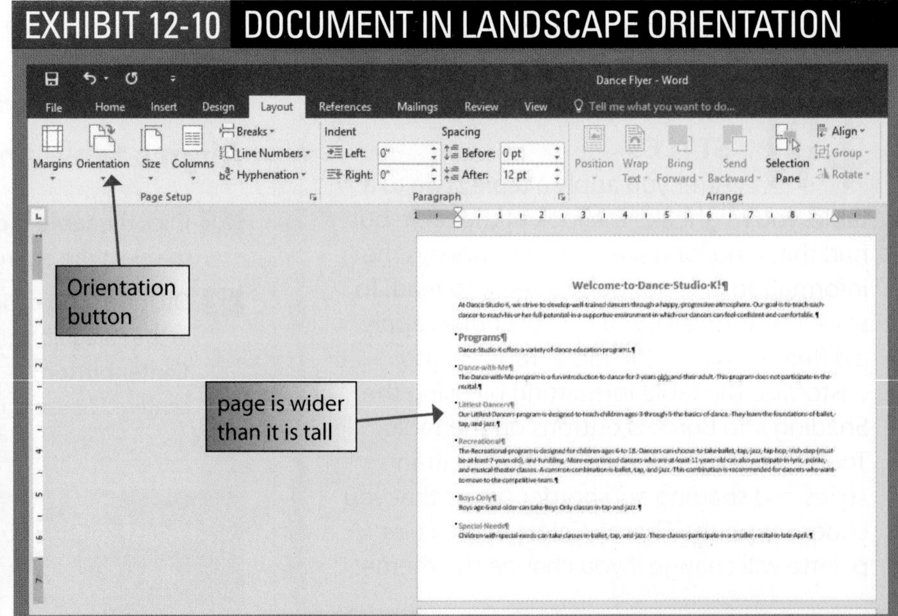

12-3 DIVIDING A DOCUMENT INTO SECTIONS

A **section** is a part of a document that can have its own page-level formatting and properties. For example, you can format one section in a document with 1-inch margins and portrait orientation, and the next section with 2-inch margins and landscape orientation. Each section in a document can also have different headers and footers, or a new section can restart the page numbering.

Every document has at least one section. To divide a document into multiple sections, you insert a **section break**. The four types of section breaks are:

- **Next Page**—inserts a section break, and forces a new page to start after the section break.
- **Continuous**—inserts a section break without starting a new page.
- **Even Page**—inserts a section break, and forces a new page to start on the next even-numbered page.
- **Odd Page**—inserts a section break, and forces a new page to start on the next odd-numbered page.

If you delete a section break, the formatting from the section below the deleted section break is applied to the section above the deleted section break. The formatting information for the last section in a document, or in a document with no section breaks, is contained in the last paragraph mark in the document.

12-3a Inserting a Section Break

You use the Breaks button in the Page Setup group on the Layout tab to select the type of section break you want to insert. See Exhibit 12-11. The Page Breaks section of the menu includes options for controlling how the text flows from page to page. The Section Breaks section includes the four types of section breaks.

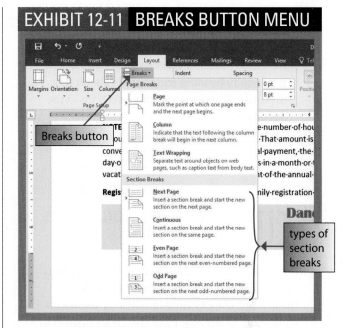

EXHIBIT 12-11 BREAKS BUTTON MENU

Breaks button

types of section breaks

When nonprinting characters are displayed, a section break is indicated by a double dotted line with the words *Section Break* in the center of it, followed by the type of section break. See Exhibit 12-12.

Begin Activity

Insert a section break.

1. Change the zoom to **120%**.
2. Scroll down to the bottom of page 3. Place the insertion point to the left of *Dance Studio K* above the address in the shaded box.
3. On the ribbon, click the **Layout tab**, if necessary. In the Page Setup group, click the **Breaks button**. The Breaks menu opens. Refer to Exhibit 12-11.
4. In the Section Breaks section, click **Next Page**. A Next Page section break is inserted. Refer to Exhibit 12-12. The text after the insertion point moves to the top of the new page 4.

TIP: To delete a section break, click the line representing the break, and then press the Delete key.

EXHIBIT 12-12 NEXT PAGE SECTION BREAK

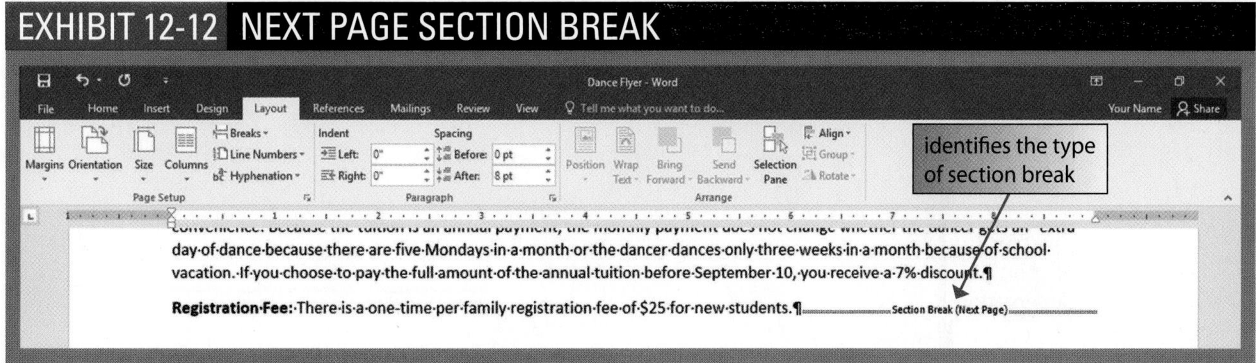

5 Scroll down to see page 4. On page 4, below the shaded box containing the address, place the insertion point before the Faculty heading, and then insert another **Next Page section break**. The Faculty heading and the text after it move to page 5. There are now three sections in the document.

End Activity

FYI VIEWING SECTION BREAKS IN DRAFT VIEW

A section break at the end of a line might be hidden. To see hidden section breaks, switch to Draft view, which displays the text of the document without showing its layout. To do this, click the Draft button in the Views group on the View tab. To switch back to Print Layout view, click the Print Layout button in the Views group on the View tab or click the Print Layout button on the status bar.

12-3b Formatting a Section Differently from the Rest of the Document

Once you have inserted a section break, you can format each section separately. When you change the page-level formatting of a section, the other sections in the document remain unchanged. See Exhibit 12-13.

Begin Activity

Format a section.

1 Change the zoom to **60%**. Scroll so that you can see the section break on page 4 and the top of page 5.

2 Click **anywhere on page 5** (which is in section 3), if necessary.

3 On the Layout tab, in the Page Setup group, click the **Orientation button**, and then click **Portrait**. Section 3, which consists of page 5, changes to portrait orientation. Section 1, which consists of pages 1–3, and section 2, which consists of page 4, remain in landscape orientation. Compare your screen to Exhibit 12-13.

End Activity

12-3c Adding Different Headers and Footers in Sections

One advantage of dividing a document into sections is that the headers and footers in each section can differ. For example, if the document includes a cover page, and you want the page numbering to begin on the first page after the cover page, you can insert a section break after

EXHIBIT 12-13 SECTIONS FORMATTED WITH DIFFERENT ORIENTATIONS

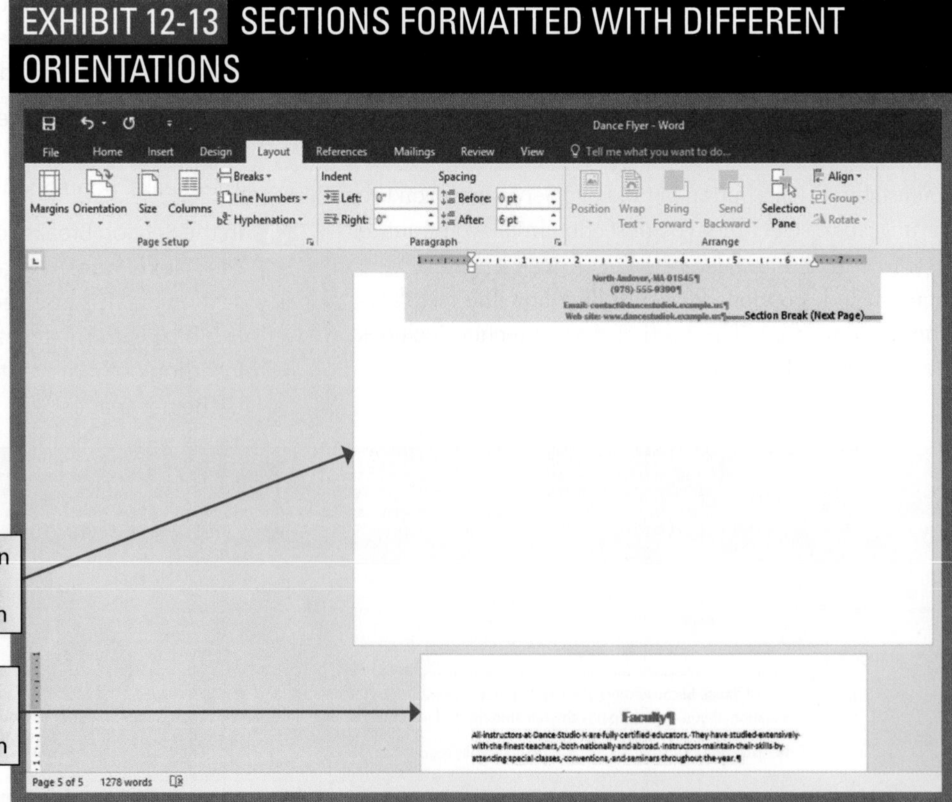

the cover page, and then have the page numbers start and appear only in section 2. That's actually what happens when you use the Cover Page button in the Pages group on the Insert tab—a section break is inserted automatically after the cover page.

Begin Activity

Add different headers and footers in sections.

1 Change the zoom to **120%**, and make sure the insertion point is still on page 5.

2 On the ribbon, click the **Insert tab**. In the Header & Footer group, click the **Footer button**, and then below the gallery, click **Edit Footer**. The insertion point moves to the footer area on page 5. On the left, the Footer area is labeled Footer –Section 3–, and on the right, the footer is labeled Same as Previous.

3 Type your name.

4 Scroll up to see the bottom of page 4. The footer area on this page is labeled Footer –Section 2–, and your name appears here as well. See Exhibit 12-14.

End Activity

The Same as Previous tab on headers and footers in sections means that the header or footer in that section is linked to the previous section. The Same as Previous tab does not appear in section 1 because there is no previous section to link to. To unlink the sections, make sure the insertion point is in the header or footer that you want to unlink, and then deselect the Link to Previous button in the Navigation group on the Header & Footer Tools Design tab.

Begin Activity

Unlink section headers and footers.

1 Scroll down, and make sure the insertion point is still in the footer area for section 3.

2 On the Header & Footer Tools Design tab, in the Navigation group, click the **Link to Previous button.** The button is no longer selected, and the Same as Previous tab on the footer disappears.

3 Scroll up so you can see the top of page 5 and the bottom of page 4. Notice that the section 3 header area on page 5 still contains the Same as Previous tab because the headers in the two sections are still linked.

4 On page 4, click after your name in the footer, press the **Tab key** twice, and then type **DRAFT**. The text is right-aligned at the default Right Tab stop in the headers and footers—the 6.5-inch mark. Because the page has landscape orientation, the right margin is at the 9-inch mark.

5 Drag the **Right Tab stop** to the right to move it on top of the Right Indent marker at the 9-inch mark on the ruler.

6 Scroll down so you can see the footer on page 5. The footer on page 5 is unchanged and does not include the word *DRAFT* because you unlinked the footer in section 3 from the footer in the previous section.

7 Double-click anywhere in the document outside the header or footer areas. Header and Footer view closes.

End Activity

EXHIBIT 12-14 FOOTER AND HEADER IN DIFFERENT SECTIONS

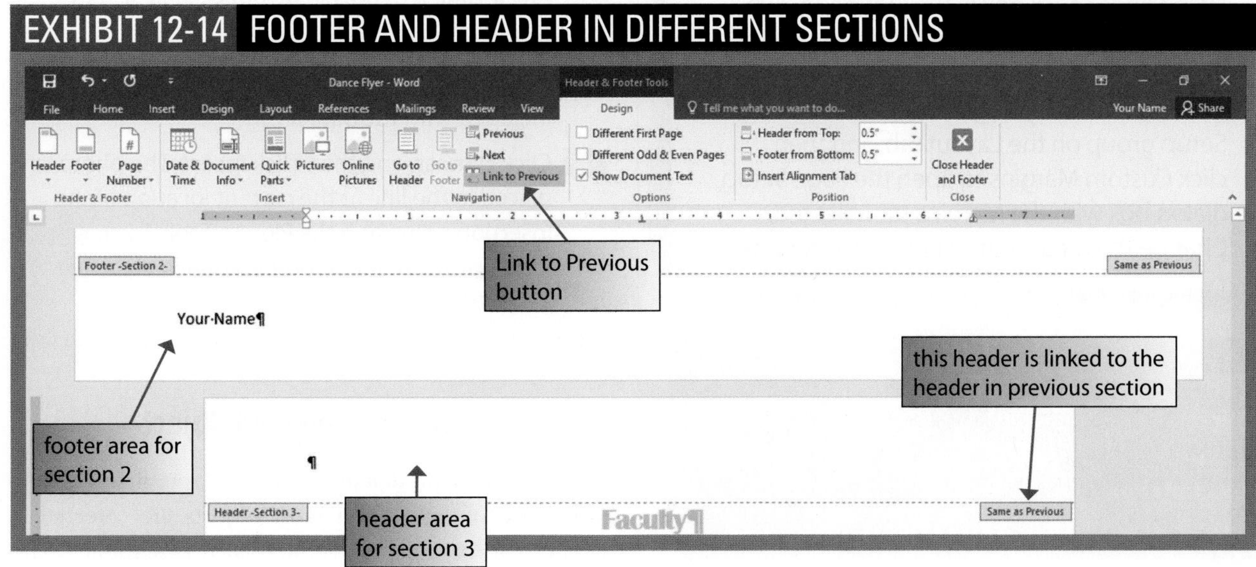

FYI ODD AND EVEN PAGES

Most professionally produced books and reports are printed on both sides of the paper and then bound. When you open a bound book or report, odd-numbered pages appear on the right and even-numbered pages appear on the left. The margin on the inside of each page, where the pages are bound together, is called the gutter. Often, the odd-numbered pages have different headers and footers than the even-numbered pages. For instance, the page numbers might appear on the outside edge of the footer, which is the right side on odd-numbered pages and the left side on even-numbered pages.

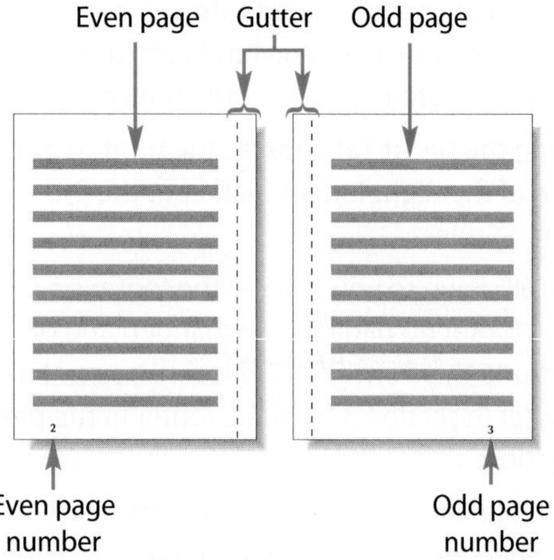

You can set up a multiple-page document with odd and even pages. After you insert a header or footer, select the Different Odd & Even Pages check box in the Options group on the Header & Footer Tools Design tab. To increase the width of the gutter to allow for binding, click the Margins button in the Page Setup group on the Layout tab, and then click Custom Margins to open the Page Setup dialog box with the Margins tab selected. Change the measurement in the Gutter box.

graphic A picture, shape, design, graph, chart, or diagram.

object Anything in a document or other file that can be treated as a whole.

selection box The box that surrounds an object when it is selected.

12-4 INSERTING AND MODIFYING GRAPHICS

A **graphic** is a picture, shape, design, graph, chart, or diagram. You can include many types of graphics in your documents, including photographs, drawings, and graphics created using other programs. You can also create graphics using drawing tools in Word.

Graphics are available in a variety of file types, including JPEG, which is the file type of most photos, and PNG, which is a file type often used for drawings. Some graphics are called clip art, which usually means drawn images stored in collections often stored on a Web site.

A graphic is an example of an **object**. An object is anything in a document or other file that can be treated as a whole. For example, a table is an object. Objects can be added, deleted, moved, formatted, and resized.

12-4a Inserting Pictures

You can add pictures to documents. To do this, click the Pictures button in the Illustrations group on the Insert tab. This opens the Insert Picture dialog box.

Begin Activity

Insert picture.

1. Place the insertion point on page 1 to the left of the first word in the *Welcome to Dance Studio K!* paragraph.
2. On the ribbon, click the **Insert tab**. In the Illustrations group, click the **Pictures button**. The Insert Picture dialog box opens. This dialog box is similar to the Open and Save As dialog boxes.
3. Navigate to the **Chapter 12\Chapter folder** included with the data files.
4. Click **Dancer**, and then click **Insert**. The photo is placed in the line at the current location of the insertion point, and the Picture Tools Format tab appears on the ribbon and is selected. See Exhibit 12-15.

End Activity

12-4b Examining a Selected Object

To work with or delete an object, you first need to select the object. When most objects are selected, a **selection box** surrounds the object. In Exhibit 12-15,

EXHIBIT 12-15 PICTURE INSERTED IN THE DOCUMENT

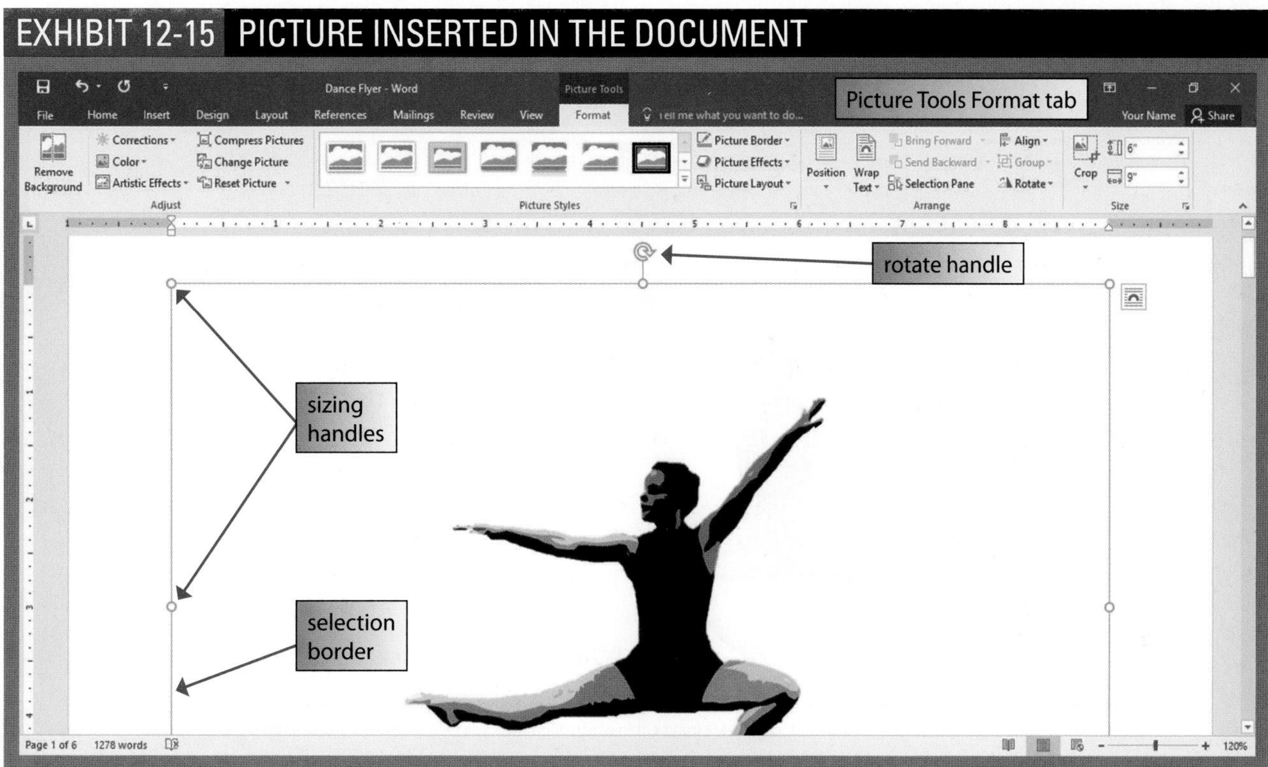

the photo is selected. The small circles at each corner of the selection boxes and in the center of each side are **sizing handles** that you can drag to change the size of the selected object. For some selected objects, like the photo you inserted, a circle appears above the top-middle sizing handle of the selected object. This is the **rotate handle**, which you can drag to rotate the object in either direction.

When an object is selected, a contextual tab appears on the ribbon with options for formatting, editing, moving, and resizing that object. For tables, as you have already seen, the two Table Tools contextual tabs appear. When you select most images, the Picture Tools Format tab appears (refer back to Exhibit 12-15). However, some images are treated as drawings, so the Drawing Tools Format tab appears when they are selected. The Picture Tools Format tab and the Drawing Tools Format tab contain similar commands.

12-4c Cropping a Picture

If you want to cut off part of a graphic, you can **crop** it. For example, you could crop an illustration of an ice cream cone by cropping off the cone, leaving only the ice cream itself. To crop a photo, select it, and then click the Crop button in the Size group on the Picture Tools Format tab. When the Crop button is selected, crop handles appear just inside of the sizing handles. You can drag the crop handles to crop off those parts of the photo. See Exhibit 12-16.

The Crop button appears only on the Picture Tools Format tab. There is no Crop button on the Drawing Tools Format tab.

Begin Activity

Crop a photo.

1. On the ribbon, click the **Picture Tools Format tab**, if necessary. In the Size group, click the **Crop button.** The Crop button is selected, and black crop handles appear inside the sizing handles on the photo's selection border.
2. Scroll the document so you can see the top of the photo and the sizing and crop handles on the sides of the photo.

sizing handle A small circle that appears at the corner or on the side of a selection box.

rotate handle A small circle that appears attached to the side of a selected object that you can drag to rotate the object in either direction.

crop To cut off part of a graphic.

EXHIBIT 12-16 CROPPED PHOTO

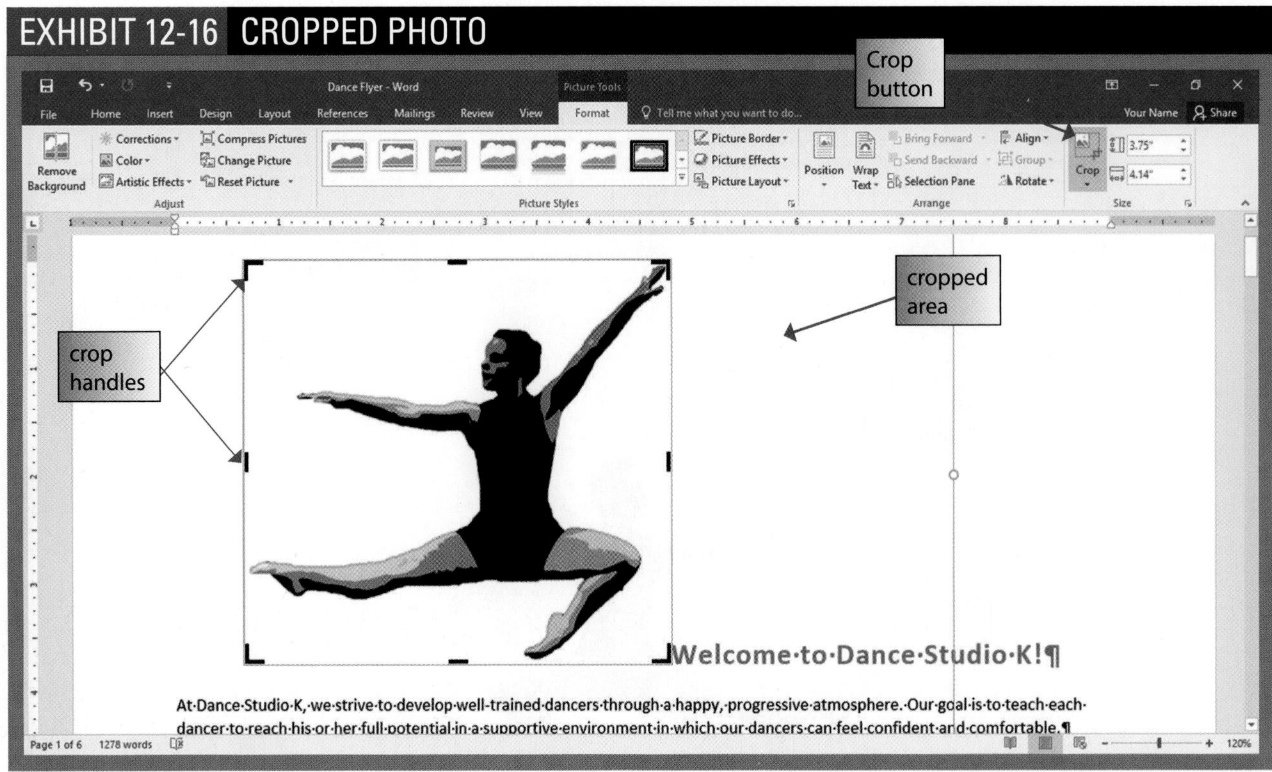

3 Point to the **top-middle crop handle**. The pointer changes to .

4 Press and hold down the mouse button and drag down a little. The pointer changes to +.

5 Drag down about one inch to just above the dancer's left hand, and then release the mouse button. The selection box and crop handles appear around the portion of the photo that will remain visible when you are finished cropping.

> **PROBLEM?** If the entire photo moves, release the mouse button, click the Undo button on the Quick Access Toolbar, and then repeat Steps 3–5, pausing slightly before dragging the crop handle.

6 Drag the **bottom-middle crop handle** up about one inch to just below the dancer's left foot.

7 Drag the **right-middle crop handle** to the left about two and a half inches to just to the right of the dancer's left hand.

> **TIP:** You can also drag the photo inside the crop area to reposition it.

8 Drag the **left-middle crop handle** to the right about two inches so it is just to the left of the dancer's right foot. Refer to Exhibit 12-16. Adjust the crop, if necessary, to match the Exhibit.

9 On the Picture Tools Format tab, in the Size group, click the **Crop button**. The Crop button is deselected, and the crop handles and the cropped portions of the photo disappear.

End Activity

FYI SPECIALIZED CROP COMMANDS

You can use commands on the Crop button menu (shown here) to crop to specific shapes or proportions. On the Picture Tools Format tab, in the Size group, click the Crop button arrow to open the Crop button menu. To crop a photo to a shape, which means trimming the edges of a graphic so it fits into a star, oval, arrow, or other shape, click the Crop button arrow, point to Crop to Shape, and then click a shape on the menu that appears. To crop to specific proportions, click the Crop button arrow, point to Aspect Ratio, and then select a ratio on the list.

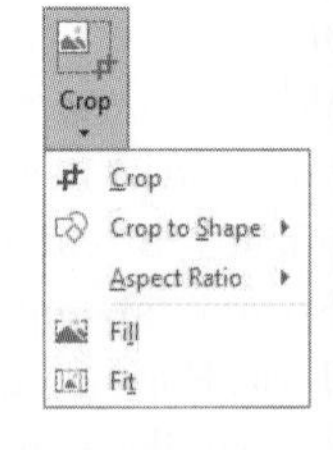

EXHIBIT 12-17 RESIZED PICTURE

12-4d **Resizing a Picture**

You can change the size of graphics you insert. The easiest way to do this is to drag the sizing handles. You can also change a graphic's measurements using the Shape Height and Shape Width boxes in the Size group on the Picture Tools or Drawing Tools Format tab.

Pictures and other objects that cause the Picture Tools Format tab to appear when selected have their aspect ratios locked by default. **Aspect ratio** specifies an object's height relative to its width. When you resize a graphic with its aspect ratio locked, dragging a corner sizing handle or changing one dimension in the Size group on the Picture Tools Format tab changes the other dimension by the same percentage. However, dragging one of the sizing handles in the middle of the graphic's border overrides the locked aspect ratio setting and resizes the object only in the direction you drag. Generally, you do not want to override the aspect ratio setting when resizing photos because the images will be distorted.

Begin Activity

Resize a picture.

1. On the selected photo, point to the **upper-right sizing handle**. The pointer changes to ⤢.
2. Press and hold the mouse button, and then start dragging down. The pointer changes to +. Because you are dragging a corner sizing handle, both the height and width change proportionally.
3. Continue dragging the **sizing handle** down and to the left. As you drag, the overall size of the photo shrinks but the photo stays centered in its position. This means the pointer moves away from the sizing handle as you drag.
4. When the photo is approximately **1.5-inches high**, release the mouse button. After you release the mouse button, look at the measurement in the Shape Height box in the Size group on the Picture Tools Format tab.
5. If the measurement in the Shape Height box is not 1.5", click in the **Shape Height box** to select the measurement, type **1.5**, and then press the **Enter key**. The height of the photo is changed to 1.5 inches and the width is resized proprtionately to maintain the aspect ratio. Compare your screen to Exhibit 12-17.

PROBLEM?
If the photo flipped so it is facing the other way, you dragged the pointer past the photo. Click the Undo button on the Quick Access Toolbar, and then repeat Steps 1–4, making sure you do not drag the pointer past the photo.

End Activity

12-4e **Formatting a Picture**

Like text and tables, pictures can have a style applied to them. A picture style can consist of a border, a shape, or an effect such as a shadow, reflection, or three-dimensional effect. To apply a style to a picture, select a style in the Picture Styles gallery on the Picture Tools Format tab. If you want to modify part of the style definition, you can use the Picture Border and Picture Effects buttons in the Picture Styles group on the Picture Tools Format tab, or you can open the Format Picture task pane and use commands there to modify the style. See Exhibit 12-18.

aspect ratio The proportion of an object's height to its width.

EXHIBIT 12-18 FORMAT PICTURE TASK PANE WITH FILL & LINE BUTTON SELECTED

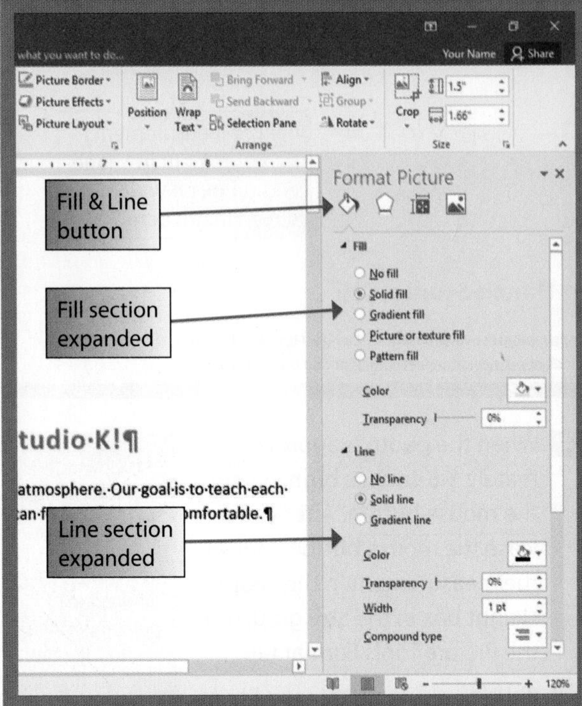

Begin Activity

Format a picture.

1 On the Picture Tools Format tab, in the Picture Styles group, click the **More button** .

2 Point to the various styles, and observe the Live Preview of the picture styles on the photo.

3 In the Picture Styles gallery, click the **Reflected Rounded Rectangle style**. The gallery closes, and the style you selected is applied. This style applies a rectangular background with rounded corners, a gray fill, and no border, and a slight reflection below the image. You can modify this style.

TIP: If file size is a concern, select a picture, click the Compress Pictures button in the Adjust group on the Picture Tools Format tab, and then select a lower resolution.

4 In the Picture Styles group, click the **Picture Border button arrow**, point to **Weight**, and then click **1 pt**. A 1-point, black border is added around the photo.

5 In the Picture Styles group, click the **Dialog Box Launcher** . The Format Picture task pane appears to the right of the document. In the task pane, the Effects tab is selected, indicated by the selected Effects button .

6 In the Format Picture task pane, click the **Fill & Line button** . The Fill & Line tab is active and the Fill and Line sections appear in the task pane.

7 In the task pane, if the Fill and Line sections are not expanded and the expand arrow appears next to Fill and Line, click **Fill**, and then click **Line**. When the sections are expanded, options for changing the fill and line of the selected photo appear under each section name, and the collapse arrow appears next to the section names. Refer to Exhibit 12-18.

8 In the task pane, in the Fill section, click the **No fill option**. In the task pane, the options for changing the solid fill disappear. In the photo, the gray fill is removed.

9 In the task pane, in the Line section, click the **No line option**. In the task pane, the options for changing the line disappear. In the photo, the border you had added using the Picture Border button is removed.

10 In the task pane, click the **Close button** . The task pane closes. Compare your screen to Exhibit 12-19.

End Activity

FYI

REMOVING A PHOTO'S BACKGROUND

One specialized technique for editing photos allows you to remove the background of a photo, leaving only the foreground image. For example, you can edit a photo of a bird in the sky to remove the sky, leaving only the image of the bird. To edit a photo to remove the background, use the Remove Background button in the Adjust group on the Picture Tools Format tab. Removing a photo's background can be tricky, especially if you are working on a photo with a background that is not clearly differentiated from the foreground image. For example, you might find it difficult to remove a white, snowy background from a photo of an equally white snowman.

EXHIBIT 12-19 FORMATTED PICTURE

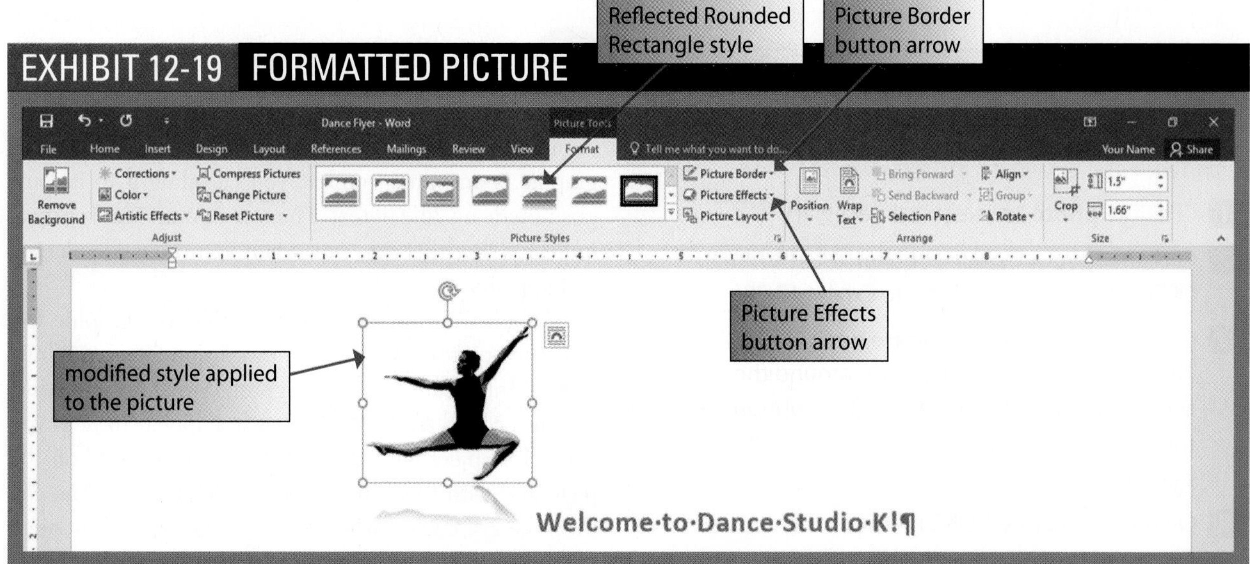

12-5 WRAPPING TEXT AROUND GRAPHICS

Graphic objects in a document are either inline or floating. An **inline object** (often called an **inline graphic**) is located in a specific position in a line of text, and the object moves with the text. For example, if you type text to the left of an inline object, the object moves right to accommodate the new text. You can drag the object to another position in the document, but it appears in a line of text wherever you drop it. When you format a paragraph that contains an inline object, the inline object is also formatted. For example, if you right-align the paragraph, the inline graphic will be right-aligned with the paragraph. The photo you inserted is an inline object.

A **floating object** (often called a **floating graphic**) can be positioned anywhere in the document, and the text will flow—wrap—around the object or float on top of or behind text. The wrap settings for graphics are:

- **Square**—text flows around the straight edges of an object's border.
- **Tight**—text flows around the contours of the object itself.
- **Through**—text flows around the contours of the object itself and also fills any open spaces in the graphic.
- **Top and Bottom**—text stops at the top border of an object and resumes below the bottom border.
- **Behind Text**—text flows over the graphic.
- **In Front of Text**—text flows behind the graphic.

To change the wrap properties of an object, select the graphic, and then click the Layout Options button that appears next to the selected graphic to open a menu of wrap options. See Exhibit 12-20. Select the wrap option you want to use. These same options are available on the Wrap Text button menu in the Arrange group on the Picture Tools Format tab.

EXHIBIT 12-20 LAYOUT OPTIONS MENU

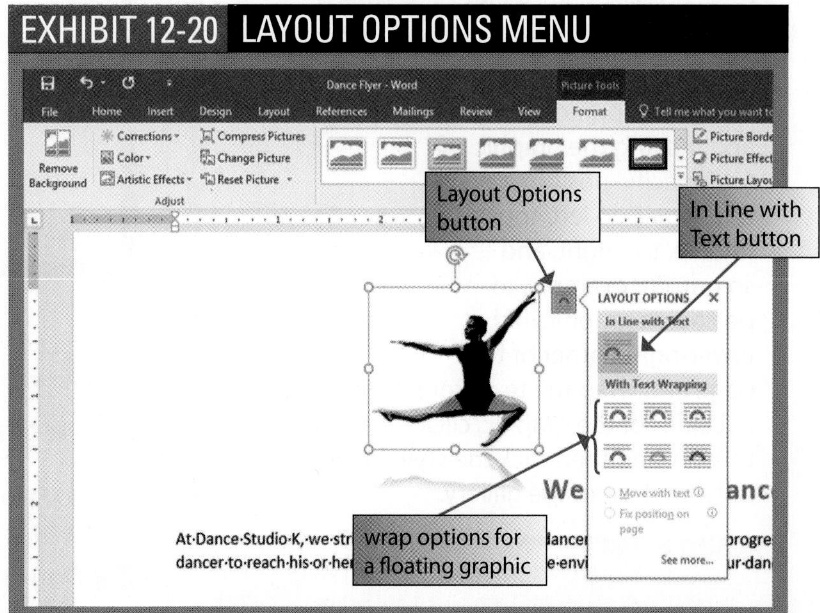

inline object (inline graphic) A graphic that is positioned in a line of text and moves along with the text.

floating object (floating graphic) A graphic that can be positioned anywhere in a document.

Begin Activity

Change a graphic's text wrap properties.

1. Click the **photo** to select it, if necessary.
2. Click the **Layout Options button** . The LAYOUT OPTIONS menu opens. Refer to Exhibit 12-20.
3. On the menu, click the **Square option** . The text in the document wraps around the photo on both sides, and the Square option on the menu is now shaded to indicate that it is selected.
4. On the LAYOUT OPTIONS menu, click the **Close button** [X]. The LAYOUT OPTIONS menu closes.

End Activity

FYI

USING THE POSITION BUTTON

The Position button in the Arrange group on the Picture Tools Format tab is a shortcut to formatting a graphic as a floating graphic with the Square wrapping option and moving the graphic to a specific position on the page (top left, top middle, top right, and so on). For example, to position a graphic in the lower-right corner of the page and wrap the text around the top and left sides of the graphic, click the Position button, and then click the style in the bottom right of the gallery.

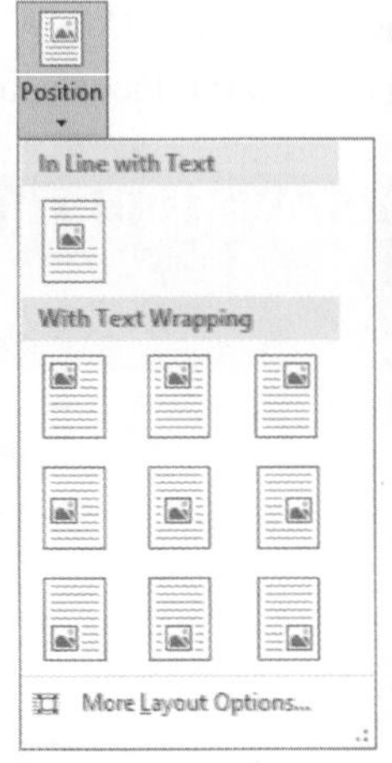

alignment guide A green horizontal or vertical line that appears when you drag a floating object in a document to help you position the object.

12-6 MOVING GRAPHICS

To move a graphic, you drag it to its new position. If the graphic is an inline graphic, you can drag it to its new position in any line of text. The same pointer and vertical indicator line that you saw when you dragged selected text appears.

When you drag a floating graphic, the graphic follows the pointer, and the text flows around it as you drag. As you drag floating graphics, green horizontal and vertical lines called **alignment guides** appear to help you align the object with the text and other objects on the page and with the margins. See Exhibit 12-21. You can drop the graphic anywhere on the page. You might need to make small adjustments in the graphic's position if the text doesn't wrap as you expect.

EXHIBIT 12-21 MOVING AN OBJECT

Begin Activity

Move graphics.

1. Point to the **photo** so that the pointer changes to .
2. Drag the **photo** to the left and down so that the green vertical alignment guides indicate that the left edge of the photo aligns with the left margin and the top edge of the photo aligns with the top of the paragraph below the *Welcome to Dance Studio K!* heading. Refer back to Exhibit 12-21.

End Activity

12-7 ADDING TEXT EFFECTS AND WORDART TEXT BOXES

Text effects are special formatting effects, such as an outline, a shadow, reflection, or glow effect, you can apply to text. A **text box** is an object that contains text. Like the photo you inserted, text boxes are objects that have a selection border, sizing handles, and a rotate handle. **WordArt** is formatted, decorative text in a text box.

12-7a Applying Text Effects

To apply text effects to text, click the Text Effects and Typography button in the Font group on the Home tab. The menu that opens includes a gallery of styles you can apply and a list of effect categories that contain submenus. See Exhibit 12-22. When you apply text effects, you are treating each character more like a shape that has an outline and an inside—a fill—color. To change the inside color, you simply change the font color.

EXHIBIT 12-22 TEXT EFFECTS AND TYPOGRAPHY BUTTON MENU

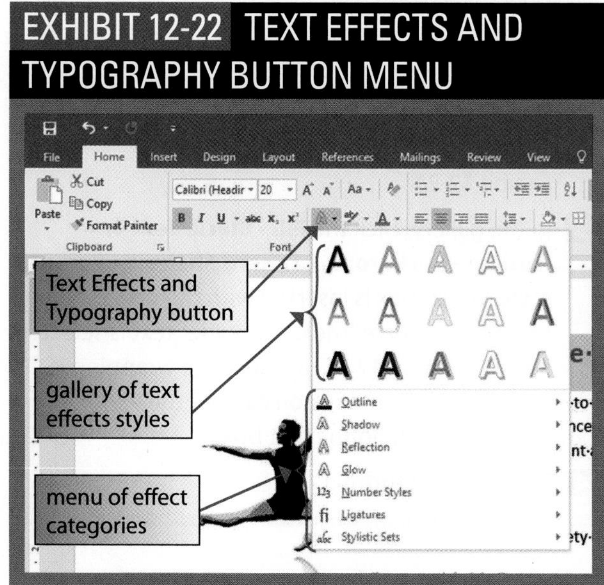

You can modify text effects by clicking one of the commands below the gallery of Text Effects styles and then choosing options on the submenus. If you want to customize effects further, you can click the Options command at the bottom of the submenus to open the Format Text Effects task pane. See Exhibit 12-23.

Begin Activity

Format text with text effects.

1 On page 1, select all of the text in the first paragraph (*Welcome to Dance Studio K!*).

EXHIBIT 12-23 FORMAT TEXT EFFECTS TASK PANE

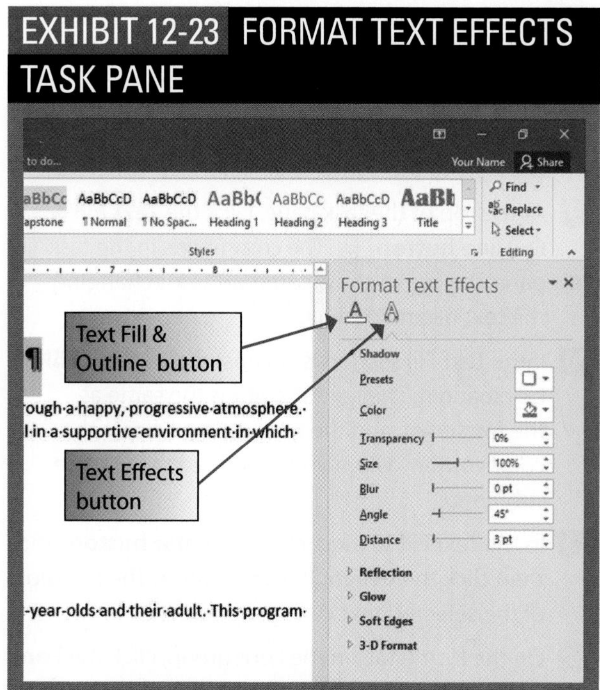

2 On the ribbon, click the **Home tab**. In the Font group, click the **Text Effects and Typography button**. A menu of styles and categories of effects opens. Refer to Exhibit 12-22.

3 In the gallery of styles, click the **Fill - Black, Text 1, Outline - Background 1, Hard Shadow - Accent 1 style** in the last row. The style is applied to the selected text.

4 Click the **Text Effects and Typography button**, and then point to **Outline**. In the color palette in the submenu, the White, Background 1 color is selected. This is the outline color that is part of the style you applied to the text.

5 On the Text Effects and Typography menu, point to **Shadow**. In the submenu, nothing is selected because the shadow applied as part of the style is not one of the preset shadow styles.

6 On the Shadow submenu, click **Shadow Options**. The menu closes and the Format Text Effects task pane opens with the Text Effects button selected and the Shadow category expanded. Refer to Exhibit 12-23.

text effects Special decorative, formatting effects that you can apply to text

text box An object that contains text.

WordArt Formatted, decorative text in a text box.

7 In the task pane, click the **Color button**. On the palette, the Blue, Accent 5 color is selected.

8 In the palette, click the **Blue, Accent 5, Lighter 40% color**. The shadow color of the selected text changes to the lighter blue color you selected.

9 At the top of the task pane, click the **Text Fill & Outline button** [A]. The commands in the task pane change to show commands for changing the text fill and outline.

10 If the Text Fill section is collapsed, click **Text Fill** to expand it. The text fill color is the same as the font color, and the text outline color is the color you saw when you examined the Outline submenu.

11 In the Text Fill section, click the **Color button**, and then click the **Green, Accent 6 color**. The fill color of the selected text changes to green.

12 On the Home tab, in the Font group, click the **Font Color button arrow** [A ▾], and then click the **Blue, Accent 5, Darker 25% color**. The fill color of the text changes to the blue color.

13 In the task pane, click the **Close button** [✕]. The task pane closes.

End Activity

12-7b Inserting and Formatting WordArt Text Boxes

To insert a text box, you use the Text Box button in the Text group on the Insert tab. After you create a text box, you can apply WordArt styles and other formatting to it. To insert a text box that has a WordArt style applied to it, use the WordArt button in the Text group on the Insert tab. When you click this button, a gallery of styles opens, as shown in Exhibit 12-24. This is the same gallery of styles as on the Text Effects button menu. However, when you insert WordArt, you don't simply format text; you create a text box containing text formatted with the style you choose.

When you insert a WordArt text box, it contains placeholder text *Your text here*, as shown in Exhibit 12-25. You can also select text in the document, and then use the WordArt button to create WordArt from the selected text.

Text boxes and WordArt that you create from selected text are inserted as floating objects with the wrapping set to Square. When you create a WordArt text box without first selecting text, the wrapping is set to In Front of Text.

EXHIBIT 12-24 WORDART BUTTON MENU

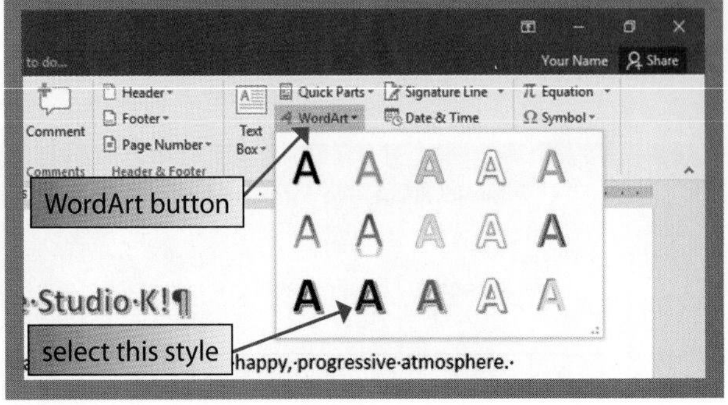

Begin Activity

Insert a WordArt text box.

1 On page 1, place the insertion point before the first character in the first paragraph (*Welcome to Dance Studio K!*).

TIP: If you select text before you click the WordArt button, the WordArt text box will contain the selected text.

2 On the ribbon, click the **Insert tab**. In the Text group, click the **WordArt button**. The gallery of WordArt styles appears. Refer back to Exhibit 12-24.

3 In the gallery, click the **Fill - Black, Text 1, Outline - Background 1, Hard Shadow - Accent 1 style**. A text box is inserted with the placeholder text *Your text here*. The placeholder text is selected. Refer to Exhibit 12-25. Because the wrapping is set to In Front of Text, you can see the text in the document behind the text box.

4 Type **Dance Studio K.**

End Activity

The Drawing Tools Format tab appears on the ribbon when a text box is selected. This tab is similar to the Picture Tools Format tab. Most of the commands in the WordArt Styles group format the text in the text box. The styles in the styles gallery are the same styles you saw when you created the WordArt. The commands in the Shape Styles group format the text box itself.

You can format the text in a text box just as you would any text in a document using the commands in the Font group on the Home tab, including adding text effects. In addition, text in a text box can be formatted with 3D effects and transformed into waves, circles, and

EXHIBIT 12-25 WORDART TEXT BOX INSERTED

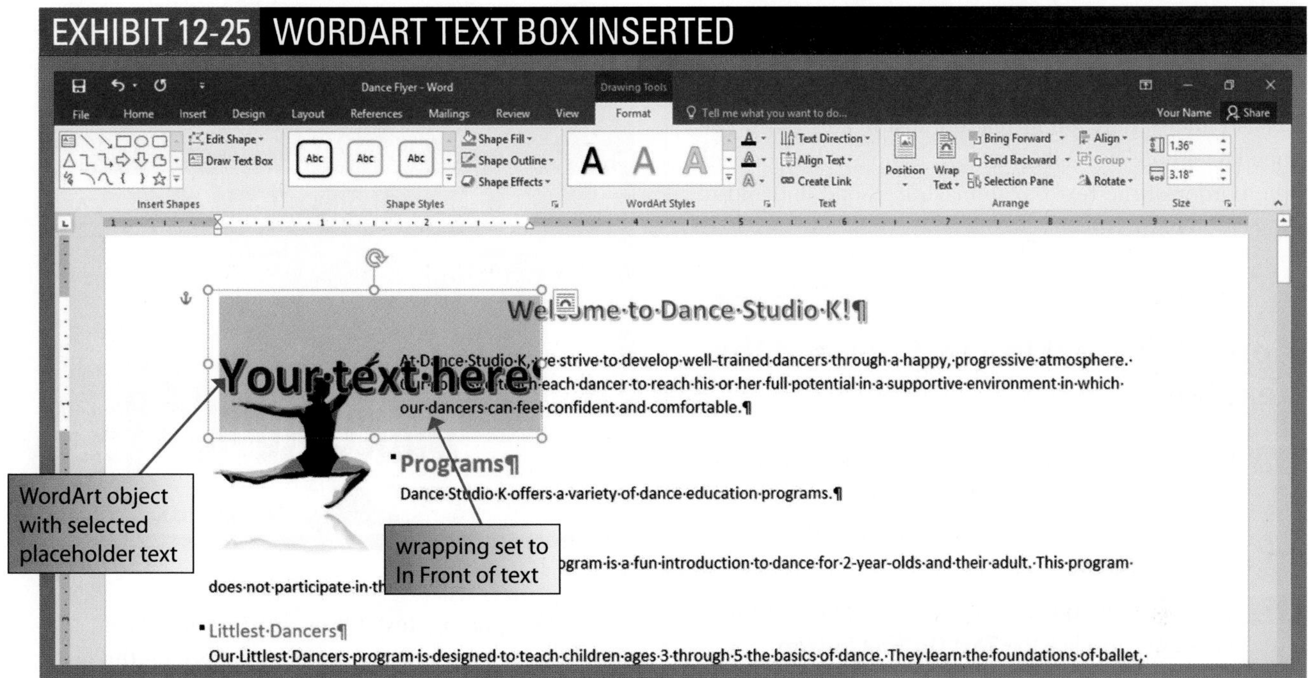

other shapes. Exhibit 12-26 shows the Transform submenu on the Text Effects button menu. The menu of text effects contains the same options that appear on the Text Effects and Typography button menu in the Font group on the Home tab plus two additional options: 3-D Rotation and Transform. These last two options are available only for text boxes.

You can also format the object itself—the container holding the text. You can change the outline and fill color (the inside color) of the container, or apply a style or the

EXHIBIT 12-26 COMMANDS ON THE DRAWING TOOLS FORMAT TAB

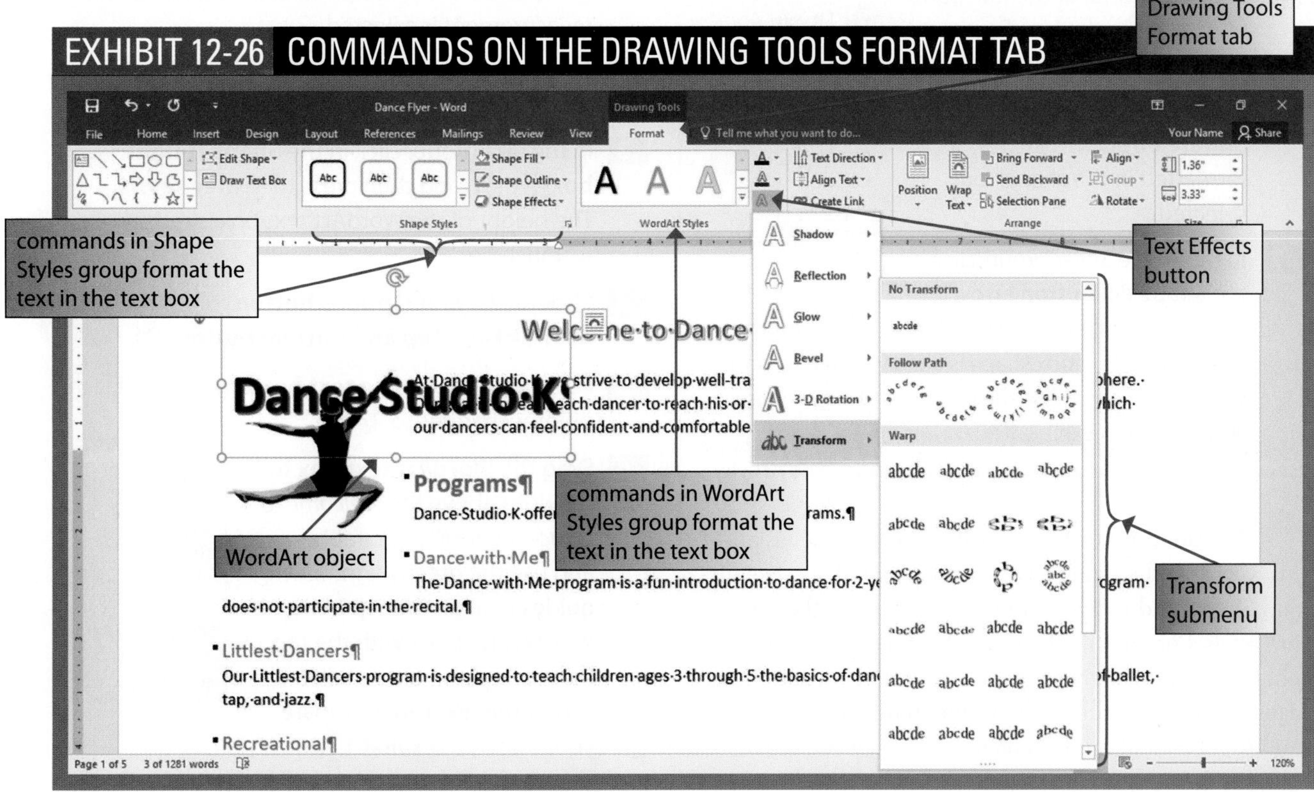

same effects that you can apply to photos. When the insertion point is in a text box, the border is a dashed line. When the entire text box is selected, the border is a solid line. When you format the text in a text box, you need to either select all of the text in the text box, or click the border of the text box to make it a solid line and to select the entire text box.

Begin Activity

Format the text in a text box and the text box.

1. Point to the **WordArt text box border** so that the pointer changes to ✥, and then click the border. The border changes to a solid line, and the text box is selected.
2. On the Drawing Tools Format tab, in the WordArt Styles group, click the **Text Outline button arrow** . The color palette opens.
3. In the color palette, click the **Blue, Accent 5, Darker 50% color**. The outline of the text in the text box changes to dark blue.
4. In the WordArt Styles group, click the **Text Effects button** , and then point to **Transform**. The gallery of transform effects appears. Refer back to Exhibit 12-26.
5. Point to several of the transform effects to see the Live Preview on the WordArt.
6. In the Warp section, click the **Square effect**. The text is formatted in the shape you selected.
7. In the Shape Styles group, click the **Shape Fill button arrow**. In the color palette, click the **White, Background 1 color**. The text box shape is filled with white, and you can no longer see the text behind it. Compare your screen to Exhibit 12-27.

TIP: If you deselect a text box with a transform or 3D effect applied and then click it to edit the text, the effect is removed temporarily.

End Activity

You can resize text boxes in the same manner as photos: you drag the sizing handles or use the Shape Height and Shape Width boxes in the Size group on the Drawing Tools Format tab. The aspect ratio for text boxes is not locked, so changing one dimension will not automatically change the other. When a text box is selected, Left and Right Indent markers on the ruler indicate the margins inside the text box.

EXHIBIT 12-27 FORMATTED WORDART TEXT BOX

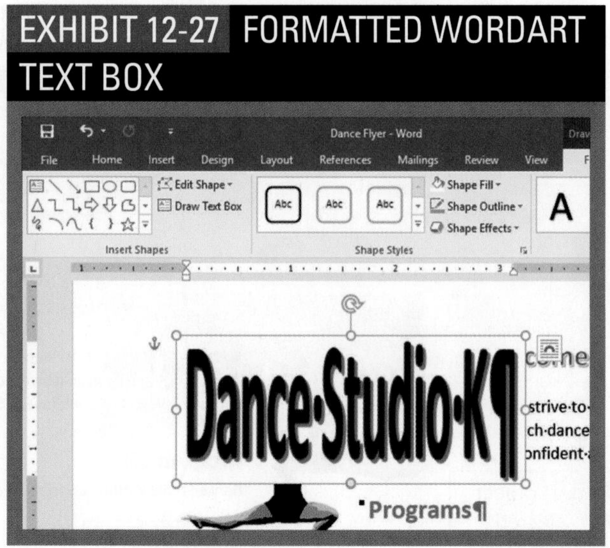

Unlike photos, text boxes are inserted as floating objects so you can position them anywhere on the page. Text boxes created using the WordArt button have the In Front of Text wrapping option applied.

Begin Activity

Resize a text box, change its wrapping option, and move it.

1. On the Drawing Tools Format tab, in the Size group, click in the **Shape Width box**. The current measurement is selected.
2. Type **6**, and then press the **Enter key**. The WordArt text box is resized to 6 inches wide.
3. In the Size group, click in the **Shape Height box**, type **1**, and then press the **Enter key**. The height of the WordArt text box is resized to 1 inch.
4. Click the **Layout Options button** , and then click the **Top and Bottom button** .
5. Point to the **solid line text box border** so that the pointer changes to ✥.
6. Drag the **WordArt text box** to the right above the *Welcome to Dance Studio K!* paragraph, and use the green alignment guides to align the top of the WordArt text box with the top margin and to horizontally center the text box. Compare your screen to Exhibit 12-28.

PROBLEM? If the green guides do not appear, use Exhibit 12-28 as a guide for where to place the text box.

End Activity

EXHIBIT 12-28 RESIZED AND REPOSITIONED WORDART TEXT BOX

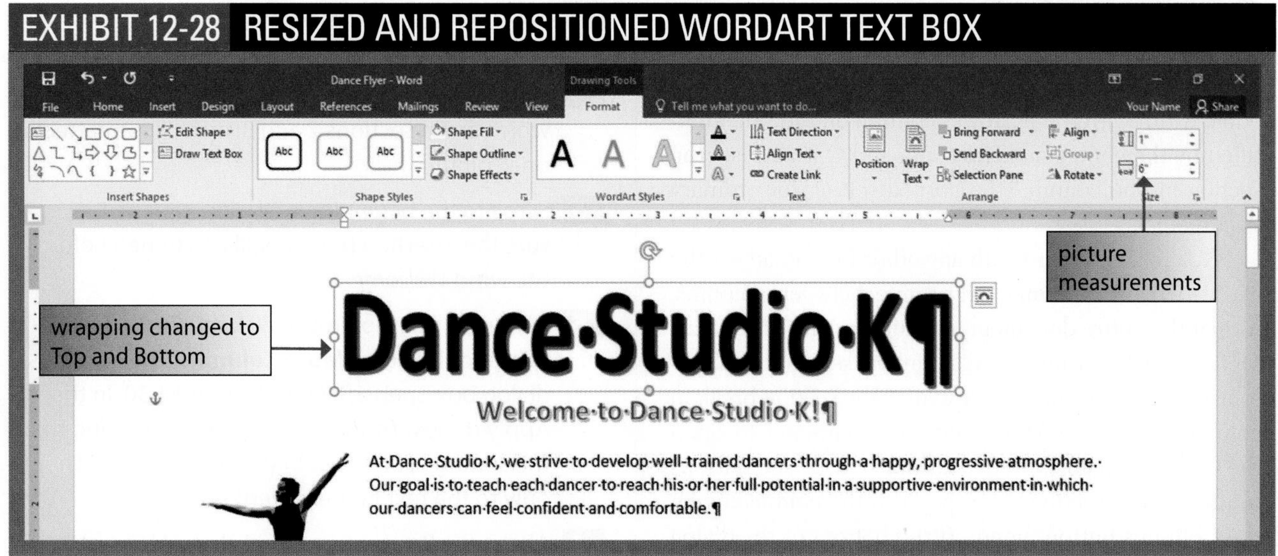

FYI MORE ABOUT TEXT BOXES

You can insert text boxes containing ordinary text—that is, text that is not WordArt. To do this, click the Text Box button in the Text group on the Insert tab. Click one of the styles in the gallery to insert a formatted text box containing placeholder text, or click Draw Text Box to insert an empty text box. You can format the text in a text box just as you would any text. You can also format the text box itself by adding or changing the fill color or the color or weight of the border. Text boxes are inserted as floating objects. Click the first style to insert a text box containing placeholder text formatted with the Normal style, or click another style to insert a text box formatted with colors and borders. If the text you want to place in the text box is already in the document, you can select it first and then create a text box that contains the text you selected.

12-8 WORKING WITH COLUMNS

Columns allow the eye to take in a lot of text and to scan quickly for interesting information. Formatting text in multiple columns also allows you to fit more text on a page than if the text were in only one column.

12-8a Creating Columns

You can format an entire document or only a section of a document in columns. To format the current section (or an entire document if it does not contain any section breaks) in columns, click the Columns button in the Page Setup group on the Layout tab, and then select a command on the Columns menu, shown in Exhibit 12-29.

EXHIBIT 12-29 COLUMNS BUTTON MENU

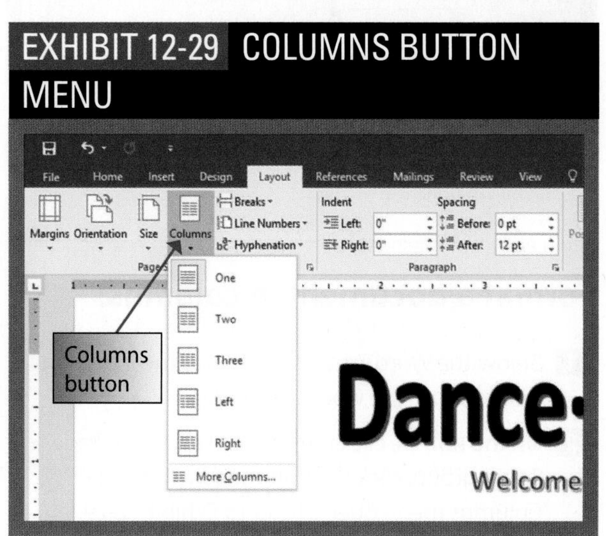

Selecting Two or Three formats the section in the corresponding number of columns of equal width. Selecting Left or Right formats the section in two columns of unequal width with the narrower column on the side identified by the command. The command One formats the section in one column (the normal setting for ordinary documents).

To create columns with any other format, adjust the width between columns, add a line between columns, format the entire document in columns when it contains section breaks, or insert a Continuous section break automatically and format the text after the section break in columns, click the More Columns command to open the Columns dialog box. See Exhibit 12-30. The buttons in the Presets section correspond to the commands on the Columns button menu. At the bottom of the dialog box, the Apply to box indicates what part of the document will be formatted with this column setting—the current section, the entire document, or from the insertion point forward.

EXHIBIT 12-30 COLUMNS DIALOG BOX

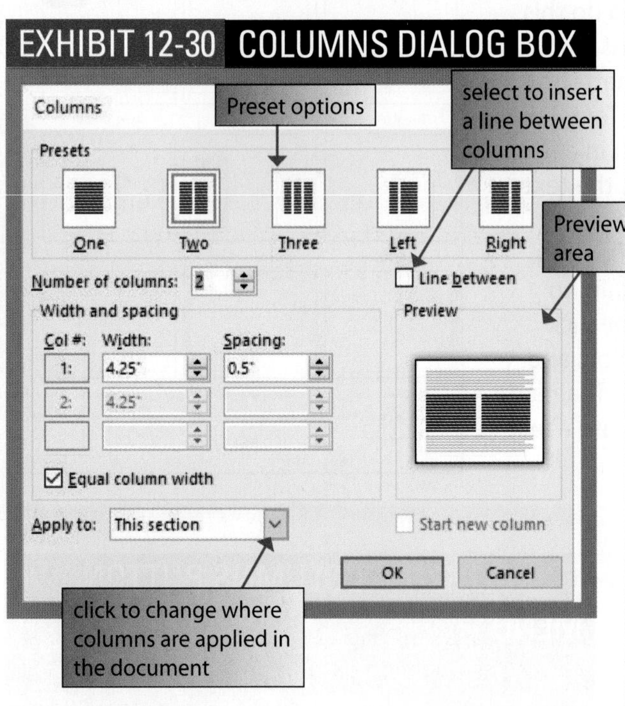

Begin Activity

Format a document in columns.

1. Below the WordArt text box, place the insertion point before the word *Welcome*.
2. On the ribbon, click the **Layout tab**. In the Page Setup group, click the **Columns button**. The Columns menu opens. Refer to Exhibit 12-29.
3. Click **Two**. All the text in section 1 after the insertion point is formatted in two columns.
4. Scroll down and view pages 4 and 5. These pages, which are in sections 2 and 3, are still formatted in one column.
5. Scroll to the beginning of the document. Make sure the insertion point is still positioned before the word *Welcome*.
6. In the Page Setup group, click the **Columns button**, and then click **More Columns**. The Columns dialog box opens. Refer to Exhibit 12-30. In the Apply to box, *This section* appears, indicating that the settings you select in this dialog box will apply only to the text in the current section.
7. Above the Preview section, click the **Line between check box** to select it. A vertical line appears in the Preview area separating the two columns.
8. Click **OK**. The Columns dialog box closes. A vertical line is inserted between the two columns.
9. Scroll up so you can see the WordArt text box. The vertical line behind the text box is not visible because you filled the text box with white. Compare your screen to Exhibit 12-31.

End Activity

> **FYI**
>
> **INSERTING A PAGE BORDER**
> A page border adds interest to a document by decorating/embellishing the edges/boundary of a page. On the Design tab, in the Page Background group, click the Page Borders button. The Borders and Shading dialog box opens with the Page Border tab selected. Select any of the line styles in the Style list, or click the Art arrow and then select a graphic to use as the border. If you are working with a document that contains section breaks, make sure the Apply to box contains the correct setting (Whole document or This section).

12-8b Balancing Columns

Balancing columns—that is, making the columns on pages in a section the same length—creates a professional-looking document. To automatically balance columns,

EXHIBIT 12-31 DOCUMENT FORMATTED IN TWO COLUMNS

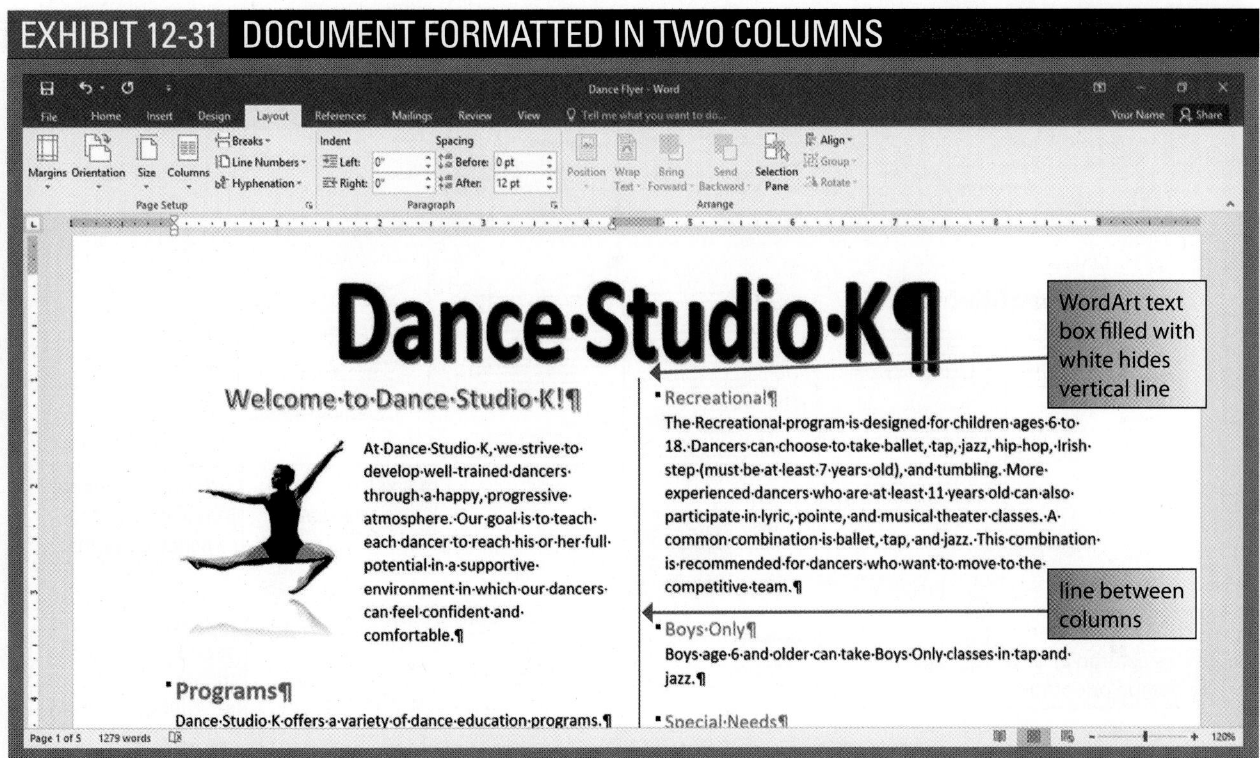

you insert a Continuous section break at the end of the last column on the last page in the section. The columns will remain balanced no matter how much material you add or remove from either column.

If you want a column to end at a specific point, or you want to manually balance the columns, insert a column break using the Breaks button in the Page Setup group on the Layout tab.

Begin Activity

Balance columns.

1. Scroll down so that you can see the end of the second column on page 3. (The last paragraph starts with *Registration Fee.*)
2. In the second column, in the last line, place the insertion point between the paragraph mark and the dotted line that indicates the Next Page section break you inserted earlier.
3. On the Layout tab, in the Page Setup group, click the **Breaks button**. The Breaks menu opens.
4. In the Section Breaks section, click **Continuous.** A Continuous section break is inserted at the insertion point, and the columns on the last page are balanced. Now there are two section breaks in a row; the Continuous section break you just inserted is immediately followed by the Next Page section break you inserted before the address on page 4. Section 1 is everything before the Continuous section break, section 2 is essentially blank because nothing appears between the two section breaks, section 3 is page 4, and section 4 is page 5.
5. Scroll down so you can see the footer on page 3 and the header area on page 4.
6. On page 3, double-click in the footer area. The tab on the footer identifies the footer as section 1, and the header on page 4 is identified as section 3.
7. Double-click anywhere outside the footer or header area.
8. On the ribbon, click the **View tab**. In the Zoom group, click the **Multiple Pages button**.
9. Change the zoom to **40%**. Compare your screen to Exhibit 12-32.

End Activity

EXHIBIT 12-32 FINAL FLYER

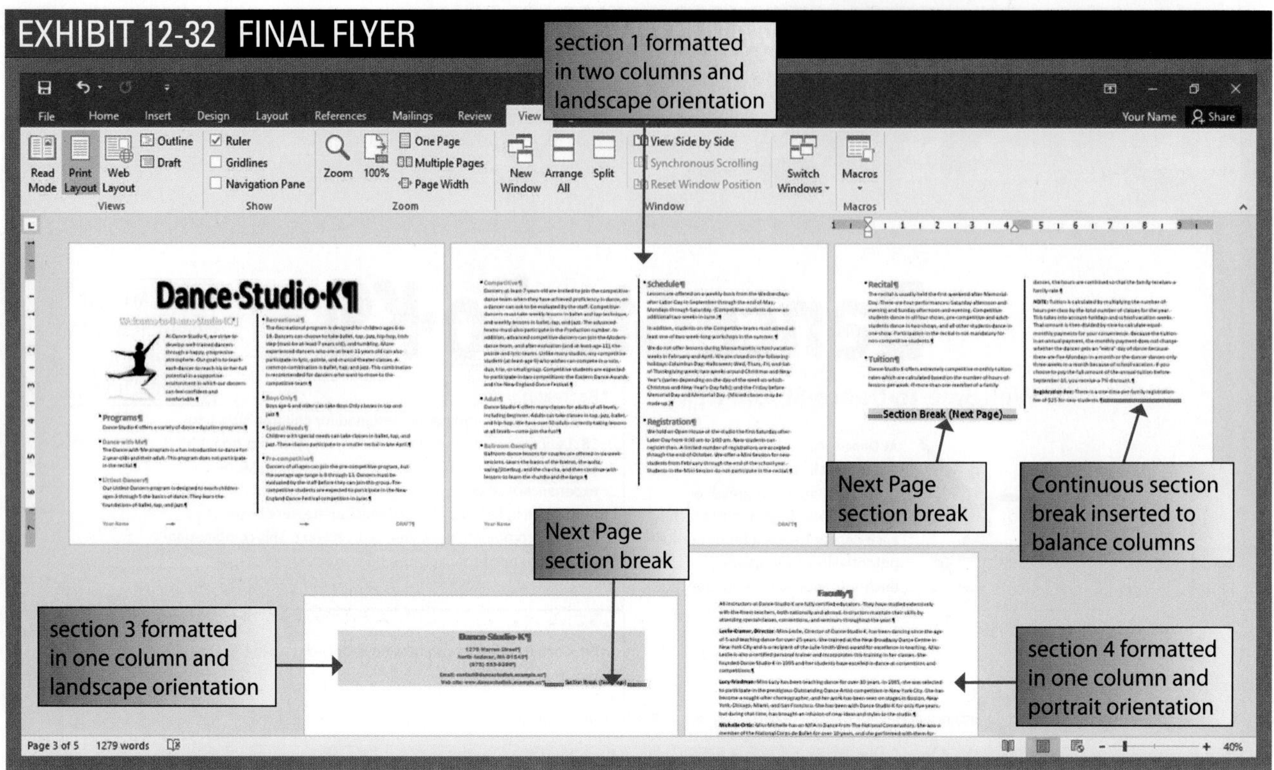

12-9 WORKING WITH BUILDING BLOCKS

Building blocks are parts of a document that are stored and reused. Word has many predesigned building blocks for a wide variety of items, including cover pages, calendars, numbering, text boxes, and more. You used building blocks when you added formatted headers and footers. Also, you can create custom building blocks from either plain text or formatted text and graphics.

Building blocks are stored in galleries. For example, the predesigned choices listed on the Header button menu are building blocks stored in the Headers gallery. If you save a custom building block to another gallery, it will be available when you access that gallery along with the built-in building blocks in that gallery. For example, if you create a custom footer and then save it to the Footers gallery, you can click the Footer button in the Header & Footer group on the Insert tab to see your custom footer in the Footers gallery.

building block A part of a document that is stored and reused.

Quick Part A building block stored in the Quick Parts gallery.

12-9a Creating Quick Parts

Building blocks that are stored in the Quick Parts gallery in the Text group on the Insert tab are called **Quick Parts**. There are no predefined Quick Parts; you need to create these. For example, you might make your signature block for a letter ("Sincerely," several blank lines, your name, and your title) a Quick Part so you can quickly insert that text without typing it every time. Or, you might create a Quick Part that contains a company name and logo.

To create a Quick Part, select the formatted text you want to save, click the Quick Parts button in the Text group on the Insert tab, and then click Save Selection to Quick Part Gallery. In the Create New Building Block dialog box that opens, you can type the name of the Quick Part. See Exhibit 12-33.

The building blocks that come with Word are stored in the global Building Blocks template, which is available to all Word documents created on the computer. When you create a custom building block in a document, it is stored in the Building Blocks template so that it can be used in all documents created on your computer. If the document was based on a custom template, or if you create the custom building block in a template, the custom building block is stored with the template so that it will be available to anyone who uses the template on any computer to which the template is copied.

EXHIBIT 12-33 CREATING A QUICK PART

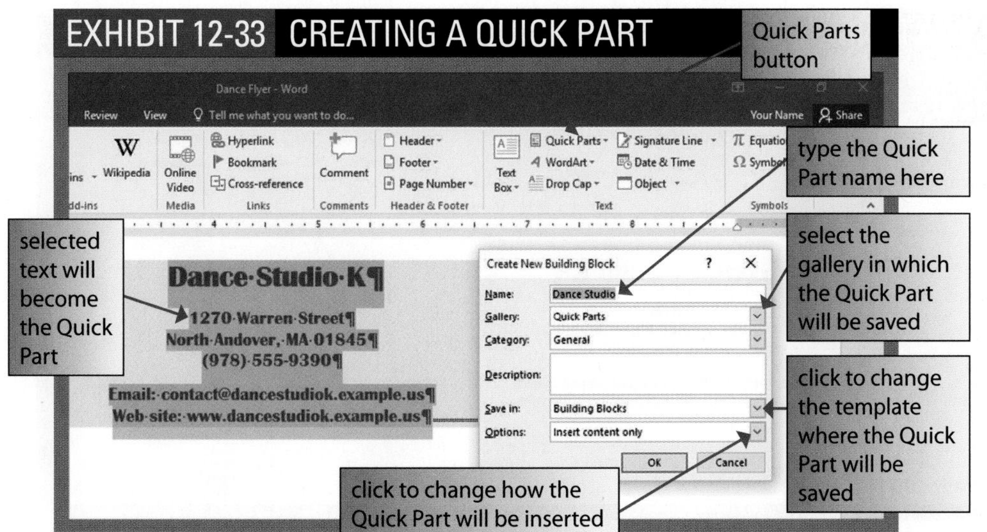

12-9b Inserting Quick Parts

After you create a Quick Part, it appears on the Quick Parts button menu as shown in Exhibit 12-34, and it is available for you to insert into other documents. To insert a Quick Part, click the Quick Parts button in the Text group on the Insert tab, and then click the Quick Part on the menu.

You can also choose the gallery in which to save a custom building block. Unless you are creating a specialty custom building block, such as a customized header, the Quick Parts gallery is a good choice. To further organize Quick Parts, you can click the Category arrow in the Create New Building Block dialog box, and then click Create New Category.

Finally, when you save the custom building block, you can choose how the content will be inserted. The default is for only the content of the custom building block to be inserted, but you can also choose to insert the content in its own paragraph or on its own page.

Begin Activity

Create Quick Parts.

1. Change the zoom to **120%**.
2. On page 4, select all of the text from **Dance Studio K** through the **paragraph mark after the Web site address**. Do *not* select the section break.
3. On the ribbon, click the **Insert tab**. In the Text group, click the **Quick Parts button**, and then click **Save Selection to Quick Part Gallery**. The Create New Building Block dialog box opens. Refer to Exhibit 12-33. The building block will be saved in the Quick Parts gallery and in the Building Blocks template.

   TIP: Right-click a Quick Part on the Quick Parts menu to open a shortcut menu containing additional ways to insert the Quick Part.
4. In the Name box, type **Contact Info**.
5. Click **OK**. The dialog box closes, and the formatted contact information is saved as a custom building block.

End Activity

EXHIBIT 12-34 QUICK PARTS MENU

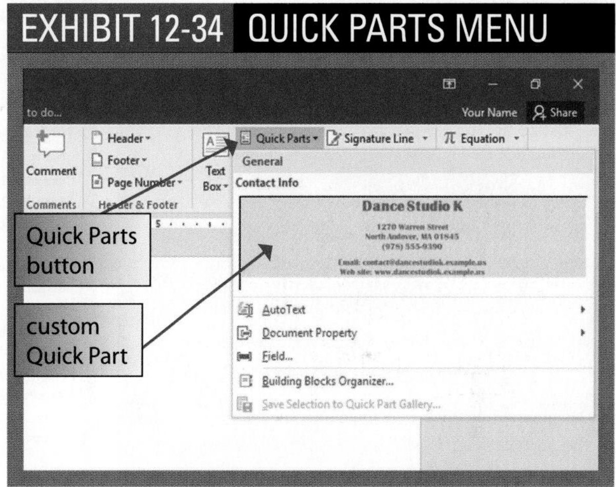

Begin Activity

Insert a Quick Part.

1. Switch to the **Class Table** document. Position the insertion point at the beginning of the document (before the word *August*).
2. On the ribbon, click the **Insert tab**. In the Text group, click the **Quick Parts button**. The Quick Part you created, Contact Info, appears on the Quick Parts menu. Refer to Exhibit 12-34.
3. Click the **Contact Info Quick Part**. The menu closes, and the contact information is inserted in its own paragraph at the insertion point. Compare your screen to Exhibit 12-35.
4. In the closing of the letter, replace *Leslie Kramer* with your name.
5. Save and close the document.

End Activity

EXHIBIT 12-35 QUICK PART INSERTED IN A DOCUMENT

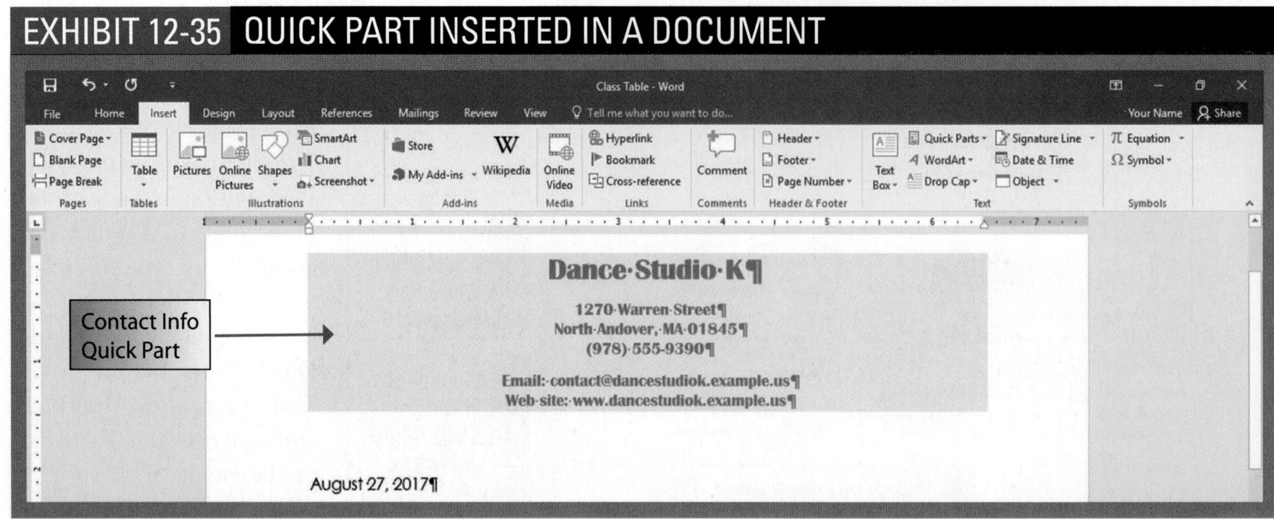

AVOID USING THEME FONTS AND COLORS FOR QUICK PARTS

Because you usually want formatted text that you save as a Quick Part to be inserted with the same formatting every time, make sure the formatted text is not formatted with theme fonts or colors or styles with definitions that include theme elements.

EXHIBIT 12-36 BUILDING BLOCKS ORGANIZER DIALOG BOX

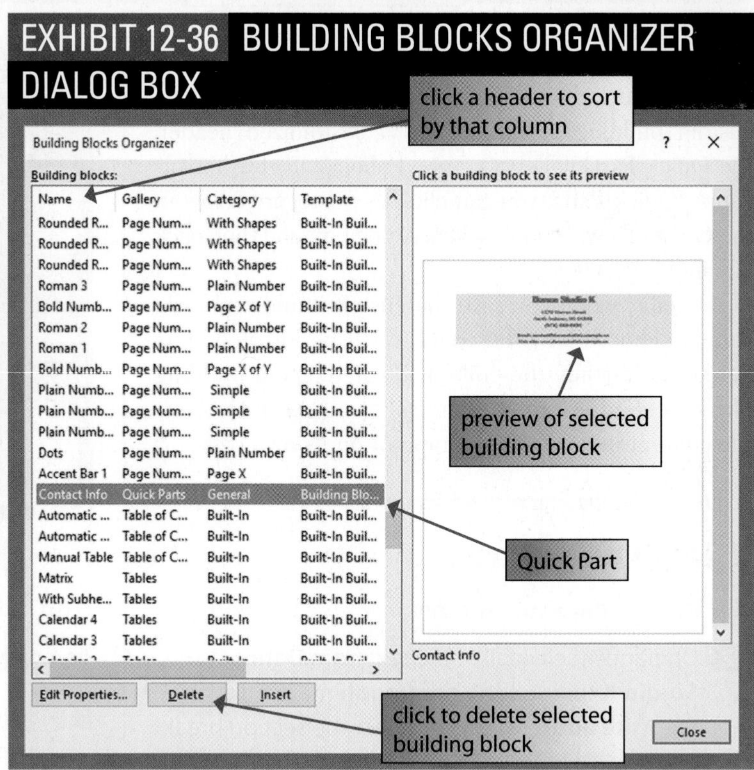

12-9c Managing Building Blocks

The Building Blocks Organizer dialog box lists all of the building blocks in the global Building Blocks template and in the current template. See Exhibit 12-36. In the Building Blocks Organizer dialog box, you can sort the building blocks by their names, gallery location, categories, or template location. You can also use the Building Blocks Organizer to insert a building block, edit the properties of a building block, or delete a building block.

Begin Activity

Use the Building Blocks Organizer and delete Quick Parts.

1. On the Insert tab, in the Text group, click the **Quick Parts button**, and then click **Building Blocks Organizer**. The Building Blocks Organizer dialog box opens.
2. Click the **Name column header**. The list is sorted in alphabetical order by name.
3. Click the **Gallery column header**. The list is sorted in alphabetical order by gallery.
4. Scroll down until you see the entry in the Quick Parts gallery, and then click the **Contact Info building block**. The selected building block appears in the preview pane. Refer to Exhibit 12-36.

TIP: To open the Building Blocks gallery with a Quick Part selected in the Building blocks list in the dialog box, right-click the Quick Part on the Quick Parts menu, and then on the shortcut menu, click Organize and Delete.

5 Below the Building blocks list, click **Delete**. A dialog box opens, asking if you are sure you want to delete the selected building block.

6 Click **Yes**. The dialog box closes, and the Contact Info custom building block is deleted from the computer.

7 At the bottom of the dialog box, click **Close**. The Building Blocks Organizer dialog box closes.

8 Save and close the **Dance Flyer document**, and exit Word. A dialog box opens asking if you want to save changes to Building Blocks. If you had not deleted the Quick Part you created and you wanted to save it for use in the future, you would click Save. Because you deleted the Quick Part, it doesn't matter if you save changes to the Building Blocks template.

9 Click **Don't Save**. The dialog box closes, and Word exits.

End Activity

STUDY TOOLS 12

READY TO STUDY? IN THE BOOK, YOU CAN:

- ☐ Rip out the Chapter Review Card, which includes key terms and key chapter concepts.

ONLINE AT WWW.CENGAGEBRAIN.COM, YOU CAN:

- ☐ Review key concepts from the chapter in a short video.
- ☐ Explore enhancing a document with the Interactive Infographic.
- ☐ Practice what you've learned with more Practice It and On Your Own exercises.
- ☐ Prepare for tests with quizzes.
- ☐ Review the key terms with flashcards.

QUIZ YOURSELF

1. In a table, what is the intersection of a column and a row called?
2. When a table is formatted with banded rows, what does it mean?
3. Explain the difference between portrait and landscape orientation.
4. What is a section?
5. How many sections does a document have if it does not contain a section break?
6. What is a sizing handle?
7. What happens to a photo when you crop part of it?
8. What is WordArt?
9. Explain the difference between an inline graphic and a floating graphic.
10. When you click one of the options on the Columns button menu, what part of the document is the column formatting applied to?
11. How do you balance columns without inserting manual column breaks?
12. What is a building block?
13. Where are Quick Parts stored?
14. How do you insert a Quick Part?
15. Describe the Building Blocks Organizer.

PRACTICE IT

Practice It 12-1

1. Use the Open command in Backstage view to open the data file **Newsletter** located in the Chapter 12\ Practice It folder. (Do not double-click the file in a File Explorer window to open it.) Open the Save As dialog box. Notice that the Save as type is Word Template so the Quick Part you will create will be included in your solution file. Type **Library Newsletter** in the File name box. Click Save.
2. In the blank paragraph at the end of the document, insert a table with two columns and five rows.
3. Enter the following data in the table:

Area	**Purchase**
Technology	**Tablets for Teen Center and Children's Room**
Technology	**Noise-reducing headsets**
Book acquisitions	**E-books, audio books, and print books**
Bulletin boards	**Maps and posters**

4. Insert a new last column, and then type **Date** in the first row in the new column.
5. Insert a new second column, and then enter the following data:

   Budget
   $7500
   $3000
   $4200
   $500

6. Insert a new row above the Book acquisitions row with the following data in the first three cells:

   Supplies
   $500
   Spine labels, spine tape, laser printer cartridge

7. Delete the row containing *Bulletin boards* and the column labeled *Date*.
8. AutoFit all of the columns.
9. Increase the width of the first column to 1.5 inches, AutoFit the Budget column, and then increase the width of the Purchase column so the right border is at the 5.5-inch mark on the ruler. (*Hint*: Make sure no text in the table is selected before resizing the columns.)
10. Format the table with the Grid Table 4 – Accent 1 table style. Apply special formatting to the header row, remove special formatting from the first column, and use banded rows.
11. Center the table horizontally on the page, and then right-align the dollar values under the Budget heading.
12. Insert a continuous section break before the third line of the document, then format all the text in the second section in two columns. Include a line between the two columns.
13. Insert a Next Page section break before the Donations heading above the table you inserted at the end of the document. Then balance the columns

by inserting a Continuous section break between the paragraph mark below the Volume 0! heading and the section break.

14. Change the formatting of the last section in the document (the section containing the Donations heading and the table) so that it is one column and in landscape orientation.
15. On page 2, use the Edit Header command on the Header button menu to insert a header, and then unlink the header on page 2 from the previous section.
16. In the header on page 2, type your name so that it is left-aligned, type **Newsletter** aligned under the Center Tab stop, and then type **page 2** aligned under the Right Tab stop. Move the Right Tab stop to the 9.25-inch mark on the ruler, and then move the Center Tab stop to the 4.5-inch mark.
17. At the top of page 1, in the paragraph under the New Labels for Children's Books heading, place the insertion point before *The*, and then insert the picture **Books** located in the Chapter 12\Practice It folder.
18. Crop the photo from the right so that there is about one-eighth of an inch of space between the bottom book and the edge of the photo, and then resize the cropped photo so it is one inch high.
19. Format the photo using the Drop Shadow Rectangle picture style, and then apply a 5 Point soft edge (using the Soft Edges submenu on the Picture Effects button menu).
20. Change the photo to a floating graphic using the Square wrapping option. Position it to the left of the first paragraph under the New Labels for Children's Books heading and so that according to the green alignment guides, the top edge is aligned with the top of the paragraph and the left edge is aligned with the left margin.
21. Place the insertion point before the word *Newsletter* at the beginning of the document. Insert a WordArt text box using the Fill – White, Outline, Accent 1, Shadow style. Type **Rutland Library Friends** as the text in the text box.
22. Change the fill color of the text in the WordArt text box to Brown, Accent 3, and change the Text Outline color of the text in the WordArt text box to White, Background 1. (Make sure the entire text box is selected.)
23. Apply the Triangle Up transform effect to the WordArt. Reposition the WordArt text box so it is centered above the Newsletter title and so the bottom border of the WordArt text box touches the top of the word *Newsletter*.
24. Save the entire paragraph containing *Newsletter* (including the paragraph mark) as a Quick Part named **Title** in the Library Newsletter template. (Make sure Library Newsletter appears in the Save in box in the Create New Building Block dialog box.)
25. Save and close the document.

Practice It 12-2

1. Open the data file **Notice** located in the Chapter 12\Practice It folder. Save the document as **Trip Notice**.
2. Insert continuous section breaks before the Nature Adventure heading and before the Registration Required heading. Format all of the text in the second section in three columns.
3. Insert a column break at the bottom of the first column before the Wildflower Adventure heading.
4. Insert another column break at the bottom of the second column before the Birds and Trees Adventure heading.
5. In the blank paragraph at the beginning of the document, insert a WordArt text box using the style in the last row that contains Teal as part of its style name. Type **Adventure Trek** as the text in the text box. Resize the text box so it is 0.9 inches high and 3.5 inches wide.
6. Change the fill of the text in the text box to Teal, Accent 5, Darker 50%. Change the color of the outline of the text in the text box to Gray-50%, Accent 6.
7. Apply the Stop transform effect to the WordArt text box.
8. Position the WordArt above the top line of text in the document. Make sure the vertical alignment guide shows that the text box is center-aligned and a horizontal alignment guide shows that the top of the text box is aligned with the top margin.
9. At the beginning of the first paragraph, insert the photo **Adventure**, located in the Chapter 12\Practice It folder.
10. Resize the picture so it is 1.7 inches tall, and change the text wrapping to Square. Position the photo to the left of the WordArt text box and the first paragraph so that it is left-aligned with the left margin and top-aligned with the top margin. Move the WordArt to the right so it is centered above the first paragraph.
11. Add your name as a left-aligned footer.
12. Save the document, and then close it.

ON YOUR OWN

On Your Own 12-1

1. Use the Open command in Backstage view to open the data file **Brochure** located in the Chapter 12\ On Your Own folder. (Do not double-click the file in a File Explorer window to open it.) Save the file as **Auction Brochure** leaving the Save as type set to Word Template so the Quick Part you will create will be included in your solution file.
2. Change the orientation of the document to Landscape.
3. Select all the text in the document except for the first paragraph containing *Raise the Funds*, and then convert the selected text into a table with three columns. (*Hint*: Use the Convert Text to Table command on the Table button menu. Adjust the number of columns to 3, and make sure the Paragraphs option button is selected in the Separate text at section.)
4. Add a new row to the top of the table with the labels **Item**, **Value**, and **Includes**.
5. Change the Theme Colors to Paper, and then apply the List Table 4 – Accent 4 table style to the table. Format the header row and the first column with special formatting, and use banded rows. (*Hint:* You will need to reapply bold formatting to *Item*.)
6. Adjust the column widths so that the first column is 2 inches wide, the second column is AutoFit, and the third column stretches to the right margin (the 9-inch mark). (*Hint:* If the table gridlines are not visible, click the View Gridlines button in the Table group on the Table Tools Layout tab.)
7. Center all the text in the Value column using the Align Top Center command.
8. Select the first paragraph (containing *Raise the Funds*), including the paragraph mark, and convert it to a WordArt text box using the Gradient Fill – Gray style. Apply the Perspective Diagonal Upper Left shadow effect to the text in the text box.
9. Position the WordArt as a floating graphic above the table, centered between the left and right margins and top-aligned with the top margin.
10. Use the keyword **auction** to search for an online picture using the Bing search engine, and choose an appropriate image. (*Hint:* Use the Online Pictures button in the Illustrations group on the Insert tab.)
11. Crop off part of the image if it would look better.
12. Change the wrap properties of the image to Tight. Position it in the upper-right corner of the document. Change the zoom to One Page, and then reduce the size of the image as needed so that the picture fits above the table and the table and the blank paragraph after the table fit on one page.
13. Save the WordArt as a Quick Part in the Auction Brochure template. Name the Quick Part **Auction Heading**.
14. Save the document, and then close it.

CAPSTONE

WORD: CREATE A FLYER

1. Plan a flyer for an upcoming event, such as a sale. Identify the content you will include on the flyer, such as listing the items for sale, a description of each item, the original cost of each item, the sale price for each item, and the location, date, and time of the sale (for this project, you can use real or fictional data). Decide how the document should be organized and formatted.
2. Create a new document for the flyer.
3. Enter the text for the flyer.
4. Use a WordArt text box to create an attractively formatted title for the flyer. Be sure to use a descriptive title that accurately describes the content of your flyer.
5. Create a table that has at least four rows and three columns. Enter descriptive column headers for each column, and then enter appropriate data in each row.
6. Format the table with a style. Make sure it is clear and easy to read.
7. Include at least one image to add interest to the flyer. Use appropriate keywords to find images related to your flyer's content.
8. Position, size, and orient the image attractively on the flyer.
9. Change the style set of the flyer to anything other than the default style set. Change the theme of the flyer to any theme other than the Office theme.
10. Use styles to format some of the text on the flyer, such as the date and time.
11. Modify the formatting of the text with styles applied so that the text looks better in your flyer, and then update the definitions of the styles with the new formatting.
12. Format the rest of the flyer by changing fonts, font sizes, font colors, borders, and so forth as needed to make the flyer attractive and easy to read.
13. Change the margins and page orientation as needed to fit the flyer on one page.
14. Format the flyer for your printer. Include headers and footers that display the file name, your name, and the date on which the flyer is printed.
15. Use the spell checker to check the spelling and grammar of the document, and then proofread it.
16. Preview the document in Backstage view to be sure that it will print as expected, and then print it.
17. Save the document, and then close it.

Office Online

USING WORD ONLINE

Office Online provides free versions of Office programs that are available to anyone with a free Microsoft account. The online versions do not make all of the features of the full version of the program installed on your computer available. You do not need to have Microsoft Office 2016 programs installed on your computer to access and use Office Online.

There are two ways to work with files using Word Online: You can view a file in View mode, or you can edit it in Edit mode. In View mode, you are limited to using the Find and Translate commands and changing the zoom level. In Edit mode, you can enter and edit text, apply basic direct font and paragraph formatting and styles, use the spell checker, and insert tables and pictures. Exhibit 1 shows a document in View mode in Word Online. Exhibit 2 shows the same document in Edit mode.

EXHIBIT 1 DOCUMENT IN WORD ONLINE IN VIEW MODE

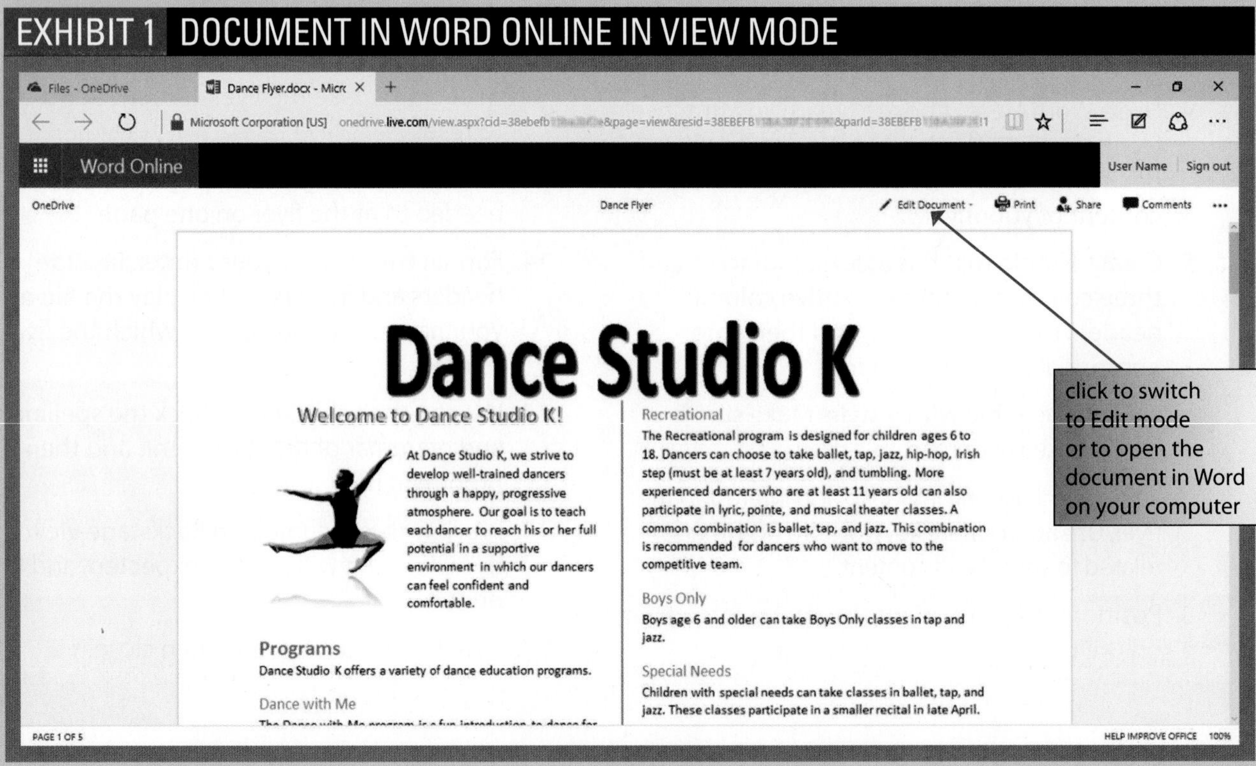

EXHIBIT 2 DOCUMENT IN WORD ONLINE IN EDIT MODE

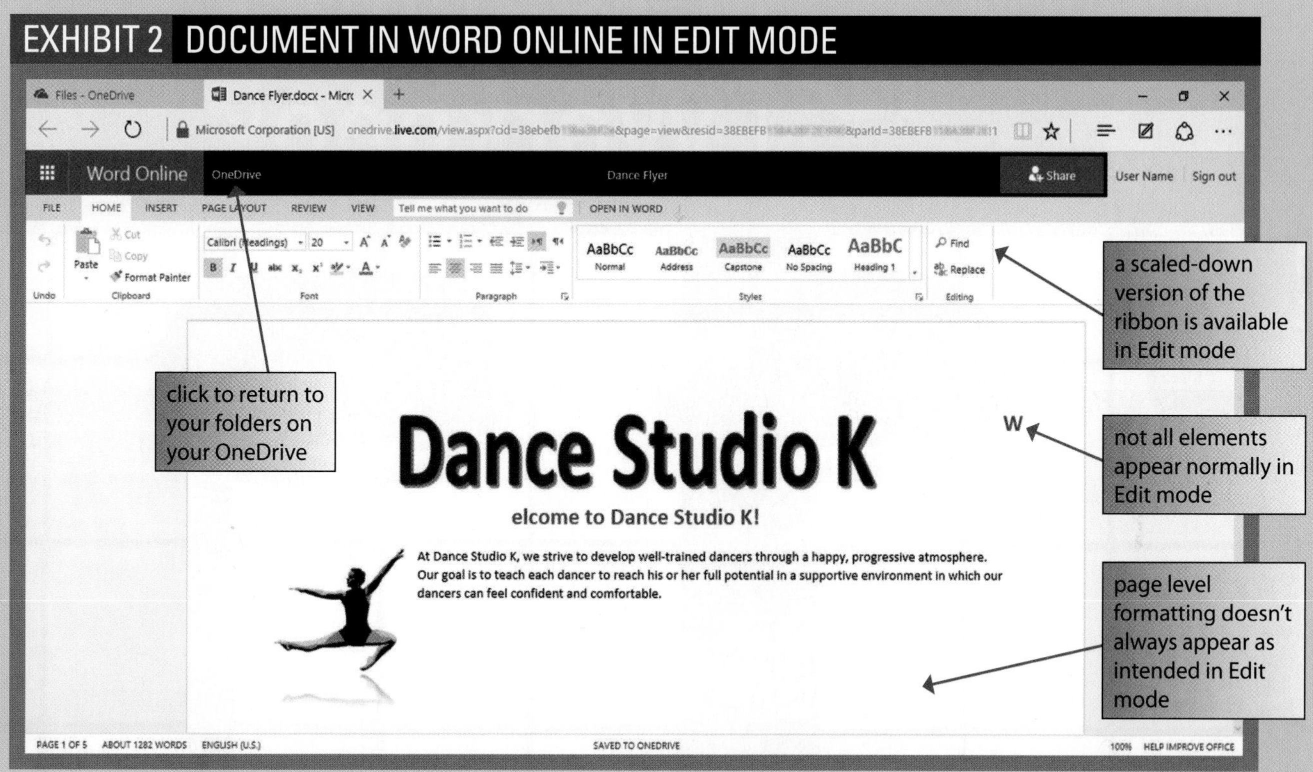

To use Word Online to view or edit a document, the document must be stored on your OneDrive or someone else must have shared it with you on their OneDrive. Open the folder on OneDrive containing the document you want to view or edit, and then click it to open it in View mode. To edit the document, click the Edit Document button on the ribbon. To create a new document in Word Online (or a new Excel, PowerPoint, or OneNote file), click the New button at the top of the window in OneDrive, and then click Word document. See Exhibit 3.

EXHIBIT 3 NEW MENU IN ONEDRIVE

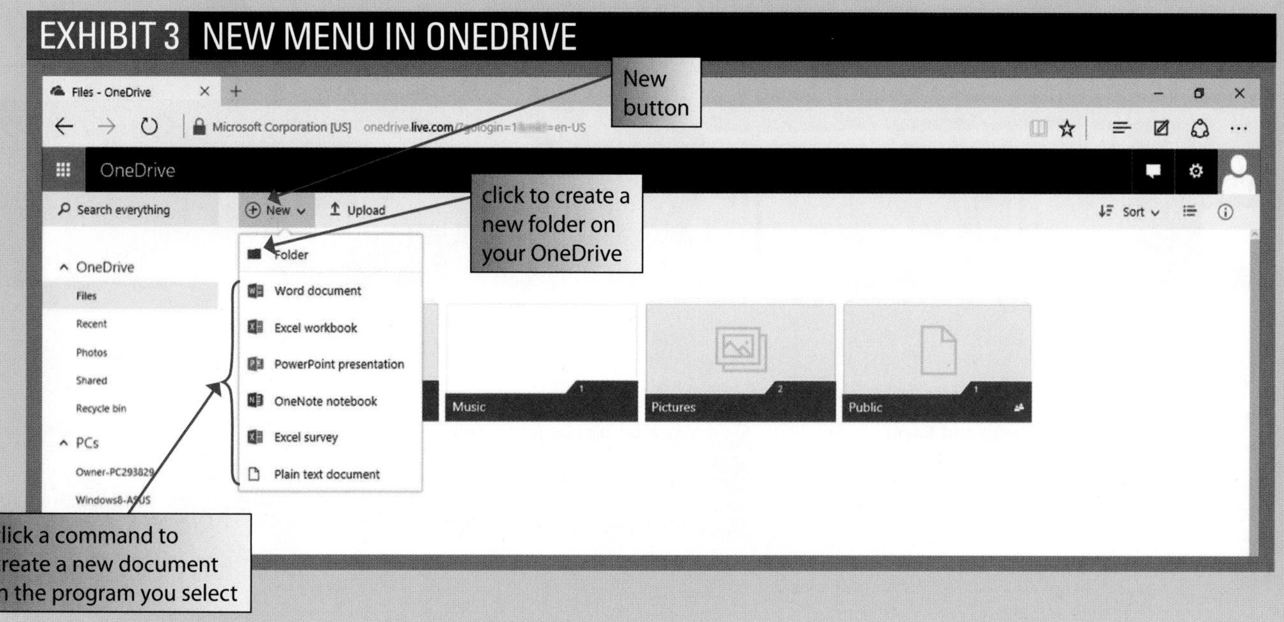

Part 7
EXCEL 2016

13 | Creating a Workbook

© Thomas Barwick/Getty Images

LEARNING OBJECTIVES After studying the material in this chapter, you will be able to:

13-1 Understand spreadsheets and Excel

13-2 Enter and format data

13-3 Edit cell content

13-4 Work with columns and rows

13-5 Work with cells and ranges

13-6 Enter simple formulas and functions

13-7 Preview and print a workbook

After finishing this chapter, go to **PAGE 407** for **STUDY TOOLS**.

13-1 UNDERSTANDING SPREADSHEETS AND EXCEL

A spreadsheet is a group of values and other data organized into rows and columns. You can create a spreadsheet using **Microsoft Excel 2016** (or just **Excel**), which is used to enter, analyze, and present quantitative data. Exhibit 13-1 shows a cash flow report in a spreadsheet. The spreadsheet records the estimated and actual cash flow for the month of June. Each line, or row, displays a different value, such as the starting cash balance or cash sales for the month. Each column displays the budgeted or actual numbers or text that describes those values.

EXHIBIT 13-1 SPREADSHEET DATA IN EXCEL

	A	B	C
1	**Cash Flow Comparison**		
2	**Budgeted vs. Actual**		
3			6/1/2017
4		**Budgeted**	**Actual**
5	**Cash reserves (start of month)**	$ 4,500.00	$ 4,500.00
6	**Cash receipts**		
7	Cash sales	$ 12,600.00	$ 14,688.00
8	**Cash expenditures**		
9	Advertising	$ 1,200.00	$ 1,425.00
10	Wages	$ 7,200.00	$ 7,850.00
11	Supplies	$ 3,600.00	$ 4,350.00
12	Total cash expenditures	$ 12,000.00	$ 13,625.00
13	**Net cash flow**	$ 600.00	$ 1,063.00
14	**Cash balance (end of month)**	$ 5,100.00	$ 5,563.00

calculated values using values in other cells

The total cash expenditures in row 12 in the spreadsheet, the net cash flow in row 13, and the closing cash balance for the month in row 14 are not entered directly but are calculated from other numbers in the spreadsheet. For example, the total cash expenditure is equal to the sum of expenditures on advertising, wages, and supplies in rows 9 through 11.

13-1a Parts of the Excel Window

In addition to the common elements found in all Office 2016 applications, including the title bar, ribbon, scroll bars, and status bar, the Excel window contains features that are unique to Excel, as shown in Exhibit 13-2.

Excel files are called **workbooks**. The workbook that is currently being used is the active workbook. The name of the workbook appears in the title bar of the Excel window. Each workbook is made up of individual **sheets**. Each sheet is identified by a sheet name, which is displayed in its sheet tab. A **worksheet** is a sheet that contains data laid out in a grid of rows and columns. A **chart sheet** is a sheet that contains a visual representation of spreadsheet data. Charts can also be embedded within worksheets, so you can view both the data and the charts in one sheet.

Each workbook can contain multiple worksheets and chart sheets. You can add sheets to a workbook as needed. This capability enables you to better organize data and focus each worksheet on one area of data. For example, a sales report workbook might have a different worksheet for each sales region and another worksheet that summarizes the results from all the regions. A chart sheet might contain a chart that graphically compares the sales results from all of the regions.

Worksheets are laid out in rows and columns. Row headers identify each row with a number, ranging from 1 to 1,048,576. Column headers identify each column with a letter. The first 26 are columns A through Z. After Z, the next column headers are labeled AA, AB, AC, and so forth until you reach the last possible column, which is labeled XFD (which means a maximum of 16,384 columns).

Rows and columns intersect in a single **cell**; all data entered in a worksheet is placed in cells. Each cell is identified by a **cell reference**, which indicates its column and row location. For example, the cell reference B6 indicates the cell located where column B intersects row 6.

Microsoft Excel 2016 (Excel) A computer application used to enter, analyze, and present quantitative data.

workbook An Excel file that stores spreadsheets.

sheet An individual page in a workbook.

worksheet A sheet that contains data laid out in a grid of rows and columns.

chart sheet A sheet that contains a visual representation of spreadsheet data.

cell The location in a worksheet where a row and column intersect.

cell reference The column letter and row number of a cell used to identify the location of a specific cell.

EXHIBIT 13-2 PARTS OF THE EXCEL WINDOW

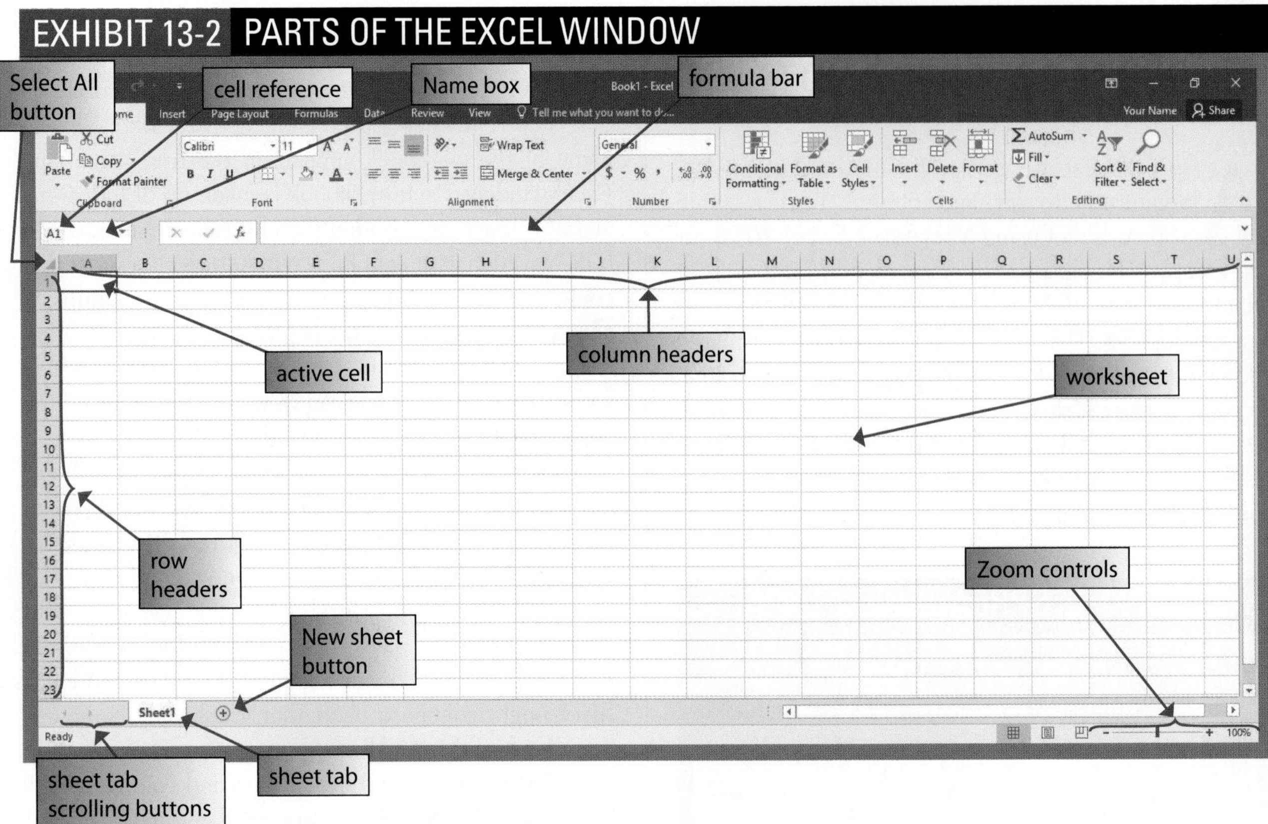

Begin Activity

Start Excel, and save a workbook.

1. Start **Excel**. The Recent screen opens in Backstage view.
2. Click the **Blank workbook tile**. The Excel window opens, displaying a blank worksheet in an untitled workbook. Refer back to Exhibit 13-2.
3. If the Excel window is not maximized, click the **Maximize button** ▣.
4. Change the zoom level of the worksheet to **120%**.
5. On the Quick Access Toolbar, click the **Save button** 🖫. Because this is the first time you are saving the workbook, the Save As screen appears.
6. Save the workbook as **Frame Up Inventory**.

End Activity

active cell The selected cell in a worksheet.

Name box The location where the active cell reference is displayed.

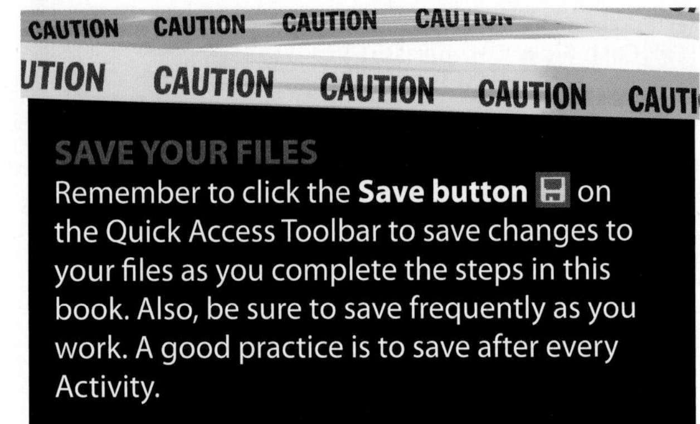

SAVE YOUR FILES

Remember to click the **Save button** 🖫 on the Quick Access Toolbar to save changes to your files as you complete the steps in this book. Also, be sure to save frequently as you work. A good practice is to save after every Activity.

13-1b Moving the Active Cell

The cell in which you are currently working is the **active cell**. Excel distinguishes the active cell by outlining it with a green box. In Exhibit 13-2, cell A1 is the active cell. The cell reference for the active cell appears in the **Name box** located in the upper-left corner of the worksheet.

You can click a cell to make it the active cell, or you can press the arrow keys to move from one cell to another. Exhibit 13-3 identifies the keys you can use to move around a worksheet. You can also move directly to a specific cell by typing its cell reference in the Name box, and then pressing the Enter key. Scrolling the worksheet does not change the location of the active cell.

EXHIBIT 13-3 EXCEL NAVIGATION KEYS

Press	To move the active cell
Arrow keys	Up, down, left, or right one cell
Home	To column A of the current row
Ctrl+Home	To cell A1
Ctrl+End	To the last cell in the worksheet that contains data
Enter	Down one row or to the start of the next row of data
Shift+Enter	Up one row
Tab	One column to the right
Shift+Tab	One column to the left
Page Up, Page Down	Up or down one screen
Ctrl+Page Up, Ctrl+Page Down	To the previous or next sheet in the workbook

Begin Activity

Move the active cell.

1. Point to the **worksheet area**. The pointer changes to ✚. A1 appears in the Name box because cell A1 is the active cell. The column header for column A and the row header for row 1 are shaded and those column and row labels are green to help you locate the active cell.
2. Click **cell A5**. Cell A5 now has a green box around it to indicate that it is the active cell, the cell reference in the Name box changes to A5, and the row header for row 5 is shaded and contains green text instead of the row header for row 1.
3. Press the **Tab key**. The active cell moves one cell to the right to cell B5.
4. Press the **Page Down key**. The active cell moves down one full screen.
5. Click in the **Name box**. The active cell reference in the Name box is selected.
6. Type **D4**. The cell reference you typed replaces the selected reference.
7. Press the **Enter key**. Cell D4 is now the active cell.
8. Press the **Ctrl+Home keys**. The active cell returns to the first cell in the worksheet, cell A1.

End Activity

13-1c Inserting and Deleting Sheets

New workbooks contain one worksheet named Sheet1. If you need more worksheets, you can add them. When you add a new worksheet, it is named with the next consecutive sheet number, such as Sheet2. You can also delete unneeded worksheets that were added to the workbook.

Begin Activity

Insert and delete sheets.

1. To the right of the Sheet1 sheet tab, click the **New sheet button** ⊕. A new worksheet named Sheet2 is inserted to the right of the last sheet tab.
2. Click the **New sheet button** ⊕. A new worksheet named Sheet3 is inserted to the right of the last sheet tab.
3. Right-click the **Sheet3 sheet tab**. On the shortcut menu, click **Delete**. The Sheet3 worksheet is deleted.

End Activity

13-1d Switching Between Sheets

The sheet currently displayed in the workbook window is the **active sheet**. Its sheet tab has a green border on the bottom, and the sheet name is in bold, green text. The sheet tabs for inactive sheets do not have a bottom border, and the sheet name is in normal black text. An inactive sheet becomes active when you click its sheet tab. In Exhibit 13-4, Sheet1 is the active sheet.

For workbooks that contain more sheet tabs than can be displayed at the same time in the workbook window, you can scroll through the sheet tabs using the sheet tab scrolling buttons to the left of the first sheet tab (refer back to Exhibit 13-2).

EXHIBIT 13-4 ACTIVE AND INACTIVE SHEETS

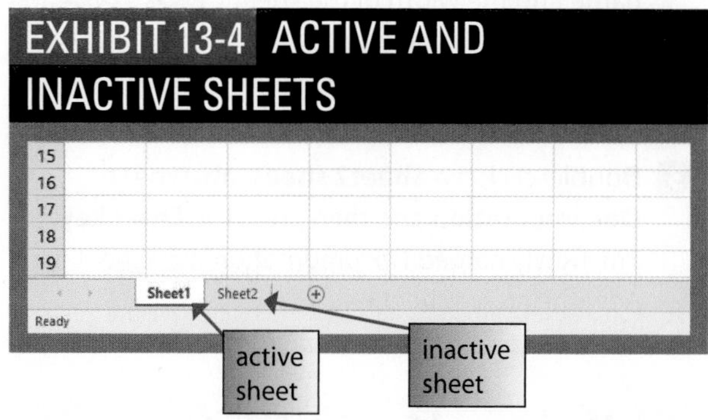

active sheet The sheet currently displayed in the workbook window.

Begin Activity

Switch the active sheet.

1 Click the **Sheet1 sheet tab.** The Sheet1 worksheet becomes the active sheet. Refer back to Exhibit 13-4.

2 Click the **Sheet2 sheet tab** to make the second worksheet active.

3 In Sheet2, change the zoom to **120%**.

End Activity

13-1e Renaming Sheets

The default worksheet names, Sheet1, Sheet2, and so on, are not very descriptive. You can rename sheets with more meaningful names so that you know what they contain. The width of the sheet tab will adjust to the length of the name you enter. Exhibit 13-5 shows Sheet1 renamed.

EXHIBIT 13-5 RENAMED SHEET

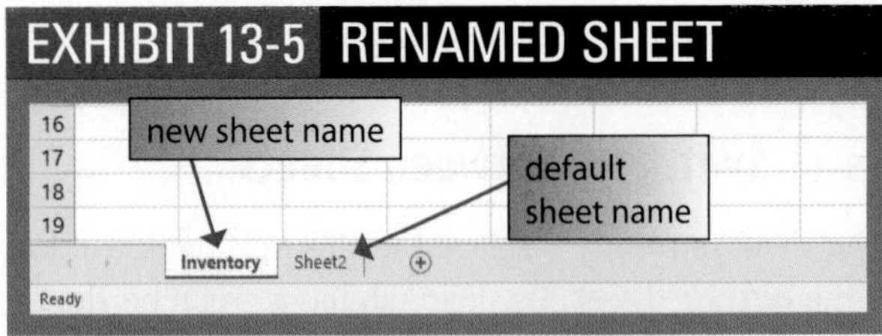

Begin Activity

Rename sheets.

1 Double-click the **Sheet1 sheet tab**. The sheet name is selected in the sheet tab.

2 Type **Inventory**, and then press the **Enter key**. The text you type replaces the selected sheet name and the width of the sheet tab expands as you type to accommodate the longer sheet name. Refer back to Exhibit 13-5.

TIP: Sheet names cannot exceed 31 characters, including blank spaces.

3 Double-click the **Sheet2 sheet tab**, type **Documentation** and then press the **Enter key**. The newly named Documentation worksheet is now the active sheet.

End Activity

13-1f Moving and Copying Sheets

You can change the placement of the sheets in a workbook. A good practice is to place the most important sheets at the beginning of the workbook (the leftmost sheet tabs) and less important sheets toward the end (the rightmost tabs).

The quickest way to move a sheet is to use drag and drop to drag its sheet tab to the new location. As you drag a sheet tab, the pointer changes to [move pointer] and a triangle indicates where the sheet tab will be dropped when you release the mouse button. See Exhibit 13-6. To copy rather than move a sheet, press and hold the Ctrl key as you drag and drop the sheet tab. The copy is placed where you drop the sheet tab; the original sheet remains in its initial position.

EXHIBIT 13-6 SHEET TAB BEING MOVED

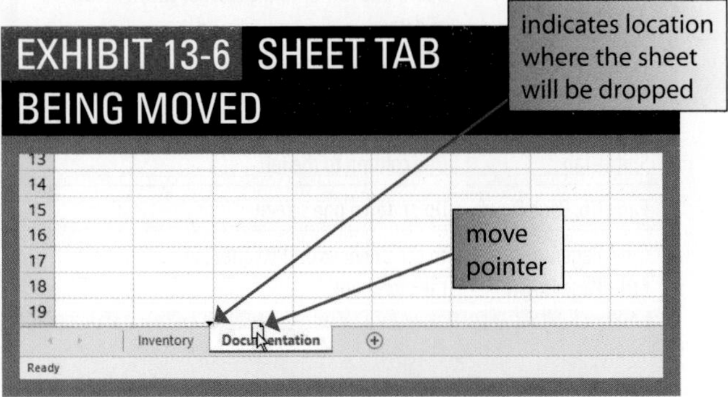

Begin Activity

Move a sheet.

1 Click the **Documentation sheet tab**, but don't release the mouse button. The pointer changes to [move pointer], and a small black triangle appears in the upper-left corner of the sheet tab. Refer back to Exhibit 13-6.

2 Drag left until the small black triangle is at the left edge of the Inventory sheet tab.

3 Release the mouse button. The Documentation worksheet is now the first sheet in the workbook.

End Activity

FYI **ENTERING DATA**

Text you type is not entered into the worksheet until you accept it. The easiest way to accept data is to press the Enter key, the Tab key, or an arrow key. You can also click the Enter button [✓], which appears between the formula bar and the Name box.

13-2 ENTERING AND FORMATTING DATA

You enter data by typing it into the active cell. When you finish typing, you need to press the Enter or Tab key or click the Enter button ✓ to complete the data entry and move to the next cell in the worksheet. As you enter data into the worksheet, it appears in both the active cell and in the formula bar. The **formula bar** displays the contents of the active cell, which can be data or, as you'll see later, the underlying formulas used to create a calculated value.

13-2a Entering Text

Text data is a combination of letters, numbers, and symbols. When you enter text data into a cell, the text is left-aligned unless you change it.

If a text entry is too long to fit in a cell, it will flow into the next cell to the left as long as that cell is empty. If the cell to the left is not empty, the long text will look like it is cut off.

When creating a worksheet, you should make sure its intent and content are clear to others. One way to do this is to create a documentation sheet, which documents why you created the workbook and what it contains. It is also a good way to relay the workbook's purpose and content to others with whom you share the workbook. The documentation sheet shown in Exhibit 13-7 includes text data with the company name (Frame Up), the worksheet's author, and the worksheet's purpose.

EXHIBIT 13-7 DOCUMENTATION SHEET WITH TEXT DATA

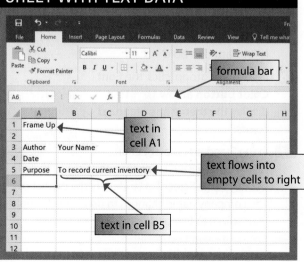

Begin Activity

Enter text.

1. In the Documentation worksheet, in cell A1, type **Frame Up**. As you type, the text appears in both cell A1 (the active cell) and in the formula bar.
2. Press the **Enter key**. The text is entered, and the active cell moves down one cell to cell A2.
3. Press the **Enter key** to move the active cell down one cell to cell A3.
4. Type **Author** and then press the **Tab key**. The text is entered, and the active cell moves one cell to the right to cell B3.
5. Type your name, and then press the **Enter key**. The text is entered, and the active cell moves one cell down and one cell to the left to cell A4.
6. Type **Date** and then press the **Tab key**. The text is entered, and the active cell moves one cell to the right to cell B4, where you will later enter the date you created the workbook.
7. Click **cell A5** to make it the active cell, type **Purpose** and then press the **Tab key**. The active cell moves one cell to the right to cell B5.
8. Type **To record current inventory** and then press the **Enter key**. This cell entry is too long to fit in cell B5, but because cell C5 is empty, the text flows into cell C5 and you can see all of the entry. Refer back to Exhibit 13-7.
9. Click the **Inventory sheet tab** to make it the active sheet. Cell A1 is the active cell.
10. Type **Inventory Date** and then press the **Enter key**. The label is entered in the cell, and cell A2 is the active cell.
11. Enter the following column labels in row 2, pressing the **Tab key** after each entry:

cell A2:	**Artist**
cell B2:	**Print**
cell C2:	**# in Stock**
cell D2:	**Unit Cost**
cell E2:	**Inventory Value**

formula bar A bar used to enter, edit, or display the contents of the active cell.

text data Any combination of letters, numbers, and symbols.

12 Click **cell A3**, the start of the next row where you want to begin entering the customer data.

13 Type **Klimt** in cell A3, press the **Tab key** to move to the next cell, type **The Tree of Life, Stoclet Frieze** in cell B3, and then press the **Enter key**. You have entered the first artist and print title and moved the active cell to cell A4.

> **TIP:** To place text on separate lines within the same cell, press the Alt+Enter keys to create a line break within the cell.

14 Enter the following text in **cells A4** through **B7**.

cell A4:	**Warhol**	cell B4:	**Campbell Soup I: Tomato**
cell A5:	**Miro**	cell B5:	**Singing Fish**
cell A6:	**Rothko**	cell B6:	**White Center**
cell A7:	**Lichtenstein**	cell B7:	**Sunrise**

15 Click **cell A7**. Notice that the entry in cell A7 is too wide to fit in the cell, but because there is an entry in cell B7, it looks like the entry in cell A7 was cut off. However, in the formula bar, which shows the contents of the active cell, shows the complete entry. Compare your screen to Exhibit 13-8.

End Activity

EXHIBIT 13-8 TEXT DATA ENTERED IN CELLS

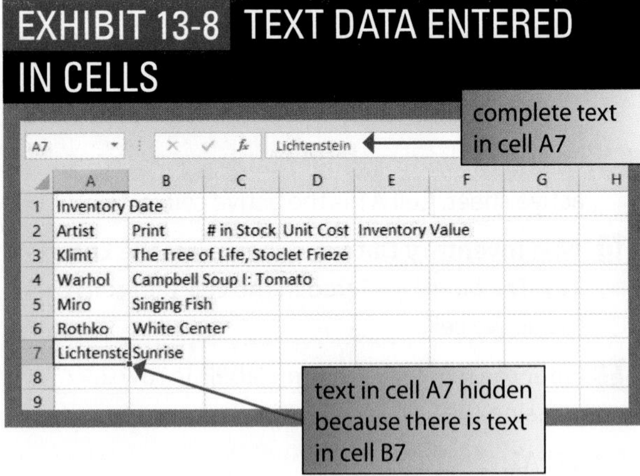

13-2b Formatting Text

The default format for any data you enter in a cell is the General format. When text is entered, this means, as mentioned ealier, that the entry is left-aligned.

You can change the way text looks by changing fonts, font sizes, font styles, and color. These text formatting options are the same as those you worked with in Word. They are available in the Font group on the Home tab. Remember that fonts and colors are organized into theme and non-theme fonts and colors, so if you want to format text with a font or a color that will not change when the theme is changed, use a non-theme font and color.

> **FYI**
> **USING AUTOCOMPLETE**
> As you enter text in a worksheet, Excel tries to anticipate what you are about to enter by displaying text that begins with the same letters as a previous entry in the same column. This feature, known as AutoComplete, helps make entering repetitive text easier. To accept the suggested text, press the Tab key or the Enter key. To override the suggested text, continue to type the text you want to enter in the cell.

Begin Activity

Format text.

1 Make the **Documentation worksheet** the active sheet. Click **cell A1**.

2 On the Home tab, in the Font group, click the **Font box arrow** [Calibri].

3 At the top of the Font list, click **Calibri Light (Headings)**. The company name in cell A1 changes to the Calibri Light font, the default headings font in the Office theme.

4 In the Font group, click the **Font Size box arrow** [11], and then click 24. The company name changes to 24 points.

5 In the Font group, click the **Bold button** [B]. The company name is formatted in bold.

6 In the Font group, click the **Font Color button arrow** [A] to display the theme and standard colors.

7 In the Standard Colors section, click the **Dark Blue color**. Remember to use the ScreenTip to identify the correct color. The company name changes to dark blue. Compare your screen to Exhibit 13-9.

> **TIP:** If you want to change the format of only some of the text in a cell, double-click the cell, and then drag to select the text you want to format.

End Activity

EXHIBIT 13-9 FORMATTED TEXT IN CELL A1

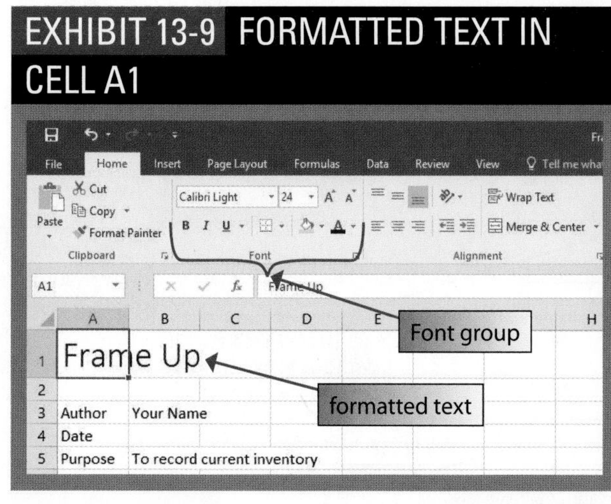

4. Enter the following inventory values and unit costs into **cells C4** through **D5**:

cell C4:	**13**	cell D4:	**12.99**
cell C5:	**24**	cell D5:	**16.99**

5. Click **cell C6**, type **3**, press the **Tab key**, type **18.50** in cell D6, and then to the left of the formula bar, click the **Enter button** ✓. The value you typed in cell D4 is changed to 18.5, without the ending zero.

6. Make **cell D6** the active cell, if necessary. Compare your screen to Exhibit 13-10.

End Activity

13-2c Entering Numbers

Number data is any numerical value that can be used in a mathematical calculation. In Excel, numbers can be integers such as 378, decimals such as 1.95, or negatives such as –5.2. By default, numbers are right-aligned in cells.

If a number is too wide to fit in a cell, it does not flow into the next cell if the next cell is empty or look like it is cut off. Instead, the column will automatically widen to fit the number. If the number still doesn't fit, a series of pound signs (#) appears in the cell instead of the number. The entire number still appears in the formula bar, however, when the cell is active.

EXHIBIT 13-10 NUMBER DATA ENTERED IN A WORKSHEET

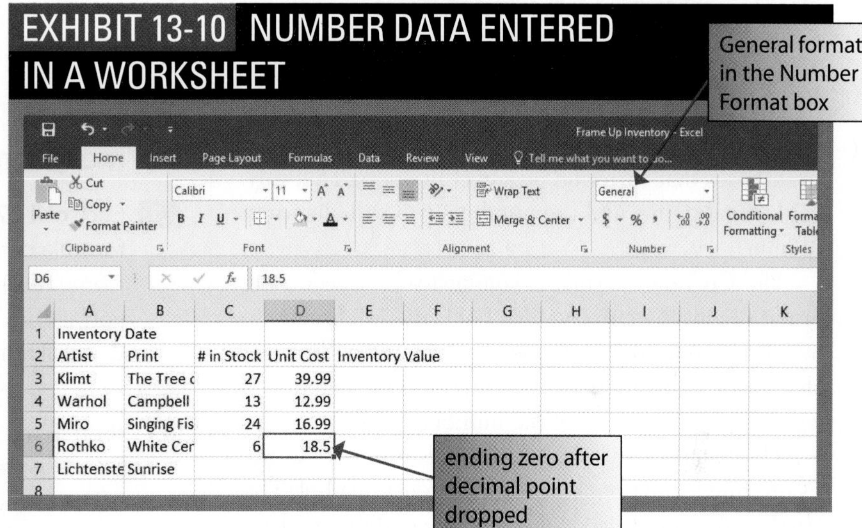

Begin Activity

Enter number data.

1. Click the **Inventory sheet tab**, and then click **cell C3**. Although it looks like cell C3 contains the text, this is the overflow text from cell B3, and you can see in the formula bar that cell C3 is empty.

2. Type **27**, and then to the left of the formula bar, click the **Enter button** ✓. The inventory quantity for the Klimt print is entered in cell C3. Now that cell C3 contains data, the excess text from cell B3 cannot flow over cell C3.

3. Click **cell D3**, type **39.99**, and then press the **Enter key**. The number you typed is entered into cell D3.

13-2d Formatting Numbers

You can format values using a number format, which displays the values in a way that makes them easier to understand and interpret. Changing the number format has absolutely no effect on the value stored in the workbook. The default format when numbers are entered is the General format, which, for the most part, displays values exactly as they are typed by the user. To make numbers easier to interpret, you can:

- Set how many digits appear to the right of the decimal point.
- Add commas to act as a thousands separator for large values.

number data Any numerical value that can be used in a mathematical calculation.

- Include currency symbols to identify the monetary unit being used.
- Display percentages using the % symbol.

The most common number formats are Accounting, Currency, Number, and Percentage. The Accounting format adds a dollar sign (or the currency symbol you select) one space from the left edge of the cell, inserts a comma as a thousands separator, sets two decimal places, aligns numbers by their decimal points one space from the right end of the cell, and encloses negative numbers in parentheses. The spaces between the dollar sign and the left edge of the cell and between the last number and the right edge of the cell leave room on either end for the parentheses that surround negative numbers. That way, the decimal points and the numbers will still align in a column.

The Currency format is similar to the Accounting format except the currency symbol is placed directly to the left of the number, numbers are aligned at the right edge of the cell, and negative values are indicated by a negative sign to the left of the number.

The Comma Style button formats numbers in the Accounting format but without a currency symbol. The Number format is used for general numbers, and includes two decimal places and negative signs. Percentage format changes the value to the decimal equivalent in hundreds, adds the % symbol after the number, and removes all decimal places. For example, if you enter 1 in a cell and then apply the Percentage format, the value is changed to 100%.

Whatever format is applied to a number, you can change the number of decimal places displayed. When you decrease the number of decimal places shown, the values are rounded using standard rounding practices: If the number is five or higher, the value is rounded up and the number to its left is increased by one. If the number is four or lower, the value is rounded down and the number to its left remains the same.

The options for changing the number format are all available in the Number group on the Home tab. Note that changing the number format has no effect on the value stored in the workbook. For example, Excel treats a currency value such as $87.25 as the number 87.25 and a percentage such as 95% as the number 0.95. See Exhibit 13-11.

EXHIBIT 13-11 NUMBER FORMATTED AS CURRENCY

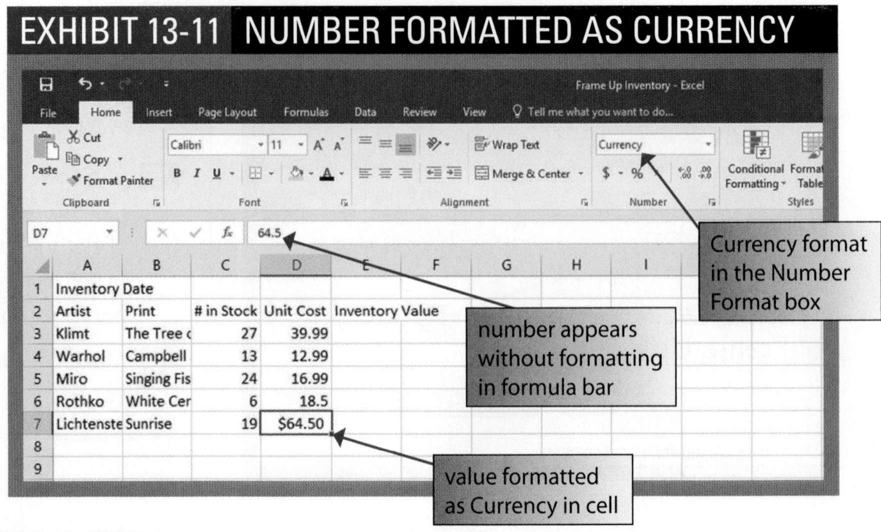

Begin Activity

Format numbers.

1 Click **cell C7**, type **19**, and then to the left of the formula bar, click the **Enter button** ✓. On the Home tab, in the Number group, the Number Format box identifies the numbers as having the General number formats.

2 Click **cell D7**, type **$64.50**, and then to the left of the formula bar, click the **Enter button** ✓. In the formula bar, the value is 64.5, without the dollar sign or ending zero. In the Number Format box, Currency is selected. The Currency format was automatically applied because you typed the dollar sign. Refer back to Exhibit 13-11.

TIP: When you type the dollar sign to apply the Currency format instead of applying the Currency format directly, negative numbers are in parentheses and in red.

3 In the Number group, click the **Accounting Number Format button** $. The format of the cell changes to the Accounting format and the dollar sign shifts to the left edge of the cell.

TIP: To select other currency symbols, click the Accounting Number Format button arrow $ ▾ in the Number group on the Home tab, and then click a currency symbol.

4 In the Number group, click the **Decrease Decimal button** .00→.0 twice. Both decimal places are removed and the number in the cell is rounded up to $65. In the formula bar, the value is still 64.5. All you have done is change the format of the number; you have not changed its value.

5 In the Number group, click the **Increase Decimal button** [icon] twice to redisplay the currency with two decimal places.

6 On the Home tab, in the Clipboard group, double-click the **Format Painter button**, and then click **cell D3**. The Accounting format is copied from cell D7 to cell D3. The Format Painter is still selected.

7 Click **cells D4**, **D5**, and **D6**, and then in the Clipboard group, click the **Format Painter button** to deselect it. All the number values in column D are formatted with the Accounting format. Compare your screen to Exhibit 13-12.

End Activity

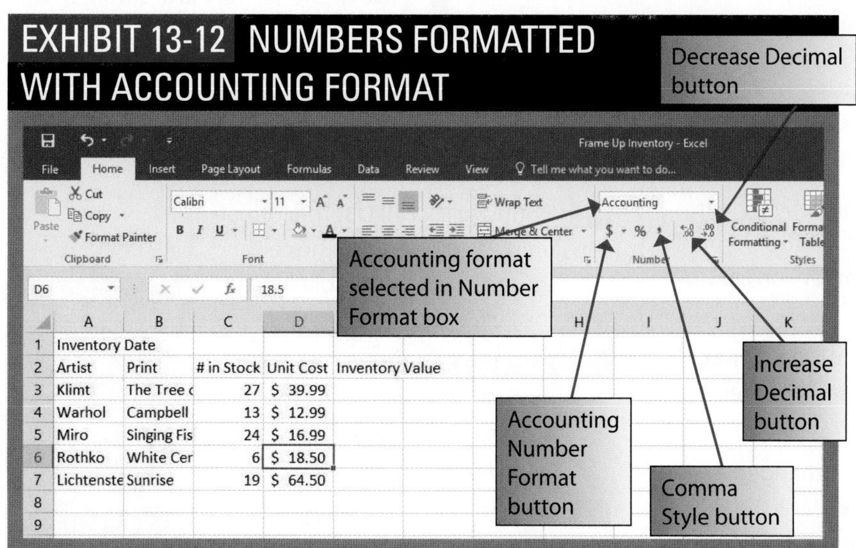

EXHIBIT 13-12 NUMBERS FORMATTED WITH ACCOUNTING FORMAT

13-2e Entering Dates

Date data is commonly recognized formats for date and time values. When you enter a date in a cell, such as April 6, 2017, Excel interprets it as a date and not as text and formats it appropriately. You can enter dates in any of the standard formats, including the following date formats (as well as many others), and Excel recognizes each format as representing the same date:

- 4/6/2017
- 4/6/17
- 4-6-2017
- April 6, 2017
- 6-Apr-17

No matter how you enter dates, Excel alters the date format to one of two default formats. If you use numbers separated by slashes or hyphens, Excel displays the date with the four-digit year value. For example, if you enter the date 4/6/17, Excel changes it to 4/6/2017. If you use text for the month, for example, April 6, 2017, Excel converts the date to the format 6-Apr-17.

In Excel, dates are actually numbers that are formatted to appear as text. This allows you to perform calculations with dates, such as determining the elapsed time between two dates. Because they are numbers, dates and times are right-aligned in the cell.

Begin Activity

Enter dates.

1 On the Inventory worksheet, click **cell B1**.

2 Type **June 22, 2017** and then press the **Tab key**. The date you typed appears in cell B1 but is reformatted as 22-Jun-17.

3 Click **cell B1**. In the formula bar, the value in the cell is 6/22/2017.

4 Make the **Documentation worksheet** the active sheet.

5 Click **cell B4**, type **6-22-17**, and then next to the formula bar, click the **Enter button** [icon]. The date appears in the cell and in the formula bar as 6/22/2017.

End Activity

13-2f Formatting Dates

Because Excel stores dates and times as numbers and not as text, when you apply different formats the date and time values are not changed. The format that is applied when you enter a date using numbers and slashes, *mm/dd/yyyy*, is the Short Date format. The Long Date format displays the day of the week and the full month name in addition to the day of the month and the year. To change a date format to the Short or Long Date format, you use the Number Format box arrow in the Number group on the Home tab, as shown in Exhibit 13-13.

date data Text or numbers in commonly recognized formats for date values.

EXHIBIT 13-13 NUMBER FORMAT MENU

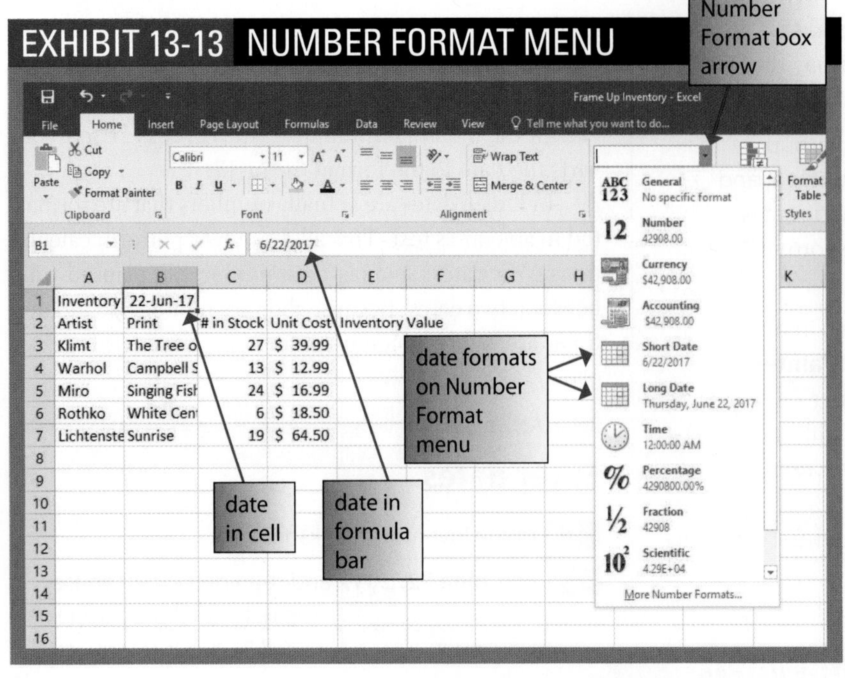

- Double-click the cell.
- Select the cell, click anywhere in the formula bar, and then click in the cell.
- Select the cell, and then press the F2 key.

When editing content directly in a cell, some of the keyboard shortcuts work differently because now they apply only to the text within the selected cell. For example, pressing the Home key moves the insertion point to the beginning of the cell's content, and pressing the Left Arrow key or the Right Arrow key moves the insertion point backward or forward through the cell's content.

Begin Activity

Format dates.

1. Make the **Inventory worksheet** the active sheet, and then click **cell B1**, if necessary. On the Home tab, in the Number group, the Number Format box displays Custom.
2. In the Number group, click the **Number Format box arrow** to display commonly used number formats. Refer to Exhibit 13-13.
3. Click **Short Date**. The date format is changed to the Short Date number format, 6/22/2017. Because the date in the Short Date format is too wide to fit in the cell, a series of pound signs (#) appears in the cell instead. You will fix this later.

End Activity

13-3 EDITING CELL CONTENT

As you work, you might make mistakes that you want to correct or undo, or you might need to replace a value based on more current information. You could simply make the cell active and then type the new entry or delete the value in the cell and then type the correct value. If you need to edit only a portion of an entry rather than change the entire contents of a cell, you can edit the contents of a selected cell in the formula bar, or you can do one of the following to edit the cell contents directly in the cell:

Begin Activity

Edit cell content.

1. Double-click **cell D3**. The formatting disappears from the cell and the insertion point is blinking in the cell.
2. Press the **Right Arrow key** as many times as necessary to move the insertion point to the end of the cell, after the second 9.
3. Press the **Backspace key** twice to delete 99, type **5**, and then press the **Enter key**. The unit cost value in cell D3 changes to $39.50.

PROBLEM?
If you make a mistake as you edit, press the **Esc key** or click the **Cancel button** ✕ on the formula bar to cancel those edits.

End Activity

13-4 WORKING WITH COLUMNS AND ROWS

You can modify a worksheet to make it easier to read and include more data. To do this, you can change the column widths and row heights, insert columns and rows, and delete columns and rows.

13-4a Selecting Columns and Rows

In order to work with columns and rows, you need to know how to select them. To select a column, you click its column header. Likewise, to select a row, you click its row header. To select adjacent columns or rows, you can drag across the column or row headers, or you can click the first header, press and hold the Shift key, and then click the last header. To select nonadjacent columns or rows, press and hold the Ctrl key as you click the column or row headers. Finally, you can select all the columns and rows in a worksheet by clicking the Select All button in the upper-left corner of the worksheet.

Begin Activity

Select columns and rows.

1. Point to the **column A header** so that the pointer changes to ⬇, and then click the **mouse button**. The entire column A is selected.
2. Press and hold the **Shift key**, click the **column C header**, and then release the **Shift key**. Columns A through C are selected.
3. Press and hold the **Ctrl key**, click the **column F header**, and then release the **Ctrl key**. Columns A through C and column F are selected.
4. Click the **column A header**, but do not release the mouse button. Without releasing the mouse button, drag to the **column B header**, and then release the **mouse button**. Both columns A and B are selected.
5. Point to the **row 2 header** so that the pointer changes to ➡, and then click the **row 2 header**, but do not release the mouse button.
6. Drag down to the **row 7 header**, and then release the **mouse button**. Rows 2 through 7 are selected.
7. Click anywhere in the worksheet to deselect the rows.

End Activity

13-4b Changing Column Widths and Row Heights

The default sizes of the columns and rows in a worksheet might not always accommodate the information you need to enter. For example, on the Inventory sheet, the text in cell E2 is so long that it seems to overflow into cell F2. When you enter more text than can fit in a cell, the additional text is visible in the adjacent cells as long as they are empty. If the adjacent cells also contain data, Excel displays only as much text as fits into the cell, cutting off the rest of the text entry. For example, all of the titles in cells B3 through B6 are cut off because the adjacent cells in column C contain data. The complete text is still entered in the cell; it's just not displayed.

To make the cell content easier to read or fully visible, you can resize the columns and rows in the worksheet. Column widths are expressed in terms of either the number of characters the column can contain or the size of the column in pixels. A pixel is a single point, or the smallest colorable area, on a computer monitor or printout. The default column width allows you to type about eight or nine characters in a cell before that entry is either cut off or overlaps the adjacent cell. The default column width is 8.43 characters or 64 pixels. Of course, if you decrease the font size of characters, you can fit more text within a cell. Row heights are expressed in points—the same unit of measurement that is used for font sizes—or pixels. The default row height is 15.00 points or 20 pixels.

If the default column width is too narrow, you can widen it by dragging the column border. When you drag the column border, a ScreenTip appears, identifying the width of the column in characters, followed in parentheses by the width of the column in pixels. Exhibit 13-14 shows column B being resized by dragging the column border. Rather than resizing each column or row separately, you can select multiple columns or rows and resize them at the same time.

EXHIBIT 13-14 CHANGING THE COLUMN WIDTH BY DRAGGING

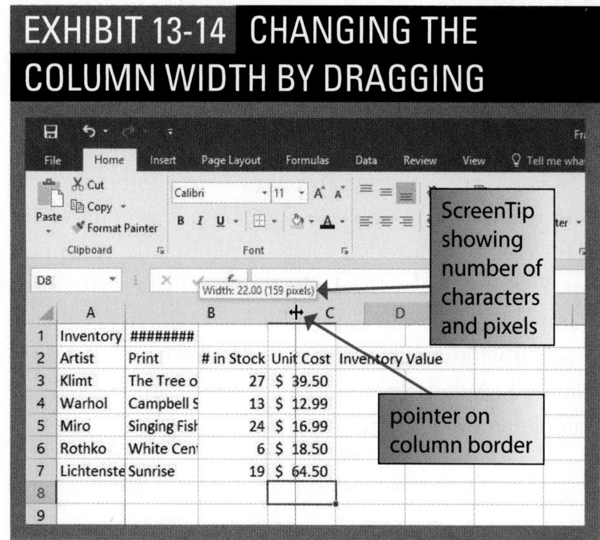

Another option is to AutoFit a column or row to its content. **AutoFitting** eliminates any empty space by matching the column to the width of its longest cell entry or a row to the height of its tallest entry. If the

AutoFit In Excel, to resize a column by matching its width to the width of its longest cell entry or resize a row to the height of its tallest cell entry.

column is blank, Excel restores the column to its default width. The simplest way to AutoFit a column is to double-click its right border. To AutoFit a row, double-click its bottom border.

Finally, you can use the commands on the Format button menu in the Cells group on the Home tab to resize columns and rows. Exhibit 13-15 shows the Format button menu. The top five commands on this menu, in the Cell Size section, provide options for adjusting column width and row height.

EXHIBIT 13-15 FORMAT BUTTON MENU

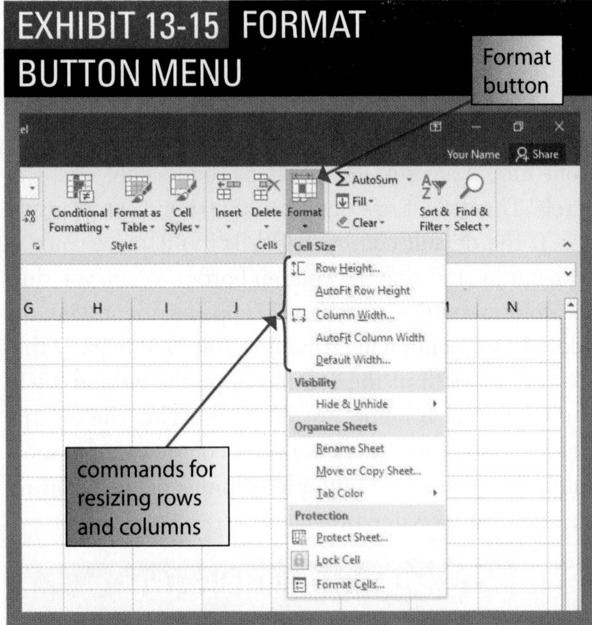

If you enter an integer with more digits than can fit in a cell, the column width automatically widens to accommodate the number. If you resize a column narrower after you enter a number and the number no longer fits in the cell, you see ###### in the cell instead of the number. You can display the entire number by increasing the column width. If you enter a decimal value in a cell and it is too wide to fit in the cell, the decimal places are rounded so that the number fits. You can still see the complete number in the formula bar.

Begin Activity

Change column widths.

TIP: You can also click the Format button in the Cells group on the Home tab, click Column Width, and then type the width you want (in characters) in the Column Width dialog box.

1. Point to the **column B header right border** so that the pointer changes to ✛.
2. Drag to the right until the ScreenTip identifies the width of the column as about **22 characters**, but do not release the mouse button. Refer back to Exhibit 13-14.
3. Release the **mouse button**. The width of column B expands to 22 characters, and all of the titles in column B except the title in cell B3 fit and are now visible. The date in cell B1 is now also visible.
4. Point to the **column A header right border** so that the pointer changes to ✛, and then double-click. The width of column A AutoFits to 13.57 characters, which displays all of the text in cell A1, the widest entry in the column.
5. Select **column C** and **column D**.
6. Drag the **right border** of the column D header to the right until the column width changes to about **12 characters**, and then release the **mouse button**. Both of the selected columns are now 12 characters wide.
7. Select **column E**. On the Home tab, in the Cells group, click the **Format button**. A menu of commands opens. Refer back to Exhibit 13-15.
8. Click **AutoFit Column Width**. The width of the selected column—column E—Auto Fits to its content.
9. Click anywhere in the worksheet to deselect the column.

End Activity

FYI

SETTING COLUMN WIDTHS PROPERLY

You should set column widths based on the maximum number of characters you want to display in the cells rather than pixel size. Pixel size is related to screen resolution, and a cell might be too narrow under a different resolution. This might come into play if you work on multiple computers or share your workbooks with others.

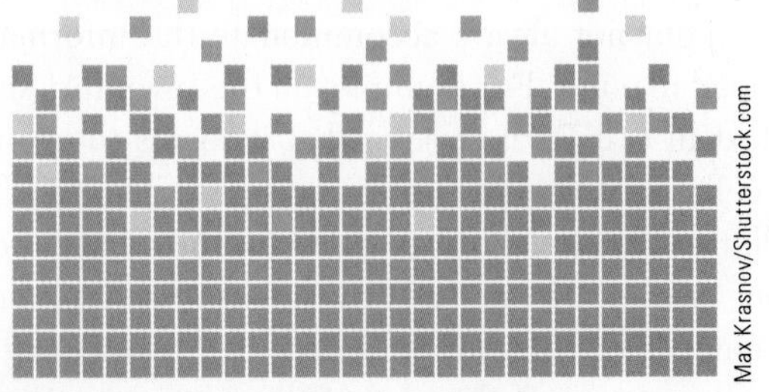

13-4c **Inserting a Column or Row**

You can insert a new column or row anywhere within a worksheet. When you insert a new column, the existing columns shift to the right, and the new column has the same width as the column directly to its left. When you insert a new row, the existing rows shift down, and the new row has the same height as the row above it. You can insert a column or row using the Insert button in the Cells group on the Home tab, and then selecting the appropriate command on the menu. Exhibit 13-16 shows the Insert button menu. If you select a row or column first, you can click the Insert button instead of opening the menu. If a column is selected, clicking the button inserts a new column; if a row is selected, clicking the button inserts a new row.

EXHIBIT 13-16 INSERT BUTTON MENU

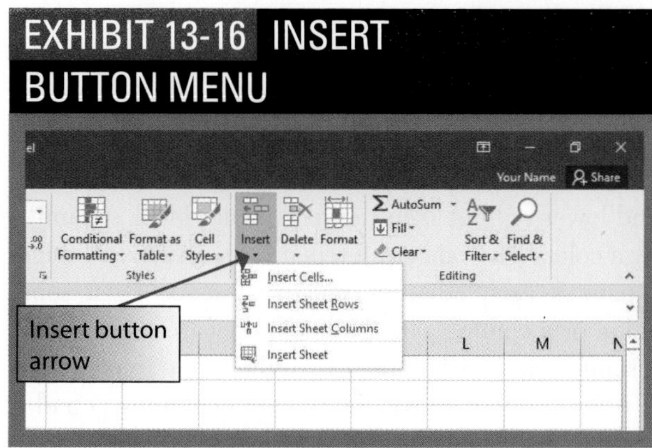

Begin Activity

Insert columns and rows.

1. Click **cell C1**. On the Home tab, in the Cells group, click the **Insert button arrow**. The Insert button menu opens. Refer back to Exhibit 13-16.
2. Click **Insert Sheet Columns**. The menu closes and a new column C is inserted into the worksheet, shifting the columns to the right of the new column. The new column has the same width as the column to its left, column B.

> **TIP:** The Insert Options button that appears when you insert a column or row lets you choose how the inserted column or row is formatted.

3. Click **cell C2**, type **Stock Number** and then press the **Enter key**. The new column label is entered, and cell C3 is the active cell.
4. Enter the following data in **cells C3** through **C7**:

   cell C3: **K-1837**
   cell C4: **W-3015**
   cell C5: **M-9271**
   cell C6: **R-5392**
   cell C7: **L-0372**

5. AutoFit the contents of **column C**.
6. Click the **row 2 header**. The entire second row is selected.
7. On the Home tab, in the Cells group, click the **Insert button.** A new row 2 is inserted, and the remaining rows shift down. Compare your screen to Exhibit 13-17.

End Activity

EXHIBIT 13-17 COLUMN AND ROW ADDED TO WORKSHEET

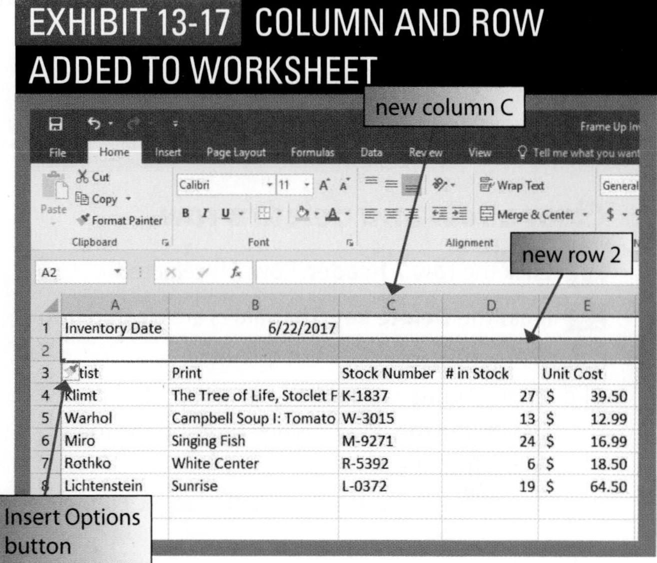

13-4d **Clearing or Deleting a Row or Column**

Adding new data to a workbook is common, as is removing old or erroneous data. You can remove data in two ways: clearing and deleting.

- **Clearing**—Removes data from a worksheet but leaves the blank cells
- **Deleting**—Removes both the data and the cells from the worksheet

When you delete a column, the columns to the right shift left to fill the vacated space. Similarly, the

clear To remove data from cells but leave the blank cells in the worksheet.

delete In Excel, to remove both the data and the cells from a worksheet.

rows below a deleted row shift up to fill the vacated space. Deleting a column or row has the opposite effect of inserting a column or row.

You can delete entire columns or rows by selecting them, and then clicking the Delete button in the Cells group on the Home tab. To clear data from a column or row without deleting the column or row itself, select the columns or rows with data to clear, and then press the Delete key.

You'll first clear data from the worksheet and then delete the row that contained the data. Usually, you would do this in one step by simply deleting the row, but this activity highlights the difference between clearing and deleting.

Begin Activity

Clear a row and delete a row.

1 Click the **row 7 header**. Row 7 is selected.

2 Press the **Delete key**. The values are cleared from row 7, and row 7 remains selected.

3 On the Home tab, in the Cells group, click the **Delete button**. Row 7 is deleted, and the rows below it shift up.

End Activity

13-5 WORKING WITH CELLS AND RANGES

A group of cells is called a **cell range** or **range**. Ranges can be either adjacent or nonadjacent. An adjacent range is a single rectangular block of cells. All of the artist data entered in cell A3 through cell A7 is an adjacent range because it forms one rectangular block of cells. A nonadjacent range consists of two or more distinct adjacent ranges. In Exhibit 13-18, the artist data in cell A3 through cell A7 are an adjacent range, and the inventory and unit costs in cell D3 through cell E7 together are another adjacent range. The two selected ranges are nonadjacent ranges.

cell range (range) A group of cells.

range reference The location and size of a range.

EXHIBIT 13-18 NONADJACENT RANGE

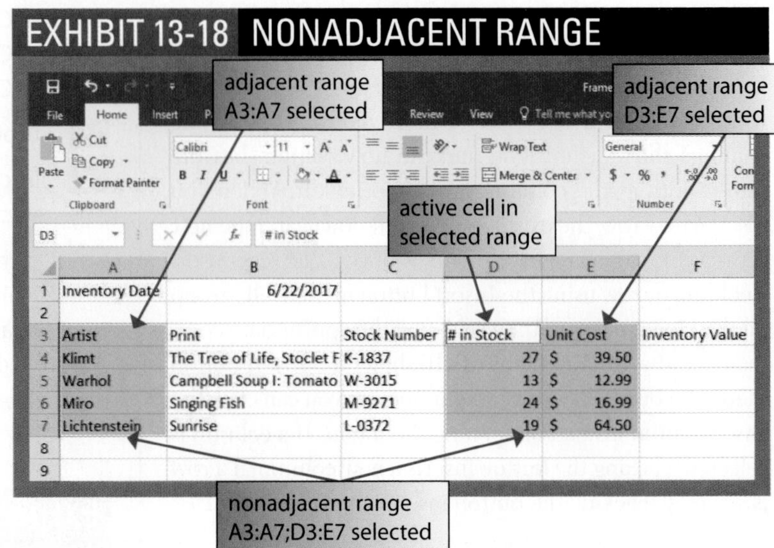

Just as a cell reference indicates the location of an individual worksheet cell, a **range reference** indicates the location and size of a range. For adjacent ranges, the range reference specifies the locations of the upper-left and lower-right cells in the rectangular block separated by a colon. The range reference for nonadjacent ranges separates each adjacent range reference by a semicolon or a comma. (In this book, they are separated by a semicolon.). In Exhibit 13-18, the range in column A is referenced as A3:A7, the range in columns D and E is referenced as D3:E7, and the selected nonadjacent range is referenced as A3:A7;D3:E7.

13-5a Selecting a Range

You select adjacent and nonadjacent ranges of cells by dragging the pointer over the cells. Selecting a range enables you to work with all of the cells in the range as a group. This means you can do things like move the cells, delete them, or clear their contents at the same time.

Begin Activity

Select ranges.

1 Click **cell A1**, but do not release the mouse button. This cell will be the cell in the upper-left corner of the range A1:F7.

2 Drag the pointer to **cell F7**, and then release the **mouse button**. The cells you drag over are shaded (except cell A1) and surrounded by a green border. Cell F7 is the cell in the lower-right corner of the adjacent range A1:F7. The first cell you clicked, cell A1, remains white to indicate that it is the active cell in the worksheet.

3 Click **any cell** in the worksheet to deselect the range.

4 Select the adjacent **range A3:A7**.

5 Press and hold the **Ctrl key**, select the adjacent **range D3:E7**, and then release the **Ctrl key**. All of the cells in the nonadjacent range A3:A7;D3:E7 are selected. Refer back to Exhibit 13-18.

TIP: You can enter a range reference in the Name box to select that range in the worksheet.

6 Click **any cell** in the worksheet to deselect the nonadjacent range.

7 Select the adjacent **range A3:F3**. Because more than one cell is selected, any formatting you apply will affect all of the cells in the range.

8 On the Home tab, in the Font group, click the **Bold button** **B**. The entries in the selected range are formatted as bold.

9 Click **any cell** in the worksheet to deselect the range.

End Activity

13-5b Moving and Copying a Cell or Range

One way to move a cell or range is to select it, position the pointer over the bottom edge of the selection, and then drag the selection to a new location, as shown in Exhibit 13-19. A green box indicates where the selected range will be dropped. You can also use drag and drop to copy a cell or range by pressing the Ctrl key as you drag the selected range to its new location.

EXHIBIT 13-19 RANGE BEING MOVED WITH DRAG AND DROP

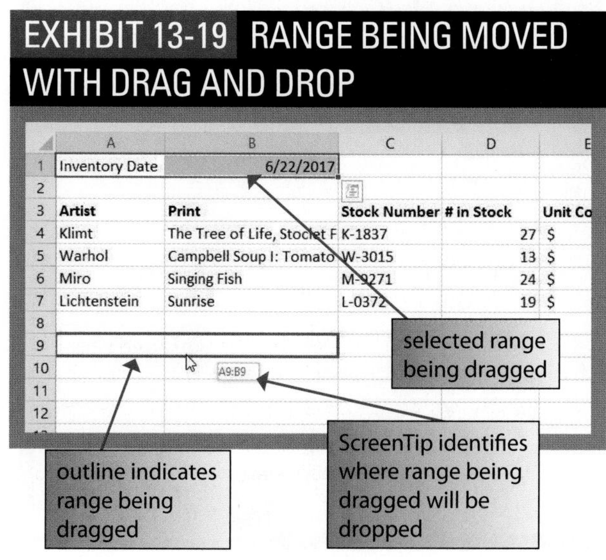

Drag and drop can be a difficult and awkward way to move or copy a selection, particularly if the worksheet is large and complex. In those situations, it is often more efficient to use the Cut or Copy and Paste commands. When you cut or copy a range, the selected cells are surrounded by a blinking border, indicating that the selection is stored on the Clipboard. The blinking border remains until you paste a cut range or start entering data in another cell. After the blinking border disappears, the selection is no longer stored on the Clipboard and you cannot paste it.

To make pasting a range easier, you can select only the upper-left cell of the range in the new location rather than the exact range where you want to paste. Excel will paste the entire range on the Clipboard with the same pattern of cells in the new location. Be aware that the pasted data will overwrite any data already in those cells.

Begin Activity

Move a range and a cell.

1 Select the **range A1:B1**.

2 Move the **pointer** over the bottom border of the selected range so that the pointer changes to the move pointer.

3 Press and hold the **left mouse button** to change the pointer to the arrow pointer.

4 Drag the selection down eight rows to row 9, but do not release the mouse button. A ScreenTip appears, indicating the new range reference for the selected cells—A9:B9. Refer back to Exhibit 13-19.

TIP: If the new location is not visible, drag the selected range to the edge of the worksheet in the direction you want to scroll.

5 When the ScreenTip displays the range A9:B9, release the **mouse button**. The selected cells move to the new location.

6 Make sure the **range A9:B9** is selected.

7 On the Home tab, in the Clipboard group, click the **Cut button**. The selected range is surrounded by a blinking border, which indicates that its contents are stored on the Clipboard.

8 Click **cell A1**. This cell is the upper-left corner of the range where you want to paste the data.

9 In the Clipboard group, click the **Paste button**. Excel pastes the contents of the range A9:B9 into the range A1:B1. The blinking border disappears and the Paste button is gray as visual clues that the Clipboard is now empty.

End Activity

13-5c Inserting and Deleting a Cell or Range

If you click the Insert button in the Cells group on the Home tab while one cell is selected, a cell is inserted and the selected cell and the cells below it move down one row. If you select a range and then click the Insert button, the selected range shifts down when the selected range is wider than it is long, and shifts right when the selected range is longer than it is wide, as illustrated in Exhibit 13-20.

If you click the Insert button arrow, you can use the Insert Cells command on the menu to open the Insert dialog box shown in Exhibit 13-21. This allows you to specify whether you want to shift the existing cells right or down, or whether to insert an entire row or column. The selected option is Excel's best guess of which way you want the current cells to shift.

If you no longer need a specific cell or range in a worksheet, you can delete those cells and any content they contain. To delete a range, select the range, and then click the Delete button in the Cells group on the Home tab. As with deleting a row or column, cells adjacent to the deleted range either move up or left to fill in the vacancy left by the deleted cells. To specify how the adjacent cells shift, or if you want to delete the entire row or column, click the Delete button arrow, and then click Delete Cells to open the Delete dialog box, which is similar to the Insert dialog box.

Begin Activity

Insert and delete ranges.

1 Select the **range B3:C4**.

2 On the Home tab, in the Cells group, click the **Insert button arrow** to open the Insert button menu.

3 On the Insert button menu, click **Insert Cells**. The Insert dialog box opens. Refer back to Exhibit 13-21. The Shift cells down option button is selected because this is the most likely action you will take for the selected range.

4 Click **OK**. The dialog box closes, four cells are inserted, and the selected cells move down two rows.

EXHIBIT 13-20 CELLS INSERTED WITHIN A RANGE

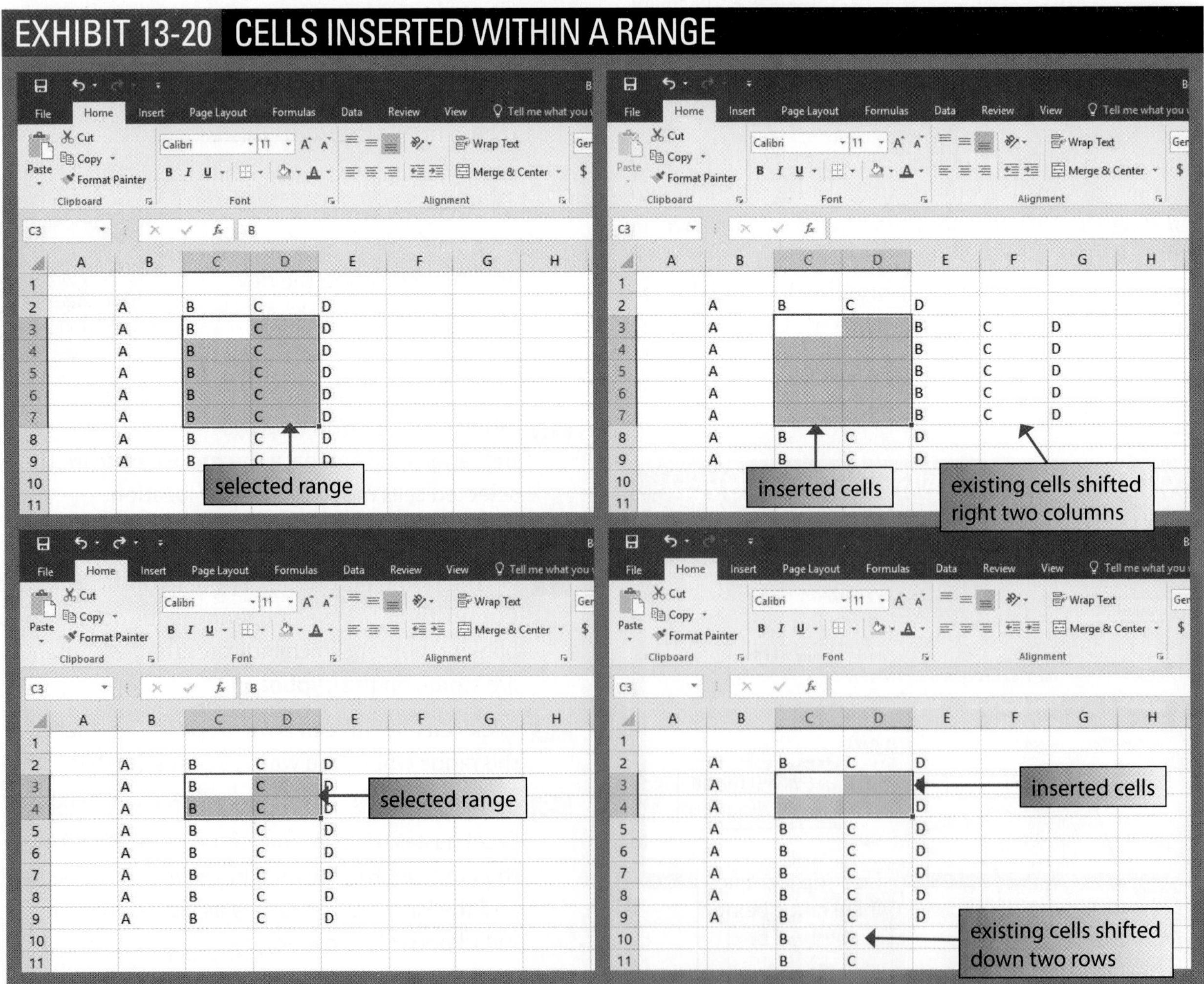

EXHIBIT 13-21 INSERT DIALOG BOX

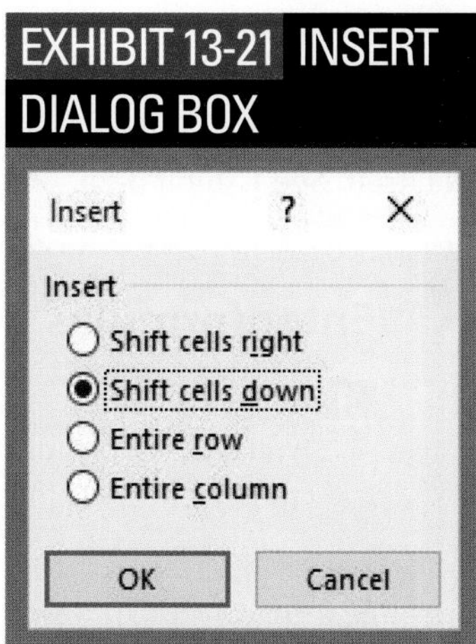

5 Make sure the **range B3:C4** is still selected.

6 In the Cells group, click the **Delete button arrow** to open the Delete button menu.

7 On the Delete button menu, click **Delete Cells**. The Delete dialog box opens. The Shift cells up option button is selected by default.

8 Click **OK**. The dialog box closes, the selected cells are deleted, and the cells below the selected cells move up two rows.

End Activity

13-5d Wrapping Text Within a Cell

You can force text that extends beyond a cell's border to fit within the cell. First, make the cell with text that is cut off the active cell. Then, click the Wrap Text button in the Alignment group on the Home tab. As shown in Exhibit 13-22, the row height increases as needed to wrap all the text within the cell. You can click the Wrap Text button again to turn off the text wrapping within the active cell.

EXHIBIT 13-22 CELL WITH TEXT WRAPPING

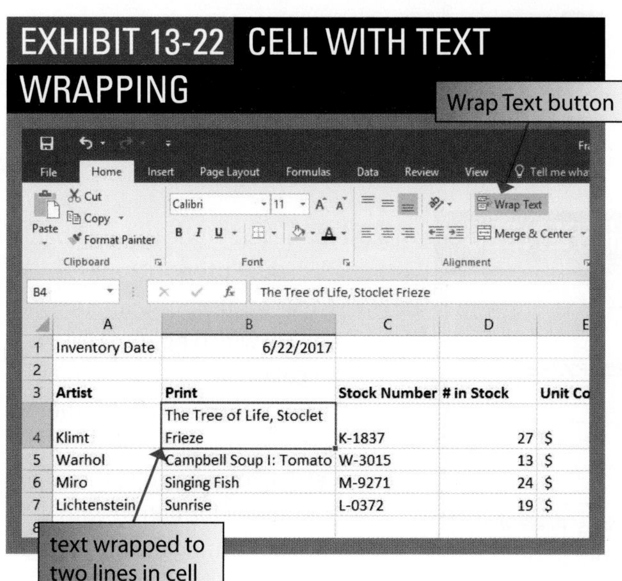

Begin Activity

Wrap text within a cell.

1 Make **cell B4** the active cell. The title of the Klimt print extends past the right border of cell B4.

2 On the Home tab, in the Alignment group, click the **Wrap Text button.** The button is selected, the text in cell B4 wraps to a second line so that the entire title is visible, and the row height increases so you can see both lines of text within cell B4. Refer back to Exhibit 13-22.

End Activity

13-6 ENTERING SIMPLE FORMULAS AND FUNCTIONS

Up to now, you have entered only text, numbers, and dates in the worksheet. However, the main reason for using Excel is to display values calculated from data. For example, the workbook has all the data needed to determine the total inventory Frame Up has in stock and the value of the current inventory. Such calculations are added to a worksheet using formulas and functions.

13-6a Entering a Formula

A **formula** is a mathematical expression that returns a value. In most cases, this is a number, although it can also be text or a date. Every Excel formula begins with an equal sign (=) followed by an expression that describes the operation to be done. A formula is written using **operators** that combine different values, returning a single value that is then displayed in the cell. The most commonly used operators are arithmetic operators that perform addition, subtraction, multiplication, division, and exponentiation. For example, the following formula uses the + operator to add 5 and 7, returning a value of 12:

= 5+7

Most formulas in Excel contain references to cells that store numbers rather than the specific values. For example, the following formula returns the result of adding the values in cells A1 and B2:

= A1+B2

formula A mathematical expression that returns a value.

operator A mathematical symbol used to combine values.

If the value 5 is stored in cell A1 and the value 7 is stored in cell B2, this formula would also return a value of 12. Exhibit 13-23 describes the different arithmetic operators and provides examples of formulas.

After a formula has been entered into a cell (by pressing the Enter or Tab key or clicking the Enter button ✓), the cell displays the *results* of the formula and not the formula itself. See Exhibit 3-25.

EXHIBIT 13-23 ARITHMETIC OPERATORS

Operation	Arithmetic Operator	Example	Description
Addition	+	=10+A1	Adds 10 to the value in cell A1
		=B1+B2+B3	Adds the values in cells B1, B2, and B3
Subtraction	–	=C9–B2	Subtracts the value in cell B2 from the value in cell C9
		=1–D2	Subtracts the value in cell D2 from 1
Multiplication	*	=C9*B9	Multiplies the values in cells C9 and B9
		=E5*0.06	Multiplies the value in cell E5 by 0.06
Division	/	=C9/B9	Divides the value in cell C9 by the value in cell B9
		=D15/12	Divides the value in cell D15 by 12
Exponentiation	^	=B5^3	Raises the value of cell B5 to the third power
		=3^B5	Raises 3 to the value in cell B5
<>	Not equal to	A1<>B1	Tests whether the value in cell A1 *is not equal to* the value in cell B1

To enter a formula in a cell, start by typing an equal sign. This indicates that you are entering a formula rather than data. If you are using numbers in the formula, type the first number. If you are using a cell reference, you can type the cell reference or you can click the cell you want to reference to add that reference to the formula. Clicking a cell reduces the possibility of error caused by typing an incorrect cell reference. When you add a cell reference to a formula, the reference is colored blue and a blue border appears around the corresponding cell in the worksheet. Next you type the operator you want to use, and then you type the next number or cell reference or click the next cell you want to reference. Exhibit 13-24 shows a formula typed in cell F4 that references cells D4 and E4.

Begin Activity

Enter formulas.

1 Make **cell F4** the active cell. You will enter a formula to calculate the inventory value of the Klimt print.

2 In cell F4, type = to begin the formula. The equal sign indicates that you are entering a formula rather than data.

> **TIP:** Remember, formulas always begin with = (an equal sign).

3 After the equal sign, type **D** so that the formula so far is *=D*. A list of Excel function names starting with the letter *D* appears below the cell. You can ignore this for now; you'll learn more about Excel functions shortly.

4 Type **4** so that the formula so far is *=D4*. The function list closes because no function name begins with *D4*. Cell D4 is surrounded by a blue border and is shaded to visually indicate which cell you are referencing in the formula. The corresponding cell reference D4 in the formula you are typing is colored the same blue. Cell D4 contains the current inventory of the Klimt print.

5 Type * to enter the multiplication operator.

6 Type **E4**. Cell E4 has a red border and shading, and the cell reference E4 in the formula changes to the same red. Cell E4 contains the unit cost for each Klimt print. Refer back to Exhibit 13-24.

EXHIBIT 13-24 FORMULA WITH TWO CELL REFERENCES

	A	B	C	D	E	F	G
1	Inventory Date	6/22/2017					
2							
3	Artist	Print	Stock Number	# in Stock	Unit Cost	Inventory Value	
4	Klimt	The Tree of Life, Stoclet Frieze	K-1837	27	$ 39.50	=D4*E4	
5	Warhol	Campbell Soup I: Tomato	W-3015	13	$ 12.99		
6	Miro	Singing Fish	M-9271	24	$ 16.99		
7	Lichtenstein	Sunrise	L-0372	19	$ 64.50		
8							

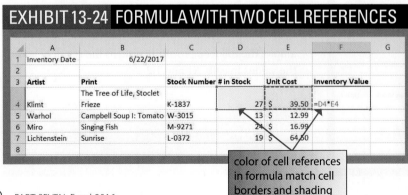

color of cell references in formula match cell borders and shading

7 To the left of the formula bar, click the **Enter button** ✓. The formula is entered in cell F4, which now displays the calculated value $1,066.50. The result is formatted with the Accounting format because cell E4, referenced in the formula, is formatted with the Accounting format. In the

EXHIBIT 13-25 CELL AND FORMULA BAR AFTER ENTERING A FORMULA

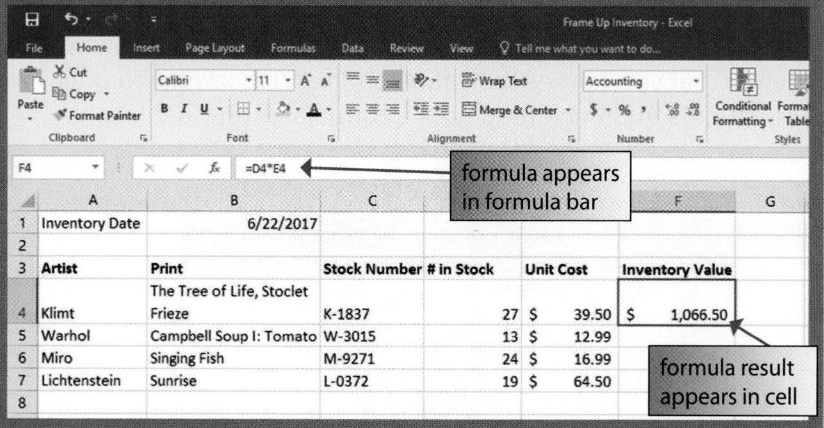

formula bar, the formula appears rather than the calculated value. This is because the formula bar always displays the actual content of the cell. Refer back to Exhibit 13-25.

8 Click **cell F5**, and then type = to begin the formula.

9 Click **cell D5**. The cell reference is inserted into the formula.

10 Type * to enter the multiplication operator, and then click **cell E5** to enter its cell reference in the formula.

11 To the left of the formula bar, click the **Enter button** ✓ to enter the formula. Cell F5 displays the value $168.87, which is the total value of the Warhol print inventory. In the formula bar, the formula appears, not the result.

12 Click in the **formula bar**. The cell displays the formula again, the colored boxes appear around each cell referenced in the formula, and the cell references in the formula bar are colored with the same colors so that you can quickly match the cell references with their locations in the worksheet. This would also happen if you double-clicked in the cell or made the cell active and then pressed the F2 key.

13 Press the **Esc key** to remove the focus from the formula bar and redisplay the calculated value in cell F4.

End Activity

13-6b Copying and Pasting Formulas

Sometimes, you need to repeat the same formula for several rows of data. Rather than retyping the formula, you can copy the formula and then paste it into the remaining rows.

Pasting a formula is different from pasting a value. When you paste a copied or cut formula, Excel adjusts the cell references used in the formula to reflect the new location of the formula in the worksheet. For example, if a formula in cell C3 contains a cell reference to cell B1, it contains a cell reference to the cell two cells above and one cell to the left of the cell containing the formula. You could copy this formula and then paste it into cell E5, and the cell reference in the formula would automatically change to cell D3, the cell that is two cells above and one cell to the left of the cell containing the formula. Excel does this automatically because you want to replicate the actions of a formula rather than duplicate the specific value the formula generates. In Exhibit 13-26, the formula =D4*E4 was copied from cell F4 and pasted in cell F6. When it was pasted, it was changed to =D6*E6.

EXHIBIT 13-26 FORMULA COPIED AND PASTED

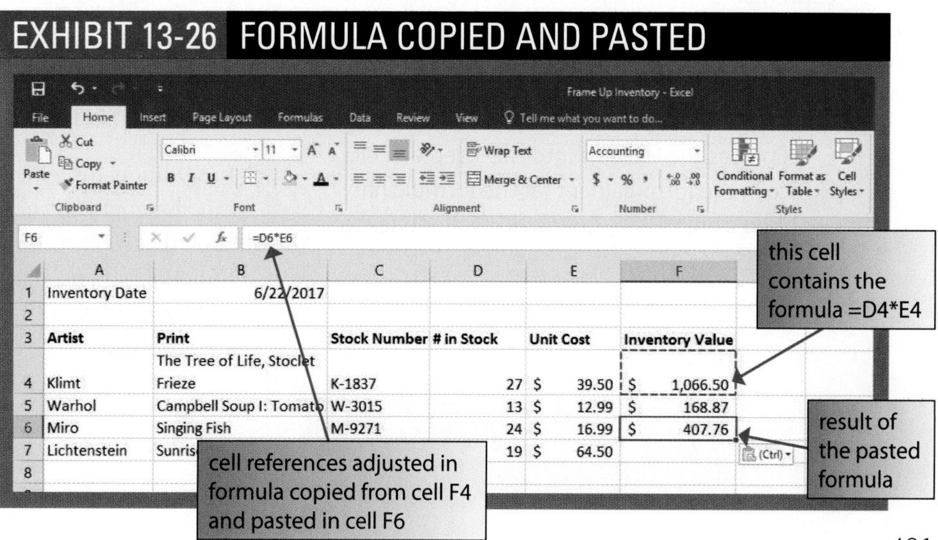

FYI VIEWING WORKSHEET FORMULAS

In some cases you might want to view the formulas used to develop the workbook. For example, if you encounter unexpected results and you want to examine the underlying formulas. When you display the formulas in a worksheet instead of the resulting values, the columns containing formulas temporarily widen so that you can see the entire formulas. To view the formulas, click the Show Formulas button in the Formula Auditing group on the Formulas tab.

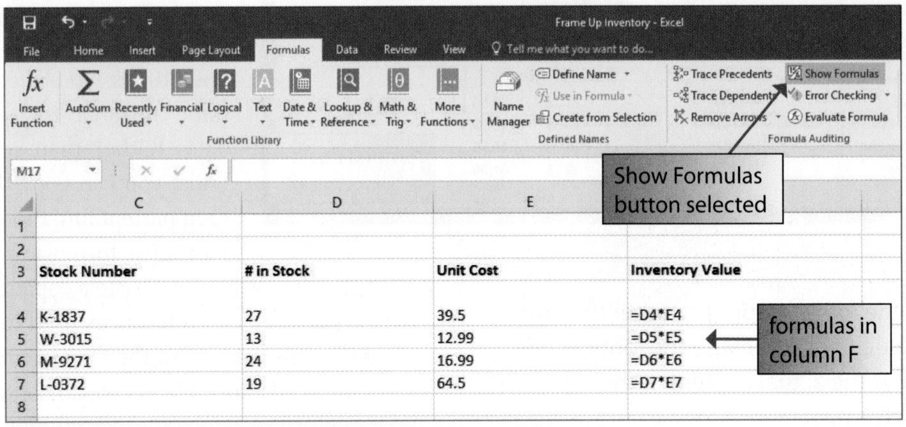

Show Formulas button selected

	C	D	E
1			
2			
3	Stock Number	# in Stock	Unit Cost	Inventory Value
4	K-1837	27	39.5	=D4*E4
5	W-3015	13	12.99	=D5*E5
6	M-9271	24	16.99	=D6*E6
7	L-0372	19	64.5	=D7*E7
8				

formulas in column F

Begin Activity

Copy and paste formulas.

1 Make **cell F4** the active cell. This cell contains the formula to copy.

2 On the Home tab, in the Clipboard group, click the **Copy button**. The formula is copied to the Clipboard. A moving, dashed border surrounds cell F4, indicating that you can paste the cell contents.

3 Click **cell F6**. This is the cell in which you want to paste the formula.

4 In the Clipboard group, click the **Paste button**. Excel pastes the formula into the selected cell. Notice in the formula bar that the formula has changed from *=D4*E4* to *=D6*E6*. Refer back to Exhibit 13-26.

5 Make **cell F7** the active cell, and then paste the contents of the Clipboard into the cell. You can paste the formula without recopying because the moving, dashed line border still surrounds the cell whose contents you copied to the Clipboard. The formula is adjusted again to =D7*E7.

TIP: It's a good idea to check the cell references in a copied formula to ensure the cell references changed as you expected.

6 Press the **Esc key** to remove the moving border from cell F7.

End Activity

13-6c Entering a Function

In addition to cell references and operators, formulas can also contain functions. A **function** is a named operation that replaces the action of an arithmetic expression. Functions are used to simplify formulas. For example, to add the values in the range A1:A9, you could enter the long formula:

=A1+A2+A3+A4+A5+A6+A7+A8+A9

Or, you could use the SUM function:

=SUM(A1:A9)

function A named operation that replaces the action of an arithmetic expression.

In both cases, Excel adds the values in cells A1 through A9, but the SUM function is faster and simpler to enter and less prone to a typing error. You should always use a function, if one is available, in place of a long, complex formula.

There are many ways to enter a function in a worksheet. One way is to type it. Because a function is part of a formula, type an equal sign to start the formula, and then type the function name. For the SUM function, the next thing you need to type is the range whose values you want to add. These values are placed between parentheses. Exhibit 13-27 shows the SUM function in cell D8 that adds the values in the range D4:D7.

EXHIBIT 13-27 SUM FUNCTION IN CELL D8

D8 fx =SUM(D4:D7)

	A	B	C	D
1	Inventory Date	6/22/2017		
2				
3	Artist	Print	Stock Number	# in Stock
4	Klimt	The Tree of Life, Stoclet Frieze	K-1837	27
5	Warhol	Campbell Soup I: Tomato	W-3015	13
6	Miro	Singing Fish	M-9271	24
7	Lichtenstein	Sunrise	L-0372	19
8				=SUM(D4:D7)

SUM function entered in cell

Begin Activity

Enter a function.

1 Make **cell D8** the active cell.

2 Type = to begin the formula.

3 Type **SUM** to enter the function name. As when you entered the formula, a list of functions opens listing functions that begin with the letters you typed.

4 Type **(**. The list of functions closes, and a ScreenTip appears, showing how the SUM function should be written.

5 Select the **range D4:D7**. The function changes to include the cells you selected, and a moving, dashed border surrounds the selected range.

TIP: You can also type a range reference directly in a function.

6 Type **)** to complete the function. The moving, dashed border changes to a solid blue line, the range reference in the function changes to blue text, and the complete function, =SUM(D4:D7), appears in cell D8. Refer back to Exhibit 13-27.

7 Press the **Tab key** to enter the function. The calculated value of the SUM function appears in cell D8, indicating that the total inventory is 83 prints.

End Activity

FYI

EXCEL FUNCTIONS

Excel supports over 300 different functions from the fields of finance, business, science, and engineering. For example, the PMT function calculates the amount of the loan payments based on an interest rate and a payment schedule; and the CONVERT function converts a number in one unit of measurement system to another unit of measurement. Functions are not limited to numbers. Excel also provides functions that work with text and dates, such as LOWER, which converts all the characters in a cell to lowercase letters, or NETWORKDAYS, which calculates the number of workdays between two dates. You can see the function categories in the Function Library group on the Formulas tab.

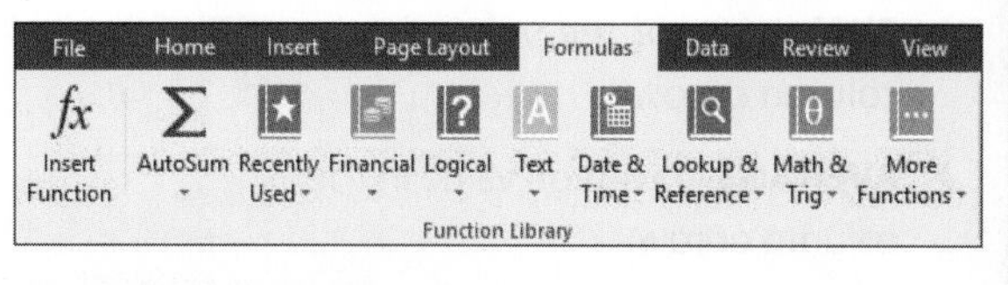

13-6d Using AutoSum

A quick and easy way to enter commonly used functions is with the AutoSum feature. **AutoSum** inserts one of five common functions and a range reference that Excel determines by examining the layout of the data and choosing

AutoSum A feature that inserts the SUM, AVERAGE, COUNT, MIN, or MAX function.

the most likely range. For example, if you use AutoSum with the SUM function in a cell that is below a column of numbers, Excel assumes that you want to summarize the values in the column. Similarly, if you use AutoSum with the SUM function in a cell to the right of a row of values, Excel assumes you want to summarize the values in that row. If the range reference is incorrect, you can change it.

To use AutoSum with the SUM function, click the AutoSum button in the Editing group on the Home tab or click the AutoSum button in the Function Library group on the Formulas tab.

Begin Activity

Use AutoSum.

1 Make **cell F8** the active cell.

2 On the Home tab, in the Editing group, click the **AutoSum button**. The SUM function with the range reference F4:F7 is entered in cell F8.

3 Press the **Enter key** to accept the formula. The total inventory value, $2,868.63, is displayed in cell F8.

TIP: To change the range reference, drag any sizing handle on the selected range, select a different range in the worksheet, or type a different range reference directly in the formula.

End Activity

FYI

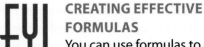

MORE AUTOSUM FUNCTIONS

You can use AutoSum to insert the five functions described below:

- **SUM**—sum of the values in the column or row.
- **AVERAGE**—average value in the column or row.
- **COUNT**—total count of numeric values in the column or row.
- **MAX**—maximum value in the column or row.
- **MIN**—minimum value in the column or row.

To use AutoSum with a function other than the SUM function, click the AutoSum button arrow in the Editing group on the Home tab or in the Function Library group on the Formulas tab, and then select one of the functions in the list.

CREATING EFFECTIVE FORMULAS

You can use formulas to quickly perform calculations on data. To use formulas effectively, keep in mind the following:

- **Keep formulas simple.**
  Use functions in place of long, complex formulas whenever possible. For example, use the SUM function instead of entering a formula that adds individual cells. This makes it easier to confirm that the formula is accurate.
- **Do not place important data in formulas.**
  The worksheet displays only formula results rather than the actual formulas with that important data. For example, the formula =0.05*A5 calculates a 5% sales tax on a price in cell A5, but hides the 5% tax rate. Instead, you should enter the tax rate in another cell, such as cell A4, with an appropriate label and use the formula =A4*A5 to calculate the sales tax. Readers can then see the tax rate as well as the resulting sales tax.
- **Break up formulas to show intermediate results.**
  Complex calculations should be split so that the different parts of the computation are easily distinguished and understood. For example, the formula =SUM(A1:A10)/SUM(B1:B10) calculates the ratio of two sums but hides the two sum values. Instead, enter each SUM function in a separate cell, such as cells A11 and B11, and use the formula =A11/B11 to calculate the ratio. Readers can see both sums and the value of their ratio in the worksheet and better understand the final result.

13-7 PREVIEWING AND PRINTING A WORKBOOK

When you have finished the final edit of the workbook, you might want to print a hard copy. However, before you print the workbook, you should preview it to ensure that it will print correctly.

EXHIBIT 13-28 WORKSHEET DISPLAYED IN PAGE LAYOUT VIEW

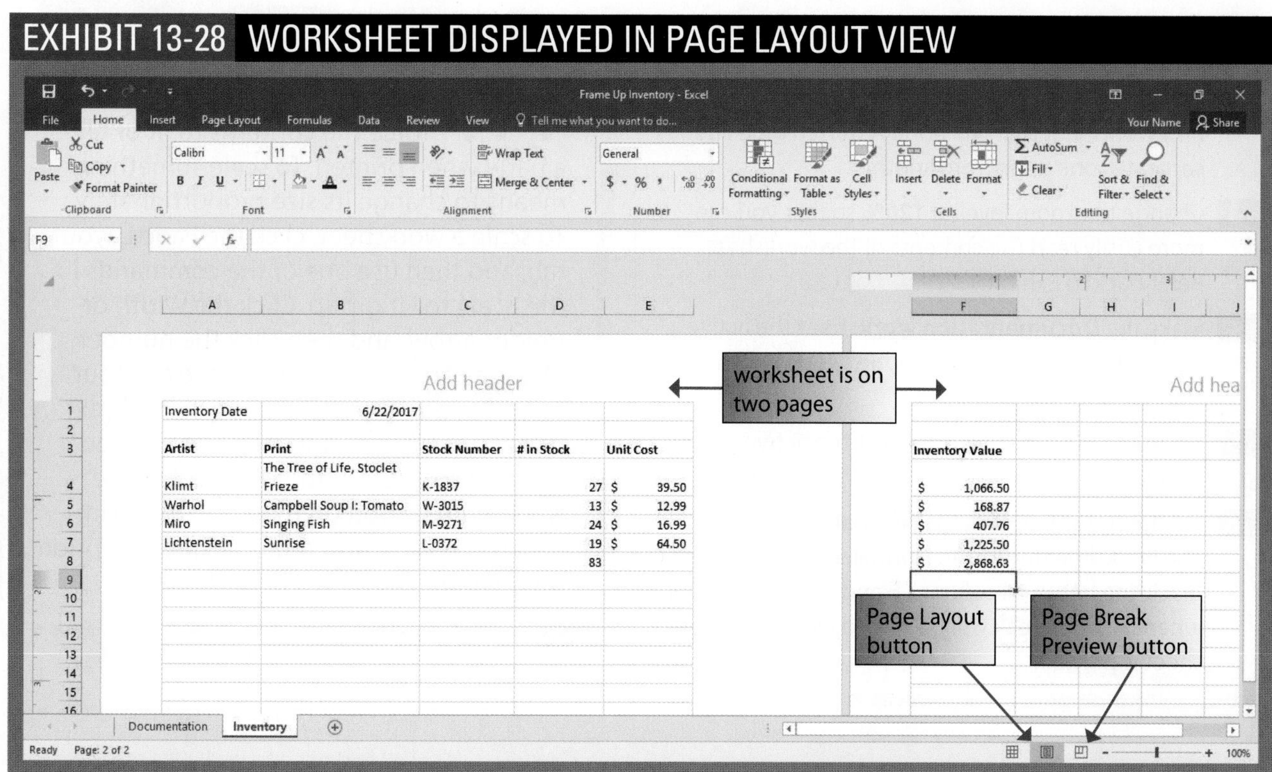

13-7a Changing Worksheet Views

You can view a worksheet in three ways. **Normal view**, which you have been using, simply shows the contents of the sheet. **Page Layout view**, shown in Exhibit 13-28, shows how the sheet will look when printed. **Page Break Preview**, shown in Exhibit 13-29, displays the location of page breaks within the worksheet. This is particularly useful when a worksheet will span several printed pages and you want to control what content appears on each page. The view buttons are located on the right edge of the status bar. You can also change the view by clicking the appropriate button in the Workbook Views group on the View tab.

EXHIBIT 13-29 WORKSHEET DISPLAYED IN PAGE BREAK PREVIEW

	A	B	C	D	E	F	G
1	Inventory Date	6/22/2017					
2							
3	Artist	Print	Stock Number	# in Stock	Unit Cost	Inventory Value	
4	Klimt	The Tree of Life, Stoclet Frieze	K-1837	27	$ 39.50	$ 1,066.50	
5	Warhol	Campbell Soup I: Tomato	W-3015	13	$ 12.99	$ 168.87	
6	Miro	Singing Fish	M-9271	24	$ 16.99	$ 407.76	
7	Lichtenstein	Sunrise	L-0372	19	$ 64.50	$ 1,225.50	
8				83		2,868.63	
9							
10							

Begin Activity

Change worksheet views.

1 On the right end of the status bar, click the **Page Layout button**. The page layout of the worksheet appears in the workspace. The data appears on two pages. Refer back to Exhibit 13-28.

Normal view The Excel view that shows the contents of the current sheet.

Page Layout view The Excel view that shows how the current sheet will look when printed.

Page Break Preview The Excel view that displays the location of page breaks within the worksheet.

2 On the status bar, click the **Page Break Preview button** [icon]. The view switches to Page Break Preview, which shows only those parts of the current worksheet that will print. A dotted blue line separates one page from another.

3 Change the zoom level to **120%** so that you can more easily read the contents of the worksheet. Refer back to Exhibit 13-29.

4 Make the **Documentation worksheet** the active sheet. The Documentation worksheet is still in Normal view.

5 Make the **Inventory worksheet** the active sheet.

6 On the status bar, click the **Normal button** [icon]. The worksheet returns to Normal view. The dotted black line between columns E and F indicates where a page break will be placed when the worksheet is printed.

End Activity

13-7b Changing the Orientation

You can adjust the worksheet so that it prints on a single page. The simplest way to accomplish this is to change the page orientation. By default, Excel displays pages in portrait orientation, where the page is taller than it is wide. In many cases, however, you will want to print the page in landscape orientation, where the page is wider than it is tall.

Begin Activity

Change the page orientation.

1 On the ribbon, click the **Page Layout tab.**

2 In the Page Setup group, click the **Orientation button.**

3 On the menu, click **Landscape.** The page orientation changes to landscape, and the dotted line moves to between columns I and J to indicate the new page break.

4 On the status bar, click the **Page Layout button** [icon]. The Inventory worksheet content now fits on one page.

5 On the status bar, click the **Normal button** [icon]. The worksheet is again in Normal view.

End Activity

FYI

SCALING A PRINTOUT

You can scale a worksheet to force the contents to fit or fill a page when printed. To scale something means to change its size proportionately. To scale a worksheet, click the Page Layout tab, and then use one of the commands in the Scale to Fit group. Click the Width or Height arrow, and then click the number of pages on which you want the printout to fit. Change the percentage in the Scale box to specify a custom percentage. You can also scale a printout by clicking the No Scaling button on the Print screen in Backstage view, and then clicking an option on the menu.

13-7c Previewing and Printing a Workbook

You can print the contents of a workbook using the Print screen in Backstage view. As shown in Exhibit 13-30, the Print screen provides options for choosing what and how to print. For example, you can specify the number of copies to print and which printer to use. You can print only the selected cells, the active sheets, or all of the worksheets in the workbook that contain data. The printout includes only the data in the worksheet. The other elements in the worksheet, such as the row and column headings and the gridlines around the cells, do not print. You also see a preview of the workbook so you can check exactly how the printed pages will look with the settings you selected before you print.

Begin Activity

Preview and print a workbook.

1 On the ribbon, click the **File tab.** In the navigation bar, click **Print.** The Print screen appears in Backstage view. Refer to Exhibit 13-30.

2 At the top of the left column, in the Copies box, make sure **1** appears so that only one copy of the workbook will print.

3 If the printer to which you want to print is not already listed in the Printer button, click the **Printer button,** and then click the desired printer.

EXHIBIT 13-30 PRINT SCREEN IN BACKSTAGE VIEW

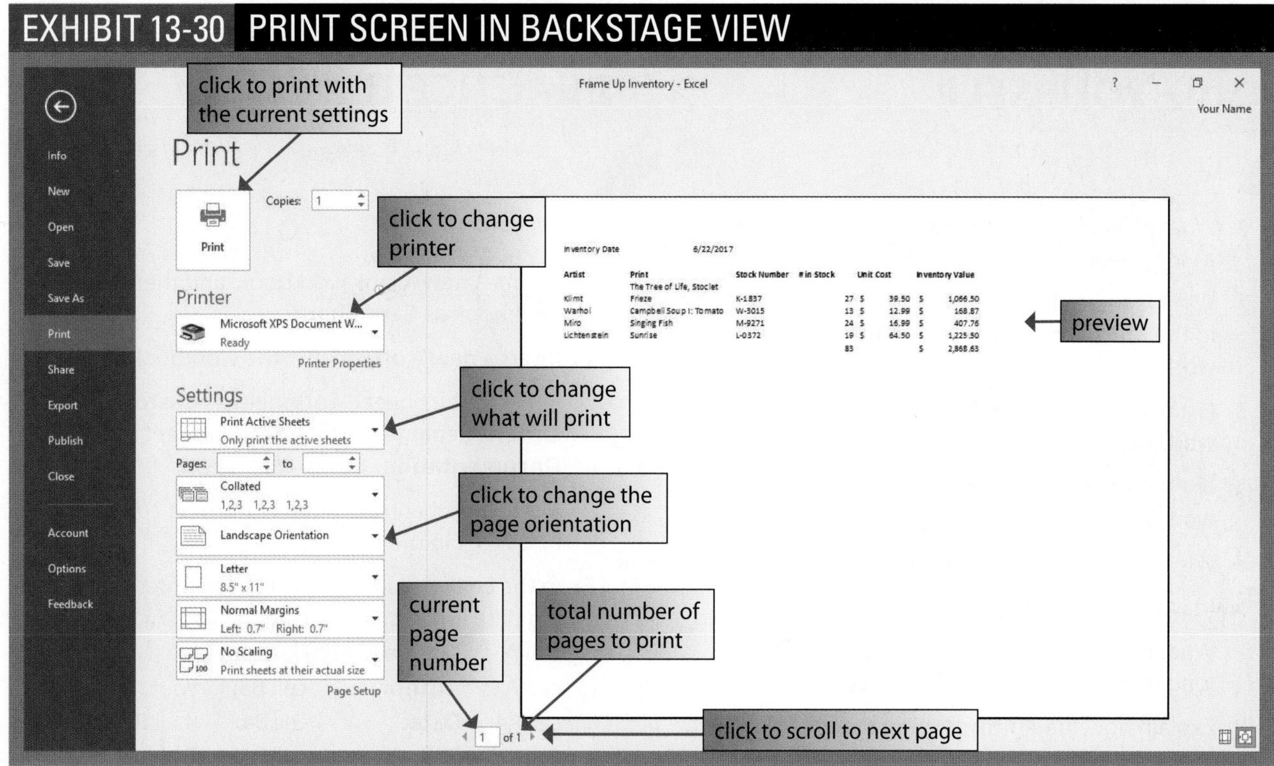

4 In the Settings group, click the **Print Active Sheets button**, and then click **Print Entire Workbook**. The preview changes to show the Documentation worksheet as the first page to be printed of two pages, and at the bottom, the page number indicator changes to show that there are now two pages to print. The Documentation worksheet is still in portrait orientation.

TIP: You can also choose to print only the selected cells, the active sheet (or sheets), or all the worksheets in the workbook that contain data.

5 Below the preview, click the **Next Page button** ▸. The second page—the Inventory worksheet in landscape orientation—appears in the preview. Refer to Exhibit 13-30.

6 At the top of the Print screen, click the **Print button**. The workbook is sent to the printer, and Backstage view closes.

PROBLEM? If you don't want to print the workbook, click the Back button at the top of the navigation bar.

7 Save and close the workbook.

End Activity

STUDY TOOLS 13

READY TO STUDY? IN THE BOOK, YOU CAN:

- ☐ Rip out the Chapter Review Card, which includes key terms and key chapter concepts.

ONLINE AT WWW.CENGAGEBRAIN.COM, YOU CAN:

- ☐ Review key concepts from the chapter in a short video.
- ☐ Explore creating a workbook in Excel with the interactive infographic.
- ☐ Practice what you've learned with more Practice It and On Your Own exercises.
- ☐ Prepare for tests with quizzes.
- ☐ Review the key terms with flashcards.

QUIZ YOURSELF

1. What is the difference between a workbook and a worksheet?
2. What is the cell reference for the cell located in the fourth column and seventh row of a worksheet?
3. List two ways of identifying the active cell in the worksheet.
4. List the three types of data you can enter into a worksheet.
5. Why would you want to format a worksheet?
6. In what two places can you edit cell content?
7. What happens when text entered in a cell is too long to be fully displayed in that cell?
8. Explain how the AutoFit feature works.
9. Describe the difference between clearing data and deleting data.
10. Describe the two types of cell ranges in Excel.
11. What is the range reference for cells A1 through A5 and cells F1 through G5?
12. How can you force text that extends beyond a cell's border to fit within the cell?
13. What is a formula?
14. Write the formula that adds the values in cells C4 and E9 and then divides the sum by the value in cell A2.
15. What is a function? Why are functions used?
16. What formula would you enter to add the values in cells C4, C5, and C6? What function would you enter to achieve the same result?
17. What view shows how the sheet will look when printed?

PRACTICE IT

Practice It 13-1

1. Create a new, blank workbook, and then save the workbook as **Card Shark**.
2. Insert a new worksheet in the workbook.
3. Rename the Sheet1 worksheet as **Customer Orders**. Rename the Sheet2 worksheet as **Documentation**.
4. Move the Documentation worksheet so it is the first sheet in the workbook.
5. In the Documentation worksheet, enter the following data in the cells specified:
   cell A1: **The Card Shark**
   cell A3: **Author:** cell B3: your name
   cell A4: **Date:** cell B4: the current date
   cell A5: **Purpose:** cell B5: **To track online customer orders**
6. Format cell A1 so the text is 20-point Calibri Light (Headings), bold, and the Blue standard color.
7. In the Customer Orders worksheet, enter the following labels in the cells specified:
   cell A1: **Last Name**
   cell B1: **First Name**
   cell C1: **Cards**
   cell D1: **Price per Card**
   cell E1: **Total Charge**
8. In the Customer Orders worksheet, enter the following customer names:
   cell A2: **Landers** cell B2: **Nellie**
   cell A3: **Maxwell** cell B3: **Sam**
   cell A4: **Jones** cell B4: **Frank**
   cell A5: **Neemer** cell B5: **Macey**
   cell A6: **Parker** cell B6: **Tracy**
9. In the Customer Orders worksheet, enter the following order quantities and charges:
   cell C2: **14** cell D2: **2.99**
   cell C3: **22** cell D3: **3.49**
   cell C4: **2** cell D4: **3.79**
   cell C5: **8** cell D5: **3.99**
   cell C6: **37** cell D6: **2.39**

10. Format the values in the range D2:D6 in the Accounting format.
11. Edit the contents of cell C1 to **Number of Cards**. Edit the contents of cell C2 to **17**.
12. Insert a new column A.
13. Enter the following data into the new column A (make sure you do not type a period after the abbreviation for August):
    cell A1: **Order Date**
    cell A2: **July 30, 2017**
    cell A3: **Aug 4, 2017**
    cell A4: **Aug 8, 2017**
    cell A5: **Aug 9, 2017**
    cell A6: **Aug 17, 2017**
14. Format the dates in the range A2:A6 in the Short Date format.
15. Set the width of columns A, B, and C to 14 characters. AutoFit the contents of columns D, E, and F.
16. Clear the data from row 4, and then delete the row.
17. Select the range A1:F5. Use drag and drop or cut and paste to move the selected range to range A4:F8.
18. In cell A1, enter **Online Customer Orders**. In cell A2, enter **July 30 to August 17**.
19. Wrap the text in cell A2.
20. Format the range A4:F4 as bold.
21. In cell F5, enter a formula that multiplies the number of cards in cell D5 by the price per card in cell E5 to calculate the total charge for the customer in row 5.
22. Copy the formula in cell F5, and then paste it into cells F6, F7, and F8.
23. In cell D9, enter the SUM function to add the total number of cards ordered.
24. In cell F9, use AutoSum to enter the SUM function to calculate the total charge for all of the customer orders.
25. View the worksheet in Page Layout view and Page Break Preview. Return to Normal view.
26. Change the page orientation of the Customer Orders worksheet to landscape.
27. Print the entire workbook.
28. Save the workbook, and then close it.

Practice It 13-2

1. Open the data file **Eco-Harvest** located in the Chapter 13\Practice It folder. Save the workbook as **Eco-Harvest Paper**.
2. At the top of the Sheet1 worksheet, insert three new rows.
3. In cell A1, enter the text **Eco-Harvest Paper Company Income Statement***. (The asterisk is a footnote reference to the note in cell A27.)
4. In cell A2, enter the text **For the years ending December 31, 2015 through December 31, 2017**.
5. In the range C6:E7, enter the following net sales and cost of sales:
    cell C6: **20320**
    cell C7: **6423**
    cell D6: **17518**
    cell D7: **6159**
    cell E6: **15293**
    cell E7: **5460**
6. In the range C11:E14, enter the following expenses:
    cell C11: **2018**
    cell C12: **3357**
    cell C13: **733**
    cell C14: **702**

    cell D11: **1832**
    cell D12: **2678**
    cell D13: **607**
    cell D14: **522**

    cell E11: **1684**
    cell E12: **2261**
    cell E13: **574**
    cell E14: **299**
7. In the nonadjacent range C18:E18;C20:E20; C24:E24, enter the following values for Other Income, Income Taxes, and Shares:
    cell C18: **629**
    cell D18: **513**
    cell E18: **303**

    cell C20: **1706**
    cell D20: **1435**
    cell E20: **1086**

    cell C24: **4037**
    cell D24: **3037**
    cell E24: **2783**
8. Format the values you entered in the range C6:E7;C11:E14;C18:E18;C20:E20 in the Accounting format with no decimal places. Format the values in the range C24:E24 in the Comma Style format with no decimal places.

9. Expand column A to 17 characters, and then AutoFit column B.
10. In the range C8:E8, enter a formula to calculate the gross margin for each year, where the gross margin is equal to the net sales minus the cost of sales.
11. In the range C15:E15, enter the SUM function to calculate the total operating expenses for each year, where the total operating expenses equal the sum of the four expense categories.
12. In the range C17:E17, enter a formula to calculate the operating income for each year, where operating income is equal to the gross margin minus the total operating expenses.
13. In the range C19:E19, enter a formula to calculate the pretax income for each year, where pretax income is equal to the operating income plus other income.
14. In the range C22:E22, enter a formula to calculate the company's net income for each year, where net income is equal to the pretax income minus income taxes.
15. In the range C25:E25, enter a formula to calculate the earnings per share for each year, where earnings per share is equal to the net income divided by the number of shares. Format the results with the Accounting format and two decimal places.
16. AutoFit columns C, D, and E.
17. Edit the contents of cell A18 to capitalize the word *income*.
18. Format cell A1 so it is 12-point Arial Rounded MT Bold. Format cell A2 with italics. Format the nonadjacent range A4:A25;C4:E4 with bold.
19. Rename the Sheet1 worksheet as **Income Statement**.
20. Insert a new sheet, rename the worksheet as **Documentation**, and then move it to the beginning of the workbook.
21. In the Documentation worksheet, enter the following text and values:

cell A1:	**Eco-Harvest Paper Company**		
cell A3:	**Author:**	cell B3:	your name
cell A4:	**Date:**	cell B4:	the current date
cell A5:	**Purpose:**	cell B5:	**To create an income statement for Eco-Harvest Paper Company for 2015 through 2017**

22. Format the company name in cell A1 so it is 20-point Arial Rounded MT Bold and the Green, Accent 6, Darker 25% color. Format the date in cell B4 with the Long Date format.
23. View each worksheet in Page Layout view, making sure each worksheet fits on one page in portrait orientation. Do not switch back to Normal view.
24. Print the entire workbook.
25. Save the workbook, and then close it.

ON YOUR OWN

On Your Own 13-1

1. Open the data file **Pizza** located in the Chapter 13\On Your Own folder. Save the workbook as **Pizza Palace**.
2. Rename the Sheet1 worksheet as **Pizza Sales**.
3. Insert 12 rows at the top of the Pizza Sales worksheet. (*Hint:* Select rows 1 through 12 before using the Insert command.)
4. Increase the width of column A to 18 characters and increase the width of columns B through G to 14 characters.
5. Copy the contents of the range B13:G13. Paste the contents of the Clipboard in the range B7:G7.
6. In the range A8:A11, enter the following data:
   cell A8: **Pizza Sales**
   cell A9: **Average per Month**
   cell A10: **Maximum**
   cell A11: **Minimum**
7. Select the range B26:G26, and then use AutoSum to calculate the sum of the pizzas sales in each of the six restaurants.
8. Drag and drop the calculated values that are in the range B26:G26 to the range B8:G8. Notice that the formulas still show the original results because the cell references in the function did not change when you moved the range.

9. Select the range B26:G26, and then use AutoSum to calculate the average sales of pizzas served in each of the six restaurants. (*Hint:* Click the AutoSum button arrow to access additional functions.)
10. Drag and drop the calculated values that are in the range B26:G26 to the range B9:G9.
11. Select the range B26:G26, and then use AutoSum to calculate the maximum sales of pizzas served in each of the six restaurants. Move the calculated values in the range B26:G26 to the range B10:G10.
12. Select the range B26:G26, and then use AutoSum to calculate the minimum sales of pizzas served in each of the six restaurants. Move the calculated values in the range B26:G26 to the range B11:G11.
13. Enter the following data:
    cell A1: **Pizza Palace**
    cell A2: **Annual Sales Report**
    cell A3: **Year:**
    cell A4: **Total Sales**
    cell B3: **2016**
14. In cell B4, use the SUM function to add the values in the range B8:G8.
15. Format the nonadjacent range B7:G7;B13:G13;A8:A25 with bold.
16. Change the theme to Berlin, and then format cell A1 so it is 20 points and the Brown, Text 2 color.
17. Insert a new worksheet. Rename the worksheet as **Restaurant Directory**.
18. In the Restaurant Directory worksheet, enter the following data:
    cell A1: **Pizza Palace**
    cell A2: **Restaurant Directory**
19. In the range A4:D9, enter the following data:

Restaurant	**Manager**	**Location**	**Phone**
1	**Quinn Stevens**	**58 Maple Drive**	**555-3585**
2	**Eva Langdon**	**4514 Carroll Avenue**	**555-3728**
3	**Ari Silverton**	**525 Sandy Street**	**555-4093**
4	**Gretchen Smith**	**3654 Foster Lane**	**555-7831**
5	**Ellen Izzary**	**1087 Capital Boulevard**	**555-6117**

20. Format the labels in row 4 as bold.
21. Set the widths of columns A through D so that all of the data is visible. (*Hint:* Column A should be wide enough to display the Restaurant heading in row 3 but not fit the contents in cells A1 and A2.
22. Copy the formatting of cell A1 in the Pizza Sales worksheet to cell A1 in the Restaurant Directory worksheet.
23. Insert a new worksheet in the workbook. Rename the inserted sheet as **Documentation**. Move the Documentation worksheet to be the first sheet in the workbook.
24. In the Documentation worksheet, enter appropriate data to record the company name, yourself as the author, the current date, and the purpose of the workbook.
25. View each sheet in the workbook in Page Layout view, and change the page orientation as needed so that each sheet fits on a single page. Do not switch back to Normal view.
26. Print the entire workbook.
27. Save the workbook, and then close it.

Part 7
EXCEL 2016

14 | Working with Formulas and Functions

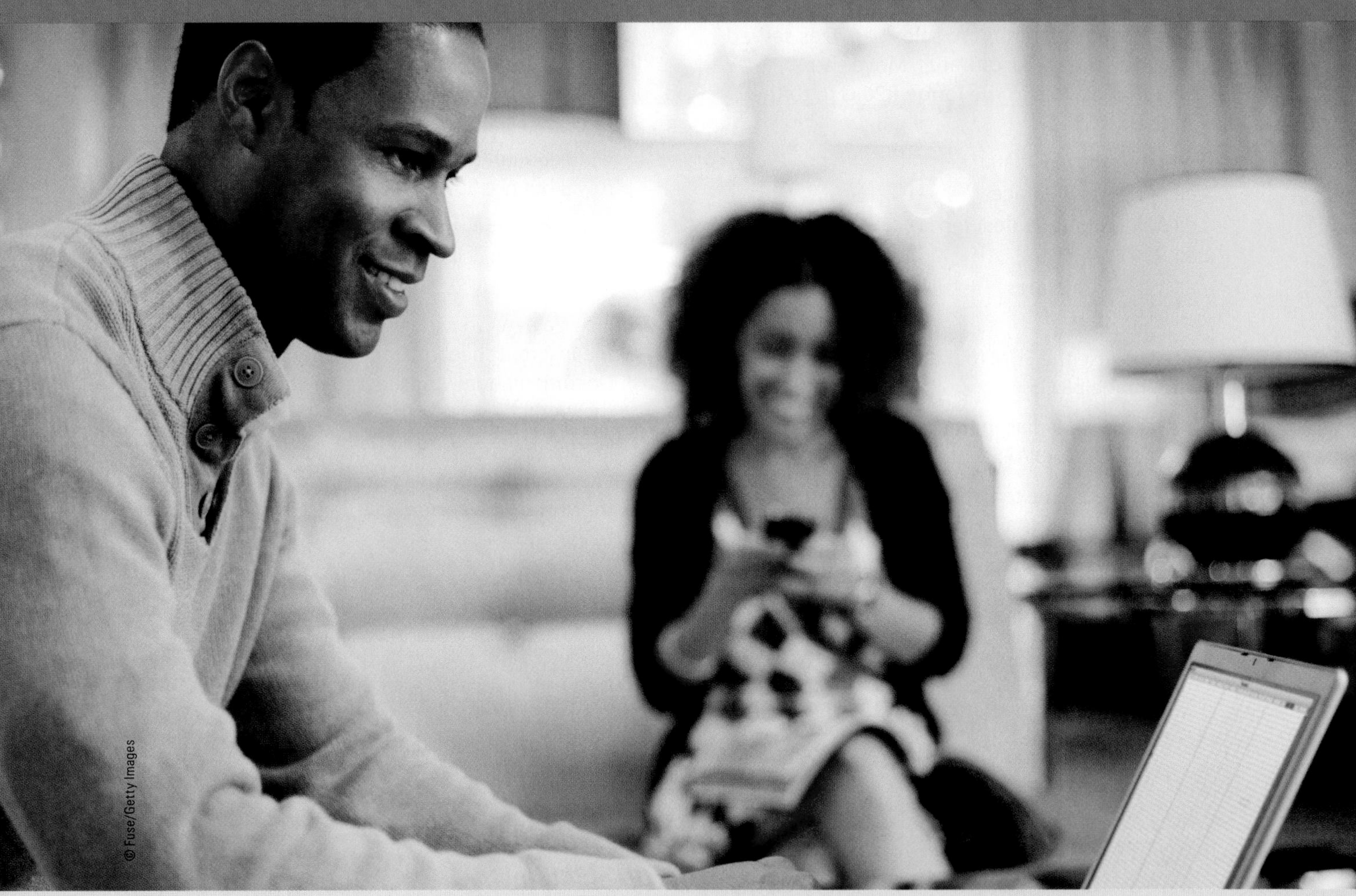

© Fuse/Getty Images

LEARNING OBJECTIVES After studying the material in this chapter, you will be able to:

- 14-1 Use relative, absolute, and mixed cell references in formulas
- 14-2 Enter functions
- 14-3 Use AutoFill
- 14-4 Work with date functions
- 14-5 Work with the PMT financial function
- 14-6 Use references to another worksheet
- 14-7 Edit formulas and functions
- 14-8 Format cells and ranges

After finishing this chapter, go to **PAGE 444** for **STUDY TOOLS**.

14-1 USING RELATIVE, ABSOLUTE, AND MIXED CELL REFERENCES IN FORMULAS

Most Excel workbooks are created to record and analyze data. Formulas and functions make it simpler and more accurate to perform this analysis. To do this effectively, you enter data in cells in a worksheet and then reference those cells in formulas that perform calculations on that data, such as adding a column of numbers as part of a budget. Referencing cells prevents errors that could occur if you retype data. Referencing cells also means that you can change data in one place and the new data is automatically used in calculations that reference that data.

One of the most powerful aspects of Excel is being able to copy formulas between cells. This allows you to enter a formula one time and then use that same formula throughout a workbook. When you paste the formula, sometimes you will want the cell references in the formula to change according to the new location in the spreadsheet. Other times, you will want the cell references to stay the same as they were in the original formula. You can control whether cell references change by how you enter them.

Begin Activity

Use cell references in a formula.

1. Open the data file **Budget** located in the Chapter 14\Chapter folder. Save the workbook as **Willis Budget**.
2. In the **Documentation worksheet**, enter your name in **cell B3** and the date in **cell B4**.
3. Make the **Budget worksheet** the active sheet. Set the zoom to **120%**, if necessary, and then review its contents.
4. Select the **range B9:C9**.
5. On the Home tab, in the Editing group, click the **AutoSum button**. The SUM function is inserted in both cells, and the estimated income is calculated for the school and summer months. Compare your screen to Exhibit 14-1.

TIP: Remember to save frequently as you work through the chapter. A good practice is to save after every Activity.

End Activity

EXHIBIT 14-1 MONTHLY INCOME ESTIMATES

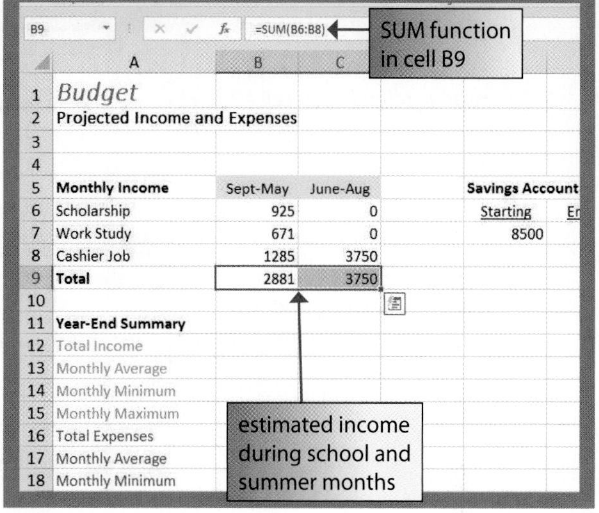

	A	B	C		
1	Budget				
2	Projected Income and Expenses				
3					
4					
5	Monthly Income	Sept-May	June-Aug		Savings Account
6	Scholarship	925	0		Starting	Er
7	Work Study	671	0		8500
8	Cashier Job	1285	3750		
9	Total	2881	3750		
10					
11	Year-End Summary				
12	Total Income				
13	Monthly Average				
14	Monthly Minimum				
15	Monthly Maximum				
16	Total Expenses				
17	Monthly Average				
18	Monthly Minimum				

14-1a Using Relative References

So far, you have used relative cell references in formulas. A **relative reference** is always interpreted in relation, or relative, to the location of the cell containing the formula. For example, when you entered the formula in cell B9 to sum the income for the school months, Excel interprets the cell references in that formula relative to the location of cell B9. In other words, Excel interprets the formula =SUM(B6:B8) as adding the values entered in the three cells directly above cell B9.

If the formula is moved or copied to other cells, Excel uses this same interpretation of the cell references. You saw this in Chapter 13 when you copied the formula that calculated the value of the inventory value of a print and then pasted the copied formula into other cells in the column to calculate the values of the inventory of the rest of the prints.

Exhibit 14-2 illustrates how a relative reference in a formula changes when the formula is copied to another group of cells. In this figure, the formula =A2 entered in cell C5 displays 10, which is the value entered in cell A2. When pasted to a new location, each of the pasted formulas contains a reference to a cell that is three rows up and three rows to the left of the current cell's location.

relative reference A cell reference that is interpreted in relation to the location of the cell containing the formula.

EXHIBIT 14-2 FORMULAS USING RELATIVE REFERENCES

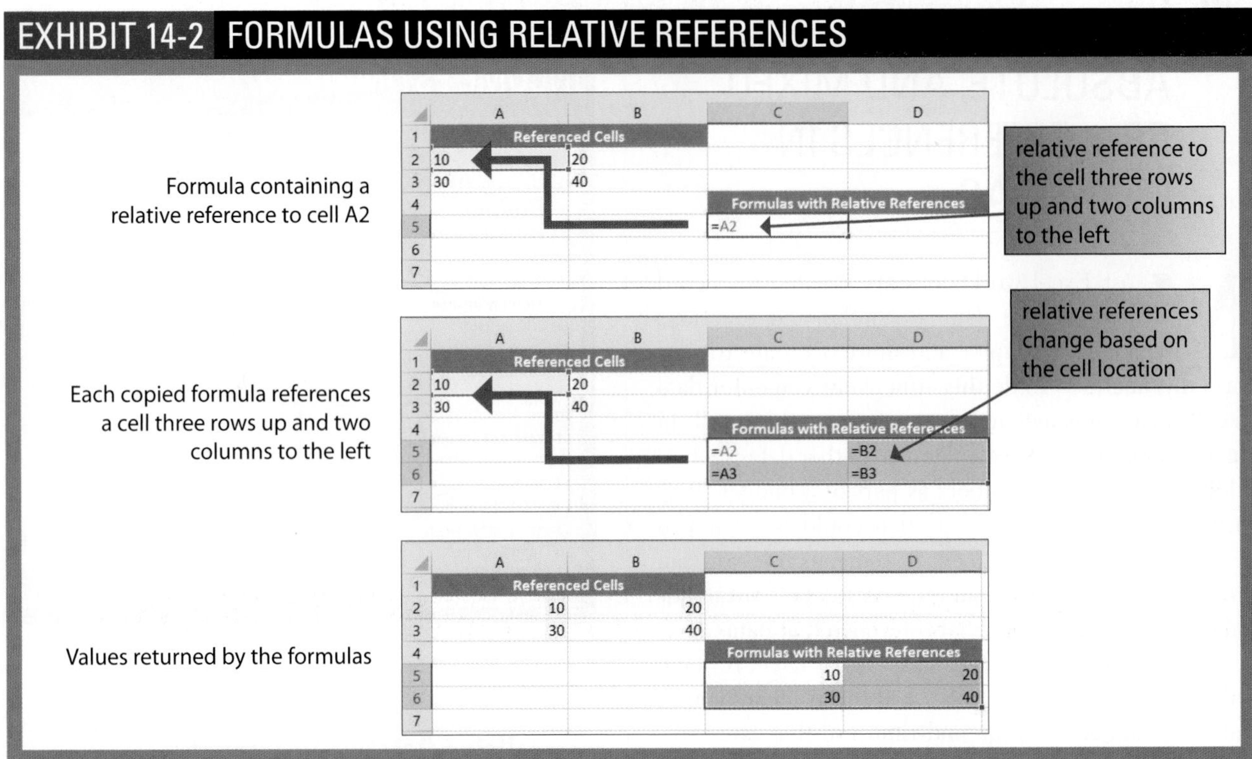

Begin Activity

Use relative references in formulas.

1 Scroll down to view the **range A26:M34**. This range lists the estimated monthly expenses by category for the coming year.

2 In **cell B34**, enter the formula **=SUM(B26:B33)**. Cell B34 displays −9270, January's estimated expenses.

TIP: You can type the SUM function or use the AutoSum button.

3 Copy the formula in **cell B34** to the Clipboard. You can copy cell contents to more than one cell at once.

4 Select the **range C34:M34**. On the Home tab, in the Clipboard group, click the **Paste button**. The formula in cell B34 is pasted in each of the cells in the selected range to calculate the estimated monthly expenses for the rest of the year. Compare your screen to Exhibit 14-3.

5 Review the total expenses for each month. Notice that January and August are particularly expensive months because the expenses include both tuition and the purchase of books for the upcoming semester.

6 Click each cell in the **range B34:M34** and review the formula entered in the cell. The formulas all calculate the sums of the values in the cells above them, so the cell references are different in each formula. For example, the formula =SUM(C26:C33) was inserted in cell C34, the formula =SUM(D26:D33) was inserted in cell D34, and so forth.

End Activity

FYI

LISTING EXPENSES AS NEGATIVE NUMBERS

In a checkbook ledger, most people list expenses (that is, money spent) as positive numbers that they subtract from the running total. In a worksheet, however, it is usually better practice to list expenses as negative numbers. Whether the expenses are entered as positive or negative numbers, you can add all of the expenses to calculate the total. If the expenses are entered as positive numbers, you need to subtract the expenses from the income to calculate the difference between income and expenses. If the expenses are entered as negative numbers, you can add the negative expenses to the positive income to calculate the difference between them.

EXHIBIT 14-3 TOTAL MONTHLY EXPENSES

C34 =SUM(C26:C33)

	A	B	C	D	E	F	G	H	I	J	K	L	M
21	Income / Expenses	Jan	Feb	Mar	Apr	May	Jun	Jul	Aug	Sep	Oct	Nov	Dec
22	Scholarship												
23	Work Study												
24	Cashier Job												
25	Total												
26	Rent	-785	-785	-785	-785	-785	-785	-785	-785	-785	-785	-785	-785
27	Food	-285	-285	-285	-285	-285	-285	-285	-285	-285	-285	-285	-285
28	Utilities	-115	-105	-90	-85	-70	-75	-80	-75	-70	-70	-90	-105
29	Internet	-145	-145	-145	-145	-145	-145	-145	-145	-145	-145	-145	-145
30	Clothes	-50	-50	-50	-50	-150	-50	-50	-250	-50	-50	-150	-50
31	Tuition	-6575	0	0	0	0	-1350	0	-5900	0	0	0	0
32	Books & Supplies	-1095	0	0	0	0	-475	0	-875	0	0	0	0
33	Travel/Entertainment	-220	-160	-170	-520	-170	-190	-920	-550	-155	-225	-315	-385
34	Total	-9270	-1530	-1525	-1870	-1605	-3355	-2265	-8865	-1490	-1560	-1770	-1755
35	Balance												
36													

monthly totals

EXHIBIT 14-4 FORMULAS USING ABSOLUTE REFERENCES

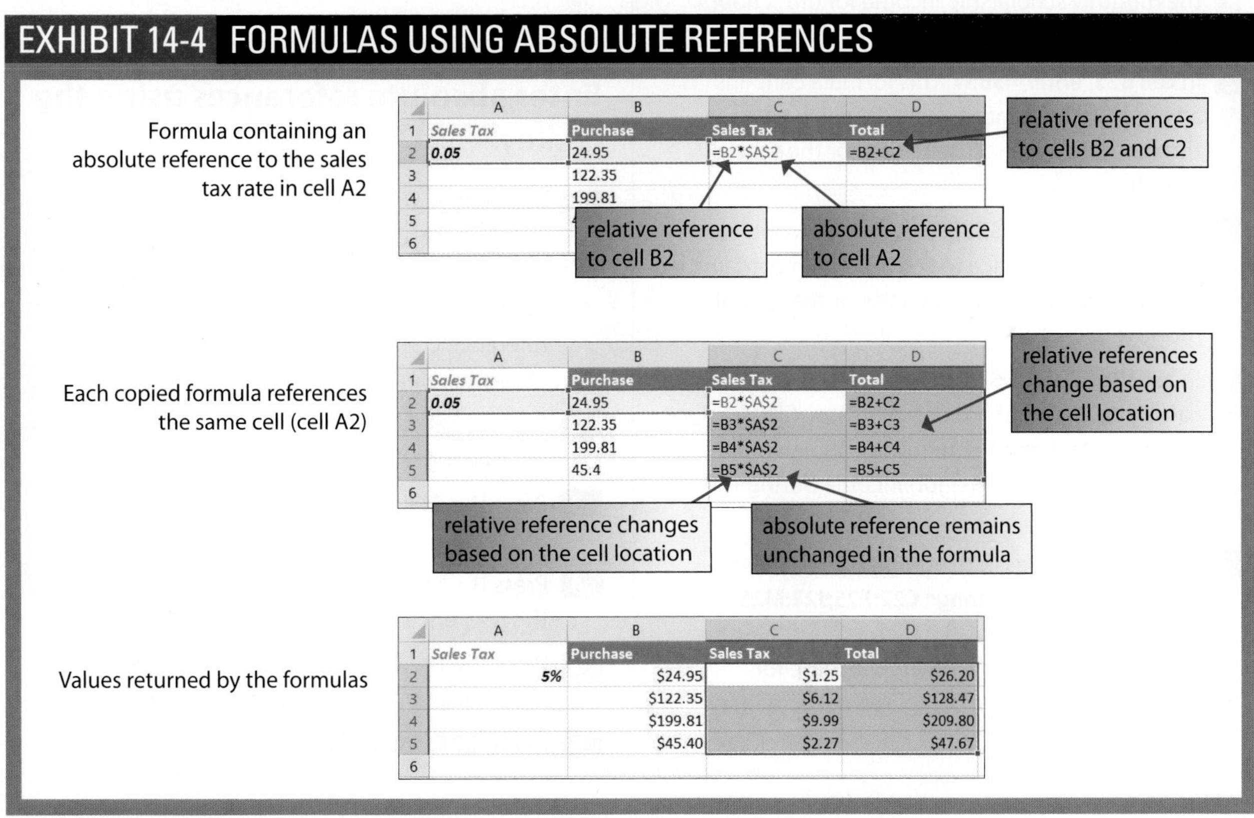

14-1b Using Absolute References

Cell references that remain fixed when a formula is copied to a new location are called **absolute references**. In Excel, absolute references have a $ (dollar sign) before each column and row designation. For example, B8 is a relative reference to cell B8, but $B$8 is an absolute reference to cell B8. When you copy a formula that contains an absolute reference to a new location, the reference does not change.

Exhibit 14-4 shows an example of how copying a formula with an absolute reference results in the same cell reference being pasted in different cells regardless of their location. In this figure, the sales tax of different purchases is calculated and displayed. All items have

absolute reference A cell reference that remains fixed when copied to a new location.

the same 5 percent tax rate, which is stored in cell A2, applied to the purchase. The sales tax and the total cost of the first item are calculated in cells C2 and D2, respectively. When those formulas are copied and pasted to the remaining purchases, the relative references in the formulas change to point to the new location of the purchase cost; the sales tax rate continues to point to cell A2, regardless of the cell in which the formula is pasted.

Begin Activity

Use absolute references in formulas.

1. In **cell B22**, enter **=$B$6**. This formula contains an absolute reference to cell B6, which contains the monthly scholarship income for the school months.
2. In **cell B23**, enter **=$B$7**. This formula contains an absolute reference to cell B7, which contains the monthly work study income for the school months.
3. In **cell B24**, enter **=$B$8**. This formula contains an absolute reference to cell B8, which contains the monthly restaurant income for the school months.
4. In **cell B25**, enter **=SUM(B22:B24)**. This formula calculates the total projected income for January by adding the monthly scholarship, work study, and cashier job income during the school months.
5. Copy the formulas in the **range B22:B25**, and paste them into the **range C22:F25;J22:M25**. February through May and September through December show the estimated income for those school months. Compare your screen to Exhibit 14-5.
6. Click each cell in the **range C22:F24;J22:M24**, and verify that the copied formulas contain the absolute cell references $B$6, $B$7, and $B$8.

End Activity

Instead of entering an absolute reference in a cell by typing dollar signs, you can type just the column letter and row number, and then press the F4 key to change the reference to an absolute reference. Pressing the F4 key adds a dollar sign in front of both the column letter and row number to change both references to absolute. If you continue to press the F4 key, first the dollar sign is removed from in front of the column letter, then the dollar sign is added back in front of the column reference, but it is removed from in front of the row reference, then the dollar signs are removed completely.

Begin Activity

Enter absolute references using the F4 key.

1. In **cell G22**, type **=C6** and then press the **F4 key**. Cell C6 contains the income from work study during the summer months. The cell reference changes to =$C$6, an absolute reference.
2. Press the **F4 key** again. The reference changes to =C$6.
3. Press the **F4 key** again to change the reference to =$C6.
4. Press the **F4 key** again to change the reference to =C6.
5. Press the **F4 key** once more to change the reference back to =$C$6. Press the **Enter key**.
6. In **cell G23**, enter **=$C$7**.

PROBLEM?
If the cell reference did not change to an absolute reference, press the **F Lock key**, and then press the **F4 key** again. If the cell reference still does not change, retype it by typing the dollar signs.

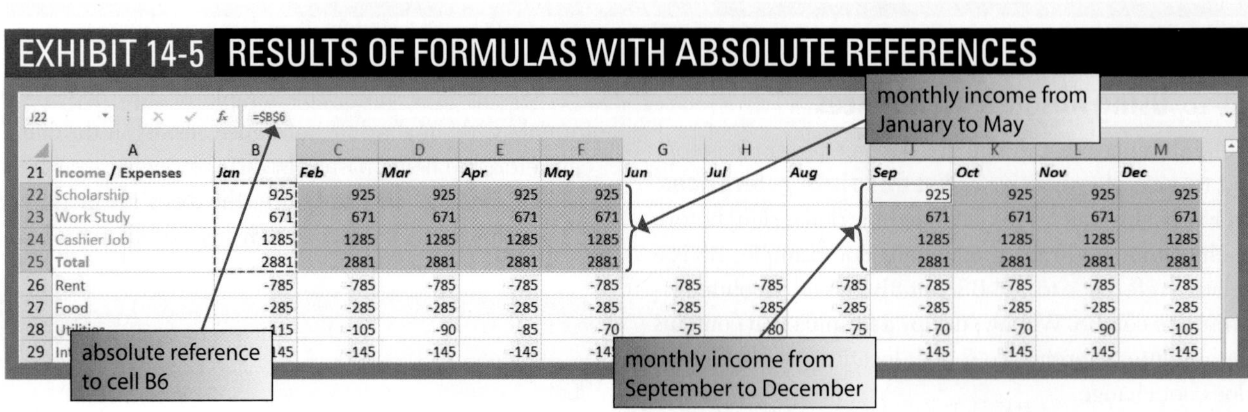
EXHIBIT 14-5 RESULTS OF FORMULAS WITH ABSOLUTE REFERENCES

J22 =$B$6

	A	B	C	D	E	F	G	H	I	J	K	L	M
21	Income / Expenses	Jan	Feb	Mar	Apr	May	Jun	Jul	Aug	Sep	Oct	Nov	Dec
22	Scholarship	925	925	925	925	925				925	925	925	925
23	Work Study	671	671	671	671	671				671	671	671	671
24	Cashier Job	1285	1285	1285	1285	1285				1285	1285	1285	1285
25	Total	2881	2881	2881	2881	2881				2881	2881	2881	2881
26	Rent	-785	-785	-785	-785	-785	-785	-785	-785	-785	-785	-785	-785
27	Food	-285	-285	-285	-285	-285	-285	-285	-285	-285	-285	-285	-285
28	Ut	115	-105	-90	-85	-70	-75	80	-75	-70	-70	-90	-105
29	In	45	-145	-145	-145	-14				-145	-145	-145	-145

7 In **cell G24**, enter **=$C$8.**

8 In **cell G25**, enter the formula **=SUM(G22:G24).** This formula adds the work study, scholarship, and restaurant income during June to calculate a total of 3750.

9 Copy the **range G22:G25** to the Clipboard. Paste the copied formulas into the **range H22:I25**. The total income is added for the months of June through August.

End Activity

FYI WHEN TO USE RELATIVE, ABSOLUTE, AND MIXED REFERENCES

An important part of effective formula writing is using the correct type of cell reference. Keep in mind the following when choosing whether to use relative, absolute, or mixed cell references:

- **Relative references**—use relative references, such as L17, when you want to repeat the same formula with cells in different locations on your worksheet. Relative references are commonly used when copying a formula that sums a column of numbers or that calculates the cost of several items by multiplying the item cost by the quantity being purchased.
- **Absolute references**—use absolute references, such as $L$17, when you want different formulas to refer to the same cell. This usually occurs when a cell contains a constant value, such as a tax rate, that will be used in formulas throughout the worksheet.
- **Mixed references**—mixed references, such as $L17 and L$17, are seldom used other than when creating tables of calculated values such as a multiplication table in which the values of the formula or function can be found in the initial rows and columns of the table.

14-1c Using Mixed References

When you pressed the F4 key the second and third time in the previous Activity, you created cell references that contained both a relative reference and an absolute reference. This is called a **mixed reference**. In a mixed reference, the reference to the part of the reference with the dollar sign in front of it is absolute, and the reference to the part of the reference without the dollar sign in front of it is relative. For example, in the mixed reference A$2, the column reference is relative and the row reference is absolute, and in the mixed reference $A2, the column reference is absolute and the row reference is relative. When you copy and paste a formula with a mixed reference to a new location, the absolute portion of the cell reference remains fixed and the relative portion shifts.

Exhibit 14-6 shows an example of using mixed references to complete a multiplication table. The first cell in the table, cell B3, contains the formula =$A3*B$2, which multiplies the first column entry (A3) by the first row entry (B2), returning 1. When this formula is copied to another cell, the absolute portions of the cell references remain unchanged and the relative portions of the references change. For example, if the formula is copied to cell E6, the first mixed cell reference changes to $A6 because the column reference is absolute and the row reference is relative, and the second cell reference changes to E$2 because the row reference is absolute and the column reference is relative. The result is that cell E6 contains the formula =$A6*E$2 and returns 16. Other cells in the multiplication table are similarly modified so that each entry returns the multiplication of the row and column headings.

Begin Activity

Enter formulas with mixed references.

1 Make the **Savings Plan worksheet** the active sheet.

2 In **cell B5**, enter **=$A5*B$4.** This formula uses mixed references to calculate the amount of savings generated by saving $50 per month (cell B4) for 12 months (cell A5). The calculated value $600 is displayed. The value is formatted as Currency with no decimal places because the value in cell B4 is formatted that way.

mixed reference A cell reference that contains both an absolute reference and a relative reference.

EXHIBIT 14-6 MULTIPLICATION TABLE USING MIXED REFERENCES

Formula with mixed cell references multiplies the first row by the first column

	A	B	C	D	E	F
1	Multiplication Table					
2		1	2	3	4	5
3	1	=$A3*B$2				
4	2					
5	3					
6	4					
7	5					
8						

Each copied formula multiplies the first row entries by the first column entries

	A	B	C	D	E	F
1	Multiplication Table					
2		1	2	3	4	5
3	1	=$A3*B$2	=$A3*C$2	=$A3*D$2	=$A3*E$2	=$A3*F$2
4	2	=$A4*B$2	=$A4*C$2	=$A4*D$2	=$A4*E$2	=$A4*F$2
5	3	=$A5*B$2	=$A5*C$2	=$A5*D$2	=$A5*E$2	=$A5*F$2
6	4	=$A6*B$2	=$A6*C$2	=$A6*D$2	=$A6*E$2	=$A6*F$2
7	5	=$A7*B$2	=$A7*C$2	=$A7*D$2	=$A7*E$2	=$A7*F$2
8						

Values returned by the formulas

	A	B	C	D	E	F
1	Multiplication Table					
2		1	2	3	4	5
3	1	1	2	3	4	5
4	2	2	4	6	8	10
5	3	3	6	9	12	15
6	4	4	8	12	16	20
7	5	5	10	15	20	25
8						

3 Copy the formula in **cell B5** to the Clipboard. You need to paste this formula into the range B6:B7 and the range C5:G7. Instead, you can select the cell that contains the formula you are copying as part of the range you will paste to.

4 Select the **range B5:G7**, and then in the Clipboard group, click the **Paste button**. The pasted formulas calculate total savings over 12, 24, and 36 months for deposits ranging from $50 to $200 per month.

5 Click the **Esc key** to remove the contents of the Clipboard. Compare your screen to Exhibit 14-7.

End Activity

syntax A set of rules.

argument The numbers, text, or cell references used by a function to return a value.

optional argument An argument that is not required for the function to return a value but provides more control over how the returned value is calculated.

EXHIBIT 14-7 COMPLETED SAVINGS PLAN

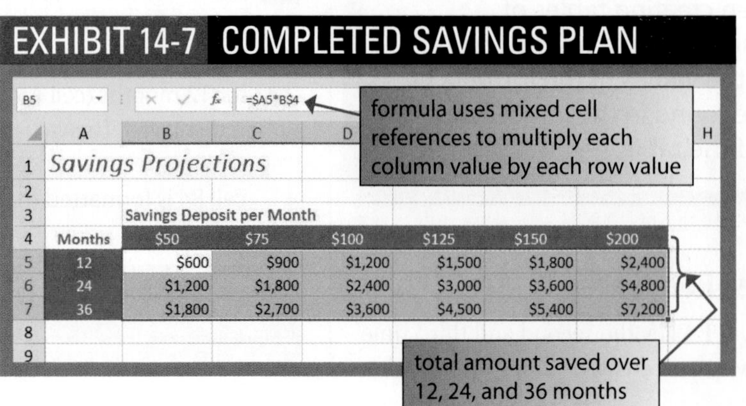

	A	B	C	D	E	F	G
1	Savings Projections						
2							
3		Savings Deposit per Month					
4	Months	$50	$75	$100	$125	$150	$200
5	12	$600	$900	$1,200	$1,500	$1,800	$2,400
6	24	$1,200	$1,800	$2,400	$3,000	$3,600	$4,800
7	36	$1,800	$2,700	$3,600	$4,500	$5,400	$7,200

14-2 ENTERING FUNCTIONS

Remember from Chapter 13 that a function is a named operation that replaces the action of an arithmetic expression. Some functions provide a shorter way to enter common formulas, such as the SUM function for adding numbers, the AVERAGE function for calculating the average value of a group of numbers, and so forth. Other functions perform complex calculations based on the data you enter. For example, Excel has a function you can use to determine loan payments based on the parameters you enter.

Every function follows a set of rules, or **syntax**, which specifies how the function should be written. The general syntax of Excel functions is

FUNCTION(argument1,argument2,...)

where *FUNCTION* is the name of the function, and *argument1*, *argument2*, and so forth are **arguments**, which are the numbers, text, or cell references used by the function to return a value. When you use multiple arguments within a function, they are separated by a comma.

You have already worked with the SUM function with one argument. For that function, the function name is SUM, and the range reference that appears between the parentheses is the single argument.

Not all functions have arguments. Some functions have **optional arguments**, which are not required for the function to return a value but can be included to provide more control over how Excel calculates the returned value. If an optional argument is not included, Excel assumes a default value for it. This chapter shows optional arguments within square brackets along with the argument's default value:

FUNCTION(argument1[,argument2=value2,...])

In this function, *argument1* is required, *argument2* is an optional argument, and *value2* is the default value used for *argument2*. Optional arguments are always placed last in the argument list.

The hundreds of available Excel functions are organized into the 13 categories described in Exhibit 14-8.

The SUM function is one of the most commonly used Math & Trig functions. Exhibit 14-9 describes the SUM function as well as some of the other common Math, Trig, and Statistical functions used in workbooks.

For example, the AVERAGE function calculates the average value from a collection of numbers. The syntax of the AVERAGE function is

AVERAGE(*number1*[,*number2*,*number3*,...])

EXHIBIT 14-8 EXCEL FUNCTION CATEGORIES

Category	Description
Compatibility	Functions available in earlier versions of Excel that have been replaced with new functions that provide the same actions
Cube	Functions that retrieve data from multidimensional databases involving online analytical processing (OLAP)
Database	Functions that retrieve and analyze data stored in databases
Date & Time	Functions that analyze or create date and time values and time intervals
Engineering	Functions that analyze engineering problems
Financial	Functions that have financial applications
Information	Functions that return information about the format, location, or contents of worksheet cells
Logical	Functions that return logical (true-false) values
Lookup & Reference	Functions that look up and return data matching a set of specified conditions from a range
Math & Trig	Functions that have math and trigonometry applications
Statistical	Functions that provide statistical analyses of a set of data
Text	Functions that return text or evaluate text
Web	Functions that provide information on Web-based connections

EXHIBIT 14-9 COMMON MATH, TRIG, AND STATISTICAL FUNCTIONS

Function	Category	Description
AVERAGE(*number1* [,*number2*, *number3*,...]),	Statistical	Calculates the average of a collection of numbers, where *number1*, *number2*, and so forth are either numbers or cell references. Only *number1* is required. For more than one cell reference or to enter numbers directly into the function, use the optional arguments *number2*, *number3*, and so forth.
COUNT(*value1* [,*value2*, *value3*,...])	Statistical	Counts how many cells in a range contain numbers, where *value1*, *value2*, and so forth are text, numbers, or cell references. Only *value1* is required. For more than one cell reference or to enter numbers directly into the function, use the optional arguments *value2*, *value3*, and so forth.
COUNTA(*value1* [,*value2*, *value3*,...])	Statistical	Counts how many cells are not empty in ranges *value1*, *value2*, and so forth, or how many numbers are listed within *value1*, *value2*, and so forth.
INT(*number*)	Math & Trig	Displays the integer portion of a number, *number*.
MAX(*number1* [,*number2*, *number3*,...])	Statistical	Calculates the maximum value of a collection of numbers, where *number1*, *number2*, and so forth are either numbers or cell references.
MEDIAN(*number1* [,*number2*, *number3*,...])	Statistical	Calculates the median, or middle, value of a collection of numbers, where *number1*, *number2*, and so forth are either numbers or cell references.
MIN(*number1* [,*number2*, *number3*,...])	Statistical	Calculates the minimum value of a collection of numbers, where *number1*, *number2*, and so forth are either numbers or cell references.
RAND()	Math & Trig	Returns a random number between 0 and 1.
ROUND(*number*, *num_digits*)	Math & Trig	Rounds a number to a specified number of digits, where *number* is the number you want to round and *num_digits* specifies the number of digits to round the number.
SUM(*number1* [,*number2*, *number3*,...])	Math & Trig	Adds a collection of numbers, where *number1*, *number2*, and so forth are either numbers or cell references.

where *number1*, *number2*, *number3*, and so forth are either numbers or cell references to numbers. The formula

=AVERAGE(1,2,5,8)

uses the AVERAGE function to calculate the average of 1, 2, 5, and 8, returning the value 4.

You can replace the values used as arguments with cell references. So, if the range A1:A4 contains the values 1, 2, 5, and 8, the following formula also returns 4:

=AVERAGE(A1:A4)

14-2a Inserting a Function Using the Insert Function Dialog Box

The Insert Function dialog box allows you to search for a function and organizes the functions by category. To open the Insert Function dialog box, you can click the Insert Function button to the left of the formula bar or in the Function Library group on the Formulas tab. Exhibit 14-10 shows the Insert Function dialog box with the SUM function selected in the Select a function box.

After you select a function, the Function Arguments dialog box opens, listing all of the arguments associated with that function. (If you know the function's category and name, you can select that function by clicking the appropriate category button in the Function Library group on the Formulas tab, and then clicking the function you want to open the Function Arguments dialog box for that function.) In the Function Arguments dialog box, required arguments are in bold type; optional arguments are in normal type. Exhibit 14-11 shows the Function Arguments dialog box for the SUM function.

EXHIBIT 14-11 FUNCTION ARGUMENTS DIALOG BOX FOR THE SUM FUNCTION

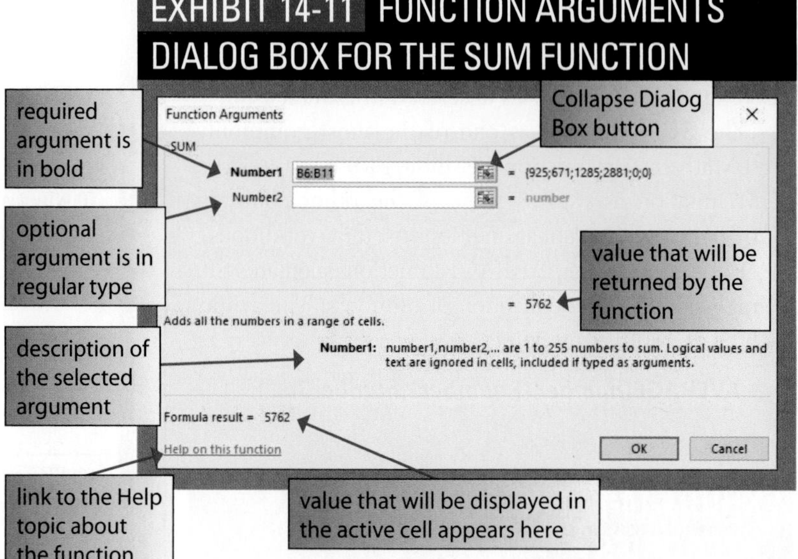

To add cell references as arguments, you can type the cell reference in the argument box, or you can click in the argument box in the dialog box, and then click the cell or range reference in the worksheet. When you do this, the Function Arguments dialog box collapses to show only the selected argument box. See Exhibit 14-12.

EXHIBIT 14-10 SUM FUNCTION SELECTED IN THE INSERT FUNCTION DIALOG BOX

Insert Function ? ×

Search for a function: Type a brief description of what you want to do and then click Go — Go

Or select a category: Most Recently Used

Select a function: IF, SUM, PMT, TODAY, MIN, AND, DATE

SUM(number1,number2,...)

Adds all the numbers in a range of cells.

Help on this function — OK — Cancel

type a description of the function you want to find

selected function

syntax and description of the SUM function

click to select a different function category

link to the Help topic about this function

Begin Activity

Insert the SUM function using the Insert Function dialog box.

1. Make the **Budget worksheet** the active sheet. Select **cell B12**.
2. To the left of the formula bar, click the **Insert Function button** *fx*. The Insert Function dialog box opens with the text in the Search for a function box selected, and an equal sign is inserted in cell B12. Most Recently Used appears in the Or select a category box.
3. In the Select a function box, click **SUM**. The syntax and a description of the SUM function appear below the Select a function box. Refer back to Exhibit 14-10.

PROBLEM?
If the SUM function is not listed in the Select a function box, type **SUM** in the Search for a function box, and then click **Go**.

EXHIBIT 14-12 FUNCTION ARGUMENTS DIALOG BOX COLLAPSED

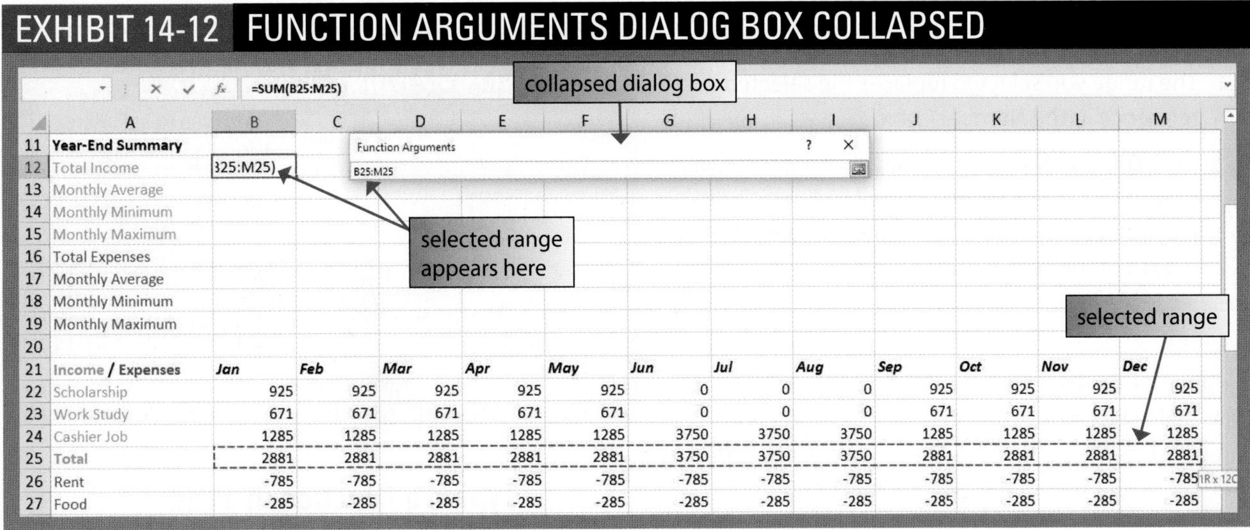

4 Click **OK**. The Function Arguments dialog box opens, listing the arguments for the SUM function. Depending on the surrounding data, the Number1 box shows Excel's best guess of the range you want to sum. In this case, either B6:B11 or nothing appears in the Number1 box. Refer back to Exhibit 14-11. This formula in cell B12 needs to calculate the total income for the year, so it needs to add the values in the range B25:M25.

5 Click **any cell** in the worksheet. The selected cell has a blinking border to indicate it is selected for the formula, and the cell reference of the cell you clicked appears in the Number1 box in the Function Arguments dialog box.

6 Click **cell B25**, but do not release the mouse button. B25 appears in the Number1 box.

7 Drag to select the **range B25:M25**, but do not release the mouse button. As you drag, the dialog box collapses to show just its title bar and the Number1 box. Refer back to Exhibit 14-12.

8 Release the **mouse button.** The dialog box expands to its full size and the range reference B25:M25 appears as the value of the Number1 argument. The values of the cells in the range reference are listed to the right of the Number1 box, and the result of the function appears in the bottom-left of the dialog box.

> **PROBLEM?** If the dialog box is blocking cell B25 or you cannot see row 25 because the worksheet is scrolled, drag the dialog box out of the way by its title bar or use the vertical scroll bar to scroll row 25 into view.

9 Click **OK**. The formula =SUM(B25:M25) is entered in cell E10, as shown in the formula bar. The calculated value 37179, which is the estimated total annual income, appears in the cell.

End Activity

If you don't see the function you want to use in the Select a function list in the Insert Function dialog box, you can use the search feature to search for a function that performs a particular calculation. This is helpful when you don't know the category or name of a function.

Begin Activity

Insert the MIN function using the Insert Function dialog box.

1 Select **cell B14**. To the left of the formula bar, click the **Insert Function button** f_x. The Insert Function dialog box opens.

2 In the Search for a function box, type **Display the smallest number in a set of values** and then click **Go**. The list of functions in the Select a function box changes to functions that match the phrase you typed.

> **TIP:** To learn more about the function selected in the Select a function box, click the Help on this function link.

3 In the Select a function box, click **MIN** if it is not already selected, and then click **OK**. The Function Arguments dialog box appears with the arguments for the MIN function. The reference for the range B12:B13 is selected in the Number1 box.

4 With the range reference in the Number1 box selected, select the **range B25:M25** in the worksheet. The range you selected replaces the selected reference in the Number1 box.

5 Click **OK**. The dialog box closes, and the formula =MIN(B25:M25) is entered in cell B14, which displays 2881—the lowest estimated income for any month of the year.

End Activity

One of the categories available in the Insert Functions dialog box is the Most Recently Used category. This category lists the most recently used functions, sorted in order of recent use, in the Select a function box.

Begin Activity

Insert recently used functions with the Insert Function dialog box.

1 Select **cell B16**, and then, to the left of the formula bar, click the **Insert Function button** . The Insert Function dialog box appears with the Most Recently Used category selected. The MIN function followed by the SUM function appear at the top of the Select a function box because these are the two functions you have used most recently.

PROBLEM? If Most Recently Used is not the current category, click the **Or select a category arrow,** and then click **Most Recently Used.**

2 In the Select a function box, click **SUM**, and then click **OK**. The Function Arguments dialog box for the SUM function appears.

3 In the worksheet, select the **range B34:M34**. The range with the estimated monthly expenses appears in the Number1 box.

4 In the Function Arguments dialog box, click **OK**. The formula =SUM(B34:M34) is inserted in cell B16, which displays −36860—the total projected expenses for the upcoming year. Compare your screen to Exhibit 14-13.

TIP: Click the Collapse Dialog Box button to shrink the Function Arguments dialog box to its title bar and the currently selected argument box. The button changes to the Expand Dialog Box button , which you can click to restore the dialog box.

End Activity

EXHIBIT 14-13 VALUES AFTER ENTERING THE SUM AND MIN FUNCTIONS

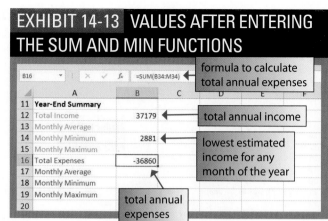

formula to calculate total annual expenses

total annual income

lowest estimated income for any month of the year

total annual expenses

14-2b Typing a Function in a Cell

After you become familiar with a function, it can be faster to type the function directly in a cell rather than using the Insert Function dialog box, as you did in Chapter 13 when you typed the SUM function in a cell. As with any formula, first type = (an equal sign). Then start typing the function name. As you type, a list of functions that begin with the letters you typed appears. As shown in Exhibit 14-14, when you type A, the list shows all of the functions starting with the letter A; when you type AV, the list shows only those functions starting with the letters AV, and so forth. This helps to ensure that you are entering a legitimate Excel function name. If you don't know what a specific function does, you can select the function in the list to display a ScreenTip with a description of that function.

EXHIBIT 14-14 FUNCTIONS LIST IN THE WORKSHEET

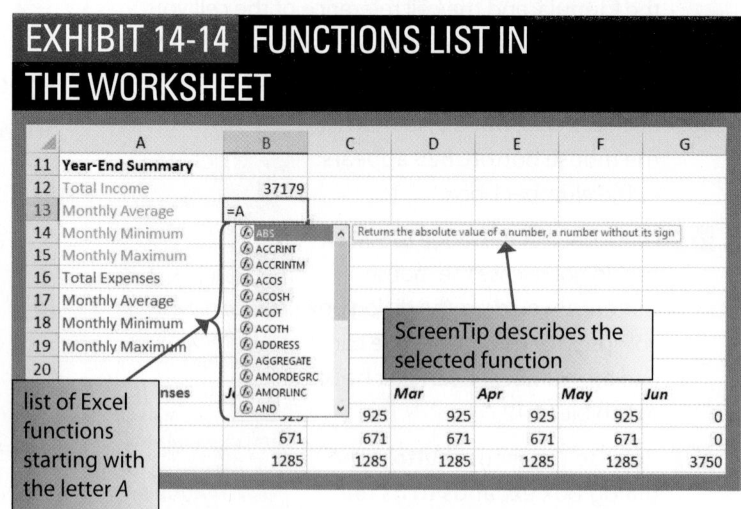

To insert a function in the active cell, press the Tab key or double-click the function name in the list to insert the function name and the opening parenthesis. You could also continue typing it and then type the opening parenthesis. After the opening parenthesis is added, a ScreenTip appears showing the function's syntax. See Exhibit 14-15. To

EXHIBIT 14-15 FUNCTION IN CELL WITH SCREENTIP SHOWING THE SYNTAX

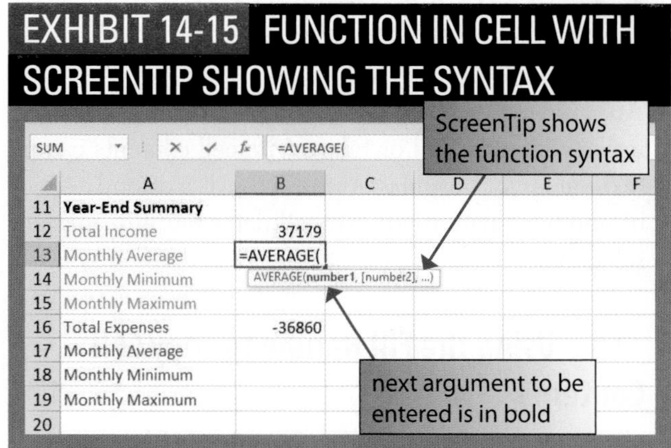

add the first argument, you can select a cell or range or type the appropriate reference or argument. After you enter all the arguments, type the closing parenthesis to ensure that Excel interprets the formula correctly, and then enter it in the cell by pressing the Enter or Tab key or by clicking the Enter button ✓ to the left of the formula bar.

Begin Activity

Type functions in cells.

1 Select **cell B13**.

2 Type **=A**. As you type a formula, a list with function names starting with the letter A opens. Refer back to Exhibit 14-14.

3 Type **V**. The list shows only those functions starting with the letters *AV*.

> **TIP:** You can also click a category button in the Function Library group on the Formulas tab and then clicking the function you want to use.

4 In the list, click **AVERAGE** to select the name of the function you want to use. A ScreenTip appears, describing the selected function.

5 Press the **Tab key**. The AVERAGE function with its opening parenthesis is inserted into cell B13, and a ScreenTip shows the syntax for the function. At this point, you can either type the range reference or select the range with your mouse. Refer back to Exhibit 14-15.

6 Select the **range B25:M25**. The range reference is added to the formula.

7 Type **)** (the closing parenthesis), and then click the **Enter button** ✓. The formula =AVERAGE(B25:M25) is entered in cell B13, which displays 3098.25—the average estimated monthly income.

> **PROBLEM?** If #NAME? appears in the cell, you probably mistyped the function name. Edit the formula to correct the misspelling.

8 In **cell B15**, type **=M**, double-click **MAX** to insert the function, drag to select the **range B25:M25**, type **)** and then press the **Enter key**. The number 3750—the highest estimated income for any month of the year—appears in cell B15.

9 Enter the following functions, using any method and using the **range B34:M34** as the argument. When you are finished, compare your screen to Exhibit 14-16.

cell B17: **AVERAGE**
cell B18: **MIN**
cell B19: **MAX**

End Activity

EXHIBIT 14-16 YEAR-END SUMMARY VALUES

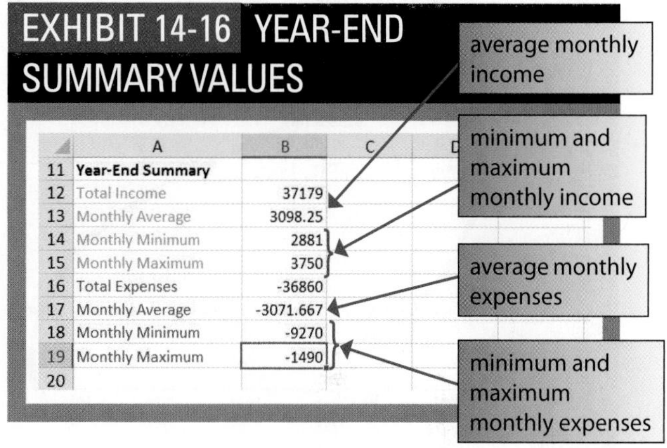

Note that the minimum and maximum monthly expense values are correct mathematically—the negative number −9270 is smaller than the negative number −1490. However, as cash values, the minimum value −9270 is actually the largest (maximum) expense, and the maximum value −1490 is actually the smallest (minimum) expense. In a real budget that uses negative numbers to track expenses, you would use the Minimum function to find the largest expense and the Maximum function to find the smallest expense.

14-2c Modifying Data Used in a Formula

Formulas provide the greatest flexibility for working with data that changes. By entering data values in cells and then referencing those cells in formulas, you can quickly change a value and immediately see the new formula results. This allows you to use Excel to change one or more values in a spreadsheet and then immediately see how those changes affect calculated values. For example in the Budget worksheet, if you change any of the values entered in the range B6:C8, the values that contain formulas that reference those cells—B22:M24—are changed. This causes the values in the cells that reference those cells—B25:M25—to change, and therefore the values in any cells that contain references to those cells to change. Exhibit 14-17 illustrates this.

EXHIBIT 14-17 REVISED INCOME PROJECTION AFFECTS CALCULATED VALUES

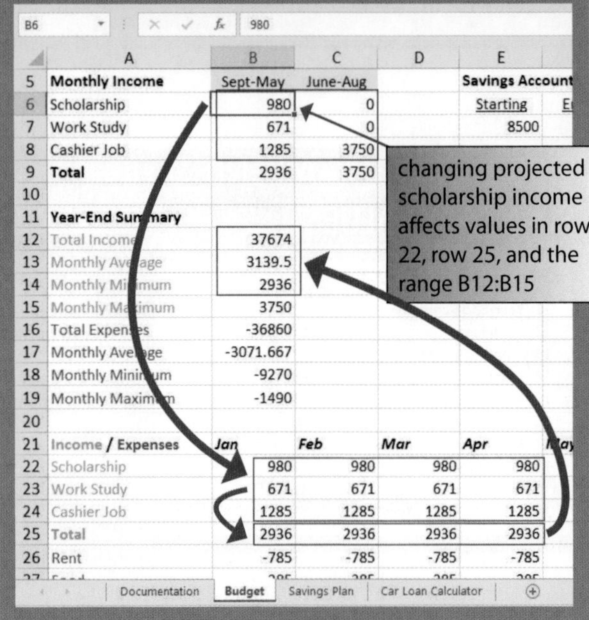

Begin Activity

Modify data used in a formula.

1 Make **cell B6** the active cell. You will change the monthly income earned from work study during the school months.

2 Type **980**, and then click the **Enter button** ✓. Refer back to Exhibit 14-17. (You will need to scroll to see all the cells shown in the Exhibit.)

End Activity

AutoFill An Excel feature that copies content and formats from a cell or range into an adjacent cell or range.

fill handle A box in the lower-right corner of a selected cell or range that you drag over an adjacent cell or range to copy the content and formatting from the original cells into the adjacent range.

14-3 USING AUTOFILL

AutoFill copies content and formats from a cell or range into an adjacent cell or range. The cell contents can be text, values, or formulas. AutoFill can also extend a series of numbers, patterned text, and dates into the adjacent selection.

14-3a Using the Fill Handle to Copy Cell Contents

After you select a cell or range, the **fill handle** ■ appears in the lower-right corner of the selection. See Exhibit 14-18. When you drag the fill handle over an adjacent range, AutoFill copies the content and formats from the original cell into the adjacent range.

EXHIBIT 14-18 FILL HANDLE ON A CELL CONTAINING A FORMULA

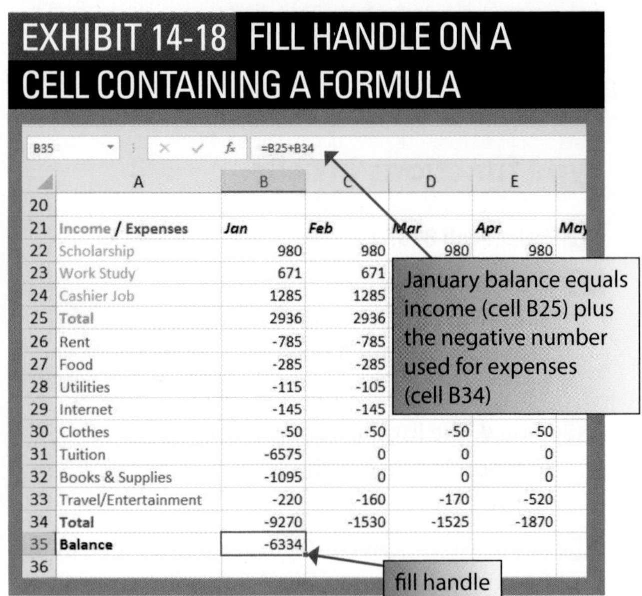

Begin Activity

Enter a formula to calculate the difference between income and expenses.

1 In **cell B35**, type the formula **=B25+B34**. Because the expenses were entered as negative numbers, to calculate the difference between total income and total expenses, you need to add the positive total income value and the negative total expenses value for January.

TIP: If the expenses had been entered as positive numbers, to calculate the difference, you would enter the formula =B25-B34 to subtract the total expenses from the total income.

2 To the left of the formula bar, click the **Enter button** ✓. Refer back to Exhibit 14-18. The result, 26334, indicates a projected shortfall for January. This is due to the cost of tuition and books that occur in that month.

End Activity

Now that you entered a formula in cell B35, you can use the fill handle to quickly copy the formula to the range C35:M35. After you release the mouse button, the contents of the cell whose fill handle you dragged are pasted into the cells over which you dragged. See Exhibit 14-19.

Begin Activity

Use a cell's fill handle to copy the cell contents.

1 Make sure **cell B35** is the active cell. The fill handle appears in the lower-right corner of the cell.

2 Point to the **fill handle** ■ in the lower-right corner of the cell. The pointer changes to +.

3 Click the **fill handle** ■, and without releasing the mouse button, drag over the **range C35:M35**. A green border appears around the range.

4 Release the **mouse button**. The selected range is filled with the formula in cell B35. The Auto Fill Options button appears below the lower-right corner of the selected range. Refer to Exhibit 14-19.

5 Review the formula that calculates each month's balance to confirm that AutoFill correctly copied the formula into the selected range. These calculations provide a picture of how the balance varies from month to month. Only in January and August, when tuition payments for the semesters are due, do expenses exceed income.

End Activity

You can also drag the fill handle of a selected range. After you release the mouse button, the contents of each cell are copied to the corresponding cells in the same row or column.

Begin Activity

Use a range's fill handle to copy the range contents.

1 In **cell B38**, enter **=E7** to retrieve the value in cell E7, which is the balance in the savings account at the beginning of the year.

EXHIBIT 14-19 FORMULAS PASTED WITH AUTOFILL

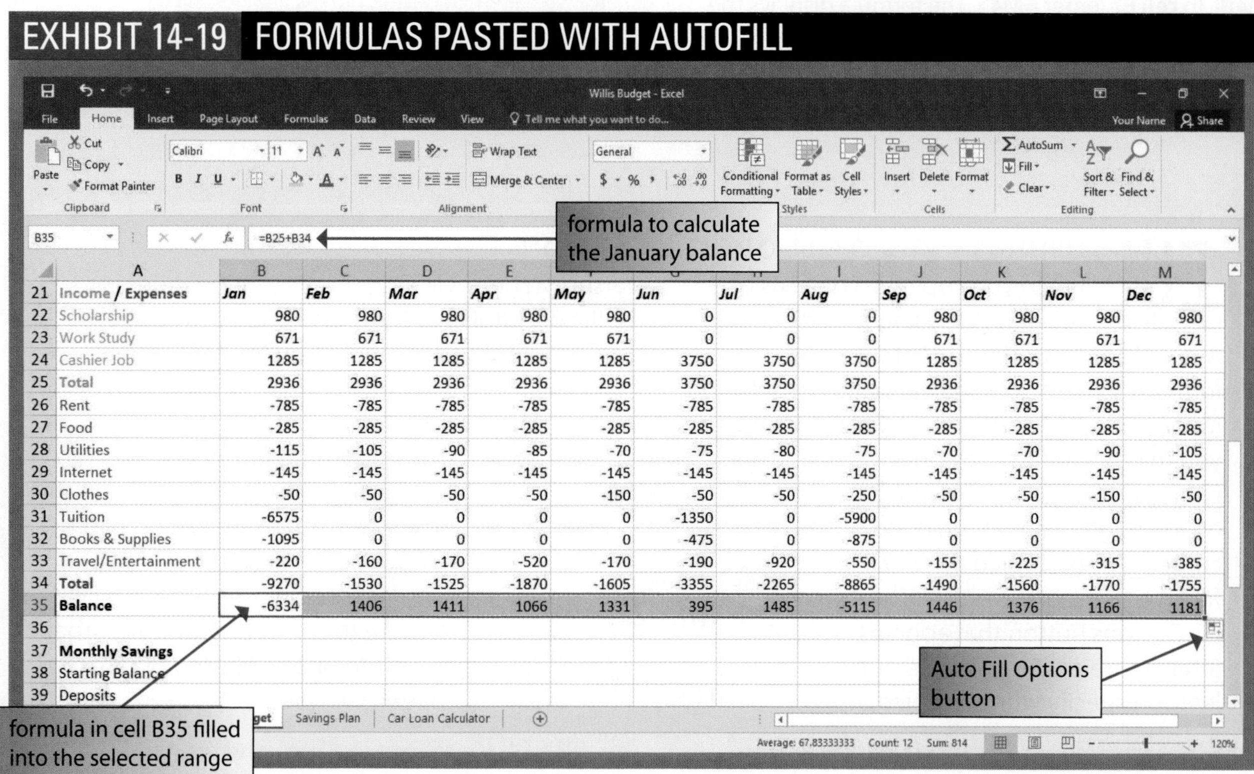

	A	B	C	D	E	F	G	H	I	J	K	L	M
21	Income / Expenses	Jan	Feb	Mar	Apr	May	Jun	Jul	Aug	Sep	Oct	Nov	Dec
22	Scholarship	980	980	980	980	980	0	0	0	980	980	980	980
23	Work Study	671	671	671	671	671	0	0	0	671	671	671	671
24	Cashier Job	1285	1285	1285	1285	1285	3750	3750	3750	1285	1285	1285	1285
25	Total	2936	2936	2936	2936	2936	3750	3750	3750	2936	2936	2936	2936
26	Rent	-785	-785	-785	-785	-785	-785	-785	-785	-785	-785	-785	-785
27	Food	-285	-285	-285	-285	-285	-285	-285	-285	-285	-285	-285	-285
28	Utilities	-115	-105	-90	-85	-70	-75	-80	-75	-70	-70	-90	-105
29	Internet	-145	-145	-145	-145	-145	-145	-145	-145	-145	-145	-145	-145
30	Clothes	-50	-50	-50	-50	-150	-50	-50	-250	-50	-50	-150	-50
31	Tuition	-6575	0	0	0	0	-1350	0	-5900	0	0	0	0
32	Books & Supplies	-1095	0	0	0	0	-475	0	-875	0	0	0	0
33	Travel/Entertainment	-220	-160	-170	-520	-170	-190	-920	-550	-155	-225	-315	-385
34	Total	-9270	-1530	-1525	-1870	-1605	-3355	-2265	-8865	-1490	-1560	-1770	-1755
35	Balance	-6334	1406	1411	1066	1331	395	1485	-5115	1446	1376	1166	1181
36													
37	Monthly Savings												
38	Starting Balance												
39	Deposits												

2 In **cell B39**, enter **=B25** to display the value in cell B25, which is the January total income.

3 In **cell B40**, enter **=B34** to display the value in cell B34, which is the January total expenses. These relative references will change when you copy the formula to other months.

4 In **cell B41**, use the **SUM function** to add the contents of the **range B38:B40**. This calculates the ending balance for the savings account. Cell B41 displays 2166, which is the projected balance in the savings account at the end of January.

5 Select the **range B38:B41**, and then drag the **fill handle** ■ over the **range C38:C41** to calculate the ending balance for February. However, the starting balance value for February in cell C38 is incorrect. It should be the same as the ending balance in January.

6 In **cell C38**, change the formula to **=B41**. Now the February starting balance for the savings account is based on the January ending balance. When you copy this formula, the starting balance for each month will equal the ending balance of the month before.

7 Select the **range C38:C41**, and then drag the **fill handle** ■ over the **range D38:M41**. The formulas and formatting from February are copied into the remaining months of the year.

8 In **cell F7**, enter **=M41**. The formula displays the ending balance of the savings account in December—9314.

End Activity

14-3b Creating a Series

AutoFill can also be used to create a series of numbers, dates, or text based on a pattern. To create a series of numbers, you enter the initial values in the series in a selected range and then use AutoFill to complete the series. Exhibit 14-20 shows how AutoFill can be used to insert the numbers from 1 to 10 in a selected range. The first few numbers in the range were entered to establish the pattern—in this case, consecutive positive integers 1 through 3 in the range A1:A3. Then, you select the range, and drag the fill handle over the cells where you want the pattern continued; in this case, over the range A4:A10. Excel fills in the rest of the series.

EXHIBIT 14-20 AUTOFILL EXTENDS A SEQUENCE

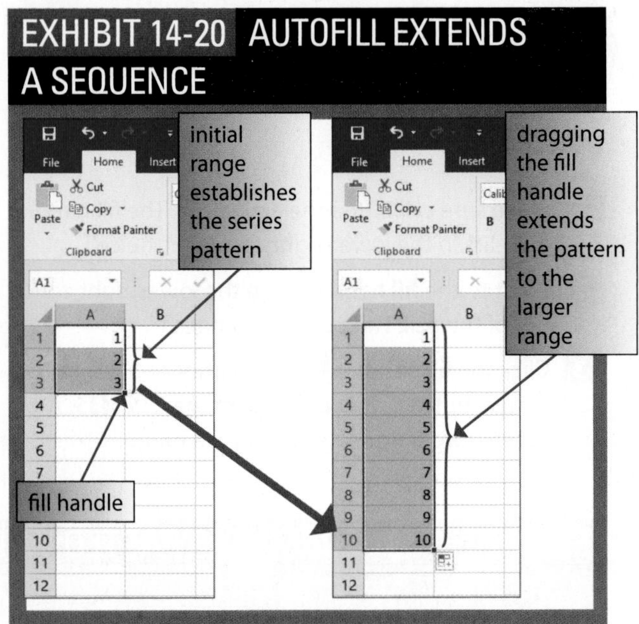

FYI USING THE AUTO FILL OPTIONS BUTTON

When you copy the contents of a cell or range using the fill handle, AutoFill copies both the content and the formatting of the original range to the selected range or fills the series. However, sometimes you might want to copy only the content or only the formatting, or you might want to force the contents to be copied instead of filling a series or vice versa. The Auto Fill Options button that appears after you release the mouse button lets you specify what is copied. As shown here, clicking this button provides a list of AutoFill options. The Copy Cells option copies both the content and the formatting. The Fill Series option continues the pattern of data. The Fill Formatting Only option copies the formatting into the selected cells but not any content. The Fill Without Formatting option copies the content but not the formatting. The last option uses the Flash Fill feature to copy content from other cells into one cell based on the pattern you set.

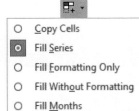

- Copy Cells
- Fill Series
- Fill Formatting Only
- Fill Without Formatting
- Fill Months

AutoFill can extend a wide variety of series, including dates and times and patterned text. Exhibit 14-21 shows examples of some series that AutoFill can generate. For example, a text pattern that includes text and a number, such as Region 1, Region 2, and so on, can be extended using AutoFill. In each case, you must provide enough information for AutoFill to identify the pattern. AutoFill can recognize some patterns from only a single value, such as Jan or January to create a series of month names or abbreviations, or Mon or Monday to create a series of the days of the week.

EXHIBIT 14-22 SCREENTIP WHEN AUTOFILLING MONTH ABBREVIATIONS

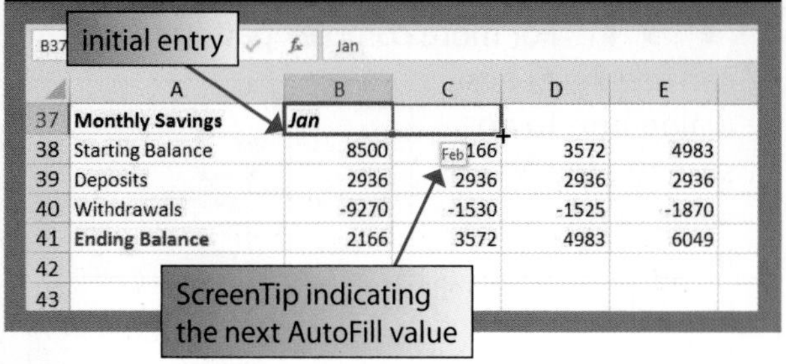

	A	B	C	D	E
37	**Monthly Savings**	***Jan***			
38	Starting Balance	8500	Feb 166	3572	4983
39	Deposits	2936	2936	2936	2936
40	Withdrawals	-9270	-1530	-1525	-1870
41	**Ending Balance**	2166	3572	4983	6049
42					
43					

initial entry

ScreenTip indicating the next AutoFill value

EXHIBIT 14-21 AUTOFILL APPLIED TO VALUES, DATES AND TIMES, AND PATTERNED TEXT

Type	Initial pattern	Extended series
Values	1, 2, 3	4, 5, 6, ...
	2, 4, 6	8, 10, 12, ...
Dates and times	Jan	Feb, Mar, Apr, ...
	January	February, March, April, ...
	14-Jan, 14-Feb	14-Mar, 14-Apr, 14-May, ...
	12/30/2016	12/31/2016, 1/1/2017, 1/2/2017, ...
	12/31/2016, 1/31/2017	2/28/2017, 3/31/2017, 4/30/2017, ...
	Mon	Tue, Wed, Thu, ...
	Monday	Tuesday, Wednesday, Thursday, ...
	11:00AM	12:00PM, 1:00PM, 2:00PM, ...
Patterned text	1st period	2nd period, 3rd period, 4th period, ...
	Region 1	Region 2, Region 3, Region 4, ...
	Quarter 3	Quarter 4, Quarter 1, Quarter 2, ...
	Qtr3	Qtr4, Qtr1, Qtr2, ...

As you drag a fill handle over a range, a ScreenTip appears showing how AutoFill will fill the series. For example, if a cell contains Jan, the abbreviation for January, the next cell will be filled with Feb, the abbreviation for February. See Exhibit 14-22.

Begin Activity

Use AutoFill to enter a series.

1. In **cell B37**, enter **Jan**. (Do not enter the period.) This is the first value in the series.
2. Select **cell B37** if necessary.
3. On the Home tab, in the Font group, click the **Bold button** B, and then click the **Italic button** *I*. The text in cell B37 is formatted in bold and italics.
4. Drag the **fill handle** over **cell C37**, but do not release the mouse button. A ScreenTip appears showing the month abbreviation for the next cell in the series. In this case, the ScreenTip shows the abbreviation Feb for cell C37. Refer back to Exhibit 14-22.
5. Continue dragging over the **range D37:M37**, and then release the **mouse button**. AutoFill enters the three-letter abbreviations for each of the remaining months of the year. It also copies the bold and italic formatting that you applied to cell B37. Compare your screen to Exhibit 14-23.

End Activity

EXHIBIT 14-23 MONTH SERIES COMPLETED WITH AUTOFILL

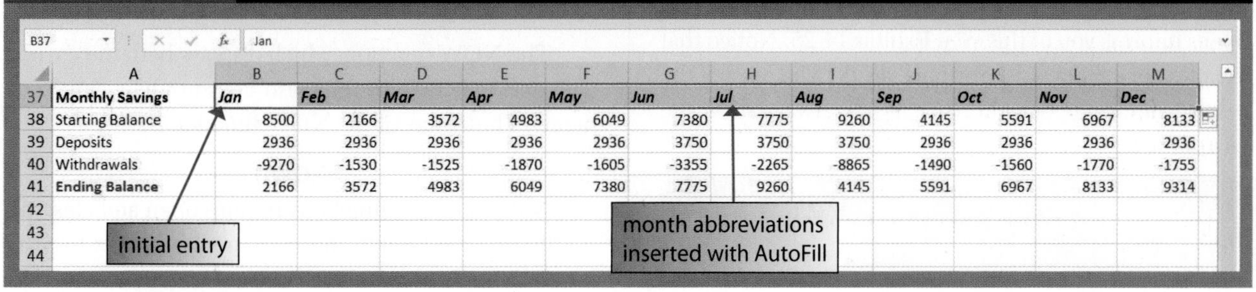

	A	B	C	D	E	F	G	H	I	J	K	L	M
37	**Monthly Savings**	***Jan***	***Feb***	***Mar***	***Apr***	***May***	***Jun***	***Jul***	***Aug***	***Sep***	***Oct***	***Nov***	***Dec***
38	Starting Balance	8500	2166	3572	4983	6049	7380	7775	9260	4145	5591	6967	8133
39	Deposits	2936	2936	2936	2936	2936	3750	3750	3750	2936	2936	2936	2936
40	Withdrawals	-9270	-1530	-1525	-1870	-1605	-3355	-2265	-8865	-1490	-1560	-1770	-1755
41	**Ending Balance**	2166	3572	4983	6049	7380	7775	9260	4145	5591	6967	8133	9314
42													
43													
44													

initial entry

month abbreviations inserted with AutoFill

FYI CREATING A SERIES WITH A COMPLEX PATTERN

For more complex patterns, you can use the Series dialog box. To do so, enter the first value of the series in a worksheet cell, select the entire range that will contain the series, click the Fill button in the Editing group on the Home tab, and then click Series. The Series dialog box opens. You can use the Series dialog box to specify a linear or growth series for numbers; a Date series for dates that increase by day, weekday, month, or year; or an AutoFill series for patterned text. With numbers, you can also specify the step value (indicating how much each number increases over the previous entry) and a stop value (to specify the endpoint for the entire series).

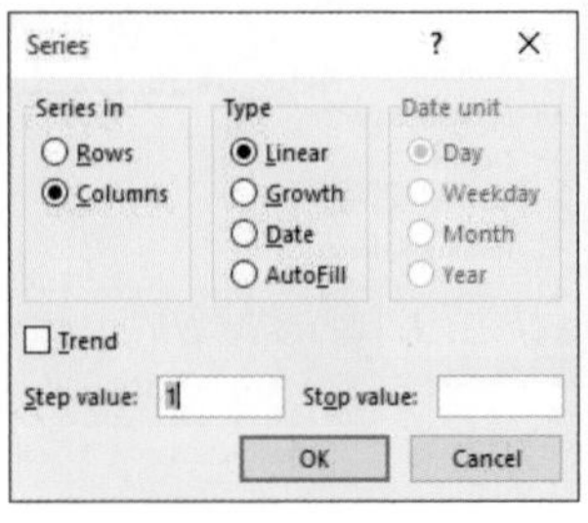

14-4 WORKING WITH DATE FUNCTIONS

A **date function** is a function that inserts or calculates dates and times. Exhibit 14-24 describes seven of the date functions supported by Excel. You can use these functions to help with scheduling or to determine on what days of the week certain dates occur.

Perhaps the most commonly used date function is the TODAY function, which displays the current date. The syntax of the TODAY function is:

=TODAY()

The TODAY function doesn't have any arguments. If you enter the TODAY function using the Insert Function dialog box, the Function Arguments dialog box that opens informs you of this. See Exhibit 14-25. Notice that Volatile appears next to Formula result. This means the result will change—in this case, it will always show the current date.

date function A function that inserts or calculates dates and times.

EXHIBIT 14-24 DATE AND TIME FUNCTIONS

Function	Description
NOW( )	Displays the current date and time
TODAY( )	Displays the current date
DATE (*year,month,day*)	Creates a date value for the date represented by the *year*, *month*, and *day* arguments
DAY(*date*)	Extracts the day of the month from the *date* value
MONTH(*date*)	Extracts the month number from the *date* value where 1=January, 2=February, and so forth
YEAR(date)	Extracts the year number from the *date* value
WEEKDAY (*date*[*,return_type*])	Calculates the day of the week from the *date* value, where 1=Sunday, 2=Monday, and so forth; to choose a different numbering scheme, set the optional *return_type* value to "1" (1=Sunday, 2=Monday, ...), "2" (1=Monday, 2=Tuesday), or "3" (0=Monday, 1=Tuesday, ...)

EXHIBIT 14-25 FUNCTION ARGUMENTS DIALOG BOX FOR THE TODAY FUNCTION

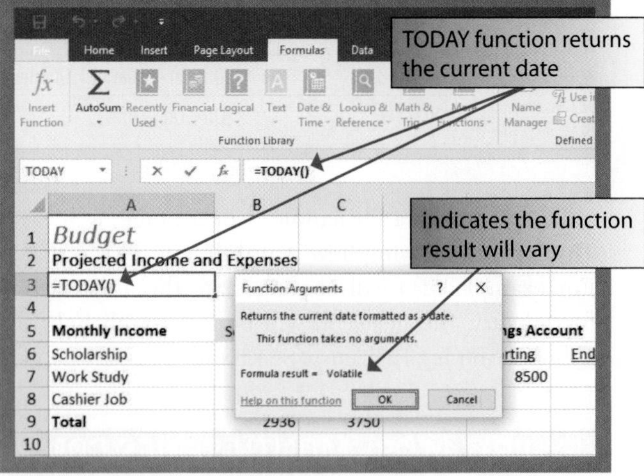

The NOW function, which displays both the current date and the current time, also does not have any arguments. The syntax of the NOW function is:

=NOW()

Note that both functions require open and close parentheses even though there are no arguments to place inside them.

FYI EXCEL DATES AND TIMES AS NUMERIC VALUES

Although dates and times entered into a cell usually are displayed as text, they are actually stored by Excel as numbers measuring the interval between the specified date and time and January 1, 1900 at 12:00 a.m. For example, the date May 1, 2016 is stored as 42,491, which is the number of days between January 1, 1900 and May 1, 2016. Times are stored as fractional parts of one day. The time 6:00 a.m. is stored as 0.25 because that represents one-fourth of a 24-hour day (starting the day from 12:00 a.m.). Similarly, the date and time of May 1, 2016 at 6:00 a.m. is stored as 42,491.25.

Excel stores dates and times as numbers to make it easier to calculate time intervals. For example, to calculate the difference between one date and another, you subtract the earlier date from the later date. If you subtract the date and time of April 30, 2016 at 12:00 a.m. from May 1, 2016 at 6:00 p.m., Excel displays 1.75—or one and three-quarters of a day. You can always view the actual date and time by selecting the cell that contains the date/time entry and applying the General number format or by switching the workbook window to Formula view.

The values returned by the TODAY and NOW functions are updated automatically whenever you reopen the workbook or enter a new calculation.

Begin Activity

Enter a date function.

1. In the **Budget worksheet**, select **cell A3**.
2. On the ribbon, click the **Formulas tab**. In the Function Library group, click the **Date & Time button**. A menu of date functions opens.
3. In the date functions list, click **TODAY**. The TODAY function is entered in cell A3, and the Function Arguments dialog box appears. Refer back to Exhibit 14-25.
4. Click **OK**. The Function Arguments dialog box closes, and the formula =TODAY() is entered into cell A3. The formula appears in the formula bar, and the current date appears in cell A3.

End Activity

14-5 WORKING WITH THE PMT FINANCIAL FUNCTION

A **financial function** is a function related to monetary calculations, such as loans and payments. Excel provides a wide range of financial functions. Exhibit 14-26 describes some of Excel's financial functions that are often used to develop budgets. These financial functions are the same as those widely used in business and accounting to perform various financial calculations, such as depreciation of an asset, the amount of interest paid on an investment, and the present value of an investment.

14-5a Understanding Loan Factors

One commonly used financial function is the **PMT function**, which is used to calculate a payment schedule required to completely repay a loan. The cost of a loan to the borrower is largely based on three factors: the principal, the time required to repay the loan, and the interest. **Principal** is the amount of money being loaned.

The length of time required to repay the loan is usually specified as the number of payments. To calculate the number of payments, you need to know the length of the loan in years and the number of payments

financial function A function related to monetary calculations, such as loans and payments.

PMT function A financial function that calculates the payment schedule required to repay a loan.

principal The amount of money being loaned.

EXHIBIT 14-26 FINANCIAL FUNCTIONS FOR LOANS AND INVESTMENTS

Function	Description
FV(*rate,nper,pmt*[,*pv*=0][,*type*=0])	Calculates the future value of an investment, where *rate* is the interest rate per period, *nper* is the total number of periods, *pmt* is the payment in each period, *pv* is the present value of the investment, and *type* indicates whether payments should be made at the end of the period (0) or the beginning of the period (1)
PMT(*rate,nper,pv*[,*fv*=0][,*type*=0])	Calculates the payments required each period on a loan or investment, where *fv* is the future value of the investment
IPMT(*rate,per,nper,pv*[,*fv*=0][,*type*=0])	Calculates the amount of a loan payment devoted to paying the loan interest, where *per* is the number of the payment period
PPMT(*rate,per,nper,pv*[,*fv*=0][,*type*=0])	Calculates the amount of a loan payment devoted to repaying the principal of a loan
PV(*rate,nper pmt*[,*fv*=0][,*type*=0])	Calculates the present value of a loan or investment based on periodic, constant payments
NPER(*rate,pmt,pv*[,*fv*=0][,*type*=0])	Calculates the number of periods required to repay a loan or investment
RATE(*nper,pmt,pv*[,*fv*=0][,*type*=0])	Calculates the interest rate of a loan or investment based on periodic, constant payments

required per year, and then you multiple these numbers. For example, a 10-year loan that is paid monthly—that is, 12 times per year—has 120 payments (10 years × 12 months per year). If that same 10-year loan is paid quarterly—that is, four times per year—it has 40 payments (10 years × 4 quarters per year). The length of time between each payment is the **payment period**, or just **period**.

Interest is the amount added to the principal by the lender. Think of interest as a kind of "user fee" because the borrower is paying for the right to use the lender's money for a length of time. Generally, the interest rate is expressed at an annual percentage rate, or APR. For example, an 8 percent APR means that the annual interest rate on a loan is 8 percent of the amount owed to the lender. To calculate how much interest a borrower owes each payment period—the interest rate per period—the annual interest rate is divided by the number of payments per year (often monthly or quarterly). So, if the 8 percent annual interest rate is paid monthly, the resulting monthly interest rate is 1/12 of 8 percent, which is about 0.67 percent per month. If payments are made quarterly, then the interest rate per quarter would be 1/4 of 8 percent, which is 2 percent per quarter.

payment period (period) The length of time between each loan payment.

interest The amount added to the principal by the lender.

14-5b Entering the PMT Function

To calculate the costs associated with a loan, you need the following information:

- Annual interest rate
- Number of payments or payment periods per year
- Length of the loan
- Principal amount

With this information, you can use the PMT function to determine the loan payments for a specific amount. The syntax of the PMT function is

PMT(*rate,nper,pv*[,*fv*=0][,*type*=0])

where *rate* is the interest rate for each payment period, *nper* is the total number of payments required to repay the loan, and *pv* is the present value of the loan or the principal. The optional argument *fv* is the future value of the loan. Because the intent with most loans is to repay them completely, the future value is equal to 0 by default. The optional *type* argument specifies when the interest is charged on the loan, either at the end of the payment period (type=0)—for example, at the end of every month—or at the beginning of the payment period (type=1). The default is type=0.

For example, if you borrowed $10,000 to buy a car, you could use the PMT function to calculate your monthly payment over a five-year period, payable monthly, at an annual interest rate of 9 percent. The APR is 9 percent; therefore the rate argument—the interest rate per period—is 9 percent divided by 12 monthly payments, which is 0.75 percent per month. The nper argument—the total number of payments or payment periods—is equal to the number of years (five) multiplied by the number of payments per year (12), or 60. The pv argument—the principal—is $10,000. Because the loan will be repaid completely and payments will be made at the end of the month, you can accept the default values for the fv and type arguments. The resulting PMT function

=PMT(0.75,60,10000)

returns a value of –$207.58, which means you would need to pay $207.58 every month for five years before the loan and the interest are completely repaid. The value is negative because the payment is an expense to the borrower. Essentially, the loan is money the borrower subtracts from his or her funds to repay the loan.

Of course, one of the benefits of using Excel is that you can have Excel calculate the interest rate per period (the rate argument) and the number of payments or payment periods (the nper argument). To do this, you could use formulas as the arguments and rewrite the PMT function as:

=PMT(0.09/12,5*12,10000)

Another way to do this is to set up a worksheet in which you directly enter the values you know—the annual interest rate (APR), the number of payments per year, the number of years of the loan, and the loan amount—into cells, and then add formulas to calculate the interest rate per period and the number of payments. Then you can reference the cells containing the calculated rate and number of payments and the cell containing the loan amount as the arguments in the PMT function.

The calculated result of the PMT function is automatically formatted as a negative number with the Currency format. The number is negative because it is an amount the user will be paying out to someone else. However, instead of displaying the negative number with a minus sign in front of it, the number is displayed within parentheses and is red. This is one of the options for displaying negative numbers formatted as Currency.

Begin Activity

Set up a worksheet to use the PMT function to calculate a monthly payment.

1 Make the **Car Loan Calculator worksheet** the active sheet. Make **cell B3** the active cell.

2 On the ribbon, click the **Home tab**. In the Number group, click the **Percent Style button** %. Now you can type the percentage as a whole number rather than a decimal number.

3 Type **6**, and then press the **Enter key**. 6% appears in cell B3.This is the annual interest rate for the loan.

4 In **cell B4**, enter **12** as the number of payments per year because the loan needs to be paid monthly.

5 In **cell B5**, enter the formula **=B3/B4** to calculate the interest per period. This is the rate argument for the PMT function. The calculated value is 0.50 percent per month. The formula result did not pick up the percentage formatting from cell B3.

6 Make **cell B5** the active cell. On the Home tab, in the Number group, click the **Percent Style button** %. The value is formatted as a percentage and appears as 1% because the percent format does not show any decimal places. Any calculations that reference this value will use the value stored in the cell—0.5%—so you don't need to change the format. However, it is confusing to someone looking at the worksheet, so you will change the format to show one decimal place.

7 In the Number group, click the **Increase Decimal button**. The value in cell B5 changes to 0.5%. This is the correct interest rate per period.

TIP: To see a more precise interest rate per period for loans, continue clicking the Increase Decimal button to add additional decimal places.

8 In **cell B6**, enter **5**. This is the length of the loan in years.

9 In **cell B7**, enter the formula **=B4*B6** to multiply the number of payments per year by the number of years. This calculates the total number of monthly payments—60.

10 In **cell B8**, enter **20000** for the amount of the loan.

End Activity

Once you have set up the worksheet, you can add the PMT function. Instead of typing the values of the arguments directly in the function, you will reference the corresponding cells in the worksheet. Exhibit 14-27 shows the Function Arguments dialog box for the PMT function with cell references instead of values in the boxes that contain the arguments.

EXHIBIT 14-27 FUNCTION ARGUMENTS DIALOG BOX FOR THE PMT FUNCTION

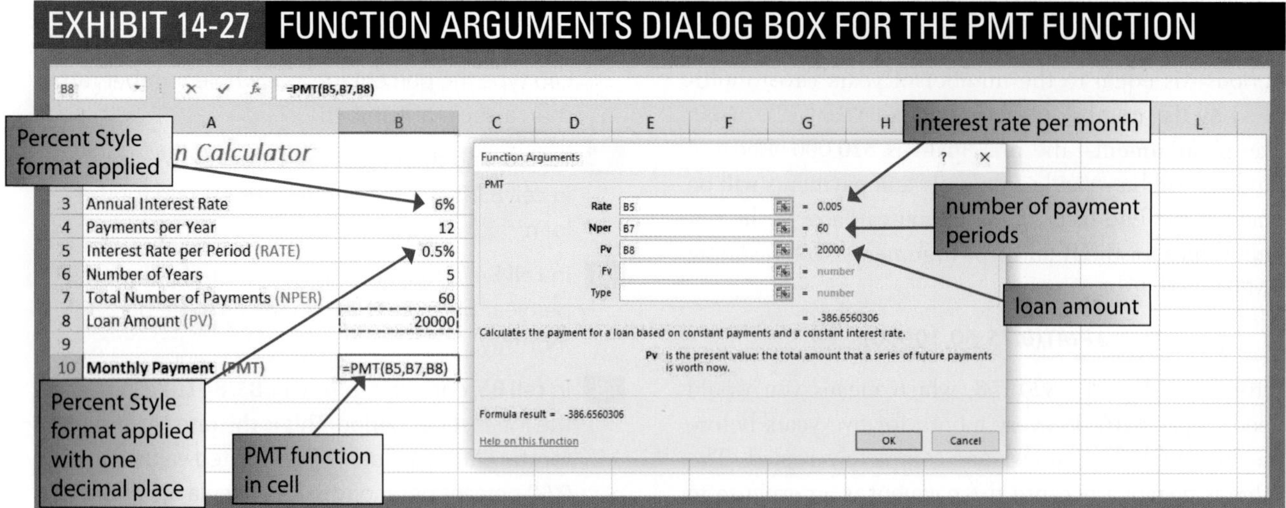

Begin Activity

Insert the PMT function to calculate a monthly payment.

1 Select **cell B10**. To the left of the formula bar, click the **Insert Function button** *fx*. The Insert Function dialog box opens. In the Or select a category box, Date & Time appears because that was the last function category you used.

2 Click the **Or select a category box arrow**, and then click **Financial**. Financial functions appear in the Select a function box.

3 Scroll down the alphabetical list until you see the PMT function, click **PMT**, and then click **OK**. The Function Arguments dialog box for the PMT function opens. The PMT function requires three arguments—rate, nper, and pv. You can add two optional arguments—fv and type. The insertion point is in the Rate box.

4 In the worksheet, click **cell B5**, the cell that contains the interest rate per month.

5 Click in the **Nper box**, and then click **cell B7**, the cell that contains the total number of monthly payments required to repay the loan. (*Nper* stands for *Number Per.*)

6 Click in the **Pv box**, and then click **cell B8**, the cell that contains the present value of the loan. In cell B10, the complete formula =PMT(B5,B7,B8) appears. Refer to Exhibit 14-27.

7 Click **OK**. The value ($386.66) appears in cell B10 in red. The value is formatted as a negative number in the Currency format because it is a payment. Compare your screen to Exhibit 14-28.

8 Double-click **cell B10**. Instead of the calculated result, the function appears in cell B10. Notice that each cell reference listed as an argument is a different color, and the cells referenced have colored borders and shading that correspond to the colors of the cells' references in the function.

9 Press the **Esc key** to exit Edit mode.

End Activity

EXHIBIT 14-28 PMT FUNCTION USED TO CALCULATE LOAN PAYMENTS

B10 =PMT(B5,B7,B8)

	A	B
1	Car Loan Calculator	
2		
3	Annual Interest Rate	6%
4	Payments per Year	12
5	Interest Rate per Period (RATE)	0.5%
6	Number of Years	5
7	Total Number of Payments (NPER)	60
8	Loan Amount (PV)	20000
9		
10	Monthly Payment (PMT)	($386.66)
11		
12		

PMT function calculates loan payments
annual interest rate
number of payments per year
interest rate per month
length of the loan in years
length of the loan in months
total loan amount
value calculated by the PMT function

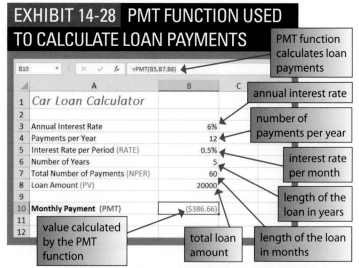

what-if analysis An examination of how changing values entered directly in a worksheet affect calculated values.

14-5c Performing What-If Analysis

One key benefit of Excel is its ability to do a **what-if analysis**, which lets you examine how changing values entered directly in a worksheet, such as the interest rate, the length of the loan, or the amount borrowed, affect the calculated values. By setting up a worksheet with these values and then using cell references in the function, you can easily change the known values to see the effect on the result of the PMT function.

For example, what would the monthly payment be if you changed the length of the loan? The only value you need to change to see this result is the value in cell B6, the number of years of the loan. By changing this value, you will change the calculated value in cell B7, which is the total number of payments—the nper argument in the PMT function—and therefore the result of the PMT function in cell B10.

Begin Activity

Analyze other loan options.

1 Click **cell B6**, type **4**, and then press the **Enter key**. By reducing the number of years from five to four, the amount of the monthly payment increases to $469.70.

2 In **cell B8**, change the value to **18,000**. For this smaller loan, the monthly payment drops to $422.73 per month.

End Activity

14-6 USING REFERENCES TO ANOTHER WORKSHEET

In addition to referencing cells on a worksheet, you can reference cells on another worksheet. The reference to a cell or range on another worksheet begins with the sheet name followed by an exclamation point and then the cell reference. If the sheet name has spaces in it, the sheet name is enclosed in single quotation marks. For example, if the Budget worksheet contained a reference to cell B10 on the Car Loan Calculator worksheet, it would appear as ='Car Loan Calculator'!B10. See Exhibit 14-29. As with references to cells on the same worksheet, you can add the cell or range reference by typing or clicking.

Begin Activity

Insert a reference to a cell on another worksheet.

1 Switch to the **Budget worksheet**, and then click **cell A34**.

EXHIBIT 14-29 WORKSHEET WITH A REFERENCE TO A CELL ON ANOTHER WORKSHEET

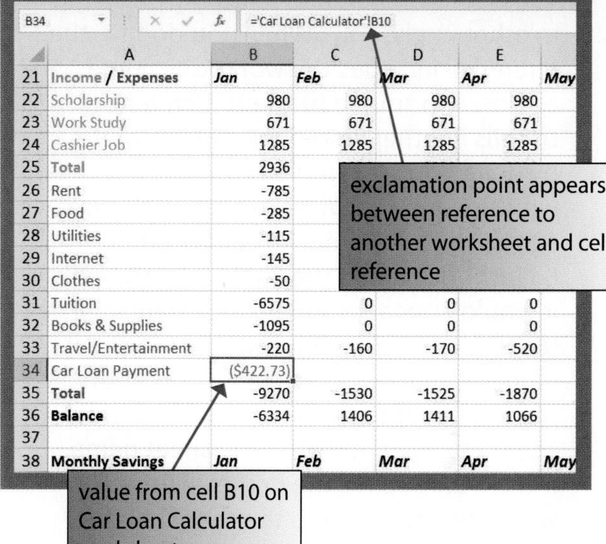

	A	B	C	D	E	
21	Income / Expenses	Jan	Feb	Mar	Apr	May
22	Scholarship	980	980	980	980	
23	Work Study	671	671	671	671	
24	Cashier Job	1285	1285	1285	1285	
25	Total	2936				
26	Rent	-785				
27	Food	-285				
28	Utilities	-115				
29	Internet	-145				
30	Clothes	-50				
31	Tuition	-6575	0	0	0	
32	Books & Supplies	-1095	0	0	0	
33	Travel/Entertainment	-220	-160	-170	-520	
34	Car Loan Payment	($422.73)				
35	Total	-9270	-1530	-1525	-1870	
36	Balance	-6334	1406	1411	1066	
37						
38	Monthly Savings	Jan	Feb	Mar	Apr	May

2 On the Home tab, in the Cells group, click the **Insert button arrow**, and then click **Insert Sheet Rows**. A new row 34 is inserted.

3 In **cell A34**, enter **Car Loan Payment**.

4 In **cell B34**, type = (an equal sign).

5 Click the **Car Loan Calculator sheet tab**, and then click **cell B10**. In the formula bar, the formula appears as ='Car Loan Calculator'!B10. This indicates that the cell being referenced is on another worksheet—in this case, the worksheet named Car Loan Calculator.

6 To the left of the formula bar, click the **Enter button** ✓. The Budget worksheet is the active sheet and the value ($422.73) appears in cell B34. Refer back to Exhibit 14-29.

7 In the formula bar, double-click **B10**, and then press the **F4 key**. The cell reference changes to an absolute reference to cell B10 on the Car Loan Calculator worksheet.

8 To the left of the formula bar, click the **Enter button** ✓.

9 Copy the formula in **cell B34** to the **range C34:M34**.

End Activity

FYI USING REFERENCES TO CELLS IN ANOTHER WORKBOOK

You can also reference cells on worksheets in other workbooks. When you do this, the reference includes the workbook name enclosed in square brackets. References to cells in other workbooks are absolute by default. For example, if the Budget worksheet in the Willis Budget workbook contained a reference to cell A1 on the Loan worksheet in the Banking workbook, it would appear as =[Banking]Loan!$A$1. If either the workbook name or the sheet name contains spaces, single quotation marks appear to the left of the first square bracket and after the sheet name. If the workbook name in the example was Banking Final and the sheet name was Loan Amounts, the reference to cell A1 would be ='[Banking Final]Loan Amounts'!$A$1.

EDITING FORMULAS AND FUNCTIONS

If you need to change a formula or function after it is entered, you can edit it just as you would edit a cell containing data. If a formula or function contains a range reference, you can double-click the cell containing the formula or function to make the formula appear in the cell and to highlight the range used in the formula. Then you can select the range again, drag a handle on the border of the shading to change the reference, or edit the reference by typing. See Exhibit 14-30.

Begin Activity

Insert a reference to a cell on another worksheet.

1 In the Budget worksheet, double-click **cell B35**. The formula in this cell appears in the cell instead of the calculated value, and the cells in the range referenced in the formula are shaded blue. Refer to Exhibit 14-30.

EXHIBIT 14-30 EDITING A CELL CONTAINING A FORMULA

2 In cell B35, click after **B33**, press the **Backspace key**, and then type **4**. Cell B34 is now included in the shaded blue range.

3 Press the **Tab key**. The total in cell B35 is recalculated to –9692.731.

4 Double-click **cell C35**. The formula appears in the cell, and the cells in the range referenced in the formula are shaded blue.

5 In **cell C33**, position the pointer on top one of the **bottom-right fill handle** on the border around the shaded range so that the pointer changes to ↖↘.

6 Press and hold the **mouse button**, drag the border of the shaded range down one row so that it includes cell C34, and then release the **mouse button.** The formula in cell C35 changes to =SUM(C26:C34).

7 To the left of the formula bar, click the **Enter button** ✓. The result in cell C35 is now –1952.731.

8 Copy the formula in **cell C35** to the **range D35:M35.** The formulas in the range B35:M35 that calculate the total expenses now include the row you added to insert the monthly car loan payment.

End Activity

FORMATTING CELLS AND RANGES

A workbook often contains several cells that store the same type of data. For example, each worksheet might have a cell that contains the sheet title, or a range of financial data might have several cells containing summary totals. A good design practice is to apply the same format to worksheet cells that contain the same type of data.

You can format the appearance of individual cells by modifying the alignment of text within the cell, indenting cell text, or adding borders of different styles and colors to individual cells or ranges.

14-8a Using the Format Cells Dialog Box

The buttons in the Font and Alignment groups on the Home tab provide access to the most common formatting choices. Using these buttons has the same effect as in Word. As you have already seen, you can also use the buttons in the Number group to format cell values.

If you need to make more formatting changes to cell contents, you can open the Format Cells dialog box. See Exhibit 14-31.

EXHIBIT 14-31 NUMBER TAB IN THE FORMAT CELLS DIALOG BOX WITH THE CURRENCY CATEGORY SELECTED

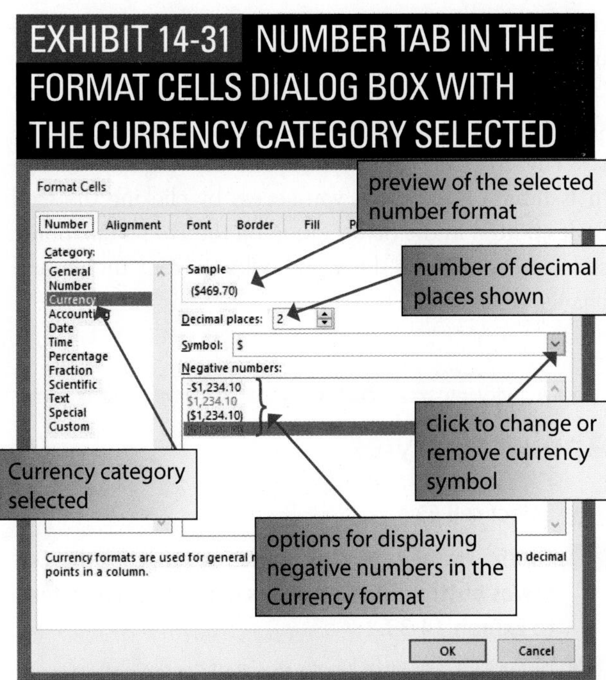

The Format Cells dialog box has the following six tabs, each focusing on a different set of formatting options:

- **Number**—options for formatting the appearance of numbers, including dates and numbers treated as text such as telephone or Social Security numbers.
- **Alignment**—options for how data is aligned within a cell.
- **Font**—options for selecting fonts, font sizes, font styles, underlining, font colors, and font effect.
- **Border**—options for adding and removing cell borders as well as selecting a line style and color.
- **Fill**—options for creating and applying background colors and patterns to cells.
- **Protection**—options for locking or hiding cells to prevent other users from modifying their contents.

Begin Activity

Use the Format Cells dialog box.

1 In the Budget worksheet, select the **range B34:M34**. These cells are formatted with the Currency number format. A standard accounting practice is to display a currency symbol in only the first and total entries within a column of values.

2 On the Home tab, in the Number group, click the **Dialog Box Launcher**. The Format Cells dialog box opens with the Number tab selected. Currency is selected in the Category box. Refer back to Exhibit 14-31. In the Category list, Currency is selected. This is the same format that appears in the Number Format box in the Number group on the Home tab. In the Negative numbers list, the last option is selected. This is why the negative number appears as red and between parentheses. When you apply the Currency format directly, the default choice for negative numbers is the first option in the list—with a minus sign before the number and with black text.

TIP: You can also open the Format Cells dialog box by right-clicking a cell or selected range, and then clicking Format Cells on the shortcut menu.

3 In the Category box, click **Accounting**. The dialog box changes to show the options for the Accounting format—in this case, two decimal places and a dollar sign as the symbol.

4 Click the **Decimal places box down arrow** twice. The value in the box changes to 0 and the decimal places are removed from the number in the Sample box.

5 Click the **Symbol box arrow**, and then click **None**. The dollar sign is removed from the number in the Sample box.

TIP: You could also click the Comma Style button in the Number group on the Home tab to format cells with the Accounting format with no currency symbol.

6 Click **OK**. The selected cells are formatted with the Accounting Number format with no symbol and zero decimal places.

7 Format the **nonadjacent range B23:M24;B27:M33** with the **Accounting format** but with **zero decimal places** and **no symbol**.

8 Format the **nonadjacent range B22:M22;B25:M26;B39:M39;B42:M42** with the **Accounting format** but with **zero decimal places**. (This range should have the dollar sign.)

9 Format the **nonadjacent range B6:C6;E7:F7;B9:C9;B12;B16** with the **Accounting format** and **zero decimal places**, then modify the format of the **nonadjacent range B7:C8;B13:B15;B17:B19** with the **Accounting format** with **zero decimal places** and **no symbol**.

End Activity

Recall that if you enter an integer with more digits than can fit in a cell, the column width automatically widens to accommodate the number. However, if you enter a decimal value in a cell and it is too wide to fit in the cell, the decimal places are rounded so that the number fits. And if you resize a column narrower after you enter a number and the number no longer fits in the cell, or if you apply a format that makes the number larger, such as adding decimal places, and the number no longer fits in the cell, ###### appears in the cell instead of the number. The number is still in the cell as it was entered or formatted, and you see the complete number in the formula bar. You can also display the entire number by increasing the column width or changing the number format.

Begin Activity

Format additional cells with the Accounting format.

1 Select the **nonadjacent range B35:M36;B40:B41**.

2 On the Home tab, in the Number group, click the **Accounting Number Format button** [$]. The Accounting format is applied to the range. In several of the selected cells, ######## appears instead of the value.

3 In the Number group, click the **Decrease Decimal button** [.00 →.0] twice. The decimal places are removed, and the numbers fit in the column. Notice that the values in several of the cells, including cell B35, are within parentheses. This is how the Accounting format displays negative values.

TIP: If pound signs (#) appear in a cell, you can increase the column width to display a value.

4 Select the **range B40:M41**. In the Number group, click the **Comma Style button** [,]. The Accounting format with no symbol is applied.

5 In the Number group, click the **Decrease Decimal button** [.00 →.0] twice. Compare your screen to Exhibit 14-32. You will need to scroll to see all the rows on your screen.

End Activity

14-8b Applying Cell Styles

Similar to styles you apply to text in Word, you can apply styles to change how a cell and its contents are formatted. For example, you can create a style to display titles in a bold, white, 20-point Calibri font on a blue background. You can then apply that style to any cell with a title in the workbook. As in Word, if you revise the style, the appearance of any cell formatted with that style is updated automatically.

Excel has a variety of built-in styles to format worksheet titles, column and row totals, and cells with emphasis. These are available in the Cell Styles gallery shown in Exhibit 14-33, which you access by clicking the Cell Styles button in the Styles group on the Home tab. Some styles are based on the workbook's current theme and change if the theme is changed.

Begin Activity

Apply cell styles.

1 Select **cell E5**.

2 On the Home tab, in the Styles group, click the **Cell Styles button**. The Cell Styles gallery opens. Refer to Exhibit 14-33.

3 Point to several styles in the Cell Styles gallery to see the Live Preview of the style on cell E5.

4 In the Themed Cell Styles section, click the **Accent5 style**. The gallery closes, and the text in cell E5 is formatted as 11-point, white text, and the cell is filled with a blue background. The text overflows into cell F5. You cannot see the overflow text because it is now formatted as white, and cell F5 is filled with white; white text on a white background is not visible. You'll fix this shortly.

5 Select the **nonadjacent cells A5;A11;A21;A38**, and then apply the **Accent5 style** to the selected cells.

6 Select the **nonadjacent range B25:M25;B42:M42**.

EXHIBIT 14-32 BUDGET WORKSHEET WITH FORMATTED NUMBERS

	A	B	C	D	E	F	G	H	I	J	K	L	M
5	**Monthly Income**	Sept-May	June-Aug		**Savings Account**								
6	Scholarship	$ 980	$ -		Starting	Ending							
7	Work Study	671	-		$ 8,500	$ 4,241							
8	Cashier Job	1,285	3,750										
9	**Total**	$ 2,936	$ 3,750										
10													
11	**Year-End Summary**												
12	Total Income	$ 37,674											
13	Monthly Average	3,140											
14	Monthly Minimum	2,936											
15	Monthly Maximum	3,750											
16	Total Expenses	$ (41,933)											
17	Monthly Average	(3,494)											
18	Monthly Minimum	(9,693)											
19	Monthly Maximum	(1,913)											
20													
21	Income / Expenses	*Jan*	*Feb*	*Mar*	*Apr*	*May*	*Jun*	*Jul*	*Aug*	*Sep*	*Oct*	*Nov*	*Dec*
22	Scholarship	$ 980	$ 980	$ 980	$ 980	$ 980	$ -	$ -	$ -	$ 980	$ 980	$ 980	$ 980
23	Work Study	671	671	671	671	671	-	-	-	671	671	671	671
24	Cashier Job	1,285	1,285	1,285	1,285	1,285	3,750	3,750	3,750	1,285	1,285	1,285	1,285
25	Total	$ 2,936	$ 2,936	$ 2,936	$ 2,936	$ 2,936	$ 3,750	$ 3,750	$ 3,750	$ 2,936	$ 2,936	$ 2,936	$ 2,936
26	Rent	$ (785)	$ (785)	$ (785)	$ (785)	$ (785)	$ (785)	$ (785)	$ (785)	$ (785)	$ (785)	$ (785)	$ (785)
27	Food	(285)	(285)	(285)	(285)	(285)	(285)	(285)	(285)	(285)	(285)	(285)	(285)
28	Utilities	(115)	(105)	(90)	(85)	(70)	(75)	(80)	(75)	(70)	(70)	(90)	(105)
29	Internet	(145)	(145)	(145)	(145)	(145)	(145)	(145)	(145)	(145)	(145)	(145)	(145)
30	Clothes	(50)	(50)	(50)	(50)	(150)	(50)	(50)	(250)	(50)	(50)	(150)	(50)
31	Tuition	(6,575)	-	-	-	-	(1,350)	-	(5,900)	-	-	-	-
32	Books & Supplies	(1,095)	-	-	-	-	(475)	-	(875)	-	-	-	-
33	Travel/Entertainment	(220)	(160)	(170)	(520)	(170)	(190)	(920)	(550)	(155)	(225)	(315)	(385)
34	Car Loan Payment	(423)	(423)	(423)	(423)	(423)	(423)	(423)	(423)	(423)	(423)	(423)	(423)
35	**Total**	$ (9,693)	$ (1,953)	$ (1,948)	$ (2,293)	$ (2,028)	$ (3,778)	$ (2,688)	$ (9,288)	$ (1,913)	$ (1,983)	$ (2,193)	$ (2,178)
36	**Balance**	$ (6,757)	$ 983	$ 988	$ 643	$ 908	$ (28)	$ 1,062	$ (5,538)	$ 1,023	$ 953	$ 743	$ 758
37													
38	**Monthly Savings**	*Jan*	*Feb*	*Mar*	*Apr*	*May*	*Jun*	*Jul*	*Aug*	*Sep*	*Oct*	*Nov*	*Dec*
39	Starting Balance	$ 8,500	$ 1,743	$ 2,727	$ 3,715	$ 4,358	$ 5,266	$ 5,239	$ 6,301	$ 763	$ 1,786	$ 2,740	$ 3,483
40	Deposits	2,936	2,936	2,936	2,936	2,936	3,750	3,750	3,750	2,936	2,936	2,936	2,936
41	Withdrawals	(9,693)	(1,953)	(1,948)	(2,293)	(2,028)	(3,778)	(2,688)	(9,288)	(1,913)	(1,983)	(2,193)	(2,178)
42	Ending Balance	$ 1,743	$ 2,727	$ 3,715	$ 4,358	$ 5,266	$ 5,239	$ 6,301	$ 763	$ 1,786	$ 2,740	$ 3,483	$ 4,241

EXHIBIT 14-33 CELL STYLES GALLERY

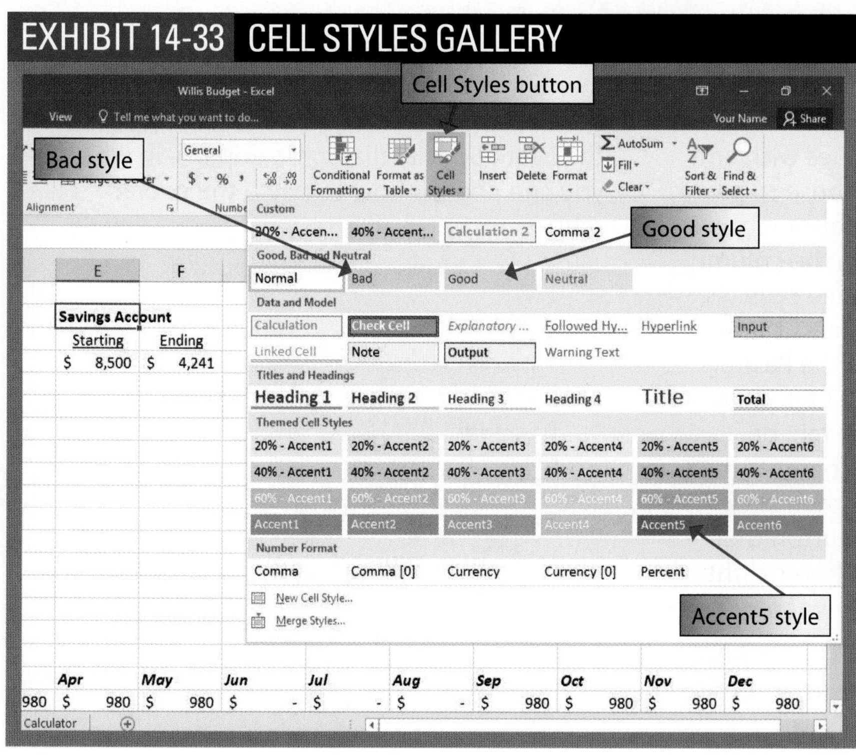

7 In the Styles group, click the **Cell Styles button**. In the Good, Bad and Neutral section, click the **Good style**. Each cell in the selected range is formatted with green text on a light green background.

8 Select the **range B35:M35**.

9 In the Styles group, click the **Cell Styles button**. In the Good, Bad and Neutral section, click the **Bad style**. The expense values are formatted with red text on a light red background.

10 Click **any cell** in the worksheet to deselect the range. Compare your screen to Exhibit 14-34.

End Activity

EXHIBIT 14-34 BUDGET WORKSHEET WITH CELL STYLES APPLIED

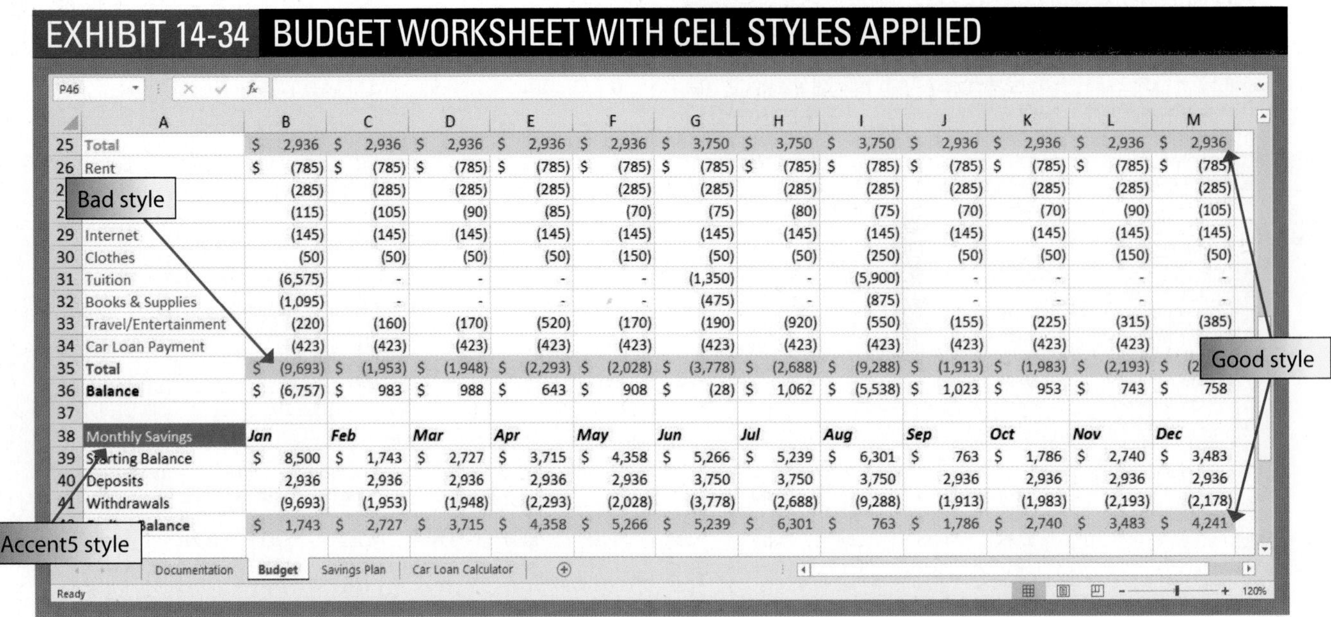

	A	B	C	D	E	F	G	H	I	J	K	L	M
25	Total	$ 2,936	$ 2,936	$ 2,936	$ 2,936	$ 2,936	$ 3,750	$ 3,750	$ 3,750	$ 2,936	$ 2,936	$ 2,936	$ 2,936
26	Rent	$ (785)	$ (785)	$ (785)	$ (785)	$ (785)	$ (785)	$ (785)	$ (785)	$ (785)	$ (785)	$ (785)	$ (785)
2		(285)	(285)	(285)	(285)	(285)	(285)	(285)	(285)	(285)	(285)	(285)	(285)
2		(115)	(105)	(90)	(85)	(70)	(75)	(80)	(75)	(70)	(70)	(90)	(105)
29	Internet	(145)	(145)	(145)	(145)	(145)	(145)	(145)	(145)	(145)	(145)	(145)	(145)
30	Clothes	(50)	(50)	(50)	(50)	(150)	(50)	(50)	(250)	(50)	(50)	(150)	(50)
31	Tuition	(6,575)	-	-	-	-	(1,350)	-	(5,900)	-	-	-	-
32	Books & Supplies	(1,095)	-	-	-	-	(475)	-	(875)	-	-	-	-
33	Travel/Entertainment	(220)	(160)	(170)	(520)	(170)	(190)	(920)	(550)	(155)	(225)	(315)	(385)
34	Car Loan Payment	(423)	(423)	(423)	(423)	(423)	(423)	(423)	(423)	(423)	(423)	(423)	
35	Total	$ (9,693)	$ (1,953)	$ (1,948)	$ (2,293)	$ (2,028)	$ (3,778)	$ (2,688)	$ (9,288)	$ (1,913)	$ (1,983)	$ (2,193)	$ (2
36	Balance	$ (6,757)	$ 983	$ 988	$ 643	$ 908	$ (28)	$ 1,062	$ (5,538)	$ 1,023	$ 953	$ 743	$ 758
37													
38	Monthly Savings	Jan	Feb	Mar	Apr	May	Jun	Jul	Aug	Sep	Oct	Nov	Dec
39	Starting Balance	$ 8,500	$ 1,743	$ 2,727	$ 3,715	$ 4,358	$ 5,266	$ 5,239	$ 6,301	$ 763	$ 1,786	$ 2,740	$ 3,483
40	Deposits	2,936	2,936	2,936	2,936	2,936	3,750	3,750	3,750	2,936	2,936	2,936	2,936
41	Withdrawals	(9,693)	(1,953)	(1,948)	(2,293)	(2,028)	(3,778)	(2,688)	(9,288)	(1,913)	(1,983)	(2,193)	(2,178)
	Balance	$ 1,743	$ 2,727	$ 3,715	$ 4,358	$ 5,266	$ 5,239	$ 6,301	$ 763	$ 1,786	$ 2,740	$ 3,483	$ 4,241

14-8c Aligning Cell Content

Text in a cell is horizontally left-aligned by default, and numeric values (including dates) are right-aligned. The default vertical alignment for cell contents is bottom-aligned. You might want to change these alignments to make the cell content more readable or visually appealing. In general, you should center column titles and left-align other cell text and align numbers within a column by the decimal point. The buttons to set these alignment options are located in the Alignment group on the Home tab. Exhibit 14-35 describes the actions of these buttons.

FYI COPYING AND PASTING FORMATS

The Paste Options button in Excel is similar to the Paste Options button in Word. However, in Excel, it includes many more options than in Word. For example, you can paste values with and without formatting, you can choose to paste calculated results instead of a formula, or you can paste values and retain the column width from the source cells. As in Word, you can access these options by clicking the Paste button arrow in the Clipboard group on the Home tab, or you can paste cell contents in the worksheet and then click the Paste Options button that appears below the lower-right corner of the range where you pasted the items.

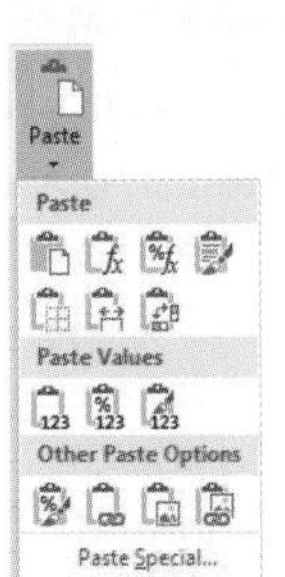

In Excel, you can also use the Paste Special command on the Paste button menu to control how content is pasted from the Clipboard. When you click Paste Special, the Paste Special dialog box opens, in which you can choose how to paste the copied range.

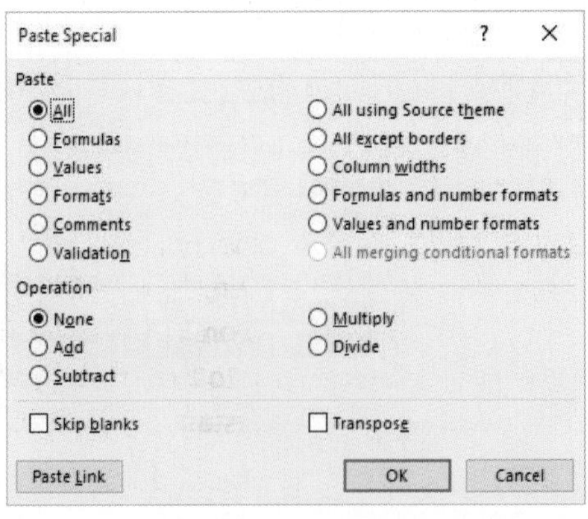

EXHIBIT 14-35 ALIGNMENT BUTTONS

Button	Name	Description
	Top Align	Aligns the cell content with the cell's top edge
	Middle Align	Centers the cell content vertically within the cell
	Bottom Align	Aligns the cell content with the cell's bottom edge
	Align Left	Aligns the cell content with the cell's left edge
	Center	Centers the cell content horizontally within the cell
	Align Right	Aligns the cell content with the cell's right edge
	Decrease Indent	Decreases the size of the indentation used in the cell
	Increase Indent	Increases the size of the indentation used in the cell
	Orientation	Rotates the cell content to any angle within the cell
	Wrap Text	Forces the cell text to wrap within the cell borders
	Merge & Center	Merges the selected cells into a single cell, and centers the content horizontally within the merged cell

Begin Activity

Align cell content.

1. Select **cell A3**.
2. On the Home tab, in the Alignment group, click the **Align Left button**. The date is left-aligned in the cell. This makes the header information on the worksheet easier to read.
3. Select the **nonadjacent range B21:M21;B38:M38.**
4. In the Alignment group, click the **Center button**. The selected column labels are centered.
5. Select the **nonadjacent range A9;A25;A35:A36;A42.** These rows all contain calculated totals.
6. In the Alignment group, click the **Align Right button**. The selected labels are right-aligned in their cells.

TIP: For cells taller than the height of their contents, you can change the vertical alignment from the default bottom-alignment so the contents are middle- or top-aligned.

End Activity

14-8d Indenting Cell Content

Sometimes you want a cell's content indented a few spaces from the cell's left edge. This is particularly useful for entries that are considered subsections of a worksheet. For example, the monthly deposits and withdrawals in rows 39 and 40 of the Budget worksheet can be considered a subsection. They would be easier to identify if the labels were indented a few spaces. Each time you click the Increase Indent button in the Alignment group on the Home tab, you increase the indentation by roughly one character space. To decrease or remove an indentation, click the Decrease Indent button.

Begin Activity

Indent cell content.

1. Select the **range A40:A41**.
2. On the Home tab, in the Alignment group, click the **Increase Indent button** twice. The contents of the selected cells indent to the right two character spaces.
3. In the Alignment group, click the **Decrease Indent button**. Each label moves left one character space. See Exhibit 14-36.

End Activity

14-8e Merging Cells

Merging combines two or more cells into one cell. You can merge cells horizontally and vertically. When you merge cells, only the content from the upper-left cell in the range is retained, and the cell reference for the merged cell is the original upper-left cell reference. For example, if you merge cells A1 and A2, the merged cell reference is cell A1, and if you merge cells A1, A2, B1, and B2, the merged cell reference is still cell A1.

To merge selected cells and center the content, use the Merge button in the Alignment group on the Home tab. If you click the Merge button arrow, you can choose from the following merge options:

- **Merge & Center**—merges the range into one cell, and horizontally centers the content.

merge To combine two or more cells into one cell.

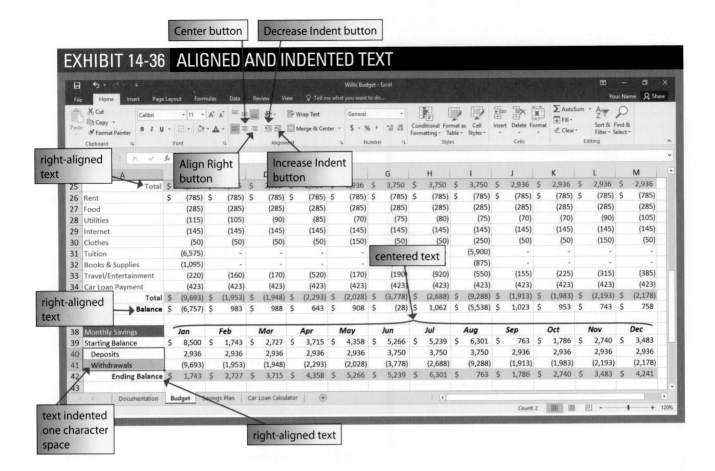

EXHIBIT 14-36 ALIGNED AND INDENTED TEXT

Center button

Decrease Indent button

right-aligned text

Align Right button

Increase Indent button

centered text

right-aligned text

text indented one character space

right-aligned text

- **Merge Across**—merges each of the rows in the selected range across the columns in the range.
- **Merge Cells**—merges the range into a single cell, but does not horizontally center the cell content.
- **Unmerge Cells**—reverses a merge, returning the merged cell back into a range of individual cells.

After you merge a range into a single cell, you can change the alignment of its content.

Begin Activity

Merge and center cells.

1. Select the **range E5:F5.**
2. On the Home tab, in the Alignment group, click the **Merge & Center button.** The range E5:F5 merges into one cell. The merged cell reference is E5, and the text is centered within the merged cell. The formatting from cell E5 is applied to the new merged cell. Compare your screen to Exhibit 14-37.

TIP: After merging cells with formatting, you might need to reapply formatting or the cell style.

End Activity

EXHIBIT 14-37 MERGED CELLS

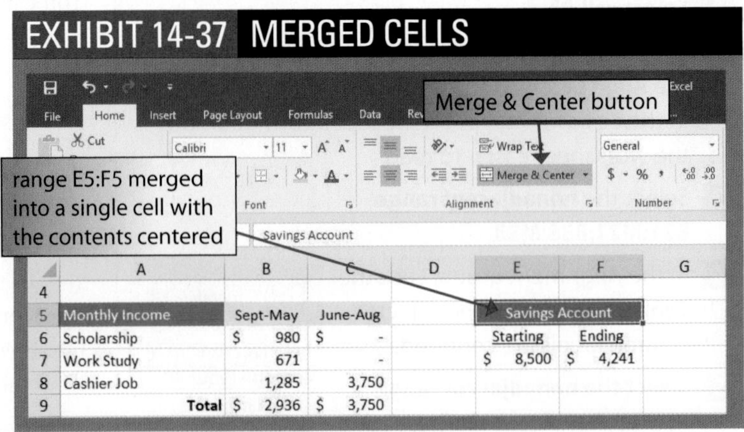

14-8f Adding Cell Borders

Sometimes you want to include lines along the edges of cells to improve the readability of the rows and columns of data. One way to do this is by adding a border to a cell or range. A line that you add along an edge of a

FYI ROTATING CELL CONTENT

Text and numbers are usually displayed within cells horizontally. However, you can rotate cell text to save space or to provide visual interest to a worksheet. This is commonly used as a way to label narrow columns or identify rows in a category. For example, the Budget worksheet you are working on could be reorganized to include category labels in a merged cell to the left of each category that are rotated in the merged cells so that they read vertically from bottom to top, as shown in the illustration. You can choose from the following Orientation options, which you access by clicking the Orientation button in the Alignment group on the Home tab:

- **Angle Counterclockwise**—rotates cell content to a 45-degree angle to the upper-right corner of the merged cell.
- **Angle Clockwise**—rotates cell content to a 45-degree angle to the lower-right corner of the merged cell.

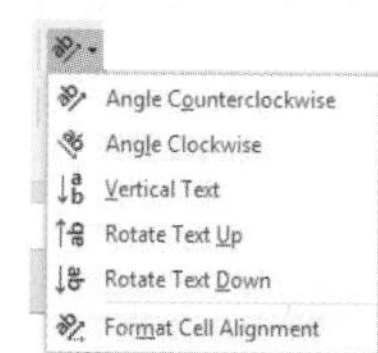

- **Vertical Text**—rotates cell content to appear stacked from the top of the cell to the bottom.
- **Rotate Text Up**—rotates cell content 90 degrees counterclockwise so that text is placed sideways in the cell and read from the bottom of the cell to the top.
- **Rotate Text Down**—rotates cell content 90 degrees clockwise so that text is placed sideways in the cell and read from the top of the cell to the bottom.

After you rotate cell content, you may need to resize the column width or row height to eliminate excess space or add more space so that the cell contents are completely visible.

cell is called a **border**. You can add borders to the left, top, right, or bottom of a cell or range; around an entire cell; or around the outside edges of a range. A standard accounting practice is to add a single top border and a double bottom border to the total rows to clearly differentiate them from financial data. You can also specify the thickness of and the number of lines in the border. All of these border options are available from the Borders button in the Font group on the Home tab, as shown in Exhibit 14-38.

Borders are different from the gridlines that surround the cells in each worksheet. **Gridlines** are the lines that divide the columns and rows on the worksheet and define the structure of the worksheet. When a worksheet is printed, the gridlines are not printed unless you specify that they should be. Borders are always printed.

Begin Activity

Add cell borders.

1. Select the **range B9:C9**. This row shows the total monthly income during school and summer.
2. On the Home tab, in the Font group, click the **Borders button arrow** to display a list of available borders and options. Refer back to Exhibit 14-38.

EXHIBIT 14-38 BORDERS BUTTON MENU

Borders button

Top and Double Bottom Border command

border A line added along an edge of a cell.

gridlines In a worksheet, lines that divide columns and rows in a worksheet and define the structure of the worksheet.

3 Click **Top and Double Bottom Border**. The borders on the selected cells change to black lines. Notice that the Borders button changed to [icon] to match the selection you just made.

4 Select the **nonadjacent range B25:M25;B35:M35;B42;M42**. These rows show the total monthly income, expenses, and account balance.

TIP: You can use the Total cell style to make cell text bold and add colored top and double bottom borders to selected cells.

5 In the Font group, click the **Borders button** [icon]. The selected cells now have a single top border and a double bottom border, following standard accounting practice.

6 Select the **range A1:C1**.

7 On the Home tab, in the Font group, click the **Borders button arrow** [icon], and then click **More Borders**. The Format Cells dialog box opens with the Border tab displayed. See Exhibit 14-39.

8 In the Line section, in the Style box, click the **thickest line** (the sixth line in the second column).

EXHIBIT 14-39 BORDER TAB IN THE FORMAT CELLS DIALOG BOX

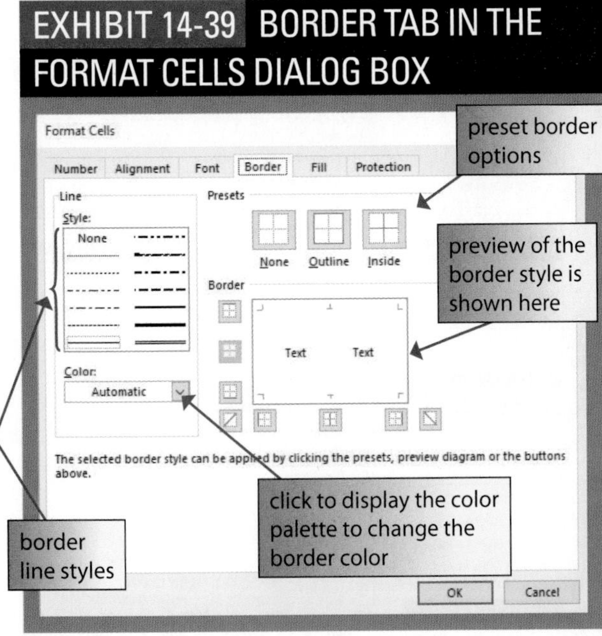

fill color A color added to cells or shapes.

9 In the Line section, click the **Color arrow** to display the color palette. Click the **Blue, Accent 5, Darker 25% color**.

10 In the Border section, click the **bottom border** of the preview. A thick, dark blue bottom border appears in the preview.

11 Click **OK**. The dialog box closes, and the selected cells have a thick, dark blue bottom border.

End Activity

14-8g Changing Cell Background Color

Another way to distinguish sections of a worksheet is by formatting the cell background. You can change the color of cells by adding background colors, also known as **fill colors** because you are filling the cell with colors. You already added fill colors when you used the styles to format the category labels and the total rows. If you don't like any of the styles with fill colors in the Cell Styles gallery, you can select any background color you like by clicking the Fill Color button arrow in the Font group on the Home tab.

If you add a dark fill color to cells, black text can be harder to read than text formatted with a light or white font color. The Accent5 cell style that you applied to the category labels in the Budget worksheet changed the font color in these cells to white as part of the style. If you change the fill color of cells using the Fill Color button, you might then need to change the font color in those cells.

Begin Activity

Change the fill color.

1 Select the **range E6:F7**.

2 On the Home tab, in the Font group, click the **Fill Color button arrow** [icon] to display the color palette.

3 In the Theme Colors section, click the **Orange, Accent 2, Lighter 60% color**. The background color of the cells is now light orange, hiding the gridlines. Compare your final worksheet to Exhibit 14-40.

4 Save the workbook, and then close it.

End Activity

EXHIBIT 14-40 FINAL BUDGET WORKSHEET WITH BORDER AND FILL COLORS

	A	B	C	D	E	F	G	H	I	J	K	L	M
1	*Budget*												
2	**Projected Income and Expenses**												
3	10/15/2015												
4													
5	Monthly Income	Sept-May	June-Aug		Savings Account								
6	Scholarship	$ 980	$ -		Starting	Ending							
7	Work Study	671	-		$ 8,500	$ 4,241							
8	Cashier Job	1,285	3,750										
9	**Total**	$ 2,936	$ 3,750										
10													
11	Year-End Summary												
12	Total Income	$ 37,674											
13	Monthly Average	3,140											
14	Monthly Minimum	2,936											
15	Monthly Maximum	3,750											
16	Total Expenses	$ (41,933)											
17	Monthly Average	(3,494)											
18	Monthly Minimum	(9,693)											
19	Monthly Maximum	(1,913)											
20													
21	Income / Expenses	*Jan*	*Feb*	*Mar*	*Apr*	*May*	*Jun*	*Jul*	*Aug*	*Sep*	*Oct*	*Nov*	*Dec*
22	Scholarship	$ 980	$ 980	$ 980	$ 980	$ 980	$ -	$ -	$ -	$ 980	$ 980	$ 980	$ 980
23	Work Study	671	671	671	671	671	-	-	-	671	671	671	671
24	Cashier Job	1,285	1,285	1,285	1,285	1,285	3,750	3,750	3,750	1,285	1,285	1,285	1,285
25	Total	$ 2,936	$ 2,936	$ 2,936	$ 2,936	$ 2,936	$ 3,750	$ 3,750	$ 3,750	$ 2,936	$ 2,936	$ 2,936	$ 2,936
26	Rent	$ (785)	$ (785)	$ (785)	$ (785)	$ (785)	$ (785)	$ (785)	$ (785)	$ (785)	$ (785)	$ (785)	$ (785)
27	Food	(285)	(285)	(285)	(285)	(285)	(285)	(285)	(285)	(285)	(285)	(285)	(285)
28	Utilities	(115)	(105)	(90)	(85)	(70)	(75)	(80)	(75)	(70)	(70)	(90)	(105)
29	Internet	(145)	(145)	(145)	(145)	(145)	(145)	(145)	(145)	(145)	(145)	(145)	(145)
30	Clothes	(50)	(50)	(50)	(50)	(150)	(50)	(50)	(250)	(50)	(50)	(150)	(50)
31	Tuition	(6,575)	-	-	-	-	(1,350)	-	(5,900)	-	-	-	-
32	Books & Supplies	(1,095)	-	-	-	-	(475)	-	(875)	-	-	-	-
33	Travel/Entertainment	(220)	(160)	(170)	(520)	(170)	(190)	(920)	(550)	(155)	(225)	(315)	(385)
34	Car Loan Payment	(423)	(423)	(423)	(423)	(423)	(423)	(423)	(423)	(423)	(423)	(423)	(423)
35	Total	$ (9,693)	$ (1,953)	$ (1,948)	$ (2,293)	$ (2,028)	$ (3,778)	$ (2,688)	$ (9,288)	$ (1,913)	$ (1,983)	$ (2,193)	$ (2,178)
36	**Balance**	$ (6,757)	$ 983	$ 988	$ 643	$ 908	$ (28)	$ 1,062	$ (5,538)	$ 1,023	$ 953	$ 743	$ 758
37													
38	Monthly Savings	*Jan*	*Feb*	*Mar*	*Apr*	*May*	*Jun*	*Jul*	*Aug*	*Sep*	*Oct*	*Nov*	*Dec*
39	Starting Balance	$ 8,500	$ 1,743	$ 2,727	$ 3,715	$ 4,358	$ 5,266	$ 5,239	$ 6,301	$ 763	$ 1,786	$ 2,740	$ 3,483
40	Deposits	2,936	2,936	2,936	2,936	2,936	3,750	3,750	3,750	2,936	2,936	2,936	2,936
41	Withdrawals	(9,693)	(1,953)	(1,948)	(2,293)	(2,028)	(3,778)	(2,688)	(9,288)	(1,913)	(1,983)	(2,193)	(2,178)
42	Ending Balance	$ 1,743	$ 2,727	$ 3,715	$ 4,358	$ 5,266	$ 5,239	$ 6,301	$ 763	$ 1,786	$ 2,740	$ 3,483	$ 4,241
43													

STUDY TOOLS 14

READY TO STUDY? IN THE BOOK, YOU CAN:

- ☐ Rip out the Chapter Review Card, which includes key terms and key chapter concepts.

ONLINE AT WWW.CENGAGEBRAIN.COM, YOU CAN:

- ☐ Review key concepts from the chapter in a short video.
- ☐ Explore working with functions and formulas in Excel with the interactive infographic.
- ☐ Practice what you've learned with more Practice It and On Your Own exercises.
- ☐ Prepare for tests with quizzes
- ☐ Review the key terms with flashcards.

QUIZ YOURSELF

1. Explain the difference between a relative reference, an absolute reference, and a mixed reference.
2. What are the relative, absolute, and mixed cell references for cell H9?
3. What is the general syntax of all Excel functions?
4. In a function, what is an argument?
5. Describe how to type a function directly in a cell.
6. What is AutoFill?
7. How do you use the fill handle?
8. Describe how to use AutoFill to create a series of numbers.
9. What is a date function?
10. Which date function returns the current date?
11. What is the PMT function?
12. What is the syntax of the PMT function?
13. Most interest rates are presented as an annual interest rate. How do you determine the interest rate per month?
14. Write the formula to determine the monthly payment for a $50,000 loan with an annual interest rate of 4 percent that will be repaid in three years.
15. Why does the PMT function return a negative value?
16. Why would you use a cell style?
17. Unless you change the alignment, how is text aligned within a cell, and how are values aligned within a cell?
18. If the range A1:C5 is merged into a single cell, what is the cell reference of this merged cell?
19. What is a border?
20. What is a fill color? When would you use fill colors?
21. Where can you access all of the formatting options for worksheet cells?

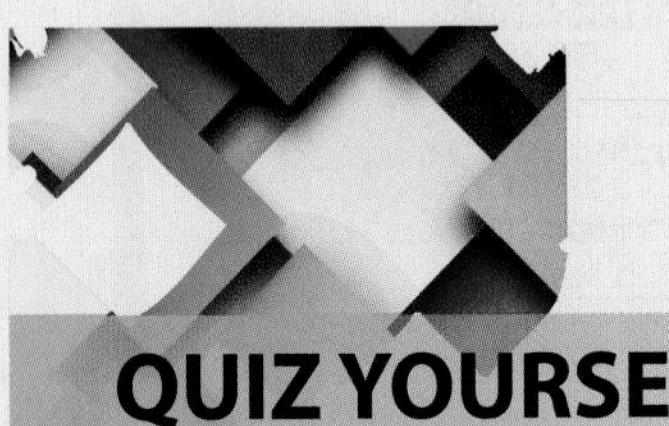

PRACTICE IT

Practice It 14-1

1. Open the data file **Loan** located in the Chapter 14\ Practice It folder. Save the workbook as **Personal Loan**.
2. In the Documentation worksheet, enter your name in cell B3. Enter the TODAY function in cell B4 to display the current date. Widen column B to 9.50 characters, and then left-align the date.
3. Make the Budget worksheet the active sheet. In cell B11, enter **Jan** (without a period).
4. In the range C11:M11, use AutoFill to fill the range with *Feb* through *Dec*.
5. In cell B17, use the SUM function to calculate total January expenses in the range B13:B16. (*Hint*: Do not include the January total income in the calculation.)
6. In cell B18, enter a formula that calculates the difference between January expenses and the total January income.
7. Copy the formulas in the range B17:B18 to the range C17:M18.
8. In cell B3, enter the SUM function to calculate the total monthly income for the entire year in the range B12:M12.
9. In cell C3, enter the AVERAGE function to calculate the average monthly income for the year.
10. In cell D3, enter the MAX function to calculate the maximum monthly income for the year.
11. In cell E3, enter the MIN function to calculate minimum monthly income for the year.
12. Select the range B3:E3, and then copy the formulas in the selected range to the range B4:E9 to complete the Year-End Summary table.
13. On the Loan worksheet, format cells B4 and B6 with the Percent Style, and show two decimal places.
14. In the range B4:B9, enter the following data and formulas:

    cell B4: **4.68**
    cell B5: **12**
    cell B6: **=B4/B5**
    cell B7: **3**
    cell B8: **=B7*B5**
    cell B9: **19000**

15. In cell B11, enter the PMT function to calculate the monthly payment required to repay the loan.
16. On the Budget worksheet, insert a new row 8, and then insert a new row 18. In cell A8 and in cell A18, enter **Personal Loan**. In cell B18, enter the formula **=Loan!B11** to display the results of the PMT function on the Loan worksheet for the January loan payment.
17. Edit the formula in cell B18 to use an absolute reference.
18. Copy the formula in cell B18 into the range C18:M18. Verify that the values in the range B18:M18 match the monthly payment for the loan.
19. Edit the formula in cell B19 so that it includes adding the value in cell B18. Copy the revised formula in cell B19 to the range C19:M19.
20. Copy the formulas in the range B7:E7 to the range B8:E8.
21. Format the numbers in the nonadjacent range B3:E3;B9:E9;B13:M14;B19:M20 with the Accounting format with no decimal places.
22. Format the nonadjacent range B4:E8;B15:M18 with the Accounting format with no decimal places and no currency symbol.
23. Apply the Accent2 cell style to cell A2.
24. Apply the following cell styles to the ranges specified:

    range B13:M13: 40% - Accent2
    range B19:M19: 60% - Accent6
    range B20:M20: 40% - Accent5

25. Select the range C1:E1. Merge and center the cells, and then apply the Explanatory cell style to the range.
26. Center and bold the text in the nonadjacent range B2:E2;B12:M12.
27. Select the range A14:A18, and then indent the text one space.
28. Add a Top and Double Bottom Border to the nonadjacent range B13:M13;B19:M19.
29. Apply the White, Background 1, Darker 5% fill color to the merged cell C1.

30. On the Loan worksheet, in cell B4, change the annual interest rate to **4.02%**. In cell B7, change the total years of the loan to **4**. Verify that the monthly loan payment amounts in row 18 on the Budget worksheet changed to the new payment amount shown in cell B12 on the Loan worksheet.
31. Save the workbook, and then close it.

Practice It 14-2

1. Open the data file **Cloud** located in the Chapter 14\Practice It folder. Save the workbook as **Cloud Backup Services**.
2. In the Documentation worksheet, enter your name in cell B3, and enter the TODAY function in cell B4. Left-align the date in cell B4.
3. In the Price Comparison worksheet, use AutoFill to enter the labels **Month 1**, **Month 2**, and so forth through **Month 12** in the range B12:M12 and the range B17:M17.
4. Format the nonadjacent range B8:C10;F8:G10; J8:K10 as Currency. Format the nonadjacent range B13:N15;B18:N20 as Currency also.
5. Add the following formulas:

cell C8:	a formula to display the setup fee value from cell B8
cell C9:	a formula that multiplies an absolute reference to the monthly timeframe in cell B5 by a relative reference to the monthly fee in cell B9
cell C10:	a formula that multiplies an absolute reference to the number of gigabytes to back up in cell B3 by an absolute reference to the yearly timeframe in cell B4 and by a relative reference to the annual fee per gigabyte in cell B10

6. Copy the formulas in the range C8:C10 to the range G8:G10 and the range K8:K10 to calculate the costs for vendors 2 and 3.
7. In cell B13, enter a formula to add the setup fee, the monthly fee, and the annual fee per gigabyte from the Rate column multiplied by the number of gigabytes to back up for the first vendor. Enter similar formulas in cells B14 and B15 to calculate the Month 1 cost for the first year for the second and third vendors.
8. In the range C13:C15, enter formulas to retrieve the monthly fees shown in the Rate column as the Month 2 cost. Be sure to use an absolute reference to the cell in each formula so you can copy the formulas.
9. Copy the formulas in the range C13:C15 to the range D13:M15.
10. In the range B18:B20, enter formulas to add the monthly fee and the annual fee per gigabyte from the Rate column multiplied by the number of gigabytes to back up for the corresponding vendor to calculate the first month cost for each additional year.
11. In the range C18:C20, enter formulas using absolute values to retrieve the monthly fees shown in the Rate column as the Month 2 cost. Copy the formulas in the range C18:C20 to the range D18:M20.
12. In the range N13:N15;N18:N20, use the SUM function to total the first year and additional year costs for each vendor.
13. Merge the following cells, leaving them left-aligned: range D8:E8, range D9:E9, range D10:E10, range H8:I8, range H9:I9, and range H10:I10. (*Hint*: Click the Merge Cells option on the Merge & Center button menu.)
14. Format the following ranges as directed:

range A7:C7;A13;A18	Accent4 cell style
range A8:C10,B13:N13; B18:N18	20% - Accent4 cell style
range D7:G7;A14;A19	Accent5 cell style
range D8:G10;B14:N14; B19:N19	40% - Accent5 cell style
range H7:K7;A15;A20	Accent6 cell style
range H8:K10;B15:N15; B20:N20	20% - Accent6 cell style

15. Bold and center the labels in the range A12:N12;A17:N17.
16. Add a thick border outline around the range A3:B5 using the fifth style in the second column in the Style box on the Border tab in the Format Cells dialog box, and add thin borders between the cells inside this range.
17. Save the workbook, and then close it.

ON YOUR OWN

On Your Own 14-1

1. Open the data file **Lakeview** located in the Chapter 14\On Your Own folder. Save the workbook as **Lakeview Jazz**.
2. In the Documentation worksheet, enter your name in cell B3, and enter the NOW function in cell B4. Left-align the date.
3. In the Building Fund worksheet, enter the three-letter month abbreviations (Jan, Feb, and so on) for each year (rows 7, 20, 32) in columns C through N. For example, for 2017, enter the month abbreviations in the range C7:N7.
4. On the Calculator worksheet, in the range C3:C8, enter the loan conditions for the PMT function to calculate the monthly payment required to repay a **$1,200,000** loan (principal) in **20** years at an annual rate of **3.8%** that is paid monthly. Format the cells appropriately. Enter the PMT function in cell C10 using the conditions that you just entered.
5. On the Building Fund worksheet, in cell C11, enter a formula with an absolute reference that retrieves the principal of the loan you used in the PMT function.
6. In cell C15 (the Jan 2017 column in the Loan Payment row), enter a formula with an absolute reference to the loan payment returned by the PMT function on the Calculator worksheet. Copy this formula to the rest of the months in 2017, and then to the Loan Payment rows for 2018 and 2019.
7. For each year, use the SUM function to calculate total income per month and total expenses per month.
8. In column O, use the SUM function to calculate the total for each row that contains numeric data.
9. For each year, enter a formula to calculate the net income per month. (Do not calculate the total net income for the year in column O.)
10. In cell C18, enter a formula that adds the starting cash available (retrieved using an absolute reference to cell C3) and the January net cash (retrieved from cell C17) to calculate the January 2017 cash available.
11. In cell D18, enter a formula that adds the cash available from the previous month and the net cash for the current month. Copy this formula to the remaining months in 2017.
12. Copy the 2017 cash available formulas to the other two years. Then edit the January 2018 and 2019 cash available formulas to add the cash available from the last month of the previous year to the net cash for the current month.
13. Merge and center the range A7:A18, and then rotate the text up and middle-align it. Repeat for the range A20:A30 and the range A32:A42.
14. Change the theme to the Dividend theme. (*Hint*: The command is on the Page Layout tab.)
15. On the Building Fund worksheet, format the numeric values with the Accounting format using standard accounting practices. Show two decimal places. Use AutoFit to widen columns as needed.
16. Apply cell styles to the merged cells in column A to fill the merged cells with three different colors.
17. Use a cell style to apply standard accounting borders to the numeric values in the two rows for each year that calculate totals. Right-align the row labels for the two total rows for each year and make them bold.
18. Center the month column labels and the Total headings, and make them bold and underlined.
19. Add a thick border around each of the three ranges that contain the information about each year using the fifth style in the right column in the Style box on the Border tab in the Format Cells dialog box.
20. Save the workbook, and then close it.

Part 7
EXCEL 2016

15 | Creating an Advanced Workbook

© Hero Images/Getty Images

LEARNING OBJECTIVES After studying the material in this chapter, you will be able to...

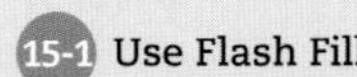

- 15-1 Use Flash Fill
- 15-2 Enter formulas with multiple calculations
- 15-3 Fix error values
- 15-4 Work with the IF logical function
- 15-5 Create a nested IF function
- 15-6 Add conditional formatting
- 15-7 Hide rows and columns
- 15-8 Format a worksheet for printing

After finishing this chapter, go to **PAGE 467** for **STUDY TOOLS**.

15-1 USING FLASH FILL

Excel has a variety of tools to help you create more advanced workbooks and analyze the data in them. **Flash Fill** enters text based on patterns it finds in the data. Usually, you need to enter at least one value and then start typing the next value for Flash Fill to suggest content. Exhibit 15-1 shows Aspen, Colorado entered in cell A12 and Flash Fill–generated content for the rest of column A based on the pattern used for cell A12—the city name from column B, a comma, and then the state name from column D. To accept the suggested content, press the Enter key. If you don't want to accept the suggested content, continue typing. You can also press the Esc key to make the suggested content disappear.

EXHIBIT 15-1 TEXT BEING ENTERED WITH FLASH FILL

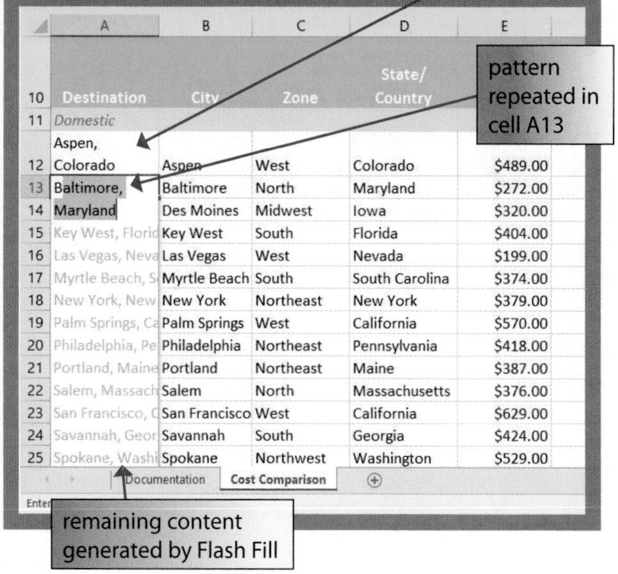

pattern set in cell A12

pattern repeated in cell A13

	A	B	C	D	E
10	Destination	City	Zone	State/ Country	
11	Domestic				
12	Aspen, Colorado	Aspen	West	Colorado	$489.00
13	Baltimore,	Baltimore	North	Maryland	$272.00
14	Maryland	Des Moines	Midwest	Iowa	$320.00
15	Key West, Floric	Key West	South	Florida	$404.00
16	Las Vegas, Neva	Las Vegas	West	Nevada	$199.00
17	Myrtle Beach, S	Myrtle Beach	South	South Carolina	$374.00
18	New York, New	New York	Northeast	New York	$379.00
19	Palm Springs, Ca	Palm Springs	West	California	$570.00
20	Philadelphia, Pe	Philadelphia	Northeast	Pennsylvania	$418.00
21	Portland, Maine	Portland	Northeast	Maine	$387.00
22	Salem, Massach	Salem	North	Massachusetts	$376.00
23	San Francisco, C	San Francisco	West	California	$629.00
24	Savannah, Geor	Savannah	South	Georgia	$424.00
25	Spokane, Washi	Spokane	Northwest	Washington	$529.00

Documentation | Cost Comparison

remaining content generated by Flash Fill

After you accept Flash Fill entries, the Flash Fill Options button appears to the right of the first cell containing suggested content. If you click the Flash Fill Options button, the menu that opens provides options to undo Flash Fill, accept the suggestions, and select all the changed cells.

Flash Fill works best when the pattern is clearly recognized from the values in the data. Be sure to enter the data pattern in the column or row right next to the related data. The data used to generate the pattern must be in a rectangular grid and cannot have blank rows or columns. Also, Flash Fill enters text, not formulas. If you edit or replace an entry originally used by Flash Fill, the content generated by Flash Fill will not be updated.

Begin Activity

Use Flash Fill to enter text.

1. Open the data file **Vacation**, located in the Chapter 15\Chapter folder. Save the workbook as **Vacation Getaways**.
2. In the **Documentation** worksheet, enter your name in **cell B3** and the current date in **cell B4**.
3. Make the **Cost Comparison worksheet** the active worksheet. Change the zoom to **120%**, if necessary.
4. Select **cell A12**, type **Aspen, Colorado** to begin the pattern, and then press the **Enter key**.
5. In cell **A13**, type **B** Flash Fill generates the remaining entries in the column based on the pattern you used in cell A12. Refer back to Exhibit 15-1.
6. Press the **Enter key** to accept the suggested entries. The columns specifying City and State/Country are no longer needed now that the destinations appear in column A.
7. Delete the **nonadjacent range B10:B34;D10:D34**. Make sure you delete the cells, not just the contents. The duplicate data is removed from the worksheet, and the remaining data shifts to the left to fill the space.

TIP: Remember to save frequently as you work through the chapter. A good practice is to save after every activity.

PROBLEM? If Flash Fill did not generate the entries, finish typing **Baltimore, Maryland**, press the **Enter key**, and then type **D** in cell A14.

End Activity

15-2 ENTERING FORMULAS WITH MULTIPLE CALCULATIONS

In Chapter 14, you created simple formulas to perform a single calculation. Formulas can also be used to perform multiple calculations. If a formula contains more than one arithmetic operator, Excel performs the calculation using the same order of operations you might already

Flash Fill An Excel feature that enters text based on patterns that it finds in the data.

FYI CREATING AN EXCEL TABLE

When a range contains related data, such as the trip comparison data, you can format it as an Excel table. An **Excel table** is a range of data that is treated as a distinct object in a worksheet. An Excel table makes it easier to identify, manage, and analyze related data. For example, you can quickly sort the data, filter the data to show only those rows that match specified criteria, and add formulas to an entire column. In addition, the entire table is formatted using a single table style, which specifies formats for the entire table, including font color, fill color, and borders. Excel tables can include optional elements such as a header row that contains titles for the different columns in the table and a total row that contains formulas summarizing the values in the table's data. They can also have banded rows, which format every other row in the table with a fill color, making the data easier to read. If you later add or delete a row from the table, the banded rows are adjusted to maintain the alternating row colors. You can create more than one Excel table in a worksheet.

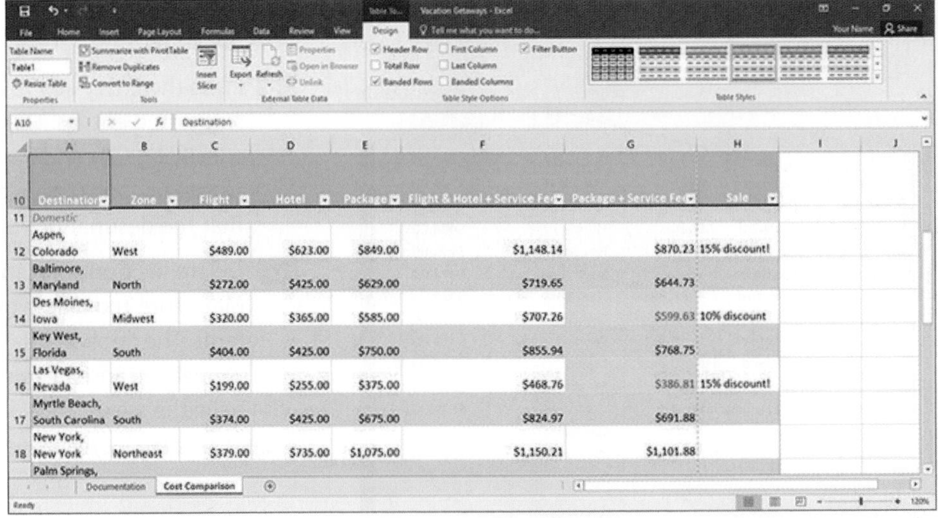

	Destination	Zone	Flight	Hotel	Package	Flight & Hotel + Service Fee	Package + Service Fee	Sale
11	Domestic							
12	Aspen, Colorado	West	$489.00	$623.00	$849.00	$1,148.14	$870.23	15% discount!
13	Baltimore, Maryland	North	$272.00	$425.00	$629.00	$719.65	$644.73	
14	Des Moines, Iowa	Midwest	$320.00	$365.00	$585.00	$707.26	$599.63	10% discount
15	Key West, Florida	South	$404.00	$425.00	$750.00	$855.94	$768.75	
16	Las Vegas, Nevada	West	$199.00	$255.00	$375.00	$468.76	$386.81	15% discount!
17	Myrtle Beach, South Carolina	South	$374.00	$425.00	$675.00	$824.97	$691.88	
18	New York, New York	Northeast	$379.00	$735.00	$1,075.00	$1,150.21	$1,101.88	
	Palm Springs,							

When you create an Excel table, arrows appear next to each column label. You can click an arrow to change the way the data in the table is displayed by sorting it or hiding rows that contain certain data. If you scroll the table above the column headings, the text of the header row replaces the letters in the column headers, making it easier to track which columns you are viewing.

When you add a formula in one cell of a table, the formula is automatically entered in the other cells in that column. You can also enter summary functions for each column in the Total row. When you click in the Total row, an arrow button appears. When you click the arrow button, a list of the most commonly used functions—SUM, AVERAGE, COUNT, MIN, and MAX—opens.

have seen in math classes. The **order of operations** is a set of predefined rules used to determine the sequence in which operators are applied in a calculation:

- First, exponentiation (^) is calculated.
- Second, multiplication (*) and division (/) are calculated in any order.
- Third, addition (+) and subtraction (–) are calculated.

For example, the formula

=3+4*5

returns 23 because multiplication occurs before addition, even though it appears second in the expression. So first, the operation 4*5 is performed to return 20, and then the addition operation is performed to add 3 to that value to return 23.

To change the order of operations, you can enclose parts of the formula within parentheses. Any expression

Excel table A range of data that is treated as a distinct object in a worksheet.

order of operations A set of predefined rules used to determine the sequence in which operators are applied in a calculation—first, exponentiation (^); second, multiplication (*) and division (/); and third, addition (+) and subtraction (–).

within a set of parentheses is calculated before the rest of the formula. So, the formula

=(3+4)*5

first calculates the value of the expression inside the parentheses—in this case, adding 3+4 to return 7. This result is then multiplied by 5 to return 35.

Note that formulas containing more than one multiplication and division operation and formulas containing more than one addition and subtraction operation return the same result no matter what order you perform the operations. For example, the formula

=4*10/8

returns 5 whether you first multiply 4*10 to get 40 and then divide by 8 to get a final result of 5 or you first divide 10 by 8 to get 1.25, and then multiply this value by 4.

The order of operations has a big impact on how Excel calculates the results of a formula. As you can see in Exhibit 15-2, including or moving parentheses within a formula can greatly affect the results.

EXHIBIT 15-2 RESULTS OF FORMULAS USING DIFFERENT ORDERS OF OPERATIONS

Formula	Result
=50+10*5	100
=(50+10)*5	300
=50/10–5	0
=50/(10–5)	10
=50/10*5	25
=50/(10*5)	1

An important skill you need when creating a workbook is translating an equation into an Excel formula. In the Cost Comparison worksheet in the Vacation Getaways workbook, you need to create a formula to calculate the cost of purchasing an airline ticket and hotel room separately. The total cost is the airfare plus the cost of the hotel added to the service fee that Vacation Getaways adds to each transaction. The service fee differs depending on the type of service and the cost. To book airfare and hotel rooms, they charge a 3.5% fee. The equation to calculate the total air and hotel cost is:

(Air + Hotel)* x *Service Fee + Air + Hotel

To convert this equation into an Excel formula, you need to replace Air and Hotel with their corresponding base prices for each destination, and Service Fee with the service fee percentage for Air & Hotel. The service fee is stored in cell B4 in the worksheet. For the first destination—Aspen, Colorado—the Air and Hotel base prices are stored in cells C12 and D12, respectively. The resulting Excel formula is:

=(C12+D12)*B4+C12+D12

Following the order of operations, Excel will first add the base prices in cells C12 and D12, and then multiply the total base price by the service fee percentage in cell B4. The resulting service fee is then added to the base prices in cells C12 and D12. This is shown in Exhibit 15-3.

EXHIBIT 15-3 FORMULA USING THE ORDER OF OPERATIONS

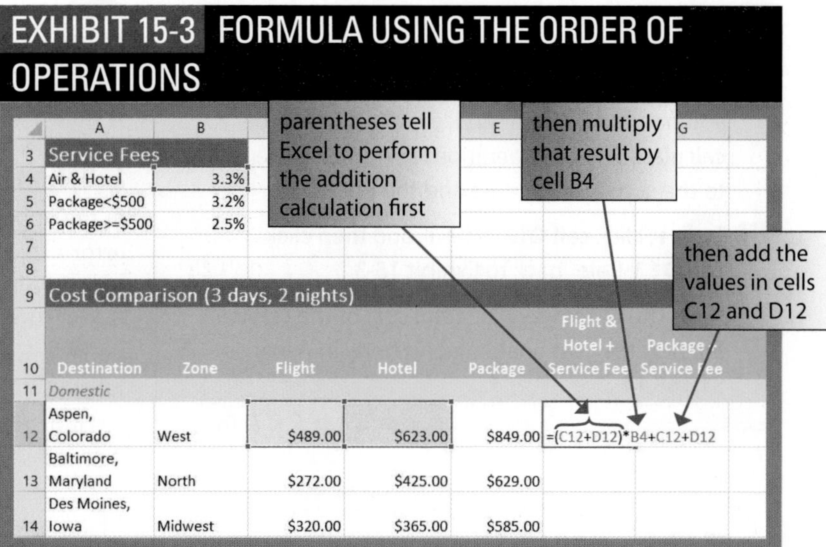

Begin Activity

Enter a formula using the order of operations.

1 Select **cell F12**. You need to create a formula to calculate the total price of airfare and hotel in Aspen by first calculating the service fee and then adding that result to the sum of the airfare and the hotel cost.

2 Type =(, click **cell C12**, type +, click **cell D12**, and then type). This first part of the formula adds the base price of airfare to Aspen to the hotel cost in Aspen. To calculate the service fee, you need to multiply that sum by the Air & Hotel service fee percentage.

TIP: To be certain you obtain the results you want, use parentheses to indicate which operation in a formula should be calculated first.

3 Type * to insert the multiplication sign, and then click **cell B4** to select the Air & Hotel service fee. Finally, to calculate the total price for the customer, you need to add the service fee, which will be calculated by the operations currently in the cell, to the sum of the airfare and the hotel cost.

4 Type +, click **cell C12**, type +, and then click **cell D12**. Refer back to Exhibit 15-3.

5 Press the **Enter key**. The total cost of the service fee plus the cost of airfare and hotel in Aspen is $1,148.14.

End Activity

FYI USING CONSTANTS IN FORMULAS

A **constant** is a value in a formula that doesn't change. A constant can be entered directly in a formula or placed in a separate worksheet cell and referenced in the formula. The location you select depends on the constant being used, the purpose of the workbook, and the intended audience. In the Cost Comparison worksheet, the service fees in the range B4:B6 are constants. Placing constants in separate cells that you reference in the formulas can help users better understand the worksheet because no values are hidden within the formulas. Also, when a constant is entered in a cell, you can add explanatory text next to each constant to document how it is being used in the formula. On the other hand, you don't want a user to inadvertently change the value of a constant and throw off all the formula results. You need to evaluate how important it is for other people to immediately see the constant and whether the constant requires any explanation for other people to understand the formula.

Usually, if you reference a cell that contains a constant, you should use an absolute reference. Then, if you copy the formula containing the reference, the reference to the cell containing the constant will not change.

constant A value in a formula that doesn't change.

error indicator A small green triangle that appears in the upper-left corner of a cell with a possible error.

error value A message that appears in a cell that indicates some part of a formula is preventing Excel from returning a calculated value.

15-3 FIXING ERROR VALUES

If some part of a formula is preventing Excel from returning a calculated value, Excel flags the possible error with an **error indicator** (a small green triangle) that appears in the upper-left corner of the cell. Some errors cause an error value to appear instead of the formula results. An **error value** is a message indicating the type of error in the cell. Error values begin with a pound sign (#) followed by an error name that indicates the type of error. Exhibit 15-4 describes common error values that you might see instead of the results from formulas and functions.

EXHIBIT 15-4 ERROR VALUE MESSAGES

Error Value	Description
#DIV/0!	The formula or function contains a number divided by 0.
#NAME?	Excel doesn't recognize text in the formula or function, such as when the function name is misspelled.
#N/A	A value is not available to a function or formula, which can occur when a workbook is initially set up prior to entering actual data values.
#NULL!	A formula or function requires two cell ranges to intersect, but they don't.
#NUM!	Invalid numbers are used in a formula or function, such as text entered in a function that requires a number.
#REF!	A cell reference used in a formula or function is no longer valid, which can occur when the cell used by the function was deleted from the worksheet.
#VALUE!	The wrong type of argument is used in a function or formula. This can occur when you reference a text value for an argument that should be strictly numeric.

Error values appear based on the error-checking rules selected in the Excel Options dialog box shown in Exhibit 15-5. For example, one rule checks for formulas that refer to empty cells. If the rule is selected, an error value appears when a formula uses a cell that is blank. If the rule is not selected, a formula that uses a blank cell does not result in an error value.

EXHIBIT 15-5 FORMULAS TAB IN THE EXCEL OPTIONS DIALOG BOX

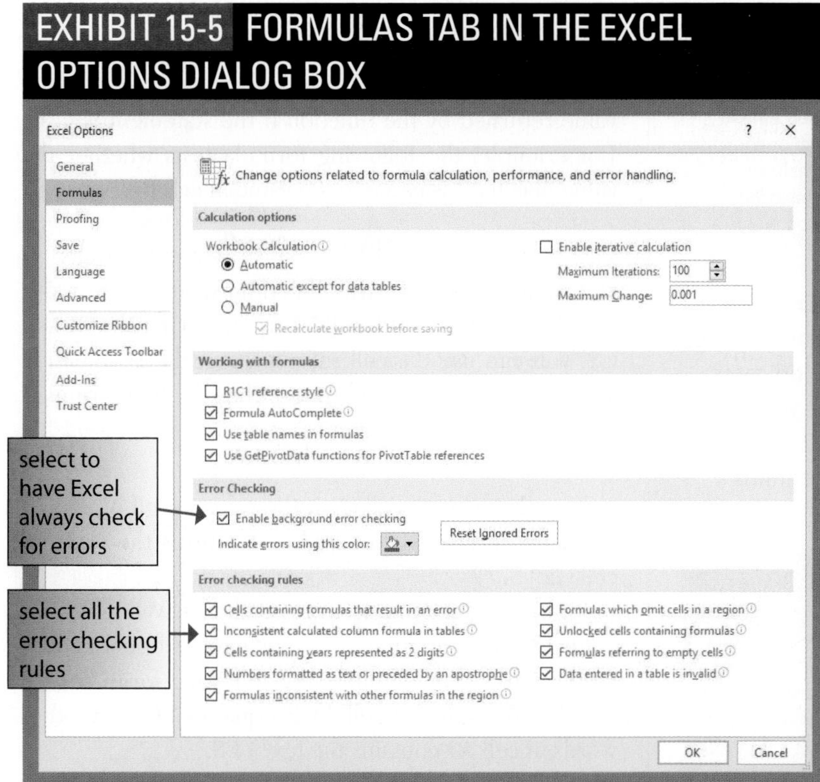

Begin Activity

Verify the Error Checking settings.

1 On the ribbon, click the **File tab**. In the navigation bar, click **Options**. The Excel Options dialog box opens.

> TIP: You can also click the Error Checking button next to a cell with an error indicator, and then click Error Checking Options to open the Formulas tab in the Excel Options dialog box.

2 In the navigation bar of the dialog box, click **Formulas**. The Formulas tab in the Excel Options dialog box appears.

3 In the Error Checking section, click the **Enable background error checking check box** to select it if it is not already selected.

4 In the Error checking rules section, click any check boxes that are not selected. Now all types of errors will be flagged. Refer to Exhibit 15-5.

5 Click **OK**. The dialog box closes.

End Activity

Cells that contain possible errors have a small green triangle in the upper-left corner. When the cell containing the error is the active cell, the Error Checking button appears to the left of the cell. To obtain more information about the source of the error, you can point to the Error Checking button to display a ScreenTip with a description of the possible error. Exhibit 15-6 shows a worksheet with errors in several cells.

Begin Activity

Enter a formula that produces an error value.

1 Copy the formula in **cell F12** to the **range F13:F18**. The small green triangle that indicates a possible error is in the upper-left corner of the cells in the range F15:F18, and in cell F18, the error message #VALUE! appears.

2 Select **cell F15**. To the left of cell F15, the Error Checking button appears.

3 To the left of cell F15, point to the **Error Checking button**. The button change to , and a ScreenTip appears, identifying the error. Refer back to Exhibit 15-6. In this case, the formula refers to cells that are currently empty. In the formula bar, the formula is =(C15+D15)*B7+C15+D15. Cell B7 is the empty cell. The original formula in

EXHIBIT 15-6 CELLS WITH ERRORS

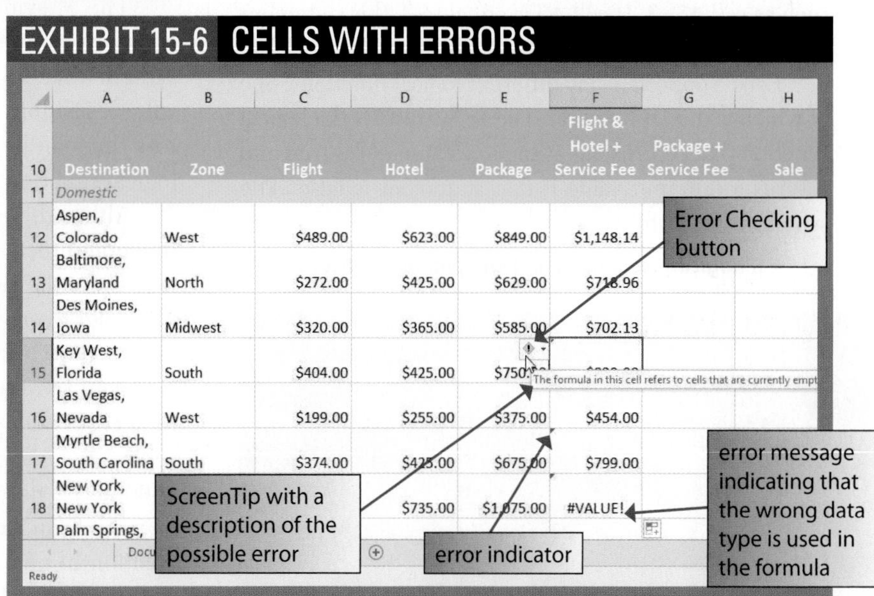

cell F12 should have used an absolute reference to cell B4. Although cells F13 and F14 do not contain the green triangle that indicates an error, the formulas in these cells are also incorrect because they reference cells B5 and B6 instead of cell B4.

TIP: Click the Error Checking button to open a menu with options to help you resolve the error.

4 Click **cell F18**, and then point to the **Error Checking button**. Cell F18 contains the error message #VALUE!, and the ScreenTip indicates that a value used in the formula is the wrong data type. In the formula bar, the reference to the cell in column B is B10. Cell B10 contains text, not a number.

5 Select **cell F12**. In the formula bar, click **B4**, press the **F4 key** to change the reference to an absolute reference, and then click the **Enter button**.

6 Copy the formula in **cell F12** to the nonadjacent **range F13:F28;F30:F34**. This time, no error indicators appear.

PROBLEM? If pressing the F4 key did not change the cell reference to an absolute reference, press the **F-Lock key,** and then press the **F4 key**.

End Activity

15-4 WORKING WITH THE IF LOGICAL FUNCTION

A **logical function** is a function that works with statements that are either true or false. Consider a statement such as *cell A5=3*. If cell A5 is equal to 3, this statement is true; if cell A5 is not equal to 3, this statement is false.

Excel supports many different logical functions, one of which is the IF function. The **IF function** is a logical function that returns one value if a statement is true and returns a different value if that statement is false. The syntax of the IF function is

IF(*logical_test*[,*value_if_true*][,*value_if_false*])

logical function A function that works with statements that are either true or false.

IF function A logical function that tests a condition and then returns one value if the condition is true and another value if the condition is false.

comparison operator A symbol that indicates the relationship between two values.

where *logical_test* is a statement that is either true or false, *value_if_true* is the value returned by the IF function if the statement is true, and *value_if_false* is the value returned by the function if the statement is false. For example, the following formula tests whether the value in cell A1 is equal to the value in cell B1:

=IF(A1=B1,100,50)

If it is, the formula returns 100; otherwise, it returns 50.

If the values of 100 and 50 are stored in cells C1 and C2, you can use the cell references in the IF function arguments instead of the values. The resulting formula

=IF(A1=B1,C1,C2)

returns the value of cell C1 if the value in cell A1 equals the value in cell B1; otherwise, it returns the value of cell C2.

The IF function also works with text. When you include text in an argument, you need to enclose it in quotation marks. For example, the following formula tests whether the value of cell A1 is equal to YES—in other words, if cell A1 contains the text *YES*.

=IF(A1="YES","DONE","")

If the value of cell A1 is equal to YES, the formula returns the text *DONE*; otherwise, it returns nothing as indicated by the opening and closing quotation marks. You can also use calculations as the *value_if_true* and *value_if_false* arguments. For example, in the function

=IF(A1="YES",(B1*B2),"No")

if cell A1 contains YES, the formula returns the result of multiplying cell B1 by cell B2; otherwise, it returns the text *No*.

The = symbol in the logical test argument is a comparison operator. A **comparison operator** is a symbol that indicates the relationship between two values. Exhibit 15-7 describes the comparison operators that can be used in the logical test argument in a logical function.

Although you could type the formula with the IF function directly in a cell, the Function Arguments dialog box for the IF function, shown in Exhibit 15-8, makes it simpler to enter each part of the formula.

In the Cost Comparison worksheet, you need to calculate the total cost of packages in column G. The total cost is the package price plus the service fee. The service fee is 3 percent if the package price is less than \$500 and 2 percent if the cost of the package is \$500 or more. You can use an IF function to make this calculation in one formula. For Aspen, the logical test is whether the value in cell E12 is less than \$500. The

EXHIBIT 15-7 COMPARISON OPERATORS

Operator	Relationship	Example	Description
=	Equal to	A1=B1	Tests whether the value in cell A1 *is equal to* the value in cell B1
>	Greater than	A1>B1	Tests whether the value in cell A1 *is greater than* the value in cell B1
<	Less than	A1<B1	Tests whether the value in cell A1 *is less than* the value in cell B1
>=	Greater than or equal to	A1>=B1	Tests whether the value in cell A1 *is greater than or equal to* the value in cell B1
<=	Less than or equal to	A1<=B1	Tests whether the value in cell A1 *is less than or equal to* the value in cell B1
<>	Not equal to	A1<>B1	Tests whether the value in cell A1 *is not equal to* the value in cell B1

EXHIBIT 15-8 FUNCTION ARGUMENTS DIALOG BOX FOR THE IF FUNCTION

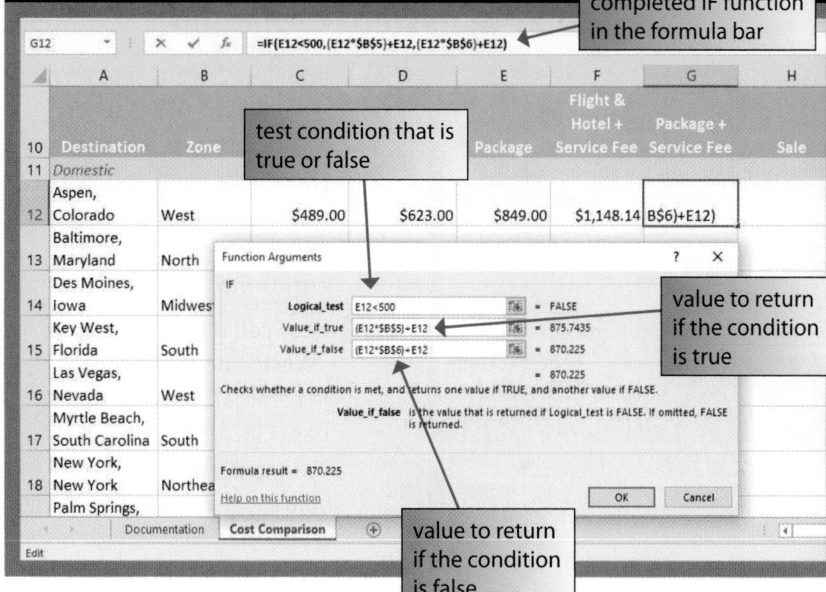

value_if_true argument is a calculation that multiplies the package price in cell E12 by the service fee percentage in cell B5, which contains the service fee for packages that cost less than $500, and then adds that result to the package price in cell E12. The *value_if_false* argument is a calculation that multiplies the package price in cell E12 by the service fee percentage in cell B6, which contains the service fee for packages that cost $500 or more, and then adds that result to the package price in cell E12. This results in the following formula:

=IF(E12<500,(E12*$B$5)+E12,(E12*$B$6)+E12)

Begin Activity

Insert an IF function.

1 Select **cell G12**. To calculate the service fee for the package, you first need to know whether the cost of the package is less than $500.

2 On the ribbon, click the **Formulas tab**. In the Function Library group, click the **Logical button**, and then click **IF** in the list of logical functions. The Function Arguments dialog box for the IF function opens, and the IF function and its parentheses appear in cell G12. The insertion point is in the Logical_test box in the dialog box. The logical test for this function is whether the price of the Aspen package is less than $500.

3 Click **cell E12**, and then type **<500**. This creates the equation E12<500. Next, you need to enter the calculation to be performed if the condition in the Logical_test box is true—that is, if the value in cell E12 is less than $500.

4 Click in the **Value_if_true box**, type **(**, click **cell E12**, type *****, and then click **cell B5**. You're going to copy this formula, so you need to change the reference to cell B5 to an absolute reference.

5 Press the **F4 key**, type **)+**, and then click **cell E12**. The final formula of (E12*$B$5)+E12 multiplies the service fee percentage for packages that cost less than $500 (cell B5) by the base package price (cell E12) to determine the service fee, and then adds the calculated fee to the base price of the package (cell E12). Note that you do not need to add the parentheses around the multiplication operation because it would be performed first anyway; however, using the parentheses makes it easier to understand the formula. Now you need to enter the calculation to be performed if the condition in the Logical_test box is false—in other words, if the package price is $500 or more.

6 Click in the **Value_if_false box**, type (, click **cell E12**, type *, click **cell B6**, press the **F4 key**, type **)+**, and then click **cell E12**. The final formula of (E12*$B$6)+E12 multiplies the service fee percentage for packages that cost $500 or more (cell B6) by the base package price (cell E12) to determine the service fee, and then adds the calculated fee to the base price of the package (cell E12). Refer back to Exhibit 15-8.

7 Click **OK**. The value $870.225 is displayed in cell G12. Because the package price for Aspen is $849, which is more than $500, the value_if_false calculation was performed—the package price was multiplied by 2.5% (the value in cell B6) and the resulting service fee was added to the base package price to calculate the total package price. Compare your screen to Exhibit 15-9.

8 Format **cell G12** as **Currency**, and then copy the formula in **cell G12** to the **nonadjacent range G13:G28;G30:G34**.

End Activity

EXHIBIT 15-9 PACKAGE PRICE PLUS SERVICE FEE

G12 =IF(E12<500,(E12*$B$5)+E12,(E12*$B$6)+E12)

IF function calculates the package price plus the corresponding service fee

formula returns the price for the package plus a 2% service fee

	A	B	C	D	E	F	G	H
3	Service Fees							
4	Air & Hotel	3.3%						
5	Package<$500	3.2%						
6	Package>=$500	2.5%						
7								
8								
9	Cost Comparison (3 days, 2 nights)							
10	Destination	Zone	Flight	Hotel	Package	Flig[…] Hotel + Service Fee	Package + Service Fee	Sale
11	*Domestic*							
12	Aspen, Colorado	West	$489.00	$623.00	$849.00	$1,148.14	870.225	
13	Baltimore, Maryland	North	$272.00	$425.00	$629.00	$719.65		
14	Des Moines, Iowa	Midwest	$320.00	$365.00	$585.00	$707.26		
	Key West,							

15-5 CREATING A NESTED IF FUNCTION

Functions can also be placed inside another function, or **nested**. If a formula contains several functions, Excel starts with the innermost function and then moves outward. For example, the following formula first calculates the average of the values in the range A1:A100 using the AVERAGE function, then extracts the integer portion of that value using the INT function, and then tests whether cell A5 is equal to that value:

=IF(A5=INT(AVERAGE(A1:A100)),"Average","")

If cell A5 is equal to the integer portion of the result of the AVERAGE function, the formula returns the text Average; otherwise, it returns no text.

You can use multiple IF functions to test for several conditions. In the Cost Comparison worksheet, the Sale column should contain text that indicates which packages are currently on sale. Trips to the West are on sale for 15% off, trips to the Midwest are on sale for 10% off, and international trips are on sale for 20% off. You can create a nested IF function to add the correct text to each cell.

nest To place one item, such as a function, inside another.

Begin Activity

Create a nested IF function.

1 In **cell H12**, type **=IF(** to start the function. First you need to enter the first condition to check if the content of cell B12 is West. When you enter text as a condition, you need to enclose it in quotation marks.

2 Click **cell B12**, type =, type **"West"** and then type **,** (a comma). In the formula bar, =IF(B12="West", appears. Next you need to enter the value_if_true. If the region is categorized as West, there is a 15% discount with the current sale.

3 Type **"15% discount!"** and then type **,** (a comma). The next part of an IF function is the value_if_false. In this case, if the first condition—checking to see if West appears in cell B12—is false, you want to check to see if the value in the cell equals Midwest. This means the value_if_false calculation will be a second IF statement.

4 Type **IF(** to start the second IF statement, click **cell B12**, type =, type **"Midwest"** and then type **,** (a comma). This is the second condition that will be tested. Now you need to type the value_if_true for this second IF statement.

EXHIBIT 15-10 NESTED IF FUNCTION

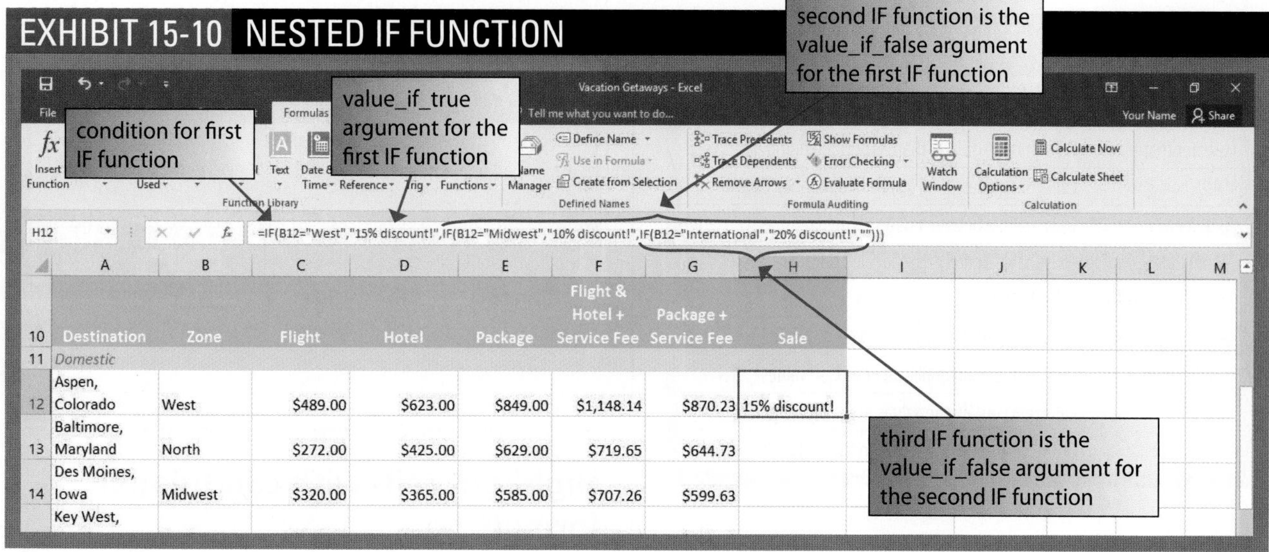

5 Type **"10% discount!"** and then type **,** (a comma). The value_if_false for the second IF statement will be a third IF statement.

6 Type **IF(B12= "International", "20% discount!"** and then type **,** (a comma). Now you need to type the value_if_false for the third IF statement.

7 Type **""** (two quotation marks with nothing between them). This specifies to Excel not to insert any text in the cell. The result of this nested IF is that if the value in cell B12 is not West, not Midwest, and not International, nothing will be entered in the cell.

8 Type **)))** to add the closing parentheses for all three IF statements.

9 To the left of the formula bar, click the **Enter button** ✓. The text *15 discount!* appears in cell H2, the cell containing the nested IF functions, because cell B12 contains *West*. Compare your screen to Exhibit 15-10.

10 Copy the contents of **cell H12** to the nonadjacent range **H13:H28;H30:H34**.

End Activity

15-6 ADDING CONDITIONAL FORMATTING

Conditional formatting applies formatting only when a cell's value meets a specified condition. This can help you analyze data. For example, conditional formatting is often used to highlight important trends and values of interest.

With conditional formatting, the format applied to a cell depends upon the value or content of the cell. For example, conditional formatting can format negative numbers as red and positive numbers as black. Conditional formatting is dynamic—if the cell's value changes, the cell's format also changes as needed. Each type of conditional formatting has a set of rules that defines how the formatting should be applied and under what conditions the format will be changed.

To apply a conditional format, you need to create a conditional formatting rule that specifies the type of condition (such as formatting cells greater than a specified value), the type of formatting when that condition occurs (such as light red fill with dark red text), and the cell or range to which the formatting is applied.

15-6a Highlighting a Cell Based on Its Value

Cell highlighting changes a cell's font color or background fill color or both based on the cell's value. Excel provides built-in conditional formatting rules that allow you to highlight cells that meet specific criteria. Exhibit 15-11 describes some of the ways that cells can be highlighted with conditional formatting.

If you apply more than one rule that affects a cell or range, the rules are applied in the order you created them (unless you change that order later). That means, for example, that if a range contains the values 80, 90, 100, 110, 120, and 130, and you create a rule that fills cells with red if the values in those cells are greater than 100, the cells

conditional formatting Formatting that is applied to a cell only when the cell's value meets a specified condition.

EXHIBIT 15-11 HIGHLIGHTING RULES

Rule	Highlights
Greater Than	Cells that are greater than a specified number
Less Than	Cells that are less than a specified number
Between	Cells that are between two specified numbers
Equal To	Cells that are equal to a specified number
Text That Contains	Cells that contain specified text
A Date Occurring	Cells that contain a specified date
Duplicate Values	Cells that contain duplicate or unique values
Top 10%	Cells that contain the values in the top 10 percent
Bottom 10%	Cells that contain the values in the bottom 10 percent

containing 110, 120, and 130 will be filled with red. Then, if you create a rule that formats the top five values in the range with yellow, the cells containing the top five values will be filled with yellow (meaning all the cells except the one containing 80), overriding the red formatting for cells whose values are greater than 100.

To apply conditional formatting to cells, you first select the range that you want to highlight. Click the Conditional Formatting button in the Styles group on the Home tab to display the conditional formatting options shown in Exhibit 15-12.

EXHIBIT 15-12 CONDITIONAL FORMATTING BUTTON MENU

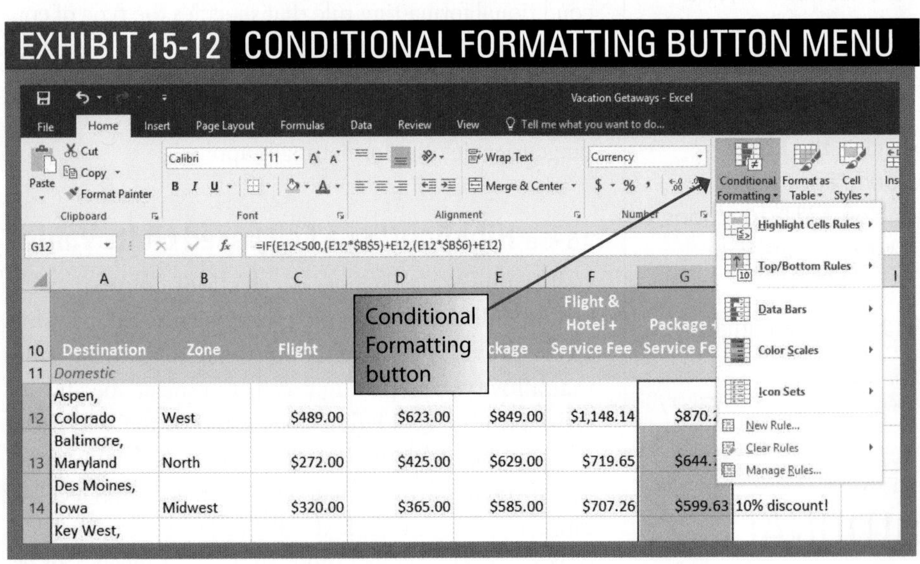

To apply one of the built-in cell highlighting rules, point to Highlight Cells Rules or Top/Bottom Rules to display the available options, and then click the type of condition you want to create for the rule, such as Less Than. A dialog box opens so you can specify the formatting to use for that condition. Exhibit 15-13 shows the Less Than dialog box.

EXHIBIT 15-13 LESS THAN DIALOG BOX

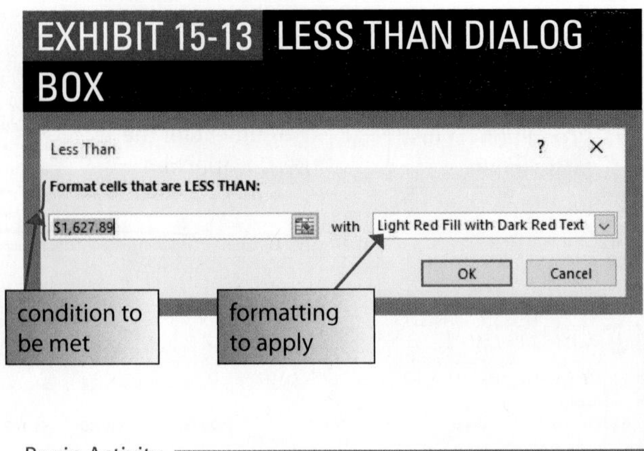

Begin Activity

Highlight cells with conditional formatting.

1. Select the **range G12:G28;G30:G34**.
2. On the ribbon, click the **Home tab**. In the Styles group, click the **Conditional Formatting button**. Refer back to Exhibit 15-12.
3. Point to **Highlight Cells Rules**. A submenu lists the available highlighting rules.
4. Click **Less Than**. The Less Than dialog box opens. The default condition specifies that cells in the selected range with a value less than $1,627.89 will be filled with a light red fill and the text formatted as dark red. Refer back to Exhibit 15-13.
5. Delete the current entry in the Format cells that are LESS THAN box, and then type **600**.
6. Click the **with arrow**, and then click **Green Fill with Dark Green Text**. All cells in the selected range with a value less than $600 will be highlighted with green text on a green background.
7. Click **OK** to apply the highlighting rule, and then scroll to see the highlighted cells. Cells G14, G16, G27, and G30 are highlighted.
8. Make sure the **range G12:G28;G30:G34** is still selected. In the Styles group, click the **Conditional Formatting button**, point to **Top/Bottom Rules**,

and then click **Bottom 10 Items**. The Bottom 10 Items dialog box, which is similar to the Less Than dialog box, opens. The number 10 in the left box in the dialog box specifies the number of items to highlight.

9 Select the **10** in the left box, and then type **3**.

10 Click the **with arrow**, and then click **Yellow Fill with Dark Yellow Text**. The three cells containing the lowest prices are filled with light yellow and contain dark yellow text.

11 Click **OK**. The cells with the three lowest prices—cells G16, G27, and G30—are filled with yellow and contain dark yellow text. Because this rule affects three of the same cells affected by the rule you previously applied, only one of the cells is still shaded green.

12 Make sure the **range G12:G28;G30:G34** is still selected. In the Styles group, click the **Conditional Formatting button**, point to **Top/Bottom Rules**, and then click **Top 10 Items**. The Top 10 Items dialog box opens.

13 Select the **10** in the left box, and then type **3**, and then click **OK**.

14 Select **any cell that is not in column G** to deselect the range, and then scroll down. The three cells containing the highest prices (cells G31, G32, and G33) are filled with light red and contain dark red text. The cells containing the three lowest values are still shaded yellow, and cell G14, the only cell containing a price less than $600 but not one of the three lowest prices, is still shaded green. Exhibit 15-14 shows rows 14 through 33 after applying the conditional formatting.

End Activity

EXHIBIT 15-14 CELLS HIGHLIGHTED WITH CONDITIONAL FORMATTING

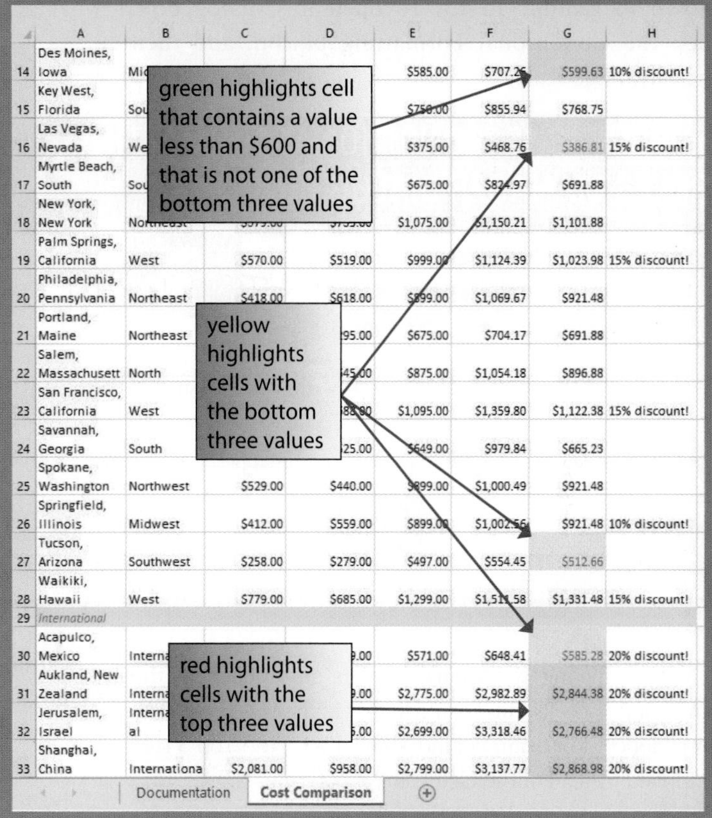

15-6b **Managing Conditional Formatting Rules**

If you want to modify conditional formatting rules, or you no longer want to highlight cells using the conditional formatting, you can remove, or clear, the current highlighting rule. You can clear all of the rules from a selected range or an entire worksheet. These commands are available by clicking the Conditional Formatting button and then pointing

FYI

USING THE QUICK ANALYSIS TOOL

The **Quick Analysis tool** provides access to some of the most commonly used formatting and analysis tools, including conditional formatting. Whenever you select a range of data, the Quick Analysis button appears next to the lower-right corner of the range. Click the Quick Analysis button to open the Quick Analysis tool. Click the conditional formatting you want to apply to open the corresponding dialog box. Click Clear to remove the conditional formatting from the selected range.

Quick Analysis tool A button that appears next to a selected range that provides access to commonly used formatting and analysis tools.

to Clear Rules. If you want to delete only some of the conditional formatting rules, you need to use the Conditional Formatting Rules Manager dialog box shown in Exhibit 15-15. To open this dialog box, click the Conditional Formatting button, and then click Manage Rules.

EXHIBIT 15-15 CONDITIONAL FORMATTING RULES MANAGER DIALOG BOX

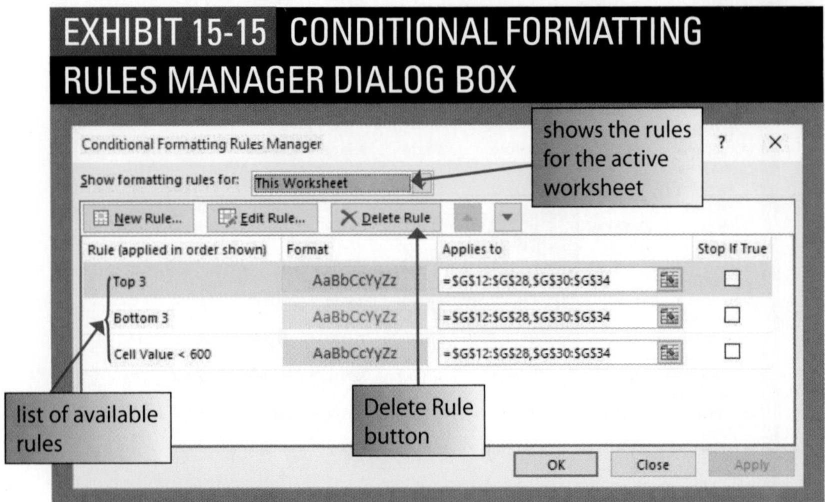

If conflicting conditional formats are applied to the same range of cells, rules listed higher in the dialog box take precedence. For example, in Exhibit 15-15, the Top 3 rule is applied instead of the Cell Value <600 rule.

Begin Activity

Clear a conditional formatting rule.

1 On the Home tab, in the Styles group, click the **Conditional Formatting button**, and then click **Manage Rules**. The Conditional Formatting Rules Manager dialog box opens. The rules you created are not listed because the active cell is not in the range for which the rules were created.

> **PROBLEM?** If the dialog box lists the three rules, the active cell is in the range G12:G28; G30:G34. This is fine. You will not see a difference in the dialog box after completing Step 2.

2 At the top of the dialog box, click the **Show formatting rules for arrow**, and then click **This Worksheet**. The three rules you created are now listed in the dialog box. Refer to Exhibit 15-15.

3 Click the **Bottom 3 rule** to select it.

> **TIP:** To clear all conditional formatting rules from a range or worksheet, click the Conditional Formatting button, point to Clear Rules, and then click the appropriate Clear command in the submenu.

4 Near the top of the dialog box, click the **Delete Rule button**. The selected rule is deleted from the list.

5 Click **OK**. The dialog box closes, and the yellow shading is removed from the cells containing the lowest three percentages. Now that the Bottom 3 rule is deleted, the effect of the first rule you created is applied to all of the cells that contain prices lower than $600 again, and cells G14, G16, G27, and G30 are all shaded green.

End Activity

15-7 HIDING ROWS AND COLUMNS

Sometimes a worksheet contains so much data that it doesn't fit in the worksheet window. One way to manage the contents of a large worksheet is to selectively hide (and later unhide) rows and columns containing extraneous information. This allows you to focus your attention on only a select few data points. You can also hide rows or columns before printing if you don't want others to see the contents of those rows or columns or be distracted by their content. For example, before printing the Trip Comparison worksheet for customers, you might want to hide the rows containing the service fee percentages. The values are not important for marketing purposes, as long as the service fee is disclosed to the customer somewhere. You can tell rows or columns are hidden because the numbers or letters are no longer consecutive, and a double border appears between the rows or columns. Exhibit 15-16 shows rows 2 through 9 hidden in the Trip Comparison worksheet.

Hiding rows, columns, and worksheets is a good way to manage a large volume of information, but it should never be used to hide data that is crucial to understanding a workbook. Note that hiding a row or column does not affect the other formulas in the workbook. Formulas still show the correct value even if they reference a cell in a hidden row or column.

Begin Activity

Hide and unhide worksheet data.

1 Select **row 2** through **row 9**.

2 On the Home tab, in the Cells group, click the **Format button**, and then point to **Hide & Unhide**. A submenu opens, listing the commands for hiding and unhiding the selected rows, columns, or sheet.

EXHIBIT 15-16 ROWS HIDDEN IN THE WORKSHEET

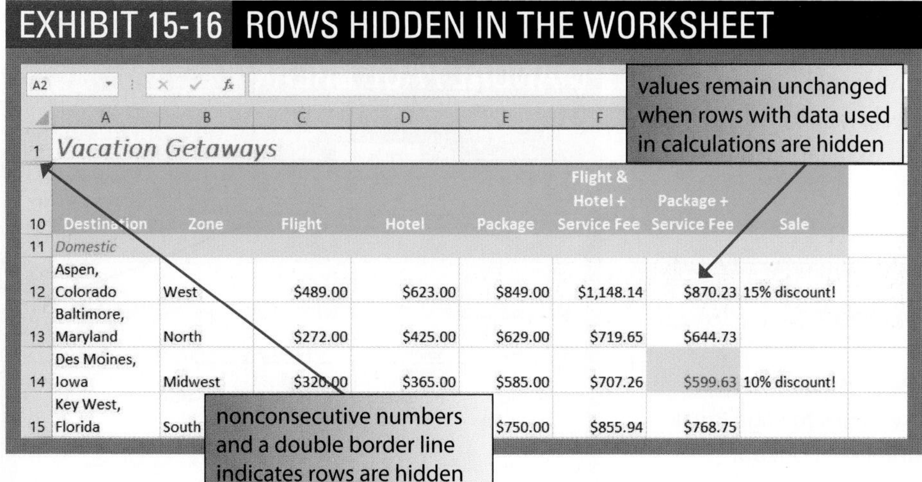

3 On the submenu, click **Hide Rows**. Rows 2 through 9 are hidden, and the row numbers in the worksheet jump from row 1 to row 10. Notice that the trip comparison data does not change even though its formulas use data from the hidden rows. Refer to Exhibit 15-16.

TIP: You can also hide or unhide a row or column by right-clicking the selected row or column header and clicking Hide or Unhide on the shortcut menu.

4 Select **row 1** and **row 10**, which are the rows before and after the hidden rows.

5 On the Home tab, in the Cells group, click the **Format button**, point to **Hide & Unhide**, and then click **Unhide Rows**. Rows 2 through 9 reappear.

6 Hide **row 3** through **row 8**.

End Activity

15-8 FORMATTING A WORKSHEET FOR PRINTING

You should take as much care in formatting the printed output as you do in formatting the contents of the electronic file. Excel has a variety of print settings that you can use to specify what prints and how it appears on the printed pages. Print settings can be applied to an entire workbook or to individual sheets.

15-8a Inserting and Removing Page Breaks

Often the contents of a worksheet do not fit onto a single page. By default, Excel prints as much of the content that fits on a single page without resizing the content and then inserts **automatic page breaks** to continue printing the remaining worksheet content on successive pages. This can result in page breaks that leave a single column or row on a separate page or split worksheet content in awkward places such as within range of related data. Automatic page breaks appear as dotted blue lines in Page Break Preview. See Exhibit 15-17.

One way to fix this problem is to scale the printout by reducing the font size to fit on a single sheet of paper. However, if you have more than one or two columns or rows to fit onto the page, the resulting text is often too small to read comfortably. A better fix is usually to split the worksheet into logical segments, which you can do by inserting **manual page breaks** that specify where

EXHIBIT 15-17 WORKSHEET WITH AUTOMATIC PAGE BREAKS

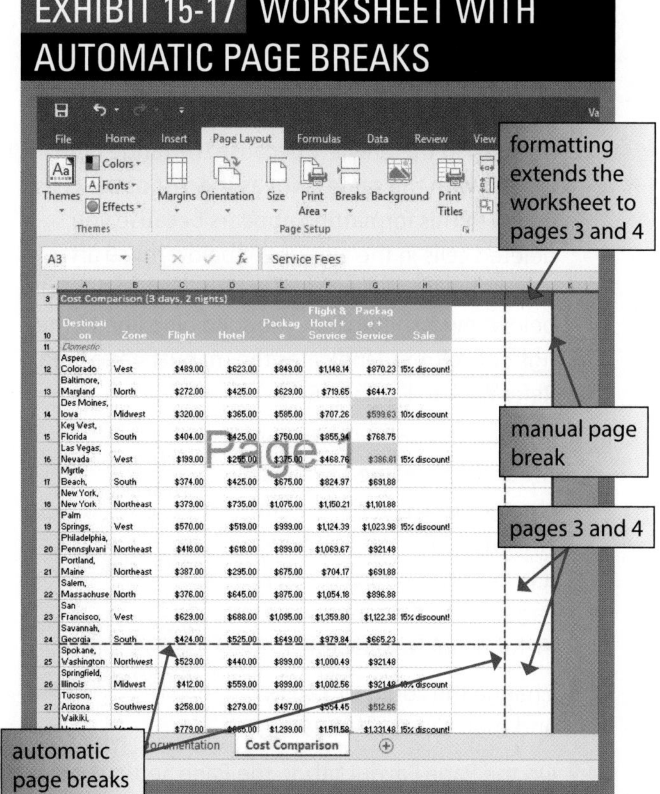

automatic page break A page break Excel inserts when no more content will fit on the page.

manual page break A page break you insert to specify where a page break occurs.

the page breaks occur. A page break is inserted directly above and to the left of a selected cell, directly above a selected row, or to the left of a selected column. Remember that automatic page breaks appear as dotted blue lines in Page Break Preview. Manual page breaks appear as solid blue lines.

Begin Activity

Move and insert page breaks.

1 On the status bar, click the **Page Break Preview button** [icon]. The worksheet switches to Page Break Preview. The worksheet's contents fit on four pages, and the trip comparison data breaks across pages.

2 On the ribbon, click the **Page Layout tab**. In the Page Setup group, click the **Orientation button**, and then click **Landscape**. The page orientation changes to landscape, making each page wide enough to display all of the columns in each table and fitting the contents on two pages. There is a page 3 and a page 4 in the preview because the range I9:J9 is filled with the same color as the rest of the cells in row 9. This formatting appears because you deleted cells in the worksheet below row 9 after using the Flash Fill feature, and the rest of the cells below row 9 shifted left. The solid blue line to the right of column J indicates the manual page break. Refer back to Exhibit 15-17.

TIP: You can set the gridlines or the row and column headings to print by clicking the Print check boxes in the Sheet Options group on the Page Layout tab.

3 Position the pointer on top of the **solid blue line** so that it changes to ↔, and then drag **the line** to the left to position it between columns H and I. Pages 3 and 4 no longer are included in the preview.

TIP: To remove a manual page break, click the cell below or to the right of the page break, click the Breaks button, and then click Remove Page Break.

4 Change the zoom to **120%,** and then select **cell A29**.

5 On the Page Layout tab, in the Page Setup group, click the **Breaks button**, and then click **Insert Page Break**. A solid blue line appears above row 29. Compare your screen to Exhibit 15-18.

print area The region of the active sheet that is sent to the printer.

EXHIBIT 15-18 WORKSHEET WITH MANUAL PAGE BREAK

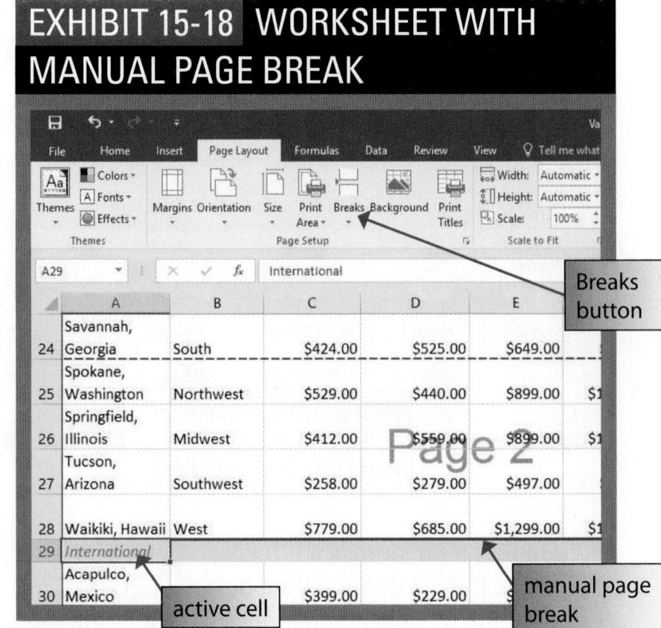

6 On the ribbon, click the **File tab**. In the navigation bar, click **Print**. The preview on the Print screen shows the first page of the current worksheet.

7 Below the preview, click the **Next Page button** [▶]. The second page of the worksheet containing the rest of the domestic data appears. Notice that the column headings in row 10 do not appear on this page.

8 Click the **Next Page button** [▶]. The third page of the worksheet appears. The international trip comparison data is on the third page.

9 In the navigation bar, click the **Back button** [←] to close Backstage view and redisplay the worksheet with the Page Layout tab selected on the ribbon.

End Activity

15-8b Setting the Print Area

By default, all cells in the active worksheet containing text, formulas, or values are printed. The region of the active sheet that is sent to the printer is known as the **print area**. To print part of a worksheet, you can define the print area, overriding the default setting. A print area can cover an adjacent or nonadjacent range in the current worksheet. The rest of the worksheet content is gray to indicate that it will not be part of the printout. See Exhibit 15-19.

The easiest way to set the print area is in Page Layout view or Page Break Preview. For example, to print only the trip comparison in the Monthly Sales worksheet, you could set the print area to cover that range while in Page Break Preview.

EXHIBIT 15-19 PRINT AREA SET IN PAGE BREAK PREVIEW

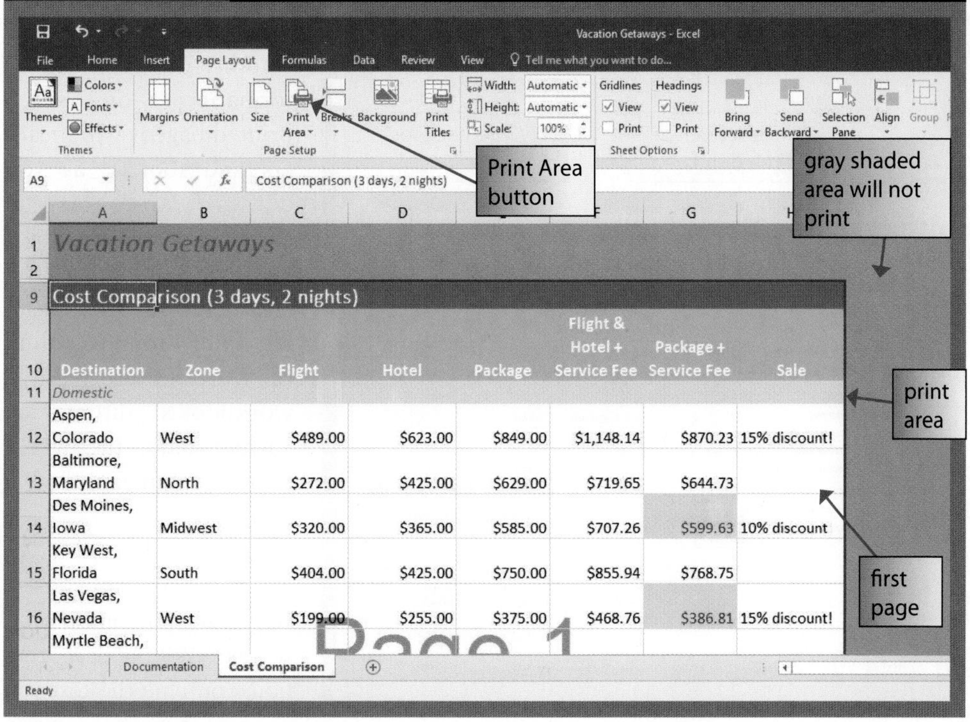

Print Area button

gray shaded area will not print

print area

first page

Destination	Zone	Flight	Hotel	Package	Flight & Hotel + Service Fee	Package + Service Fee	Sale
Domestic							
Aspen, Colorado	West	$489.00	$623.00	$849.00	$1,148.14	$870.23	15% discount!
Baltimore, Maryland	North	$272.00	$425.00	$629.00	$719.65	$644.73	
Des Moines, Iowa	Midwest	$320.00	$365.00	$585.00	$707.26	$599.63	10% discount
Key West, Florida	South	$404.00	$425.00	$750.00	$855.94	$768.75	
Las Vegas, Nevada	West	$199.00	$255.00	$375.00	$468.76	$386.81	15% discount!
Myrtle Beach,							

15-8c Adding Print Titles

A good practice is to include descriptive information such as the company name, logo, and worksheet title on each page of a printout in case a page becomes separated from the other pages. You can repeat information in the worksheet by specifying which rows or columns in the worksheet act as **print titles**. If a worksheet contains a large range of data, you can print the column and row labels on every page of your printout by designating those initial columns and rows as print titles. You do this on the Sheet tab in the Page Setup dialog box. See Exhibit 15-20.

Begin Activity

Set and clear the print area.

1. Select the **range A9:H28**. This range includes the header row containing Cost Comparison and the data for domestic travel only.
2. On the Page Layout tab, in the Page Setup group, click the **Print Area button**, and then click **Set Print Area**. The print area changes to cover only the selected range A9:H28.
3. Select **cell A9**. Any worksheet content that is not included in the print area is shaded gray to indicate that it will not be part of the printout. Refer back to Exhibit 15-19.
4. On the ribbon, click the **File tab**. In the navigation bar, click **Print**. On the Print screen, below the preview, the page numbers indicate that now only two pages will print.
5. Below the preview, click the **Next Page button** ▶. The second page of the worksheet containing the rest of the domestic data appears.
6. In the navigation bar, click the **Back button** to close Backstage view and redisplay the worksheet with the Page Layout tab selected on the ribbon.

End Activity

Begin Activity

Create print titles.

1. Switch to **Normal view**.
2. On the Page Layout tab, in the Page Setup group, click the **Print Titles button**. The Page Setup dialog box opens with the Sheet tab selected.
3. In the Print titles section, click in the **Rows to repeat at top box**.
4. Click in the worksheet, and then select **row 10**. The row reference $10:$10 appears in the Rows to repeat at top box, indicating that the print title range starts and ends with row 10. A blinking border appears around row 10 in the worksheet, indicating that the contents of these rows will be repeated on each page of the printout. Refer to Exhibit 15-20.

print title Information from a workbook that appears on every printed page.

EXHIBIT 15-20 SHEET TAB IN THE PAGE SETUP DIALOG BOX

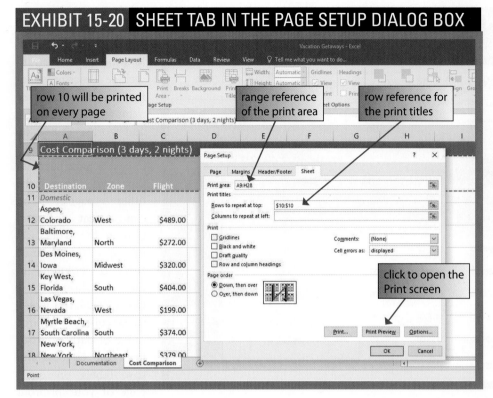

row 10 will be printed on every page

range reference of the print area

row reference for the print titles

click to open the Print screen

15-8d Creating Headers and Footers

Another way to repeat information on each printed page is with headers and footers, as you did in Word. You can add headers and footers that contain helpful and descriptive text usually not found within the worksheet, such as the workbook's author, the current date, the workbook file name, and page numbers.

The header and footer each have a left section, a center section, and a right section. Within each section, you type the text you want to appear or insert elements such as the worksheet name or the current date and time. These header and footer elements are dynamic; if you rename the worksheet, for example, the name is automatically updated in the header or footer.

5 At the bottom of the dialog box, click **Print Preview**. The dialog box closes, and the Print screen appears in Backstage view.

6 Below the preview, click the **Next Page button** ▶. The second page of the worksheet containing the rest of the domestic data appears. The column headings from row 10 appear at the top of the page. Compare your screen to Exhibit 15-21.

7 In the navigation bar, click the **Back button** to close Backstage view and redisplay the worksheet with the Page Layout tab selected on the ribbon.

End Activity

Begin Activity

Insert a header and a footer.

1 On the status bar, click the **Page Layout button**.

2 Scroll so that you can see the top margin of the worksheet, and then point to **Add header**. A light border surrounds the entire header section, and a dark border surrounds the middle section of the header.

EXHIBIT 15-21 PRINT TITLES ADDED TO THE PRINTOUT

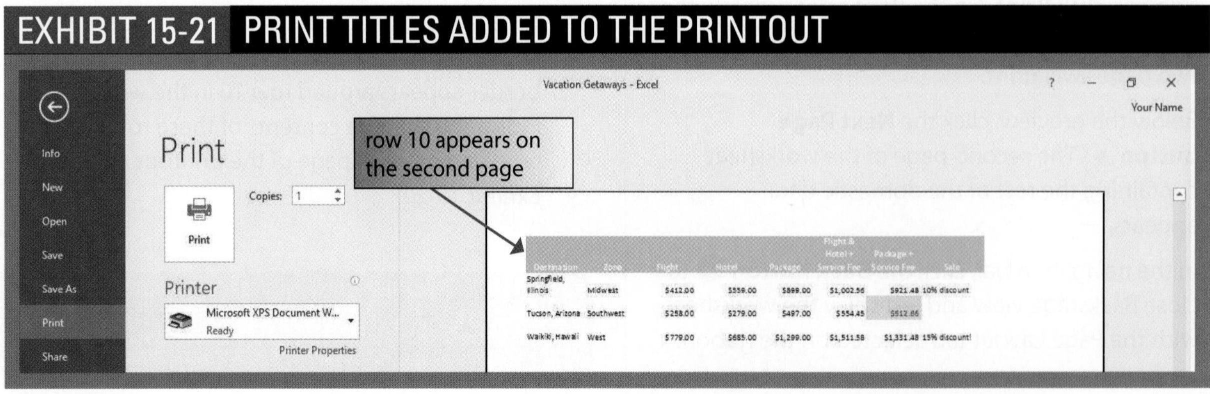

3 Click the **left section** of the header. The dark border appears around the left section, the insertion point appears in the left section, and the Header & Footer Tools Design tab appears on the ribbon.

4 On the ribbon, click the **Header & Footer Tools Design tab**, if necessary.

5 In the left section of the header, type **File name:** and then press the **Spacebar**.

6 On the Header & Footer Tools Design tab, in the Header & Footer Elements group, click the **File Name button**. The code &[File], which displays the file name of the current workbook, is added to the left section of the header.

7 Click the **right section** of the header. In the left section, the &[File] code is replaced with the workbook file name, *Vacation Getaways*.

8 On the Header & Footer Tools Design tab, in the Header & Footer Elements group, click the **Current Date button**. The code &[Date] is added to the right section of the header. See Exhibit 15-22.

9 On the Header & Footer Tools Design tab, in the Navigation group, click the **Go to Footer button**. The worksheet scrolls so you can see the footer, and the insertion point is in the right section of the footer.

10 Type **Prepared by:**, press the **Spacebar**, and then type your name.

11 In the footer, click in the **center section**. Type **Page** and then press the **Spacebar**.

TIP: To quickly enter commonly used header or footer text, in the Header & Footer group, click the Header or Footer button, and then click the text you want.

12 In the Header & Footer Elements group, click the **Page Number button**. The code &[Page] is added after the text in the center section of the footer.

13 Press the **Spacebar**, type **of** and then press the **Spacebar**.

14 In the Header & Footer Elements group, click the **Number of Pages button**. The text *Page &[Page] of &[Pages]* appears in the center section of the footer. Compare your screen to Exhibit 15-23.

PROBLEM? If the footer shows a different page number, the active cell in your worksheet is in another location.

15 Click the **File tab**, and then in the navigation bar, click **Print**. The header and footer you added appear in the preview.

End Activity

FYI — PRINT OPTIONS ON THE SHEET TAB

The Sheet tab in the Page Setup dialog box provides other print options, such as printing the gridlines or row and column headings. You can also print the worksheet in black and white or in draft quality. For a multiple page printout, you can specify whether the pages are ordered by going down the worksheet and then across, or across first and then down.

EXHIBIT 15-22 HEADER WITH CONTENT

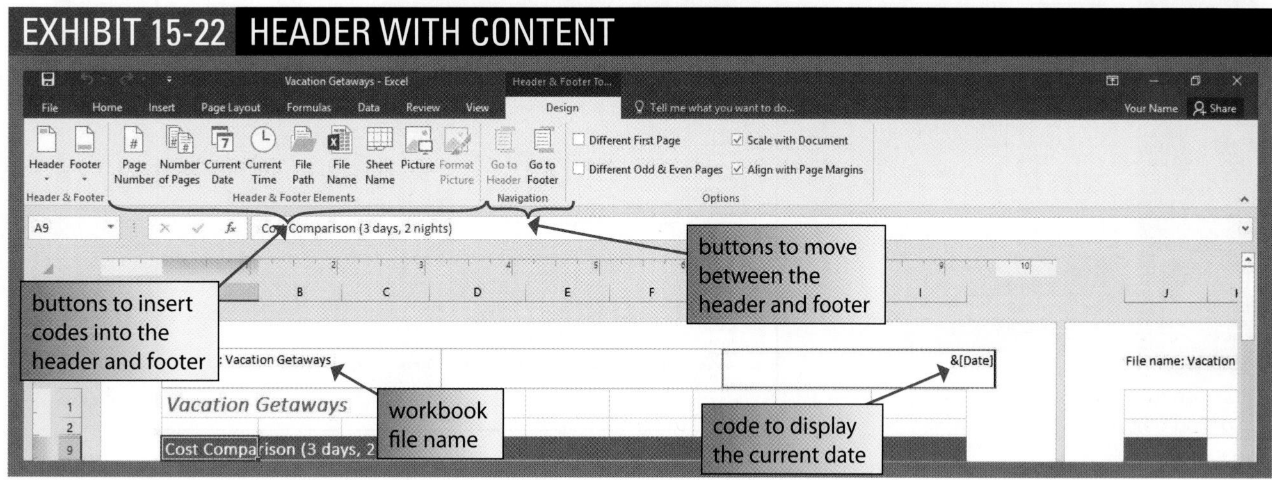

EXHIBIT 15-23 FOOTER WITH CONTENT

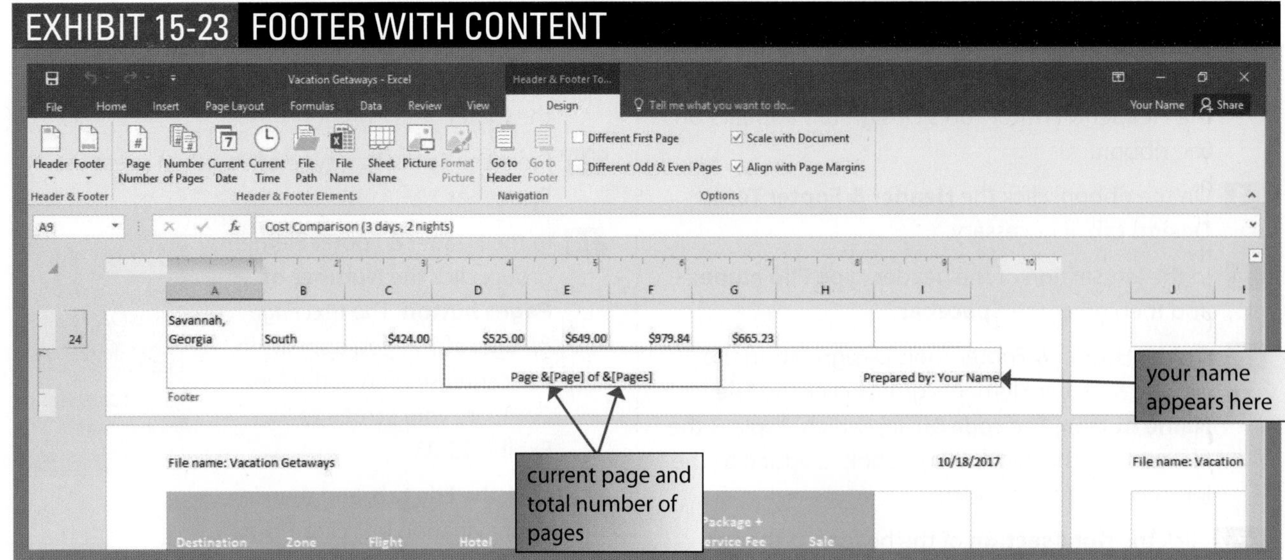

15-8e Setting the Page Margins

Another way to fit a large worksheet on a single page is to reduce the size of the page margins. A margin is the space between the page content and the edges of the page. In a new worksheet, the page margins are set to 0.7 inches on the left and right and 0.75 inches on the top and bottom with 0.3-inch margins around the page header and footer. You can change these margins as needed by selecting from a set of predefined margin sizes, which are available on the Print screen. See Exhibit 15-24. You can also specify your own margins. For example, you might need narrower margins to fit all of the columns on a page or wider margins to accommodate the page binding. You use the Margins tab in the Page Setup dialog box to set custom margins. See Exhibit 15-25.

Begin Activity

Set the page margins.

1 On the Print screen, click the **Normal Margins button**. A menu opens with a list of predefined margins. Refer to Exhibit 15-24.

EXHIBIT 15-24 NORMAL MARGINS MENU ON THE PRINT SCREEN

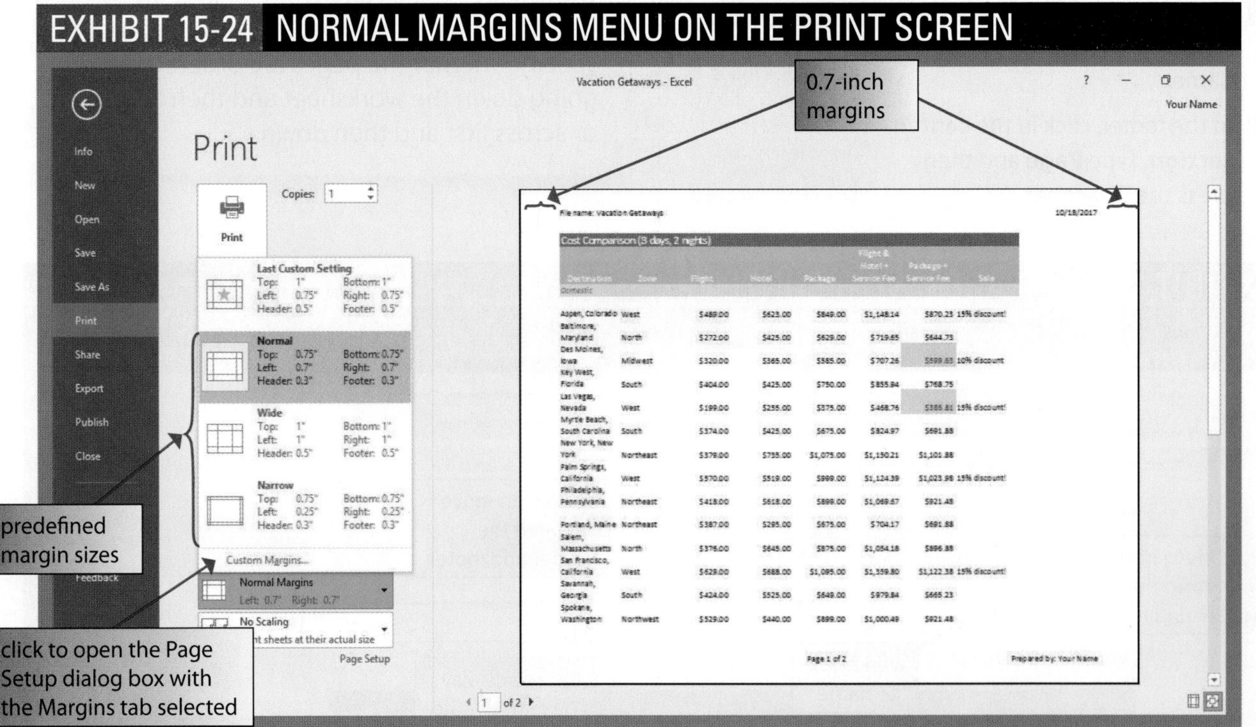

2 Click **Wide**. The menu closes, and the margins are changed to set 1-inch margins around the printed content with 0.5-inch margins above the header and below the footer. The size of the margins around the page increases but does not affect how the content fits on the pages. In the preview, notice that the Sale column no longer fits on page 1 and the preview now consists of four pages.

TIP: You can also set the margins by clicking the Margins button in the Page Setup group on the Page Layout tab.

3 Click the **Wide Margins button**, and then click **Custom Margins**. The Page Setup dialog box opens with the Margins tab selected. Refer to Exhibit 15-25.

EXHIBIT 15-25 MARGINS TAB IN THE PAGE SETUP DIALOG BOX

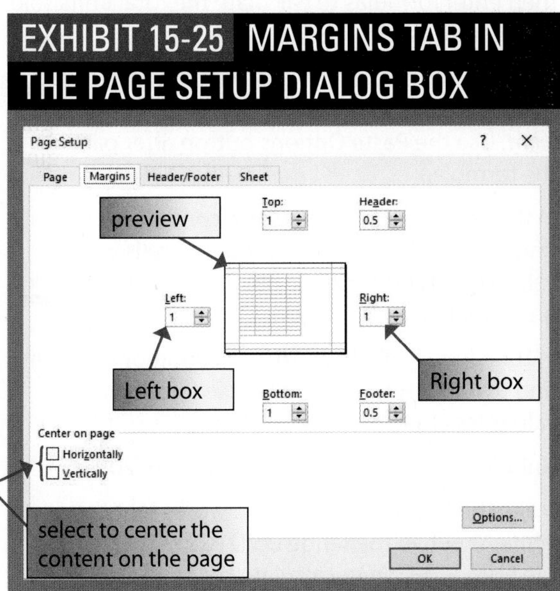

4 Click the **Left box down arrow**. The value in the Left box changes from 1 to 0.75.

5 Change the value in the **Right box** to **0.75**.

6 Click **OK**. The dialog box closes, and the margins in the preview are adjusted. The Sale column again fits on page 1.

7 Print the worksheet, if requested, or click the **Back button** to close Backstage view and return to Page Layout view.

End Activity

FYI CENTERING CONTENT ON THE PAGE

Worksheet content is printed on pages starting from the left and top margins. This can leave a lot of empty space on the right and top sides of the pages. To center the content on the page, click the Dialog Box Launcher in the Page Setup group on the Page Layout tab to open the Page Setup dialog box, click the Margins tab, and then select the Horizontally and Vertically check boxes to center the content of the current sheet on the page.

STUDY TOOLS 15

READY TO STUDY? IN THE BOOK, YOU CAN:

- ☐ Rip out the Chapter Review Card, which includes key terms and key chapter concepts.

ONLINE AT WWW.CENGAGEBRAIN.COM, YOU CAN:

- ☐ Review key concepts from the chapter in a short video.
- ☐ Explore using the IF function in Excel with the interactive infographic.
- ☐ Practice what you've learned with more Practice It and On Your Own exercises.
- ☐ Prepare for tests with quizzes.
- ☐ Review the key terms with flashcards.

QUIZ YOURSELF

1. Why should you document the contents of a workbook?
2. What does Flash Fill do?
3. How does Excel determine how to perform a calculation that contains more than one arithmetic operator?
4. What is an error value, and when does it appear?
5. What is the IF function?
6. Write the formula that tests whether the value in cell S2 is equal to the value in cell P7 and then returns 75 if it is, but otherwise returns 150.
7. What is conditional formatting?
8. How would you highlight the top 10 values in the range A1:C20?
9. How does clearing a conditional formatting rule affect the cell contents?
10. Why would you hide some rows or columns in a worksheet?
11. Why would you define a print area?
12. Describe the difference between automatic and manual page breaks.
13. What are print titles?
14. Describe how to add the workbook file name in the center section of the footer on every page of a printout.

PRACTICE IT

Practice It 15-1

1. Open the data file **Saw** located in the Chapter 15\ Practice It folder. Save the workbook as **Saw House**.
2. In the Documentation worksheet, enter your name in cell B3 and the date in cell B4.
3. Use Flash Fill to enter the first and last names of the staff in the range B7:B11. Then, delete the contents of the range C7:E11.
4. Make the Units Sold by Model worksheet the active sheet. Enter a formula in the range E4:E8 and the range E12:E16 to calculate the percent increase in units sold for each model. (*Hint*: Subtract the units sold in 2016 from the units sold in 2017 to calculate the increase in sales, and then divide that increase by the units sold in 2016 to calculate the percent increase in units sold for each model. Remember the order of operations.) Make sure these ranges are formatted with Percent style and no decimal places.
5. Select the nonadjacent range C9:D9;C17:D17, and then enter formulas to calculate the total units sold per year for gas chainsaws and electric chainsaws.
6. Copy the formula in cell E4 to cells E9 and E17, pasting only the formula and number formatting. (*Hint*: Use the Paste Options button after pasting the formula.)
7. In the range E4:E8;E12:E16, use conditional formatting to add a Highlight Cells Rule to cells with values greater than 25% with a green fill and dark green text.
8. In the range E4:E8;E12:E16, use conditional formatting to add a Highlight Cells Rule to cells with values less than 0% with red text.
9. Unhide rows 18–21, and then hide row 20.
10. Make the Units Sold by Month worksheet the active sheet. In the range D5:D16;J5:J16, enter the SUM function to calculate the total units sold for all chainsaws by month.
11. In the range B17:D17;H17:J17, use the SUM function to add the total of each column.
12. In cell E5, enter a formula to calculate the total of all gas and electric chainsaws sold in January 2016. (This will be the same result as the result in cell D5.)
13. In cell E6, enter a formula to calculate the total of all gas and electric chainsaws sold in February 2016, and then add that to the total chainsaws sold in January 2016 (cell E5).
14. Copy the formula in cell E6 to the range E7:E16. Copy the formulas in the range E5:E16 to the range K5:K16.
15. In cell F5, enter an IF function that tests whether the number of all chainsaws sold in January 2017 is greater than the number of chainsaws sold in January 2016. If it is, the formula should return the text "*" (that is, an asterisk between quotation marks); otherwise, it should return no text.

(*Hint*: Enter **" "** to specify no text, and enter "*" for the asterisk so it is treated as text and not the multiplication sign.)

16. Copy the formula in cell F5 to the range F6:F16.
17. View the worksheet in Page Break Preview.
18. Set the print area to the range A3:K17. Set the print titles to repeat row 1 at the top of each page. Change the page break so it occurs between column E and column F.
19. For the Units Sold by Model and Units Sold by Month worksheets, create headers and footers that display your name in the left section of the header, display the current date in the right section of the header, the workbook file name in the left section of the footer, and the sheet name in the right section of the footer.
20. Save the workbook, and then close it.

Practice It 15-2

1. Open the data file **Clear Talk** located in the Chapter 15\Practice It folder. Save the workbook as **ClearTalk Cell**.
2. In the Documentation worksheet, enter your name in cell B3 and the date in cell B4.
3. In the Cell Phone Sales worksheet, enter a formula in cell C5 that adds the sales of all phones in January in Zone 1.
4. Copy the formula in cell C5 to the range C5:G16 to find the total sales for each month in each region.
5. Use conditional formatting to highlight the top 10 items in the nonadjacent range C19:G30;C33:G44;C47:G58 with a green fill and dark green text.
6. Use conditional formatting to highlight the top 10% of cells in the range C5:G16 with a red border.
7. Enter a formula in cell C3 that calculates Zone 1's percentage of the total sales. To do this, add the total sales in Zone 1 and then divide that amount by the total sales in all zones. Format the results as a percentage with no decimal places.
8. Copy the formula in cell C3 to the range D3:G3 to find the percentage of total sales for each region. (*Hint*: Make sure you used an absolute reference in the formula you copied.)
9. In cell C2, use a nested IF function to test whether the percentage of total sales in 2017 for Zone 1 is greater than or equal to 20%. If it is, then formula returns **Met Goal**; otherwise, test whether the percentage of total sales for Zone 1 is greater than 10%. If it is, the formula returns **Good Effort**; otherwise, it leaves the cell blank.
10. Copy the IF function to the range D2:G2.
11. Use conditional formatting to add a Highilght Cells rule to the range C2:G2 that formats cells that are equal to **Met Goal** with fill using the Standard Color Yellow. (*Hint:* Do not put quotation marks around the text; click Custom Format on the menu you use to add formatting in the Equal To dialog box, and then use the Fill tab in the Format Cells dialog box.)
12. View the Cell Phone Sales worksheet in Page Layout view. Set the margins to Wide, and set the page orientation to landscape.
13. View the Cell Phone Sales worksheet in Page Break Preview. Insert page breaks so that each table of data prints on a separate page.
14. Repeat rows 1,2, and 3 of the worksheet on every printed page.
15. Center each page both horizontally and vertically on the paper.
16. Display your name in the left header, display **Page** *page number* **of** *number of pages* in the right header, display the file name in the left footer, and then display the current date in the right footer.
17. Save the workbook, and then close it.

ON YOUR OWN

On Your Own 15-1

1. Open the data file **Property** located in the Chapter 15\On Your Own folder. Save the workbook as **Property Management**.
2. In the Documentation worksheet, enter your name in cell B3 and the date in cell B4.
3. In the Yearly Rates worksheet, in the % Increase column, enter formulas to calculate the percentage the income increased between 2016 and 2017 and the percentage the vacancies increased between 2016 and 2017. Remember the order of operations.
4. Format the results appropriately, using symbols and an appropriate number of decimal places.

5. In the range G6:G13;B17:G24, use IF functions to test whether the corresponding cells in column F are positive. If they are, display the contents of cell H1; if not, display the contents of cell I1.
6. Edit cell H1 to **Increase**, and edit cell I1 to **Decrease**.
7. Hide columns H and I in the worksheet.
8. Use conditional formatting to add a Highilght Cells rule to the range G6:G13;G17:G24 that formats cells that are equal to **Increase** so that the font is bold and White and so that the cell is filled with the Standard Color Purple, and formats cells that are equal to **Decrease** so that the text is bold and Red. (*Hint*: Do not put quotation marks around the text; click Custom Format on the menu you use to add formatting in the Equal To dialog box, and then use the Fill tab in the Format Cells dialog box.)
9. In the Monthly Rates worksheet, hide the Units Vacant in 2016 and the Units Vacant in 2017 data.
10. In the Net Increase data, use conditional formatting to highlight the top 10% of vacancies and the bottom 10% of vacancies with two different formats, and then clear or delete the rule that formatted the cells containing 0 with a red border.
11. Format the Net Increase data as an Excel Table using the Table Style Medium 16 style. (*Hint:* Select the data below the *Net Increase* header row, use the Table button on the Insert tab, and then change the style on the Table Tools Design tab.)
12. On the Monthly Rates worksheet, add a Total Row to the Excel Table to calculate the total number of vacancies in each column. (*Hint:* Use the Total Row check box in the Table Style Options group on the Table Tools Design tab, and then click in each cell in the total row and click the arrow that appears.)
13. Add your name to the left header, the current date to the right header, and the file name to the middle footer.
14. View each worksheet in Page Layout view or on the Print screen in Backstage view, and then change the print area, margins, orientation, print titles, and page breaks as needed to ensure that the printout is easily read and interpreted.
15. Save the workbook, and then close it.

Part 7
EXCEL 2016

16 | Inserting and Formatting Charts

© Pressmaster/Shutterstock.com

LEARNING OBJECTIVES After studying the material in this chapter, you will be able to:

16-1 Create a chart

16-2 Move and resize a chart

16-3 Modify a chart

16-4 Create an exploded pie chart

16-5 Create a column or bar chart

16-6 Create a line chart

16-7 Edit chart data

16-8 Insert and format sparklines

16-9 Insert and modify data bars

After finishing this chapter, go to **PAGE 499** for **STUDY TOOLS**.

16-1 CREATING A CHART

A **chart**, or **graph**, is a visual representation of a set of data values. Charts provide a way to illustrate numbers. Because many people are overwhelmed by tables of numbers, you can use charts to show trends or relationships in data that are easier to see than by looking at the actual numbers. For example, it can be difficult to identify in which range of months a mutual fund performed exceptionally well simply looking at numbers, whereas a chart can make that relationship easy to see.

Begin Activity

Review chart data.

1. Open the data file **Virginia Beach** located in the Chapter 16\Chapter folder. Save the workbook as **Virginia Beach Real Estate**.
2. In the **Documentation worksheet**, enter your name in **cell B3** and the date in **cell B4**.
3. Left-align the date in **cell B4**.
4. Review the contents of each worksheet.

End Activity

The Summary Report worksheet will summarize data and facts about Virginia Beach real estate. The Historical Prices worksheet lists real estate prices from 2013 through 2017. The Metro Population worksheet lists the populations of Virginia cities. The Structure Types worksheet shows the breakout of Virginia Beach structure types compared to the entire United States. The Population History worksheet shows population changes in Virginia cities between 1987 and 2017. Much of this numerical data would be easier to understand as charts.

16-1a Selecting a Data Source

Each chart has a **data source**, which is the range that contains the data to display in the chart. A data source includes one or more **data series**, which is the set of values represented in a chart. The data series includes one or more **categories**, which are the sets of values that represent the data for the same item. The **category values** provide descriptive labels for each data series, and the **data series values** contain the actual numbers plotted on the chart.

Category values are usually located in the first column or first row of the data source. The data series values are usually placed in subsequent columns or rows. However, you can select category and data series values from anywhere within a workbook.

The data source shown in Exhibit 16-1 includes two columns. The category values are located in the first column, and the one and only data series is located in the second column. The first row of this data source contains labels that identify the category values (City) and the data series (Population).

EXHIBIT 16-1 DATA SOURCE SELECTED FOR A CHART

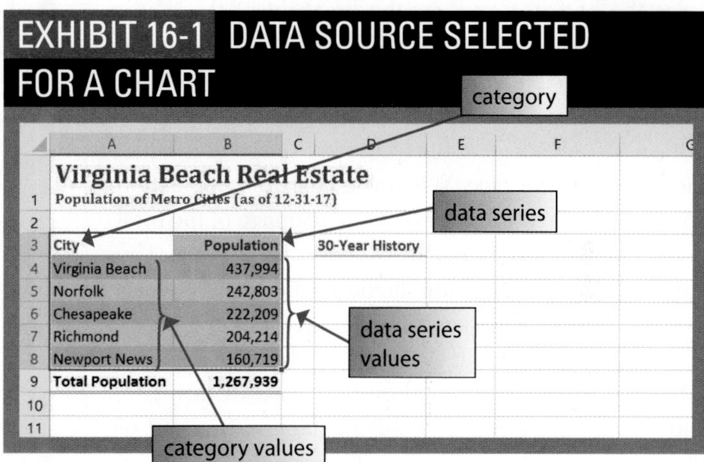

Begin Activity

Select the data source for a chart.

1. Make the **Metro Population worksheet** the active sheet.
2. Select the **range A3:B8**. The data source in this range has one data series, named Population, that includes one category, named City. The category values in the range A4:A8 list the different cities. The data series values in the range B4:B8 contain the population numbers to be charted. Refer back to Exhibit 16-1.

End Activity

chart (graph) A visual representation of a set of data values.

data source The range that contains the data to display in a chart.

data series A set of values represented in a chart.

category A set of values that represent data for one item in a chart.

category values The row or column of a data source that provides the descriptive labels for each data series.

data series values The actual numbers plotted on a chart.

16-1b Selecting a Chart Type

In Excel, you can choose from a variety of charts to create the type of chart that best illustrates the data. Excel includes 15 chart types described in Exhibit 16-2. Each chart type includes variations of the same chart type, which are called chart subtypes. You can also create custom chart types based on the built-in charts.

You should select the type of chart that makes the data easiest to interpret. For example, a pie chart provides the best way to show the breakout of the population data you selected. A **pie chart** is a chart in the shape of a circle divided into slices like a pie. Each pie slice represents one data series value and shows that value as a percentage of the whole. The larger the value, the larger the pie slice. When you chart the population data, each slice will represent the percentage of the total population from one of the five cities in Virginia. The data source for a pie chart should include only the category values and the data series values, not any row or column totals because Excel will treat those totals as another category to be plotted on the chart. In this case, you will not include the Total Population row as part of the data source, because it is not a population category and should not be included in a pie chart.

EXHIBIT 16-2 EXCEL CHART TYPES

Chart type	Description
Column	Compares values from different categories. Values are indicated by the height of the columns.
Line	Compares values from different categories. Values are indicated by the height of the line.
Pie	Compares relative values of different categories to the whole. Values are indicated by the size of the pie slices.
Bar	Compares values from different categories. Values are indicated by the length of the bars.
Area	Compares values from different categories. Similar to the line chart except that areas under the lines contain a fill color.
X Y (Scatter)	Shows the patterns or relationship between two or more sets of values.
Stock	Displays stock market data, including the high, low, opening, and closing prices of a stock.
Surface	Compares three sets of values in a three-dimensional chart.
Radar	Compares a collection of values from several different data sets.
Treemap	Compares the size of the elements of a hierarchy.
Sunburst	Displays all the levels of a hierarchy to make it easy to see.
Waterfall	Used with a series of positive and negative values to show individual values compared to the whole.
Histogram	Shows the distribution of values to show how many data points are within specific ranges.
Box & Whisker	Highlights the middle set of values.
Combo	Combines two or more data types to make the data easy to visualize, especially when the data is widely used.

16-1c Inserting a Pie Chart

The chart types are available in the Charts group on the Insert tab. To create a chart from the selected data source, you click the button that corresponds to the type of chart you want to insert, which opens a gallery of chart subtypes. You can point to each subtype in the gallery to see a Live Preview of the selected data source in that chart subtype. Exhibit 16-3 shows the Pie charts gallery. Just click a chart subtype to insert that chart in the worksheet.

When you create or select a chart, two Chart Tools tabs appear on the ribbon. The Design tab provides commands to set the chart's overall design, including changing the chart type, and to work with individual elements of the chart such as the chart's title. The Format tab provides commands to change the appearance of graphic shapes in the chart such as the chart's border or markers placed in the chart.

EXHIBIT 16-3 PIE CHARTS GALLERY

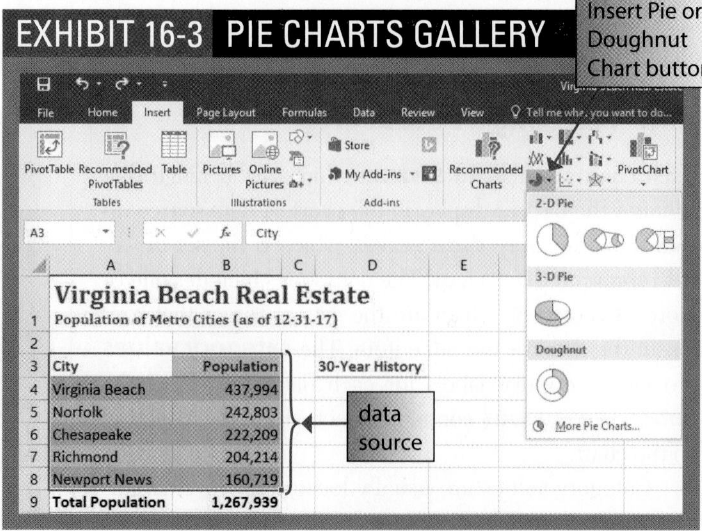

pie chart A chart in the shape of a circle divided into slices like a pie that shows the data values as a percentage of the whole.

FYI SELECTING A RECOMMENDED CHART

The Quick Analysis tool provides a list of recommended charts for the selected data source. After you select the range you want to use as a chart's data source, the Quick Analysis button appears in the lower-right corner of the selected range. Click the Quick Analysis button, and then click Charts to display a list of recommended charts. You can point to the different charts to see how the data would appear in the chart style. If you want to use a chart style, click that option. If not, you can click the More button to open the Insert Chart dialog box, which has two tabs: The Recommended Charts tab shows the different types of charts that Excel has determined are most appropriate for the data. The All Charts tab provides access to all of the different chart types and subtypes. You can also open the Insert Chart dialog box with the Recommended Charts tab displayed by clicking the Recommended Charts button in the Charts group on the Insert tab.

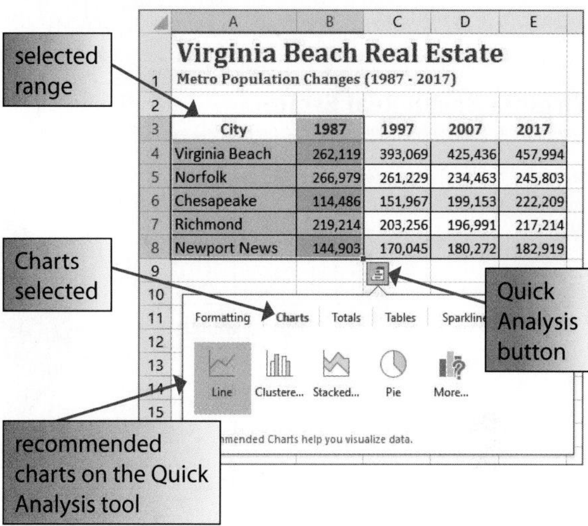

Three buttons appear to the right of the selected chart. The Chart Elements button is used to add, remove, or change elements displayed in the chart. The Chart Styles button sets the style and color scheme of the chart. The Chart Filters button lets you edit the data displayed in the chart.

Begin Activity

Insert a pie chart.

1. On the ribbon, click the **Insert tab**.
2. In the Charts group, click the **Insert Pie or Doughnut Chart button**. The Pie charts gallery opens. Refer back to Exhibit 16-3.
3. Point to the different pie chart subtypes.
4. In the 2-D Pie section, click the **Pie chart** (the first pie chart). The pie chart is inserted in the Metro Population worksheet; three buttons appear next to the chart and two Chart Tools tabs appear on the ribbon. Compare your screen to Exhibit 16-4.

End Activity

16-1d Selecting Chart Elements

Chart elements are individual parts of a chart such as the chart area, the chart title, the plot area, data markers, and a legend. See Exhibit 16-5. The **chart area** contains the chart and all of the other chart elements. The **chart title** is a descriptive label or name for the chart. The **plot area** is the part of the chart that contains the graphical representation of the data series. Each value in a data series is represented by a **data marker** such as a pie slice. A **legend** is a rectangular area that identifies the data markers associated with the data series. You can choose which of these elements to include in the chart as well as where each element is placed and how each element looks.

chart element An individual part of a chart.

chart area The area that contains the chart and all of the other chart elements.

chart title A descriptive label or name for the chart.

plot area The part of the chart that contains the graphical representation of the data series.

data marker An object in a chart that represents a value in a data series, such as a pie slice or column.

legend A rectangular area that identifies the data markers associated with the data series.

EXHIBIT 16-4 PIE CHART INSERTED INTO THE WORKSHEET

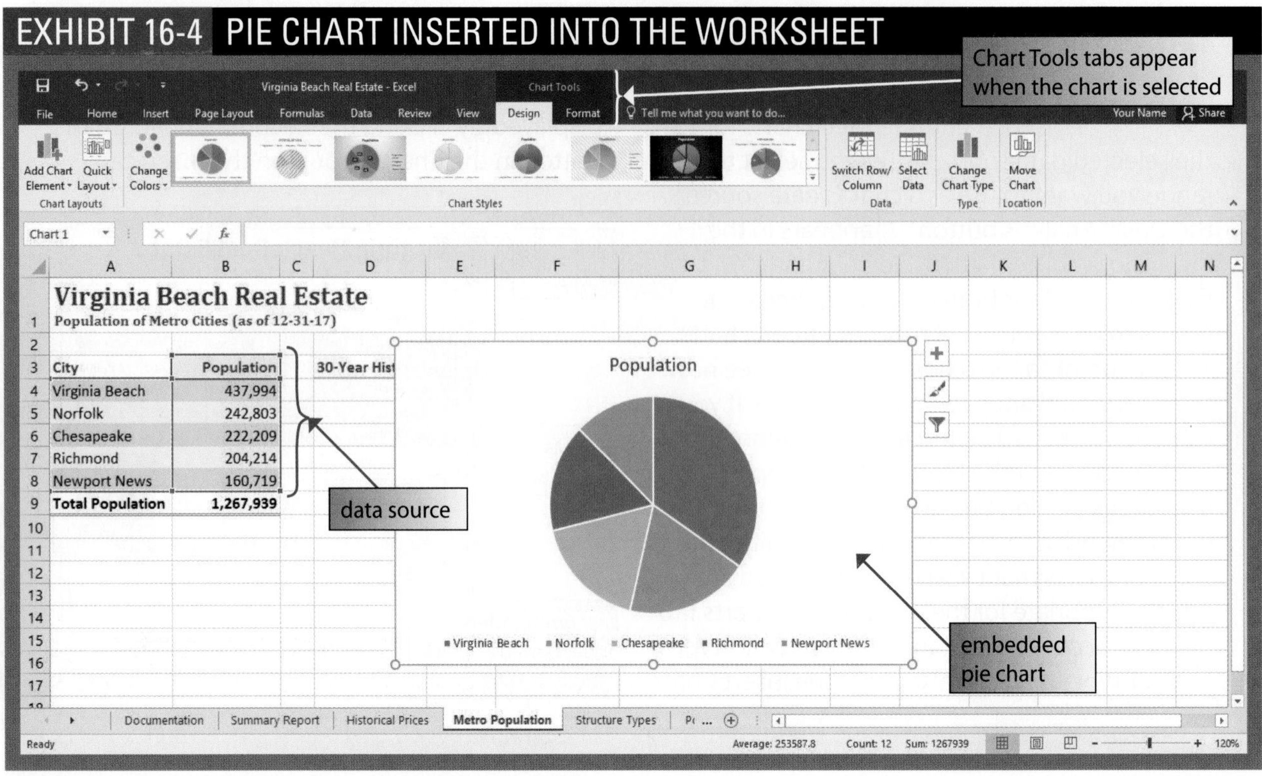

EXHIBIT 16-5 CHART ELEMENTS

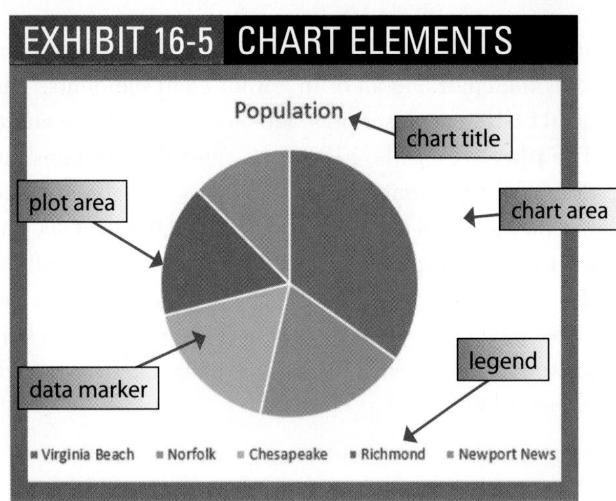

Before you can work with a chart element, you must select it. The simplest way to select a chart element is to click it. To ensure that you are clicking the right element, point to the element and check that the correct element name appears in the ScreenTip. The name of the selected element appears in the Chart Elements box located in the Current Selection group on the Chart Tools Format tab. You can also use this box to select chart elements. Click the Chart Elements box arrow, and then select the appropriate chart element in the list. A selection box with sizing handles, which you use to reposition or resize the element, surrounds the selected element. See Exhibit 16-6.

Begin Activity

Select chart elements.

1. Point to an empty area of the selected chart. The pointer changes to ✥ and the ScreenTip *Chart Area* appears, indicating that the pointer is over the chart area.
2. In the chart area above the pie chart, point to **Population**. The ScreenTip *Chart Title* appears, indicating that the pointer is over the chart title.
3. Click **Population**. A selection box appears around the chart title, indicating that it is selected.
4. On the ribbon, click the **Chart Tools Format tab**. In the Current Selection group, notice that *Chart Title* appears in the Chart Elements box.
5. Click the **Chart Elements box arrow** to display a list of elements in the current chart. Refer to Exhibit 16-6.
6. In the Chart Elements list, click **Plot Area**. The selection box surrounds the pie chart.
7. Select the **chart area**.

> **PROBLEM?**
> If you don't see the Chart Tools Format tab, the chart is not selected. In the Metro Population worksheet, click any part of the **chart** to select it, and then repeat Step 4.

End Activity

EXHIBIT 16-6 CURRENT SELECTION LIST

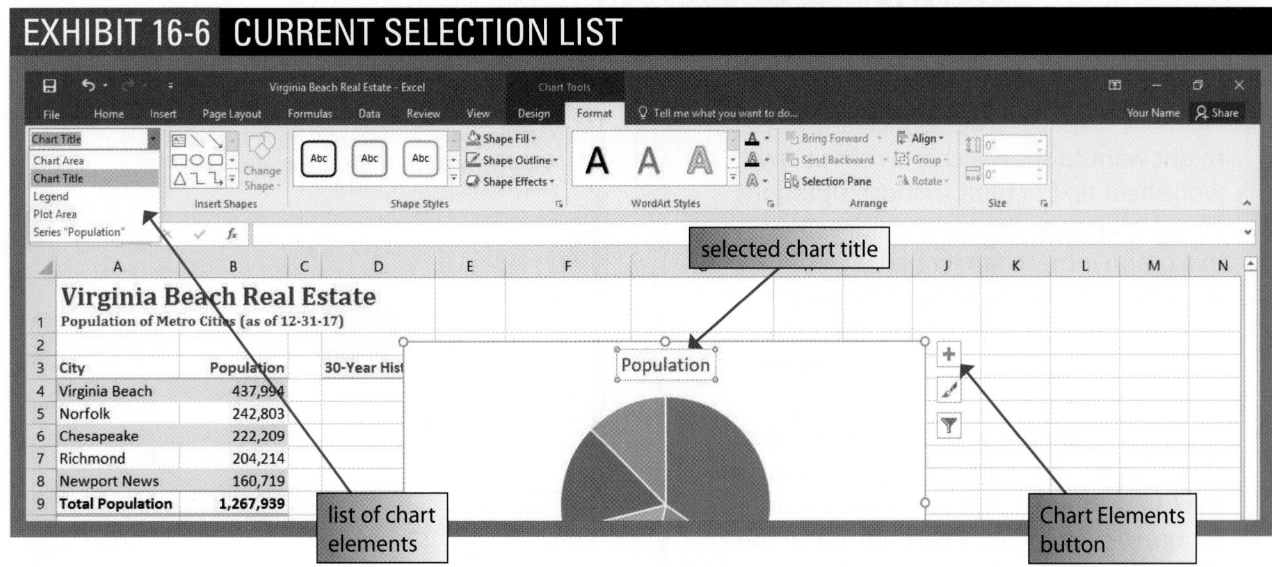

16-2 MOVING AND RESIZING A CHART

Each chart you create is inserted as an embedded chart in the worksheet that contains its data source. An **embedded chart** is an object in a worksheet. For example, the pie chart is embedded in the Metro Population worksheet. The advantage of an embedded chart is that you can display the chart alongside its data source or any text or graphics that can explain the chart's meaning and purpose. However, an embedded chart might cover worksheet cells that hide data and formulas. To avoid hiding data, you can move an embedded chart to a different sheet in the workbook, you can reposition it on the worksheet, or you can resize the chart.

16-2a Moving a Chart to a Different Sheet

You can move an embedded chart to a different worksheet in the workbook, or you can move it to a **chart sheet** (a sheet that contains only the chart and no worksheet cells). Likewise, you can move a chart from a chart sheet and embed it in any worksheet you select. Click the Move Chart button in the Location group on the Chart Tools Design tab to open the Move Chart dialog box, which provides options for moving charts between worksheets and chart sheets. See Exhibit 16-7. You can also cut and paste a chart to a new location in the workbook.

Begin Activity

Move a chart to another sheet.

1 On the ribbon, click the **Chart Tools Design tab.**

EXHIBIT 16-7 MOVE CHART DIALOG BOX

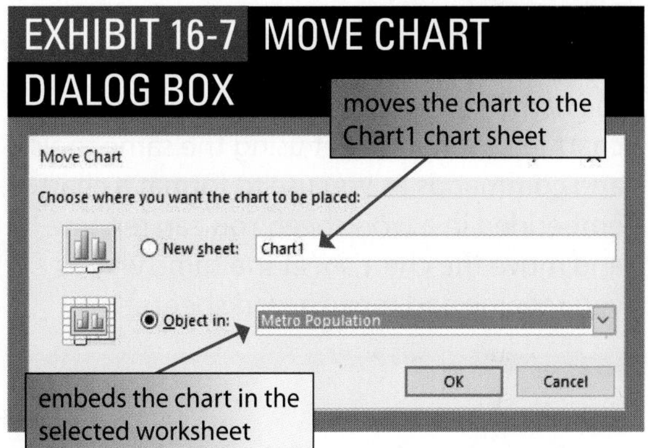

2 In the Location group, click the **Move Chart button.** The Move Chart dialog box opens. Refer back to Exhibit 16-7.

3 Click the **Object in box arrow** to display a list of worksheets in the active workbook, and then click **Summary Report.**

4 Click **OK.** The embedded pie chart moves from the Metro Population worksheet to the Summary Report worksheet and remains selected.

TIP: To move a chart to a chart sheet, in the Move Chart dialog box, click the New sheet option button, type a name for the chart sheet in the box, and then click OK.

End Activity

embedded chart A chart that is an object in a worksheet.

chart sheet A sheet in a workbook that contains only a chart and no worksheet cells.

FYI CREATING A CHART SHEET

Detailed charts might need more space to be seen clearly or you might want to show a chart without any worksheet text or data. In those situations, you may want to devote an entire sheet to a graph rather than embed it within a worksheet. To create a chart that covers an entire sheet, you move the chart to a chart sheet. Chart sheets do not contain worksheet cells.

To move an embedded chart to a chart sheet, select the chart in the worksheet. On the Chart Tools Design tab, in the Location group, click the Move Chart button. In the Move Chart dialog box, click the New sheet option button, type a name for the chart sheet in the box, and then click OK. The chart is moved to a new chart sheet with the name you specified. You can format the chart in the chart sheet using the same tools and commands as you use to format a chart embedded in a worksheet. You can rename and move the chart sheet the same way as you rename and move a worksheet.

16-2b Repositioning and Resizing a Chart

An embedded chart might cover other data in the worksheet or be placed in an awkward location. You can reposition and resize the embedded chart to better fit on the worksheet. To do so, first select the chart. A selection box, which you use to reposition or resize the object, surrounds the chart. To reposition the chart, drag the selection box to a new location in the worksheet. To resize the chart, drag a sizing handle on the selection box to change the object's width and height. See Exhibit 16-8.

Begin Activity

Reposition and resize a chart.

1 Point to an **empty part of the chart** until the pointer changes to ✥ and the ScreenTip *Chart Area* appears.

EXHIBIT 16-8 PIE CHART REPOSITIONED AND RESIZED

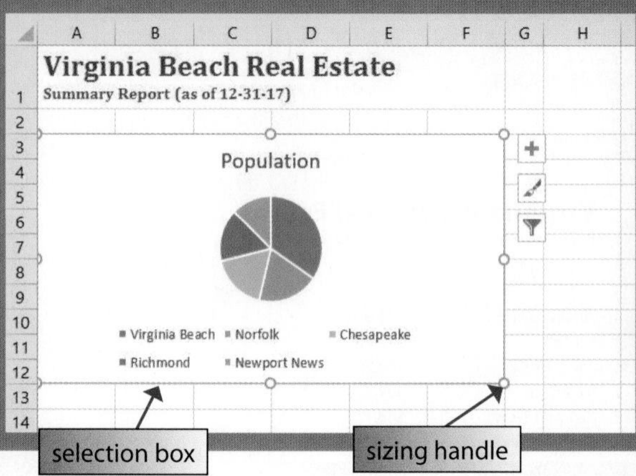

2 Click the **chart area**, drag to the left until the chart's upper-left corner is in cell A3, and then release the mouse button. The chart moves to a new location.

3 Point to the **sizing handle** in the lower-right corner of the chart until the pointer changes to ⤡.

4 Drag the **sizing handle** up to cell F12. The chart resizes to cover the range A3:F12 and remains selected. Refer back to Exhibit 16-8.

PROBLEM? If the chart resizes or other chart elements move, undo your last action, and then repeat Steps 1 and 2, being sure to drag the pie chart from the chart area.

TIP: To maintain the aspect ratio of the chart as you resize it, hold down the Shift key as you drag the sizing handle.

End Activity

16-3 MODIFYING A CHART

After you create a chart, you can change its style and layout. You can also choose which chart elements to include with the chart and change how each element is formatted. This flexibility enables you to create a chart that best conveys its data. It also lets you create a chart with a look and feel that suits your intended readers.

16-3a Changing the Chart Style

When you create a chart, the chart is formatted with the default chart style for that chart type. For example, the default pie chart style applies a solid color to each slice. You can modify the appearance of a chart by applying a different **chart style** to the chart.

chart style A style that formats an entire chart at one time.

The chart styles are located in the Chart Styles gallery, which is available on the Chart Tools Design tab or by clicking the Chart Styles button next to the selected chart. See Exhibit 16-9. There are both two-dimensional and three-dimensional chart styles. The 3-D chart styles provide the illusion of depth and distance, which makes the charts appear to stand out on the page and add visual interest. Live Preview shows how each of the selected charts will look with the different chart styles.

EXHIBIT 16-9 CHART STYLES GALLERY FOR PIE CHARTS

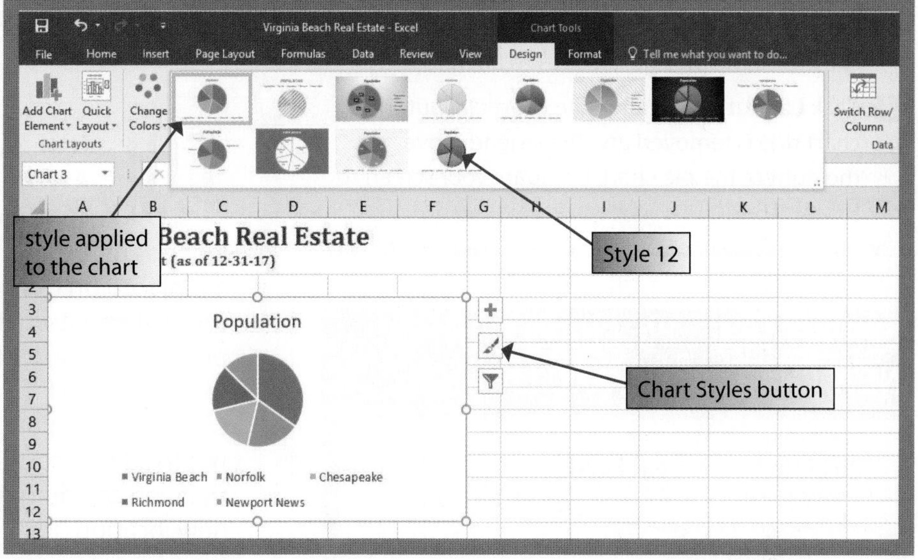

style applied to the chart

Style 12

Chart Styles button

For even more control over how a chart looks, you can select and format individual elements. To apply formatting to an individual chart element, double-click that chart element to open a pane with format options specific to the selected element.

Begin Activity

Change the chart style.

1. Make sure the **pie chart** is selected.
2. On the **Chart Tools Design tab**, in the Chart Styles group, click the **More button**. The Chart Styles gallery opens. Refer back to Exhibit 16-9.
3. Point to different styles in the gallery. Live Preview shows the impact of each chart style on the pie chart's appearance.
4. Click **Style 12**. Each pie slice now appears rounded and three-dimensional.

> **TIP:** You can also click the Chart Styles button next to the selected chart to access the chart styles.

End Activity

16-3b Changing a Chart Layout

Chart layouts provide different options for displaying and arranging chart elements. These layouts specify which chart elements are displayed and how they are formatted. The chart layouts include some of the most common ways of displaying different charts. Each chart type has its own collection of layouts. For a pie chart, the chart layout you choose may hide or display the chart title, display a chart legend or place legend labels in the pie slices, and add percentages to the pie slices. The chart layouts are available by clicking the Quick Layout button in the Chart Layouts group on the Chart Tools Design tab. See Exhibit 16-10.

EXHIBIT 16-10 QUICK LAYOUT GALLERY

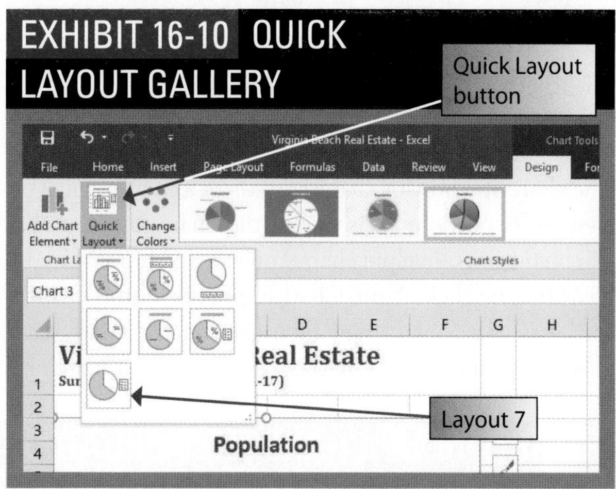

Begin Activity

Change the chart layout.

1. On the **Chart Tools Design tab**, in the Chart Layouts group, click the **Quick Layout button**. The Quick Layout gallery opens. Refer back to Exhibit 16-10.

> **chart layout** An option for displaying and arranging chart elements.

2 In the last row, point to **Layout 7**. Live Preview shows the impact of the layout on the pie chart's appearance. The chart title is removed from the chart, and the pie chart resizes to fill the space.

3 Click **Layout 7** to change the chart's layout. The chart title is removed and the legend moves to the right of the pie chart. Compare your screen to Exhibit 16-11.

End Activity

EXHIBIT 16-11 PIE CHART WITH NEW CHART STYLE AND LAYOUT

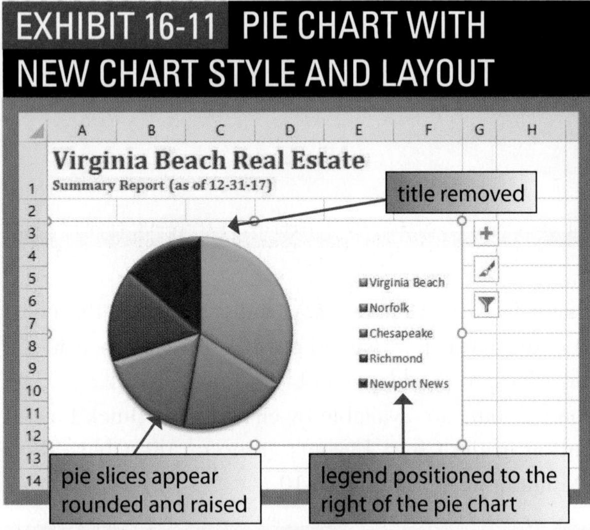

16-3c Modifying and Formatting a Chart Title

The chart title provides a description of a chart or an overview of its purpose. It is one of the chart elements that can be included in a pie chart. You can add or remove the chart title by clicking the Chart Elements button [+] next to the selected chart, and then clicking the Chart Title check box. See Exhibit 16-12. When you create a chart, Excel uses the data series label as the chart title. You can edit or replace this default chart title. You can also format the text of the chart title just like you can format any text.

> **FYI**
>
> **OVERLAYING CHART TITLES AND LEGENDS**
>
> You can overlay chart titles and legends in the chart area, which means they are placed on top of the chart. Overlaying these elements makes more space for the plot area because the chart does not resize to make room for that element. An overlaid chart element floats in the chart area and is not fixed to a particular position. This means that you can drag the chart element to a new location. To overlay a chart title, click the Chart Elements button, point to Chart Title, click the right arrow button, and then click Centered Overlay. To overlay a legend, double-click the legend to open the Format Legend pane, and then select the Show the legend without overlapping the chart check box in the Legend Options section in the Legend Options.

Begin Activity

Modify and format a chart title.

1 Click the **Chart Elements button** [+] next to the selected chart. A menu with the available chart elements for the selected chart appears. Notice that only the Legend check box is selected, as this is the only element currently on the chart.

EXHIBIT 16-12 CHART TITLE UPDATED AND FORMATTED

selected chart title
Chart Title check box
Beach Real Est
rt (as of 12-31-17)
Population
CHART ELEMENTS
Chart Title
Data Labels
Legend
Virginia Beach
Norfolk
Chesapeake
Richmond
Newport News
plot area decreases to make room for the chart title

2 Click the **Chart Title check box**. The chart title is added to the chart and a selection box appears around the chart title. Refer back to Exhibit 16-12.

3 In the **chart title**, click after *Population*, press the **Spacebar**, and then type **of Metro Cities**.

4 Click the border of the **chart title selection box** to select the entire box.

5 Change the font size to **12 points**. The chart title reduces in size, and the pie chart increases in size to fill the extra space.

End Activity

16-3d **Positioning and Formatting the Chart Legend**

EXHIBIT 16-13 LEGEND OPTIONS IN THE CHART ELEMENTS BUTTON MENU

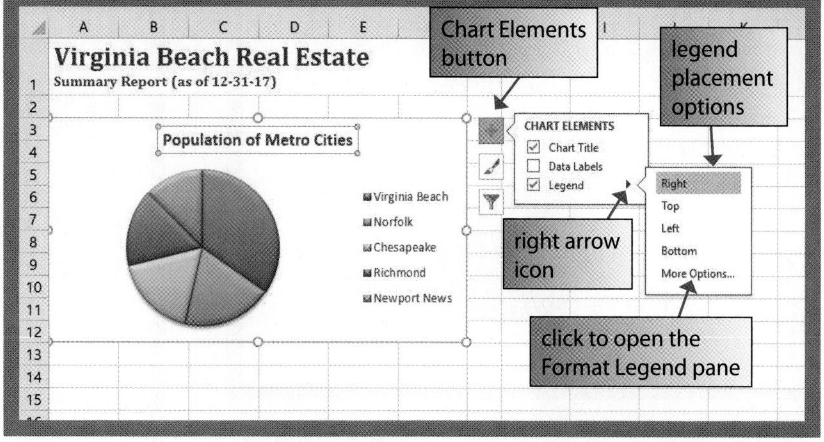

The chart legend identifies each data series in the chart. With a pie chart, the legend shows the color used for each slice and its corresponding category value. In this case, the category values are the different cities. You can choose where to position the legend. Click the Chart Elements button [+] next to the selected chart to open the CHART ELEMENTS menu, point to Legend to display the right arrow [▸] next to the Legend option, click the right arrow [▸], and then click one of the placement options—Right, Top, Left, or Bottom. Live Preview shows the legend placement when you point to an option. See Exhibit 16-13.

If you click More Options, the Format Legend pane opens at the right side of the workbook window. The Format pane provides additional options for formatting the selected element's appearance. In this case, because the legend is selected, the pane is labeled "Format Legend" and includes options for formatting the legend's fill, border, effects (shadow, glow, and soft edges), placement, and text. See Exhibit 16-14.

EXHIBIT 16-14 FORMAT LEGEND PANE

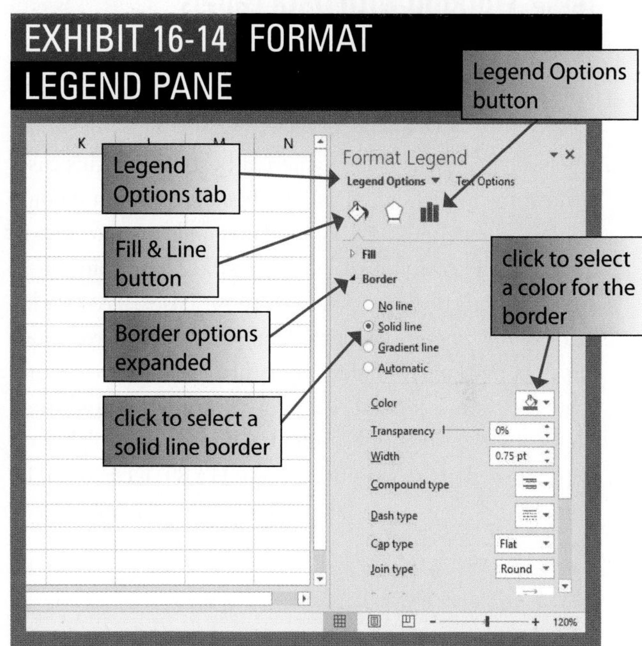

Begin Activity

Position and format the chart legend.

1 Next to the selected chart, click the **Chart Elements button** [+]. The CHART ELEMENTS menu appears next to the chart.

2 Point to **Legend** to display the right arrow [▸] next to the Legend option.

3 Click the **right arrow** [▸] to display the placement options. Refer back to Exhibit 16-13.

4 Click **Left**. The legend moves to the left side of the chart.

5 On the Legends submenu, click **More Options**. The Format Legend pane appears on the right side of the workbook window with the Legend Options tab selected. On the Legend Options tab, the Legend Options button is selected, and the Legend Options section is expanded.

> **TIP:** You can also double-click the legend to open the Format Legend pane.

6 In the Format Legend pane, click the **Fill & Line button**, and then click **Border** to display the border options in the pane.

7 Click the **Solid line option button**. Additional line options in the pane are now available.

8 Click the **Color button** to display the color palette, and then select the **Turquoise, Accent 6 theme color**. Refer back to Exhibit 16-14. The legend now has a turquoise border, although you can't see this because the selection box appears on top of the border.

9 Click the **chart area** to deselect the legend and better see the formatted border. Compare your screen to Exhibit 16-15.

End Activity

EXHIBIT 16-15 CHART LEGEND POSITIONED AND FORMATTED

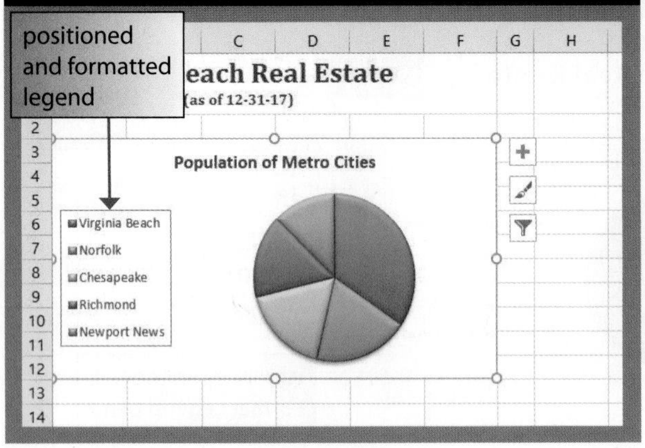

EXHIBIT 16-16 FORMAT DATA LABELS PANE

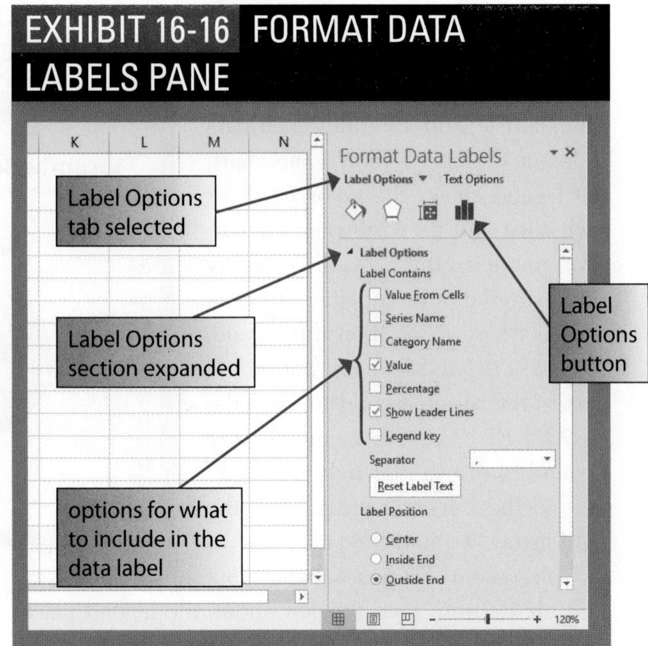

16-3e Working with Data Labels

A **data label** is text for an individual data marker, such as a pie slice. A data label can show a value or other descriptive text. When you use a chart layout that shows data labels, each label is placed where it best fits—in this case, either on the pie slice or along its side. You can change the label placement so that all data labels appear next to their pie slices. Labels placed outside of the pie might appear far from their slices. In those cases, Excel adds leader lines to connect each data label to its corresponding data marker. A leader line is not used when enough space exists in the chart area to place a label next to its slice. The data label placement options are available on the Data Labels submenu on the CHART ELEMENTS menu. Additional data label options are available in the Format Data Labels pane. See Exhibit 16-16.

Begin Activity

Format data labels.

1. Click the **Chart Elements button** + next to the selected chart, and then click **Data Labels**. Data labels are added to each pie slice.
2. Point to **Data Labels**, click the **right arrow** ▶, and then click **Outside End**. This option sets the data labels outside the pie chart.
3. On the **Data Labels submenu**, click **More Options**. The pane on the right changes to the Format Data Labels pane with the Label Options tab selected.

> **TIP:** You can also open the Format pane by double-clicking a chart element.

4. In the Format Data Labels pane, click the **Label Options button**, and then click **Label Options** below the buttons to expand that section. Refer back to Exhibit 16-16. In the Label Contains section, the Value and the Show Leader Lines check boxes are already checked because these are the default data label options. These options set the data labels to display as the values in the data source and use leader lines when needed to connect the labels with their corresponding pie slices.
5. In the Label Contains section, click the **Value check box** to deselect it. The value data labels are removed from the chart.
6. Click the **Percentage check box**. The data values are displayed as percentages of the whole. Even though the Show Leader Lines check box is selected, the lines don't appear on the chart because the chart area has enough space to place the labels close to their slices.

> **TIP:** Some of the chart styles for a pie chart add the percentage data labels to the pie slices.

7. In the Format Data Labels pane, click **Label Options** to collapse that section. Click **Number** to expand that section and display options related to formatting numbers.

data label Text for an individual data marker.

8 Click the **Category box arrow**, and then click **Percentage**. The data labels are formatted with the Percentage number style and two decimal places. Compare your screen to Exhibit 16-17.

9 Click the **chart area** to deselect the data labels and keep the chart selected.

End Activity

EXHIBIT 16-17 FORMATTED DATA LABELS

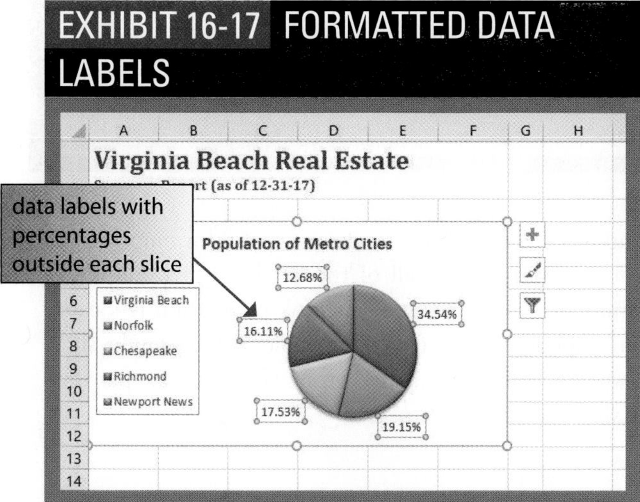

16-3f Changing the Color of a Data Series

The data series is the range of values plotted on the chart. The values in each data series are plotted as a single unit on a chart. Usually, you use one color for an entire data series. However, in a pie chart, you want each slice to have a different color or a distinct shade of the same color so that the slices are easy to distinguish.

Pie slice colors should be as distinct as possible to avoid confusion. Using distinct colors is especially important for adjacent slices. Depending on the printer quality or the monitor resolution, similarly colored slices might be difficult to distinguish. You can change all of the pie slice colors at once by clicking the Chart Styles button next to the selected chart, clicking Color at the top of the menu, and then clicking the set of colors you want to use. See Exhibit 16-18.

You can also change the color of each slice in a pie chart individually. To select an individual slice, you first click the pie chart slices to select the entire data series, and then you click the specific slice you want to select. The Format pane changes to the Format Data Point pane, and you can use the Fill options in the pane to select the fill you want to use for the selected slice. See Exhibit 16-19. You can also use the Fill Color button in the Font group on the Home tab to change the fill color.

Begin Activity

Change the color of a data series.

1 Next to the selected chart, click the **Chart Styles button**, and then click **Style**, if necessary. The menu that opens contains the same chart styles that appear in the Chart Styles gallery on the Chart Tools Design tab.

2 At the top of the menu, click **Color**. The available color schemes appear in the gallery. Refer to Exhibit 16-18.

3 Point to the different color sets to see a Live Preview on the pie chart, and then click the **Color 3 set**. The slices and the legend colors change color to reflect the selected color scheme.

4 Next to the chart, click the **Chart Styles button** to close the menu.

5 Click the **pie chart** to select the entire data series. The pane on the right changes to the Format Data Series pane.

6 Click the **dark teal Newport News slice**, which represents 12.68 percent of the pie. Only that value, or slice, is selected. The pane to the right of the worksheet window changes to the Format Data Point pane.

EXHIBIT 16-18 PIE CHART COLOR OPTIONS

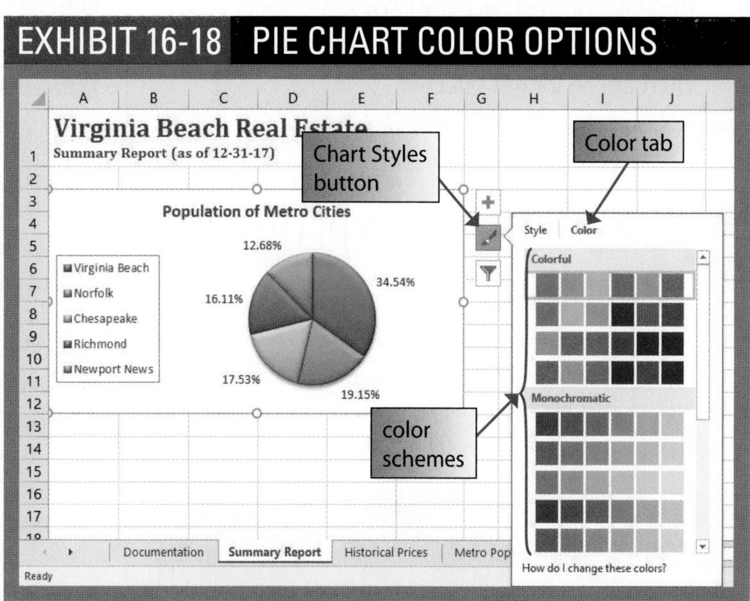

EXHIBIT 16-19 FORMAT DATA POINT PANE AND PIE SLICES WITH NEW COLORS

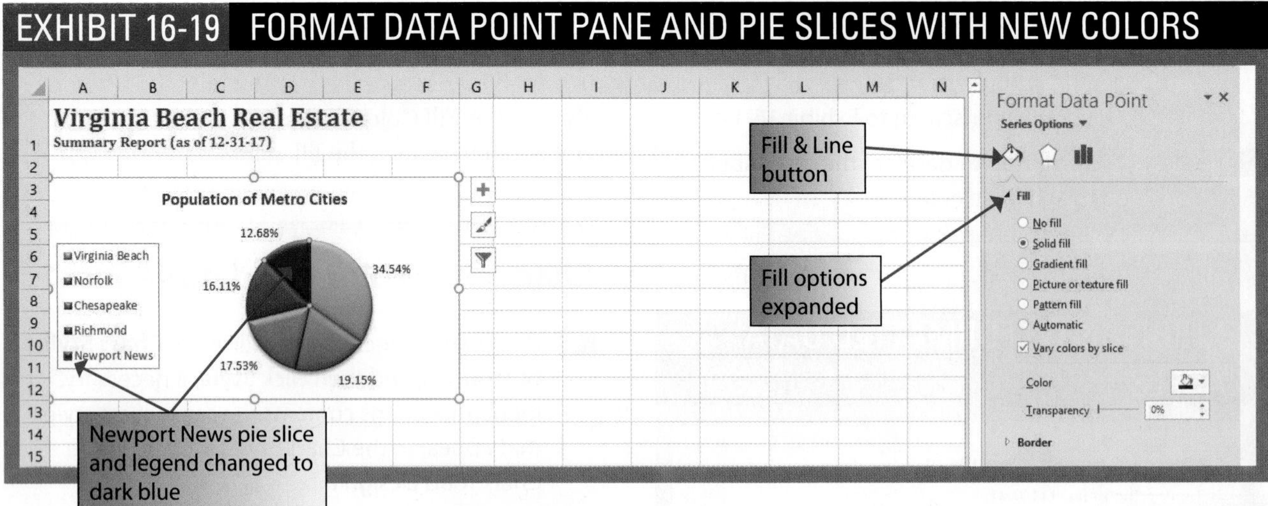

7 In the Format Data Point pane, click the **Fill & Line button**, if necessary, to display the fill and border options.

8 Click **Fill** to expand the list of fill options in the pane.

9 Click the **Solid fill option button.** The selected pie slice changes to a green color, which is the color selected on the Color button in the pane.

10 Click the **Color button** to display the color palette, and then click the **Turquoise, Accent 6, Darker 50% theme color.** The Newport News slice and legend marker change to dark blue. Refer back to Exhibit 16-19.

11 In the Format Data Point pane, click the **Close button** . The task pane closes.

12 In the worksheet, click **any cell.** The slice and the chart are no longer selected.

End Activity

TIP: You can also use the Fill Color button in the Font group on the Home tab to change the font color of a selected data series or data point.

16-4 CREATING AN EXPLODED PIE CHART

Pie slices do not need to be fixed within the pie. An **exploded pie chart** moves one slice away from the others as if someone were taking the piece away from the pie. Exploded pie charts are useful for emphasizing one category above all of the others. For example, to emphasize how much of a state's population is located in a specific city, you could explode that single slice, moving it away from the other slices in the pie. See Exhibit 16-20.

EXHIBIT 16-20 EXPLODED PIE CHART

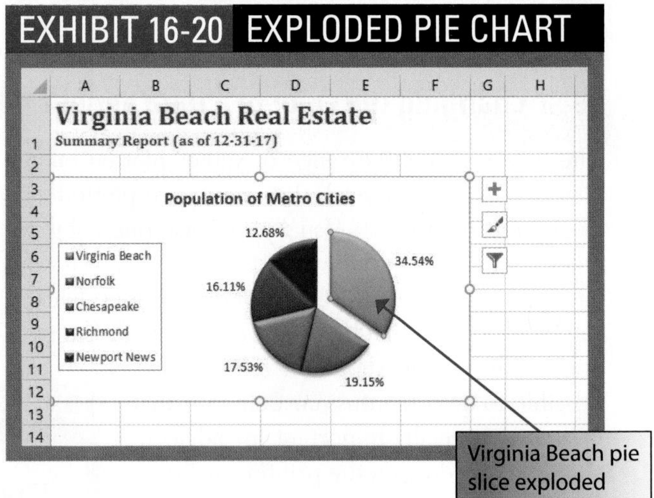

To explode a pie slice, select that slice from the pie chart and then drag the slice away from the pie. You can also explode multiple slices by selecting each slice and dragging them away. To explode all of the slices, select the entire pie and drag the pointer away from the pie's center. Each slice will be exploded and separated from the others. Although you can explode more than one slice, the resulting pie chart is rarely effective as a visual aid to the reader.

exploded pie chart A pie chart where one slice is moved away from the pie.

Begin Activity

Create an exploded pie chart.

1 Click the **pie chart**. The entire data series is selected as indicated by the sizing handles on each pie slice.

2 Click the **light green Virginia Beach slice** to select that slice.

3 Drag the selected **Virginia Beach slice** to the right approximately one-quarter inch. The slice is separated from the rest of the pie chart. Refer to Exhibit 16-20.

> **PROBLEM?**
> If a square border appears around the pie chart, you selected the plot area, not the chart itself. Click the **pie chart** again.

End Activity

16-5 CREATING A COLUMN OR BAR CHART

A **column chart** displays values in different categories as columns; the height of each column is based on its value. A **bar chart** is a column chart turned on its side so that the length of each bar is based on its value. Each data series has columns or bars of the same color.

Column and bar charts apply to a wider range of data than pie charts. For example, you can show how a set of values changes over time, such as housing prices over several years. You can also include several data series in a column or bar chart, such as the populations of five cities over several years. The values from different data series are displayed in columns side by side. Pie charts usually show only one data series.

16-5a Creating a Column Chart

The process for creating a column chart is the same as for creating any other chart. First, you select the data source. Then, you select the type of chart you want to create. After the chart is embedded in the worksheet, you can move and resize the chart as well as change the chart's design, layout, and format.

Begin Activity

Create a column chart.

1 Make the **Structures Types worksheet** the active sheet. Select the **range A3:C12**.

2 On the ribbon, click the **Insert tab**. In the Charts group, click the **Insert Column or Bar Chart button**. The gallery shows the different column charts you can create.

3 In the 2-D Column section, click the **Clustered Column chart** (the first chart). The column chart is inserted in the active worksheet, and the Chart Tools Design tab is selected on the ribbon.

4 On the Chart Tools Design tab, in the Location group, click the **Move Chart button**. The Move Chart dialog box opens.

5 Click the **Object in box arrow**, click **Summary Report**, and then click **OK**. The column chart moves to the Summary Report worksheet and is still selected.

6 In the Summary Report worksheet, drag the selected column chart down so its upper-left corner is in **cell A14**.

7 Drag the **lower-right sizing handle** until the chart covers the **range A14:F27**. The chart is resized smaller. Compare your screen to Exhibit 16-21.

End Activity

EXHIBIT 16-21 COLUMN CHART OF STRUCTURE TYPES

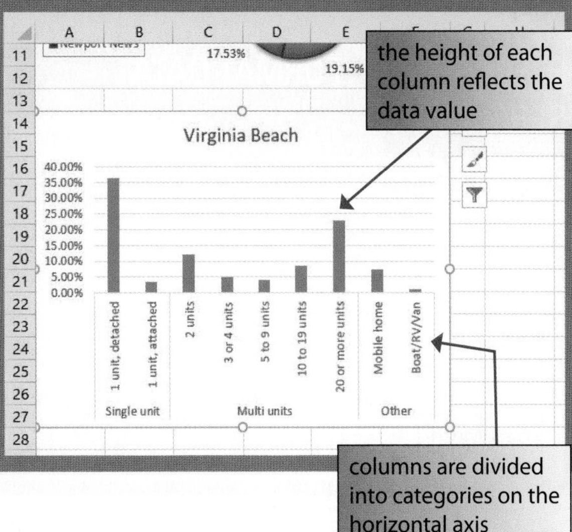

column chart A chart that displays values in different categories as columns so that the height of each column is based on its value.

bar chart A column chart that is turned on its side so that the length of each bar is based on its value.

16-5b Formatting a Column Chart

The process for formatting a chart is the same for each type of chart, although the specific formats and options available reflect the current chart type. The Chart Tools Design tab provides a gallery of column chart layouts and a gallery of column chart styles and access to the individual chart elements you can include on the column chart. The Chart Tools Format tab provides options to change the appearance of a column chart by formatting these chart elements.

You have already seen how to add and remove chart elements, change the chart color scheme, and change the color of one value in a data series. You can also format an entire data series at once. For example, in a column chart, you can change the amount of space between the columns or change the way the columns look by changing their inside color (or fill). One option is to fill the columns with a gradient—shading in which one color blends into another or varies from one shade to another. To format a data series in a column chart, double-click any column in the series you want to change to open the Format Data Series pane. You can then click the Series Options button to display the tab on which you can adjust the amount of space between the columns. See Exhibit 16-22. To change the fill color of columns, you click the Fill & Line button in the Format Data Series pane.

EXHIBIT 16-22 FORMAT DATA SERIES PANE

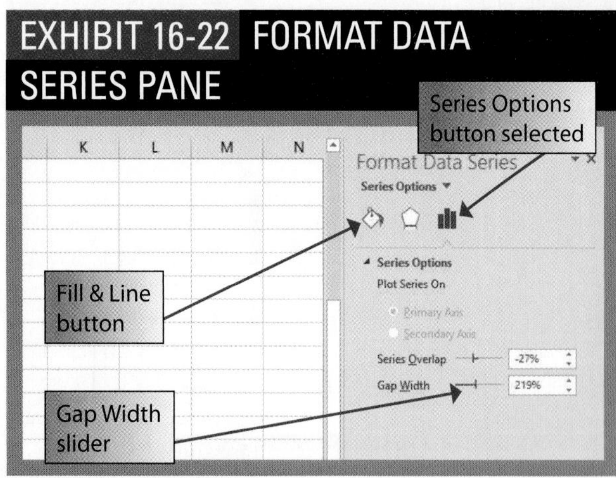

vertical (value) axis The axis along the side of the chart that shows the range of values from all of the data series plotted on the chart.

horizontal (category) axis The axis along the bottom of the chart that shows the category values from each data series.

scale The range of values along an axis.

Begin Activity

Format a column chart.

1. In the column chart, click the **chart title** to select it.
2. Change the font size of the chart title to **12 points**.
3. With the chart title still selected, type **S**. Nothing changes in the chart title text box, but the *S* you typed appears in the formula bar.
4. Type **Structure Types** so that *Structure Types* appears in the formula bar, and then press the **Enter key**. The text you typed replaces the original chart title.
5. In the column chart, double-click **any column**. All of the columns for the data series in the chart are selected, and the Format Data Series pane opens with the Series Options button selected and the Series Options section expanded. Refer back to Exhibit 16-22.
6. Drag the **Gap Width slider** to the left until the value in the Gap Width box is **50%**. The gap between adjacent columns is reduced, and the columns become wider to fill the space.
7. In the Format Data Series pane, click the **Fill & Line button**. If the fill options are not expanded, click **Fill**.
8. Click the **Gradient fill option button**. The columns are filled with a gradually changing shade of green.
9. Click the **Direction button** to display a gallery of gradient directions. Click **Linear Up** (the second option in the second row). The columns are filled with a gradient that blends to the top. Compare your screen to Exhibit 16-23.

PROBLEM?
If you cannot drag the Gap width slider to exactly 50%, select the value in the Gap Width box next to the slider, type **50**, and then press the **Enter key**.

End Activity

16-5c Changing the Axis Intervals

Chart data is plotted along axes. The **vertical (value) axis** shows the range of values from all of the data series plotted on the chart. The **horizontal (category) axis** shows the category values from each data series. The range of values, or **scale**, of an axis is based on the values in the data source. The scale usually ranges from 0 through the maximum value. If the scale includes negative values, it ranges from the minimum value through the maximum value.

EXHIBIT 16-23 FORMATTED COLUMN CHART

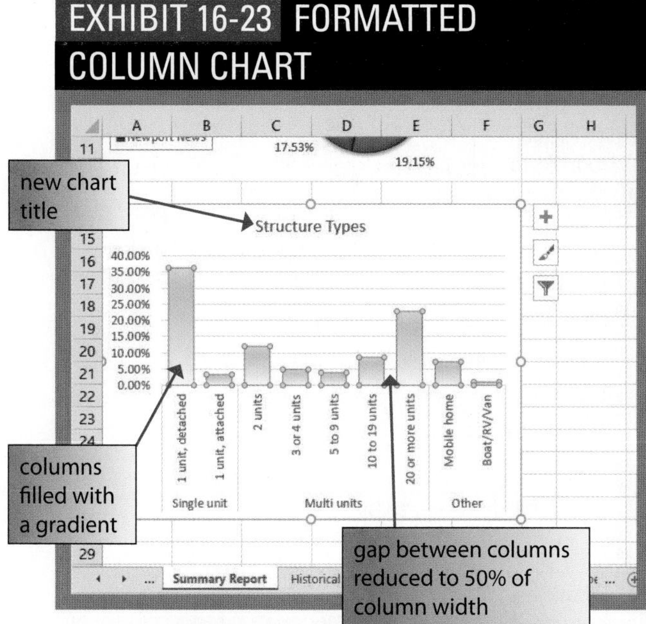

The labels on the vertical (value) axis identify intervals along the axis. For example, an axis whose scale is 0 through 50 might have labels identifying intervals every five units, as in 0, 5, 10, 15, 20, and so on. You can change this interval by changing the units. For example, you could specify that the axis labels appear every 10 units, as in 0, 10, 20, and so on. Keep in mind that more labels at smaller intervals, but fewer labels at larger intervals could make the chart less informative.

The axis options are available in the Format Axis pane. See Exhibit 16-24. The label Auto next to some options indicates that Excel set automatic values based on the values represented in the chart. The Bounds section indicates the scale, so it shows the minimum and maximum values that appear on the selected axis. The Major box in the Units section indicates the intervals at which the values appear in the chart.

EXHIBIT 16-24 AXIS OPTIONS IN THE FORMAT AXIS PANE

Auto indicates that Excel set the value

vertical axis scale ranges from 0 to 50%

vertical axis values appear at 5% intervals

Format Axis

Axis Options ▾ Text Options

Axis Options

Bounds

Minimum 0.0 Auto

Maximum 0.4 Auto

Units

Major 0.05 Auto

Minor 0.01 Auto

Horizontal axis crosses

Automatic

Axis value 0.0

Maximum axis value

Display units None

Show display units label on chart

Logarithmic scale Base 10

FYI FORMATTING A DATA POINT

In a pie chart, each slice or data marker has a different format. In a column chart, all of the columns usually have the same format because the columns are distinguished by height, not color. However, you can format individual columns in a data series to highlight a particular value. For example, you can change the color of one column, as shown here. You can also modify the appearance of the data markers in a column chart using any of the standard formatting options, including fonts, sizes, colors, and bold.

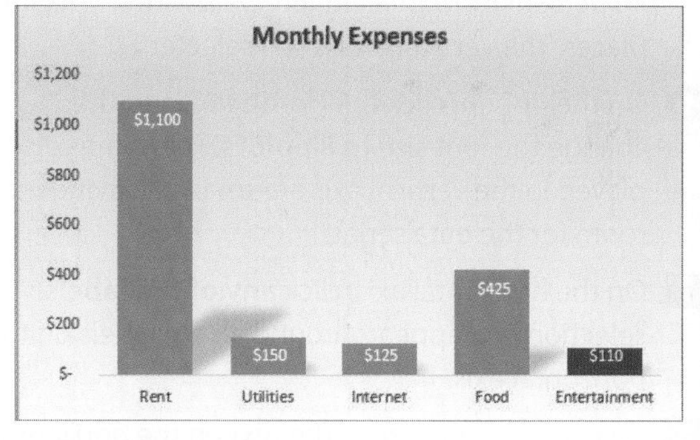

Begin Activity

Change the axis intervals and format the axis.

1 In the column chart, click **any value on the vertical axis** (the list of percentages). The Format Data Series pane changes to the Format Axis pane with the Axis Options tab selected.

TIP: If no pane is open, double-click a chart element to open its corresponding pane.

2. In the Format Axis pane, on the Axis Options tab, click the **Axis Options button**. If the Axis Options section is not expanded, click **Axis Options**. Refer back to Exhibit 16-24. In the Bounds section, the minimum value of the axis is set to 0 and the maximum value is set to 0.4, or 40 percent. This matches the values listed on the vertical axis. In the Units section, 0.05 appears in the Major box, indicating that the vertical axis values will appear every five percentage points.
3. In the Units section, select the current value in the Major box, type **0.1**, and then press the **Enter key**. The intervals between the values on the vertical axis change from 5 percent to 10 percent.
4. In the Format Axis pane, click **Axis Options** to collapse that section, and then click **Number** to expand the Number section. In the Category box, Percentage is selected. This is the current format of the numbers on the vertical axis.
5. In the Decimal places box, select **2**, type **0**, and then press the **Enter key**. The percentages on the vertical axis now show only integers. The percentages on the vertical axis range from 0 percent to 40 percent in 10 percent intervals with no decimal places. The vertical axis is still selected.
6. On the ribbon, click the **Home tab**, and then change the font size to **8 points**. The values displayed in the vertical axis are smaller, leaving more room for the data series.
7. On the horizontal axis, click **any of the labels**. A selection box appears around all the labels on the horizontal axis.
8. Change the font size of the text on the horizontal axis to **8 points**. Compare your screen to Exhibit 16-25.
9. Close the **Format Axis pane**.

End Activity

EXHIBIT 16-25 FORMATTED CHART AXES

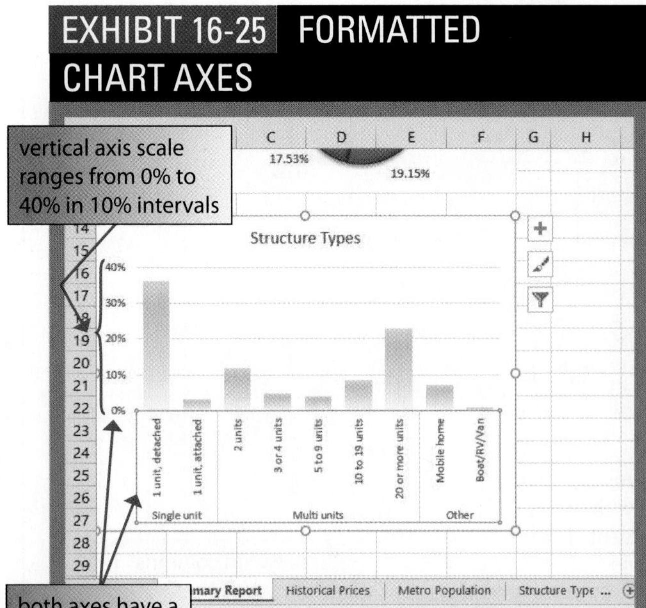

16-6 CREATING A LINE CHART

A **line chart** displays data values using a connected line rather than columns or bars. Line charts are typically used when the data consists of values drawn from categories that follow a sequential order at evenly spaced intervals, as with historical data in which the data values are recorded periodically such as monthly, quarterly, or yearly. Each data series has a different line color. Line charts are also commonly used instead of column charts when there are many data points across several data series. For example, when there are 40 data points across three data series, a column chart of this data would be difficult to read and interpret, whereas a line chart more clearly conveys this data.

line chart A chart that displays data values using a connected line rather than columns or bars.

16-6a Creating and Formatting a Line Chart

The process for creating a line chart is the same as for creating pie charts and column charts, though the specific options available differ a bit. A data marker for a line chart can appear with or without the connecting line.

Begin Activity

Create and format a line chart.

1. Make the **Historical Prices worksheet** the active sheet. Select the **range A3:D56**.
2. On the ribbon, click the **Insert tab**. In the Charts group, click **Insert Line or Area Chart button**. In the 2-D Line section, click the **Line chart**. A line chart is embedded in the Historical Prices worksheet.

3 Move the line chart to the **Summary Report worksheet.** Reposition and resize the chart to cover the **range H3:M13.**

> **PROBLEM?**
> If you don't see the chart on the Summary Report worksheet, scroll the worksheet down.

4 In the line chart, replace the **chart title** with **Price History.**

5 Change the font size of the chart title to **12 points.**

6 Click the **vertical axis** to select it, and then change its font size to **8 points.**

7 Select the **horizontal axis**, and then change its font size to **8 points.**

8 Below the horizontal axis, select the **legend**, and then change its font size to **8 points.** The line chart resizes to fill the space left by the smaller chart title, axes, and chart legend. Compare your screen to Exhibit 16-26.

End Activity

EXHIBIT 16-26 LINE CHART WITH THREE DATA SERIES

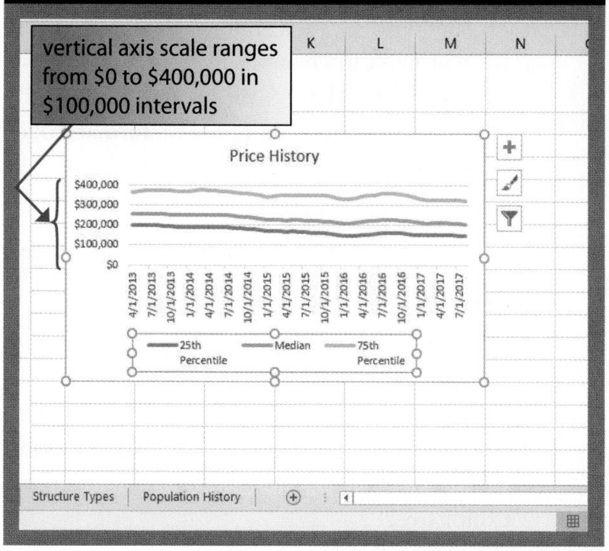

vertical axis scale ranges from $0 to $400,000 in $100,000 intervals

16-6b Editing the Axis Scale and Display Units in a Line Chart

When an axis scales from zero to a large number, it can be harder to see the difference between the data points if the values are all large. You can modify the scale of the axis to make the chart easier to understand. In addition, sometimes the axis labels can take up a lot of the available chart area and be difficult to read. You can simplify the chart's appearance by displaying units of measure more appropriate to the data values. For example, you can display the value 20 to represent 20,000 or 20,000,000. This is particularly useful when space is at a premium, such as in an embedded chart confined to a small area of the worksheet. If you change the display units, it's good practice to show the units as a label on the axis so that it is clear what values are listed. In Exhibit 16-27, the vertical axis in the Price History chart is scaled from $100,000 to $400,000 in intervals of $50,000, but because the display unit is Thousands, the labels are $100 through $400 in intervals of $50. The display unit *Thousands* is shown in a label next to the axis.

Begin Activity

Change the scale and display units of the vertical axis.

1 In the line chart, double-click the **vertical axis.** The Format Axis pane with the Axis Options tab and the Axis Options button selected and the Axis Options section expanded. (You might need to scroll up to see the Axis Options section.) In the Bounds section, the scale of the axis ranges from 0.0 to 400000.0. In the Major box in the Units section, the intervals are every 100000.

2 In the Bounds section, select the value in the Minimum box, type **100000**, and then press the **Enter key.** The scale of the vertical axis now ranges from $100,000 to $400,000, in $50,000 intervals. The value in the Display units box is None, and the Show display units label on chart check box is not selected.

3 Click the **Display units box arrow**, and then click **Thousands.** The values on the vertical axis change to $100 through $400 in intervals of $50. The Show display units label on chart check box is now selected and the display units label *Thousands* was added to the vertical axis, indicating that the values are expressed in units of 1,000. Compare your screen to Exhibit 16-27.

End Activity

EXHIBIT 16-27 RESCALED VERTICAL AXIS

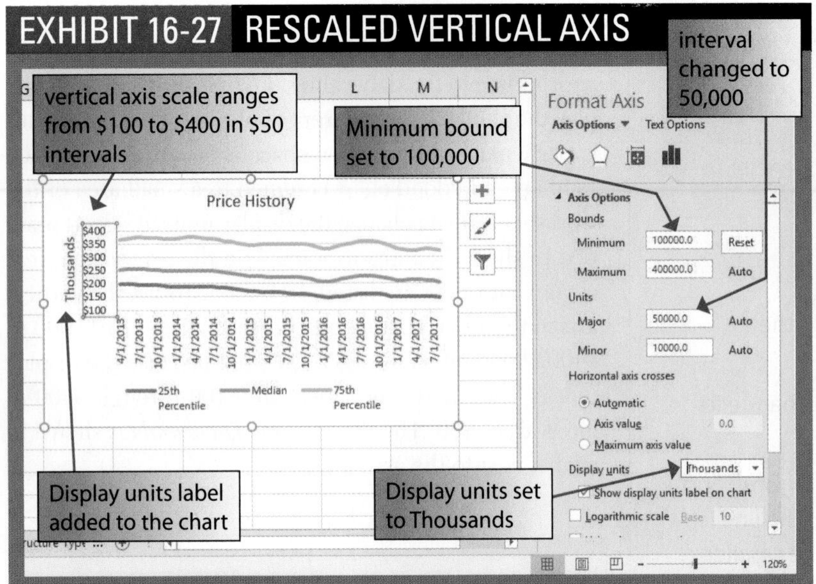

FYI COMBINING CHART TYPES

A **combination chart** combines two or more chart types in a single graph, such as a column chart and a line chart. To create a combination chart, select the data series in an existing chart that you want to appear as another chart type. On the Chart Tools Design tab, in the Type group, click the Change Chart Type button, click a chart type, and then click OK. The selected series changes to the new chart type on the chart, leaving the other data series in its original format.

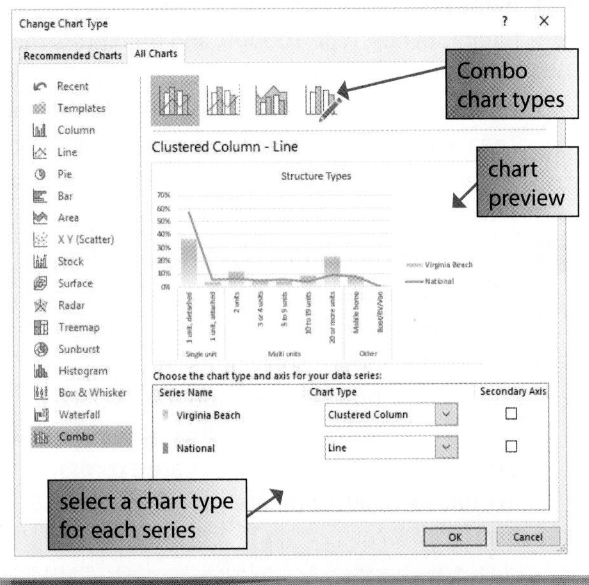

combination chart A chart that combines two or more chart types in a single graph, such as a column chart and a line chart.

16-6c Editing the Axis Scale and Labels for Dates

In addition to numbers, a scale can be based on dates, as the horizontal axis is in the Price History line chart. As with numerical scales, you can set the minimum and maximum dates to use in the scale's range. You can also set the major and minor units as days, months, or years to use for the scale's interval. This is helpful when the data source includes exact dates, but the chart trends only need to show years. Also as with numeric scales, you can specify the intervals.

Exhibit 16-28 shows the Format Axis pane with the Axis Options button selected for an axis that shows dates. You can change it from showing four months per year—currently specified by the unit 3 months in the Major row in the Units section—to any other interval and unit you specify. For example, if the axis is divided into too many units, you could specify that labels identify markers every two years.

To change the way a time or date unit is displayed, you need to change the format code. Format codes use the letters *m*, *d*, and *y* to signify month, day, and year. Examples of format codes are shown in Exhibit 16-29.

Begin Activity

Edit the axis scale and labels for dates.

1. In the line chart, click the **horizontal axis.** The Format Axis pane changes to show the options for the dates on the horizontal axis. Refer to Exhibit 16-28.
2. In the Format Axis pane, in the Units section, select the value in the **Major box**, and then type **2.**
3. Click the **Major box arrow** (the box currently contains Months), and then click **Years.** The units on the horizontal axis change to indicate every two years. Because you are using years as the labels, the months and days in the labels are not needed.

EXHIBIT 16-28 HORIZONTAL AXIS OPTIONS

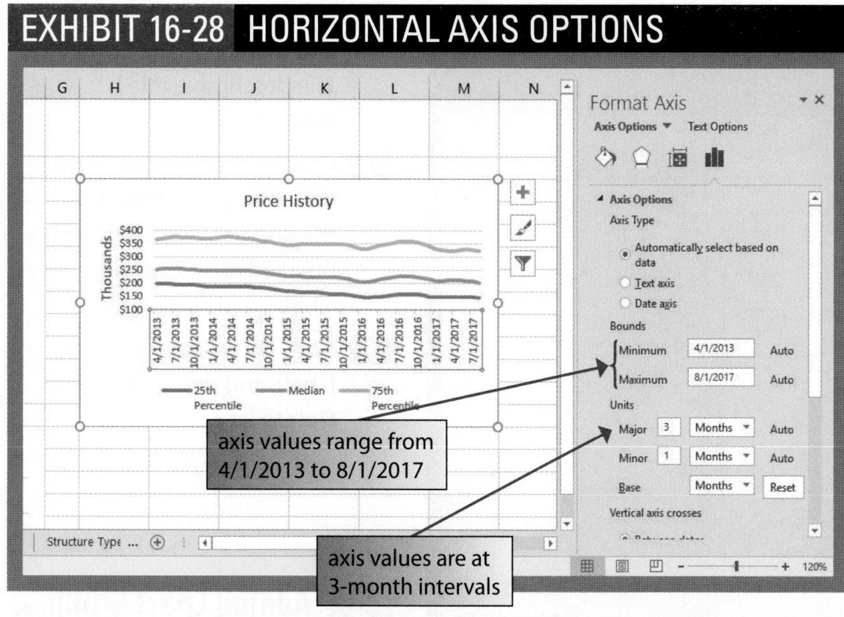

EXHIBIT 16-29 FORMAT CODES

Code	Description	Example code	Result
m (month)	m = one digit for months January through September, two digits for October through December	m/d/yy	4/1/16
	mm = two digits for all months	mm/dd/yy	04/01/16
	mmm = standard three-letter text abbreviation for month names	mmm d, yyyy	Apr 1, 2016
	mmmm = full text month name	mmmm d, yyyy	April 1, 2016
d (day)	d = one digit for day numbers 1 through 9, two digits for day numbers 10 and above	m/d/yy	4/1/16
	dd = two digits for all day numbers	mmmm dd, yyyy	April 01, 2016
y (year)	yy = two digits for all years	m/d/yy	4/1/16
	yyyy = four digits for all years	mm/dd/yyyy	04/01/2016

4 In the Format Axis pane, click **Axis Options** to collapse this section, and then click **Number** to expand that section, if necessary. In the Category box, Date is selected. In the Format Code box, *m/d/yyyy* appears, indicating the dates will be displayed in the format 4/1/2017.

5 In the Format Code box, change the code to **yyyy**, and then to the right of the Format Code box, click **Add**. The format of the dates on the horizontal axis changes to display only the year. Compare your screen to Exhibit 16-30.

6 Close the Format Axis pane.

End Activity

16-6d Adding and Formatting an Axis Title

An axis title is descriptive text that appears next to the axis values. An axis title can provide additional information that is not covered in the chart title. It can include information about the source of the data and the units in which the data is measured. By default, no titles appear next to the axes. This is fine when

FYI

CUSTOM NUMBER AND DATE FORMATS

You can create custom formats for all types of numbers. One application of a custom format is to add text to a number, which is often used to include the units of measure alongside the value, such as 10k to indicate 10,000, 20k to indicate 20,000, and so forth. To add text to a value, you use the custom format

value"text"

where *value* is the number format applied to the value, and *text* is the text to include next to the value. The text must be placed within quotation marks. For example, the format to display integers with a comma as a thousands separator is

#,##0

The # sign is a placeholder for a number; the 0 indicates that 0 will appear if a number is not in that position. To change this to a format that displays the letter *k* at the end of the value, the custom format would be

#,##0"k"

EXHIBIT 16-30 AXIS LABEL BASED ON THE FORMAT CODE

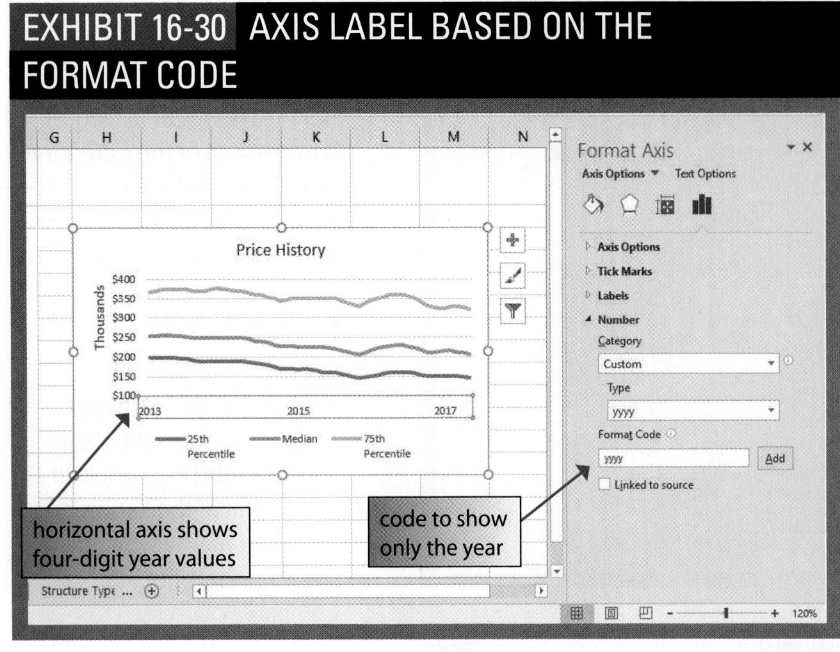

the axis labels are self-explanatory. Otherwise, you can add descriptive axis titles. In general, you should avoid adding extra chart elements such as axis titles when that information is easily understood from other parts of the chart.

You can choose how the axis title appears on the chart by clicking the Chart Elements button, pointing to Axis Titles, clicking the right arrow button ▶, and then selecting an option on the Axis Titles submenu.

Begin Activity

Add and format an axis title.

1 To the right of the line chart, click the **Chart Elements button** +. The Axis Titles check box is not selected.

2 Point to **Axis Titles**, and then click the **right arrow** ▶. Options for adding the Primary Horizontal and Primary Vertical titles appear on the submenu.

3 Click the **Primary Vertical check box.** A title is added to the vertical axis to the left of the units label, and the new axis title is selected.

4 Type **Prices in Thousands**, and then press the **Enter key**. The descriptive title is entered.

5 Change the font size of the axis title to **8 points**. With the added axis title, there is no need for the display units label.

6 Click **Thousands** (the units label), and then press the **Delete key**.

End Activity

16-6e Adding Chart Gridlines

Gridlines extend the values of the major or minor units across the plot area. By default, horizontal gridlines appear on line charts and column charts. Each gridline is aligned with a major unit on the vertical axis. You can change the gridlines so that they appear for only the minor units, appear for both the major and minor units, or do not appear at all. The horizontal axis has these same gridline options. You select which gridlines to add to a chart with the Gridlines submenu on Chart Elements button menu. See Exhibit 16-31. Gridlines are similar to borders in that you can change their color and design style as well as add drop shadows or glowing color effects. The other options are available in the Format pane.

Begin Activity

Add gridlines to a chart.

1 To the right of the line chart, click the **Chart Elements button** +, point to **Gridlines**, and then click the **right arrow** ▶. The available gridlines appear in the submenu. The Primary Major Horizontal check box is selected. This corresponds to the horizontal gridlines to the right of each dollar value in the line chart.

2 Click the **Primary Minor Vertical check box**. Faint vertical gridlines appear on the chart to indicate each year. Refer to Exhibit 16-31.

End Activity

gridlines In a chart, lines that extend the values of the major or minor units across the plot area of a chart.

EXHIBIT 16-31 GRIDLINES ADDED TO THE LINE CHART

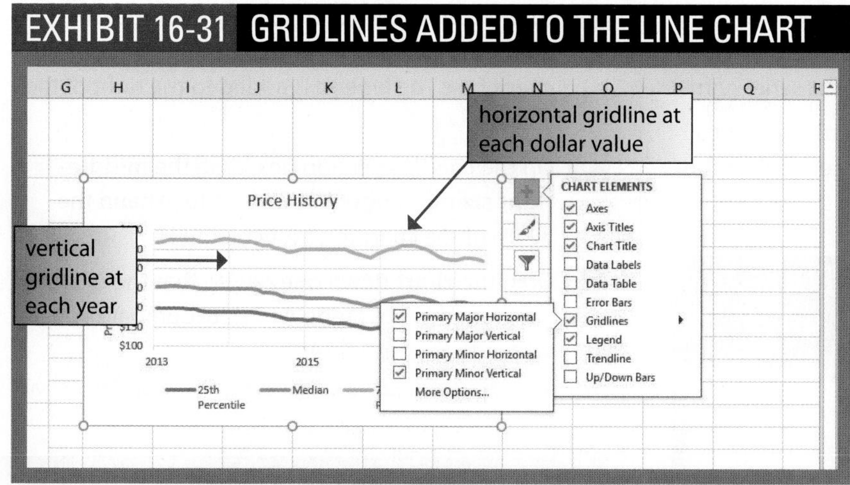

16-7 EDITING CHART DATA

Chart data can be edited and revised at any time. You do this by modifying the data range that the chart is based on, not by directly modifying the data in the chart. The change can be as simple as updating a specific value within the data source. Or it can be as involved as adding another data series to the chart.

16-7a Changing a Data Value or Label

Charts remain linked or connected to their data sources, even if they appear in different worksheets. If you change any value or label in the data source, the chart is automatically updated to show the new content. As a result, you can immediately see how changing one or more values affects the chart.

Begin Activity

Change a chart's data source.

1 In the **pie chart**, examine the **Newport News pie slice.** The data label for the slice indicates that it is 12.68% of the whole pie.

2 Make the **Metro Population worksheet** the active sheet.

3 In **cell B8**, change the value to **180000.**

4 Make the **Summary Report worksheet** the active sheet. The pie chart has been updated with the new data value, and the data label now indicates that the Newport News slice is 13.98% of the whole. Because the pie slices show percentages, not the actual data values, all the slices were updated to their new percentages.

End Activity

16-7b Adding a Data Series to a Chart

You can modify a chart by adding a new data series. The new data series appears in the chart with a different set of data markers in the same way that the line chart you created had different data markers for each of the three different series. You modify a chart from the Select Data Source dialog box. See Exhibit 16-32. The left side lists the data series displayed in the chart. The right side lists the horizontal axis labels associated with each data series. You can add, edit, or remove any of these data series from the chart.

EXHIBIT 16-32 SELECT DATA SOURCE DIALOG BOX

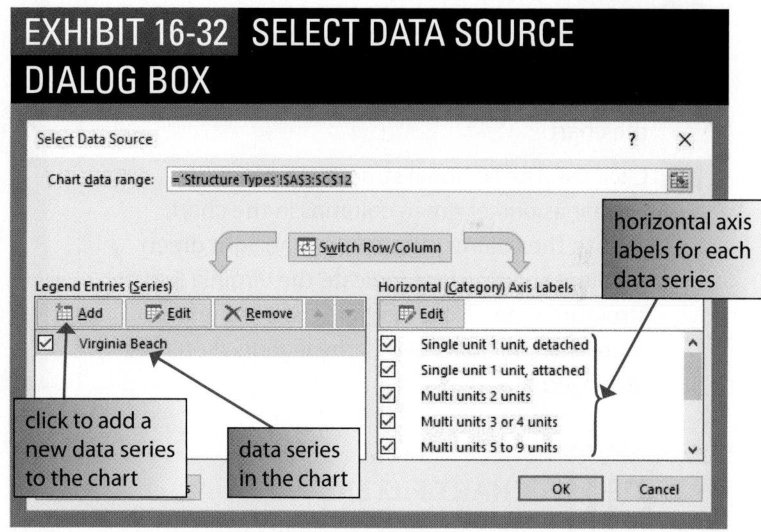

Begin Activity

Add a data series to a chart.

1 Click the **Structure Types column chart** to select it.

2 On the ribbon, click the **Chart Tools Design tab.** In the Data group, click the **Select Data button.** The Select Data Source dialog box opens. Refer back to Exhibit 16-32.

3 In the Legend Entries (Series) box, click **Add.** The Edit Series dialog box opens. In this dialog box, you specify the name of the new data series and its range of data values.

4 With the insertion point in the Series name box, click the **Structure Types sheet tab**, and then click **cell D3**, which is the cell containing the series name.

5 Press the **Tab key** to move the insertion point to the Series values box. In the worksheet, select the **range D4:D12**. See Exhibit 16-33.

EXHIBIT 16-33 EDIT SERIES DIALOG BOX

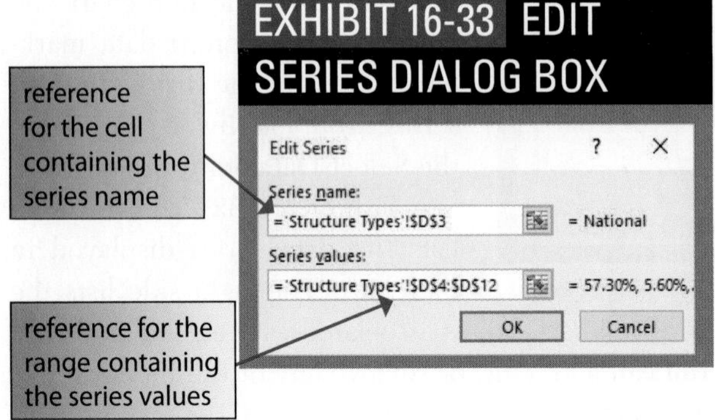

6 Click **OK**. The Edit Series dialog box closes, and the Select Data Source dialog box reappears. In the Legend Entries (Series) box, the National data series is added to the list of data series in the chart.

7 Click **OK**. The National structure type values appear as darker green columns in the chart, next to the columns containing the light green gradient shading that indicate the Virginia Beach structure types. Now that this chart contains more than one data series, the legend should be displayed.

8 To the right of the column chart, click the **Chart Elements button** +, and then click the **Legend** check box. The legend is added to the right of the chart.

9 On the chart's selection box, drag the **middle-right sizing handle** to the right to expand the width of the chart to cover column H.

10 Drag the **chart** down one row so that the chart is positioned in the range A15:H28. Compare your screen to Exhibit 16-34.

End Activity

EXHIBIT 16-34 COLUMN CHART WITH ADDED DATA SERIES

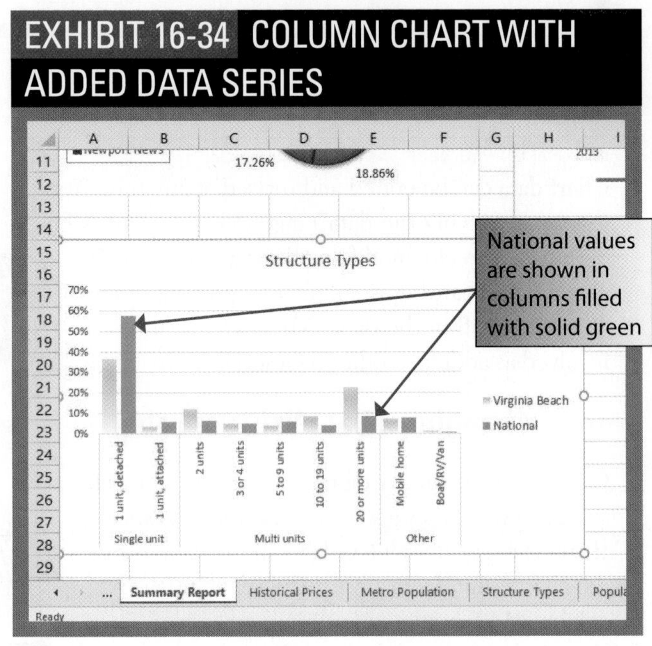

FYI CHART FILTERS

You can apply chart filters to limit what data in the chart's data source is displayed in the chart. Click the Chart Filters button next to the selected chart to display a list of the data series and category values used in the chart. Click the corresponding check boxes to deselect them and then click Apply to hide the original data from the chart. The chart is recalculated to show only the checked categories or series. Filtering is helpful when you want to focus on only a subset of the original data.

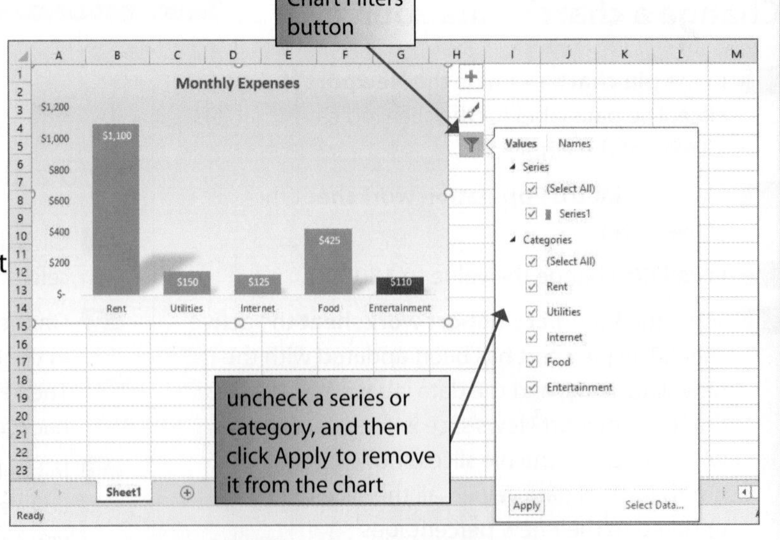

FYI

UNDERSTANDING THE SERIES FUNCTION

If you select a chart's series, the formula displayed in the formula bar uses the SERIES function. The SERIES function describes the content of a chart data series, and has the syntax

=SERIES(*name, categories, values, order*)

where *name* is the label that appears above the data in the worksheet used to create the chart, *categories* are the labels that appear on the horizontal axis of the chart, *values* are the values that Excel plots for the data series, and *order* is the order in which the series appears in the chart. For example, in the data series represented by

=SERIES(Sheet1!$B$1,Sheet1!$A$2:$A$6, Sheet1!$B$2:$B$6,1)

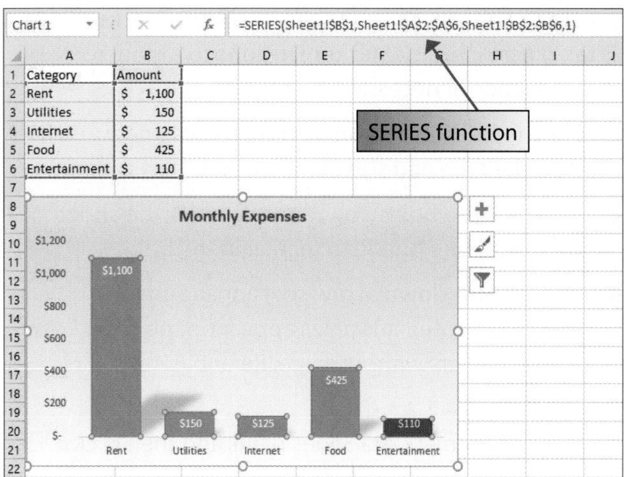

The name of the series is in cell B1 in the Sheet1 worksheet, the labels are in the range A2:A6 in the Sheet1 worksheet, the data values are in the range B2:B6 in the Sheet1 worksheet, and the series is the first data series in the chart.

Although you can edit the SERIES function within the formula bar to make quick changes to your chart, the function is tied to an existing chart. It cannot be used within a worksheet cell or referenced from another Excel formula.

16-7c Modifying Lines and Data Markers

You can change the appearance of the lines and data markers in a line chart. You do this with the Marker Options in the Format Data Series pane. See Exhibit 16-35. For example, you can remove the lines connecting categories when they have no meaning. You can also change the shape and size of the marker itself, such as changing square markers to horizontal line markers at each data point.

EXHIBIT 16-35 MARKER OPTIONS IN THE FORMAT DATA SERIES PANE

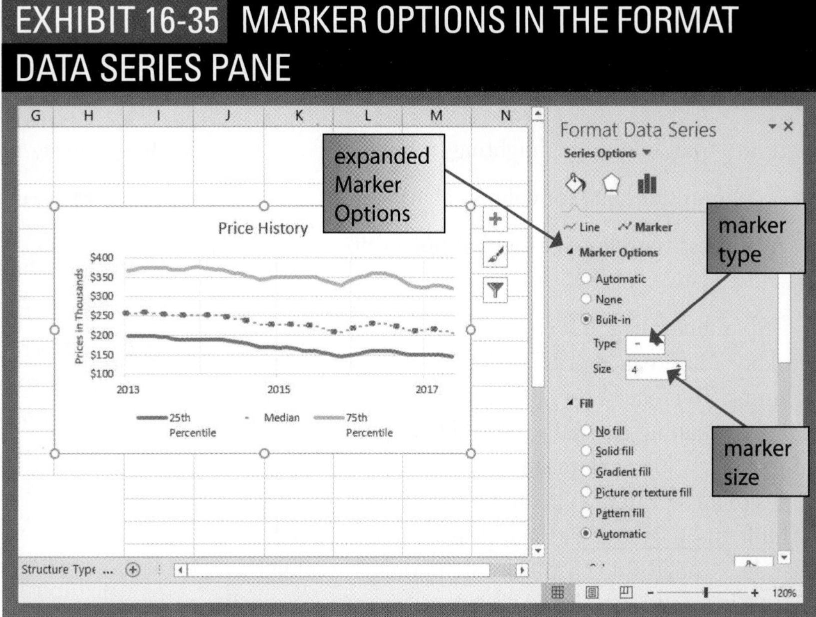

Modify lines and data markers.

1 In the **Price History line chart**, double-click the **Median data series line** (the middle line) to select it. The Format Data Series pane opens.

2 In the Format Data Series pane, click the **Fill & Line button** . The options change to show the Line tab selected and the Line options expanded.

3 Click the **No line option button**. The line is removed from the chart.

4 In the Format Data Series pane, click the **Marker tab**, and then click **Marker Options** to expand that section, if necessary.

5 Click the **Built-in option button**. You can now select the type and size of the marker.

6 Click the **Type box arrow**, and then click the **short horizontal line** (the sixth marker in the list).

7 Click the **Size down arrow** so 4 appears in the Size box. The Median values appear on the chart as data markers without a line. Refer back to Exhibit 16-35.

8 Close the Format Data Series pane, and then click **any cell** to deselect the chart.

End Activity

16-8 INSERTING AND FORMATTING SPARKLINES

A **sparkline** is a mini chart that is displayed entirely within a cell. The goal of a sparkline is to convey a large amount of graphical information within a very small space. They don't include chart elements such as legends, titles, gridlines, or axes. You can create three types of sparklines:

- A line sparkline for highlighting trends
- A column sparkline for column charts
- A win/loss sparkline for highlighting positive and negative values

Sparklines can be inserted anywhere within the workbook and can represent data from several rows or columns. To create a set of sparklines, you specify a data range containing the data you want to graph, and then you select a location range where you want the sparklines to appear in the Create Sparklines dialog box. See Exhibit 16-36. Note that the cells in which you insert the sparklines need not be blank. Sparklines are added as part of the cell background and do not replace any cell content.

sparkline A graph that is displayed entirely within a cell.

EXHIBIT 16-36 CREATE SPARKLINES DIALOG BOX

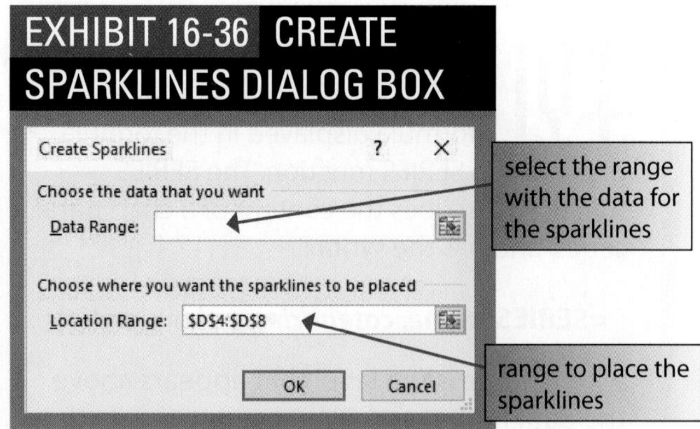

The Sparkline Tools Design tab provides options for formatting the appearance of sparklines. Sparklines can show data markers to identify the high and low points, negative points, first and last point, and all points. Just select the check boxes for the markers you want to display in the Show group. As with other charts, the Style gallery in the Style group provides built-in styles for sparklines. In addition, you can specify the sparkline color and the marker color, which are also available in the Style group. The only other feature you can add to a sparkline is an axis, which for sparklines is simply a horizontal line that separates positive values from negative values. Click the Axis button in the Group group, and then click Show Axis. To remove sparklines from the worksheet, select the sparkline or sparklines to delete. On the Sparkline Tools Design tab, in the Group group, click the Clear button.

Begin Activity

Insert and format sparklines.

1 Make the **Metro Population worksheet** the active sheet. Select the **range D4:D8**.

2 On the ribbon, click the **Insert tab**. In the Sparklines group, click the **Line button**. The Create Sparklines dialog box opens with the insertion point in the Data Range box. The location range is already entered because you selected it before opening the dialog box. Refer Exhibit 16-36.

3 With the insertion point in the Data Range box, click the **Population History sheet tab**, and then select the **range B4:E8** to enter the range that contains the data to chart.

PROBLEM?
If you don't see the Population History sheet tab, to the left of the sheet tabs, click the **Next sheet button** as many times as needed to scroll the sheet tabs.

4 Click **OK**. The dialog box closes, and the Metro Population sheet tab is the current tab again. Sparklines are inserted into each cell in the selected location range D4:D8. The Sparkline Tools Design tab appears on the ribbon and is the active tab.

5 On the Sparkline Tools Design tab, in the Show group, click the **High Point check box** and the **Low Point check box** to display markers for the high and low points within each sparkline.

6 On the Sparkline Tools Design tab, in the Style group, click the **More button**. In the Style gallery, in the last row, click **Sparkline Style Colorful #3.** The line changes to light green and the High Point markers change to a darker green. Compare your screen to Exhibit 16-37.

TIP: On the Sparkline Tools Design tab, in the Style group, click the Sparkline Color button to change the sparkline color and click the Marker Color button to change the data marker color.

End Activity

EXHIBIT 16-37 SPARKLINES WITH DATA MARKERS

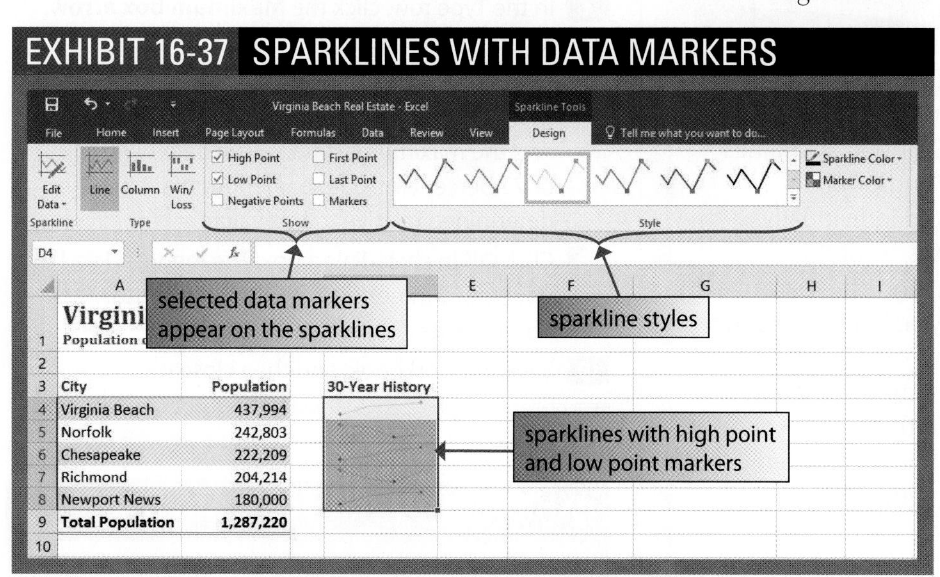

16-9 INSERTING AND MODIFYING DATA BARS

A **data bar** is conditional formatting that adds a horizontal bar to the background of a cell containing a number. When applied to a range of cells, the data bars have the same appearance as a bar chart with each cell containing one bar. The lengths of data bars are based on the values in the selected range. Cells with larger values have longer bars; cells with smaller values have shorter bars. See Exhibit 16-38.

EXHIBIT 16-38 DATA BARS ADDED TO THE STRUCTURE TYPES WORKSHEET

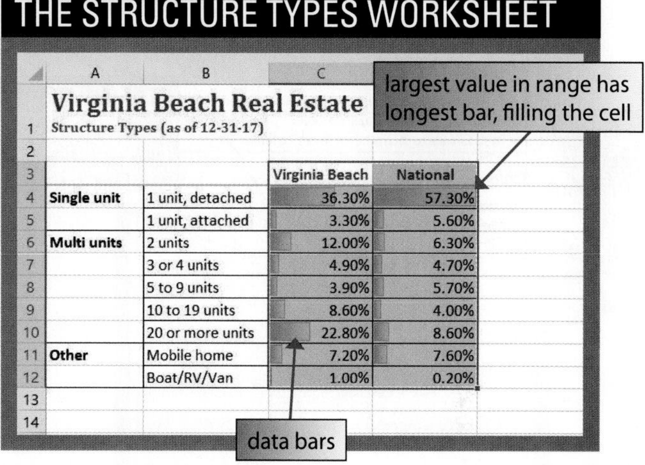

Data bars are dynamic, which means that if one cell's value changes, the lengths of the data bars in the selected range are automatically updated. When data bars are used with negative values, the data bars originate from the center of the cell with negative bars extending to the left and positive bars extending to the right.

The lengths of the data bars are determined based on the values in the selected range. The cell with the largest value contains a data bar that extends across the entire width of the cell, and the lengths of the other bars in the selected range are determined relative to that bar. In some cases, this means that the longest data bar overlaps the cell's data value, making it difficult to read. You can modify the length of the data bars by altering the conditional formatting rule in the Edit Formatting Rule dialog box. See Exhibit 16-39.

Data bars are always placed in the cells containing the value they represent, and each cell represents only a single bar.

data bar Conditional formatting that adds a horizontal bar to a cell's background that is proportional.

EXHIBIT 16-39 EDIT FORMATTING RULE DIALOG BOX

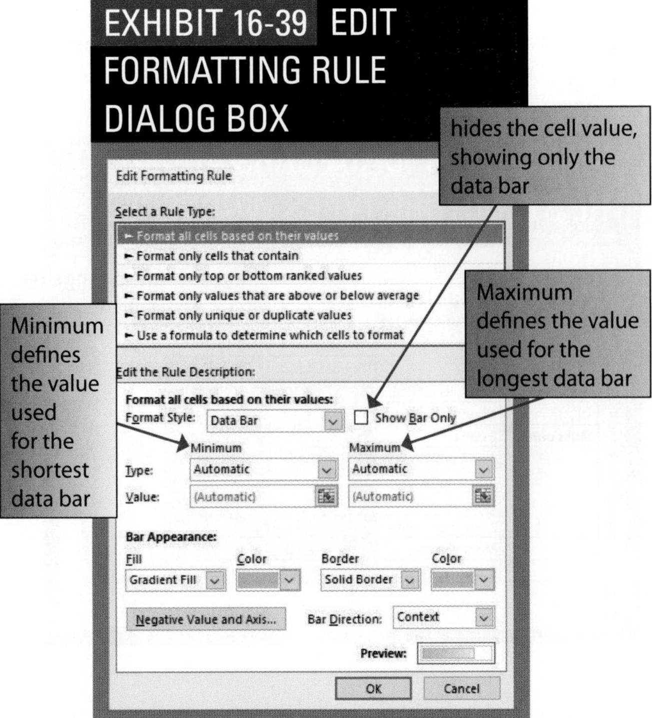

FYI

SPARKLINE GROUPS

Sparklines can be grouped or ungrouped. Grouped sparklines share a common format. Ungrouped sparklines can be formatted individually. When you create sparklines, all of the sparklines in the location range are part of a single group. Clicking any cell in the location range selects all of the sparklines in the group. Similarly, any formatting you apply affects all the sparklines in the group. This ensures that all the sparklines for related data are formatted consistently.

You can differentiate one sparkline in a group by formatting that sparkline differently. First, select the individual sparkline you want to format. Then, on the Sparkline Tools Design tab, in the Group group, click the Ungroup button. The selected sparkline is split from the rest of the sparklines in the group. Finally, apply a unique format to the selected sparkline. To regroup the sparklines, select all of the cells in the location range containing sparklines, and then click the Group button in the Group group.

Begin Activity

Add data bars.

1. Make the **Structure Types worksheet** the active sheet. Select the **range C4:D12**.
2. On the Home tab, in the Styles group, click the **Conditional Formatting button**, and then point to **Data Bars** to display the Data Bars gallery.
3. In the Gradient Fill section, click the **Orange Data Bar style**. The data bars are added to the selected cells. Refer back to Exhibit 16-38. These data bars present essentially the same information as the column chart you created earlier.
4. On the Home tab, in the Styles group, click the **Conditional Formatting button**, and then click **Manage Rules**. The Conditional Formatting Rules Manager dialog box opens. In the Show formatting rules for box, Current Selection appears.
5. Click **Edit Rule**. The Edit Formatting Rule dialog box opens. Refer back to Exhibit 16-39. You want to modify the data bar rule to proportionally reduce the lengths of the data bars.
6. In the Type row, click the **Maximum box arrow**, and then click **Number**.
7. In the Value row, click in the **Maximum box**, and then replace the value with **0.75**. The rule now sets the maximum value for the data bar to 0.75, or 75 percent. All data bar lengths will then be determined relative to this value.
8. Click **OK** in each dialog box. The longest data bar now spans three-fourths of the cell width. Compare your screen to Exhibit 16-40.
9. Save the workbook, and then close it.

End Activity

EXHIBIT 16-40 EDITED DATA BARS

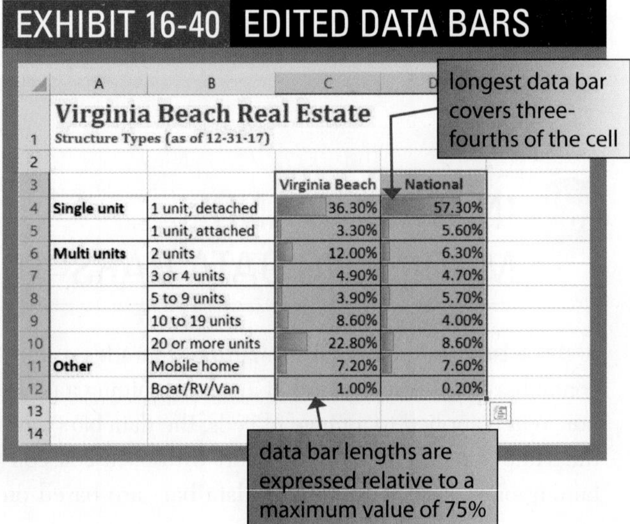

	A	B	C	D
1	Virginia Beach Real Estate Structure Types (as of 12-31-17)			
2				
3			Virginia Beach	National
4	Single unit	1 unit, detached	36.30%	57.30%
5		1 unit, attached	3.30%	5.60%
6	Multi units	2 units	12.00%	6.30%
7		3 or 4 units	4.90%	4.70%
8		5 to 9 units	3.90%	5.70%
9		10 to 19 units	8.60%	4.00%
10		20 or more units	22.80%	8.60%
11	Other	Mobile home	7.20%	7.60%
12		Boat/RV/Van	1.00%	0.20%
13				
14				

STUDY TOOLS 16

READY TO STUDY? IN THE BOOK, YOU CAN:

- ☐ Rip out the Chapter Review Card, which includes key terms and key chapter concepts.

ONLINE AT WWW.CENGAGEBRAIN.COM, YOU CAN:

- ☐ Review key concepts from the chapter in a short video.
- ☐ Explore creating a chart in Excel with the interactive infographic.
- ☐ Practice what you've learned with more Practice It and On Your Own exercises.
- ☐ Prepare for tests with quizzes.
- ☐ Review the key terms with flashcards.

QUIZ YOURSELF

1. What is the difference between a data source and a data series?
2. What is the difference between the chart area and the plot area?
3. In what two locations can you place a chart?
4. If a data series contains values divided into 10 categories, would this data be better displayed as a pie chart or a column chart? Why?
5. What is a column chart, and how is a bar chart different?
6. Why would you change the scale of a chart axis?
7. What are major units and minor units?
8. When should you use a line chart instead of a column chart?
9. What is a combination chart? Describe how to create a combination chart.
10. What does it mean to overlay a chart title or legend?
11. How do you update a chart after editing the chart data?
12. How do you add a data series to an already existing chart?
13. What are sparklines? Describe the three types of sparklines.
14. What are data bars?
15. How do data bars differ from sparklines?

PRACTICE IT

Practice It 16-1

1. Open the data file **Slippers Peak** located in the Chapter 16\Practice It folder. Save the workbook as **Slippers Peak Resort**.
2. In the Documentation worksheet, enter your name in cell B3 and the date in cell B4. Left-align the date.
3. In the Usage Data worksheet, select the range B4:E4;B17:E17. Insert a pie chart using the Pie chart type in the 2-D Pie section in the gallery.
4. Move the embedded pie chart to the Summary Charts worksheet. Reposition and resize the chart to cover the range A3:F14.
5. Change the chart style of the pie chart to Style 3.
6. Change the chart title to **Total Annual Usage**. Change the font size of the chart title to 14 points.
7. Position the legend to the left of the pie chart. Change the border of the legend to a solid line using the Blue-Gray, Text 2 theme color.
8. Change the data labels so they appear using the Best Fit option.
9. In the Usage Data worksheet, select the range A4:E16. Insert a column chart using the 3-D Clustered Column chart type in the 3-D Column section in the gallery.
10. Move the embedded column chart to the Summary Charts worksheet. Reposition and resize the embedded column chart to cover the range A16:N32.
11. Change the chart style of the column chart to Style 3.
12. Change the chart layout of the column chart to Layout 3.
13. Change the chart title to **Amenities Usage by Month**. Set the font size of the chart title to 14 points.
14. Add a primary vertical axis title to the column chart. Enter **Attendance** as the vertical axis title.
15. Change the intervals on the vertical axis of the column chart to 250.
16. In the Usage Data worksheet, change the month labels in the range A5:A16 to the full month names. Change the value in cell E5 to **796**. In the Summary Charts worksheets, make sure the charts are updated to reflect the full month names and the new totals.
17. In the Usage Data worksheet, select the range A4:A16;F4:F16. Insert a line chart using the Line chart type in the 2-D Line section in the gallery.

18. Move the embedded line chart to the Summary Charts worksheet. Reposition and resize the embedded column chart to cover the range H3:N14.
19. Change the vertical axis scale of the line chart so that it ranges from 750 to 6,750.
20. Change the chart style of the line chart to Style 2.
21. Change the chart title to **Total Monthly Usage**. Set the font size of the chart title to 14 points.
22. In the Usage Data worksheet, in the range G5:G16, insert line sparklines based on the data range B5:E16.
23. On the sparklines, show the high point and low point markers.
24. Change the sparkline style to Sparkline Style Accent 1, Darker 25%.
25. Select the range F5:F16, and then insert data bars using the Red Data Bar option in the Gradient Fill section of the gallery.
26. Save the workbook, and then close it.

Practice It 16-2

1. Open the data file **Steel** located in the Chapter 16\ Practice It folder. Save the workbook as **Steel Production**.
2. In the Documentation worksheet, enter your name in cell B3 and the date in cell B4. Left-align the date.
3. In the Production by Country worksheet, select the range A4:A10;N4:N10. Insert a pie chart using the Pie chart in the 2-D Pie section in the Charts gallery.
4. Move the embedded pie chart to the Summary Charts worksheet. Reposition and resize the chart to cover the range A4:F15.
5. Change the chart style of the pie chart to Style 7.
6. Change the chart layout of the pie chart to Layout 6.
7. Enter **Crude Steel Production by Country** as the chart title. Change the font size of the chart title to 12 points.
8. Position the legend below the pie chart.
9. In the Production by Country worksheet, select the range A4:M10. Insert a column chart using the Clustered Column chart in the 2-D Column section in the gallery.
10. Move the embedded column chart to the Summary Charts worksheet. Reposition and resize the embedded column chart to cover the range A17:K33.
11. Change the chart style of the column chart to Style 6.
12. Change the chart title to **Steel Production by Country and Month**. Set the font size of the chart title to 12 points.
13. In the column chart, change the Asia data series (the data series with the largest values), and the Africa and Middle East data series (the two data series with the smallest values) to lines on another axis. (*Hint*: Select the Asia data series. On the Chart Tools Design tab, in the Type group, click the Change Chart Type button. In the Change Chart Type dialog box, on the All Charts tab with Combo selected on the left, scroll down the box at the bottom, click the box arrows next to each of the three data series, click Line, then click the Secondary Axis check boxes next to each series.)
14. In the Summary Charts worksheet, in the merged cell H6, insert a line sparkline based on the data range B11:M11 in the Production by Country worksheet. (*Hint*: The Location Range in the Create Sparklines dialog box should be an absolute reference to H6.)
15. On the sparkline, show the high point and low point markers.
16. Change the sparkline style to Sparkline Style Colorful #2.
17. Change the sparkline type to Column. (*Hint*: On the Sparkline Tools Design tab, in the Type group, click the Column button.)
18. Save the workbook, and then close it.

ON YOUR OWN

On Your Own 16-1

1. Open the data file **Fairbanks** located in the Chapter 16\On Your Own folder. Save the workbook as **Fairbanks Skies**.
2. In the Documentation worksheet, enter your name in cell B3 and the date in cell B4. Left-align the date.
3. In the Weather worksheet, based on the data in the range A4:M7, insert an appropriate chart to show the data in a clear manner. Move the embedded chart to a chart sheet named **Average Days Chart**.
4. Format the chart using an appropriate chart layout and chart style.
5. Insert an appropriate chart title for the chart, and then change the font size as needed.
6. Add appropriate axis titles, and change the font sizes as needed.
7. Position the legend appropriately, and change its font size, border color, fill color, and so forth as desired.
8. Change the axis scale as needed to eliminate blank areas of the chart.
9. Change the color of the data series using anything except the default set of colors.
10. In the Weather worksheet, edit the text in cell A6 to **Partly Sunny**.
11. In the Weather worksheet, based on the data in the range A4:A7;N4:N7, insert a pie chart. Title the chart **ANNUAL AVERAGES**, and then reposition and resize the chart attractively on the Weather worksheet.
12. Format the pie chart attractively, using the chart layout, chart style, chart title, legend, and data labels of your choice. Make sure the chart shows the percentage of each pie slice.
13. In the Weather worksheet, in the range E1:G1, insert a line or column sparkline for each of the following data: Clear (range B5:M5), Partly Sunny (range B6:M6), and Overcast (range B7:M7). Format the sparklines appropriately and enter labels in the range E2:G2 to identify each sparkline. Format the labels so they look different from the other text in the worksheet.
14. In the Weather worksheet, insert data bars in the range N5:N7.
15. Save the workbook, and then close it.

CAPSTONE

Excel: Create a Budget

1. Plan a budget workbook. Identify the workbook's purpose or goal. Figure out the data you need to collect and enter in the workbook (for this project, you can use real or fictional data). Determine what calculations you need to enter in the workbook. Decide how the workbook should be organized and formatted.
2. Create a new workbook for the financial data. Use the first worksheet as a documentation sheet that includes your name, the date on which you start creating the workbook, and a brief description of the workbook's purpose. Format the worksheet appropriately.
3. Use a second worksheet to create the budget. Enter appropriate labels to identify the data the budget will include. Include a section to enter values that remain consistent from month to month, such as monthly income and expenses. You can then reference these cells in formulas.
4. In the budget worksheet, enter the data on which the budget will be based. Be sure to enter realistic earnings for each month of the year and realistic expenses for each month. Apply appropriate number formats and styles to the values.
5. In the budget worksheet, enter formulas and functions to calculate the total earnings each month, the average monthly earnings, and the total earnings for the entire year. Also, calculate the total expenses for each month, the average monthly expenses, and the total expenses for the year.
6. Calculate the monthly net cash flow (the value of total income minus total expenses).
7. Use the cash flow values to track the savings throughout the year. Use a realistic amount for savings at the beginning of the year. Use the monthly net cash flow values to add or subtract from this value. Project the end-of-year balance in savings under your proposed budget.
8. Format the budget worksheet by changing fonts, font sizes, font colors, borders, cell styles, fill colors, and so forth as needed to make the worksheet attractive, ensure it is easy to read and interpret, and has a uniform appearance.
9. Use conditional formatting to automatically highlight negative net cash flow months.
10. Insert a pie chart that compares the monthly expenses for the categories.
11. Insert a column chart that charts all of the monthly expenses regardless of the category.
12. Insert a line chart or sparkline that shows the change in the savings balance throughout the 12 months of the year.
13. Insert new rows at the top of the worksheet and enter titles that describe the worksheet's contents.
14. Use a third worksheet to plan for a major purchase, such as a car or a computer. Determine the amount of the purchase and the current annual interest rate charged by your local bank. Provide a reasonable length of time to repay the loan, such as five years for a car loan or 20 to 30 years for a home loan. Use the PMT function to determine how much you would have to spend each month on the payments for your purchase. You can do these calculations in a separate worksheet.
15. Add the loan information to the monthly budget and evaluate the impact of the purchase of this item on the budget. Examine other possible loans and evaluate their impact on the budget. If the payment exceeds the budget, reduce the estimated price of the item being purchased until you determine an affordable monthly payment.
16. Format the worksheets for your printer. Include headers and footers that display the workbook file name, the workbook's author, and the date on which the report is printed. If the report extends across several pages, repeat appropriate print titles on all of the pages, set page breaks and orientation as needed, and include page numbers and the total number of pages on every printed page.
17. Save the workbook, and then close it.

Office Online

WORKING WITH EXCEL ONLINE

Similar to Word Online, you can use Excel Online to view or edit Excel workbooks on OneDrive. See Exhibit 1. When you edit a workbook in Excel Online, you can apply basic formatting, perform calculations, and create charts. You can functions; however, the Formulas tab and the Function Arguments dialog box are not available.

EXHIBIT 1 EXCEL WORKBOOK OPEN IN EXCEL ONLINE

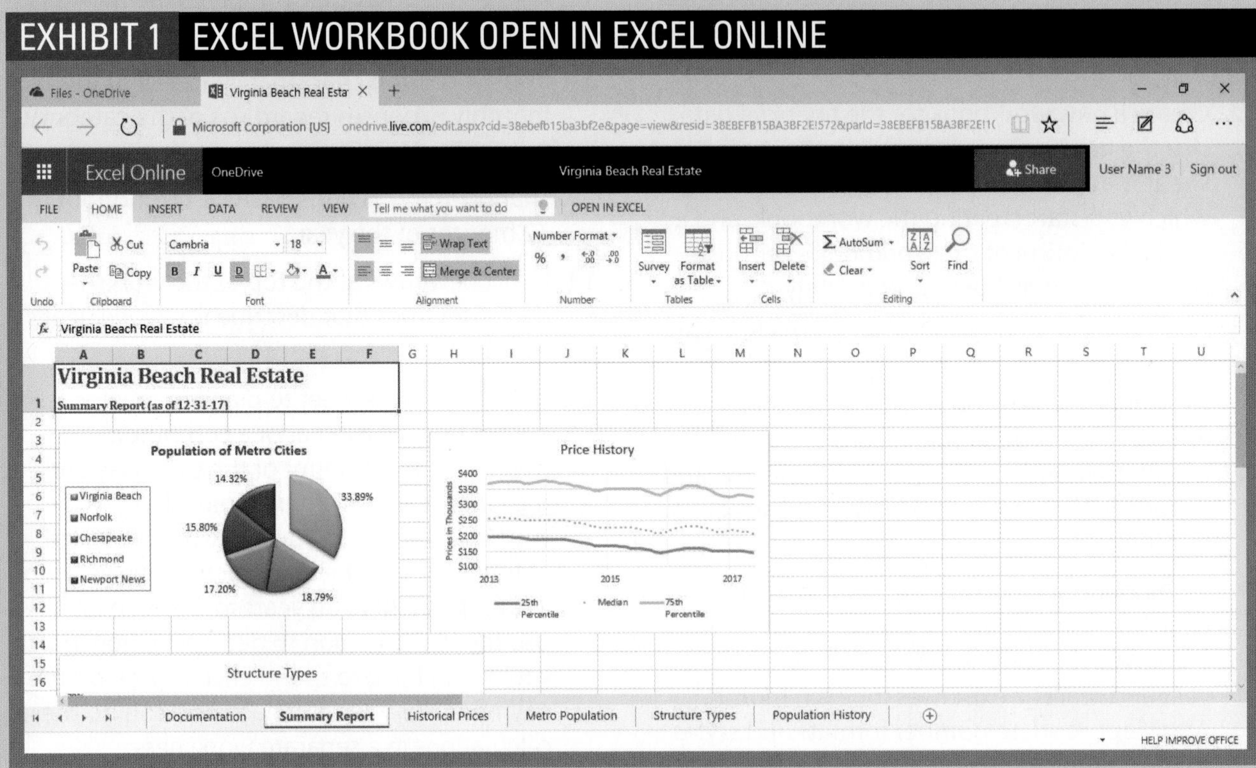

Excel Online provides a template for creating Excel surveys. To use this feature, click the Survey button in the Tables group on the Home or Insert tab in Excel Online, and then click New Survey. (You can also click the New button on your OneDrive page, and then click Excel survey.) A window opens in which you can create questions. Type a title for the survey in the Enter a title for your survey here box. Then, you click in the Enter your first question here box to open a dialog box in which you can create questions. Type the question in the top box. The default response type is Text. You can click the Response Type box arrow to choose from the response types shown in Exhibit 2. Some of the response types change the bottom part of the dialog box. For example, if you select Choice, a box appears in which you list the three choices from which respondents must select their answers.

To distribute the survey, click Share Survey after you finish creating the questions. A new window opens with a Create link button in it. Click this to create a web address for your survey. Click the link to select it, right-click the selected link, and then click Copy on the shortcut menu. Then you can paste it in an email message or to a social media site or in any location where your respondents can access it. Although you need a Microsoft account in order to create the survey, people responding to the survey do not need one in order to complete the survey.

EXHIBIT 2 WINDOW THAT OPENS WHEN YOU CREATE A NEW SURVEY

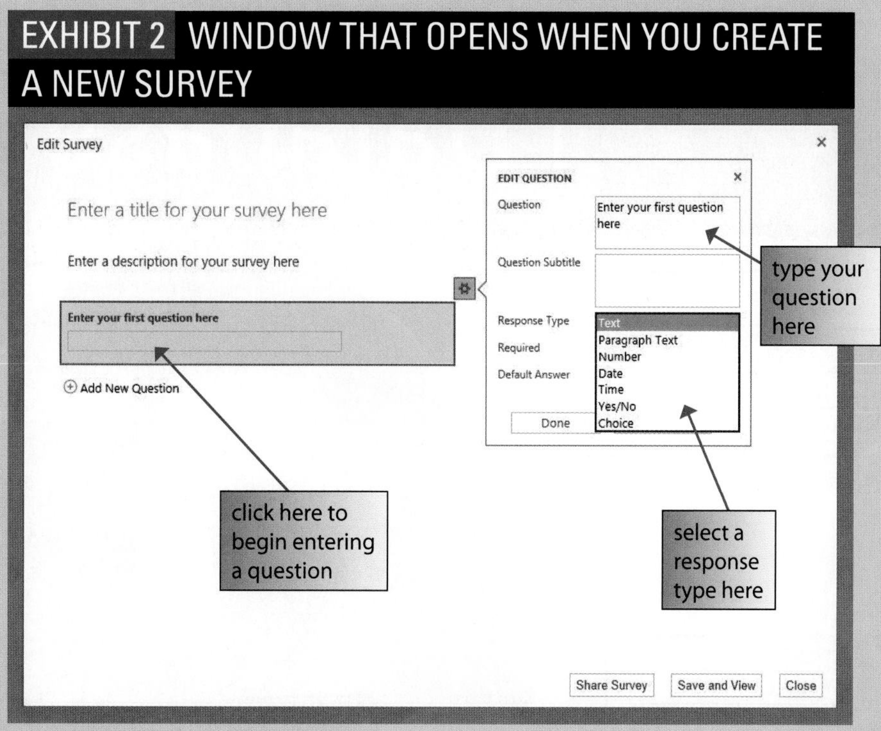

As people submit their completed surveys, the responses are automatically tabulated in the Excel survey worksheet that is created and stored in the open workbook on your OneDrive when you create the survey. The responses are tabulated whether the workbook is open or closed. See Exhibit 3.

EXHIBIT 3 FOUR RESPONSES TO A SURVEY

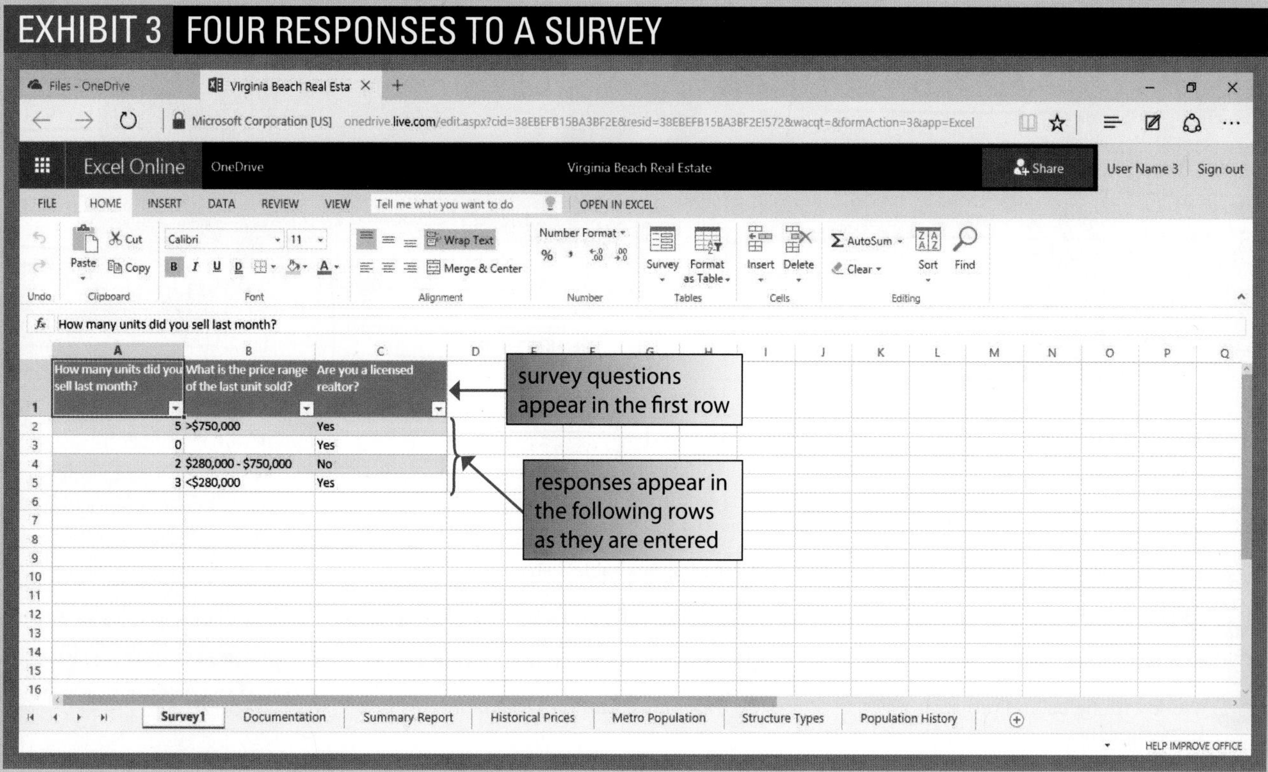

Part 8
ACCESS
2016

17 | Creating a Database

LEARNING OBJECTIVES After studying the material in this chapter, you will be able to:

- 17-1 Understand database concepts
- 17-2 Create a database
- 17-3 Use Datasheet view
- 17-4 Work with fields and properties in Design view
- 17-5 Modify a table's structure
- 17-6 Close and open objects and databases
- 17-7 Create simple queries, forms, and reports
- 17-8 Compact and repair a database

After finishing this chapter, go to **PAGE 532** for **STUDY TOOLS**.

17-1 UNDERSTANDING DATABASE CONCEPTS

Data is a valuable resource to any business. Important data for many businesses includes customer's names and addresses, as well as contract amounts and dates. Organizing, storing, maintaining, retrieving, and sorting this type of data are critical activities that enable a business to find and use information effectively. A database is an organized collection of related data. **Microsoft Access 2016** (or simply **Access**) is used to enter data into databases, maintain databases, and retrieve data from databases.

Each piece of data in a database—that is, a single characteristic or attribute of a person, place, object, event, or idea—is stored in a **field**. For example, a database named BusinessInfo that contains information about a business's customers might include fields that contain the following customer data: ID number, first name, last name, company name, street address, city, state, ZIP code, and phone number.

A **table** is a collection of related fields. Exhibit 17-1 shows a table with the following fields that contain information about customers: CustomerID, LastName, FirstName, and Phone.

The content of a field is the **field value**. In Exhibit 17-1, the field values in the first row for CustomerID, LastName, FirstName, and Phone are, Sanders, Lily, and (408) 555-3999.

Each row in a table contains all the fields about a single person, place, object, event, or idea, and this is called a **record**. The table shown in Exhibit 17-1 contains five records.

A database that contains more than one related table is a **relational database**. In a relational database, the tables are related to each other using a **common field**, which is simply a field that appears in more than one table. For example, a relational database that included the table of customer information shown in Exhibit 17-1 might also contain a table named Contracts that stores data about customer contracts and a table named Invoices that stores data that is used to create customer invoices. To track the information for each customer, each of the three tables needs to have at least one field in common.

In a relational database, each record in a table must be unique. To ensure that each record in a table is unique, at least one field in each table is designated as the primary key. A **primary key** is a field, or a collection of fields, whose value uniquely identifies each record in a table. No two records can contain the same value for the primary key field. For example, a table named Customers might have, in addition to FirstName and LastName fields for customer names, a CustomerID field. The CustomerID field would be the primary key field. Usually a field such as the CustomerID field is designated as the primary key because no two customers will have the same Customer ID number. Two customers might, however, have the same last name, so you would not select the LastName field as the table's primary key because the last name alone might not uniquely identify each record in the table.

To form a relationship between two tables—that is, to connect two tables—the two tables must contain

EXHIBIT 17-1 A DATABASE TABLE

CustomerID	LastName	FirstName	Phone
1	Sanders	Lily	(408) 555-3999
2	Runyon	Seth	(707) 555-7032
3	Bayers	Jillian	(707) 555-4309
4	Heinen	Aisha	(408) 555-3323
5	Chung	Mike	(408) 555-4428

Microsoft Access 2016 (Access) A computer application used to enter, maintain, and retrieve related data in a format known as a database.

field A part of a database that contains a single characteristic or attribute of a person, place, object, event, or idea.

table In Access, a collection of related fields.

field value The content of a field.

record All the fields in a table about a single person, place, object, event, or idea; that is, a row in a table.

relational database A database that contains a collection of related tables.

common field A field that appears in more than one table.

primary key A field, or a collection of fields, whose value uniquely identifies each record in a table.

EXHIBIT 17-2 DATABASE RELATIONSHIP BETWEEN TABLES

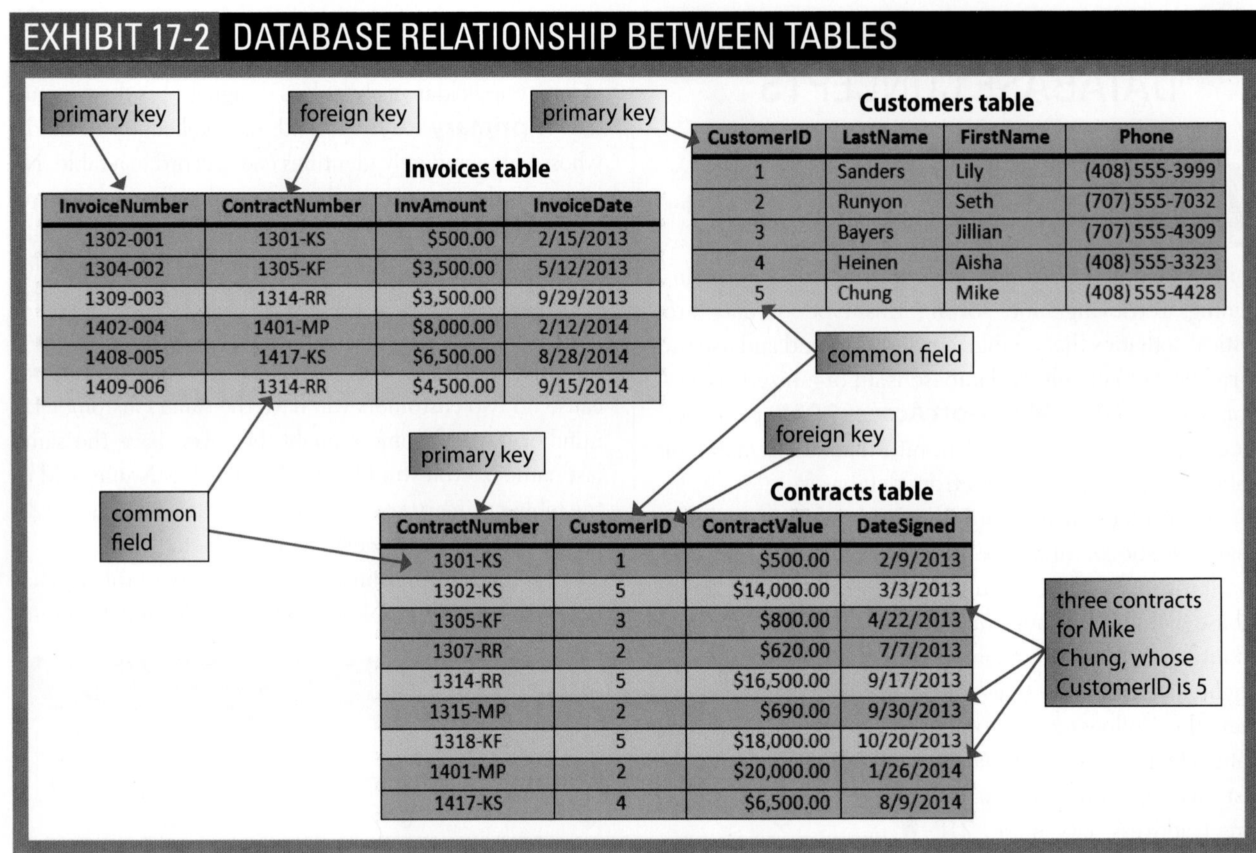

Invoices table

InvoiceNumber	ContractNumber	InvAmount	InvoiceDate
1302-001	1301-KS	$500.00	2/15/2013
1304-002	1305-KF	$3,500.00	5/12/2013
1309-003	1314-RR	$3,500.00	9/29/2013
1402-004	1401-MP	$8,000.00	2/12/2014
1408-005	1417-KS	$6,500.00	8/28/2014
1409-006	1314-RR	$4,500.00	9/15/2014

Customers table

CustomerID	LastName	FirstName	Phone
1	Sanders	Lily	(408) 555-3999
2	Runyon	Seth	(707) 555-7032
3	Bayers	Jillian	(707) 555-4309
4	Heinen	Aisha	(408) 555-3323
5	Chung	Mike	(408) 555-4428

Contracts table

ContractNumber	CustomerID	ContractValue	DateSigned
1301-KS	1	$500.00	2/9/2013
1302-KS	5	$14,000.00	3/3/2013
1305-KF	3	$800.00	4/22/2013
1307-RR	2	$620.00	7/7/2013
1314-RR	5	$16,500.00	9/17/2013
1315-MP	2	$690.00	9/30/2013
1318-KF	5	$18,000.00	10/20/2013
1401-MP	2	$20,000.00	1/26/2014
1417-KS	4	$6,500.00	8/9/2014

a common field, and the common field must be the primary key in at least one of the tables being related. This is how the database knows which record in one table is related to which record or records in the other table or tables.

When the primary key from one table is included in another table, it is called a **foreign key**. In the Contracts table, the CustomerID field is a foreign key. Although a table may have only one primary key, it can have many foreign keys.

Exhibit 17-2 shows the relationship between three tables in a database. CustomerID, which is the primary key in the Customers table, is included in the Contracts table so that we can identify the contracts for each customer. The CustomerID field is not the primary key in the Contracts table because a customer might have signed more than one contract. ContractNumber, which is the primary key in the Contracts table, is included in the Invoices table so that each invoice is associated with a specific contract. ContractNumber is not the primary key in the Invoices table because one contract might result in several invoices being created.

foreign key A field in a table that is a primary key in another table and that is included to form a relationship between the two tables.

Datasheet view The Access view that shows a table's contents as a datasheet.

datasheet Rows and columns in which a table's contents are displayed.

17-2 CREATING A DATABASE

After you create or open a database, the Navigation Pane appears along the left side of the Access window and displays all of the tables, reports, and other objects in the database. The Navigation Pane is the main control center for opening and working with database objects.

Any open table, report, or other object appears in the right pane with a tab that displays its name. You can open more than one object at a time and click the tabs to switch between them.

CAUTION CAUTION CAUTION
CAUTION CAUTION
SAVE YOUR FILES
Remember to save your files to the drive and folder where you are storing the files you create as you complete the steps in this book.

Begin Activity

Create a new, blank database.

1 Start **Access**. The Recent screen appears in Backstage view.

2 Click the **Blank desktop database tile**. A dialog box opens. See Exhibit 17-3.

3 To the right of the File Name box, click the **Browse button** [folder icon]. The File New Database dialog box opens.

4 Navigate to the **Chapter 17\Chapter folder** or to the drive and folder in which you store the files you create in this book.

TIP: To create a database that contains objects found in common databases, type keywords in the Search box at the top of the Recent screen.

5 In the File name box, select all of the text, and then type **Energy**.

6 Click **OK**. The dialog box closes. Energy.accdb appears in the File Name box. The file extension .accdb identifies the file as an Access database.

7 Click the **Create button**. Access creates the new database, and then opens an empty table named Table1 in Datasheet view. The Table1 table is listed in the Navigation Pane. See Exhibit 17-4.

8 If the Access program window is not maximized, click the **Maximize button** [icon].

PROBLEM? If the Property Sheet pane is open on the right, on the Table Tools Design tab on the ribbon, in the Show/Hide group, click the **Property Sheet button** to close the pane.

End Activity

EXHIBIT 17-3 BLANK DESKTOP DATABASE DIALOG BOX

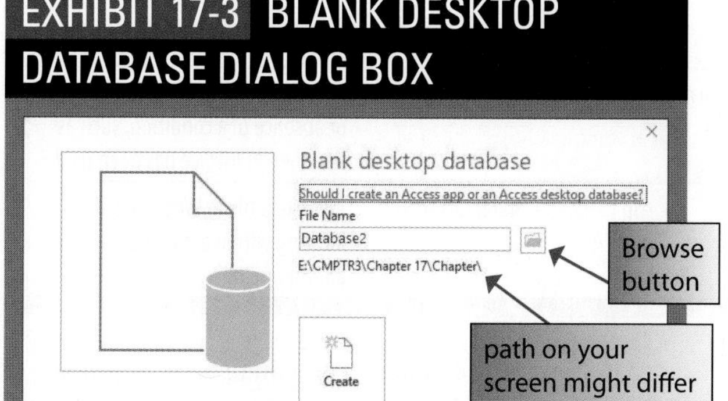

17-3 USING DATASHEET VIEW

To create your database, you need to design a table and enter data into it. One way to create and work with tables is to work in Datasheet view. **Datasheet view** shows the table's contents as a datasheet. A **datasheet** displays the table's contents in rows and columns, similar to a Word table or an Excel worksheet. In Access, each column is a field, and each row is a record. In Datasheet

EXHIBIT 17-4 ACCESS WINDOW WITH AN EMPTY TABLE IN DATASHEET VIEW

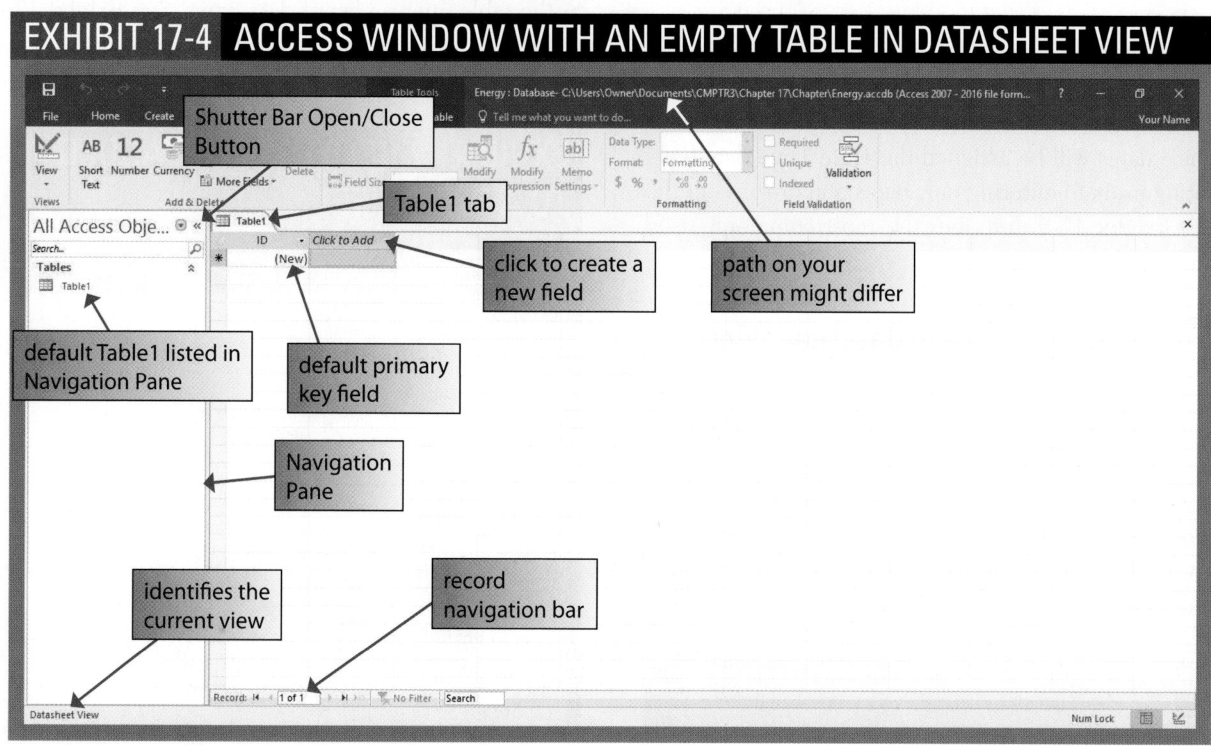

view, you can create fields and enter records, much like you enter data in a Word table or an Excel worksheet. When you first create a new database, an empty table opens in Datasheet view. Refer to Exhibit 17-4.

When you create a table, keep in mind that you should divide all information into its smallest useful part. For example, instead of including a person's full name in one field, separate the first name and the last name into separate fields. When you name a field, you should choose a name that describes the purpose or contents of the field so you and other users can quickly tell what the field stores. For example, you might use CustomerID, FirstName, LastName, and Phone as field names. A field name must be unique within a table, but it can be used again in another table in the same database.

In Access, each field must be assigned a data type. A **data type** specifies the type of data that may be entered for that field—such as text, numbers, currency, and dates and times. For example, a field that will store invoice dates will be assigned the Date/Time data type, limiting users to entering only dates and/or times in the field. Exhibit 17-5 describes the most commonly used data types.

EXHIBIT 17-5 COMMON DATA TYPES

Data type	Description	Field size	Use for
Short Text	Letters, digits, spaces, and special characters	0 to 255 characters; default is 255	Names, addresses, descriptions, and numbers not used in calculations
Long Text	Letters, digits, spaces, and special characters	1 to 65,535 characters; exact size is determined by entry	Long comments and explanations
Number	Positive and negative numbers that can contain digits, a decimal point, commas, and a plus or minus sign	1 to 15 digits	Fields that will be used in calculations, except those involving money
Date/Time	Dates and times from January 1, 100 to December 31, 9999	8 bytes	
Currency	Monetary values	Accurate to 15 digits on the left side of the decimal point and to 4 digits on the right side	
AutoNumber	Unique integer created by Access for every record; can be sequential or random numbering	9 digits	The primary key in any table
Yes/No	Values that are yes or no, on or off, and true or false	1 character	Fields that indicate the presence or absence of a condition, such as whether an invoice has been paid
Hyperlink	Text used as a hyperlink address	Up to 65,535 characters total	A link to a file or Web page, a location within a file or Web page, another field

17-3a Creating a Table in Datasheet View

When you create a table in Datasheet view, you first need to create the empty table structure. A blank table is created automatically when you start Access and create a new database, as was shown in Exhibit 17-4. If you need to create a new, blank table in Datasheet view, click the Table button in the Tables group on the Create tab.

data type The type of data that can be entered for a field.

After creating a blank table, you need to add fields to it. To define a new field, you assign a data type and enter a field name. Clicking the Click to Add column heading in the table opens a list of data types. See Exhibit 17-6. Click a data type to assign it to the new field. After you select a data type, you can type the field name.

EXHIBIT 17-6 FIELD BEING ADDED TO A DATASHEET

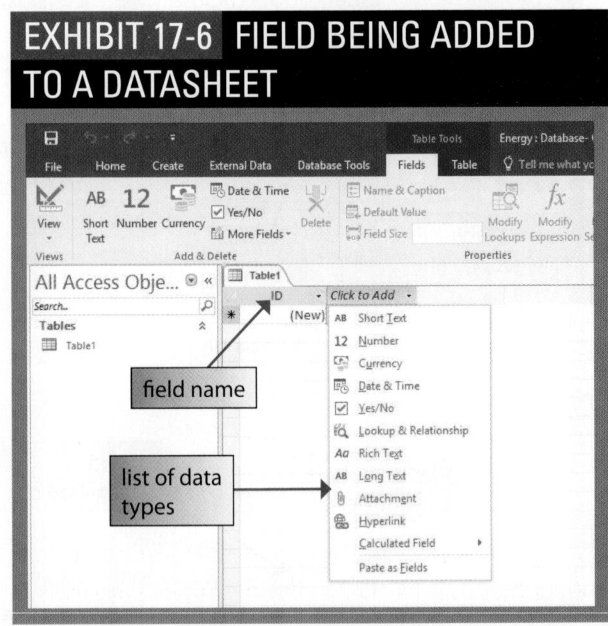

If a field name is not completely visible in a datasheet because the column is too narrow, you can resize the column using the same techniques you used for columns in Word tables and Excel worksheets: double-click the column border to AutoFit the contents or drag a column border to change the column width to any size you want.

When you first create a table in Datasheet view, the first field in the datasheet is named ID and is identified as the primary key for the table. This field is assigned the AutoNumber data type, which will add a unique number, beginning with 1, to the ID field as you enter each record in the table. If you want, you can rename the primary key field, change its data type, and then type your own values for the primary key.

Begin Activity

Create a table in Datasheet view.

1 In the datasheet, click the **Click to Add column heading**. The list of available data types appears. Refer back to Exhibit 17-6.

2 Click **Short Text** to select the type of data to store in the field. A new field is added to the table, and its placeholder name, Field1, is selected in the column heading.

> **TIP:** You can also add a field by clicking the appropriate data type button in the Add & Delete group on the Table Tools Fields tab.

3 Type **FirstName** as the field name, and then press the **Enter key**. The list of available data types appears for the next field so you can quickly add another field.

4 Select **Short Text** as the data type, type **LastName** as the field name, and then press the **Tab key**. The list of available data types appears for the next field.

5 Select **Date & Time** as the data type, type **Since** as the field name, and then press the **Tab key**. The list of available data types appears for the next field.

6 Right-click the field name **Since**. On the shortcut menu, click **Rename Field**. The Since field name is selected.

7 Type **ClientSince** and then press the **Tab key**. The list of available data types appears for the next field.

> **TIP:** To change a field's data type in Datasheet view, click the field, click the Data Type arrow in the Formatting group on the Table Tools Fields tab, and then click the new data type.

8 Right-click the field name **ID**. On the shortcut menu, click **Rename Field**. The ID field name is selected.

9 Type **ClientID** and then press the **Tab key**.

End Activity

17-3b Saving a Table

A table is not stored in the database until you save it. When you save a table, you are saving its structure—the number of fields, the field names, the column widths in the datasheet, and so on. The first time you save a table, you should give it a descriptive name that identifies the information it contains. To save the table, you click the Save button on the Quick Access Toolbar.

If you store your database on a removable drive, such as a USB drive, you should never remove the drive while the database file is open. If you do, Access will encounter problems that might damage the database when it tries to save the database.

> **FYI**
>
> **SAVING A DATABASE**
>
> Unlike other Office programs, you do not need to save the database after you add or delete records. Access automatically saves changes to the active database when you change or add a record or close the database. Clicking the Save button saves the design and format of an Access object, such as a table. For example, if you add or delete fields, or change the width of a column in a datasheet, you need to save these changes.

Begin Activity

Save and name a table.

1 On the Quick Access Toolbar, click the **Save button**. The Save As dialog box opens with the default table name Table1 selected in the Table Name box.

> **TIP:** You can also use the Save and Save As commands in the navigation bar in Backstage view.

2 In the Table Name box, type **Clients** and then click **OK**. The Clients table is saved in the database, and the table name is updated in the Navigation Pane and on the table's tab. Compare your screen to Exhibit 17-7.

End Activity

EXHIBIT 17-7 TABLE SAVED WITH A NEW NAME

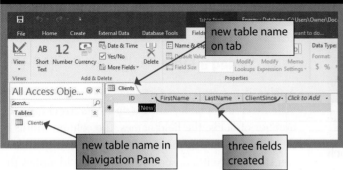

new table name on tab

new table name in Navigation Pane

three fields created

17-3c Entering Records

After you create the structure of a table by naming fields and assigning data types, you can enter records. To enter records in a table datasheet, you type the field values below the column headings for the fields. When you start typing a value in a field, a pencil symbol appears in the row selector at the beginning of the row for the new record. The pencil symbol indicates that the record is being edited. See Exhibit 17-8.

EXHIBIT 17-8 FIRST FIELD VALUE ENTERED

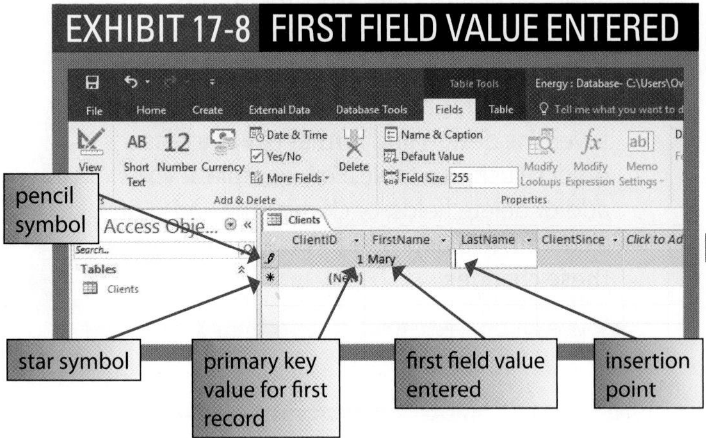

One way a datasheet differs from Word tables and Excel worksheets is that when you add a record to a table, you can enter it only in the next available row. You cannot insert a row between existing records for the new record. A star symbol appears at the beginning of the next available row for a new record.

If you mistype a field value or need to change it, you can correct it. Click in the field to position the insertion point, use the Backspace key or Delete key to delete incorrect text, type the correct text, and then press the Tab key or the Enter key. Note that you cannot edit the values in a field that has the AutoNumber data type.

Begin Activity

Enter records in a table.

1. In the first row of the datasheet, click in the **FirstName column**. The FirstName column header is highlighted, and the insertion point appears in the FirstName column for the first record, ready for you to enter the field value.
2. Type **Mary** and then press the **Tab key**. The field value is entered, and the insertion point moves to the LastName column for the first record. Access assigns the first primary key value. Refer to Exhibit 17-8.
3. Type **Watson** and then press the **Tab key**. Access enters the field value and moves the insertion point to the ClientSince column.
4. Type **2/27/17** and then press the **Tab key**. The year changes to 2017 even though you entered only the final two digits of the year because the ClientSince field has the Date/Time data type, which formats dates with four-digit years. The first record is entered into the table, and the insertion point appears in the ClientID field for the second record. The pencil symbol is removed from the first row because the record in that row is no longer being edited.

PROBLEM?
If you see another date format for the ClientSince field, your Windows date setting is different. Continue with Step 5; this difference will not cause any problems.

5. Press the **Enter key** to move to the FirstName field in the second row, type **Carlos**, press the **Enter key** to move to the LastName field, type **Ramos**, press the **Enter key** to move to the ClientSince field, type **4-4-17**, and then press the **Enter key**. The second record is entered, the number 2 was assigned to the ClientID field in the second row, and the third row is active, ready for a new record. Again, the ClientSince date you entered was changed to match the Date/Time format.
6. Press the **Tab key** to move to the FirstName field in the third row, enter **Jillian** as the first name, **Bayers** as the last name, and **6/15/2017** as the ClientSince date.

PROBLEM?
If you enter a value in the wrong field, a menu might open with options for addressing the problem. If this happens, click the **Enter new value option** to highlight the field with the incorrect value, and then type the correct value.

FYI NAMING TABLES AND FIELDS

Each table in a database and each field in a single table must have a unique name. Be sure to use descriptive names that indicate what the field or table stores. For example, you might use Customers as a table name and CustomerID, FirstName, and LastName as field names because these names describe their contents. In addition, when naming fields, keep in mind the following guidelines:

- A field name can have up to 64 characters, including letters, numbers, spaces, and special characters, except for a period (.), exclamation mark (!), accent grave ('), and square brackets ([ ]).
- A field name cannot begin with a space.
- Capitalize the first letter of each word in a field name that combines multiple words (for example, InvoiceDate).
- Use standard abbreviations, such as Num for Number, Amt for Amount, and Qty for Quantity.
- Avoid using spaces in field names (even though Access allows them) because they can cause errors when you perform other tasks.

7 Click the field containing **Bayers**. The insertion point appears in the field.

8 Delete all of the text in the field, type **Connor,** and then press the **Enter key.**

9 Enter the following data for the fourth and fifth records:

FirstName	LastName	ClientSince
Aisha	**Heinen**	**10-5-16**
Mike	**Chung**	**6/13/2017**

End Activity

17-4 WORKING WITH FIELDS AND PROPERTIES IN DESIGN VIEW

Each field in a table is defined by a variety of attributes, or characteristics, called properties. A **property** describes one characteristic of a field. A field name and its data type are properties.

The properties for a field depend on the field's data type. In addition to the field name and the data type, the following are common additional properties for different fields:

- **Description**—an optional property for describing a field; usually used only when the field name is not descriptive enough or the field has a special function such as a primary key.
- **Field Size**—the maximum storage size for Short Text, Long Text, Number, and AutoNumber fields.
- **Format**—describes how the value is displayed; for example, with the Date/Time data type, you can choose an existing format or enter a custom format using the same custom codes as you used in Excel.
- **Decimal Places**—the number of decimal places that are displayed to the right of the decimal point in a field defined with the Number or Currency data type.
- **Caption**—the field name as it will appear in database objects, such as in the table in Datasheet view. For example, you might use the field name CustNum in the table's design but set the Caption property to display Customer Number as the field's caption to enhance readability in datasheets and forms.
- **Default Value**—the value automatically entered in a field. For example, if every customer in a Customers table live in a certain state, you might set the Default Value property for the State field to the state's abbreviation.

property One characteristic or aspect of a field, such as its name or data type.

EXHIBIT 17-9 TABLE IN DESIGN VIEW

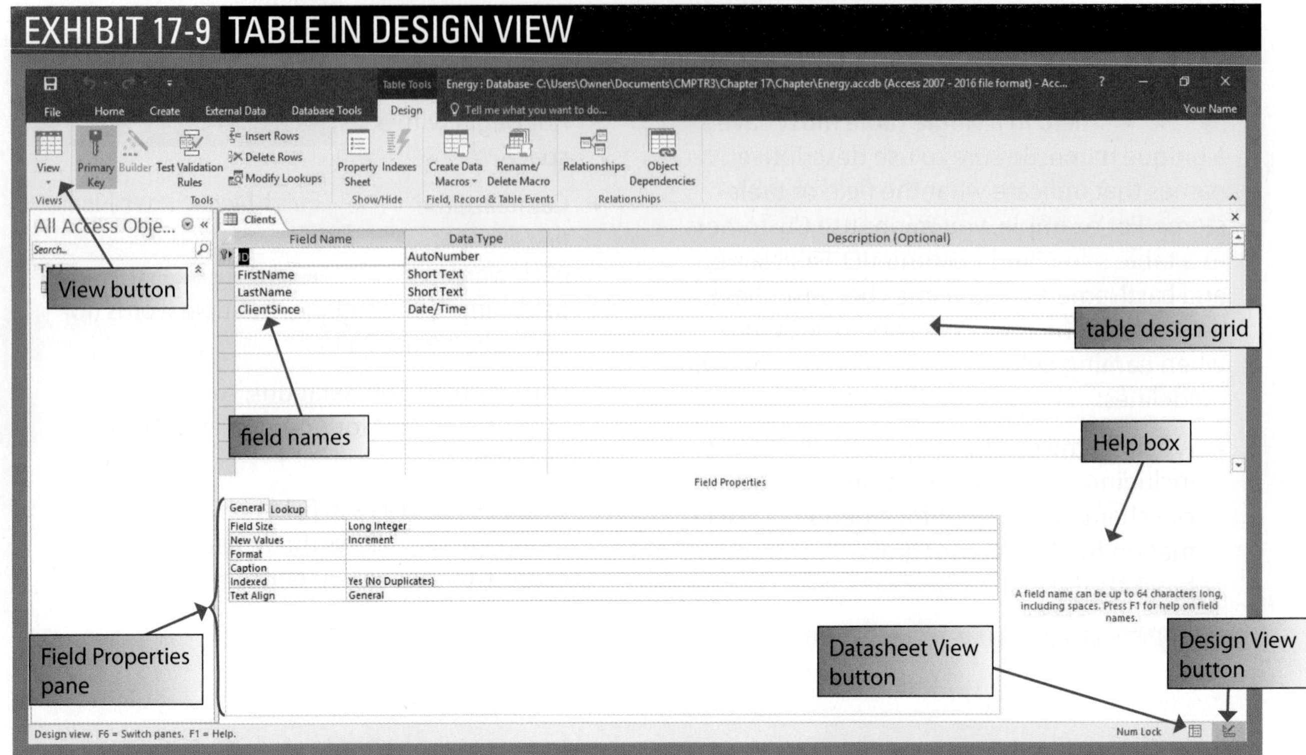

The field name and data type properties are available on the ribbon on the Table Tools Fields tab in Datasheet view, but more properties are available in Design view. **Design view** shows a listing of a table's fields and field properties. See Exhibit 17-9. A table design grid in the top portion of the window lists the field names and data types. The table design grid also includes a description of each field. At the bottom of the window in Design view, the Field Properties pane lists the additional properties available for the field currently selected in the table design grid, and the Help box displays information about the currently selected property. In Design view, you can create and modify fields, but you cannot enter records.

To switch between Datasheet view and Design view, you can use the View button on the ribbon. This button appears in three places on the ribbon. It appears in the Views group on the Home tab; in Datasheet view, it appears in the Views group on the Table Tools Fields tab; and in Design view, it appears in the Views group on the Table Tools Design tab. The icon on the View button changes to reflect the view that you will switch to; that is, in Datasheet view, the icon shows that clicking it will switch you to Design view, and vice versa in Design view. If you can switch to more than one view, you can click the View button arrow to display a menu of available views. You can also use buttons on the status bar to switch among views, similar to the view buttons on the status bars in Word and Excel.

Design view The Access view that shows the underlying structure of a database object and allows you to modify that structure.

17-4a Changing Field Properties in Design View

When you first create a field, most properties are assigned default values. You can change these values to match the field's content or purpose. To do this, you change the values in the Field Properties pane in Design view. Often you can change a property by typing the new value in the property's box. For some properties, when you click the box in the Field Properties pane, an arrow appears at the right end of the box. This indicates that in addition to typing the new value, you can click the arrow and then choose from a list of predesigned formats or values for that property. Generally, it's a good idea to create the structure of a table and change field properties before you enter any data so that values you have already entered do not change unexpectedly when a property changes.

FYI FIELD SIZE PROPERTY FOR NUMBER FIELDS

When you use the Number data type to define a field, you should set the Field Size property based on the largest value you expect to store in that field. Access processes smaller data sizes faster, using less memory, so you can optimize the database's performance and its storage space by selecting the correct field size for each field. Number fields have the following Field Size property settings:

- **Byte**—stores whole numbers (numbers with no fractions) from 0 to 255 in one byte
- **Integer**—stores whole numbers from –32,768 to 32,767 in two bytes
- **Long Integer** (default)—stores whole numbers from –2,147,483,648 to 2,147,483,647 in four bytes
- **Single**—stores positive and negative numbers to precisely seven decimal places and uses four bytes
- **Double**—stores positive and negative numbers to precisely 15 decimal places and uses eight bytes
- **Replication ID**—establishes a unique identifier for replication of tables, records, and other objects in databases created using Access 2003 and earlier versions and uses 16 bytes
- **Decimal**—stores positive and negative numbers to precisely 28 decimal places and uses 12 bytes

Begin Activity

Change field properties in Design view.

1 On the status bar, click the **Design View button** . The table switches to Design view. Refer back to Exhibit 17-9. The table design grid lists the fields you entered in Datasheet view. The Field Properties pane lists the available properties for the selected ClientID field, and a description of the selected property (field name) appears in the Help box.

PROBLEM? If the Property Sheet pane is open on the right, on the Table Tools Design tab on the ribbon, in the Show/Hide group, click the **Property Sheet button** to close the pane.

2 In the table design grid, in the Field Name column, click **FirstName**. The field is selected in the table design grid, and its properties appear in the Field Properties pane. The number 255 appears in the Field Size box. This is the maximum number of characters allowed for a Short Text field.

TIP: To change a field property in Datasheet view, use the buttons in the Formatting group on the Table Tools Fields tab.

3 In the Field Properties pane, select the value in the **Field Size box**, and then type **20**. Now the maximum number of characters allowed for a client's first name is 20. The description in the Help box changed to describe the currently selected property.

4 In the table design grid, in the Field Name column, click **ClientSince**. The properties for the ClientSince field appear in the Field Properties pane. A Date/Time field does not have a Field Size property, so that property is not listed.

5 In the Field Properties pane, click in the **Format box**. An arrow appears at the right end of the Format box.

6 Click the **Format box arrow** . A list of date formats opens.

7 In the list, click **Long Date**. The format is changed.

8 On the Quick Access Toolbar, click the **Save button** to save the changes to the design of the Client table. Because you reduced the Field Size property of the FirstName field from 255 characters to 20 characters, a dialog box appears, indicating that some data may be lost because the field size was decreased. If you click Yes and any value in the FirstName field contains more than 20 characters, any characters after the twentieth will be deleted. In this case, none of the values in the FirstName field in your table have more than 20 characters.

9 Click **Yes**. The table is saved.

10 On the Table Tools Design tab, in the Views group, click the **View button**. The table returns to Datasheet view. The date no longer fits in the ClientSince column because the Long Date format that you selected as the field's Format property displays many more characters than the default Short Date format.

11 Double-click the **Client Since column header right border**. The column widens to fit the widest entry. The dates in that field now appear in the Long Date format. Compare your screen to Exhibit 17-10. Note that the property change to the FirstName field is not apparent because none of the names entered have more than 20 characters.

12 Save the **Clients table**.

End Activity

EXHIBIT 17-10 RECORDS WITH THE LONG DATE FORMAT

ID	FirstName	LastName	ClientSince
1	Mary	Watson	Monday, February 27, 2017
2	Carlos	Ramos	Tuesday, April 04, 2017
3	Jillian	Connor	Thursday, June 15, 2017
4	Aisha	Heinen	Wednesday, October 05, 2016
5	Mike	Chung	Tuesday, June 13, 2017

17-4b Creating a Table and Setting Properties in Design View

Because you can set additional properties for fields in Design view, it can be a good idea to create a table in Design view. Then, after you have named all the fields and modified the field properties, you can switch to Datasheet view to enter records. To create a new, blank table in Design view, switch to Design view immediately after creating a new database. Or, if a table already exists and you need to create a new one, click the Table Design button in the Tables group on the Create tab. You can also create a table in Datasheet view and then switch to Design view, but you must save the table before switching views.

When you first create a table in Design view, the insertion point appears in the table design grid in the first row's Field Name box, ready for you to begin defining the first field in the table. To name a field, type it in the Field Name box. To assign a data type to a field, click in the Data Type box, click the arrow that appears, and then select the data type. See Exhibit 17-11.

Begin Activity

Create a table in Design view.

1 On the ribbon, click the **Create tab**. In the Tables group, click the **Table Design button**. The view switches to Design view, and a new, blank table named Table1 is created. This table will contain contract data, and its first field will contain the unique number that identifies each contract.

FYI

INPUT MASK PROPERTY

The Input Mask property can be used to display data in a specific format. For example, you might use the Input Mask property to format a field that stores phone numbers with the area code enclosed in parentheses and a dash to separate the other seven digits. The user can then type just the digits of the phone number, and the input mask formats the field value. If you change the display of the phone numbers, you need to change only the Input Mask property, and all of the phone numbers would immediately use the new formatting.

If you add an input mask to a field, you need to keep the big picture in mind. For instance, if the customer list for a company includes international customers, an input mask that restricts a phone number field to the format (000) 0000000 would cause problems because other countries use different formats and number of digits to display their phone numbers.

© HannaMonika/Shutterstock.com

EXHIBIT 17-11 NEW TABLE IN DESIGN VIEW AFTER ENTERING THE FIRST FIELD NAME

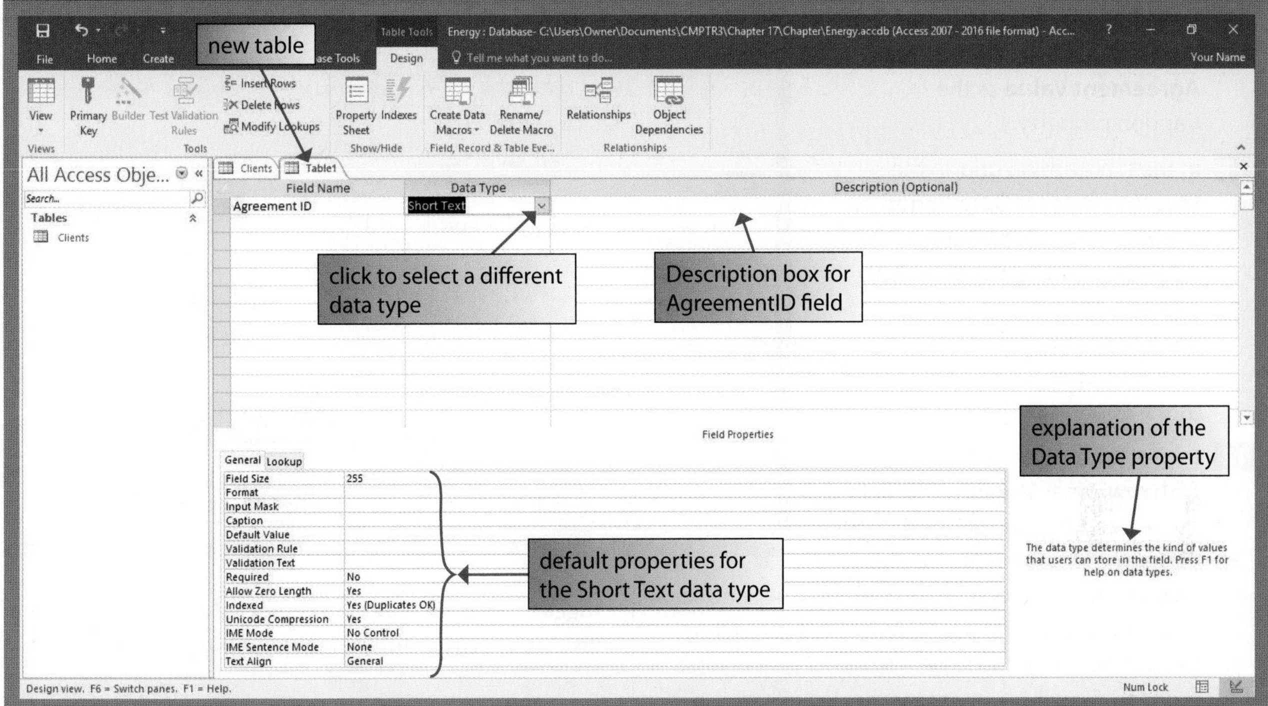

2 In the table design grid, in the Field Name column, in the first row, type **AgreementID** and then press the **Tab key** to select the Data Type box. The default data type, Short Text, appears highlighted in the Data Type box, which now also contains an arrow, and the field properties for a Text field appear in the Field Properties pane. Refer to Exhibit 17-11. The Help box provides an explanation for the current property, Data Type. Agreement ID numbers at this company are two digits that identify the year, followed by two numbers that identify the actual contract number, a hyphen, and the initials of the salesperson at the company who completed the contract. Therefore, the default Short Text data type is appropriate.

3 Press the **Tab key** to accept Short Text as the data type and to move the insertion point to the Description box.

4 In the Description box, type **Primary key**. The description you entered will appear on the status bar when you view the table in Datasheet view. (Note that specifying Primary key as the Description property does not set the current field as the primary key; you will set the primary key shortly.)

5 In the Field Properties pane, change the **Field Size property** to **7**.

6 In the Field Properties pane, click in the **Caption box**, and then type **Agreement Number**. This value is what will appear in Access objects, including tables. When you look at a table in Datasheet view, you will see this caption as the field name for this field instead of AgreementID.

> **TIP:** You can press the F6 key to move the insertion point from the table design grid to the Field Properties pane.

7 In the table design grid, click in the **Field Name column in the second row**, type **ClientID** as the field name, and then press the **Tab key**. Short Text is selected as the data type.

8 Click the **Short Text box arrow**, and then click **Number** to specify the data type.

9 Press the **Tab key**, and then type **Foreign key** as the description. In the Field Properties pane, click in the **Caption box**, and then type **Client ID** as the Caption property. The ClientID field is the field that will connect (relate) the Agreements table to the Clients table you already created. The related field in the Clients table is also named ClientID, and it has the AutoNumber data type. The data type of a foreign key must be compatible with the data type of the primary key in the original table.

10 In the table design grid, in the **third row**, enter **AgreementValue** as the field name, **Currency** as the data type, **Total value of the agreement** as the description, and **Agreement Value** as the Caption property.

11 In the table design grid, in the **fourth row**, enter **DateSigned** as the field name, **Date/Time** as the data type, **Date agreement was signed** as the description, **Short Date** as the Format property, and **Date Signed** as the Caption property.

12 In the table design grid, in the **fifth row**, enter **Signed** as the field name, **Yes/No** as the data type, and **Signed?** as the Caption property. This field can have only two values: Yes (the contract was signed) or No (it hasn't been signed yet). In the Default Value box, the value is No. Until the contract is signed, No will be entered as the default value in the Signed field in all new records. Because the default appearance for the Yes/No data type is a check box, this means the check box will be unchecked for new records. Compare your screen to Exhibit 17-12.

End Activity

EXHIBIT 17-12 NEW TABLE IN DESIGN VIEW

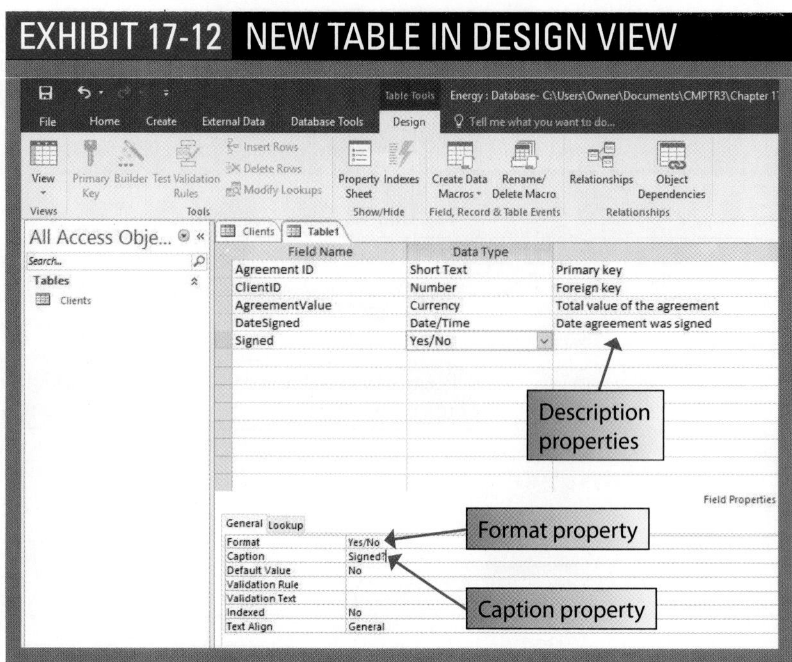

17-4c Specifying the Primary Key

You can choose which field to use as the primary key in Design view. See Exhibit 17-13. The Primary Key button in the Tools group on the Table Tools Design tab is a toggle. Click the button to remove the key symbol if you want to specify a different field as the primary key.

Begin Activity

Specify a primary key.

1 In the table design grid, click in the **AgreementID row** to make it the current field.

2 On the Table Tools Design tab, in the Tools group, click the **Primary Key button**. A key symbol appears in the row selector for the AgreementID row, indicating that the AgreementID field is the table's primary key. Refer to Exhibit 17-13.

End Activity

FYI

CHANGING THE DEFAULT PRIMARY KEY FIELD

When you create a new table in Datasheet view, Access creates the ID field as the table's default primary key. You can rename the ID field to better reflect the contents of the field you want to use for the primary key. Right-click the ID field, click Rename Field on the shortcut menu, type a new name, and then click in the next row.

The renamed primary key field still retains the properties of the default field, including its data type. The default ID primary key field is assigned the AutoNumber data type. For primary keys that contain a mix of letters and numbers, such as contract numbers, select the Short Text data type. However, you can also change the data type. In Datasheet view, you use the Data Type box for changing the data type. On the Fields tab, in the Formatting group, click the column, click the Data Type box arrow, and then click the new data type.

EXHIBIT 17-13 FIELD SELECTED AS THE PRIMARY KEY

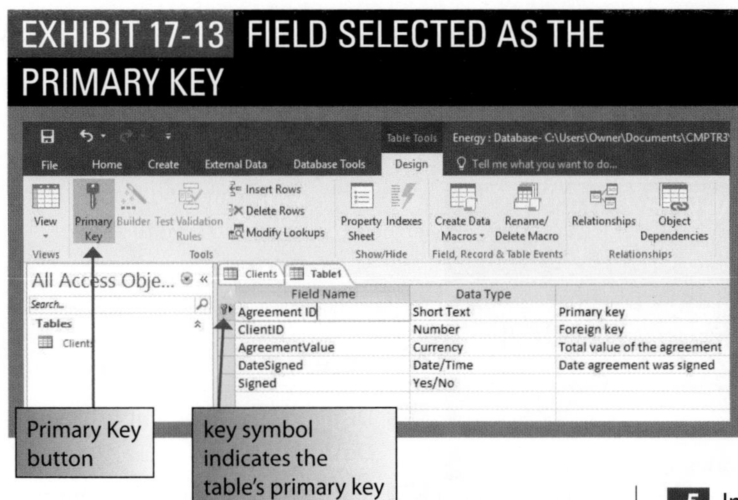

17-4d Saving the Table Design and Entering Records

After you design a table, you need to save it. To enter records into the new table, you need to switch to Datasheet view. You can use the Save button, or you can let Access remind you to save the table when you switch to Datasheet view.

Begin Activity

Save the table design and enter records.

1. On the Table Tools Design tab, in the Views group, click the **View button**. A dialog box opens telling you that you must first save the table.
2. Click **Yes**. The Save As dialog box opens with Table1 selected in the Table Name box.
3. Type **Agreements** and then click **OK**. The Agreements table is added to the Tables list in the Navigation Pane, and the Agreements table is displayed in Datasheet view.
4. Double-click the right borders of each column in the datasheet to change the widths of each column to just fit the widest entry, which in this case, is the field name.
5. In the first row of the datasheet, type **1704-RR** as the Agreement ID, and then press the **Tab key**.
6. Type **5** as the Client ID, press the **Tab key**, type **710** as the Agreement Value, and then press the **Tab key**. The contract value amount is displayed with a dollar sign and two decimal places to match the default format for the Currency data type even though you didn't type them. To the right of the Date Signed field, a calendar icon appears.
7. In the Date Signed field, type **1/16/17** and then press the **Tab key**. The Signed? field is selected.
8. Press the **Spacebar**. A check mark appears in the check box.

TIP: To use the mouse to enter the date, click the calendar icon and then select the date.

TIP: To use the mouse to select the check box, click it.

FYI COPYING RECORDS FROM ANOTHER ACCESS DATABASE

After you created the Clients table, you entered records directly into the table's datasheet. You can also enter records in a table by copying and pasting records from a table in the same database or in a different database. To use this method, however, the tables must have the same structure—that is, the tables must contain the same fields, with the same design and characteristics, in the same order.

To insert records from another table, first select the records you want to copy. If the records are in a second database, you need to open the second database file. Next, copy the records to the Clipboard. Then, with the table where you want to paste the data open in Datasheet view, select the next available row for a new record, making sure the entire row is selected. Finally, paste the records into the table by clicking the Paste button arrow in the Clipboard group on the Home tab, and then clicking Paste Append. When a dialog box opens asking you to confirm that you want to paste all the records, click Yes. The dialog box closes, and the records are pasted.

9 Press the **Tab key** to move to the second record. Compare your screen to Exhibit 17-14.

10 Save the Agreements table.

End Activity

EXHIBIT 17-14 RECORD ENTERED IN THE AGREEMENTS TABLE

17-5 MODIFYING A TABLE'S STRUCTURE

Even a well-designed table might need to be modified. Some changes you can make to a table's structure in Design view are changing the order of fields, adding fields, and deleting fields.

17-5a Moving a Field in Design View

To move a field in Design view, you first select the field's row in the table design grid. To do this, click the box to the left of the row, which is called a row selector or record selector. After a row is selected, you can drag it up or down to its new location in the grid. See Exhibit 17-15. This is similar to dragging headings in the Navigation pane or in Outline view in Word.

Although you can move fields in Datasheet view by dragging a field's column heading to a new location, doing so rearranges only the display of the table's fields; the table structure is not changed. To move a field permanently, you must display the table in Design view. After you modify the table's structure, be sure to save the table.

Begin Activity

Move a field in a table.

1 Display the Agreements table in **Design view**.

2 In the table design grid, point to the **DateSigned row selector**. The pointer changes to ➡. Click the **DateSigned row selector** to select the row.

3 Press and hold the **mouse button**. The pointer changes to the move pointer. Drag down until the dark line indicating the drop location for the field appears below the Signed field. Refer back to Exhibit 17-15.

4 Release the **mouse button**. The DateSigned field now appears below the Signed field.

5 Save the Agreements table, and then click the **Clients tab** to display the Clients table.

6 Display the Clients table in **Design view**.

7 Move the **LastName Field** above the FirstName field.

8 Save the **Clients table**, and then switch to **Datasheet view** to confirm that the LastName field appears to the left of the FirstName field.

PROBLEM?
If LastName does not appear to the left of FirstName, right-click the **Clients tab**, click **Close**, and then double-click **Clients** in the Navigation Pane.

End Activity

EXHIBIT 17-15 FIELD BEING MOVED IN THE TABLE STRUCTURE

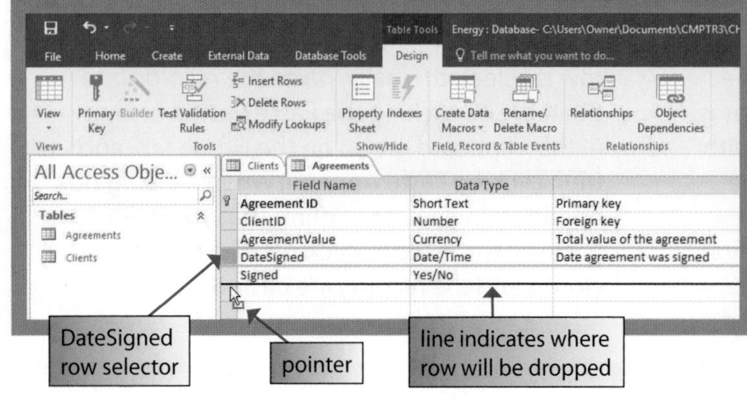

17-5b Adding a Field

You can add a new field to a table at any time. If the field will be the last field in the table, you can add the field the same way as when you add fields to a new table. If you decide the field belongs in a different location, you can always move it to its proper position.

You can also insert a new field between existing fields. In Datasheet view, select the field to the left of where you want the new field to be inserted. Then, in the Add & Delete group on the Table Tools Fields tab, click the button for the data type of the field you want to insert. Exhibit 17-16 shows a new field inserted to the right of the FirstName field in Datasheet view.

EXHIBIT 17-16 TABLE WITH NEW FIELD IN DATASHEET VIEW

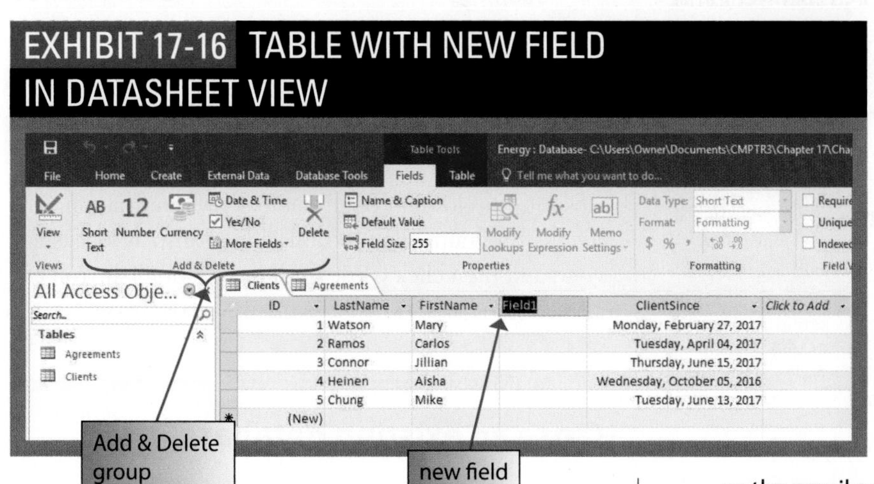

You can also insert new fields between other fields in Design view. In the table design grid, select the row below where you want the new field to be inserted. Then, in the Tools group on the Table Tools Design tab, click the Insert Rows button. You then enter the field name, data type, optional description, and any additional field properties for the new field as usual. Exhibit 17-17 shows a new field inserted above the Email field in Design view.

EXHIBIT 17-17 TABLE WITH NEW FIELD IN DESIGN VIEW

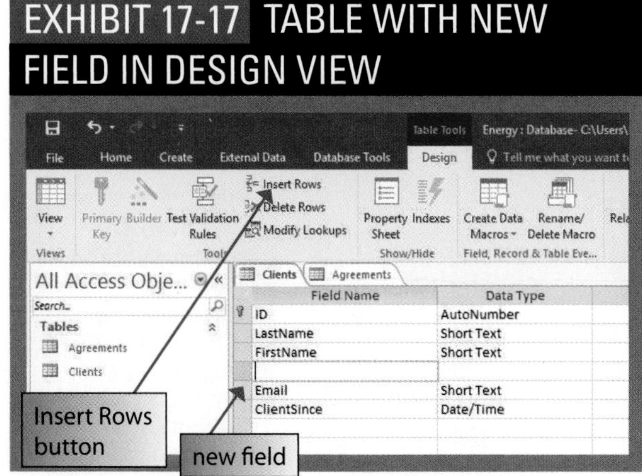

Keep in mind that the new field does not contain data for any existing records. If you want to add data to the new field in existing records, you need to go back to each existing record in Datasheet view, click in the column for that record, and type the new data.

Begin Activity

Add a field to a table.

1. In Datasheet view for the Clients table, click the **FirstName column header** to select the field.
2. On the ribbon, click the **Table Tools Fields tab.** In the Add & Delete group, click the **Short Text button**. A new field is inserted to the right of the selected FirstName field with the temporary field name Field1 selected. Refer to Exhibit 17-16.
3. Type **Email** as the field name, and then press the **Enter key**. The ClientID field value for the first record is selected.
4. In the first record, click in the **Email column**, type **mwatson@example.com** as the email address, and then press the **Tab key**. Resize the **Email column** to fit the widest value.
5. Switch the table to **Design view**. In the table design grid, in the Field Name column, click **Email**.
6. On the Table Tools Design tab, in the Tools group, click the **Insert Rows button.** A new, blank row appears above the current Email field. The insertion point is in the Field Name box, ready for you to type the name for the new field. Refer to Exhibit 17-17.
7. Type **InvoiceItem** as the field name, and keep the Data Type as **Short Text.**
8. Save the Clients table.

End Activity

17-5c Deleting a Field

After you have created a table, you might need to delete a field. When you delete a field, you also delete all the values for that field from the table. So, before you delete a field, make sure that you really want to do so and that you choose the correct field to delete. You can delete one field at a time, or you can select and delete a group of fields at the same time.

You can delete fields in either Datasheet view or Design view. In Datasheet view, select the field to delete, and then click the Delete button in the Add & Delete group on the Table Tools Fields tab. In Design view, click the Field Name box for the field to delete, and then click the Delete Rows button in the Tools group on the Table Tools Design tab.

Begin Activity

Delete a field from a table.

1 In the table design grid, in the Field Name column, click **InvoiceItem** to make it the current field.

2 On the Table Tools Design tab, in the Tools group, click the **Delete Rows button.** A dialog box appears, confirming that you want to permanently delete the selected field and all of the data in that field.

TIP: You can also select the column header in Datasheet view and then click the Delete button in the Add & Delete group on the Table Tools Fields tab.

3 Click **Yes.** The selected InvoiceItem field is removed from the Clients table.

4 Save the Clients table.

End Activity

17-6 CLOSING AND OPENING OBJECTS AND DATABASES

Unlike other programs, you need to open and close the tables and other objects in a database. A database can be open but have all its objects closed.

17-6a Closing a Table

When you are done working with a table, you should close it. You close the selected table by clicking the Close button [X] in the upper-right corner of the pane. Note that the ScreenTip for the Close button shows the name of the tab that will close as part of the button name, such as Close 'Table1'. If you changed the table structure but didn't save it, a dialog box appears reminding you to save. It is a good idea to work in an object and then save and close it as you go.

Begin Activity

Close a table.

1 If it is not already selected, click the **Clients tab.**

2 In the upper-right corner of the pane, to the right of the tabs, click the **Close 'Clients' button** [X]. The Clients table closes, and the Agreements table is displayed.

3 Right-click the **Agreements tab.** On the shortcut menu, click **Close.** The Agreements table closes, and the main portion of the Access window is now blank because no table or other database object is open.

PROBLEM? If a dialog box appears asking if you want to save the changes to the layout of the Agreements table, click **Yes.**

End Activity

17-6b Closing a Database

When you are done working with a database, you should close it. To close an open database without closing the Access program, click the File tab to display Backstage view, and then click Close in the navigation bar. You can also close Access, which also closes the database.

Begin Activity

Close an existing database.

1 On the ribbon, click the **File tab.** Backstage view appears with the Info screen displayed.

2 In the navigation bar, click **Close.** The Energy database closes, and the blank Access window appears.

End Activity

17-6c Opening a Database

You open an existing database from Backstage view by clicking Open in the navigation bar and then using the Open dialog box to navigate to and open the database.

Begin Activity

Open an existing database.

1 Open the data file **Energy17** located in the Chapter 17\Chapter folder. The Energy17 database opens. This database contains three objects: the Agreements, Clients, and Invoices tables.

PROBLEM? If the Security Warning bar appears, click the **Enable Content** button to close it. If the Security Warning dialog box opens asking if you want to make this file a Trusted Document, click **Yes** to prevent the Security Warning bar from appearing again, or click **No** to have the Security Warning bar appear the next time you open the database.

2 Click the **File tab.** In the navigation bar, click **Save As** to display the Save As screen in Backstage view.

3 Under File Types, make sure **Save Database As** is selected.

4 Under Save Database As on the right, make sure **Access Database** is selected.

5 Click the **Save As button**. The Save As dialog box opens.

6 Save the database as **SolarEnergy17** to the location where you are saving your files.

End Activity

17-6d **Opening a Table**

All of the tables (as well as any queries, forms, or reports) in a database are listed in the Navigation Pane. You open a table or other object by double-clicking its name in the Navigation Pane.

EXHIBIT 17-18 THREE TABLES OPEN

All Access Obje... «
Search...
Tables
Agreements
Clients
Invoices

three objects in the database

Clients | Agreements | Invoices

three open tables

Invoice Number	Agreement ID	Invoice Date	Amount	Paid?
1602-001	1601-TM	2/18/2016	$500.00	☑
1604-002	1603-MP	4/1/2016	$1,150.00	☑
1604-003	1604-MP	4/29/2016	$1,200.00	☑
1605-004	1602-TM	5/10/2016	$12,500.00	☑
1605-005	1606-MP	5/15/2016	$1,100.00	☑
1605-006	1605-KF	5/30/2016	$800.00	☑
1606-007	[illegible]	6/9/2016	$1,500.00	☑
1607-008	[illegible]	7/15/2016	$620.00	☑
1608-009	[illegible]	8/28/2016	$450.00	☑
1608-010	[illegible]	8/29/2016	$800.00	☑
1609-011	1611-TM	9/15/2016	$5,100.00	☑
1609-012	1612-KF	9/15/2016	$2,500.00	☑
1609-013	1610-MP	9/29/2016	$17,800.00	☑
1609-014	1613-RR	9/29/2016	$550.00	☑
1610-015	1615-MP	10/15/2016	$690.00	☑
1610-016	1614-RR	10/15/2016	$3,500.00	☑
1611-017	1617-KF	11/12/2016	$8,500.00	☑
1611-018	1615-MP	11/12/2016	$4,100.00	☑
1611-019	1616-RR	11/15/2016	$6,500.00	☑
1611-020	1619-RR	11/15/2016	$7,800.00	☑
1611-021	1611-TM	11/15/2016	$20,400.00	☑
1611-022	1612-KF	11/15/2016	$22,500.00	☑
1611-023	1610-MP	11/29/2016	$45,600.00	☑
1612-024	1619-RR	12/15/2016	$12,480.00	☑
1612-025	1618-KF	12/21/2016	$15,000.00	☐

Record: 1 of 82 No Filter Search

Primary key

Begin Activity

Open a table.

1 In the Navigation Pane, double-click **Clients** to open the Clients table in Datasheet view. Examine the fields in the Clients table.

2 In the Navigation Pane, double-click **Agreements** to open the Agreements table in Datasheet view. Examine the fields in the Agreements table.

TIP: You can click the Shutter Bar Open/Close Button « to hide the Navigation Pane and display more of the datasheet.

3 Open the **Invoices table**, and then examine the fields in the Invoices table. See Exhibit 17-18.

4 Close the **Clients** and **Agreements tables**.

End Activity

17-6e **Moving Around a Datasheet**

You move around a datasheet using many of the same techniques you learned when you worked with Word tables and Excel worksheets. You can click in a field to make it the active field, or you can use the Tab key or the arrow keys to move to a different field. Access databases can contain thousands of records. When a table contains many records, only some of the records are visible on the screen at one time. You can use the navigation buttons on the record navigation bar, shown in Exhibit 17-19, to move through the records and to see the number of the current record as well as the total number of records in the table.

EXHIBIT 17-19 RECORD NAVIGATION BAR

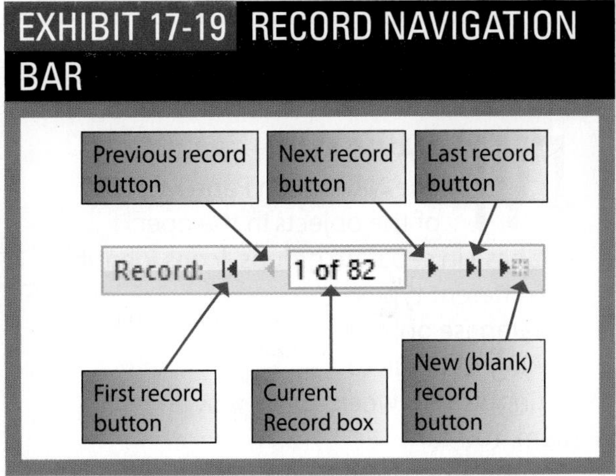

Begin Activity

Move around a datasheet.

1 In the Invoices table, click anywhere in the **second record** except in the Paid field (this would change the value of the check box). On the record navigation bar, the Current Record box shows that record 2 is the current record and there are 82 records in the table.

2 On the record navigation bar, click the **Next record button** ▶. The third record is now highlighted, identifying it as the current record, and the Current Record box changed to display 3 of 82 to indicate that the third record is the current record.

3 Click the **Last record button** ▶|. The last record in the table, record 82, is now the current record.

4 In the vertical scroll bar, drag the **scroll box** to the top of the bar. Although the first records are now visible, record 82 is still the current record, as indicated in the Current Record box.

5 On the record navigation bar, click the **Previous record button** . Record 81 is now the current record.

6 On the record navigation bar, click in the **Current Record box**, press the **Backspace key** twice to delete 81, type **1**, and then press the **Enter key**. The first record is selected.

7 On the record navigation bar, click the **New (blank) record button** . The first field in the next available blank record (record 83) is selected.

8 On the record navigation bar, click the **First record button** . The first record is now the current record and is visible on the screen.

End Activity

FYI **NAVIGATION PANE** The Navigation Pane lists all of the objects in the open database in separate groups. Icons identify the different types of database objects, making it simple to distinguish between them. You can click the arrow on the title bar of the Navigation Pane to display a menu with options for various ways to group and display objects in the Navigation Pane. In addition, you can use the Search box to enter text to find in the listed objects. For example, you could search for all objects that contain the word *Invoice* in their names. Note that Access searches for objects only in the categories and groups currently displayed in the Navigation Pane.

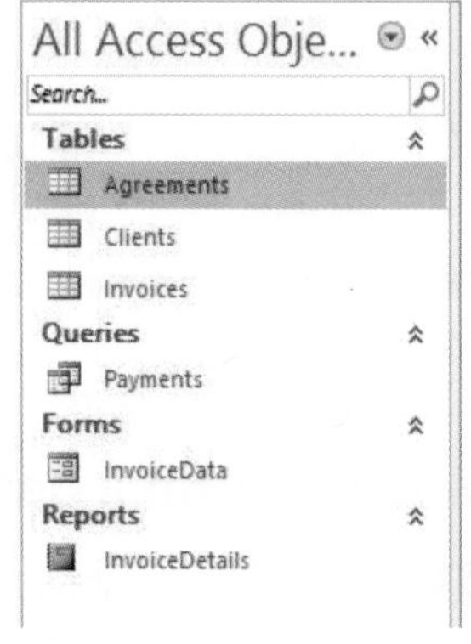

query A question about the data stored in a database.

17-7 CREATING SIMPLE QUERIES, FORMS, AND REPORTS

The data in a database becomes even more useful when you can extract specific information and display it in a format that is easy to read and understand. You can do this by creating simple queries, forms, and reports based on the tables and other queries in a database.

17-7a Creating a Simple Query

A **query** is a question about the data stored in a database. When you create a query, you specify which fields to use to answer the question. Then Access displays only the records that fit, so you don't have to navigate through the entire database. In the Invoices table, for example, you might create a query to display only the invoice numbers and the invoice dates.

You can use the Simple Query Wizard to create a query based on the records and fields in a table. (A *wizard* is a series of dialog boxes that takes you step-by-step through a process.) After you start the Simple Query Wizard, you select the table or another query on which to base the new query, and then you select which fields to include in the query. Exhibit 17-20 shows the dialog box in the Simple Query Wizard in which you make these selections.

EXHIBIT 17-20 FIRST SIMPLE QUERY WIZARD DIALOG BOX

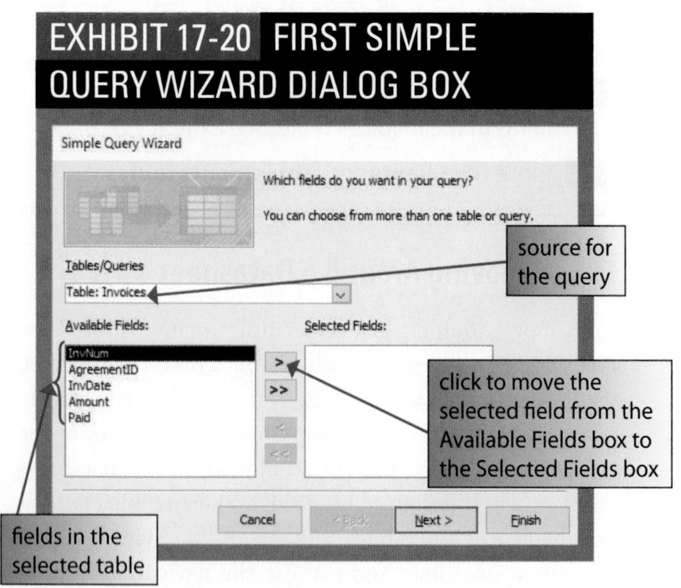

If values in one of the selected fields can be used in calculations, such as the Amount field, the next dialog box that appears asks whether you want a detail or summary query. The default is a **detail query**, which shows every field of every record.

Query results are not stored in the database. However, the query design is stored in the database with the name you specified. You can redisplay the query results at any time by opening the query again.

Begin Activity

Create a query using the Simple Query Wizard.

1. On the ribbon, click the **Create tab**. In the Queries group, click the **Query Wizard button**. The New Query dialog box opens with Simple Query Wizard selected in the list.
2. Click **OK**. The first Simple Query Wizard dialog box opens. Table: Invoices is selected in the Tables/Queries box, and the fields in the Invoices table are listed in the Available Fields box. The first field in the list is selected. Refer back to Exhibit 17-20.

PROBLEM? If the Microsoft Access Security Notice dialog box opens warning you that the content might contain unsafe content, click **Open**.

3. Click the **Tables/Queries box arrow**. All three objects in the database are listed. The Invoices table is selected because it was the selected table in the Navigation Pane before you started the Simple Query Wizard.
4. Click **Table: Invoices**.
5. With InvNum selected in the Available Fields box, click [>]. The InvNum field moves to the Selected Fields box.
6. In the Available Fields box, click **Paid**, and then click [>] to move the Paid field to the Selected Fields box.

TIP: You can also double-click a field to move it from the Available Fields box to the Selected Fields box.

7. Click **Next**. The second Simple Query Wizard dialog box appears, asking whether you want a detail or summary query. The Detail option button is selected.
8. Click **Next**. The final Simple Query Wizard dialog box appears, asking what title you want to use for the query. The suggested query title is based on the name of the table you are using.
9. In the What title do you want for your query? box, change the suggested name to **Payments**. Near the bottom of the dialog box, the Open the query to view information option button is selected.
10. Click **Finish**. The query results appear on a new tab named Payments in Datasheet view, and the query is added to the Navigation Pane. Compare your screen to Exhibit 17-21. The query lists all the records but shows only the InvNum and Paid fields as you specified in the first dialog box in the Simple Query Wizard.
11. Close the **Payments query**.

PROBLEM?
If a dialog box opens asking if you want to save the changes to the layout of the query, you changed the query layout in some way, such as by resizing a column. If the change is intentional, click **Yes**; otherwise, click **No**.

End Activity

EXHIBIT 17-21 QUERY RESULTS

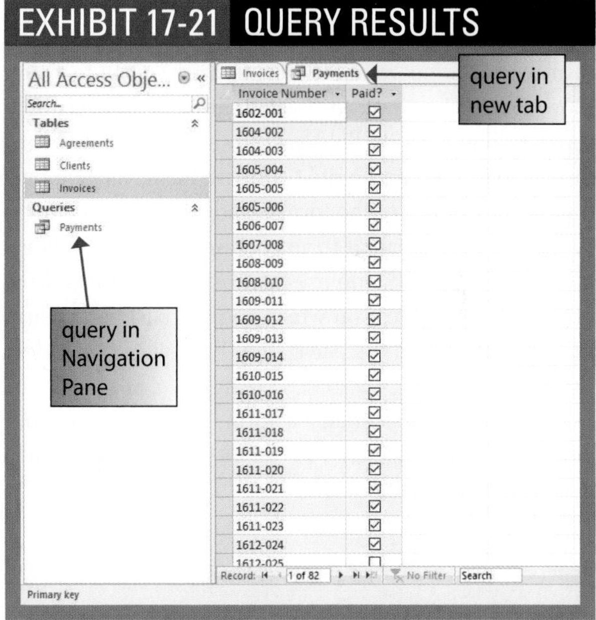

17-7b Creating a Simple Form

You use a **form** to enter, edit, and view records in a database. Although you can perform these same functions with tables and queries, forms can present data in customized and helpful ways. In a simple form, the fields

detail query A query that shows every field of every record as defined by the query criteria.

form A database object used to enter, edit, and view records in a database.

EXHIBIT 17-22 FORM CREATED BY THE FORM TOOL

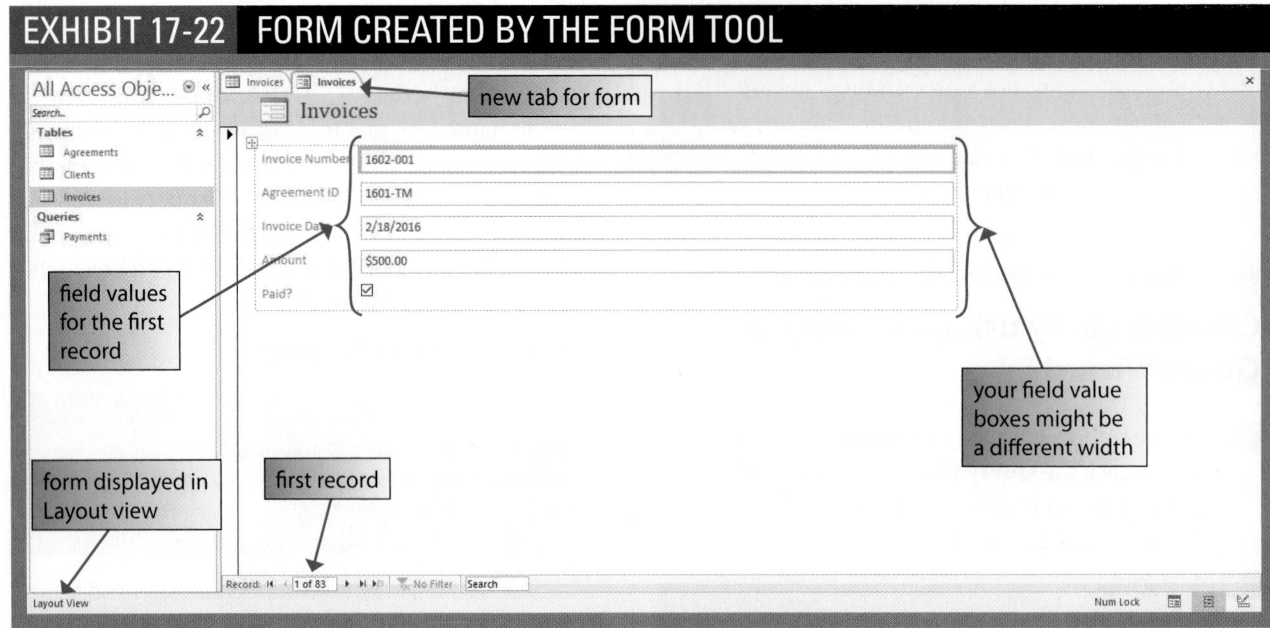

from the table or query on which the form is based are displayed one record at a time, allowing you to focus on the values for one record. Each field name appears on a separate line with its field value for the current record displayed in a box to the right. You use the navigation buttons at the bottom of the form to move between records.

To quickly create a form containing all of the fields in a table (or query), you use the Form tool. The table or other database object on which you are basing the form must be selected in the Navigation Pane when you select the Form tool.

When you first create a form, it opens in Layout view. See Exhibit 17-22. You use **Layout view** to make design changes to the form.

Begin Activity

Create a simple form.

1 In the Navigation Pane, click the **Invoices table** to select it. Note that you must click it even if it looks like it is selected because the first field in the Payments query was selected.

2 On the Create tab, in the Forms group, click the **Form button**.

TIP: You can also select a query in the Navigation Pane to create the form based on the query you select.

Because the Invoices table is selected in the Navigation Pane, a simple form showing every field in the Invoices table is created. Refer to Exhibit 17-22. The name on the tab is the same as the table name on which the form is based, and the fields in the form display the Caption properties set for the fields. The field values for the first record appear in the form, and a border appears around the value for the first field in the form, Invoice Number, indicating that it is selected. The form is in Layout view.

3 On the record navigation bar, click the **Next record button**. The values for the second record in the Invoices table appear in the form.

4 On the record navigation bar, click the **New (blank) record button**. A blank form is created, and 83 of 83 appears in the Current Record box on the record navigation bar.

5 Next to the Invoice Number field name, click the **empty field box**. It is highlighted with an orange border.

6 Type any character. Nothing happens because the form is in Layout view.

7 On the Quick Access Toolbar, click the **Save button**. The Save As dialog box opens.

8 In the Form Name box, type **InvoiceData** and then click **OK**. The form's tab now displays the name InvoiceData, and the form is added to the Navigation Pane.

End Activity

Layout view The Access view in which you can make design changes to database objects such as forms and reports.

17-7c **Entering Data in a Form**

After you create a form, you can use it to enter data in the table. To do this, you need to switch from Layout view to Form view.

Begin Activity

Enter data in a form.

1 On the Form Layout Tools Design tab, in the Views group, click the **View button**. The form appears in Form view. The insertion point is blinking in the first field, Invoice Number.

2 Type **1712-056** and then press the **Tab key**. The insertion point moves to the next field.

3 Enter the following data, pressing the **Tab key** after entering each field value:

Agreement ID	**1714-TM**
Invoice Date	**12/18/17**
Amount	**7500**
Paid?	**No (that is, unchecked)**

Compare your screen to Exhibit 17-23.

4 Close the **InvoiceData form**, saving if requested. The Invoices table is displayed in Datasheet view.

End Activity

EXHIBIT 17-23 FORM IN FORM VIEW WITH NEW DATA

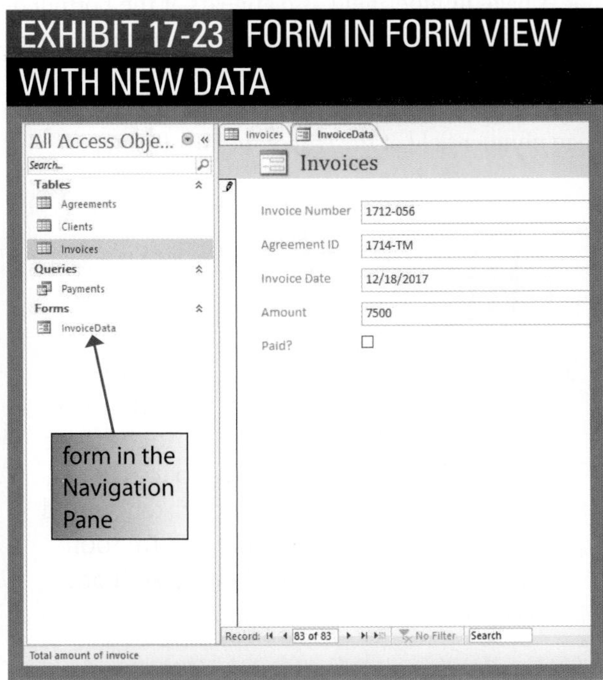

When you add data using one object, such as a form, and the table you added the data to is open, you need to refresh the table before you can see the data you added using the form in the datasheet.

Begin Activity

Refresh data.

1 On the record navigation bar, click the **Last record button** ▶|. There are still only 82 records in the datasheet; the record you entered using the form isn't included.

2 On the Home tab, in the Records group, click the **Refresh All button**. The datasheet is refreshed, and the first record is selected.

3 Display the last record in the datasheet. The datasheet now contains 83 records; the record you added using the form is the last record.

4 Close the **Invoices table**.

End Activity

17-7d **Creating a Simple Report**

A **report** is a formatted printout or screen display of the contents of one or more tables or queries. A report shows each field in a column with the field values for each record in a row, similar to a datasheet. However, the report has a more visually appealing format for the data—column headings are in a different color, borders appear around each field value, a graphic of a report is included in the upper-left corner of the report, and the current day, date, and time appear in the upper-right corner. Dotted horizontal and vertical lines mark the edges of the page and show where text will be printed on the page. Exhibit 17-24 shows a simple report created from the Invoices table.

You can use the Report tool to quickly create a report based on all of the fields from a selected table or query. The Report tool also generates summaries and totals in the report automatically.

Begin Activity

Create a simple report using the Report tool.

1 In the Navigation Pane, click the **Invoices table**.

report A database object that shows a formatted printout or screen display of the contents of the table or query objects on which the report is based.

EXHIBIT 17-24 REPORT CREATED BY THE REPORT TOOL

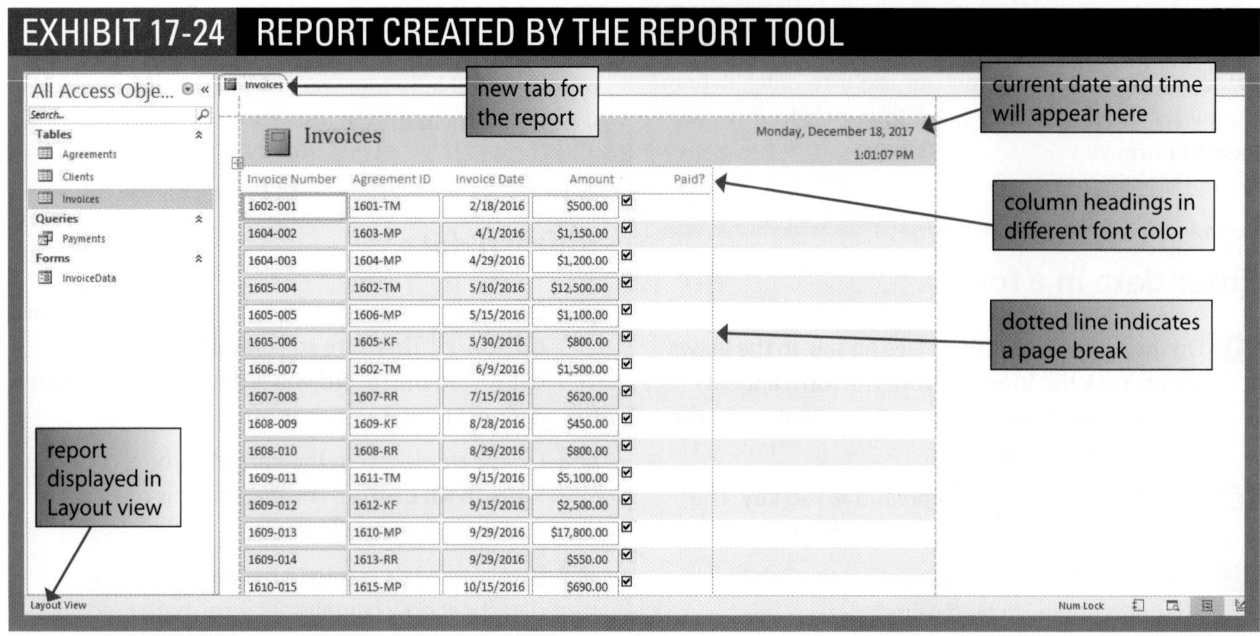

2 On the ribbon, click the **Create tab**. In the Reports group, click the **Report button**. A simple report showing every field in the Invoices table is created. Refer to Exhibit 17-24. The name on the tab is Invoices, because the report is based on the Invoices table. The report opens in Layout view. On the ribbon, the Report Layout Tools tabs appear and the Design tab is selected.

End Activity

17-7e Formatting a Report

The report is displayed in Layout view. In Layout view, you can change the format of the report. One way is to resize columns to better fit the data and ensure that all values will be printed. Also note that the page area, the area that will print, is defined by the dotted lines. Anything outside of the page area will not be printed.

Begin Activity

Format a report.

1 In the Paid? column, click **any field value**. The field you clicked has a dark orange border; the rest of the field values in the Paid? column are highlighted with lighter orange boxes.

2 In the Paid? column, point to the **right border** of any field value. The pointer changes to ↔.

3 Drag the **right border of any field value in the Paid? column** until the column is just wide enough to fit the Paid? column heading. The column is now narrower, better fitting the values. Compare your screen to Exhibit 17-25.

End Activity

Reports are generally intended to be printed and distributed. When a table or query on which a report is based includes a field that can be used in calculations, the total of this field is calculated and displayed at the end of the report below a horizontal rule. If this field is not useful in your report, you can delete it.

A page number field also appears at the bottom of each page in a report. If you don't like the placement of a page number field, you can drag it to a new position. Exhibit 17-26 shows the calculated field and the page number field at the end of the Invoices report.

> **FYI**
>
> **WHEN TO SAVE DATABASE OBJECTS**
>
> In general, it is best to save a database object—query, form, or report—only if you anticipate using the object frequently or if it is time-consuming to create because all objects use storage space on your disk. For example, you most likely would not save a form created with the Form tool because you can re-create it easily with one mouse click.

EXHIBIT 17-25 REPORT AFTER RESIZING COLUMNS

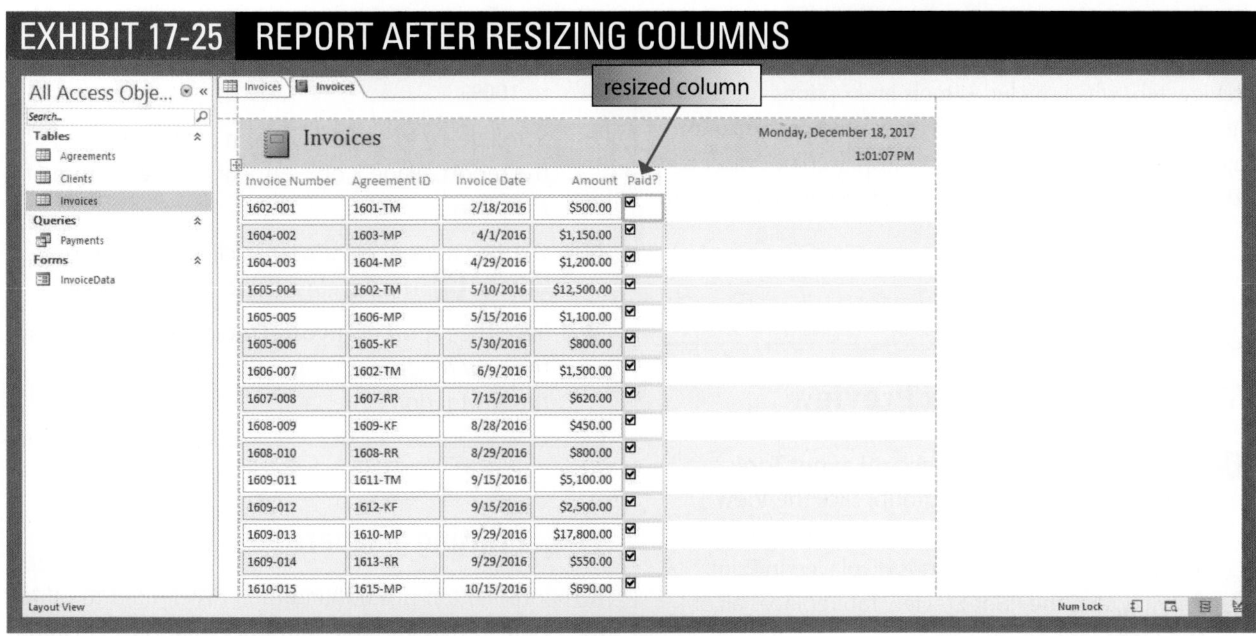

EXHIBIT 17-26 CALCULATED FIELD AND PAGE NUMBER FIELD AT THE END OF THE REPORT

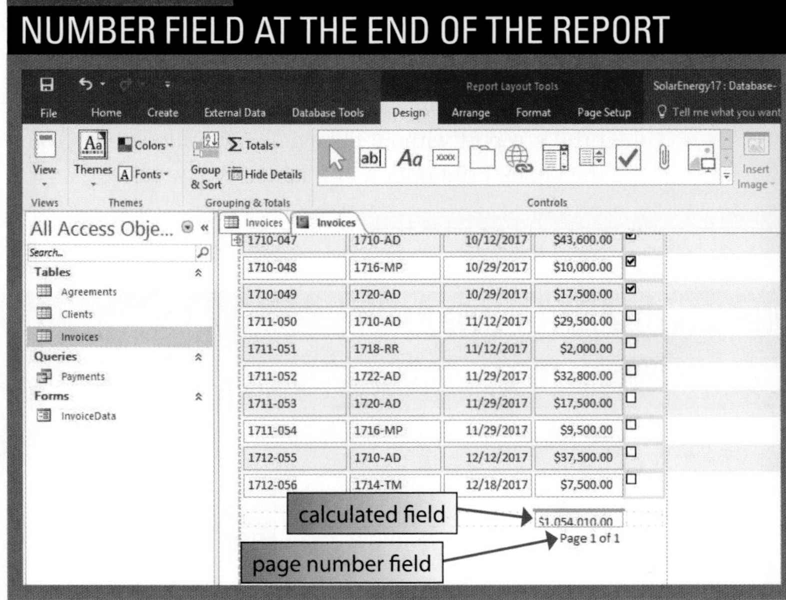

Begin Activity

Delete a calculated field in a report.

1. Scroll to the bottom of the report. A calculated Amount Total field containing a total dollar amount was added at the bottom of the Amount column. Refer to Exhibit 17-26.
2. Click the **Amount Total field** ($1,054,010.00), and then press the **Delete key**. The field is deleted from the report, and the report scrolls back to the top of the page.
3. Scroll to the bottom of the report, click the **field above the page number field** (with one border as a solid line), and then press the **Delete key**.
4. Scroll back to the bottom of the page. The stray blank line was deleted.
5. Click the **page number field**. An orange box surrounds the field.
6. Point to the **selected page number field** so that the pointer changes to ⁺✥. Drag the **page number field** to the left as far as it will go.
7. On the ribbon, click the **Report Layout Tools Format tab**. In the Font group, click the **Align Left button** ☰. The text in the selected field is left aligned.

End Activity

17-7f Viewing a Report in Print Preview

In Layout view, the report doesn't show how many pages the report includes. To see this, you need to switch to Print Preview. **Print Preview** shows exactly how the

Print Preview The Access view that shows exactly how a report will look when printed.

report will look when printed. When you switch to Print Preview, the ribbon changes to include only the Print Preview tab, which includes tools and options for printing the report as well as for changing the page size, the page layout, and how the report is displayed in Print Preview. Exhibit 17-27 shows the report at One Page zoom in Print Preview.

Begin Activity

View a report in Print Preview.

1. On the ribbon, click the **Report Layout Tools Design tab**. In the Views group, click the **View button arrow**, and then click **Print Preview**. The first page of the report is displayed in Print Preview, and the Print Preview tab replaces all of the other tabs on the ribbon.
2. On the Print Preview tab, in the Zoom group, click the **One Page button** (even if it is already selected). Refer back to Exhibit 17-27.
3. On the page navigation bar, click the **Next Page button** twice. The second and then the third page of the report are displayed in Print Preview.
4. On the Print Preview tab, in the Zoom group, click the **Zoom button**. The zoom level changes back to 100%.
5. Scroll down to see the bottom of the third page of the report. "Page 3 of 3" appears at the bottom of the page.
6. On the Quick Access Toolbar, click the **Save button**. The Save As dialog box opens.
7. Save the report as **InvoiceDetails**. The tab displays the new report name, and the report appears in the Navigation Pane.

End Activity

17-7g Printing a Report

A report is often printed and then distributed to others to review. Although table and query datasheets can be printed, they are usually used for viewing and entering data; reports are generally used for printing the data in a database. You can change the print settings in the Print dialog box, which you open by clicking the Print button in the Print group on the Print Preview tab or by clicking Print on the Print tab in Backstage view. You can also print a report without changing any print settings using the Quick Print option in Backstage view.

EXHIBIT 17-27 FIRST PAGE OF THE REPORT IN PRINT PREVIEW

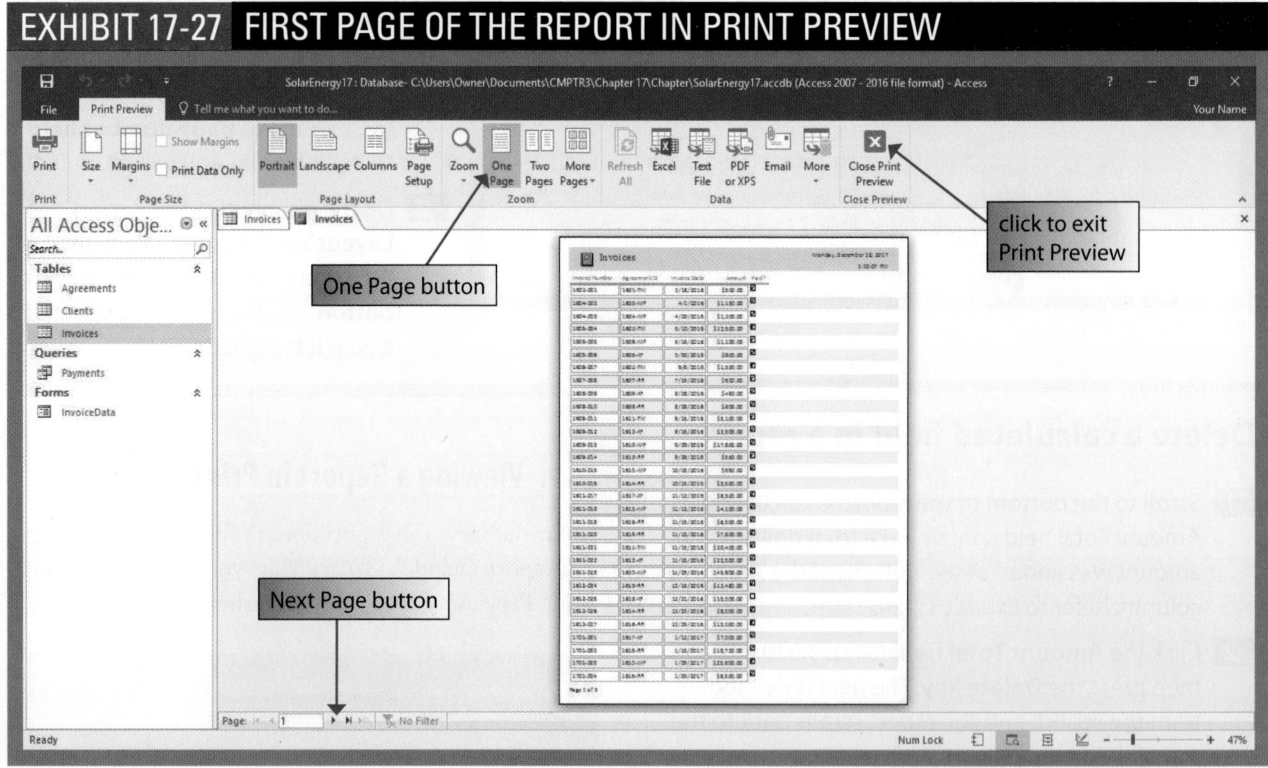

Begin Activity

Print a report.

1. On the Print Preview tab, in the Print group, click the **Print button**. The Print dialog box opens.

TIP: You can also click the File tab, click Print in the navigation bar, and then click Print on the Print screen.

2. Check the printer name in the Name box. If it is not correct, click the **Name box arrow**, and then click the printer you want to use.
3. If you want to print the report, click **OK;** if you don't want to print the report, click **Cancel**. The dialog box closes, and the report prints with the default print settings.
4. Close the report.

End Activity

EXHIBIT 17-28 COMPACTING A DATABASE

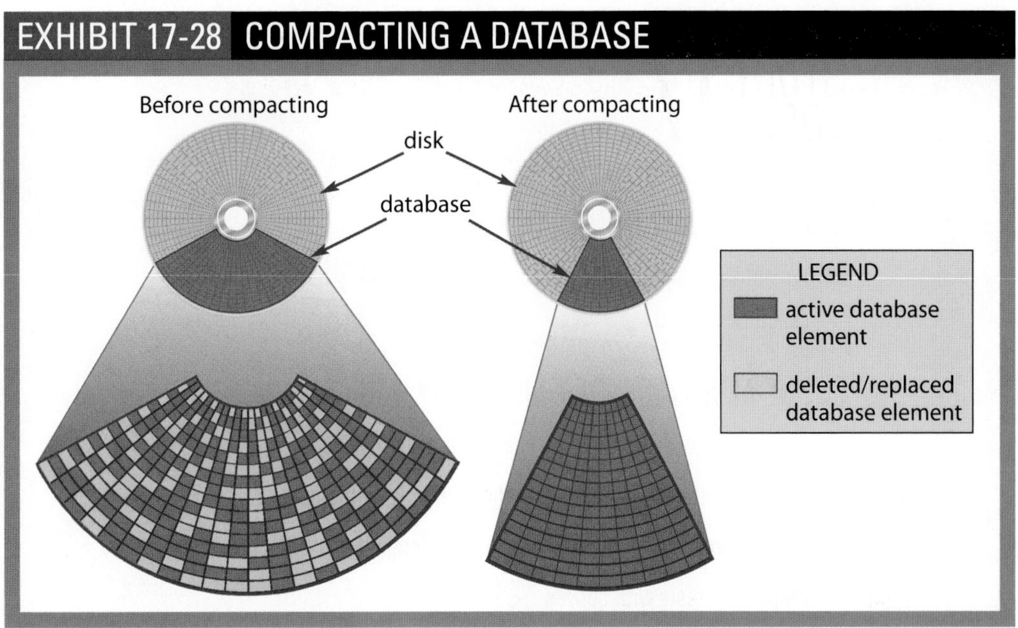

17-8 COMPACTING AND REPAIRING A DATABASE

Each time you open and work in a database, the size of the database increases. In addition, when you delete records or when you delete or replace database objects—such as queries, forms, and reports—the space they occupied does not become available for other records or objects until you compact the database. As illustrated in Exhibit 17-28, **compacting** a database rearranges the data and objects in a database to decrease its file size, making more space available and letting you open and close the database more quickly.

When you compact a database, Access repairs the database at the same time. In many cases, Access detects that a database is damaged when you try to open it and gives you the option to compact and repair it at that time. For example, the data in a database might become damaged, or corrupted, if you close Access suddenly by turning off your computer. If you think your database might be damaged because it is behaving unpredictably, you can use the Compact & Repair Database option to fix it.

Begin Activity

Compact and repair a database.

1. On the ribbon, click the **File tab**. Backstage view opens with the Info screen displayed.
2. Click the **Compact & Repair Database button**. Backstage view closes, and the database is compacted and repaired.
3. Close the database.

TIP: To compact and repair a database every time you close the file, click the File tab, click Options, click Current Database, and then select the Compact on Close check box.

End Activity

compact To rearrange data and objects in a database to decrease its file size.

STUDY TOOLS 17

READY TO STUDY? IN THE BOOK, YOU CAN:

- ☐ Rip out the Chapter Review Card, which includes key terms and key chapter concepts.

ONLINE AT WWW.CENGAGEBRAIN.COM, YOU CAN:

- ☐ Review key concepts from the chapter in a short video.
- ☐ Explore creating a database with the interactive infographic.
- ☐ Practice what you've learned with more Practice It and On Your Own exercises.
- ☐ Prepare for tests with quizzes.
- ☐ Review the key terms with flashcards.

QUIZ YOURSELF

1. What is a field?
2. What is a record?
3. How are tables related in a relational database?
4. Explain the difference between a primary and a foreign key.
5. What does the Data Type property do?
6. Describe how the data in a table is displayed in Datasheet view.
7. Describe how a table's contents appear in Design view.
8. When you create a new table in Datasheet view, which field does Access create, by default, as the primary key field for the new table, and what are its default field name and data type?
9. In Datasheet view, what do the pencil symbol and the star symbol at the beginning of a record represent?
10. What is a property?
11. What does the Caption property do?
12. What is a query?
13. What is a form?
14. What is a report?
15. When you create a form using the Form tool, in which view does the form open?
16. What happens when you compact a database?

PRACTICE IT

Practice It 17-1

1. Start Access, and create a new, blank database named **Customers.**
2. Add the following fields to the table in the order shown, leaving the first field named ID:

Short Text	**Company**
Short Text	**FirstName**
Short Text	**LastName**
Short Text	**Phone**
Date/Time	**CustomerSince**

3. Resize the CustomerSince column width so it fits the column name.
4. Save the table as **Customers**.
5. Enter the following records in the Customers table:

	Record 1	Record 2
Company	**Waterville Electric**	**Singing Creek Resort**
FirstName	**Mina**	*your first name*
LastName	**Laleek**	*your last name*
Phone	**207-555-6869**	**207-555-3132**
CustomerSince	**1/12/2016**	**11/29/2017**

6. Save the table, and then switch to Design view. For each field, set the following field size or format and caption:

	Field Size/Format	Caption
Company	**150**	
FirstName	**20**	**First Name**
LastName	**25**	**Last Name**
Phone	**15**	
CustomerSince	**Long Date**	**Customer Since**

7. Add a new field as the last field in the Customers table with the field name **CallAM**, the Yes/No data type, a Format property of Yes/No, and a Caption property of **Call before 9?**. Make sure the Default Value property is No.
8. Add the following descriptions to the Description property for each of the fields listed below:

ID	**Primary key**
CallAM	**Indicates whether customer has given permission for us to call before 9:00 am**

9. Save the table, and then switch the table to Datasheet view. Resize all the columns so that each column is wide enough to display the widest entry in the column.
10. In the Call before 9? column, select the check boxes for both records.
11. Save and close the table, and then compact and repair the database.
12. Close the database.
13. Open the data file **Tree17** located in the Chapter 17\Practice It folder. Save the database as **TreeRemoval17**.
14. In the ServiceContracts table, set the ContractNum field to be the primary key, and then save and close the table.
15. In Design view for the Invoices table, move the Paid field so it follows the InvAmt field, and then save and close the table.
16. In Design view for the Customers table, add a new Short Text field named **Email** between the FirstName and Phone fields, and then save and close the table.
17. Create a query named **AllAmounts** that includes the ContractNum and ContractAmt fields from the ServiceContracts table. Close the query.
18. Create a form based on the ServiceContracts table, and then enter the following as a new record in the form:

Contract Number	**1737**
Client ID	**39**
Amount	**2900**
Contract Date	**12/22/17**
Service Type	**Commercial**

19. Save the form as **ContractsForm**. Display the ServiceContracts table to see the new record, and then close the table and the form.
20. Create a report based on the ServiceContracts table. Resize the Client ID field so it is slightly wider than the field name.
21. At the bottom of the report, delete the calculated ContractAmount Total field and the field that contains the horizontal line. Then drag the page number field as far left as possible, and left-align the contents of that field.
22. Display the report in Print Preview, and then print it if instructed.
23. Save the report as **ContractsReport**, and then close it.
24. Compact and repair the database.
25. Close the database.

Practice It 17-2

1. Start Access, and create a new, blank database named **Classes**.
2. Add the following fields to the table in the order shown, leaving the first field named ID:

Short Text	**SessionName**
Yes/No	**Teens**
Currency	**Cost**
Number	**Length**

3. Save the table as **Sessions**.
4. Enter the following records in the Sessions table:

	Record 1	Record 2
SessionName	**Watercolor I**	*your first and last names*
Teens	**Yes**	**No**
Cost	**75**	**100**
Length	**45**	**60**

5. Resize columns in the datasheet so that the widest value in each field just fits, and then save the table.
6. Switch to Design view, and then for the SessionName field, change the Field Size property to **45** and the Caption property to **Session Name**.
7. Add a new field as the last field in the Class table with the field name **Level**, the Short Text data type, a Description property of **Beginning, Intermediate, or Advanced**, and a Field Size property of **20**. Set the Default Value property to **Beginning**.
8. Add the following descriptions to the Description property for each of the fields listed below:

ID	**Primary key**
Teens	**Does the session allow teen participation?**
Length	**Class duration in minutes**

9. Save and close the table, compact and repair the database, and then close the database.
10. Open the data file **Studio17** located in the Chapter 17\Practice It folder. Save the database as **StudioClasses17**.
11. In the Sessions table, specify that the following classes accept teens: 123-PA, 125-PA, 203-DR, 204-DR, 205-DR, 392-CL, 394-CL, and 410-PH.
12. In Design view, move the Cost field so it follows the Length field. Delete the Level field. Save and close the table.
13. Create a query named **Cost** based on the Sessions table that includes the SessionName, Cost, and Length fields (in that order). Close the query.
14. Create a form based on the Sessions table, and then enter the following as a new record in the Sessions table using the form.

Session ID	**412-PH**
Session Name	**Photography III**
Teens	**No**
Length	**120**
Cost	**300**

15. After entering the record, save the form as **SessionsForm** and then close it.
16. Create a report based on the Sessions table. Resize each field so it is slightly wider than the longest entry (either the field name itself or an entry in the field).
17. Delete the total field and the horizontal line that was added at the bottom. Align the page number field so its right edge is aligned with the right edge of the page (the dashed line). Change the alignment of the text in the page number field so it is right-aligned.
18. Display the report in Print Preview, and then print it.
19. Save the report as **SessionsReport**, and then close it.
20. Close all open objects, and then compact and repair the database.
21. Close the database.

ON YOUR OWN

On Your Own 17-1

1. Open the data file **ContributionsTable17** located in the Chapter 17\On Your Own folder. Save the database as **ContributionsTable17Modified**.
2. Open the Contributions table, and then switch to Design view.
3. Rename the ID field as **OrganizationID**.
4. Set the ContributionID field as the primary key.
5. Set appropriate values for the ContributionID field's Description, Field Size, and Caption properties. (*Hint*: To determine the field size of the ContributionID field, look at the records in the datasheet.)
6. Change the Field Size and Caption properties for the rest of the fields (use the Short Date format for the ContributionDate field, leave the Description field size at 255, use **Pick up?** as the caption for PickUp, and make sure the default value for PickUp is No). Save the table.
7. In Datasheet view, resize the columns as needed so that all of the columns are just wide enough to display the widest values. Save the table, and then close it.
8. In the Navigation Pane, select the Contributions table. Copy the Contributions table to the Clipboard.
9. Open the data file **Contributions17** located in the Chapter 17\On Your Own folder. Save the database as **ContributionsList17**.

10. In ContributionsList17, paste the contents of the Clipboard. In the Paste Table As dialog box that opens, change the table name to **Contributions**, make sure the Structure and Data option button is selected, and then click OK.
11. Open the Organizations table, and then delete the Fax and Notes fields from the table. Save and close the table.
12. Use the Simple Query Wizard to create a query that includes all the fields in the Contributors table except the ContributorID field. Save the query as **ContributorPhoneList**.
13. Sort the query results by the Last Name column. (*Hint*: Make the Last Name column the current field, and then click the appropriate button on the Home tab in the Sort & Filter group.)
14. Save and close the query.
15. Create a form based on the Contributors table.
16. In the new form, navigate to record 24. In Form view, change the first name to your first initial and your last name (for example, *JSmith*). Click in another box, and then click the AutoCorrect Options button that appears. On the menu, click the command that changes the name back so that your last name begins with an uppercase letter.
17. In Layout view, change the font style of each of the labels (Contributor ID, First Name, Last Name, and Phone) to bold.
18. Print the form for the current record only.
19. Save the form as **ContributorInfo**, and then close it.
20. Create a report based on the Contributors table.
21. In Layout view, resize each field so it is slightly wider than the longest entry (either the field name itself or an entry in the field).
22. At the bottom of the report, make adjustments as necessary so that there are no extra fields and so that the page number is left-aligned.
23. Save the report as **ContributorList**.
24. Display the report in Print Preview, and verify that the fields and page number fit within the page area. Print the report, and then close it.
25. Compact and repair the database, and then close it. If a dialog box opens asking if it is OK to empty the Clipboard, click Yes.
26. Open the **ContributionsTable17Modified** database, compact and repair it, and then close it. If a dialog box opens asking if it is OK to empty the Clipboard, click Yes.

Part 8
ACCESS
2016

18 Maintaining and Querying a Database

© Blend Images/Getty Images

LEARNING OBJECTIVES After studying this chapter, you will be able to:

18-1 Maintain database records

18-2 Work with queries in Design view

18-3 Sort and filter data

18-4 Define table relationships

18-5 Create a multitable query

18-6 Add criteria to a query

18-7 Create a copy of a query

18-8 Add multiple criteria to queries

18-9 Create a calculated field

18-10 Use a property sheet

18-11 Use functions in a query

After finishing this chapter, go to **PAGE 560** for **STUDY TOOLS**.

18-1 MAINTAINING DATABASE RECORDS

Designing and creating a database is just the beginning. Once the database structure is developed, the ongoing work of record keeping begins. Data is constantly changing. People regularly get new phone numbers and email addresses. Invoices are sent and then paid. Customer activity is ongoing, and tracking this accurately leads to developing new strategies for promoting services. So, no matter what kind of information the database contains—customer, contract, invoice, or asset data, to name just a few—the information must be accurate and current to be of value. This requires continual and diligent entering and updating of records. Maintaining a database involves adding new records, updating the field values of existing records, and deleting outdated records to keep the database current and accurate.

18-1a Editing Field Values

Records often need to be edited to update or correct a field value. For example, information, such as a phone number or email address, might have changed, or the original record might have been entered inaccurately, and as a result, it contains an error. To replace a field value, you select it in the table datasheet and then type the new entry. To edit a field value, position the insertion point in the field value, and use standard editing techniques to delete and insert text as needed.

FYI **NAVIGATE AND EDIT FIELDS**

The F2 key is a toggle that you use to switch between navigation mode and editing mode. In navigation mode, Access selects an entire field value. The entry you type while in navigation mode replaces the highlighted field value. In editing mode, you can insert or delete characters in a field value. You can use the mouse or the keyboard to move the location of the insertion point, as you have done in Word and Excel.

F2

© deepspacedave/Shutterstock.com

Begin Activity

Move around the datasheet, and modify records.

1. Open the data file **Energy18** located in the Chapter 18\Chapter folder. Save the database as **SolarEnergy18**.
2. In the Navigation Pane, double-click the **Clients table**. The table opens in Datasheet view. In the first record, the field value for the first field—the Client ID field—is selected.
3. Press the **Ctrl+End keys**. The last field—the Email field—in the last record—record 35—in the Clients table is selected.
4. Press the **Up Arrow key**. The Email field value for record 34, the second to last record, is now selected.
5. Press the **Shift+Tab keys**. The Phone field value for record 34 is selected.
6. Click at the end of the **Phone field value for record 34** to position the insertion point to the right of the phone number. Press the **Backspace key** to delete the 0, type **4** as the new final digit of the phone number, and then press the **Enter key**. The Phone field value for record 34 is updated.

   TIP: Remember that changes to field values are saved when you move to a new field or another record or when you close the table.

7. Press the **Home key**. The Client ID field value for record 34 is now selected.
8. Press the **Ctrl+Home keys**. The Client ID field value for the first record is selected.
9. Press the **Down Arrow key** twice, and then press the **Tab key** to select the Last Name field value for the third record.
10. Type **Blake**. Press the **Tab key** to select the First Name field value for the third record, type **David**, and then press the **Tab key** to move to the next field.

End Activity

18-1b Finding and Replacing Data

As a database grows, the number of records becomes numerous—too numerous to scroll and search for a specific record that you need to update or delete. Instead of scrolling the table datasheet to find the field value you need to change or delete, you can use the Find and

Replace dialog box to locate a specific field value in a table, query datasheet, or form. See Exhibit 18-1. In the Find and Replace dialog box, you specify the value you want to find, where to search for that value, and whether to locate all or part of a field value. You also can choose to search up or down from the currently selected record. If you want to substitute a different field value, you can enter that value on the Replace tab.

EXHIBIT 18-1 FIND AND REPLACE DIALOG BOX

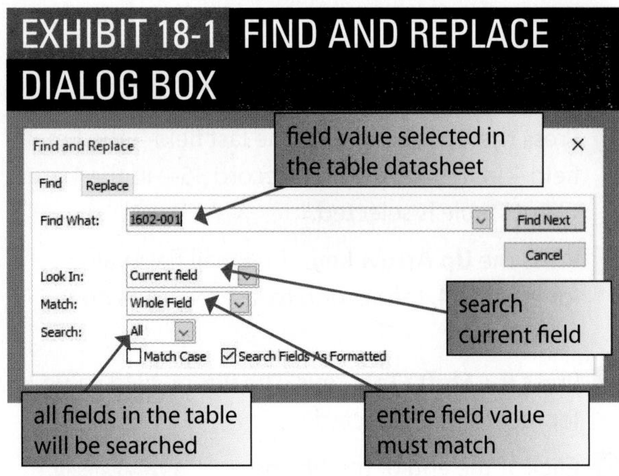

Begin Activity

Find data.

1 Open the **Invoices table** in Datasheet view. The Invoice Number field value for the first record is selected. This is the field you want to search.

2 On the Home tab, in the Find group, click the **Find button**. The Find and Replace dialog box opens with the value in the Find What box selected. This value is the Invoice Number field value for the first record in the Invoices table. Refer back to Exhibit 18-1.

3 In the Find What box, type **1706-033** to replace the selected value. You want to find the record for invoice number 1706-033.

4 Click **Find Next**. The datasheet scrolls to the record for invoice number 1706-033 (record number 63) and selects the Invoice Number field value.

5 In the Find and Replace dialog box, click **Cancel**. The Find and Replace dialog box closes.

6 For invoice number 1706-033, click in the **Amount box**, and then edit the value to **$14,750.00**.

7 Close the **Invoices table**.

End Activity

18-1c Deleting a Record

Deleting a record removes all of the field values for that record from the database. Before you delete a record, you must select the entire row for the record in the datasheet. Then, you can delete the selected record using the Delete button in the Records group on the Home tab or the Delete Record command on the shortcut menu. Keep in mind that the deletion of a record is permanent and cannot be undone.

Begin Activity

Delete a record.

1 In the Clients table, find the record for the client with the last name **Velazquez**.

2 Click **the row selector** to select the entire record for the client with the last name Velazquez.

3 On the Home tab, in the Records group, click the **Delete button**. A dialog box appears, confirming that you want to delete the record and reminding you that you cannot undo this deletion.

4 Click **Yes**. The dialog box closes, and the record is removed from the table.

5 Close the **Clients table**.

End Activity

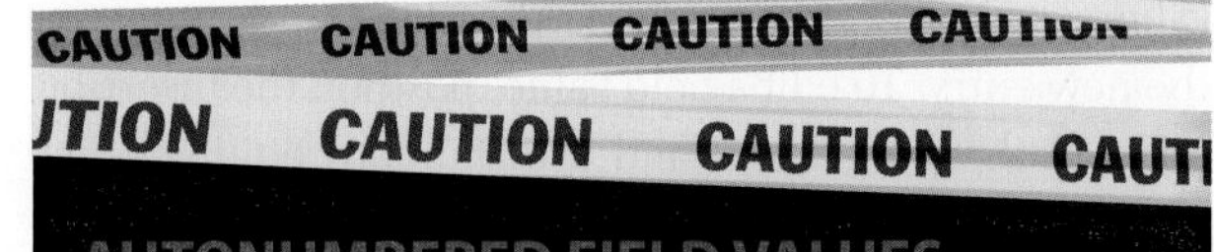

AUTONUMBERED FIELD VALUES

Each value generated by a field is unique. When you use the AutoNumber data type to define the primary key field, the AutoNumber data type ensures that all primary key field values are unique. When you delete a record that has an AutoNumber field, the corresponding value is also deleted and cannot be reused. After deleting a record with an AutoNumber field, you might see gaps in the numbers used for the field values.

18-2 WORKING WITH QUERIES IN DESIGN VIEW

Database records can also be used to monitor and analyze other aspects of the business by creating and using queries to retrieve information from the database.

Queries can also be saved so anyone can run the queries at any time, modify them as needed, or use them as the basis for designing new queries to meet additional information requirements. You have used the Simple Query Wizard to create a query based on one table. You can also create queries in Design view. When you do this, you are constructing a query by example. **Query by example (QBE)** retrieves the information that precisely matches the example you provide of the information being requested. Queries can be based on one table, on multiple tables, on other queries, or on a combination of tables and queries. For example, you might use a query to find records in the Clients table for only those clients who have unpaid invoices as recorded in the Invoices table.

FYI

DESIGNING QUERIES VS. USING A QUERY WIZARD

More specialized, technical queries, such as finding duplicate records in a table, are best created using a Query Wizard. A Query Wizard prompts you for information by asking a series of questions and then creates the appropriate query based on your answers. You used the Simple Query Wizard to display only some of the fields in the Invoices table. The other Query Wizards can create more complex queries. For common, informational queries, it is often easier to design the query yourself than to use a Query Wizard.

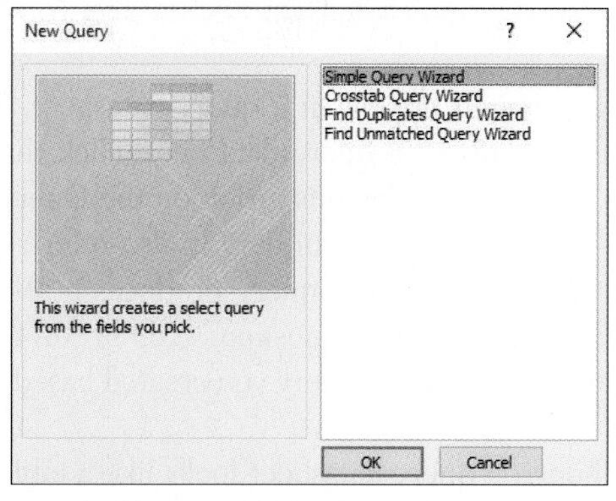

18-2a Designing a Select Query

Most questions about data are general queries in which you specify the fields and records you want to select. These common requests for information, such as "Which clients are located in Berkeley?" or "How many invoices have been paid?", are select queries. A **select query** is a query in which you specify the fields and records you want Access to select. The answer to a select query is returned in a query datasheet.

When you design a query in Design view, you specify which fields to include in the query. To begin, you click the Query Design button in the Queries group on the Create tab. This opens a new Query window in Design view with the Show Table dialog box open. See Exhibit 18-2.

EXHIBIT 18-2 SHOW TABLE DIALOG BOX

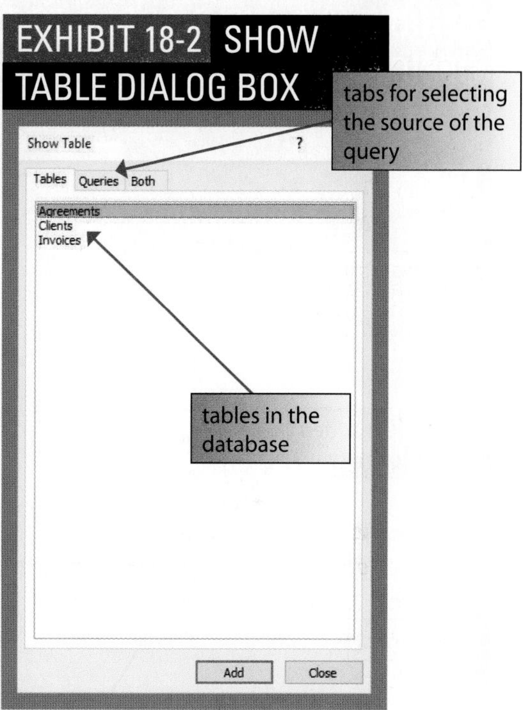

In this dialog box, click the table and query names of the tables and queries on which you are basing your query, and then click Add to add the field lists from those tables and queries to the top portion of the Query window. The bottom portion of the Query window contains the **design grid**, which is the area to which you add the fields and record-selection criteria

query by example (QBE) A query that retrieves the information that precisely matches the example you provide of the information being requested.

select query A query in which you specify the fields and records you want Access to select.

design grid The bottom portion of the Query window in Design view to which you add the fields and record-selection criteria for a query.

for your query. Each column in the design grid contains specifications about a field being used in the query. Exhibit 18-3 shows the field list from the Clients table added to the top portion of the Query window and the ClientID field added to the design grid. In the design grid, the field name appears in the Field box, and the table name that contains the field appears in the Table box. The selected Show check box indicates that the field will be displayed in the datasheet after you run the query.

EXHIBIT 18-3 FIELD ADDED TO THE DESIGN GRID

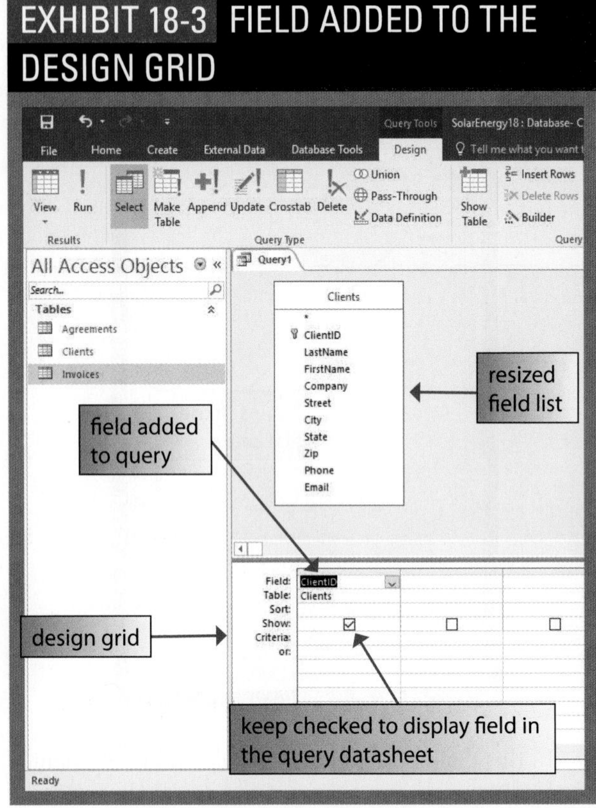

Begin Activity

Design a select query.

1 On the ribbon, click the **Create tab**. In the Queries group, click the **Query Design button**. The Query window opens in Design view. The Show Table dialog box opens with the Tables tab selected. The three tables in the database are listed on the Tables tab. Refer back to Exhibit 18-2.

recordset The result of a query, which is a set of records that answers the question.

2 In the list, click **Clients**, and then click **Add**. The field list for the Clients table is added to the Query window.

PROBLEM? If the wrong table is added to the Query window, click **Close** in the dialog box, right-click **the table name** in the field list in the Query window, and then click **Remove Table**. Click the **Show Table button** in the Query Setup group on the Query Tools Design tab, and then repeat Step 2.

3 In the Show Table dialog box, click **Close**. The Show Table dialog box closes.

4 Point to the **bottom border** of the Clients field list to change the pointer to ⇕, and then drag the **bottom border** of the Clients field list down until the vertical scroll bar in the field list disappears and all of the fields are visible. (Email is the last field in the list.)

5 In the Clients field list, double-click **ClientID**. The field is placed in the Field box in the first column of the design grid. Refer back to Exhibit 18-3.

6 In the Clients field list, click **Company**, and then drag Company down to the **second column Field box** in the design grid. When the pointer changes to ⊞, release the mouse button. The Company field is placed in the Field box in the second column in the design grid.

PROBLEM? If you add the wrong field, click anywhere in that field's column in the design grid, and then click the **Delete Columns button** in the Query Setup group on the Query Tools Design tab.

7 Add the **FirstName**, **LastName**, **City**, **Email**, and **Phone** fields to the third through seventh columns in the design grid.

End Activity

Query results appear in a query datasheet. To see the query results in a query datasheet, click the View or Run button in the Results group on the Query Tools Design tab. The result of a query is also referred to as a **recordset** because the query produces a set of records that answers your question. Exhibit 18-4 shows the query results for the query you created based on the Clients table.

Although a query datasheet looks like a table datasheet, a query datasheet is temporary. Its contents are based on the criteria specified in the query design grid. In contrast, a table datasheet shows the permanent data in a table. Data in a query datasheet is not duplicated; it is the same data that is contained in the table datasheet displayed in a different way. If you update data in a query datasheet, the data in the underlying table will be updated with those changes.

EXHIBIT 18-4 QUERY DATASHEET WITH QUERY RESULTS

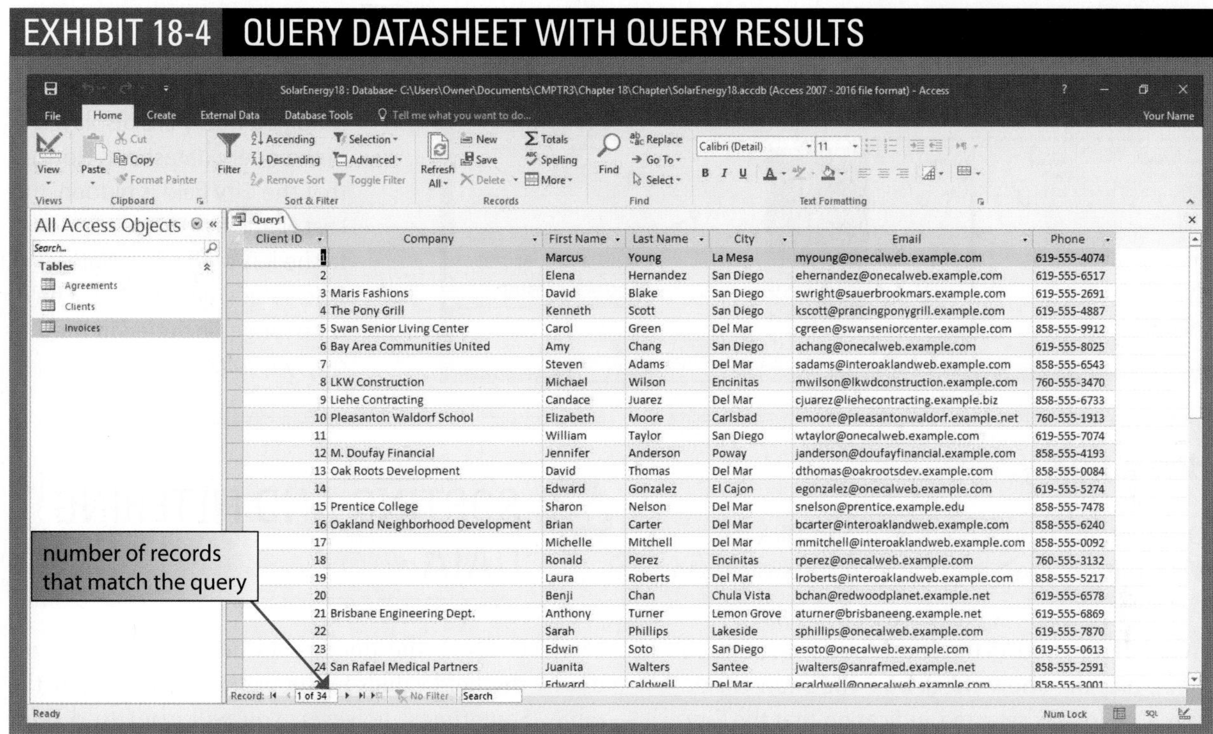

Begin Activity

Run and save a query.

1 On the ribbon, on the Query Tools Design tab, in the Results group, click the **Run button**. The query runs, and the results are displayed in Datasheet view. The fields you added to the design grid appear in the datasheet in the same order as in the design grid. The records are displayed in order based on the values in the primary key field, Client ID. A total of 34 records are displayed in the datasheet. Refer back to Exhibit 18-4.

2 On the Quick Access Toolbar, click the **Save button**. The small Save As dialog box opens.

3 In the Query Name box, type **ClientContact**, and then click **OK**. The query name appears on the tab for the query object and also in the Queries group in the Navigation Pane.

End Activity

18-2b Modifying a Query

If the results of a query are not what you expected or require, you can make changes to the query. For example, you can hide a field's values in the query results, change the order in which the fields appear in the query results, or add fields to or remove fields from the query.

Sometimes, you might want to hide a field in a query's results. For example, if a query lists all clients who live in San Francisco, you don't need to see the City field listing the same value—San Francisco—for every record. To hide a field in the query results, click the Show check box in that field's column in the design grid to deselect it.

Keep in mind that hiding a field's values does not remove the field from the query design. To delete a field from the query design, click in its column and then click the Delete Columns button in the Query Setup group on the Query Tools Design tab.

If you want the fields to appear in a different order in the query results, you can change the order of the fields in the design grid. To move a field, first select the field's column in the design grid. The thin bar above each column in the design grid is the **field selector**, and you click the field selector to select the entire column in the design grid. After a field is selected, you can drag it left or right and drop it when the vertical line is in the location where you want the field to be inserted, as shown in Exhibit 18-5.

field selector The thin bar above each column in the design grid in a Query window that you click to select the entire field.

EXHIBIT 18-5 SELECTED FIELD BEING MOVED IN THE DESIGN GRID

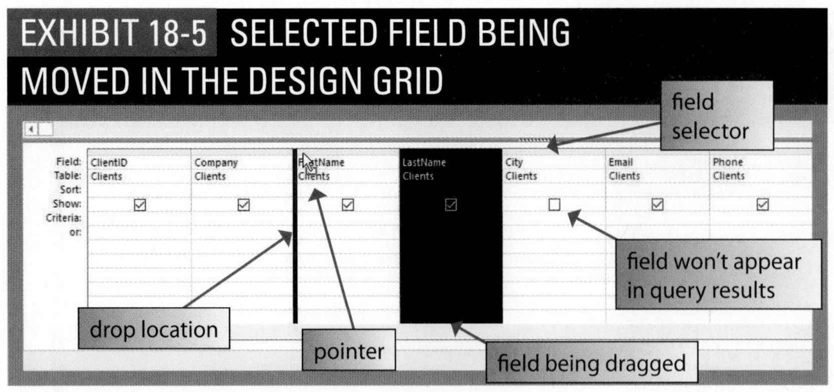

Begin Activity

Modify a query.

1 On the Home tab, in the Views group, click the **View button**. The ClientContact query switches to Design view.

2 In the design grid, in the Show row for the City column, click the **Show check box**. The Show check box is no longer selected, indicating that the City field will still be included in the query but will not appear in the results.

3 Point to the **LastName field selector** so that the pointer changes to ⬇, and then click. The entire field is selected.

4 Point to the **LastName field selector** so that the pointer is ⇖, and then drag the selected field to the left until the vertical line to the left of the FirstName field is highlighted. Refer back to Exhibit 18-5.

5 Release the mouse button. The LastName field moves to the left of the FirstName field.

6 In the design grid, click in the **Email column**. On the Query Tools Design tab, in the Query Setup group, click the **Delete Columns button**. The Email field is removed from the query design.

TIP: You can also click a field selector to select that column and then press the Delete key to delete a field from a query design.

7 On the Query Tools Design tab, in the Results group, click the **Run button**. The results of the modified query are displayed in the query datasheet. Notice that the City field is hidden, the Last Name field values appear to the left of the First Name field values, and the Email field is no longer included in the query results.

End Activity

sort The process of rearranging records in a specified order or sequence.

sort field The field used to determine the order of records in the datasheet.

filter A set of restrictions placed on records in a datasheet or form to temporarily isolate a subset of the records.

18-3 SORTING AND FILTERING DATA

The records in the query datasheet are listed in order by the field values in the primary key field for the table. Sometimes, however, you will want to display the records in a specific order, such as in alphabetical order by city. Other times, you will want to display a subset of the records, such as only the records for a certain city. To make these changes, you can sort and filter the data.

Sorting is the process of rearranging records in a specified order or sequence. For example, you might sort client information by the Last Name field to more easily find specific clients, or you might sort agreements by the Agreement Value field to monitor the financial aspects of a business. When you sort data in a query, only the records in the query datasheet are rearranged; the records in the underlying tables remain in their original order.

To sort records, you must select the **sort field**, which is the field used to determine the order of records in the datasheet. You sort records in either ascending (increasing) or descending (decreasing) order, as described in Exhibit 18-6.

A **filter** is a set of restrictions you place on the records in a datasheet or form to temporarily isolate a subset of the records. A filter lets you view different subsets of displayed records so that you can focus on only the data you need. Unless you save the object with a filter applied, the filter is not available the next time you open the object.

18-3a Sorting in Datasheet View

In Datasheet view, you can click the arrow ▾ on a column heading in the datasheet to open a menu

EXHIBIT 18-6 SORT RESULTS FOR DIFFERENT DATA TYPES

Data type	Ascending sort results	Descending sort results
Short Text, Long Text*	A to Z	Z to A
Number	Lowest to highest numeric value	Highest to lowest numeric value
Date/Time	Oldest to most recent date	Most recent to oldest date
Currency	Lowest to highest numeric value	Highest to lowest numeric value
AutoNumber	Lowest to highest numeric value	Highest to lowest numeric value
Yes/No	Yes (check mark in check box) then No values	No then Yes values

**Note that Long Text fields are sorted on only the first 255 characters*

of options for sorting and filtering field values. Exhibit 18-7 shows the menu that appears when you click the arrow on the Last Name column heading. The first two commands sort the values in the current field in ascending or descending order. You can also click the Ascending and Descending buttons in the Sort & Filter group on the Home tab to sort the data based on the current field. When records are sorted, an arrow appears on the right side of the column heading, indicating the sort order. If you sort in ascending order, the arrow points up. If you sort in descending order, the arrow points down.

EXHIBIT 18-7 MENU THAT APPEARS WHEN YOU CLICK A COLUMN HEADING ARROW

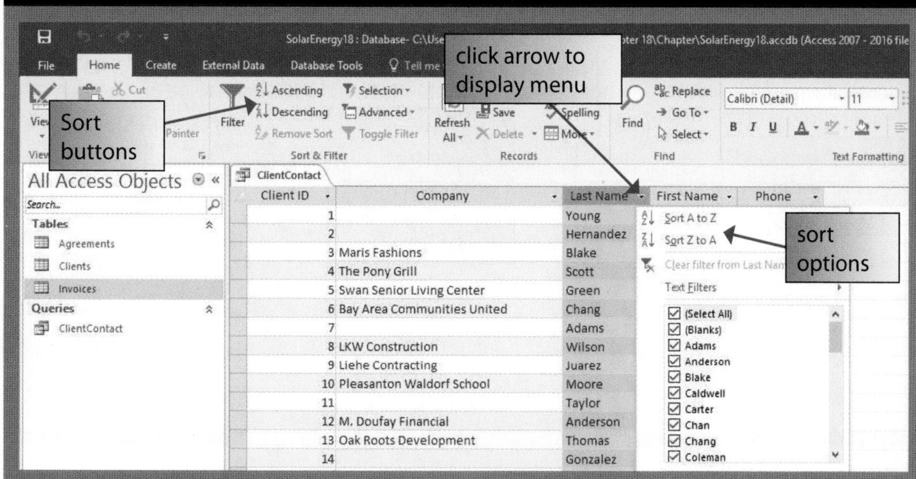

Begin Activity

Use AutoFilter to sort data.

1 In the ClientContact datasheet, click the **Last Name column heading arrow** . A menu opens. Refer to Exhibit 18-7.

2 On the menu, click **Sort A to Z.** The records are rearranged in ascending alphabetical order by last name, as indicated by the up arrow on the right side of the Last Name column heading arrow .

TIP: You can also use the Ascending and Descending buttons in the Sort & Filter group on the Home tab to sort records based on the selected field in a datasheet.

End Activity

18-3b Sorting Multiple Fields in Design View

Sometimes you need to sort using more than one field. The first field you sort by is the primary sort field, the second field you sort by is the secondary sort field, and so on. For example, you might sort a list of clients alphabetically by city. To make it easier to locate a specific name within a city, you can then sort alphabetically by Last Name within each city. In this case, City is the primary sort field, and Last Name is the secondary sort field.

You can select as many as 10 different sort fields. For example, you might sort invoices based on whether they are paid or unpaid. Then you could sort each group of invoices by the invoice date. And finally, you could sort the invoices for each date by the invoice amount.

To sort by two fields in Datasheet view, first apply a sort to the secondary field, and then apply a sort to the primary field. For queries, you can also sort fields in Design view. In Design view, the leftmost sort field in the design grid is the primary sort field, and each remaining sort field is applied from left to right. Exhibit 18-8 shows a query with two sort fields specified.

EXHIBIT 18-8 QUERY WITH TWO SORT FIELDS

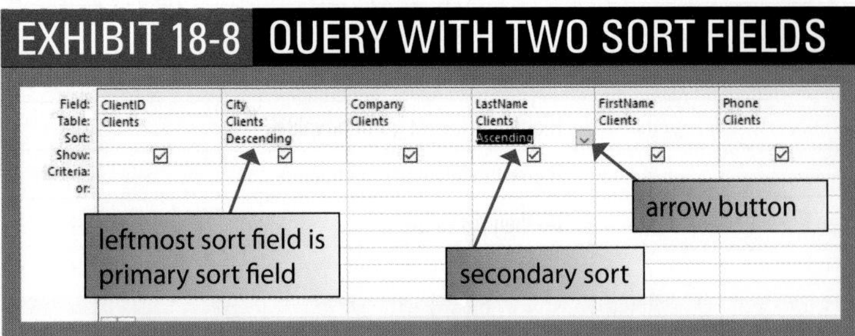

Begin Activity

Sort multiple fields in Design view.

1 On the Home tab, in the Views group, click the **View button**. The ClientContact query switches to Design view. You will sort the query results in reverse alphabetical order by city and then within each city, in alphabetical order by last name.

2 In the design grid, in the City field, click the **Show check box** to select it. The field will again be displayed in the query results.

3 Move the **City field** to the left of the Company field. The City field will appear to the left of the Company field in the query results. This will be the primary sort field.

4 In the design grid, click in the **City column Sort box**. An arrow button appears at the right end of the City column Sort box.

5 Click the **City column Sort box arrow button** to display the sort options, and then click **Descending**. The City field now has a descending sort order. Because the City field is a Short Text field, the field values will be displayed in reverse alphabetical order.

6 Click the **LastName Sort box**, click the **arrow button** , and then click **Ascending**. The LastName field, which will be the secondary sort field because it appears to the right of the primary sort field (City) in the design grid, now has an ascending sort order. Refer back to Exhibit 18-8.

7 On the Query Tools Design tab, in the Results group, click the **Run button**. In the query datasheet, the records appear in descending order based on the values in the City field. Records with the same City field value appear in ascending order by the values in the Last Name field. Compare your screen to Exhibit 18-9.

8 Save the **ClientContact query**. All the design changes—including the sort fields—are saved with the query.

End Activity

EXHIBIT 18-9 QUERY DATASHEET SORTED ON TWO FIELDS

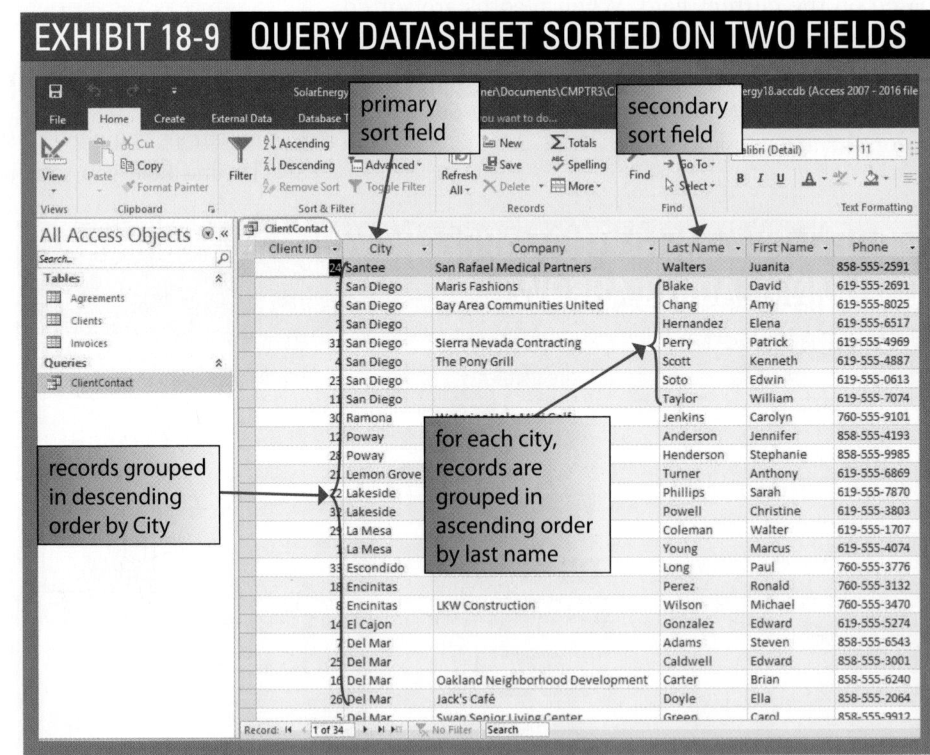

18-3c Filtering Data

There are several methods you can use to filter data.

- **Common filters**—filters the datasheet based on a field value. They are listed on the menu that appears when you click the arrow on the column heading in Datasheet view.

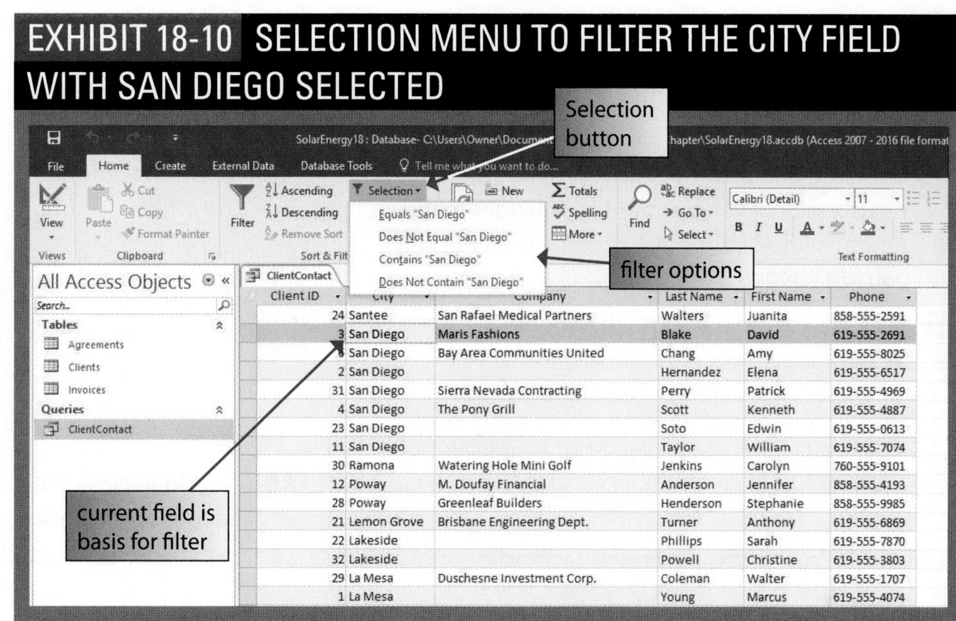

EXHIBIT 18-10 SELECTION MENU TO FILTER THE CITY FIELD WITH SAN DIEGO SELECTED

- **Filter by selection**—filters the datasheet based on a selected field value in a datasheet or form. Exhibit 18-10 shows the Selection menu when San Diego is selected in the CLI City field. The commands on the menu change depending on the data type of the selected field. In this case, you can choose to display records with a City field value that equals the selected value (in this case, San Diego); does not equal the value; contains the value somewhere within the field; or does not contain the value somewhere within the field.
- **Filter by form**—changes the datasheet to display blank fields so that you can choose a value for any blank field to apply a filter that selects only those records containing that value.

When a datasheet has been filtered, *Filtered* appears on the status bar and a Filtered button appears to the right of the navigation buttons. Also, as shown in Exhibit 18-11, the arrow on the column heading for the filtered field changes to a filter icon. To remove the filter and redisplay all the records, click the Toggle Filter button in the Sort & Filter group on the Home tab.

Begin Activity

Filter records by selection.

1. In the ClientContact query datasheet, locate the first occurrence of a City field containing the value **San Diego**, and then click anywhere within that field value.
2. On the Home tab, in the Sort & Filter group, click the **Selection button**. A menu opens with options for the type of filter to apply. Refer back to Exhibit 18-10. You want to display all the records whose City field value equals *San Diego*.
3. In the Selection menu, click **Equals "San Diego"**. The filtered results appear in the datasheet, and the filter icon appears in the column heading for the City field. Only seven records have a City field value of *San Diego*. Refer back to Exhibit 18-11.
4. On the Home tab, in the Sort & Filter group, click the **Toggle Filter button**. The filter is removed, and all 34 records are redisplayed in the query datasheet.

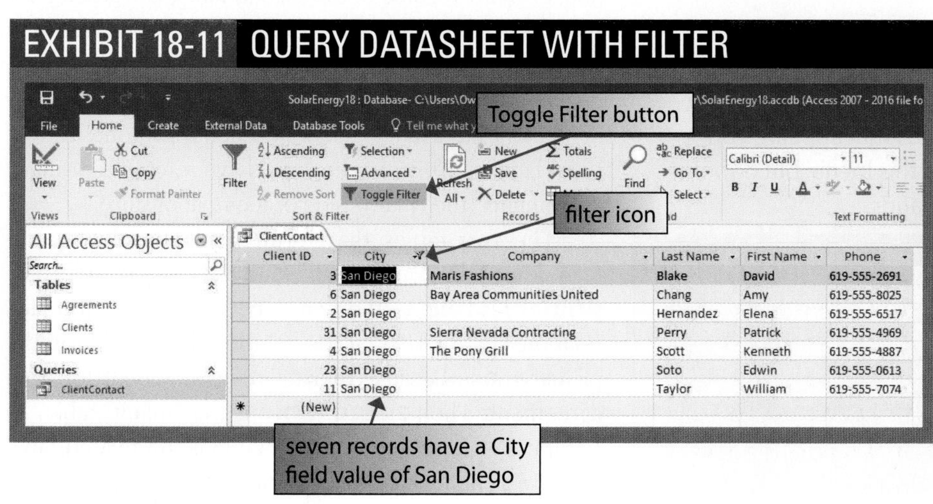

EXHIBIT 18-11 QUERY DATASHEET WITH FILTER

5 On the Home tab, in the Sort & Filter group, click the **Toggle Filter button** again. The filter is reapplied and only the records with San Diego in the City field appear.

6 Close the **ClientContact query**. A dialog box appears, asking if you want to save changes to the design of the query which now includes the filter you just created.

7 Click **Yes** to save and close the query.

End Activity

You can apply more than one filter to a datasheet. When you apply the second filter, that filter is applied only to the records displayed as a result of applying the first filter.

Begin Activity

Apply two filters to a datasheet.

1 Open the **Invoices table**.

2 In the datasheet, click in the **Invoice Date field** for any record.

3 On the Home tab, in the Sort & Filter group, click the **Selection button**. In the Selection menu, click **Between**. The Between Dates dialog box opens.

4 In the Oldest box, type **1/1/2017**. In the Newest box, type **12/31/2017**.

5 Click **OK**. The filter is applied to the query datasheet, which now shows the 85 records of invoices dated 2017.

6 In the datasheet, click in the **Amount field for the first record**.

7 On the Home tab, in the Sort & Filter group, click the **Selection button**. The menu that opens contains commands to display values related to the value in the selected field.

8 Click the **Selection button** again to close the menu. In the datasheet, click the **Amount column heading arrow**, and then point to **Number Filters**. The same commands that appeared on the Selection menu are on this menu, but no value appears next to the commands.

9 On the submenu, click **Greater Than**. The Custom Filter dialog box opens with the insertion point in the Amount is greater than or equal to box.

10 Type **100,000**, and then click **OK**. The datasheet now shows only one record—one invoice dated 2017 with an amount greater than $100,000.

11 On the Home tab, in the Sort & Filter group, click the **Toggle Filter button**. The filters are removed.

12 Close the **Invoices table**. A dialog box appears, asking if you want to save changes to the design of the table which now included the filter you just created.

13 Click **No** to close the table without saving the changes to the design.

End Activity

18-4 DEFINING TABLE RELATIONSHIPS

One of the most powerful features of a relational database management system is its ability to define relationships between tables. You use a common field to relate one table to another. The process of relating tables is often called joining tables. When you join tables that have a common field, you can use data from them as if they were one larger table. For example, you can join the Clients and Agreements tables by using the ClientID field in both tables as the common field. Then you can use a query, a form, or a report to display selected data from each table, even though the data is contained in two separate tables. See Exhibit 18-12.

A **one-to-many relationship** exists between two tables when one record in the first table matches zero, one, or many records in the second table, and when each record in the second table matches at most one record in the first table. For example, as shown in Exhibit 18-12, client 13 has two agreements in the Agreements table. Every agreement has a single matching client (the "one" side of the relationship), and a client can have zero, one, or many agreements (the "many" side of the relationship).

The two tables that form a relationship are referred to as the primary table and the related table. The **primary table** is the "one" table in a one-to-many relationship. In Exhibit 18-12, the Clients table is the primary table because there is only one client for each agreement. The **related table** is the "many" table. In Exhibit 18-12, the Agreements table is the related table because a client can have zero, one, or many agreements.

one-to-many relationship A connection between two tables when one record in the primary table matches zero, one, or many records in the related table, and when each record in the related table matches at most one record in the primary table.

primary table The "one" table in a one-to-many relationship.

related table The "many" table in a one-to-many relationship.

EXHIBIT 18-12 ONE-TO-MANY RELATIONSHIP AND QUERY

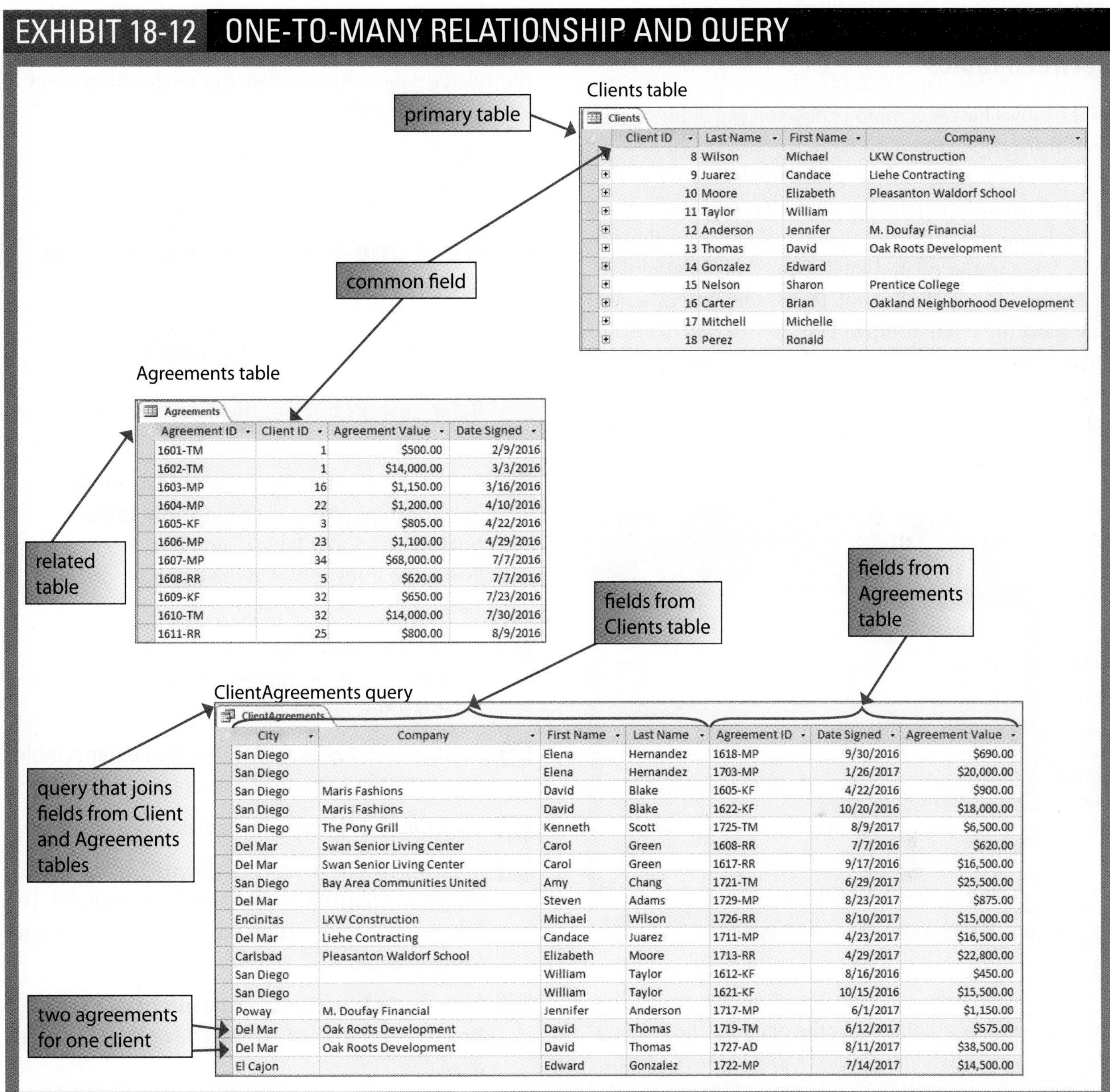

Clients

Client ID	Last Name	First Name	Company
8	Wilson	Michael	LKW Construction
9	Juarez	Candace	Liehe Contracting
10	Moore	Elizabeth	Pleasanton Waldorf School
11	Taylor	William	
12	Anderson	Jennifer	M. Doufay Financial
13	Thomas	David	Oak Roots Development
14	Gonzalez	Edward	
15	Nelson	Sharon	Prentice College
16	Carter	Brian	Oakland Neighborhood Development
17	Mitchell	Michelle	
18	Perez	Ronald	

Agreements

Agreement ID	Client ID	Agreement Value	Date Signed
1601-TM	1	$500.00	2/9/2016
1602-TM	1	$14,000.00	3/3/2016
1603-MP	16	$1,150.00	3/16/2016
1604-MP	22	$1,200.00	4/10/2016
1605-KF	3	$805.00	4/22/2016
1606-MP	23	$1,100.00	4/29/2016
1607-MP	34	$68,000.00	7/7/2016
1608-RR	5	$620.00	7/7/2016
1609-KF	32	$650.00	7/23/2016
1610-TM	32	$14,000.00	7/30/2016
1611-RR	25	$800.00	8/9/2016

ClientAgreements

City	Company	First Name	Last Name	Agreement ID	Date Signed	Agreement Value
San Diego		Elena	Hernandez	1618-MP	9/30/2016	$690.00
San Diego		Elena	Hernandez	1703-MP	1/26/2017	$20,000.00
San Diego	Maris Fashions	David	Blake	1605-KF	4/22/2016	$900.00
San Diego	Maris Fashions	David	Blake	1622-KF	10/20/2016	$18,000.00
San Diego	The Pony Grill	Kenneth	Scott	1725-TM	8/9/2017	$6,500.00
Del Mar	Swan Senior Living Center	Carol	Green	1608-RR	7/7/2016	$620.00
Del Mar	Swan Senior Living Center	Carol	Green	1617-RR	9/17/2016	$16,500.00
San Diego	Bay Area Communities United	Amy	Chang	1721-TM	6/29/2017	$25,500.00
Del Mar		Steven	Adams	1729-MP	8/23/2017	$875.00
Encinitas	LKW Construction	Michael	Wilson	1726-RR	8/10/2017	$15,000.00
Del Mar	Liehe Contracting	Candace	Juarez	1711-MP	4/23/2017	$16,500.00
Carlsbad	Pleasanton Waldorf School	Elizabeth	Moore	1713-RR	4/29/2017	$22,800.00
San Diego		William	Taylor	1612-KF	8/16/2016	$450.00
San Diego		William	Taylor	1621-KF	10/15/2016	$15,500.00
Poway	M. Doufay Financial	Jennifer	Anderson	1717-MP	6/1/2017	$1,150.00
Del Mar	Oak Roots Development	David	Thomas	1719-TM	6/12/2017	$575.00
Del Mar	Oak Roots Development	David	Thomas	1727-AD	8/11/2017	$38,500.00
El Cajon		Edward	Gonzalez	1722-MP	7/14/2017	$14,500.00

Referential integrity is a set of rules to maintain consistency between related tables when data in a database is updated. The referential integrity rules are:

- You cannot add a record to a related table unless a matching record already exists in the primary table, preventing the possibility of **orphaned records**.
- You cannot change the value of the primary key in the primary table if matching records exist in a related table. However, you can select the Cascade Update Related Fields option, which updates the corresponding foreign keys when you change a primary key field value, eliminating the possibility of inconsistent data.
- You cannot delete a record in the primary table if matching records exist in the related table. However, you can select the Cascade Delete Related Records option to delete the record in the primary table as well as all records in the related table that have matching foreign key field values. This option is rarely used because it often leads to related records being unintentionally deleted from the database.

referential integrity A set of rules to maintain consistency between related tables when data in a database is updated.

orphaned record A record in a related table that has no matching record in the primary table.

18-4a Defining a One-to-Many Relationship Between Tables

When tables have a common field, you can define a relationship between them in the Relationships window. To create a relationship, first add the field list for each table in the relationship to the Relationships window. To form the relationship, drag the common field from the primary table to the related table. The Edit Relationships dialog box, shown in Exhibit 18-13, then opens so you can select the relationship options for the two tables. To enforce referential integrity, select that check box. To override the rule that prevents you from changing the value of a primary key in the primary table, select the Cascade Update Related Fields option.

EXHIBIT 18-13 EDIT RELATIONSHIPS DIALOG BOX

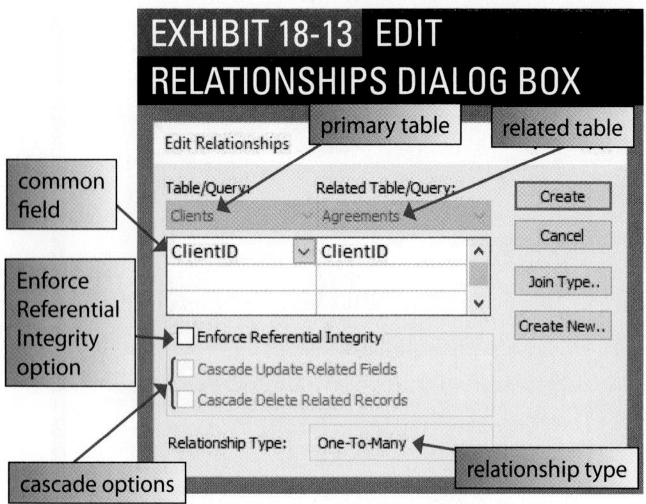

After you close the Edit Relationships dialog box, the relationship is defined. In the window, the relationship is shown with a line—called a join line—connecting the two tables. See Exhibit 18-14. The "1" above the end of the join line attached to the primary table and the infinity symbol above the end of the join line attached to the related table indicate that the relationship is set to enforce referential integrity.

EXHIBIT 18-14 DEFINED RELATIONSHIP IN THE RELATIONSHIPS WINDOW

Begin Activity

Define a one-to-many relationship between tables.

1. On the ribbon, click the **Database Tools tab**. In the Relationships group, click the **Relationships button**. The Relationships window opens.
2. On the Relationship Tools Design tab, in the Relationships group, click the **Show Table button**. The Show Table dialog box opens, listing the three tables in the database on the Tables tab.
3. In the Show Table dialog box, double-click **Clients**. The Clients table's field list is added to the Relationships window.
4. Double-click **Agreements**. The Agreements table's field list is added to the Relationships window.
5. Click **Close**. The Show Table dialog box closes.
6. In the Clients field list, click **ClientID**, and then drag it to **ClientID** in the Agreements field list. The Edit Relationships dialog box opens. Refer back to Exhibit 18-13.
7. Click the **Enforce Referential Integrity check box** to select it. The two cascade options become available.
8. Click the **Cascade Update Related Fields check box** to select it.
9. Click **Create**. The Edit Relationships dialog box closes, and the one-to-many relationship between the two tables is defined. The completed relationship appears in the Relationships window, with the join line connecting the common field of ClientID in each table. Refer back to Exhibit 18-14. In this relationship, Clients is the primary table and Agreements is the related table.
10. On the Quick Access Toolbar, click the **Save button** to save the layout in the Relationships window.
11. Close the **Relationships window**.

End Activity

EXHIBIT 18-15 SUBDATASHEET WITH RELATED RECORDS

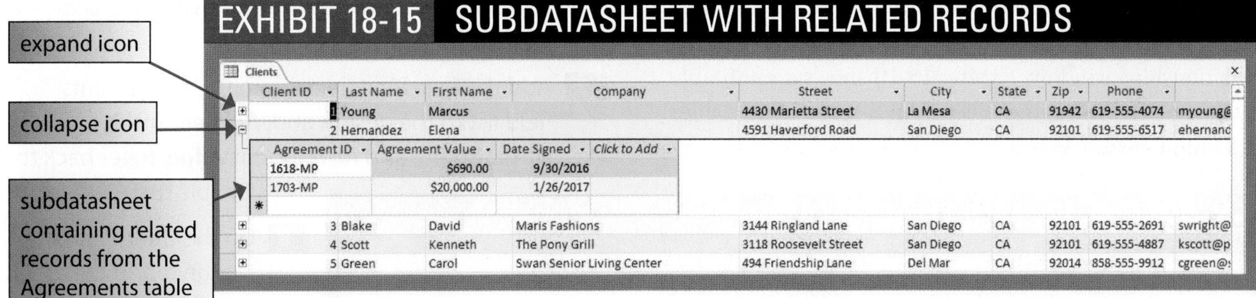

18-4b Working with Related Data in a Subdatasheet

After you define a one-to-many relationship between tables with a common field, the primary table in the relationship contains a **subdatasheet** that displays the records from the related table. Exhibit 18-15 shows the subdatasheet for the second record in the Clients table. When you open the primary table, the subdatasheet for each record in the primary table is collapsed until you expand it by clicking the expand button [−].

If you did not select the option to cascade deletions to related records when you created a relationship between two tables, you cannot delete a record in a primary table that has matching records in a related table. If you want to delete a record from the primary table, you first must delete the related records in the related table. Although you could open the related table and then find and delete the related records, a simpler way is to delete the related records from the primary table's subdatasheet, which deletes the records from the related table.

Begin Activity

Work with related data in a subdatasheet.

1. Open the **Clients table** in Datasheet view. Because this is the primary table in a relationship, expand buttons [+] appear next to each record.
2. To the left of Client ID 2, click the **expand button** [+]. The subdatasheet for this client appears, listing the related records from the Agreements table, and the expand icon changes to a collapse icon [−]. Refer back to Exhibit 18-15.
3. Select the entire row for **Client ID 2**. On the Home tab, in the Records group, click the **Delete button**. A dialog box opens, indicating that you cannot delete the record because the Agreements table contains records that are related to the current client. This occurs because you enforced referential integrity and did not select the option to cascade deletions to related records.
4. Click **OK** to close the dialog box.
5. If necessary, to the left of Customer ID 2, click the **collapse button** [−]. The subdatasheet for that record collapses.
6. Display the **Client ID 3 subdatasheet**. Two related records from the Agreements table for this client appear in the subdatasheet.
7. In the subdatasheet, for Agreement Number 1605-KF, edit the Agreement Value field value to **$900.00**.
8. Collapse the **Client ID 3subdatasheet**.
9. Open the **Agreements table**, find the record for Agreement Number **1605-KF**, and then verify that the agreement value is now $900.00.
10. Close the **Clients** and **Agreements tables**.

End Activity

18-5 CREATING A MULTITABLE QUERY

A **multitable query** is a query based on more than one table. To create a query that retrieves data from multiple tables, the tables must have a common field. Because you established a relationship between the Clients (primary) and Agreements (related) tables based on the common ClientID field that exists in both tables, you can now create a query to display data from both tables at the same time. The one-to-many relationship between

subdatasheet A datasheet that displays the records from a related table in the primary table's datasheet.

multitable query A query based on more than one table.

two tables is shown in the Query window with a join line, which is the same way the relationship is indicated in the Relationships window. Exhibit 18-16 shows a multitable query created using the Clients and Agreements tables in Design view.

EXHIBIT 18-16 MULTITABLE QUERY

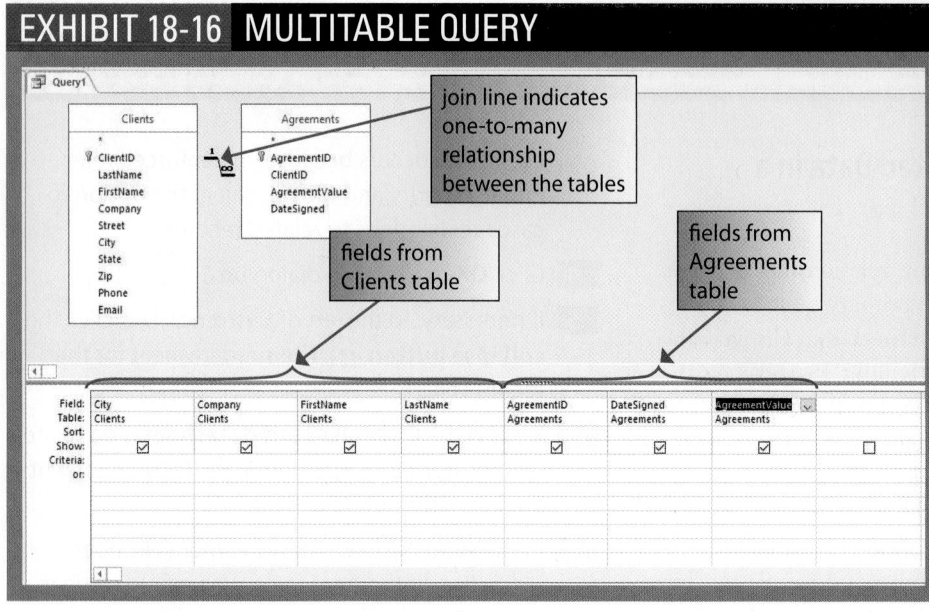

Begin Activity

Create and run a multitable query.

1 On the ribbon, click the **Create tab**. In the Queries group, click the **Query Design button**. The Show Table dialog box appears.

2 Double-click **Clients**, and then double-click **Agreements**. The field lists for the Clients and Agreements tables appear in the Query window with a join line indicating the one-to-many relationship between the tables.

3 In the Show Table dialog box, click **Close**. The dialog box closes.

4 Resize the **Clients field list** so that all the fields in the table are displayed.

5 In the Clients field list, double-click **City** to place this field in the first column of the design grid.

6 Add the following fields from the Clients field list to the design grid: **Company**, **FirstName**, and **LastName**.

7 Add the following fields from the Agreements field list to the design grid: **AgreementID**, **DateSigned**, and **AgreementValue**. Refer back to Exhibit 18-16.

8 On the Query Tools Design tab, in the Results group, click the **Run button**. The query runs, and the results appear in Datasheet view. The selected fields from both the Clients table and the Agreements table appear in the query datasheet. Compare your screen to Exhibit 18-17. The records are displayed in order according to the values in the ClientID field because it is the primary key field in the primary table, even though this field is not included in the query datasheet.

9 Save the query as **ClientAgreements**, and then close it.

End Activity

EXHIBIT 18-17 RESULTS OF A MULTITABLE QUERY

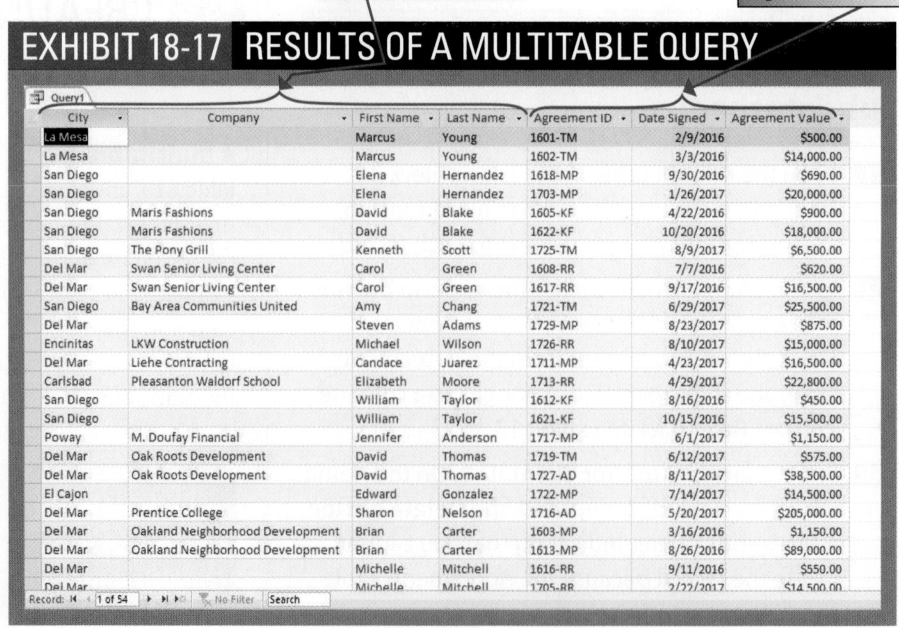

City	Company	First Name	Last Name	Agreement ID	Date Signed	Agreement Value
La Mesa		Marcus	Young	1601-TM	2/9/2016	$500.00
La Mesa		Marcus	Young	1602-TM	3/3/2016	$14,000.00
San Diego		Elena	Hernandez	1618-MP	9/30/2016	$690.00
San Diego		Elena	Hernandez	1703-MP	1/26/2017	$20,000.00
San Diego	Maris Fashions	David	Blake	1605-KF	4/22/2016	$900.00
San Diego	Maris Fashions	David	Blake	1622-KF	10/20/2016	$18,000.00
San Diego	The Pony Grill	Kenneth	Scott	1725-TM	8/9/2017	$6,500.00
Del Mar	Swan Senior Living Center	Carol	Green	1608-RR	7/7/2016	$620.00
Del Mar	Swan Senior Living Center	Carol	Green	1617-RR	9/17/2016	$16,500.00
San Diego	Bay Area Communities United	Amy	Chang	1721-TM	6/29/2017	$25,500.00
Del Mar		Steven	Adams	1729-MP	8/23/2017	$875.00
Encinitas	LKW Construction	Michael	Wilson	1726-RR	8/10/2017	$15,000.00
Del Mar	Liehe Contracting	Candace	Juarez	1711-MP	4/23/2017	$16,500.00
Carlsbad	Pleasanton Waldorf School	Elizabeth	Moore	1713-RR	4/29/2017	$22,800.00
San Diego		William	Taylor	1612-KF	8/16/2016	$450.00
San Diego		William	Taylor	1621-KF	10/15/2016	$15,500.00
Poway	M. Doufay Financial	Jennifer	Anderson	1717-MP	6/1/2017	$1,150.00
Del Mar	Oak Roots Development	David	Thomas	1719-TM	6/12/2017	$575.00
Del Mar	Oak Roots Development	David	Thomas	1727-AD	8/11/2017	$38,500.00
El Cajon		Edward	Gonzalez	1722-MP	7/14/2017	$14,500.00
Del Mar	Prentice College	Sharon	Nelson	1716-AD	5/20/2017	$205,000.00
Del Mar	Oakland Neighborhood Development	Brian	Carter	1603-MP	3/16/2016	$1,150.00
Del Mar	Oakland Neighborhood Development	Brian	Carter	1613-MP	8/26/2016	$89,000.00
Del Mar		Michelle	Mitchell	1616-RR	9/11/2016	$550.00
Del Mar		Michelle	Mitchell	1705-RR	2/22/2017	$14,500.00

18-6 ADDING CRITERIA TO A QUERY

You can refine a query to display only selected records by specifying criteria. **Criteria** are conditions for selecting records. For example, you could create a query that displays client names and invoice numbers for all clients, and add a criterion to select only those records with unpaid invoices. You specify criteria in a field's Criteria box in the design grid in the Query window.

To add criteria to a query, you need to create expressions to specify the conditions. To do this, you use one of the operators shown in Exhibit 18-18. You add a condition in the Criteria box in the appropriate column in the design grid. When you do this, the field value in each record is compared to the value you enter after the comparison operator, and only those records for which that condition is true are displayed in the query results. For example, if you type *San Francisco* in the Criteria box in the City column in the design grid, when you run the query, only those records in the Clients table with the value *San Francisco* in the City field would be displayed. (Note that this example uses the Equals to comparison operator, but you do not need to type it.) Similarly, if you type <> *San Francisco* in the Criteria box, the query results would include all the records except for the ones with *San Francisco* in the City field. Exhibit 18-19 shows a query that includes the Paid field and will include only records where the paid field is equal to No—that is, the check box in the Paid field is not selected.

EXHIBIT 18-18 OPERATORS FOR CREATING CRITERIA IN ACCESS

Operator	Description	Example
=	Equal to (optional; default operator)	"Hall"
<>	Not equal to	<>"Hall"
<	Less than	<#1/1/99#
<=	Less than or equal to	<=100
>	Greater than	>"C400"
>=	Greater than or equal to	>=18.75
Between ...	Between two values	Between 50
And ...	(inclusive)	And 325
In ()	In a list of values	In ("Hall", "Seeger")
Like	Matches a pattern that includes wildcards	Like "706*"

EXHIBIT 18-19 CRITERIA ADDED TO THE DESIGN GRID

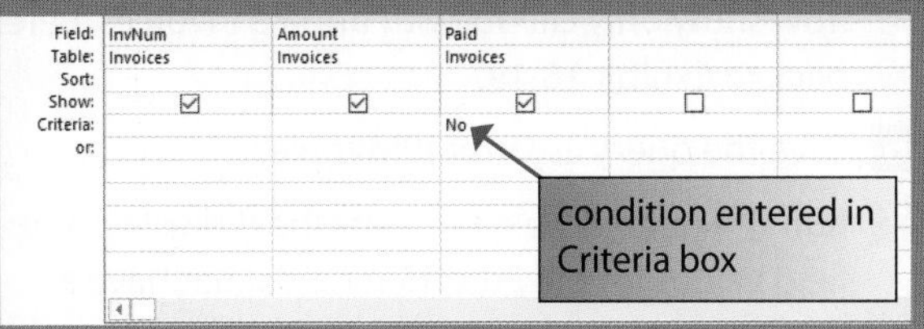

FYI FORMATTING A DATASHEET

You can format a datasheet using many of the same features you learned in Word and Excel. For example, you can change the font, font size, and font color using the buttons in the Text Formatting group on the Home tab. You can also change the alternate row color in a datasheet by using the Alternate Row Color button in the Text Formatting group on the Home tab.

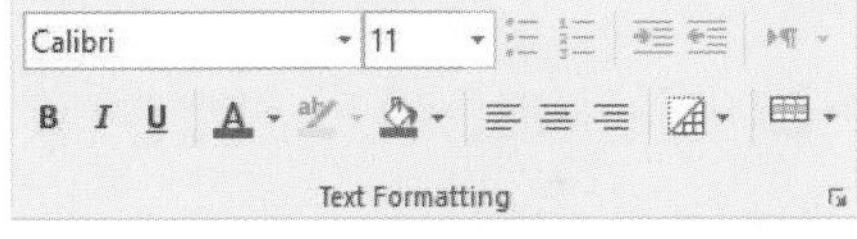

Begin Activity

Create queries with one criterion.

1. Create a new query in Design view.
2. Add the **Invoices table** to the Query window.
3. Add the following fields from the Invoices table to the design grid: **InvNum**, **Amount**, and **Paid**.
4. In the design grid, click in the **Paid field Criteria box**, and then type **No**. This tells Access to retrieve only the records for unpaid invoices. As soon as you type the letter *N*, a menu appears with options for entering various functions for the criteria. You don't need to enter a function, so you can close this menu.

criteria Conditions that determine which records are selected in a query.

5 Press the **Esc key** to close the menu. You must close the menu so that you don't enter a function, which would cause an error. The query results will now show only clients with unpaid invoices. Refer back to Exhibit 18-19.

6 Save the query as **UnpaidInvoices**.

7 Run the query. The query datasheet displays the field values for only the 15 records that have a Paid field value of No. Compare your screen to Exhibit 18-20.

8 Close the **UnpaidInvoices query**.

End Activity

EXHIBIT 18-20 QUERY RESULTS SHOWING ONLY UNPAID INVOICES

All Access Objects

Search...

Tables: Agreements, Clients, Invoices

Queries: ClientAgreements, ClientContact, UnpaidInvoices

UnpaidInvoices

Invoice Number	Amount	Paid?
1612-028	$15,000.00	☐
1701-006	$3,000.00	☐
1706-029	$1,150.00	☐
1709-056	$875.00	☐
1710-065	$6,500.00	☐
1710-067	$7,500.00	☐
1711-076	$29,500.00	☐
1711-077	$2,000.00	☐
1711-078	$9,800.00	☐
1711-079	$4,000.00	☐
1711-080	$14,325.00	☐
1711-081	$32,800.00	☐
1711-082	$17,500.00	☐
1711-083	$9,500.00	☐
1712-084	$37,500.00	☐
*		☐

18-7 CREATING A COPY OF A QUERY

When the design of the query you need to create is similar to an existing query, you can create a copy of the query and then rename the copy. This process is faster than creating a new query from scratch. You can copy and paste the query in the Navigation Pane, or you can use the Save As command to save a copy of the query design.

Begin Activity

Create copies of database objects.

1 In the Navigation Pane, in the Queries group, right-click **UnpaidInvoices**, and then on the shortcut menu, click **Copy**.

2 At the bottom of the Navigation Pane, right-click an empty area, and then on the shortcut menu, click **Paste**. The Paste As dialog box opens with Copy Of UnpaidInvoices selected in the Query Name box.

3 In the Query Name box, type **UnpaidFees** as the name for the new query, and then click **OK**. The dialog box closes, and the new query appears in the Queries section of the Navigation Pane.

4 In the Navigation Pane, double-click the **ClientAgreements query** to open, or run, the query. The query datasheet opens.

5 Switch to **Design view**. You are saving a copy of the query design, not the query results.

6 On the ribbon, click the **File tab**. In the navigation bar, click **Save As**. The Save As screen appears.

7 Under File Types, click **Save Object As**, and then click the **Save As button**. A small Save As dialog box opens, similar to the Save dialog box that appears when you save a table or query. In the As box, Query is displayed.

8 In the Save 'ClientAgreements' to box, type **TopAgreementValues** as the new query name.

9 Click **OK**. The new query is saved with the name you specified and appears in the Navigation Pane.

End Activity

Once you've created a copy of a query, you can open the copy and modify the existing design just as you would modify any query. You can modify the TopAgreementValues query design to list only those agreements with a value of $25,000 or more. Exhibit 18-21 shows the comparison operator greater than or equal to in the expression >=25000 in the AgreementValue column. The query results will contain only records with a value of $25,000 or more in the AgreementValue field.

EXHIBIT 18-21 CRITERIA ENTERED FOR THE AGREEMENTVALUE FIELD

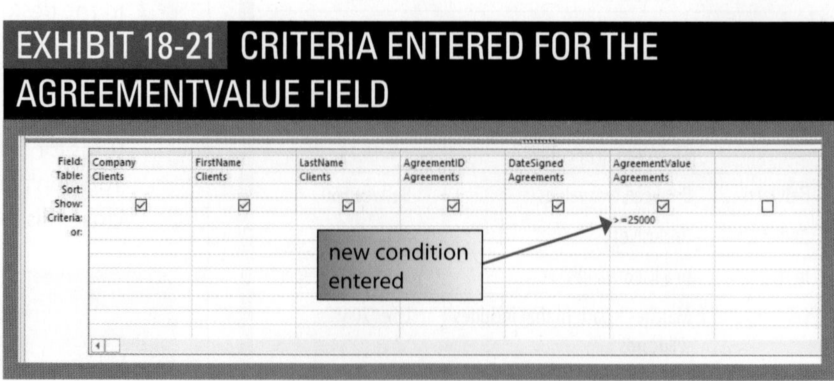

Begin Activity

Create a query with a comparison operator.

1. In the design grid, delete the **City field**.
2. In the design grid, click in the **AgreementValue field Criteria box**, and then type **>=25000**. The condition specifies that a record will be selected only if its AgreementValue field value is $25,000 or greater. Refer back to Exhibit 18-21.
3. Run the query. The query datasheet displays the selected fields for only those 20 records with an AgreementValue field value that is greater than or equal to $25,000. Compare your screen to Exhibit 18-22.
4. Save the **TopAgreementValues query**, and then close the query.

End Activity

PROBLEM?

If a dialog box opens indicating that you entered an expression containing invalid syntax, you might have typed a comma in the amount. Commas are not allowed in selection criteria for Currency fields. Click **OK**, and then delete the comma from the AgreementValue Criteria box.

EXHIBIT 18-22 QUERY RESULTS LISTING RECORDS WITH AN AGREEMENT VALUE GREATER THAN OR EQUAL TO $25,000

TopAgreementValues

Company	First Name	Last Name	Agreement ID	Date Signed	Agreement Value
Chen Builders	Marie	Patterson	1607-MP	7/7/2016	$68,000.00
Oakland Neighborhood Development	Brian	Carter	1613-MP	8/26/2016	$89,000.00
Jack's Café	Ella	Doyle	1614-TM	9/3/2016	$25,500.00
San Rafael Medical Partners	Juanita	Walters	1615-KF	9/4/2016	$25,000.00
	Edward	Caldwell	1620-RR	10/15/2016	$32,500.00
	Edward	Caldwell	1623-RR	11/7/2016	$39,000.00
Greenleaf Builders	Stephanie	Henderson	1701-KF	1/12/2017	$30,800.00
Chen Builders	Marie	Patterson	1702-TM	1/16/2017	$34,000.00
	Edward	Caldwell	1704-RR	2/18/2017	$138,000.00
Greenleaf Builders	Stephanie	Henderson	1708-MP	3/26/2017	$165,000.00
Sierra Nevada Contracting	Patrick	Perry	1712-AD	4/29/2017	$37,000.00
Prentice College	Sharon	Nelson	1716-AD	5/20/2017	$205,000.00
Sierra Nevada Contracting	Patrick	Perry	1718-RR	6/4/2017	$46,000.00
Bay Area Communities United	Amy	Chang	1721-TM	6/29/2017	$25,500.00
Happy Skies Day Care	Dennis	Ross	1723-RR	7/26/2017	$37,250.00
	Ronald	Perez	1724-MP	7/30/2017	$35,000.00
Oak Roots Development	David	Thomas	1727-AD	8/11/2017	$38,500.00
	Edward	Caldwell	1728-AD	8/17/2017	$50,000.00
	Edward	Caldwell	1730-AD	9/2/2017	$41,000.00
Yamada Architects, Inc.	Paul	Long	1731-AD	9/9/2017	$132,000.00
*					

18-8 ADDING MULTIPLE CRITERIA TO QUERIES

Some queries require more than one criterion. To create these more complex queries that have multiple criteria, you need to combine two or more conditions. You can specify that the records meet all of the conditions you define or one or the other of the conditions. When you want the records in the query results to meet all of your conditions, you use the **And operator**. For example, you might want to display all the records that have a City field value of *Del Mar* and have an AgreementValue field value greater than $25,000. When you want the records in the query results to meet at least one of the specified conditions, you use the **Or operator**. For example, you could create a query that displays all records that have a City field value of *Del Mar* or have an AgreementValue field value greater than $25,000.

18-8a Using the And Logical Operator

To create a query with the And logical operator, you specify all of the conditions in the same Criteria row of the design grid. The query will then display records only if all of the conditions are met. If even one condition is not met, the record is not included in the query results. Exhibit 18-23 shows two conditions in the Criteria row in the design grid. The query results for this query will display only records that have a value of *Del Mar* in the City field and a value greater than $25,000 in the AgreementValue field.

Begin Activity

Use the And logical operator in a query.

1. Create a new query in Design view.
2. Add the **Clients table** and **Agreements table** to the Query window.
3. Add the following fields from the Clients field list to the design grid: **Company**, **FirstName**, **LastName**, and **City**.
4. Add the following fields from the Agreements field list to the design grid: **AgreementValue** and **DateSigned**.

And operator The operator used to select records only if all of the specified conditions are met.

Or operator The operator used to select records if at least one of the specified conditions is met.

EXHIBIT 18-23 QUERY WITH AND LOGICAL OPERATOR

Field:	Company	FirstName	LastName	City	AgreementValue	DateSigned	
Table:	Clients	Clients	Clients	Clients	Agreements	Agreements	
Sort:							
Show:	☑	☑	☑	☑	☑	☑	☐
Criteria:				"Del Mar"	>25000		
or:							

And logical operator; conditions entered in same row

5 In the design grid, click in the **City field Criteria box**, type **Del Mar** and then press the **Tab key**. The first condition is entered, and the insertion point moves to the AgreementValue field Criteria box. Notice that quotation marks were added around the condition because the City field is a Short Text field.

6 In the **AgreementValue field Criteria box**, type **>25000** and then press the **Tab key**. The second condition is entered. Refer back to Exhibit 18-23. Because both conditions appear in the same Criteria row, both conditions must be met for a record to appear in the query results.

7 Run the query. The query datasheet includes only the 11 records for clients who meet both conditions: a City field value of *Del Mar* and an AgreementValue field value greater than $25,000. Compare your screen to Exhibit 18-24.

8 Save the query as **TopDelMarClients** and then close the query.

End Activity

EXHIBIT 18-24 QUERY RESULTS LISTING RECORDS WITH THE CITY EQUAL TO DEL MAR AND AN AGREEMENT VALUE GREATER THAN $25,000

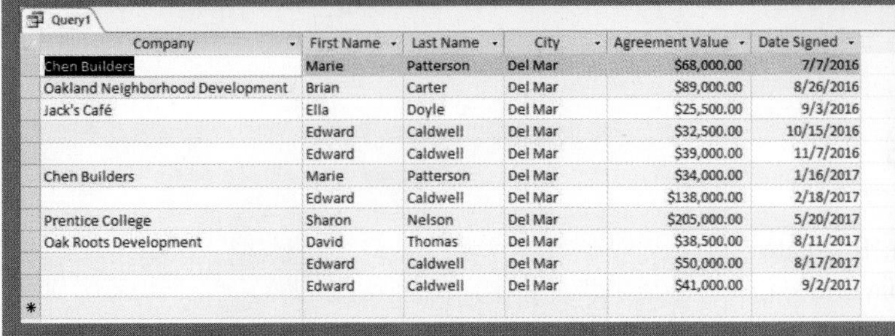

Query1

Company	First Name	Last Name	City	Agreement Value	Date Signed
Chen Builders	Marie	Patterson	Del Mar	$68,000.00	7/7/2016
Oakland Neighborhood Development	Brian	Carter	Del Mar	$89,000.00	8/26/2016
Jack's Café	Ella	Doyle	Del Mar	$25,500.00	9/3/2016
	Edward	Caldwell	Del Mar	$32,500.00	10/15/2016
	Edward	Caldwell	Del Mar	$39,000.00	11/7/2016
Chen Builders	Marie	Patterson	Del Mar	$34,000.00	1/16/2017
	Edward	Caldwell	Del Mar	$138,000.00	2/18/2017
Prentice College	Sharon	Nelson	Del Mar	$205,000.00	5/20/2017
Oak Roots Development	David	Thomas	Del Mar	$38,500.00	8/11/2017
	Edward	Caldwell	Del Mar	$50,000.00	8/17/2017
	Edward	Caldwell	Del Mar	$41,000.00	9/2/2017

18-8b Using the Or Logical Operator

To create a query with the Or logical operator, you specify each condition in a different Criteria row. The query will display records if any of the conditions are met. Exhibit 18-25 shows one condition in the Criteria row in the design grid and a second condition in the "or" row. The query results for this query will display records that have a value of less than $10,000 in the AgreementValue field and a value in the DateSigned field between January 1, 2017 and March 31, 2017.

EXHIBIT 18-25 QUERY WINDOW WITH THE OR LOGICAL OPERATOR

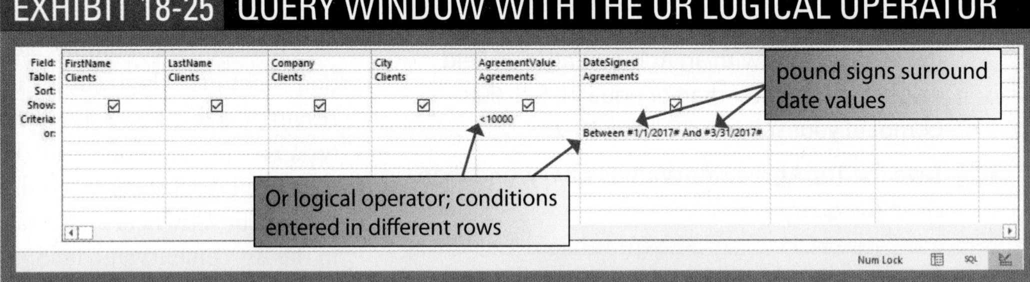

Begin Activity

Use the Or logical operator in a query.

1 Create a new query in Design view.

2 Add the **Clients table** and the **Agreements table** to the Query window.

3 Add the following fields from the Clients field list to the design grid: **FirstName**, **LastName**, **Company**, and **City**.

4 Add the following fields from the Agreements field list to the design grid: **AgreementValue** and **DateSigned**.

5 Click in the **AgreementValue field Criteria box**, type **<10000** and then press the **Tab key**. The first condition—to select agreements with amounts less than $10,000—is specified, and the Criteria box for the DateSigned field is selected.

6 Press the **Down Arrow key** to select the DateSigned field "or" box. Entering a condition in the "or" box creates a query using the Or logical operator.

7 In the **DateSigned field or box**, type **Between 1/1/2017 And 3/31/2017** and then press the **Tab key**. The second condition—to select agreements when the DateSigned field value is between 1/1/2017 and 3/31/2017—is specified.

8 In the design grid, point to the top of the **DateSigned right column border** so that the pointer changes to ✛, and then double-click to resize the DateSigned column so that the entire condition is visible. Refer back to Exhibit 18-25. Note that Access automatically places pound signs (#) around date values in the condition to distinguish them from the operators.

PROBLEM?
To make the pointer change shape, make sure you point to the top of the column border next to the field selector.

9 In the design grid, click in the **DateSigned field Sort box**, click the **arrow button** ⌄, and then click **Descending**. The query results will appear in descending order by DateSigned to create a logical order in which to analyze the data.

10 Run the query. The query results include the selected fields for the 27 records that meet one or both of the following conditions: an AgreementValue field value of less than $10,000 or a DateSigned field value between 1/1/2017 and 3/31/2017. The records in the query datasheet appear in descending order based on the values in the DateSigned field. Compare your screen to Exhibit 18-26.

11 Save the query as **SmallOrQ1Agreements** and then close the query.

End Activity

EXHIBIT 18-26 RESULTS OF QUERY USING THE OR LOGICAL OPERATOR

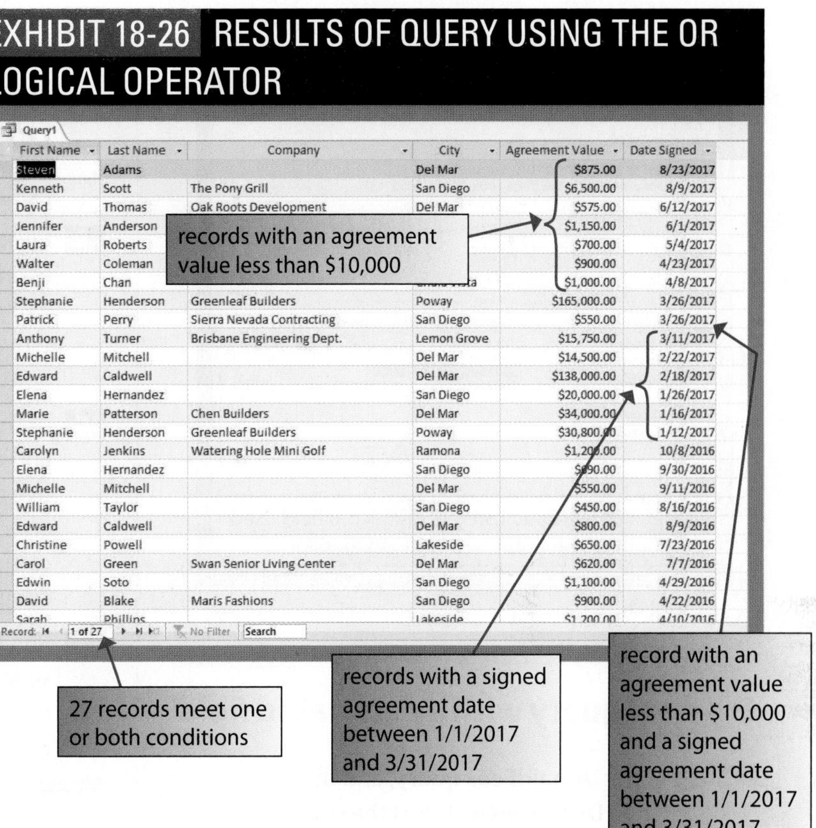

First Name	Last Name	Company	City	Agreement Value	Date Signed
Steven	Adams		Del Mar	$875.00	8/23/2017
Kenneth	Scott	The Pony Grill	San Diego	$6,500.00	8/9/2017
David	Thomas	Oak Roots Development	Del Mar	$575.00	6/12/2017
Jennifer	Anderson			$1,150.00	6/1/2017
Laura	Roberts			$700.00	5/4/2017
Walter	Coleman			$900.00	4/23/2017
Benji	Chan		[illegible]	$1,000.00	4/8/2017
Stephanie	Henderson	Greenleaf Builders	Poway	$165,000.00	3/26/2017
Patrick	Perry	Sierra Nevada Contracting	San Diego	$550.00	3/26/2017
Anthony	Turner	Brisbane Engineering Dept.	Lemon Grove	$15,750.00	3/11/2017
Michelle	Mitchell		Del Mar	$14,500.00	2/22/2017
Edward	Caldwell		Del Mar	$138,000.00	2/18/2017
Elena	Hernandez		San Diego	$20,000.00	1/26/2017
Marie	Patterson	Chen Builders	Del Mar	$34,000.00	1/16/2017
Stephanie	Henderson	Greenleaf Builders	Poway	$30,800.00	1/12/2017
Carolyn	Jenkins	Watering Hole Mini Golf	Ramona	$1,2[illegible].00	10/8/2016
Elena	Hernandez		San Diego	$[illegible]90.00	9/30/2016
Michelle	Mitchell		Del Mar	$550.00	9/11/2016
William	Taylor		San Diego	$450.00	8/16/2016
Edward	Caldwell		Del Mar	$800.00	8/9/2016
Christine	Powell		Lakeside	$650.00	7/23/2016
Carol	Green	Swan Senior Living Center	Del Mar	$620.00	7/7/2016
Edwin	Soto		San Diego	$1,100.00	4/29/2016
David	Blake	Maris Fashions	San Diego	$900.00	4/22/2016
Sarah	Phillips		Lakeside	$1,200.00	4/10/2016

18-9 CREATING A CALCULATED FIELD

To perform a calculation in a query, you add a calculated field to the query. A **calculated field** displays the results of a mathematical expression. When you run a query that contains a calculated field, Access evaluates the expression in the calculated field and displays the resulting value in the query datasheet, form, or report.

To enter an expression for a calculated field, you type it in an empty Field box in the design grid. You can also use the Expression Builder to enter the expression. Expression Builder is an Access tool that makes it easy for you to create a mathematical expression. When you click the Builder button in the Query Setup group on the Query Tools Deisgn tab, the Expression Builder dialog box opens. In the dialog box, the Expression Categories box lists the fields from the query so you can include them in the expression, and the Expression Elements box contains other elements you can use in the expression, including functions, constants, and operators. Exhibit 18-27 shows the Expression Builder dialog box with an expression in it to calculate five percent of the value in the Amount field.

calculated field A field that displays the results of a mathematical expression.

EXHIBIT 18-27 EXPRESSION BUILDER DIALOG BOX

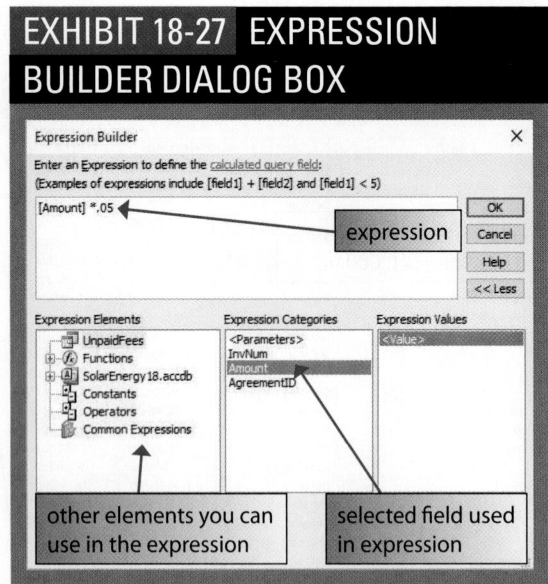

Begin Activity

Create a query with a calculated field.

1 Open the **UnpaidFees query**, and then switch to **Design view**. This is the copy of the UnpaidInvoices query.

2 Add the **AgreementID field** from the Invoices table field list to the fourth column in the design grid.

3 Click the **Paid field Show check box** to remove the check mark. The query name indicates that the data is for unpaid invoices, so you don't need to include the Paid field values in the query results.

4 Save the **UnpaidFees query**.

5 Click the **blank Field box** to the right of the AgreementID field. This field will contain the calculated expression.

TIP: A query must be saved and named in order for its fields to be listed in the Expression Categories box of the Expression Builder.

6 On the Query Tools Design tab, in the Query Setup group, click the **Builder button**. The Expression Builder dialog box opens. The insertion point is in the large box at the top of the dialog box, ready for you to enter the expression.

7 In the Expression Categories box, double-click **Amount**. The field name is added to the expression box and placed within brackets and followed by a space.

8 Type * (an asterisk) to enter the multiplication operator, and then type **.05** for the constant. The expression you entered for the calculated field will multiply the Amount field values by .05 (which represents a five percent late fee). Refer back to Exhibit 18-27.

9 Click **OK**. The Expression Builder dialog box closes, and the expression is added to the design grid in the Field box for the calculated field as *Expr1: [Amount]*0.05*. The text before the colon will appear as the field name in the query results.

10 At the beginning of the expression, select **Expr1**, and then type **Late Fee** to specify a more descriptive name for the field. Be sure to leave the colon after the field name; it is needed to separate the calculated field name from the expression. The complete expression is *Late Fee: [Amount]*0.05*.

11 Run the query. The query datasheet contains the specified fields and the calculated field with the column heading Late Fee. Compare your screen to Exhibit 18-28.

End Activity

EXHIBIT 18-28 DATASHEET DISPLAYING THE CALCULATED FIELD

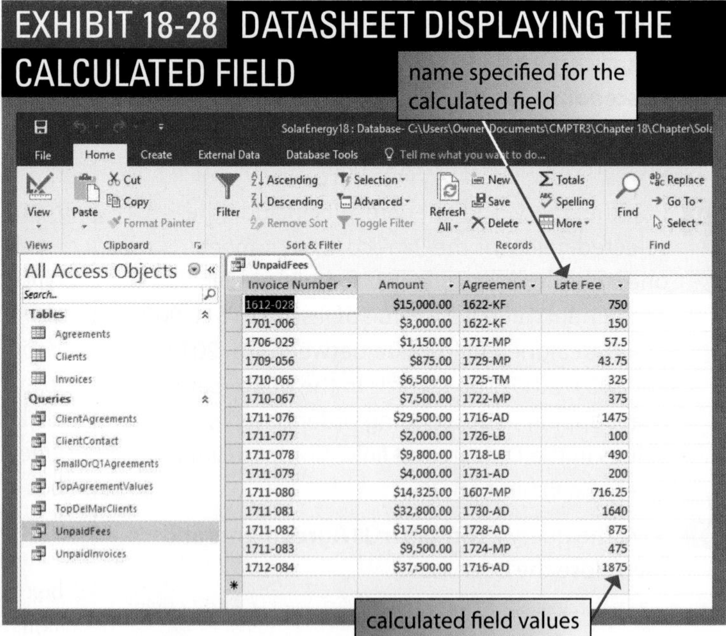

18-10 USING A PROPERTY SHEET

In the query results for the UnpaidFees query, the amounts listed in the Late Fee column are not formatted as currency. You can specify a format for a calculated field, just as you can for any field, by modifying its properties. As you have seen, when you work with tables, some of the field properties appear in the Field Properties pane at the bottom of the window in Design view. You can see additional properties by opening the Property Sheet. When you are working with queries, you need to open the Property Sheet to adjust any of the field properties. Exhibit 18-29 shows the Property Sheet for the calculated field in the UnpaidFees query.

EXHIBIT 18-29 PROPERTY SHEET FOR THE CALCULATED FIELD

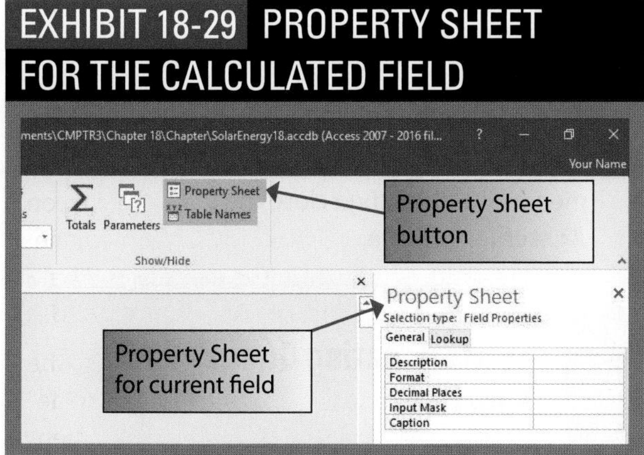

Begin Activity

Format a calculated field.

1. Switch the UnpaidFees query to **Design view**.
2. In the design grid, click the **Late Fee calculated field Field box**.
3. On the Query Tools Design tab, in the Show/Hide group, click the **Property Sheet button**. The Property Sheet for the calculated field appears on the right side of the Query window. Refer back to Exhibit 18-29.

TIP: You can also right-click a field in the design grid, and then click Properties on the shortcut menu to open the Property Sheet for that field.

4. In the Property Sheet, click the **Format box**, click the **arrow button** to display a list of available formats, and then click **Currency**. The Format property is set to Currency, which displays values with a dollar sign and two decimal places.
5. In the Property Sheet, click the **Close button**. The Property Sheet closes.
6. Run the query. The amounts in the Late Fee calculated field are now displayed with dollar signs and two decimal places.
7. Save the **UnpaidFees query**, and then close it.

End Activity

FYI

CALCULATED FIELDS

The Calculated Field data type, which is available only for tables in Datasheet view, lets you store the result of an expression as a field in a table. However, database experts caution against storing calculations in a table for the following reasons:

- **Storing calculated data in a table consumes space and increases the size of the database.** The preferred approach is to use a calculated field in a query; with this approach, the result of the calculation is not stored in the database—it is produced only when you run the query—and it is always current.
- **Using the Calculated Field data type provides limited options for creating a calculation.** A calculated field in a query provides more functions and options for creating expressions.
- **Including a field in a table whose value is dependent on other fields in the table violates database design principles.** To avoid problems, create a query that includes a calculated field to perform the calculation you want, instead of creating a field in a table that uses the Calculated Field data type.

18-11 USING FUNCTIONS IN A QUERY

You can use a table or query datasheet to perform calculations, such as sums, averages, minimums, and maximums, on the displayed records. To do this, you use functions to perform arithmetic operations on selected records in a database. These are the same functions that are available in Excel. Exhibit 18-30 lists the most frequently used functions.

18-11a Using the Total Row in a Datasheet

To perform a calculation using a function in a table or query datasheet, you can add a Total row at the bottom of the datasheet. In the Total row, you can then choose

EXHIBIT 18-30 FREQUENTLY USED FUNCTIONS

Function	Determines
Average	Average of the field values for the selected records
Count	Number of records selected
Maximum	Highest field value for the selected records
Minimum	Lowest field value for the selected records
Sum	Total of the field values for the selected records

one of the functions for a field in the datasheet, and the results of the calculation will be displayed in the Total row for that field. Exhibit 18-31 shows the menu that appears when you click a field in a Total row.

EXHIBIT 18-31 MENU OF FUNCTIONS IN THE TOTAL ROW

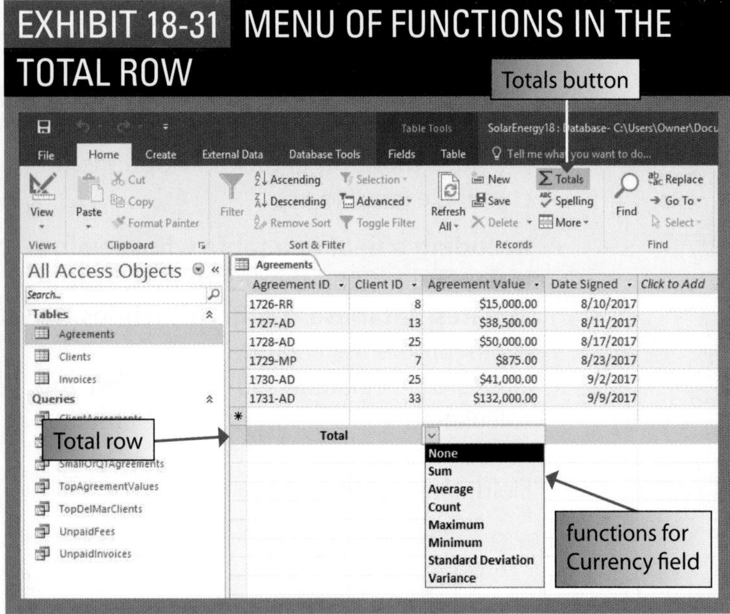

You can add or remove the Total row from the datasheet by clicking the Totals button in the Records group on the Home tab; this button works as a toggle to switch between the display of the Total row and the results of any calculations in the row, and the display of the datasheet without this row.

Begin Activity

Use the Total row.

1 Open the **Agreements table** in Datasheet view.

2 On the Home tab, in the Records group, click the **Totals button**. A Total row appears at the bottom of the datasheet.

3 Scroll to the bottom of the datasheet to view the Total row.

4 In the Total row, click in the **Agreement Value column**, and then click the **arrow button** that appears on the left side of the field to display a menu of functions. Refer back to Exhibit 18-31. The available functions depend on the data type of the current field. In this case, the menu provides functions for a Currency field.

5 On the menu, click **Sum**. Access adds all the values in the Agreement Value column and displays the total $1,555,410.00 in the Total row for the column.

6 Save the changes to the Agreements table, and then close the **Agreements table**.

TIP: Click the selected Totals button in the Records group on the Home tab to remove the Totals row.

End Activity

18-11b Creating Queries with Functions

Functions can operate on the records that meet a query's selection criteria. You specify a function for a specific field, and the appropriate operation applies to that field's values for the selected records. For example, you can use the Minimum, Average, and Maximum functions for the AgreementValue field to display the minimum, average, and maximum of all the amounts in the Agreements table. For each calculation you want to perform on the same field, you need to add the field to the design grid.

After you run the query, the query datasheet uses a default column name that includes the function and the field name, such as MinOfAgreementValue, for the field. You can change the datasheet column name to a more descriptive or readable name by entering that name in the Field box followed by a colon and the field name, such as Minimum Agreement Value: AgreementValue. See Exhibit 18-32.

EXHIBIT 18-32 TOTAL ROW INSERTED IN THE DESIGN GRID

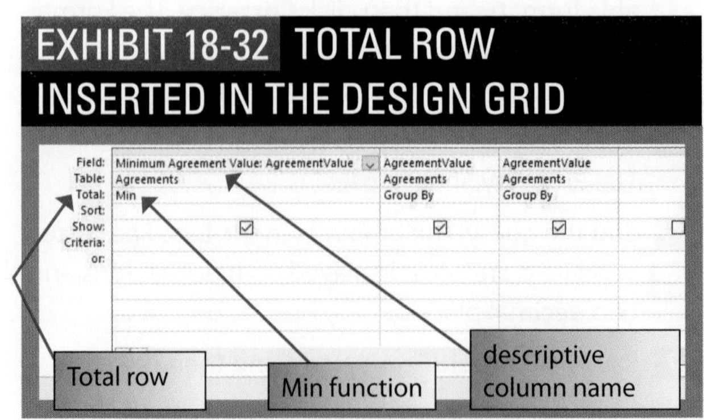

Begin Activity

Create a query with functions.

1 Create a new query in **Design view**.

2 Add the **Agreements table** to the Query window.

3 In the Agreements field list, double-click **AgreementValue** three times to add three copies of the field to the design grid.

4 On the Query Tools Design tab, in the Show/Hide group, click the **Totals button**. The Total row appears between the Table and Sort rows in the design grid. The default function Group By appears in the Total boxes.

5 In the design grid, click in the **first AgreementValue column Total box**, click the **arrow button**, and then click **Min** to specify the function to use for the field. This function will calculate the minimum amount of all the AgreementValue field values.

6 Click in the **first AgreementValue column Field box**, and then press the **Left Arrow key** to position the insertion point to the left of AgreementValue. Type **Minimum Agreement Value:** (including the colon), and then press the **Spacebar**. The Field box now contains *Minimum Agreement Value: AgreementValue*.

7 In the design grid, resize the first column so you can see all of the text in the Field box. Refer back to Exhibit 18-32.

8 Click in the **second AgreementValue column Total box**, click the **arrow button**, and then click **Max**. This function will calculate the maximum amount of all the AgreementValue field values.

9 Click in the **second AgreementValue Field box**, position the insertion point to the left of AgreementValue, type **Maximum Agreement Value:** and then press the **Spacebar**.

10 Click in the **third AgreementValue column Total box**, click the **arrow button**, and then click **Avg**. This function will calculate the average of all the AgreementValue field values.

11 Click in the **third AgreementValue Field box**, position the insertion point to the left of AgreementValue, type **Average Agreement Value:** and then press the **Spacebar**.

12 Run the query. The query datasheet includes one record with the results of the three calculations. These calculations are based on all of the records selected for the query—in this case, all 54 records in the Agreements table.

13 Resize all of the columns to their best fit so that the column names are fully displayed. Compare your screen to Exhibit 18-33.

14 Save the query as **AgreementValueStats**, and then close the query.

End Activity

EXHIBIT 18-33 RESULT OF QUERY USING FUNCTIONS

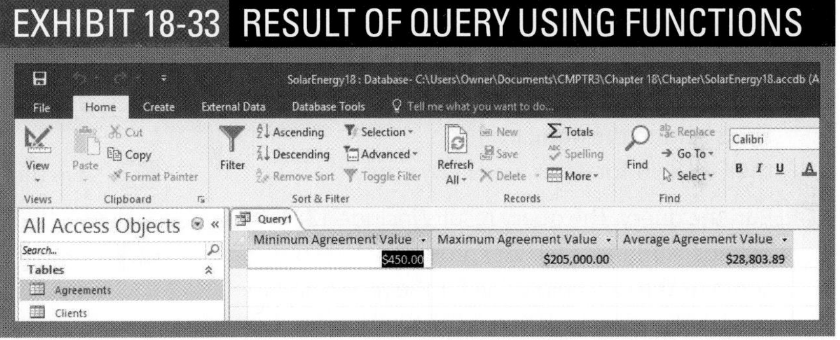

18-11c Creating Calculations for Groups of Records

In addition to calculating statistical information on all or selected records in selected tables, you can calculate statistics for groups of records. For example, you can determine the number of clients in each city or the average agreement amount by city. The **Group By operator** divides the selected records into groups based on the values in the specified field. Those records with the same value for the field are grouped together, and the datasheet displays one record for each group. Functions, which appear in the other columns of the design grid, provide statistical information for each group.

Begin Activity

Create a query with the Group By operator.

1 Create a copy of the **AgreementValueStats query**. Name the copy **AgreementValueStatsByCity**.

2 Open the **AgreementValueStatsByCity query**, and then switch to **Design view**.

Group By operator An operator that divides selected records into groups based on the values in the specified field.

3 On the Query Tools Design tab, in the Query Setup group, click the **Show Table button**. The Show Table dialog box appears.

4 Add the **Clients table** to the Query window, and then close the **Show Table dialog box**.

5 In the Clients field list, drag the **City field** to the **first column in the design grid**. The City field appears in the first column, and the existing fields shift to the right. In the City field Total box, Group By appears.

6 Run the query. The query results include 13 records—one for each City group. Each record contains the City field value for the group and the results of each calculation using the Min, Max, and Avg functions. The summary statistics represent calculations based on the 54 records in the Agreements table. Compare your screen to Exhibit 18-34.

EXHIBIT 18-34 RECORDS GROUPED BY CITY

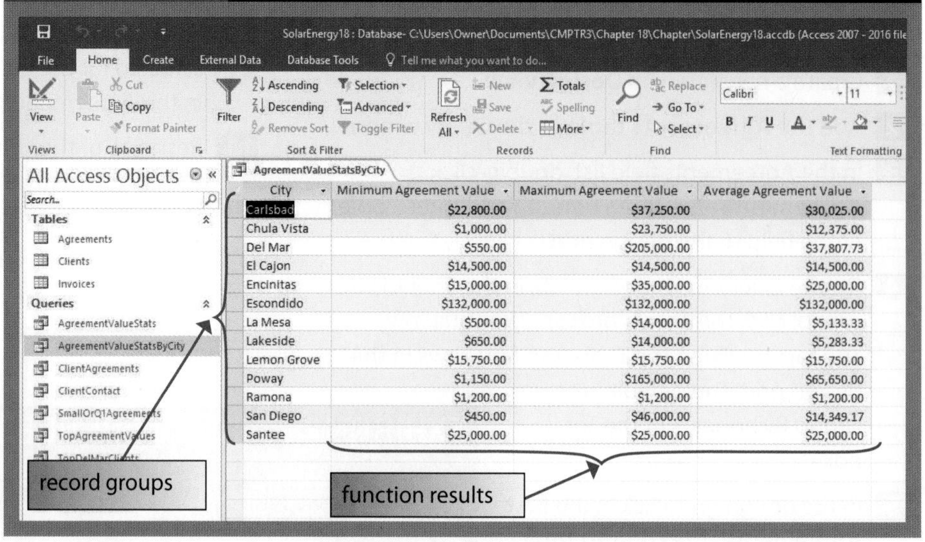

AgreementValueStatsByCity

City	Minimum Agreement Value	Maximum Agreement Value	Average Agreement Value
Carlsbad	$22,800.00	$37,250.00	$30,025.00
Chula Vista	$1,000.00	$23,750.00	$12,375.00
Del Mar	$550.00	$205,000.00	$37,807.73
El Cajon	$14,500.00	$14,500.00	$14,500.00
Encinitas	$15,000.00	$35,000.00	$25,000.00
Escondido	$132,000.00	$132,000.00	$132,000.00
La Mesa	$500.00	$14,000.00	$5,133.33
Lakeside	$650.00	$14,000.00	$5,283.33
Lemon Grove	$15,750.00	$15,750.00	$15,750.00
Poway	$1,150.00	$165,000.00	$65,650.00
Ramona	$1,200.00	$1,200.00	$1,200.00
San Diego	$450.00	$46,000.00	$14,349.17
Santee	$25,000.00	$25,000.00	$25,000.00

record groups

function results

7 Save the **AgreementValueStatsByCity query**, and then close it.

8 Compact and repair the SolarEnergy18 database, and then close the database.

PROBLEM?
If a dialog box opens warning you that this action will cause the Clipboard to be emptied and asking if you want to continue, click Yes.

End Activity

STUDY TOOLS 18

READY TO STUDY? IN THE BOOK, YOU CAN:

- ☐ Rip out the Chapter Review Card, which includes key terms and key chapter concepts.

ONLINE AT WWW.CENGAGEBRAIN.COM, YOU CAN:

- ☐ Review key concepts from the chapter in a short video.
- ☐ Explore maintaining and querying a database with the interactive infographic.
- ☐ Practice what you've learned with more Practice It and On Your Own exercises.
- ☐ Prepare for tests with quizzes.
- ☐ Review the key terms with flashcards.

QUIZ YOURSELF

1. In Datasheet view, what is the difference between navigation mode and editing mode?
2. Describe the field list and the design grid in the Query window in Design view.
3. What is a select query?
4. How are a table datasheet and a query datasheet similar? How are they different?
5. Describe how records are organized when you select multiple sort fields.
6. What is a filter?
7. When does a one-to-many relationship exist between tables?
8. What is referential integrity?
9. How do you create a multitable query?
10. What is a condition, and when do you use it?
11. In the design grid, where do you place the conditions for two different fields when you use the And logical operator?
12. In the design grid, where do you place the conditions for two different fields when you use the Or logical operator?
13. How do you perform a calculation in a query?
14. How do you calculate statistical information, such as sums, averages, minimums, and maximums, on the records displayed in a table datasheet or selected by a query?
15. Explain what the Group By operator does.

PRACTICE IT

Practice It 18-1

1. Open the data file **Tree18** located in the Chapter 18\Practice It folder. Save the database as **TreeRemoval18**.
2. Open the Customers table in Datasheet view. For CustomerID 1, change the field values in the First Name and Last Name columns to your first and last names.
3. Find the record with the Company field value of **Hanford Fashion**. Change the Phone field value to **207-555-8743**. Close the Customers table.
4. Open the ServiceContracts table, find the record for Contract Number **1736**, and then delete the record. Close the ServiceAgreements table.
5. Create a query in Design view based on the Customers table. Include the following fields in the query: Company, FirstName, LastName, and Phone. Save the query as **CustomerPhoneList**, and then run the query.
6. Modify the CustomerPhoneList query in Design view to sort the query results in ascending order by the Company field and then in ascending order by the LastName field. Save the modified query, run the query, and then close it.
7. Create a one-to-many relationship between the primary Customers table and the related ServiceContracts table based on the CustomerID field. Enforce referential integrity, and select the Cascade Update Related Fields check box.
8. Create a one-to-many relationship between the primary ServiceContracts table and the related Invoices table based on the ContractNum field. Enforce referential integrity, and select the Cascade Update Related Fields check box. Save the layout in the Relationships window, and then close the window.
9. Open the ServiceContracts table in Datasheet view, find the record for Contract Number **1716**, display the subdatasheet, change the record for invoice number 1709-049 to paid by selecting the Paid? check box, and then close the table.
10. Create a query in Design view based on the ServiceContracts and Invoices tables. Select the ContractNum, ContractAmt, and ServiceType fields from the ServiceContracts table, and then select the InvNum and InvAmt fields from the Invoices table. Sort the query results in descending order based on the ContractAmt. Select only those records for business customers by entering **Commercial** in the ServiceType Criteria box. Do not display the ServiceType field values in the query results. Save the query as **CommercialContracts**, run the query, and then close it.
11. Create a copy of the CommercialContracts query and name the copy **ResidentialContracts**. Open the ResidentialContracts query in Design view, and then edit it so that the ServiceType criteria is **Residential**. Save and run the query, and then close it.

12. Create a query in Design view that lists all unpaid invoices that are dated between 1/1/2017 and 12/31/2017. Include the following fields from the Invoices table in the query: InvNum, InvAmt, InvDate, and Paid. Sort the InvDate field in ascending order. Do not show the Paid field in the query results. Save the query as **UnpaidInvoices**, run the query, and then close it.
13. Create a query in Design view that lists clients located in Waterville or service agreements for less than $1,000. Include the Company, City, FirstName, and LastName fields from the Customers table and the ContractNum and ContractAmt fields from the ServiceContracts table. Sort the query in ascending order by the City field and then in descending order by the ContractAmt field. Save the query as **WatervilleOrSmallContracts**, run the query, and then close it.
14. Create a copy of the UnpaidInvoices query. Name the copy **UnpaidInvoicesCashDiscount**. Open the UnpaidInvoicesCashDiscount query in Design view, and then add a calculated field to the fifth column in the design grid that calculates a six percent discount based on the InvAmt field values. (*Hint*: Multiply the InvAmt field by 0.06.) Change the field's column name to **Cash Discount** and format it as Currency. Save and run the query, and then close it as.
15. Create a query in Design view that calculates the minimum, maximum, and average contract amounts for all service contract amounts using the field names **Lowest**, **Highest**, and **Average**, respectively. Save the query as **ContractStats**. Run the query, and then close it.
16. Create a copy of the ContractStats query. Name the copy **ContractStatsByCity**. Modify the ContractStatsByCity query so that the records are grouped by the City field in the Customers table. Sort the query in ascending order by the City field. The City field should appear first in the query datasheet. Save the query, run the query, and then close it.
17. Compact and repair the TreeRemoval18 database, and then close it.

Practice It 18-2

1. Open the data file **Studio18** located in the Chapter 18\Practice It folder. Save the database as **StudioClasses18**.
2. In the Faculty table, for Faculty ID CC-1201, change the value in the First Name and Last Name columns to your first and last names.
3. In the Instructors table, find the record with the last name of **Weigel**, and then change the value in the Hire Date column to **8/12/2015**. Close the Faculty table.
4. Create one-to-many relationships between the primary Faculty table and the related Sessions table using the FacultyID field, and between the primary Sessions table and the related Students table using the SessionID field. In each relationship, enforce referential integrity, and select the option to cascade updates to related fields. Save and close the Relationships window.
5. In the Faculty table, find the record with the Instructor ID DR-9123, delete the related record in the subdatasheet for this instructor, and then delete the record for this instructor. Close the Faculty table.
6. Create a query in Design view based on the Students table that includes the LastName, FirstName, and Phone fields. Sort the query in ascending order by LastName. Save the query as **StudentPhoneNumbers**, and then run the query.
7. In the StudentPhoneNumbers query results, change the phone number for Christa Harris to **740-555-2235**. Close the query.
8. Create a query in Design view based on the Faculty and Sessions tables. Add the LastName and FacultyID fields from the Faculty table. Add the SessionID, SessionName, Teens, Length, and Cost fields from the Sessions table. Sort in ascending order on the LastName field, and then sort in ascending order by the SessionID field. Save the query as **SessionsByInstructor**, run it, and then close it.
9. Create a copy of the SessionsByInstructor query named **TeenSessions**. Modify the TeenSessions query to display all classes taught by instructors who allow teens to participate. Do not include the Teens field in the query results. Save the query, run it, and then close it.
10. Create a copy of the TeenSessions query named **TeenSessionsLowCost**. Modify the TeenSessionsLowCost query to display only those classes taught by instructors who allow teens to participate and that cost $100 or less. Do not include the Teens field values in the query results. Save the query, and then run it.
11. In the TeenSessionsLowCost query datasheet, calculate the average cost of the classes selected by the query. Save and close the query.
12. Compact and repair the StudioClasses18 database, and then close it.

ON YOUR OWN

On Your Own 18-1

1. Open the data file **Contributions18** located in the Chapter 18\On Your Own folder. Save the database as **ContributionsList18**.
2. In the Contributor table, for Donor ID 2017-001, change the First Name field value to your first name, and change the Last Name field value to your last name.
3. Create one-to-many relationships between the primary Organizations table and the related Contributions table, and between the primary Contributors table and the related Contributions table. For each relationship, enforce referential integrity, and cascade updates to related fields. Save and close the Relationships window.
4. In the Contributors table, delete the record for Contributor ID 2017-028. (Be sure to delete the related record first.)
5. Create a query based on the Organizations table that includes the Organization, FirstName, LastName, and City fields. Save the query as **OrganizationsByCity**, and then run it.
6. Modify the OrganizationsByCity query design so that it sorts records in ascending order first by City and then in ascending order by Organization. The query results should display the fields in the following order: Organization, FirstName, LastName, and City fields. (*Hint*: Add the Organization field to the query twice to achieve the correct sort order, and hide the extra copy of the field.) Save and run the query.
7. In the OrganizationsByCity query datasheet, change the contact for the SeniorCare to **Mary Sheehan**. Close the query.
8. Create a query in Design view that displays the ContributorID, FirstName, and LastName fields from the Contributors table, and the Description and ContributionValue fields from the Contributions table for all donations with a value over $100. Sort the query in descending order by ContributionValue. Save the query as **BigContributors**. Run the query, and then close it.
9. Create a copy of the BigContributors query named **BigCashContributors**. Modify the BigCashContributors query to display only records with cash donations of more than $100. Do not include the Description field values in the query results. In the query datasheet, calculate the sum of the donations. Save and close the query.
10. Create a query in Design view that displays the Organization field from the Organizations table, and the ContributionID, ContributionDate, and Description fields from the Contributions table. Run the query.
11. Use the Selection button in the Sort & Filter group on the Home tab to filter the datasheet for the query you created in Step 10 to display only the records for contributions to Wyoming Family Services. Save the query as **WFSContributions.**
12. Format the WFSContributions query datasheet to use an alternate row color of the Olive Green, Accent 3, theme color. (*Hint*: Use the Alternate Row Color button in the Text Formatting group on the Home tab.) Resize the columns to best fit the complete field names and values. Save and close the WFSContributions query.
13. Create a copy of the WFSContributions query named **BooksOrToys**. Modify the BooksOrToys query by deleting the ContributionDate from the query design grid, and then display donations of only books or toys. Then list the Organization ID instead of the Organization name. Change the order of the fields so that the Description field appears first, then the OrganizationID, then the ContributionID. Sort the records in ascending order first by Description and then in ascending order by OrganizationID. Run the query, adjust the column widths, save the query, and then close it.
14. Create a query in Design view that displays the ContributorID, Organization, Description, and ContributionValue fields for all donations that require a pickup. Do not display the Pickup field in the query results. Save the query as **PickupCharge**. Create a calculated field named **Net Contribution** that displays the results of subtracting $5.50 from the ContributionValue field values. Display the results in ascending order by ContributionValue. Format the calculated field with the Currency format. Run the query, resize the columns in the query datasheet to their best fit, save the query, and then close it.
15. Create a query in Design view based on the Contributions table that displays the total and average of the ContributionValue field for all contributions. Then add a function that counts the number of records used to calculate the query results. (*Hint*: Use the Count function to count the

number of rows.) Enter appropriate column names for each field. Format the sum and average values as Currency. Save the query as **ContributionStats**, and then run the query. In the query datasheet, resize the columns to their best fit, save the query, and then close it.

16. Create a copy of the ContributionStats query named **ContributionStatsByOrganization**. Modify the ContributionStatsByOrganization query to display the sum, average, and count of the ContributionValue field for all contributions grouped by Organization, with Organization appearing as the first field. Sort the records in descending order by the value of the total contribution. Save the query, run the query, and then close it.

17. Compact and repair the ContributionsList18 database, and then close it. (Do not save the contents of the Clipboard.)

Part 8
ACCESS
2016

19 Creating Forms and Reports

LEARNING OBJECTIVES After studying the material in this chapter, you will be able to:

19-1 Create a form using the Form Wizard

19-2 Modify a form's design in Layout view

19-3 Find data using a form

19-4 Create a form based on related tables

19-5 Preview and print selected form records

19-6 Create a report using the Report Wizard

19-7 Modify a report's design in Layout view

After finishing this chapter, go to **PAGE 585** for **STUDY TOOLS**.

19-1 CREATING A FORM USING THE FORM WIZARD

Forms provide a simpler, more intuitive layout for displaying, entering, and changing data. You have already used the Form tool to create a simple form to enter, edit, and view records in a database. The Form tool creates a form automatically, using all the fields in the selected table or query. You can also create a form using the Form Wizard, which guides you through the process of creating a form. In the Form Wizard dialog boxes, you select the tables or queries on which to base the form, choose which fields to include in the form, and specify the order in which the selected fields should appear in the form. See the first dialog box in Exhibit 19-1. You then select a form layout, which can be Columnar, Tabular, Datasheet, and Justified. The Tabular and Datasheet layouts display the fields from multiple records at one time. The Columnar and Justified layouts display the fields from one record at a time. See the center dialog box in Exhibit 19-1. Finally, you enter a title for the form and choose whether to open the form in Form view so you can work with data or in Design view so you can modify the form's design. See the third dialog box in Exhibit 19-1.

Begin Activity

Create a form using the Form Wizard.

1 Open the data file **Energy19** located in the Chapter 19\Chapter folder. Save the database as **SolarEnergy19**.

2 In the Navigation Pane, select the **Clients table**.

3 On the ribbon, click the **Create tab**. In the Forms group, click the **Form Wizard button**. The first Form Wizard dialog box opens. The Clients table is selected in the Tables/Queries box, and the fields from the Clients table are listed in the Available Fields box. Refer to the first dialog box shown in Exhibit 19-1.

> **PROBLEM?**
> If the Microsoft Access Security Notice dialog box opens warning you that the file might contain unsafe content, click **Open**.

4 Click >> to move all the fields to the Selected Fields box.

5 In the Selected Fields box, click **Email**, and then click < to move the Email field back to the Available Fields box. In the Selected Fields box, the Phone field is selected. The next field you add will be added below the selected Phone field.

EXHIBIT 19-1 DIALOG BOXES IN THE FORM WIZARD

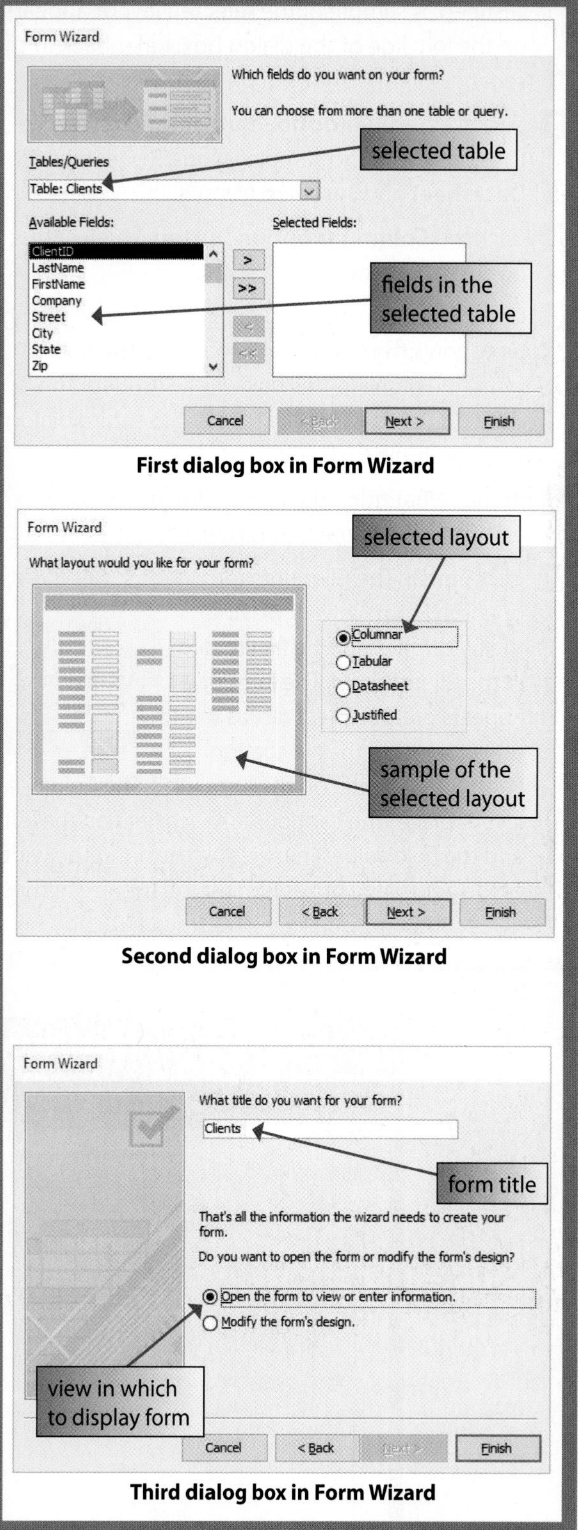

6 With the Email field selected in the Available Fields box, click >. The Email field is added back to the Selected Fields box below the Phone field.

ACCESS 2016

7. Click **Next** to display the second Form Wizard dialog box, which provides the available layouts for the form: Columnar, Tabular, Datasheet, and Justified. A sample of the selected layout appears on the left side of the dialog box. Refer back to the second dialog box in Exhibit 19-1.
8. Click the **Tabular option button**, and review the corresponding sample layout. Review the **Datasheet** and **Justified** layouts.
9. Click the **Columnar option button** to select that layout for the form.
10. Click **Next**. The third and final Form Wizard dialog box shows the Clients table name as the default form title name in this box will be used for the form object as well. Refer back to the third dialog box in Exhibit 19-1.
11. In the "What title do you want for your form" box, edit the form name to **ClientInfo**.
12. Click **Finish**. The ClientInfo form opens in Form view, displaying the field values for the first record in the Clients table. The form title appears on the object tab, as the object name in the Navigation Pane, and as a title on the form itself. The Columnar layout places the captions for each field on the left and the field values in boxes on the right. The width of the field value boxes is based on the size of the field. Compare your screen to Exhibit 19-2.

TIP: You can close the Navigation Pane to display more of the Form window.

End Activity

EXHIBIT 19-2 CLIENTINFO FORM IN FORM VIEW

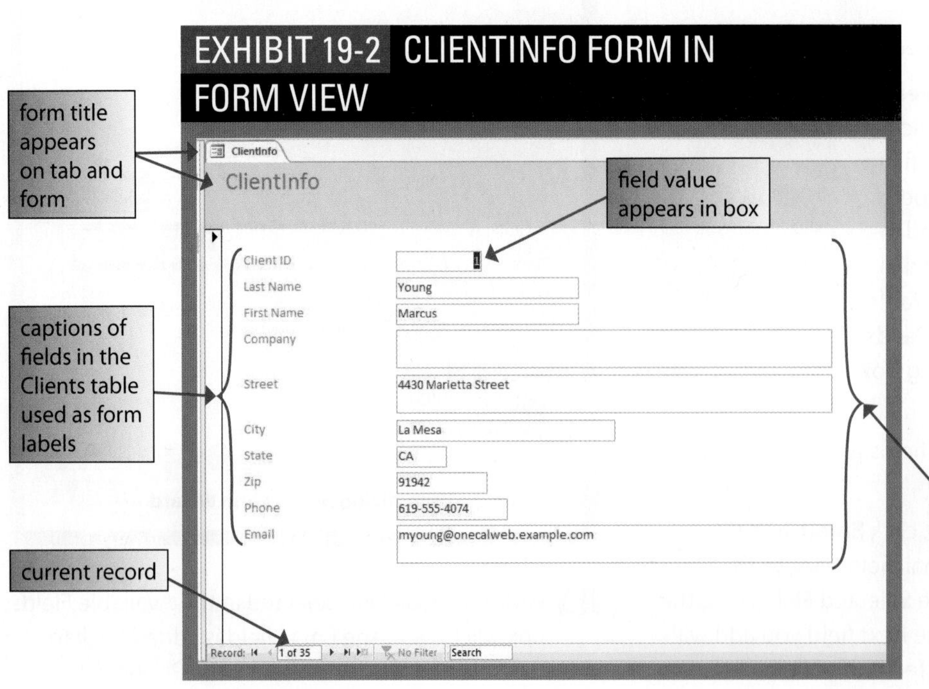

19-2 MODIFYING A FORM'S DESIGN IN LAYOUT VIEW

After you create a form, it opens in Form view. If you need to improve its appearance or to make the form easier to use, you need to switch to Layout view. In Layout view, you can see a record in the form and change its layout at the same time, which lets you easily see the results of any design changes you make. You can continue to make changes, undo modifications, and rework the design in Layout view to achieve the look you want for the form. For example, you might change the font, font size, or font color of the labels; add a picture; or modify other form elements such as the type of line used for the field value boxes. To make one of these changes, you must select an object. In Layout view, a solid orange outline identifies the currently selected object on the form.

Keep in mind that some changes to the form design must be done in Design view, which gives you a more detailed view of the form's structure.

19-2a Applying a Theme to a Form

You can quickly change the look of a form by applying a different theme, which determines the design scheme for the colors and fonts used in the form. Forms are originally formatted with the Office theme, but you can apply a different theme in Layout view. The theme you select is applied to all of the objects in the database unless you specify to apply the theme to the current object only or to all matching objects, such as all forms. To change the theme, you use the Themes button in the Themes group on the Form Layout Tools Design tab, as shown in Exhibit 19-3.

EXHIBIT 19-3 FORM IN LAYOUT VIEW

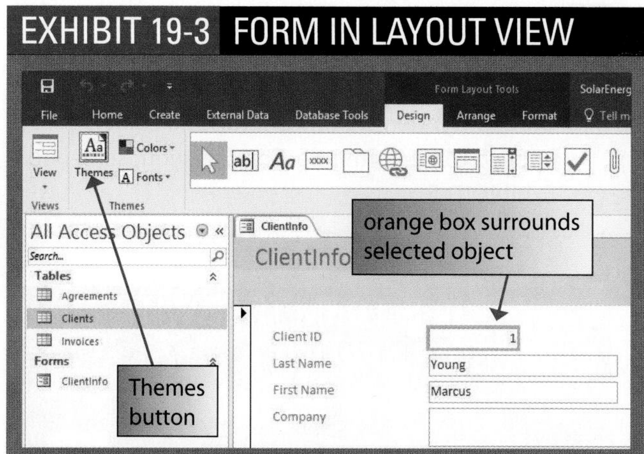

4. In the Themes gallery, right-click the **Facet theme**. A shortcut menu appears with options for applying the theme to all matching objects, applying the theme to this object only (the ClientInfo form), or making the theme the default for all objects in the database.

5. On the shortcut menu, click **Apply Theme to This Object Only**. The gallery closes, and the ClientInfo form is formatted with the Facet theme. Compare your screen to Exhibit 19-4.

End Activity

Begin Activity

Apply a theme to a form.

1. Display the form in **Layout view**. The Form Layout Tools tabs appear on the ribbon, and the field value box for the Client ID field is selected, as indicated by the orange border.
2. If necessary, click the **Form Layout Tools Design tab**. If a pane is open on the right, click the **Close button** [X] to close the pane. Refer to Exhibit 19-3.
3. In the Themes group, click the **Themes button**. The Themes gallery appears, showing the available themes for the form.

EXHIBIT 19-4 FORM WITH FACET THEME APPLIED

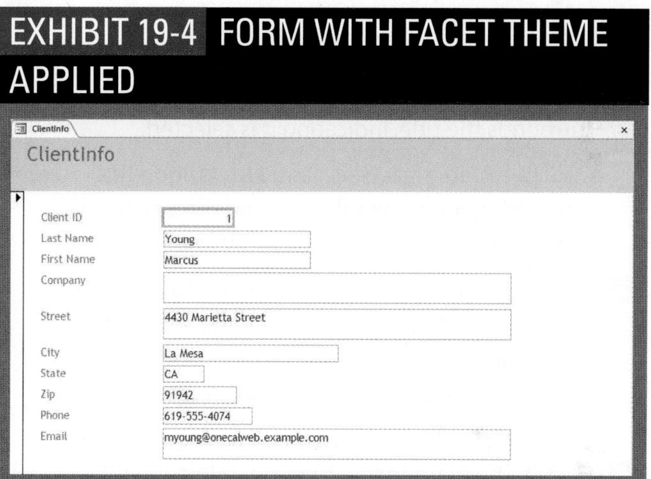

FYI WORKING WITH THEMES IN DATABASES

Themes provide a quick way to format the objects in a database consistently. You can choose to apply a theme to the current object or to all matching objects, such as all forms in the database. You can also choose to make a theme the default theme for the database, which means any existing objects and any new objects you create in the database will be formatted with the selected theme. Instead of clicking a theme in the Themes gallery, you right-click the theme and then click the option you want on the shortcut menu.

When you apply a theme to all matching objects in the database or make the theme the default for the database, Access applies that theme to both new and existing objects in the database. Although this approach ensures design consistency, it can also introduce formatting problems with existing objects.

A better approach is to select the Apply Theme to This Object Only option on the shortcut menu for a theme in the Themes gallery, for each existing form and report. If the new theme causes problems for that form or report, you can simply reapply the previous theme to return the object to its original design.

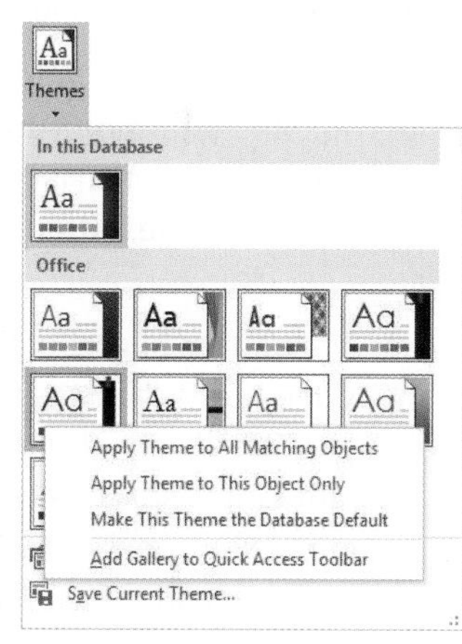

19-2b Changing the Form Title's Text and Appearance

A form's title should be descriptive and indicate the form's purpose. To make the form's purpose clearer, you can edit or replace the form's current title. You can also format it to change its appearance. For example, you can make text bold, italic, and underlined; change the font, font color, and font size; and change the alignment of text. These options are located in the Font group on the Form Layout Tools Format tab.

Begin Activity

Change the appearance of a form title.

1. Click the **ClientInfo form title**. An orange box surrounds the title, indicating it is selected.
2. Click between the letters *t* and *I* to position the insertion point in the title text, and then press the **Spacebar**. The form title is now *Client Info*.
3. Press the **Right Arrow key** four times to move the insertion point to the end of the title, and then type **rmation**. The form title is now *Client Information,* and the word *Information* appears on a second and third line.
4. Click in the **main form area** to deselect the title. Click **Client Information** to reselect the title. The orange outline appears around the title.
5. Position the **pointer** on top of the **right edge of the orange outline** around the title so that the pointer changes to ↔.
6. Press and hold the **mouse button,** drag the **border** about one-eighth of an inch to the right, and then let go of the **mouse button.** All of the letters in *Information* now appear on one line.
7. Drag the **bottom border of the orange outline** up about one-half inch so the bottom border is below the word *Information*. There should be about the same amount of space between the word *Information* and the bottom border as there is between the word *Client* and the top border.
8. On the ribbon, click the **Form Layout Tools Format tab.** In the Font group, click the **Font Color button arrow** A, and then click the **Blue-Gray, Text 2 theme color.** The color is applied to the form title. Compare your screen to Exhibit 19-5.

End Activity

EXHIBIT 19-5 FORM TITLE WITH NEW COLOR APPLIED

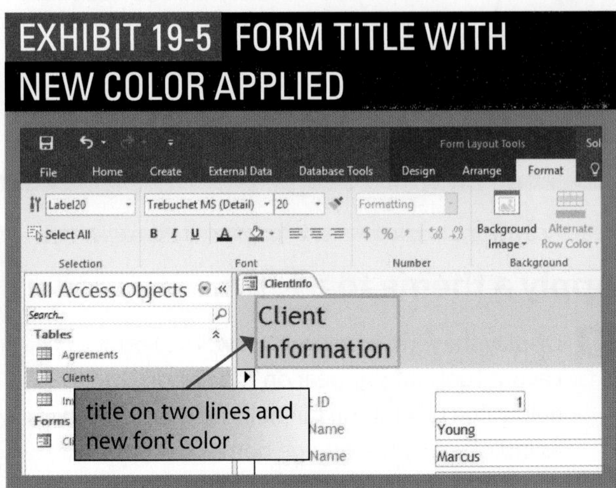

19-2c Adding a Logo to a Form

A logo can be used to provide color and visual interest in a form. A logo is one of many controls you can use in a form. A **control** is an item in a form, report, or other database object that you can manipulate to modify the object's appearance. The controls you add and modify in Layout view are available on the Form Layout Tools Design tab in the Controls group and the Header/Footer group.

When you add a logo or other control to a form, it is placed in a **control layout**, which is a set of controls grouped together in a form or report so that you can manipulate the set as a single control. Exhibit 19-6 shows a logo inserted on the ClientInfo form in its control layout. The dotted outline indicates the control layout is selected. You can remove a control from the control layout so you can move the control independently of the control layout.

Begin Activity

Add a picture to a form.

1. On the ribbon, click the **Form Layout Tools Design tab**. In the Header/Footer group, click the **Logo button**. The Insert Picture dialog box opens.
2. Click the data file **Panels** located in the Chapter 19\Chapter folder, and then click **OK**. A

control An item in a form, report, or other database object that you can manipulate to modify the object's appearance.

control layout A set of controls grouped together in a form or report so that you can manipulate the set as a single control.

EXHIBIT 19-6 FORM WITH PICTURE

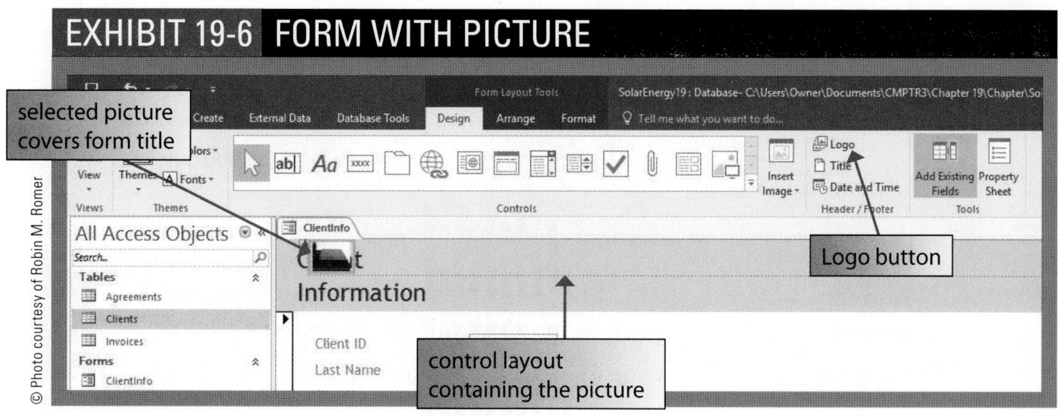

picture of solar panels appears on top of the form title. A solid orange outline surrounds the picture, indicating it is selected, and a dotted outline surrounds the control layout. Refer to Exhibit 19-6.

3 Right-click the **selected picture** to display the shortcut menu, point to **Layout**, and then click **Remove Layout**. The picture is removed from the control layout.

4 Drag the **picture** to the right of the title so that it does not block any part of the form title.

5 Drag a **corner of the orange box** to enlarge the picture to fit within the shaded title area. Compare your screen to Exhibit 19-7 and adjust the size and position of the picture if necessary.

End Activity

EXHIBIT 19-7 FORM WITH REPOSITIONED AND RESIZED PICTURE

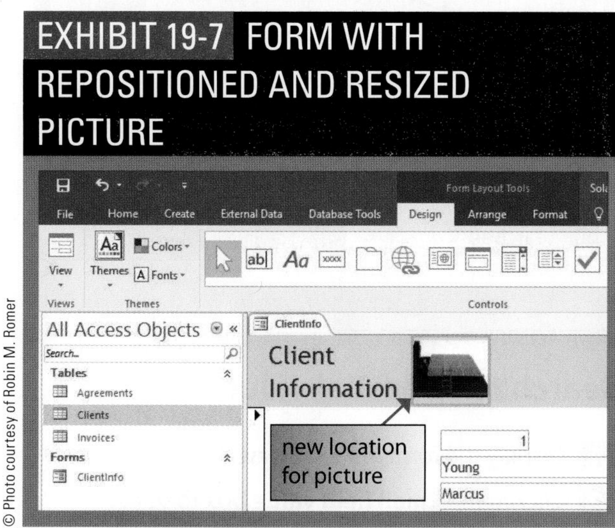

19-2d Changing the Lines in a Form

Each field value in the form is displayed in a field value box. The field value boxes are made up of solid lines, which, depending on the theme, might overshadow the field values and make them difficult to read. Fortunately, the lines are another type of control that you can modify in Layout view. The Control Formatting group on the Form Layout Tools Format tab provides options for changing the thickness, type, and color of any line in a form. See Exhibit 19-8. You can change the line type for each field value box in the form one at a time. Or, you can select all of the field value boxes and apply a new line type to all of them at the same time.

Begin Activity

Change the lines in a form.

1 Click the **Client ID field value box**, which contains the field value 1. An orange outline appears around the field value box to indicate it is selected.

2 On the ribbon, click the **Form Layout Tools Format tab**. In the Control Formatting group, click the **Shape Outline button**. The Shape Outline gallery opens with options for changing the line color, line thickness, and line type.

3 Point to **Line Type** to display a submenu with line formats. Refer to Exhibit 19-8.

4 Click the **Dash Dot line type**, and then click a **blank area of the main form**. The line around the Client ID field value box is now alternating dashes and dots.

5 Click the **Last Name field value box**, press and hold the **Shift key**, click each remaining field value box below the Last Name field value box, and then release the **Shift key**. All of the field value boxes except the Client ID field value box are selected.

6 On the Form Layout Tools Format tab, in the Control Formatting group, click the **Shape Outline button**, and then point to **Line Type**.

7 Click the **Dash Dot line type**, and then click a **blank area of the main form**. The line type for each box is now dotted.

8 Save the form.

End Activity

EXHIBIT 19-8 LINE TYPE SUBMENU

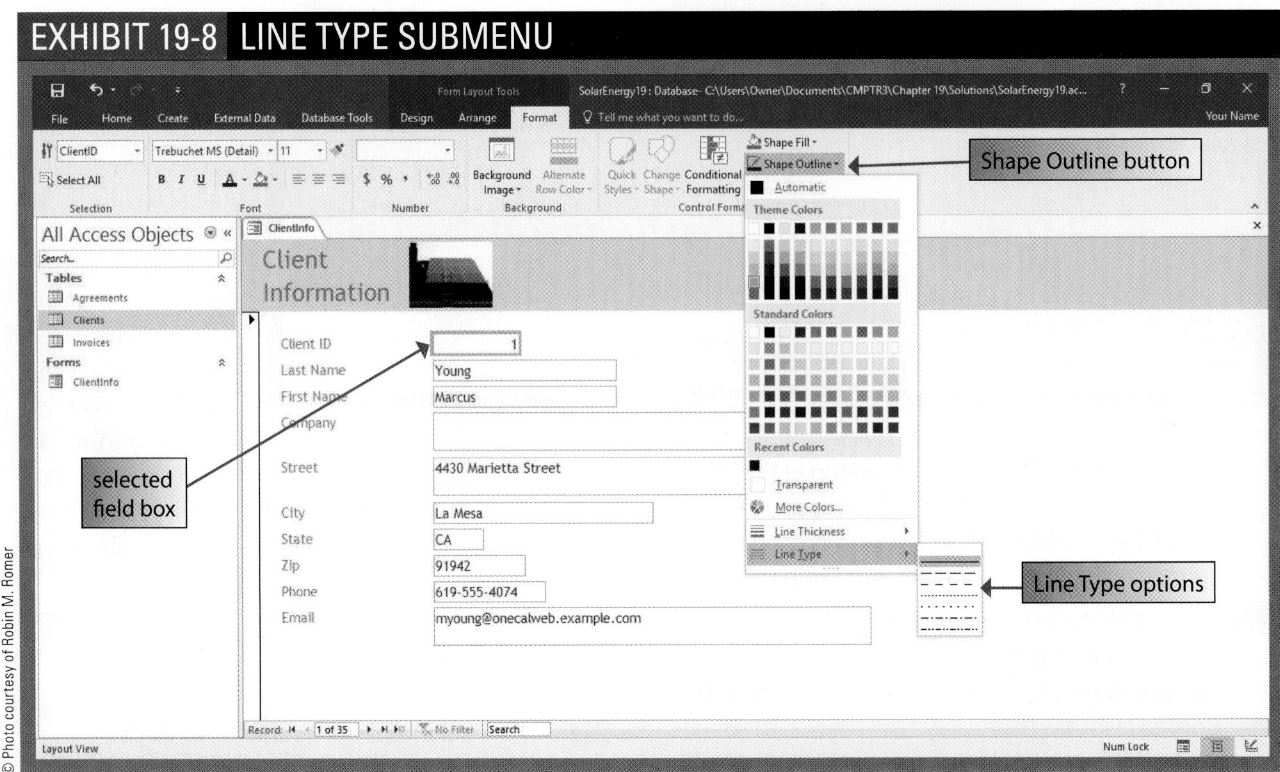

19-3 FINDING DATA USING A FORM

You can use the Find and Replace dialog box to search for data in a form. As you did when using the Find and Replace dialog box to search a datasheet, you choose a field to base the search on by making that field the current field, and then you enter the value you want to match. The record you want to view is then displayed in the form.

19-3a Searching for a Partial Value

Instead of searching for an entire field value, you can search for a record that contains part of the value anywhere in that field. Performing a partial search such as this is often easier than matching the entire field value and is useful when you don't know or can't remember the entire field value. For example, you can search for part of a company's name.

To search fields for values, use the Find and Replace dialog box as shown in Exhibit 19-9. When you open this dialog box, the default is to search in the current field, so you should click in the field in which you want to search before you open the dialog box. Another default is that the entire field must match the search text unless you change the option in the Match box to Any Part of Field.

EXHIBIT 19-9 FIND AND REPLACE DIALOG BOX

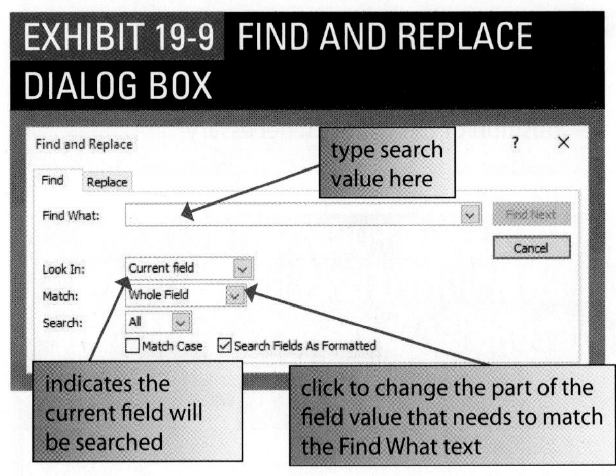

Begin Activity

Search for a partial value.

1. Display the form in **Form view.**
2. Click in the **Email field value box** to select Email as the current field and as the field to search.
3. On the Home tab, in the Find group, click the **Find button**. The Find and Replace dialog box opens. The Look In box shows that the current field (in this case, Email) will be searched. Refer to Exhibit 19-9.

4 In the Find What box, type **more** to search for records that contain the text *more* in the email address.

5 Click the **Match arrow** to display the list of matching options, and then click **Any Part of Field** to find records that contain the text *more* in any part of the Email field.

6 Click **Find Next**, and then drag the Find and Replace dialog box by its title bar so you can see the field value boxes in the form. The ClientInfo form now displays record 10, which is the record for Elizabeth Moore. The text *more* is selected in the Email field value box because you searched for this string of characters.

7 Click in the **form area** to make the form active. The Find and Replace dialog box remains open.

8 Click in the **Email field value box** between the *m* and the *o* at the beginning of the email address, and then type **o** to add a second *o*. The contact's email address is now correct.

End Activity

TIP: Unless you select the Match Case check box, Access will find any record containing the search text with any combination of uppercase and lowercase letters.

19-3b Searching with Wildcards

Instead of entering an exact value to find when you search for text with the Find and Replace dialog box, you can use wildcards. A **wildcard character** is a placeholder you use when you know only part of a value or when you want to start or end with a specific character or match a certain pattern. Exhibit 19-10 lists wildcard characters.

For example, you might want to view the records for customers with phone numbers beginning with the area code 760. You could search for any field containing the digits 760 in any part of the field, but this search would also find records with the digits 760 in other parts of the phone number. To find only those records with the 760 area code, you can use the * wildcard character.

Begin Activity

Search with a wildcard character.

1 In the ClientInfo form, click in the **Phone field value box**. This is the field you want to search.

2 Click the **Find and Replace dialog box** to make it active. The Look In box setting is still Current field, which is now the Phone field; this is the field that will be searched.

3 Click in the Find What box to select **more**, and then type **760***.

4 Click the **Match arrow**, and then click **Whole Field**. Because you are using a wildcard character in the search value, you want to search the whole field.

5 Click **Find Next**. The search process starts from the point of the previously displayed record in the form, which was record 10, and then finds records in which any field value in the Phone field begins with 760. Record 18 is the first record found for a customer with the area code 760.

6 Click **Find Next** three more times. Records 27, 30, and 33 are the next records found for customers with the area code 760.

7 Click **Find Next** again. The next record found is record 8. Because record 10 was the current record when you started the search, the search process cycled back through the beginning of the records.

EXHIBIT 19-10 WILDCARD CHARACTERS

Wildcard Character	Purpose	Example
*	Match any number of characters. It can be used as the first and/or last character in the character string.	th* finds the, that, this, therefore, and so on
?	Match any single alphabetic character.	a?t finds act, aft, ant, apt, and art
[]	Match any single character within the brackets.	a[fr]t finds aft and art but not act, ant, and apt
!	Match any character not within brackets.	a[!fr]t finds act, ant, and apt but not aft and art
-	Match any one of a range of characters. The range must be in ascending order (a to z, not z to a).	a[d-p]t finds aft, ant, and apt but not act and art
#	Match any single numeric character.	#72 finds 072, 172, 272, 372, and so on

wildcard character A placeholder you use when you know only part of a value, or when you want to start or end with a specific character or match a certain pattern.

8 Click **Find Next** again. Record 10, the record you started with appears. This is because this record has a phone number that has the area code 760.

9 Click **Find Next** one more time. A dialog box appears, indicating that the search is finished.

10 Click **OK** to close the dialog box.

11 Click **Cancel** to close the Find and Replace dialog box.

End Activity

19-3c Maintaining Table Data Using a Form

Maintaining data using a form in Form view is often easier than using a datasheet because you can focus on all the changes for one record at one time. For example, you can add a new record to the table. Exhibit 19-11 shows the ClientInfo form in Form view after clicking the New button in the Records group on the Home tab or the New (blank) record button on the record navigation bar. In Form view, you can also edit the field values for a record or delete a record from the underlying table. If you know the number of the record you want to edit or delete, you can enter the number in the Current Record box to move to that record.

EXHIBIT 19-11 FORM FOR A NEW RECORD

ClientInfo

Client Information

Client ID is an AutoNumber field so the number will be added by Access

Client ID (New)
Last Name
First Name
Company
Street
City
State
Zip
Phone
Email

Record: 36 of 36 No Filter Search

Begin Activity

Maintain table data using a form.

1 In the record navigation bar at the bottom of the form, click in the **Current Record box**, delete **10**, type **8** and then press the **Enter key**. Record 8 (LKW Construction) is now current.

2 In the Street field value box, drag to select the **4457 Water Street**, and then type **6195 South Main Street**. The address is updated.

3 On the Home tab, in the Records group, click the **New button**. Record 36, the next available new record, becomes the current record. All field value boxes are empty, and the insertion point is positioned in the Client ID field value box. Refer back to Exhibit 19-11.

4 Press the **Tab key**, and then type your last name in the Last Name field.

5 Press the **Tab key**, and type your first name in the First Name field.

6 Press the **Tab key** seven times to move the insertion point to the Email field, and then press the **Tab key** once more. A new record 37, the next available new record, becomes the current record, and the record for Customer ID 36 is saved in the Clients table.

7 Close the **ClientInfo form**.

End Activity

19-4 CREATING A FORM BASED ON RELATED TABLES

Forms can display data from two or more related tables at the same time, offering a more complete picture of the information in the database. For example, a form might show data about customers and their associated contracts, which are stored in separate tables. A form based on two tables requires the tables to have a defined relationship. For example, defining a relationship between a Clients (primary) table and a Agreements (related) table enables you to create a form based on both tables. When you use related tables in a form, the form includes a main form and a subform. A **main form** displays the data from the primary table. A **subform** displays the data from the

main form The part of a form that displays data from the primary table in a defined relationship.

subform The part of a form that displays data from a related table in a defined relationship.

related table. Access uses the defined relationship between the tables to join them automatically through the common field that exists in both tables.

19-4a Creating a Form with a Main Form and a Subform

When creating a form based on two tables, first you choose the primary table and select the fields to include in the main form. Then you choose the related table and select the fields to include in the subform.

To create a form and a subform, you use the Form Wizard. If you select fields from two tables in the first dialog box, a new second dialog box appears, as shown in Exhibit 19-12. In this dialog box, you choose whether to create a main form with a subform or a linked form. In a linked form, only the main form fields are displayed, and a button with the subform's name on it appears on the main form. You can click this button to display the associated subform records.

EXHIBIT 19-12 FORMATS FOR THE MAIN FORM AND SUBFORM

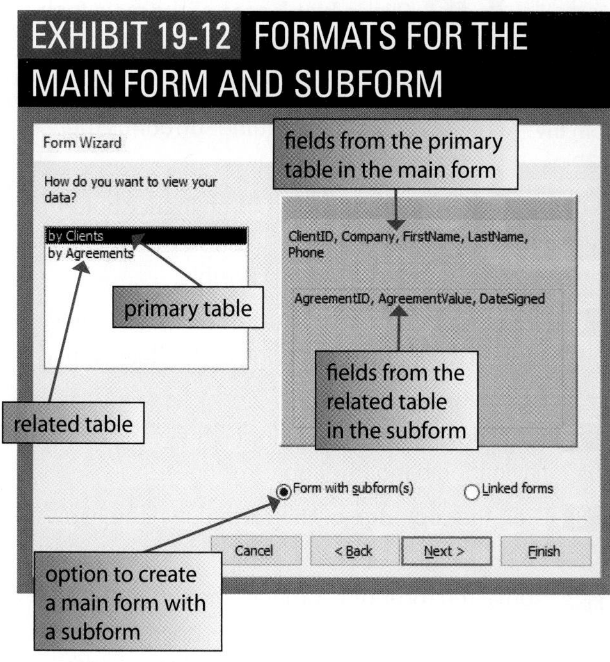

Begin Activity

Create a form with a main form and a subform.

1. On the ribbon, click the **Create tab**. In the Forms group, click the **Form Wizard button**. The first Form Wizard dialog box opens.
2. If necessary, click the **Tables/Queries arrow**, and then click **Table: Clients**.
3. Move the following fields from the Available Fields box to the Selected Fields box in the order listed: **ClientID**, **Company**, **FirstName**, **LastName**, and **Phone**.
4. Click the **Tables/Queries arrow**, and then click **Table: Agreements**. The fields from the Agreements table appear in the Available Fields box.
5. Move all the fields in the Agreements table to the Selected Fields box. The table name (Agreements) is included in the ClientID field name to distinguish it from the same field (ClientID) in the Clients table.
6. Move the **Agreements.ClientID** field back to the Available Fields box.
7. Click **Next**. The second Form Wizard dialog box appears. The Form with subform(s) option button is selected. The left box shows the order in which the data will be displayed—first data from the primary Clients table, and then data from the related Agreements table. The preview on the right shows how the form will appear—fields from the Clients table at the top in the main form and fields from the Agreements table at the bottom in the subform. Refer back to Exhibit 19-12.
8. Click **Next**. The third Form Wizard dialog box opens, in which you choose the subform layout. The Tabular layout displays subform fields as a table. The Datasheet layout displays subform fields as a table datasheet.
9. Click the **Datasheet option button** if it is not already selected, and then click **Next**. The fourth Form Wizard dialog box opens, in which you choose titles for the main form and the subform.
10. In the **Form box**, click to the right of the last letter in the word *Clients,* press the **Backspace** key to delete the *s*, and then type **Agreements**. The main form name is now *ClientAgreements*.
11. In the **Subform box**, delete the space between the two words so that the subform name is *AgreementsSubform*.

TIP: You can double-click a field to move it between the Available Fields box and the Selected Fields box.

12 Click **Finish**. The completed form opens in Form view formatted with the Office theme. The main form displays the fields from the first record in the Clients table in a columnar format. The records in the main form appear in primary key order by Client ID. Client ID 1 has two related records in the Agreements table, which appear in the subform in the datasheet format. Compare your screen to Exhibit 19-13.

End Activity

19-4b Modifying a Main Form and Subform in Layout View

You can modify a form with a main form and a subform, just as you can a form based on one table. For example, you can edit the form title, resize the subform, and resize columns to fully display their field values. You can make these types of changes in Layout view or Design view.

EXHIBIT 19-13 MAIN FORM WITH SUBFORM IN FORM VIEW

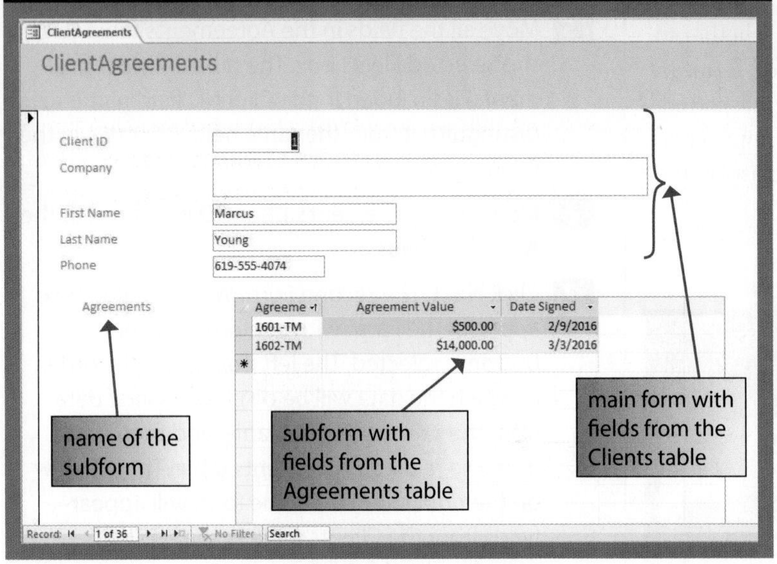

Begin Activity

Modify a main form and subform in Layout view.

1 Display the **ClientAgreements form** in **Layout view.**

2 In the shaded title area at the top of the form, select and then edit the **form title** so that the title in the form is *Client Agreements.*

3 Click a **blank area** of the main form to deselect the title.

4 Click the **subform** to select it. An orange outline surrounds the subform.

5 Resize each column in the subform datasheet so that the widest entry in each column is visible.

6 Drag the **right edge of the subform** to the left to align it with the right edge of the Date Signed column.

7 Scroll down so that you can see the record navigation bar of the subform, if necessary.

8 Drag the **top edge of the form** down three rows. The table resizes so it is shorter.

9 Above the top-right corner of the subform, drag the **table move handle** up until the pointer is to the right of the label Agreements. After you release the mouse button, the subform moves up and you can see the entire subform in the window without needing to scroll. Compare your screen to Exhibit 19-14.

10 Save the **ClientAgreements form**, and then switch to **Form view.**

End Activity

FYI

MAIN FORM AND SUBFORM NAMES

The main form name (ClientAgreements, in this case) appears on the object tab and as the form title. The subform name (Agreements, in this case) appears to the left of the subform. Access displays only the table name for the subform, but uses the complete object name, AgreementsSubform, in the Navigation Pane. The subform designation is necessary in a list of database objects, so that you can distinguish the AgreementsSubform from other objects, such as the Agreements table. The subform designation is not needed in the ClientAgreements form; only the table name is required to identify the table containing the records in the subform.

EXHIBIT 19-14 MODIFIED FORM IN LAYOUT VIEW

Enter key. Record 25 in the Clients table (for Jack's Café) becomes the current record in the main form. The subform shows that this customer has six agreements, and the first agreement is selected.

4 At the bottom of the subform, on the record navigation bar, click the **Next record button** ▸. The second agreement in the subform, AgreementID 1620-LB, is selected in the subform.

5 At the bottom of the subform, on the record navigation bar, click the **Last record button** ▸|. Agreement ID 1730-AD in the Agreements table becomes the current record in the subform.

End Activity

19-4c **Displaying Records in a Main Form and a Subform**

A form with a main form and subform includes two sets of navigation buttons. The navigation buttons at the bottom of the Form window select records from the primary table in the main form. The navigation buttons at the bottom of the subform select records from the related table in the subform. The subform navigation buttons may not be visible until you scroll to the bottom of the main form. If you enter data in the main form, the primary table is updated. If you enter data in the subform, the related table is updated.

Begin Activity

Navigate main form and subform records.

1 At the bottom of the main Form window, on the record navigation bar, click the **Last record button** ▸|. Record 36 in the Clients table (your information) becomes the current record in the main form. The subform shows that this customer currently has no agreements.

2 Click the **Previous record button** ◂ twice. Record 34 in the Clients table (for Chen Builders) becomes the current record in the main form. The subform shows that this customer has two agreements.

3 At the bottom of the main Form window, on the record navigation bar, click in the **Current Record box,** select **34**, type **25** and then press the

19-5 PREVIEWING AND PRINTING SELECTED FORM RECORDS

When you print a form, Access prints as many form records as can fit on a printed page. If only part of a form record fits on the bottom of a page, the remainder of the record prints on the next page. You can choose to print all pages or a range of pages. In addition, you can print only the currently selected form record. Before printing, you should always preview the form using Print Preview to see how it will look when printed, as shown in Exhibit 19-15.

Begin Activity

Preview the form.

1 On the ribbon, click the **File tab**. In the navigation bar, click **Print**. The Print screen in Backstage view has three options: Quick Print, Print, and Print Preview.

2 Click **Print Preview**. The Print Preview window opens, showing the records for the ClientAgreements form. Each record appears in its own form, and shading distinguishes one record from the next. Refer to Exhibit 19-15.

EXHIBIT 19-15 FORM RECORDS DISPLAYED IN PRINT PREVIEW

3. On the ribbon, on the Print Preview tab, in the Close Preview group, click the **Close Print Preview button**. Print Preview closes, and you return to the ClientAgreements form in Form view with the record for Jack's Café still displayed in the main form.

End Activity

You can print the data of a single record. To do this, you need to open the Print dialog box from the Print screen in Backstage view. See Exhibit 19-16. You can also open the Print dialog box by clicking the Print button in the Print group on the Print Preview tab; however, the option to print only selected records does not appear in the Print dialog box when you use this method.

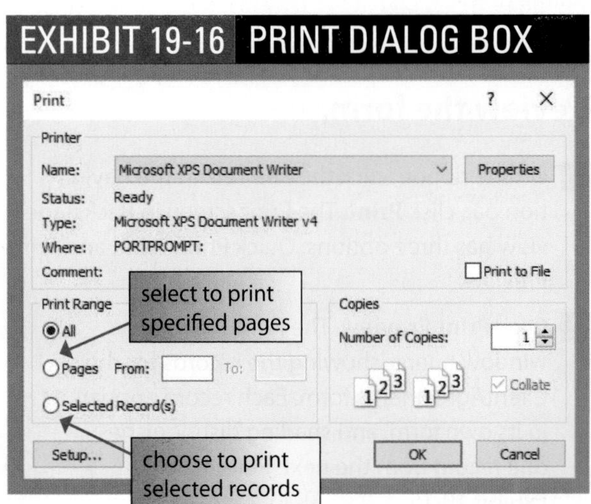

Begin Activity

Print the current record.

1. On the ribbon, click the **File tab**. In the navigation bar, click **Print**. On the Print screen, click **Print**. The Print dialog box appears. Refer to Exhibit 19-16.
2. Click the **Selected Record(s) option button**. Now only the current form record (record 25) will print.
3. Click **OK** to close the dialog box and print the selected record, or click **Cancel** to close the dialog box without printing.
4. Close the **ClientAgreements form**.

End Activity

19-6 CREATING A REPORT USING THE REPORT WIZARD

Reports provide a formatted printout or screen display of the data in a database. For example, a database might include a formatted report of customer and contract data that staff can use for market analysis and strategic planning for selling services to customers. You can design your own reports, or you can use the Report Wizard to create them. The Report Wizard guides you through the process of creating a report. You choose which fields to display from tables and queries as well as how to group and sort the records in the report, the page orientation, and the report's title. As with a form, you can change the report's design after you create it.

19-6a Creating a Report

When you create a report with the Report Wizard, you first choose the table or query on which to base the report and then select the fields you want to include in the report. You can select fields from more than one table as long as the tables are related, such as the Clients and Agreements tables.

In the Report Wizard, the second dialog box lets you choose whether to show the data in the report grouped by table or ungrouped. See the top dialog box in Exhibit 19-17. A grouped report places the data from the first table in one group followed by the related records. For example, each customer record will appear in its own group followed by the related agreement records for that customer. An example of an ungrouped report would be a report of records from the Clients and Agreements tables in order by AgreementsID. Each agreement and its associated customer data would appear together on one or more lines of the report, not grouped by table.

EXHIBIT 19-17 DIALOG BOXES IN THE REPORT WIZARD

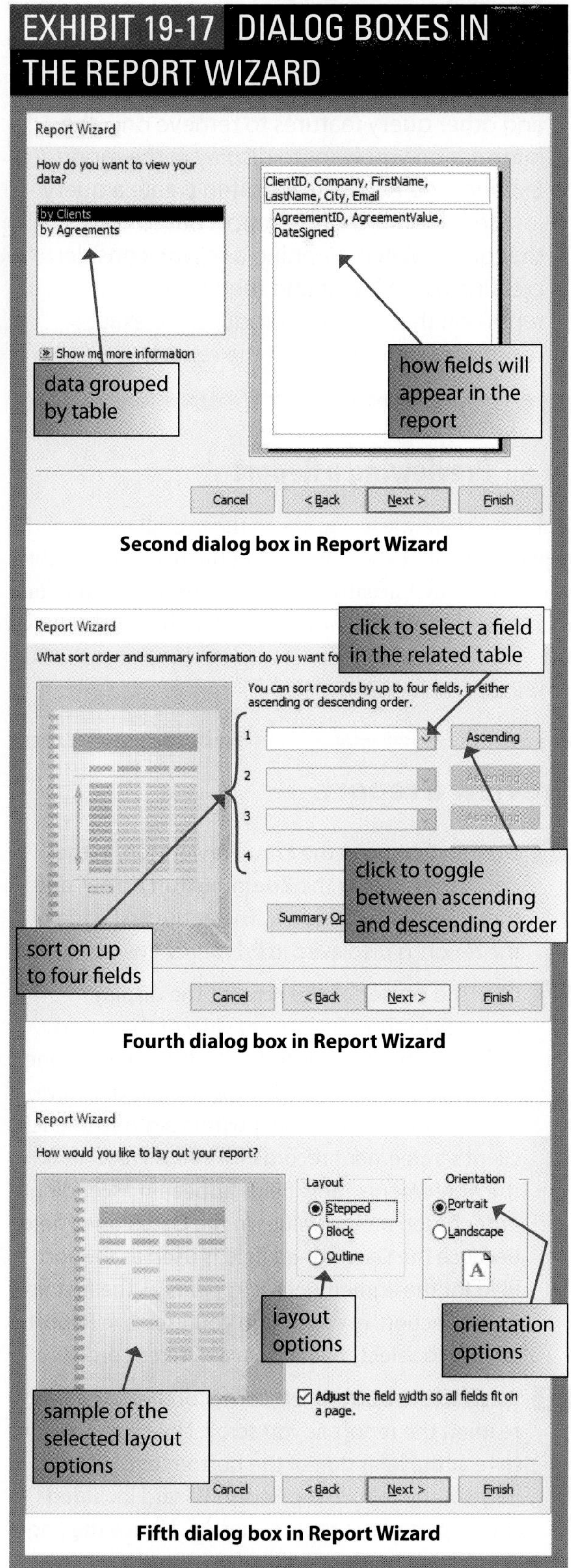

Second dialog box in Report Wizard

Fourth dialog box in Report Wizard

Fifth dialog box in Report Wizard

Whether the report is grouped or ungrouped, the next dialog box in the Report Wizard lets you select grouping levels to add to the report. Grouping levels are useful for reports with multiple levels, such as those containing monthly, quarterly, and annual totals, or for those containing city and country groups.

The next dialog box that appears lets you choose the sort order for the detail records. See the center dialog box in Exhibit 19-17. You can sort the detail records for the report by up to four fields, choosing ascending or descending order for each field.

In the next dialog box, you select a layout and the page orientation for the report. See the bottom dialog box in Exhibit 19-17.

Begin Activity

Create a report using the Report Wizard.

1 On the ribbon, click the **Create tab**. In the Reports group, click the **Report Wizard button**. The first Report Wizard dialog box opens. You select the table or query and then add fields to use in the report.

2 If necessary, click the **Tables/Queries arrow**, and then click **Table: Clients**.

3 Move the following fields from the Available Fields box to the Selected Fields box in the order listed: **ClientID**, **Company**, **FirstName**, **LastName**, **City**, and **Email**. The fields will appear in the report in the order you select them.

4 Click the **Tables/Queries arrow**, and then click **Tables: Agreements**. The fields from the Agreements table appear in the Available Fields box.

5 Move all of the fields from the Available Fields box to the Selected Fields box.

6 Move the **Agreements.ClientID** field from the Selected Fields box back to the Available Fields box. The ClientID field will appear on the report with the customer data, so you do not need to include it in the detail records for each agreement.

7 Click **Next**. The second Report Wizard dialog box appears, in which you select whether the report is grouped by table or ungrouped. Refer to the top dialog box shown in Exhibit 19-17. You will leave the report grouped by the Clients table.

> **TIP:** You can display tips for creating reports and examples of reports by clicking the Show me more information button.

8 Click **Next**. The third Report Wizard dialog box opens, in which you can choose additional grouping levels. Two grouping levels are shown: one for a client's data, and the other for a client's agreements.

9 Click **Next**. The fourth Report Wizard dialog box opens, in which you can choose the sort order for the detail records. The records from the Agreements table for a client represent the detail records for the report. Refer back to the center dialog box shown in Exhibit 19-17.

10 Click the **1 arrow**, and then click **DateSigned**. The Ascending option is selected, so the agreements will be shown in chronological order.

> **TIP:** To change the sort order to descending, click the Ascending button.

11 Click **Next**. The fifth Report Wizard dialog box opens, in which you choose a layout and page orientation for the report. Refer back to the bottom dialog box shown in Exhibit 19-17.

12 In the Layout section, click the **Outline option button** to select the Outline layout.

13 In the Orientation section, click the **Landscape option button**. This page orientation provides more space across the page to display longer field values.

14 Click **Next**. The sixth and final Report Wizard dialog box opens. The report title you enter in this dialog box also serves as the name for the report object in the database.

15 In the box for the title, edit the title to **ClientsAndAgreements**. You entered the report name as one word so that the report object is named appropriately.

16 Click **Finish**. The Report Wizard creates the report, saves the report as an object in the database, and opens the report in Print Preview.

End Activity

> **FYI**
>
> **CREATE A REPORT BASED ON A QUERY**
>
> You can create a report based on one or more tables or queries. When you base a report on a query, you can use criteria and other query features to retrieve only the information you want to display in the report. Experienced Access users often create a query just so they can create a report based on that query. When planning a report, consider creating a query first and then basing the report on that query to produce the exact results you want to see in the report.

19-6b Previewing a Report

In Print Preview, you can check the overall layout of the report, as well as zoom in to read the text. This enables you to find any formatting problems or other issues and make the necessary corrections. Exhibit 19-18 shows the ClientsAndAgreements report in Print Preview zoomed in.

Begin Activity

Preview a report.

1 On the ribbon, on the Print Preview tab, in the Zoom group, click the **Zoom button arrow**, and then click **Fit to Window**. The entire first page of the report is displayed in Print Preview.

2 Click the **center of the report**. The display changes to show a close-up view of the report. Refer to Exhibit 19-18. Shading distinguishes one client's record from the next, as well as one agreement record from the next within a group of each client's agreement records. The detail records for the Agreements table fields appear in ascending order based on the values in the DateSigned field. Because the DateSigned field is used as the sort field for the agreements, it appears as the first field in this section, even though you used the Report Wizard to select the fields in a different order.

3 Scroll to the bottom-left corner of the first page, reading the report as you scroll. Notice the current date at the left edge of the bottom of the first page of the report; the Report Wizard included this as part of the report's design. Notice the page number at the right edge of the footer.

EXHIBIT 19-18 CLOSE-UP VIEW OF THE REPORT

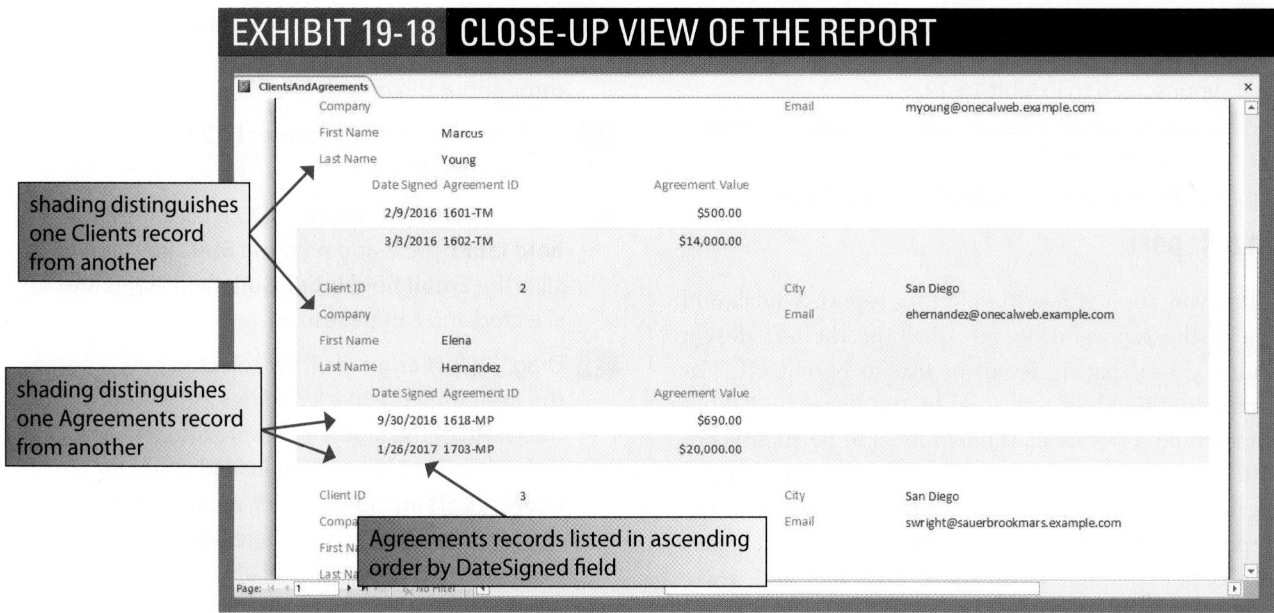

4 Click the report to zoom back out, and then use the navigation buttons to review the 12 pages of the report.

5 On the Print Preview tab, in the Close Preview group, click the **Close Print Preview button.** Print Preview closes and the report is displayed in Design view.

PROBLEM? If you see blank pages every other page, the text of the page number might be outside the page border. You'll fix this soon.

End Activity

19-7 MODIFYING A REPORT'S DESIGN IN LAYOUT VIEW

You modify a report's design in Layout view or in Design view. Many of the same options that are available for forms are also provided for reports.

19-7a Changing a Report's Appearance

You can change the text of the report title as well as the font and color of text in a report to enhance its appearance. The same themes available for forms are also available for reports. You can choose to apply a theme to the current report object only, or to all reports in the database. When you point to a theme in the Themes gallery, a ScreenTip displays the names of the database objects that use the theme. You can also add a picture to a report for visual interest or to identify a particular section of the report.

Begin Activity

Change a report's appearance.

1 Display the report in **Layout view**. The Report Layout Tools tabs appear on the ribbon.

2 If a pane opens on the right, at the top of the pane, click the **Close button** ✕.

3 On the ribbon, click the **Report Layout Tools Design tab**. In the Themes group, click the **Themes button**, right-click the **Facet theme**, and then click **Apply Theme to This Object Only**. The gallery closes, and the theme is applied to the report.

4 At the top of the report, select the **report title,** and then edit the text to **Clients and Agreements**.

5 Click in the **report** to deselect the report title, and then select the **report title** again.

6 On the ribbon, click the **Report Layout Tools Format tab**. In the Font group, click the **Font Color button arrow**, and then click the **Blue-Gray, Text 2 theme color**. The color is applied to the report title.

7 On the ribbon, click the **Report Layout Tools Design tab**. In the Header/Footer group, click the **Logo button**.

8 Double-click the data file **Panels** located in the Chapter 19\Chapter folder. The picture is inserted in the upper-left corner of the report, partially covering the report title.

9 Drag the selected **picture** to the right of the report title within the shaded title area. Compare your screen to Exhibit 19-19.

End Activity

19-7b Resizing Fields and Field Values in a Report

After you apply a new theme to a report, you should check the report to be sure that the theme's design didn't cause spacing issues or text to be cut off. For example, the larger font used by the Facet theme has caused the Agreement ID field label to be slightly cut off. Working in Layout view, you can resize and reposition labels and fields to improve the appearance of the report or to address the problem of some field values not being completely displayed. To select and resize multiple fields, you press the Shift key as you select the different fields. You should also check the page number in the footer to make sure it fits completely on the page.

Begin Activity

Resize field labels and field value boxes.

1 In the report, click the first **Agreement ID field label** to select it. When you select a field label in Layout view, all of the labels for that field are selected in the report. Any changes you make to a single selected field will also be made to the other labels for that field.

2 Resize the **Agreement ID field label** until the entire field label is visible. The change is made throughout the report.

3 Find the record for **Customer ID 21,** Brisbane Engineering Dept.

4 In the record for Customer ID 21, click the **City field label**, press and hold the **Shift key**, and then click the **Email field label**. Both field labels are selected and can be resized.

5 Drag the **left edge** of either selected field label to the right until the black outlines indicating the width of the labels are approximately one inch wide. The City and Email field labels for the entire report are now smaller, moving them closer to their values. Compare your screen to Exhibit 19-20.

6 Scroll the report to the bottom, and view the page number text. If the page number in the footer is not completely within the page border, select the **page number,** and then drag the **orange box** to the left until the page number text is within the page border.

End Activity

19-7c Using Conditional Formatting in a Report

You can add conditional formatting to a report or form. As when you used conditional formatting in Excel, special formatting is applied to field values that meet the condition or conditions you set. For example, you might

EXHIBIT 19-19 REPORT WITH INSERTED PICTURE

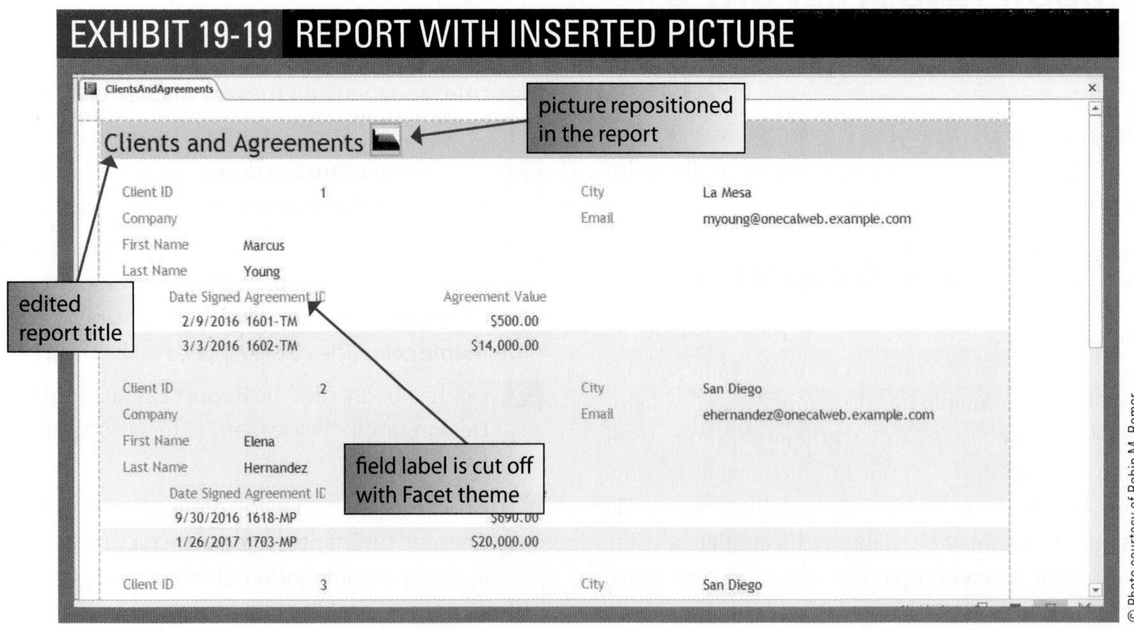

EXHIBIT 19-20 REPORT WITH RESIZED FIELD LABELS AND FIELD VALUE BOXES

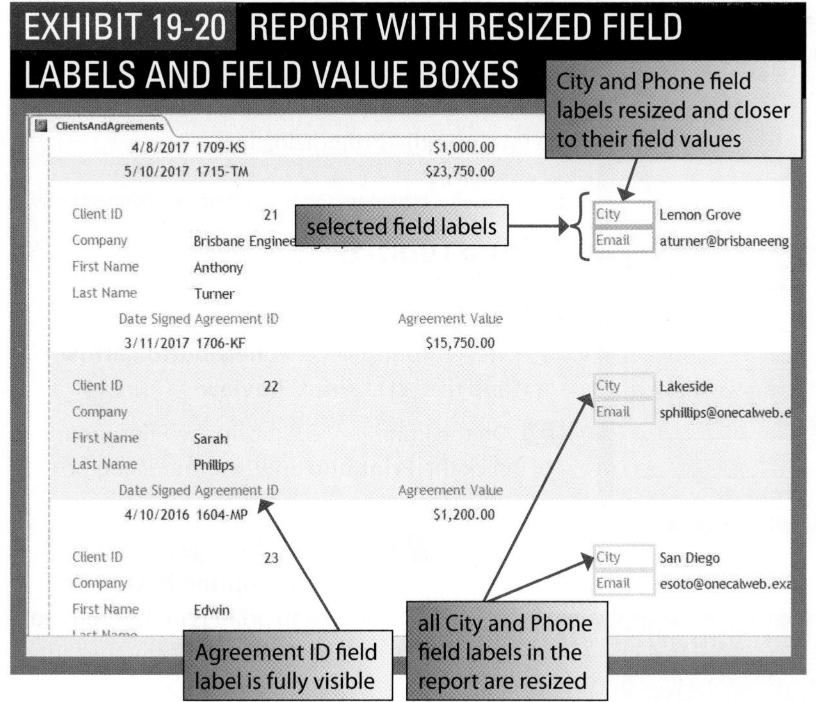

use conditional formatting in a report to format agreement amounts that are greater than or equal to $25,000 in a bold, red font.

Begin Activity

Use conditional formatting in a report.

1 In the record for Client ID 34, click the **Agreement Value field value for Agreement ID 1607-MP**. An orange outline appears around the field value box, and a lighter orange outline appears around the other Agreement Value field value boxes in the report. The conditional formatting you specify will affect all the values for the field.

> **TIP:** You must select a field *value box,* and not the field *label,* before applying a conditional format.

2 On the ribbon, click the **Report Layout Tools Format tab**. In the Control Formatting group, click the **Conditional Formatting button**. The Conditional Formatting Rules Manager dialog box opens. The field selected in the report, AgreementValue, appears in the Show formatting rules for box. No conditional formatting rules are set for the selected field.

3 In the dialog box, click the **New Rule button**. The New Formatting Rule dialog box opens. The selected rule type specifies that Access will check field values in the selected field to determine if they meet the condition. You enter the condition in the Edit the rule description box. The Field Value Is setting means that the conditional format you specify will be applied only when the value for the selected AgreementValue field meets the condition. See Exhibit 19-21.

4 On the box that contains the word *between,* click the **arrow**, and then click **greater than or equal to**.

5 Click in the empty box to the right of the box containing *greater than or equal to,* and then type **25000**. The condition is set to format cells where the field value is greater than or equal to 25,000.

6 In the Preview section, click the **Font color button arrow** [A], and then click the **Red color**.

7 In the Preview section, click the **Bold button** [B]. Any field value that meets the condition will be formatted in bold, red text.

8 Click **OK**. The new rule you specified appears in the Rule section of the Conditional Formatting Rules Manager dialog box as *Value >= 25000*. The Format section on the right shows the conditional formatting (red, bold font) that will be applied based on this rule. See Exhibit 19-22.

9 Click **OK**. The conditional formatting is applied to the AgreementValue field values. Compare your screen to Exhibit 19-23.

End Activity

EXHIBIT 19-21 NEW FORMATTING RULE DIALOG BOX

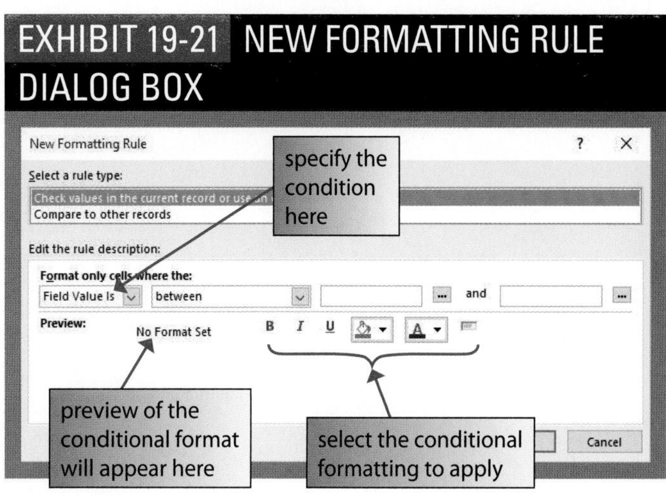

EXHIBIT 19-22 CONDITIONAL FORMATTING RULES MANAGER DIALOG BOX

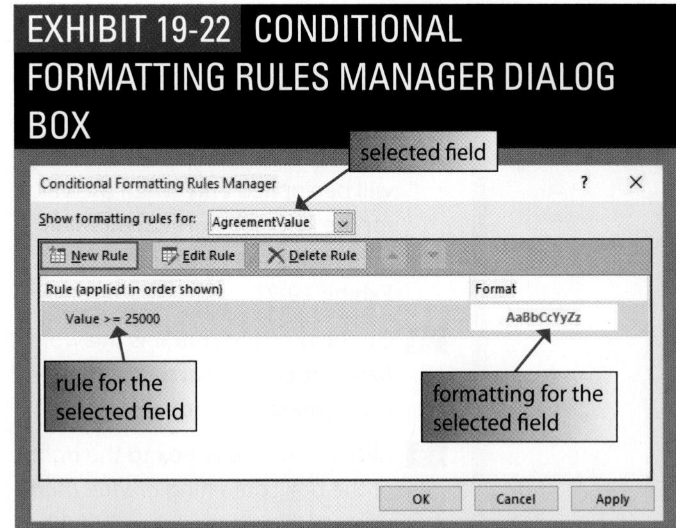

EXHIBIT 19-23 PRINT PREVIEW OF REPORT WITH CONDITIONAL FORMATTING

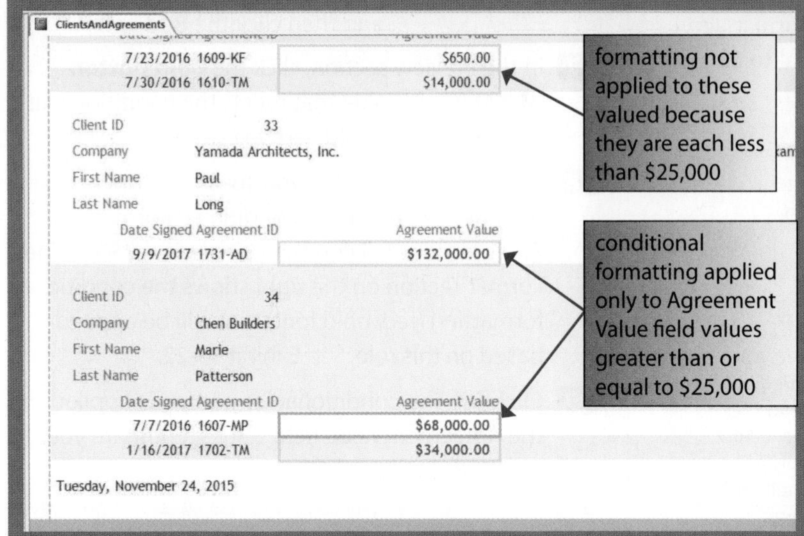

19-7d Printing a Report

When you print a report, you can specify whether to print the entire report or select pages to print. You do this from the Print dialog box.

Begin Activity

Print a report.

1. On the ribbon, click the **Home tab**. In the Views group, click the **View button arrow**, and then click **Print Preview**.
2. On the Print Preview tab, in the Print group, click the **Print button**. The Print dialog box opens.
3. In the Print Range section, click the **Pages option button**. The insertion point is in the From box so that you can specify the range of pages to print.
4. In the From box, type **1**, press the **Tab key** to move to the To box, and then type **1**. These settings specify that only page 1 of the report will be printed.
5. Click **OK** to print the first page of the report, or click **Cancel** to close the Print dialog box without printing.
6. Save the **ClientsAndAgreements report**, and then close it.
7. Compact and repair the **SolarEnergy19 database**, and then close the database.

End Activity

STUDY TOOLS 19

READY TO STUDY? IN THE BOOK, YOU CAN:

- ☐ Rip out the Chapter Review Card, which includes key terms and key chapter concepts.

ONLINE AT WWW.CENGAGEBRAIN.COM, YOU CAN:

- ☐ Review key concepts from the chapter in a short video.
- ☐ Explore creating forms and reports with the interactive infographic.
- ☐ Practice what you've learned with more Practice It and On Your Own exercises.
- ☐ Prepare for tests with quizzes.
- ☐ Review the key terms with flashcards.

QUIZ YOURSELF

1. Describe the difference between creating a form using the Form tool and creating a form using the Form Wizard.
2. How do you apply a theme to an existing form?
3. What is a control?
4. What is a wildcard character?
5. Which wildcard character matches any single alphabetic character?
6. In a form that contains a main form and a subform, what data is displayed in the main form and what data is displayed in the subform?
7. Describe the navigation buttons used to move through a form containing a main form and a subform.
8. Describe how to print only the current record displayed in a form.
9. What are detail records?
10. Describe how to resize a field in a report.
11. When working in Layout view for a report, how do you select multiple fields in the report?
12. How do you apply conditional formatting to a report?

PRACTICE IT

Practice It 19-1

1. Open the data file **Tree19** located in the Chapter 19\Practice It folder. Save the database as **TreeRemoval19**.
2. Use the Form Wizard to create a form based on the Customers table. Select all fields for the form, use the Columnar layout, and specify the title **CustomerContactInfo** for the form.

3. Display the form in Layout view, and then apply the Wisp theme to the CustomerContactInfo form only.
4. Edit the form title so that it appears as **Customer Contact Info** (three words). Widen the box so that the title fits on one line. Change the font color of the form title to the Olive Green, Accent 4, Darker 25% theme color.
5. Insert the data file **Tree** located in the Chapter 19\Practice It folder as a logo in the CustomerContactInfo form. Remove the picture from the control layout, move the picture to the right of the form title, and then resize it to be the same height as the shaded title area.
6. Change the line type for all of the field value boxes to the Dash Dot type.
7. Switch to Form view, and use the Customer Contact Info form to update the Customers table as follows:
    a. Use the Find command to search for **pony** anywhere in the Company field to display the record for the Pony Grill (Client ID 19). Change the Street field value in this record to **4640 Willow Way**.
    b. Add a new record with your first and last names in the First Name and Last Name fields.
8. Save and close the form.
9. Use the Form Wizard to create a form containing a main form and a subform based on the Customers and ServiceContracts tables. Select all fields from the Customers table for the main form, and select ContractNum, ContractDate, and ContractAmt from the ServiceContracts table for the subform. Use the Datasheet layout. Specify the title **CustomerAndServiceContracts** for the main form and **ServiceContractsSubform** for the subform.
10. Change the form title text to **Customer Service Contracts**.
11. Resize all columns in the subform to their best fit. Save and close the CustomerAndServiceContracts form.
12. Use the Report Wizard to create a report based on the primary ServiceContracts table and the related Invoices table. Select all the fields from the ServiceContracts table, and select the InvNum, InvDate, InvAmt, and Paid fields from the Invoices table. Do not specify any additional grouping levels, and sort the detail records by the Paid field in ascending order. Choose the Outline layout and Landscape orientation. Specify the title **InvoicesByContract** for the report.
13. Display the report in Layout view. Change the report title text to **Invoices by Contract**.
14. Apply the Wisp theme to the InvoicesByContract report only. Widen the outline around the title if needed.
15. Change the color of the report title text to the Olive Green, Accent 4, Darker 25% theme color.
16. Resize the Service Type label box so it just fits the label, and resize the Amount field value box in the main form so the value in it is right-aligned with the values in the CustomerID and Contract Date field value boxes.
17. In the subform, resize the Amount field label box and the Amount field value box from the left so that the boxes are about half the size they were.
18. Drag the right edge of the Invoice Date field label box about one-quarter inch to the right, and then drag the left edge of the the Invoice Date field label box to the left so the label just fits inside the box.
19. Drag the right edge of the Invoice Number field label box to the right so the box is large enough to just fit the label.
20. Drag the left edge of the Paid? label box to the left about one-eighth of an inch so that the Paid? label fits in the box.
21. Apply conditional formatting so that the Invoice Date field values less than 1/1/2017 are bold Red.
22. Preview each page of the report, verifying that all the fields fit on the page. If necessary, return to Layout view and make changes so the report prints within the margins of the page and so that all field names and values are completely displayed.
23. Save the InvoicesByContract report, print only page 3 of the report, and then close the report.
24. Compact and repair the TreeRemoval19 database, and then close it.

Practice It 19-2

1. Open the data file **Studio19** located in the Chapter 19\Practice It folder. Save the database as **StudioClasses19**.
2. Use the Form Wizard to create a form based on the Students table. Select all the fields for the form and the Columnar layout. Specify the title **StudentData** for the form.
3. Apply the Ion theme to the StudentData form only.
4. Edit the form title so that it appears as **Student Data** (two words) on one line, and change the font

color of the form title to the Blue-Gray, Accent 5, Darker 25% theme color.

5. Use the Find command to display the record for Richard Collins, and then change the Address field value for this record to **210 Boston Street**.
6. Use the StudentData form to add a new record to the Students table using the Student ID **ZD4762**, the Session ID **129-PA**, and your first and last names in the First Name and Last Name fields.
7. Save and close the StudentData form.
8. Use the Form Wizard to create a form containing a main form and a subform. Select all the fields from the Faculty table for the main form, and select the SessionID, SessionName, and Teens fields from the Sessions table for the subform. Use the Datasheet layout. Specify the title **SessionsByInstructor** for the main form and the title **SessionsSubform** for the subform.
9. Change the form title text for the main form to **Sessions by Instructor**.
10. Change the line type for all the field value boxes in the main form except for the Full Time? check box to Dashes.
11. Move through the records in the main form and until you see the session name Clay Handbuilding and Sculpture in the subform, and then resize the all the columns in the subform to their best fit. Resize the subform so the subform just fits horizontally within the border.
12. Save and close the SessionsByInstructor form.
13. Use the Report Wizard to create a report based on the primary Sessions table and the related Students table. Select all fields from the Sessions table, and select the FirstName, LastName, and BirthDate fields from the Students table. Do not select any additional grouping levels, and sort the detail records in ascending order by LastName. Choose the Outline layout and Landscape orientation. Specify the title **StudentSessions** for the report.
14. Apply the Ion theme to the StudentClasses report only.
15. Edit the report title so that it appears as **Student Sessions** (two words); and change the font color of the title to the Blue-Gray, Accent 5, Darker 25% theme color.
16. In Layout view, make the Length and Cost field label boxes about half as wide as their current widths by resizing them from the left, then change the width of the Cost field value box so the value in it is right-aligned with the value in the Length field value box.
17. Insert the data file **Paint** located in the Chapter 19\Practice It folder as a logo in the report. Move the picture to the right of the report title.
18. Apply conditional formatting so that any Cost field value greater than or equal to 200 appears as bold and with the text color as Green.
19. Preview the entire report to confirm that it is formatted correctly. If necessary, return to Layout view, and make changes so that all field labels and field values are completely displayed. When you are finished, save the report, print the first page, and then close the report.
20. Compact and repair the StudioClasses19 database, and then close it.

ON YOUR OWN

On Your Own 19-1

1. Open the data file **Contributions19** located in the Chapter 19\On Your Own folder. Save the database as **ContributionsList19**.
2. Use the Form Wizard to create a form based on the Contributions table. Select all the fields for the form and the Columnar layout. Specify an appropriate title for the form.
3. Apply a different theme to the form only.
4. Edit the form title as needed so that spaces separate each word. Change the font color of the form title to a color that is easy to read with the theme you applied to the form.
5. Use the appropriate buttons in the Font group on the Form Layout Tools Format tab to underline the form title and make it bold. Resize the title, as necessary, so that all of the title text appears on the same line. If the height of the shaded area behind the title changes to just fit the height of the title, drag the bottom border of the title down so that the box is about twice as high as the height of the title.
6. Use the form to update the Contributions table. Search for records that contain the word **animals** anywhere in the Description field. Find the record with the field value Stuffed animals (and the Contribution ID 192), and then change the Contribution

Value for this record to **50.00**. Save and close the form.

7. Use the Form Wizard to create a form containing a main form based on the Contributors table and a subform based on the Contributions table that lists the ContributorID, each donor's first and last names, a description of the contribution, and the contribution value. Use the Datasheet layout, and specify appropriate titles for the main form and the subform.
8. Apply the same theme you applied in Step 3 to this form only.
9. Edit the form title so that each word is separated by a space and uses correct capitalization. Make the same changes you made to the format of the title that you made in Steps 4 and 5.
10. Use the appropriate button in the Font group on the Form Layout Tools Format tab to apply a background color of your choice to all the field value boxes in the main form.
11. Use the appropriate button in the Control Formatting group on the Form Layout Tools Format tab to change the outline of all the main form field value boxes to a line thickness of two points.
12. Resize each column in the subform to its best fit. Navigate through the records in the main form to find the value *Garden equipment* in the subform, and then resize the Description column in the subform as necessary. Save the form.
13. Use the Report Wizard to create a report based on the primary Organizations table and the related Contributions table that shows the organization name, the organization phone number, the contribution and contributor ID numbers, the contribution date, the description of the contribution, and the contribution value. In the third Report Wizard dialog box, add ContributorID as an additional grouping level. Sort the detail records in descending order by ContributionValue. Choose the Outline layout and Portrait orientation. Specify the name **OrganizationContributions** for the report.
14. Apply the same theme you applied in Step 3 to this report only.
15. Edit the report title appropriately, and then make the same formatting changes to the report title that you made in Steps 4 and 5. If the height of the shaded area behind the title changes to just fit the height of the title, drag the bottom border of the title down so that the box is about twice as high as the height of the title.
16. Resize the field labels and field value boxes for the contribution value, contribution ID, contribution date, and description to fully display their values and so that the field values for the contribution value, contribution ID, and contribution date are centered below their labels. (Leave the field value below the label *Description* left-aligned below its label stay under the labels.) Resize the field value for the contributor ID so it is left-aligned below the field values for the organization names and phone numbers.
17. Insert the data file **CharityLogo** located in the Chapter 19\On Your Own folder in the report. Place the picture appropriately in the report. Resize it larger to fill the space.
18. Apply conditional formatting to the Contribution Value field to format values greater than or equal to $100 with formatting different from the rest of the values.
19. Preview the report to confirm that it is formatted correctly and all field labels and field values are fully visible. Save the report, print one page that shows the conditional formatting you applied, and then close the report.
20. Compact and repair the ContributionsList19 database, and then close it.

CAPSTONE

ACCESS: CREATE A DATABASE

1. Plan a database to track data for an organization, an event, or a project (either real or fictional). Determine how many tables you need and what data will go into each table. Identify the layout of the columns (fields) and rows (records) for each table. Determine the field properties you need for each field.
2. Create a new database to contain the data you want to track.
3. Create at least two tables in the database that can be joined through a one-to-many relationship.
4. Define the properties for each field in each table. Include a mix of data types for the fields (for example, do not include only Text fields in each table).
5. Specify a primary key for each table.
6. Define the necessary one-to-many relationships between the tables in the database with referential integrity enforced.
7. Enter at least 10 records in each table.
8. Create three to four queries based on single tables and multiple tables. The queries should include some or all of the following: exact match conditions, comparison operators, and logical operators.
9. For some of the queries, use sorting and filtering techniques to display the query results in various ways. Save these queries with the sort and/or filter applied.
10. Create at least one calculated field in one of the queries.
11. Use at least one function to produce a summary statistic based on the data in at least one of the tables.
12. Create at least one form for each table in the database. Enhance each form's appearance with pictures, themes, line colors, and so on.
13. Create at least one form with a main form and subform based on related tables in the database. Enhance the form's appearance appropriately.
14. Create at least one report based on each table in the database. Enhance each report's appearance with pictures, themes, color, and so on.
15. Apply conditional formatting to the values in at least one of the reports.
16. Compact and repair the database, and then close it.

Part 9
POWERPOINT
2016

20 | Creating a Presentation

© Hero Images/Getty Images

LEARNING OBJECTIVES After studying the material in this chapter, you will be able to:

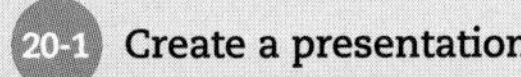

- 20-1 Create a presentation

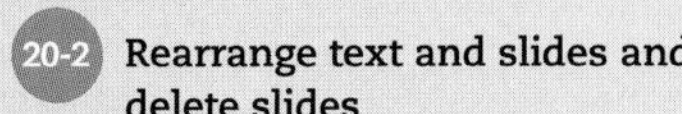

- 20-2 Rearrange text and slides and delete slides
- 20-3 Add speaker notes
- 20-4 Run a slide show
- 20-5 Add animations
- 20-6 Add transitions
- 20-7 Add footers and headers
- 20-8 Review, preview, and print a presentation

After finishing this chapter, go to **PAGE 618** for **STUDY TOOLS**.

20-1 CREATING A PRESENTATION

Microsoft PowerPoint 2016 (or simply **PowerPoint**) is a powerful presentation graphics program used to create slides that can contain text, charts, pictures, sound, movies, and so on. Files created in PowerPoint are called **presentations**. PowerPoint presentations consist of slides, which are similar to pages in a document. You can show these presentations as slide shows on a computer monitor, project them onto a screen, share them over the Internet, or publish them to a Web site. You can also create documents from the presentation by printing the slides, outlines, or speaker notes.

When you create a blank presentation in PowerPoint, the presentation appears in Normal view. See Exhibit 20-1. **Normal view** displays slides one at a time and displays thumbnails of all the slides in the **Slides pane** on the left. You click a slide thumbnail in the Slides pane to display it so that you can work with the text and graphics on the slide. If the Notes button on the status bar is selected, the Notes pane appears below the displayed slide. The **Notes pane** contains notes for the presenter to refer to when delivering the presentation.

As you create presentations, you will work extensively with these different panes and tabs. They provide you the flexibility to work with and view the presentation in a variety of ways, enabling you to create the most effective presentation for conveying the slide show's purpose and goals to the intended audience.

Begin Activity

Start PowerPoint.

1. Start **PowerPoint**. The Recent screen appears in Backstage view.
2. Click the **Blank Presentation tile**. A new, blank presentation appears in the PowerPoint window.
3. If the PowerPoint program window is not maximized, click the **Maximize button** ☐. Your screen should look like Exhibit 20-1.
4. On the Quick Access Toolbar, click the **Save button** 🖫. Because this is the first time this presentation has been saved, the Save As screen appears.
5. Save the presentation as **Gourmet**.

End Activity

CAUTION CAUTION CAUTION CAUTION

SAVE YOUR FILES

Remember to save your files to the drive and folder where you are storing the files you create as you complete the steps in this book. Also, be sure to save frequently as you work. A good practice is to save after every Activity.

20-1a Creating a Title Slide

The first slide in a PowerPoint presentation is usually the **title slide**, which typically contains the title of the presentation and a subtitle, often the presenter's name. The blank title slide contains two objects called text placeholders. A **placeholder** is a region of a slide reserved for inserting text or graphics. A **text placeholder** is a placeholder designed to contain text. Text placeholders usually display text that describes the purpose of the placeholder and instructs you to click so that you can start typing in the placeholder. The larger text placeholder on the title slide is designed to hold the presentation title, and the smaller text placeholder is designed to contain a subtitle. Once you enter text into a text placeholder, it is no longer a placeholder and becomes an object called a **text box**.

To add text to a text placeholder, you click in it, and then type. When you click in a placeholder, the placeholder text disappears, and the insertion point, which

Microsoft PowerPoint 2016 (PowerPoint) A presentation graphics program used to create a collection of slides that can contain text, charts, pictures, sound, movies, and so on.

presentation A file created in PowerPoint.

Normal view The PowerPoint view that includes slide thumbnails in the Slides pane and displays the selected slide.

Slides pane The area of the PowerPoint window that shows a column of slide thumbnails.

Notes pane The area of the PowerPoint window that contains notes for the presenter to refer to when delivering the presentation.

title slide The first slide in a presentation; typically contains the presentation title and a subtitle.

placeholder A region of a slide reserved for inserting text or graphics.

text placeholder A placeholder designed to contain text.

text box An object that contains text.

EXHIBIT 20-1 BLANK PRESENTATION IN THE POWERPOINT WINDOW IN NORMAL VIEW

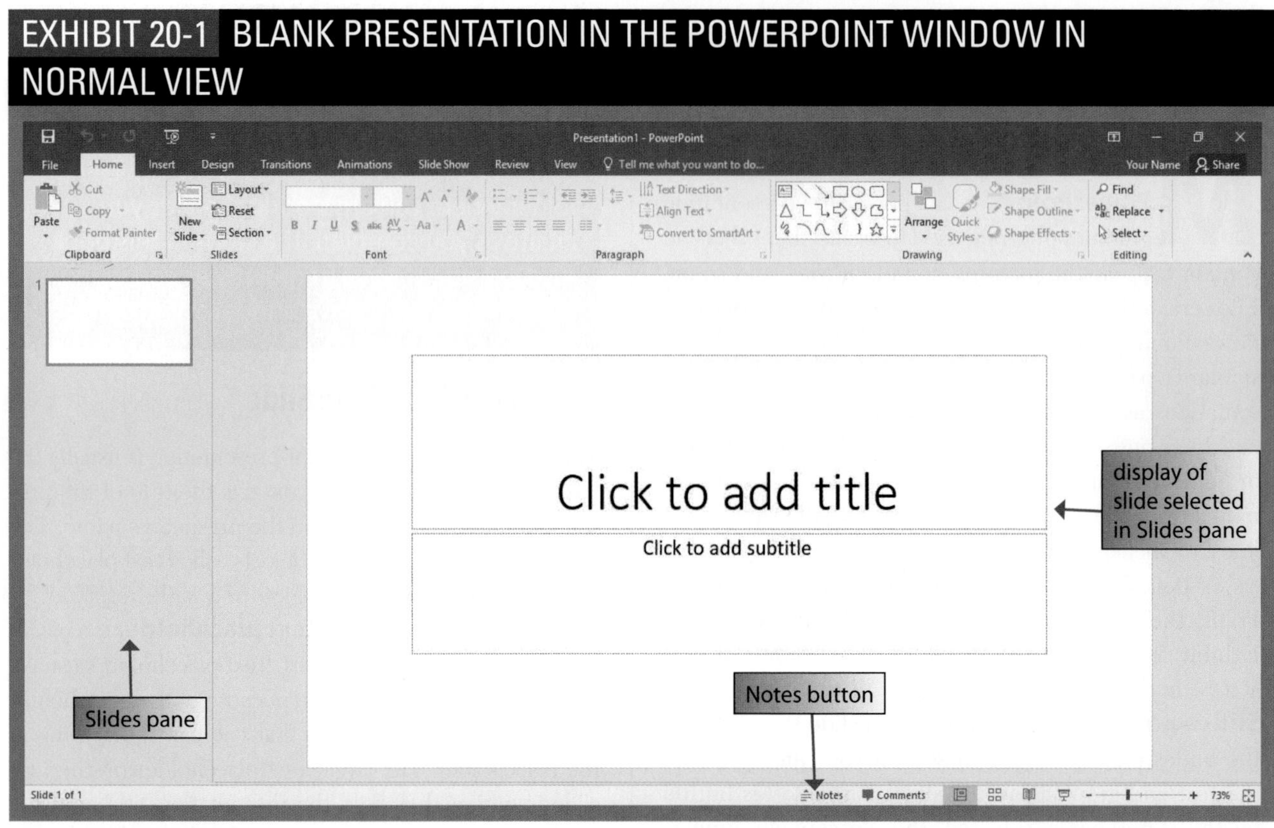

indicates where text will appear when you start typing, appears as a blinking line in the center of the placeholder. This means the placeholder is active, and any text you type will appear in the placeholder. In addition, a contextual tab, the Drawing Tools Format tab, appears on the ribbon. See Exhibit 20-2.

EXHIBIT 20-2 TITLE TEXT PLACEHOLDER ACTIVE ON THE TITLE SLIDE

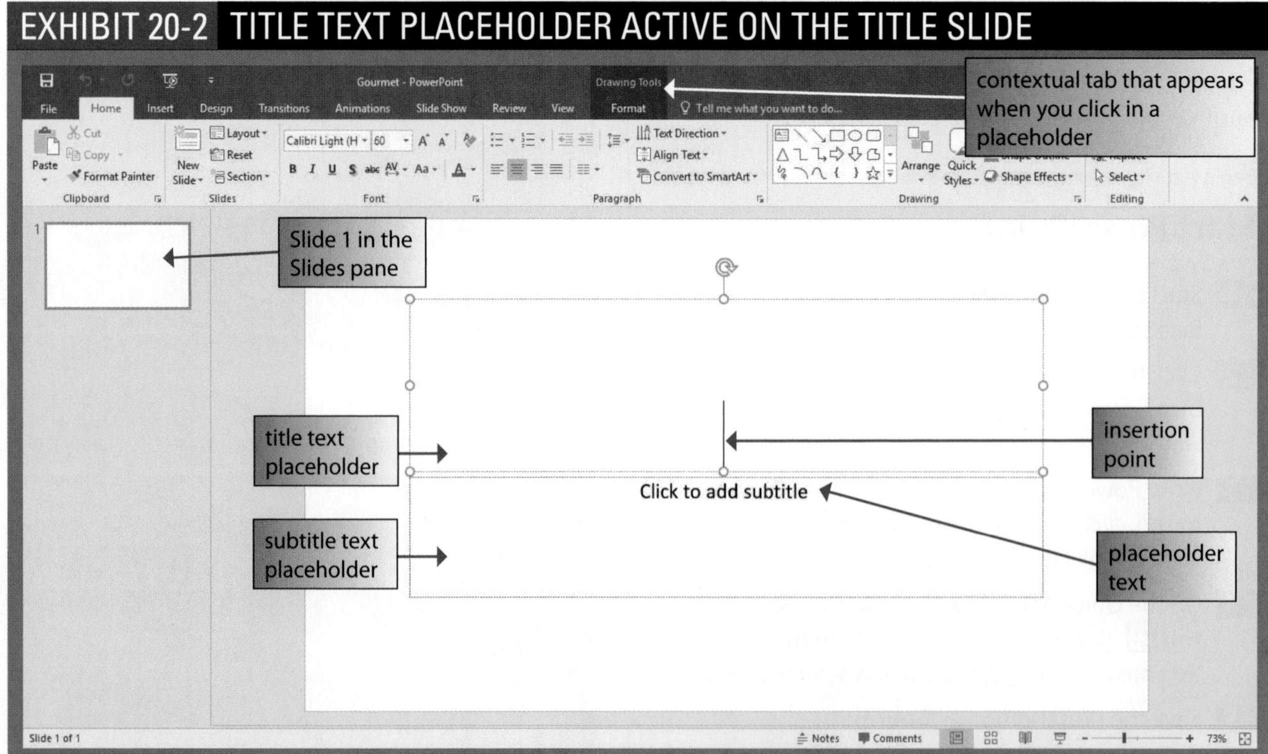

Begin Activity

Add text to text placeholders.

1 Click anywhere in the **Click to add title box**, which is the title text placeholder. The title text placeholder text disappears, and the insertion point appears in the box. Refer to Exhibit 20-2.

2 Type **Gourmet: Delivered** as the title.

3 Click a **blank area** of the slide. The border of the title text placeholder disappears, and the text you typed appears in place of the placeholder text. The thumbnail in the Slides pane also contains the text you typed.

4 Click in the **Click to add subtitle box**, which is the subtitle text placeholder.

5 Type your first and last name, and then click anywhere else on the slide except in the title text box.

End Activity

20-1b Adding a New Slide and Choosing a Layout

After the title slide, you need to add more slides to the presentation. When you add a new slide, the slide is formatted with a **layout**, which is a predetermined way of organizing the objects on a slide, including title text and other content (bulleted lists, photographs, charts, and so forth). PowerPoint provides nine built-in layouts, as described in Exhibit 20-3. All layouts, except the Blank layout, include placeholders to help you create a presentation.

Slides can include several types of placeholders, but the most common are text and content placeholders. You have already seen text placeholders on the title slide. Most layouts include a title text placeholder to contain the slide title. A **content placeholder** is intended to contain the slide content, which can be text or a graphic object, such as a table, a chart, a diagram, a picture, clip art, or a video. If you click in a content placeholder and then add text, the content placeholder is no longer a placeholder and becomes a text box. Exhibit 20-4 shows a slide with the Title and Content layout applied.

To insert a new slide, you use the New Slide button in the Slides group on the Home tab. If you are inserting a new slide after the title slide and you click the New Slide button, the new slide is created using the Title and Content layout. Otherwise, the new slide is created using the same layout as the current slide. If you want to choose a different layout, click the New Slide button arrow, and then select the layout you want to use from the menu that opens. Exhibit 20-5 shows the layouts on the New Slide button arrow.

You can also change the layout of a slide after it is created. To do this, click the Layout button in the Slides group on the Home tab, and then select the layout you want to use.

EXHIBIT 20-3 BUILT-IN LAYOUTS IN POWERPOINT

Layout	Description
Title Slide	Contains the presentation title and a subtitle; is usually used as the first slide in a presentation
Title and Content	Contains either a bulleted list or a graphic in addition to the slide title
Section Header	Contains a section title and text that describes the presentation section
Two Content	The same as the Title and Content layout, but with two side-by-side content placeholders, each of which can contain a bulleted list or a graphic
Comparison	The same as the Two Content layout, but includes text placeholders above the content placeholders to label the content
Title Only	Includes only a title text placeholder for the slide title
Blank	Does not contain any placeholders
Content with Caption	Contains a content placeholder, a title text placeholder to identify the slide or the content, and a text placeholder to describe the content; suitable for photographs or other graphics that need an explanation
Picture with Caption	Similar to the Content with Caption layout, but with a picture placeholder instead of a content placeholder

layout A predetermined way of organizing the objects on a slide.

content placeholder A placeholder designed to hold any type of slide content—text, a graphic, or another object.

EXHIBIT 20-4 NEW SLIDE WITH THE TITLE AND CONTENT LAYOUT

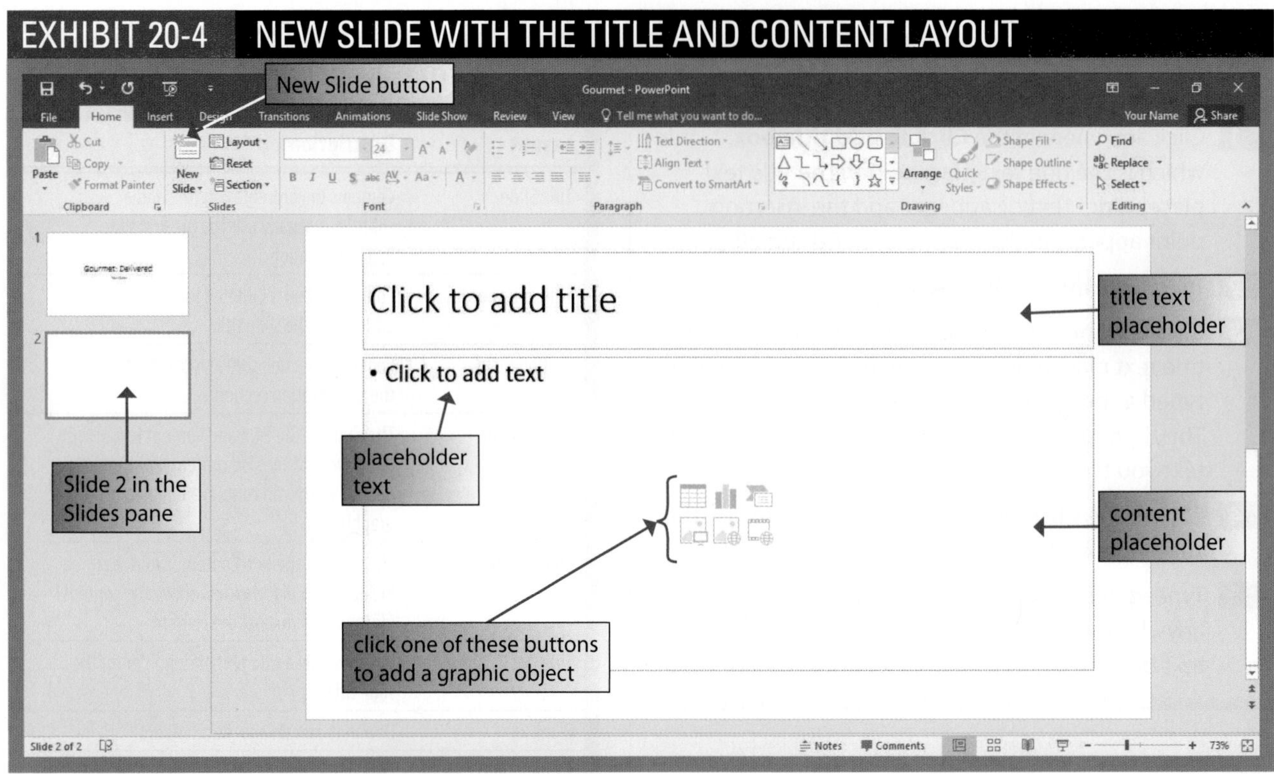

EXHIBIT 20-5 LAYOUTS ON THE NEW SLIDE BUTTON MENU

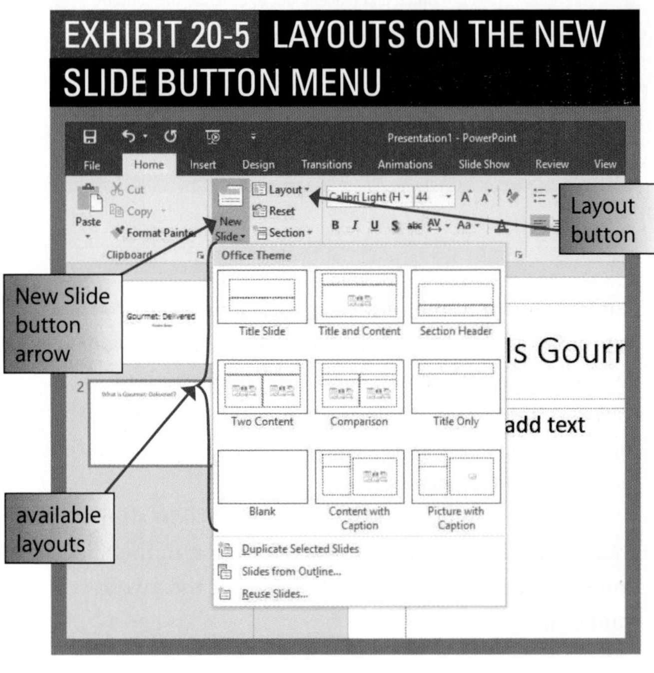

Begin Activity

Create new slides, and change the layout.

1 On the Home tab, in the Slides group, click the **New Slide button**. A new Slide 2 appears with the Title and Content layout applied. Refer back to Exhibit 20-4. The content placeholder contains placeholder text that you can click to insert your own text and six icons that you can click to insert the specific item identified by each icon.

2 Click anywhere in the **title text placeholder**, and then type **What Is Gourmet: Delivered?**

3 On the Home tab, in the Slides group, click the **New Slide button arrow**. The New Slide gallery opens, displaying the nine layouts available. Refer to Exhibit 20-5.

4 In the gallery, click the **Two Content layout**. Slide 3 is created with the Two Content layout, which consists of three placeholders: the title text placeholder and two content placeholders side by side.

5 Click anywhere in the **title text placeholder**, and then type **Contact Us**.

6 On the Home tab, in the Slides group, click the **Layout button**. The same gallery of layouts you saw on the New Slide gallery appears.

7 In the gallery, click the **Title and Content layout**. The layout of Slide 3 changes to the layout you selected.

End Activity

20-1c Moving Between Slides in Normal View

As you work on a presentation, you will need to move from one slide to another. In Normal view, you can click a slide thumbnail in the Slides pane to display that slide. You can also use the vertical scroll bar next to the slide to scroll from slide to slide, or you can click the Next Slide [button] or Previous Slide [button] button at the bottom of the vertical scroll bar next to the slide.

Begin Activity

Move from one slide to another.

1. In the Slides pane, click the **Slide 1 thumbnail**. The title slide appears.
2. At the right side of the window, drag the **scroll box** to the bottom of the scroll bar. As you drag, a ScreenTip appears, identifying the slide that will appear when you release the mouse button.
3. Release the **mouse button**. Slide 3 ("Contact Us") appears.
4. At the bottom of the scroll bar, click the **Previous Slide button** [button]. Slide 2 ("What Is Gourmet: Delivered?") appears.

End Activity

20-1d Working with Lists

Often, text on a slide is in the form of bulleted lists to emphasize important points to the audience. Items in a list can appear at different levels. A **first-level item** is a main item in a list; a **second-level item**—sometimes called a **subitem**—is an item beneath and indented from a first-level item. Usually, the font size—the size of the text—in subitems is smaller than the size used for text in the level above.

A **bulleted list** is a list of "paragraphs" (words, phrases, sentences, or paragraphs) with a special symbol such as a dot, dash, circle, box, star, or other character to the left of each paragraph. A bulleted item is one paragraph in a bulleted list. If the symbol to the left of each item in a list is a number, the list is referred to as a **numbered list**. And if no symbol appears, the list is referred to as an **unnumbered list**.

To add a bulleted list to a slide, click the placeholder text in a content placeholder. When you do this, the placeholder text disappears, the insertion point appears in its place, and a light gray bullet symbol appears. See Exhibit 20-6. Notice that on the Home tab, in the Font group, in the Font Size box, the font size of this first-level bullet is 28 points.

EXHIBIT 20-6 INSERTION POINT IN THE CONTENT PLACEHOLDER

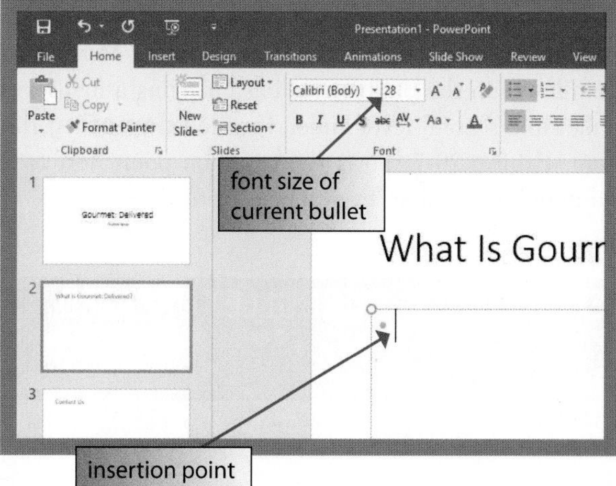

After you type the text of a bulleted item, press the Enter key to move the insertion point to the next line. This creates a new bulleted item. If you don't type anything next to a bullet, the bullet will not appear on the slide.

Begin Activity

Create a bulleted list.

1. In **Slide 2** ("What Is Gourmet: Delivered?"), in the content placeholder, click the placeholder text, **Click to add text**. Refer to Exhibit 20-6.
2. Type **Gourmet meals delivered to your home** and then press the **Enter key**. A new bullet that is lighter than the first bullet appears. It will darken as soon as you start typing text.
3. Type **Meals are ready for** and then press the **Enter key**. A third bullet is added to the slide.

End Activity

first-level item A main item in a list.

second-level item (subitem) An item beneath and indented from a first-level item.

bulleted list A list of paragraphs with a special symbol to the left of each paragraph.

numbered list A list of paragraphs with a sequential numbers to the left of each paragraph.

unnumbered list A list of paragraphs that do not have any symbol to the left of each paragraph.

You can change a first-level bulleted item into a subitem, and you can change a subitem into a first-level bulleted item. As in Word, moving an item to a higher level, such as changing a second-level bullet to a first-level bullet, is called **promoting** the item. Moving an item lower in the outline, such as changing a first-level bullet to a second-level bullet, is called **demoting** the item. Exhibit 20-7 shows the insertion point next to a subitem below a first-level item.

EXHIBIT 20-7 SUBBULLET CREATED

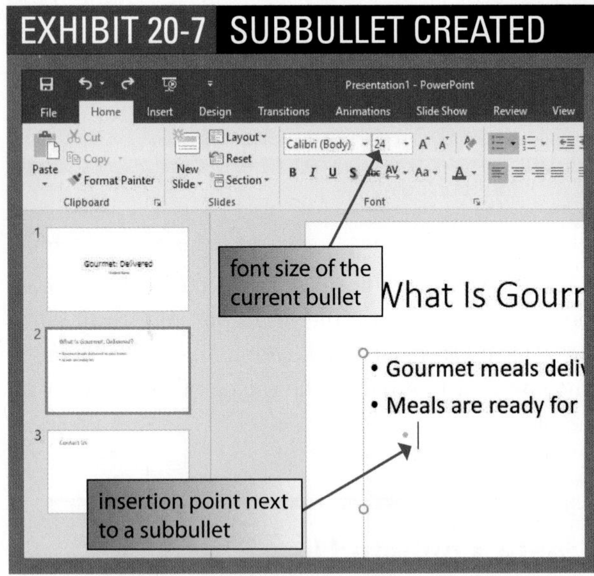

Begin Activity

Add subitems to a bulleted list.

1 Press the **Tab key**. The new bullet is demoted and indented to become a subitem. The font size of the subitem is 24 points, which is smaller than the font size used in the first-level bullets on the slide. Refer back to Exhibit 20-7.

2 Type **Serving** and then press the **Enter key**. A second subitem is created.

3 Type **Freezing** and then press the **Enter key** to create a third subitem.

4 Press the **Shift+Tab keys**. The subitem is promoted and changes to a first-level bullet.

5 Type **Select from a variety of dishes** as the bullet text.

6 Click a **blank area** of the slide outside the content text box. The dashed line border of the text box disappears.

End Activity

Sometimes, you will want to create a new line within a bulleted item without creating a new bullet. This is helpful when you include an address as a bullet item and want to split the address on two lines of the same bullet. To create a new line, press the Shift+Enter keys. This moves the insertion point to the next line without creating a new paragraph.

Begin Activity

Create a new line without creating a new bullet.

1 Display **Slide 3** ("Contact Us"). Click to the right of the bullet in the content placeholder, and then type **Phone:** as the bullet text.

2 Press the **Shift+Enter keys**. The insertion point moves to the next line without creating a new bullet.

3 Type **210-555-3800** and then press the **Enter key**. A new bullet is created.

4 Type **Address:** and then press the **Shift+Enter keys**.

5 Type **4301 Commercial St.** and then press the **Shift+Enter keys**. Type **San Antonio, TX 78056**. The address is entered on two lines under the Address bullet without creating new bullets.

6 Save the presentation, and then close it.

TIP: To change a bulleted list into a numbered list, select the bulleted items, and then click the Numbering button in the Paragraph group on the Home tab; to change it to a list without any bullets, click the Bullets button to deselect it.

End Activity

20-1e Using AutoFit

As you add text to a content placeholder, **AutoFit** makes adjustments if you add more text than will fit in the placeholder. First it reduces the spacing between lines, and then it reduces the font size of the text. AutoFit is

promote To move an item to a higher level in an outline.

demote To move an item to a lower level in an outline.

AutoFit A PowerPoint feature that automatically changes the line spacing and the font size of text if you add more text than will fit in a placeholder.

turned on by default. When you start typing the next bullet, you will see AutoFit adjust the text to make it fit. If AutoFit adjusts the text in a text box, the AutoFit Options button appears on the slide below and to the left of the placeholder. You can click the AutoFit Options button and select an option on the menu to control the way AutoFit works. See Exhibit 20-8. If you select the option to turn off AutoFit for a text box, you can turn it back on later.

EXHIBIT 20-8 AUTOFIT OPTIONS BUTTON MENU

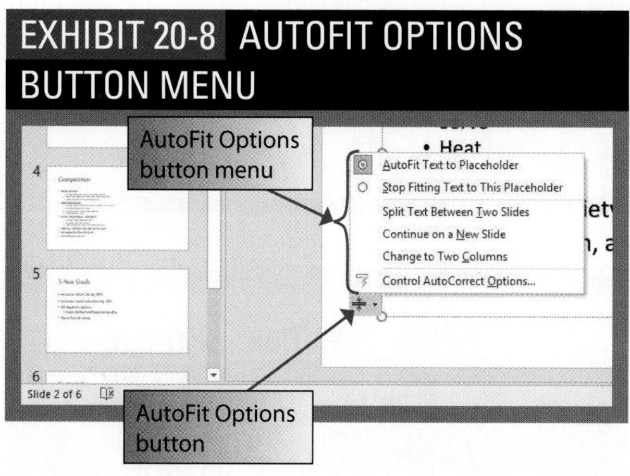

Begin Activity

Use the AutoFit feature.

1. Open the data file **Expansion** located in the Chapter 20\Chapter folder. Save the file as **Expansion Goals**.
2. On Slide 1 (the title slide), click in the **subtitle text box** and then type your name.
3. Display **Slide 2** ("What Is Gourmet: Delivered?").
4. In the last bulleted item, click after the word *available*, and then press the **Enter key**. A new first-level bullet is created.
5. Type **M**. After you type the first character in this new bullet, the line spacing in the text box tightens up slightly, and the AutoFit Options button appears next to the lower-left corner of the text box.
6. Click the **AutoFit Options button**. The AutoFit Options button menu appears. The default option, AutoFit Text to Placeholder, is selected. Refer back to Exhibit 20-8.
7. Click **anywhere on the slide** to close the AutoFit Options button menu without changing the selected default option.

TIP: You can also press the Esc key to close a menu without selecting a command or option.

8. In the last bulleted item, click immediately after *M*, and then type **enus change seasonally** to complete the bulleted item.
9. Click a **blank area** of the slide to deselect the list.

End Activity

20-1f Changing Themes

Plain white slides with a common font (such as black Times New Roman or Calibri) often fail to hold an audience's attention. Audiences expect more interesting color schemes, fonts, graphics, and other effects. You can easily change the fonts and color used for the background, title text, body text, accents, and graphics in a presentation as well as the style used in a presentation by changing the theme. In a presentation, the Headings theme font is used for the slide titles and the Body theme font is used for text in content placeholders. Some PowerPoint themes include graphics as part of the slide background. In PowerPoint, each theme has several variants with different coordinating colors and sometimes slightly different backgrounds. A theme and its variants are called a **theme family**. To see the available themes, click the More button in the Themes group in the Design tab. See Exhibit 20-9.

By default, new, blank presentations have the Office theme applied. PowerPoint comes with several installed themes, and many more themes are available online at Office.com. In addition, you can use a custom theme stored on your computer or network. When you apply a different theme, be aware that some themes use a font size much smaller than 28 points for first-level items in a bulleted list.

Begin Activity

Change the theme.

1. On the ribbon, click the **Design tab**. In the Themes group, the first theme displayed in the group is always the currently applied theme.
2. In the Themes group, point to the **first theme**, which has an gray border around it. A ScreenTip identifies the theme, which, in this case, is the Office Theme. After the currently applied theme, the rest of the available themes are listed.

theme family A theme and its variants.

EXHIBIT 20-9 THEMES ON THE DESIGN TAB

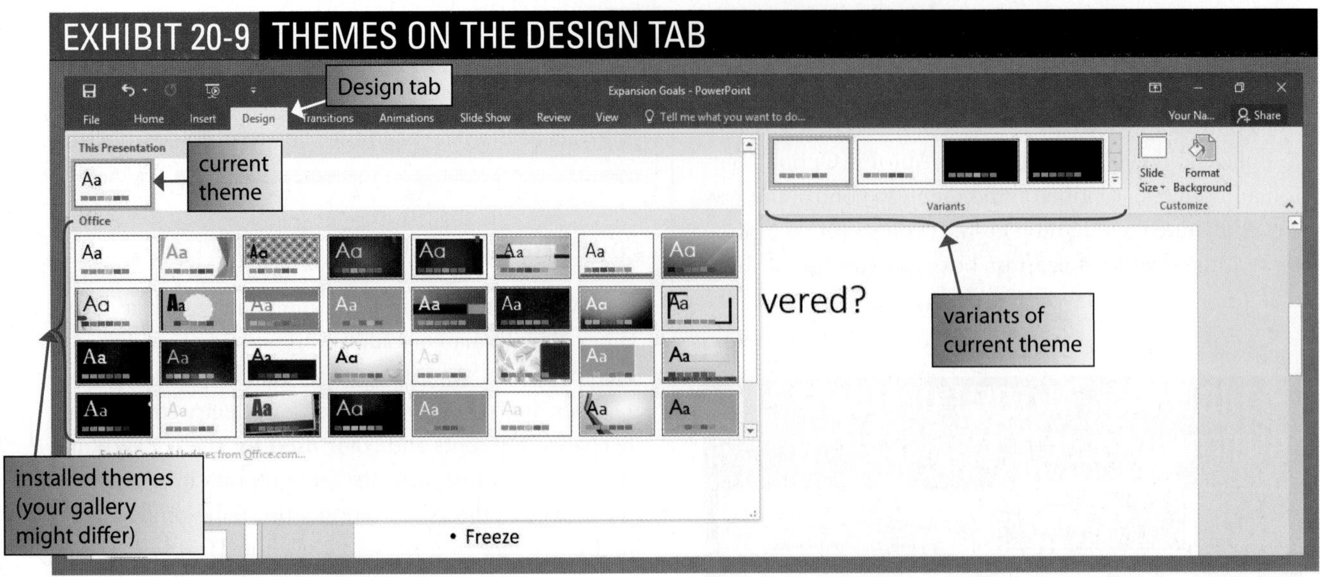

3 In the Themes group, click the **More button**. The Themes gallery opens. Refer back to Exhibit 20-9.

4 Point to several of the themes to see the Live Preview on Slide 2.

5 Using the ScreenTips, locate the **Wisp theme** in the second row, and then click it. The design and colors of the slides in the presentation change to those of the default variant of the Wisp theme.

6 In the Variants group, point to each variant to see the Live Preview. Note that the ScreenTips are the same as the theme name.

7 In the Variants group, click the **second variant**. The background and font colors change to match the ones used in this variant. Compare your screen to Exhibit 20-10.

End Activity

CAUTION

DUPLICATED THEMES

There might be two copies of the first nine themes in the gallery. If you want to use one of these themes, click the first copy. The second copy will not retain its formatting.

Sometimes when you change the theme, the font size of the text on the slides changes size. You should examine the slides after changing theme. You can change the font size of text by selecting the individual text items or you can select the entire text box and change the size of all the text in the text box at the same time. To select the entire text box, you click the text box border. If the text in bulleted list items is different sizes, when you select the entire text box, the smallest font size used in the

EXHIBIT 20-10 SECOND VARIANT OF THE WISP THEME APPLIED TO THE PRESENTATION

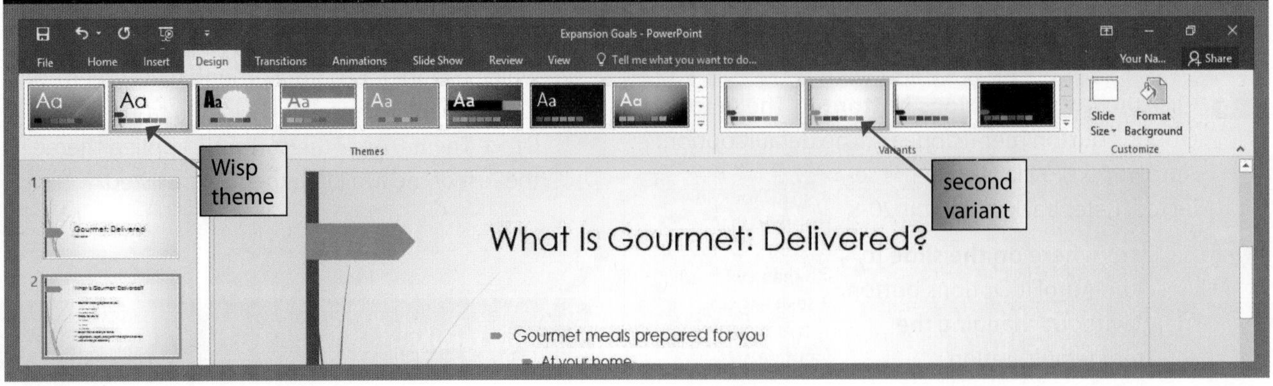

bulleted list appears in the Font Size box and a plus sign appears after the font size. See Exhibit 20-11. You can click the Increase Font Size button [A] or the Decrease Font Size button [A] to increase or decrease the size of the text in bulleted items by one or two points.

EXHIBIT 20-11 SELECTED TEXT BOX

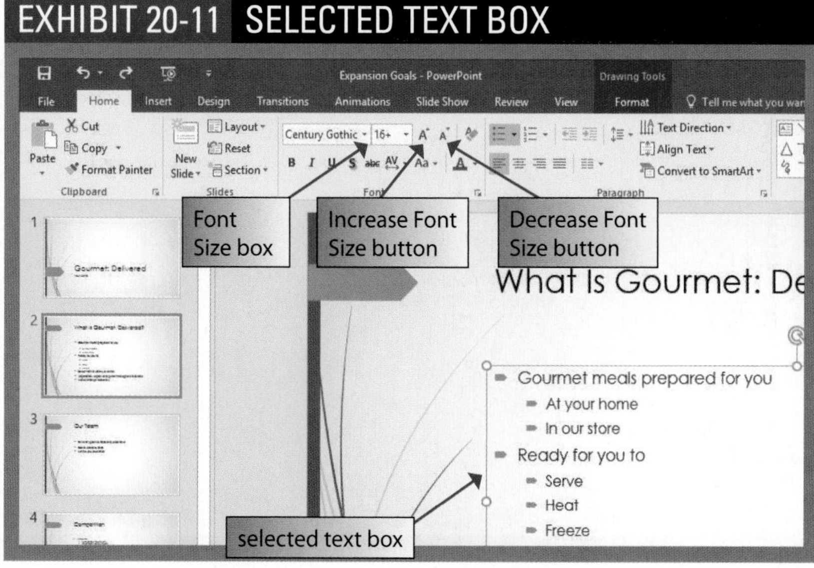

Begin Activity

Change the font size of text in bulleted lists.

1 On the ribbon, click the **Home tab**. On Slide 2 ("What Is Gourmet: Delivered?"), click anywhere on the **first bulleted item**. The dotted line border of the text box appears, and in the Font group, 18 appears in the Font Size group, so the text in first-level items in this text box is 18 points.

2 Click anywhere in the **second bulleted item**. As shown in the Font group, the text in the second-level items in this text box is 16 points.

3 Position the pointer on top of the **text box border** so that the pointer changes to ✥, and then click the **text box border**. The dotted line border changes to a solid line. Now the entire text box is selected, and formatting changes will affect all of the text in the box. On the Home tab, in the Font group, 16+ appears in the Font Size box. Refer to Exhibit 20-11.

4 In the Font group, click the **Increase Font Size button** [A]. In the Font Size box, 18+ now appears, indicating that the smallest font size in the selected text box is now 18 points.

5 Click anywhere in the **first bulleted item**. The text in this bulleted item is now 20 points.

6 In the Slides pane, click the **Slide 3 thumbnail**.

7 On Slide 3 ("Our Team"), click on the **bulleted list**, click the **text box border**, and then in the Font group, click the **Increase Font Size button** [A] twice. The font size of the text in the bulleted list changes to 24 points.

8 Display **Slide 5** ("5-Year Goals"), and then increase the font size of the text in the bulleted list so that the first-level items are 24 points and the second-level items are 20 points.

9 Display **Slide 6** ("Contact Us"), and then increase the font size of the text in the bulleted list so that the first-level items are 24 points.

End Activity

20-1g Modifying Text and Changing Bullet Levels in Outline View

Outline view displays the outline of the entire presentation in the Outline pane, which is similar to the Slides pane. See Exhibit 20-12. Slide titles appear at the top level in the outline, and the slide content—that is, the bulleted lists—are indented below the slide titles. When you view the outline in the Outline pane, you see only the text of the slide titles and the text in content placeholders; you do not see any graphics on the slides or any text that is not in a content placeholder.

You can modify the text of a slide in the Outline pane in Outline view as well as on the slide. You also promote and demote items in the Outline pane using the same techniques you use on a displayed slide. Any changes you make in the Outline pane appear on the slide.

If you need to move bulleted items from one slide to another, or change a bulleted item to a new slide title, it can be easier to do this in Outline view than in Normal view.

Outline view The PowerPoint view that displays the text of the slides in the Outline pane.

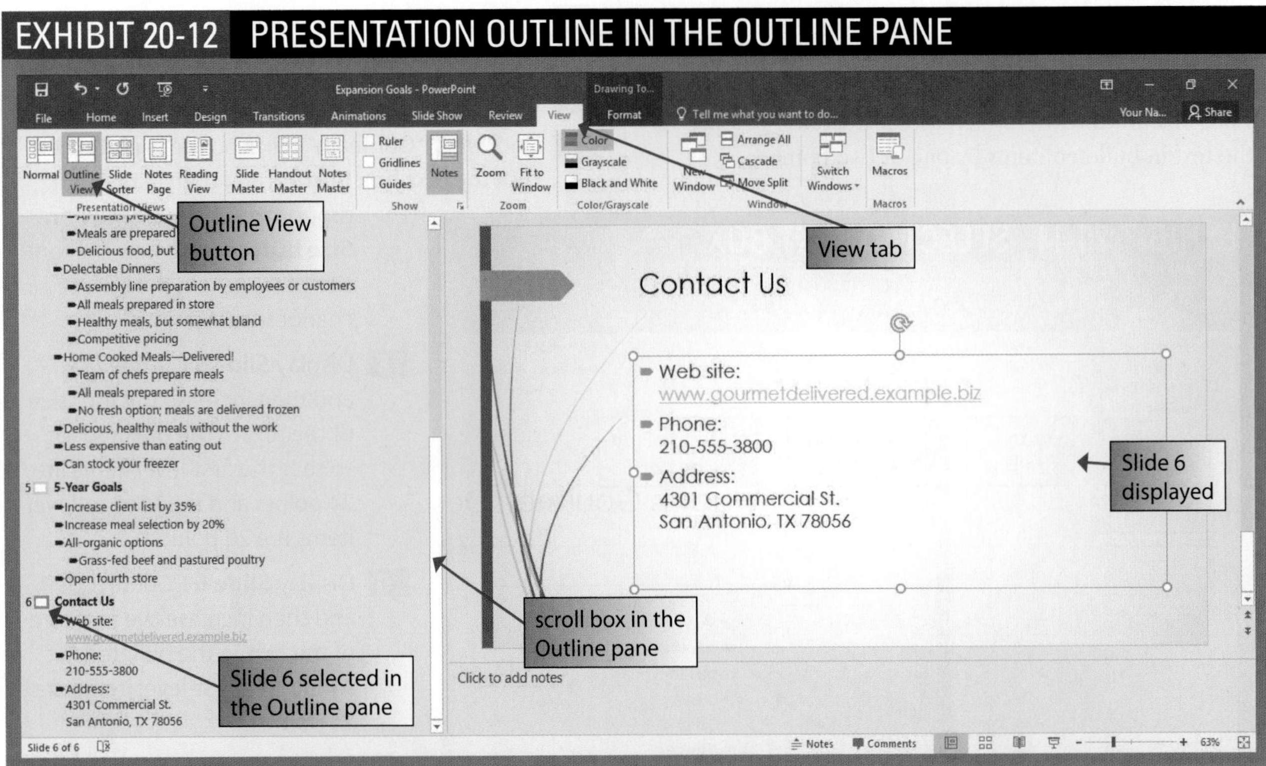

EXHIBIT 20-12 PRESENTATION OUTLINE IN THE OUTLINE PANE

Begin Activity

Modify text in the Outline pane.

1 On the ribbon, click the **View tab**. In the Presentation Views group, click the **Outline View button**. The presentation is displayed in Outline view, and the outline of the presentation is in the Outline pane. Because Slide 6 is displayed, the slide icon next to Slide 6 in the Outline pane is outlined in orange. Also, the Notes pane appears below the displayed slide. Refer to Exhibit 20-12.

2 In the Outline pane, scroll up until **Slide 4** ("Competition") is at the top of the Outline pane.

3 In the Outline pane, click anywhere on the text in **Slide 4** ("Competition"). Slide 4 is displayed.

4 In the Outline pane, in the fourth first-level bullet in Slide 4, click immediately before the word *Delicious*, and then press the **Enter key**. A new line is created above the current bulleted item in both the Outline pane and on the slide.

5 Press the **Up Arrow key**. The insertion point moves up to the new line, and the bullet appears in the new line.

6 Type **Advantages**. The text you typed appears in the Outline pane and on the slide.

7 In the Outline pane, in Slide 5 ("5-Year Goals"), point to the ***All-organic options* bullet** so that the pointer changes to ✥, and then click. The All-organic options bulleted item and its subitem are selected.

8 On the ribbon, click the **Home tab**. In the Paragraph group, click the **Increase List Level button**. The selected first-level bulleted item is demoted—it is indented and becomes a second-level bulleted item—and its subitem becomes a third-level bulleted item.

PROBLEM?

If the subitem is not indented as a third-level item, you selected only the All-organic options item without selecting its subitem. Skip Steps 9 and 10.

9 In the Outline pane, in Slide 5 ("5-Year Goals"), click the **Grass-fed beef and pastured poultry bullet**.

10 On the Home tab, in the Paragraph group, click the **Decrease List Level button**. The selected third-level bulleted item is promoted to the second level.

11 On the slide, click **All-organic options**. In the Font Size box, 22 appears. When you promote or demote items in the Outline pane, the font size may not match other items at the same level.

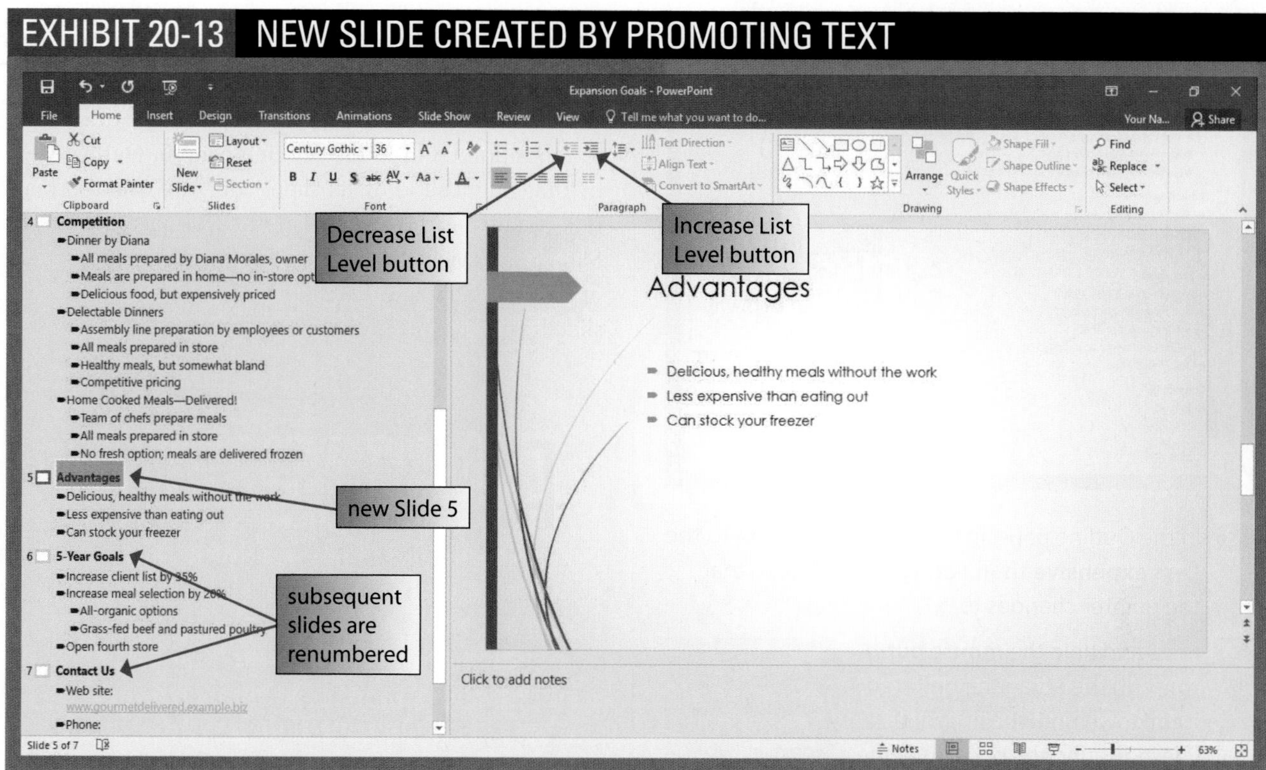

EXHIBIT 20-13 NEW SLIDE CREATED BY PROMOTING TEXT

12 On the slide, select **All-organic options**, and then in the Font group, click the **Decrease Font Size button** [A]. The text is now the same size as the other second-level bulleted item.

13 In the Outline pane, in Slide 4 ("Competition"), click the **Advantages bullet**.

14 On the Home tab, in the Paragraph group, click the **Decrease List Level button** [icon]. The selected first-level bulleted item is promoted to a slide title for a new Slide 5, and the three bulleted items below it are now first-level bulleted items on the new Slide 5. Compare your screen to Exhibit 20-13.

End Activity

20-2 MOVING TEXT AND SLIDES, AND DELETING SLIDES

You can move bulleted items to new positions on slides or from one slide to another, and you can rearrange the slides themselves. To move bulleted items, you must work in the Outline pane or on the slide. To move slides, you can work in the Slides or Outline pane in Normal view or in Slide Sorter view. **Slide Sorter view** displays all the slides in the presentation as thumbnails to provide you with a visual overview of the presentation.

20-2a Moving Bulleted Items

Bulleted items should be placed in a logical order, such as most to least important, alphabetically, or chronologically. You can move a bulleted item to a new position in the outline by using drag and drop. You drag the bulleted item by its bullet. As you drag, a horizontal line follows the pointer to show you where the bulleted item will be positioned after you release the pointer. See Exhibit 20-14.

Begin Activity

Move bulleted items.

1 If Slide 5 ("Advantages") is not the current slide, in the Outline pane, click the **Slide 5 slide icon** [icon]. Slide 5 is displayed.

2 On the slide, click anywhere on the **bulleted list**, and then click the **text box border**. On the Home tab, in the Font group, click the **Increase Font Size button** [A] twice to change the font size of the text in the bulleted list to 24 points.

Slide Sorter view The PowerPoint view that displays all the slides in a presentation as thumbnails to provide a visual overview of the presentation.

EXHIBIT 20-14 BULLETED ITEM BEING DRAGGED IN THE OUTLINE PANE

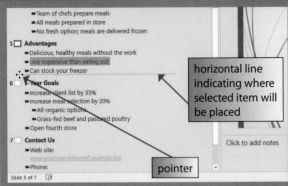

Team of chefs prepare meals
All meals prepared in store
No fresh option; meals are delivered frozen
5 Advantages
Delicious, healthy meals without the work
Less expensive than eating out
Can stock your freezer
6 5-Year Goals
Increase client list by 35%
Increase meal selection by 20%
All-organic options
Grass-fed beef and pastured poultry
Open fourth store
7 Contact Us
Web site:
www.gourmetdelivered.example.biz
Phone:
Slide 5 of 7
Click to add notes
horizontal line indicating where selected item will be placed
pointer

3 In the Outline pane, in the Slide 5 text, point to the **Less expensive than eating out bullet** so that the pointer changes to ✥.

4 Press and hold the **mouse button**, and then drag the **bulleted item** down until the horizontal line indicating the position of the item you are dragging appears below the Can stock your freezer bullet on Slide 5. Refer back to Exhibit 20-14.

> **TIP:** You can also use the Cut, Copy, and Paste commands to move text or slides.

5 With the horizontal line positioned below the Can stock your freezer bullet, release the **mouse button**. The bulleted item you dragged is now the last bulleted item on Slide 5, both in the Outline pane and on the slide.

End Activity

20-2b Rearranging Slides

As you develop a presentation, you might want to change the order in which the slides appear. You can drag slides to reposition them in the Outline pane in Outline view by dragging a slide by its slide icon. You can also rearrange slides in the Slides pane in Normal view and in Slide Sorter view. See Exhibit 20-15. In the Slides pane in Normal view and in Slide Sorter view, you move a slide by dragging its thumbnail.

> **FYI**
>
> **DUPLICATING SLIDES**
>
> As you create a presentation, you might want to create a slide that is similar to another slide. Starting with a copy of a slide that already exists can save time. To duplicate a slide, right-click the slide thumbnail in the Slides pane in Normal view, and then click Duplicate Slide on the shortcut menu. You can also use the ribbon to duplicate one or multiple slides. In the Slides group on the Home tab, click the New Slide button arrow, and then click Duplicate Selected Slides. If you select more than one slide before you use the Duplicate Selected Slides command, all of the selected slides will be duplicated.

EXHIBIT 20-15 SLIDE SORTER VIEW

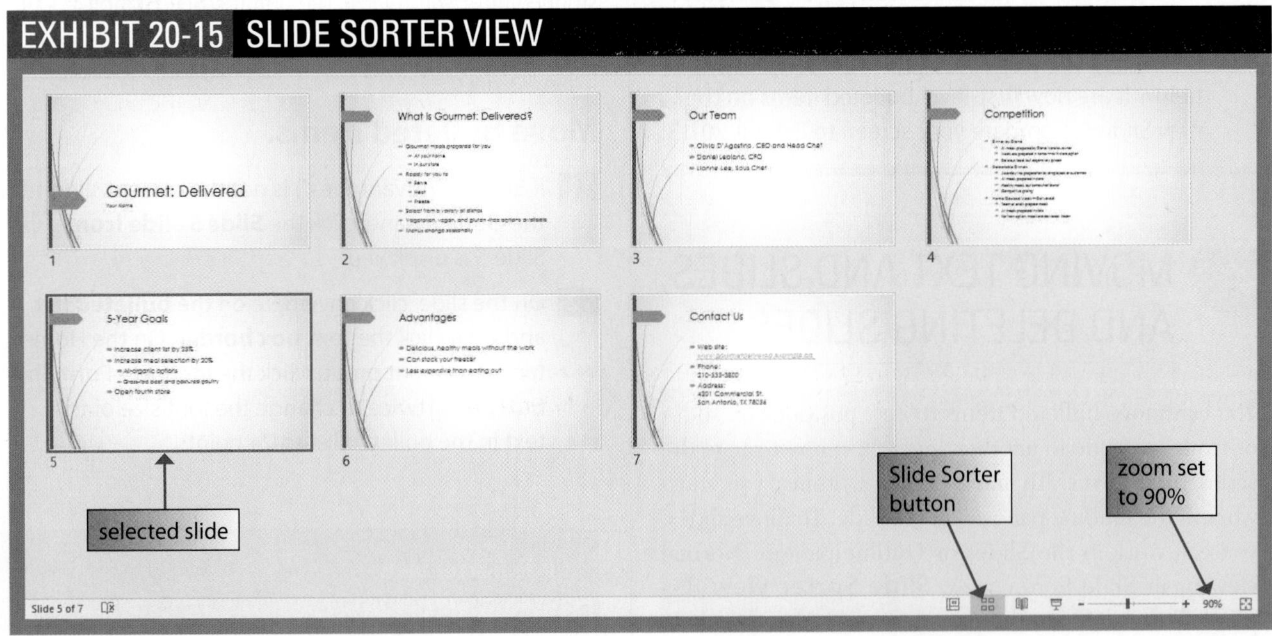

Begin Activity

Rearrange slides.

1 In the Outline pane, drag the **Slide 6 slide icon** (the slide titled "5-Year Goals") up until the horizontal line indicating the new position of the slide appears just above the slide title for Slide 5 ("Advantages"). The slide titled "5-Year Goals" is now Slide 5 and the slide titled "Advantages" is now Slide 6.

2 On the status bar, click the **Slide Sorter button**. The presentation appears in Slide Sorter view. An orange border appears around the Slide 5 thumbnail, indicating that the slide is selected.

3 If necessary, change the zoom level to **90%** so you can see four slides in the first row and three slides in the second row. Refer back to Exhibit 20-15.

> **PROBLEM?**
> If only three slides appear in the first row, change the zoom to **70%** and then back to **90%**.

4 Drag the **Slide 3 thumbnail** (the "Our Team" slide) down to position it between the Slide 6 ("Advantages") and the Slide 7 ("Contact Us") thumbnails. As you drag, the other slides move out of the way. The slide titled "Our Team" is now Slide 6.

5 Double-click the **Slide 6 thumbnail** (the "Our Team" slide). The presentation appears in the previous view it was in before you switched to Slide Sorter view—in this case, Outline view—with Slide 6 displayed.

6 On the status bar, click the **Normal button**. The slide thumbnails appear in the Slides pane, and the Notes pane is now visible below the slide.

End Activity

20-2c Deleting Slides

As you develop a presentation, you will sometimes need to delete slides. You can delete slides in the Slides and Outline panes in Normal view and in Slide Sorter view. To delete a slide, right-click the thumbnail in the Slides pane or Slide Sorter view, and then click Delete Slide on the shortcut menu. You can also click its thumbnail in the Slides pane or Slide Sorter view or click the slide icon in the Outline pane, and then press the Delete key. It is a good idea to verify that you are deleting the correct slide by first displaying that slide.

Begin Activity

Delete a slide.

1 In the Slides pane, click the **Slide 3 thumbnail**. Slide 3 ("Competition") is displayed.

2 In the Slides pane, right-click the **Slide 3 thumbnail**.

3 On the shortcut menu, click **Delete Slide**. Slide 3 is deleted. The slide titled "5-Year Goals" is now Slide 3 and is displayed.

End Activity

20-3 ADDING SPEAKER NOTES

Speaker notes help the speaker remember what to say when a particular slide appears during the presentation. You use the Notes pane to add and display speaker notes. In Normal view, you can open the Notes pane below the slide by clicking the Notes button on the status bar. See Exhibit 20-16. Click the Notes button again to close the Notes pane. If you use Outline view, the Notes pane appears automatically when you switch to Outline view.

EXHIBIT 20-16 SPEAKER NOTE

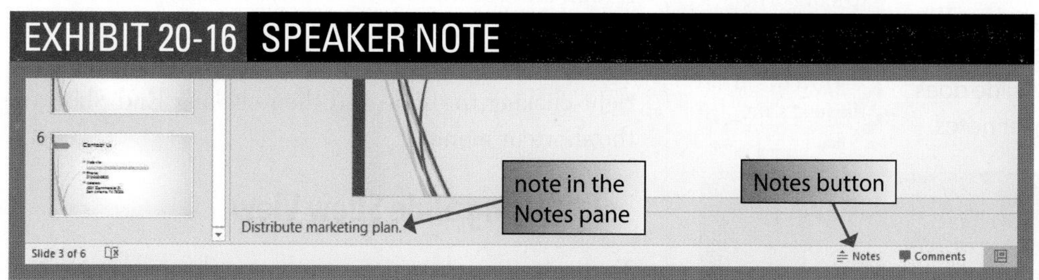

speaker notes Notes that appear in the Notes pane to remind the speaker of points to make when the particular slide appears during the slide show.

You can switch to **Notes Page view** to display each slide in the top half of the presentation window and the speaker notes for that slide in the bottom half. See Exhibit 20-17. You can also print notes pages with a picture of and notes about each slide.

EXHIBIT 20-17 SLIDE 3 IN NOTES PAGE VIEW

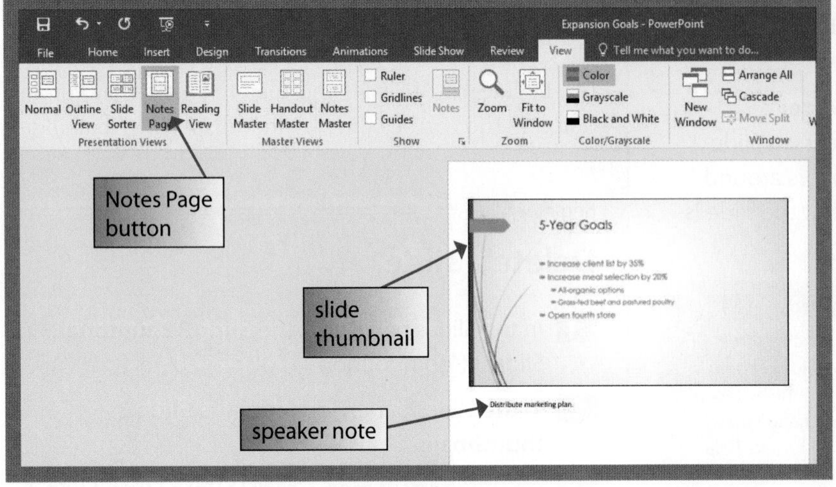

Begin Activity

Create a note and view slides in Notes Page view.

1 Make sure **Slide 3** ("5-Year Goals") is displayed.

2 Click in the **Notes pane.**

3 Type **Distribute marketing plan.** as the note. Refer back to Exhibit 20-16.

4 On the ribbon, click the **View** tab, and then in the Presentation Views group, click the **Notes Page button.** Slide 3 is displayed in Notes Page view. Refer to Exhibit 20-17.

5 At the bottom of the vertical scroll bar, click the **Next Slide button** . Slide 4 ("Advantages") appears in Notes Page view. The notes placeholder appears below the slide because this slide does not contain any speaker notes.

PROBLEM? If the Notes pane is not visible, click the **Notes button** on the status bar.

TIP: In Normal view and in Notes Page view, you can also press the Page Up key to move to the previous slide or the Page Down key to move to the next slide.

Notes Page view The PowerPoint view that displays each slide in the top half of the presentation window and the speaker notes for that slide in the bottom half.

6 At the bottom of the vertical scroll bar, click the **Next Slide button** to display Slide 5 ("Our Team"). This slide has a speaker note.

7 On the View tab, in the Presentation Views group, click the **Normal button.** Slide 5 appears in Normal view. You can clearly see the speaker note in the Notes pane.

8 On the status bar, click the **Notes button.** The Notes pane closes.

End Activity

20-4 RUNNING A SLIDE SHOW

After you have created and proofed your presentation, you should view it as a slide show to see how it will appear to your audience. You can do this in Slide Show view and Presenter view. As the presenter, you need to advance the slide show, which means you need to do something to display the next slide. To advance the slide show, you can click anywhere on the slide that is currently displayed, or you can use the keyboard by pressing the Spacebar, the Enter key, the Right Arrow key, or the Page Down key. You can also use the keyboard to move to the previous slide by pressing the Left Arrow key, the Page Up key, or the Backspace key. If you right-click the currently displayed slide during a slide show, a shortcut menu that contains commands to jump to specific slides opens. Finally, you can also use buttons on a toolbar that appears in the lower-left corner of the currently displayed slide in Slide Show view or below the currently displayed slide in Presenter view.

After you display the last slide in a slide show, the screen changes to black with a small note at the top that tells you that you have reached the end of the slide show. To end the slide show—that is, to remove the black screen and return to the view from which you started—advance the slide show once more. You can also end a slide show at any time by pressing the Esc key or by right-clicking the slide and then clicking End Show on the shortcut menu.

20-4a Using Slide Show View

To display one slide after another so that each slide fills the entire screen with no toolbars or other Windows elements visible on the screen, use **Slide Show view**. It also displays special effects applied to the text and graphics on each slide or to the slide itself. To start a slide show from the current slide in Slide Show view, click the Slide Show button on the status bar. To start a slide show from the first slide in the presentation, click the Start From Beginning button on the Quick Access Toolbar.

Begin Activity

Run a slide show in Slide Show view.

1. On the Quick Access Toolbar, click the **Start From Beginning button**. The slide show starts from the beginning, and Slide 1 fills the screen in Slide Show view.

TIP: To start the slide show from the current slide, click the Slide Show button on the status bar.

2. Click anywhere on the screen to advance the slide show. Slide 2 ("What Is Gourmet: Delivered?") appears on the screen.
3. Press the **Spacebar** to display the next slide. Slide 3 ("5-Year Goals") appears on the screen.
4. Press the **Enter key** to display the next slide. Slide 4 ("Advantages") appears on the screen.
5. Press the **Left Arrow key** to redisplay the previous slide. Slide 3 ("5-Year Goals") reappears.
6. Right-click anywhere on the screen. On the shortcut menu, click **See All Slides** to display all the slides in the presentation, similar to Slide Sorter view.

TIP: Use Reading view to view the slide show in a window that you can resize.

7. Click the **Slide 6** ("Contact Us") **thumbnail**. Slide 6 ("Contact Us") appears on the screen.
8. Right-click anywhere on the screen. On the shortcut menu, click **Last Viewed**. The most recently viewed slide prior to the current slide—Slide 3 ("5-Year Goals")—reappears.

End Activity

In Slide Show view, if you move the pointer on the slide, a faint row of buttons appears in the lower-left corner of the slide. See Exhibit 20-18. You can use these buttons to navigate the slide show.

EXHIBIT 20-18 NAVIGATION BUTTONS IN SLIDE SHOW VIEW

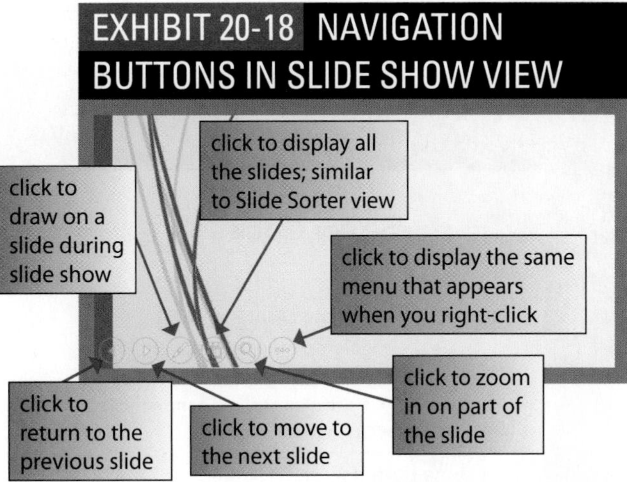

Begin Activity

Use the navigation buttons in Slide Show view.

1. Move the **pointer** without clicking. A faint row of buttons appears in the lower-left corner. Refer back to Exhibit 20-18.
2. Click the **Zoom into the slide button**. The pointer changes to a magnifier, and three-quarters of the slide is darkened.
3. Move the pointer to the title text **5-Year Goals**, and then click. The view zooms so that the part of the slide inside the bright rectangle fills the screen, and the pointer changes to a hand.
4. Point to the **lower-left corner** of the screen, press and hold the **mouse button** to change the pointer to a grabbing hand, drag up and to the right to pull another part of the zoomed-in slide into view, and then release the **mouse button**.
5. Press the **Esc key** to zoom back out to see the whole slide.
6. Move the pointer so you can see the faint row of buttons in the lower-left corner, and then click the **Advance to the next slide button**. Slide 4 ("Advantages") appears.
7. Press the **Right Arrow key** twice to advance two slides. The next two slides, Slide 5 ("Our Team") followed by Slide 6 ("Contact Us"), appear.

Slide Show view The PowerPoint view that displays one slide after another so that each slide fills the entire screen with no toolbars or other Windows elements visible on the screen and displays special effects applied to the text and graphics on each slide or to the slide itself.

EXHIBIT 20-19 SLIDE 3 IN PRESENTER VIEW

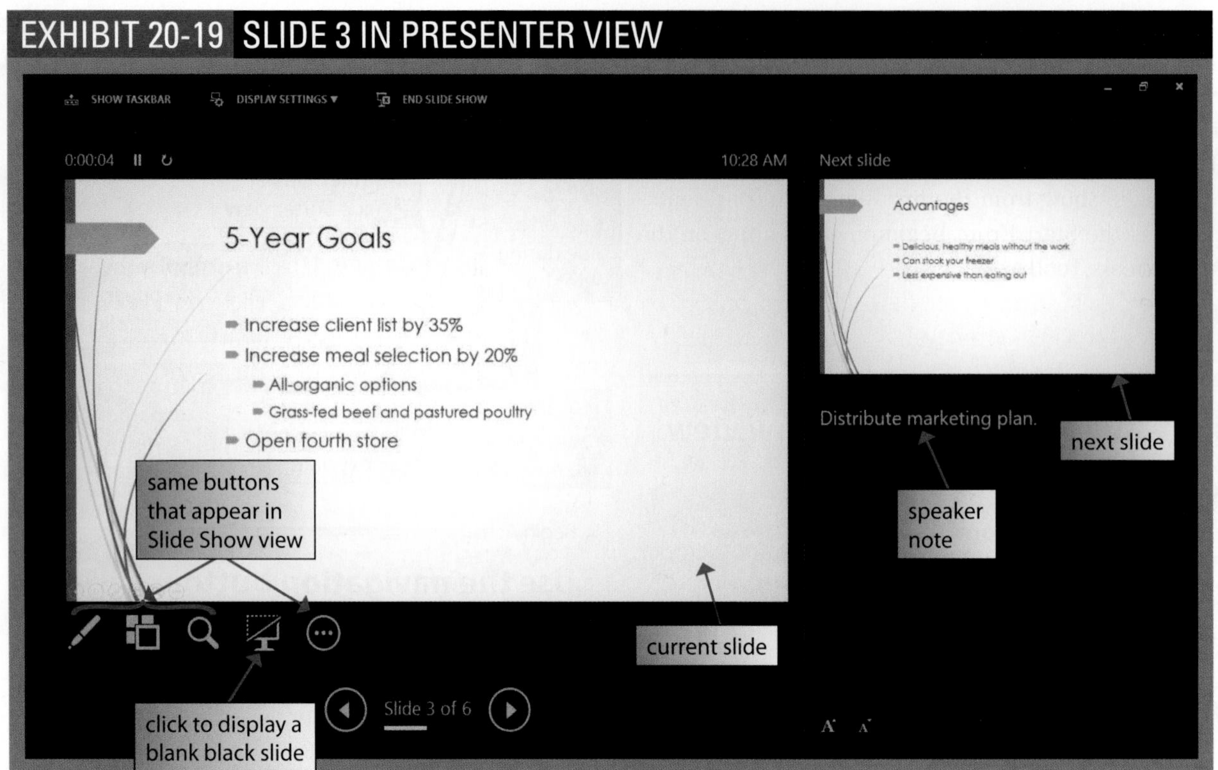

8 Click anywhere on the screen. A black screen with a message that this is the end of the slide show appears.

9 Use any method to advance the slide show. Slide Show view closes, and the presentation appears in Normal view.

End Activity

20-4b Using Presenter View

Presenter view, which was designed to make it easier to display a slide show using a second monitor or a projection screen, shows the current slide in the left pane, the next slide in the right pane, and other helpful controls and information in other areas of the screen, including speaker notes and a timer showing how long the slide show has been running. The slide in the left pane is the slide that fills the screen in Slide Show view on the second monitor or projection screen and is what the audience sees. See Exhibit 20-19.

If your computer is connected to a projector or second monitor, and you start a slide show in Slide Show view, Presenter view automatically starts on the computer, and Slide Show view appears on the second monitor or projection screen. If, for some reason, you don't want to use Presenter view in that circumstance, you can switch to Slide Show view. If you want to practice using Presenter view when your computer is not connected to a second monitor or projector, you can switch to Presenter view from Slide Show view.

Presenter view The PowerPoint view that shows the current slide, the next slide, speaker notes, a timer showing how long the slide show has been running, and other helpful controls and information; designed to make it easier to display a slide show using a second monitor or a projection screen.

Begin Activity

Run a slide show in Presenter view.

1 Display **Slide 3** ("5-Year Goals").

2 On the status bar, click the **Slide Show button**. Clicking this button starts the slide show from the current slide, so Slide 3 appears in Slide Show view.

3 Right-click **anywhere on the slide**. On the shortcut menu, click **Show Presenter View**. The presentation switches to Presenter view. Slide 3 ("5-Year Goals")—the current slide—appears in the left pane. The speaker note that you added to this slide (*Distribute marketing plan.*) appears at the bottom of the right pane, and the next slide preview appears at the top of the right pane. Refer back to Exhibit 20-19.

PROBLEM?
If the next slide does not appear at the top of the right pane, click the **Advance to the next slide button** below Slide 3, and then click the **Return to the previous slide button**.

FYI DISPLAYING A BLANK SLIDE DURING A SLIDE SHOW

Sometimes during a presentation, the audience has questions about the material, and you want to pause the slide show to respond to their questions. Or, you might want to refocus the audience's attention on you instead of on the visuals on the screen. In these cases, you can display a blank slide (either black or white). When you do this, the audience, with nothing else to look at, will shift all of their attention to you. Some presenters plan to use blank slides and insert them at specific points during their slide shows. If you did not create blank slides in your presentation file, but during your presentation you feel you need to display a blank slide, you can easily do this in Slide Show or Presenter view by pressing the B key to display a blank black slide or the W key to display a blank white slide. To remove the black or white slide and redisplay the slide that had been on the screen before you displayed the blank slide, press any key on the keyboard or click anywhere on the screen. In Presenter view, you can also use the Black or unblack slide show button to toggle a black slide on or off.

An alternative to redisplaying the slide that had been displayed prior to the blank slide is to click the Advance to the next slide button or . This can be more effective than redisplaying the slide that was onscreen before the blank slide because, after you have grabbed the audience's attention and prepared them to move on, you won't lose their focus by displaying a slide they have already seen.

4 Below the current slide, click the **Advance to the next slide button** . Slide 4 ("Advantages") appears in the left pane.

5 At the top of the screen, click the **END SLIDE SHOW button.** Presenter view closes, and the slide you started with, Slide 3 ("5-Year Goals"), appears on the slide in Normal view.

End Activity

20-5 ADDING ANIMATIONS

Animations are special effects applied to an object, such as a graphic or a bulleted list, that make the object move or change. Animations add interest to a slide show and draw attention to the text or object being animated.

Animation effects are grouped into the following four types in the Animations gallery (see Exhibit 20-20):

- **Entrance**—text and objects animate as they appear on the slide; one of the most commonly used animation types.

EXHIBIT 20-20 ANIMATION GALLERY

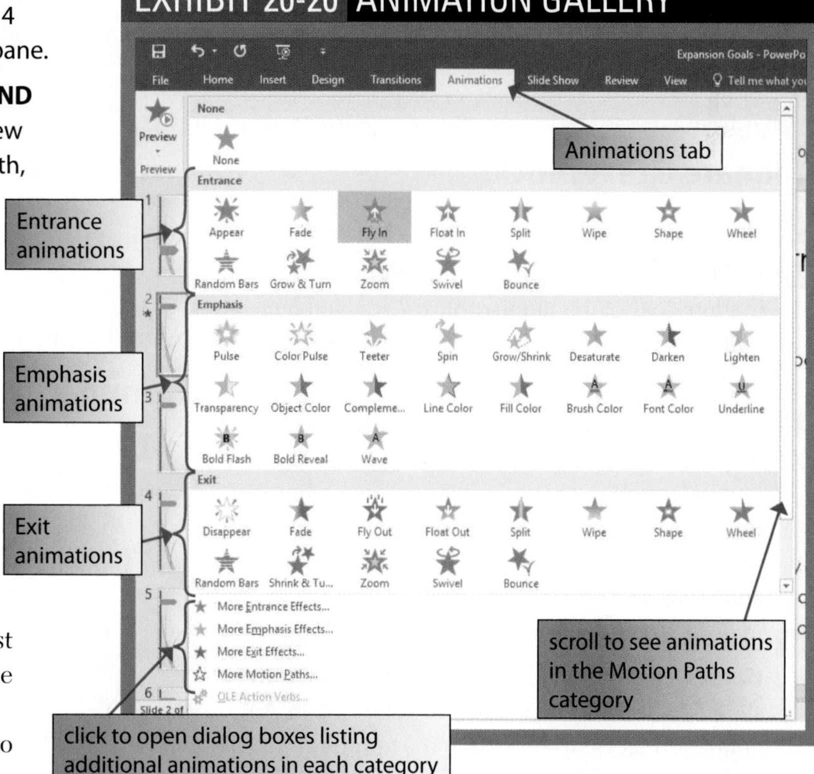

animation A special effect applied to an object that makes the object move or change.

- **Emphasis**—the appearance of text and objects already visible on the slide changes or the text or objects move in place.
- **Exit**—text and objects leave the screen before the slide show advances to the next slide.
- **Motion Paths**—text and objects move following a path on a slide.

Unless you change the behavior, animations are set to start On Click, which means when you advance the slide show—that is, when you click the screen or press the Spacebar, Enter key, or Right Arrow key.

After you apply an animation to an object on a slide, an animation sequence icon appears near the upper-left corner of the object. The number in the icon indicates the order of the animation when you advance the slide show. In other words, the item labeled with the number 1 animation sequence icon animates first, the item labeled with the number 2 animation sequence icon animates second, and so on.

20-5a Animating a Text Box

To animate a text box, you click anywhere in it, and then click an animation in the Animation group on the Animations tab.

Begin Activity

Animate a text block.

1 Display **Slide 2** ("What Is Gourmet: Delivered?").

2 On the ribbon, click the **Animations tab**. The animations in the Animation group are grayed out, indicating they are not available. This is because nothing is selected on the slide.

3 On the slide, click anywhere on the **title text**. A dotted line appears around the border of the title text box, and the animations in the Animation group are now available. All of the animations currently visible in the Animation group are entrance animations.

4 In the Animation group, click the **Fly In animation**. The animation previews on the slide and the slide title flies in from the bottom of the slide. An animation sequence icon with the number 1 in it appears next to the upper-left corner of the title text box.

5 In the Animation group, click the **More button** [▼]. The Animation gallery opens. Refer back to Exhibit 20-20.

6 In the Emphasis section, click the **Underline animation**. The gallery closes, and the animation previews on the slide by underlining the slide title from left to right. The Underline animation replaced the Fly In animation you applied previously.

7 On the Animations tab, in the Preview group, click the **Preview button**. The emphasis animation applied to the slide title previews on the slide again.

8 On the status bar, click the **Slide Show button** [icon]. Slide 2 appears in Slide Show view.

9 Advance the slide show. The animation you applied—the emphasis Underline animation—occurs, and the slide title is underlined.

10 Right-click a **blank area of the slide**. On the shortcut menu, click **End Show**.

End Activity

20-5b Animating Bulleted Lists

When you apply an animation to text, it affects all of the text in the text box. When you animate a bulleted list, sequential animation sequence numbers appear next to each bulleted item. If an item has subitems, the same animation sequence number that appears next to the first-level item appears next to the subitems. See Exhibit 20-21. This means that each first-level bulleted item along with its subitems is animated one at a time.

Begin Activity

Animate a bulleted list.

1 On **Slide 2** ("What Is Gourmet: Delivered?"), click anywhere in the **bulleted list** to make the text box active.

2 On the Animations tab, in the Animation group, click the **Fly In animation**. Each first-level bulleted item flies in from the bottom along with its subitems. The numbered animation sequence icons next to each item indicate the order of the animations. Refer to Exhibit 20-21.

3 On the status bar, click the **Slide Show button** [icon]. Slide 2 appears in Slide Show view with only the slide title visible.

4 Advance the slide show. The first animation—the Underline animation—occurs.

EXHIBIT 20-21 ANIMATION SEQUENCE ICONS FOR A BULLETED LIST WITH SUBBULLETS

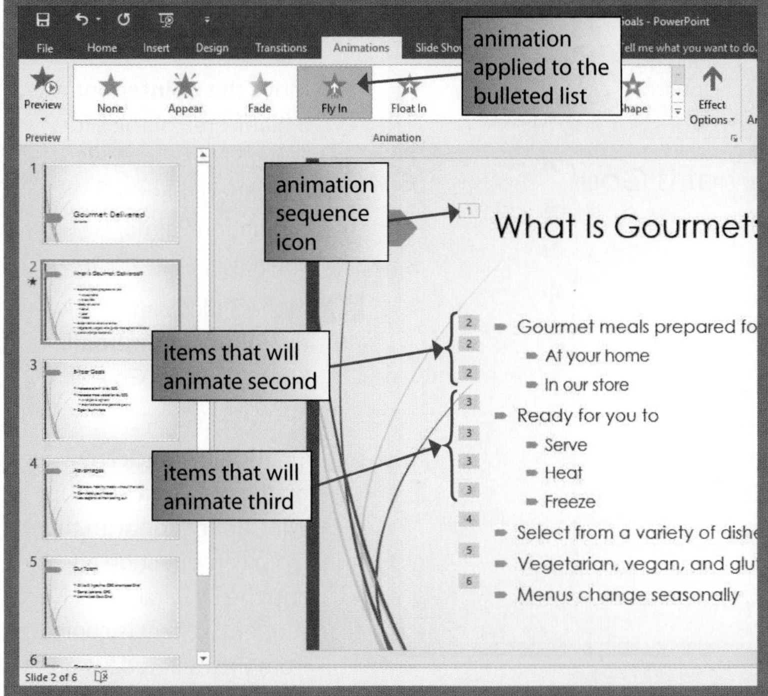

5 Advance the slide show again. The first bulleted item and its subitems fly onto the screen.

6 Advance the slide show four more times to make the rest of the bulleted items fly onto the screen.

7 Press the **Esc key** to end the slide show.

End Activity

20-5c Changing Animation Effects

Most animations have effects that you can modify. For example, the Fly In and Wipe animations can animate text or objects to fly in or wipe from different directions. In addition, you can change the sequence effects for objects made up of multiple items, such as a bulleted list. The default sequence for bulleted lists is for items to appear By Paragraph. This means that each first-level item and its subitems animates one at a time when you advance the slide show. You can change this so that the entire list animates at once as one object, or so that each first-level item animates at the same time but as separate objects.

The animation effects that you can modify appear on the Effect Options menu that appears when you click the Effect Options button in the Animation group on the Animations tab. Exhibit 20-22 shows the Direction options for the Fly In animation and the Sequence options for a bulleted list.

Begin Activity

Change animation effects.

1 On **Slide 2** ("What Is Gourmet: Delivered?"), click anywhere on the **bulleted list**, if necessary. In the Animation group, Fly In is selected.

2 In the Animation group, click the **Effect Options button.** The menu of options that you can change for the selected Fly In animation and the selected bulleted list object appears. Refer to Exhibit 20-22.

3 Click **From Left.** The animation previews and the bulleted items fly in from the left, one first-level bulleted item at a time.

4 In the Animation group, click the **Float In animation.** The animation previews and the bulleted items float in one first-level item at a time.

5 In the Animation group, click the **Effect Options button.** The sequence options are the same because a bulleted list is still the object being animated, but the Float animation has only two direction options available.

6 Click **Float Down.**

7 Click the **Effect Options button.** At the bottom of the menu, the three sequence options for a bulleted list are listed.

8 Click **As One Object.** All the bulleted items float in from the top at the same time. A single animation sequence icon appears next to the bulleted list indicating that the entire list will animate as one object.

9 Apply the **Wipe animation**, and then change the effect to **From Left.** The default sequence option, By Paragraph, is applied automatically when you applied the new animation.

10 Click the **title text.** In the Animation group, click the **Effect Options button.** The Underline animation has no effects you can modify, and the title text box has only one sequence option—As One Object.

11 Press the **Esc key** to close the menu without making a selection.

End Activity

EXHIBIT 20-22 EFFECTS FOR THE FLY IN ANIMATION

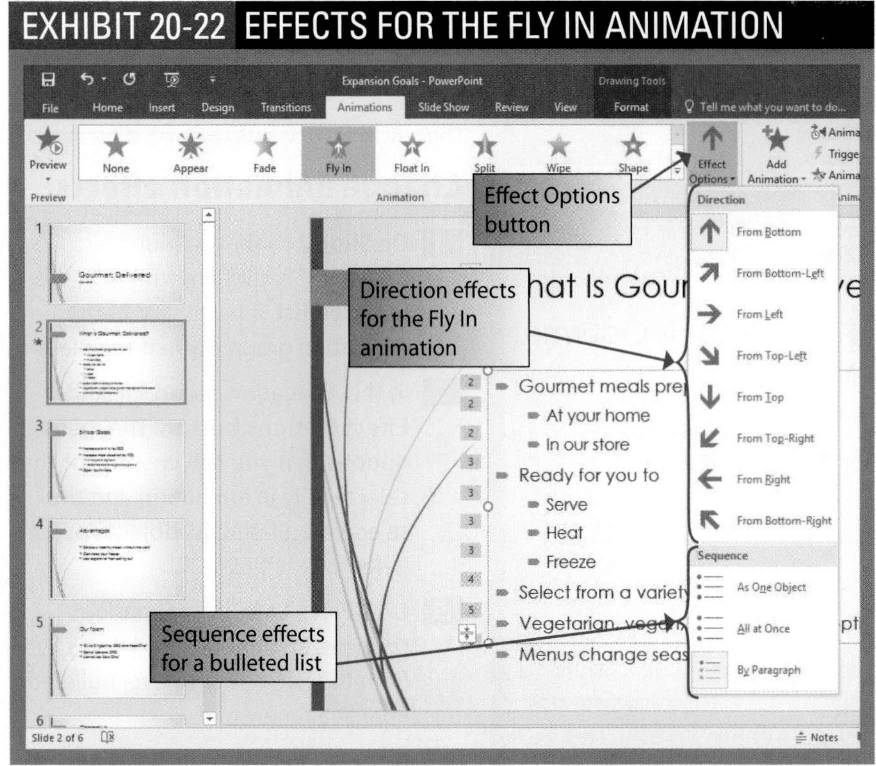

20-5d Using the Animation Painter

For consistency, you will usually want to apply the same animation to all the slide titles in the presentation. You can display each slide and repeat the same procedure to apply the same animation to each slide title. A faster and more accurate method is to use the **Animation Painter** to copy an animation from one object to another. To do so, you click the animated object, click the Animation Painter button in the Advanced Animation group on the Animations tab, click the slide containing the object you want to animate, and then click that object. If you want to copy the animation to multiple objects, double-click the Animation Painter button. You can then click as many objects as you want, and the Animation Painter will remain selected and active until you click it again or press the Esc key to turn it off.

Begin Activity

Use the Animation Painter.

1. On Slide 2 ("What Is Gourmet: Delivered?"), click anywhere on the **bulleted list**.
2. In the Advanced Animation group, click the **Animation Painter button**. The button changes to orange to indicate that it is selected.
3. Move the **pointer** onto a blank area of the slide. The pointer changes to indicating that the Animation Painter is active.
4. In the Slides pane, click the **Slide 3 thumbnail**. Slide 3 ("5-Year Goals") appears.
5. On the slide, click anywhere on the **bulleted list**. The Wipe animation with the From Left direction effect and the By Paragraph sequence effect is copied from the bulleted list on Slide 2 and applied to the bulleted list on Slide 3. The Animation Painter button is no longer selected, and the pointer returns to its default shape. The bulleted list is still selected.
6. On the Animations tab, in the Advanced Animation group, double-click the **Animation Painter button**.
7. Display **Slide 4** ("Advantages"). On the slide, click the **bulleted list**. The copied animation is applied to the bulleted list on Slide 4, but this time, the Animation Painter button remains selected, and the pointer is still .
8. Apply the copied animation to the bulleted list on Slide 5.
9. On the Animations tab, in the Advanced Animation group, click the **Animation Painter button**. The button is deselected, and the pointer returns to its usual shape.

TIP: You can also press the Esc key to deselect the Animation Painter button.

End Activity

Animation Painter A tool in PowerPoint that you can use to copy an animation from one object to another.

20-5e Removing an Animation

If you animate a slide title, make sure you consider how it will appear to the audience. You don't want to leave them wondering what type of information the next slide will contain. As you create a presentation, you might decide to remove an animation. For example, too many animations on a slide can distract an audience rather than enhance your message. If you decide that you don't want an object to be animated, you can remove its animation.

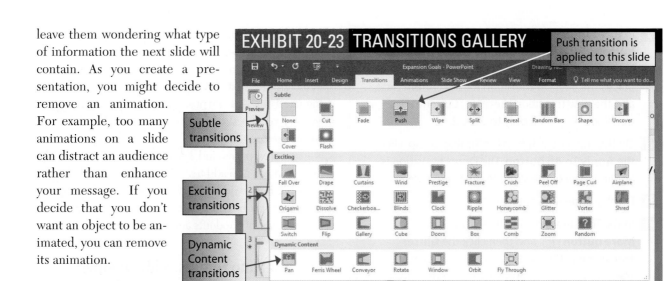

EXHIBIT 20-23 TRANSITIONS GALLERY

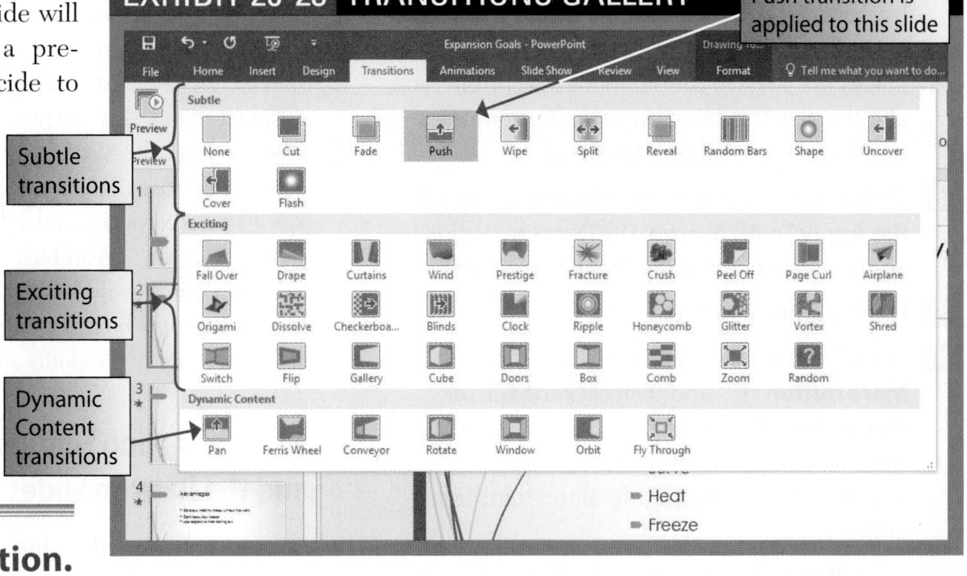

Begin Activity

Remove an animation.

1 Display **Slide 2** ("What Is Gourmet: Delivered?").

2 On the slide, click the **title text**. On the Animations tab, in the Animation group, the Underline animation is selected.

3 On the Animations tab, in the Animation group, click the **More button** [▾].

4 At the top of the gallery, click the **None animation**. The gallery closes, and the Underline animation is removed from the title text on Slide 2.

End Activity

20-6 ADDING TRANSITIONS

A **transition** is the manner in which the next slide appears on the screen in place of the previous slide during a slide show. The default is for one slide to disappear and the next slide to immediately appear on the screen. You can make the transitions more interesting by using the Transitions gallery in the Transition to This Slide group on the Transitions tab. You can modify transitions in Normal or Slide Sorter view.

In the Transitions gallery, shown in Exhibit 20-23, transitions are organized into three categories: Subtle, Exciting, and Dynamic Content. Dynamic Content transitions are a combination of the Fade transition for the slide background and a different transition for the slide content. If slides have the same background, it looks like the slide background stays in place and only the slide content moves. Similar to animations, you can modify transitions using the Effect Options button in the Transition to This Slide group. Each transition has different effects that you can apply.

Begin Activity

Add transitions to the slides.

1 On the ribbon, click the **Transitions tab**. In the Transition to This Slide group, click the **Push transition**. The Push transition is applied to the current slide, and you see a preview of it.

2 On the Transitions tab, in the Preview group, click the **Preview button**. The transition is again previewed.

3 In the Transition to This Slide group, click the **More button** [▾]. The gallery of transitions opens. Refer back to Exhibit 20-23.

4 In the first row in the Exciting section, click the **Peel Off transition** to apply the Peel Off transition to the current slide. The transition previews by peeling Slide 1 from the lower-right corner of the screen to the upper-left corner.

5 In the Transition to This Slide group, click the **Effect Options button**. The Peel Off transition has only two effects from which you can choose.

6 Click **Right**. The transition previews by peeling Slide 1 from the lower-left corner of the screen to the upper-right corner.

transition The manner in which the next slide appears on the screen in place of the previous slide during a slide show.

7 In the Transition to This Slide group, click the **More button** [icon], and then click the **Doors transition** in the Exciting group. The Doors transition replaces the Peel Off transition for the current slide, and the new transition previews. Currently, the transition is applied only to Slide 2.

8 On the Transitions tab, in the Timing group, click the **Apply To All button.** The Doors transition is applied to all of the slides in the presentation.

9 Display **Slide 6** ("Contact Us").

10 In the Transition to This Slide group, click the **More button** [icon], and then click the **Glitter transition** in the Exciting section. The Glitter transition is applied only to the current slide, Slide 6, and a preview of the Glitter transition appears.

11 Display **Slide 4** ("Advantages"). On the status bar, click the **Slide Show button** [icon]. Slide 4 transitions onto the screen with the Doors transition.

12 Advance the slide show twice to animate and display all of the content on Slide 4 and transition to Slide 5 ("Our Team") with the Doors transition.

13 Advance the slide show twice to animate and display all of the content on Slide 5 and transition to Slide 6 ("Contact Us") with the Glitter transition.

14 End the slide show.

End Activity

20-7 ADDING FOOTERS AND HEADERS

Sometimes it can be helpful to have information on each slide such as the title of the presentation or the company name. It can also be helpful to have the slide number and the date displayed on each slide. In common usage, a footer is any text that appears at the bottom of every page in a document or every slide in a presentation. However, in PowerPoint, a **footer** is specifically the text that appears in a Footer text box designated for this purpose. This text box can appear anywhere on the slide; in some themes the footer appears at the top of slides.

For notes pages and **handouts**—printouts of the slides—you can also add text in a header text box. Similar to a footer, in PowerPoint, a **header** is text that appears in a Header text box. The Header text box appears in the top-left corner of handouts and notes pages.

footer In PowerPoint, text that appears in a Footer text box, which can appear anywhere on a slide depending on the theme, or at the bottom of handouts and notes pages.

handout A printout of the slides in a presentation.

header In PowerPoint, text that appears at the top of handouts and notes pages in a document.

20-7a Inserting Footers, Slide Numbers, and the Date on Slides

To add a footer, the slide number, and the date to slides, you need to open the Slide tab on the Header and Footer dialog box by clicking the Header & Footer button in the Text group on the Insert tab. See Exhibit 20-24. When you add this information, you can choose to add it only to the current slide or to all the slides. There is also a Preview area in the dialog box that shows where the footer, slide number, and date will appear on the slide.

EXHIBIT 20-24 SLIDE TAB IN THE HEADER AND FOOTER DIALOG BOX

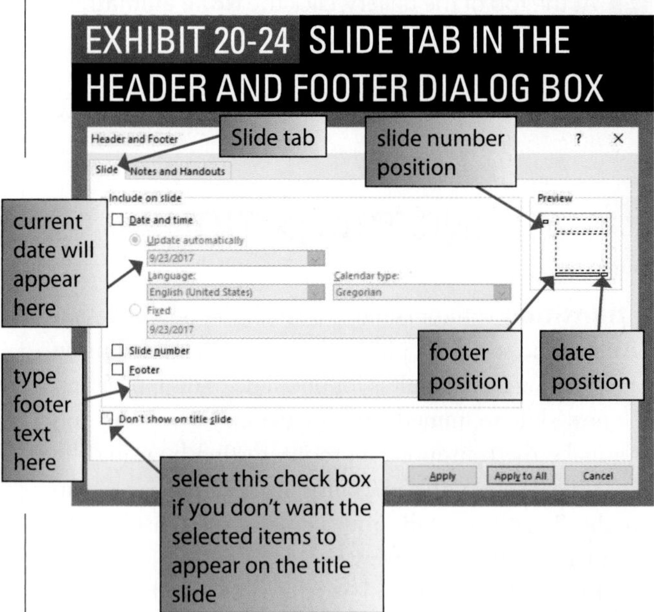

Often, presenters do not want the footer, slide number, and date to appear on the title slide. You can specify that these elements appear on all slides except the title slide by selecting the Don't show on title slide check box. When you do this, any slide other than Slide 1 must be displayed.

Begin Activity

Insert footers, slide numbers, and the date on slides.

1 With **Slide 4** ("Advantages") displayed, on the ribbon, click the **Insert tab**. In the Text group, click the **Header & Footer button**. The Header and Footer dialog box opens with the Slide tab on top. In the upper-right corner of the dialog box, the Preview box shows a preview slide with rectangles that identify where the footer, date, and slide number will appear. Their exact positions change depending on the current theme. Refer back to Exhibit 20-24.

> **TIP:** Clicking the Date & Time button or the Slide Number button also opens the Header and Footer dialog box.

2 Click the **Footer check box** to select it. In the Preview box, the rectangle at the lower-left of the slide turns black to indicate that the footer will appear on the slides.

3 Click in the **Footer box**, and then type **Gourmet: Delivered**.

4 Click the **Slide number check box** to select it. The rectangle at the upper-right of the Preview box turns black to indicate that the slide number will appear in this location on each slide.

5 Click the **Date and time check box**. The rectangle at the lower-right of the Preview box turns black, and the options under this check box darken so you can choose one of them.

6 If necessary, click the **Update automatically option button**. The current date will appear on the slides every time the presentation is opened.

> **TIP:** To have a specific date always appear on the slides, select the Fixed option button on the Slide tab in the Header and Footer dialog box, and then type a date in the Fixed box.

7 Click the **Don't show on title slide check box** to select it.

8 Click **Apply to All**. The dialog box closes, and all the slides except the title slide contain the footer and today's date at the bottom of the slides and the slide number in the upper-left corner of the slides. Compare your screen to Exhibit 20-25.

9 Display **Slide 1** (the title slide). Verify that the footer, slide number, and date do not appear on the slide.

End Activity

20-7b Inserting Headers and Footers on Notes Pages and Handouts

If you plan to print notes for your reference or distribute handouts to the audience, you might want to add information to the header and footer in these printouts. The footer that appears on the slides does not appear on the notes pages or the handouts. You need to open the Notes and Handouts tab in the Header and Footer dialog box

EXHIBIT 20-25 FOOTER, DATE, AND SLIDE NUMBER ON SLIDE 4

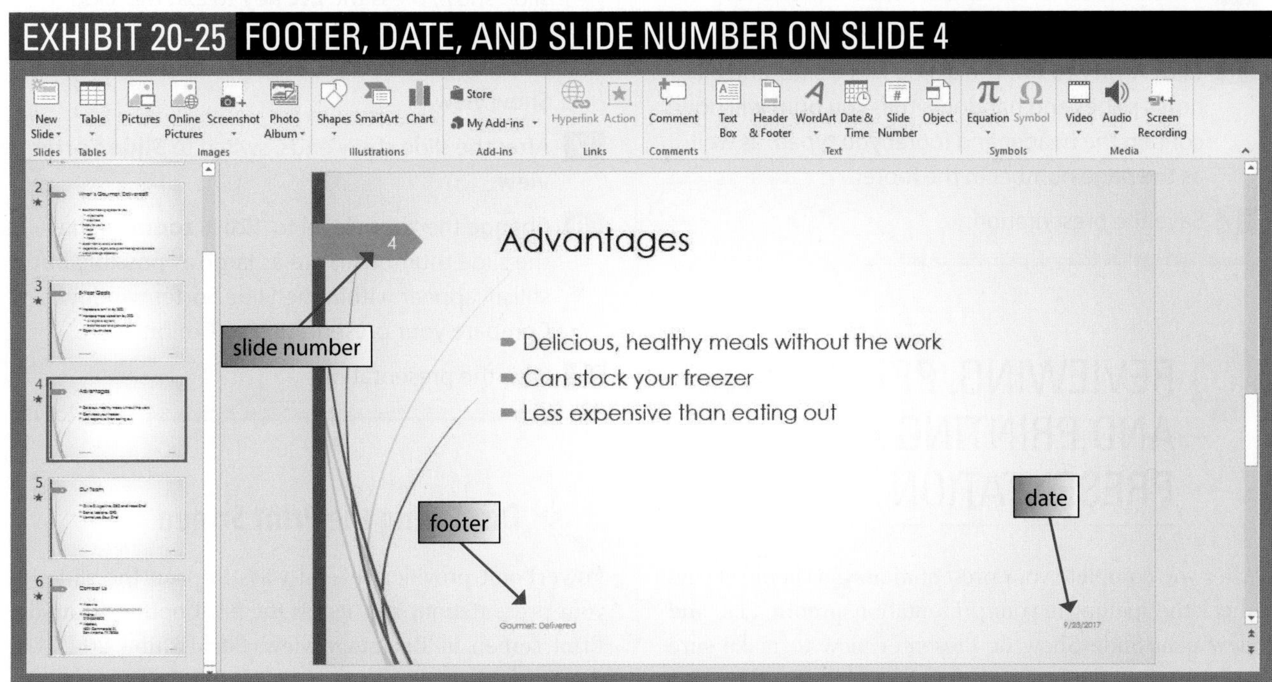

to set the options for both headers and footers on notes and handouts. The page number appears in the footer of notes and handouts by default.

Begin Activity

Add a header and footer to the notes pages and handouts.

1. On the Insert tab, in the Text group, click the **Header & Footer button**. The Header and Footer dialog box opens with the Slide tab on top.
2. Click the **Notes and Handouts tab**. In addition to the Date and time and Footer check boxes, this tab contains a Page number check box instead of a Slide number check box, as well as a Header check box and a box in which to type a header. The Page number check box is selected by default, and the thick black border around the box in the lower-right corner of the preview indicates that this is where the page number will appear. Note that the footer you added to the slides does not appear in the Footer box on the Notes and Handouts tab.
3. Click the **Header check box** to select it. A thick border appears around the placeholder in the upper-left corner of the Preview. That is where the header will appear.
4. Click in the **Header box**, and then type **Expansion Plans**.
5. Click the **Footer check box**, click in the Footer box, and then type **Presentation to Investors**.
6. Click **Apply to All**. The dialog box closes, and all notes pages and handouts that you print will now contain the header and footer you typed, as well as the page number in the footer.
7. Save the presentation.

End Activity

20-8 REVIEWING, PREVIEWING, AND PRINTING A PRESENTATION

After you complete your presentation, you should always check the spelling in your presentation, proofread it, and view it in Slide Show or Presenter view to make sure everything works as expected.

20-8a Checking and Reviewing a Presentation

You should always check the spelling in a presentation and proofread it for errors. Using the spell checker in PowerPoint is similar to using the spell checker in Word—click the Spelling button, examine any flagged words, and decide whether to change the word or ignore the suggested correction. After you check the spelling, you should run the slide show to verify that all of your animations and transitions work as you expect and to review the contents of each slide.

Begin Activity

Check and review the presentation.

1. On the ribbon, click the **Review tab**. In the Proofing group, click the **Spelling button**.
2. Ignore all instances of the two names flagged as misspelled on Slide 5 ("Our Team"). After you ignore the second name, a dialog box opens, telling you that the spelling check is complete.
3. Click **OK**.
4. Display **Slide 1** (the title slide).
5. On the status bar, click the **Slide Show button** . The slide show starts in Slide Show view.
6. Advance through the slide show. If you see any problems while you are watching the slide show, press the **Esc key** to exit the slide show and return to Normal view, make the necessary corrections, and then return to Slide Show view.
7. After the slide show ends, switch to **Slide Sorter view**.
8. Change the zoom level to **120% zoom** so that the slide thumbnails are as large as possible but still all appear within the Slide Sorter window. Compare your presentation to Exhibit 20-26.
9. Save the presentation.

End Activity

20-8b Displaying the Print Screen

PowerPoint provides several ways to print the slides in your presentation. You access the print options from the Print screen in Backstage view. See Exhibit 20-27. In the Settings section, you can click the Full Page Slides

EXHIBIT 20-26 COMPLETED PRESENTATION IN SLIDE SORTER VIEW

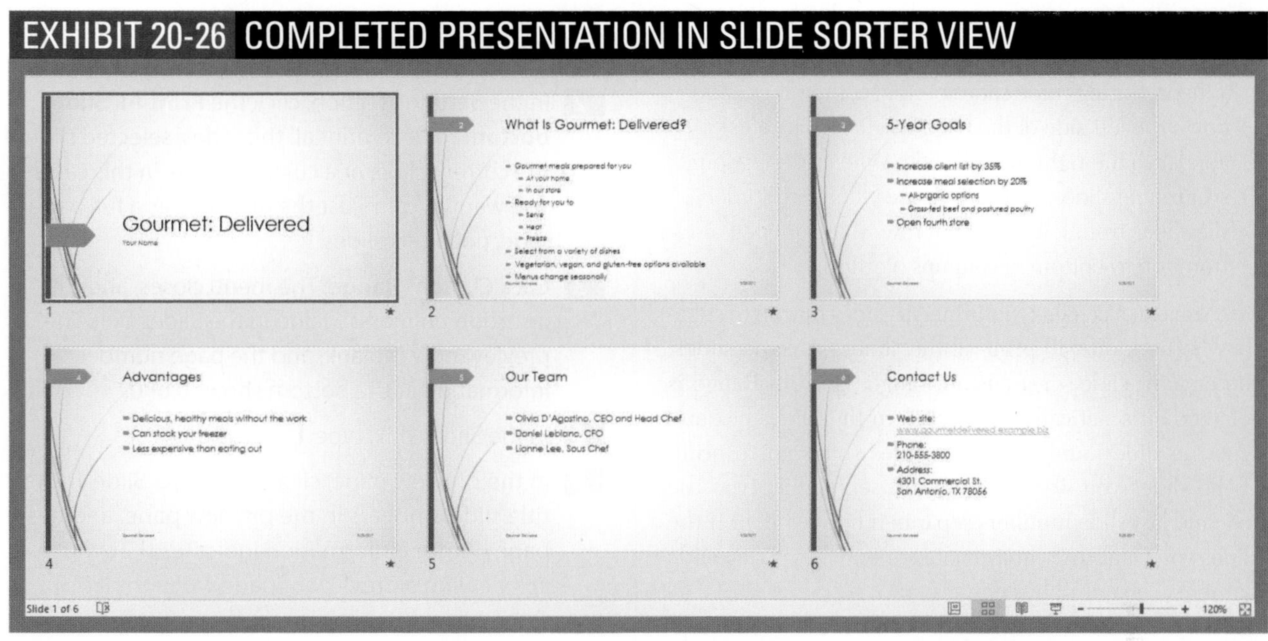

EXHIBIT 20-27 PRINT SCREEN IN BACKSTAGE VIEW

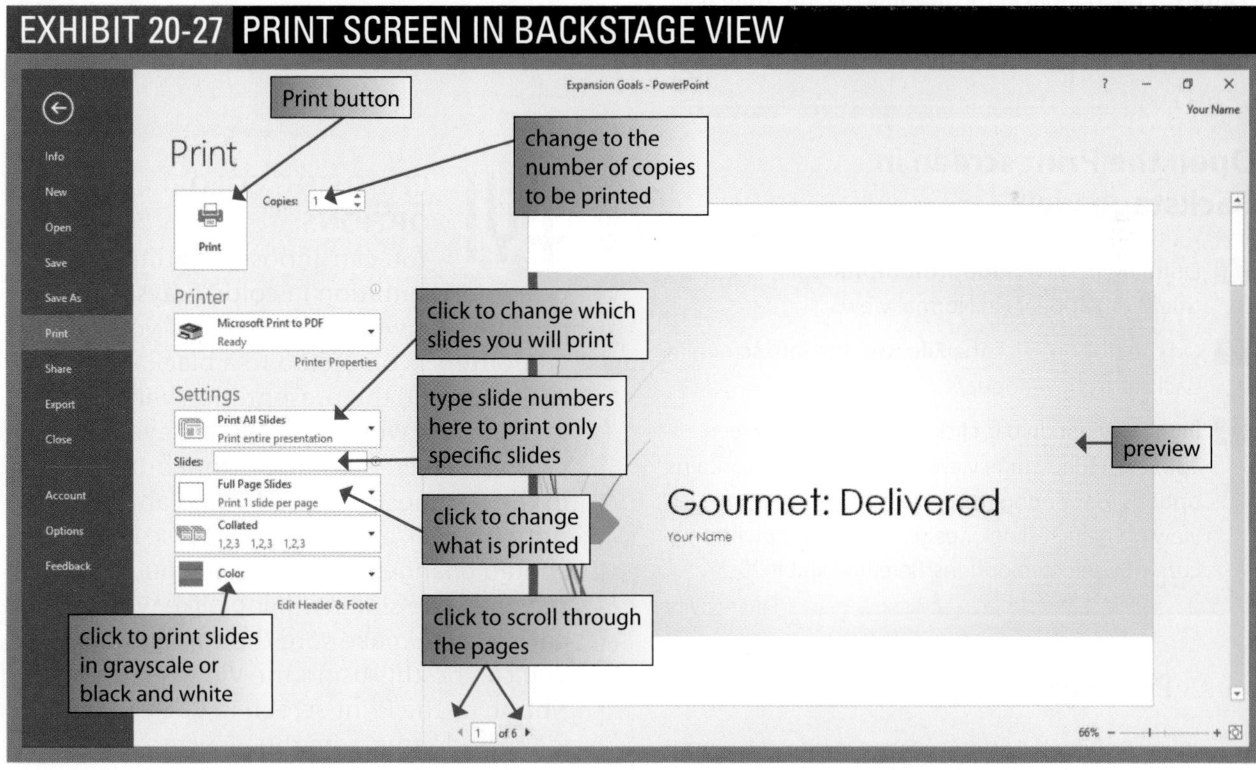

button to choose from the following options for printing the presentation:

- **Full Page Slides**—prints each slide full size on a separate piece of paper; speaker notes are not printed.
- **Notes Pages**—prints each slide as a notes page, with the slide at the top of the page and speaker notes below the slide, similar to how a slide appears in Notes Page view.
- **Outline**—prints the text of the presentation as an outline.

- **Handouts**—prints the presentation with one, two, three, four, six, or nine slides on each piece of paper. When printing three slides per page, the slides appear down the left side of the page and lines for notes appear to the right of each slide. When printing four, six, or nine slides, you can choose whether to order the slides from left to right in rows (horizontally) or from top to bottom in columns (vertically).

You can also click the Print All Slides button to specify whether you will print all the slides, selected slides, the current slide, or a custom range. Custom Range is selected automatically if you click in the Slides box and type the slide numbers of the slides you want to print. If the slides you want to print are sequential, type the first and last slide numbers separated by a hyphen. If the slides you want to print are not sequential, type the slide numbers separated by commas.

A preview of the presentation using the print options you select appears on the right side of the Print tab. You can click the Next Page ▶ and Previous Page ◀ buttons at the bottom of the preview to scroll from page to page, or you can drag the scroll bar.

Begin Activity

Open the Print screen in Backstage view.

1. Double-click the **Slide 1 thumbnail**. Slide 1 (the title slide) appears in Normal view.
2. On the ribbon, click the **File tab**. The Info screen in Backstage view appears.
3. In the navigation bar, click **Print**. The Print screen appears in Backstage view. The Print screen contains options for printing the presentation, and a preview of the first slide or page as it will print with the currently selected options. Refer to Exhibit 20-27.

End Activity

20-8c Printing Full Page Slides

The default option for printing a presentation is to print all the slides as full page slides, one slide per page.

Begin Activity

Print the title slide as a full page slide.

1. If the second button in the Settings section is not labeled "Full Page Slides," click it, and then click **Full Page Slides**. At the bottom of the preview pane, the page number information indicates that you are viewing Slide 1 of 6 slides to print.
2. In the Settings section, click the **Print All Slides button**. You can print all the slides, selected slides, the current slide, or a custom range. In this case, you want to print just the title slide as a full page slide, not all six slides.
3. Click **Custom Range**. The menu closes, and the insertion point is blinking in the Slides box. The preview now is blank, and the page number information at the bottom shows 0 of 0.
4. In the Slides box, type **1**.
5. In the preview pane, click anywhere. Slide 1 (the title slide) appears in the preview pane, and the page number information indicates that you are viewing a preview of page 1 of a total of 1 page to print.
6. At the top of the Print section, click the **Print button**. Backstage view closes, and Slide 1 prints.

End Activity

FYI

CHOOSING COLOR OPTIONS

You can choose whether to print a presentation in color, grayscale, or black and white. Obviously, if your computer is connected to a black and white printer, the presentation will print in black and white or grayscale even if Color is selected in the bottom button in the Settings section. If you plan to print in black and white or grayscale, you should change this setting so you can see what the slides will look like without color and to make sure they are legible. You can do this using the View tab on the ribbon or the Print screen in Backstage view. To do this from the View tab, click the Grayscale or Black and White button in the Color/Grayscale group. To do this from the Print screen, click the Color button, and then click Grayscale or Pure Black and White. The preview will change to show the presentation in grayscale or black and white.

20-8d Printing Handouts

If you print a presentation as handouts, you can fit multiple slides on a page. To choose the number of slides per page, click the Full Page Slides button, and then select one of the options in the Handouts section. See Exhibit 20-28.

EXHIBIT 20-28 MENU LISTING PRINT OPTIONS ON THE PRINT SCREEN

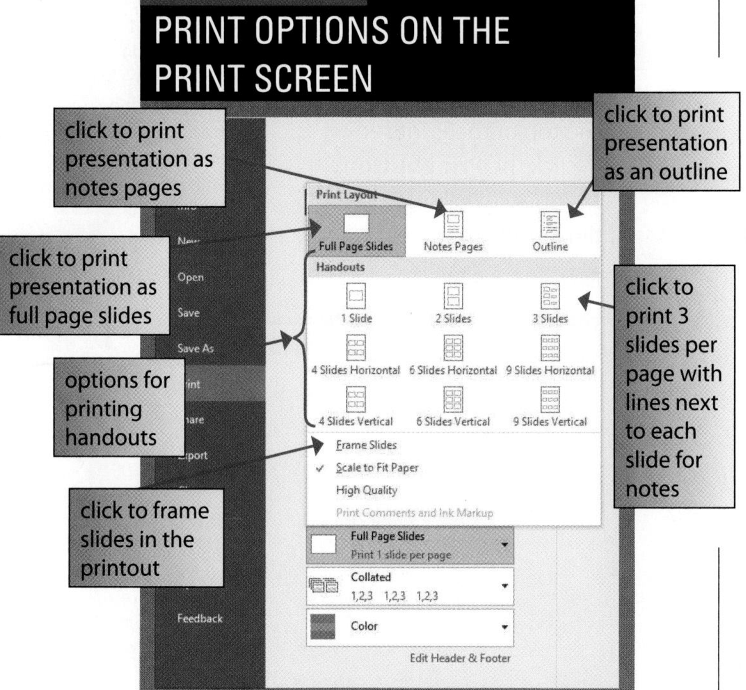

Begin Activity

Print handouts.

1. On the ribbon, click the **File tab**. In the navigation bar, click **Print**. The Print screen appears in Backstage view.
2. In the Settings section, click the **Full Page Slides button**. A menu opens with choices for printing the presentation. At the bottom of the menu, Frame Slides does not have a check mark next to it because the default for Full Page Slides, the currently selected option, is to not frame the slides on the page. Refer back to Exhibit 20-28.
3. In the Handouts section, click **6 Slides Horizontal**. The preview changes to show Slide 1 smaller and in the upper-left corner of the page.

TIP: If you select 3 Slides to print handouts as three slides per page, the slides print with horizontal lines to the right of each slide to make it easier for someone to take notes.

4. In the Settings section, click the **6 Slides Horizontal button**. The Frame Slides command now has a check mark next to it because the default for handouts is to frame the slides. You can click this command at any time to toggle it on or off.
5. Click a **blank area** of the screen to close the open menu.
6. Below the Custom Range button, click in the **Slides box**, and then press the **Delete key** or the **Backspace key** to delete the 1. The button above the Slides box changes from Custom Range to Print All Slides, and all six slides appear on the page in the preview, arranged in order in three rows from left to right.
7. At the top of the Print section, click the **Print button**. Backstage view closes, and the handout prints.

End Activity

20-8e Printing Notes Pages

You can print the slides as notes pages to include any speaker notes. Click the second button under Settings, and then click Notes Pages. Then you can scroll through the preview to see which slides contain notes. If you want to print only the slides that contain notes, click in the Slides box, and then type the slide numbers.

Begin Activity

Print slides containing speaker notes.

1. Open the **Print screen** in Backstage view.
2. In the Settings section, click the **6 Slides Horizontal button**. The button is labeled "6 Slides Horizontal," one of the options for printing handouts, because that was the last printing option selected.
3. In the Print Layout section of the menu, click **Notes Pages**. The menu closes, and the preview shows Slide 1 as a notes page. Notice the header and footer that you entered in the Header and Footer dialog box appear in the preview. You will verify that Slides 3 and 5 contain speaker notes.
4. Below the preview, click the **Next Page button** twice to display Slide 3 ("5-Year Goals") in the preview, and then click the **Next Page button** two more times to display Slide 5 ("Our Team"). These slides contain speaker notes.

5 In the Settings section, click in the **Slides box**, type **3,5** to specify the slides to print, and then click a blank area of the Print screen. Only the two specified pages will print.

6 Scroll through the preview to confirm that Slides 3 and 5 will print.

7 Click the **Print button**. Slides 3 and 5 print as notes pages.

End Activity

20-8f Printing the Presentation as an Outline

You can also print the presentation as an outline. The printout matches the text you see in the Outline pane in Normal view.

Begin Activity

Print the presentation as an outline.

1 Open the **Print screen** in Backstage view.

2 In the Settings section, click the **Notes Pages button**, and then click **Outline**. Slides 3 and 5 appear as an outline in the preview pane.

3 Click the **Custom Range button**, and then click **Print All Slides**. The entire outline appears in the preview.

4 At the top of the Print section, click the **Print button**. Backstage view closes, and the outline prints.

5 Close the presentation.

TIP: If an outline is a bit longer than one page, you can click the Outline button, and then click Scale to Fit Paper to try to force the outline to fit on one page.

End Activity

STUDY TOOLS 20

READY TO STUDY? IN THE BOOK, YOU CAN:

- ☐ Rip out the Chapter Review Card, which includes key terms and key chapter concepts.

ONLINE AT WWW.CENGAGEBRAIN.COM, YOU CAN:

- ☐ Review key concepts from the chapter in a short video.
- ☐ Explore creating a presentation with the interactive infographic.
- ☐ Practice what you've learned with more Practice It and On Your Own exercises.
- ☐ Prepare for tests with quizzes.
- ☐ Review the key terms with flashcards.

QUIZ YOURSELF

1. Which view displays all the slide thumbnails on the screen at once?
2. What is a placeholder?
3. What is a text box?
4. What is a layout?
5. What does AutoFit do?
6. What is included in a theme family?
7. What happens when you demote a slide title one level?
8. How can you move a slide from one position to another?
9. How do you create speaker notes?
10. After you have created and proofed your presentation, why should you view it as a slide show?
11. Describe Slide Show view.
12. Describe Presenter view.
13. What is an animation?
14. What tool can you use to copy animation from one object to another?
15. What is a transition?
16. In PowerPoint, what is a footer?
17. When you add a footer and slide number to slides, how do you prevent them from appearing on the title slide?
18. What are the four ways you can print the content of a presentation?

PRACTICE IT

Practice It 20-1

1. Start PowerPoint, and then save the new, blank presentation as **Bookstore Plan**.
2. In Slide 1, add the title **Book Corner**, and add your name as the subtitle.
3. Add a new Slide 2 using the Title and Content layout.
4. Add the slide title **A Bookstore for Booklovers** and then add the following first-level bulleted items:
   - **Independent bookseller**
   - **Skilled staff**
   - **Events**
5. Below the Events bullet item, add the following second-level bulleted items:
   - **Book clubs**
   - **Author signings**
   - **Book launch parties**
6. Add a new Slide 3 using the Comparison layout, and then add the slide title **Contact Us**.
7. Change the layout of Slide 3 ("Contact Us") to Title and Content.
8. In the content placeholder on Slide 3, add the first-level bulleted item **Address**, add a second bulleted item **400 Oak St.**, and then add **Atlanta, GA 30313** on a new line without creating a new subitem.
9. Save the presentation, and then close it. Open the data file **Bookstore** located in the Chapter 20\Practice It folder. Save the presentation as **Bookstore Growth**.
10. Display Slide 6 ("A Bookstore for Booklovers"). Below the first-level item "Skilled staff," add the following subitems, allowing the text to AutoFit in the text box:
    - **Genre specialists**
    - **Invested in the community**
11. Display Slide 2 ("About Us"), and then change the theme of the presentation to the Integral theme. (Make sure you use the Integral theme in the first row.) Apply the eighth variant. Increase the font size of the text in the bulleted lists on all the slides by two points.
12. Switch to Outline view. In the Outline pane, on Slide 6, add **New Ideas** as a new, first-level bulleted item before the "Webinars and online chats with authors" item.
13. In the Outline pane, on Slide 6, promote the "New Ideas" bulleted item so it becomes a new Slide 7.
14. On the new Slide 7 ("New Ideas"), create a third bulleted item, and then type **"Staff Picks" list**. Drag the "Staff Picks" list bulleted item up so it appears as the second item in the list above the "Add pastries to coffee shop" bulleted item.
15. In the Outline pane, on Slide 4 ("Why a New Store?"), under the "Sales have risen steadily" first-level bulleted item, demote the "At least 15% increase each quarter" bulleted item to a subitem. If necessary, promote the "Marked increase after coffee shop" opened bulleted item back to a second-level bulleted item.

16. Rearrange the slides so that Slide 2 ("About Us") becomes Slide 6, Slide 5 ("A Bookstore for Booklovers") becomes Slide 2, Slide 3 ("Contact Us") becomes Slide 7, and Slide 6 ("New Ideas") becomes Slide 5.
17. Delete Slide 4 ("Join Us for the Party!").
18. On Slide 2 ("A Bookstore for Booklovers"), animate the slide title using the Bold Reveal animation in the Emphasis category.
19. On Slide 2 ("A Bookstore for Booklovers"), animate the bulleted list using the Fly In animation in the Entrance category. Change the direction effect to From Left.
20. Copy the animation applied to the bulleted list on Slide 2 to the bulleted lists on Slides 3 through 5.
21. On Slide 2 ("A Bookstore for Booklovers") remove the animation applied to the title text.
22. Apply the Page Curl transition in the Exciting category to all of the slides. Apply the Cover transition in the Subtle category to only Slide 1 (the title slide).
23. On Slide 4 ("New Ideas"), add **Ideas were solicited from customers and staff.** as a speaker note. On Slide 6 ("Contact Us"), add **Mention that the Web site is being redesigned.** as a speaker note.
24. Add the footer **Book Corner New Store Proposal** to all the slides except the title slide, and then display the slide number on all the slides except the title slide.
25. On the notes and handouts, add **Book Corner** as a header and **New Store Presentation** as a footer.
26. Check the spelling in the presentation, making any corrections necessary. Review each slide in the presentation.
27. View the entire slide show. Make sure the animations and transitions work as you expect, and look carefully at each slide and check the content. If you see any errors or formatting problems, press the Esc key to end the slide show, fix the error, and then start the slide show again from the current slide.
28. Add your name as the subtitle on Slide 1, and then save the presentation. Print the title slide as a full page slide. Print the entire presentation as handouts, six slides per page, and as an outline. Print Slides 4 and 6 as notes pages.
29. Close the presentation.

Practice It 20-2

1. Open the data file **Customer** located in the Chapter 20\Practice It folder. Save the presentation as **Customer Presentation**.
2. In the title slide, add **Nevada Cleaning Pros** as the title, press the Enter key, and then type **Office Cleaning Specialists**. Add your name as the subtitle.
3. Delete Slide 3 ("Our Cleaning Staff").
4. Move Slide 6 ("Weekly Services") so it becomes Slide 3.
5. On Slide 3 ("Weekly Services"), at the end of the bulleted list, add **Polish floors** as a new first-level bulleted item.
6. On Slide 3, add **Pause for questions from the audience.** as the speaker note.
7. On Slide 2 ("Daily Services"), at the end of the bulleted list, add **Clean and disinfect restrooms** as a new first-level bulleted item.
8. On Slide 2 ("Daily Services"), in the second first-level bulleted item, make the words *Sinks and countertops* a new first-level bullet below "Clean kitchen and lounge area including", and then demote the bulleted items "Sinks and countertops" and "Microwave and toasters" to second-level bullets so that two second-level bulleted items now appear under "Clean kitchen and lounge area including."
9. On Slide 4 ("Specialized Services"), drag the bulleted items to the following order:
   - Air duct cleaning
   - Carpet cleaning
   - Clean light fixtures, baseboards, millwork, etc.
   - Pressure washing
   - Sanitizing all lavatory fixtures, sinks, partitions, walls, etc.
   - Stripping and refinishing
   - Wash windows
10. Animate the bulleted lists on Slides 2 through 5 with the Wipe entrance animation using the From Top effect.
11. On Slide 6 ("For More Information"), animate the bulleted list using the Random Bars entrance animation. Change the sequence effect so that the entire list animates as one object.
12. Add the Uncover transition with the From Top-Left effect to all of the slides, and then remove the transition from the title slide.
13. Display the footer text **Presentation for New Clients** and the slide number on all of the slides except the title slide.
14. Apply the Dividend theme, and then apply the second variant.
15. Check the spelling throughout the presentation, and then view the slide show. If you see any errors, press the Esc key to end the slide show, correct the error, and then start the slide show again from the current slide. Save the presentation.

16. Preview the presentation in grayscale, and then in pure black and white. If you have a color printer, switch back to color so the presentation will print in color.
17. Print the title slide as a full page slide, print Slides 2 through 6 as a handout with six slides per page arranged vertically, and then print Slide 3 as a notes page.
18. Close the presentation.

ON YOUR OWN

On Your Own 20-1

1. Open the data file **Sales** located in the Chapter 20\On Your Own folder. Save the presentation as **Sales Presentation**.
2. In the title slide, add **Oceanside Mini Golf and More** as the presentation title, and then add your name as the subtitle.
3. On Slide 2 ("Packages"), add **Mention that these packages can be customized.** as the speaker note.
4. On Slide 2, move the "Birthday Basics" bulleted item and its subitems to be first in the list.
5. On Slide 2, change the last three bulleted items into subitems under "Outdoor Fun" bulleted item.
6. On Slide 3 ("Mini Golf"), add **Variety of pitch speeds** as the fourth subitem under "Batting Cages," and then drag it so it is the second subitem in the list.
7. On Slide 3 ("Mini Golf"), change the Batting Cages bulleted item into a new Slide 4 with its four subitems as first-level bullets on the new Slide 4. Move the "Fun obstacles" and "Hole in One on Hole 18 wins" bulleted items back to Slide 3. (*Hint:* Make sure the bulleted list on the new Slide 4 consists of four first-level items.)
8. On Slide 7 ("Arcade"), promote the "New Games" subitem so it becomes a first-level bulleted item with three subitems.
9. Move Slide 4 ("Batting Cages") so it becomes Slide 5. Move Slide 6 ("Customer Comments") so that it becomes Slide 7.
10. Add a new Slide 7 using the Title and Content layout with the slide title **Go Carts** and the following three first-level bulleted items:
    - **Two outdoor tracks**
    - **Helmets provided**
    - **Minimum age: 15**
11. Under the "Two outdoor tracks" bulleted item, add the following subitems. (*Hint*: AutoCorrect changes the two hyphens to an em dash—a typographic character—after you press the Spacebar after the word following the second dash.)
    - **Slick--go really fast**
    - **Twist and Turn--lots of curves**
12. Change the theme to the Retrospect theme and its second variant.
13. Change the theme fonts to the Franklin Gothic theme fonts. (*Hint*: On the Design tab, in the Variants group click the More button, and then point to Fonts.)
14. In all of the lists, including the list on Slide 8, increase the point size of the text in the first-level items to 24 points and the point size of the text in the second-level items to 20 points.
15. Animate the lists on Slides 2 through 7 using the Zoom animation. Change the sequence effect so the lists animate as one object.
16. Animate the list on Slide 8 ("Customer Comments") using the Appear animation. Change the effect so that the letters appear one at a time with 0.1 seconds between each letter. (*Hint*: On the Animations tab, in the Animation group, click the Dialog Box Launcher, and then modify the Animate text option.)
17. Apply the Pan transition to all the slides, and then apply the Reveal transition to Slide 1 (the title slide).
18. Change the speed of the Reveal transition applied to Slides 1 so it takes two seconds instead of 3.4 seconds. (*Hint*: Use the Duration box in the Timing group on the Transitions tab.)
19. Display the slide number on all slides, including the title slide. Add your name as a header on the notes and handouts.
20. Check the spelling in the presentation, and view the slide show. If you see any errors, press the Esc key to end the slide show, correct the error, and then start the slide show again from the current slide. Save the presentation.
21. Preview the presentation in grayscale and then in pure black and white. If you have a color printer, switch back so the presentation will print in color.
22. Print Slides 1-8 as handouts with four slides per page arranged horizontally. Print Slide 2 ("Packages") as a notes page. Print the presentation outline on one page. (If the outline does not fit on one page even after selecting Scale to Fit Paper, print it on two pages.) Close the presentation.

Part 9
POWERPOINT 2016

21 | Enhancing a Presentation

© Caiaimage/Getty Images

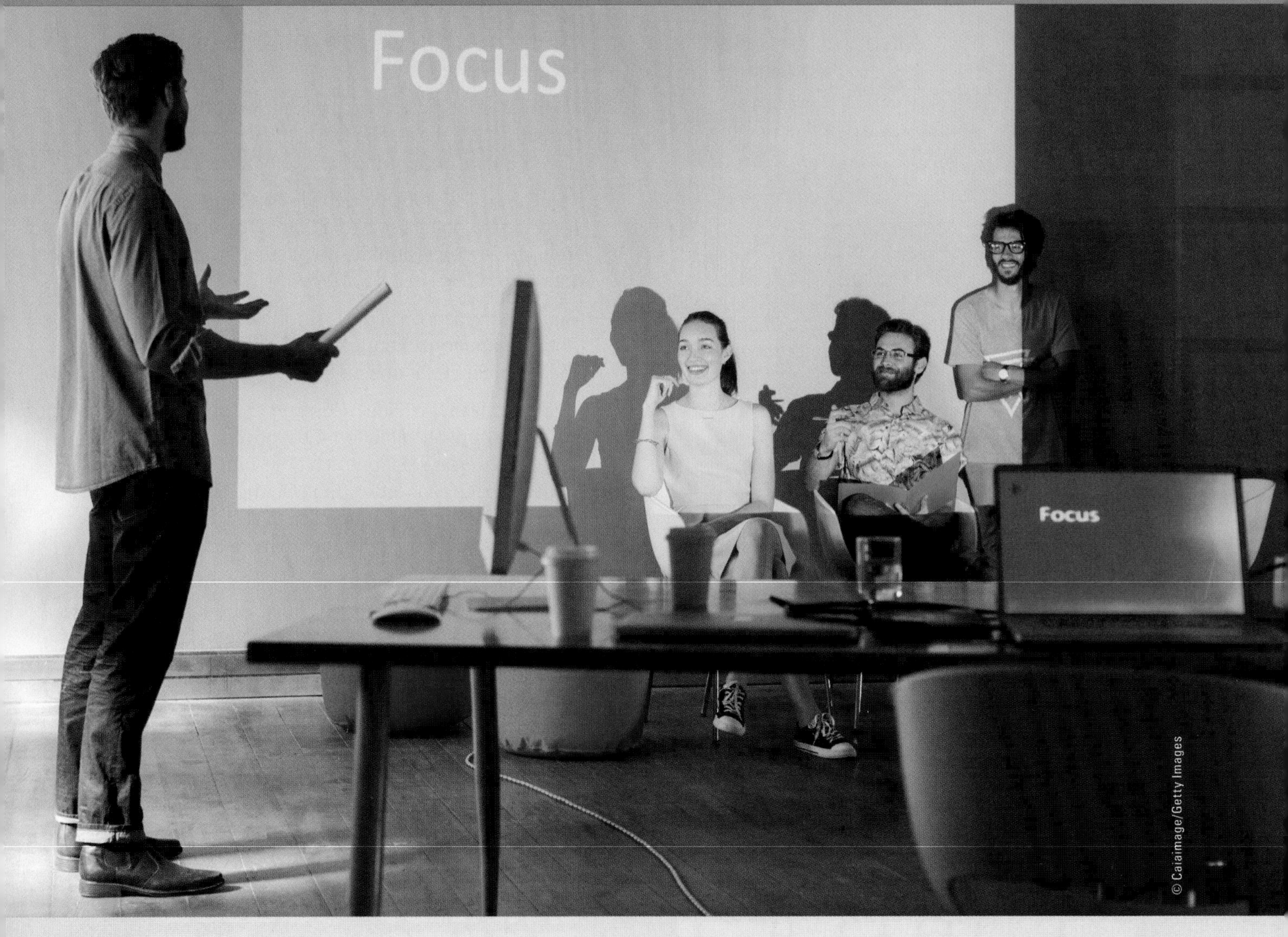

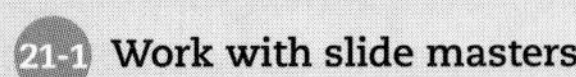

LEARNING OBJECTIVES After studying the material in this chapter, you will be able to:

21-1 Work with slide masters

21-2 Insert graphics

21-3 Create SmartArt diagrams

21-4 Apply animations to graphics

21-5 Modify animation timings

21-6 Add video

21-7 Compress pictures and media

21-8 Save a presentation for distribution

After finishing this chapter, go to **PAGE 650** for **STUDY TOOLS**.

21-1 WORKING WITH SLIDE MASTERS

The **slide master** stores theme fonts, colors, elements, and styles, as well as text and other objects that appear on all the slides in the presentation. Slide masters ensure that all the slides in the presentation have a similar appearance and contain the same elements. A slide master is associated with a theme. The **theme Slide Master** is the primary slide master, and text, graphics, and formatting on the theme Slide Master appear on all slides in the presentation. Changes made to the theme Slide Master affect all of the slides in the presentation. Each theme Slide Master has an associated **layout master** for each layout in the presentation. If you modify a layout master, the changes affect only slides that have that layout applied. For example, the Title Slide Layout master is used by slides with the Title Slide Layout applied, and the Title and Content Layout master is used by slides with the Title and Content Layout applied.

You already know how to modify the look of documents, worksheets, database forms and reports, and presentations by applying a different theme and changing the theme colors and fonts. If you want to make additional changes to the overall look of slides, it is a good idea to make this type of change in the slide masters rather than on the individual slides. For example, if you want to change the color of bullets in bulleted lists or add a graphic to every slide in a presentation, you should do this in the slide master to keep the look of the slides in the presentation consistent.

You can modify slide masters by changing the size and design of text in the content placeholders, adding or deleting graphics, changing the background, and making other modifications.

21-1a Working in Slide Master View

The components of a slide layout include not only the title and content placeholders but also background graphics and text boxes for the footer, slide number, and date, as well as any other objects included as part of the design. Exhibit 21-1 shows a slide with the Title and Content layout applied for a presentation whose theme includes background graphics. The slide contains a title text box, a bulleted list that was created in the content placeholder, a Footer text box at the bottom of the slide, and the Slide Number text box on top of the orange shape to the left of the title text placeholder. It also contains three graphics—the thin vertical rectangle on the left edge of the slide, curvy shapes meant to look like strands of tall grass, and the orange shape to the left of the title text placeholder. Note that the Date text box is not displayed. Exhibit 21-2 shows the theme Title and Content Layout master, which is the layout master for the slide shown in Exhibit 21-1.

To view the slide masters, you need to switch to **Slide Master view**. In Slide Master view, the largest thumbnail in the pane on the left is the slide master associated with the current theme.

Begin Activity

Work in Slide Master view.

1. Open the data file **Wildlife** located in the Chapter 21\Chapter folder. Save the file as **Wildlife Preserve**.
2. Add your name as the subtitle.
3. Display **Slide 5** ("Keep Nature Natural") in the Slide pane. Examine the elements on the slide. Refer to Exhibit 21-1.
4. On the ribbon, click the **View tab**. In the Master Views group, click the **Slide Master button**. In the Slides pane, drag the **scroll box** to the top. The presentation is displayed in Slide Master view. Refer to Exhibit 21-2.
5. In the Slides pane, point to the **selected layout thumbnail** (the one with the orange border). The ScreenTip identifies it as the Title and Content Layout and informs you that this layout is used by Slides 5 and 6.

TIP: You can also press and hold the Shift key and click the Normal button on the status bar to switch to Slide Master view.

slide master A slide that contains theme elements and styles, as well as text and other objects that appear on all the slides in the presentation.

theme Slide Master The primary slide master for a presentation.

layout master A slide master for a specific layout in a presentation.

Slide Master view The PowerPoint view that displays the slide masters.

EXHIBIT 21-1 TITLE AND CONTENT LAYOUT APPLIED TO SLIDE 5

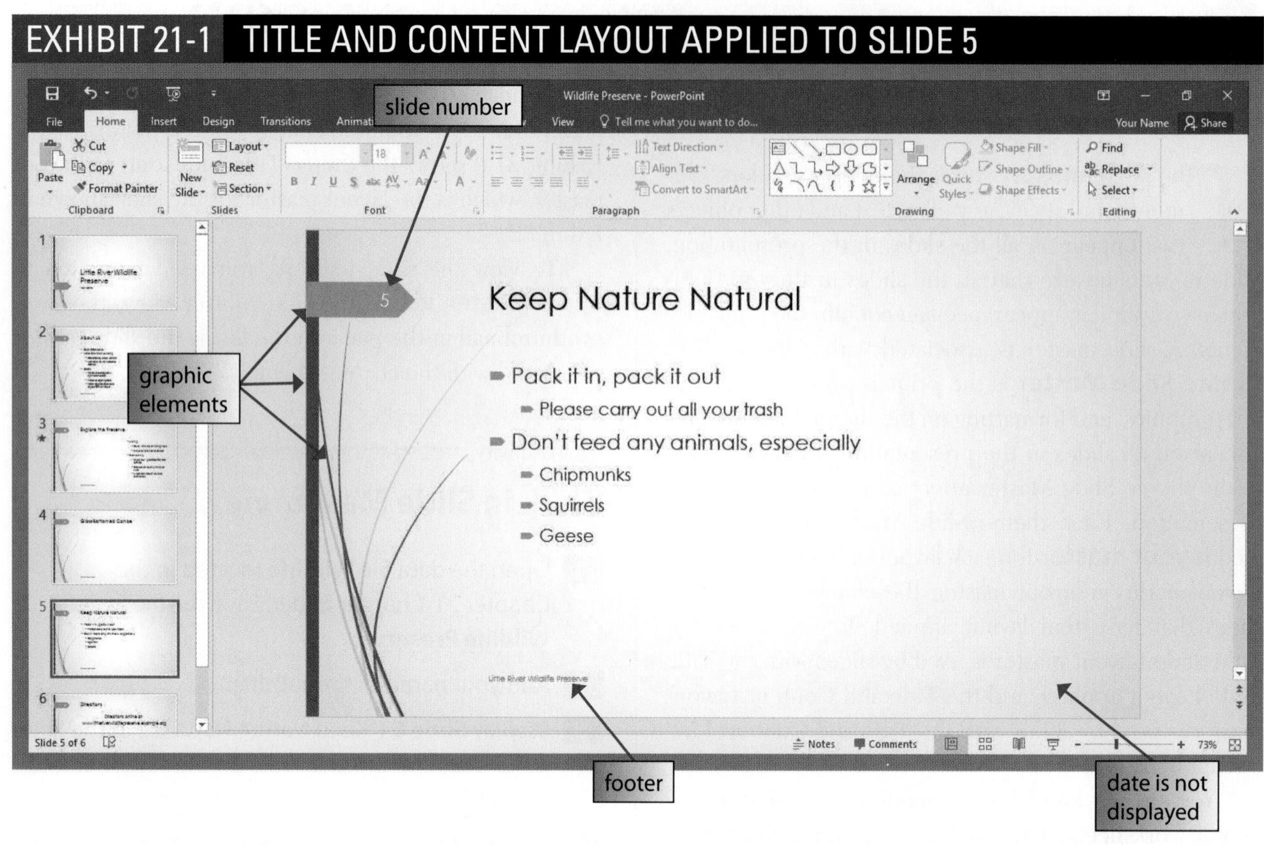

EXHIBIT 21-2 TITLE AND CONTENT LAYOUT MASTER IN SLIDE MASTER VIEW

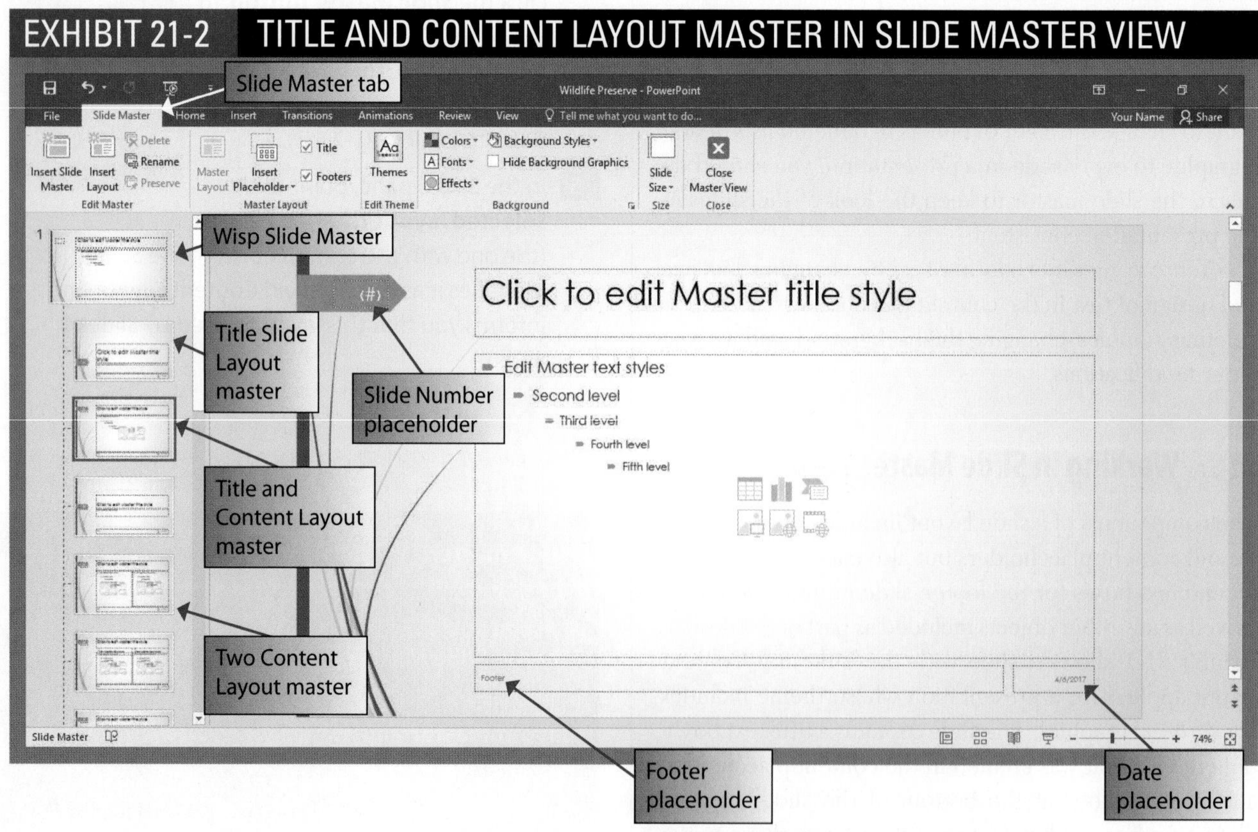

6 In the Slides pane, click the **Title Slide Layout master**. The Title Slide Layout master appears. The Title Slide Layout master contains the elements that appear on the title slide—the title text placeholder and the subtitle text placeholder. It also contains the same three graphics that appeared on the Title and Content Layout master, although the orange shape is in a different position than on the Title and Content Layout master.

7 In the Slides pane, point to the **top thumbnail**, which is slightly larger than the other thumbnails. This is the theme Slide Master; the ScreenTip identifies it as the Wisp Slide Master and informs you that it is used by Slides 1 through 6. The theme Slide Master includes the name of the theme as the first part of the Slide Master name.

8 Click the **Wisp Slide Master thumbnail** to display it. The Slide Master has the thin vertical rectangle on the left edge and the curvy shapes but not the orange shape. Any graphics that appear on the theme Slide Master appear on all the slides in the same position as on the Slide Master. The orange shape does not appear on the Wisp Slide Master because it appears in a different position on the Title Slide Layout master than on the Title and Content Layout master.

TIP: Remember to save frequently as you work through the chapter. A good practice is to save after every Activity.

End Activity

21-1b Modifying Text Placeholders in the Slide Master

You can adjust the size and position of text placeholders on slide masters. You can also delete placeholders if you want. When a text box is active, its border is a dotted line. To select a text box, you click the text box border to change it to a solid line. To change the size of a text placeholder, you drag the sizing handles, the same way you drag sizing handles to resize pictures in a Word document. To move a text box, you drag the selected text box by its border, as shown in Exhibit 21-3.

EXHIBIT 21-3 DRAGGING A TEXT BOX

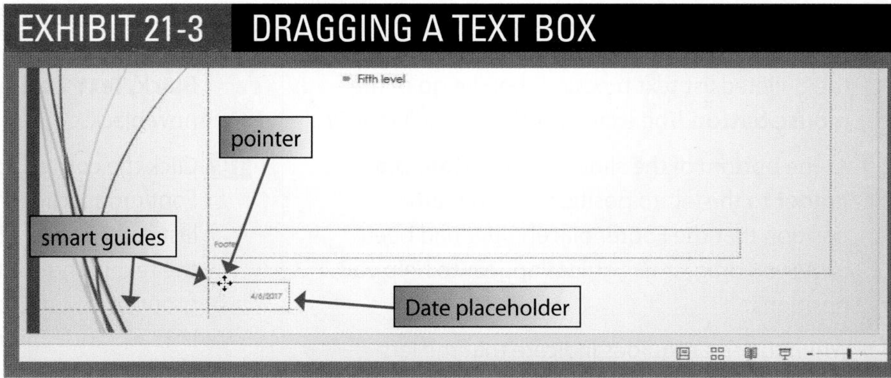

When you drag an item on slides to reposition them, dashed orange lines and arrows called **smart guides** appear, to help you align the object. These guides are similar to the alignment guides that appear when you position a floating object in a Word document.

You can also change the formatting of all the text in a text box when the entire text box is selected. For example, you can change the font or the font size.

FYI

HANDOUTS AND NOTES MASTERS

In addition to the slide masters, each presentation has a **handouts master** that contains the elements that appear on all the printed handouts and a **notes master** that contains the elements that appear on the notes pages. To display these masters, click the appropriate buttons in the Master Views group on the View tab.

Begin Activity

Modify text placeholders in the Slide Master.

1 In Slide Master view, with the **Wisp Slide Master** displayed, click the **Footer placeholder border** at the bottom of the slide.

2 Position the **pointer** on the selected border. The pointer changes to ✥.

smart guide A dashed, orange line or arrow that appears when you drag an object on a slide to help you position the object.

handouts master A master that contains the elements that appear on printed handouts.

notes master A master that contains the elements that appear on the notes pages.

3 Press and hold the **mouse button**, drag the **Footer placeholder** up to position it inside the bulleted list text box, and then let go of the **mouse button**. The exact position doesn't matter.

4 At the bottom of the slide, drag the **Date placeholder** to the left to position it in the same position that the Footer placeholder had been in. As you drag, smart guides appear to help you position it.

5 When the smart guides indicate that the left edge of the Date placeholder is aligned with the left edge of the bulleted list placeholder and the bottom of the Date placeholder is aligned with the smart guide that appears below it as shown in Exhibit 21-3, let go of the **mouse button.**

6 Drag the **Footer placeholder** to position it to the right of the Date placeholder so that the smart guides indicate that the right edge of the Footer placeholder is aligned with the right edge of the bulleted list text box and that the Footer placeholder is horizontally aligned with the Date placeholder.

7 On the ribbon, click the **Home** tab, and then in the Paragraph group, click the **Align Right** button. The placeholder text in the Footer placeholder is right-aligned in the placeholder text box.

8 With the **Footer placeholder** selected, press and hold the **Shift key**, click the **Date placeholder border**, and then let go of the **Shift key**. The two placeholders are selected.

9 On the Home tab, in the Font group, click the **Font Color button arrow**, and then click the **Black, Text 1 color**. The text in the placeholders is now black.

10 Click the **content placeholder border**. In the Font group, click the **Font Color button**. The last color applied, Black, Text 1, is applied to all of the text in the content placeholder. In the Font group, the Font Size button indicates that the text is 12+ points. This means that in the selected text box, the text that is the smallest is 12 points, and there is some text that is a larger point size.

11 In the Font group, click the **Increase Font Size button** three times. Each level of bulleted text in the content placeholder increases by two or four points each time you click the button. Now the font size of the smallest text in the content placeholder is 18 points. (If you used the Font Size button arrow to change the font size, all of the bulleted items would have been changed to the same point size.)

12 Click anywhere in the **first-level bulleted item**. The Font Size box indicates that this text is 28 points. Compare your screen to Exhibit 21-4.

13 In the Slides pane, click the **Title and Content Layout thumbnail** to display the Title and Content placeholder. The changes you made on the Wisp Slide Master are reflected on the Title and Content placeholder.

End Activity

FYI ADDING PLACEHOLDERS AND CREATING A CUSTOM LAYOUT

Although each theme comes with built-in layouts, you might find that none of them meets your needs. You know how to customize an existing layout by resizing, moving, and deleting placeholders. In addition, you can add placeholders to an existing layout master, or you can create a completely new layout master.

To insert a new placeholder, switch to Slide Master view. Click the Insert Placeholder button arrow in the Master Layout group on the Slide Master tab, select a placeholder type, and then click or drag on the slide, similar to creating a text box.

To create a new layout master, click the Insert Layout button in the Edit Master group on the Slide Master tab. A new layout identical to the Title Only Layout master is created. To create a custom layout that doesn't include any of the elements of the current slide master, click the Insert Slide Master button instead of the Insert Layout button. When you create a new layout, the default name is Custom Layout Layout. To change the name of the new layout, right-click it, and then click Rename Layout on the shortcut menu. In Normal view, the new layout will be available on the New Slide button menu and on the Layout button menu.

EXHIBIT 21-4 WISP SLIDE MASTER AFTER FORMAT CHANGES

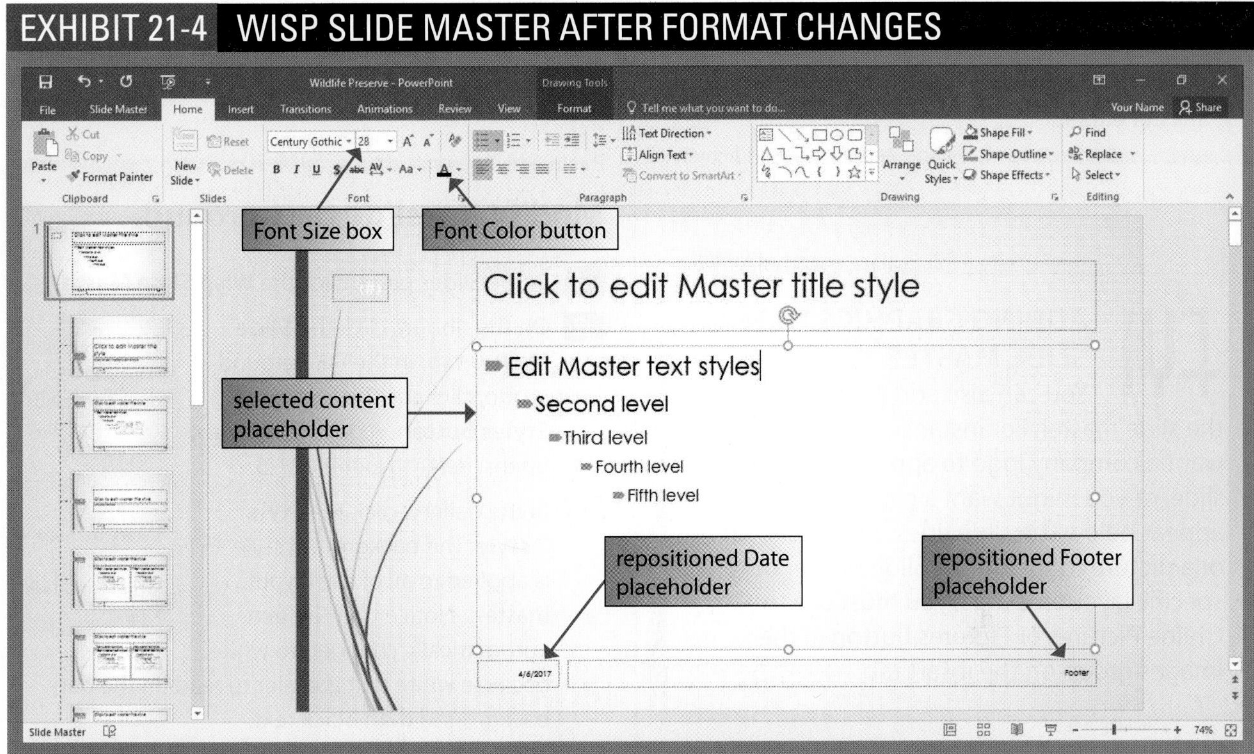

21-1c Deleting a Graphic from the Slide Master

Many themes contain graphics in the Slide Master or on individual layout masters. Often the graphics are attractive elements of the slide design. However, sometimes you might want to delete a graphic because it doesn't fit well with your content or you would rather use something else. You can do this in Slide Master view. To delete a graphic, you first need to click it to select it. Exhibit 21-5 shows the greenish gray rectangle shape graphic on the Wisp Slide Master selected.

Begin Activity

Delete a graphic from the Slide Master.

1. In the Slides pane, click the **Wisp Slide Master thumbnail**.
2. On the slide, click the **greenish gray rectangle** along the left edge of the slide. Refer to Exhibit 21-5.
3. Press the **Delete key**. The graphic is deleted from the Wisp Slide Master and from all the Layout masters.

EXHIBIT 21-5 GRAPHIC SELECTED ON THE WISP SLIDE MASTER

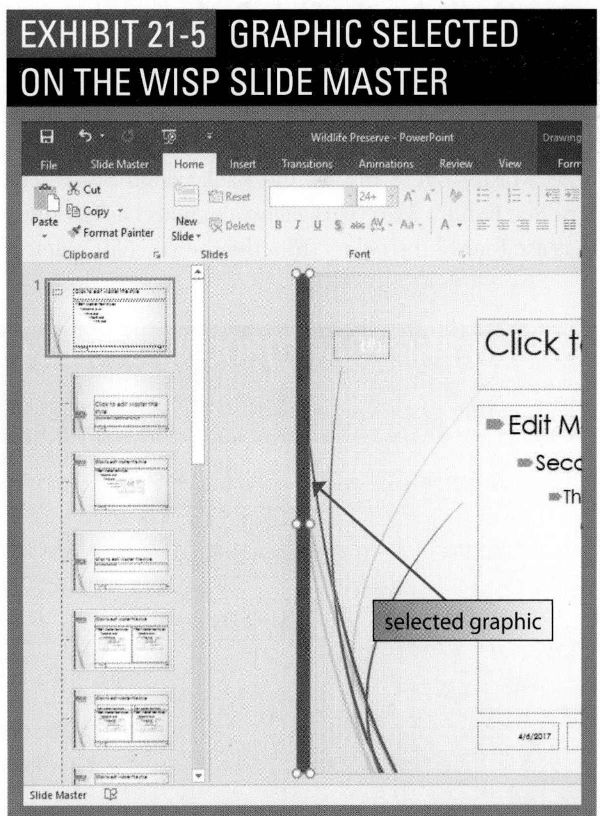

4. Click the **Title Slide Layout master** in the Slides pane. The greenish gray rectangle and the Date placeholder no longer appear on the Title Slide Layout master.

5 Click the **Title and Content Layout master** in the Slides pane. The objects you deleted from the Wisp Slide Master no longer appear on this Layout master either.

End Activity

FYI

ADDING GRAPHICS TO THE SLIDE MASTER

You can also add graphics to the slide master. For instance, you might want a company logo to appear on every slide, or you might want a colored line to appear below the slide titles. To add clip art or a picture to the theme Slide Master or to specific layout masters, you must use the Online Pictures or Pictures button in the Images group on the Insert tab.

21-1d Modifying the Slide Background

You can customize the background of slides in a presentation. To change the slide background, click the Background Styles button in the Background group on the Slide Master tab to display the Background Styles gallery. See Exhibit 21-6. This gallery contains backgrounds that use four of the colors from the theme color palette. Some of the styles have gradients applied. A **gradient** is shading in which one color blends into another or varies from one shade to another.

Begin Activity

Modify the slide background.

1 In the Slides pane, click the **Wisp Slide Master**.

2 On the ribbon, click the **Slide Master tab**. In the Background group, click the **Background Styles button**. A gallery of styles opens. Refer to Exhibit 21-6.

3 In the gallery, click the **Style 7 style**. The background style is applied to all of the layout masters. Notice that the text automatically changed to white because white text is easier to read on the dark background than black text.

TIP: To access more choices for customizing the background, click Format Background below the gallery to open the Format Background task pane.

End Activity

21-1e Closing Slide Master View

When you are finished modifying the slide master, you need to close Slide Master view and return to Normal view. You should always examine the slides in Normal view after you make changes to the slide master to make sure they look as you expected them to.

EXHIBIT 21-6 BACKGROUND STYLES GALLERY

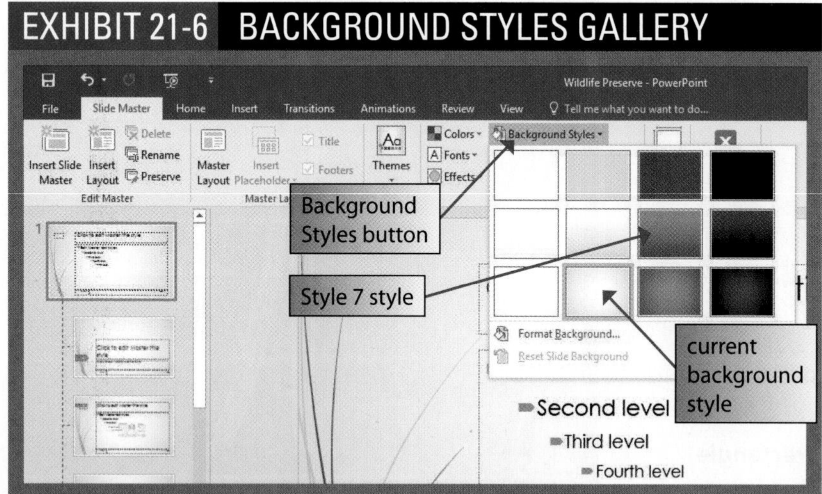

Begin Activity

Close Slide Master view and examine the results of the changes.

1 On the Slide Master tab, in the Close group, click the **Close Master View button**. Slide Master view closes, and the presentation appears in Normal view. Slide 5, which has the Title and Content layout applied, is displayed. The changes you made in Slide Master view are visible on the slide.

TIP: You can also click the Normal button on the status bar to close Slide Master view.

gradient Shading in which one color blends into another or varies from one shade to another.

2 Display **Slide 2** ("About Us") in the Slide pane. This slide has the Two Content layout applied. The changes made in Slide Master view are visible on this slide as well.

3 Display **Slide 1** (the title slide) in the Slide pane. The changes you made to the Title Layout master are visible on this slide.

End Activity

21-2 INSERTING GRAPHICS

We live in a highly visual society. Most people are exposed to multimedia daily and expect to have information conveyed visually as well as verbally. In many cases, a graphic is more effective than words for communicating an important point. For example, if a sales force has reached its sales goals for the year, a graphic of a person summiting a mountain can convey a sense of exhilaration. Judicious use of graphics and multimedia elements can clarify a point for audience members and help them remember it later.

Remember that a graphic is a picture, shape, design, graph, chart, or diagram. You can include many types of graphics in your presentation: clip art; graphics created using other programs; scanned photographs, drawings, and cartoons; other picture files stored on your computer or network; or graphics you create using drawing tools in PowerPoint.

When you insert a graphic in a PowerPoint slide (or an Excel worksheet), you do not have to set text-wrapping options like you do in Word; graphics are always floating graphics in PowerPoint slides and Excel worksheets. To reposition a graphic on a slide, drag it to its new position. In PowerPoint, objects "snap to" or align with an invisible grid when they are moved. This usually helps you align objects on a slide. If a graphic jumps from one location to another as you drag it and you can't position it exactly where you want it, press and hold the Alt key as you drag it. The Alt key temporarily disables the feature that forces objects to snap to the grid.

> **FYI**
>
> **INSERTING TABLES ON A SLIDE**
>
> To insert a table on a slide, click the Insert Table button in a content placeholder to open a dialog box in which you specify the number of columns and rows you want to insert. You can also click the Table button in the Tables group on the Insert tab to insert a table using the same grid you used in Word. After you insert a table, the steps for working with the table are the same as working with a table in a Word document.

21-2a Inserting a Picture File

You can insert graphics stored on your computer on a slide. If a slide has an empty content placeholder, as shown in Exhibit 21-7, you can click the Pictures button

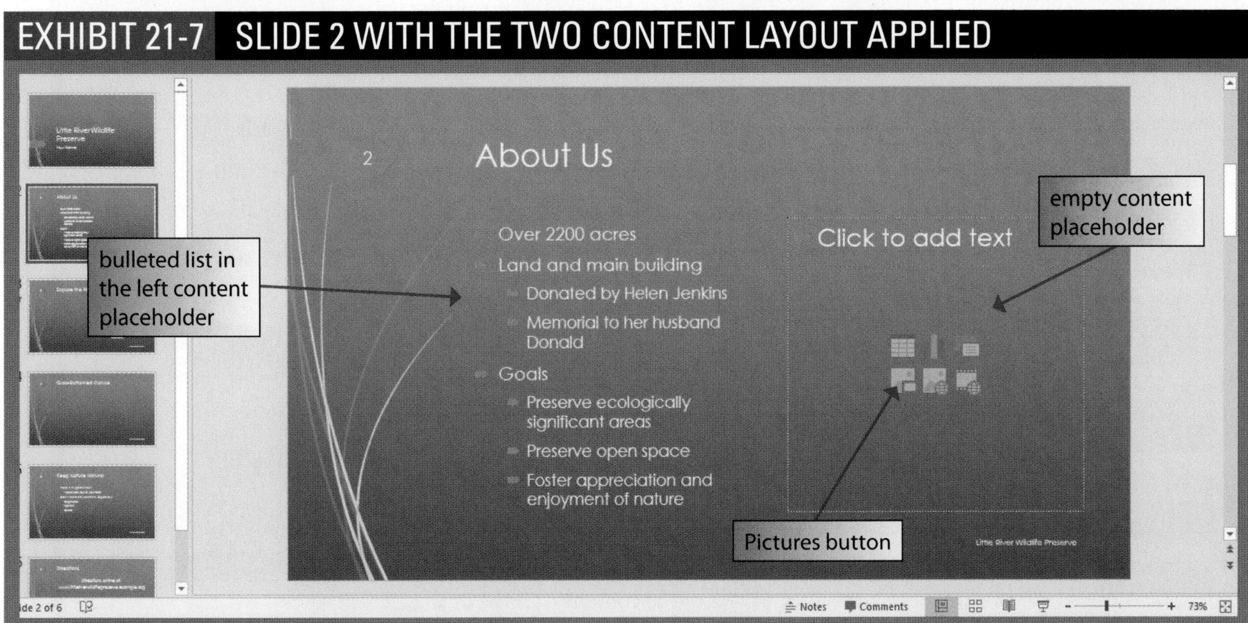

EXHIBIT 21-7 SLIDE 2 WITH THE TWO CONTENT LAYOUT APPLIED

in the content placeholder. This opens the Insert Picture dialog box, which is similar to the Open dialog box. To insert an image stored on a Web site, you would click the Online Pictures button in the content placeholder.

Begin Activity

Add a graphic from a file using a button in the content placeholder.

1 Display **Slide 2** ("About Us"). This slide has the Two Content layout applied. Refer back to Exhibit 21-7.

2 On the right side of the slide, in the content placeholder, click the **Pictures button** . The Insert Picture dialog box opens. This dialog box is similar to the Open and Save As dialog boxes.

3 Click the picture data file **Landscape** located in the Chapter 21\Chapter folder, and then click **Insert**. The dialog box closes, and the picture replaces the content placeholder on the slide. The Picture Tools Format tab appears on the ribbon and is the active tab. Compare your screen to Exhibit 21-8.

4 Display **Slide 3** ("Explore the Preserve"), and then insert the picture data file **Hikers** located in the Chapter 21\Chapter folder in place of the content placeholder.

5 Display **Slide 4** ("Glass-Bottomed Canoe"), and then insert the picture data file **Canoe** located in the Chapter 21\Chapter folder in place of the content placeholder on the left.

End Activity

If a slide does not have an empty content placeholder, you can insert a picture using the Pictures button in the Images group on the Insert tab.

If you need to resize a picture on a slide, you can drag its sizing handles. Remember to drag the corner sizing handles to maintain the aspect ratio of the picture so that the image does not become distorted.

Begin Activity

Add a graphic from a file using the ribbon, and reposition it.

1 Display **Slide 6** ("Directions").

2 On the ribbon, click the **Insert tab**. In the Images group, click the **Pictures button**. The Insert Picture dialog box opens.

3 Click the picture data file **Goose** located in the Chapter 21\Chapter folder, and then click **Insert**. The dialog box closes, and the picture of the goose appears in the center of Slide 6.

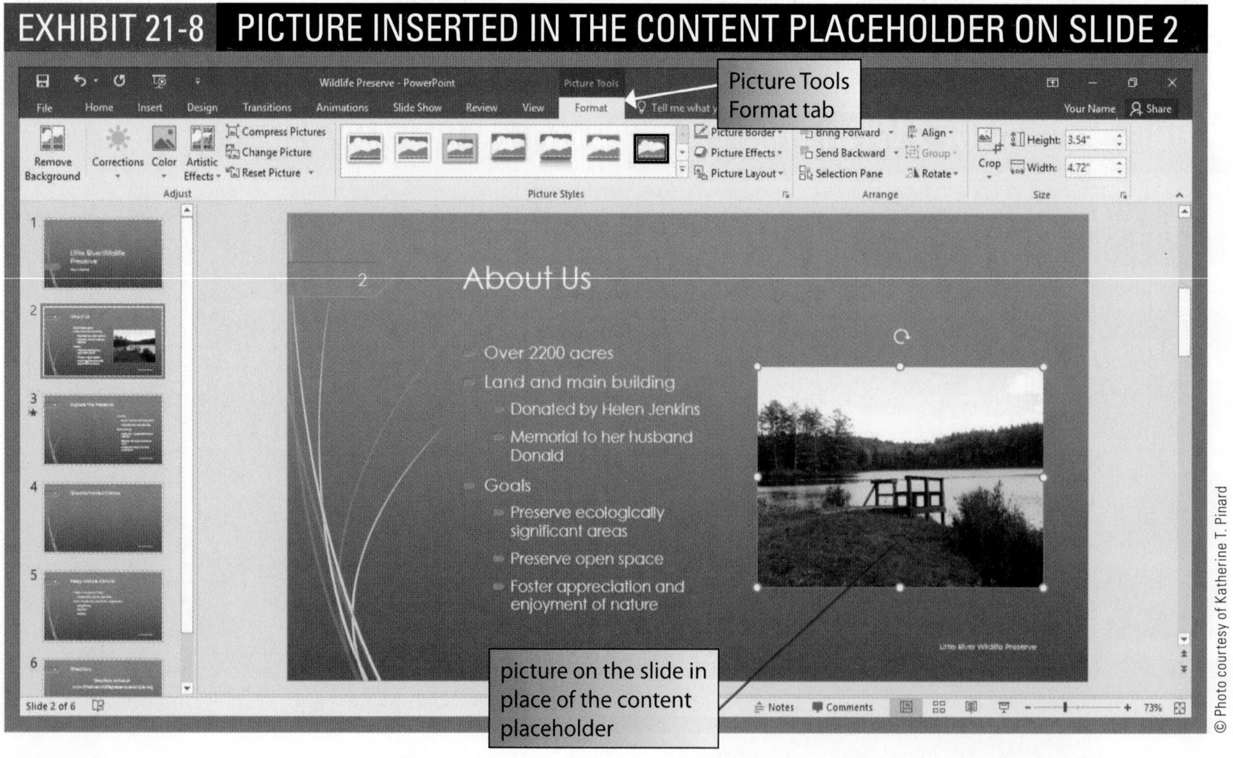

EXHIBIT 21-8 PICTURE INSERTED IN THE CONTENT PLACEHOLDER ON SLIDE 2

© Photo courtesy of Katherine T. Pinard

4 Point to the **bottom-left corner sizing handle** so that the pointer changes to ⤢. Drag the sizing handle up and to the right to resize the picture so it is approximately two inches high. After you release the mouse button, look at the measurement in the Height box in the Size group on the Picture Tools Format tab, and then click the **Height box up** or **down** arrows as needed to change the value in the box to two inches.

5 Point to the picture so that the pointer changes to ✥.

6 Drag the **goose picture** to the bottom-right of the slide so that the smart guides indicate that the right edge of the graphic is aligned with the right edge of the text box on the slide and the bottom of the graphic is aligned with the top of the Footer text box, as shown in Exhibit 21-9.

7 Click a blank area of the slide to deselect the picture.

End Activity

EXHIBIT 21-9 PICTURE REPOSITIONED USING SMART GUIDES

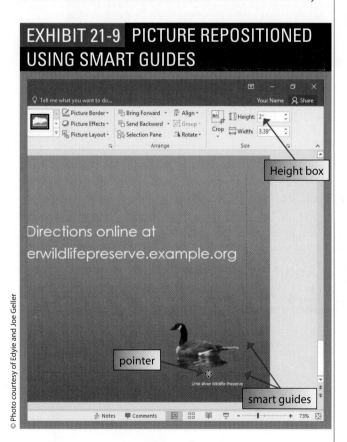

21-2b Drawing a Shape

Another way to add a graphic to a slide is to draw it using tools available in PowerPoint. You can add many shapes to a slide, including lines, rectangles, stars, and many more. To draw a shape, click the Shapes button in the Illustrations group on the Insert tab or in the Drawing group on the Home tab to display the Shapes gallery, as shown in Exhibit 21-10. (There is no icon in the content placeholders to insert a shape.) Click a shape in the gallery, and then click or drag on the slide to draw the shape.

EXHIBIT 21-10 SHAPES GALLERY

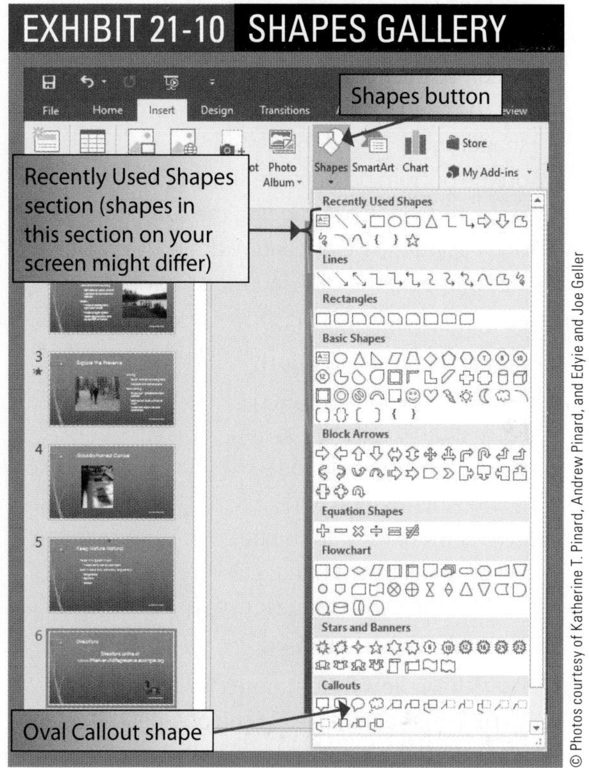

When a drawn shape is selected on a slide, the Drawing Tools Format tab appears on the ribbon. This tab contains commands similar to the commands found on the Picture Tools Format tab. You can resize a shape in the same manner as you resize other objects. You can also format it by applying styles, borders, and effects, similar to pictures, and by filling it with color. You can also add text to a selected shape.

Begin Activity

Draw a shape on a slide.

1 With **Slide 6** ("Directions") displayed, on the ribbon, click the **Insert tab**.

2 In the Illustrations group, click the **Shapes button**. The Shapes gallery opens. Refer back to Exhibit 21-10. The gallery is organized into nine categories of shapes, plus the Recently Used Shapes group at the top.

3 In the Callouts section, click the **Oval Callout shape**. The gallery closes, and the pointer changes to +.

4 In the Slide pane, point to a blank area above and to the left of the picture of the goose, and then click. A callout shape 0.67 inches high and one inch wide is inserted on the slide, and the Drawing Tools Format tab becomes the active tab on the ribbon. A selection box and sizing handles appear around the shape, and a yellow adjustment handle appears on the bottom point of the shape. You can resize the shape by dragging the sizing handles or by using the Height and Width boxes in the Size group on the Drawing Tools Format tab.

TIP: You can also press and hold the mouse button, and then drag to draw a shape any size.

5 Drag the **sizing handles** or use the **Height** and **Width boxes** on the Drawing Tools Format tab to change the size of the callout shape so it is 1.5 inches high and 2.5 inches wide. You can use the yellow adjustment handle to change the way a shape looks without changing its size.

TIP: To draw a circle, square, or equilateral triangle, hold the Shift key while you click or drag the pointer after selecting the Oval, Rectangle, or Isosceles Triangle shape, respectively.

6 Drag the **yellow adjustment handle** to the right so that the point of the callout shape is directed toward to the picture of the goose.

7 Drag the **callout shape** to position it to the left of and a little above the picture of the goose. Compare your screen to Exhibit 21-11.

End Activity

EXHIBIT 21-11 ADJUSTED AND RESIZED CALLOUT SHAPE

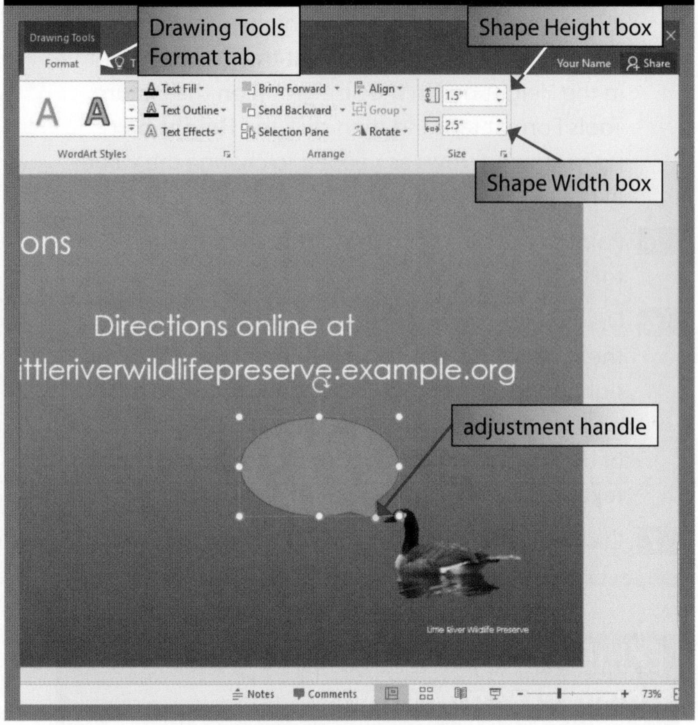

© Photo courtesy of Edyie and Joe Geller

FYI INSERTING AND FORMATTING TEXT BOXES

Sometimes, you need to add text to a slide in a location other than in one of the text box placeholders included in the slide layout. You can insert a rectangle shape and add text to it, or you can add a text box, an object designed to hold text. To insert a text box, click the Text Box button in the Text group on the Insert tab, or use the Text Box shape in the Shapes gallery. When you enter text in a text box, the text box will keep widening to accommodate the text you type. If you want the text to wrap to additional lines, drag a sizing handle to change the height of the text box object.

21-2c Adding Text to a Shape

To add text to a shape, select it, and then type. The text will be inserted at 18 points in the Body font of the selected theme. The text will wrap in the shape automatically. If you type more text than the shape can hold, you can resize the shape or change the font size to make it fit. The color of the text is black or white, depending on the fill color of the shape.

Begin Activity

Add text to a shape.

1 With the shape still selected, type **Come visit us!**. The text is white so that it is readable on the dark background.

2 Click the **callout shape dashed line border** to select the entire shape, and then change the font size to **24 points**.

End Activity

21-2d Formatting Graphics

You can apply formatting to any object on a slide. As you have seen, when a picture is selected on a slide, the Picture Tools Format tab appears on the ribbon, and when a shape is selected on a slide, the Drawing Tools Format tab appears. The commands on the two tabs are very similar.

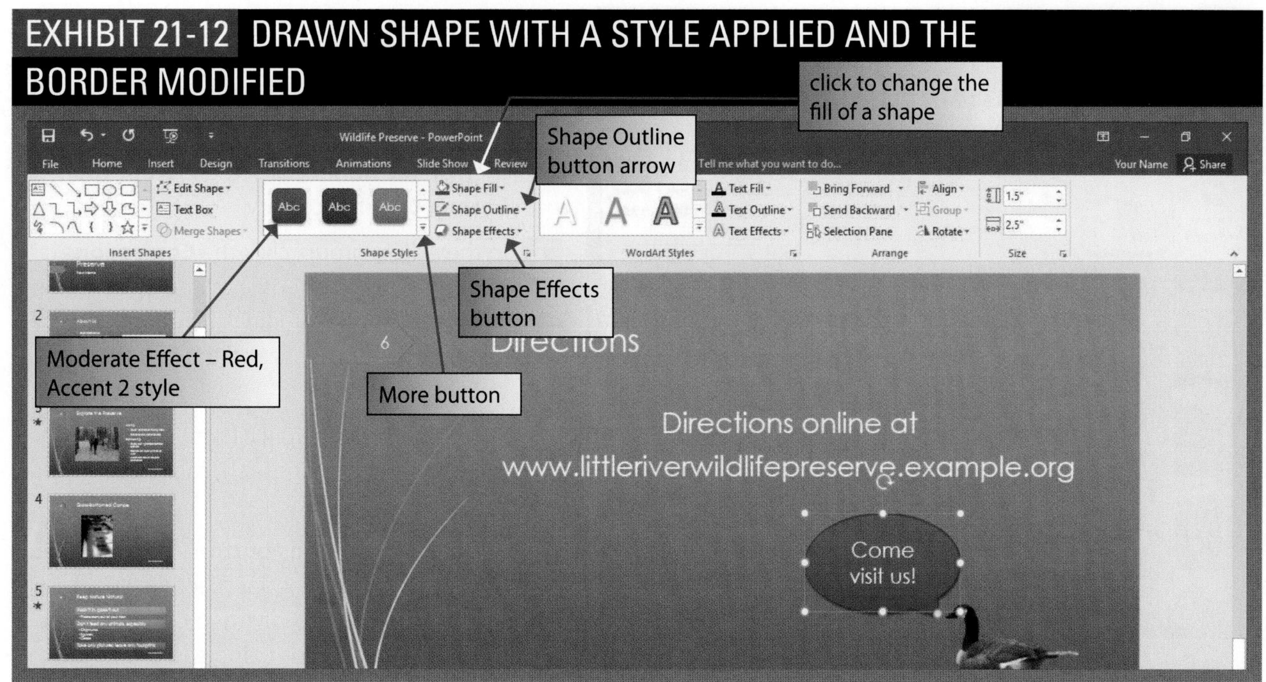

EXHIBIT 21-12 DRAWN SHAPE WITH A STYLE APPLIED AND THE BORDER MODIFIED

© Photos courtesy of Katherine T. Pinard, Andrew Pinard, and Edyie and Joe Geller

For example, you can apply a style, add or change the border or outline, and add special effects. Exhibit 21-12 shows the callout shape selected and the Drawing Tools Format tab on the ribbon. Some formatting tools are available only to one or the other type of object. For example, the Remove Background tool is available only to pictures, and the Fill command is available only to shapes. The **fill** is the formatting of the area inside a shape.

Begin Activity

Format drawings and pictures on slides.

1 If necessary, on **Slide 6** ("Directions"), select the **callout shape**.

2 On the ribbon, click the **Drawing Tools Format tab**. In the Shape Styles group, a gray border appears around one of the styles. When you draw a shape, this default style is applied.

3 In the Shape Styles group, click the **More button** . The Shape Styles gallery opens.

4 Scroll down in the gallery, and then in the Theme Styles section, click the **Moderate Effect – Red, Accent 2 style**, using the ScreenTips to locate this style. The style is applied to the callout shape.

5 In the Shape Styles group, click the **Shape Outline button arrow**. On the menu, point to **Weight**, and then click **2¼ pt.** The weight of the shape border increases to 2¼ points.

6 In the Shape Styles group, click the **Shape Effects button**, point to **Shadow**, and then, in the Outer section, click the **Offset Bottom shadow effect**. Refer to Exhibit 21-12.

7 Display **Slide 4** ("Glass-Bottomed Canoe"). On Slide 4, select the picture. The Picture Tools Format tab appears on the ribbon.

8 On the ribbon, click the **Picture Tools Format tab**. In the Picture Styles group, click the **Drop Shadow Rectangle style**. The style is applied to the picture.

9 Format the pictures on **Slide 3** ("Explore the Preserve") and **Slide 2** ("About Us") in the Slide pane with the **Drop Shadow Rectangle style**.

End Activity

If photos you want to use in a presentation are too dark or require other fine-tuning, you can use PowerPoint's photo correction tools. You can use options on the Corrections button menu to sharpen a blurry image or soften details in a photo or adjust the brightness and contrast to change the difference between dark and light areas in the photo. See Exhibit 21-13. You can also

fill The formatting of the area inside a shape.

EXHIBIT 21-13 CORRECTIONS BUTTON MENU

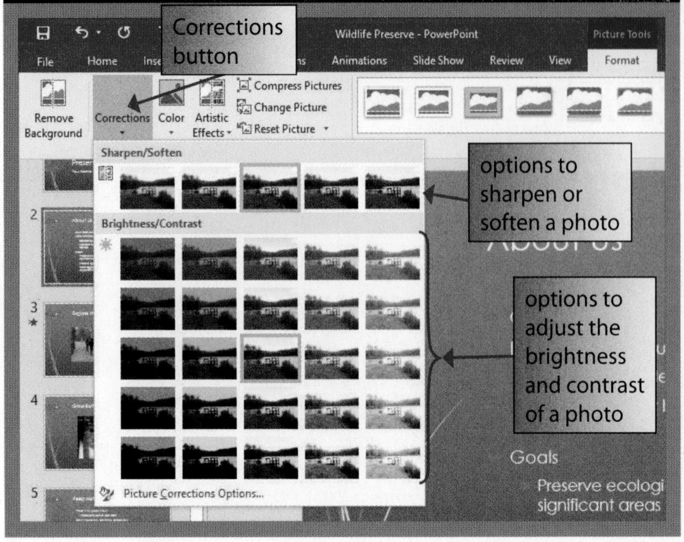

Corrections button

options to sharpen or soften a photo

options to adjust the brightness and contrast of a photo

use the options on the Color button menu to adjust the color saturation, which is the amount or intensity of color in a photo, and the color tone, which is the amount of reds and yellows or blues and greens, in a photo. See Exhibit 21-14.

EXHIBIT 21-14 COLOR BUTTON MENU

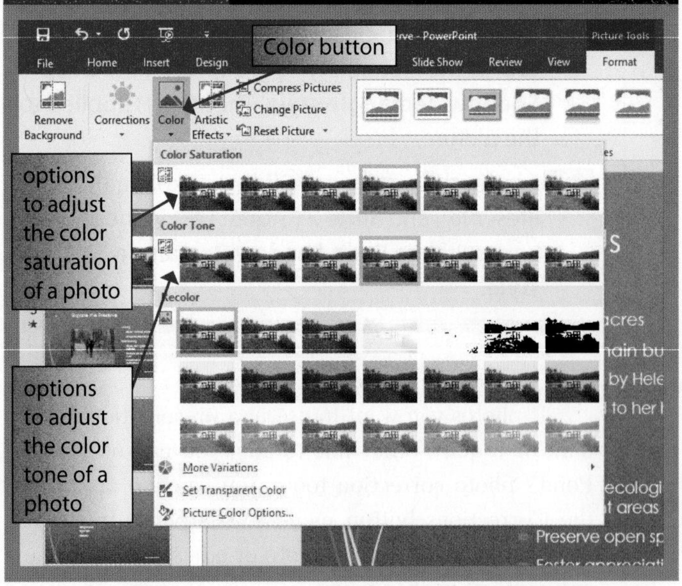

Color button

options to adjust the color saturation of a photo

options to adjust the color tone of a photo

diagram An illustration that visually depicts information or ideas and shows how they are connected.

SmartArt A diagram with a predesigned layout.

Begin Activity

Edit a photo.

1. On **Slide 2** ("About Us"), select the **photo**, and then on the ribbon, click the **Picture Tools Format tab**, if necessary.
2. In the Adjust group, click the **Corrections button**. A menu opens showing options for sharpening and softening the photo and adjusting the brightness and the contrast. Refer to Exhibit 21-13.
3. In the Sharpen section, click the **Sharpen: 50% style**. The image is sharpened so it is more in focus.
4. Click the **Corrections button** again, and then in the Brightness/Contrast section, click the **Brightness: +20% Contrast: -20% style**. The brightness of the photo increases, and the contrast decreases.
5. In the Adjust group, click the **Color button**. A menu opens with options for adjusting the saturation and tone of the photo's color. Refer to Exhibit 21-14.
6. In the Color Saturation section, click the **Saturation: 66% style**. The colors in the photo are less intense.
7. Click the **Color button**, and then in the Color Tone section, click the **Temperature: 11200 K**. More reds and yellows are added to the photo.

TIP: If you make changes to photos and then change your mind, you can click the Reset Picture button in the Adjust group on the Picture Tools Format tab.

End Activity

21-3 CREATING SMARTART DIAGRAMS

A **diagram** is an illustration that visually depicts information or ideas and shows how they are connected. You can use **SmartArt**, diagrams with predesigned layouts, to create diagrams easily and quickly. In addition to shapes, SmartArt diagrams usually include text to help describe or label the shapes. You can create the following types of diagrams using SmartArt:

- **List**—shows a list of items in a graphical representation.
- **Process**—shows a sequence of steps in a process.
- **Cycle**—shows a process that has a continuous cycle.
- **Hierarchy** (including **organization charts**)—shows the relationship between individuals or units within an organization.
- **Relationship** (including **Venn diagrams**, **radial diagrams**, and **target diagrams**)—shows the relationship between two or more elements.
- **Matrix**—shows information in a grid.
- **Pyramid**—shows foundation-based relationships.
- **Picture**—provides a location for a picture or pictures.

EXHIBIT 21-15 CHOOSE A SMARTART GRAPHIC DIALOG BOX

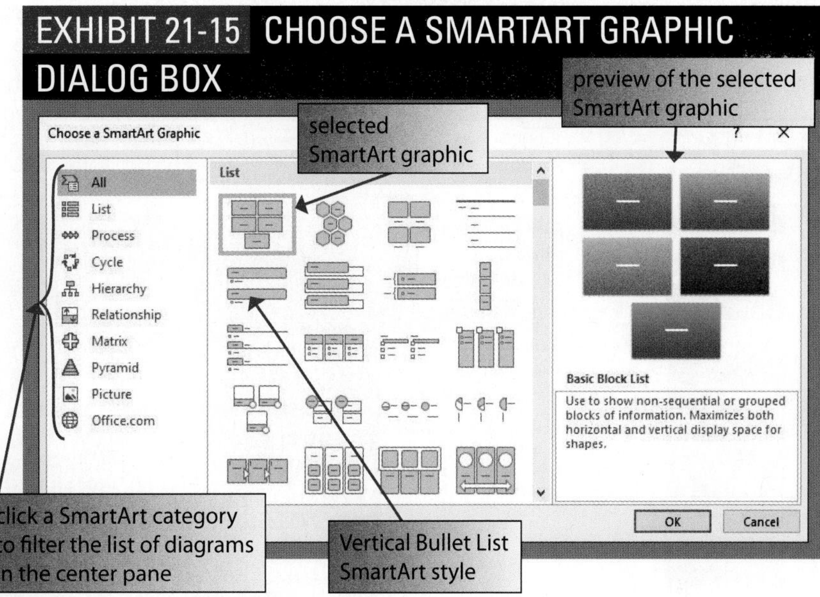

There is also an Office.com category, which, if you are connected to the Internet, displays additional SmartArt diagrams available on Office.com. You also might see an Other category, which contains SmartArt diagrams previously downloaded from Office.com.

21-3a Creating a SmartArt Diagram

To create a SmartArt diagram, you can click the Insert a SmartArt Graphic button in a content placeholder, or you can click the SmartArt button in the Illustrations group on the Insert tab to open the Choose a SmartArt Graphic dialog box. You can also convert an existing bulleted list into a SmartArt diagram by using the Convert to SmartArt button in the Paragraph group on the Home tab. The Choose a SmartArt Graphic dialog box is shown in Exhibit 21-15. To filter the diagram layouts shown, click a category in the list on the left.

Begin Activity

Create a SmartArt diagram.

1 Display **Slide 5** ("Keep Nature Natural"), and then click the bulleted list.

2 On the Home tab, in the Paragraph group, click the **Convert to SmartArt button**. A gallery of SmartArt diagram types opens.

3 Below the gallery, click **More SmartArt Graphics**. The gallery closes, and the Choose a SmartArt Graphic dialog box opens. Refer to Exhibit 21-15.

4 In the center pane, click the **Vertical Bullet List SmartArt diagram** in the second row. A preview and description of the selected diagram appear in the right pane.

5 Click **OK**. The dialog box closes, and the bulleted list on the slide is replaced with a Vertical Bullet List SmartArt diagram with the text from the bulleted list in the diagram. The SmartArt Tools Design tab is the active tab on the ribbon. You might see a text pane labeled *Type your text here* to the left of the diagram.

6 If the text pane is not visible, on the SmartArt Tools Design tab, in the Create Graphic group, click the **Text Pane button**. The button is selected, and the text pane appears to the left of the SmartArt diagram. Compare your screen to Exhibit 21-16. The SmartArt diagram consists of colored rectangles that contain the text from the first-level bullets in the original list with the second-level bullets from the original list below each one. The border around the diagram defines the borders of the entire SmartArt diagram object.

End Activity

TIP: If there is no text on a slide, you can click the Insert a SmartArt Graphic button in the content placeholder on a slide, or you can click the SmartArt button in the Illustrations group on the Insert tab.

EXHIBIT 21-16 VERTICAL BULLET LIST SMARTART DIAGRAM

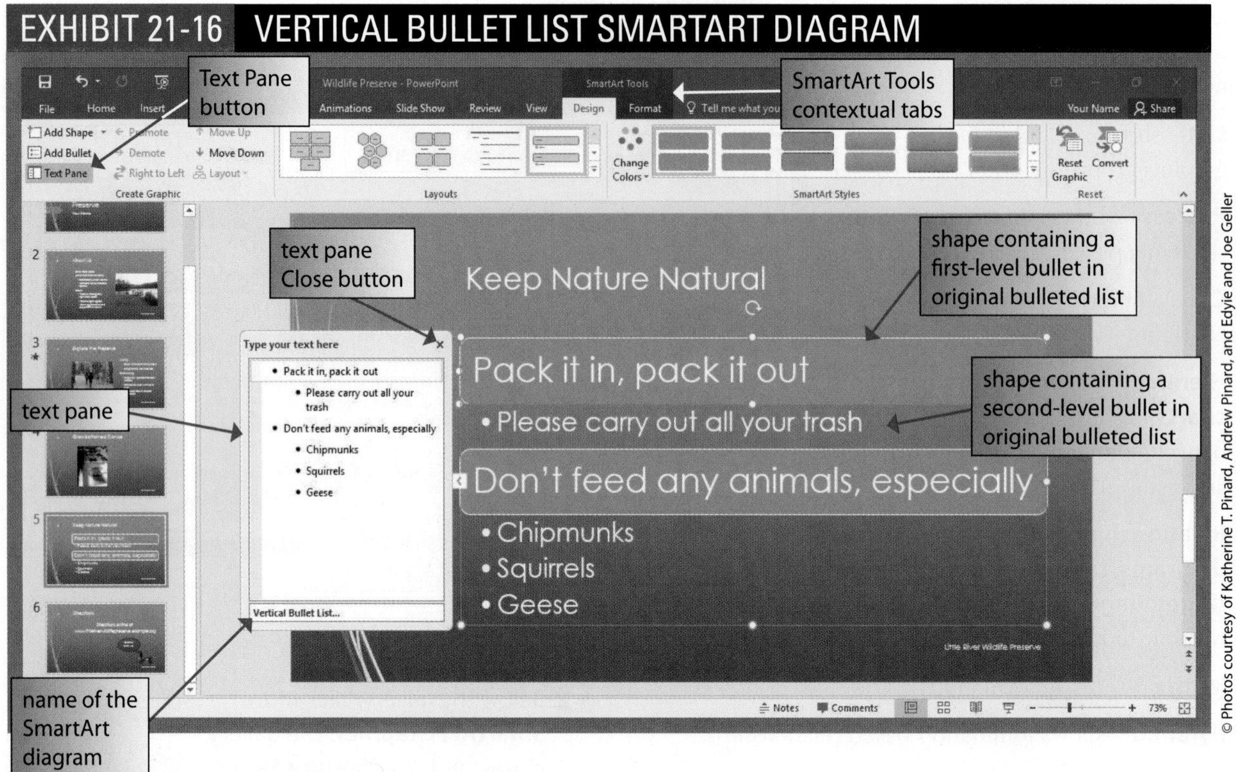

21-3b Modifying a SmartArt Diagram

A SmartArt diagram is a larger object composed of smaller objects. You can modify the diagram by adding or deleting shapes, modifying the text by changing the font format, and changing the way the shapes look. You can also modify the diagram as a whole. Exhibit 21-17 shows the SmartArt diagram after a new shape was added to it.

EXHIBIT 21-17 NEW SHAPE ADDED TO THE SMARTART DIAGRAM

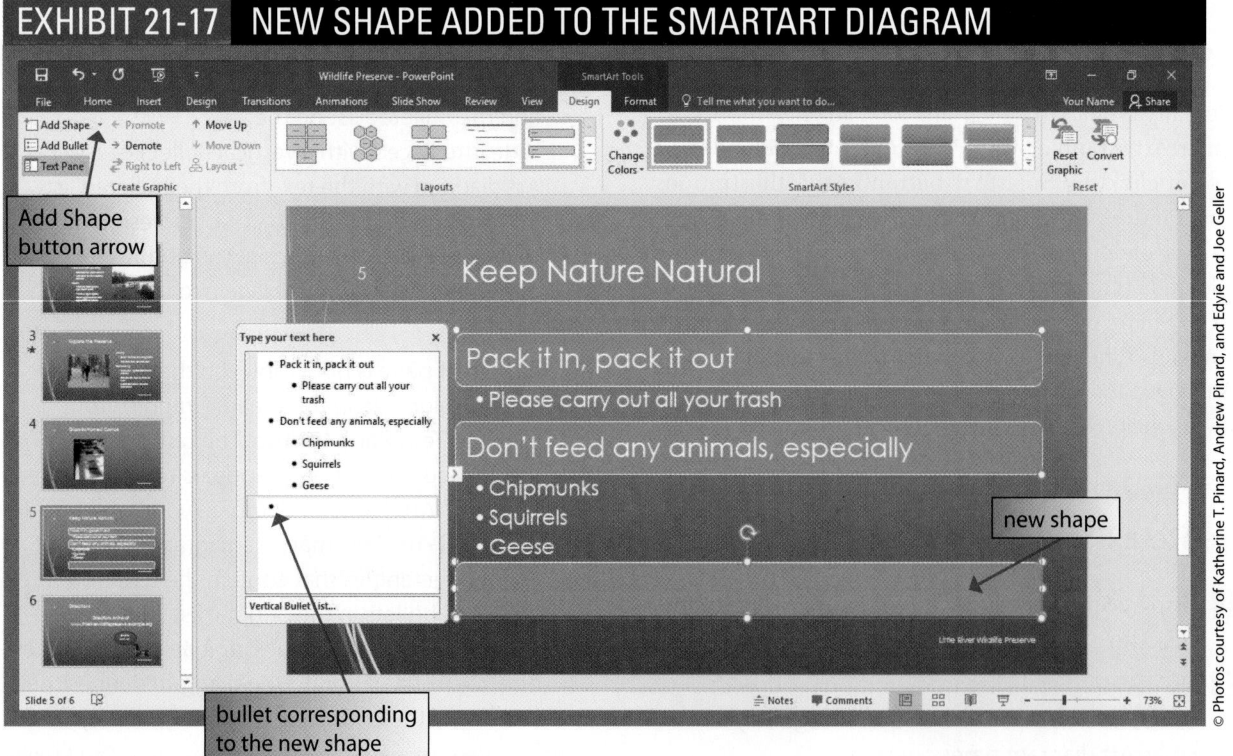

Begin Activity

Modify a SmartArt diagram.

1 In the SmartArt diagram, click the **Don't feed any animals shape**. The shape is selected, and the corresponding bulleted item in the text pane is selected as well.

2 On the SmartArt Tools Design tab, in the Create Graphic group, click the **Add Shape button arrow**. The top command on the menu is the default command that would be executed if you clicked the icon on the Add Shape button. The commands in gray on the menu are available when different SmartArt diagrams are on the slide.

3 Click **Add Shape After**. The menu closes, and a new shape is added to the diagram below the selected shape. The new shape is selected, and a corresponding bullet appears in the text pane. Refer to Exhibit 21-17.

4 Type **Leave only footprints**. The text appears in the new shape and next to the corresponding bullet in the text pane.

5 On the SmartArt Tools Design tab, in the Create Graphic group, click the **Add Shape button arrow**, and then click **Add Shape Before**. A new shape appears above the selected shape, and a new bullet appears above the last bullet in the text pane.

6 Type **Take only pictures**.

7 Click in the **Leave only footprints shape**.

8 On the SmartArt Tools Design tab, in the Create Graphic group, click the **Demote button**. The shape is changed to a bulleted item at the same level as the second-level bulleted items in the text pane.

9 In the text pane, click before **Leave only footprints**, press the **Backspace key** twice to delete the bullet and move the Leave only footprints item into the first-level bulleted item. The insertion point is between the words *pictures* and *Leave*.

> **TIP:** You can work in the text pane using the same skills you use to work with a bulleted list on a slide.

10 Type **;** (a semicolon), press the **Spacebar**, press the **Delete key** to delete *L*, and then type **l** (lowercase *L*). The last shape in the diagram now contains *Take only pictures; leave only footprints.*

11 In the upper-right corner of the text pane, click the **Close button** ✕. The text pane closes.

End Activity

21-3c Formatting a SmartArt Diagram

As with any object, you can add formatting to a SmartArt diagram using the commands on the contextual SmartArt Tools tabs. To quickly change the colors and look of a SmartArt diagram, you can use the Change Colors button and the options in the SmartArt Styles gallery on the SmartArt Tools Design tab. See Exhibit 21-18.

EXHIBIT 21-18 SMARTART GALLERY AND CHANGE COLORS BUTTON

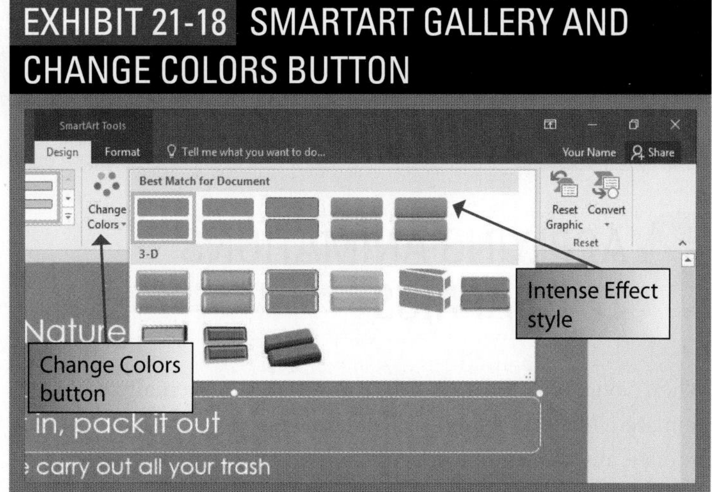

Begin Activity

Format a SmartArt diagram.

1 Click the **SmartArt diagram**, if necessary, to select the SmartArt diagram.

2 On the SmartArt Tools Design tab, in the SmartArt Styles group, click the **More button**. A gallery of styles available for the diagram opens. Refer to Exhibit 21-19.

3 In the gallery, in the Best Match for Document section, click the **Intense Effect style**. The style of the graphic changes to the one you chose.

4 In the SmartArt Styles group, click the **Change Colors button**. A gallery of color options opens.

5 In the gallery, in the Colorful section, click the **Colorful Range – Accent Colors 5 to 6 style**. The gallery closes, and the colors in the SmartArt diagram change to the style you selected. Compare your screen to Exhibit 21-19.

End Activity

EXHIBIT 21-19 FORMATTED SMARTART DIAGRAM

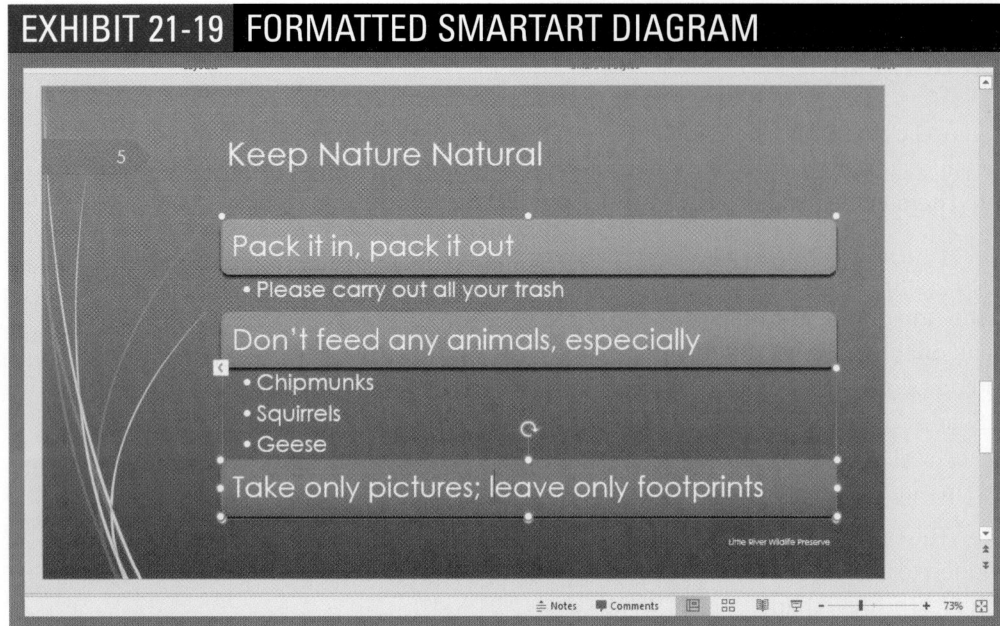

21-4 APPLYING ANIMATIONS TO GRAPHICS

When you animated text in Chapter 20, you actually animated the text boxes, which are objects. You can animate any object on a slide, including photos, shapes, and SmartArt diagrams. Because a SmartArt diagram is composed of more than one object, when you animate a SmartArt diagram, you can change the sequence effects, similar to the sequence effects you can change for a bulleted list. However, when you animate a photo or a shape, because they are single objects, there are no sequence effects that you can change.

Begin Activity

Apply animations to graphics.

1. On **Slide 5** ("Keep Nature Natural"), click the **SmartArt diagram** to select it, if necessary. On the ribbon, click the **Animations tab**.
2. In the Animation group, click the **Wipe animation**, which is an entrance animation. The animation previews, and the diagram wipes onto the slide from the bottom. A single animation sequence icon appears next to the SmartArt diagram.
3. In the Animation group, click the **Effect Options button**. The Wipe animation has four direction effects and five sequence effects from which you can choose.
4. Click **From Left**. The animation previews again, this time wiping the diagram in from the left.
5. Click the **Effect Options button** again. Because the SmartArt diagram is composed of multiple objects, Sequence effects are available, similar to the Sequence effects for bulleted lists.
6. Click **One by One**. Each shape in the diagram animates one at a time. Now there are five animation sequence icons next to the diagram.
7. Display **Slide 3** ("Explore the Preserve"), and then click the bulleted list. Animation sequence icons appear next to the items in the bulleted list, and the entrance animation Fly In is selected in the Animation group on the Animations tab.
8. Click the **photo** to select it. In the Animation group, click the **Shape button**. The animation previews and the photo fades in from the outside to the center in a circle shape. The animation sequence icon that appears next to the photo contains a 3.
9. In the Animation group, click the **Effect Options button**. The Shape animation has two types of effects you can modify—the direction from which the object will fade in and the shape of the fade. There are no Sequence effects available because the photo is a single object.
10. Under Shapes, click **Box**. The shape fades in from the outside to the center in a square shape.
11. Click the **Effect Options button**, and then click **Out**. The shape fades in from the center out in a square shape.

End Activity

21-5 MODIFYING ANIMATION TIMINGS

You can modify animation timings by changing their order, start timing, and speed. These commands are all available in the Timing group on the Animations tab. See Exhibit 21-20.

2 In the Timing group, click the **Move Earlier button**. The animation sequence number next to the photo changes to a 1, and the numbers next to the bulleted list items change to 2 and 3. Now the photo will animate first.

3 Click the **bullet symbol next to Hiking**. The first-level item and all its subitems are selected. All of the animation sequence icons next to these items are selected as well.

EXHIBIT 21-20 OPTIONS IN THE TIMING GROUP ON THE ANIMATIONS TAB

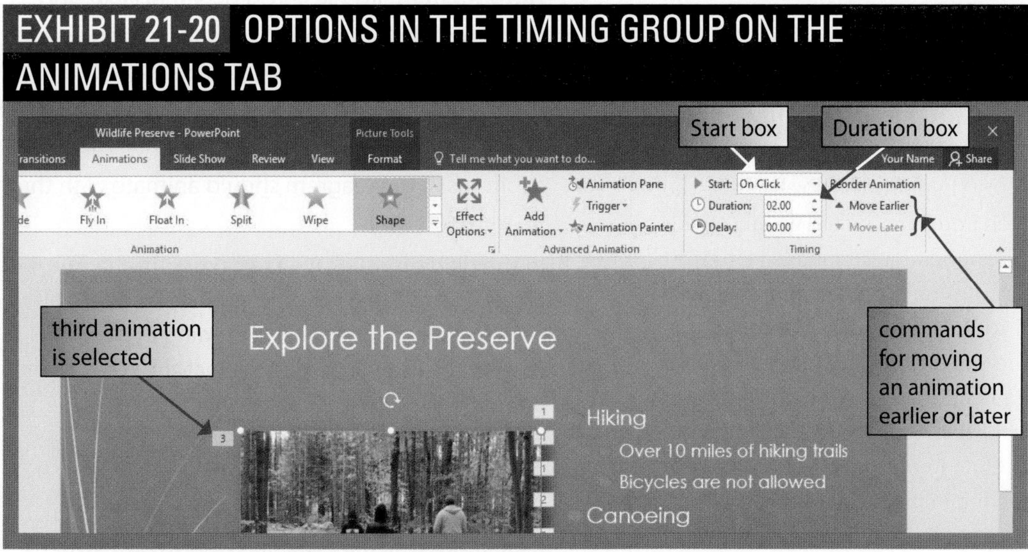

4 On the Animations tab, in the Timing group, click the **Move Earlier button**. The animation sequence numbers next to the Hiking item and its subitems change to 1, and the number next to the photo changes to 2.

5 On the status bar, click the **Slide Show button**. Slide 3 appears in Slide Show view.

6 Press the **Spacebar**. The Hiking bulleted item and its subitems fly in from the bottom.

7 Press the **Spacebar** again. The photo of people hiking fades in.

8 Press the **Spacebar** one more time. The Canoeing bulleted item and its subitems fly in from the bottom.

9 Press the **Esc key** to end the slide show.

End Activity

21-5a Modifying the Order of Animations

If objects on a slide do not animate in the order you want, you can change the order of the animations. To see the current order, display the slide in the Slide pane, click the Animations tab, and then examine the numbers in the animation sequence icons. Items labeled with lower number animation sequence icons animate before items labeled with higher number animation sequence icons. To change the animation order, click the object or the animation sequence icon associated with the item whose animation order you want to change. In the Timing group on the Animations tab, click the Move Earlier or Move Later button under the Reorder Animation label.

Begin Activity

Modify the order of animations.

1 On **Slide 3** ("Explore the Preserve"), click the **photo** to select it. The number 3 in the animation sequence icon indicates that this object will be the third object animated on the slide when you do something to advance the slide show. Refer to Exhibit 21-20.

21-5b Modifying the Start Timing of an Animation

Animations can occur when you do something to advance the slide show, or they can occur automatically. When an object animates when you advance the slide show, its start timing is set to On Click. When an object animates automatically, its start timing is set to With Previous or After Previous. When you apply an animation to a bulleted list that contains subitems, as is the case with Slide 2, the subitems animate at the same time as their first-level bullet. This is because their start timing is set to With Previous.

You can change the start timing for animations. First, select the animated bulleted item or object whose start timing you want to change, and then click the Start arrow in the Timing group on the Animations tab to change whether an animation starts when you advance the slide show (On Click), at the same time as when the previous item animates (With Previous), or automatically after the previous item animates (After Previous).

The numbers in the animation sequence icons increase by one for each item that is set to animate On Click. When an animation is set to start With Previous or After Previous, the animation sequence number does not increase. On Slide 3 ("Explore the Preserve"), the Hiking first-level bulleted item is animated when you advance the slide show. The animation sequence icons next to its subitems also have a number 1 on them because their start timing is set to With Previous. The animation sequence number is the same as the first-level bulleted item because you don't need to do anything to advance the slide show to animate this item since it will animate with the previous item. If an item is labeled with an animation sequence icon containing the number 0 (zero), the default behavior was changed, and that item will animate at the same time as or immediately after the slide transitions onto the screen.

Begin Activity

Change the start timing of animations.

1. On **Slide 3** ("Explore the Preserve"), next to the Hiking bulleted item, click the **animation sequence icon 1**. On the Animations tab, in the Timing group, On Click appears in the Start box, indicating that the Hiking bulleted item will animate when you do something to advance the slide show.
2. Next to the first subitem under Hiking, click the **animation sequence icon 1**. In the Start box, With Previous appears, indicating that the subitem will animate with the first-level item when you advance the slide show.
3. Click the **photo**. The animation sequence icon next to the photo contains a 2. In the Start box, On Click appears.
4. Click the **Start box arrow**, and then click **With Previous**. The animation sequence number next to the photo changes to 1, the same number as the animation sequence numbers next to the Hiking item and its subitems.
5. On the status bar, click the **Slide Show button** , and then press the **Spacebar**. The Hiking item and its subitems fly in from the bottom, and the photo fades in at the same time.
6. Right-click the **slide**, and then on the shortcut menu, click **See All Slides**. Thumbnails of all the slides appear.
7. Click the **Slide 5** ("Keep Nature Natural") **thumbnail** to display it in Slide Show view, and then press the **Spacebar** five times to display each of the five items in the diagram. Each shape wipes in one at a time.
8. Press the **Esc key** to end the slide show. The two subitems in the diagram should animate with their first-level items.
9. In the diagram, click **Please carry out all your trash**. The five animation sequence icons are all selected. To change the start timing of a single item in the list, you need to select the specific animation sequence icon connected to the item.
10. Click the **animation sequence icon 2**. In the Timing group, click the **Start box arrow**, and then click **With Previous**. The animation sequence icon associated with the Please carry out all your trash subitem changes to a 1 to indicate that it will animate at the same time as the other item numbered 1. The two animation sequence icons numbered 1 are stacked one on top of each other.
11. Click the **animation sequence icon 3**. In the Timing group, click the **Start box arrow**, and then click **With Previous**.
12. On the status bar, click the **Slide Show button** . Slide 5 appears in Slide Show view.
13. Press the **Spacebar**. The first shape and its subitem wipe onto the screen.
14. Press the **Spacebar** again to animate the second first-level shape and its subitem.
15. Press the **Spacebar** a third time to display the last shape.
16. Press the **Esc key** to end the slide show.

End Activity

21-5c Changing the Speed of Animations

You can adjust the speed of animations. To change the speed of an animation, you change the time in the Duration box in the Timing group on the Animations tab. To make an animation go faster, decrease the time in the Duration box; to make it go slower, increase the time.

Begin Activity

Change the speed of animations.

1. Display **Slide 3** ("Explore the Preserve"), and then click the **photo** to select it.
2. On the Animations tab, in the Timing group, click the **Duration down arrow** four times. The Shape animation applied to the photo will now take one second to complete instead of two.
3. On the status bar, click the **Slide Show button**, and then press the **Spacebar**. The photo fades in more quickly than before.
4. End the slide show.

End Activity

FYI

CHANGING THE SPEED OF TRANSITIONS

The Duration box in the Timing group on the Transitions tab allows you to change the speed of transitions in the same way you change the duration of an animation. As with animations, you decrease the value in the Duration box to make the transition faster, and increase the value to slow it down.

21-6 ADDING VIDEO

You can insert digital video in slides or in slide masters. PowerPoint supports various file formats. The most commonly used are the MPEG-4 format, the Windows Media Audio/Video format, and the Audio Visual Interleave format, which appears in Explorer windows as the Video Clip file type. After you insert a video, you can modify it by changing the length of time the video plays, changing playback options, and applying formats and styles.

21-6a Inserting a Video on a Slide

You can insert a video clip in two ways. To display the Insert Video dialog box shown in Exhibit 21-21, you can click the Video button in the Media group on the Insert tab, or you can click the Insert Video button in a content placeholder. You can choose to insert a video from a file or from the Web. When you insert video from the Web, you can search for a video using the Bing search engine, or, if you have the embed code from a Web site such as YouTube, you can paste the embed code in the From a Video Embed Code box.

EXHIBIT 21-21 INSERT VIDEO DIALOG BOX

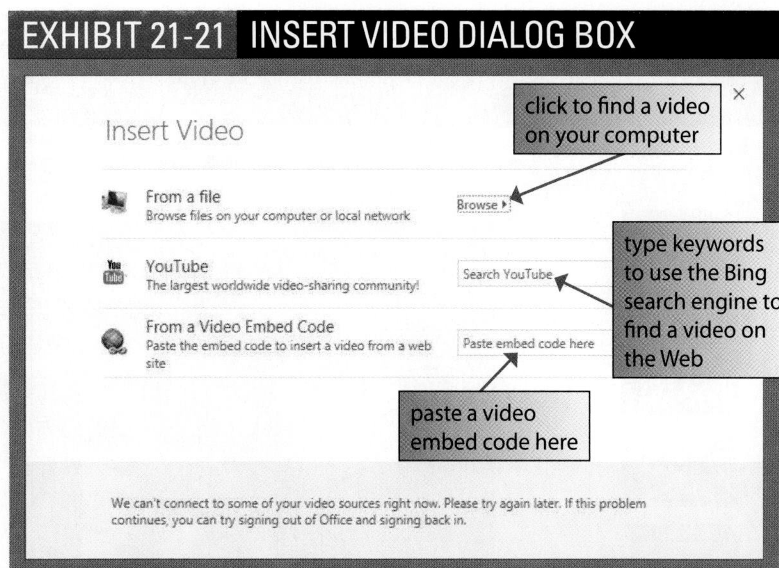

Begin Activity

Insert a video on a slide.

1. Display **Slide 4** ("Glass-Bottomed Canoe").
2. In the content placeholder on the right, click the **Insert Video button**. The Insert Video dialog box opens. Refer to Exhibit 21-21.
3. Next to From a file, click **Browse**. Another Insert Video dialog box opens. This dialog box is similar to the Open and Save As dialog boxes.
4. Click the movie data file **Canoe Video** located in the Chapter 21\Chapter folder, and then click **Insert**. The movie is inserted in place of the content placeholder. The Video Tools contextual tabs appear on the ribbon, and the Video Tools Format tab is the active tab. Compare your screen to Exhibit 21-22.
5. On the play bar below the movie, click the **Play button**, and then watch the video, which is approximately 18 seconds long. Note that this video has no sound.

End Activity

TIP: You can also click the Video button arrow in the Media group on the Insert tab, and then click Video on My PC to open the Insert Video dialog box.

EXHIBIT 21-22 VIDEO INSERTED ON SLIDE 4

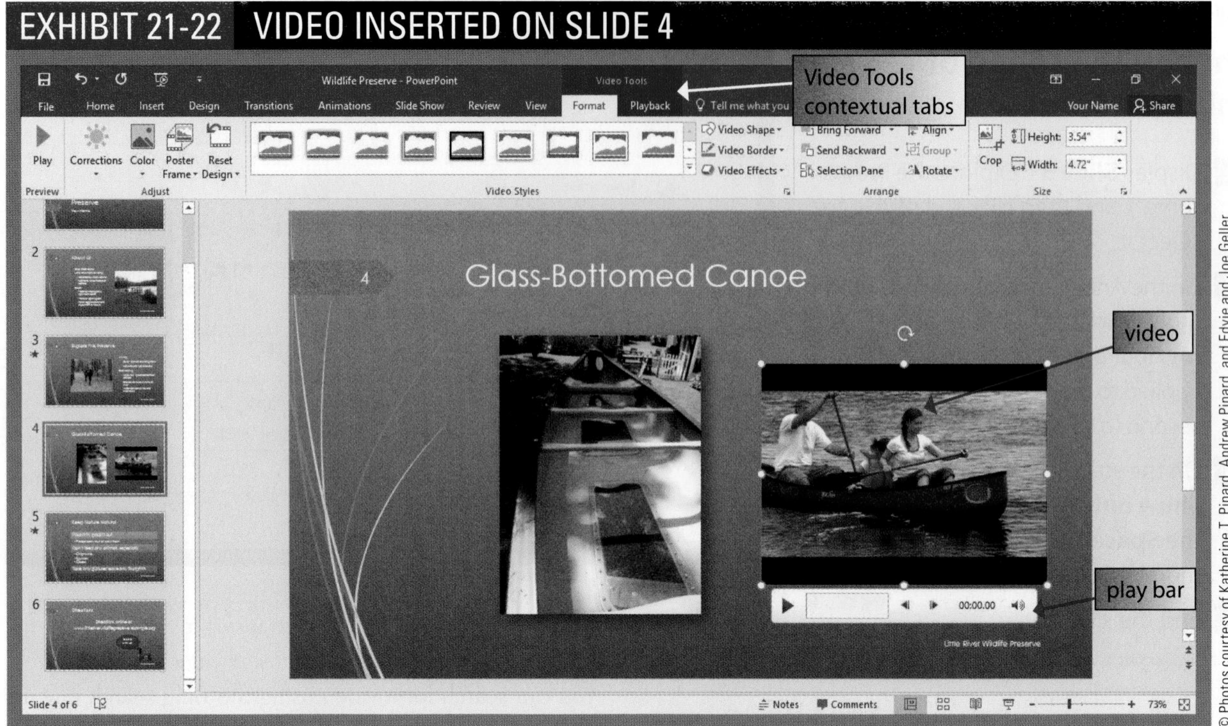

21-6b Formatting a Video

Videos can be formatted just like pictures. For example, you can crop the sides of a video or resize it by dragging the sizing handles. Be careful if you resize a video; you want to maintain the aspect ratio so you don't distort the image. You can also apply a style or special effects to a video.

Begin Activity

Format a video.

1 On **Slide 4** ("Glass-Bottomed Canoe"), if necessary, click the **video** to select it, and then click the **Video Tools Format tab**.

2 In the Size group, click the **Crop button**. Crop the black area from the top and bottom of the video, and then in the Size group, click the **Crop button** to deselect it.

3 Drag the **upper-left-corner sizing handle** up and to the left until the left edge of the video is touching the right edge of the photo.

4 Drag the **video** down and right to center it in the area to the right of the photo.

5 On the Video Tools Format tab, in the Video Styles group, click the **Video Effects button**.

6 On the menu, point to **Reflection**. In the Reflection Variations section, click the **Half Reflection, touching style**. A reflection appears below the video. Compare your screen to Exhibit 21-23.

EXHIBIT 21-23 CROPPED, RESIZED VIDEO WITH A REFLECTION STYLE APPLIED

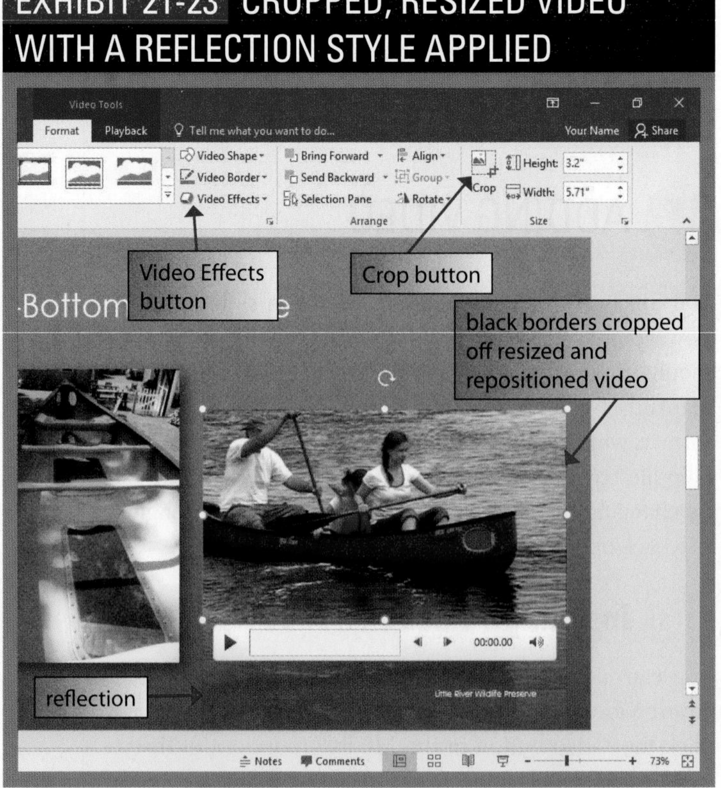

7 On the play bar below the movie, click the **Play button** ▶. The video plays in the reflection as well as in the main video window.

End Activity

21-6c Trimming a Video

If a video is too long, or if it contains parts you don't want to show during the slide show, you can trim the clip from within PowerPoint. To do this, click the Trim Video button in the Editing group on the Video Tools Playback tab to open the Trim Video dialog box. See Exhibit 21-24. Drag the green and red sliders to indicate where you want the video to start and stop.

EXHIBIT 21-24 TRIM VIDEO DIALOG BOX

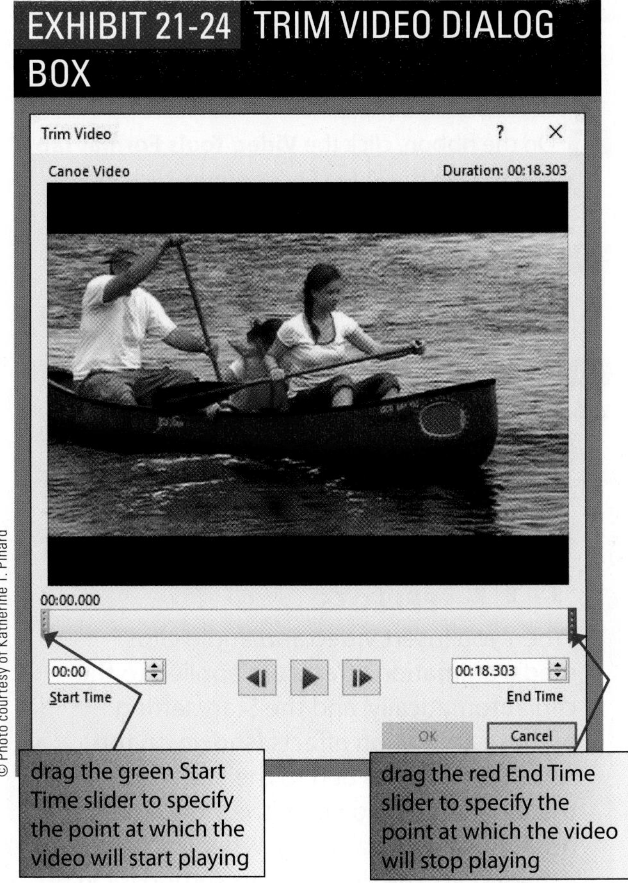

© Photo courtesy of Katherine T. Pinard

Begin Activity

Trim a video.

1 On **Slide 4** ("Glass-Bottomed Canoe"), if necessary, click the **video** to select it, and then click the **Video Tools Playback tab**.

2 In the Editing group, click the **Trim Video button**. The Trim Video dialog box opens. Refer to Exhibit 21-24.

3 On the bar below the video, drag the **green Start Time slider** to the right to approximately the 7-second mark. The time in the Start Time box changes to match the time point where you dragged the slider. The video will now start playing at this point.

4 Drag the **red End Time slider** to the left to approximately the 15-second mark. The time in the End Time box changes to match the time point where you dragged the slider. The video will stop playing at this point.

5 Click **OK**. You can watch the trimmed video in Normal view.

6 On the play bar, click the **Play button** ▶. The trimmed video—now about eight seconds long—plays.

End Activity

21-6d Changing Video Playback Options

You can change several options for how a video plays. For example, you can set a video to play automatically when the slide appears during a slide show or wait until you click the video's play button. You can also set a video to loop continuously until the next slide is displayed or to fill the screen while it is playing, covering the other objects on the slide. Video playback options are described in Exhibit 21-25, and the Video Options group on the Video Tools Playback tab is shown in Exhibit 21-26.

EXHIBIT 21-25 VIDEO PLAYBACK OPTIONS

Video Option	Function
Volume	Change the volume of the video from high to medium or low or mute it.
Start	Change how the video starts, either when the presenter advances the slide show (On Click) or automatically when the slide appears during the slide show.
Play Full Screen	When selected, the video fills the screen during the slide show.
Hide While Not Playing	When selected, the video does not appear on the slide when it is not playing; make sure the video is set to play automatically if this option is selected.
Loop until Stopped	When selected, the video will play continuously until the next slide appears during the slide show.
Rewind after Playing	When selected, the video will rewind after it plays so that the first frame or the poster frame appears again.

EXHIBIT 21-26 VIDEO OPTIONS GROUP ON THE VIDEO TOOLS PLAYBACK TAB

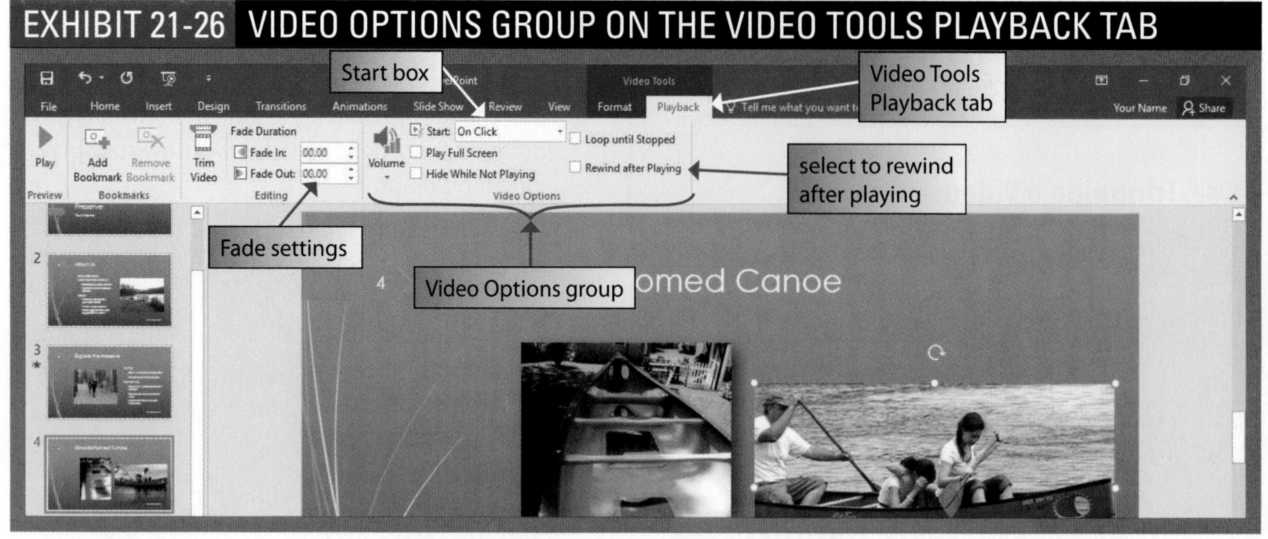

© Photos courtesy of Katherine T. Pinard and Andrew Pinard

Begin Activity

Change video playback options.

1. On **Slide 4** ("Glass-Bottomed Canoe"), if necessary, click the **video** to select it.
2. Click the **Video Tools Playback tab**. Refer to Exhibit 21-26.
3. In the Video Options group, click the **Rewind after Playing check box** to select it. Now the video will rewind to the beginning after playing in the slide show.
4. In the Video Options group, click the **Start box arrow**, and then click **Automatically**. Now the video will play automatically when the slide is displayed during a slide show.
5. On the status bar, click the **Slide Show button** . Slide 4 appears in Slide Show view, and the video plays. The way the video started and stopped is a little abrupt. Also, the reflection effect makes the video look more jumpy.
6. End the slide show.
7. On the Video Tools Playback tab, in the Editing group, click the **Fade In box up arrow**, and then click the **Fade Out box up arrow** to change the values in both boxes to **00.25**, or one-quarter second.
8. On the ribbon, click the **Video Tools Format tab**, and then in the Video Styles group, click the **Center Shadow Rectangle style**.
9. Play the slide show from the current slide. Now there is a brief, one-quarter second fade at the start and end of the video.
10. Press the **Esc key** to end the slide show.

End Activity

TIP: To play the video so that it fills the entire screen, select the Play Full Screen check box in the Video Options group on the Video Tools Playback tab.

TIP: To set the volume for a video, click the Volume button in the Video Options group on the Video Tools Playback tab or use the Volume control on the play bar.

FYI UNDERSTANDING VIDEO AND AUDIO ANIMATION EFFECTS

When you insert video and audio clips, media animation effects are applied to the clip automatically, and the Start setting of these animation effects (shown on the Animations tab) is tied to the Start setting of the media clip (shown on the Video Tools or Audio Tools Playback tab). When you insert a media clip, the default Start setting is On Click. A Play animation is also automatically applied to the clip, and it too is set to start On Click. If you insert audio or video on a slide that contains other animations, and the animations and media do not play as you expect during a slide show, remember to check the Animations tab to see if the Play animation settings are in conflict with the settings on the Playback tab.

EXHIBIT 21-27 SETTING A POSTER FRAME

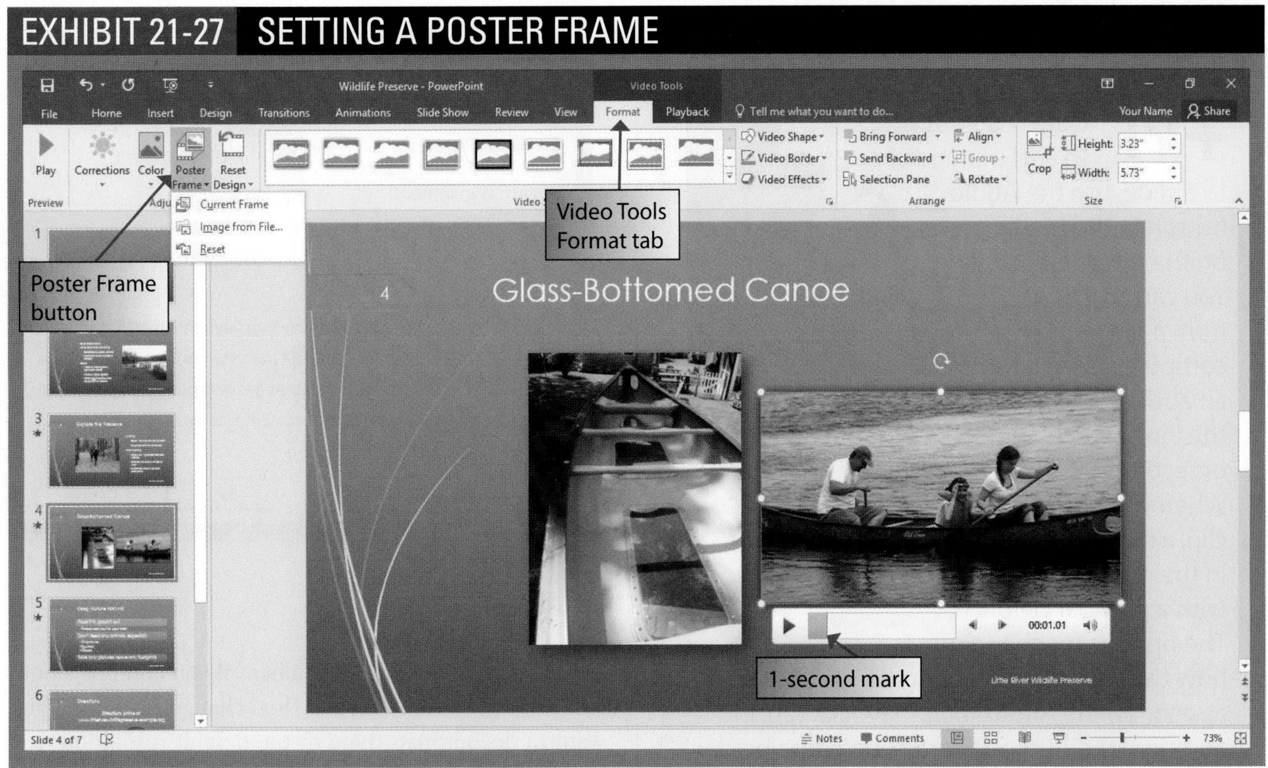

© Photos courtesy of Katherine T. Pinard, Andrew Pinard, and Edyie and Joe Geller

21-6e Setting a Poster Frame

A **poster frame**, sometimes called a **preview frame**, is the image that appears before the video starts playing. The default poster frame for a video is the first frame of the video. You can change this so that any frame from the video or any image stored in a file is the poster frame. To set the poster frame to a specific frame in the video, click the playbar at the point the frame appears, and then click the Poster Frame button in the Adjust group on the Video Tools Format tab. See Exhibit 21-27. Click Current Frame to set the poster frame to the currently displayed frame.

Begin Activity

Set the poster frame for a video.

1 On **Slide 4** ("Glass-Bottomed Canoe"), if necessary, click the **video** to select it.

2 On the ribbon, click the **Video Tools Format tab**.

3 On the slide, point to the **play bar** so that you see a ScreenTip identifying the time at the point where the pointer is positioned.

PROBLEM?
If you don't see the ScreenTip, click a **blank area of the slide**, click the **video** again, and then repeat Step 2.

4 Move the **pointer** until it is at approximately the 1-second mark, and then click. The gray indicator in the play bar moves to the 1-second mark.

5 On the Video Tools Format tab, in the Adjust group, click the **Poster Frame button**. A menu opens. Refer to Exhibit 21-27.

6 On the menu, click **Current Frame**. The menu closes, and a note appears in the play bar indicating that this will be the poster frame.

7 On the status bar, click the **Slide Show button** . Slide 4 appears in Slide Show view, and the video plays. When the video is finished, it rewinds and displays the poster frame again.

8 Press the **Esc key** to end the slide show.

End Activity

poster frame (preview frame) In a video object, the image that appears before the video starts playing.

mikeledray/Shutterstock.com

FYI **ADDING A SOUND CLIP TO A SLIDE** To add a sound clip to a slide, use the Audio button in the Media group on the Insert tab. You can add audio from a file on your computer, search for an audio clip using the Bing search engine, or record new audio. When you add an audio clip, a sound icon appears in the middle of the slide with a play bar below it. The options for changing how the sound plays during the slide show appear on the Audio Tools Playback tab. In addition, the Audio Styles group contains the Play in Background button. When you select this, the Play Across Slides, Loop until Stopped, and Hide During Show check boxes in the Audio Options group become selected. The audio clip will play continuously as you display the rest of the slides in the presentation.

21-7 COMPRESSING PICTURES AND MEDIA

When you save a presentation that contains photos, PowerPoint automatically compresses the photos to a resolution of 220 pixels per inch (ppi). (For comparison, photos printed in magazines are typically 300 ppi.) Compressing photos reduces the size of the presentation file, although it also reduces the quality of the photos. To change the compression settings, select a photo, and then in the Adjust group on the Picture Tools Format tab, click the Compress Pictures button to open the Compress Pictures dialog box. See Exhibit 21-28.

If you insert additional photos or crop a photo after you applied compression settings, you will need to reapply the settings. Photo compression is not permanent until you close the file. This means if you compress photos to a lower resolution and then change your mind and want to decompress them to the default resolution, you can do this as long as you have not closed the file. Once the compression settings are permanently applied, you cannot undo them because the extra information has been discarded.

EXHIBIT 21-28 COMPRESS PICTURES DIALOG BOX

Compress Pictures

deselect to compress all the pictures in the presentation

Compression options:

☑ Apply only to this picture

☑ Delete cropped areas of pictures

Target output:

○ HD (330 ppi): good quality for high-definition (HD) displays

○ Print (220 ppi): excellent quality on most printers and screens

○ Web (150 ppi): good for web pages and projectors

○ E-mail (96 ppi): minimize document size for sharing

◉ Use document resolution

OK Cancel

select compression level

Begin Activity

Modify the compression of pictures.

1. On **Slide 4** ("Glass-Bottomed Canoe"), click the **photo** to select it.
2. On the ribbon, click the **Picture Tools Format tab**.
3. In the Adjust group, click the **Compress Pictures button**. The Compress Pictures dialog box opens. Refer to Exhibit 21-28.
4. Click the **E-mail (96 ppi) option button**. This setting compresses the photos to the smallest possible size. At the top of the dialog box under Compression options, the Delete cropped areas of pictures check box is already selected. This option is not applied to cropped photos until you open this dialog box and then click the OK button to apply it. To make the presentation file size as small as possible, leave this selected. The Apply only to this picture check box is also selected; to apply the settings to all the photos in the file, you need to deselect it.
5. Click the **Apply only to this picture check box** to deselect it.

6 Click the **OK button.** The dialog box closes, and the compression settings are applied to all the photos in the presentation.

End Activity

As with pictures, you can compress media files. If you need to send a file via email or you need to upload it, you should compress media files to make the final PowerPoint file smaller. To do this, click the File tab to display the Info screen in Backstage view, and then click the Compress Media button. See Exhibit 21-29. The more you compress files, the smaller the final presentation file will be, but also the lower the quality. When you compress videos, any parts of videos that you trimmed off will be deleted, similar to deleting the cropped portions of photos.

EXHIBIT 21-29 COMPRESS MEDIA MENU ON THE INFO SCREEN IN BACKSTAGE VIEW

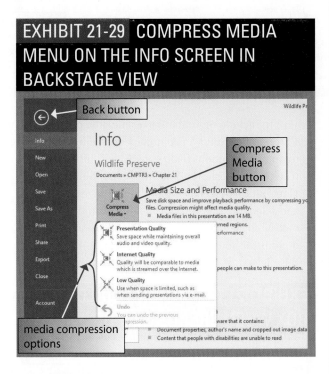

Begin Activity

Compress media.

1 Click the **File tab.** Backstage view appears, displaying the Info screen.

2 Click the **Compress Media button.** A menu opens listing your compression choices. Refer to Exhibit 21-29.

TIP: If the Info screen in Backstage view contains an Optimize Media button as well as the Compress Media button, click the Optimize Media button first to prevent any potential problems playing the video on the slide.

3 Click **Low Quality.** The menu closes, and a dialog box opens listing the video file in the presentation, with a progress bar appearing next to it in the Status column to show you the progress of the compression. After the file is compressed, the progress bar is replaced by a message indicating that compression for the file is complete and stating how much the video file size was reduced. The Cancel button at the bottom changes to the Close button.

4 Click the **Close button.** Next to the Compress Media button on the Info screen, the bulleted list tells you that the presentation's media was compressed to Low Quality and that you can undo the compression if the results are unsatisfactory.

5 At the top of the navigation bar, click the **Back button** ←. Slide 4 ("Glass-Bottomed Canoe") appears.

6 Save the presentation.

End Activity

21-8 SAVING A PRESENTATION FOR DISTRIBUTION

PowerPoint lets you save presentations in several formats that allow others to view the presentation but does not allow them to make any changes to it. Each method produces a different type of file for you to distribute. Before distributing a presentation, you should consider checking it for hidden or private information. To do this, click the Check for Issues button on the Info screen in Backstage view, and then click Inspect Document.

- **Video**—you can save a presentation as a video in the MPEG-4 format. After you have created the video, you can play it in Windows Media Player or any other video player. To save the presentation as a video, click Export in the navigation tab in Backstage view, and then click Create a Video.
- **Picture Presentation**—you can save a presentation as a picture presentation, which saves each slide as an image file in the JPEG format and then places that image on a slide in a new presentation so that it fills the entire slide. This format prevents other people from modifying it or copying complex animations, backgrounds, or

other features. To save a presentation as a picture presentation, on the Export screen in Backstage view, click Change File Type, and then click PowerPoint Picture Presentation under Presentation File Types.

- **Individual Image Files**—you can save slides as individual image files. To do this, on the Export screen in Backstage view, click Change File Type, and then click PNG Portable Network Graphics or JPEG File Interchange Format under Image File Types. You can save only the current slide or all the slides.
- **PowerPoint Show**—you can save a presentation as a PowerPoint Show file, which causes the presentation to open only in Slide Show view. To save a presentation as a PowerPoint Show, on the Export screen in Backstage view, click Change File Type, and then click PowerPoint Show under Presentation Files Types.
- **Package Presentation for CD**—you can package a presentation for CD, which saves all the files needed to run the presentation in a folder or to a CD. If you package a presentation to a CD, when the CD is inserted in the computer and starts running, the user is offered the opportunity to download Viewer, a free program that allows you to run a slide show but not edit it. You can also search the Microsoft Web site for this program and install it on any computer that does not already have PowerPoint installed on it. To package a presentation for CD, on the Export screen in Backstage view, click Package Presentation for CD.
- **Portable Document Format (PDF)**—you can save a presentation as a PDF file and then open it using the Reader app. When you save a presentation as a PDF file, each slide becomes a page in the PDF file, or you can change this so that the PDF looks like a handout with the number of slides per page that you specify. To do this, on the Export screen in Backstage view, click Create PDF/XPS Document, and then click the Create PDF/XPS button. This opens the Publish as PDF or XPS dialog box. See Exhibit 21-30. Navigate to the folder where you want to save the PDF file, and type the file name you want to use in the File name box. To make the PDF file size smaller, click the Minimum size (publishing online) option button to select it. If you want to open the PDF automatically after creating it, select the Open file after publishing check box.

EXHIBIT 21-30 PUBLISH AS PDF OR XPS DIALOG BOX

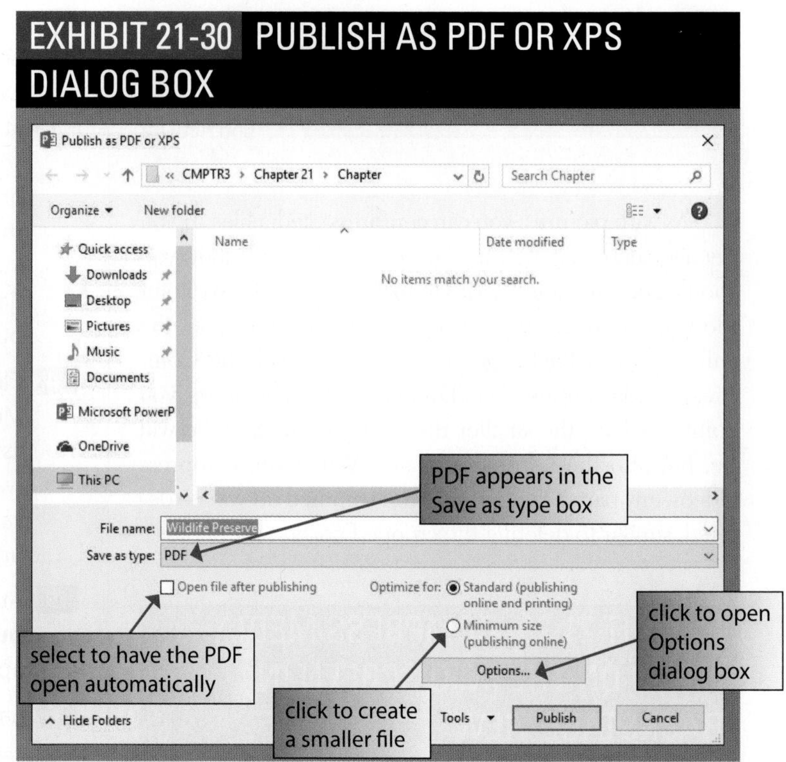

To include more than one slide on a page in the PDF, similar to PowerPoint handouts, click Options to open the Options dialog box. See Exhibit 21-31. Click the Publish what box arrow, and then click Handouts. Then click the Slides per page box arrow, and select the number of slides you want to appear on each page in the PDF. You can also choose other options for how the slides will appear in the PDF in this dialog box.

EXHIBIT 21-31 OPTIONS DIALOG BOX WHEN CREATING A PDF

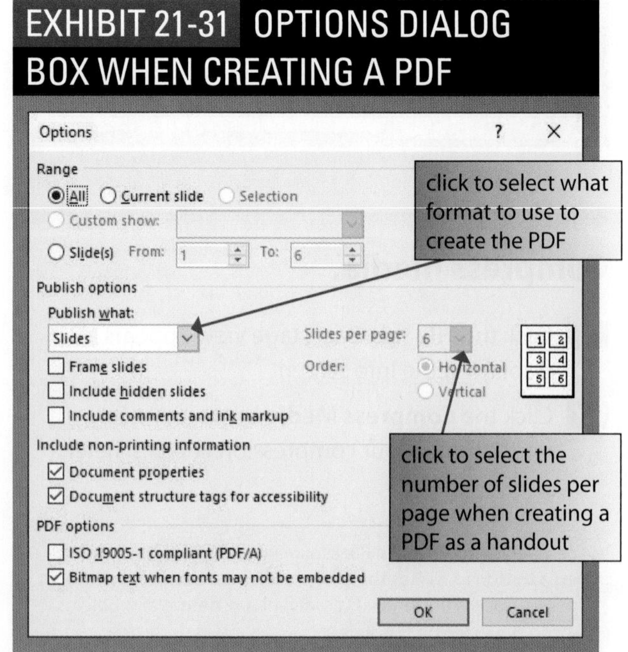

Begin Activity

Save a presentation as a PDF.

1. On the ribbon, click the **File** tab, and then on the navigation bar, click **Export**. The Export screen appears with Create PDF/XPS Document selected.
2. Click the **Create PDF/XPS button**. The Publish as PDF or XPS dialog box opens with PDF in the Save as type box. Refer to Exhibit 21-30.
3. Navigate to the location where you are saving your files, if necessary, and then change the name in the File name box to **Wildlife Preserve PDF**.
4. Click the **Minimum size (publishing online) option button**.
5. Click **Options**. The Options dialog box opens. Refer to Exhibit 21-31.
6. In the Publish options section, click the **Publish what arrow**, and then click **Handouts**. The Slides per page box becomes available and 6 appears in the box. There are only six slides in the presentation, so this is fine.
7. Click **OK**. The Options dialog box closes.
8. In the Publish PDF or XPS dialog box, if the **Open file after publishing check box** is selected, click it to deselect it.
9. Click **Publish**. The dialog box closes and the PDF file is created.

End Activity

PROBLEM?
If XPS appears in the Save as type box, click the **Save as type box**, and then click **PDF**.

FYI

USING OFFICE MIX

Office Mix is a PowerPoint add-in used to create a mix. An **add-in** is software that you can install to add new commands and features to PowerPoint. A **mix** is an interactive video created from a PowerPoint presentation using Office Mix and posted to a Web site. When you use Office Mix, you can record just your voice as you give your presentation and describe your slides, or you can record video of yourself as you speak. The audio and video become part of the mix. The video can fill the screen or appear in a small box on each slide as people view the mix. You can also record annotations (notes and drawings) that you add to slides while they are displayed, and you can add links to Web sites that viewers can click when they watch the mix. In addition, you can add quizzes to your mix that cause the video to pause and ask viewers questions that test their understanding of the content presented in the mix. After you create a mix, you upload it to a Microsoft Web site using your Microsoft account, and anyone with the link can view the mix.

Office Mix A PowerPoint add-in used to create a mix.

add-in Software that you can install to add new commands and features to an Office application.

mix An interactive video created from a PowerPoint presentation using Office Mix and posted to a Web site.

STUDY TOOLS 21

READY TO STUDY? IN THE BOOK, YOU CAN:

- ☐ Rip out the Chapter Review Card, which includes key terms and key chapter concepts.

ONLINE AT WWW.CENGAGEBRAIN.COM, YOU CAN:

- ☐ Review key concepts from the chapter in a short video.
- ☐ Explore enhancing a presentation with the interactive infographic.
- ☐ Practice what you've learned with more Practice It and On Your Own exercises.
- ☐ Prepare for tests with quizzes.
- ☐ Review the key terms with flashcards.

QUIZ YOURSELF

1. What is the difference between the theme Slide Master and a layout master?
2. Describe the two ways you can add a picture stored in a file on your computer to a slide.
3. How do you add a shape to a slide?
4. How do you add text to a shape on a slide?
5. What is a diagram?
6. Describe how to convert a bulleted list into a SmartArt diagram.
7. How do you modify animation effects?
8. How do you modify an animation so that it starts automatically at the same time as the previous animation?
9. How do you change the speed of an animation?
10. What happens during playback when you add a reflection effect to a video?
11. How do you shorten a video's playback?
12. What is a poster frame?
13. How do you increase the compression of all the photos in a presentation?
14. How do you save a presentation in other file formats?

PRACTICE IT

Practice It 21-1

1. Open the data file **Geese** located in the Chapter 21\Practice It folder. Add your name as the subtitle. Save the presentation as **Geese Problem**.
2. Switch to Slide Master view.
3. Display the Berlin Slide Master.
4. Delete the thin black rectangles on either side of the slide.
5. Click the border of the Date placeholder to select it, and then delete the Date placeholder.
6. Resize the Footer placeholder by dragging one of the right sizing handles to the right so that the Footer placeholder is the same width as the content placeholder above it. Then change the alignment of the text in the Footer placeholder so that it is center-aligned.
7. Increase the font size of the text in the content placeholder on the Berlin Slide Master so that the text size of the first-level bulleted item is 28 points and the smallest text size in the list is 18 points. Repeat this on the Title and Content Layout master.
8. Apply the Style 3 background style to all the slides.
9. On the Berlin Slide Master, draw a Rounded Rectangle shape (in the Basic Shapes section of the Shapes gallery) in the upper-right corner of the slide, and then type **Macon Road Neighborhood Association** in the shape. Resize the shape so it is 0.3 inches high and 4.5 inches wide. Position the shape so its right edge is aligned with the right edge of the title text box and so that its top edge is aligned with the smart guide that appears about one-eighth of an inch from the top of the slide.
10. Apply the Subtle Effect - Lime, Accent 1 shape style to the shape.
11. Close Slide Master view.
12. Display Slide 5 ("Possible Solutions"). In place of the content placeholder on the right, insert the picture data file **Barrier** located in the Chapter 21\Practice It folder. Apply the Compound Frame, Black style to the picture. Increase the brightness of the picture by 40% and increase the contrast by 20%.
13. Display Slide 6 ("Hidden River: Alternate Nesting Site"). In place of the content placeholder on the right, insert the picture data file **Geese Photo** located in the Chapter 21\Practice It folder. Apply the Compound Frame, Black style to the picture, increase the color saturation by 200%, and decrease the contrast by 20%.
14. Display Slide 4 ("Why Geese Stay"). Convert the bulleted list on the slide to the Target List SmartArt diagram (located in the List category).
15. Add a new shape after the People feed shape in the SmartArt diagram. Add the words **Grass is cut** to the shape.
16. Change the colors of the diagram to the Dark 1 Outline style (in the Primary Theme Colors section on the Change Colors menu). Change the style of the SmartArt diagram to the Cartoon style.
17. Animate the SmartArt diagram with the Fade entrance animation. Change the Sequence effect to One by One, and change the duration to one-quarter second.
18. On Slide 5 ("Possible Solutions"), animate the photo with the Split entrance animation and the Vertical Out effect. Change the order of the animations on Slide 5 so that the photo is the second item to animate.
19. Change the Start timing of the photo animation to With Previous so it animates with the *Build barriers* item.
20. Display Slide 3 ("Listen!") in the Slide pane. Insert the video data file **Geese Video** located in the Chapter 21\Practice It folder.
21. Crop the black borders on the sides of the video. Apply the Compound Frame, Black style to the video.
22. Set the video to rewind after playing.
23. Trim the video so it ends at approximately the 8-second mark.
24. Use the frame at approximately the 4.5-second mark (showing two geese side by side) as the poster frame.
25. Compress all the photos in the presentation to 96 ppi. Compress the media using the Low Quality setting.
26. Save the presentation. Then save the presentation as a PDF handout with nine slides per page using the Minimum size option. Name the PDF **Geese Problem PDF**.

Practice It 21-2

1. Open the data file **Round Lake** located in the Chapter 21\Practice It folder. Add your name as the subtitle, and then save the file as **Round Lake Resort**.
2. On the Vapor Trail Slide Master, modify the title text so the text is bold, and then change the font size of the text in the content placeholder so the text in the first-level bulleted item is 28 points and the text in the fifth-level bulleted item is 20 points.
3. On the Vapor Trail Slide Master, delete the Date placeholder text box. Then move the Slide Number placeholder down to position it to the right of the Footer placeholder (where the Date placeholder was before you deleted it).
4. On the Title Slide Layout master, delete the graphic at the bottom of the slide.
5. On Slide 2 ("Why Build at Round Lake?"), insert the video data file **Lake** located in the Chapter 21\Practice It folder.
6. Crop the black edges from the video. Change the size of the video so it is four inches high, maintaining the aspect ratio, and then position the video so its top edge is aligned with the top edge of the bulleted list and its right edge is aligned with the right edge of the title text box.
7. Trim the video so that it starts at approximately the 4-second mark and ends at the 18-second mark.
8. Set the video to start automatically, and then set a one-half-second fade at both the start and the end of the video.
9. On the Video Tools Playback tab, change the volume of the video to Low. Set the video to loop until stopped and to rewind after playing.
10. Apply the Beveled Perspective Left video style (in the Intense section in the Video Styles gallery) to the video.
11. On Slide 2, insert a Rounded Rectangle shape below the video that is the same width as the video and is 0.3 inches high.
12. Add the text **Property Today** to the rectangle.
13. Format the shape using the Transparent - Black, Dark 1 shape style (in the Presets section).
14. On Slide 4 ("Benefits"), insert the picture **Property After**, located in the Chapter 21\Practice It folder. Increase the brightness of the photo by 20% and decrease the contrast by 20%. Change its color saturation to 66%.
15. On Slide 4, apply the Bevel Perspective Left, White effect to the picture. Use a command on the Picture Border button menu to remove the border.
16. On Slide 5 ("Plan"), convert the bulleted list to a Step Up Process SmartArt diagram.
17. After the Submit proposal to council shape, add a new shape containing the text **Begin lake cleanup**.
18. Change the color of the SmartArt diagram to Colored Fill – Accent 2 (in the Accent 2 section). Change the style to the Subtle Effect SmartArt style.
19. Animate the SmartArt diagram with the Darken emphasis animation. Modify the SmartArt animation so that the shapes darken one by one, and then change the speed of the SmartArt animations to one-quarter second.
20. On Slide 6 ("Round Lake Resort"), insert the picture data file **Logo** located in the Chapter 21\Practice It folder. Resize the logo so it is 3.5 inches high, maintaining the aspect ratio. Position the logo so it is center-aligned on the slide and so its top edge is aligned with the bottom edge of the title text box.
21. Select the photo on Slide 4, and then compress all the photos in the presentation to 96 ppi. Compress the media to Low Quality.
22. Save the presentation, and then save the presentation as a PDF handout using the Minimum sizing option with six slides per page. Name the PDF file **Round Lake Resort PDF**.

ON YOUR OWN

On Your Own 21-1

1. Open the data file **Landmarks** located in the Chapter 21\On Your Own folder. Save the file as **Landmarks Quiz**.
2. Add the following as a footer on all slides except the title slide: **Click the correct answer.** (including the period).
3. On the Banded Slide Master, change the alignment of the title text placeholder so that it is centered.
4. On the Banded Slide Master, change the font size of the text in the Footer placeholder to 28 points and format it as bold. Then change the size of the

Footer placeholder box to 0.8 inches high and 4.4 inches wide. Position the Footer placeholder box so it is aligned with the top and left edges of the slide. Change the alignment of the text in the Footer placeholder so that it is left-aligned.

5. On the Banded Slide Master, change the font size of the text in the content placeholder so that the size of the text in the first-level item is 28 points and the size of the text in the fifth-level bulleted item is 20 points. Do the same thing to the content placeholders on the Two Content Layout master.
6. In the content placeholders on Slide 2, insert the photo **Arc de Triomphe**; on Slide 3, insert the photo **Easter Island**; and then on Slide 4, insert the photo **Parthenon**. The three photos are located in the Chapter 21\On Your Own folder.
7. On Slide 4, resize the photo so it is 3 inches high, and then position it so its right edge is aligned with the right edge of the title text box and so it is center aligned with the bulleted list.
8. Apply the Drop Shadow Rectangle style to each photo.
9. On Slides 2, 3, and 4, change the bullet symbols to a lettered list from A to C.
10. On Slide 2 ("Question 1"), draw a rectangle, and then resize it to 0.6 inches high and 1.3 inches wide. Center this rectangle between the third lettered item and the photo. Use the Shape Outline button to remove its outline, and then use the Shape Fill button to fill it with the Lime, Accent 2 color.
11. Copy the rectangle to the Clipboard. Paste copies of the rectangle to the right of the first and second lettered items. The three rectangles should align vertically in the space between the text and the photo.
12. Select all three rectangles, and then copy them to Slides 3 and 4. On both slides, position the rectangles to the right of each lettered list item.
13. On Slide 2, add the text **Incorrect** to the top two rectangles, and then add the text **Correct** to the bottom rectangle. Change the font size of the text in all three rectangles to 20 points, and format it as bold.
14. On Slide 3, add the text **Correct** to the top rectangle, and then add the text **Incorrect** to the middle and bottom rectangles. Format the text in the rectangles to match the formatting of the text in the rectangles on Slide 2.
15. On Slide 4, add the text **Correct** to the middle rectangle, and then add the text **Incorrect** to the top and bottom rectangles. Format the text in the rectangles to match the formatting of the text in the rectangles on Slides 2 and 3.
16. On Slide 4, draw another rectangle, and then resize it so it is 0.7 inches high and 1.4 inches wide. Change its outline to No Outline. Leave its fill as yellow.
17. Position the yellow rectangle so it is on top of one of the green rectangles, hiding it completely. Copy the yellow rectangle to the Clipboard, and then paste the copied rectangle twice. Position the copied rectangles on top of the other two green rectangles on the slide.
18. Select the three yellow rectangles, and then apply the exit animation Wipe. (Make sure you choose the Wipe animation in the Exit section, not in the Entrance section.)
19. Copy the selected three rectangles to the Clipboard. Display Slide 3, paste the copied rectangles, and then position the pasted rectangles on top of the three green rectangles. Do the same on Slide 2.
20. On Slide 2, draw a Rounded Rectangle 0.5 inches high and 6 inches wide on top of the letter C and the last item in the lettered list. Change the fill of this shape to the Blue, Accent 4 color. Copy this rectangle, and then paste a copy on top of the lettered item B. Paste a second copy on top of the lettered item A.
21. On Slide 2, select the top yellow rectangle. On the Animations tab, set the Rounded Rectangle on top of the first lettered item as the trigger for this animation. (*Hint:* Use the Trigger button in the Advanced Animation group on the Animations tab, and then point to On Click of. Select the Rounded Rectangle with the highest number in the list.) Set the Rounded Rectangle surrounding the second lettered item as the trigger for the middle yellow rectangle. (Select the Rounded Rectangle with the second lowest number in the list.) Set the Rounded Rectangle surrounding the third lettered item as the trigger for the bottom yellow rectangle. (Select the Rounded Rectangle with the lowest number in the list.)
22. Click the top yellow rectangle , and then use the Shape Fill command to fill it with the same color as the slide background. (*Hint:* Use the Eyedropper command.)
23. With the rectangle still selected, use the Format Painter to copy its formatting to the other two yellow rectangles on the slide. If you see any of the green rectangle beneath the rectangles that are the same gray color as the background, reposition the gray rectangles, or, if necessary, change the size of a gray rectangle so that it is 0.65 inches high.

24. Right-click the top blue Rounded Rectangle, and then click Format Shape to open the Format Shape pane. In the pane, click Fill. Change the Transparency to 100%. In the pane, click Line, and then select the No line option.
25. With the transparent Rounded Rectangle still selected, use the Format Painter to copy its formatting to the other two blue Rounded Rectangles on the slide.
26. On Slides 3 and 4, repeat Steps 20 through 25 to set the blue rectangles as triggers for the corresponding yellow rectangles, and to change the fill of all of the rectangles. As needed, adjust the height and width of the blue rectangles you create on each slide so that they do not overlap the green rectangles and so that they cover all the text in the lettered list. The first blue rectangle you draw on each slide will have the lowest number in the Trigger list.
27. On Slide 5 ("Presented by"), draw a rectangle large enough to cover *Click the correct answer.* at the top of the slide. Change its fill and outline so you cannot see the rectangle.
28. On Slide 5, add your name in the content placeholder, and then save the presentation.
29. Run the presentation in Slide Show view. On Slides 2, 3, and 4, click each lettered item to see the answers. Close the presentation when you're finished.

CAPSTONE

POWERPOINT: PREPARE A PRESENTATION

1. Plan a presentation about a topic of your choosing. For example, you can create a presentation to train others how to do a job; convey information about a person, place, or thing; influence others to buy or do something; or create a slide show of photographs around a specific topic, event, or person. Develop the basic outline of the presentation, and decide what content will go on each slide.
2. Create a new PowerPoint presentation, and apply an appropriate theme. Make sure you choose a theme that is relevant to your presentation and intended audience.
3. On Slide 1, add an appropriate title for the presentation. Add your name as a subtitle.
4. On the theme Slide Master, add a digital image that is related or relevant to the presentation you are creating.
5. Look at each layout master, and make sure the digital image is appropriately placed on it. If not, remove the digital image from the theme Slide Master, and then add it and position it appropriately on each layout master.
6. Create a presentation based on your plan.
7. Where needed, create bulleted lists to provide details or information about the topic.
8. Add clip art or graphics to illustrate your points. Use at least one SmartArt diagram. (*Hint:* Examine the diagrams in the Picture category.)
9. On at least one slide, insert a shape, such as a rectangle, triangle, circle, arrow, or star.
10. If appropriate, add video and audio clips. Trim the clips as needed, and set appropriate playback and formatting options.
11. On at least one slide, do not use a bulleted list; use only an image, clip art, a video, SmartArt, or another graphic element, with animation if appropriate. Make sure the effect during the slide show conveys your planned spoken message.
12. Examine the presentation outline. Are you using too many words? Can any of your bulleted lists be replaced with a graphic?
13. Re-evaluate the theme you chose. Do you think it is still appropriate? Does it fit the content of the presentation? If not, apply a different theme, or modify the colors or fonts.
14. Add appropriate transitions and animations. Remember that the goal is to keep audience members engaged without distracting them.
15. Check the spelling, including contextual spelling, of the presentation, and then proofread it.
16. Rehearse the presentation. Consider your appearance, and decide on appropriate clothing to wear. Practice in front of a mirror and friends or family. If possible, create a video of yourself giving the presentation. Notice and fine-tune your body language, tone of voice, and fluency to fully engage your audience.

Office Online

WORKING WITH POWERPOINT ONLINE

As with Word and Excel Online, you can use PowerPoint Online to view or edit PowerPoint presentations stored on OneDrive. When you open a presentation in PowerPoint Online in View mode, it appears in the browser window similar in Reading view. See Exhibit 1. If you use the buttons on the navigation bar, when you scroll through the presentation, you will see the presentation as it appears in Reading or Slide Show view in PowerPoint 2016 with a few exceptions. Some transitions and animations are not supported and video clips might be distorted.

EXHIBIT 1 PRESENTATION IN VIEW MODE IN POWERPOINT ONLINE

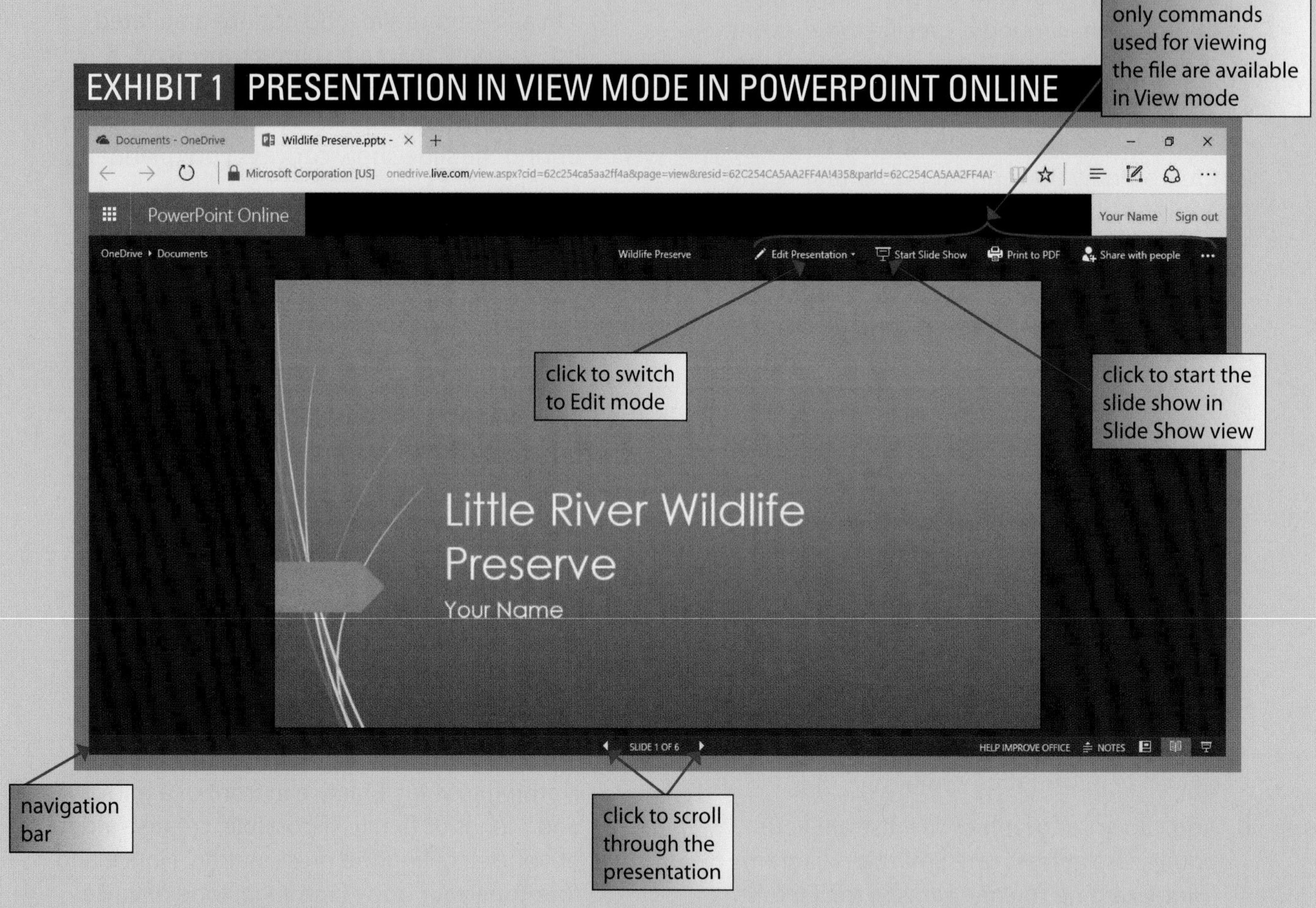

If you open a presentation in PowerPoint Online in Edit mode, you can do almost everything you can do in PowerPoint 2016; however, you have access to only a few transitions and animations. See Exhibit 2.

From both View mode and Edit mode, you can switch to Slide Show view. (Note that if your pop-up blocker is set to block most pop-ups, you might need to allow pop-ups from the onedrive.live.com Web site.) See Exhibit 3. As with Edit mode, some transitions and animations are not supported, although more than are supported in Edit mode. Also, video might be distorted. Note that in Slide Show view in PowerPoint Online, the shortcut menu that appears when you right-click contains only a few of the commands that appear when you right-click during a slide show in PowerPoint 2016. Also, the Slide Show toolbar contains only the Next Slide and Previous Slide buttons, as well as a button that you can click to end the slide show.

EXHIBIT 2 PRESENTATION IN EDIT MODE IN POWERPOINT ONLINE

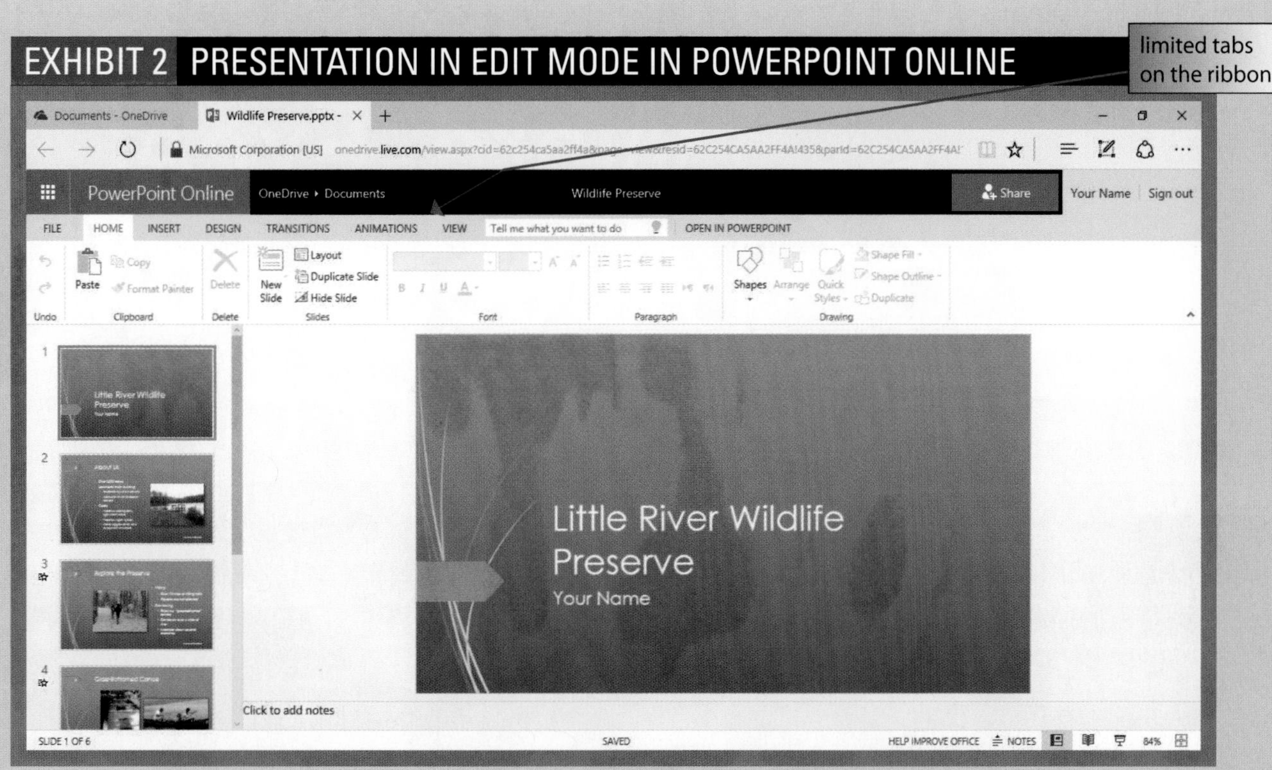

EXHIBIT 3 PRESENTATION IN SLIDE SHOW VIEW IN POWERPOINT ONLINE

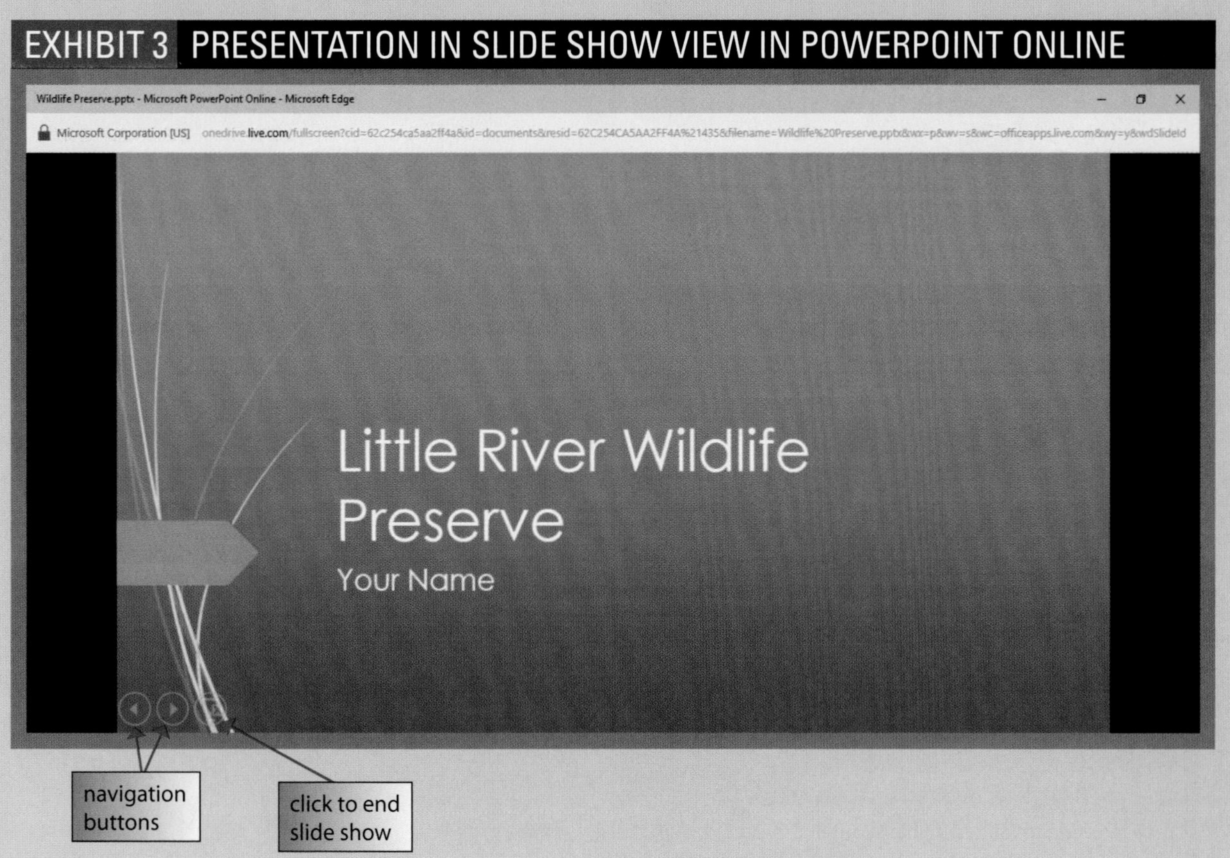

Part 10
INTEGRATION

22 Integrating Word, Excel, Access, and PowerPoint

© nopporn/Shutterstock.com

LEARNING OBJECTIVES After studying the material in this chapter, you will be able to:

22-1 Understand object linking and embedding

22-2 Import and export data

22-3 Use the Object command to insert text from a file

22-4 Copy and paste among Office programs

22-5 Create PowerPoint slides from a Word outline

22-6 Create form letters with mail merge

After finishing this chapter, go to **PAGE 682** for **STUDY TOOLS**.

22-1 OBJECT LINKING AND EMBEDDING

In many business, people work together on teams to complete projects. Individuals might be asked to prepare or focus on a specific aspect of a project, report, or event. Each person can use the particular application to create the needed files. The files are then integrated to create an in-depth and complete product, with each part of the file having been created in the program that best fits that data. The ability to integrate Microsoft Office documents allows people to share info and create complex docs even if they're not in the same location, an important consideration in our global society.

Remember that an object is anything that can be manipulated as a whole; in other words, it is the specific information that you want to share between programs and can be anything from a chart or a table to a picture, video, sound clip, or almost anything else you can create on a computer. The program used to create the object you want to integrate into another program is the **source program**; the file that initially contains the object is the **source file**. The program used to create the file where you want to insert the object is called the **destination program**; the file where you want to insert the object is called the **destination file**.

When you **embed** an object, a copy of the object along with a link to the source program become part of the destination file, and you can edit the object using the source program's commands. There is no connection between an embedded object and its source file, which means that changes made to the object in the source file do not appear in the destination file. You must have access to the source program to edit an embedded object; you do not need access to the source file.

When you **link** an object, a direct connection is created between the source and destination files. The object exists in only one place—the source file—but the link displays the object in the destination file as well. You must have access to the source file if you want to make changes to the linked source object. If you edit a linked object in the source file, the link ensures that the changes appear in the destination file. If you edit a linked object in the destination file, the changes do not appear in the source file. The next time the link is updated, the changes made in the destination file will be overwritten with the linked data from the source file.

Both linking and embedding involve inserting an object into a destination file; the difference lies in where their respective objects are stored. The advantage of embedding an object instead of linking it is that the source file and the destination file can be stored separately. You can use the source program commands to make changes to the object in the destination file, and the source file will be unaffected. The disadvantage is that the destination file size is somewhat larger than it would be if the object was simply pasted as a picture or text, or if it was linked. The advantage of linking an object instead of embedding it is that the linked object remains identical in the source and destination files, and the destination file size does not increase as much as if the object were embedded. The disadvantage is that the source and destination files must be stored together. When you need to copy information from one program to another, consider which option is the best choice for your needs.

Exhibit 22-1 illustrates the difference between linking and embedding. Exhibit 22-2 summarizes embedding and linking and compares their advantages and disadvantages.

22-1a Creating an Embedded Excel Chart in Word or PowerPoint

If you want to embed a chart in a Word document or PowerPoint slide, and the chart or the data to create it does not already exist in a separate Excel file, you can create the chart from within the Word or PowerPoint file. To do this, in either program, click the Chart button in the Illustrations group on the Insert tab to open the Insert Chart dialog box. After you select the type of chart you want to create, a spreadsheet with sample data opens, and a chart based on the sample data and the chart style you selected appears in the document or slide.

source program The program used to create an object.

source file The file that contains an object that you want to integrate into another file.

destination program The program used to create the file where you want to insert an object created in a different file.

destination file The file into which you want to insert an object created in another file.

embed To copy an object along with a link to the source program in a destination file.

link To establish a direct connection between a source file and a destination file.

EXHIBIT 22-1 EMBEDDING CONTRASTED WITH LINKING

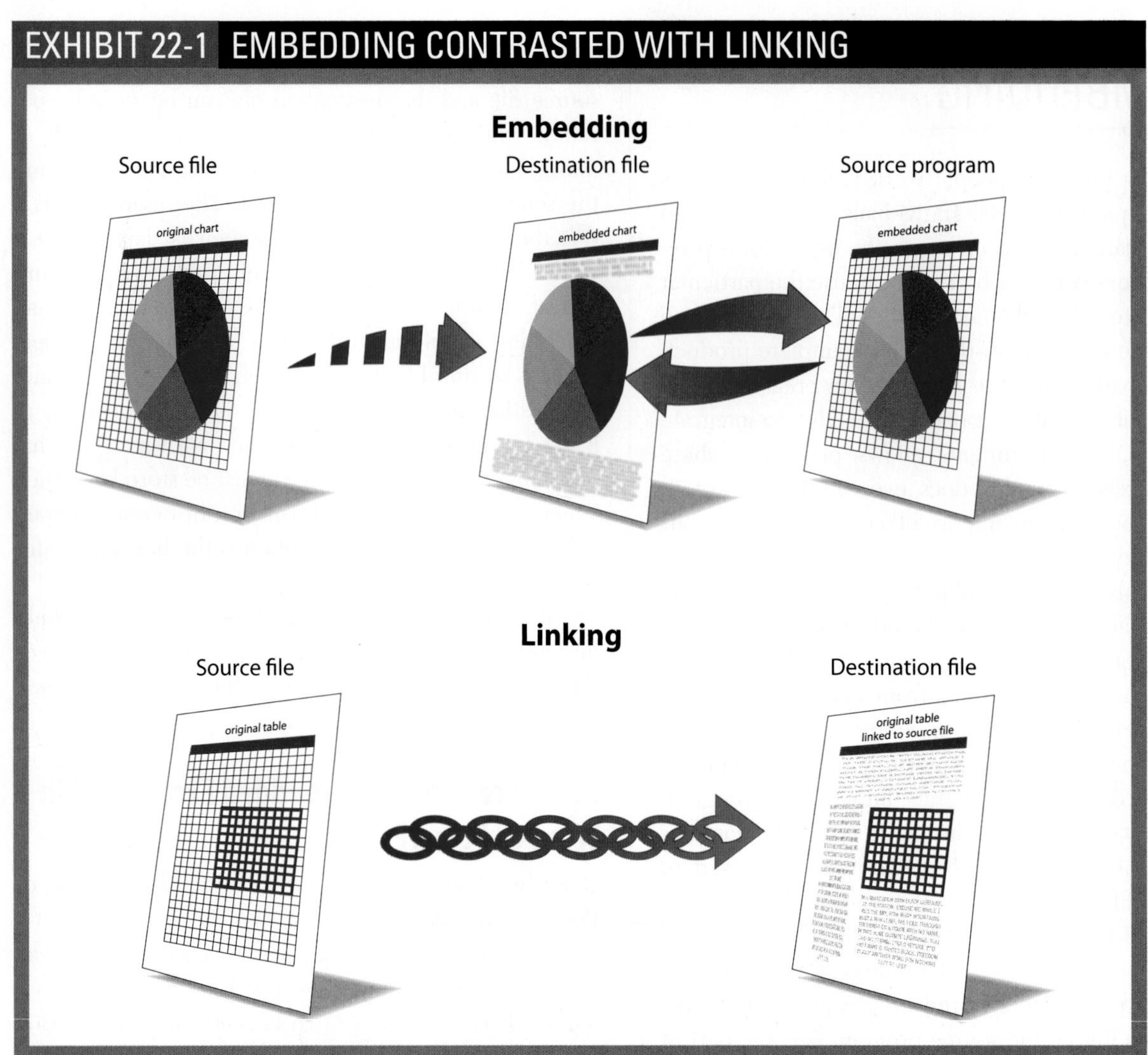

EXHIBIT 22-2 COMPARING INTEGRATION METHODS

	Embedding	Linking
Description	Displays and stores an object in the destination file.	Displays an object in the destination file along with the source file's location; stores the object in the source file.
Use if you want to	Include the object in the destination file, and edit the object using the source program without affecting the source file.	Edit the object in the source file and have the changes appear in the destination file.
Advantages	The source file and destination file can be stored separately. You can use source program commands to make changes to the object in the destination file.	The destination file size remains fairly small. The source file and the object in the destination file remain identical.
Disadvantages	The destination file size increases to reflect the addition of the object from the source file.	The source and destination files must be stored together.

Once you insert the chart, you can modify the sample data in the spreadsheet so that it contains your data. The chart will adjust as you edit the spreadsheet.

Begin Activity

Create an embedded chart in a Word document.

1 Open the Word data file **Brochure** located in the Chapter 22\Chapter folder. Save the document as **EcoFlooring Brochure**.

2 At the bottom of page 1, after *Prepared by:*, type your name. If necessary, change the zoom to **120%**.

3 On page 2, delete the **yellow highlighted text**. The insertion point is in the now empty paragraph.

4 On the ribbon, click the **Insert tab**. In the Illustrations group, click the **Chart button**. The Insert Chart dialog box opens. Column is selected in the list of chart types.

5 Click **OK**. The dialog box closes, a column chart with sample data appears in the document and a spreadsheet with sample data appears above it. Colored borders appear around the cells that are included in the chart. Compare your screen to Exhibit 22-3.

End Activity

> **TIP:** You can create an embedded chart in a PowerPoint slide using the Chart button in the Illustrations group on the Insert tab, or by clicking the Insert Chart button in a Content placeholder.

Begin Activity

Modify data in a spreadsheet.

1 In the spreadsheet, click **cell A2**, type **Ash** and then press the **Down Arrow key**. The text you type replaces the placeholder text in the cell and below the first set of columns in the chart in the Word window.

2 In **cell A3**, type **Bamboo**, and then press the **Down Arrow key**.

3 In **cell A4**, type **Beech**, and then press the **Down Arrow key**.

4 In **cell A5**, type **Cherry birch**, and then press the **Down Arrow key**. Cell A6, which doesn't contain placeholder text, is selected.

5 In **cell A6**, type **Hevea**, and then press the **Down Arrow key**. The colored borders in the spreadsheet expand to row 6, and a new label is added to the horizontal axis on the chart.

> **TIP:** If the data on which a chart will be based exists in an Excel worksheet, you can copy the data to the Excel worksheet that opens when you click the Chart button in the Word or PowerPoint file.

EXHIBIT 22-3 SPREADSHEET AND COLUMN CHART WITH SAMPLE DATA IN WORD WINDOW

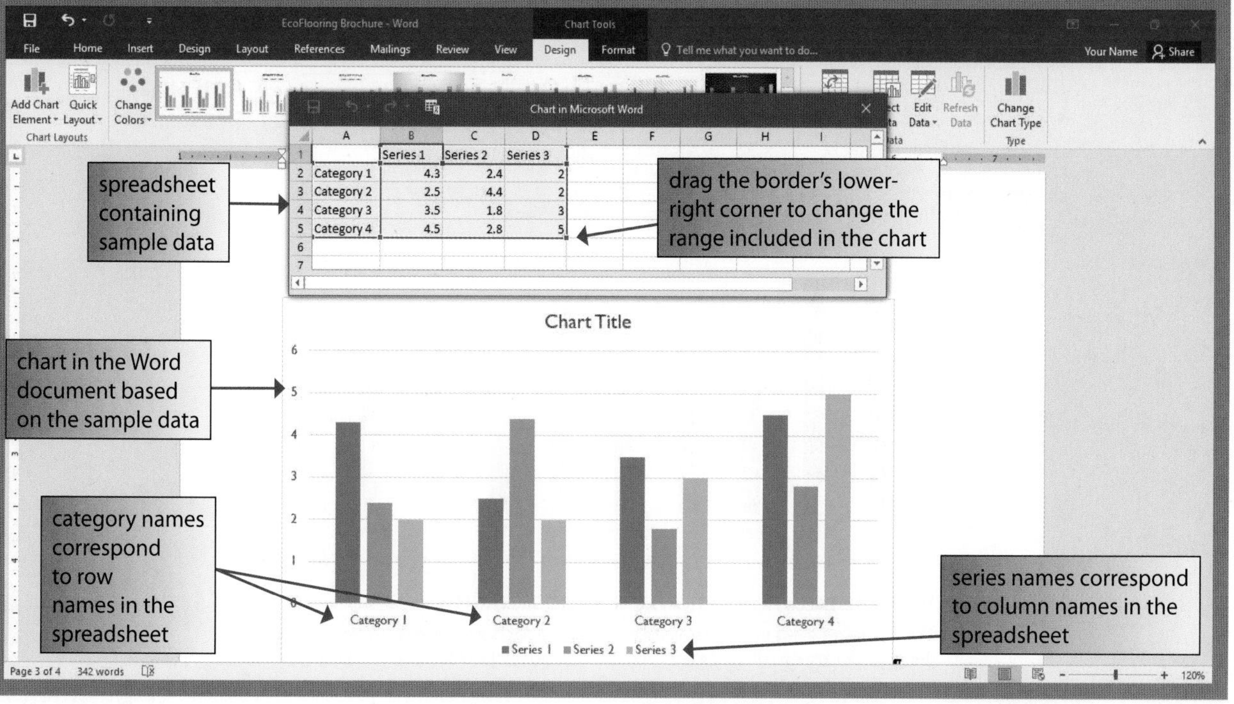

6 In the **range A7:A10**, type the following:

Kempas

Maple

Oak

Walnut

7 In the Chart in Microsoft Word window, click **cell B2**, type **3.8** and then press the **Enter key**. The first green column in the chart shortens to the 3.8 mark.

8 In the **range B3:B10**, enter the following values:

6.1

3.1

3.1

4.3

5.6

2.9

4.2

3.6

9 In the spreadsheet, drag the **lower-right blue border corner** to the left two columns so that the blue border surrounds the range B2:B10. The blue and yellow columns in the chart in the Word window disappear.

10 In the spreadsheet, click the **Close button**. The spreadsheet closes. In the Word document, the chart is selected, and the Chart Tools Design tab is selected.

11 To the right of the chart, click the **Chart Elements button**, and then click the **Legend check box** to deselect it. The legend is removed from the chart.

12 In the chart, click the **Series 1 title**, and then type **Janka Rating for Common Woods** as the new title. Compare your screen to Exhibit 22-4.

13 Save the document.

End Activity

22-1b Embedding a Chart Created in an Excel Worksheet in Word or PowerPoint

If a chart already exists in an Excel worksheet, you can copy it from there and then embed it in the document or slide. You can then use Excel commands to modify the chart from within the document or slide. Your changes, however, will not appear in the original file.

Remember that when you use the Paste command, you have access to several options to paste the object in different ways. If you click the Paste button arrow instead of clicking the Paste button, a menu with Paste Options buttons appears. You can point to each button to see a Live Preview of the pasted object. Exhibit 22-5 shows the Live Preview when a chart is on the Clipboard and you are pointing to the Use Destination Theme & Embed Workbook button. For most objects, you can choose whether to keep the source file formatting or use the destination file formatting. For some objects, such as pasting an Excel chart into a Word document,

EXHIBIT 22-4 COMPLETED COLUMN CHART IN WORD DOCUMENT

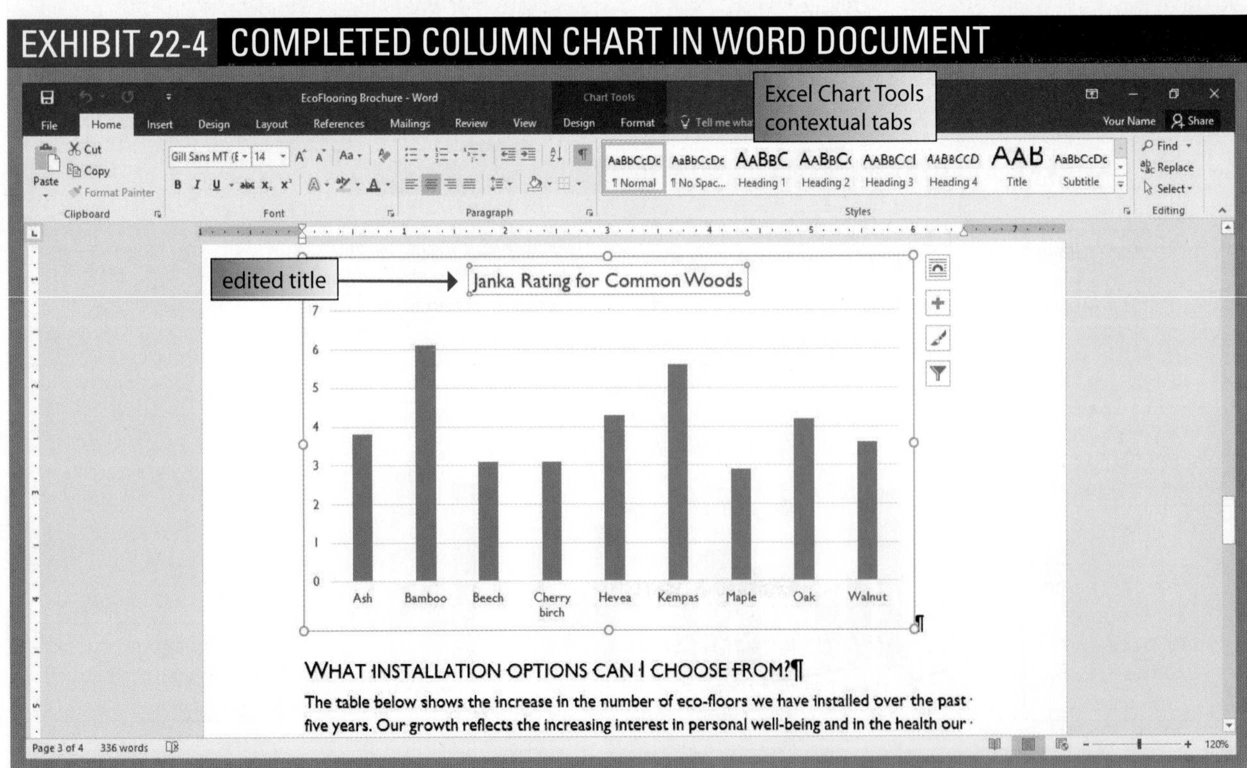

EXHIBIT 22-5 PASTE BUTTON MENU WITH PASTE OPTIONS AND LIVE PREVIEW OF THE CHART

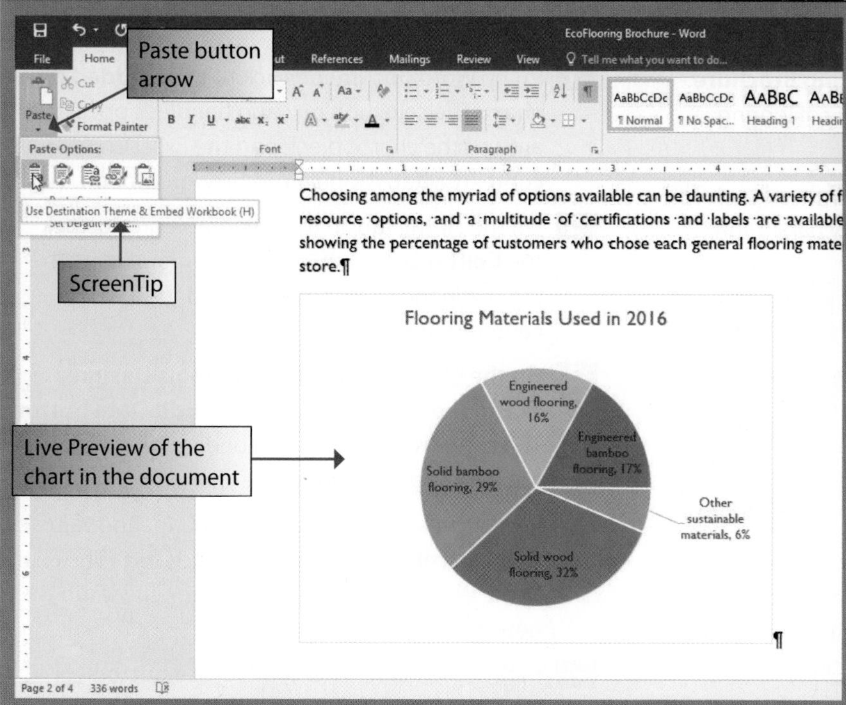

you can also choose to embed or link the object or paste it as a picture. Remember, if you click the Paste button, you can change the way an object is pasted by clicking the Paste Options button that appears below and to the right of the pasted object to access the same menu of options.

Begin Activity

Embed a chart created in an Excel worksheet in a Word document.

1 Open the Excel data file **Data** located in the Chapter 22\Chapter folder. Save the document as **EcoFlooring Data**. On the taskbar, a Microsoft Excel button appears next to the Microsoft Word button. This workbook contains three worksheets.

FYI

EMBEDDING EXCEL WORKSHEET DATA IN WORD AND POWERPOINT FILES

When you copy worksheet data, the first two buttons on the Paste button menu are Keep Source Formatting and Use Destination Styles. Selecting either of these two buttons converts the data to an ordinary Word or PowerPoint table. You can then format the table using the usual methods. If you want to embed worksheet data in either a Word document or a PowerPoint slide instead of pasting it as a table or linking it to the Excel worksheet, you need to use the Paste Special command. To do this, click the Paste button arrow, and then click Paste Special to open the Paste Special dialog box. With the Paste option button selected, click Microsoft Excel Worksheet Object in the As list, and then click OK. The table is placed into the document or the slide with a selection box and sizing handles around it. You cannot edit the data in an embedded table as you do an ordinary Word or PowerPoint table. Instead, you double-click the embedded table to access Excel editing commands. When you double-click the embedded table, instead of the worksheet appearing in a separate Excel window, a copy of the entire workbook from which you copied the table appears within a dashed line border and the Excel ribbon tabs completely replace the Word or PowerPoint ribbon tabs.

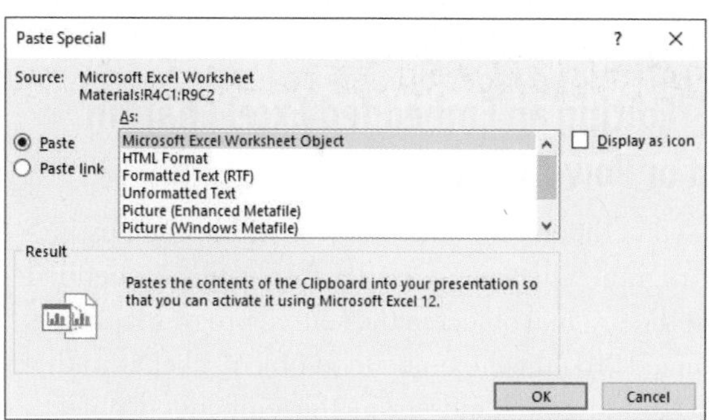

2 On the Materials worksheet, click the **pie chart** to select it.

3 On the Home tab, in the Clipboard group, click the **Copy button**. The chart is copied to the Clipboard.

4 On the taskbar, click the **EcoFlooring Brochure - Word button** to return to the EcoFlooring Brochure document.

5 On page 2, delete the **green highlighted text**. The insertion point is in the now empty paragraph.

6 On the Home tab, in the Clipboard group, click the **Paste button arrow**. A menu of Paste options appears.

7 In the Paste button menu, point to the **Use Destination Theme & Embed Workbook button** (the first button). The chart appears in the document at the insertion point using the theme colors and fonts in the Word document file. Refer again to Exhibit 22-5. This is the default option.

> TIP: The same options appear on the Paste button arrow in the PowerPoint window when an Excel chart has been copied to the Clipboard.

8 In the Paste button menu, point to the **Keep Source Formatting & Embed Workbook button** (the second button). The chart changes to use the theme colors and fonts from the source file.

9 In the Paste button menu, point to the other three buttons, noting the change in the chart in the document and reading their ScreenTips, and then click the **Use Destination Theme & Embed Workbook button** (the first button). The chart is pasted in the document as an inline object using the document theme colors and fonts.

> TIP: To change the default paste option, click Set Default Paste on the Paste menu, and then make your selections in the Cut, copy, and paste section of the Advanced page of the Word Options dialog box that opens.

End Activity

22-1c Editing an Embedded Excel Chart in Word or PowerPoint

When you edit an embedded object within the destination program, the changes affect only the embedded object; the original object in the source program remains unchanged. To edit the embedded object, click it to display tabs and commands from the embedded object's source program on the ribbon. You can then use these to modify the embedded object.

Begin Activity

Edit an embedded chart in a Word document.

1 In the Word document, click the **embedded pie chart**. The selection box and handles appear around the chart object, and the Excel Chart Tools contextual tabs appear on the Word ribbon.

2 On the Home tab, in the Paragraph group, click the **Center button**. The paragraph containing the inline chart object is formatted so it is centered horizontally.

3 On the ribbon, click the **Chart Tools Design tab**. In the Data group, click the **Edit Data button**. The spreadsheet for the embedded pie chart appears above or below the chart.

4 In the spreadsheet, in **cell B5**, change the value to **30**. In **cell B7**, change the value to **18**. The chart in the Word document changes to reflect the new data.

5 In the spreadsheet, click the **Close button**. The spreadsheet closes.

6 On the taskbar, click the **EcoFlooring Materials - Excel button** to switch to the Excel window. Notice the values in cells B5 and B7 on the Materials worksheet in the EcoFlooring Data workbook are unchanged.

7 Switch back to the **EcoFlooring Brochure document**, view the document in **One Page view**, and then scroll through the document.

8 Save the document, and then close it.

End Activity

22-1d Linking Excel Chart Data to a Word Document or PowerPoint Presentation

If a chart exists in an Excel worksheet and you think you might update the data on which the chart is based in the future, you can link it to a Word document or PowerPoint slide instead of embedding it. Then when you modify the data in the Excel file, the changes will appear in the destination file. To link Excel chart data to a Word document or PowerPoint presentation, copy the chart in the Excel file, and then use one of the Link buttons on the Paste button menu. You must leave the Excel workbook open while you paste, or the Paste button menu will offer only options to embed the chart or paste it as an image.

When you link an Excel chart using one of the Link buttons on the Paste button menu, you are actually linking only the data used to create the chart. This means that if you change the data on which the chart is based, the linked chart will change to reflect the modified data. But, if you modify the chart in the Excel workbook, such as by changing the chart colors or adding or removing chart elements, those changes will not be reflected in the linked chart. If you want to link both the data and the chart itself, you need to use the Paste Special command on the Paste button menu.

Begin Activity

Link an Excel worksheet to a PowerPoint presentation.

1. Open the PowerPoint data file **EcoPresentation** located in the Chapter 22\Chapter folder. Save the presentation as **EcoFlooring Presentation**.
2. On the title slide, add your name as the subtitle.
3. Switch to the Excel workbook **EcoFlooring Data,** and then click the **Growth sheet tab.**
4. Select the **column chart**, and then copy it to the Clipboard.
5. Switch to the PowerPoint presentation **EcoFlooring Presentation**, and then display **Slide 2** ("Growth Chart").
6. On the Home tab, in the Clipboard group, click the **Paste button arrow**. The same buttons that appeared when you embedded the Excel chart in the Word document appear.
7. Click the **Use Destination Theme & Link Data button** . The chart object is pasted into the slide and is linked to the Excel workbook.
8. On the ribbon, click the **Chart Tools Design tab**, and then in the Chart Styles group, click the **Style 8 style**.
9. In the Chart Styles group, click the **Change Colors button**, scroll up to the top of the menu, and then click the **Color 3 color palette**.
10. Resize and center the **chart** to fill the space below the title. Compare your screen to Exhibit 22-6.

End Activity

22-1e Linking Excel Worksheet Data to Word or PowerPoint

When you copy Excel worksheet data and then click the Paste button arrow in a PowerPoint presentation, none of the buttons on the menu are Link commands. To link copied data to in a Word document or to a PowerPoint slide, you need to use the Paste Special command to open the Paste Special dialog box. In the Paste Special dialog box, click the Paste link option button. The As list changes to include link options including Microsoft Excel

EXHIBIT 22-6 LINKED EXCEL CHART IN A POWERPOINT SLIDE

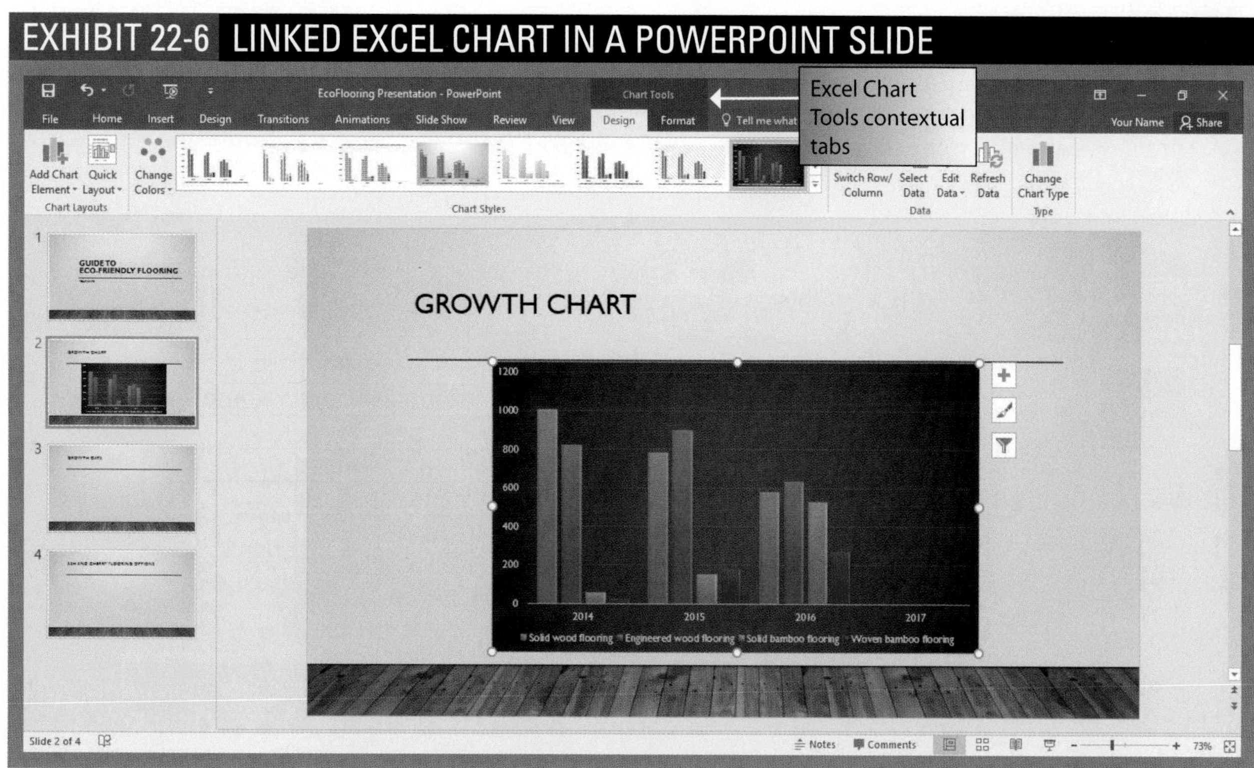

Worksheet Object, as shown in Exhibit 22-7. Then, just like with a linked chart, you can edit the source file, and the edits will appear in the destination file.

EXHIBIT 22-7 PASTE SPECIAL DIALOG BOX WITH PASTE LINK OPTIONS

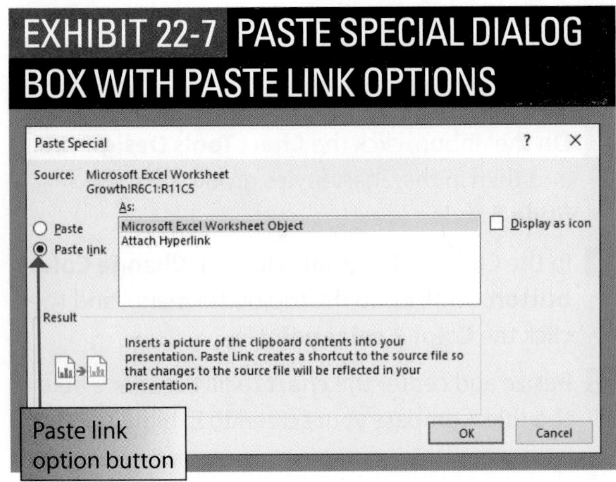

Begin Activity

Link Excel worksheet data to a PowerPoint slide.

1. Switch to the Excel workbook **EcoFlooring Data,** and make sure the **Growth worksheet** is selected.
2. Select the **range A6:E11**, and then copy it to the Clipboard.
3. Switch to the PowerPoint presentation **EcoFlooring Presentation**, and then display **Slide 3** ("Growth Data").
4. On the Home tab, in the Clipboard group, click the **Paste button arrow**. Point to each Paste Options button, watching the worksheet change on the slide and reading the ScreenTip. The set of buttons on the Paste button menu are different than the sets of Paste buttons you have seen until now. None of the buttons on the Paste button menu allow you to link the worksheet data.
5. On the menu, click **Paste Special**. The Paste Special dialog box opens. The Paste option button is selected, and a list of format options for the copied worksheet data appears.
6. Click the **Paste link option button**. The As list changes and Microsoft Excel Worksheet Object is selected in the list. Refer again to Exhibit 22-7.
7. Click **OK**. The dialog box closes, and the worksheet data appears on the slide.
8. Resize the **worksheet object** to fill the space below the slide title. Compare your screen to Exhibit 22-8.

End Activity

EXHIBIT 22-8 LINKED EXCEL WORKSHEET DATA ON A POWERPOINT SLIDE

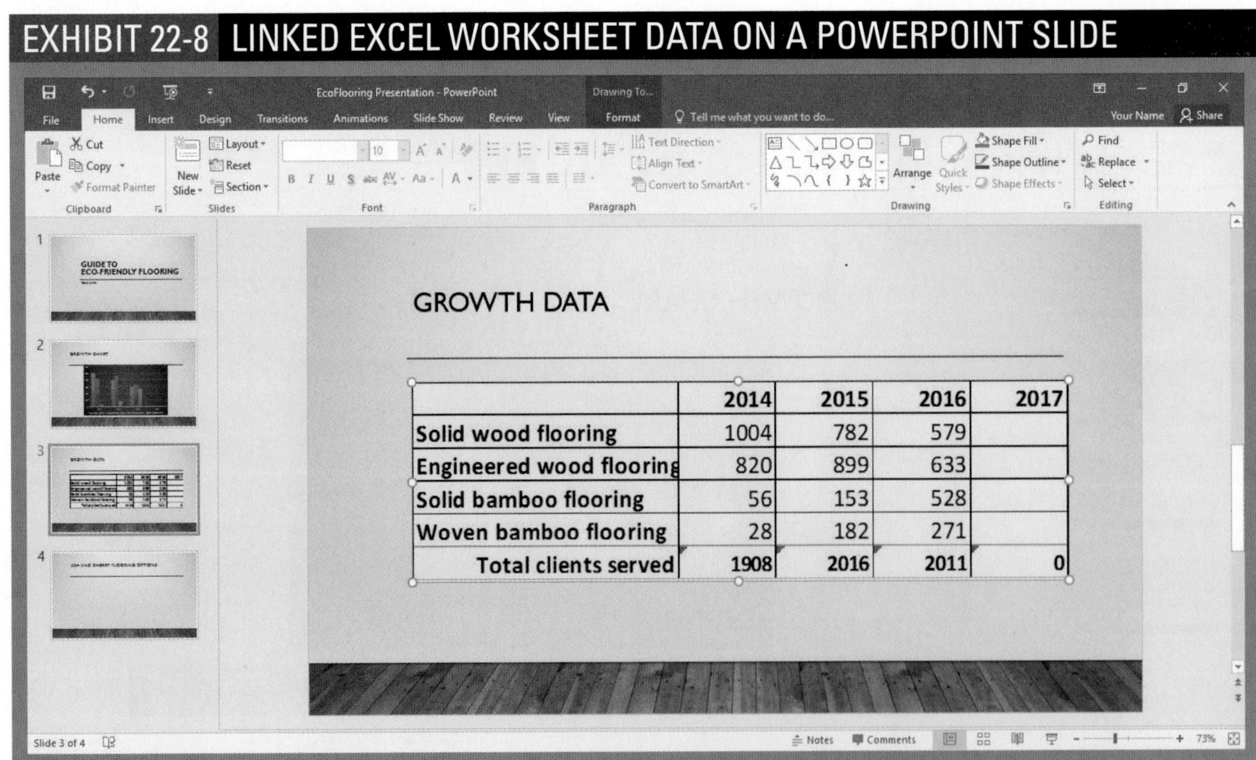

FYI **PASTE OPTIONS VS. THE PASTE SPECIAL DIALOG BOX** Using one of the buttons on the Paste button menu (or on the Paste Options button that appears after you paste an object) allows you to choose to keep the source file theme and formatting or apply the theme and formatting in the destination file, in addition to letting you choose between pasting, embedding, and linking. Using the commands in the Paste Special dialog box offers additional choices for pasting. For example, if you want to paste an Excel table as text, you can choose to paste it as formatted or unformatted text; and if you want to paste a table or chart as an image, you can choose from a few additional file types. You cannot, however, choose to use the source or destination theme formatting. If you choose a formatted option, the copied object will be pasted with the source file formatting; if you choose an unformatted option, the copied object will be pasted as unformatted text or data. Ultimately, the method you use will be determined by exactly what you want to appear in your destination document.

22-1f Updating Linked Objects When the Destination File Is Open

When an object is linked from a source file to a destination file, you can edit the information in the source file, and the changes will appear in the destination file. If both files are open, the changes appear instantaneously. Sometimes linked data does not automatically update, even if both files are open. If the linked object is a chart, you can click the Refresh Data button in the Data group on the Chart Tools Design tab. If the linked object is a worksheet, right-click the linked object in the destination file to open a shortcut menu, and then click Update Link.

Begin Activity

Update linked objects.

1. In the PowerPoint presentation, display **Slide 2** ("Growth Chart") in the Slide pane, and then select the **linked chart**.
2. On the ribbon, click the **Chart Tools Design tab**. In the Data group, click the **Edit Data button**. The original worksheet from which you copied the data, the Growth worksheet in the EcoFlooring Data workbook, becomes the active window.
3. In the Excel window, click **cell E7**, type **613** and then press the **Enter key**. A bar is added to the chart in the Excel worksheet.
4. Switch to the **PowerPoint window**. The new bar containing the data on solid wood flooring for 2017 was added to the chart on Slide 2.
5. Display **Slide 3** ("Growth Data") in the Slide pane. The value you typed in the source file appears in the table on Slide 3.

PROBLEM? If the chart did not update, click the **chart** in the slide, and then on the Chart Tools Design tab, in the Data group, click the **Refresh Data button.**

PROBLEM? If the table did not update, right-click the **table**, and then on the shortcut menu, click **Update Link.**

End Activity

22-1g Updating Linked Objects When the Destination File Is Closed

When you link objects to a file, they are set to update automatically or manually. When you open a destination file that contains a linked object that is set to update automatically, a dialog box opens asking if you want to update the linked data. See Exhibit 22-9. If the linked object is set to be updated manually, no dialog box appears when you open the file, but you can refresh the data or update the link.

EXHIBIT 22-9 MICROSOFT POWERPOINT SECURITY NOTICE DIALOG BOX

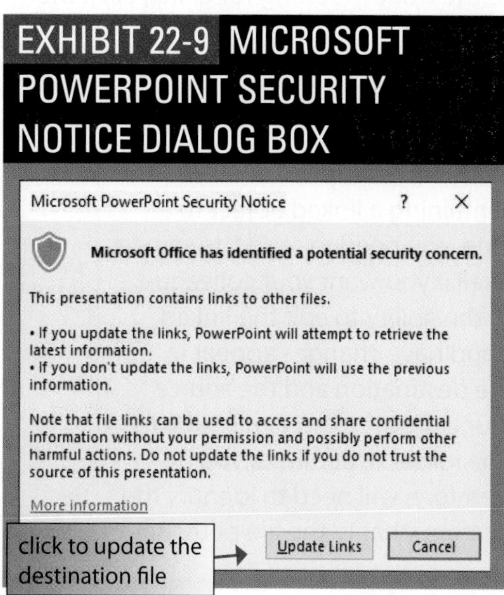

Begin Activity

Edit the linked object when the destination files are closed.

1 Save the PowerPoint file **EcoFlooring Presentation**, and then close it. The Growth worksheet in the EcoFlooring Data workbook becomes the active document.

2 On the Growth worksheet, in **cell E8**, enter **974**, in **cell E9**, enter **279**, and then in **cell E10**, enter **387**.

3 Save the Excel file.

4 Open the PowerPoint file **EcoFlooring Presentation.** A dialog box opens notifying you that the presentation contains links to other files. Refer again to Exhibit 22-9.

5 Click **Update Links.** The dialog box closes and the presentation opens.

6 Display **Slide 3** ("Growth Data") in the Slide pane. The worksheet data is updated with the new values.

7 Display **Slide 2** ("Growth Chart") in the Slide pane. The new columns do not appear above the 2017 label in the chart.

PROBLEM?
If the table did not update, right-click the **table**, and then on the shortcut menu, click **Update Link**.

8 Click the **chart** to select it. On the ribbon, click the **Chart Tools Design tab**. In the Data group, click the **Refresh Data button**. Three bars are added to the 2016 data. Compare your screen to Exhibit 22-10.

9 Save the **EcoFlooring Presentation file.**

End Activity

FYI

USING THE LINKS DIALOG BOX

By default, linked objects are supposed to update automatically; however, sometimes this is not the case. To see if a link is set to update automatically or manually, you can open the Links dialog box. To do this, click the File tab in the destination file to display the Info screen in Backstage view. At the bottom on the right, in the Related Documents section, click the Edit Links to Files link. The Links dialog box opens listing all the links in the file. To change the update setting for a link, click the appropriate setting at the bottom of the dialog box.

You can also use the Links dialog box to change the location of a linked object's source file. For example, if you send a file containing a linked object to a colleague, you need to send the source file as well if you want your colleague to have the ability to edit the linked object and have changes appear in both the destination and the source files. Your colleague likely will not have the same folder structure as you do and, therefore, will need to identify the new location (that is, the file path) of the source file. To do this, in the list of links in the Links dialog box, click the link whose location has changed, click Change Source, and then navigate to the new location of the source file.

Finally, you can break a link in the Links dialog box. This is a good idea if you plan to send the file to someone who will not have access to the linked object's source file. After you break a link, users who open the destination file will not get a message asking if they want to update the links—an impossible task if the users do not have access to the source file. To break a link, select the link in the list in the dialog box, and then click Break Link.

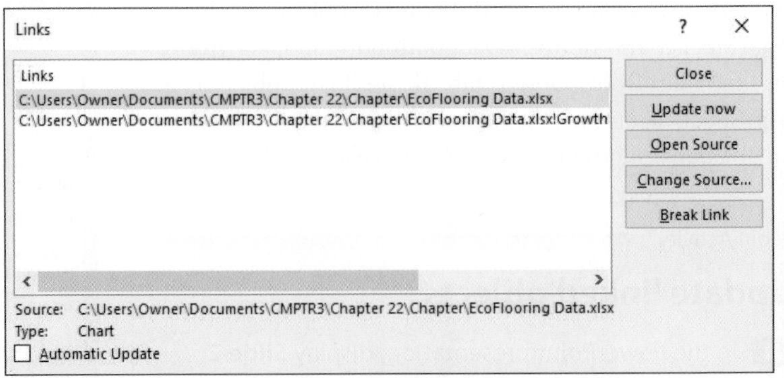

EXHIBIT 22-10 UPDATED LINKED CHART IN THE POWERPOINT PRESENTATION

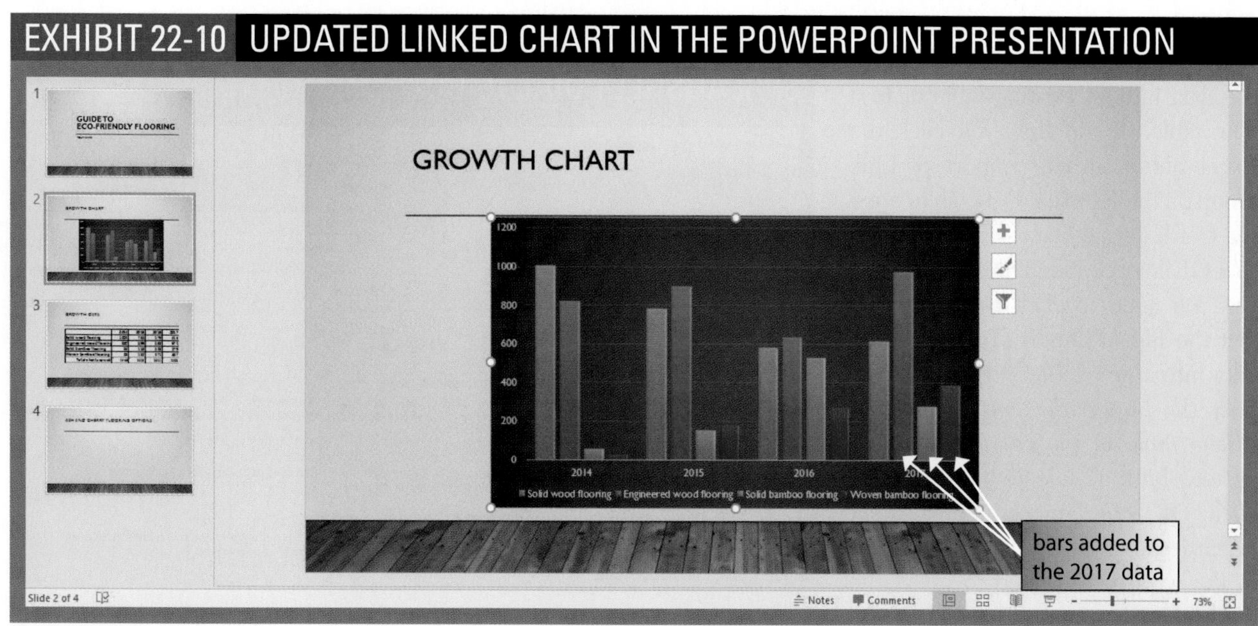

22-2 IMPORTING AND EXPORTING DATA

You might want to use Access commands to analyze data stored in a list in a text file or an Excel worksheet. You cannot embed or link data in an Access datasheet. Instead, you can import data from these files to build a table in Access. Then, you can create forms, reports, queries, and other Access objects based on the tables. You cannot import data directly from a Word file, only from a plain text file. So if data already exists in a Word file, save the file as a plain text file using the Save as type arrow in the Save As dialog box.

22-2a Importing an Excel List into an Access Table

You can only import data that is in the form of a list—a series of paragraphs or worksheet rows that contain related data, such as product names and prices or client names and phone numbers. Before you import the list, you should check the format of the data. The first row of data will become the field names in the new table, so it is important that every column have a heading. Each row of data becomes a record in the database, so there should not be any rows above the column heads and there should not be any blank rows.

Begin Activity

Import an Excel list to an Access table.

1 Switch to the **EcoFlooring Data workbook,** and then click the **Types sheet tab**.

2 Delete **rows 1–3**.

3 In **cell A1**, enter **Species**. Compare your screen to Exhibit 22-11.

4 Save and close the file, and exit Excel.

End Activity

EXHIBIT 22-11 WORKSHEET PREPPED TO IMPORT INTO ACCESS

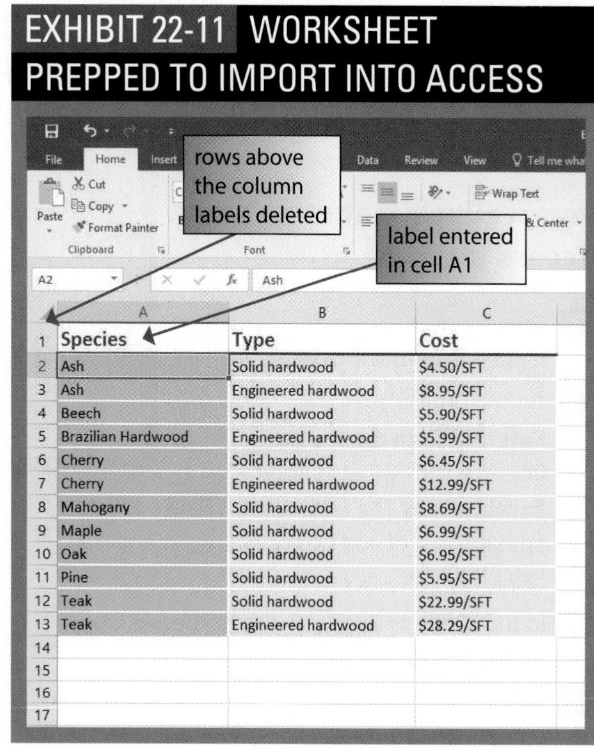

	A	B	C
1	Species	Type	Cost
2	Ash	Solid hardwood	$4.50/SFT
3	Ash	Engineered hardwood	$8.95/SFT
4	Beech	Solid hardwood	$5.90/SFT
5	Brazilian Hardwood	Engineered hardwood	$5.99/SFT
6	Cherry	Solid hardwood	$6.45/SFT
7	Cherry	Engineered hardwood	$12.99/SFT
8	Mahogany	Solid hardwood	$8.69/SFT
9	Maple	Solid hardwood	$6.99/SFT
10	Oak	Solid hardwood	$6.95/SFT
11	Pine	Solid hardwood	$5.95/SFT
12	Teak	Solid hardwood	$22.99/SFT
13	Teak	Engineered hardwood	$28.29/SFT

Once you have prepared the worksheet, you can start Access and import the data into an existing table or to a new table. To do this, you click the Excel button in the Import & Link group on the External Data tab to open the Get External Data – Excel Spreadsheet dialog box. See Exhibit 22-12.

You need to click Browse to select the file to import. To import the data into a new table in the database, keep the *Import the source data into a new table in the current database* option button selected. After you click OK, the Import Spreadsheet Wizard starts. In the first dialog box in the wizard, you need to select the worksheet that contains the data you want to import. The data in the selected worksheet previews in a table at the bottom of the dialog box. See Exhibit 22-13. In the second dialog box in the wizard, you specify whether the first row in the worksheet contains headings. The headings will become the field names in the Access table. After you make this specification, click Next in the next two dialog boxes to accept the defaults. In the last wizard dialog box, you can specify the name for the Access table.

EXHIBIT 22-12 GET EXTERNAL DATA – EXCEL SPREADSHEET DIALOG BOX

Get External Data - Excel Spreadsheet

Select the source and destination of the data

Specify the source of the definition of the objects.

File name: C:\Users\Owner\Documents\

Browse...

Specify how and where you want to store the data in the current database.

Import the source data into a new table in the current database.
If the specified table does not exist, Access will create it. If the specified table already exists, Access might overwrite its contents with the imported data. Changes made to the source data will not be reflected in the database.

Append a copy of the records to the table: Table1
If the specified table exists, Access will add the records to the table. If the table does not exist, Access will create it. Changes made to the source data will not be reflected in the database.

Link to the data source by creating a linked table.
Access will create a table that will maintain a link to the source data in Excel. Changes made to the source data in Excel will be reflected in the linked table. However, the source data cannot be changed from within Access.

OK Cancel

your path might differ

click to browse to the location of the file you want to import

data will be imported into a new table in the database

EXHIBIT 22-13 FIRST DIALOG BOX IN THE IMPORT SPREADSHEET WIZARD

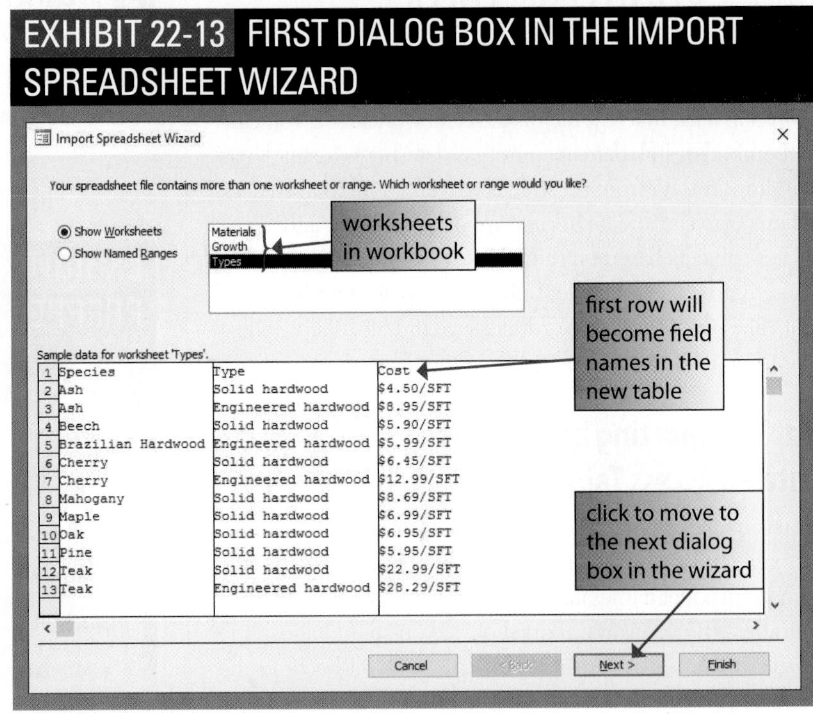

Begin Activity

Import Excel data to an Access table.

1 Create a new Access database named **EcoFlooringTypes**.

2 On the ribbon, click the **External Data tab**. In the Import & Link group, click the **Excel button**. The Get External Data – Excel Spreadsheet dialog box opens. Refer again to Exhibit 22-12.

3 In the dialog box, click **Browse**. The File Open dialog box opens.

4 Navigate to the location where you are storing your files, click the Excel file **EcoFlooring Data**, and then click **Open**. EcoFlooring Data.xlsx and its path are listed in the File name box in the Get External Data – Excel Spreadsheet dialog box. The *Import the source data into a new table in the current database* option button is selected, so the data will be imported into a new table in the database.

5 Click **OK**. The first dialog box in the Import Spreadsheet Wizard opens. At the top, the Show Worksheets option button is selected, and the names of the worksheets in the EcoFlooring Data workbook are listed.

> **PROBLEM?**
> If a Microsoft Access Security Notice dialog box opens warning you that a potential security concern has been identifies, click **Open**.

6 In the list of worksheets, click **Types**. The data below the worksheet list changes to the data in the Types worksheet. Refer again to Exhibit 22-13.

7 Click **Next**. The second dialog box in the wizard opens. The first row in the Excel worksheet contains column headings, so you need to select that option.

8 If it is not already selected, click the **First Row Contains Column Headings check box**. The first row in the table is shaded to indicate that it contains headings.

9 Click **Next**. In the third dialog box in the wizard, you could specify information about the fields you are importing, including the data type of each field.

10 Click **Next** to accept the default field names and other information. The next dialog box in the wizard lets you assign a primary key to the data. The Let Access add primary key option button is selected. Because the worksheet you are importing does not contain information you can convert to a primary key, you will let Access add one to the table.

11 Click **Next** to let Access add a primary key. The final dialog box in the Import Spreadsheet Wizard opens. In the Import to Table box, Types appears, and the *I would like a wizard to analyze my table after importing the data* check box is deselected.

12 Click **Finish**. The Get External Data – Excel Spreadsheet dialog box appears again, displaying the Save Import Steps screen. If you were going to import this table again, you could save the choices you made when you went through the wizard. You don't need to do that in this case, so you'll leave the Save import steps check box unchecked.

13 In the dialog box, click **Close**. The new table appears in the Navigation Pane.

14 In the Navigation Pane, double-click **Types** to open the Types table. The Excel data has been imported into the new Access table. The Excel column headings are converted to field names and the rows to records. Compare your screen to Exhibit 22-14.

15 Close both tables.

End Activity

EXHIBIT 22-14 EXCEL DATA IMPORTED INTO AN ACCESS TABLE

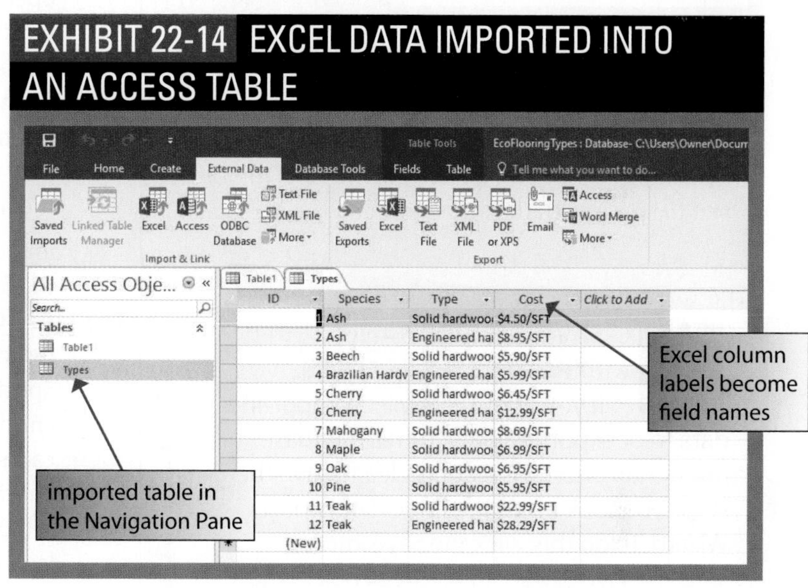

22-2b Exporting Access Data to a Word File

Recall from your work with Access that you use a query to extract information from a database. The query results are stored in a datasheet. You can export the query results to a new text document or Excel worksheet.

Begin Activity

Create a query.

1 Create a query named **AshCherry** that lists only the records with a species of ash or cherry, and shows the Species, Type, and Cost fields for those records.

2 Run the query, and then widen the **Type column** to fit the widest entry. See Exhibit 22-15.

End Activity

EXHIBIT 22-15 RESULTS OF THE ASHCHERRY QUERY

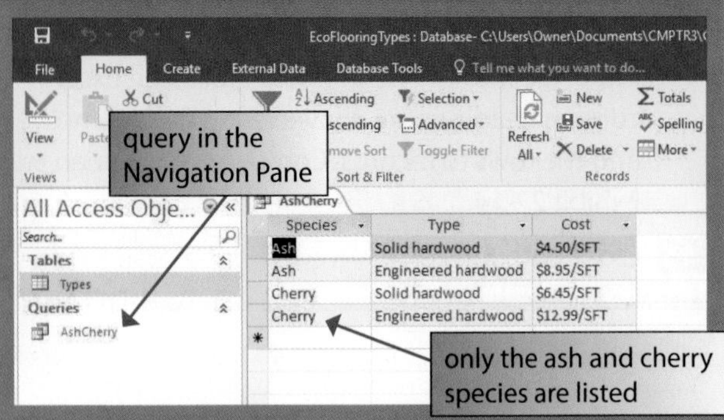

Now that the query is created, you can export the results to a text file. To export to a text file, you can choose the Text file type, which creates a document with unformatted text, or **Rich Text Format (RTF)**, a text format that preserves the formatting and layout of data.

FYI SAVING IMPORT AND EXPORT STEPS IN ACCESS

If you know you will be importing data to or exporting data from a database more than once, it is a good idea to save the steps you took using the Import or Export Wizard. To do this, click the Save import steps or Save export steps check box in the corresponding screen in the Get External Data or Export dialog boxes. When you select this check box, the dialog box changes to display boxes that allow you to name the saved operation and add a description to remind you of the details of the operation. After you have saved a set of import or export steps, you can access them by clicking the External Data tab, and then clicking the Saved Imports button in the Import & Link group or the Saved Exports button in the Export group. When you do, the Manage Data Tasks dialog box opens. You can then click the Saved Imports or Saved Exports tab to see each list of saved operations. To run the selected operation, click Run in the dialog box.

Rich Text Format (RTF) A text format that preserves the formatting and layout of data.

Begin Activity

Export the Access data to a Word file.

1. In the Navigation Pane, click the **AshCherry query** to select it.
2. On the ribbon, click the **External Data tab**. In the Export group, click the **More button**, and then click **Word**. The Export – RTF File dialog box opens. It is similar to the dialog box that opened when you imported data from Excel. In the File name box, the path is to the location where you are storing your files, and the file name of the new file is AshCherry.rtf.

TIP: If you don't need to preserve the layout of your data, export the table or query to a plain text file by clicking the Text File button in the Export group on the External Data tab.

3. In the File name box, change the file name AshCherry.rtf to **Ash Cherry Table.rtf** (leave the rest of the file path as is). Under Specify export options, the first check box is selected and you cannot click it to remove the check mark. With this check box selected, the formatting and layout of the data in the query datasheet will be preserved. You cannot change it because you are exporting to an RTF document, so the layout and formatting will remain as originally designed.

PROBLEM? If you can't see the last character because the path is too long, click anywhere in the File name box, and then press and hold the **Right Arrow key** until the insertion point moves to the end of the file name.

4. Click the **Open the destination file after the export operation is complete check box** to select it. Now the new file will open automatically after you close this dialog box.
5. Click **OK**. Access converts the query results into an RTF file and opens the new file in Word.
6. Close the **Word file**. The Export – RTF File dialog box is still open in Access with the Save Export Steps screen displayed. As in the Save Import Steps screen you saw earlier, you can click the Save export steps check box, and then save the steps you took to export the query. You don't need to do this.
7. Click **Close**. The dialog box closes.

End Activity

USING THE OBJECT COMMAND IN WORD, EXCEL, AND POWERPOINT

The Object button in the Text group on the Insert tab in Word, Excel, and PowerPoint allows you to insert the contents of one file into another file. If you use the Object command and then click the Create from File tab, you can select a file and then choose to embed or link that file. If you do this, the entire file is inserted as an object in the destination file. Note that in Word, you can also use the Text from File command on the Object button menu to insert only the text of another text file into the destination document.

Begin Activity

Insert the text of a file into a different Word file.

1 Open the Word data file **Letter**, located in the Chapter 22\Chapter folder. Save it as **EcoFlooring Letter**. Change the zoom to **120%**, if necessary.

2 In the body of the letter, delete the **yellow highlighted text**.

3 On the ribbon, click the **Insert tab**. In the Text group, click the **Object button arrow**, and then click **Text from File**. The Insert File dialog box opens.

4 Navigate to the folder where you are storing the files you create, click **Ash Cherry Table**, and then click **Insert**. The Query results are inserted into the document as a table.

TIP: You could also open the RTF file in a Word window, copy the table, and then paste it into the destination document.

5 Click anywhere in the **table**.

6 On the ribbon, click the **Table Tools Design tab**. In the Table Style Options group, select the **Header Row check box**, and deselect the **Banded Rows** and **Banded Columns check boxes**.

7 Apply the **List Table 4 – Accent 6 table style** (the last style in the fourth row under List Tables in the Table Styles gallery).

8 Select the **table**, and then center the table horizontally.

9 Delete **one of the blank paragraphs** below the table. Compare your screen to Exhibit 22-16.

10 In the closing at the end of the letter, replace *Aaron Greenburg* with your name, and then save the document.

End Activity

COPYING AND PASTING AMONG OFFICE PROGRAMS

If you want to use Access data in a PowerPoint slide, you cannot export it directly to a slide. You can, however, use Copy and Paste commands to copy data from a datasheet, and then paste it to a PowerPoint slide as a table.

Begin Activity

Copy and paste Access data to a PowerPoint slide.

1 Switch to the Access database **EcoFlooringTypes**. The AshCherry query is still open.

2 To the left of the Species column heading, click the **selector box** ▢. All the records in the query results datasheet are selected.

EXHIBIT 22-16 QUERY RESULTS INSERTED AS A TABLE IN THE BROCHURE

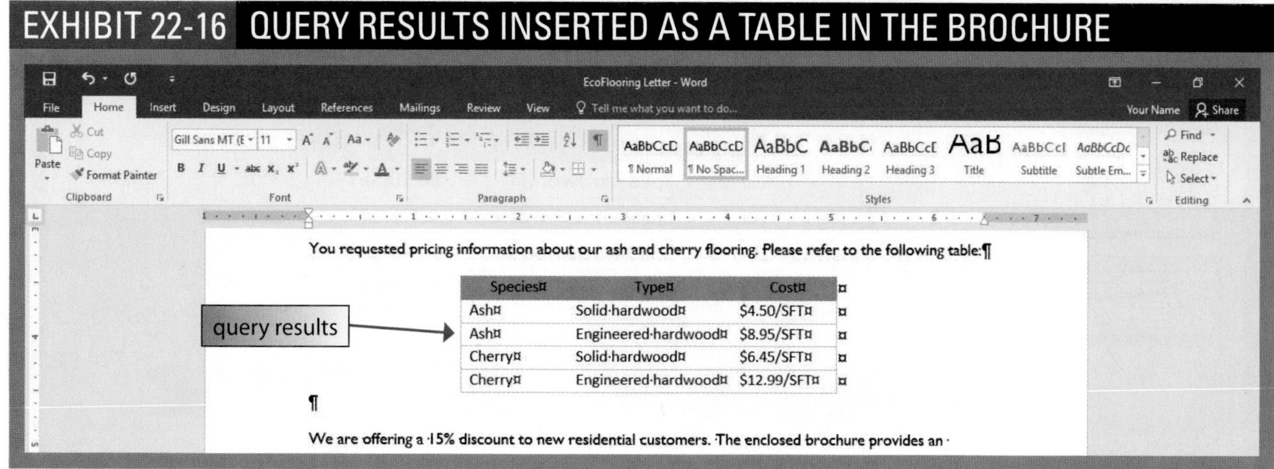

3 On the ribbon, click the **Home tab**. In the Clipboard group, click the **Copy button**. The selected query results are copied to the Clipboard.

4 Switch to the PowerPoint file **EcoFlooring Presentation**. Display **Slide 4** ("Ash and Cherry Flooring Options") in the Slide pane.

5 In the Slide pane, click in the **blank area below the title**.

6 On the Home tab, in the Clipboard group, click the **Paste button arrow**, point to each button to see its effect, and then click the **Use Destination Theme button** . PowerPoint inserts the query results in a table on the slide.

> **TIP:**
> Remember that you can use the Office Clipboard to collect text and objects from various files so that you can paste them later.

7 In the table, click in the **first row** (containing *AshCherry*).

8 On the ribbon, click the **Table Tools Layout tab**. In the Rows & Columns group, click the **Delete button**, and then click **Delete Rows**. The first row in the table is deleted.

9 Click the **table border** to select the entire table. Change the font size of the table text to **28 points**.

10 Specify that the **Header row** is to be treated differently, and then apply the **Medium Style 1 – Accent 1 table style**.

11 AutoFit each column in the table. Center the table in the area under the slide title. Compare your screen to Exhibit 22-17.

> **PROBLEM?**
> If you can't AutoFit the third column by double-clicking the right border of the column, click in the **third column**, then on the Table Tools Layout tab, in the the Cell Size group, click in the **Width box**, type **2.2**, and then press the **Enter key.**

12 Save the presentation.

13 Switch to the Access database **EcoFlooring Types**, close the **AshCherry query**, saving changes if prompted, and then exit Access.

End Activity

22-5 CREATING POWERPOINT SLIDES FROM A WORD OUTLINE

If you have an outline in a Word document, you can use that outline to create PowerPoint slides. When you create slides from a Word outline, PowerPoint uses the heading styles in the Word document to determine how to format the text. Each paragraph formatted with the Heading 1 style becomes the title of a new slide, each

EXHIBIT 22-17 FORMATTED DATA FROM THE ACCESS QUERY ON THE POWERPOINT SLIDE

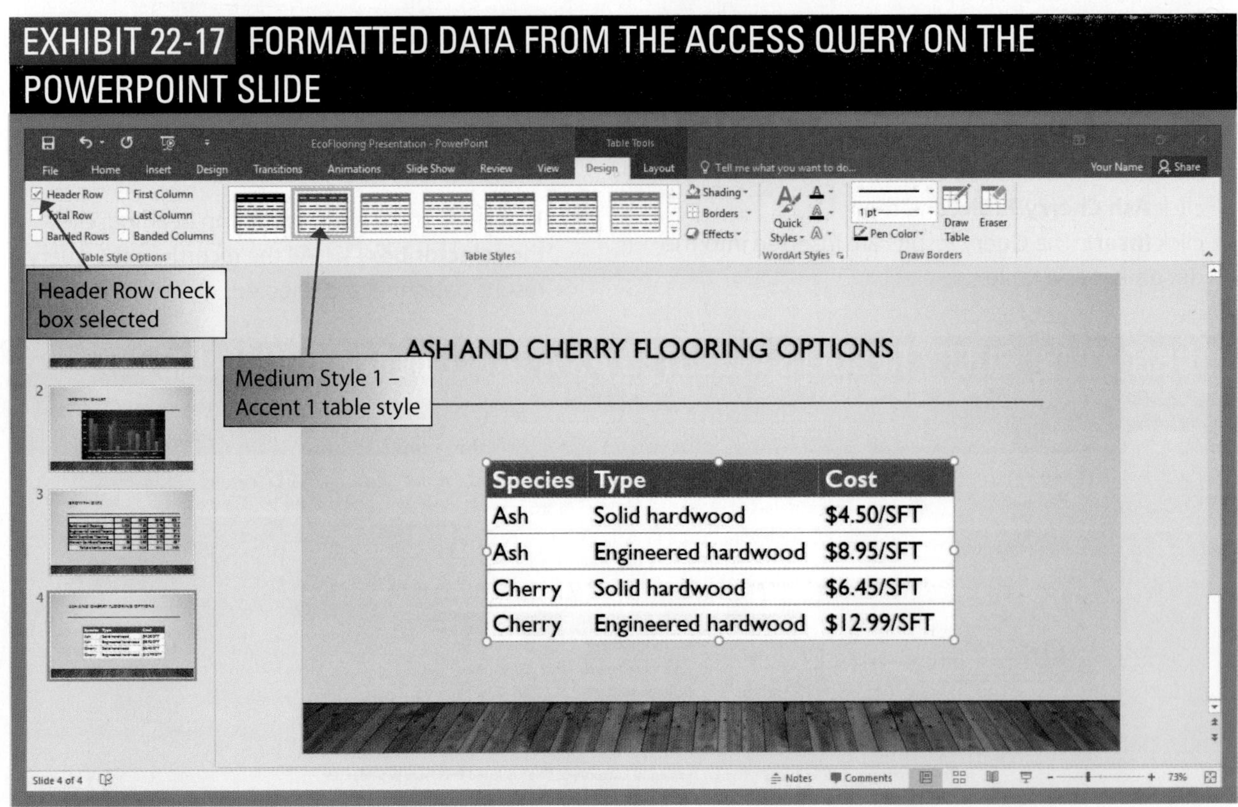

paragraph formatted with the Heading 2 style becomes a first level bulleted item on a slide, and so on.

When you create slides from an outline, PowerPoint inserts them after the current slide. If the document containing the outline is formatted with a theme different from the theme applied to the presentation, you might need to reset the slides to force them to use the theme formatting in the presentation. When you reset slides, you reset the position, size, and formatting of the slide placeholders to match the settings in the slide masters.

Begin Activity

Create PowerPoint slides from a Word outline.

1. Open the Word data file **EcoOutline** located in the Chapter 22\Chapter folder.
2. Switch to **Outline view**. Examine the structure of the document. Close the **EcoOutline document**.
3. Switch to the PowerPoint file **EcoFlooring Presentation**. Display **Slide 1** (the title slide).
4. On the Home tab, in the Slides group, click the **New Slide button arrow**, and then click **Slides from Outline**. The Insert Outline dialog box opens.
5. Navigate to the **Chapter 22\Chapter folder**, click **EcoOutline**, and then click **Insert**. PowerPoint inserts and formats the text of the Word outline to create Slides 2 through 9.
6. Display **Slide 9** in the Slide pane. Slide 9 does not contain any text because there was a blank paragraph at the end of the Word outline.
7. In the Slides pane, right-click the **Slide 9 thumbnail**, and then click **Delete Slide**. The blank slide is deleted.
8. Display **Slide 8** ("Summary") in the Slide pane. The slide text is a different color and style than the text on the other slides. This is because the document containing the outline was formatted with a different theme than the presentation.
9. Press and hold the **Shift key**, and then scroll up in the Slides pane and click the **Slide 2 thumbnail**. Slides 2 through 8 are selected.
10. On the Home tab, in the Slides group, click the **Reset button**. The slides are reformatted with the theme used in the presentation.
11. Rearrange the slides in the presentation as follows:
    - Move **Slide 10** ("Growth Data") so it becomes **Slide 3**.
    - Move the new **Slide 10** ("Growth Chart") so it becomes **Slide 4**.
    - Move **Slide 11** ("Ash and Cherry Flooring Options") so it becomes **Slide 7**.
12. Switch to **Slide Sorter view**. Change the zoom level to **70%**. Compare your screen to Exhibit 22-18.
13. Save the presentation, and then close the presentation and exit PowerPoint.

End Activity

EXHIBIT 22-18 FINAL PRESENTATION IN SLIDE SORTER VIEW

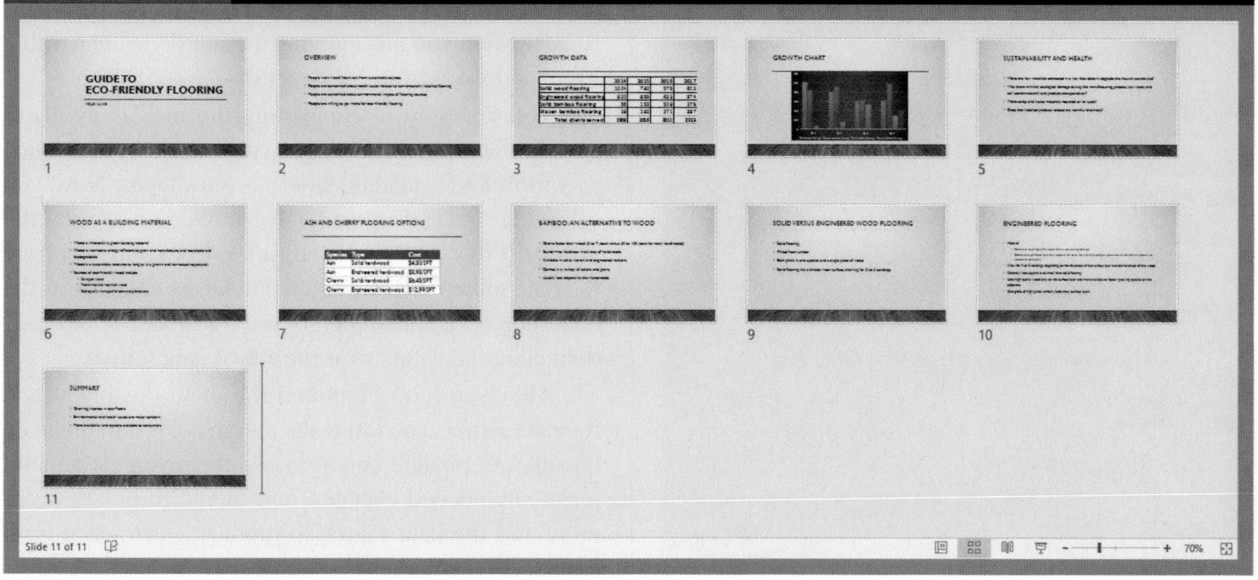

EXHIBIT 22-19 PLAN FOR THE FORM LETTER

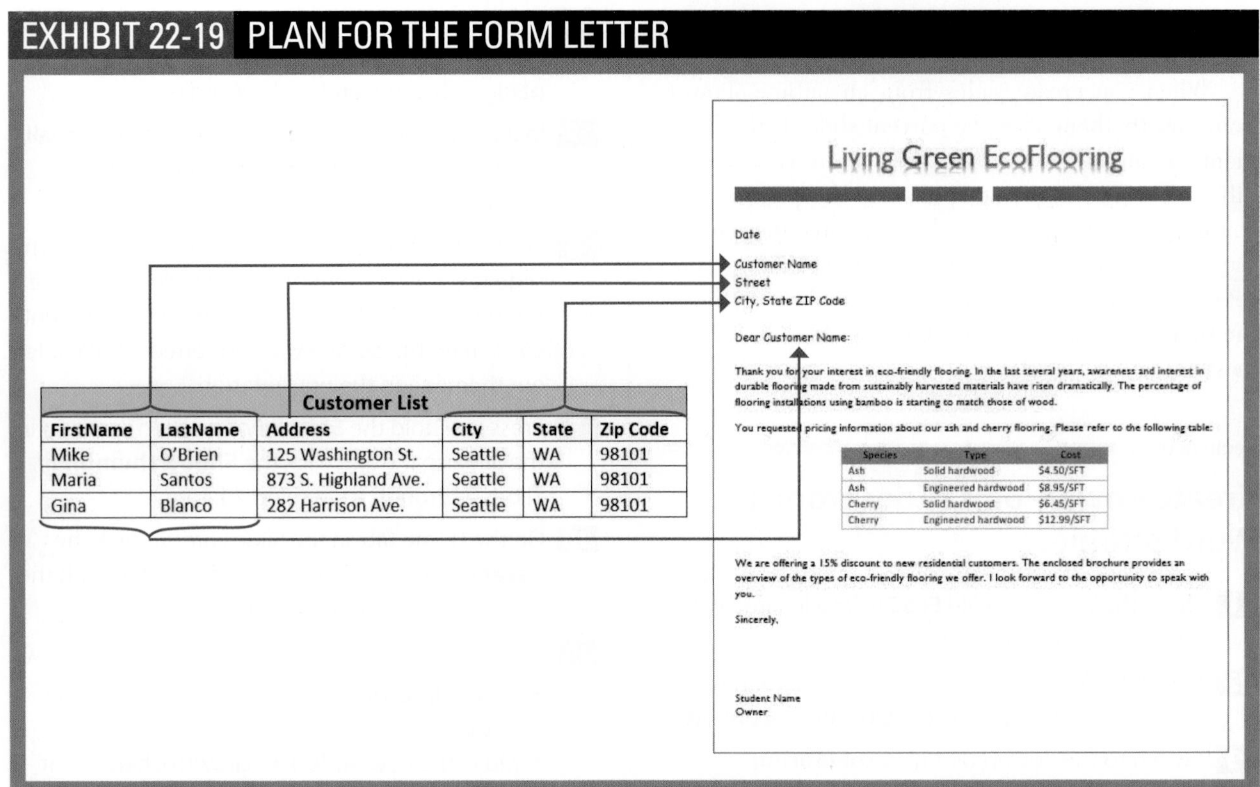

Customer List					
FirstName	LastName	Address	City	State	Zip Code
Mike	O'Brien	125 Washington St.	Seattle	WA	98101
Maria	Santos	873 S. Highland Ave.	Seattle	WA	98101
Gina	Blanco	282 Harrison Ave.	Seattle	WA	98101

Living Green EcoFlooring

Date

Customer Name
Street
City, State ZIP Code

Dear Customer Name:

Thank you for your interest in eco-friendly flooring. In the last several years, awareness and interest in durable flooring made from sustainably harvested materials have risen dramatically. The percentage of flooring installations using bamboo is starting to match those of wood.

You requested pricing information about our ash and cherry flooring. Please refer to the following table:

Species	Type	Cost
Ash	Solid hardwood	$4.50/SFT
Ash	Engineered hardwood	$8.95/SFT
Cherry	Solid hardwood	$6.45/SFT
Cherry	Engineered hardwood	$12.99/SFT

We are offering a 15% discount to new residential customers. The enclosed brochure provides an overview of the types of eco-friendly flooring we offer. I look forward to the opportunity to speak with you.

Sincerely,

Student Name
Owner

22-6 CREATING FORM LETTERS WITH MAIL MERGE

A **form letter** is a Word document that contains standard paragraphs of text and a minimum of variable text, such as the names and addresses of the letter's recipients. The **main document** of a form letter contains the text and other information (including punctuation, spaces, and graphics) that you want to keep the same in each letter. It also includes **merge fields**, which contain instructions for replacing the field placeholder with the variable information that changes from one letter to another. The variable information is contained in a **data source**, which can be a Word table, an Access database, or another source. When you **merge** the main document with the data source, Word replaces the merge fields with the appropriate information from the data source. See Exhibit 22-19. The term **mail merge** is used when you are merging a main document with a list of addresses from a data source.

The first step in completing the mail merge is to specify the type of document you want to create, such as a form letter, mailing labels, or envelopes. Next, you select the main document, which Word also calls the **starting document**. Then, you select recipients from the data source. When you use an Access database as the data source for a mail merge, you select a table or query defined in the database as the actual data source.

After you have identified the main document and the data source, you insert the merge fields into the main document. Finally, you preview the main document, make any needed changes, and merge the main document and the data source to produce customized form letters.

form letter A Word document that contains standard paragraphs of text and a minimum of variable text.

main document A document that contains the text and other information that you want to keep the same in each form letter.

merge field A field that contains instructions to be replaced with the variable information that changes from one letter to another.

data source In a mail merge, a file that contains the variable information for form letters.

merge To combine, such as a main document with a data source.

mail merge To merge a main document with a list of addresses from a data source.

starting document The main document in a Word mail merge.

To perform a mail merge, you can use buttons on the Mailings tab on the ribbon or you can use the Mail Merge Wizard, which appears in a task pane to the right of the Word window. The Mail Merge wizard is helpful; but if you work from left to right on the Mailings tab, you should have no trouble creating a main document with the correct merge fields, and then performing the merge.

22-6a Selecting a Main Document and Data Source

The main document of a mail merge can be a new or an existing Word document. In this case, the starting document is the letter to potential customers. You will begin by starting Word and opening the main document, and selecting the list of recipients.

Begin Activity

Select the main document and data source for a mail merge.

1 If necessary, on the taskbar, click the **EcoFlooring Letter - Word button** to display the **EcoFlooring Letter**. Scroll to the top of the document.

2 On the ribbon, click the **Mailings tab**. Notice that only a few buttons on the Mailings tab are available. The other buttons will become available as you set up the mail merge.

3 In the Start Mail Merge group, click the **Start Mail Merge button**. A menu opens with Normal Word Document selected. You want to merge a letter, but you can also create email messages, envelopes, labels, or a directory of all the names in the data source.

TIP: To be guided step-by-step through the mail merge process, click the Start Mail Merge button in the Start Mail Merge group on the Mailings tab, and then click Step-by-Step Mail Merge Wizard.

4 Click **Letters** to specify that you want to merge a letter. The next step is to select the recipients of the letter. You want to select recipients from an existing list in an Access database.

5 In the Start Mail Merge group, click the **Select Recipients button**, and then click **Use an Existing List**. The Select Data Source dialog box opens, displaying a list of possible data sources.

6 Navigate to the **Chapter 22\Chapter folder**, click the Access file **Clients**, and then click **Open**. Because the data source is an Access database, the Select Table dialog box opens listing all the objects in the selected database (this database contains one table and one query). You need to choose a table or query in the selected database as the data source. If the database contained only one table, the Select Table dialog box would not open; instead, the Mail Merge Recipients dialog box would open immediately after you selected the database.

7 Click the **Clients table** to select it, and then click **OK**. The dialog box closes and the Edit Recipient List button, as well as several others, is now available on the ribbon.

End Activity

You can edit the recipient list before completing the merge. To do this, click the Edit Recipient List button in the Start Mail Merge group on the Mailings tab to open the Mail Merge Recipients dialog box. See Exhibit 22-20.

EXHIBIT 22-20 MAIL MERGE RECIPIENTS DIALOG BOX

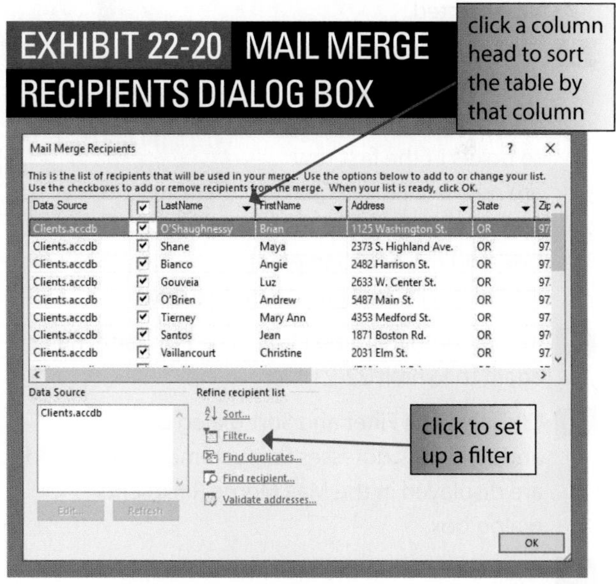

In this dialog box, you can narrow the list by deselecting records individually. You can also sort the list or filter it to include only records that meet specific criteria of recipients. To sort the list by a single column, you can click the column heading arrow and then click one of the Sort commands. To filter the list, click the Filter link at the bottom of the dialog box to open the Filter and Sort dialog box. In this dialog box, you select the field on which you want to filter, select the comparison operator, and then fill in the text in which to compare the field value. See Exhibit 22-21.

EXHIBIT 22-21 FILTER RECORDS TAB IN THE FILTER AND SORT DIALOG BOX

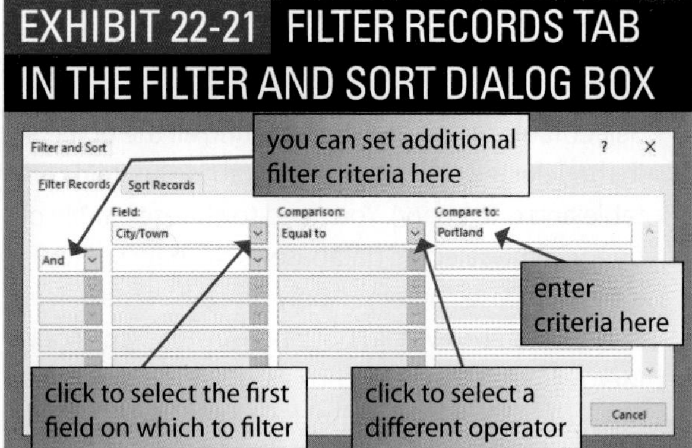

Begin Activity

Edit the recipient list.

1 In the Start Mail Merge group, click the **Edit Recipient List button**. The Mail Merge Recipients dialog box opens. Refer again to Exhibit 22-20.

2 At the bottom of the dialog box, click the **Filter link**. The Filter and Sort dialog box opens with the Filter Records tab selected.

3 Click the **Field arrow**, and then click **City/Town**. The Comparison and Compare to boxes in the first row are now available. Equal to appears in the Comparison box, and the insertion point is blinking in the Compare to text box.

4 In the Compare to text box, type **Portland**. Refer again to Exhibit 22-21.

5 Click **OK**. The Filter and Sort dialog box closes and only the addresses for customers in Portland are displayed in the Mail Merge Recipients dialog box.

6 Click **OK** to close the Mail Merge Recipients dialog box.

End Activity

22-6b Inserting the Merge Fields

As noted earlier, a merge field is a special instruction that tells Word where to insert the variable information from the data source into the main document. For example, right now the letter does not have an inside address (the address for the recipient) at the top, as business letters usually do, so you will insert a merge field to tell Word what information to pull from the data source. You will insert the Address block and Greeting line merge fields in the EcoFlooring Letter document. You then will check the merge fields to make sure they correspond with the fields in the Customer table.

The Address Block merge field inserts each recipient's first and last names, address, city and state in a single merge field. It can also include the recipient's company name. When you click the Address Block button in the Write & Insert Fields group on the Mailings tab, the Insert Address Block dialog box opens, as shown in Exhibit 22-22.

EXHIBIT 22-22 INSERT ADDRESS BLOCK DIALOG BOX

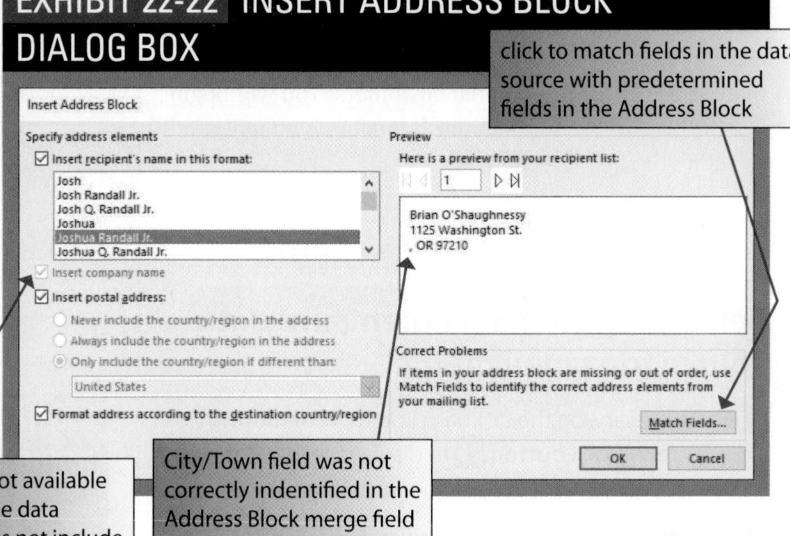

You use this dialog box to choose the format of the recipient's name and to specify whether to include the company name and country in the address. The Preview box on the right shows you a preview of how the address block will look with data from your recipient list. The default format of first and last name is selected in the list on the left. Word tries to match fields in a recipient list with predetermined fields in the Address Block, but sometimes you need to explicitly identify a field. If Word cannot match the fields, you need to click Match Fields to open the Match Fields dialog box. See Exhibit 22-23. On the left are the fields Word expects in the Address Block. On the right are the fields in the data source. Click an arrow in the list on the right and select the correct field in the list.

Begin Activity

Insert merge fields into a main document.

1 Below the date in the letter, click in the **blank paragraph**. This is where the recipient's name and address will appear.

EXHIBIT 22-23 MATCH FIELDS DIALOG BOX

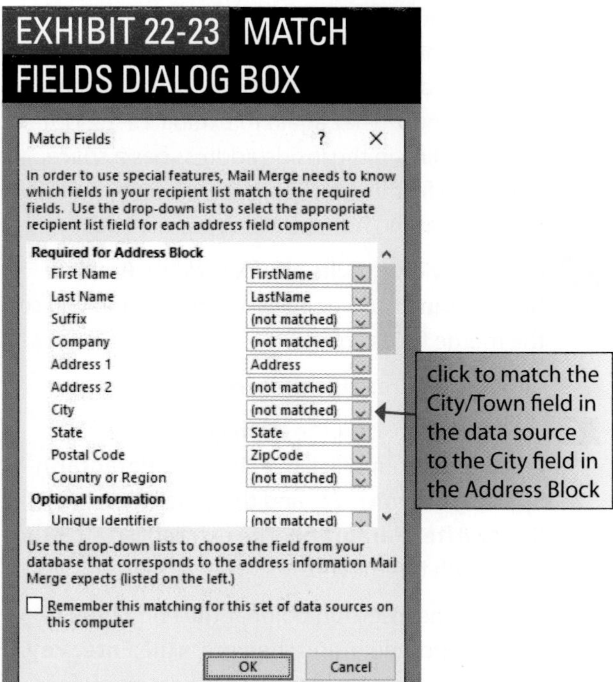

2 On the Mailings tab, in the Write & Insert Fields group, click the **Address Block button**. The Insert Address Block dialog box opens. Refer again to Exhibit 22-22. In this case, Word did not find a match for the City field in the Address Block.

> **TIP:** Click the Insert Merge Field button to insert merge fields individually instead of a block of fields, as with the Address Block and Greeting Line fields.

3 In the Correct Problems section of the dialog box, click **Match Fields**. The Match Fields dialog box opens. Refer again to Exhibit 22-23. You want to match the City field in the Address Block with the City/Town field in the Access table.

4 Click the **City arrow**, and then click **City/Town**.

5 Click **OK**. The Match Fields dialog box closes. The Preview area in the Insert Address Block dialog box now displays the city as part of the address.

> **PROBLEM?**
> If a dialog box opens warning the built-in Unique Identifier field might be available to people who read your document, click **Yes**.

6 Click **OK** to close the Insert Address Block dialog box. The Address block merge field appears in the main document between double chevrons (« »). Now that there is a merge field in the letter, a few more buttons on the Mailings tab are available.

> **PROBLEM?**
> If the Address block merge field appears between curly braces and includes additional text, such as {ADDRESSBLOCK \f}, field codes are displayed. Click the **File tab**, click **Options** in the navigation bar, click **Advanced** in the navigation pane, scroll down the list on the right, and then, in the Show document content section, deselect the **Show field codes instead of their values check box**.

End Activity

Next you need to insert a greeting line to personalize the salutation. When you click the Greeting Line button in the Write & Insert Fields group on the Mailings tab, the Insert Greeting Line dialog box opens. See Exhibit 22-24. The Greeting line format and the Preview at the bottom of the dialog box show how Word will insert the salutation. The Greeting line for invalid recipient names box shows how the greeting will appear if a name is missing from the data source.

EXHIBIT 22-24 INSERT GREETING LINE DIALOG BOX

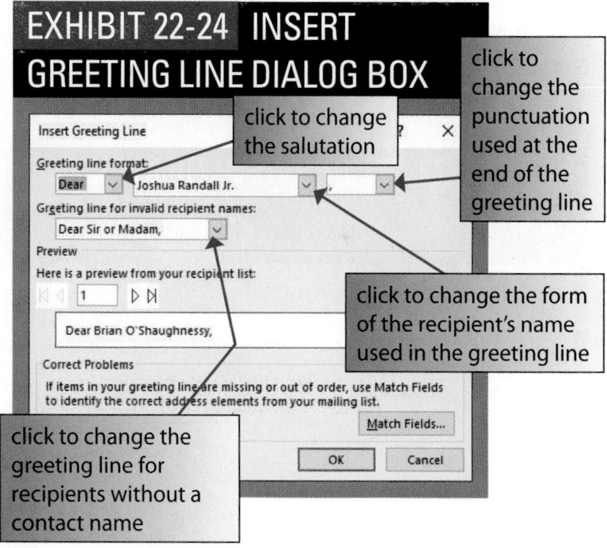

Begin Activity

Insert the Greeting Line merge field.

1 In the salutation, delete **Dear Sustainable Partner:** (including the colon).

2 On the Mailings tab, in the Write & Insert Fields group, click the **Greeting Line button**. The Insert Greeting Line dialog box opens. Refer again to Exhibit 22-24. The Greeting line format and the Preview at the bottom of the dialog box show that Word will insert *Dear* followed by the recipient's entire name, and then a comma.

3 In the Greeting line format section, click the **third arrow**, and then click : (the colon). The change is reflected in the Preview section. You can accept the other options in the Greeting Line dialog box to begin the salutation with *Dear* and to use *Dear Sir or Madam* for records in the Clients table that do not include a contact name.

4 Click **OK**. Word inserts the Greeting Line merge field in the main document.

5 Save the document.

End Activity

22-6c Previewing the Mail Merge and Checking for Errors

With the starting document and merge fields in place, you're ready to perform the mail merge. First you should preview the merge. To do this, click the Preview Results button in the Preview Results group on the Mailings tab. If the Address Block merge field is inserted in a paragraph that has extra space after it, the results will show the inside address with space between each line. See Exhibit 22-25. To fix this, you need to change the format of the paragraph containing the Address Block merge field.

EXHIBIT 22-25 PREVIEW OF MAIL MERGE

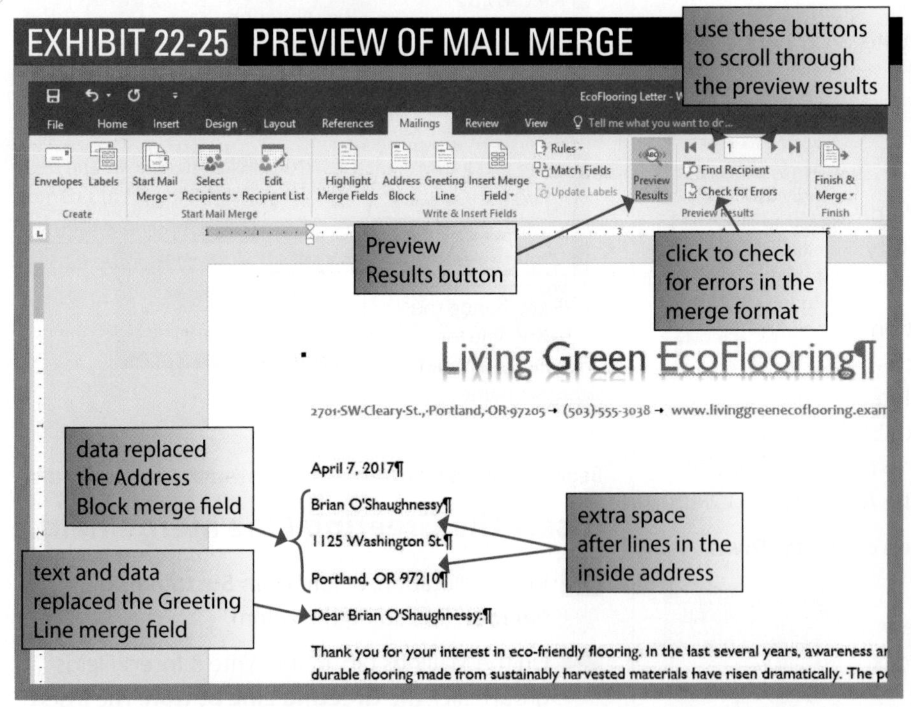

Begin Activity

Preview a merged document and fix the Address Block paragraph formatting.

1 On the Mailings tab, in the Preview Results group, click the **Preview Results button**. The first merged form letter appears with Brian O'Shaughnessy as the first recipient. This is the first letter, as indicated by the "1" in the Preview Results group. Refer again to Exhibit 22-25. Notice that each line in the inside address has a space after it. To fix this, you'll turn off the preview and then format the Address Block merge field.

2 In the Preview Results group, click the **Preview Results button**. The preview turns off and you see the merge fields again.

3 Click the **Address Block merge field**.

4 On the ribbon, click the **Home tab**. In the Paragraph group, click the **Line and Paragraph Spacing button**, and then click **Remove Space After Paragraph**. The extra space after the paragraph is removed.

5 Position the insertion point at the end of the Address Block line, and then press the **Enter key**. This inserts a single blank line (a paragraph formatted with no extra space after it) between the last line of the inside address and the salutation.

6 On the ribbon, click the **Mailings tab**. In the Preview Results group, click the **Preview Results button**. Brian O'Shaughnessy's information appears in the letter properly formatted.

7 In the Preview Results group, click the **Next Record button** to preview the next recipient. The letter to Maya Shane appears.

End Activity

It is also a good idea to use the Check for Errors command to check the main document for errors. When you select this command, a dialog box opens in which you choose to simulate the merge and list the errors in a new document or to complete the merge, reporting each error as it is found in a new document after the merge is completed. See Exhibit 22-26. The option that simulates the merge is the safest as it allows you to easily modify the main document to correct the errors.

EXHIBIT 22-26 CHECKING AND REPORTING ERRORS DIALOG BOX

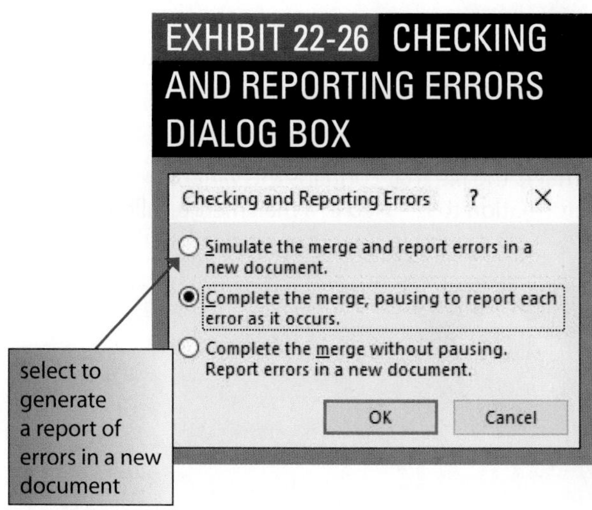

Begin Activity

Check a main document for errors.

1 On the Mailings tab, in the Preview Results group, click the **Check for Errors button**. The Checking and Reporting Errors dialog box opens. Refer again to Exhibit 22-26.

2 Click the **Simulate the merge and report errors in a new document option button**.

3 Click **OK**. After a moment, another dialog box opens reporting that no mail merge errors were found.

4 Click **OK** to close the dialog box.

End Activity

22-6d Finishing the Mail Merge

After you have inserted all of the merge fields, previewed the merge, and checked the document for errors, you can finish the merge. To do this, you click the Finish & Merge button in the Finish group on the Mailings tab. On the menu that opens, you can choose to print the form letters, send them as email messages, or save the completed letters to a new document so that you can print them later. If you merge the letters to a new Word document, you can proofread the final letters before printing all of them.

Begin Activity

Finish a mail merge.

1 On the Mailings tab, in the Finish group, click the **Finish & Merge button**, and then click **Edit Individual Documents**. The Merge to New Document dialog box opens.

2 If it is not already selected, click the **All option button**, and then click **OK**. A new document opens with the temporary name "Letters" followed by a number. This 13-page document contains one letter for each contact who lives in Portland.

3 Scroll through the merged document to see the merged addresses and salutations.

4 Save the document as **Merged Letters**.

5 Close the document. The EcoFlooring Letter main letter document is the current document again.

6 On the Mailings tab, in the Preview Results group, click the **Preview Results button** to toggle it off.

7 Save the document, close it, and then exit Word.

End Activity

FYI

PERFORMING A MAIL MERGE WITH AN EMAIL MESSAGE

You can make the most of your email correspondence by merging your Outlook Contacts with an email message. To do this, on the Mailings tab, in the Start Mail Merge group, click E-mail Messages on the Start Mail Merge button menu, click the Select Recipients button, and then click Choose from Outlook Contacts. Using the Mail Merge Recipients dialog box, you can filter the contacts to include only those people to whom you want to send your message. After you compose your message, click the Finish & Merge button, and then click Send E-mail Messages. This opens the Merge to E-mail dialog box in which you can type the subject for your email message. After you click OK, Word creates new email messages addressed to each person in your recipients list and places them in your Outlook Outbox, ready to send the next time you send email messages.

©U.P.images_vector/Shutterstock.com

STUDY TOOLS 22

READY TO STUDY? IN THE BOOK, YOU CAN:

- ☐ Rip out the Chapter Review Card, which includes key terms and key chapter concepts.

ONLINE AT WWW.CENGAGEBRAIN.COM, YOU CAN:

- ☐ Review key concepts from the chapter in a short video.
- ☐ Explore integrating Word, Excel, Access, and PowerPoint with the interactive infographic.
- ☐ Practice what you've learned with more Practice It and On Your Own exercises.
- ☐ Prepare for tests with quizzes.
- ☐ Review the key terms with flashcards.

QUIZ YOURSELF

1. What is the difference between embedding an object and linking an object?
2. When an object is embedded, how many copies of the object exist?
3. If an Excel chart is linked to a Word document, which is the source program?
4. What happens if you make changes to a linked object in the destination file?
5. How do you use Excel data in an Access table without using the Copy and Paste commands?
6. What does RTF stand for?
7. How do you insert text from a text file into another Word file without using the Copy and Paste commands?
8. How can you use data from an Access datasheet in a PowerPoint slide without first exporting it to another file format?
9. Describe the slide or slides that PowerPoint would create from a Word outline that has one Level 1 paragraph and three Level 2 paragraphs.
10. After importing a Word outline, how do you change the format of a slide so that it matches the theme used in the presentation?
11. In a mail merge, what is a merge field?
12. What is the file that contains the variable information to be used in a mail merge called?

PRACTICE IT

Practice It 22-1

1. Open the Word data file **CC Flyer** located in the Chapter 22\Practice It folder. Save the document as **Coastline CC Flyer.**
2. In the fourth paragraph, replace the yellow highlighted text with an embedded pie chart that you create from within the Word document. Use the following as data for the chart:

Biology	**359**
Business	**1645**
Chemistry	**471**
English	**1012**
Health	**724**
Hospitality & Tourism	**549**

3. In the chart object in the Word document, change the chart title to **Distribution of Students by Department**. Add data labels to the center of the pie slices that identify the percentage of each slice, and display the legend on the right.
4. Open the Excel data file **CC Info** located in the Chapter 22\Practice It folder. Save the workbook as **Coastline CC Info.**
5. On the Student Data worksheet, copy the column chart to the Clipboard.
6. In the Word document Coastline CC Flyer, delete the green highlighted text, and then insert the chart as an embedded object using the destination theme. Horizontally center the chart in the paragraph.
7. Edit the data in the embedded worksheet that contains the column chart so that the number of students who completed the program in two years and who graduated in 2014 (cell B14) is **590**. Save and close the document.

8. Open the PowerPoint data file **CC Presentation** located in the Chapter 22\Practice It folder. Add your name as the subtitle, and then save the presentation as **Coastline CC Presentation.**
9. Link the line chart data on the Student Data worksheet in the Excel file Coastline CC Info to Slide 2 ("Number of Students Chart") in the PowerPoint file Coastline CC Presentation using the destination theme. Resize the chart so it is four inches high and 6.7 inches wide, and then position it so it is centered in the space below the slide title.
10. Link the worksheet data in cells A31 through B36 in the Student Data worksheet in the Excel file Coastline CC Info to Slide 3 ("Number of Students") in the PowerPoint file Coastline CC Presentation. Resize the linked worksheet data so the object is 3.5 inches high and 5.15 inches wide.
11. Edit the data in cell B36 in the Student Data worksheet in the Excel file Community CC Number so that number enrolled in credit courses in 2016 is **4550**. Update the chart and datasheet in the PowerPoint presentation if necessary.
12. Save the PowerPoint file, and then close it.
13. Edit cell B35 in the Student Data worksheet in the Excel file Coastline CC Info so that number enrolled in credit courses in 2015 is **4000**.
14. Re-open the PowerPoint file **Coastline CC Presentation**. Examine both Slides 2 and 3, and manually update the links if necessary.
15. In the Excel file Coastline CC Info, switch to the Courses worksheet, and then prepare the worksheet to be imported into Access by deleting the rows above the column labels and adding the label **Dept.** above the data in column A.
16. Save the workbook, and then close it and exit Excel.
17. Open the Access database named **Coastline** located in the Chapter 22\Practice It folder. Save it as **CoastlineCC**.
18. Import the Courses worksheet in the Excel file Coastline CC Info into the CoastlineCC Access file to create a new table named **Courses**. Make sure you indicate that the first row contains headers, and let Access set the primary key.
19. Create a query named **Business** that lists only classes in the Business department. Show only values in the Class field. Resize the column to fit its widest entry.
20. Export the query results to a Word Rich Text File named **Business Courses**.
21. Open the Word data file **CC Letter** located in the Chapter 22\Practice It folder. Replace the name in the signature (*Susan Oh*) with your name. Save the document as **Coastline CC Letter.**
22. In the empty paragraph in the body of the letter, insert the text of the Word file **Business Courses**. Format the table with the Grid Table 4 – Accent 2 table style with the Header Row treated differently and the Banded Rows option set. Center the table horizontally, and delete one of the empty paragraphs below the table.
23. In the CoastlineCC Access file, copy the Business query results to the Clipboard, and then paste the query results using the destination theme to Slide 4 ("Business Courses") in the PowerPoint file Coastline CC Presentation. Remove the first row in the pasted table, and then change the font size of the text in the table to 24 points. Apply the table style Medium Style 1 – Accent 6 with the Header Row treated differently and with banded rows. Change the width of the column to six inches, and then center the table in the blank area on the slide. Exit Access.
24. In the Coastline CC Presentation file, import the Word outline stored in the file **CC Outline** in the Chapter 22\Practice It folder so that the slides created from the outline appear after Slide 4 ("Business Courses") in the PowerPoint file Coastline CC Presentation.
25. Reset the new Slides 5–10, and then delete the blank Slide 10.
26. In the PowerPoint file Coastline CC Presentation, move Slide 5 ("Student Population") so that it becomes Slide 2.
27. In the Word file Coastline CC Letter, start a mail merge and select the Letters main document type.
28. Select the Student table in the Access file CoastlineCC as the data source.
29. Edit the recipient list by filtering it so that only students with an interest in Business are included in the mail merge.
30. Insert the Address Block and Greeting Line merge fields at the beginning of the document below the date. Match fields as needed. In the Greeting Line merge field, use Dear as the salutation, choose just the first name as the name to be used in the greeting line, and choose a comma at the end of the line.
31. Preview the document. Adjust the spacing after the Address Block merge field as needed.

32. Check the document for errors by simulating the merge.
33. Complete the merge by merging all the records to a new file. (There should be six letters.) Save the file as **Coastline CC Merged Letters**.
34. Close the merged document Coastline CC Merged Letters. Turn the Preview off in the document Coastline CC Letter, and then save and close the Coastline CC Letter document.
35. Close all open files, saving if prompted.

Practice It 22-2

1. Open the Excel data file **Spa Services** located in the Chapter 22\Practice It folder. Save the workbook as **Salon Services**.
2. Open the PowerPoint data file **Spa Presentation** located in the Chapter 22\Practice It folder. Enter your name as the subtitle. Save the presentation as **Salon Presentation**.
3. Embed the chart in the Excel file Salon Services in Slide 2 ("Price Comparison") of the PowerPoint file Salon Presentation using the destination theme. Resize the chart so it is 12.06 inches wide (so that the left and right edges of the chart align with the left and right edges of the title text box), and so that the chart is 4.5 inches high. Apply the Style 4 style (on the Chart Tools Design tab) to the embedded chart object.
4. In the embedded chart, change the price of One Process Color in cell C7 to **$55** and change the price of Full Foil in cell C8 to **$95**.
5. In the Excel file Salon Services, copy Sheet1 to a new worksheet. In the new worksheet, delete the chart, and then prepare the data on Sheet1 (2) to be exported to an Access table. (*Hint*: Make sure a label appears in every cell in column A for all rows that contain data.) Label column B **Service** and column C **Price**.
6. Save and close the Excel file Salon Services.
7. Create a new Access database named **Salon**.
8. In the Access database Salon, import the data from Sheet1 (2) in the Excel file Salon Services to a new table named **Services**. Make sure you indicate that the first row contains headers, and let Access set the primary key.
9. In the Services table, change the price of One Process Color to $55, and then change the price of Full Foil to $95.
10. Create a query named **Hair** that lists the service and price for all services of the type Hair, but do not show the Type field. Resize columns as needed in the query results. (*Hint*: If you get only one result, close the query, and then delete the query and the Services table. Reopen the Excel file **Salon Services**, and add a label to each row, as explained in the Hint in Step 5. Then repeat Steps 8 and 9.)
11. Export the results of the query to a Rich Text File named **Hair Services**.
12. In the PowerPoint file Salon Presentation, create new slides after Slide 2 by importing the outline in the Word data file **Spa Outline**, located in the Chapter 22\Practice It folder. Reset the imported slides. Move Slide 2 ("Price Comparison") so it becomes Slide 4, and then move Slide 7 (a blank slide) so it becomes Slide 5.
13. Add the title **Hair Services** to Slide 5, and then change the layout to Title Only.
14. Use the Object button in the Text group on the Insert tab to embed the **Hair Services** file into Slide 5.
15. Double-click the embedded table to open a Word window in the Slide, select all the text and data in the table, and then increase the font size of all the text in the table to 20 points. Format the table with the Grid Table 3 – Accent 3 table style, and then AutoFit each column. Click a blank area of the slide, and then resize the object so it is about 9.5 inches wide and 4.2 inches high. Position the table so it is visually centered in the blank area on the slide. (The table object will not be centered and part of it will be off the slide to the right.)
16. Change the layout of Slide 3 to the Two Content layout. Move the last first-level bulleted item and its subitems to the content placeholder on the right. Change the size of the text in the bulleted lists on Slide 2, 3, 6, and 7 so the first-level items are 24 points and the second level items are 20 points.
17. Close all open files, saving when prompted.

ON YOUR OWN

On Your Own 22-1

1. Open the Excel data file **Zoo Data** located in the Chapter 22\On Your Own folder. Save the workbook as **Zoo Combined Data**.

2. Open the PowerPoint data file **Zoo Presentation** located in the Chapter 22\On Your Own folder. Add your name as the subtitle, and then save the presentation as **Zoo Slide Show**.
3. In the Visitors worksheet in the Excel file Zoo Combined Data, copy the column chart to the Clipboard.
4. Link the data of the copied chart to Slide 2 ("Number of Visitors") in the Zoo Slide Show presentation using the destination theme. Resize the chart object so it is 4.5 inches high and 8.5 inches wide, and then center it in the blank area of the slide.
5. In the Visitors worksheet in the Excel file Zoo Combined Data, add the following data as the number of visitors in 2016: **648**, **1411**, **220**, and **99**.
6. Save the changes to the Excel file Zoo Combined Data, and then update the chart in the PowerPoint file Zoo Slide Show if needed.
7. Open the Word data file **Zoo Letter** located in the Chapter 22\On Your Own folder. Replace the name *Karl Croston* in the signature with your name. Save the document as **Zoo Member Letter**.
8. In the Visitors worksheet Excel file Zoo Combined Data, copy the column chart to the Clipboard.
9. In the Word document Zoo Member Letter, delete the yellow highlighted text, and then link the data of the copied chart to the document using the destination theme. Resize the chart so that it is 2.5 inches high and 6.5 inches wide.
10. In the Excel file Zoo Combined Data, change the number of Adult visitors in 2016 to **710** and then change the number of Families who visited in 2016 to **1500**. Save the file.
11. Prepare the Animals worksheet in the Excel file Zoo Combined Data file for importing into Access. Add **Species** as the column A label. Save and close the file.
12. Open the Access database **ZooMembers**, and then save it as **ZooData-base**. Import the Animals worksheet in the Excel file Zoo Combined Data to a new table named **Animals**.
13. Create four queries, each listing all the animals in one species (Mammal, Bird, Amphibian, and Reptile). Do not show the Species field. Save each query with the plural name of the species included (Mammals, Birds, Amphibians, and Reptiles). Resize columns as needed in the query results.
14. Open the Office Clipboard, and then copy the query results for each of the four queries to the Office Clipboard.
15. Paste each query into the appropriate slide in the PowerPoint file Zoo Slide Show so that the animals are listed on each slide as a bulleted list. (*Hint*: On each slide, select the Keep Text Only option after you paste the object. Then delete the Type item at the top of the list, copy the rest of the items in the list, paste the copied items into the content placeholder, and then delete the text box on top of the bulleted list.)
16. Use the Word file Zoo Member Letter to create a form letter using the Members table in the Access file ZooDatabase as the data source.
17. Edit the recipient list by sorting the customers alphabetically by last name.
18. Insert the Address Block and Greeting Line merge fields, matching fields if necessary. In the Greeting Line merge field, change the form of the name to the first name, and change the form of greeting line for records with an invalid recipient name to **Dear Guest,**.
19. In the body of the letter, replace the green highlighted text with the DateVisited merge field.
20. Preview the merged document, and then correct any spacing issues.
21. In the closing, replace *Karl Croston* with your name.
22. Turn the preview off, merge only the first and second letter of the mail merge to a new document, and then save the new document as **Zoo Merged Letters**.
23. Close all open documents, saving when prompted.

ANSWERS TO QUIZ YOURSELF

CHAPTER 1

1. A computer is a programmable, electronic device that accepts data, performs operations on that data, presents the results, and stores the data or results as needed.
2. The four primary operations of a computer are input, processing, output, and storage.
3. Data is raw, unorganized facts. Information is data that has been processed or modified into a meaningful form.
4. A Web browser is software because it is a program that tells the computer what to do. Hardware includes the physical parts of a computer.
5. A programmer writes the programs that computers use.
6. A smart TV is a TV that is capable of delivering Internet content, such as YouTube videos and Netflix movies.
7. A smartphone is a mobile phone that includes Internet capabilities and can run mobile apps.
8. A notebook computer is a personal computer because it is designed to be used by one person at a time.
9. A mainframe computer is a powerful computer used to manage large amounts of centralized data and perform a variety of processing tasks for many users. Supercomputers are faster and more powerful and focus on running one program at a time as fast as possible.
10. Home networks can be used to share a single printer, share an Internet connection, and exchange files.
11. The Internet is the largest and most well-known computer network in the world.
12. The Internet is the physical Internet network while the World Wide Web is a collection of documents called Web pages available through the Internet.
13. The most common types of Internet addresses are IP addresses and domain names (to identify computers), URLs (to identify Web pages), and email addresses (to identify people).
14. In the email address jsmith@cengage.com, jsmith is the username and cengage.com is the domain name.
15. A copyright protects an original artistic, musical, or literary work.
16. Unethical acts are not always illegal because ethics refers to overall standards of moral conduct, not laws.
17. Repetitive stress injuries (RSIs) are caused by performing the same physical movements over and over again, such as with extensive keyboard and mouse use.
18. Examples of e-waste related to computer use include paper, used toner cartridges, obsolete or broken hardware, and discarded CDs, DVDs, and other storage media.

CHAPTER 2

1. Data must be in binary form, such as represented by 0s and 1s.
2. A bit is the smallest unit of data that a computer can recognize (a 0 or a 1).
3. A byte is a group of eight bits.
4. The main circuit board inside the system unit is the motherboard.
5. The main processing device for a computer is the CPU (central processing unit).
6. A multi-core CPU has the processing components or cores of multiple independent processors in a single CPU.
7. The purpose of RAM is to store programs and data while the computer is using them.
8. A blue USB port indicates that the port adheres to a USB 3 standard.
9. The ALU is the part of a CPU or CPU core that performs logical operations and integer arithmetic.
10. A storage medium is the hardware where data is actually stored. A storage medium is inserted into its corresponding storage device in order to be read from or written to.
11. Advantages of SSDs over magnetic hard drives include the fact that SSDs are not subject to mechanical failures like magnetic hard drives and are, therefore, more resistant to shock and vibration. They also consume less power, generate less heat, make no noise, and are much faster.
12. A hybrid hard drive contains both magnetic hard disks and flash memory media.
13. Flash memory cards are the most common type of external storage media for smartphones and other portable devices.

14. The biggest advantage of cloud computing is the ability to access your data from any location with any Internet-enabled device.
15. The most common pointing device is the mouse.
16. QR barcodes are most commonly read by smartphones.
17. OLED displays are more energy efficient than LCDs because they emit a visible light and so do not use backlighting.
18. Laser printers and ink-jet printers are both nonimpact printers.

CHAPTER 3

1. System software controls a computer and allows you to use it. It enables the computer to boot, to launch application programs, and to facilitate important jobs, such as transferring files from one storage medium to another and configuring the computer to work with the hardware connected to it.
2. Multitasking allows you to have more than one program open at one time.
3. Most modern operating systems use a graphical user interface (GUI) in which the user clicks icons, buttons, or other graphical objects to issue instructions to the computer.
4. An iPhone would use iOS, the mobile operating system for the Apple iPhone, iPad, and iPod touch.
5. The type of utility program used to make duplicate copies of files is a backup program.
6. Application software or apps includes all the programs that allow you to perform specific tasks or applications on a computer, such as writing a letter or viewing a Web page.
7. A software license specifies the conditions under which the buyer can use the software, such as the number of computers on which it may be installed.
8. Shareware programs are distributed on the honor system and are often available to try free of charge but usually require a fee if you choose to continue to use the program. Freeware programs do not require a fee for use.
9. Installed software must be installed on a device before it can be used. Cloud software is not installed on the device; instead it is run via the Internet. Cloud software requires an Internet connection, whereas installed software does not.
10. Office suites typically contain word processing software, spreadsheet software, database software, and presentation graphics software.
11. The Microsoft Office program most appropriate for creating a memo is Microsoft Word, a word processing program.
12. Painting and drawing programs are graphics software.
13. Media players are programs designed to play audio and video files available via a computer, such as music CDs, downloaded music, or video streamed from the Internet.
14. Advantages of using a Web publishing program or Web site builder include the ability to create a complete Web site, that the program automatically generates Web pages as the user specifies the desired content and appearance, the ability to apply a consistent theme to all pages in the site, and the ability to publish the site directly to a Web server.
15. The type of software used to create a design of a new building or product is computer-aided design (CAD) software.
16. The type of software that enables a group of individuals to work together on a project is collaboration software.

CHAPTER 4

1. A computer network is a collection of computers and other hardware devices that are connected so users can share hardware, software, and data as well as communicate with each other electronically.
2. Telecommuting allows individuals to work from a remote location (typically their homes) and communicate with their places of business and clients via networking technologies.
3. The three most common network topologies are star, bus, and mesh.
4. A client-server network uses servers to process requests from client devices. In a peer-to-peer network, the devices access each other directly.
5. A small network designed to connect the personal devices for an individual is a personal area network (PAN).
6. The world's largest WAN is the Internet.
7. A virtual private network (VPN) is a private, secure path across a public network (usually the Internet). It can be used to allow authorized users private, secure access to the company network or to enable individuals to surf safely at public hotspots.
8. In a digital signal, data is represented by 0s and 1s. In an analog signal, data is represented by continuous waves. Computers use digital signals.

9. The three most common types of cables used to create wired networks are twisted-pair cable, coaxial cable, and fiber-optic cable.
10. TCP/IP is the communications protocol used for transferring data over the Internet.
11. The most widely used standard for wired networks is Ethernet.
12. Wi-Fi is used to wirelessly connect devices, such as to connect devices to the Internet via a router, to connect a computer to a printer, or to connect a smartphone to a smart appliance.
13. The 4G standard is a cellular standard and so is used to communicate over cellular networks.
14. Bluetooth is designed for very short-range connections, such as to connect a mouse to a computer.
15. A wireless router is used to connect devices on a LAN; it also typically connects those devices to the Internet.
16. A bridge is used to connect two LANs.
17. A repeater is a device that amplifies signals along a network.
18. The purpose of an antenna is to increase the range of a wireless networking device, such as a wireless router.

CHAPTER 5

1. ARPANET is the predecessor of the Internet, named after the Advanced Research Projects Agency (ARPA), which sponsored its development.
2. An Internet service provider is a business or other organization that provides Internet access to others, typically for a fee.
3. The three decisions typically involved before you connect to the Internet are (1) determining the type of device you will use to access the Internet, (2) deciding which type of connection you want, and (3) selecting the Internet service provider to use.
4. No, most Internet connections are direct Internet connections, but not all are. For example, dial-up Internet connections, such as conventional dial-up connections, are also available.
5. Satellite Internet is a better option for rural areas. DSL is only available to users who are relatively close (within three miles) to a telephone switching station so it is usually only available in urban areas.
6. A Wi-Fi hotspot is a location that provides wireless Internet access.
7. Search site databases are typically updated by small, automated programs (often called spiders or webcrawlers) that use the hyperlinks located on Web pages to jump continually from page to page and record important data about each page.
8. To perform a search, you type one or more keywords in the search box on the search site.
9. To avoid plagiarizing Web page content, you need to credit Web page sources—as well as any other Internet resources—when you use them in papers, on Web pages, or in other documents.
10. The advantage of Web-based email is you can access your email from any device with an Internet connection.
11. An SMS text message contains only text, while an MMS text message contains a photo, audio, or video.
12. A blog is a Web page usually created and updated by one individual while a wiki is collaborative and intended to be modified by multiple individuals.
13. A podcast is a recorded audio or video file that can be downloaded via the Internet.
14. The biggest advantage of VoIP is cost savings. One of the biggest disadvantages of VoIP is that it does not function during a power outage or if your Internet connection goes down.
15. A Webinar is a seminar presented via the Web.
16. Facebook is a social networking site.
17. No, online music is often accessed via streaming online music, such as via Pandora.
18. E-commerce is the act of performing financial transactions online.

CHAPTER 6

1. Unauthorized access occurs when an individual gains access to a resource without permission. Unauthorized use is using a resource for unauthorized activities.
2. The typical motivation for hacking is to steal data, sabotage a computer system, or perform some other type of illegal act.
3. War driving is the act of driving in a car looking for unsecured Wi-Fi networks to access.
4. A biometric access system uses a physical characteristic, such as a fingerprint.
5. A firewall is used to protect a computer by essentially creating a barrier between a computer or network and the Internet to protect against unauthorized access.

6. You would encrypt a file when you want to protect it from being viewed by unauthorized individuals.
7. Malware refers to any type of malicious software.
8. A Trojan horse is a malicious program that is disguised as something else, usually an application program.
9. Phishing tries to trick the recipient into revealing sensitive personal information that then can be used in identity theft and other fraudulent activities.
10. The best way to avoid phishing schemes is to never click a link in an unsolicited message.
11. The two most common way individuals are harrassed online are cyberbullying and cyberstalking.
12. Full-disk encryption is a technology that encrypts everything stored on a storage medium without any user interaction.
13. A ruggedized device would be used when more protection is needed from physical abuse, such as drops, extreme temperatures, or wet conditions.
14. Information privacy refers to the rights of individuals and companies to control how information about them is collected and used.
15. Electronic profiling is the use of electronic means to collect a variety of in-depth information about an individual, such as name, address, income, and buying habits.
16. Computer-monitoring software records keystrokes, logs the programs or Web sites accessed, or otherwise monitors someone's computer activity.
17. You can use a throw-away email address for activities that typically lead to junk email to protect your private email address from spam.
18. Opting out refers to following a predesignated procedure to remove yourself from marketing lists or otherwise preventing your personal information from being obtained by or shared with others. Opting in refers to requesting participation in a particular marketing activity.

CHAPTER 7

1. To start an app, click its tile on the Start menu, or click the Start button or the Search the web and Windows box, type the name of the app, and then click the app in the list of results, or click the Start button, click All apps, and then scroll through the alphabetical list of apps and click the app you want to start.
2. To manually resize a window, point to a window border until the pointer changes to the two-headed arrow, and then drag the border.
3. To switch between open windows, click in the window you want to make active or click the button on the taskbar that corresponds to the window you want to make active.
4. The left pane in a File Explorer window is called the navigation pane.
5. To change the view in a File Explorer window, click one of the view buttons on the status bar or click the View tab on the ribbon, and then in the Layout group, click the desired view button.
6. The root directory is the topmost folder in a computer, and it stores the folders and files that the computer needs when you turn it on.
7. A path shows the location of a file on a computer.
8. When you use the left mouse button to drag a file or folder from one location to another on a drive, the file or folder is moved. When you drag a file or folder from one drive to another, the file or folder is copied.
9. To copy a file or folder from one location to another on the same drive, you can press and hold the Ctrl key and then drag the file or folder, or you can drag the file or folder using the right mouse button, and then on the shortcut menu, click Copy here.
10. A file name can have 255 characters.
11. You can identify a compressed folder by the zipper on the folder icon.
12. No, a file is not deleted from a compressed folder when you extract it.
13. To permanently delete files in the Recycle Bin from a drive, do one of the following: right-click the Recycle Bin, and then click Empty Recycle Bin on the shortcut menu; or double-click the Recycle Bin, click the file you want to permanently delete, click the Recycle Bin Tools Manage tab on the ribbon, and then the Empty Recycle Bin button.
14. To close a window, click the Close button on the title bar, right-click the window's button on the taskbar and then click Close window, or point to the window's button on the taskbar, point to the window's thumbnail, and then click the Close button on the thumbnail.
15. Shutting down a computer closes all open apps, including Windows itself, and then completely turns off the computer.

CHAPTER 8

1. The start page is the page that appears when you start a browser.
2. A home page on a Web site is the main page on a Web site.
3. To conduct a search using the default search engine, you type keywords in the Address bar, and then press the Enter key to begin the search. The hits are displayed on the search site set for your version of Edge.
4. A tab is the object on which Web pages are displayed in Edge.
5. The history is a list that tracks the Web pages you visit in Edge during multiple browsing sessions.
6. If you visit a Web page frequently, you can pin it to the Start menu so you can open the Web page directly from the Start menu without first starting Edge.
7. A favorite is a shortcut to a Web page saved in the Favorites list in Edge.
8. A reading list is a list of links to Web pages saved in the Reading list in Edge.
9. With a Web Note, you can save a Web page with your handwritten or typed notes and highlights, and clip a section of the Web page to save.
10. It is a good idea to preview Web pages before you print them because Web pages are not usually designed with printing in mind.
11. When you reply to an email message, the email address of the original sender is entered in the To box. When you forward an email message, the To box is left empty so you can add the email address of the person to whom you want to forward the message.
12. An attachment is a file that you send with an email message.
13. When you delete an email message, it is moved to the Deleted Items folder.
14. You use the People app to store information about the people and businesses with whom you communicate.

CHAPTER 9

1. Backstage view contains commands that allow you to manage application files and options.
2. The ribbon is organized into tabs, and each tab is organized into groups.
3. An object is anything in a document that can be manipulated as a whole.
4. A text box is an object that contains text.
5. A toggle button is a button that you click once to turn a feature on and click again to turn it off.
6. Live Preview shows the results that would occur in your file if you clicked an option in a gallery or on a menu.
7. A dialog box is a window in which you enter or choose settings for performing a task.
8. A task pane is a narrow window that appears to the left or right of the workspace in which to enter or choose settings for performing a task.
9. The Mini toolbar appears when you select text with the mouse or right-click in the application window.
10. To undo your most recent action, click the Undo button on the Quick Access Toolbar or press the Ctrl+Z keys.
11. You need to save files that you create in Office applications because as you create and modify an Office file, your work is stored only in the computer's temporary memory. If you exit the application without saving, turn off your computer, or experience a power failure, your work would be lost.
12. To close a file without exiting the application, click the Close command in Backstage view. If more than one file is open in an application, you can also click the Close button in the application window title bar.
13. The system Clipboard contains only the item that was most recently cut or copied and is available to all Windows 8 apps and applications. The Office Clipboard contains up to 24 cut or copied items and is available only to Office applications.
14. When you click the Tell me what you want to do button and then type key words, a list of commands related to the key words appears, and you can click a command to execute it. You can also click Get Help on "*key words*" on the menu to open the Help window containing links to information about the key words.
15. To exit an Office application, click the Close button in the application window title bar; if more than one file is open, click the Close button in each window's title bar.

CHAPTER 10

1. Nonprinting characters are characters that do not print and that control the format of the document. To display them, click the Show/Hide ¶ button in the Paragraph group on the Home tab.
2. To insert symbols not included in the AutoCorrect list, use the Symbol button in the Symbols group on the Insert tab.

3. When you use drag and drop to move text, you cannot next use the Paste command to paste that text somewhere else because text moved or copied using drag and drop is not placed on the Clipboard.
4. A font is the design of a set of characters.
5. A point is the unit of measurement used for type equal to 1/72 of an inch.
6. The default paragraph spacing in a Word document is zero points before a paragraph and 8 points after it. The default line spacing in a Word document is 1.08.
7. Justified text is a type of text alignment in which both sides of the text are aligned along the margins.
8. The default tab stops are positioned every half-inch. When you insert a new tab stop, all of the default tab stops before it are deleted.
9. When you create a bulleted or a numbered list, a tab character is inserted between the bullet symbol or the number and the text, and the paragraph is formatted with a hanging indent.
10. To indent a paragraph one-half inch from the left margin, click the Increase Indent button in the Paragraph group on the Home tab, or drag the Left Indent marker to the .5-inch mark on the ruler.
11. The buttons on the Paste Options menu control the formatting of the pasted text.
12. The Format Painter copies the format of a block of text to another block of text.
13. When you type text in the Search Document box in the Navigation Pane, all instances of the search text is immediately highlighted in the document.
14. Possible spelling errors, contextual spelling errors, and grammatical errors are flagged in a document with wavy underlines: red for spelling errors, blue for possible misused words and grammatical errors.
15. The Print screen in Backstage view shows a preview of the document as it will look when it is printed.

CHAPTER 11

1. When you use the Replace All command, all instances of the text in the Find what box are replaced with the text in the Replace with box.
2. The style applied to text if you do nothing to change it is the Normal style.
3. The template on which all Word documents are based is the Normal template.
4. A character style affects only selected text. A paragraph style affects the entire paragraph. But you can apply a linked style only to selected text or to an entire paragraph.
5. To apply a style from the Styles gallery to text already in a document, first select the text or paragraph, and then click the style in the Styles gallery on the Home tab.
6. A theme is a coordinated set of colors, fonts, and effects.
7. When you apply a different style set to a document, the style definitions are changed to match those of the new style set.
8. When you promote a paragraph in an outline, the paragraph is moved up to a higher level in the outline.
9. To move a heading up or down in a document in both the Navigation Pane and in Outline view, click it to select it (in Outline view, click its outline symbol), and then drag it to its new position.
10. The default setting for margins in a new document is one inch all around.
11. An automatic page break is created when you fill a page with text and a new page is automatically created. A manual page break is created when you use the Page Break command to force text after the break to a new page.
12. When you use the Page Number command to insert page numbers in a document, you actually insert a field.
13. A header is text that appears at the top of every page in a document. A footer is text that appears at the bottom of every page in a document.
14. A content control is a placeholder for text you insert or designed to contain a specific type of text, such as a date.
15. A source is anything you use to research your topic.
16. You need to cite your sources to avoid charges of plagiarism or trying to pass off someone else's thoughts as your own.
17. When you use the Bibliography command to create the list of works cited, you insert every source in the Current List in the Source Manager dialog box, even if the source is not cited.
18. A footnote appears at the foot or bottom of a page, and an endnote appears at the end of a document.

CHAPTER 12

1. The intersection of a column and a row is a cell.
2. When a table is formatted with banded rows, every other row is shaded.
3. Portrait orientation describes a page taller than wide. Landscape orientation describes a page wider than tall.
4. A section is a part of a document that has its own page-level formatting and properties.
5. If a document does not contain a section break, it contains one section.
6. Sizing handles are the small circles at each corner of a selection box and in the center of each side of a selection box that you can drag to change the size of the selected object.
7. When you crop part of a photo, you cut off the part that you crop.
8. WordArt is formatted, decorative text in a text box.
9. An inline graphic is a graphic that is positioned in a line of text and moves along with the text. A floating graphic is a graphic that can be positioned anywhere in a document.
10. When you click one of the options on the Columns button menu, the column formatting is applied to the current section.
11. To balance columns without inserting manual column breaks, insert a Continuous section break at the end of the last column.
12. A building block is a part of a document that is stored and reused.
13. Quick Parts are stored in the Quick Parts gallery.
14. To insert a Quick Part, select it on the Quick Parts button menu.
15. The Building Blocks Organizer lists all the Quick Parts in the current template and stored on the computer. You can select a building block in the list and delete it in the Building Blocks Organizer.

CHAPTER 13

1. A workbook is an Excel file, which stores a spreadsheet. A worksheet is an individual page or sheet in a workbook that contains data laid out in a grid of rows and columns.
2. The cell reference for the cell located in the fourth column and seventh row of a worksheet is D7.
3. The active cell is outlined with a green border and its cell reference appears in the Name box.
4. The three types of data you can enter into a worksheet are text, dates and times, and numbers.
5. You format a worksheet to make it easier to read and understand the data.
6. You can edit cell content in the formula bar or directly in the cell.
7. When text entered in a cell is too long to be fully displayed in that cell, Excel displays only as much text as fits into the cell, cutting off the rest of the text entry; although the complete text is still entered in the cell, it is not displayed.
8. The AutoFit feature eliminates any empty space by matching the column to the width of its longest cell entry or the height of a row to its tallest cell entry.
9. Clearing removes data from a worksheet but leaves the blank cells. Deleting removes both the data and the cells from the worksheet.
10. An adjacent range is a single rectangular block of cells. A nonadjacent range consists of two or more distinct adjacent ranges.
11. The range reference for cells A1 through A5 and cells F1 through G5 is: A1:A5;F1:G5.
12. To force text that extends beyond a cell's border to fit within the cell, make the cell with cut-off text the active cell, and then click the Wrap Text button in the Alignment group on the Home tab.
13. A formula is a mathematical expression that returns a value.
14. The formula that adds the values in cells C4 and E9 and then divides the sum by the value in cell A2 is =(C4+E9)/A2.
15. A function is a named operation that replaces the action of an arithmetic expression. Functions are used to simplify formulas, reducing what might be a long expression into a compact statement.
16. The formula to add the values in cells C4, C5, and C6 is =C4+C5+C6. The function that achieves the same result is =SUM(C4:C6).
17. Page Layout view shows how the sheet will look when printed.

CHAPTER 14

1. A relative reference is a cell reference that is interpreted in relation to the location of the cell containing the formula. An absolute reference is a cell reference that remains fixed when copied to a new location; it includes $ in front of both the column letter and row number. A mixed reference

is a cell reference that contains an absolute row reference or an absolute column reference, such as $A2 or A$2.

2. For cell H9, the relative reference is H9, the absolute reference is $H$9, and the mixed reference is either $H9 or H$9.
3. The general syntax of all Excel functions is FUNCTION(argument1,argument2,...) where FUNCTION is the name of the function, and argument1, argument2, and so forth are arguments.
4. In a function, arguments are the numbers, text, or cell references used by the function to return a value.
5. To type a function directly in a cell, first type an equal sign. As you begin to type a function name, a list of functions that begin with the letters you typed appears. To insert a function in the active cell, press the Tab key or double-click its function name. You can then either select a cell or range or type the appropriate reference or argument. When the function is complete, you enter it into the cell as usual.
6. AutoFill is an Excel feature that copies content and formats from a cell or range into an adjacent cell or range. AutoFill can also extend a series of numbers, patterned text, and dates into the adjacent selection.
7. After you select a cell or range, the fill handle appears in the lower-right corner of the selection. When you drag the fill handle over an adjacent range, AutoFill copies the content and formats from the original cell into the adjacent range.
8. To create a series of numbers with AutoFill, you enter the initial values in the series, such as the first few consecutive integers, in a selected range to establish the pattern for AutoFill to use, select the range, and then drag the fill handle over the cells where you want the pattern continued.
9. A date function is a function that inserts or calculates dates and times.
10. The TODAY function returns the current date.
11. The PMT function is a financial function that calculates the monthly payment required to repay a loan.
12. The syntax of the PMT function is

    PMT(rate,nper,pv[,fv=0][,type=0])

    where rate is the interest rate for each payment period, nper is the total number of payment periods required to repay the loan, pv is the present value of the loan or the amount that needs to be borrowed, fv is the future value of the loan, and type specifies when the interest is charged on the loan.
13. To determine the interest rate per month, divide the annual interest rate by 12.
14. The formula to determine the monthly payment for a $50,000 loan with an annual interest rate of 4% that will be repaid in three years is:

    =PMT(0.04/12,3*12,50000).
15. The PMT function returns a negative value because the payment is an expense to the borrower.
16. A cell style lets you apply the same collection of formatting options to multiple cells within the workbook, ensuring consistency throughout the workbook.
17. Unless you change the alignment, text is aligned with the left and bottom borders of a cell and values are aligned with the right and bottom borders of a cell.
18. If the range A1:C5 is merged into a single cell, the cell reference of this merged cell is A1.
19. A border is a line you add along an edge of a cell.
20. A fill color is a background color that is added to worksheet cells. Fill colors are useful for differentiating parts of a worksheet or highlighting data.
21. You can access all the formatting options for worksheet cells in the Format Cells dialog box.

CHAPTER 15

1. You should document the contents of a workbook to make it accessible to its intended users, avoid errors and confusion, and make it easier for others to understand.
2. Flash Fill enters text based on patterns it finds in the data.
3. If a formula contains more than one arithmetic operator, Excel performs the calculation using the order of operations—first, exponentiation (^); second, multiplication (*) and division (/); and third, addition (+) and subtraction (–).
4. An error value is a message indicating that some part of a formula is preventing Excel from returning a calculated value. An error value appears instead of the formula results.
5. The IF function is a logical function that returns one value if a statement is true and returns a different value if that statement is false.
6. The formula that tests whether the value in cell S2 is equal to the value in cell P7, and then returns 75 if it is, but returns 150 otherwise is =IF(S2=P7,75,150).

7. Conditional formatting is formatting that is applied to a cell only when the cell's value meets a specified condition.
8. To highlight the top 10 values in the range A1:C20, first select the range, then click the Conditional Formatting button in the Styles group on the HOME tab, point to Highlight Cells Rules, point to Top/Bottom Rules, and then click Top 10. Select the format, and then click OK.
9. Clearing a conditional formatting rule doesn't affect the contents of the cells.
10. You might hide some rows or columns in a worksheet to remove extraneous information from view.
11. You would define a print area to specify what part of a worksheet should be printed.
12. Excel prints as much of the content that fits on a single page without resizing the content and then inserts automatic page breaks to continue printing the remaining worksheet content on successive pages. A manual page break is one you insert to specify exactly where the page break occurs.
13. Print titles are information from a workbook that appears on every printed page.
14. To add the workbook file name in the center section of the footer on every page of a printout, switch to Page Layout view, scroll down until you see the footer, click in the center section of the footer, and then click the File Name button in the Header & Footer Elements group on the Header & Footer Tools Design tab.

CHAPTER 16

1. A data source is the range that contains the data being displayed in a chart. A data source is a collection of one or more data series, which is a range of values that is plotted as a single unit on a chart.
2. The chart area contains the chart and all of the other chart elements. The plot area is the part of the chart that contains the graphical representation of the data series.
3. You can place a chart in a worksheet as an embedded chart or you can place a chart into a chart sheet, which contains only the chart and no worksheet cells.
4. A data series that contains values divided into 10 categories would be better displayed as a column chart because a pie chart is more effective with six or fewer categories.
5. A column chart displays values in different categories as columns; the height of each column is based on its value. A bar chart is a column chart turned on its side so that the length of each bar is based on its value.
6. You would change the scale of a chart axis to make the chart easier to read.
7. Major units identify the main intervals on a chart axis. Minor units identify smaller intervals between the major units.
8. You should use a line chart instead of a column chart when the data consists of values drawn from categories that follow a sequential order at evenly spaced intervals, as with historical data in which the data values are recorded periodically such as monthly, quarterly, or yearly.
9. A combination chart combines two or more chart types in a single graph, such as a column chart and a line chart. To create a combination chart, first select the data series in an existing chart that you want to appear as another chart type. Then, on the Chart Tools Design tab, in the Type group, click the Change Chart Type button, click the chart type you want to apply to the selected series, and then click OK.
10. Overlaying a chart title or legend means they are placed on top of the chart in the chart area.
11. A chart is automatically updated when its data source is edited.
12. To add a data series to an existing chart, select the chart, click the Select Data button in the Data group on the Chart Tools Design tab, click the Add button in the Select Data Source dialog box, click in the Series name box in the Edit Series dialog box, select the range with the new data series. Click OK in each dialog box.
13. A sparkline is a graph that is displayed within a cell. The three types of sparklines are line sparklines, column sparklines, and win/loss sparklines.
14. A data bar is conditional formatting that adds a horizontal bar to the background of a cell containing a number.
15. Data bars differ from sparklines in that the bars are always placed in the cells containing the value they represent and each cell represents only a single bar from the bar chart. By contrast, a column sparkline can be inserted anywhere within the workbook and can represent data from several rows or columns.

CHAPTER 17

1. A field is a single characteristic of a person, place, object, event, or idea.

2. A record is all the fields about a single person, place, object, event, or idea collected in a row in a table.
3. Tables in a relational database are related through common fields.
4. The primary key, whose values uniquely identify each record in a table, is called a foreign key when it is placed in a second table to form a relationship between the two tables.
5. The Data Type property restricts the type of data that can be entered in a field.
6. In Datasheet view, a table's contents are displayed in rows and columns.
7. In Design view, you see the structure of a table, including field names, data types, and properties, but no data.
8. When you create a new table in Datasheet view, the first field is the primary key field. It is named ID, and its data type is AutoNumber.
9. The pencil symbol indicates that the record is being edited. The star symbol indicates the next row available for a new record.
10. A property is one characteristic or aspect of a field, such as its name or data type.
11. The Caption property is what appears in tables and other objects in place of the field name.
12. A query is a question about the data stored in a database.
13. A form is a database object used to enter, edit, and view records in a database.
14. A report is a database object that shows a formatted printout or screen display of the table or query objects on which the report is based.
15. When you create a form with the Form tool, the form opens in Layout view.
16. When you compact a database, you rearrange data and objects in a database to decrease its file size and repair any errors.

CHAPTER 18

1. In navigation mode, the entire field value is selected, and anything you type replaces the field value; in editing mode, you can insert or delete characters in a field value based on the location of the insertion point.
2. The field list contains the table name at the top of the list and the table's fields listed in the order in which they appear in the table; the design grid displays columns that contain specifications about a field you will use in the query.
3. A select query is a general query in which you specify the fields and records you want Access to select.
4. A table datasheet and a query datasheet look the same, appearing in Datasheet view, and can be used to update data in a database. A table datasheet shows the permanent data in a table, whereas a query datasheet is temporary and its contents are based on the criteria you establish in the design grid.
5. Each additional sort field organizes the records within the higher-level sort.
6. A filter is a set of restrictions you place on the records in an open datasheet or form to temporarily isolate a subset of the records.
7. A one-to-many relationship exists between two tables when one record in the primary table matches zero, one, or many records in the related table, and when each record in the related table matches at most one record in the primary table.
8. Referential integrity is a set of rules to maintain consistency between related tables when data in a database is updated.
9. The process for creating a multitable query is similar to creating a query with one table. First, the tables must have a common field with an established relationship. Then, you open the tables in the Query window and add fields from any of the field lists for the open tables to the design grid.
10. A condition is a criterion, or rule, that determines which records are selected. You specify a condition as part of a query to refine the query to display only selected records.
11. In the design grid, when you use the And logical operator, you place the conditions for two different fields in the same Criteria row.
12. In the design grid, when you use the Or logical operator, you place the two different fields in different Criteria rows.
13. To perform a calculation in a query, you add a calculated field to the query, which displays the results of an expression (a combination of database fields, constants, and operators).
14. To calculate statistical information, such as sums, averages, minimums, and maximums, on the records displayed in a table datasheet or selected by a query, you use functions to perform arithmetic operations on selected records in a database.
15. The Group By operator divides selected records into groups based on the values in a field.

CHAPTER 19

1. The Form tool creates a form using all the fields in the selected table or query. The Form Wizard allows you to choose some or all of the fields in the selected table or query, choose fields from other tables and queries, and display fields in any order on the form.
2. To apply a theme to a form, display the form in Layout view, click the Themes button in the Themes group on the Design tab, and then click the theme in the displayed gallery to apply it to all objects or right-click the theme and choose to apply it to the current object only.
3. A control is an item on a form, report, or other database object that you can manipulate to modify the object's appearance.
4. A wildcard character is a placeholder you use when you know only part of a value or when you want to start or end with a specific character or match a certain pattern.
5. The question mark (?) wildcard character matches any single alphabetic character.
6. The main form displays the data from the primary table, and the subform displays the data from the related table.
7. The navigation buttons in the subform are used to navigate and display records from the related table in the subform. The navigation buttons in the Form window are used to navigate and display records from the primary table in the main form.
8. To print only the current record displayed in a form, you open the Print dialog box, click the Selected Record(s) option button, and then click OK .
9. Detail records are the field values for the records from the related table when you create a report based on two tables that are joined in a one-to-many relationship.
10. To resize a field on a report, display the report in Layout view, click the field you want to resize to select it, and then drag an edge of the orange outline surrounding the field to the size you want.
11. When working in Layout view for a report, hold down the Shift key as you click different fields to select multiple fields on the report.
12. To apply conditional formatting to a report, display the report in Layout view, select the field value box for the field you want to format conditionally, click the Conditional Formatting button in the Control Formatting group on the Report Layout Tools tab, click the New Rule button in the Conditional Formatting Rules Manager dialog box, specify the condition and formatting in the New Formatting Rule dialog box, and then click OK in each dialog box.

CHAPTER 20

1. The view that displays all the slide thumbnails on the screen at once is Slide Sorter view.
2. A placeholder is a region of a slide, or a location in an outline, reserved for inserting text or graphics.
3. A text box is a container that holds text.
4. A layout is a predetermined way of organizing the objects on a slide including title text and other content (bulleted lists, photographs, charts, and so forth).
5. AutoFit automatically changes the line spacing and the font size of the text in a text box if you add more text than will fit.
6. A theme family includes a theme and its variants.
7. When you demote a slide title one level, it becomes a first-level bulleted item.
8. To move a slide from one position to another, you can drag its thumbnail in the Slides in Normal view or in Slide Sorter view.
9. To create speaker notes, click in the Notes pane, and then type.
10. After you have created and proofed your presentation, you should view it as a slide show to see how it will appear to your audience.
11. Slide Show view displays one slide after another so that each slide fills the entire screen with no toolbars or other Windows elements visible on the screen and displays special effects applied to the text and graphics on each slide or to the slide itself.
12. Presenter view displays each slide in a small window that floats on top of the program window, and you can display each slide, one after the other in the small window to see how it will appear during the slide show.
13. An animation is a special effect applied to an object that makes the object move or change.
14. The Animation Painter is the tool you can use to copy animation from one object to another.
15. A transition is a special effect that changes the way an entire slide appears during a slide show.
16. In PowerPoint, a footer is text that appears in a Footer text box, which can appear anywhere on a slide depending on the theme, or at the bottom of handouts and notes pages.

17. To prevent a footer and slide number from appearing on the title slide, select the Don't show on title slide check box in the Header and Footer dialog box.

18. You can print a presentation as full page-sized slides, handouts, notes pages, and an outline.

CHAPTER 21

1. The theme Slide Master is the primary slide master for a presentation. A layout master is a slide master for a specific layout in a presentation.
2. To add a picture stored in a file on your computer to a slide, you can use the Pictures button in a content placeholder, or you can use the Pictures command in the Images group on the Insert tab.
3. To add a shape to a slide, select the shape on the Shapes button menu, and then drag on the slide.
4. To add text to a shape, select the shape, and then type.
5. A diagram is an illustration that visually depicts information or ideas and shows how they are connected.
6. To covert a bulleted list to a SmartArt diagram, select a bulleted list, and then click the Convert to SmartArt button in the Paragraph group on the Home tab.
7. To modify animation effects, select the animated object, click the Effect Options button in the Animation group on the Animations tab, and then select the effect you want to change.
8. To modify an animation so that it starts automatically at the same time as the previous animation, change the Start setting to With Previous.
9. To change the speed of an animation, increase the value in the Duration box in the Timing group on the Animations tab to slow down the animation, or decrease the value in the Duration box to speed up the animation.
10. When a reflection effect is applied to a video, the video plays in the reflection during playback.
11. To shorten a video's playback, use the Trim Video command.
12. A poster frame is the image that appears in a video object before the video starts playing.
13. To increase the compression of photos in a presentation, select a photo, click the Compress Pictures button in the Adjust group on the Picture Tools Format tab, and then select the new compression setting in the dialog box that opens; to apply the new settings to all the photos in the presentation, deselect the check box that specifies the settings will be applied only to the selected picture.
14. Open Backstage view, display the Export screen, and then select the file format you want to save the presentation in.

CHAPTER 22

1. Embedding stores a copy of the object in the destination file, and any changes made to the source file do not appear in the destination file; linking stores the object in the source file and displays it in the destination file, and any changes to the object in the source file appear in the destination file.
2. When an object is embedded, two copies of the object exist, one in the source file and one in the destination file.
3. If an Excel chart is linked to a Word document, the source program is Excel.
4. If you make changes to a linked object in the destination file, the changes you make appear in the destination file; however, if you update the linked object, the data in the source file will overwrite the changes you made to the linked object in the destination file.
5. To use Excel data in an Access table without using the Copy and Paste commands, prepare the Excel worksheet so that there are no blank rows and no rows above the column headings, and then import the worksheet into Access.
6. RTF stands for Rich Text Format.
7. To insert text from a text file into another Word file without using the Copy and Paste commands, use the Text from File command on the Object menu.
8. To use data from an Access datasheet in a PowerPoint slide without first exporting it to another file format, copy the data on the datasheet, and then paste it onto the slide.
9. If you create PowerPoint slides from a Word outline that has one Level 1 paragraph and three Level 2 paragraphs, the outline will create one slide with a title and three first-level bulleted items.
10. After importing a Word outline, to change the format of a slide so that it matches the theme used in the presentation, select the slides whose format need to be changed, and then click the Reset button in the Slides group on the Home tab.
11. In a mail merge, a merge field contains instructions for replacing the field placeholder with the variable information that changes from one letter to another.
12. The file that contains the variable information to be used in a mail merge is called the data source.

INDEX

D

E

F

G

H

I

J

K

L

M

N

Q

R

S

T

U

V

W

Z

CHAPTER REVIEW 1

Introduction to Computers and the Internet *Concepts*

LEARNING OBJECTIVES

- 1-1 Explain what computers do
- 1-2 Identify types of computers
- 1-3 Describe computer networks and the Internet
- 1-4 Understand how computers impact society

KEY CONCEPTS

1-1

Explain what computers do

- A **computer** is a programmable, electronic device that accepts data, performs operations on that data, presents the results, and stores the data or results as needed.
- **Input**—entering data into the computer
- **Processing**—performing operations on the data
- **Output**—presenting the results
- **Storage**—saving data, programs, or output
- When a computer processes **data** into meaningful form, it becomes **information**.
- The physical parts of a computer are called **hardware**; the instructions the hardware follows is called **software**.

1-2

Identify types of computers

- An **embedded computer** is a tiny computer designed to perform specific tasks for a product.
- A **mobile device** is a small device, such as a **smartphone** or tablet, that has built-in computing or Internet capability.
- A **personal computer (PC)** is a small computer, such as a **desktop** or **notebook computer**, designed for use by one person at a time.
- A **server** is a computer used to host programs and data for a network.
- A **mainframe computer** is a powerful computer that runs multiple programs simultaneously and is used to manage large amounts of centralized data.
- A **supercomputer** is the fastest and most powerful type of computer available and generally runs one program at a time as fast as possible.

KEY TERMS

Go to CMPTR³ Online for a full list of key terms and definitions.

communications The transmission of data from one device to another.

computer A programmable, electronic device that accepts data input, performs processing operations on that data, and outputs and stores the results.

computer network Computers and other devices that are connected to share hardware, software, and data.

copyright The legal right to sell, publish, or distribute an original artistic or literary work; it is held by the creator of a work as soon as it exists in physical form.

domain name A text-based Internet address used to uniquely identify a computer on the Internet.

email address An Internet address consisting of a username and domain name that uniquely identifies a person on the Internet.

ergonomics The science of fitting a work environment to the people who work there.

ethics Overall standards of moral conduct.

e-waste Electronic trash, such as discarded computer components.

green computing The use of computers in an environmentally friendly manner.

hardware The physical parts of a computer.

input The process of entering data into a computer; can also refer to the data itself.

Internet The largest and most well-known computer network, linking billions of computers all over the world.

IP address A numeric Internet address that uniquely identifies a computer on the Internet.

output The process of presenting results of processing; can also refer to the results themselves.

processing Performing operations on data that has been input into a computer, such as to convert that input to output.

smartphone A mobile device based on a mobile phone that includes Internet capabilities and can run mobile apps.

software Programs or instructions used to tell the computer what to do.

storage The operation of saving data, programs, or output for future use.

tablet computer A portable computer about the size of a notebook that is designed to be used with a digital pen, or touch input.

trademark A word, phrase, symbol, or design that identifies a good or service.

virtualization The creation of virtual versions of a computing resource.

Web server A computer continually connected to the Internet that stores Web pages accessible through the Internet.

World Wide Web (Web) The collection of Web pages available through the Internet.

CHAPTER 1 REVIEW

KEY CONCEPTS, *cont.*

1-3

Describe computer networks and the Internet

- A **computer network** is a collection of computers and other devices connected to share hardware, software, and data as well as to communicate electronically.
- The **Internet** is the largest computer network in the world.
- The **World Wide Web (Web)** is a vast collection of **Web pages**, connected with **hyperlinks** and viewed with a Web **browser**, available via the Internet.
- Computers are identified on the Internet via **IP addresses** and **domain names**, Web pages are identified by **URLs**, and people are identified by **email addresses**.

1-4

Understand how computers impact society

- Although technology benefits our society, there are risks that can impact our security and privacy as well.
- **Intellectual property rights** include **copyrights, trademarks,** and **patents** and protect the creators of intellectual property.
- **Ethics** refer to standards of moral conduct; **computer** and **business ethics** guide the behavior of individuals and the policies of businesses, respectively.
- Computer use can cause physical conditions including eyestrain, headaches, backaches, and **repetitive stress injuries (RSIs)** like **carpal tunnel syndrome** and **De Quervain's tendonitis**.
- **Green computing** refers to using computers in an environmentally friendly manner, including reducing the use of natural resources such as energy and paper, and proper disposal of **e-waste**.

DIGITAL BACKPACK

- **Practice It:** Practice It 1-3—Discuss the pros and cons of using technology in your daily life.
- **On Your Own:** On Your Own 1-2—Discuss your opinion about campus gossip sites.
- **Collect StudyBits:** Use your highlighted StudyBits from CMPTR[3] Online to create notes, rate your understanding, and create practice quizzes.
- **Quiz:** Take the practice quizzes on key concepts in the chapter to prepare for tests.
- **Key Terms:** Review key terms and definitions with flashcards, and create your own flashcards from your StudyBits.
- **Videos:** Watch the videos to learn more about the topics taught in this chapter.

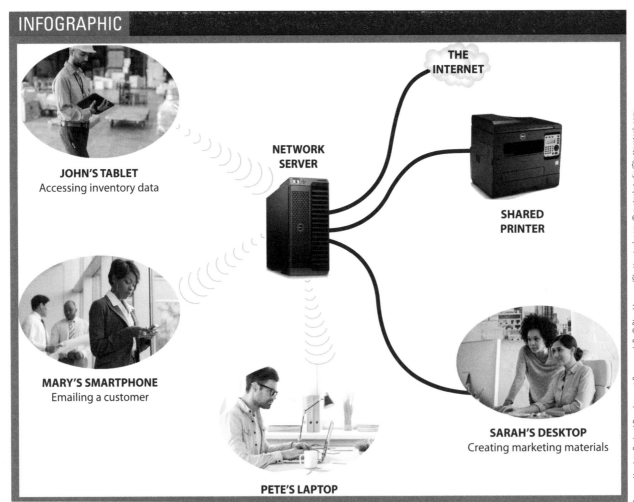

INFOGRAPHIC

CHAPTER REVIEW 2
Computer Hardware *Concepts*

LEARNING OBJECTIVES

- **2-1** Understand how data is represented to a computer
- **2-2** Identify the hardware located inside the system unit
- **2-3** Explain how the CPU works
- **2-4** Describe different types of storage systems
- **2-4** Identify and describe common input devices
- **2-4** Identify and describe common output devices

KEY CONCEPTS

2-1
Understand how data is represented to a computer

- Computers can understand only two (binary) states represented by 0 and 1 (on and off).
- A **bit** is the smallest unit of data a computer can recognize, represented by a 0 or a 1.
- A group of eight bits is a **byte**.
- A **file** is a named collection of bytes, such as a written document, computer program, or a photo.

2-2
Identify the hardware located inside the system unit

- The **system unit** houses the processing hardware for a device as well as other components, such as storage devices and cooling fans.
- The **motherboard** inside the system unit connects the components together and to external devices via **buses** and **ports**.
- The **central processing unit (CPU)** performs most of the processing for a computer as well as controls the operations.
- The primary **memory** used by the computer while it is powered up is **RAM (random access memory)**.
- External devices often connect to the system unit via a **USB** port.

KEY TERMS

Go to CMPTR³ Online for a full list of key terms and definitions.

bit The smallest unit of data that a computer can recognize.

byte Eight bits grouped together.

central processing unit (CPU) The main processor for a computer.

circuit board A thin board containing computer chips and other electronic components.

cloud computing To use Internet-based computing resources, such as data, software, and storage.

control unit The part of a CPU core that coordinates its operations.

display device An output device that presents visual output on a screen.

flash memory Nonvolatile chips that can be used for storage by a computer or a user.

memory Locations, typically inside the system unit, that the computer uses for temporary storage.

mouse A common pointing device that the user slides along a flat surface to move the on-screen pointer and manipulate objects.

multifunction device (MFD) An output device that can copy, scan, fax, and print documents.

optical disc A circular plastic disk used to store data and that is read from and written to using a laser beam.

port A connector on the exterior of the system unit case that is used to connect an external hardware device.

scanner An input device that captures an image of an object and then transfers that data to a computer.

solid-state drive (SSD) A hard drive that uses flash memory chips instead of magnetic hard disks.

Universal Serial Bus (USB) A versatile bus architecture widely used for connecting peripheral devices.

USB-C The newest, and most versatile, type of USB connector.

USB flash drive A small storage device that contains flash memory media and plugs into a USB port.

2-3
Explain how the CPU works

- Most CPUs have multiple cores and each core includes an **arithmetic/logic unit** (ALU), a **floating point unit (FPU)**, a **control unit**, a **prefetch unit**, a **decode unit**, and a **bus interface unit** as well as **registers** and internal **cache memory** for temporary storage.
- A **system clock,** located on the motherboard, synchronizes all of a computer's operations.
- A **machine cycle** occurs whenever the CPU processes a single basic instruction.

2-4
Describe different types of storage systems

- Storage systems provide nonvolatile storage, making it possible to save programs, data, and processing results for later use.
- Storage systems include a **storage medium** (the hardware where data is stored) and a **storage device** (the hardware where a storage medium is inserted to be read from or written to).
- **Hard drives** store most programs and data for a device and can be **magnetic hard drives, solid-state drives (SSDs)**, or **hybrid hard drives (SSHDs)**.

CHAPTER 2 REVIEW

KEY CONCEPTS, *cont.*

• **Optical drives** store data on **optical discs** using lasers and include CDs, DVDs, and Blu-ray Discs.
• Other storage systems include **flash memory cards** and **USB flash drives, network** and **cloud storage, smart cards,** and large storage systems.

2-5
Identify and describe common input devices

• An **input device** is any piece of equipment used to enter data into the computer.
• Common input devices are **keyboards, pointing devices** (such as **mice** and **styluses**), touch devices (such as **touch screens** and **touch pads**), **scanners**, and the readers used to read **barcodes, RFID tags**, and biometric characteristics.
• Audio input includes **speech recognition systems** used to dictate content to the device being used as well as control that device.

2-6
Identify and describe common output devices

• An **output device** presents the results of processing to the user.
• The most common output device is the **display device**, which can be a **CRT monitor,** but is typically a **flat panel display** like an **LCD, LED,** or **OLED display**.
• **Printers** produce output on paper and are usually **laser** or **ink-jet printers**, although printers that produce barcodes or 3D output are also available.
• Speakers, headphones, headsets, and earbuds also produce audio output.

DIGITAL BACKPACK

• **Practice It:** Practice It 2-3—Research and recommend a new personal printer to purchase.
• **On Your Own:** On Your Own 2-2—Discuss the benefits and drawbacks of cloud storage services.
• **Collect StudyBits:** Use your highlighted StudyBits from CMPTR3 Online to create notes, rate your understanding, and create practice quizzes.
• **Quiz:** Take the practice quizzes on key concepts in the chapter to prepare for tests.
• **Key Terms:** Review key terms and definitions with flashcards, and create your own flashcards from your StudyBits.
• **Videos:** Watch the videos to learn more about the topics taught in this chapter.

INFOGRAPHIC

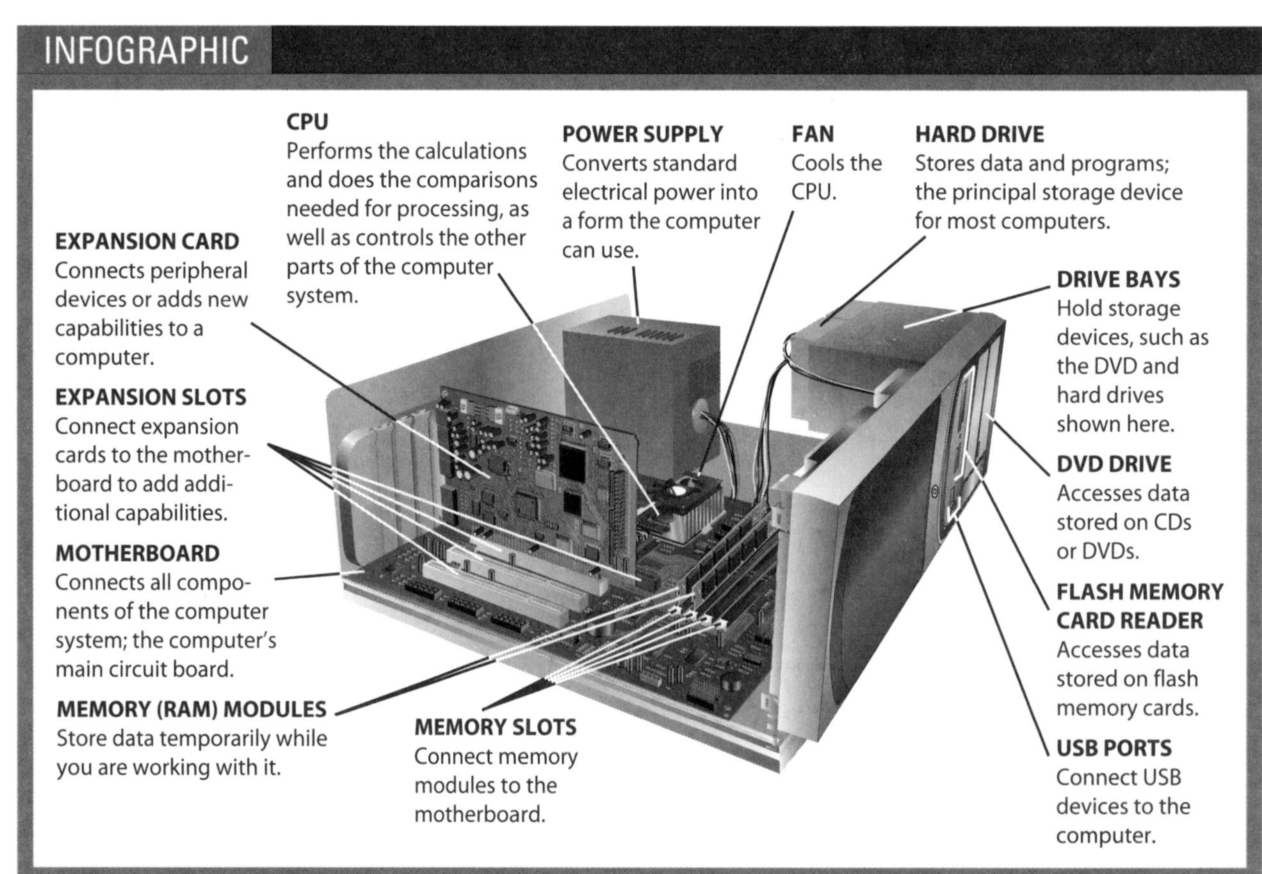

CPU
Performs the calculations and does the comparisons needed for processing, as well as controls the other parts of the computer system.
POWER SUPPLY
Converts standard electrical power into a form the computer can use.
FAN
Cools the CPU.
HARD DRIVE
Stores data and programs; the principal storage device for most computers.
EXPANSION CARD
Connects peripheral devices or adds new capabilities to a computer.
EXPANSION SLOTS
Connect expansion cards to the motherboard to add additional capabilities.
MOTHERBOARD
Connects all components of the computer system; the computer's main circuit board.
MEMORY (RAM) MODULES
Store data temporarily while you are working with it.
MEMORY SLOTS
Connect memory modules to the motherboard.
DRIVE BAYS
Hold storage devices, such as the DVD and hard drives shown here.
DVD DRIVE
Accesses data stored on CDs or DVDs.
FLASH MEMORY CARD READER
Accesses data stored on flash memory cards.
USB PORTS
Connect USB devices to the computer.

CHAPTER REVIEW 3

Computer Software *Concepts*

LEARNING OBJECTIVES

3-1 Explain system software and operating systems

3-2 Identify operating systems used with personal computers, mobile devices, and servers

3-3 Identify types of utility programs and explain their purpose

3-4 Describe common characteristics of application software

3-5 Describe application software used for business

3-6 Identify types of software used for working with multimedia

3-7 Describe other types of application software

KEY TERMS

Go to CMPTR³ Online for a full list of key terms and definitions.

Android A Linux-based operating system designed for mobile devices developed by the Open Handset Alliance.

application software (apps) The programs that allow you to perform specific tasks on a computer.

boot process The actions taken, including loading the operating system, when a computer is powered up.

device driver (driver) A small program used to communicate with a peripheral device, such as a monitor, printer, portable storage device, or keyboard.

file management program A utility program that enables the user to perform file management tasks, such as copying and deleting files.

graphic An image, such as a digital photograph, clip art, a scanned drawing, or an original image created using a software program.

multiprocessing A processing technique in which multiple processors or multiple processing cores in a single computer each work on a different job.

operating system A collection of programs that manages and coordinates the activities taking place within the computer.

parallel processing A processing technique in which multiple processors or multiple processing cores in a single computer work together to complete one job more quickly.

shareware program Software that is distributed on the honor system; consumers should either pay for it or uninstall it after the trial period.

software license An agreement that specifies the conditions under which a program can be used.

software suite A collection of related software programs bundled together and sold as a single software package.

system software Programs, such as the operating system and utility programs, that control a computer and its devices and enable it to run application software.

virtual memory A memory management technique that uses a portion of the computer's hard drive as additional RAM.

Windows The predominant operating system for personal computers.

KEY CONCEPTS

3-1
Explain system software and operating systems

- **System software** includes the **operating system** and **utility programs** that control a computer and allow you to use it.
- The operating system is loaded into memory during the **boot process** and manages and coordinates the activities taking place within the computer, including managing hardware, processing, memory, files, and interfacing with the user.
- Most operating systems today use a **graphical user interface (GUI)** and can be designed for personal computers, network servers, mobile devices, or embedded systems.

3-2
Identify operating systems used with personal computers, mobile devices, and servers

- The original operating system for personal computers was **DOS**; the most widely used today are **Windows**, **OS X,** and **Linux**.
- Mobile devices most commonly use a version of **Windows**, **iOS**, or **Android**.
- Servers, mainframes, and supercomputers sometimes use an operating system specifiically designed for that system.

3-3
Identify types of utility programs and explain their purpose

- A **utility program** is a software program that performs a specific task, usually related to managing or maintaining the computer system.
- Common types of utility programs include **file management**, **diagnostic**, **disk management**, **backup**, and **security programs.**

3-4
Describe common characteristics of application software

- **Application software (apps)** includes all of the programs that allow you to perform specific tasks on a computer.

CHAPTER 3 REVIEW

KEY CONCEPTS, *cont.*

- Application software can be **commercial**, **shareware**, **freeware**, or **public domain**.
- Mobile devices usually require mobile software.
- Software can be installed on a computer or run directly from the Internet as **cloud software**.

3-5

Describe application software used for business

- Related software programs can be sold bundled as a **software suite**.
- Programs usually in office suites include **word processing**, **spreadsheet**, **database**, and **presentation software**.
- Businesses and individuals often use office suites to create, modify, save, and print documents, as well as to share them via the Web.
- Common office suites include Microsoft Office, Corel WordPerfect Office, Apple iWork, LibreOffice, Apache OpenOffice, and Google Docs.

3-6

Identify types of software used for working with multimedia

- **Graphics** are digital representations of images; **multimedia** refers to any application that contains more than one type of data, such as audio and video.
- Software used with graphics and multimedia include **graphics software**, audio capture and editing software, video editing and DVD authoring software, and **media players**.

3-7

Describe other types of application software

- Other types of software include **desktop publishing** software; **educational**, **entertainment**, and **reference software**; **note taking software**; **CAD software**; **accounting** and **personal finance software**; and **project management**, **collaboration**, and **remote access software**.

DIGITAL BACKPACK

- **Practice It:** Practice It 3-3—Consider the advantages and disadvantages of cloud applications.
- **On Your Own:** On Your Own 3-2—Research and discuss freeware.
- **Collect StudyBits:** Use your highlighted StudyBits from CMPTR[3] Online to create notes, rate your understanding, and create practice quizzes.
- **Quiz:** Take the practice quizzes on key concepts in the chapter to prepare for tests.
- **Key Terms:** Review key terms and definitions with flashcards, and create your own flashcards from your StudyBits.
- **Videos:** Watch the videos to learn more about the topics taught in this chapter.

INFOGRAPHIC

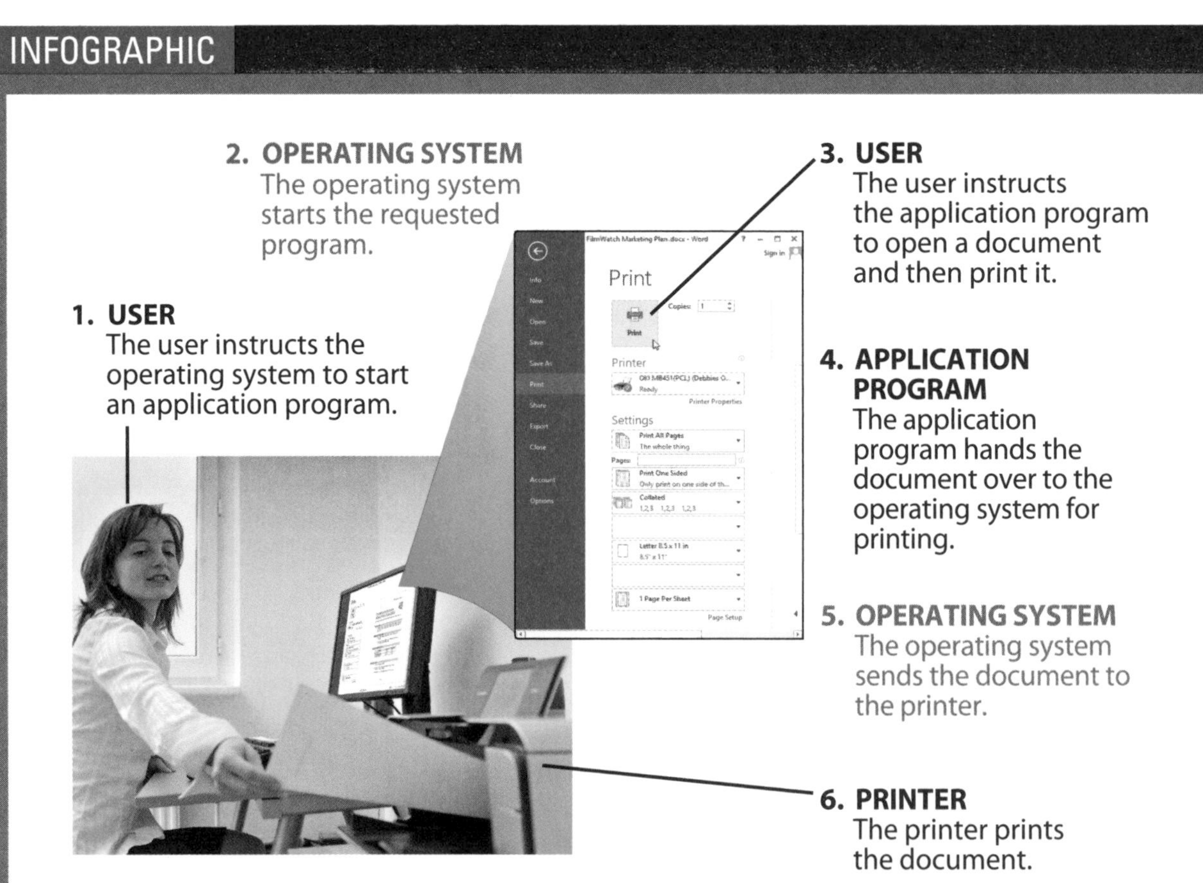

1. USER
The user instructs the operating system to start an application program.
2. OPERATING SYSTEM
The operating system starts the requested program.
3. USER
The user instructs the application program to open a document and then print it.
4. APPLICATION PROGRAM
The application program hands the document over to the operating system for printing.
5. OPERATING SYSTEM
The operating system sends the document to the printer.
6. PRINTER
The printer prints the document.
Print
Printer
Settings

CHAPTER REVIEW 4

Computer Networks
Networks and the Internet

LEARNING OBJECTIVES

- **4-1** Explain what networks are and some common networking applications
- **4-2** Identify network characteristics
- **4-3** Understand how data is transmitted over a network
- **4-4** Describe common types of network media
- **4-5** Identify communications protocols and networking standards
- **4-6** Describe networking hardware

KEY CONCEPTS

4-1
Explain what networks are and some common networking applications

- Businesses use computer networks to share resources, access the Internet, and enable individuals to communicate with each other.
- Individuals use networks to also share multimedia among the networked devices in a home as well as to locate information and stay in touch with others while they are on the go.
- Other types of communications networks are those used for television and radio broadcasting, **mobile phone** calls, and the **GPS** system.

4-2
Identify network characteristics

- Networks can be **wired networks** or **wireless networks**; wireless networks can be private or public **hotspots**.
- The physical topology of a network can be a **star**, **bus**, or **mesh network**.
- Networks can be **client-server networks** in which **client** devices request resources from **servers** or **peer-to-peer (P2P) networks** where users have direct access to all network devices.
- Networks vary in size from **personal area networks (PANs)** and **local area networks (LANs)** to **wide area networks (WANs)**.
- A **virtual area network (VPN)** is a private, secure path over a public network, usually the Internet.

KEY TERMS

Go to CMPTR[3] Online for a full list of key terms and definitions.

bandwidth The amount of data that can be transferred, such as via a bus or over a networking medium, in a given time period.

Bluetooth A networking standard for very short-range wireless connections.

client In a client-server network, a computer or other device that requests and uses network resources.

client-server network A network that includes both client devices and the servers that process client requests.

communications protocol A set of rules that determine how devices on a network communicate.

computer network Computers and other devices that are connected to share hardware, software, and data.

download To retrieve files from a server.

dual-mode phone A mobile phone that can be used with more than one communications network, such as with both a cellular and a Wi-Fi network.

Ethernet (802.3) The most widely used standard for wired networks.

fiber-optic cable A networking cable that contains hundreds of thin, transparent fibers over which lasers transmit data as light.

hotspot A location that provides wireless Internet access.

Internet of Things (IoT) The network of everyday physical objects that can communicate with each other via the Internet.

network interface card (NIC) A network adapter in the form of an expansion card.

server In a client-server network, a computer that is dedicated to processing client requests.

smart home A home that uses smart appliances and/or other smart features to automate household tasks.

TCP/IP A networking protocol that uses packet switching to facilitate the transmission of messages; the protocol used with the Internet.

telemedicine The use of networking technology to provide medical information and services.

upload To transfer files to a server.

virtual private network (VPN) A private, secure path over the Internet used for accessing a private network.

wide area network (WAN) A network that connects devices located in a large geographical area.

Wi-Fi (802.11) A widely used networking standard for medium-range wireless networks.

4-3
Understand how data is transmitted over a network

- **Bandwidth** is the amount of data that can be transferred over a networking medium in a given period of time; **throughput** is the amount of data actually transferred.
- Data sent over a network can use either **digital** or **analog signals**; it can also be sent using either **serial** or **parallel transmission**.
- Networks can use **circuit switching**, **packet switching**, or **broadcasting** to deliver data across a network.

CHAPTER 4 REVIEW

KEY CONCEPTS, *cont.*

4-4

Describe common types of networking media

• Wired networking media include **twisted-pair cables**, **coaxial (coax) cables**, or **fiber-optic cables**.

• Wireless networks use primarily radio signals, such as **cellular radio transmissions** sent to and from cell towers and **microwave** signals sent to and from **microwave stations** and **communications satellites**.

4-5

Identify communications protocols and networking standards

• **TCP/IP** is used to transfer data over the Internet.

• HTTP (Hypertext Transfer Protocol) and HTTPS (Secure Hypertext Transfer Protocol) are used to display Web pages.

• **Ethernet (802.3)** is the most widely used standard for wired networks.

• **Wi-Fi (802.11)** is the most common standard used with wireless networks.

• The most common cellular standards include 3G (such as HSDPA/UMTS and EV-DO) and 4G (such as LTE) standards.

• Wireless standards used for short-range networking include **Bluetooth**, Wi-Fi Direct, Wi-Gig, Wireless HD, ZigBee, and Z-Wave.

4-6

Describe networking hardware

• To connect to a network, a **network adapter** or **modem** is used.

• To connect devices and networks, a **switch**, **router**, or **bridge** is used.

• Other networking hardware include **repeaters**, **range extenders**, and **antennas**.

DIGITAL BACKPACK

• **Practice It:** Practice It 4-3—Create a wired home network scenario.

• **On Your Own:** On Your Own 4-2—Discuss possible solutions to the problem of interference with wireless devices and who should be responsible for fixing the problem.

• **Collect StudyBits:** Use your highlighted StudyBits from CMPTR[3] Online to create notes, rate your understanding, and create practice quizzes.

• **Quiz:** Take the practice quizzes on key concepts in the chapter to prepare for tests.

• **Key Terms:** Review the key terms and definitions with flashcards, and create your own flashcards from your StudyBits.

• **Videos:** Watch the videos to learn more about the topics taught in this chapter.

INFOGRAPHIC

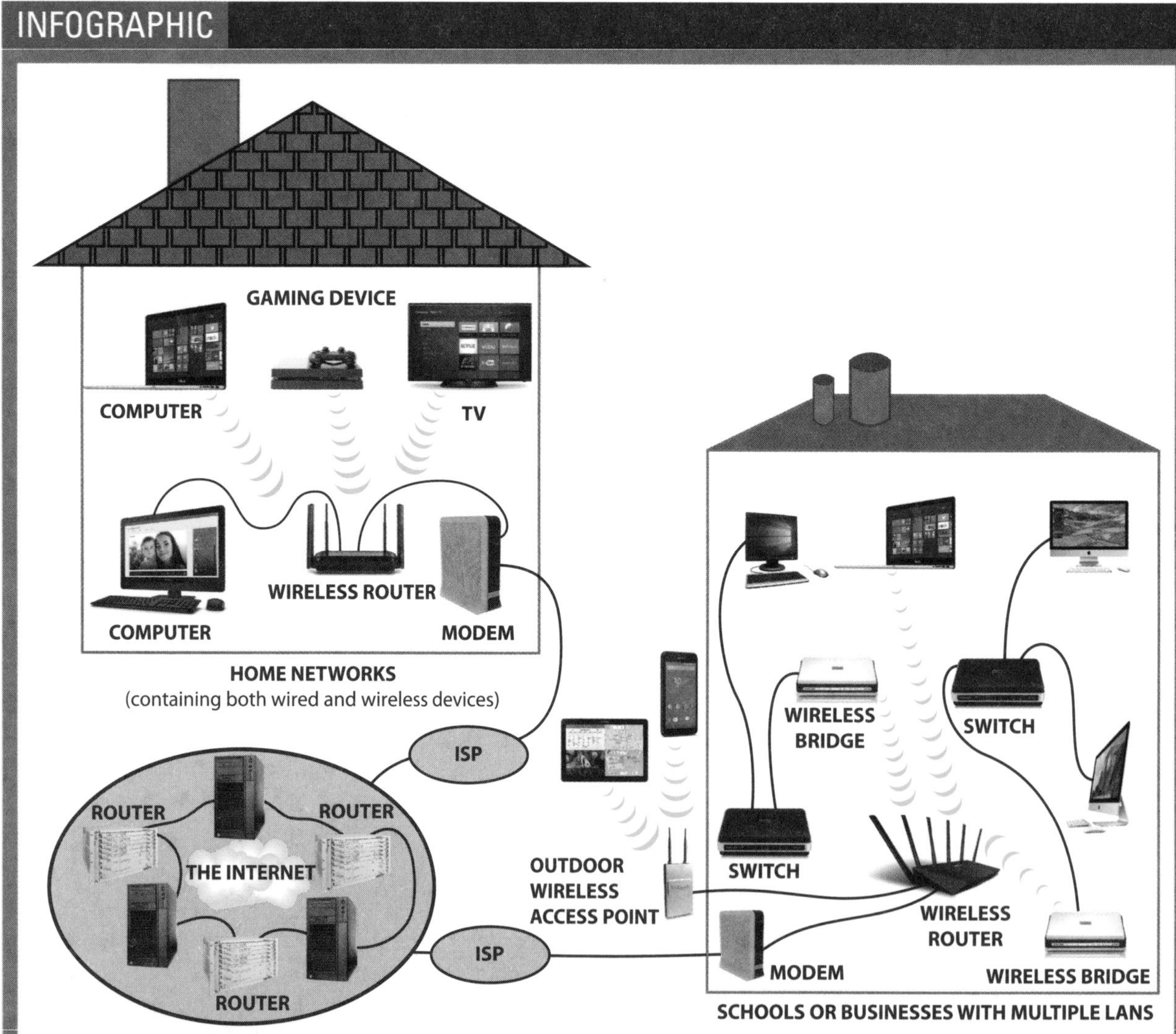

CHAPTER REVIEW 5

The Internet and Email
Networks and the Internet

LEARNING OBJECTIVES

5-1 Understand how the Internet evolved

5-2 Set up your computer to use the Internet

5-3 Understand how to search the Internet for information

5-4 Understand email and other types of messaging

5-5 Describe common Internet activities

KEY TERMS

Go to CMPTR³ Online for a full list of key terms and definitions.

ARPANET The predecessor to the Internet; named after the Advanced Research Projects Agency (ARPA), which sponsored its development.

augmented reality A technology that overlays computer-generated images on top of real-time, real life images.

blog A Web page that contains short, frequently updated entries in chronological order, typically by just one individual.

DSL (Digital Subscriber Line) Internet access Fast, direct Internet access via standard telephone lines.

e-commerce The act of performing financial transactions online.

Internet The largest and most well-known computer network, linking billions of computers all over the world.

mobile wireless Internet access Internet access via a mobile phone network.

net neutrality The basic concept that all content on the Internet is equal.

podcast A recorded audio or video file that can be played or downloaded via the Web.

search engine A software program used by a search site to retrieve matching Web pages from a search database.

social networking site A site that enables individuals to connect and interact with other individuals.

Web conference A face-to-face meeting that takes place via the Web.

Wi-Fi hotspot A location that provides wireless Internet access to the public.

KEY CONCEPTS

5-1
Understand how the Internet evolved

- **ARPANET**, the predecessor of the Internet, was created in 1969 as an experiment to enable researchers to communicate and to send data over a variety of paths.
- In 1989, Tim Berners-Lee proposed the **World Wide Web** as a way to organize information using Web pages.
- The Mosaic Web browser, released in 1993, provided a graphical user interface, allowing users to display images and increasing the use of the Web dramatically.
- The Web is the most widely used part of the Internet today.
- The Internet community includes users, **Internet service providers (ISPs)**, **Internet content providers, application service providers (ASPs)**, infrastructure companies, hardware and software companies, governments, and Internet organizations.

5-2
Set up your computer to use the Internet

- You can access the Internet using a variety of devices, such as a personal computer, a smartphone, or a smart TV.
- Connection types can be dial-up connections like **conventional dial-up Internet access**, but most are direct connections like **cable**, **DSL**, **satellite**, **fixed wireless**, or **broadband over fiber (BoF) Internet access**.
- **Wi-Fi hotspots** can be used to connect to the Internet from many locations.
- If you are using your own Internet connection, you will need to select an appropriate ISP based on your type of device, budget, location, and other factors.
- Some Internet setups require professional installation; others you can do on your own.

5-3
Understand how to search the Internet for information

- **Search sites** are Web sites designed to help users find information on the Web.
- Most search sites use a **search engine** (a software program) along with a database of information about Web pages to help users find Web pages.
- To conduct a search, you type one or more **keywords** into the search box on a search site; its search engine uses those keywords to return **hits** for Web pages that match your search criteria.
- To avoid plagiarizing Web page content, you need to credit Web page sources and other Internet resources when you use them in papers, on Web pages, or in other documents.

5-4
Understand email and other types of messaging

- You can send email messages from any Internet-enabled device to any email address.
- The sent message travels from your device, through the Internet, to your mail server then continues through the Internet to the recipient's mail server, and then to the recipient's device.

CHAPTER 5 REVIEW

- Email can be sent and received via an installed email program or via Web mail.
- Other types of messaging include **instant messaging (IM)** sent via messaging apps, **text messages** sent from one mobile phone to another, and messages sent via social networks.

5-5

Describe common Internet activities

- Other types of online communication include **blogs**, **wikis**, **forums**, **podcasts**, **Voice over Internet Protocol (VoIP)**, **Web conferences**, and **Webinars**.
- Online education includes **Web-based training (WBT)** and **distance learning**, both of which usually progress at the user's own pace.
- **Social media** is the collection of **social networking sites** and other online platforms used to transmit or share information with a broad audience.
- Other online activities include listening to music, watching online TV, and other forms of online entertainment; online shopping and other types of e-commerce; and obtaining product, corporate, and government information.

DIGITAL BACKPACK

- **Practice It:** Practice It 5-3—Consider the ethics of paid or sponsored blog posts.
- **On Your Own:** On Your Own 5-2—Evaluate the pros and cons of allowing defendants and witnesses to participate remotely in court proceedings.
- **Collect StudyBits:** Use your highlighted StudyBits from CMPTR[3] Online to create notes, rate your understanding, and create practice quizzes.
- **Quiz:** Take the practice quizzes on key concepts in the chapter to prepare for tests.
- **Key Terms:** Review the key terms and definitions with flashcards, and create your own flashcards from your StudyBits.
- **Videos:** Watch the videos to learn more about the topics taught in this chapter.

INFOGRAPHIC

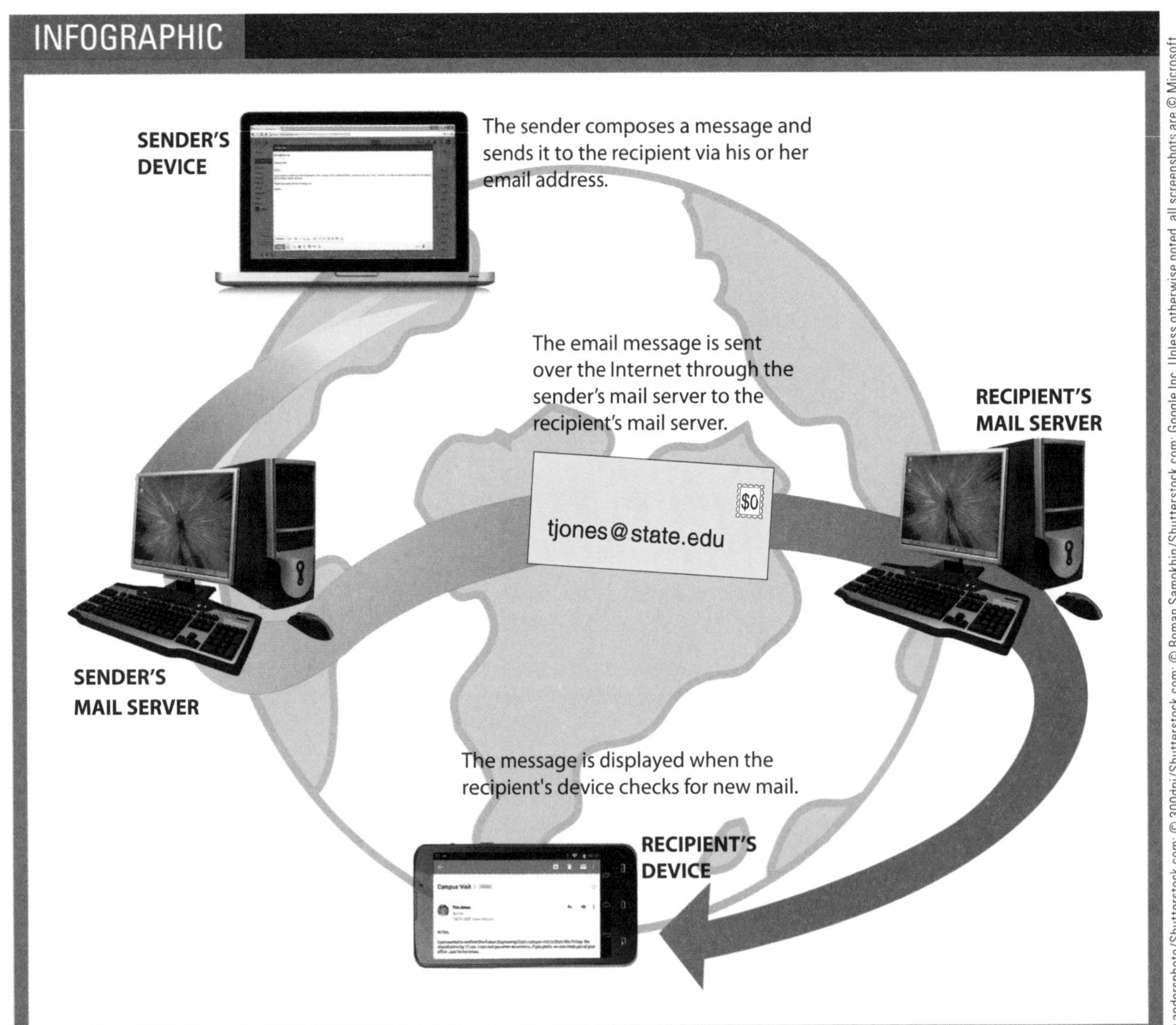
SENDER'S DEVICE
The sender composes a message and sends it to the recipient via his or her email address.
The email message is sent over the Internet through the sender's mail server to the recipient's mail server.
RECIPIENT'S MAIL SERVER
$0
tjones@state.edu
SENDER'S MAIL SERVER
The message is displayed when the recipient's device checks for new mail.
RECIPIENT'S DEVICE

CHAPTER REVIEW 6

Security and Privacy
Networks and the Internet

LEARNING OBJECTIVES

6-1 Explain the importance of network and Internet security

6-2 Define unauthorized access and use and list some precautions

6-3 Define computer sabotage and list some precautions

6-4 Describe online theft, online fraud, and other dot cons and list some precautions

6-5 Describe cyberstalking and other personal safety concerns and list some precautions

6-6 List some personal computer security risks and identify some precautions

6-7 Identify privacy concerns and list some precautions

6-8 Discuss current security and privacy legislation

KEY TERMS

Go to CMPTR³ Online for a full list of key terms and definitions.

antivirus software Software used to detect and eliminate computer viruses and other types of malware.

bot A computer that is controlled by a hacker or other computer criminal.

computer virus A software program installed without the user's knowledge that is designed to alter the way a computer operates or to cause harm to the computer system.

cyberstalking Repeated threats or harassing behavior between adults carried out via email or another Internet communications method.

electronic profiling Using electronic means to collect a variety of in-depth information about an individual, such as name, address, income, and buying habits.

encryption A method of scrambling content to make it unreadable if an unauthorized user intercepts it.

firewall A collection of hardware and/or software that protects a computer or computer network from unauthorized access.

kill switch A software program or app that enables a device owner to disable that device remotely.

phishing The use of electronic communications (typically email messages) to gain credit card numbers and other personal data to be used for fraudulent purposes.

surge suppressor A device that protects a computer system from damage due to electrical fluctuations.

two-factor authentication Using two different methods to authenticate a user.

wipe To permanently destroy the data on a device so it cannot be recovered.

KEY CONCEPTS

6-1
Explain the importance of network and Internet security

- **Computer crime (cybercrime)** includes any illegal act involving a computer.
- Some security concerns are just annoyances, but others have much more serious consequences.

6-2
Define unauthorized access and use and list some precautions

- Criminals gain access to data, files, and other content by **hacking** into a computer or network or via the Internet.
- To protect against unauthorized access and use, access controls systems can be used.
- Using a **firewall** creates a barrier between a computer or network and the Internet.
- To protect data from being viewed by unauthorized individuals, **private key** or **private key encryption** can be used.

6-3
Define computer sabotage and list some precautions

- **Computer sabotage** includes any act of malicious destruction to a computer or computing resource.
- Types of computer sabotage include **botnets; computer viruses, computer worms, Trojan horses,** and other types of **malware; denial of service (DoS)** attacks, and alteration of data, programs, or Web sites.
- **Antivirus software** and other **security software** can help protect against malware.

6-4
Describe online theft, online fraud, and other dot cons and list some precautions

- **Dot cons** include **data, information,** or **identity theft; phishing, spear phishing, pharming,** and **social media hacking; online auction fraud;** and other Internet scams.
- To help protect against dot cons, guard your personal information, use common sense, and don't click links in unsolicited messages.

6-5
Describe cyberstalking and other personal safety concerns and list some precautions

- Cybercrime can be physically dangerous.
- Types of online harassment include **cyberbullying** and **cyberstalking**.
- To help protect yourself, be discreet and nonprovocative online.

CHAPTER 6 REVIEW

KEY CONCEPTS, *cont.*

6-6

List some personal computer security risks and identify some precautions

- Common personal security concerns include hardware theft, loss, or damage as well as **system failure**.
- To protect against hardware loss, you can use doors and equipment, encrypt files or use a **self-encrypting hard drive**, and use tracking software.
- To protect against hardware damage, you can use **ruggedized devices**, a **surge protector**, and keep your devices away from dust, heat, static electricity, and moisture.

6-7

Identify privacy concerns and list some precautions

- **Privacy** is the state of being concealed or free from unauthorized intrusions; **information privacy** is the right to control how information about yourself is collected and used.
- Information can be located in **marketing** and **government** databases, which can result in **electronic profiling** and **spam**.
- Most businesses and Web sites that collect personal information have a **privacy policy**.
- Electronic surveillance includes **computer-monitoring software, video surveillance, employee monitoring**, and **presence technology**.
- To protect your privacy, **wipe** or otherwise destroy storage media being disposed of and avoid putting too many personal details online.
- To avoid spam, use a **throw-away email address** for activities that may result in spam, use a **spam filter**, and consider **opting out** of marketing activities.

6-8

Discuss current security and privacy legislation

- New legislation is passed periodically to address the latest computer crimes, but it is difficult for the legal system to keep pace with the rate at which technology changes.
- Some federal laws pertaining to computer or Internet security and privacy have been passed.

DIGITAL BACKPACK

- **Practice It:** Practice It 6-3—Research risks related to using a W-Fi hotspot and identify precautions you can take.
- **On Your Own:** On Your Own 6-2—Consider the ethics of including instruction on writing computer viruses in computer classes.
- **Collect StudyBits:** Use your highlighted StudyBits from CMPTR³ Online to create notes, rate your understanding, and create practice quizzes.
- **Quiz:** Take the practice quizzes on key concepts in the chapter to prepare for tests.
- **Key Terms:** Review the terms and definitions with flashcards, and create your own flashcards from your StudyBits.
- **Videos:** Watch the videos to learn more about the topics taught in this chapter.

INFOGRAPHIC

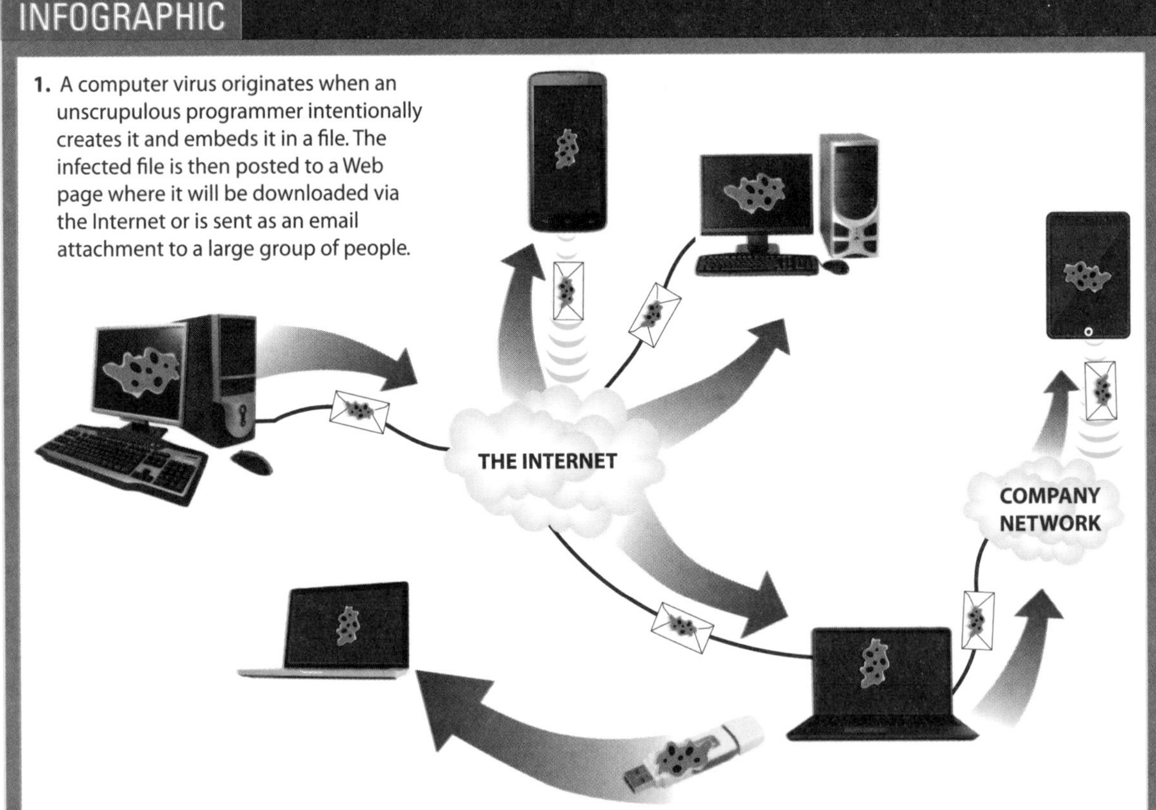

1. A computer virus originates when an unscrupulous programmer intentionally creates it and embeds it in a file. The infected file is then posted to a Web page where it will be downloaded via the Internet or is sent as an email attachment to a large group of people.
THE INTERNET
COMPANY NETWORK
2. When the infected file is opened, the virus copies itself to that device's hard drive and the device is infected. The virus may then email itself to people in the newly infected device's email address book or copy itself to any removable storage medium inserted into that device.
3. A virus can spread very quickly because every device that comes in contact with the virus—whether through an infected removable storage medium, infected downloaded file, or infected email attachment—becomes infected, unless antivirus software is used to prevent it.

CHAPTER REVIEW 7

Exploring Windows 10 and Managing Files
Windows 10

LEARNING OBJECTIVES

- 7-1 Use the Windows 10 desktop
- 7-2 Work with windows on the desktop
- 7-3 Work with the Windows file system
- 7-4 Work with files
- 7-5 Delete files and work with the Recycle Bin
- 7-6 Close apps and windows
- 7-7 Get help in Windows
- 7-8 Shut down Windows

KEY CONCEPTS

7-1
Use the Windows 10 desktop

- If the lock screen appears when you start Windows, click anywhere on the screen or press any key.
- On the Sign in screen, click your user name, type your password if you have one, and then press the Enter key.
- To start an app, click the Start button, click All apps if necessary, and then click the app name in the left pane or click the app tile in the right name. Or type the app name in the Search the web and Windows box.

7-2
Work with windows on the desktop

- Drag a window to a new position on the desktop by dragging it by its title bar.
- To resize a window, drag one of its edges.

7-3
Work with the Windows file system

- At the top of the hierarchy is the root directory, which usually is drive C.
- Folders can contain subfolders.
- To open a File Explorer window, click the File Explorer button on the taskbar.
- Double-click drives and folders in File Explorer windows until the contents of the folder you want to view are listed.

KEY TERMS

Go to CMPTR[3] Online for a full list of key terms and definitions.

active window The window to which the next keystroke or command is applied.

Address bar A bar in a File Explorer window that lists the location of the currently displayed folder.

button An object that you click to execute a command or perform a task.

click To press the left mouse button and immediately release it.

Clipboard A temporary storage area in Windows on which objects are stored when you copy or move them.

desktop The work area for using applications designed to run in Windows and where you manage files and folders.

dialog box A window that opens when you need to enter or choose settings for how you want to perform a task.

double-click To click the left mouse button twice in quick succession.

drag To position the pointer on top of an item, and then press and hold the left mouse button while moving the pointer.

file A named collection of bytes stored on a drive.

folder A container that helps to organize files on a computer.

menu A group or list of commands that you click to complete tasks.

navigation pane An area on the left side of File Explorer windows that contains icons and links to locations on your computer and your network.

path The notation that indicates a file's location on a computer.

point To position the pointer directly on top of an item.

pointer A small object, such as an arrow, that moves on the screen when you move your mouse.

Quick Access Toolbar An area at the left side of the title bar that contains buttons for frequently used commands.

ribbon An area at the top of File Explorer and some application windows that contains commands for working with the contents of the window.

right-click To click the right mouse button and immediately release it.

ScreenTip A box that appears when you point to an item that displays information about the item, such as its name or purpose.

shortcut menu A menu that lists actions you can take with the item you right-clicked.

shut down To close all running apps and Windows before completely turning off power to the computer.

Start button A button you use to start apps, access files, adjust settings on your computer, and other tasks.

subfolder A folder contained within another folder.

taskbar The horizontal bar containing buttons that provide quick access to common tools and running programs and buttons to start some programs.

title bar A banner at the top of a window that displays the window title and contains the Close button and sizing buttons.

window A rectangular work area on the desktop that contains an app, text, files, or other data and tools for performing tasks.

CHAPTER 7 REVIEW

KEY CONCEPTS, *cont.*

7-4
Work with files
- To create a compressed folder, select the files and folders you want to compress. Click the Share tab, and then click the Zip button.
- To create a folder, on the Quick Access Toolbar, click the New folder button.
- To move a file or folder into a folder, drag the file or folder on top of another folder.
- To copy a file or folder, press and hold the Ctrl key as you drag the file or folder on top of another folder.
- To rename a file or folder, right-click it, and then click Rename.

7-5
Delete files and work with the Recycle Bin
- Drag files and folders to the Recycle Bin from the hard drive to store them in the Recycle Bin.
- Drag files and folders to the Recycle Bin from removable storage, such as a USB drive, to permanently delete those files and folders.
- Right-click the Recycle Bin, and then click Empty Recycle Bin to permanently delete the files and folders in it.

7-6
Close apps and windows
- Click the Close button in the title bar.

7-7
Get help in Windows
- Type a search phrase in the Search the web and Windows box.
- Use the Contact Support app.

7-8
Shut down Windows
- Shut down to close all open apps, shut down Windows, and turn off your computer.

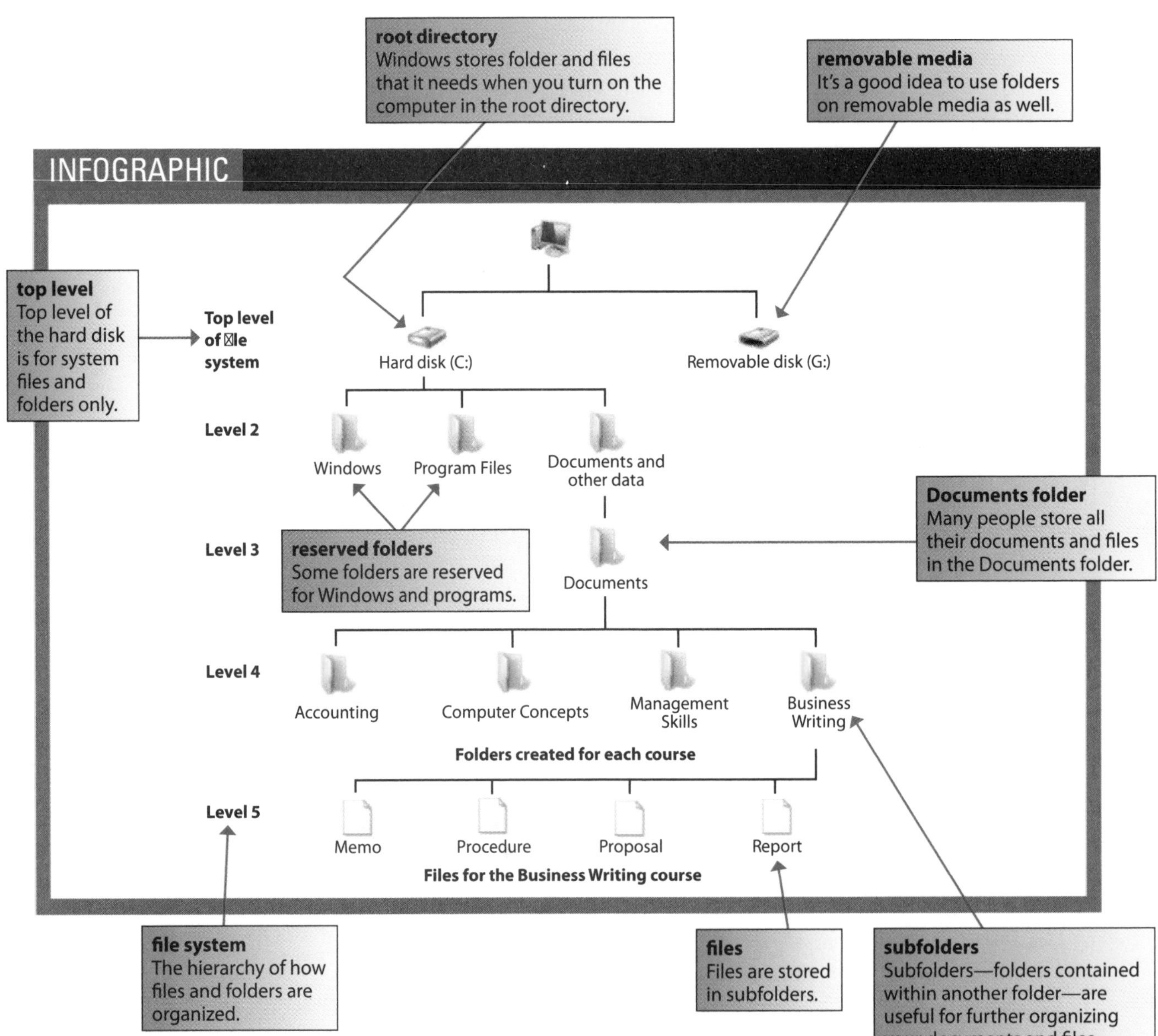
root directory
Windows stores folder and files that it needs when you turn on the computer in the root directory.
removable media
It's a good idea to use folders on removable media as well.
INFOGRAPHIC
top level
Top level of the hard disk is for system files and folders only.
Top level of file system
Hard disk (C:)
Removable disk (G:)
Level 2
Windows
Program Files
Documents and other data
Level 3
reserved folders
Some folders are reserved for Windows and programs.
Documents
Documents folder
Many people store all their documents and files in the Documents folder.
Level 4
Accounting
Computer Concepts
Management Skills
Business Writing
Folders created for each course
Level 5
Memo
Procedure
Proposal
Report
Files for the Business Writing course
file system
The hierarchy of how files and folders are organized.
files
Files are stored in subfolders.
subfolders
Subfolders—folders contained within another folder—are useful for further organizing your documents and files.

CHAPTER REVIEW 8

Using Edge, Mail, and People

Browser and Email

LEARNING OBJECTIVES

- 8-1 Browse the Web with Edge
- 8-2 Save links to Web pages
- 8-3 Create Web notes
- 8-4 Print Web pages and Web notes
- 8-5 Clean up the Hub and unpin Web pages
- 8-6 Exit Edge
- 8-7 Use the Mail app
- 8-8 Add information to the People app

KEY TERMS

Address bar The bar at the top of the Edge window that contains the Web address of the displayed Web page.

attachment A file that is sent with an email message.

contact Each person or organization with whom you communicate and about whom you store information.

conversation In Mail, an original email and its replies.

favorite A link to a Web page saved in the Favorites.

history A list that tracks the Web pages you visit over multiple browsing sessions.

home page The main page of a Web site.

keyword A word typed in a search box on a search site or other Web page to locate information related to that keyword.

link Text or a graphic formatted to load a Web page, jump to another location on the same Web page, or open a document when it is clicked.

load To copy a Web page from a server to a computer.

Mail A Windows 10 app used to send, receive, and manage email.

Microsoft Edge (Edge) The default Web browser in Windows 10.

People A Windows 10 app used to store information about the people and businesses with whom you communicate.

profile The collected information about a contact.

reading list A collection of links to Web pages.

search engine A software program used by a search site to retrieve Web pages containing the keywords from a search database.

search phrase Multiple keywords.

search results A list of links to Web pages that contain the keywords entered in a search engine.

search site A Web site designed to help users search for Web pages that contain keywords.

start page The page that appears when Edge starts.

tab An object that displays a Web page within Edge.

Web note A Web page that you save as an image with drawn or typed notes and highlights.

KEY CONCEPTS

8-1

Browse the Web with Edge

- To start Edge, on the task bar, click the Microsoft Edge button.
- To display a Web page, click in the Address bar or, on the Start page or on a new tab, click in the Search or enter web address box, type the Web address of the Web page, and then press the Enter key.
- To display a page previously visited during the current session, click the Back button to the left of the Address bar.
- To open a new tab, click the New Tab button to the right of the tabs.

8-2

Save links to Web pages

- To pin a Web page to the Start menu, click the More button, and then click Pin this page to Start.
- To save a Web page as a favorite or an entry on the reading list, click the Add to favorites or reading list button, click the Favorites or Reading List button, and then click Add.

8-3

Create Web notes

- To the right of the Address bar, click the Make a Web Note button.
- To draw on the page, on the purple bar, click the Pen button, click a color, and then drag the pointer on the page.
- To highlight something on the page, on the purple bar, click the Highlighter, and then drag on the screen.
- To add a typed note on the page, on the purple bar, click the Add a typed note button, click on the page, and then type the note.
- To save the Web note, on the purple bar, click the Save Web Note button, click the OneNote button, the Favorites button, or the Reading list button, and then click the Save button.
- To close a Web note, on the purple bar, click the Exit button.

8-4

Print Web pages and Web notes

- To print a Web page, click the More button, and then click Print.

CHAPTER 8 REVIEW

KEY CONCEPTS, *cont.*

8-5
Clean up the Hub and unpin Web pages

- To delete a favorite or an entry in the reading list, display the list, right-click the item, and then click Delete.
- To unpin a Web page from the Start menu, right-click the tile, and then click Unpin from Start.

8-6
Exit Edge

- To exit Edge, click the Close button in the upper-right corner.

8-7
Use the Mail app

- To start Mail, on the taskbar, click the Start button, and then on the Start menu, click the Mail tile.
- To create a new email message, in the top-left corner of the screen, click the New mail button.
- To reply to a message, select it, at the top of the right pane, and then click the Reply or Reply all button.
- To forward a message, select it, at the top of the right pane, and then click the Forward button.
- To attach a file to a message, at the top of the right pane, click Insert, click the Attach button, click the file, and then click Open.

8-8
Use the People app

- To start the People app, on the taskbar, click the Start button, and then on the Start menu, click the People tile.
- To create a new contact, in the left pane, click the New contact button, add the contact information, and then click the Save button.
- To delete a contact, in the top-right corner of the window, click the See more button, click Delete, and then click Delete in the dialog box.

DIGITAL BACKPACK

- **Practice It and On Your Own**—online
- **Quiz:** Take the practice quizzes on key concepts in the chapter to prepare for tests.
- **Key Terms:** Review key terms and definitions with flashcards, and create your own flashcards from your StudyBits.
- **Videos:** Watch the videos to learn more about the skills taught in this chapter.
- **Collect StudyBits:** Use your highlighted StudyBits from CMPTR Online to create notes, rate your understanding, and create practice quizzes.

Back and Forward buttons
Redisplays the previously viewed Web page and the Web page displayed after the current page.
active tab
The tab containing the currently displayed Web page.
Close tab button
Closes the tab.
New tab button
Opens a new tab.
Address bar
The bar at the top of the Edge window that contains the Web address of the displayed Web page.
Hub button
Click to open the pane that contains the Favorites, Reading list, and History list.
INFOGRAPHIC
Favorites bar
Contains favorites you want to access frequently.
favorite
A link to a Web page saved in the Favorites list.
links
Text or graphics formatted so that when you click them, another Web page loads in the browser window, you jump to another location on the same Web page, or you open a document stored on your computer or on a Web server.
National Park Service
About Us
What We Do
FAVORITES

CHAPTER REVIEW 9
Introducing Microsoft Office 2016
Office 2016

LEARNING OBJECTIVES

- **9-1** Explore common elements of Office application windows
- **9-2** Use the ribbon
- **9-3** Select text and use the Mini toolbar
- **9-4** Undo and redo
- **9-5** Zoom and scroll
- **9-6** Work with Office files
- **9-7** Use the Clipboard
- **9-8** Get Help
- **9-9** Exit Office applications

KEY CONCEPTS

9-1
Explore common elements of Office application windows
- Click the Start button or the Search the web and Windows box, type the name of the application you want to start, and then click it in the list of results.

9-2
Use the ribbon
- Click a tab on the ribbon to display its buttons.
- Remember that contextual tabs appear only when an object is selected.
- Position the pointer on top of a button to see a ScreenTip with its name and keyboard shortcut (if it has one).
- To display Backstage view, click the File tab on the ribbon.
- Click Dialog Box Launchers to open dialog boxes or panes containing additional commands.

9-3
Select text and use the Mini toolbar
- To select text using the mouse, click before the first character, press and hold the mouse button, and then drag over the text.
- To select text using the keyboard, position the insertion point before the first, press and hold the Shift key, and then press the arrow key pointing in the direction you want to select.
- To select text using the mouse and the keyboard, click before the first character, press and hold the Shift key, and then click after the last character.
- To select nonadjacent text, select the first block of text, press and hold the Ctrl key, and then drag to select other blocks of text.
- To access the Mini toolbar, select text using the mouse or right-click.

9-4
Undo and redo
- To undo an action, click the Undo button on the Quick Access Toolbar.
- To redo an action, click the Redo button on the Quick Access Toolbar

9-5
Zoom and scroll
- Use the zoom controls at the right end of the status bar or the commands in the Zoom group on the View tab to change the zoom of a file.
- Use the horizontal and vertical scroll bars to slide another part of the file into view.

KEY TERMS

Backstage view A screen that contains commands to manage application files and options.

Clipboard A temporary storage area in Windows on which text or other objects are stored when you copy or cut them.

copy To duplicate selected text or an object and place it on the Clipboard.

cut To remove selected text or an object from the original location and place it on the Clipboard.

database An Access file.

document A Word file.

gallery A menu or grid that shows visual representations of the options available for a button.

Live Preview A feature that shows the results that would occur if you clicked the option to which you are pointing in a gallery.

menu A list of commands that appears when you click a button.

Microsoft Office 2016 (Office) A collection of Microsoft programs.

Mini toolbar A toolbar with buttons for commonly used formatting commands that appears next to the pointer when you select text using the mouse or you right-click.

navigation bar The left pane in Backstage view.

object Anything in a file that can be manipulated as a whole.

paste To insert a copy of the text or object on the Clipboard in a file.

presentation A PowerPoint file.

Protected View A view of a file in an Office application in which you can see the file contents, but you cannot edit, save, or print them until you enable editing.

text box An object that contains text.

toggle button A button that you click once to turn a feature on and click again to turn it off.

workbook An Excel file.

KEY CONCEPTS, *cont.*

9-6
Work with Office files
- The Save command saves the file using the same file name and in the same location.
- The Save As command saves a copy of the file; you can type a new name and choose a new location.
- To close a file, click the Close button in the upper-right corner.
- To open a file, click the File tab, click Open, click Browse, navigate to the folder containing the file you want to open, click the file, and then click Open.

9-7
Use the Clipboard
- Use the Cut and Copy commands to place items on the Clipboard; use the Paste command to place an item on the Clipboard in the file.
- To use the Office Clipboard to collect up to 24 items, click the Dialog Box Launcher in the Clipboard group on the Home tab.

9-8
Get Help
- Click in the Tell me what you want to do box on the ribbon, and then type key words related to the command or topic you want help with.

9-9
Exit Office applications
- To exit an Office application, click the Close button in the upper-right corner of the application window.

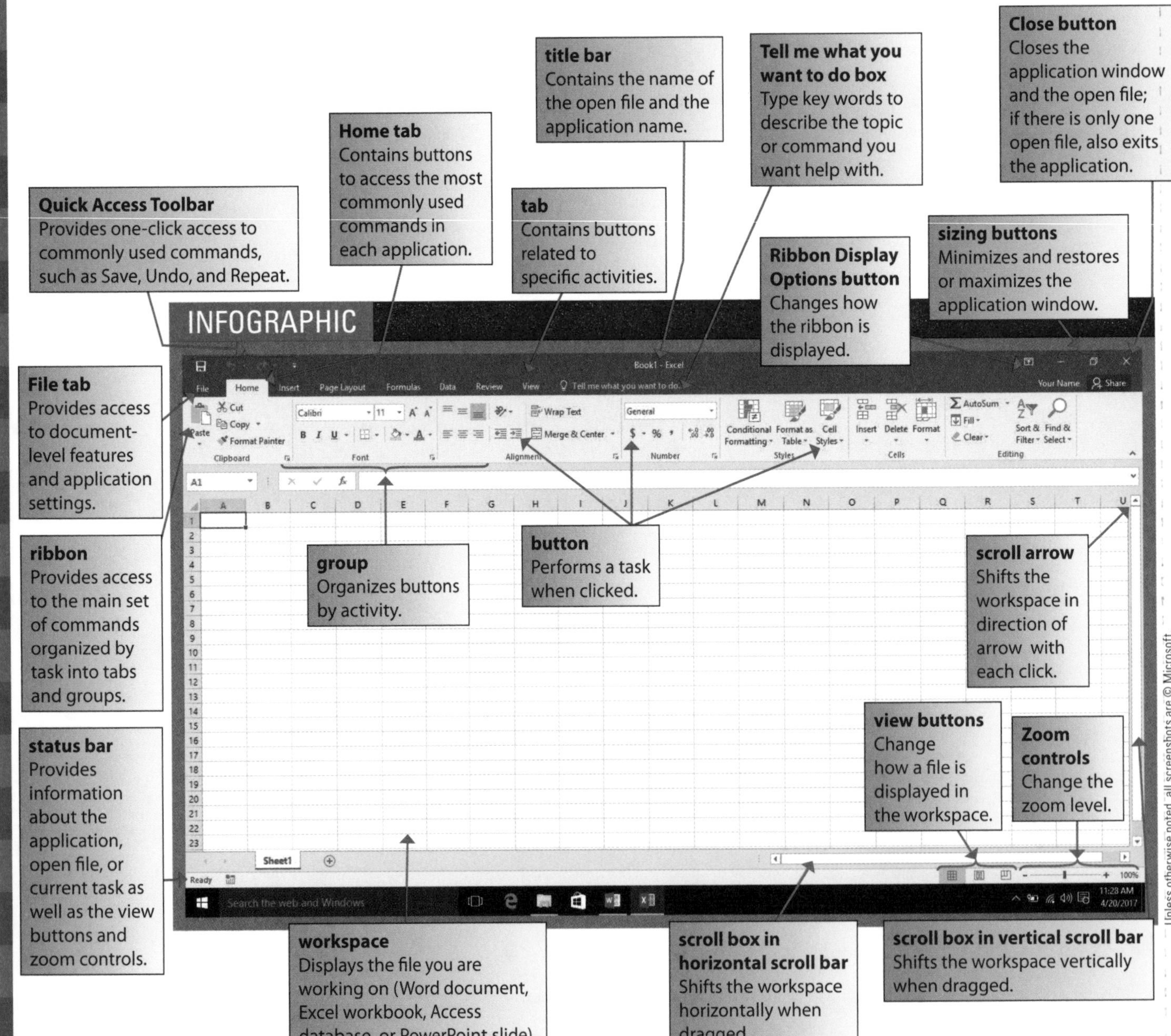

INFOGRAPHIC
title bar Contains the name of the open file and the application name.
Tell me what you want to do box Type key words to describe the topic or command you want help with.
Close button Closes the application window and the open file; if there is only one open file, also exits the application.
Home tab Contains buttons to access the most commonly used commands in each application.
Quick Access Toolbar Provides one-click access to commonly used commands, such as Save, Undo, and Repeat.
tab Contains buttons related to specific activities.
Ribbon Display Options button Changes how the ribbon is displayed.
sizing buttons Minimizes and restores or maximizes the application window.
File tab Provides access to document-level features and application settings.
ribbon Provides access to the main set of commands organized by task into tabs and groups.
group Organizes buttons by activity.
button Performs a task when clicked.
scroll arrow Shifts the workspace in direction of arrow with each click.
status bar Provides information about the application, open file, or current task as well as the view buttons and zoom controls.
view buttons Change how a file is displayed in the workspace.
Zoom controls Change the zoom level.
workspace Displays the file you are working on (Word document, Excel workbook, Access database, or PowerPoint slide).
scroll box in horizontal scroll bar Shifts the workspace horizontally when dragged.
scroll box in vertical scroll bar Shifts the workspace vertically when dragged.
Book1 - Excel

CHAPTER REVIEW 10
Creating a Document
Word 2016

LEARNING OBJECTIVES

- 10-1 Enter text
- 10-2 Create documents based on existing documents
- 10-3 Edit text
- 10-4 Switch to another open document in Word
- 10-5 Format text
- 10-6 Format paragraphs
- 10-7 Copy formats
- 10-8 Check spelling and grammar
- 10-9 Preview and print documents

KEY CONCEPTS

10-1
Enter text
- To enter text, type in a document, pressing the Enter key only to start a new paragraph.
- To insert a date with AutoComplete, press the Enter key when the date appears in a ScreenTip.
- To insert a symbol, click the Symbol button in the Symbols group on the Insert tab, and then click More Symbols. Click a symbol, click Insert, and then click Close.

10-2
Create documents based on existing documents
- To save a document with a new name, click Save As in Backstage view, and then click the Browse button or the folder name. In the Save As dialog box, type a new file name, and then click Save.

10-3
Edit text
- To replace text, select it and type.
- To move text, drag selected text to a new location.

KEY TERMS

Go to CMPTR³ Online for a full list of key terms and definitions.

AutoComplete A feature that automatically inserts dates and other regularly used items.

AutoCorrect A feature that automatically corrects certain misspelled words and typing errors.

bulleted list A group of related paragraphs with a symbol to the left of each paragraph.

center To position paragraph text evenly between the left and right margins with ragged edges along both margins.

double spaced Line spacing that has a blank line between each line of text in a paragraph

drag and drop A technique for moving or copying selected text or objects to a new location.

first-line indent A paragraph in which the first line is indented from the left margin.

font The design of a set of characters.

format To change the appearance of a file's content.

Format Painter A tool that is used to copy formatting from one location to another, such as from one block of text to another.

hanging indent A paragraph in which all the lines are indented from the left margin except the first line.

justify To align paragraph text along both the left and right margins.

leader line A line that appears between two elements, such as between tabbed text.

left-align To align paragraph text along the left margin with ragged edges along the right margin.

line spacing The amount of space between lines of text within a paragraph.

Microsoft Word 2016 (Word) Application software used to create and format documents.

nonprinting character A character that does not print and that controls the format of a document.

numbered list A group of related paragraphs that have a particular order with sequential numbers to the left of each paragraph.

paragraph spacing The space above and below a paragraph.

point The unit of measurement used for type; equal to 1/72 of an inch.

ragged Uneven, such as text with an uneven appearance along a margin.

right-align To align paragraph text along the right margin with ragged edges along the left margin.

single spaced Line spacing that has no extra space between lines of text in a paragraph.

spell check To check a file for spelling and grammatical errors using the Spelling and Grammar Checker.

tab stop A location on the horizontal ruler where the insertion point moves when you press the Tab key.

CHAPTER 10 REVIEW

KEY CONCEPTS, *cont.*

10-4

Switch to another open document in Word

- To switch to another open document in Word, click the View tab. In the Window group, click the Switch Windows button, and then click the file name of the document you want to switch to.

10-5

Format text

- You can format text by changing the font, size, style, and color.

10-6

Format paragraphs

- You can format paragraphs by changing the line spacing, paragraph spacing, alignment, borders, and shading, and by creating bulleted and numbered lists.
- To create a tab stop, click the tab selector to select a tab style, and then click on the horizontal ruler to add a tab stop.
- To create first-line, hanging, right, and left paragraph indents, use the indent markers on the horizontal ruler.

10-7

Copy formats

- To copy the format of text and apply it to other text, select the text. On the Home tab, in the Clipboard group, click the Format Painter button, and then click or select the text you want to format.
- To copy text and keep its formatting, click the Paste button arrow in the Clipboard group on the Home tab, and then click the Keep Source Formatting button.

10-8

Check spelling and grammar

- Misspelled words have a red wavy underline. Contextual spelling errors have a blue wavy underline. Grammar errors also have a blue wavy underline.
- Right-click a flagged word, and then click the correction on the shortcut menu.
- To check spelling in the entire document, on the Review tab, in the Proofing group, click the Spelling & Grammar button.

10-9

Preview and print documents

- Click the File tab, and then in the navigation bar, click Print.
- In the right pane, review the preview.
- In the left pane, set the print options.
- Click the Print button.

DIGITAL BACKPACK

- **Practice It and On Your Own** - online
- **Quiz:** Take the practice quizzes on key concepts in the chapter to prepare for tests.
- **Key Terms:** Review key terms and definitions with flashcards, and create your own flashcards from your StudyBits.
- **Videos:** Watch the videos to learn more about the skills taught in this chapter.
- **Collect StudyBits:** Use your highlighted StudyBits from CMPTR Online to create notes, rate your understanding, and create practice quizzes.

INFOGRAPHIC

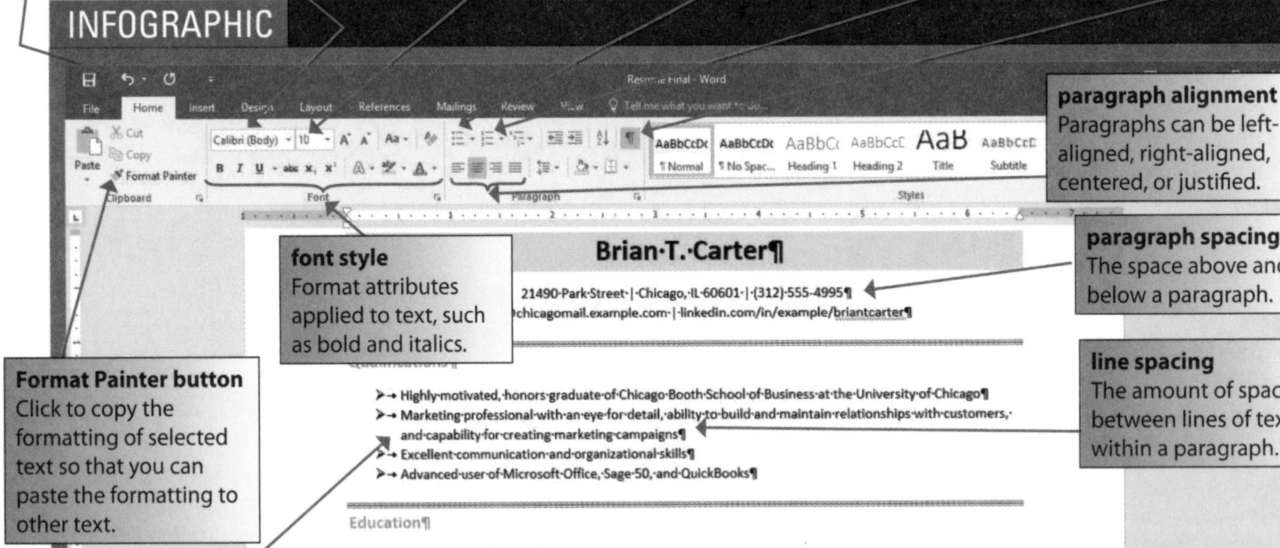
Undo button Click to undo the last action.
font The design of a set of characters.
point The unit of measurement for type; equal to 1/72 of an inch.
Bullets button Click to format the selected paragraphs as a bulleted list.
Numbering button Click to format the selected paragraphs as a numbered list.
Show/Hide ¶ button Click to display or hide nonprinting characters.
paragraph alignment Paragraphs can be left-aligned, right-aligned, centered, or justified.
paragraph spacing The space above and below a paragraph.
font style Format attributes applied to text, such as bold and italics.
line spacing The amount of space between lines of text within a paragraph.
Format Painter button Click to copy the formatting of selected text so that you can paste the formatting to other text.
hanging indent A paragraph in which all the lines are indented from the left margin except the first line.
nonprinting characters Characters that do not print and that control the format of a document.
tab character A hidden character that moves the text after it to the next tab stop on the horizontal ruler.
Brian·T.·Carter¶
21490·Park·Street·|·Chicago,·IL·60601·|·(312)·555-4995¶
Highly·motivated,·honors·graduate·of·Chicago·Booth·School·of·Business·at·the·University·of·Chicago¶
Marketing·professional·with·an·eye·for·detail,·ability·to·build·and·maintain·relationships·with·customers,·and·capability·for·creating·marketing·campaigns¶
Excellent·communication·and·organizational·skills¶
Advanced·user·of·Microsoft·Office,·Sage·50,·and·QuickBooks¶
Education¶
University·of·Chicago—Chicago,·IL¶
BA·magna·cum·laude,·Business,·June,·2017¶
Concentration:·Marketing,·Minor:·Psychology¶
Experience¶
Internship
Zisk·Media·Corporation,·September·2016–June·2017¶
Assisted·the·marketing·manager·with·daily·tasks·and·long-term·projects,·and·participated·in·weekly·staff·

CHAPTER REVIEW 11

Formatting a Long Document
Word 2016

LEARNING OBJECTIVES

- 11-1 Find and replace text
- 11-2 Work with styles
- 11-3 Work with themes
- 11-4 Scroll through a long document
- 11-5 Work with the document outline
- 11-6 Change the margins
- 11-7 Insert a manual page break
- 11-8 Add page numbers, headers, and footers
- 11-9 Create citations and a list of works cited
- 11-10 Create footnotes and endnotes

KEY CONCEPTS

11-1
Find and replace text

- To find text, click the Find button in the Editing group on the Home tab.
- To replace text, click the Replace button in the Editing group on the Home tab.

11-2
Work with styles

- To apply a style, on the Home tab, in the Styles group, click the More button, and then click a style in the styles gallery.
- To create a new style, select the text with the formatting you want, in the styles gallery, click Create a Style, type a style name, and then click OK.

11-3
Work with themes

- To change the theme, on the Design tab, in the Document Formatting group, click the Themes button, and then click a theme.

KEY TERMS

Go to CMPTR[3] Online for a full list of key terms and definitions.

automatic page break (soft page break) A page break that is created when content fills a page and a new page is created automatically.

character style A style type that includes instructions for formatting only text.

citation A formal reference to the work of others.

content control A special field used as a placeholder for text you insert or designed to contain specific type of text.

demote To move an item to a lower level in an outline.

direct formatting Formatting that overrides the style currently applied.

endnote An explanatory comment or reference that appears at the end of a section or at the end of a document.

field In Word, a placeholder for variable information that includes an instruction to insert the specific information.

footer Text that appears at the bottom of every page.

footnote An explanatory comment or reference that appears at the bottom of a page.

header Text that appears at the top of every page.

linked style A style type that acts as a paragraph style if applied to a paragraph and as a character style if applied to text.

list of works cited, references, or **bibliography** A list of sources cited in a document or consulted while researching a topic.

manual page break (hard page break) A page break that you insert to force content after the break to appear on a new page.

margin The blank area above or below text, or to the left or right of text between the text and the edge of the page.

Normal template The template on which all Word documents are based.

paragraph style A style type that includes instructions for formatting text and paragraphs.

promote To move an item to a higher level in an outline.

property Identifying information about a file that is saved with the file.

reference marker A small, superscript number to the right of text that corresponds to the footnote or endnote.

source Anything you use to research your topic.

style A named set of formatting instructions.

style set A coordinated group of style definitions.

template A file that that contains a set of styles that can be used to format documents based on that template.

theme A coordinated set of colors, fonts, and effects.

title tab A tab on a content control that indicates the control is selected and usually contains the name of the content control.

CHAPTER 11 REVIEW

KEY CONCEPTS, *cont.*

• To change a style definition, apply the style, modify the format of the text, right-click the style in the Styles gallery, and then click Update *Style* to Match Selection.

11-4

Scroll through a long document

• Click the page count indicator on the status bar to open the Navigation pane with the Pages tab selected.

11-5

Work with the document outline

• You can view a document's structure in the Navigation pane and then browse by the document's headings.
• In the Navigation pane, when browsing by heading, you can collapse or expand, promote or demote, and move headings.
• Outline view shows the document's heading levels as an outline. You can promote or demote and move headings to reorganize the document.

11-6

Change the margins

• To change the margins, click the Margins button in the Page Setup group on the Layout tab.

11-7

Insert a manual page break

• To insert a manual page break, click the Page Break button in the Pages group on the Insert tab.

11-8

Add margins, page numbers, headers, and footers

• To add page numbers to a document, on the Insert tab, in the Header & Footer group, click the Page Number button, and then click a page number style.
• To add text as a header or footer, double-click in the header or footer area, type text and format it as needed, and then click in the document area.

11-9

Create citations and a list of works cited

• On the References tab, in the Citations & Bibliography group, click the Style box arrow, and then click a style, such as MLA Seventh Edition.
• To enter a new source, in the Citations & Bibliography group, click the Insert Citation button, click Add New Source, enter source information, and then click OK.
• To insert a citation to an existing source, click the Insert Citation button, and then click the source.
• To generate a bibliography, click the Bibliography button, and then select a format.

11-10

Create footnotes or endnotes

• On the References tab, in the Footnotes group, click the Insert Footnote button or the Insert Endnote button, and then type the note text.

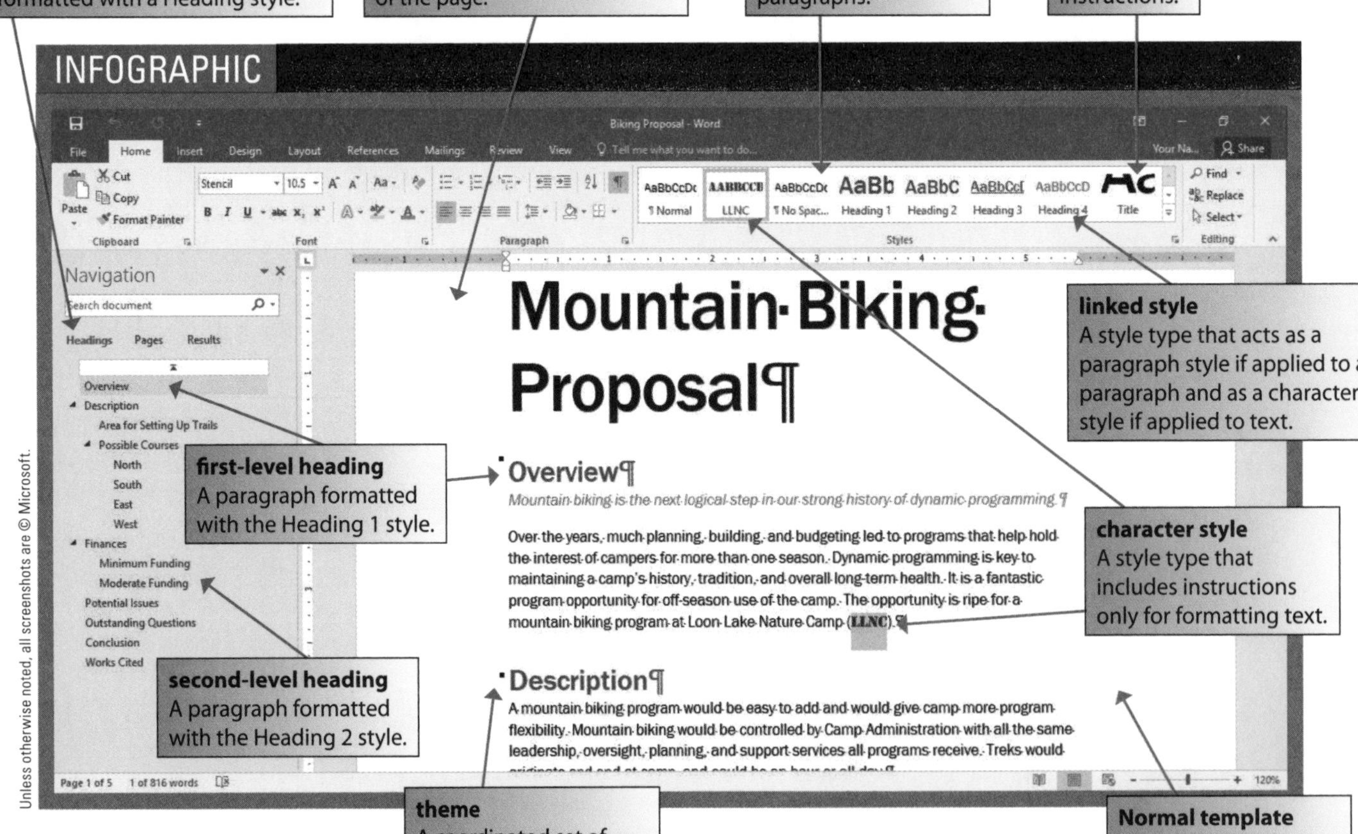

CHAPTER REVIEW 12

Enhancing a Document
Word 2016

LEARNING OBJECTIVES

12-1 Organize information in tables

12-2 Change the page orientation

12-3 Divide a document into sections

12-4 Insert and modify graphics

12-5 Wrap text around graphics

12-6 Move graphics

12-7 Add text effects and WordArt text boxes

12-8 Work with columns

12-9 Work with building blocks

KEY CONCEPTS

12-1
Organize information in tables

• To create a table, on the Insert tab, in the Tables group, click the Tables button, and then click the box in the grid that represents the lower-right corner of the table.
• To insert or delete rows and columns, click in the appropriate row or column, and then on the Table Tools Layout tab, in the Rows & Columns group, click the corresponding button.
• To format a table, on the Table Tools Design tab, in the Table Styles group, click the More button, and then click a table style.

12-2
Change the page orientation

• On the Layout tab, in the Page Setup group, click the Orientation button, and then click an orientation.

12-3
Divide a document into sections

• The four types of section breaks are Next Page, Continuous, Even Page, and Odd Page.
• You can format each section separately.
• To insert a section break, on the Layout tab, in the Setup group, click the Breaks button, and then click a section break.

12-4
Insert and modify graphics

• To resize a graphic, drag a sizing handle on the selection box.
• To crop a photo, on the Picture Tools Format tab, in the Size group, click the Crop button, drag a crop handle, and then click the Crop button again.
• To format a picture, on the Picture Tools Format tab, in the Picture Styles group, use the appropriate buttons.

KEY TERMS

alignment guide A green horizontal or vertical line that appears when you drag a floating object in a document to help you position the object.

aspect ratio The proportion of an object's height to its width.

banded rows/banded columns Formatting that displays alternate rows (or columns) in a table with different fill colors.

building block A part of a document that is stored and reused.

cell The intersection of a column and a row in a table.

crop To cut off part of a graphic.

floating object (floating graphic) A graphic that can be positioned anywhere in a document.

graphic A picture, shape, design, graph, chart, or diagram.

header row The top row in a table that contains the column labels.

inline object (inline graphic) A graphic that is postioned in a line of text and moves along with the text.

landscape orientation A page that is wider than it is tall.

object Anything in a document that can be treated as a whole.

orientation The way a page is turned.

portrait orientation A page that is taller than it is wide.

Quick Part A building block stored in the Quick Parts gallery.

Quick Table A table template with sample text and formatting.

rotate handle A small circle that appears attached to the side of a selected object that you can drag to rotate the object in either direction.

section A part of a document that can have its own page-level formatting and properties.

section break A formatting mark in a document that indicates the start of a new section.

selection box The box that surrounds an object when it is selected.

sizing handle A small circle that appears at the corner or on the side of a selection box.

table A grid of horizontal rows and vertical columns.

text box An object that contains text.

text effects Special decorative, formatting effects that you can apply to text.

WordArt Formatted, decorative text in a text box.

KEY CONCEPTS, *cont.*

12-5
Wrap text around graphics

- To change a picture from an inline graphic to a floating graphic, click the Layout Options button next to the graphic, and then select a wrap option.

12-6
Move graphics

- To move a graphic, drag it to a new location.

12-7
Add text effects and WordArt text boxes

- To insert a WordArt text box, on the Insert tab, in the Text group, click the WordArt button, select a style, and then type text.
- To format WordArt, on the Drawing Tools Format tab, click the appropriate buttons to change the styles, size, etc.

12-8
Work with columns

- To format a document in columns, on the Page Layout tab, in the Page Setup group, click the Columns button, and then click a column option.
- To balance text in columns, insert a continuous section break.

12-9
Work with building blocks

- To create a building block, select the text. On the Insert tab, in the Text group, click the Quick Parts button, and then click Save Selection to Quick Part gallery.

DIGITAL BACKPACK

- **Practice It and On Your Own**—online
- **Quiz:** Take the practice quizzes on key concepts in the chapter to prepare for tests.
- **Key Terms:** Review key terms and definitions with flashcards, and create your own flashcards from your StudyBits.
- **Videos:** Watch the videos to learn more about the skills taught in this chapter.
- **Collect StudyBits:** Use your highlighted StudyBits from CMPTR Online to create notes, rate your understanding, and create practice quizzes.

INFOGRAPHIC

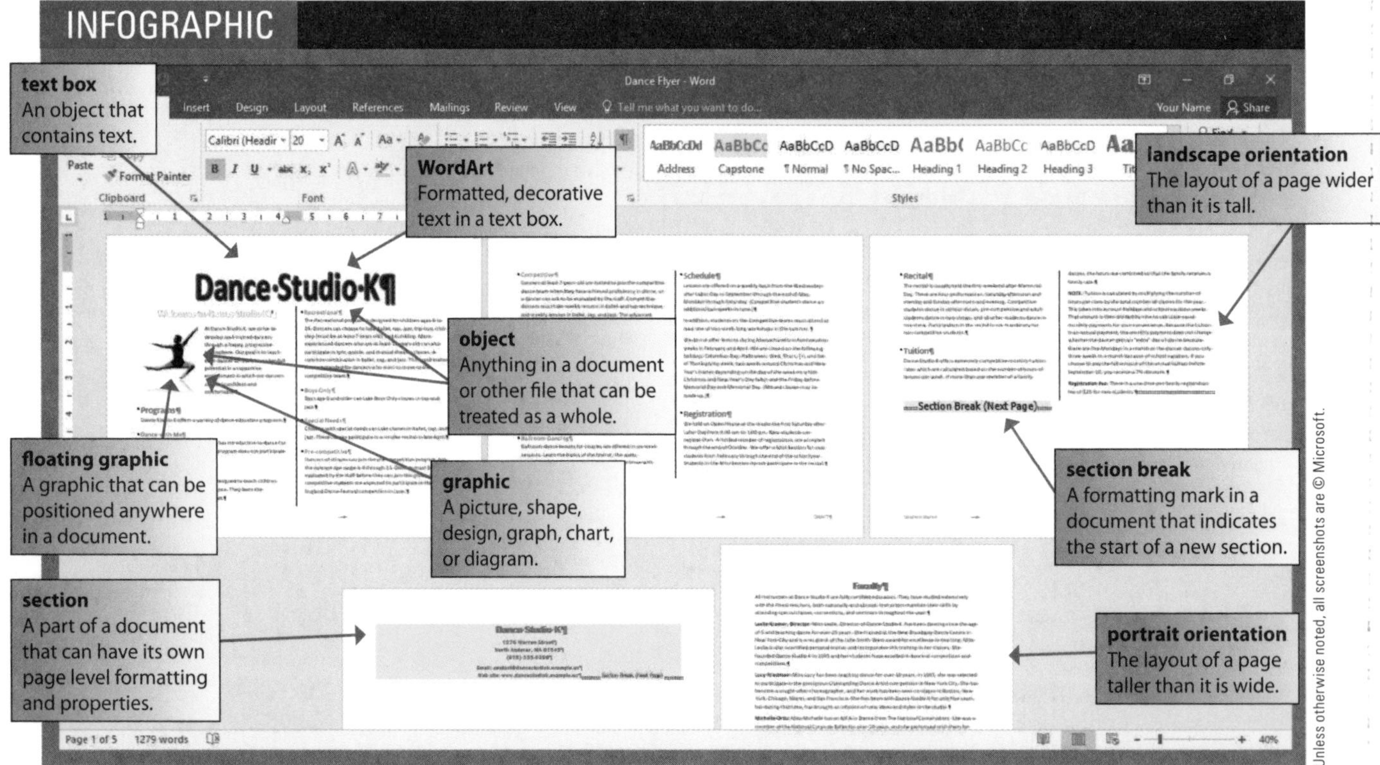

text box
An object that contains text.
WordArt
Formatted, decorative text in a text box.
landscape orientation
The layout of a page wider than it is tall.
object
Anything in a document or other file that can be treated as a whole.
floating graphic
A graphic that can be positioned anywhere in a document.
graphic
A picture, shape, design, graph, chart, or diagram.
section break
A formatting mark in a document that indicates the start of a new section.
section
A part of a document that can have its own page level formatting and properties.
portrait orientation
The layout of a page taller than it is wide.
Dance Flyer - Word
Dance·Studio·K¶
Section Break (Next Page)
Page 1 of 5
1279 words

CHAPTER REVIEW 13

Creating a Workbook
Excel 2016

LEARNING OBJECTIVES

13-1 Understand spreadsheets and Excel

13-2 Enter and format data

13-3 Edit cell content

13-4 Work with columns and rows

13-5 Work with cells and ranges

13-6 Enter simple formulas and functions

13-7 Preview and print a workbook

KEY CONCEPTS

13-1

Understand spreadsheets and Excel

- To move the active cell, click a new cell, use a keyboard shortcut, or type the cell reference in the Name box, and then press the Enter key.
- To insert a sheet, click the New sheet button.
- To switch between sheets, click the sheet tab.
- To delete a sheet, right-click the sheet tab, and then on the shortcut menu, click Delete.
- To rename a sheet, double-click the sheet tab, type the new name, and then press the Enter key.
- To move a sheet, drag its sheet tab. To copy a sheet, press and hold the Ctrl key while dragging.

13-2

Enter and format data

- To format text, on the Home tab, in the Font group, use the buttons to change fonts, font sizes, font styles, and colors.
- To format dates, on the Home tab, in the Number group, click the Number Format box arrow, and then click a date format.
- To format numbers, on the Home tab, in the Number group, use the buttons to add commas, currency symbols, and percent signs, and change the number of decimal places.

KEY TERMS

active cell The selected cell in a worksheet.

active sheet The sheet currently displayed in the workbook window.

AutoFit In Excel, to resize a column by matching its width to the width of its longest cell entry or resize a row to the height of its tallest cell entry.

AutoSum A feature that inserts the SUM, AVERAGE, COUNT, MIN, or MAX function.

cell The location in a worksheet where a row and column intersect.

cell range (range) A group of cells.

cell reference The column letter and row number of a cell used to identify the location of a specific cell.

chart sheet A sheet that contains a visual representation of spreadsheet data.

clear To remove data from cells but leave the blank cells in the worksheet.

date data Text or numbers in commonly recognized formats for date values.

delete In Excel, to remove both the data and the cells from a worksheet.

formula A mathematical expression that returns a value.

formula bar A bar used to enter, edit, or display the contents of the active cell.

function A named operation that replaces the action of an arithmetic expression.

Microsoft Excel 2016 (Excel) A computer application used to enter, analyze, and present quantitative data.

Name box The location where the active cell reference is displayed.

Normal view The Excel view that shows the contents of the current sheet.

number data Any numerical value that can be used in a mathematical calculation.

operator A mathematical symbol used to combine values.

Page Break Preview The Excel view that displays the location of page breaks within the worksheet.

Page Layout view The Excel view that shows how the current sheet will look when printed.

range reference The location and size of a range.

sheet An individual page in a workbook.

text data Any combination of letters, numbers, and symbols.

workbook An Excel file that stores spreadsheets.

worksheet A sheet that contains data laid out in a grid of rows and columns.

CHAPTER 13 REVIEW

KEY CONCEPTS, *cont.*

13-3

Edit cell content

- Double-click the cell, use the arrow keys to move the insertion point within the cell, use the Backspace key to delete characters or digits, type new characters or digits, and then press the Enter key.

13-4

Work with columns and rows

- To select a column or row, click its header.
- To select adjacent columns or rows, drag across multiple columns or rows.
- To select nonadjacent columns or rows, press and hold the Ctrl key while clicking headers.
- To insert a column or row, on the Home tab, in the Cells group, click the Insert button arrow, and then click the item you want to insert.
- To delete a column or row, select it, and then on the Home tab, in the Cells group, click the Delete button.

13-5

Work with cells and ranges

- To move a range, select it and drag it by its border.
- To insert a range, select the size of the range to insert. On the Home tab, in the Cells group, click the Insert button arrow, and click Insert Cells.
- To delete a range, select it, and then on the Home tab, in the Cells group, click the Delete button arrow, and click Delete Cells.

13-6

Enter simple formulas and functions

- To enter a formula, type = and then the formula.
- To enter the SUM function, type =SUM and then type the range between parentheses.
- To enter an AutoSum function, on the Home tab, in the Editing group, click the AutoSum button arrow, and then click a function.

13-7

Preview and print a workbook

- To preview the printed workbook, click the File tab, and then in the navigation bar, click Print.
- To view formulas in a worksheet, on the Formulas tab, in the Formula Auditing group, click the Show Formulas button.
- To change the page orientation, on the Page Layout tab, in the Page Setup group, click the Orientation button, and then click an option.

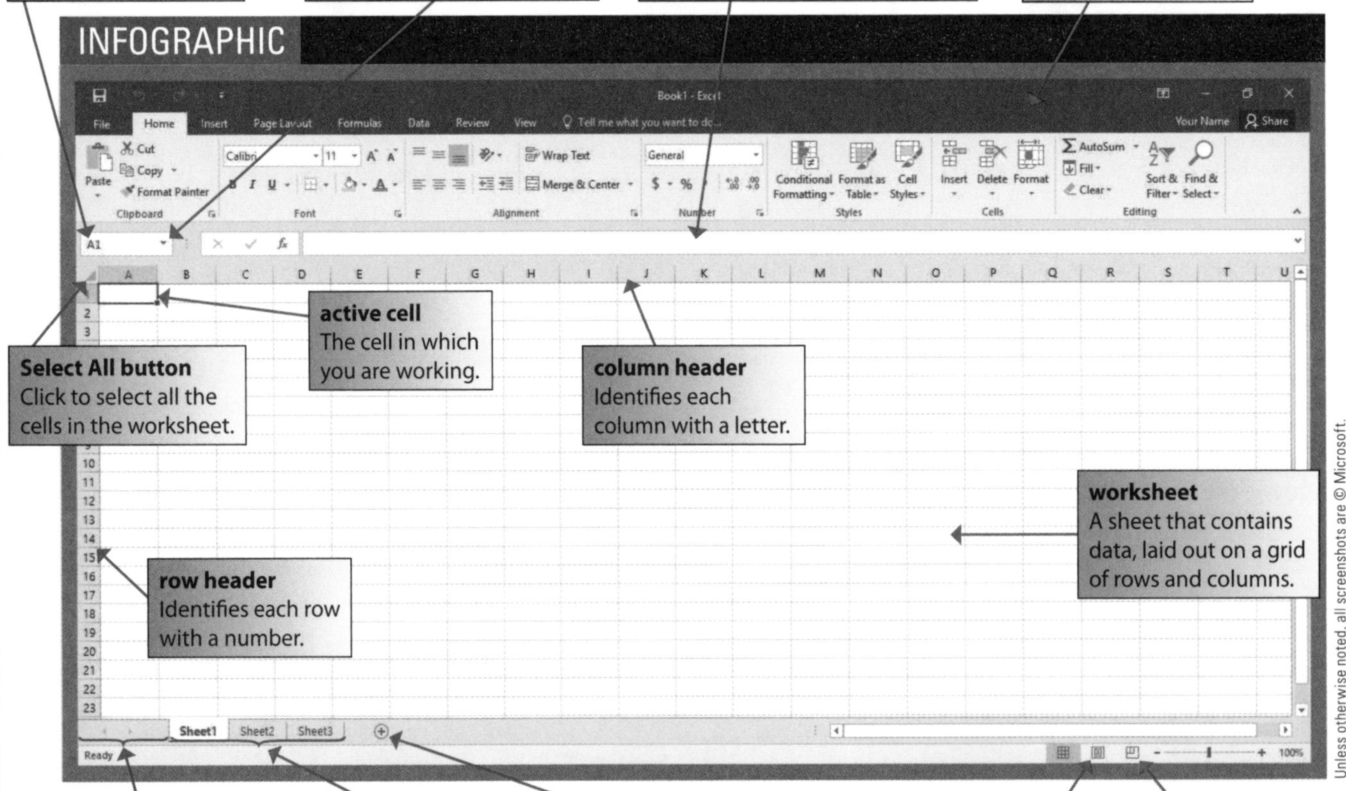

cell reference
The column letter and row number of a cell used to identify the location of a cell.
Name box
Identifies the active cell; you can type a cell reference in the Name box to make that cell the active cell.
formula bar
Displays the contents of the active cell; if the contents is a formula, displays the formula rather than the calculated value.
workbook
An Excel file, which stores a spreadsheet.
INFOGRAPHIC
active cell
The cell in which you are working.
Select All button
Click to select all the cells in the worksheet.
column header
Identifies each column with a letter.
worksheet
A sheet that contains data, laid out on a grid of rows and columns.
row header
Identifies each row with a number.
sheet tab scrolling buttons
Click to scroll additional sheet tabs into view if the worksheet contains more sheet tabs than can be displayed at the same time.
sheet tabs
Contain the name of each worksheet or chart sheet.
New sheet button
Click to create a new worksheet.
Page Layout button
Click to switch to Page Layout view to sheet how the sheet will look when printed.
Page Break Preview button
Click to switch to Page Break Preview to see the location of page breaks with the worksheet.

CHAPTER REVIEW 14
Working with Formulas and Functions
Excel 2016

LEARNING OBJECTIVES

14-1 Use relative, absolute, and mixed cell references in formulas

14-2 Enter functions

14-3 Use AutoFill

14-4 Work with date functions

14-5 Work with the PMT financial function

14-6 Use references to another worksheet

14-7 Edit formulas and functions

14-8 Format cells and ranges

KEY CONCEPTS

14-1
Use relative, absolute, and mixed cell references in formulas
- Relative references change when copied relative the location of the cell containing the formula.
- Absolute references do not change when copied.

14-2
Enter functions
- *FUNCTION(argument1[,argument2 =value2,...])*
- To open the Insert Function dialog box, to the left of the formula bar, click the Insert Function button.
- To enter a function by searching for it using the Insert Function dialog box, in the Insert Function dialog box, in the Search box, type keywords, and then click Go.
- To enter a function by using the list of recently used functions in the Insert Function dialog box, click the Or select a category arrow, click Most Recently Used, and then in the Select a function list, click the function name.
- Type = (an equal sign), type the first letter or two of the function you want to insert, click the function name in the list that appears, double-click the function name, select the range or enter, and then type) (closing parenthesis).

14-3
Use AutoFill
- Select a cell or range, and then drag the fill handle to the right or down.

14-4
Work with date functions
- To display the current date, type =TODAY().
- To display the current date and time, type =NOW().

14-5
Work with the PMT financial function
- PMT(*rate,nper,pv*[,*fv=0*][,*type=0*])

KEY TERMS

absolute reference A cell reference that remains fixed when copied to a new location.

argument The numbers, text, or cell references used by a function to return a value.

AutoFill An Excel feature that copies content and formats from a cell or range into an adjacent cell or range.

border A line added along an edge of a cell.

date function A function that inserts or calculates dates and times.

fill color A color added to cells or shapes.

fill handle A box in the lower-right corner of a selected cell or range that you drag over an adjacent cell or range to copy the content and formatting from the original cells into the adjacent range.

financial function A function related to monetary calculations, such as loans and payments.

gridlines Lines that divide columns and rows in a worksheet and define the structure of the worksheet.

interest The amount added to the principal by the lender.

merge To combine two or more cells into one cell.

mixed reference A cell reference that contains an absolute row reference or an absolute column reference.

optional argument An argument that is not required for the function to return a value, but provides more control over how the returned value is calculated.

payment period (period) The length of time between each loan payment.

PMT function A financial function that calculates the payment schedule required to pay back a loan.

principal the amount of money being loaned.

relative reference A cell reference that is interpreted in relation to the location of the cell containing the formula.

syntax A set of rules.

what-if analysis An examination of how changing values entered directly in a worksheet affect calculated values.

CHAPTER 14 REVIEW

KEY CONCEPTS, *cont.*

14-6

Use references to another worksheet

- References to a cell on another worksheet include the worksheet name and an exclamation point before the cell reference.

14-7

Edit functions and formulas

- Double-click the cell containing the formula and then edit its contents or drag sizing handles on the colored borders around the ranges referenced in the formula.

14-8

Format cells and ranges

- Open the Format Cells dialog box by clicking the Dialog Box Launcher in the Number group on the Home tab.
- Apply cell styles by using the Cell Styles button in the Styles group on the Home tab.
- Change the alignment, merge cells, and indent cell content by using the buttons in the Alignment group on the Home tab.
- Add cell borders using the Borders button in the Font group on the Home tab.
- Add fill colors to cells using the Fill Color button in the Font group on the Home tab.

DIGITAL BACKPACK

- **Practice It and On Your Own:** online
- **Quiz:** Take the practice quizzes on key concepts in the chapter to prepare for tests.
- **Key Terms:** Review key terms and definitions with flashcards, and create your own flashcards from your StudyBits.
- **Videos:** Watch the videos to learn more about the skills taught in this chapter.
- **Collect StudyBits:** Use your highlighted StudyBits from CMPTR[3] Online to create notes, rate your understanding, and create practice quizzes.

INFOGRAPHIC

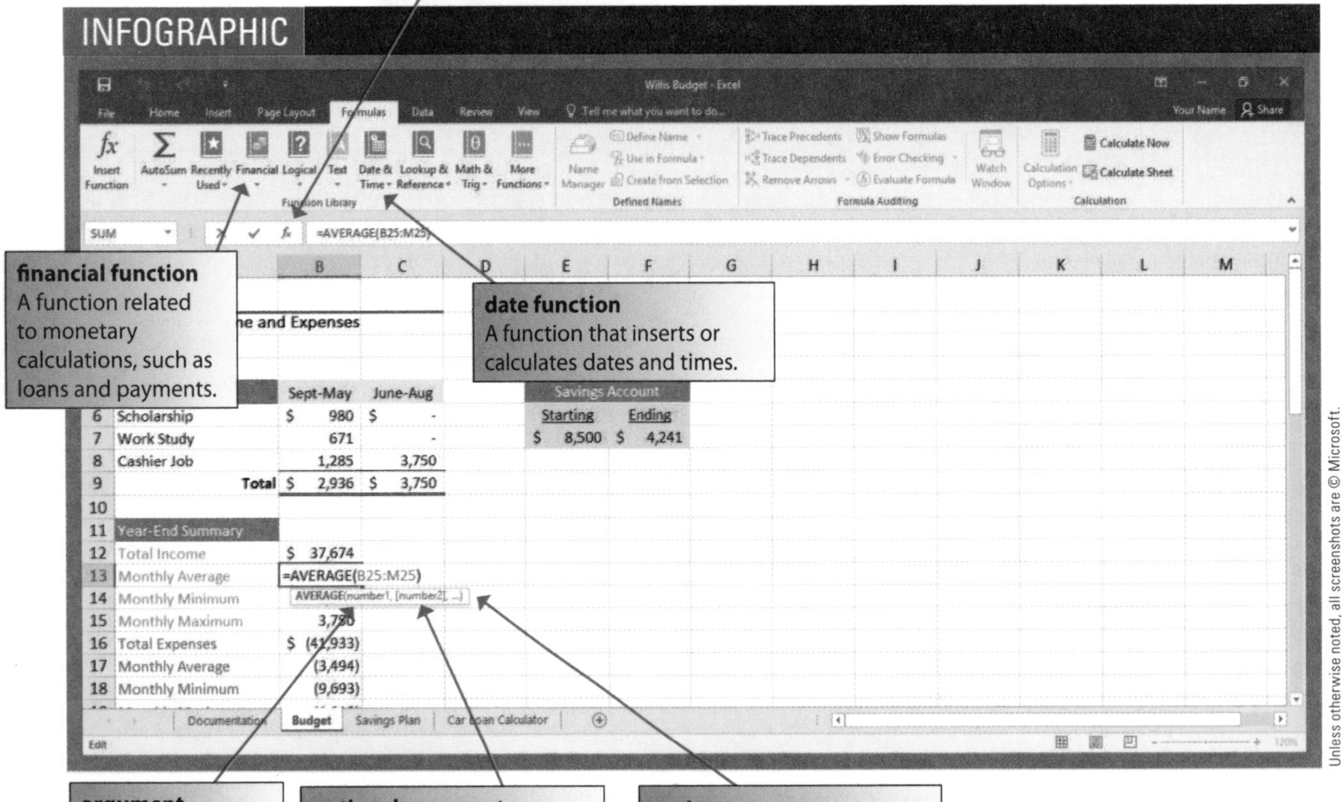
Insert Function button
Click to open the Insert Function dialog box, which organizes all of the functions by category and includes a search feature for locating a specific function.
financial function
A function related to monetary calculations, such as loans and payments.
date function
A function that inserts or calculates dates and times.
argument
The numbers, text, or cell references used by a function to return a value.
optional argument
An argument that is not required for the function to return its value, but provides more control over how the returned value is calculated.
syntax
A set of rules that shows how to write the function.
=AVERAGE(B25:M25)
AVERAGE(number1, [number2], ...)

CHAPTER REVIEW 15

Creating an Advanced Workbook
Excel 2016

LEARNING OBJECTIVES

- 15-1 Use Flash Fill
- 15-2 Enter formulas with multiple calculations
- 15-3 Fix error values
- 15-4 Work with the IF logical function
- 15-5 Create a nested IF function
- 15-6 Add conditional formatting
- 15-7 Hide rows and columns
- 15-8 Format a worksheet for printing

KEY TERMS

automatic page break A page break Excel inserts when no more content will fit on the page.

comparison operator A symbol that indicates the relationship between two values.

conditional formatting Formatting that is applied to a cell only when the cell's value meets a specified condition.

constant A value in a formula that doesn't change.

error indicator A small green triangle that appears in the upper-left corner of a cell with a possible error.

error value A message that appears in a cell that indicates some part of a formula is preventing Excel from returning a calculated value.

Excel table A range of data that is treated as a distinct object in a worksheet.

Flash Fill An Excel feature that enters text based on patterns that it finds in the data.

IF function A logical function that tests a condition and then returns one value if the condition is true and another value if the condition is false.

logical function A function that works with statements that are either true or false.

manual page break A page break you insert to specify where a page break occurs.

nest To place one item, such as a function, inside another.

order of operations A set of predefined rules used to determine the sequence in which operators are applied in a calculation—first exponentiation (^); second multiplication (*) and division (/); and third, addition (+) and subtraction (–).

print area The region of the active sheet that is sent to the printer.

print title Information from a workbook that appears on every printed page.

Quick Analysis tool A button that appears next to a selected range that provides access to commonly used formatting and analysis tools.

KEY CONCEPTS

15-1
Use Flash Fill

- Enter the first cell that reflects a pattern of combining cells in the same row, enter the second cell, and then press the Enter key to fill the rest of the cells in the range.

15-2
Enter formulas with multiple calculations

- Calculations in formulas are performed based on the order of operations—exponentiation (^); multiplication (*) and division (/); addition (=) and subtraction (-).
- To change the order of operations, enclose parts of the formula within parentheses. Any expression within a set of parentheses is calculated before the rest of the formula.
- Constants are entered directly in a formula or placed in a separate worksheet cell and referenced in the formula.

15-3
Fix error values

- Error values messages indicate the type of error that occurred in a cell.
- To obtain more information about an error, click a cell containing an error, and then point to the Error Checking button that appears to display a ScreenTip containing a description of the error.

15-4
Work with the IF logical function

- The IF function returns one value if a statement is true and a different value if the statement is false.
- IF function syntax is: IF(*Logical_test*[,*value_if_true*][,*value_if_false*]).

15-5
Create a nested IF function

- Functions can be nested inside another function. If a formula contains more than one function, the innermost function is calculated first, then the next most innermost function, and so on.

15-6
Add conditional formatting

- To apply conditional formatting, select a range, on the Home tab, in the Styles group, click the Conditional Formatting button, select a rule, and then refine the rule in the dialog box that opens.
- To clear a conditional formatting rule, click the Conditional Formatting button, click Manage Rules, select the rule, and then click Delete Rule.

CHAPTER 15 REVIEW

KEY CONCEPTS, *cont.*

15-7

Hide rows and columns

- To hide worksheet data, select the row or column to hide, on the Home tab, in the Cells group, click the Format button, point to Hide & Unhide, and then click Hide Rows or Hide Columns.
- To unhide worksheet data, select the rows or column on either side of the hidden rows and columns, on the HOME tab, in the Cells group, click the Format button, point to Hide & Unhide, and then click Unhide Rows or Unhide Columns.

15-8

Format a worksheet for printing

- To insert a manual page break, click the row below the page break location, click the Page Break Preview button on the status bar, click the tab on the ribbon, in the Page Setup group, click the Breaks button, and then click Insert Page Break.
- To set the print area, select the range to print, click the tab on the ribbon, in the Page Setup group, click the Print Area button, and then click Set Print Area.

DIGITAL BACKPACK

- **Practice It and On Your Own:** online
- **Quiz:** Take the practice quizzes on key concepts in the chapter to prepare for tests.
- **Key Terms:** Review key terms and definitions with flashcards, and create your own flashcards from your StudyBits.
- **Videos:** Watch the videos to learn more about the skills taught in this chapter.
- **Collect StudyBits:** Use your highlighted StudyBits from CMPTR[3] Online to create notes, rate your understanding, and create practice quizzes.

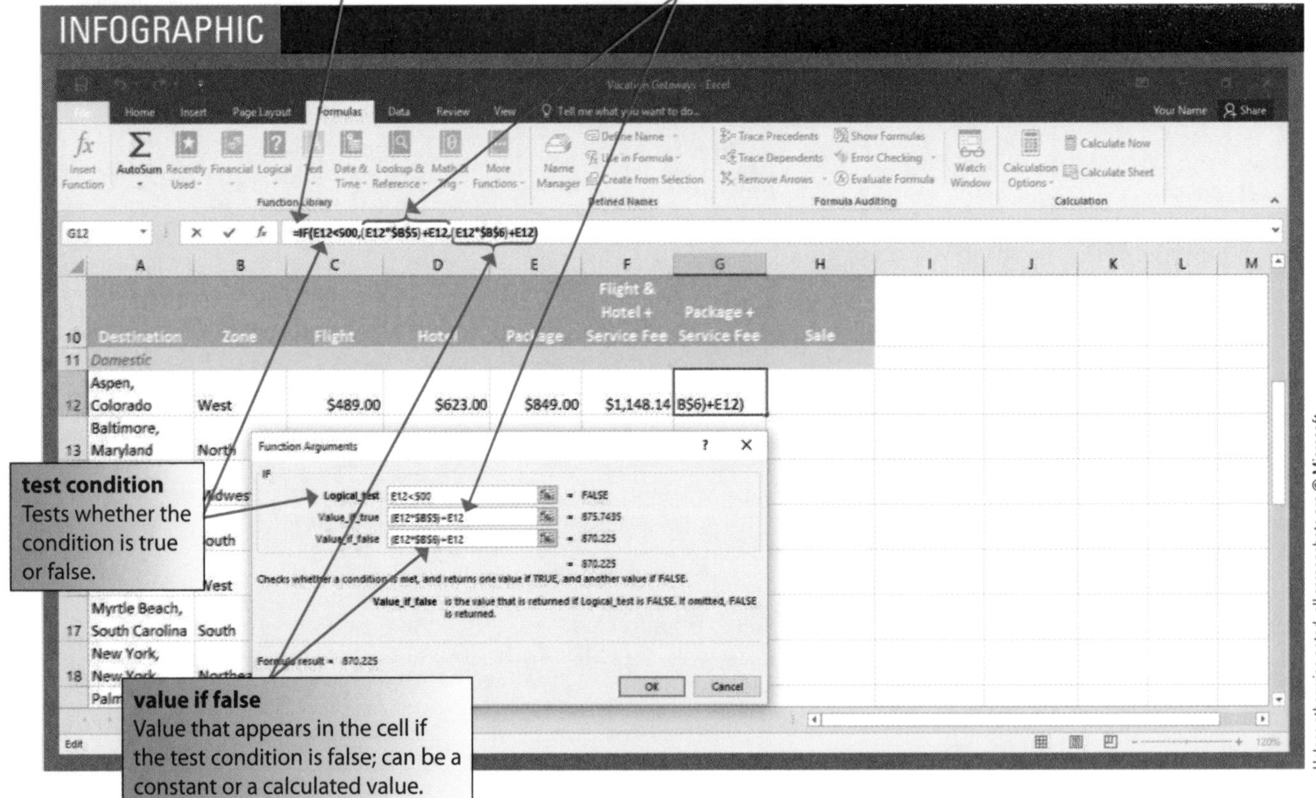
IF function
Displays one of two values depending on whether the tested condition is true or false.
value if true
Value that appears in the cell if the test condition is true; can be a constant or a calculated value.
INFOGRAPHIC
=IF(E12<500,(E12*$B$5)+E12,(E12*$B$6)+E12)
test condition
Tests whether the condition is true or false.
value if false
Value that appears in the cell if the test condition is false; can be a constant or a calculated value.

CHAPTER REVIEW 16

Inserting and Formatting Charts
Excel 2016

LEARNING OBJECTIVES

- 16-1 Create a chart
- 16-2 Move and resize a chart
- 16-3 Modify a chart
- 16-4 Create an exploded pie chart
- 16-5 Create a column or bar chart
- 16-6 Create a line chart
- 16-7 Edit chart data
- 16-8 Insert and format sparklines
- 16-9 Insert and modify data bars

KEY CONCEPTS

16-1
Create a chart
- To create a chart, select the data source range, on the Insert tab, in the Charts group, click the chart type, and then click the style.

16-2
Move and resize a chart
- To move a chart to another sheet, select the chart area, on the Chart Tools Design tab, in the Location group, click the Move Chart button; in the Move Chart dialog box, click the Object in box arrow, click the worksheet to move the chart to, and then click OK.
- To move a chart on a sheet, drag it to a new location.

16-3
Modify a chart
- To change the chart style, click the Chart Styles button next to the chart, and then click a style or color palette.
- To change the chart layout, on the Chart Tools Design tab, in the Chart Layouts group, click the Quick Layout button, and then select a layout.

KEY TERMS

bar chart A column chart that is turned on its side so that the length of each bar is based on its value.

category A set of values that represent data for one item in a chart.

category values The first column of the data range, which are the groups or categories to which the series values belong.

chart (graph) A visual representation of a set of data values.

chart area The area that contains the chart and all of the other chart elements.

chart element An individual part of a chart.

chart layout An option for displaying and arranging chart elements.

chart sheet A sheet in a workbook that contains only a chart and no worksheet cells.

chart style A style that formats an entire chart at one time.

chart title A descriptive label or name for the chart.

column chart A chart that displays values in different categories as columns so that the height of each column is based on its value.

combination chart A chart that combines two or more chart types in a single graph, such as a column chart and a line chart.

data bar Conditional formatting that adds a horizontal bar to a cell's background that is proportional in length to the cell's value.

data label Text for an individual data marker.

data marker An object in a chart that represents a value in a data series, such as a pie slice or column.

data series A set of values represented in a chart.

data series values The actual numbers plotted on a chart.

data source The range that contains the data to display in a chart.

embedded chart A chart that is an object in a worksheet.

exploded pie chart A pie chart where one slice is moved away from the pie.

gridlines In a chart, lines that extend the values of the major or minor units across the plot area of a chart.

horizontal (category) axis The horizontal axis that shows the category values from each data series.

legend A rectangular area that identifies the data markers associated with the data series.

line chart A chart that displays data values using a connected line rather than columns or bars.

pie chart A chart in the shape of a circle divided into slices like a pie that shows the data values as a percentage of the whole.

plot area The part of the chart that contains the graphical representation of the data series.

scale The range of values along an axis.

sparkline A graph that is displayed within a cell.

vertical (value) axis The vertical axis that shows the range of series values from all of the data series plotted on the chart.

CHAPTER 16 REVIEW

KEY CONCEPTS, *cont.*

• To display or hide chart elements, click the Chart Elements button to the right of the chart, and then click the check box next to the item you want to display or hide.

16-4
Create an exploded pie chart

• To create an exploded pie chart, select the pie chart, click a pie slice, and then drag the slice away from the chart.

16-5
Create a column or bar chart

• To change axis intervals, double-click the axis, click the Axis Options button in the Format Axis pane, expand the Axis Options section, and then change the value in the Major box in the Units section.

16-6
Create a line chart

• To change the axis scale, double-click the axis, click the Axis Options button in the Format Axis pane, and then change the values in the Minimum and Maximum boxes in the Bounds section.

16-7
Edit chart data

• To add a data series to a chart, click the Select Data button in the Data group on the Chart Tools Design tab, click Add, click the name of the data series, select the data series range, and then click OK in each dialog box.

16-8
Insert and format sparklines

• To insert sparklines, select the range, on the Insert tab, in the Sparklines group, click the Line button, in the Create Sparklines dialog box, in the Data Range box, select the range to chart, and then click OK.

16-9
Insert and modify data bars

• To insert data bars, select the range, on the Home tab, in the Styles group, click the Conditional Formatting button, point to Data Bars, and then select a style in the gallery.

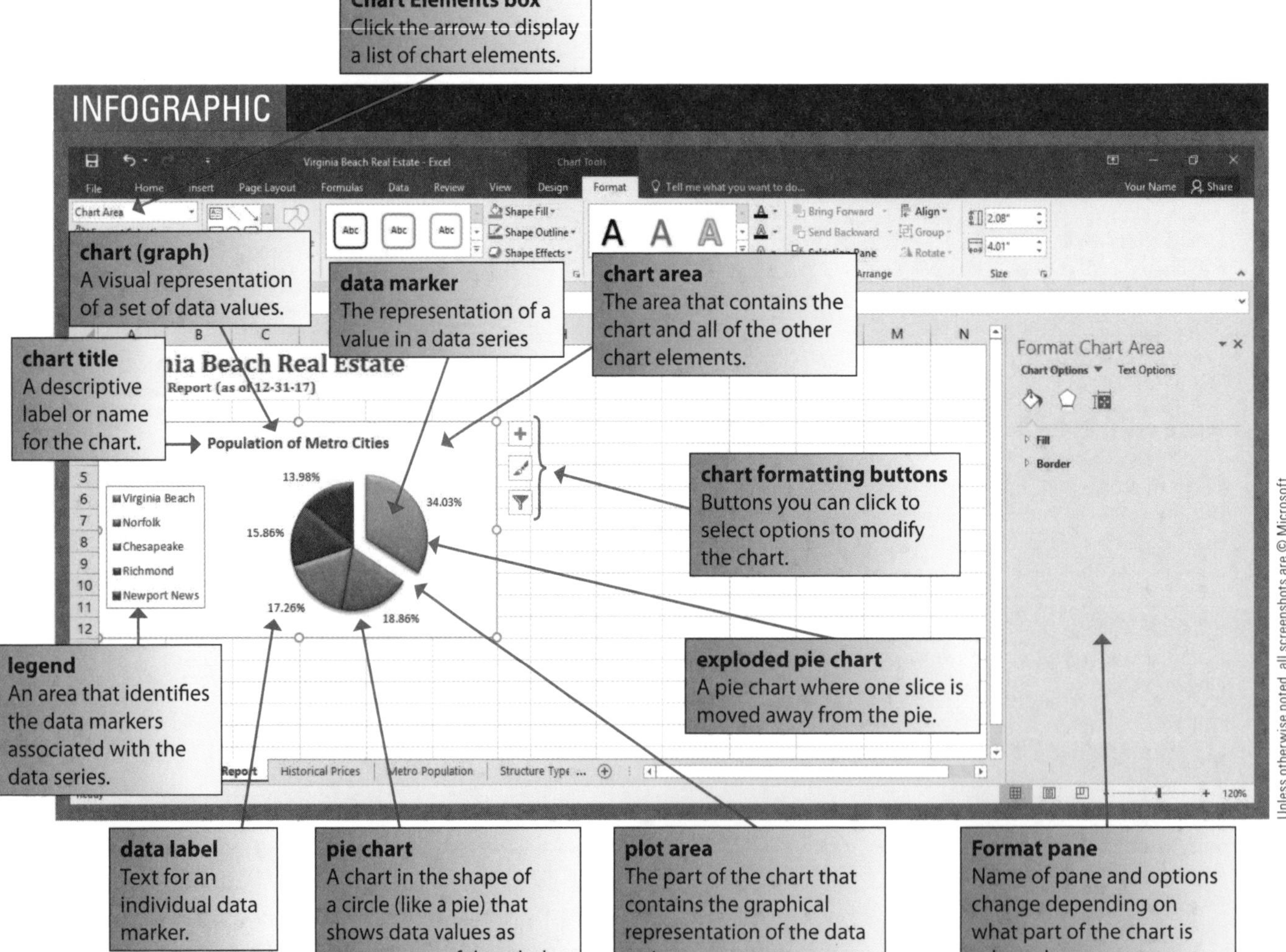

Chart Elements box
Click the arrow to display a list of chart elements.
INFOGRAPHIC
chart (graph)
A visual representation of a set of data values.
data marker
The representation of a value in a data series
chart area
The area that contains the chart and all of the other chart elements.
chart title
A descriptive label or name for the chart.
Population of Metro Cities
13.98%
34.03%
15.86%
17.26%
18.86%
Virginia Beach
Norfolk
Chesapeake
Richmond
Newport News
chart formatting buttons
Buttons you can click to select options to modify the chart.
Format Chart Area
exploded pie chart
A pie chart where one slice is moved away from the pie.
legend
An area that identifies the data markers associated with the data series.
data label
Text for an individual data marker.
pie chart
A chart in the shape of a circle (like a pie) that shows data values as percentages of the whole.
plot area
The part of the chart that contains the graphical representation of the data series.
Format pane
Name of pane and options change depending on what part of the chart is selected.

CHAPTER REVIEW 17

Creating a Database Access 2016

LEARNING OBJECTIVES

17-1 Understand database concepts

17-2 Create a database

17-3 Use Datasheet view

17-4 Work with fields and properties in Design view

17-5 Modify a table's structure

17-6 Close and open objects and databases

17-7 Create simple queries, forms, and reports

17-8 Compact and repair a database

KEY CONCEPTS

17-1
Understand database concepts
- In a relational database, each record in a table must be unique.

17-2
Create a database
- Start Access, click the Blank desktop database tile, click the Browse button to the right of the File Name box, navigate to your save location, type a file name, click OK, and then click the Create button.

17-3
Work in Datasheet view
- To create a table in Datasheet view, on the Create tab, in the Tables group, click the Table button; in the table, click Click to Add, click a data type, and then type a field name; click in the row below the field name, and then type data.

17-4
Work with fields and properties in Design view
- To create a table in Design view, on the Create tab, in the Tables group, click the Table Design button; in the table design grid, type a field name, and then press the Enter key; click the arrow that appears in the Data Type column, and then click a data type.

KEY TERMS

common field A field that appears in more than one table.

compact To rearrange data and objects in a database to decrease its file size.

data type The type of data that can be entered for a field.

datasheet Rows and columns in which a table's contents are displayed.

Datasheet view The Access view that shows a table's contents as datasheet.

Design view The Access view that shows the underlying structure of a database object and allows you to modify that structure.

detail query A query that shows every field of every record as defined by the query criteria.

field A part of a database that contains a single characteristic or attribute of a person, place, object, event, or idea.

field value The content of a field.

foreign key A field in a table that is a primary key in another table and that is included to form a relationship between the two tables.

form A database object used to enter, edit, and view records in a database.

Layout view The Access view in which you can make design changes to database objects such as forms and reports.

Microsoft Access 2016 (Access) A computer application used to enter, maintain, and retrieve related data in a format known as a database.

primary key A field, or a collection of fields, whose value uniquely identifies each record in a table.

Print Preview The Access view that shows exactly how a report will look when printed.

property One characteristic or aspect of a field, such as its name or data type.

query A question about the data stored in a database.

record All the fields in a table about a single person, place, object, event, or idea; that is, a row in a table.

relational database A database that contains a collection of related tables.

report A database object that shows a formatted printout or screen display of the contents of the table or query objects on which the report is based.

table In Access, a collection of related fields.

17-5
Modify a table's structure
- To modify field properties, in the table design grid, click a field name, in the Field Properties pane, click in the box to the right of the property, type a new property, or click the arrow that appears, and then select the new property.
- To specify a primary key, in Design view, click a field name, and then on the Table Tools Design tab, in the Tools group, click the Primary Key button.
- To delete a field from a table, in the table design grid, click the field to delete. On the Table Tools Design tab, in the Tools group, click the Delete Rows button, and then click Yes to delete the field.

KEY CONCEPTS, *cont.*

17-6

Close and open objects and databases

- To open an object, double-click it in the Navigation Pane.
- To close an object, right-click it, and then click Close on the shortcut menu.

17-7

Create simple queries, forms, and reports

- To create a simple query, click the Query Wizard button in the Queries group on the Create tab.
- To create a form, click the table on which you want to base the form in the Navigation Pane, and then on the Create tab, in the Forms group, click the Form button.
- To create a report, click the table on which you want to base the form in the Navigation Pane, and then on the Create tab, in the Reports group, click the Report button.
- To view a report in Print Preview, on the Report Layout Tools Design tab, in the Views group, click the View button arrow, and then click Print Preview.

17-8

Compact and repair a database

- On the ribbon, click the File tab. On the Info screen, click the Compact & Repair Database button.

INFOGRAPHIC

table
A collection of related fields.

primary key
A field, or a collection of fields, whose values uniquely identify each record in a table.

field
A part of a database that contains a single characteristic or attribute of a person, place, object, event, or idea.

relational database
A database that contains a collection of related tables.

table design grid
In Design view, lists the field names and data types.

data type
The type of data that can be entered for a field.

Navigation Pane
The main control center for opening and working with database objects.

Design view
The Access view that shows the underlying structure of a database object and allows you to modify that structure.

property
One characteristic or aspect of a field, such as its name or data type.

Field Properties pane
The list of properties for a field.

Help box
Displays information about the currently selected property.

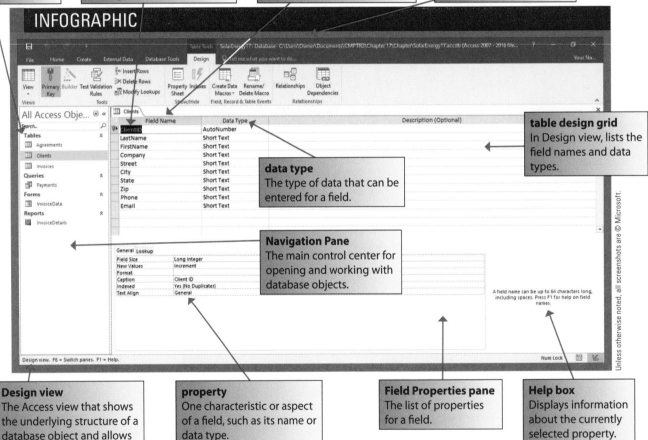

CHAPTER REVIEW 18

Maintaining and Querying a Database Access 2016

LEARNING OBJECTIVES

- 18-1 Maintain database records
- 18-2 Work with queries in Design view
- 18-3 Sort and filter data
- 18-4 Define table relationships
- 18-5 Create a multitable query
- 18-6 Add criteria to a query
- 18-7 Create a copy of a query
- 18-8 Add multiple criteria to queries
- 18-9 Create a calculated field
- 18-10 Use a property sheet
- 18-11 Use functions in a query

KEY TERMS

And operator The operator used to select records only if *all* of the specified conditions are met.

calculated field A field that displays the results of an expression (a combination of database fields, constants, and operators).

criteria Conditions that determine which records are selected in a query.

design grid The bottom portion of the Query window in Design view to which you add the fields and record-selection criteria for a query.

field selector The thin bar above each column in the design grid in a Query window that you click to select the entire field.

filter A set of restrictions placed on records in a datasheet or form to temporarily isolate a subset of the records.

Group By operator An operator that divides selected records into groups based on the values in the specified field.

multitable query A query based on more than one table.

one-to-many relationship A connection between two tables when one record in the primary table matches zero, one, or many records in the related table, and when each record in the related table matches at most one record in the primary table.

Or operator The operator used to select records if *at least one* of the specified conditions is met.

orphaned record A record in a related table that has no matching record in the primary table.

primary table The "one" table in a one-to-many relationship.

query by example (QBE) A query that retrieves the information that precisely matches the example you provide of the information being requested.

recordset The result of a query, which is a set of records that answers the question.

referential integrity A set of rules to maintain consistency between related tables when data in a database is updated.

related table The "many" table in a one-to-many relationship.

select query A query in which you specify the fields and records you want Access to select.

sort The process of rearranging records in a specified order or sequence.

sort field The field used to determine the order of records in the datasheet.

subdatasheet A datasheet in which records from a related table are displayed in the primary table.

KEY CONCEPTS

18-1
Maintain database records

• You can edit records directly, use the Find and Replace command to edit records, and add and delete records.

18-2
Work with queries in Design view

• To open a new Query window in Design view, on the Create tab, in the Queries group, click the Query Design button.
• To select tables to include in the query, in the Show Table dialog box, in the Tables list, click the table name, and then click Add.
• To add a field to the design grid, in the field list, double-click it.
• To run a query, in Design view, on the Query Tools Design tab, in the Results group, click the Run button.

18-3
Sort and filter data

• To sort on a field in Query Design view, in the design grid, in the field column of the field you want to sort on, click in the Sort row, click the arrow button, and then click the sort order.

18-4
Define table relationships

• To open the Relationships window, on the Database Tools tab, in the Relationships group, click the Relationships button.

CHAPTER 18 REVIEW

KEY CONCEPTS, *cont.*

- To add tables to the Relationships window, on the Relationship Tools Design tab, in the Relationships group, click the Show Table button, and then in the Show Table dialog box, double-click the table name.
- To establish a relationship in the Relationship window, in the table field list on the left, click the common field, and then drag it to the table field list on the right.

18-5
Create a multitable query
- Show more than one table in Design view, and then add fields from each table to the query design grid.

18-6
Add criteria to a query
- Drag fields from the displayed object to the design grid.

18-7
Create a copy of a query
- Right-click the query in the Navigation Pane, and then click Copy. Right-click in a blank area of the Navigation Pane, and then click Paste.

18-8
Add multiple criteria to queries
- To use the And logical operator, add criteria in the Criteria row in multiple fields in the design grid.
- To use the Or logical operator, add one criterion in the Criteria row in a field, and then add a second criteria in the Or row in a field.

18-9
Create a calculated field
- In Query Design view, in the design grid, click in the Field box in which you want to create an expression, and then on the Query Tools design tab, in the Query Setup group, click the Builder button.

18-10
Use a property sheet
- In the design grid, click a Field box. On the Query Tools Design tab, in the Show/Hide group, click the Property Sheet button.

18-11
Use functions in a query
- To use the Total row, in Datasheet view, on the Home tab, in the Records group, click the Totals button.
- To create a query with functions, in Design view, on the Query Tools Design tab, in the Show/Hide group, click the Totals button. In the design grid, in the Total box, click the arrow button, and then click a function.
- To create a query for groups of records, in Design view, drag a field to group by to the first column in the design grid.

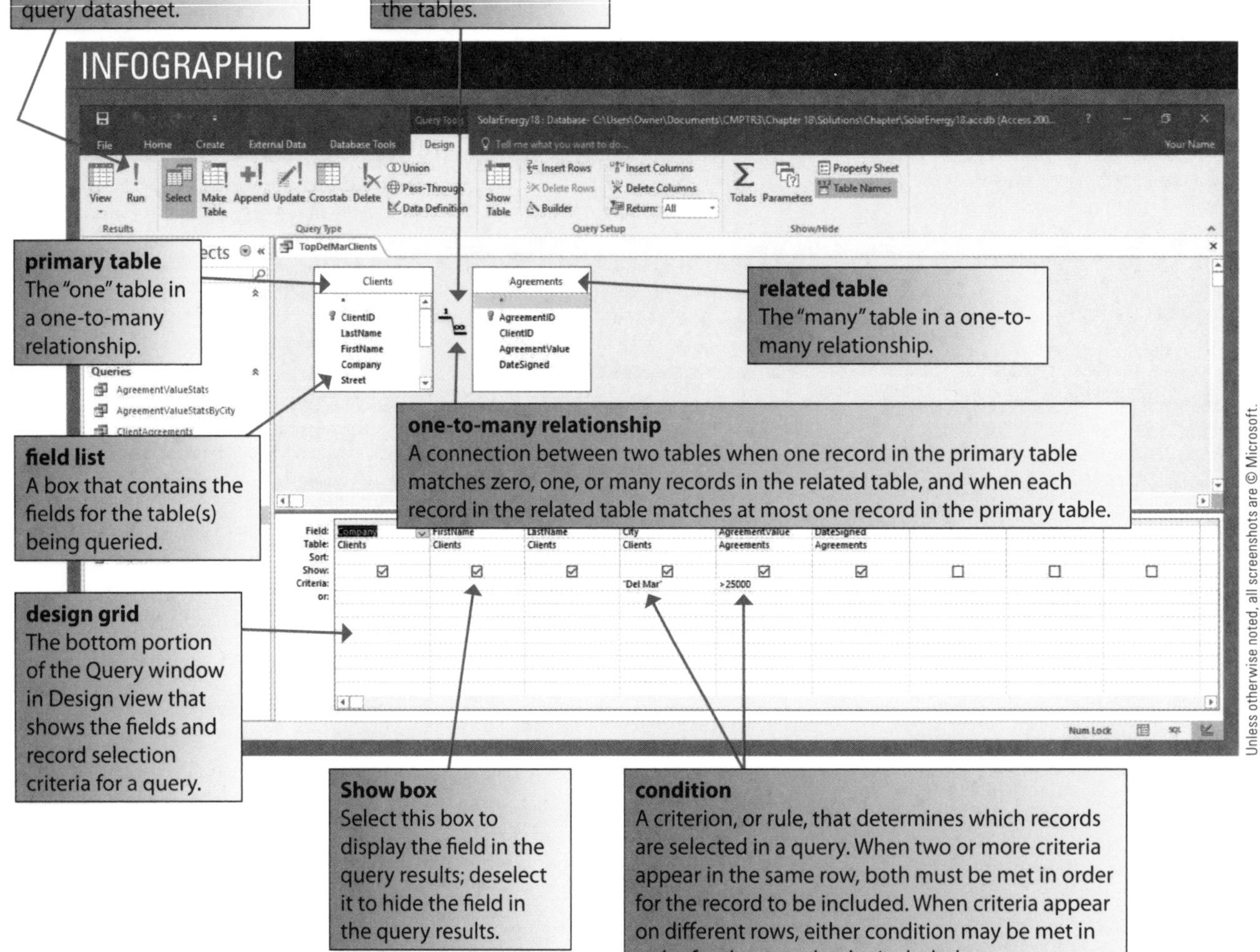

Run button
Click to run the query and display the query results in a query datasheet.
join line
Indicates one-to-many relationship between the tables.
INFOGRAPHIC
primary table
The "one" table in a one-to-many relationship.
related table
The "many" table in a one-to-many relationship.
one-to-many relationship
A connection between two tables when one record in the primary table matches zero, one, or many records in the related table, and when each record in the related table matches at most one record in the primary table.
field list
A box that contains the fields for the table(s) being queried.
design grid
The bottom portion of the Query window in Design view that shows the fields and record selection criteria for a query.
Show box
Select this box to display the field in the query results; deselect it to hide the field in the query results.
condition
A criterion, or rule, that determines which records are selected in a query. When two or more criteria appear in the same row, both must be met in order for the record to be included. When criteria appear on different rows, either condition may be met in order for the record to be included.

CHAPTER REVIEW 19

Creating Forms and Reports
Access 2016

LEARNING OBJECTIVES

- 19-1 Create a form using the Form Wizard
- 19-2 Modify a form's design in Layout view
- 19-3 Find data using a form
- 19-4 Create a form based on related tables
- 19-5 Preview and print selected form records
- 19-6 Create a report using the Report Wizard
- 19-7 Modify a report's design in Layout view

KEY TERMS

control An item on a form, report, or other database object that you can manipulate to modify the object's appearance.

control layout A set of controls grouped together in a form or report so that you can manipulate the set as a single control.

main form The part of a form that displays data from the primary table in a defined relationship.

subform The part of a form that displays data from a related table in a defined relationship.

wildcard character A placeholder you use when you know only part of a value or when you want to start or end with a specific character or match a certain pattern.

KEY CONCEPTS

19-1
Create a form using the Form Wizard
- To start the Form Wizard, on the Create tab, in the Forms group, click the Form Wizard button.
- To select the object on which to base the form, click the Tables/Queries arrow, and then click the object.
- To move fields from the Available Fields box to the Selected Fields box, click the fields, and then click the > button.
- To complete the wizard, click Next twice, in the third Form Wizard dialog box, in the Form box, type the form name, and then click Finish.

19-2
Modify a form's design in Layout view
- To open the Themes gallery, open the form in Layout view, and then on the Form Layout Tools Design tab, in the Themes group, click the Themes button.
- To apply a theme to the current object only, right-click the theme you want to apply, and then on the shortcut menu, click Apply Theme to This Object Only.
- To add a logo to a form, in Layout view, click the Form Layout Tools Design tab, and then in the Header/Footer group, click the Logo button.
- To reposition a logo on a form, right-click it, click Remove Layout, and then drag it to its new position.

19-3
Find Data using a Form
- To open the Find and Replace dialog box, in Form view, select the field you want to search, and then on the Home tab, in the Find group, click the Find button.
- To specify the field value you want to find, in the Find and Replace dialog box, in the Find What box, type the field value.
- To specify the matching options, in the Find and Replace dialog box, click the Match arrow, and then click the option you want.
- To search for the next match to the value in the Find What box, click Find Next.

19-4
Create a form based on related tables
- To start the Form Wizard, on the Create tab, in the Forms group, click the Form Wizard button.
- To select the object on which to base the main form, click the Tables/Queries arrow, and then click the object.
- To move fields from the Available Fields box to the Selected Fields box, click the fields, and then click the > button.
- To select the related object, click the Tables/Queries arrow again, click the related object, and then move the appropriate fields to the Selected Fields box.
- To complete the wizard, click Next three times, type the form and subform names in the appropriate boxes, and then click Finish.

19-5
Preview and print selected form records
- To preview a form, click the File tab, click Print, and then click Print Preview.
- To print the current records, click the Selected Record(s) option button. To print specific records, click the Pages option button.

19-6
Create a report using the Report Wizard
- To start the Report Wizard, on the Create tab, in the Reports group, click the Report Wizard button.
- In the third Report Wizard dialog box, choose additional grouping levels, if necessary, and then click Next.
- In the fourth Report Wizard dialog box, choose the sort order for the detail records, and then click Next.
- In the fifth Report Wizard dialog box, choose a layout and page orientation, and then click Next.
- In the sixth Report Wizard dialog box, edit the report title, and then click Finish.

19-7
Modify a report's design in Layout view
- To open the Conditional Formatting Rules Manager dialog box, in Layout view, click the field to format, click the Report Layout Tools Format tab, in the Control Formatting group, click the Conditional Formatting button.
- To create a rule, click the New Rule button.
- Set up the rule, and then click OK in each dialog box.

CHAPTER 19 REVIEW

field label
The Caption property of the field (or the field name if there is no Caption property) is used as the field label in the form.

form title
Identifies the form in the Navigation Pane.

field box
Displays the field value or allows you to insert values in a new record.

main form
The part of a form that displays data from the primary table in a defined relationship.

INFOGRAPHIC

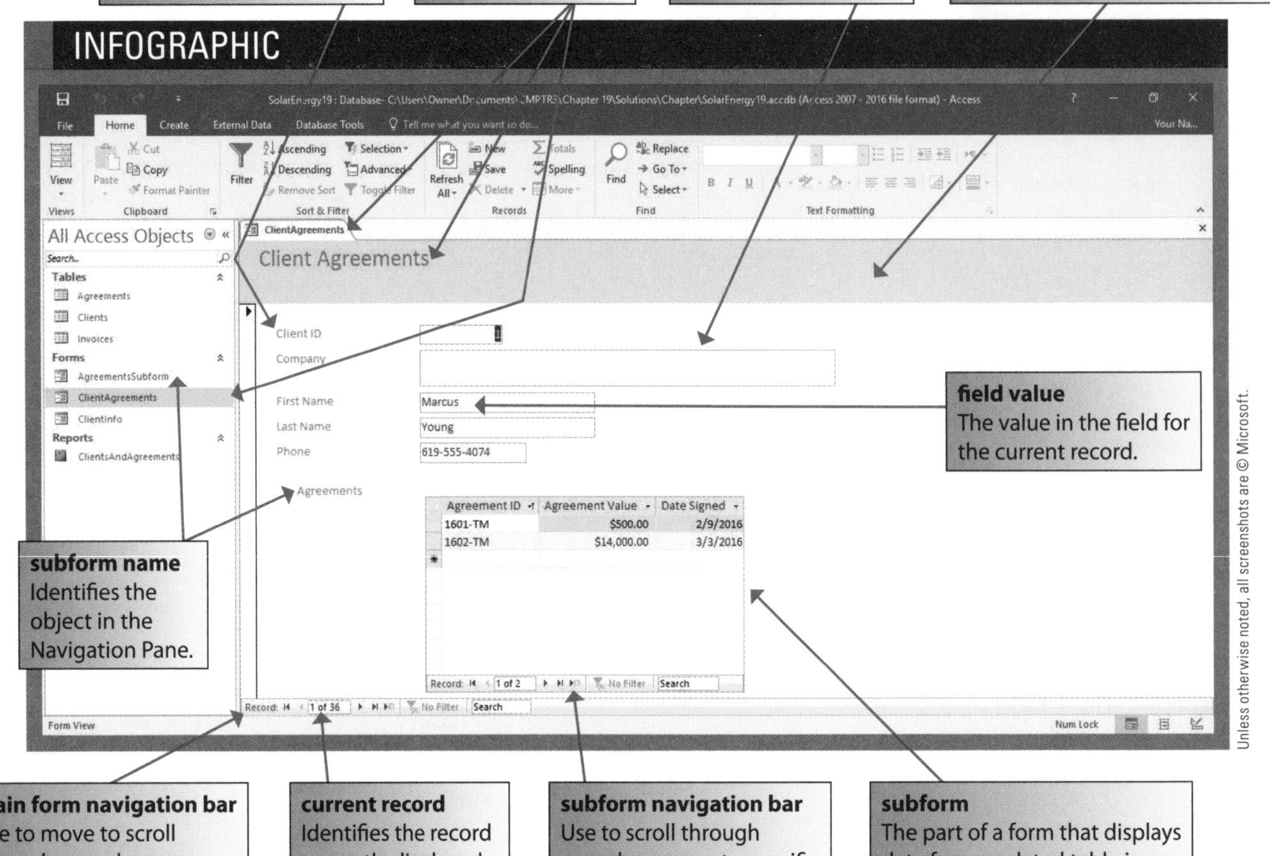

field value
The value in the field for the current record.

subform name
Identifies the object in the Navigation Pane.

main form navigation bar
Use to move to scroll through records or move to specific records using the main form.

current record
Identifies the record currently displayed in the form.

subform navigation bar
Use to scroll through records or move to specific records in the subform.

subform
The part of a form that displays data from a related table in a defined relationship.

CHAPTER REVIEW 20

Creating a Presentation PowerPoint 2016

LEARNING OBJECTIVES

20-1 Create a presentation

20-2 Move text and slides, and delete slides

20-3 Add speaker notes

20-4 Run a slide show

20-5 Add animations

20-6 Add transitions

20-7 Add footers and headers

20-8 Review, preview, and print a presentation

KEY CONCEPTS

20-1

Create a presentation

• To add a new slide with a specific layout, click the New Slide button arrow in the Slides group on the Home tab, and then click the layout you want to use.

20-2

Move text and slides, and delete slides

• Drag a slide icon in the Outline pane or drag a slide thumbnail in the Slides pane or in Outline view to a new position.

20-3

Add speaker notes

• To display the Notes pane, click the Notes button on the status bar.

20-4

Run a slide show

• To start a slide show from the current slide, click the Slide Show button on the status bar.

• To start a slide show from the first slide, on the Quick Access Toolbar, click the Start From Beginning button.

• To move forward in a slide show, click the left mouse button; or press the Spacebar, the Enter key, the Left Arrow key, or the Page Down key.

KEY TERMS

Go to your CMPTR[3] Online for a full list of key terms and definitions.

animation A special effect applied to an object that makes the object move or change.

Animation Painter A tool in PowerPoint that you can use to copy an animation from one object to another.

AutoFit A PowerPoint feature that automatically changes the line spacing and the font size of text if you add more text than will fit in a placeholder.

content placeholder A placeholder designed to hold any type of slide content—text, a graphic, or another object.

first-level item A main item in a list.

footer In PowerPoint, text that appears in a Footer text box, which can appear anywhere on a slide depending on the theme, or at the bottom of handouts and notes pages.

handout A printout of the slides in a presentation.

header In PowerPoint, text that appears at the top of handouts and notes pages in a document.

layout A predetermined way of organizing the objects on a slide.

Microsoft PowerPoint 2016 (PowerPoint) A presentation graphics program used to create a collection of slides that can contain text, charts, pictures, sound, movies, multimedia, and so on.

Notes pane The area of the PowerPoint window that contains notes for the presenter to refer to when delivering the presentation.

numbered list A list of paragraphs with a sequential numbers to the left of each paragraph.

placeholder A region of a slide reserved for inserting text or graphics.

presentation A file created in PowerPoint.

Presenter view The PowerPoint view that shows the current slide, the next slide, speaker notes, a timer showing how long the slide show has been running, and other helpful controls and information; designed to make it easier to display a slide show using a second monitor or a projection screen.

second-level item (subitem) An item beneath and indented from a first-level item.

speaker notes Notes that appear in the Notes pane to remind the speaker of points to make when the particular slide appears during the slide show.

text box An object that contains text.

transition The manner in which the next slide appears on the screen in place of the previous slide during a slide show.

unnumbered list A list of paragraphs that do not have any symbol to the left of each paragraph.

KEY CONCEPTS, *cont.*

20-5

Add animations

- Click the object, and then on the Animations tab, in the Animation group, click an animation.
- To change an animation effect, click the Effect Options button in the Animation group on the Animations tab, and then cilck an effect.

20-6

Add transitions

- To apply a transition, on the Transitions tab, in the Transition to This Slide group, click the transition you want to use.
- To apply a transition to all the slides, on the Transitions tab, in the Timing group, click the Apply to All button.

20-7

Add footers and headers

- To add a footer to the slides, on the Insert tab, in the Text group, click the Header & Footer button.
- To remove the footer from the title slide, select the Don't show on title slide check box on the Slide tab in the Header and Footer dialog box.

20-8

Review, preview, and print a presentation

- To display options for printing the presentation, click the File tab, and then in the navigation bar, click Print.
- To select the type of printout, click the Full Page Slides button, and then click Full Page Slides, Notes Pages, Outline, or one of the options under Handouts.
- To print non-sequential slides, type the slide numbers in the Slides box on the Print screen separated by commas.

New Slide button
Click to insert a new slide; click the New Slide button arrow to change the layout from the default layout.

Start From Beginning button
Click to start the slide show from the first slide.

Layout button
Click to change the layout of the current slide.

displayed slide
The currently selected slide displayed as it will look during the slide show.

INFOGRAPHIC

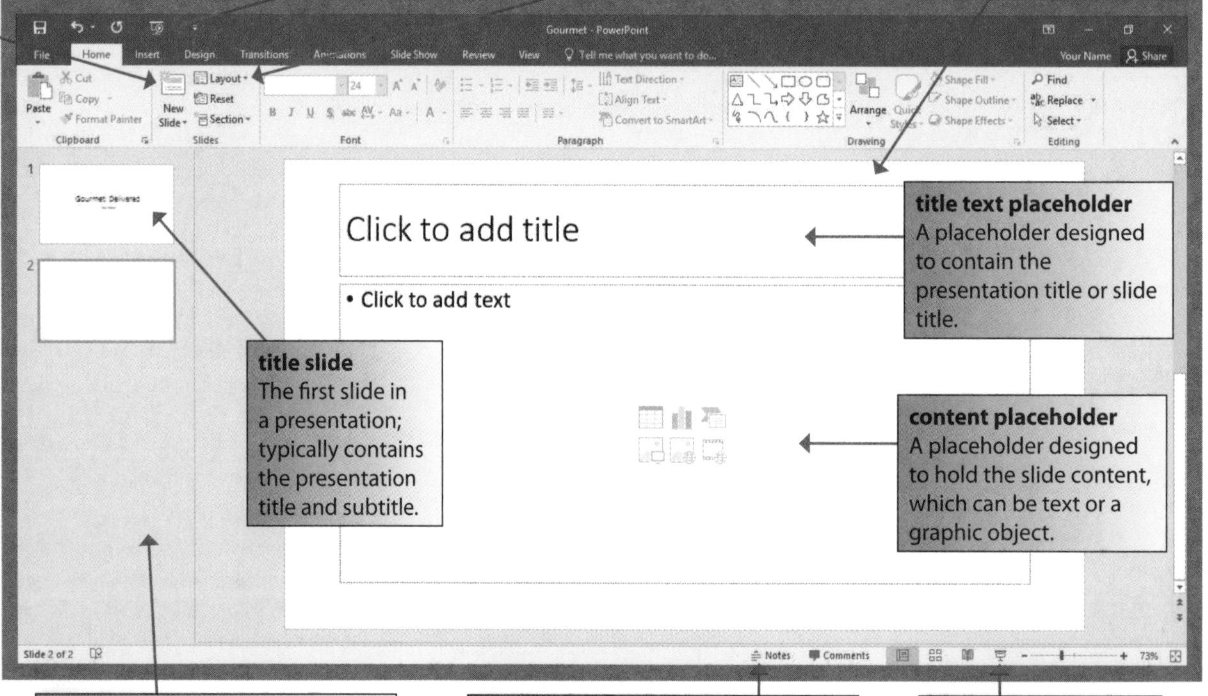

Slides pane
Shows a column of numbered slide thumbnails.

Notes button
Click to display the Notes pane below the displayed slide so that you can type notes for the presenter to refer to when delivering the presentation.

Slide Show button
Click to start the slide show from the current slide.

CHAPTER REVIEW 21

Enhancing a Presentation *PowerPoint 2016*

LEARNING OBJECTIVES

21-1 Work with slide masters

21-2 Insert graphics

21-3 Create SmartArt diagrams

21-4 Apply animations to graphics

21-5 Modify animation timings

21-6 Add video

21-7 Compress pictures and media

21-8 Save a presentation for distribution

KEY CONCEPTS

21-1

Work with slide masters

- For each theme in a presentation, the slide master includes the theme Slide Master and a layout master for each layout.
- To modify the slide master, switch to Slide Master view.
- In Slide Master view, you can modify the placeholders, fonts, colors, and slide background, and you can insert and remove graphics.

21-2

Insert graphics

- To insert a picture, click the Pictures button in a content placeholder or click the Pictures button in the Illustrations group on the Insert tab.
- To insert a shape, click the Shapes button in the Illustrations group on the Insert tab.

21-3

Create SmartArt diagrams

- To create SmartArt, click the Insert SmartArt Graphic button in a content placeholder or the SmartArt button in the Illustrations group on the Insert tab.
- To convert a bulleted list into SmartArt, click the Convert to SmartArt button in the Paragraph group on the Home tab.

21-4

Apply animations to graphics

- To apply an animation to a graphic, click the graphic, and then click the animation in the Animation gallery on the Animations tab.

KEY TERMS

add-in Software that you can install to add new commands and features to an Office application.

diagram An illustration that visually depicts information or ideas and shows how they are connected.

fill The formatting of the area inside a shape.

gradient Shading in which one color blends into another or varies from one shade to another.

handouts master A handout that contains the elements that appear on printed handouts.

layout master A slide master for a specific layout in a presentation.

notes master A note that contains the elements that appear on the notes pages.

Office Mix A PowerPoint add-in used to create a mix.

mix An interactive video created from a PowerPoint presentation using Office Mix and posted to a Web site.

poster frame (preview frame) In a video object, the image that appears before the video starts playing.

slide master A slide that contains theme elements and styles, as well as text and other objects that appear on the slides in the presentation.

Slide Master view The PowerPoint view that displays the slide masters.

smart guide A dashed, orange line or arrow that appears when you drag an object on a slide to help you position the object.

SmartArt A diagram with a predesigned layout.

theme Slide Master The primary slide master for a presentation.

21-5

Modify animation timings

- Use the Move Earlier and Move Later buttons in the Timing group on the Animations tab to change the order of animations on a slide.
- To change how an animation starts, click the Start box arrow in the Timing group on the Animations tab, and then select an option.
- To change the speed of an animation, change the time in the Duration box in the Timing group on the Animations tab.

21-6

Add video

- Insert a video by using the Insert Video button in a content placeholder or by using the Video button in the Media group on the Insert tab.
- Format video by changing options such as changing the way a clip starts and its volume. You can also trim an audio or video clip, and set a poster frame for a video clip.

21-7

Compress pictures and media

- Pictures are compressed to 220 ppi by default.
- To compress pictures further, select a picture, click the Picture Tools Format tab, and then in the Adjust group, click the Compress Pictures button. Select a compression option, deselect the Apply only to this picture check box, and then click OK.
- To compress media, click the File tab, click the Compress Media button on the Info screen, and then click one of the quality options.

21-8

Save a presentation for distribution

- To save a presentation as a PDF, click the File tab, click Export in the navigation pane in Backstage view, and then click the Create PDF/XPS button.

CHAPTER 21 REVIEW

theme Slide Master
The primary slide master for a presentation.

Slide Master view
The PowerPoint view that displays the slide masters.

slide master
A slide that contains theme elements and styles, as well as text and other objects that appear on the slides in the presentation.

Insert SmartArt Graphic button
In Normal view, click to insert a SmartArt diagram.

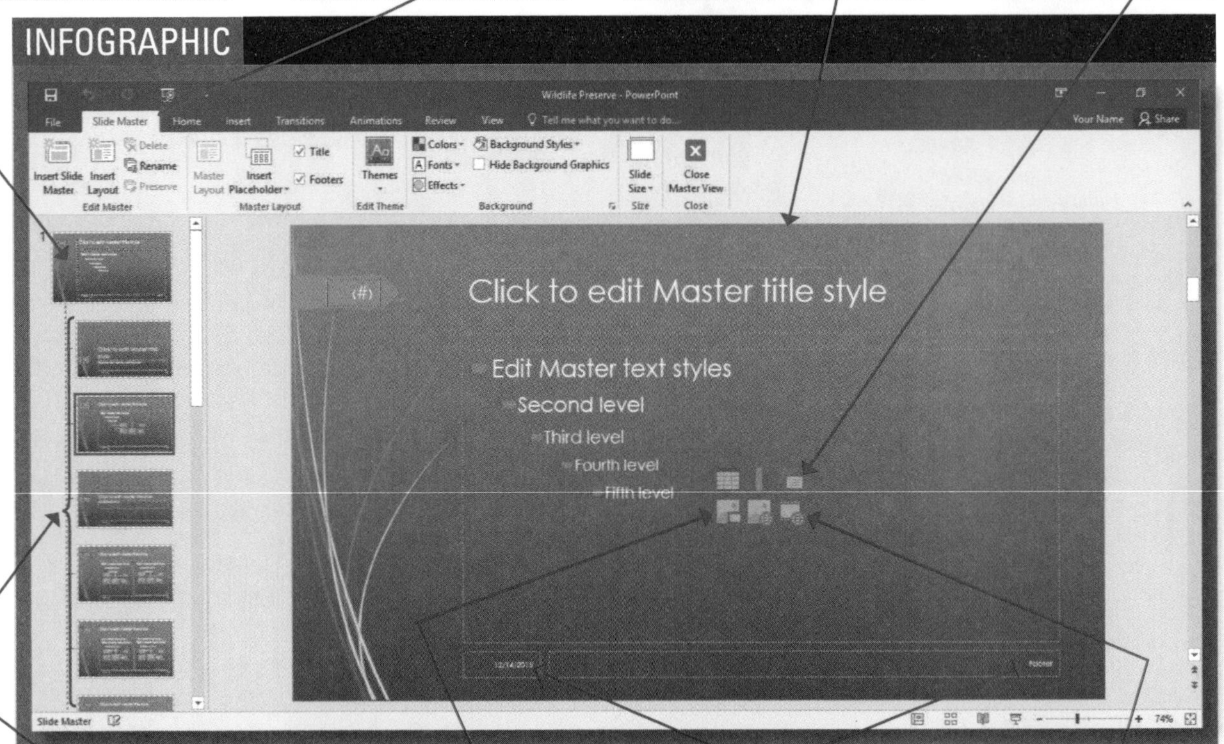

layout masters
A slide master for a specific layout in a presentation.

Pictures button
In Normal view, click to insert a picture stored on your computer or network.

placeholders
If placeholders are moved on the slide master, the change appears in Normal view.

Insert Video button
In Normal view, click to insert a video clip.

CHAPTER REVIEW 22

Integrating Word, Excel, Access, and PowerPoint
Integration

LEARNING OBJECTIVES

22-1 Understand object linking and embedding

22-2 Import and export data

22-3 Use the Object command to insert text from a file

22-4 Copy and paste among Office programs

22-5 Create PowerPoint slides from a Word outline

22-6 Create form letters with mail merge

KEY TERMS

data source A file that contains the variable information for form letters.

destination file The file into which you want to insert an object created in another file.

destination program The program used to create the file where you want to insert an object created in a different file.

embed To copy an object along with a link to the source program in a destination file.

form letter A Word document that contains standard paragraphs of text and a minimum of variable text.

link To establish a direct connection between a source and destination file.

mail merge To merge a main document with a list of addresses from a data source.

main document A document that contains the text and other information that you want to keep the same in each form letter.

merge To combine a main document with a data source.

merge field A field that contains instructions to be replaced with the variable information that changes from one letter to another.

Rich Text Format (RTF) A text format that preserves the formatting and layout of data.

source file The file that contains an object that you want to integrate into another file.

source program The program used to create an object.

starting document The main document in a Word mail merge.

KEY CONCEPTS

22-1
Object linking and embedding
- The program used to create the object you want to integrate into another file is the source program and the file that contains the object is the source file.
- The program used to create the file where you want to insert the object is the destination program and the file in which you will insert the object is the destination file.
- To embed an object means to paste it along with a link to the source program.
- To link an object means to create a connection between the source and destination file.

22-2
Import and export data
- You can import data into an Access table from another program as long as the data is in the form of a list.
- You can export data from an Access table to an Excel file, a Rich Text File, or a plain text file, and others.

22-3
Use the Object command to insert text from a file
- Use the Object command to insert the contents of one file into another file.

22-4
Copy and paste among Office programs
- Use the Copy and Paste commands to copy an object from one file to another. Use the Office Clipboard.

22-5
Create PowerPoint slides from a Word outline
- When you create a PowerPoint presentation from a Word outline, paragraphs formatted with the Heading 1 style become slide titles, paragraphs formatted with the Heading 2 style become first-level bullets, and so on.
- Slides created from a Word outline are inserted after the current slide.
- You might need to reset slides created from a Word outline to apply the theme and slide master formatting correctly.

22-6
Create form letters with mail merge
- Use the mail merge process to merge data from a data source with a letter to create personalized form letters.
- If the column labels in the data source don't match the Word field names, use the Match Fields command to manually match the fields.
- Preview the merge before printing to make sure the correct data is inserted and that paragraph spacing is correct.

CHAPTER 22 REVIEW

destination program
The program used to create the file where you want to insert an object created in a different file.

link
A direct connection between a source and destination file.

source program
The program used to create an object.

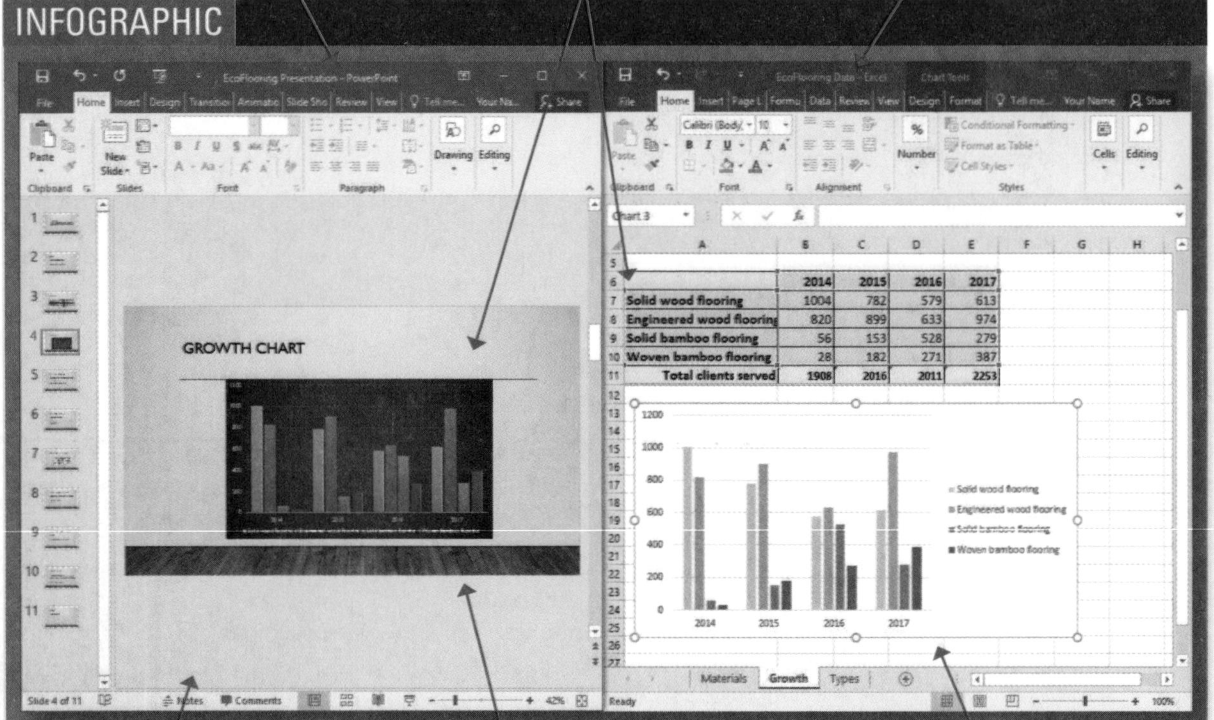

destination file
The file into which you want to insert an object created in another file.

embed
To copy an object along with a link to the source program in a destination file.

source file
The file that contains an object that you want to integrate into another file.

WORD 2016 QUICK START GUIDE

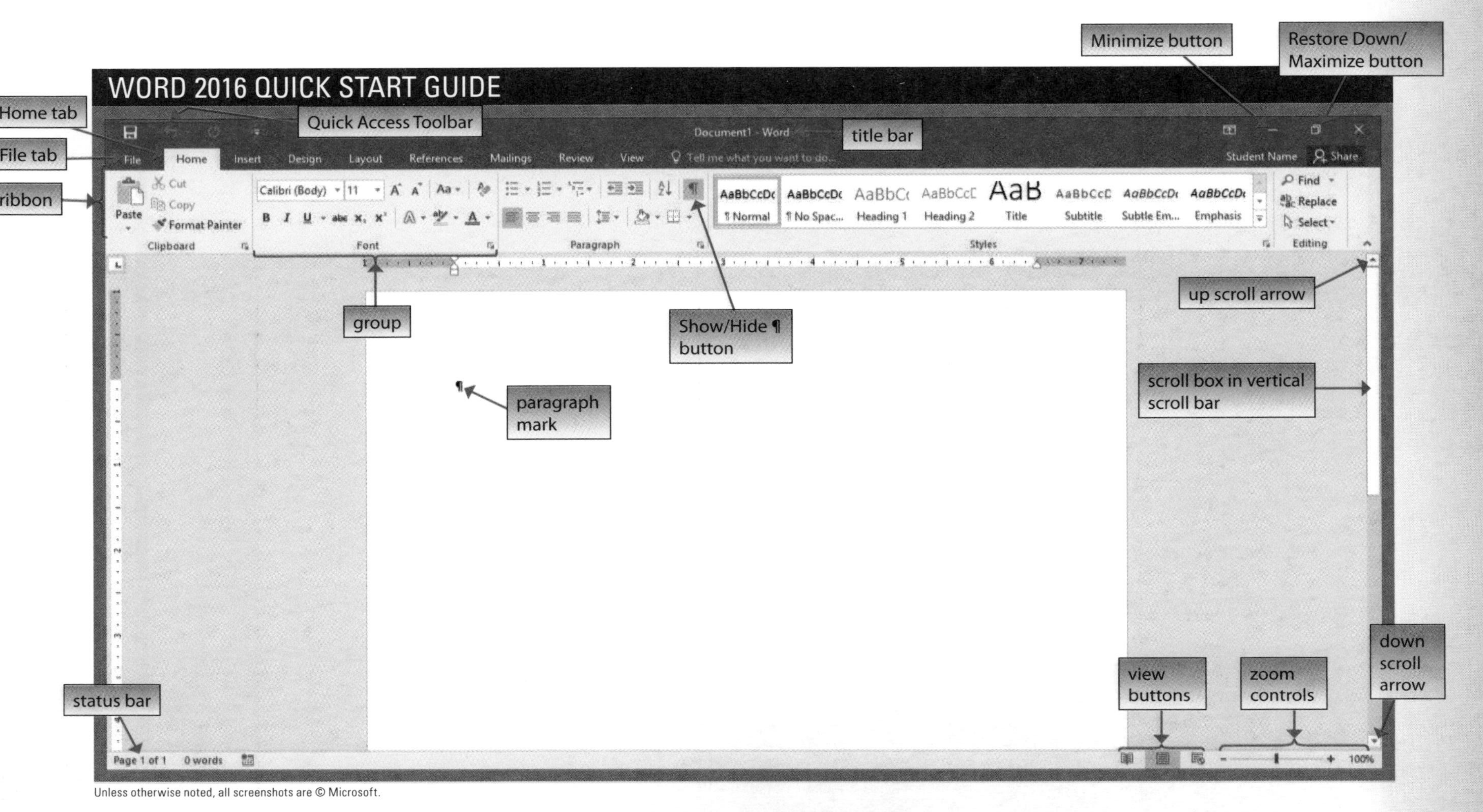

EXCEL 2016 QUICK START GUIDE

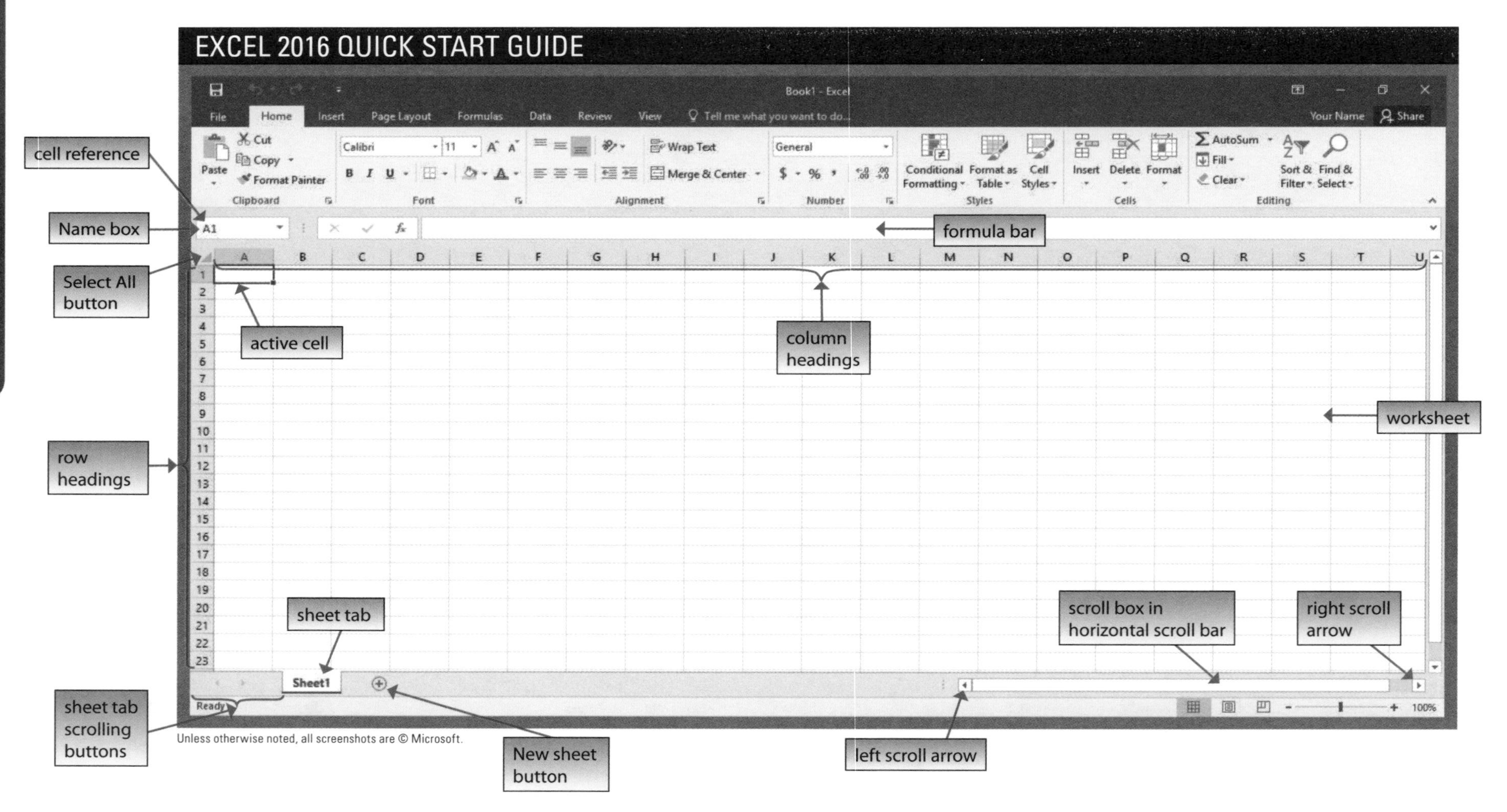

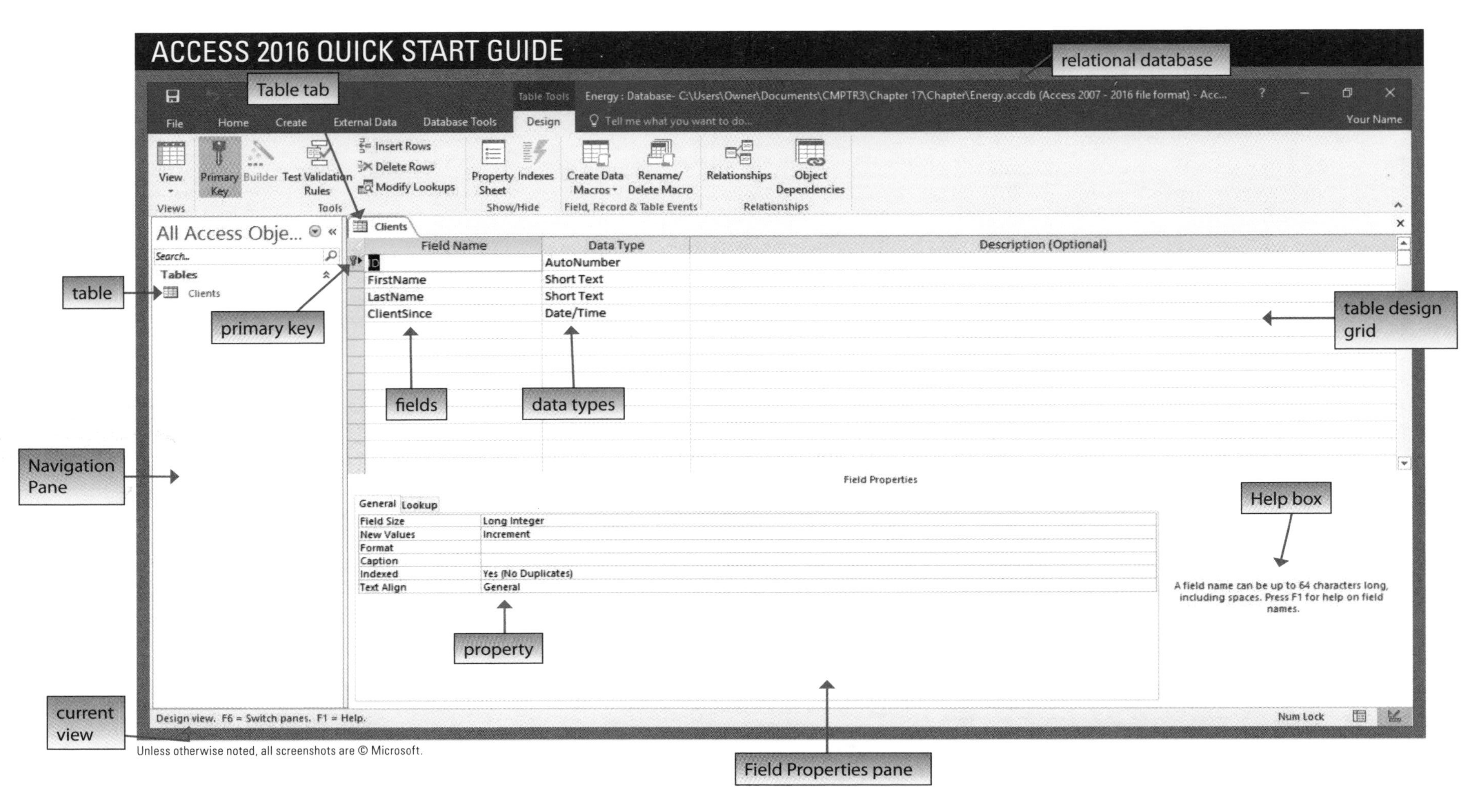

ACCESS 2016 QUICK START GUIDE
relational database
Table tab
table
primary key
fields
data types
table design grid
Navigation Pane
Help box
property
current view
Field Properties pane
Energy : Database- C:\Users\Owner\Documents\CMPTR3\Chapter 17\Chapter\Energy.accdb (Access 2007 - 2016 file format) - Acc...
File
Home
Create
External Data
Database Tools
Design
Tell me what you want to do...
Your Name
View
Primary Key
Builder
Test Validation Rules
Insert Rows
Delete Rows
Modify Lookups
Property Sheet
Indexes
Create Data Macros
Rename/ Delete Macro
Relationships
Object Dependencies
Views
Tools
Show/Hide
Field, Record & Table Events
Relationships
All Access Obje...
Search...
Tables
Clients
Field Name
Data Type
Description (Optional)
ID
AutoNumber
FirstName
Short Text
LastName
Short Text
ClientSince
Date/Time
Field Properties
General
Lookup
Field Size
Long Integer
New Values
Increment
Format
Caption
Indexed
Yes (No Duplicates)
Text Align
General
A field name can be up to 64 characters long, including spaces. Press F1 for help on field names.
Design view. F6 = Switch panes. F1 = Help.
Num Lock

POWERPOINT 2016 QUICK START GUIDE

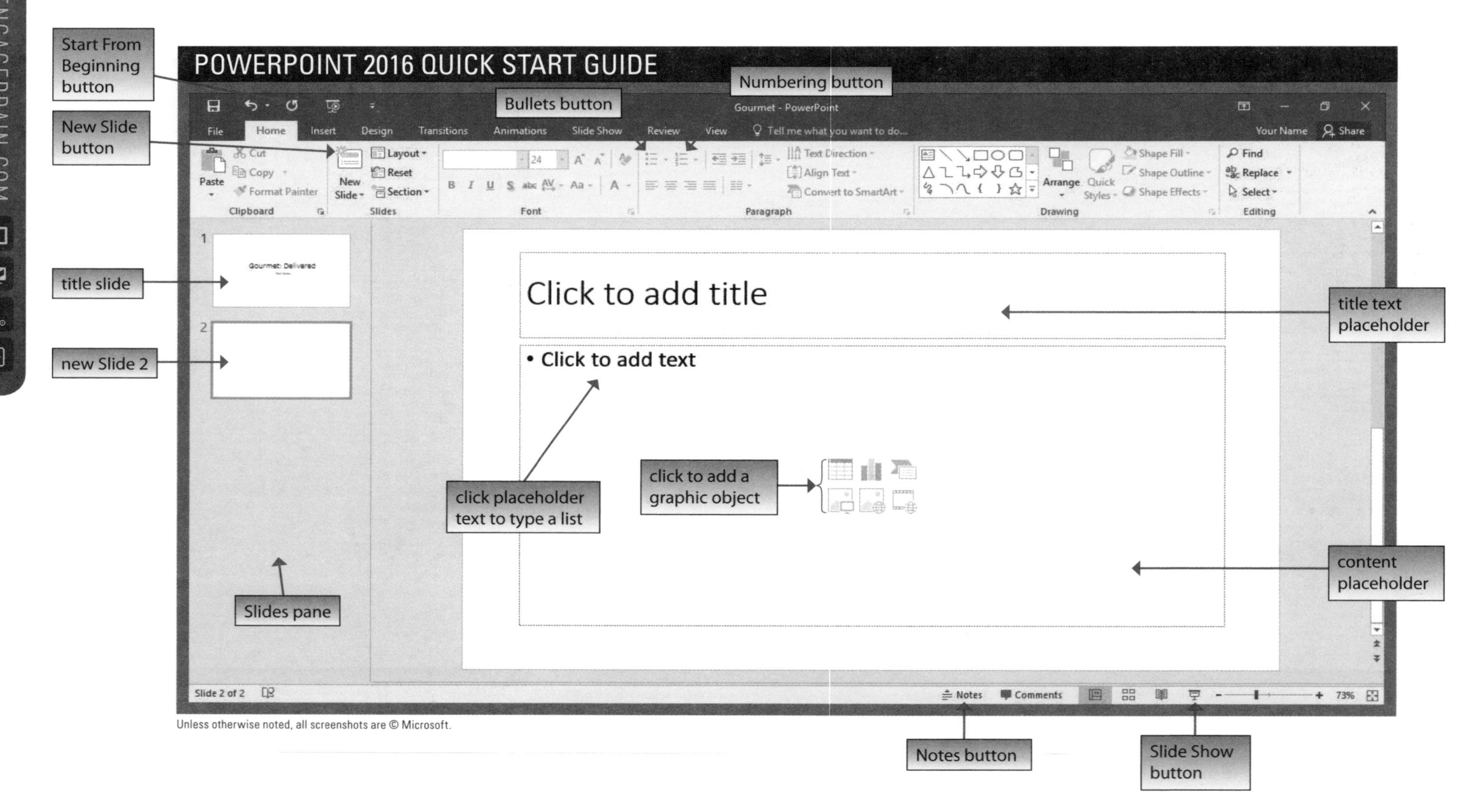

Unless otherwise noted, all screenshots are © Microsoft.